COGNITIVE NEUROSCIENCE

THE BIOLOGY OF THE MIND

Michael S. Gazzaniga

DARTMOUTH COLLEGE

Richard B. Ivry

UNIVERSITY OF CALIFORNIA,
BERKELEY

George R. Mangun

UNIVERSITY OF CALIFORNIA,
DAVIS

COGNITIVE NEUROSCIENCE

THE BIOLOGY OF THE MIND

W · W · NORTON & COMPANY

NEW YORK · LONDON

PRINTED IN THE UNITED STATES OF AMERICA

The text of this book is composed in Minion with the display set in Myriad.
Composition by TSI Graphics.
Manufacturing by R.R. Donnelley.
Editors: Howard Boyer, Steve Mosberg, and Richard Mixter
Production editor: Mary T. Kelly
Book design by Jack Meserole.
Illustrations by Frank Forney.
Cover Illustration: "Magdalena" by Sean Scully, courtesy of Mary Boone Gallery, New York.

Library of Congress Cataloging-in-Publication Data:

Gazzaniga, Michael S.
    Cognitive neuroscience : the biology of the mind / Michael S.
Gazzaniga, Richard B. Ivry, George R. Mangun.
        p.   cm.
    Includes bibliographical references and index.
    ISBN 0-393-97219-4
    1. Cognitive neuroscience.   I. Ivry, Richard B.   II. Mangun, G.
R. (George Ronald), 1956– .   III. Title.
QP360.5.G39   1998
153—dc21   97-36771
                                                                              CIP

W. W. Norton & Company, Inc., 500 Fifth Avenue, New York, NY 10110
W. W. Norton & Company Ltd., 10 Coptic Street, London WC1A 1PU

4 5 6 7 8 9 0

To

OUR FAMILIES

CONTENTS

4 Perception and Encoding 121

5 Higher Perceptual Functions 163

6 Attention and Selective Perception 207

BOXES

HOW THE BRAIN WORKS

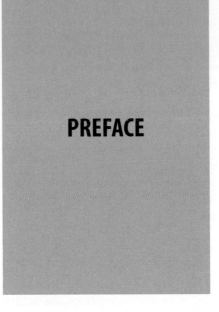

PREFACE

Cognitive neuroscience is taking the scientific community by storm. Scientists now realize that studying the mind's complex processes—perception, language, attention, memory, control of movement, feelings, and consciousness itself—has become a task that is not only scientifically tractable, but is approachable by cognitive and neural means. The disciplines of cognitive psychology, behavioral neurology, and neuroscience now feed off of each other, contributing a new view to the understanding of the mechanisms of the mind. This development has led to the emergence of the field of cognitive neuroscience.

Deciding to write a textbook is an exhilarating and terrifying decision, especially when the goal is to create the foundational text in a new field. We entered into this writing project at the urging of colleagues in the cognitive neuroscience community who are now, or will be, teaching new courses in this topic in departments of psychology, cognitive science, philosophy, neuroscience, and biology. Thanks to many of the persons acknowledged in this book, we believe we have assembled a strong first edition that meets our goals, and that contains the material and balanced viewpoints our colleagues have asked for in such a text.

The interchange of concepts among the three of us, whose interests and approaches have disparate scientific flavors, has turned out to be a significant factor in laying the foundation for this text. Each of us has come to the field with different training and add a different perspective to the study of the mind. Our individual perspectives have been woven into the fabric of this book and, we hope, offer a rich view of the study of how the brain enables the mind. The most senior of the trio (MSG) was trained as a biologist at Caltech but went on to study patients with specific surgical interventions and neurological patients with focal disease. The second author (RBI) works on the cognitive characterization of mental skills and cut his teeth on cognitive psychology. The third (GRM), started out in chemistry but then trained as a neuroscientist specializing in the brain imaging technique of event-related potentials.

All of us now practice cognitive neuroscience. All of us take on cognitive concepts and study mind/brain matters with psychophysical and brain imaging techniques such as fMRI, MR, PET, and ERPs. And all of us study patient populations. The field requires one to become knowledgeable in each of these areas and to practice several different approaches when undertaking a single study. This book is intended to prepare students of cognitive neuroscience to do just that.

What constitutes the first principles that make cognitive neuroscience distinct from physiological psychology, neuroscience, cognitive psychology or neuropsychology? This question was our first challenge in laying the groundwork for the text, and ultimately it constituted our defining point. We concluded that it is indeed a critical question—but, paradoxically, not a question at all. Cognitive neuroscience certainly overlaps with and synthesizes these traditional approaches, but the book goes beyond that function to define how cognitive neuroscientists will address the neural bases of cognition in the years ahead.

Our approach is to balance cognitive theory with neuropsychological and neuroscientific evidence, plus add examples of the use of computational techniques to complete the story. We make liberal use of patient case studies, but this is to illustrate essential points, not to provide an exhaustive description of brain disorders. In every section, we strive to include the most current information and theoretical views, supported by cutting-edge technology that is such an important part of cognitive neuroscience, such as functional brain imaging. In contrast to purely cognitive or neuropsychological approaches, this text emphasizes the convergence of evidence that is a crucial aspect of any science, particularly studies of higher mental function.

To illustrate where cognitive neuroscience has come from and how it fits into the future of brain research, we begin with a historical tour through cognitive and neural science. Then two chapters provide background information about the neuroscientific and cognitive terminology and basic principles that are used throughout the book. Chapter 2 contains a fast overview of the principles of neuroscience from the neuron to the neural system, and Chapter 3 introduces methodological approaches like cognitive logic, neuropsychological analysis of patients, and functional neuroimaging. The next eleven chapters tour the modern cognitive neuroscience of perception, attention, memory, language, hemispheric specialization, motor control, executive function, development and plasticity, evolution of cognition, and our favorite chapter, speculations on the neural bases of consciousness.

As with the construction of any effective text, we have chosen to exclude some topics in order to avoid turning the book into an encyclopedia. But with the help of our many advisors, and as an outgrowth of countless squabbles among the authors over the details as well as the big picture, we think we have come up with a consensus view of the main issues in cognitive neuroscience. We sincerely hope that students will enjoy reading it as much as we enjoyed writing it.

It should also be noted that we think learning complex material can be fun and enjoyable. Too often scientific issues are presented as if some kind of rational robot had produced the work. In fact, scientists are people too! They laugh, cry, agonize, play baseball, write novels, go to the NBA games, and all the rest. Research is a personal exploration and every scientist approaches it from a unique perspective. We decided to interview many of them and to let this human dimension of their work come forward. The interviews were so captivating, we wish we could have provided space for more and for longer discussions.

We have also made a special effort to bring cognitive neuroscience alive with color. Frank Forney, the book's artist is to be congratulated for his fine effort. Additional illustrations were provided by Conery Calhoon, Gale Mueller, Sandra Mullins, and Neil Parker. We also thank our many colleagues who have provided original artwork or scientific figures.

We are also indebted to Howard Boyer. Howard is one of those rare editors that actually gets into a book's purpose and structure. He went over every word at least three times and he cajoled, argued, reinforced, and finally gave freely of his fine editing hand. This book would be less were it not for his guidance. We are also in debt to W. W. Norton's excellent editorial staff especially to the editors Richard Mixter and Steven Mosberg, editorial assistant Peter Wei, and the project editor, Mary Kelly. Pulling together a project of this magnitude is a major achievement and all are thanked and congratulated.

In sum, this book has been an interactive effort between ourselves, our colleagues, our students, and our reviewers! The product has benefited immeasurably from these interactions and we now feel it is ready for you, the reader. And yet, we will not rest here. We stand ready to modify and improve any and all of our work. So feel free to contact us with your suggestions and questions. We live in a new age where interaction is swift and easy. We are to be found as follows: Michael.S.Gazzaniga@Dartmouth.edu; grmangun@ucdavis.edu; ivry@socrates.berkeley.edu. Good reading and learning.

Acknowledgements: We are indebted to many scientists and personal friends. Writing a textbook is a major commitment of time, intellect, and affect! Those who have helped so much are noted below. Some reviewed our words and critiqued our thoughts. Others allowed us to interview them. We owe all our deep gratitude and thanks. In addition, Chapter 8 was co-authored by Dr. Tamara Swaab (University of California, Davis). Her contributions to this section are deeply appreciated and warmly acknowledged.

Linda P. Acredolo, University of California, Davis; David G. Amaral, University of California, Davis; Horace Barlow, Cambridge University; Kathleen Baynes, University of California, Davis; Marlene Behrmann, Carnegie Mellon University; Mark Beeman, Rush Medical Center, Chicago; Ira B. Black, Robert Wood Johnson Medical School; Lindy A. Buck, Medical College of Ohio; Davina Chan, University of California, Berkeley; Valerie Clark, University of California, Davis; Clay Clayworth, VAMC Martinez, CA; Asher Cohen, Hebrew University; Michael Corballis, University Auckland; Antonio Damasio, University of Iowa; Hanna Damasio, University of Iowa; Daniel C. Dennett, Tufts University; Nina Dronkers, University of California, Davis; Martha Farah, University of Pennsylvania; Peter T. Fox, University of Texas; Karl Friston, Institute of Neurology, London; Mitchell Glickstein, University College, London and Dartmouth College; Patricia S. Goldman-Rakic, Yale University School of Medicine; Gail Goodman, University of California, Davis; Peter Hagoort, Max Planck Institute for Psycholinguistics; Todd Handy, University of California, Davis; Eliot Hazeltine, University of California, Berkeley; Jack Gallant, University of California, Berkeley; Scott Grafton, Emory University; Hans-Jochen Heinze, Magdeberg University; Steven A. Hillyard, University of California, San Diego; Joseph Hopfinger, University of California, Davis; Amishi Jha, University of California, Davis; Hermann Hinrichs, University of Madgeberg; Cindy Jordan, University of California, Berkeley; Lucy Jacobs, University of California, Berkeley; Steven Keele, University of Oregon; Robert T. Knight, University of California, Davis; Stephen M. Kosslyn, Harvard University; Neal Kroll, University of California, Davis; Leah Krubitzer, University of California, Davis; Marta Kutas, University of California, San Diego; Joseph E. Le Doux, New York University; Steven J. Luck, University of Iowa; Chris Marsolek, University of Minnesota; Nancy Martin, University of California, Davis; James L. McClelland, Carnegie Mellon University; George A. Miller, Princeton University; Ken A. Paller, Northwestern University; Steven E. Petersen, Washington University School of Medicine; Steven Pinker, Massachusetts Institute of Technology; Michael I. Posner, University of Oregon; David Presti, VA Medical Center, San Francisco; Robert Rafal, University of California, Davis; Marcus Raichle, Washington University School of Medicine; Mikko E. Sams, University of Tampere; Donatella Scabini, University of California, Davis; Daniel Schacter, Harvard University; Michael Scholz, University of Magdeberg; Art Shimamura, University of California, Berkeley; Larry Squire, University of California, San Diego; Anne M. Treisman, Princeton University; Endel Tulving, Rotman Research Institute, Baycrest Center; Marty G. Woldorff, University of Texas at San Antonio; Andrew Yonelinas, University of California, Davis.

COGNITIVE NEUROSCIENCE

THE BIOLOGY OF THE MIND

1

A Brief History of Cognitive Neuroscience

Do you wonder about big things like the meaning of life, or the meaning of meaning? Or are you the type who does not wonder about such evanescent questions? If you are the latter, do not read this book—even though you should. This is a book for those who wonder what life, mind, sex, love, thinking, feeling, moving, attending, remembering, communicating, and being are all about. And better, it is about scientific approaches to these grand issues. So prepare yourself for learning about a fantastic story still in the making.

The scientific field of cognitive neuroscience received its name in the late 1970s in the back seat of a New York City taxi. One of us (M.S.G.) was riding with the great cognitive psychologist George A. Miller on the way to a dinner meeting at the Algonquin Hotel. The dinner was being held for scientists from Rockefeller University and Cornell University, who were joining forces to study how the brain enables the mind, a subject in need of a name. Out of that taxi ride came the term *cognitive neuroscience*, which took hold in the scientific community.

Now the question is, What does it mean? In answering this ponderous question, we need to step back and look at not only the history of human thought, but also the history of the scientific disciplines of biology, psychology, and medicine.

To grasp the miraculous properties of brain function, one must bear in mind that Mother Nature built it, not a team of rational engineers. Although the earth formed approximately 5 billion years ago, and life first appeared around 3.5 billion years ago, human brains in their present form have been around only about 100,000 years. The primate brain appeared approximately 20 million years ago, and evolution took its course to build our present human brain, capable of all sorts of wondrous—and banal—feats.

During most of history, humans were too busy to think about thought. While there can be little doubt that human brains could engage in such activities, life was given over to more practical work such as surviving in tough environments, developing ways to live better by inventing agriculture or by domesticating animals, and so forth. However, as soon as civilization developed to the point when day-to-day survival did not occupy every hour of every day, our ancestors began to spend time constructing complex theories about the motives of fellow humans. Examples of attempts to understand the world and our place in it include *Oedipus Rex*, the ancient Greek play that deals with the nature of the child-parent conflict, and Mesopotamian and Egyptian theories on the nature of religion and the universe. The brain mechanisms that enabled the generation of theories about the nature of human nature thrived inside the heads of ancient humans. Yet they had one big problem: They did not have the ability to systematically explore the mind through experimentation.

In a diary entry of 1846, the brilliant philosopher Søren Kierkegaard wrote:

. . . That a man should simply and profoundly say that he cannot understand how consciousness comes into existence—is perfectly natural. But that a man should glue his eye to a microscope and stare and stare and stare—and still not be able to see how it happens—is ridiculous, and it is particularly ridiculous when it is supposed to be serious. . . . If the natural sciences had been developed in Socrates' day as they are now, all the sophists would have been scientists. One would have hung a microscope outside his shop in order to attract custom, and then would have had a sign painted saying: "Learn and see through a giant microscope how a man thinks (and on reading the advertisement Socrates would have said: 'That is how men who do not think behave')."

The Nobel Laureate Max Delbrück (1986) began his fascinating account of the evolution of the cosmos in his book *Mind from Matter?* with the foregoing quote of Kierkegaard. Delbrück is part of the modern tradition that started in the nineteenth century. Observe, manipulate, measure, and start to determine how the brain gets its job done. Armchair thinking is a wonderful thing and has produced wonderful science such as theoretical physics and mathematics. But to understand how a biological system works, a laboratory is needed and experiments have to be performed. Ideas derived from introspection can be eloquent and fascinating, but are they true? Philosophy can add perspective, but is it right? Only scientific method can move a topic along on sure footing. And just think about the rich phenomena to study. Take the perception of faces. Some say that the brain has a special system for recognizing faces. This specialized system was revealed because patients with certain brain lesions had a hard time recognizing faces of all kinds. Scientists immediately debated whether there was a specialized system. No, some said, the impairment is with object perception in general, not faces in particular. They pointed to research which suggested that people who had a hard time recognizing faces also had a hard time seeing objects or faces of animals.

But then comes a new case. A patient has a terrible time seeing everyday objects but has no problem seeing faces! In fact, if the faces are composed by arranging fruit to look like a face, the patient says he sees the face but does not realize it is made up of fruit! Incredible but true. It appears as though a special system in the brain sees faces; it is triggered to produce the percept for our conscious lives by the configuration of elements. The special face processor does not know or care about what elements it is composed of; as long as they are in proper arrangement, a face is perceived. What could be more fascinating than to study how the brain does such things?

THE BRAIN STORY

You are given a problem to solve. A hunk of biological tissue is known to think, remember, attend, solve problems, want sex, play games, write novels, exhibit prejudice, and do a zillion other things. You are supposed to figure out how it works. Before starting, you might ask a few questions. Does the blob work as a unit with each part contributing to a whole? Or is the blob full of individual processing parts, each carrying out specific functions, with the result being something that looks like it is acting as a whole unit? After all, the blob of the city of New York looks like an integrated whole from a distance, but it is actually composed of millions of individual processors, which is to say people. Perhaps people, in turn, are made of smaller, more specialized units.

This central issue—whether the whole brain working in concert or parts of the brain working independently enable mind—is what fuels much of modern research. The enigma still plagues contemporary research. As we will see, the dominant view over the past 100 years keeps changing. It all started in the nineteenth century when phrenologists, led by Franz Joseph Gall and J. G. Spurzheim (1810–1819), declared that the brain was organized around some 35 specific functions

(Figure 1.1). These functions, which ranged from cognitive basics such as language and color perception to more ephemeral capacities such as hope and self-esteem, were thought to be supported by specific brain regions. Moreover, if a person used one of the faculties with greater frequency than the others, the brain representation of that area grew. According to the phrenologists, this increase in local brain size would cause a

Figure 1.1 Left: Franz Joseph Gall. One of the founders of phrenology in the early nineteenth century. **Right:** The right hemisphere of the brain, from Gall and Spurzheim in 1810.

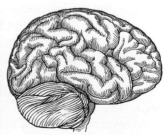

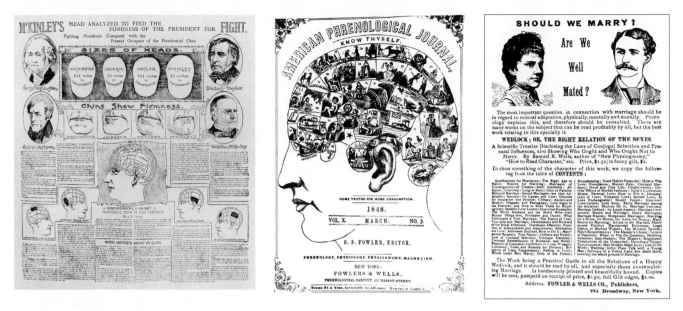

Figure 1.2 **Left:** An analysis of Presidents Washington, Jackson, Taylor, and McKinley by Jessie A. Fowler, from the *Phrenological Journal,* June 1898. **Center:** The phrenological map of personal characteristics on the skull, from the *American Phrenological Journal,* 1850. **Right:** Fowler and Wells Company publication on marriage compatibility in connection with phrenology (1888).

bump in the overlying skull. Logically, then, Gall and his colleagues believed a careful analysis of the skull could go a long way in describing the personality of the person inside the skull. He called this technique *anatomical personology* (Figure 1.2).

Gall, an Austrian physician and neuroanatomist, was not a scientist in the sense that he did not test his ideas. The best part of his life's efforts was to direct attention to the cerebral cortex, particularly to its surface, and to emphasize the idea that different brain functions are localized to discrete brain regions.

The experimental physiologist Pierre Flourens challenged Gall's localizationist view (Figure 1.3). A large group of people rejected the idea that specific processes such as language and memory were localized within circumscribed brain regions, and Flourens became their champion. He studied animals, especially birds, and discovered that brain lesions in particular brain areas did not cause certain deficits in behavior. No matter where he made a lesion in the brain, the bird recovered. He developed the notion that the whole brain participated in behavior, a view later known as the *aggregate field*. In 1824 Flourens wrote, "All sensations, all perceptions, and all volitions occupy the same seat in these (cerebral) organs. The faculty of sensation, percept and volition is then essentially one faculty."

Work on the European continent and in England helped to swing the notion back to the localizationist view. In England, for example, the neurologist John

Hughlings Jackson (Figure 1.4) began to publish his observations on the behavior of persons with brain damage. One of the key features of Jackson's writings was the incorporation of suggestions for experiments to test his observations. He noticed, for example, that during the start of their seizures, some epileptic patients moved in such characteristic ways that the seizure appeared to be stimulating a set map of the body in the brain; hence, clonic and tonic jerks in muscles, produced by the abnormal epileptic firings of neurons in the brain, progressed in an orderly way from one body part to another. This phenomenon led him to propose a

Figure 1.3 **Left:** Pierre Jean Marie Flourens (1794–1867) who supported the idea later termed the *aggregate field*. **Right:** The position described by Flourens of the pigeon deprived of its cerebral hemispheres.

Figure 1.4 John Hughlings Jackson, an English neurologist who was one of the first to recognize the localizationist view.

topographic organization in the cerebral cortex: In this view, a map of the body was represented in a particular cortical area. Jackson was one of the first to realize this essential feature of brain organization.

Although Jackson was also the first to observe that lesions on the right side of the brain affect visual-spatial processes more than do lesions on the left side, he did not maintain that specific parts of the right side of the brain were solely committed to this important human cognitive function. Jackson, being an observant clinical neurologist, noticed that it was rare for a patient to totally lose a function. For example, most people who lost their capacity to speak following a cerebral stroke could

still say some words. Patients unable to direct their hands voluntarily to specific places on their bodies could still easily scratch those places if they itched. When Jackson made these observations, he concluded that many regions of the brain contributed to a given behavior. Meanwhile, in France, perhaps the most famous neurological case in history was being reported by Paul Broca (Figure 1.5). In 1861 he treated a man who had suffered a stroke; the patient could understand language but could not speak. Consistent with Jackson's observations though, the patient could utter something—the sound "tan." Such patients also can usually speak automatically, so while they might say, "Tan, tan, tan . . ." in response to the question, "Who are you?," they might easily count from one to ten in normal fashion.

The exact part of the brain that was damaged in Broca's patient was the left frontal lobe. It has come to be called *Broca's area*. The impact of this finding was huge. Here was a specific aspect of language that was impaired by a specific lesion. This theme was picked up by the German neurologist Carl Wernicke. In 1876, when he was only 26 years old, he reported a stroke victim who could talk quite freely, unlike Broca's patient, but what he said made little sense. He also could not understand spoken or written language. Wernicke's patient had a lesion in a more posterior region of the left hemisphere, an area in and around where the temporal and parietal lobes meet. Today, these differences in how the brain responds to focal disease are well known. Every

Figure 1.5 **Left:** Pierre Paul Broca. **Right:** The connections between the speech centers from Wernicke's article on aphasia. B = Broca's area of motor speech; A = the sensory speech center of Wernicke; Pc = area concerned with language.

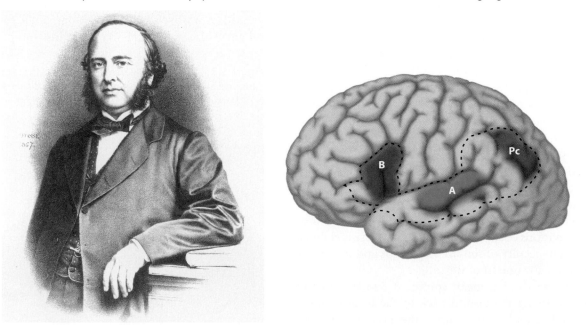

Figure 1.6 **Left:** Physiologist and anatomist Gustav Theodor Fritsch (1838–1907). **Center:** Professor of Psychiatry Eduard Hitzig (1838–1927). **Right:** The original illustration of the dog's cortex by Fritsch and Hitzig. The placement of symbols on the brain indicates areas that were stimulated, and the legend describes the bodily responses. Æ = neck muscle twitching; + = foreleg abduction; † = foreleg flexion; # = rear leg movement; x = facial twitching.

neurologist in every community hospital knows these things. But a little over a hundred years ago, Broca's and Wernicke's discoveries were earth-shattering. Philosophers, physicians, and early psychologists zeroed in on a startling point: Focal disease causes specific deficits. In those days investigators were limited in their ability to identify a patient's lesion. Physicians could observe the site of injury, for example, a penetrating head wound from a bullet, or they had to wait for the patient to die in order to determine the site of the brain lesion. The latter might take months or years, and usually was not possible: The physician would lose track of the patient after he or she recovered, and when the patient eventually died, the physician was not informed and thus could not examine the brain to correlate brain damage with the person's behavioral deficit(s). Today, the site of brain injury can be determined in a few minutes with imaging methods that scan the living brain and produce a picture. We learn about these techniques as we progress through this book. (As an interesting historical footnote, the brain of Broca's famous patient has been preserved. Recent scanning of the brain revealed the patient's lesion to be much larger than what Broca had originally described.)

As is so often the case, the study of humans leads to questions for those who work on animal models. Shortly after Broca's discovery, the German physiologists Gustav Fritsch and Eduard Hitzig electrically stimulated discrete parts of a dog brain and observed that this stimulation produced characteristic movements in the dog (Figure 1.6). This discovery led neuoanatomists to a closer analysis of the cerebral cortex and its cellular organization; they wanted support for their ideas about the importance of local regions. Because these regions performed different functions, it followed that they ought to look different at the cellular level.

Following this logic, German neuroanatomists began to analyze the brain by using microscopic methods to view the cell types in different brain regions. Per-

haps the most famous of the group was Korbinian Brodmann, who analyzed the cellular organization of the cortex and characterized fifty-two distinct regions (Figure 1.7). Brodmann used tissue stains, such as the one developed by Franz Nissl, that permitted him to visualize the different cell types in different brain regions. How cells differed between brain regions was called *cytoarchitectonics,* or cellular architecture. Soon, many now-famous anatomists, including Oskar Vogt, Vladimir Betz, Theodor Meynert, Constantin von Economo, Gerhardt von Bonin, and Percival Bailey, contributed to this work and several subdivided the cortex even further than Brodmann did. To a large extent, these investigators discovered that various cytoarchitectonically described brain areas do indeed represent functionally distinct brain regions. For example, Brodmann first distinguished between area 17 and area 18— a distinction that has proved correct. The characterization of the primary visual area of the cortex, area 17, as distinct from surrounding area 18 remarkably demonstrates the power of the cytoarchitectonic approach, as we discover in Chapter 4.

Figure 1.7 The fifty-two distinct areas described by Brodmann based on cell structure and arrangement. Adapted from Brodmann (1909).

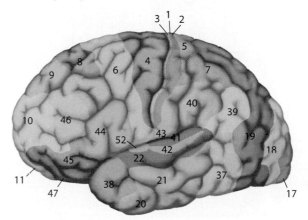

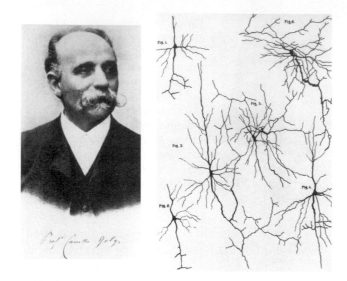

Figure 1.8 Left: Camillo Golgi (1843–1926), co-winner of the Nobel Prize in 1906. **Right:** Golgi's drawings of different types of ganglion cells in dog and cat.

Yet, the truly huge revolution in our understanding of the nervous system was happening down south, in Italy and Spain. There, an intense struggle was going on between two brilliant neuroanatomists. Oddly, it was the work of one that led to the insights of the other. Camillo Golgi, an Italian, developed a stain that impregnated individual neurons with silver (Figure 1.8). This permitted full visualization of single neurons. Using Golgi's method, Santiago Ramón y Cajal, a Spaniard, went on to find that, contrary to the view of Golgi and others, the neurons were discrete entities (Figure 1.9).

Figure 1.9 Left: Santiago Ramón y Cajal (1852–1934), co-winner of the Nobel Prize in 1906. **Right:** Cajal's drawing of the afferent inflow to the mammalian cortex.

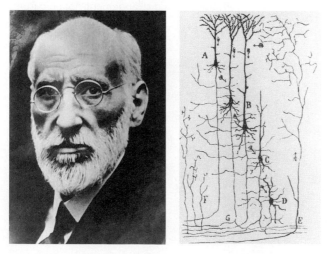

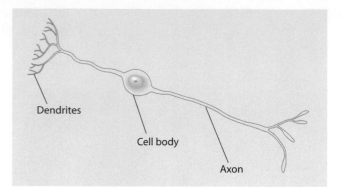

Figure 1.10 A biopolar retinal cell.

Golgi had believed that the whole brain was a syncytium, or a continuous mass of tissue that shares a common cytoplasm! Cajal extended his findings and was the first to identify not only the unitary nature of neurons but also their transmission of electrical information in only one direction, from the dendrites down to the axonal tip (Figure 1.10).

Many truly gifted scientists were involved in the early history of the neuron doctrine. For example, Johannes Evangelista Purkinje, a Czech trained in German-controlled Prague who had to travel to Poland to get a university position (Figure 1.11), not only described the first nerve cell in the nervous system, but also invented the stroboscope, described common visual phenomena, and made a host of other major discoveries.

Even Sigmund Freud got into the neuron act (Figure 1.12). As a young man he studied microscopic anatomy with the great German anatomist Ernst Brücke. Freud even wrote an essay about his subsequent and independent work with crayfish. Indeed, some of Freud's biographers suggest that he, too, had come up with the idea of the neuron as a separate and distinct physiological unit.

Hermann von Helmholtz, perhaps one of the most famous scientists of all time, also contributed to the early study of the nervous system (Figure 1.13). He was the first to suggest that invertebrates would be good models for vertebrate brain mechanisms. This was the same Helmholtz who went on to make major contributions to physics, medicine, and psychology.

The phenomenon of the famous scientist making significant contributions to several distinct fields may be a thing of the past. Not that that sort of thing does not happen today; it is just not easily recognized. Science today is an enormous enterprise, and each subdiscipline has its own cadre of heroes and villains. These guardians of a subject are loath to let a stranger enter into their debates.

Figure 1.11 Left: Johannes Evangelista Purkinje described the first nerve cell in the nervous system. **Right:** A Purkinje cell of the cerebellum.

Dendrites

Cell body

Axon

Figure 1.12 Left: Sigmund Freud (1856–1939). **Right:** From his work with crayfish, Freud published this illustration as an example of anastomosis of nerve fibers, a concept disproved by Cajal.

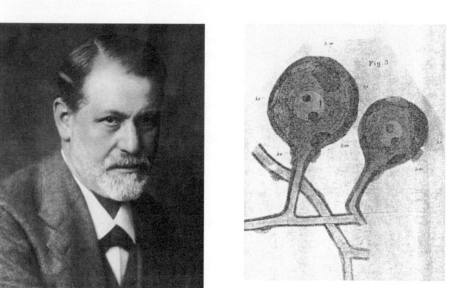

Figure 1.13 Left: Hermann Ludwig von Helmholtz (1821–94). **Right:** Helmholtz's apparatus for measuring the velocity of nerve conduction.

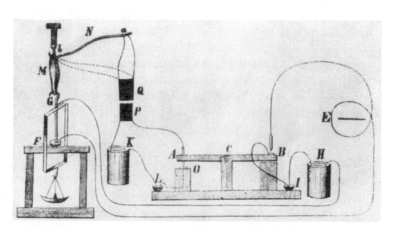

MILESTONES IN COGNITIVE NEUROSCIENCE

An Interview with Mitchell Glickstein, Ph. D.
Dr. Glickstein is a professor of Neuroanatomy and Neuroscience at University College, London. He has written extensively on the history of neuroscience.

Authors: You have taken on the task of studying a variety of issues in neuroscience from a historical point of view. What motivated this interest?

MG: Two things. One was my undergraduate education at the University of Chicago, a Baptist organization where a Jewish faculty taught Catholicism to an atheist student body. There were no textbooks (or almost none), only a syllabus of original readings. In history, for example, we read Lenin and Martov on the Russian revolution. In Chemistry we read Lavoisier. I always thought that the people who made up new ideas could teach them more effectively than textbook writers. The second influence was Harry Patton's lectures to the medical students at the University of Washington. He taught reflexes brilliantly—experiment by experiment. After his lectures you understood that the shortest pathway for the knee jerk involved only a single synapse, but the evidence that led up to that conclusion was made brilliantly clear. Patton taught not just what we know, but more importantly, how we know.

Authors: You are now caught in the modern world of textbooks, TV, magazines, and frequent conferences. All of these give rise to an image of what the important issues are in neuroscience and how they came to be. Are you suggesting that investigation of original papers and the history of ideas gives rise to a different interpretation of the present than the one most people know? If so could you give an example?

MG: There is so much to say.... For starters, consider Otto Loewi's experiment on "Vagusstoff." At the time Loewi did his critical experiment, there was the suspicion that nerves could activate muscles or other nerves by releasing a small amount of chemical substance—but no proof. Loewi set up a simple experiment in his own home after having an idea while sleeping. It was known at that time that vertebrate hearts, from frogs and even mammals, can continue to beat if removed from the body and placed in a suitable solution. Al-though hearts have a nerve supply, they can beat even when the supply is cut off. The largest of the autonomic nerves, the vagus, provides the innervation to the heart and causes slowing of the heart beat. If the vagus nerve is stimulated electrically, the heart rate slows and the force of the beat decreases. All of these facts were well known in Loewi's time. What was not known was *how* the vagus acted. Loewi stimulated a frog nerve-heart preparation at a high rate, causing the heart rate to slow. He collected the fluid from within the heart just after the electrical stimulation. He then injected it into the same heart—or a second heart—and it produced the same effect of slowing the heart rate and decreasing the pressure. When fluid was removed when the vagus had not been previously stimulated, there was no effect on the same heart or the second heart. Loewi concluded that something must have been released when the vagus nerve was stimulated, and it was that chemical that caused the slowing and decrease in force of the beat. He named it provisionally *vagusstoff,* meaning literally "vagus material." Some years later Loewi and others demonstrated that the substance was the neurotransmitter acetylcholine. Loewi at first believed that the vagusstoff—acetylcholine—was specific. Sir Henry Dale, Walter Feldberg (a student of Loewi's), and Marthe Vogt (Cecile and Otto's daughter) demonstrated that acetylcholine is also a transmitter at voluntary nerve-muscle junctions.

Consider self-observation. Wollaston (1824) described his own transient hemianopia (partial visual loss) and the more permanent hemianopia of two acquaintances, when the concept did not exist, and his description was picked up by the Boston Medical and Surgical Intelligencer as a curiosity (after which they described a boy in Philadelphia who saw a candle flame upside down!). Wollaston was one of those eighteenth-century English geniuses, working at a time when people could make contributions to several sci-

Shepherd (1992) recounted the fascinating story of Camillo Golgi and contrasted it with Cajal's. Born near Milan, Golgi, the son of a physician, received his medical degree at the age of 22 from the University of Pavia in Italy, yet he was outside the mainstream of research in Germany's great universities—a fact that haunted his career. Still, Pavia produced many spectacular scientists, like the physicist Alessandro Volta, Christopher Columbus, and a host of great biologists. Among this august group, Golgi was a well-trained physician and scientist.

ences. He had invented a kind of prism for optical work, and also developed a technique for pulling very fine wires for use in precision instruments. Prior to Wollaston's work, horse hairs had been used. Wollaston made the simplest of self-observations. He noted that he sometimes had an attack of partial loss of vision. The visual loss was the same in both eyes; half of the visual field could not be seen. Always it was the same half of the visual scene in both eyes. Wollaston gives this example: He went to see his friend—called Jackson—and looked at the name plate on Jackson's door. He said that he saw only the word "son." He was blind in the left half of the visual field in each eye. Wollaston's transient half-blindness (now called *hemianopia,* literally "half-not-seeing") was transitory, but he knew of two other individuals with the same half-blindness that was permanent. Both sorts of hemianopia are now well known to physicians. Sir Isaac Newton in his text on optics had speculated that each of the optic nerves divided in such a way that the optic nerve linking the left side of each retina went to the left side of the brain, and the optic nerve from the right went to the right side of the brain. The implications of Newton's anatomical suggestions had never been recognized, and Wollaston did not appear to be aware of them. His observation was thought to be a rare and unusual example of a visual disturbance. It was not for another 70 years that the two insights were fully integrated. Then Newton's speculations about the course of optic nerve fibers were verified, and physicians began to recognize the fact that hemianopia was all too common, and related to the underlying anatomy.

Consider the transcendent and international nature of science. It did not involve only Germans in the nineteenth century. It was a little guy, Cajal, from a backward country who set neuroanatomy on the right course for a hundred years.

These are a few of the examples of why I use historical sources. They help to get around the obscenity of 35-year-olds with five postdoctoral degrees who are brilliant at the last 5 years of research, and a bit hazy on the previous 5, and know nothing about how all of what we know came to be known. If you want to teach about science, it is not a bad choice to teach how we got here.

Authors: Surely all of that is true and more. For example, would you comment on Cajal's enunciation of the neuron doctrine? While he is largely credited as the founder, is it not really the case that the idea was in the air and many people were talking about it at the time? While Cajal was unquestionably a brilliant anatomist, perhaps the most brilliant to ever live, did he not simply crystallize and successfully market the idea of the time?

MG: Cajal was more than that. You appreciate Cajal more if you read his contemporaries (Golgi, Dogiel, Kölliker). When Cajal began his work, the dominant view was of a rather vague syncytium. Golgi thought there was an anastomosis between the axon collaterals and the brain was a fused network. I recently gave a lecture on Cajal at the Cajal Institute—a bold venture. I focused on Cajal's visit to England in 1894. I had all the documents relating to his invitation, his acceptance, and his honorary degree at Cambridge. (He was arrested briefly in Cambridge, a delightful side episode.) The reason I spent a day at the Institute was to look into a particular issue—the discovery of dendritic spines. Golgi certainly saw them, but left them out of his figures. Kölliker solemnly reviewed the question in his (1896) textbook, and concluded that the spines were an artifact. Cajal wrote a brilliant paper in which he raised the question of why should dendrites show them but not axons? Why could the Golgi method and the (mercury-based) variants show them? But to prove their validity, he said that they had to be revealed by a totally independent method. He fiddled with the methylene blue method, and got it to impregnate (to stain) as well as the Golgi method did. I went to Madrid to look at his drawings. As Cajal said, "They are there with methylene blue staining; they are really there. The matter is over." There were others. Waldeyer, for example, coined the term *neuron,* but contributed little else. I agree with Cajal who said of Waldeyer that what he had done was "…to publish my research in a weekly medical journal." How many textbooks written 100 years ago are still useful today?

Authors: Well, only time will tell if this one joins those ranks. I thank you

---

While his career started off with great promise, Golgi was forced, out of financial necessity, to take a job outside of Pavia, in the town of Abbiategrasso, where he became the resident physician at the Home for the Incurables. In such circumstances, it was highly unlikely that Golgi would continue his scientific life. But he persevered, and working by the candlelight in his kitchen, he developed the most famous cell stain in the history of the world. Golgi discovered the silver method for staining neurons—*la reazione negra,* the "black reaction."

MILESTONES IN COGNITIVE NEUROSCIENCE

Interlude

In textbook writing, authors use broad strokes to communicate milestones that have become important to our thinking over a long period of time. It would be folly, however, not to alert the reader to the complex and intriguing cultural, intellectual, and personal setting. The problems that besieged the world's first scientists remain today in full glory. Issues of authorship, ego, funding, and credit are all integral to the fabric of intellectual life. Much as teenagers never imagine that their parents once had the same interests and desires as they do, novitiates in science believe they are tackling new issues for the first time in human history. Gordon Shepherd (1992), in his riveting account *Foundations of the Neuron Doctrine,* detailed the variety of forces at work on the figures we now feature in our brief history.

Shepherd noted how the explosion of research on the nervous system started in the eighteenth century as part of the intense activity swirling around the birth of modern science. As examples, Robert Fulton invented the steam engine in 1807, and Hans Christian Øersted discovered electromagnetism. Of more interest to our concerns that, Leopoldo Nobili, an Italian physicist, invented a precursor to the galvanometer—a device that laid the foundation for studying electrical currents in living tissue. It had been many years before, in 1674, when Anton van Leeuwenhoek in Holland used a primitive microscope to view animal tissue (Figure A). One of his first observations was of a cross section of a cow's nerve in which he noted "very minute vessels." This observation was consistent with René Descartes's idea that nerves contained fluid or "spirits," and these spirits were responsible for the flow of sensory and motor information in the body (Figure B). To go farther, however, this revolutionary work would have to overcome the problems with early microscopes, not the least of which was the quality of glass used in the lens. Chromatic aberrations made them useless at higher magnification. It was not until lens makers solved this problem that microscopic anatomy again took center stage in the history of biology.

Figure A: Left: Anton van Leeuwenhoek. **Right:** One of the original microscopes used by Leeuwenhoek, which is composed of two brass plates holding the lens.

Figure B: Portrait of René Descartes by Frans Hals.

The Golgi stain became famous, as did Golgi himself. His intense interest in disease led him to several discoveries in pathobiology, and eventually he was recruited back to Pavia to be a professor. Still, his writings were not widely known outside of Italy, so he translated them, publishing them in the *Italian Archives of Biology*—which, oddly, were written in French. Golgi's reputation grew, and in 1906 he was awarded the Nobel Prize jointly with Cajal.

Meanwhile, Cajal was the rambunctious son of another physician. It was not until Cajal's ambitious father started tutoring him at home that he developed in interest in biology. From a complex childhood, Cajal emerged as what some call the "father of modern neuroscience." He is credited as the first to articulate fully the neuron doctrine.

The irony in the story, as we already mentioned, is that Cajal made many of his discoveries as a result of the Golgi stain. He first saw the stain in the Madrid home of a colleague, Don Luis Simarro, who had learned the technique while attending a meeting in Paris. Cajal said it was there, in Simarro's home laboratory—not unlike the laboratory where Golgi invented the stain—that he saw for the first time "the famous sections of the brain impregnated by the silver method of the Savant of Pavia."

Cajal's response to seeing the stain remains fascinating (translated by Sherrington, 1935):

Against a clear background stood black threadlets, some slender and smooth, some thick and thorny, in a pattern punctuated by small dense spots, stellate or fusiform. All was sharp as a sketch with Chinese ink on transparent Japanese paper. And to think that that was the same tissue which stained with carmine or logwood left the eye in a tangled thicket where sight may stare and grope for ever fruitlessly, baffled in its effort to unravel confusion and lost forever in a twilit doubt. Here, on the contrary, all was clear and plain as a diagram. A look was enough. Dumbfounded, I could not take my eye from the microscope.

And yet many years later, the scene at the Nobel Prize ceremony in Stockholm was ugly. Golgi came off as a huge egotist, set in his ways, and unwilling to acknowledge Cajal's discoveries, which by that time had established the neuron doctrine. Both were using the same stain, both were using the same microscopes, both were studying the same tissue. One saw the answer, one did not. Golgi continued to see his beloved syncytium of neurons as a single unit, whereas Cajal saw each neuron as the independent unit it has proved to be.

THE TWENTIETH CENTURY

Some scientists are chagrined to learn that the results of this early research of Cajal and others confused scientists in the first half of the twentieth century. All the work, especially when viewed in hindsight, argued for the importance of single neurons. Knowing how the nervous system worked requires understanding how single neurons interact and behave, just like understanding proteins requires a knowledge of how the constituent amino acids are organized. The vagaries of syncytial processes, of nerve nets, and of holistic processes were not needed. The nervous system is not a big blob; it is built from discrete units. If we can figure out how these units work, and describe the laws and principles of their interaction, then the problem of how the brain enables mind can be addressed, and eventually solved.

This, of course, is the ideal view; namely, that by knowing all the elements of a system we can figure out the system. Yet, the human brain is composed of billions of neurons and to think that we need to know the actions of all of them to figure out how the brain works

would be preposterous. Indeed, it took a tremendous effort to figure out how the stomatogastric ganglion of the lobster, with eight neurons, produced rhythmic activity. Advances are made by working at different levels of organization, the backbone strategy in cognitive neuroscience. By knowing what behavior is actually produced, we need not know all the possible interactions that occur with underlying elements. In this manner a problem becomes constrained and solvable. But that was not the dominant question of the early twentieth century. Even though the renowned British physiologist Sir Charles Sherrington pursued vigorously the neuron's behavior as a unit, and indeed coined the term *synapse* to describe the junction between two neurons, the scientists working on "larger" issues of brain and behavior remained committed to the belief of holistic processes. It took time for the new ideas to be widely accepted, especially when major figures of early brain science were so divided in their views. In addition, many early views were actually quite reasonable given the state of scientific knowledge at the time. Take, for example, the ideas of Broca's contemporaries, like Pierre Marie. While Broca was selling the importance of localized function, Marie was demonstrating the variability in cortical localization. Marie reported that only half of his patients displayed speech impediments when lesions were localized to the third frontal convolution of the left cerebral hemisphere—Broca's area. He also noted that several patients with lesions sparing this same area had Broca-like aphasia. Marie was both right and wrong. There is great variation in the human brain, but by looking at the underlying structure, he may well have discovered that the critical brain area was simply shifted from one place to another during development. The notion of localization, therefore, is not really challenged with the sort of observation that Marie offered.

Still, some people simply refuse to see that understanding single neuronal function or small areas of the brain can explain how the brain works. That view is as prevalent today as it was early in this century. Everybody concerned with the matter has a favorite example of the seemingly deep contradictions in this logic. During Broca's time, a German professor of physiology named Friedrich Goltz was prancing his dog around at scientific meetings (Figure 1.14). Goltz had removed large parts of the dog's cortex, and although some impairments were noted, the dog was remarkably functional. Though it turned out that the dog's lesion was smaller than claimed, the example is not uncommon. With brain-damaged humans it is common to be surprised by a patient's lack of symptoms, given the extent of lesion depicted on a brain scan.

Still, one major advance had been made. By the beginning of the twentieth century, almost everyone was willing to grant that some localization of function occurs in the cerebral cortex. Even Goltz noticed substantive differences in his animals when the occipital lobe was removed compared with when the motor cortex was removed. The critics were now claiming that it was impossible to localize "higher cortical functions" like thinking and memory, a modification of the original view that no localization of function existed in the brain. This reservation combined with the insight first articulated by Hughlings Jackson; namely, one has to distinguish between evidence for localization of *symptoms* versus the idea of localization of *function*. By this, Jackson meant that while a brain lesion might produce a bizarre symptom, it did not follow that the injured area was specialized for only that function. The lesion might well affect other structures in the brain because the lesion might have damaged neurons connected to other regions. Jackson's distinction was also an early warning that behaviors were constellations of independent activities, not a single whole unit. This distinction is crucial when analyzing modern brain imaging data, as we shall see.

Stanley Finger (1994), in his historic account *Origins of Neuroscience* of the events surrounding this key issue, provided telling quotes from antilocalizationists. At the turn of the century a broad-based movement was absorbed with gestalt processes, the idea that the whole is different from the sum of the parts. One of the movement's members, the great French biologist Claude Bernard, wrote in 1855:

Figure 1.14 **Left:** Friedrich Leopold Goltz (1834–1902). **Center:** The dog Goltz showed to the International Medical Congress in 1881. **Right:** The brain of the dog from which Goltz removed a section of cortex.

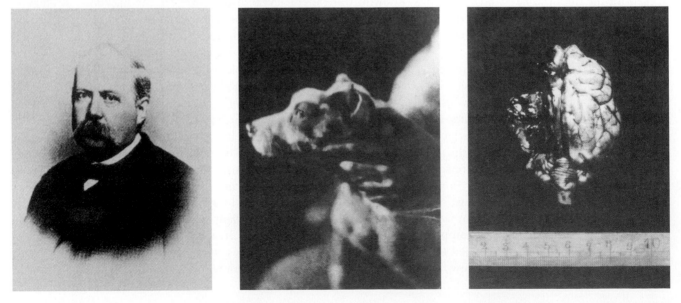

Figure 1.15   Left: Sir Henry Head and W. H. R. Rivers at St. John's College in Cambridge (1903). Head sectioned a branch of his own radial nerve and had Rivers perform experiments on his sensory loss. **Right:** Quote from Sir Henry Head.

If it is possible to dissect all the parts of the body, to isolate them in order to study them in their structure, form and connections it is not the same in life, where all parts cooperate at the same time in a common aim. An organ does not live on its own, one could often say it did not exist anatomically, as the boundary established is sometimes purely arbitrary. What lives, what exists, is the whole, and if one studies all the parts of any mechanisms separately, one does not know the way they work. In the same way, anatomically, we take the organism apart, but we cannot grasp the whole. This whole can only be seen when the organs are in motion.

This sort of thinking motivated much of the later work of Constantin von Manakow and Sir Henry Head, both of whom were neurologists (Figure 1.15). Monakow is credited with the concept of *diaschisis,* the idea that damage to one part of the brain can create problems for another, a fact that has been demonstrated time and time again. Head, who worked in London, also saw the brain as a dynamic system, interconnected and mutable. When there was injury, Head believed that the behavior resulting from a lesion was due to the whole system being out of whack. He believed that a lesioned brain was like a new system, not an old system with one part missing. To quote Head: "So far as the loss of function or negative manifestations are concerned, this response does not reveal the elements out of which the original form of behavior was composed. . . . It is a new condition, the consequence of fresh readjustment of the organism as a whole to the factors at work at the particular functional level disturbed by the local lesions."

Despite their loss of this intellectual battle, these bright scientists did formulate transcendent arguments.

The points raised by the holistic team and the reasons they put forth still have merit. With the appearance of Karl Lashley, the great experimental psychologist, the importance of single neurons and localized function was cast in doubt. His studies and writings were based on a strong academic context, bolstered by his experimental data. Lashley's point was that lesions made throughout the brain did not appear to create problems in learning or performing a task. Lashley's animal of choice was the rat, and he used a maze-learning task almost exclusively. Since then, we have learned that Lashley's conclusions contain some weaknesses. For example, the maze-learning tasks require so many modalities, which in turn involve so much of the brain, that no single lesion could produce a deficit in learning. If an animal had learned a maze task using proprioceptive and visual information, a lesion to the visual system or to the proprioceptive system might not be sufficient to create a deficit, as the other modality could compensate for the lesion. Following this logic, if the lesions made were very large and included all modalities, then deficits ought to be seen. Indeed, this is also what Lashley found. Nonetheless, the message of the holistic school still holds some valid lessons. The pendulum gradually swung back to the localizationist view as neurophysiological research began to unearth certain regularities in the organization of the cerebral cortex. Starting in the 1930s, Clinton Woolsey, Philip Bard, and others began to discover motor and sensory "maps" in the brain. Indeed, it became clear that each modality had more than one of these maps. In the 1970s and 1980s, we learned the multiple maps exist in each sensory modality, reaching a pinnacle of complexity in the primate visual system. To date, more than thirty maps

MILESTONES IN COGNITIVE NEUROSCIENCE

Female Historical Figures in Neuroscience

As in most scientific fields, until relatively recent years few women have been recognized for their contributions to neuroscience. Although it is easy to draw the conclusion that this is because of the lack of participation by women, an all too frequent alternative is that women have been involved, but have not been fully credited for their work. Consider the case of the microelectrode. The microelectrode is an important tool in electrophysiological studies today and is used to deliver discrete electrical or chemical stimulation to a cell and to record the electrical activity from within individual nerve and muscle cells. Ralph Gerard won the Nobel Prize in the 1950s, fully credited with discovery of the microelectrode among many other accomplishments. However, two notable women made significant contributions to the microelectrode's discovery, though they were not formally recognized.

In 1902, Ida Hyde (1854–1945) was the first woman to be elected to the American Physiological Society; she remained the only woman in the society until 1914. She was the first woman to be awarded a doctorate in physiology from a German university (University of Heidelberg) and to do research at Harvard Medical School. She invented the first microelectrode for intracellular work with lower organisms by combining instruments used by F. H. Pratt (1917) and M. A. Barber (1912). Hyde constructed a salt solution–filled electrode of very small diameter (3 microns or so) and connected it to a small column of mercury whose level could be altered by the introduction of varying amounts of positive or negative electrical current. This mercury in turn could force the salt solution toward or away from the tip of the capillary and also transmit electrical stimuli to the cell through the salt solution. In 1921, using this method, Hyde provided the first evidence that the re-cently discovered principle of all-or-nothing contraction was not universally true for all contractile cells. The microelectrode was subsequently lost during the war and had to be reinvented.

The first report that a microelectrode had been used to record resting potentials from the membranes of a frog muscle was published in 1942 by Judith Graham Pool (1917–1975), G. R. Carlson, and Ralph Gerard. Their electrodes (2–3 microns in diameter) were also bent capillary tubes drawn out to a tip and filled with an isotonic salt solution of potassium chloride that allowed Graham and Gerard to record resting potentials and action potentials evoked with their electrode. Although Gerard was fully credited with the microelectrode discovery because he decreased the diameter to 0.25 micron, it appears that, at the least, Graham was instrumental in its development, and according to her, she actually invented it without any credit for her achievement.

In addition to being unrecognized for their work, women have also been overshadowed by similar work done by their male contemporaries, as is exemplified by single nerve cell recording studies. Though most neuroscience textbooks discuss the work of Hodgkin and Huxley on the giant axon of the squid, a second scientist who is less recognized, Angelique Arvanitaki, made significant contributions to the study of the single neuron.

By the 1940s, neurobiologists had learned to penetrate electrically active cells with microelectrodes and wanted to study the properties of nerves from within a single cell. Although vertebrate nerves are minute and housed in a brain and nervous system, this is not true of the large nerve cells of certain invertebrates. Angelique Arvanitaki (1939) developed the ganglion preparation

---

of visual information have been found in the primate brain. Even more spectacular are the discoveries that very localized areas in the brain, such as the middle temporal area, are highly specialized for the processing of visual motion information. In short, neuroscience is continuing to reveal the startling complexity and specialization of the cerebral cortex.

Stephen Kosslyn, one of the founders of cognitive neuroscience, tidily summarized the conflict between the localizationists and holists (Kosslyn and Andersen, 1992):

The mistake of early localizationists is that they tried to map behaviors and perceptions into single locations in the cortex. Any particular behavior or perception is pro-

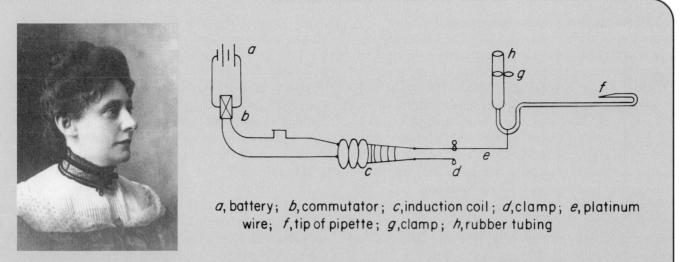

a, battery; *b*, commutator; *c*, induction coil; *d*, clamp; *e*, platinum wire; *f*, tip of pipette; *g*, clamp; *h*, rubber tubing

Left: Ida Hyde (1854–1945). The first woman elected to the American Physiological Society, 1902. **Right:** Ida Hyde's microelectrode (1921).

of large identifiable nerves in the snails *Aplysia* (sea hare) and *Helix* (land snail). Arvanitaki also discovered that in low-calcium solutions, isolated nerve fibers of the cuttlefish *Sepia* (a relative of the octopus) produced regular electrical oscillations that periodically became larger and larger, until from time to time the nerve fired a series of action potentials. She was the first to demonstrate that spontaneous, rhythmically recurring activity could be an inherent property of a single nerve without the requirement of an entire neuronal circuit to generate it. Also, she found that when two or more nerves run close together, the activity in one nerve can entrain the activity in its neighbor. Hodgkin and Huxley won the 1963 Nobel Prize in Physiology and Medicine for analyzing the ionic basis of the action potential in the squid axon and are recognized in most neuroscience textbooks, overshadowing the significant contributions to this area of study by Arvanitaki.

Since Brenda Milner's memory work in the 1960s, many women in the numerous areas of neuroscience have been recognized as being leading scientists in their field: Patricia Goldman-Rakic (neurophysiology and neuroanatomy of frontal cortex)—past president of the Society for Neuroscience; Margaret Livingstone (visual neurophysiology); Leslie Ungerleider (cortical functional neuroimaging); Carol Colby (vision and the parietal cortex); Mary Hatten (developmental cellular neurophysiology); Carla Shatz (visual neurophysiology)—past president of the Society for Neuroscience; Christine Nussellin-Volhard (molecular neurophysiology); and perhaps most well-recognized, Rita Levi-Montalcini, the neurobiologist who shared the 1986 Nobel Prize in Medicine for the discovery of nerve growth factor. Although the field of neuroscience still contains more male members than females, this inequality is quickly disappearing, as can be seen by the numbers of graduate students pursuing degrees in neuroscience.

duced by many areas, located in various parts of the brain. Thus, the key to resolving the debate is to realize that complex functions such as perception, memory, reasoning, and movement are accomplished by a host of underlying processes that are carried out in a single region of the brain. Indeed, the abilities themselves typically can be accomplished in numerous different ways, which involve different combinations of processes. . . . Any given complex ability, then, is not accomplished by a single part of the brain. So in this sense, the globalists were right. The kinds of functions posited by the phrenologists are not localized to a single brain region. However, simple processes that are recruited to exercise such abilities are localized. So in this sense, the localizationists were right. . . .

THE PSYCHOLOGICAL STORY

While the medical profession was pioneering most early studies of how the brain worked, psychologists began to lay claim that they could measure behavior and indeed study the mind. Until the start of experimental psychological science, the mind had been the province of philosophers, who wondered about the nature of knowledge, about how we come to know things. The philosophers had two main positions: empiricism and rationalism. *Empiricism* is the idea that all knowledge comes from sensory experience. Direct sensory experience produces simple ideas and concepts. When simple ideas interact and become associated with each other, complex ideas and concepts are created in an individual's knowledge system. The British philosophers—from Thomas Hobbes in the seventeenth century, up through John Locke and David Hume to John Stuart Mill in the nineteenth century—all emphasized the role of experience. It is no surprise, then, that a major school or experimental psychology arose from this associationist view.

One of the first scientists to believe in associationism was Hermann Ebbinghaus. In the late 1800s he decided that complex processes like memory could be measured and analyzed. He had taken his lead from the great psychophysicists Gustav Fechner and E. H. Weber, who were hard at work relating the physical properties of things, like light and sound, to the psychological experiences they produce in the observer. These measurements were rigorous and reproducible. Ebbinghaus was one of the first to understand that one could also measure more internal mental processes like memory (see Chapter 7).

Even more influential was Edward Thorndike, whose classic 1911 monograph *Animal Intelligence: An Experimental Study of the Associative Processes in Animals* was written at the turn of the century (Figure 1.16). In this volume, Thorndike articulated his law of effect, which was the first general statement about the nature of associations. In many ways it was so simple. Thorndike simply observed that a response that was followed by a reward would be stamped into the organism as a habitual response. If there was no reward following a response, the response would disappear. Thus, rewards were responsible for providing a mechanism for establishing a more adaptive response. This idea sounds a little like Darwin's natural selection idea and indeed, Thorndike was deeply influenced by Darwin.

And yet the father of associationist thinking in psychology mixed his terminology. *Associationism* is hardly consonant with *nativism* (that is, the idea that many forms of knowledge are built into the organism from birth). Associationism is committed to an idea widely popularized by the American psychologist John B. Watson, who promoted the notion that he could take any baby and turn him or her into anything (Figure 1.17). Learning was the key, he proclaimed, and everybody had the same neural equipment on which learning could build. American psychology was giddy with this idea. Consumed with it, all strong psychology departments in the country were run by people who held this view.

All this hubbub in behaviorist psychology went on despite the well-established position—first articulated by Descartes, Leibniz, Kant, and others—that complexity is built into the organism. Sensory information is merely data on which preexisting mental structures act. This idea, which dominates psychology today, was blithely asserted in that golden age. As the associationists took over, they ran thousands upon thousands of experiments, and thus by volume of activity stole the issue as theirs.

The behaviorists' armor started to crack, however, when gestalt psychologists, working with perceptual phenomena, reported that percepts were best understood in relation to a stimulus's emergent properties. Apparent motion, for instance, was an emergent property of real world stimuli. It existed only as a function of built-in properties of the brain. It was not learned. The gestalt psychologists developed hundreds of demonstrations making similar points.

The true end of the dominance of behaviorism and stimulus-response psychology did not come until the late 1950s. Almost overnight, psychologists began to think in terms of cognition, not behavior. George Miller, who had been a confirmed behaviorist, offered what he calls his "very personal memory" of that event (Figure

Figure 1.16 Edward L. Thorndike.

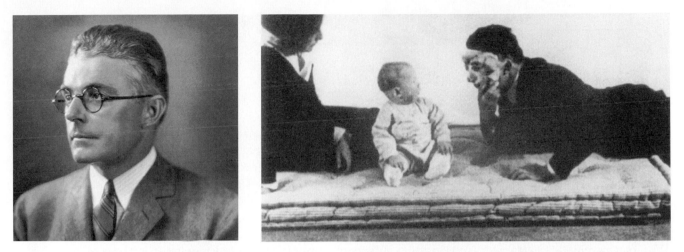

Figure 1.17 **Left:** John B. Watson. **Right:** John B. Watson and "Little Albert" during one of Watson's fear-conditioning experiments.

1.18). Miller placed the revolution in the 1950s. In 1951 he wrote an influential book entitled *Language and Communication* and noted, "The bias is behavioristic . . . ." Eleven years later he wrote another book called *Psychology, the Science of Mental Life*, a title that signals a complete rejection of the idea that psychology should study behavior. As Miller put it, "My cognitive awakening must have occurred in the 1950s."

With a little searching, Miller put the exact date at September 11, 1956, during the Second Symposium on Information Theory, held at the Massachusetts Institute of Technology (MIT). That year had been a rich one for several disciplines. In computer science, Allen Newell and Herbert Simon successfully ran Information Processing Language I, a powerful program that simulated the proof of logic theorems. The computer guru John von Neumann wrote the Silliman Lectures on neural organization. A famous meeting on artificial intelligence was held at Dartmouth College with Marvin Minsky, Claude Shannon (known as the father of information

theory), and many others in attendance.

Big things were also happening in psychology. As a result of World War II, new techniques were being applied to psychology. James Tanner and John Swets applied signal detection, servo theory, and computer technology to the study of perception. (These techniques had been developed, in large part, to help the Defense Department detect submarines.) Miller also wrote his classic paper, "The Magical Number Seven, Plus-or-Minus Two," in which he showed there was a limit on the amount of information that could be apprehended in a brief period of time. Also, the developmental psychologist Jerome Bruner was working on the problem of thinking. While he saw limited utility to associationist ideas in childhood learning, he believed in higher-level processes involved in thinking that were built upon representations and mental maps. Perhaps the most important development, however, was from Noam Chomsky's work (Figure 1.19). A preliminary version of his ideas on syntactic theories was

Figure 1.18 George A. Miller.

Figure 1.19 Noam Chomsky.

MILESTONES IN COGNITIVE NEUROSCIENCE

An Interview with George A. Miller, Ph. D. Dr. Miller is professor emeritus at Princeton University and is one of the founders of modern cognitive science.

Authors: Psychology underwent a revolutionary change in the late fifties. After years of being dominated by behaviorists there was suddenly an interest in cognition. Some say it happened in September 1956. Could you tell us a little about that?

GAM: I once picked September 11, 1956, as an appropriate birthday for cognitive science. It was the date of a meeting at the Massachusetts Institute of Technology when leading cognitivists from computer science, linguistics, and psychology all came together for the first time and began to realize they shared their interest in the human mind. The interest in cognition had been growing for at least a decade, but this was the first time we realized that these separate fields were all parts of a larger whole—even before we knew what to call it.

Authors: Was there a particular set of scientific results that students of the mind were hard pressed to explain in terms of behaviorist principles? Or were people simply becoming bored with those types of explanations?

GAM: There were many such phenomena. For example, linguists found it impossible to describe the phrase structure of a grammatical sentence in terms of a linear sequence of stimuli-response reflexes. Bruner and his collaborators found clear evidence of problem-solving strategies that looked nothing like objective stimuli, responses, or reinforcements, and Simon and Newell were actually able to program a primitive computer to tackle problems the way people did, not by some blind trial-and-error procedure. I could not explain how people could "tune" themselves to discriminate optimally among a particular set of alternative stimuli without talking about subjective expectations. Ulric Neisser pulled together some of those phenomena a few years later in his book *Cognitive Psychology* (1967). But I remember that I was personally impressed by some experiments that seemed to show that a cat's attention could be monitored in terms of the response of the auditory nerve. I think the results later turned out to have been artifactual, but at the time it was exciting to think that something as subjective as attention might be reflected in something as objective as nerve impulses. During the fifties, it became increasingly clear that behavior is simply the evidence, not the subject matter of psychology.

Authors: Interestingly, the term *psychology* has largely been abandoned, even though most universities still have departments of psychology. One hears of *cognitive science,* even though psychology is defined as the "science of mental processes and behavior." Was this both necessary and deliberate for some sociological reason?

GAM: Psychology has been defined many ways. In the nineteenth century it was thought to have three branches, which would translate today into emotion, motivation, and cognition. Behaviorism could deal with emotion and motivation, but the refusal to admit mentalism in any form made it very difficult to give a plausible behavioristic account of cognition. Some psychologists felt that a psychology without cognition was

published as Three Models of Language. Chomsky's effort transformed the study of language virtually overnight. The deep message was that learning theory—which is to say associationism, then heavily championed by B. F. Skinner—could in no way explain how language was learned. The complexity of language was built into the brain, and it ran on rules and principles that transcended all people and all languages. It was universal.

Herbert Simon and Allen Newell also publicly reported their efforts to simulate a cognitive process, presented in the context of linguistic work. A form of simple associationism was up and running once again. Remarkably, on the same day, there was an early attempt to test Donald Hebb's neuropsychological theory of cell assemblies, which is a way of suggesting any set of neurons can learn anything. Recently Hebb's ideas have been greatly advanced by computational neuroscientists. While the field gradually moves toward the importance of built-in and universal neural structures that govern cognitive and perceptual life, there are continuing efforts to demonstrate that the laws of simple association are responsible for our learning about the world. We shall return to this issue in the chapter on evolutionary perspectives.

absurd, and so began a counterrevolution. We quickly discovered allies in other disciplines, particularly in linguistics and artificial intelligence, but also in philosophy and neuroscience. Personally, I was relieved to start collaborating with these new people and their new ideas, and to stop wasting my time explaining what was wrong with behaviorism. As collaboration grew, the need to name this new enterprise grew along with it. Hence, *cognitive science*.

Authors: And now cognitive science is a major force in the study of the mind. Sophisticated models of the mind have been built as the result of experimentation. One of the motivations for the development of cognitive neuroscience was to test these models in a biological system, to test their validity. Now people tend to come to problems with what might be called the *physicist perception* or the *biologist perception*. The physicists look for a few general principles to explain complex processes and that attitude would hope for a few principles for the mind. Biologists more or less give up on this and say the biological creature is a bag of tricks, a Swiss army knife with lots of specialized functions built in. Where do you stand in this debate?

GAM: They are both right. Detailed understanding of specialized functions probably has to come first, before the general principles can become clear. The fact that we cannot intuit those principles in advance doesn't mean that they will never be understood.

Authors: OK, to take a specific example from cognitive science, you are now working on an electronic dictionary which has become a model for how the human lexicon might work in the human brain. Could you tell us a little about that and how it might lead to insight on how our own lexicon works?

GAM: It is difficult to be concise when you are as close to a problem as I am to the problem of lexical knowledge, but let me try to characterize it with an example. Years ago the English philosopher Grice noted that the two sentences "I'm out of petrol" and "There's a garage around the corner" are immediately seen as related by normally intelligent persons. The question is, How do people fill in all the unstated information in such an exchange? One answer has been phrased in terms of spreading excitation in the brain. The first sentence activates the lexical node for "petrol" and the second activates the lexical node for "garage." These activations spread until eventually they intersect on some intermediate lexical node like "car" and so a bridging sentence can be constructed: Cars are supplied with petrol at garages.

When you try to build a system that will actually do this, however, you find that spreading activation results in far too many intersections. It has been estimated that only one-tenth of the intersections resulting from an unguided spread of activity will be appropriate. Clearly, if there is such spreading excitation, the spread is guided somehow. So, what kind of information would a system need—either a brain system or a computer system—in order to be able to constrain the spread of excitation into appropriate channels?

A group of us here at Princeton have been trying to propose an answer to that question in terms of a tightly interconnected network of lexical concepts. We don't think that a brain does it the same way our computer does it, but we are gaining a much deeper appreciation of the problem that the brain must solve. Once we understand that, a cognitive neuroscientist should have a much clearer idea of what to look for.

COGNITIVE NEUROSCIENCE

The term *cognitive neuroscience* was coined in that taxi because by the late 1970s a new mission was clearly required. Neuroscientists were discovering how the cerebral cortex was organized and how it functioned in response to simple stimuli. Specific mechanisms were described, such as those relating to visual perception by David Hubel and Torsten Wiesel at Harvard. They were showing how single neurons in the visual cortex responded in a reliable way to particular forms of visual stimulation. The field had moved beyond the simple lesion method of assessing what perceptual or cognitive disorders might occur after brain damage. Neuroscientists were beginning to build models of how single cells interact to produce percepts. Most psychologists were no longer taking behaviorism seriously as a viable way to explain complex cognition. People like George Miller abandoned their earlier approach, which was totally behavioristic, and tried instead to articulate how language was represented. No longer considered the product of simple learning and associationism, language was a complex construct delivered via the brain. It was utterly biological in origin and instantiation.

The extraordinarily talented David Marr at MIT made a major effort to bridge the gap between brain mechanisms and perception. Marr, who tragically died as a young man, provided a vision of what a cognitive neuroscience might look like. As Kosslyn and Anderson (1992) put it, "At the time, Marr's work was uniquely interdisciplinary and was particularly important because it provided the first rigorous examples of cognitive neuroscience theories . . . ."

Marr stressed the idea that neural computation can be understood at multiple levels by analysis. Philosophers of science had, of course, observed long ago that a single phenomenon can be examined at multiple levels of analysis. When considering psychology, philosophers such as Jerry Fodor distinguished between a functional and physical level; the functional level ascribed roles and purposes to events, and the physical level characterized the electrical and chemical characteristics of those events.

Marr took these earlier analyses several steps further. He posited a hierarchy of levels rooted in the idea that the brain computes. He divided the functional level into two levels, one that characterizes what is computed and another that characterizes how the computation is accomplished (i.e., algorithms), and he showed how these levels related to the lowest one, the level of implementation.

Although bold and fresh, Marr's approach is not quite accurate. Marr's ideas were embraced by cognitive theorists because he suggested that we could understand the cognitive level by reason alone. Theories that purported to explain a mental skill such as language, memory, or attention required deeper analysis, including algorithms to describe how neurophysiological processes produce the cognitive state.

But the idea has not worked out entirely. The distinction between the levels, which is to say between the algorithms and implementation mechanisms of the neurons themselves, has been vague. There is not one kind of neuron in the brain; there are dozens of kinds, each with different properties, each triggered by different neurotransmitters, and so on. Any computational theory, therefore, must be sensitive to the real biology of the nervous system, constrained by how the brain actually works—and it works differently for different functions.

Not that broad generalities on nervous system function do not exist. They do, and they enable scientists to search for specific mechanisms, which has given rise to the burgeoning field of neural network research. Here, scientists build models of how the brain might work and attempt to limit how their networks function by including information from neurophysiology and neuroanatomy.

SUMMARY

By way of summarizing this chapter, we have learned how at least two rich and powerful academic fields have come together to produce yet another field of scientific research, *cognitive neuroscience*. Brain science emerged from the last century and gave us the knowledge that the brain is made up of discrete units—neurons. Cajal brought together the story about the importance of discrete entities, functioning neurons, and how they might interact to produce behavior. At a more general level, battle lines were drawn on how the brain as a whole was organized. Some researchers believed that functions were localized to discrete areas of the brain; others adamantly opposed this idea and maintained that functions were represented throughout the cerebral cortex.

As the brain localization debate continued into this century, psychologists began to think differently about their theories. Putting freudian ideas aside, the major experimental scientists working on psychological issues

believed in some form of associationism. Somehow, understanding how rewards and punishment influenced the organism would be all one needed to know to understand why and what people come to learn and remember. This belief that environmental contingencies could explain all became welded into the very fabric of thought. After all, it reflected the American Dream. Anybody could become anything in the right environment.

All of this came crashing down in the late 1950s. Empiricism failed to explain complex mental functions such as language and other perceptual functions. Scientists began to consider representations of information as being almost built into the brain at birth. Hence, the advent of cognitive psychology, which fostered the notion that processing stages and cognitive activity could be analyzed with respect to their interlinked components.

All of this activity produced a new realization, however. If one wanted to understand how the brain enabled cognition, the thinking in neuroscience was not up to the job. Likewise, in psychology per se, models were being constructed and minds were being simulated—but without concern for how the brain did the job. The field became interested in how the mind might work or how it could work but not how it does work. In this book, we explore how the brain actually does enable mind.

SUGGESTED READINGS

SHEPHERD, G. M. (1992). *Foundations of the Neuron Doctrine*. New York: Oxford University Press.

KASS-SIMON, G., and FARNES, P. (1990). *Women of Science: Righting the Record*. Bloomington, IN: Indiana University Press.

LINDZEY, G. (Ed.). A History of Psychology in Autobiography. Vol. III. Worcester, MA: The Clark University Press.

2

The Substrates of Cognition

In Chapter 1 we painted the historical canvas of modern brain science to present how psychology and biology have coalesced to form cognitive neuroscience. In so doing, we introduced the theories, thoughts, and personalities of the history of neuroscience. Although thinking about the mind and brain can be traced to pre-Christian civilizations, most of what we now consider to be the basic biology of the nervous system began from humble beginnings in the last half of the nineteenth century. Only in the last 100 years have the neurosciences laid the foundation for understanding how the human brain's cells and circuits enable behavior.

We now understand neural development, neuronal signaling, synaptic transmission, and something about the neural codes that convey and store information. Researchers have worked intensively to relate elementary molecular and cellular processes to the activity of individual neurons and to the activity of neuronal circuits. Although the precise manner by which biological events give rise to behaviors is only just beginning to be understood, there has been a vast accumulation of knowledge about events at the neuronal level. Some findings are sufficiently well understood to form a set of elementary principles of brain science. In this chapter we briefly review these first principles of neuroscience, which are necessary for comprehension of the chapters that follow. The detailed functions that brain structures enable are mentioned only cursorily, as subsequent chapters describe the myriad functions of the human brain in perception and cognition.

CELLS OF THE NERVOUS SYSTEM

Scientific investigators often adopt a reductionist strategy in the hope of understanding the whole by first identifying the parts. For example, in physics and chemistry the fundamental building blocks of matter were pursued with a vengeance over the past 400 years, a chase that led to the identification of the basic elements from which all molecules are made—and, of course, the principles of subatomic structure. This fascination with the essential building blocks of the world around us was also shared by the early biologists who in the seventeenth and eighteenth centuries, attempted to visualize the constituents of biological tissues by using a magnifying lens. Out of this effort, a fundamental principle, *the cell theory*, was derived. The idea was that the body was composed of elementary units, or *cells*. As we noted in Chapter 1, however, the idea that individual neural cells comprised the nervous system was controversial even as late as the turn of this century. In the end, Spaniard Cajal's concept of the nervous system being composed of individual neurons prevailed.

Cajal observed that although neurons are close to each other, they are separated by small gaps. From these observations Cajal defined two main principles of neurons: connectional specificity and dynamic polarization. *Connectional specificity* incorporates the ideas that cells are separate because the *cytoplasms* of neurons are not in contact, and the connections between neurons are not random—circuits pass information through specific pathways. *Dynamic polarization* is the appreciation by Cajal that some parts of neurons are specialized for taking information in, while others are specialized for sending it out to other neurons or muscles. These two principles, and the overarching theory of the neuron doctrine, provide the focus for the first part of this chapter, which reviews the cellular structure and function of the nervous system.

There are two main classes of cells in the nervous system: neurons and glial cells. Neurons share similarities with all cells, but also have unique morphological and physiological properties for special functions. The glia are a class of nonneural cells located in the nervous system that have a supportive function.

The Structure of Neurons

Neurons, the basic signaling units, are distinguished by their form, function, and location within the nervous system. As Cajal and others of his time deduced, neurons take in information, make a decision about it, and then perhaps pass it along to other neurons. These functions have close relations to the morphological specializations of neurons.

The neuron consists of a cell body or *soma* from the Greek word meaning "body" (Figure 2.1). As with most cells, the cell body contains metabolic machinery that maintains the neuron. These include a nucleus, endoplasmic reticulum, ribosomes, mitochondria, Golgi apparatus, and other intracellular organelles common to most cells. These components are surrounded by the neuronal membrane, which is composed of a lipid bilayer, and are suspended in cytoplasm, the intracellular fluid present inside all cells of the body.

In addition to the cell body, neurons also have specialized processes, dendrites and axons, that extend away from the cell body. The role of these two structures reflects the principle of dynamic polarization. *Dendrites* are (usually) large treelike processes that receive inputs from other neurons at locations called *synapses*. As a result of being located after the synapse with respect to information flow, the dendrites of a neuron are said to be *postsynaptic* (after the synapse). Although we return to this later, it is useful to point out here that neurons signal electrically, but at synapses the signal is usually mediated by chemical transmission.

Dendrites take many varied and complex forms.

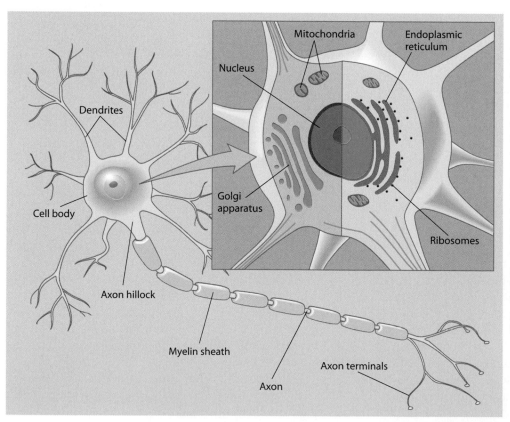

Figure 2.1 Idealized mammalian neuron. The cell body contains the cellular machinery for the production of proteins and other cellular macromolecules. Like other cells, the neuron contains a nucleus, endoplasmic reticulum, ribosomes, mitochondria, Golgi apparatus, and other intracellular organelles. These are suspended in the intracellular fluid—cytoplasm—and are contained by a cell membrane. Extending from the cell body are various processes that are extensions of the cell membrane and contain cytoplasm that is continuous with that in the cell body. These processes are called dendrites and axons.

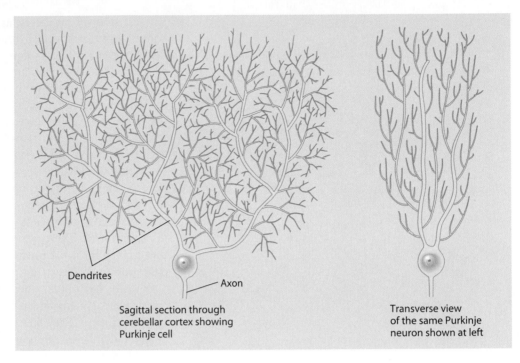

Figure 2.2 A dendritic tree of a Purkinje cell from the cerebellum. The Purkinje cells are arrayed in rows in the cerebellum. They have a large dendritic tree that is wider in one direction than the other. Adapted from Carpenter (1976).

Dendrites   Axon

Sagittal section through cerebellar cortex showing Purkinje cell

Transverse view of the same Purkinje neuron shown at left

They may appear as large arborizations like the branches and twigs of an old oak tree, as with the complex dendritic structures of the cerebellar Purkinje cells (Figure 2.2), or they may be somewhat simpler, as with the dendrites of spinal motor neurons or the neurons of the thalamus (Figure 2.3). Dendrites can also exhibit specialized processes called *spines*, little knobs attached by small necks to the surface of the dendrites; synapses are located on these spines. Synapses also are found elsewhere on neurons, including on cell bodies without spines.

The other type of process that extends away from the cell body is the *axon*. This represents the output side of the neuron, down which electrical signals can travel to synapses. These axons, and axon terminals of the neuron, are *presynaptic* because, unlike dendrites, they are located before a synapse with respect to information flow. The axon terminals have specialized morphologies and intracellular structures that enable communication via release of neurotransmitters, the chemical substances that transmit the signal between neurons at synapses. The dendrites and the axon of neurons are extensions of the cell body; their internal volume is filled with the same cytoplasm as the cell body's. Hence, the cell body, dendrites, and axon are parts of one neuron. The continuity of the intracellular space between these neuronal components is necessary for the electrical signaling that neurons perform.

The idealized neuron depicted in Figure 2.1 is modeled after a spinal motor neuron, but neurons have many forms. Indeed, the variation in the morphology of

Figure 2.3 Diagrammatic ventral horn motor neuron. The multipolar neurons are located in the spinal cord, and send their axons out the ventral root to make synapses on muscle fibers.

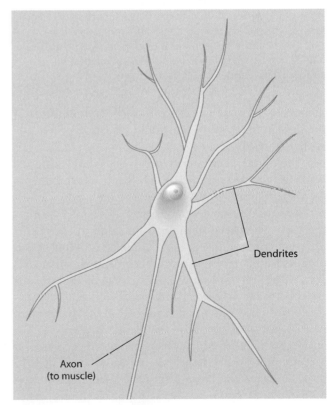

Dendrites

Axon
(to muscle)

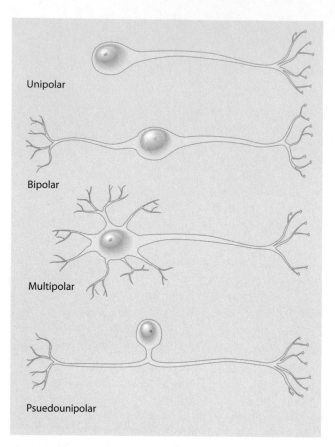

Figure 2.4 Various forms that mammalian neurons may take. Some have few and others many processes extending from their cell bodies. These diagrammatic neurons are shown with short axons, which is not intended to be illustrative of all neurons. For example, motor neurons in the spinal cord have axons that are a meter or more in length, depending on the muscle innervated or the animal or human in question. Adapted from Kandel et al. (1991).

neurons is surprising; descriptions of the multitudes in the human nervous system would take a lot of space—more than we have here. Early anatomists described this morphological variance in great detail and grouped neurons into three or four broad categories according to their shapes. These distinctions have largely to do with how the cell's dendrites and axon are oriented with respect to each other and to the soma. Figure 2.4 presents four types of neurons: unipolar, bipolar, multipolar, and pseudounipolar. Neurons with similar morphologies tend to be localized in specific regions of the nervous system and have a similar functional role, but the morphology of neurons in all areas of the nervous system varies widely.

In general, the unipolar neuron has only one process extending away from the cell body; it can branch to form dendrites and axon terminals, a pattern common in invertebrate nervous systems. Bipolar neurons partic-

ipate in sensory processes, as for example the neurons conveying information in the auditory, visual, and olfactory systems. These neurons have two processes, one axon and one dendrite, and thus might be considered the prototypical neuron: Information comes in one end via the dendrite and leaves through the other end down the axon, as, for instance, in the bipolar cells of the retina in the eye. These neurons process information within the retina and do not send projections outside it.

Pseudounipolar neurons are so named because they have the appearance of unipolar neurons but were originally bipolar sensory neurons whose dendrites and axon have fused. An example is in the dorsal root ganglia of the spinal cord. These neurons are somatosensory ones that convey information from receptors in joints, muscles, and skin into the central nervous system.

Finally, multipolar neurons exist in several areas of the nervous system and participate in motor and sensory processing. They have one axon but can have a few or many dendrites emerging from their cell bodies. The myriad of multipolar cells include spinal motor neurons, cortical sensory neurons such as stellate cells and pyramidal neurons, and some neurons of the autonomic nervous system.

The Role of Glial Cells

The other cell type in the nervous system, the neuroglial cells or simply *glia,* are more numerous than neurons and may account for more than half of the brain's volume. Neuroglial cells probably do not conduct signals themselves, but without glial cells, the functionality of neurons would be severely diminished. The term *neuroglia* means literally "nerve glue" because some anatomists in the nineteenth century believed that neuroglial cells had a role in the nervous system's structural support.

Glial cells are in the central nervous system (CNS) and the peripheral nervous system (PNS). The types of glia in each are different, though. The CNS has three main types: astrocytes, oligodendrocytes, and microglia (Figure 2.5). *Astrocytes* are large glial cells having round or radially symmetrical forms; they surround neurons and come in close contact with the brain's vasculature. Astrocytes actually make contact with blood vessels at specializations called *end-feet,* which permit the astrocyte to transport ions across the vascular wall, and to create a barrier between the tissues of the CNS and blood: the *blood-brain barrier* (BBB). This barrier prevents certain chemical compounds from leaving the blood and affecting neuronal physiology. For example, many drugs cannot cross the BBB, and certain neuroactive agents, such as dopamine and norepinephrine, do not cross the BBB when placed in the blood. This has significance for the treatment of disorders such as Parkinson's disease, in which a depletion in the neurotransmitter dopamine in the basal ganglia of the brain leads to a severe movement disorder. It is not possible to replenish the lost dopamine by injecting it into blood because of the BBB. But molecules that are precursors for the physiological synthesis of dopamine (L-dopa), when placed in the bloodstream, can cross the BBB, be taken up by neurons, and be converted to dopamine in the brain tissue. Thus, the astrocytic barrier between neuronal tissue and blood plays a vital role in protecting the CNS from blood-borne agents that might unduly affect neuronal activity.

Microglia, which are small, irregularly shaped cells, have a role to play once tissue is damaged. Microscopic analysis of tissue that has been injured reveals that the damaged region is invaded by these glial cells. They also serve a phagocytic role; they literally devour and remove damaged cells. Microglia can proliferate even in the

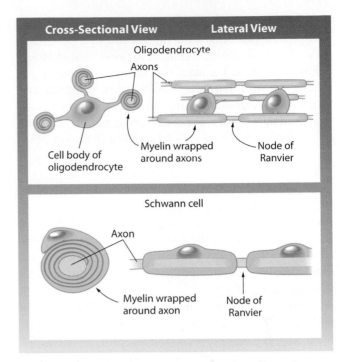

Figure 2.6 Oligodendrocytes and Schwann cells produce myelin around the axons. The oligodendrocytes in the central nervous system wrap around more than one axon to form myelin, but the Schwann cells in the peripheral nervous system wrap around a segment of only one axon. However, many of either would have to be involved to produce myelin for the length of an axon. Adapted from Netter (1991).

Figure 2.5 Various types of glial cells in the mammalian central and peripheral nervous systems. Oligodendrocytes and Schwann cells produce myelin around the axons. An astrocyte is shown with end feet attached to a blood vessel.

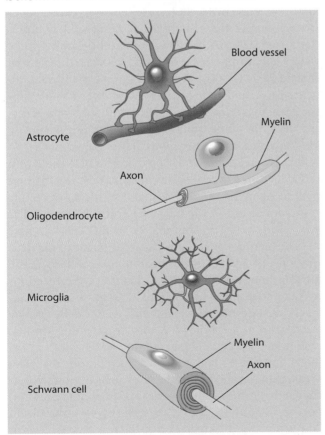

adult (as do other glial cells), whereas CNS neurons are typically prevented from so doing.

The most obvious role of glial cells in the nervous system is in the formation of myelin. *Myelin* is a fatty substance that surrounds the axons of many neurons. In the CNS, this material is the result of the action of oligodendrocytes; in the PNS, the Schwann cell is involved in the myelination of axons. Both glial cell types produce myelin by making concentric wrappings of their cell membranes around the axon during development and maturation. In the regions where the glial cell's membrane is wrapped around the axon, the cytoplasm in that portion of the glial cell is squeezed out. This leaves primarily the lipid bilayer of the glial cell membrane—hence, the characteristic appearance of myelin as a fatty-looking material (it actually looks white and shiny under normal physiological conditions). But there are differences in how oligodendrocytes and Schwann cells produce myelin.

One oligodendrocyte of the CNS can form myelin sheaths around several axons. Figure 2.6 shows the wrappings of oligodendrocytes around the axons of several adjacent neurons in a white matter tract. The analogous situation is shown for a Schwann cell in the PNS; the cell produces myelin only for a single axon in a peripheral nerve. The goal of each is similar: to provide an electrical insulation around the axon that changes the way intracellular electrical currents flow in axons. In myelinated axons (many axons are unmyelinated), the myelin is interrupted between successive patches of axon at locations called *nodes*. These nodes, first described in the late nine-teenth century by the French histologist and anatomist Louis Antoine Ranvier, are commonly referred to as the *nodes of Ranvier*. At the nodes, important membrane specializations permit the generation of action potentials that are conducted down the axon. Thus, the portions of the axon where glial cells form myelin, as well as where this is interrupted at the nodes, are significant for the way neurons are able to signal electrically.

NEURONAL SIGNALING

In reviewing the morphology of neurons we noted that their function is to analyze and transmit information, which is the goal of nervous systems. Now we turn to how neurons accomplish the transfer of information from one to another; we refer to this globally as *neuronal signaling.*

Neuronal signaling has several requirements. As with most things in the physical world, energy is a primary requirement. How do neurons provide energy for neuronal signaling? And how can one record the electrical activity of neurons and investigate the physical properties that permit them to conduct electrical current that leads to synaptic transmission, the basis of communication between neurons?

Overview of Neuronal Communication

To answer these questions, we need to know how neurons communicate. Neurons are the integral units of the nervous system, and each neuron communicates with other cells via the synapses, usually on dendrites or the cell body, or both. For outgoing information the synapses are at axon terminals. The goal of neuronal processing is to take in information, evaluate it, and pass a signal to other neurons. The process has several stages.

Neurons first receive a signal that is in either a chemical form (*neurotransmitter,* or chemical in the environment for sensations such as smell) or a physical form (such as in touch receptors in the skin, or in photoreceptors in the eye). These signals initiate changes in the membrane of the postsynaptic neuron, changes that make electrical currents flow in the neuron and generate electrical signals in the dendrites and perhaps the axon of the stimulated neuron. The current flow is mediated by ionic currents carried by electrically charged atoms (ions) such as sodium, potassium, and chloride that are dissolved in the fluid inside and outside of neurons. Long-distance signals (*action potentials*) can be generated in a region of the neuron that integrates collective currents from many synaptic inputs, or from the stimulation of a sense receptor. What results in most cases is a signal that travels down the axon to its terminal, where it eventually causes the release of neurotransmitters at synapses.

Remember that this review highlights aspects of neuronal signaling that might be considered typical, but numerous variations on this pattern are present in the nervous system. For example, many neurons communicate without ever generating a long-range signal, such as in the retina and elsewhere. And although most synapses are chemical, some are electrical, somewhat like what Golgi proposed in his theory of neural communication.

The Membrane Potential

The neuronal membrane is a bilayer of lipid molecules that separates intracellular space from extracellular space. Because the membrane is composed of lipids (fatty material), the membrane does not dissolve in the watery environments inside and outside the neuron (Figure 2.7). This is essentially how the membrane remains intact and controls the flow of water-soluble substances across its breadth. That is, the membrane generally does not allow things to cross it; it is a barrier to ions, proteins, and other molecules dissolved in the intracellular and extracellular fluid. One way to think of it is that anything that dissolves in water does not dissolve well in the membrane's lipids, and so it cannot readily cross into or out of the cell. This principle is a familiar one: oil and water do not mix.

The membrane not only keeps the inside of the neuron separate from the outside, but also can help create different internal and external chemical concentrations by the active pumping of ions. Energy-storing molecules called *adenosine triphosphate* (ATP) can be used by the neuron as a form of fuel that operates small transmembrane pumps. These pumps are enzymes (proteins) located in the neuronal membrane; they can break a chemical bond in the ATP molecule and release energy that moves sodium ions (Na^+) out of the cell and potassium ions (K^+) into the cell. Every molecule of ATP can provide enough energy to move two K^+ ions in for every three Na^+ ions extruded (Figure 2.8a).

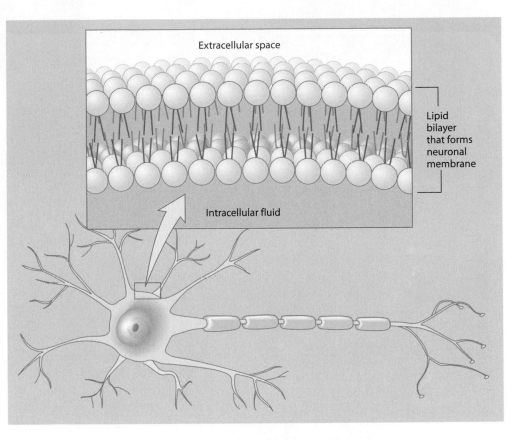

Figure 2.7 Lipid bilayer and separation of intracellular from extracellular spaces. The material of the cell membrane is composed of a lipid bilayer. The lipids (fatty material) are not water soluble, and thus form a barrier to materials in the watery solution in and out of the neuron such as Na^+ and K^+ ions and other items that are themselves water soluble.

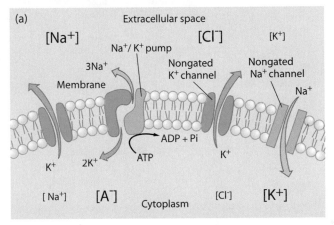

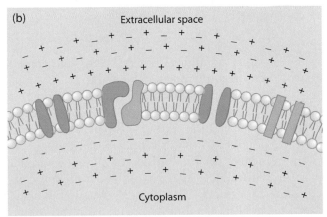

Figure 2.8 **(a)** Na^+/K^+ ATPase pump and ion concentrations inside and outside the neuron. Properties of the membrane combined with the pumping of ions across the neuronal membrane lead to ionic concentration gradients for sodium (Na^+), potassium (K^+), chloride (Cl^-), and large charged proteins (A^-) across the membrane. **(b)** The membrane selective permeability to these ions and the concentration gradients lead to a difference in electrical potential across the membrane called the resting membrane potential.

Glia, Myelin, and Disease

J.C. was 32 years old when she tripped while walking down her level, clean driveway. Embarrassed at her clumsiness, she laughed and told her friend that she should have the driveway repaired. Two weeks later she fell while walking across her living room. Six months after these seemingly trivial instances of clumsiness, some minor, but annoying visual problems developed but disappeared over the next 6 months. During the next year she experienced some strange numbness in her hands and weakness in her left leg, which prompted her to seek medical treatment. Following a series of diagnostic tests, J.C. was diagnosed with a neuromuscular disease called *multiple sclerosis* (MS). What is this disease, and why did it lead to the varied symptoms, and why was she *sometimes* clumsy?

Moment to moment, on a millisecond scale, the human nervous system processes sensory information and executes motor responses. Some of these are under voluntary control; perhaps the vast majority are reflexive or automatic in one fashion or another. For example, for standing we not only decide voluntarily whether to stand or sit, but also use reflexive systems to maintain balance and posture. To accomplish this in real time takes speed and accuracy of timing. Thus, in many ways the nervous system is a high-speed machine. The timing of this machine is compromised in some disease states when the integrity of the neurons and their component parts are destroyed. MS is one disease among many that manifests itself, in part, as a loss of coordination among information transactions within specified neural systems. Specifically, MS is manifest as damage of the myelin sheaths surrounding axons in the CNS or PNS, or both. Through mechanisms not completely understood (likely some form of autoimmune reaction of the body against the molecules in the myelin itself), the myelin is damaged, and in a spotty fashion may be broken down completely. The result for the patient can be mild or very severe. The symptoms of MS depend on which axons are affected by demyelination. If the affected axons are in the optic tract leading from an eye to the brain, then visual problems will be encountered. If demyelination happens to axons in peripheral nerves, losses of sensation or muscular control and strength may result. If the demyelination occurs in white matter tracts interconnecting regions of cerebral cortex involved in higher function, the symptoms may affect cognition or personality.

Why does damage to myelin lead to these problems? The neurons themselves are not damaged; they merely experience losses in the myelin sheaths surrounding their axons. The myelin sheath is not a part of the neuron, but rather is formed by glial cells in the nervous system. Nonetheless, it is important for the function of the neuron. Damage to myelin can lead to slowing or complete disruption of neural signaling, and hence, a loss of function in the portion of the neural circuitry affected. What function of myelin is necessary for normal neuronal conduction? In the text, the role of myelin in axonal conduction is discussed. After reading about neuronal signaling, try to deduce how intermittent damage in myelin leads to the symptoms of MS.

Over time, pumping changes the internal-to-external neuronal concentrations of Na^+ and K^+ ions and creates ionic concentration gradients across the membrane (see Figure 2.8a). The relative impermeability of the neuronal membrane keeps these ions from traveling back across the membrane, even though the natural tendency is for diffusion to push ions down their concentration gradients (from areas of high concentration to areas of low concentration) to eliminate the differential in concentration. Hence, in the resting state, a higher concentration of Na^+ is outside the neuron, and a higher concentration of K^+ is inside.

Some ions dissolved in the intracellular and extracellular fluid do cross the membrane. Thus, the neuronal membrane is actually *selectively permeable*, an important characteristic of this membrane. Selective permeability is created by the presence of nongated Na^+ channels and nongated K^+ channels, transmembrane proteins that form tunnels through the membrane. The key point of interest here is that the neuronal membrane

Figure 2.9 Intracellular recordings are used to measure the resting membrane potential and changes in the resting membrane potential that occur during electrical signaling. A small glass pipette electrode with a fine tip is used to penetrate the neuronal cell membrane without damaging it too severely. Then recordings of the transmembrane differences in voltage can be made between the electrode inside and the one outside the neuron. When the electrode enters the neuron, the voltage difference between the two electrodes reflects the membrane potential as shown in the idealized oscilloscope record.

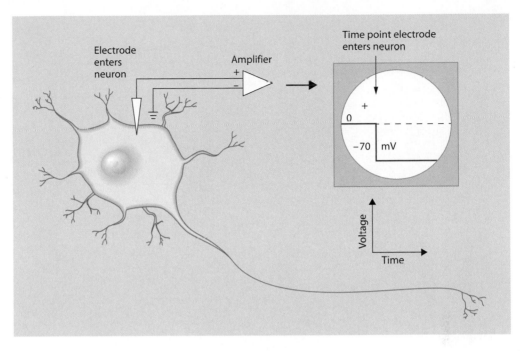

is more permeable to K^+ than to Na^+ because there are more nongated K^+ than Na^+ channels. As a result, K^+ leaks out of the neuron under the force of its concentration gradient and some Na^+ leaks into the cell. The result of K^+ leaving is a slight excess of negative charge on the inside of the membrane relative to the outside. This small separation of charge creates an electrical gradient across the membrane (see Figure 2.8b). This gradient is the basis of the *resting membrane potential*. In neurons this can range from -60 to -80 millivolts (mV) inside to outside of the neuron, a transmembrane potential that can be measured by using electrodes (Figure 2.9). In essence, the neuron now has the equivalent of a battery, that is, a form of potential energy that enables neurons to generate electrical signals.

RECORDING THE MEMBRANE POTENTIAL

Neurons have two properties important for cellular signaling. One is that they generate electrical impulses; the other is that they allow electrical current to flow through them. Let us first look at how to measure the flow of current across membranes and within neurons before delving into passive electrical properties.

In the late 1940s and early 1950s, techniques were developed to record the neuronal membrane potential. In principle the early techniques were not complex, but in practice, because of the small size of neurons (50–100 microns in diameter) and axons (1–3 microns in diameter), new techniques were needed. To record the transmembrane difference in potential, one must have a very small recording electrode (micropipette electrode) in-

side a neuron and one outside; the difference in potential between these two electrodes is defined as the membrane potential (see Figure 2.9).

A micropipette electrode is created by heating and stretching a small glass tube to a fine point (<1 micron). When the microelectrode is filled with a conductive solution, it acts as both the recording tip and a kind of harpoon for puncturing the neurons under a microscope. The difference between the voltage inside and outside of the neuron is measured as the difference between the electrode inside the cell and another located outside the cell. This difference signal can be amplified and displayed on an oscilloscope for viewing. Typically, we arbitrarily define the outside of the neuron to be at zero voltage; thus, the inside of resting neurons is observed to be a negative voltage.

This technique has also been adapted to inject current into the neuron, which is easily done by attaching a current source instead of an amplifier across the two electrodes. When electrodes are placed inside a neuron, one can inject current and record changes in the neuron's membrane potential (Figure 2.10). The action of the stimulating electrode approximates the role of synaptic inputs to a neuron, or of receptor potentials at a sensory receptor, and so we can learn about how tiny currents injected into a postsynaptic neuron affect it. Variations of this technique are now sophisticated enough to enable us to investigate the properties of ion channels, the small pores created by proteins in the neuronal membrane that permit ions to move across the membrane.

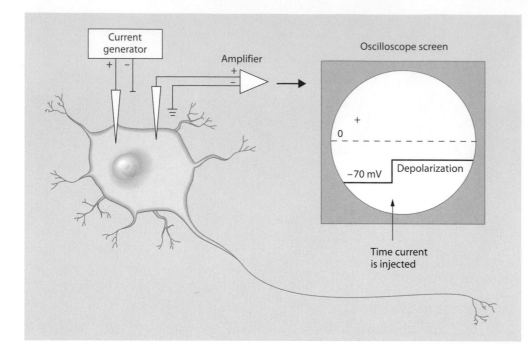

Figure 2.10 Electrodes can be attached to current-generating equipment and used to pass current into the neuron. The effect this has on the membrane potential can then be measured. Here, a depolarizing current is injected by making the tip of the electrode inside the neuron more positive. This depolarizes the membrane as the current flows out across the membrane to complete the electrical circuit with the other electrode outside the cell.

PASSIVE ELECTRICAL PROPERTIES OF NEURONS

We now know (1) the gross morphology of neurons, (2) that they have a potential difference across their membranes, and (3) that this electrical power source can be used by the neuron and measured by investigators. The next question we turn to is, How does the membrane potential permit neurons to communicate with one another? The first things to understand are the passive physical properties of neurons, and how these properties influence current flowing in their intracellular space; this is important to know because it is involved in all aspects of neuronal signaling.

Neurons are essentially sacks of electrically conductive fluid (cytoplasm), bounded by an electrical insulator (cell membrane). All this sits in a salty sea of extracellular fluid that has a conductivity similar to that of the cytoplasm. Thus, neurons and their environment can be broken down into conductors (cytoplasm and extracellular fluid) and insulators (the membranes)—the latter are structures with high but variable resistance, plus the ability to store charge briefly (capacitance). These components, plus the membrane potential and ion channels, can be modeled by using equivalent electrical circuits (see Building Neurons out of Batteries and Baling Wire, p. 34).

We can also grasp the behavior of neurons in simple, qualitative terms. The first goal is to learn how electrical currents flow passively through neurons due to sensory stimulation or synaptic activity. In so doing, we make a distinction between active processes such as those that generate action potentials, synaptic potentials, or receptor potentials, which all involve opening of ion channels, and the passive currents that these active electrical processes generate (Figure 2.11). It is how well these passive currents flow through the neuron that sets the constraints on how far a neuron can conduct, and whether and how the neuron will use action potentials to aid in communication. We will return to the action potential in the next section.

When a sensory receptor or synapse is activated, electrical current flows across the cell membrane in the receptor or dendrites of neurons (postsynaptic neuron). In neurons (and generally in the body) electrical current is *ionic;* that is, it is carried by charged atoms (i.e., ions) in solution. With neurons, the charge carriers are primarily Na^+, K^+, and Cl^- ions. Thus, we can speak of sodium currents, potassium currents, and chloride currents across the membrane, and ionic currents more generally inside or outside of the neuron. These currents typically occur when ionic species such as Na^+ or K^+ cross the neuronal membrane through ion channels that open in response to chemical or physical stimuli. This current flow across the membrane in a localized region leads to current flow that spreads passively through the neuron. This is called *electrotonic conduction.* Current must always flow so as to complete an electrical circuit; thus, movement of currents inside a neuron is accompanied by return currents outside the neuron that form the complete circuit (Figure 2.12a).

How far down a dendrite, axon, or cell body will an electrical current flow when it is not replenished by ac-

Figure 2.11 Postsynaptic currents at synapses on the neuronal cell body are conducted by electrotonic conduction through the intracellular space. These currents depolarize the membrane, and if large enough, this depolarization can trigger action potentials to be generated at the initial segment of the axon. Each action potential represents an active process that occurs when voltage-gated Na⁺ channels open in the membrane. The inward current generated during this phase of the action potential is then conducted down the axon following principles of electrotonic conduction. This leads to depolarization of adjacent regions of membrane, which can then generate another action potential, and the process continues down the axon.

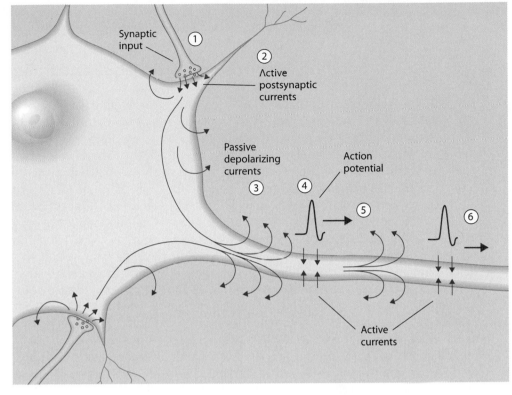

First, consider the diagrammatic axon in Figure 2.13a. Pictured is a portion of an axon viewed in mid-sagittal section. Recording electrodes are inserted into the axon at distances from the point at which a stimulating electrode is inserted into the axon. When the stimulating electrode injects positive current into the axon at that location (this means the electrode tip is made positive by a current generator), the current flows down the axon where it emerges through the axonal membrane and creates return currents that flow toward the other electrode located in the extracellular fluid, thereby completing the circuit. Near the electrode inside the axon, the current is strongest but this electrotonic current decreases with distance away from the source. If we measure the voltage across the membrane near the stimulating electrode, we see a large voltage change near the stimulating electrode, and progressively smaller voltage

tive processes (i.e., action potentials)? The distance is a function of three main physical properties of the neuron: the size of the original current, the resistivity (and capacitance) of the neuronal membrane, and the conductivity of the intracellular and extracellular fluid. We have come to understand these principles by modeling and by direct experimentation in neurons; we can record from inside neurons (if they are large enough) and can inject current into them to investigate the result (Figure 2.12b).

Figure 2.12 Diagram of currents crossing the membrane, traveling down the neuron, exiting, and returning to source **(top)**. Currents can be made to flow using an intracellular electrode attached to a current generator **(bottom)**. Adapted from Netter (1991).

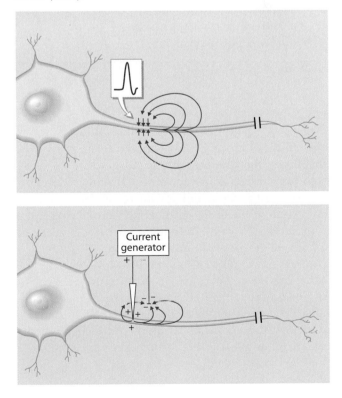

Building Neurons out of Batteries and Baling Wire

The components of the neuron have physical properties that determine how it conducts currents. These properties include the resistivities of the neuronal membrane, cytoplasm, and extracellular fluid, and the amplitude of the current generated by the power of the membrane potential. In order to model these components of the neuron to help understand the electrical behavior of dendrites, neurons, and axons, physiologists have developed the concept of "equivalent circuit." The equivalent circuit uses terminology and principles from electronics to approximate the neuron, and thus to provide quantitative values for modeling the state of the neuron given a specific set of conditions. For example, as shown in the figure, we can assign specific resistances and capacitances to the membrane, the intracellular fluid, and the extracellular fluid. Thus, diagramatically the neuronal membrane becomes a set of resistors and capacitors in parallel, while the intracellular and extracellular fluids are represented as resistors in series.

The membrane of the neuron contains variable resistors because ion channels can open and close, thereby changing the resistance of the membrane to current flow (i.e., when ions move through the ion channels). The membrane potential can be modeled as a battery across the membrane because the membrane potential represents a steady power source that can power current through the equivalent circuit.

Modeling the neuron as an electrical circuit permits quantitative predictions as to how the neuron should behave in the laboratory setting and under normal physiological conditions. By modeling the neuron in this fashion, physiologists have been able to attain theoretical explanations for the behavior of neurons from which they actually recorded data using microelectrodes. For example, the squid giant axon has a diameter of about 0.5 mm, whereas the diameter of a muscle fiber in a frog may be as small as 0.1 mm. In these two cells, the resistance of the cytoplasmic fluid is approximately equivalent, but in the larger of the two cells, the resistance inside is lower because of the greater volume, and this can be modeled by decreasing the value of the resistors in series that represent the internal resistance of the intracellular space. Thereupon, it is possible to calculate the differential effect that a given change in current at one location would have on the membrane potential at any given distance away. Experimentally, this "length constant" (see text) is known to be different, and changes in the values of the resistors in an equivalent circuit model of the neuron can effectively describe this effect.

---

changes as we move farther from the stimulating electrode. If we assume that the membrane's resistivity does not change, then the change in membrane voltage is due to the diminished amplitude of the current at more distant loci. Just as the sound of your voice, the strength of a flashlight beam, or the smell of your favorite pizza diminishes with distance from the source, so does current flowing in and around the axon.

Now, as we noted in the overview of this chapter, axons conduct information to axon terminals that release neurotransmitter, which results in synaptic transmission between neurons. The question of most interest now is whether passive electrotonic conduction is sufficient to allow this communication. The answer is a loud "No!"—with a qualifying "Yes" in many circumstances. Because the current's strength diminishes with distance from the source, such a signal is not appropriate for long-distance communication, but it can work well for short distances.

As noted, how far electrotonic currents can be effective for communication depends in part on the size of the original current. The greater the current, the farther it will conduct. In the laboratory, this can be manipulated by increasing the size of the current injected in the neuron. However, under normal physiological conditions the amplitude of the current is determined by physiological factors such as the intensity of a physical stimulus at a receptor, or the strength and number

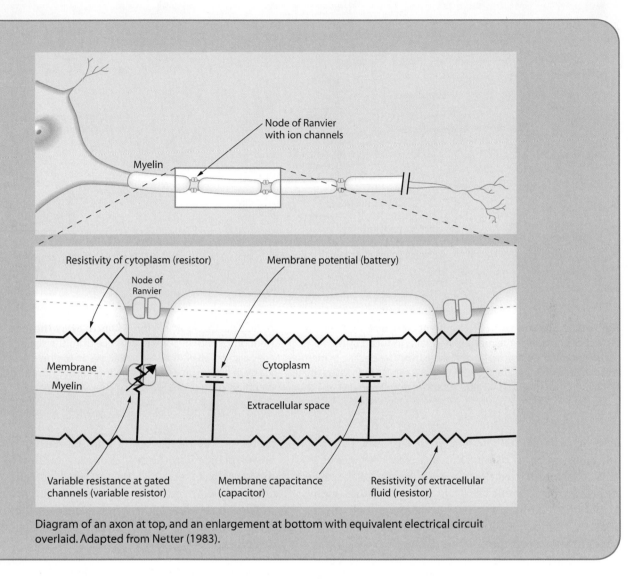

Diagram of an axon at top, and an enlargement at bottom with equivalent electrical circuit overlaid. Adapted from Netter (1983).

of synaptic inputs onto the neuron. Because sensory receptors and synaptic potentials can generate currents of differing size, the changes in membrane potential they induce are said to be *graded*. We can also ask about the influence of the membrane's resistivity on the conduction of electrotonic potentials. Put simply, as the membrane resistivity increases, more current will be shunted down the axon and less will leak out. Consider the analogy of a garden hose. If the tubing of the hose is intact (i.e., has high resistance to water crossing it), then water put in one end is forced down the hose. Yet if the hose is full of holes (i.e., has low resistance to water), the water forced in one end does not move as far down the hose because it leaks out first. If the hose is leaky enough, the

water may move only a short distance before the water pressure falls to where water no longer flows in the hose. Similarly, the resistivity of the neuronal membrane influences the distance down an axon that a current can travel.

Finally, the conductivity (resistivity = 1/conductivity) of the intracellular space also affects how far through a neuron that current will flow. Usually the intracellular and extracellular fluids have high conductivities because, as salt solutions, they are generally good conductors of electrical current (but vastly inferior to metal wire). Even so, the resistivity of dendrites, cell bodies, and axons changes as a function of their size. Returning to the garden hose analogy, we find that if the

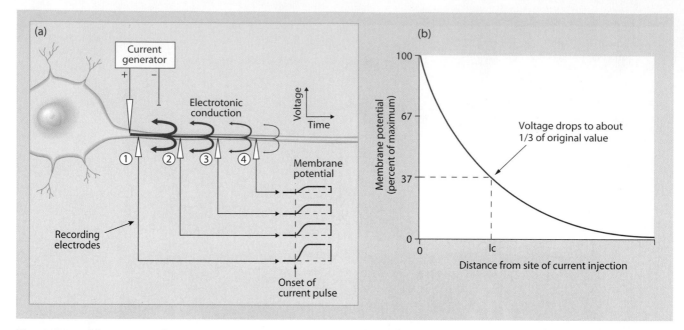

Figure 2.13 **(a)** An axon with a current electrode at one end and recording electrodes at varying distances away. The amplitude of the depolarization of the membrane that is induced by the flowing current drops with increasing distance from the site of injection of current (or of postsynaptic potentials). **(b)** The decline in membrane depolarization with distance follows an exponential function, and a value known as the length constant can be defined as the distance from the origin where the change in membrane potential reaches 37% of its original value. Adapted from Kandel et al. (1991), and Kuffler and Nicholls (1976).

hose has a large diameter, water flows easily, but in a thin hose, water pressure, and thus resistivity, rises because of the restricted flow. In a similar way, if the axon is large, the current flow is greater. Thus, high-amplitude receptor or synaptic currents, high membrane resistance, and low-resistance intracellular pathways enhance electrotonic conduction.

But under the best of conditions, how far can electrotonic conduction provide an effective means of electrical communication? Not far, generally about a millimeter. The decremental nature of passive electrical currents can be described by plotting the change in membrane potential as a function of distance from the current source to a recording site (see Figure 2.13b). What we find in this type of plot is that the recorded change in membrane potential drops exponentially. The *length constant* is defined as the distance down the axon where the potential reaches about one-third of its original value. This can be used to quantify the effectiveness of electrotonic conduction in different neurons or their parts.

A millimeter may seem too short to be effective for conducting electrical signals, but in a structure like the retina, a millimeter is enough to permit neuron-to-neuron communication. In the spinal cord, though, where axons may have cell bodies in the motor cortex of the brain, and axonal terminals on motor neurons in the spinal cord, a millimeter is too short. Under such circumstances, electrical signals down an axon might have to cover several meters; consider a giraffe, elephant, or whale! Another mechanism has evolved to conduct electrical signals long distances.

ACTIVE ELECTRICAL PROPERTIES OF NEURONS

In the preceding section we described how the physical properties of the neuron affect the way electrical currents passively flow through neurons due to synaptic inputs or sensory stimulation at receptors. We showed that electrotonic conduction is good only for short-distance communication, not for long-distance communication. Long-distance communication requires active or regenerative electrical signals called action potentials.

To understand action potentials, it is useful to appreciate that graded electrotonic potentials and action potentials involve changes in the membrane potential over time, but that these changes are different. Further, we have to remember to distinguish between the resting membrane potential and the membrane potential when current is flowing, as for example during the action potential. In addition, the membrane potential can become either more (hyperpolarized) or less (depolarized)

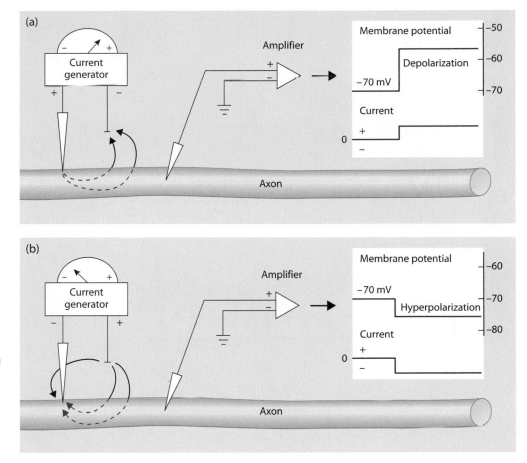

Figure 2.14 An axon with stimulating and recording electrodes placed inside. Injection of current by making the electrode tip more positive depolarizes the membrane (a), whereas current flow in the opposite direction (b) can hyperpolarize the neuronal membrane.

negative with respect to the resting membrane potentials (Figure 2.14). And finally, active processes such as action potentials are initiated by passive currents that alter the local membrane potential, thereby triggering action potentials in specific regions of the neuronal membrane. Hence, the two types of electrical conduction (passive electrotonic and active regenerative) in neurons are intimately related.

Stimulating neurons to depolarize them can generate action potentials or electrical spikes in axons. These action potentials can be observed without intracellular recording, by placing recording electrodes on the outsides of axons or bundles or axons (i.e., nerves) (Figure 2.15). To find out about the mechanisms that generate action potentials, however, researchers use intracellular recording and stimulation. In axons, if stimulation is

Figure 2.15 Extracellular stimulating and recording electrodes and recorded action potentials. A large electrode placed extracellularly can also depolarize the membrane and generate action potentials. In this figure, a peripheral nerve composed of many individual axons is being stimulated and the compound action potential (the summation of the action potentials from all the axons) is recorded using an extracellular electrode.

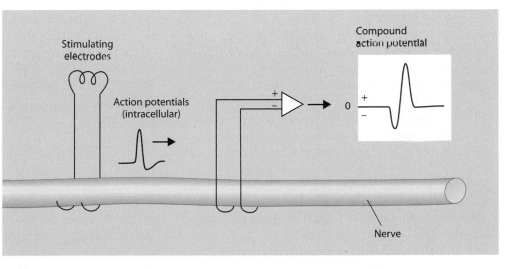

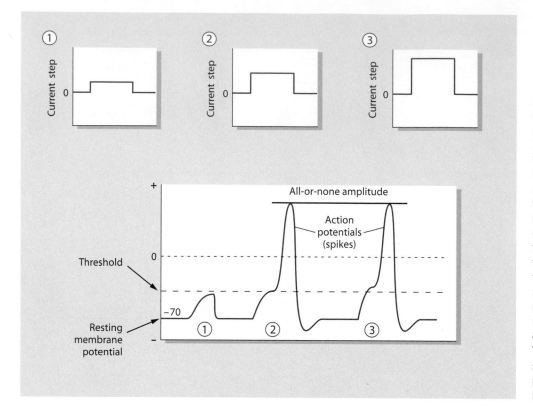

Figure 2.16 Injection of current into an axon leads to depolarization, which, if large enough, triggers an action potential. The potentials induced by injected currents are graded; that is, they can take on varying amplitudes depending on the size of the depolarizing current (1 through 3). However, when the depolarization reaches threshold, then the action potential that is generated reaches an amplitude that is not related to the size of the original depolarizing current. That is, the action potential is said to be all or none (compare 2 to 3). Adapted from Kandel et al. (1991).

continued with successively higher and higher amplitudes of current, an action potential can be elicited. The action potential is a rapid depolarization and repolarization of the membrane in a localized area. Figure 2.16 shows the depolarizations of the axonal membrane that can ultimately lead to action potentials, if large enough. The value of the membrane potential to which the axon must be depolarized to initiate an action potential is the *threshold.* Depolarizations that do not reach threshold will not elicit action potentials; those that do lead to characteristic spikes (i.e., the large positive polarity portion of the action potential resembles a spike when viewed on an oscilloscope).

The amplitude of the action potential, once initiated, does not depend on the size of the initial depolarization. Thus, if the depolarizing current is raised higher than what is needed to reach threshold, the action potential is the same size; hence, the action potential is said to be *all or none.* The reason is that the electrotonic currents that depolarize the membrane vary in amplitude (i.e., are graded), depending, for example, on the size of the stimulus or synaptic input, but the action potential is generated by active processes unrelated to the amplitude of the graded currents (as long as they are large enough to push the membrane potential to threshold).

Neuronal membranes contain ion channels that are structurally specialized to be selective to specific ionic species. As well, ion channels are distinguished by whether or not they are gated. That is, their conductivity is affected by external influences such as voltage (e.g., from passive currents), chemicals (e.g., neurotransmitters), or physical stimulation (e.g., stretch or pressure such as at sensory receptors). The gated channels have different physical states; essentially they can be open or closed, like small gates in the membrane. If the channels are open, ions can move through them by being driven by electrical and ionic concentration gradients. In contrast, the nongated ion channels are essentially always in the same, open state. An example of the latter is the nongated K^+ channel that we described earlier; this channel establishes the membrane potential by letting K^+ leak out of neurons at rest. Nongated ion channels for Na^+ and Cl^- are also present in neuronal membranes. Voltage-gated ion channels are of prime importance in generating action potentials.

Voltage-gated ion channels open and close according to the membrane potential. They are closed at the resting membrane potential but open as the membrane is depolarized. When a passive current flows across the neuronal membrane following a synaptic or receptor potential, the membrane depolarizes and affects voltage-gated Na^+ channels. At this point, some of the channels begin to admit Na^+ into the neuron and this further depolarizes the neuron. This in turn leads to fur-

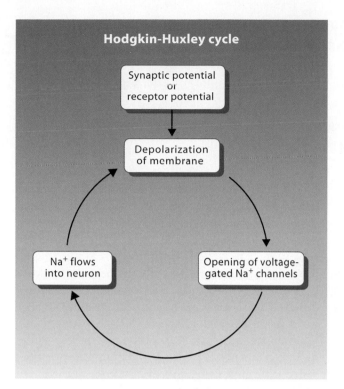

Figure 2.17 Hodgkin-Huxley cycle. Depolarization of the axonal membrane leads to the opening of voltage-gated Na⁺ channels. The inward Na⁺ current then adds to the depolarization, thereby causing even more Na⁺ channels to open. When this reaches threshold, the Na⁺ channel currents dominate the membrane potential, leading to the action potential's positive-going initial phase (see Figure 2.18).

ther opening of other voltage-gated Na⁺ channels, and thus more depolarization, which continues the cycle by opening yet more Na⁺ channels. The process, the Hodgkin-Huxley cycle, is depicted in Figure 2.17.

This rapid self-reinforcing cycle generates the large depolarization that is the first portion of the action potential (Figure 2.18). With a short delay, membrane depolarization leads to an opening of voltage-gated K⁺ channels, which allow K⁺ to flow out of the neuron and begin to repolarize it—and to reestablish the value of the resting membrane potential. This, in close temporal coincidence with the closing of the Na⁺ channels, leads to the second repolarizing phase of the action potential, which brings the membrane potential back to the level of the resting membrane potential. Because the K⁺ channels close after the resting membrane potential has been achieved, a transient period follows the action potential when the membrane is actually hyperpolarized; that is, it is even more negative inside compared to outside than when at rest. This transient hyperpolarization lasts only a couple of milliseconds as the membrane returns to the resting membrane potential.

The result of membrane hyperpolarization following the depolarization and repolarization of the action potential leaves the neuron in a state where it is temporarily more difficult to generate an action potential. This is because the membrane potential is farther away from the threshold for triggering an action potential

Figure 2.18 The relative time course of membrane voltage changes during an action potential, and the underlying causative changes in membrane conductance to Na⁺ (gNa) and K⁺ (gK). The initial depolarizing phase of the action potential is mediated by Na⁺ current, and the later repolarizing descending phase of the action potential is mediated by an increase in K⁺ conductance that occurs when the K⁺ channels open—this later phase happens during a period when the Na⁺ channels have closed. Adapted after Kuffler and Nicholls (1976).

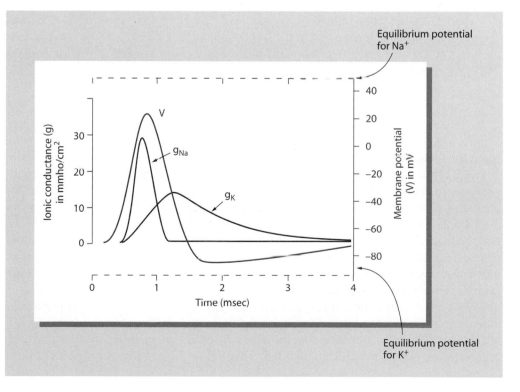

MILESTONES IN COGNITIVE NEUROSCIENCE

An Interview with Ira Black, M.D.

Dr. Black is a professor and chair of Neuroscience and Cell Biology at the Robert Wood Johnson Medical School, of the University of Medicine and Dentistry of New Jersey, and a former president of the Society for Neuroscience. Dr. Black is an authority on cellular and molecular mechanisms of neuronal plasticity.

Authors: Many neuroscientists investigate the molecular events that underlie neural processing. How will an understanding of processes such as second-messenger systems help us conceive of memory, language, or consciousness? That is, if it turned out that second-messenger systems within neurons were accomplished in a manner entirely different from what is currently being discovered, would that affect the higher-level computations that neuronal systems and neurons perform to support cognition?

IB: A satisfactory mechanistic description of any well-framed cognitive process requires that we simultaneously explain it at multiple levels of analysis. Different levels provide complementary insights to characterization and causality that are unobtainable from any single line of analysis. Considering the molecular events associated with memory may take us beyond the foregoing pat generalizations. An account of the molecular basis of a memory subtype provides the starting point. With this molecular alphabet, critical genes are identified, molecular deficits leading to dementia can be characterized, and potential therapeutic targets may be apparent. But use of the molecular al-

phabet may provide insight into the nature of memory itself. For example, an understanding of the evolution of memories may help to define neural antecedents, relationships to underlying cell biology, and the selective pressures (or lack thereof) responsible. In turn, this information may indicate whether memory is a form of a widespread, cell biological phenomenon, or whether it represents a special case fundamentally different from other processes. Molecular analysis is particularly useful in this regard, since the component processes can be traced in a convenient, rigorous, and unambiguous fashion. Ideally, this type of evolutionary analysis may define the origins of memory and the forces driving its emergence. In addition, the same strategy may be used to define relations among different forms of extant memory. Such information could help us to understand the taxonomy of memory. In turn, we could begin to understand how memory relates to other cognitive phenomena. Surprises may well occur. For example, molecular analysis can reveal occult relations among cognitive processes that seem thoroughly dissimilar behaviorally. One not-so-modest goal entails constructing a genealogy of cognition that places pro-

when the membrane is hyperpolarized. However, this is not the only factor that influences the neuron's ability to generate an action potential in the period of time immediately after one has occurred. There is a time immediately following the repolarizing phase of the action potential when the voltage-gated Na^+ channels are inactivated and unable to be opened, regardless of how much the membrane is depolarized. This *absolute refractory period* is followed by a short time, the *relative refractory period*, when the neuron can generate action potentials but only with larger-than-normal depolarizing currents. The consequence is that the neuron's speed in generating action potentials is limited. This limita-

tion of the neuron is reflected in how it can be used for temporal coding. An example is the coding of sound frequency in the auditory system. Some sounds have frequencies in the tens of thousands of cycles per second (Hertz or Hz), but the fastest neurons can follow frequencies only one-to-one up to about 1000 Hz (depending on the neuron).

We now know enough about passive and active properties of neurons to understand how action potentials can propagate down the length of even very long (several feet long) axons. The key is simply to remember that passive electrotonic currents depolarize the membrane to threshold. This triggers an action

cesses in a cognitive context and enables us to tentatively formulate a true cognitive structure. A skeletal example could indicate how different levels can and do cooperate in defining the nature of a cognitive process.

Authors: There are more glia in the brain than neurons. Can it really be the case that they have no computational role in brain processing?

IB: There are ten times as many glia in the brain as neurons. And there are about 100 billion neurons. Yet, for years we've known almost nothing about the function of these trillion or so glia. In fact, their name, which means "glue" in Greek, provides some sense of their low esteem. Early scientists thought they held the brain together. In the past few years, though, interest in glia has exploded and we know a lot more. We now know that glia produce growth factors and survival (or trophic) factors that serve as signals in the brain regulating growth, communication, and survival during maturity and development. Different glial types in the brain serve different functions. So, we are now beginning to appreciate the fact that many types of glia communicate with each other and with neurons. Instead of thinking of the neuron-neuron link as the unit of communication, we are now thinking of the neuron-glia-neuron loop. Consequently, while most scientists strongly suspect that glia are intimately involved in computations of the brain, their precise roles remain mysterious.

Authors: It has seemingly taken neuroscience many difficult years to uncover even the simplest of neural processes such as channel kinetics or transmitter system physiology. Given this, what hope do we have for understanding higher behaviors?

IB: Is the glass half empty or half full? I would reframe the question to indicate that neuroscience has made astounding progress in a few short years. For perspective, recall that the neolithic agricultural revolution took place approximately 10,000 years ago, the Renaissance commenced about 500 years ago, and the Society for Neuroscience of North America began roughly 20 years ago. Yet, in a few short years, we already have an early understanding of the chemistry of vision, the physiology of hearing and touch, the physiology of muscle movement, the biochemistry of certain emotions, and a beginning molecular biology of learning, memory, and some behaviors. Not bad for a few short years. Viewed in this light, there is every reason to be optimistic about our progress. Researchers are now beginning to elucidate the genetics of schizophrenia, the biochemistry of Alzheimer's disease, and the brain system's basis of drug addiction. For the first time in the history of humankind, we have treatments for depression, epilepsy, and stroke. We are beginning to understand the genes that control brain function, the molecular messages they use, the nature of the neurons that comprise the brain and the systems that they form, and finally, the behavioral output of these critical brain systems. We now need more neuroscientists to put all these brain and mind pieces of the puzzle together. For all these reasons, there is unparalleled excitement in neuroscience, and unparalleled opportunity.

potential that creates more passive currents which travel down the axon to depolarize new pieces of membrane to continue the process. The regeneration of action potentials is required because electrotonic currents die out quickly—regeneration has to keep the signal going. Propagation of action potentials is thus a continual interplay between electrotonic and active currents. Imagine the regeneration as a firefighter's bucket brigade; each person in the line is analogous to the action potential, and the handing off of the bucket represents the electrotonic current flowing down the axon. The analogy would be better if the firefighters threw the water out of their buckets as far as they could to the next person, but analogies and firefighters have their limitations.

Saltatory Conduction and the Role of Myelin

A key aspect of neuronal communication is the speed of signaling between neurons, or neurons and muscles. For example, as noted earlier, in animals as large as a giraffe or whale, the motor neurons located in the brain's motor cortex project axons down to the spinal cord, and therefore may have to send signals several meters. It is essential that these signals occur rapidly; otherwise coordination of motor activity would be compromised. It is not enough that the signals can travel that distance; they must do it quickly.

The physical properties of neurons affect how currents flow through them, and the resistances of the intracellular fluid and neuronal membrane are of prime importance. If the resistance of the membrane increases, or the resistance of the axon decreases, then currents flow down the axon more effectively, following the path of least resistance. Current will flow down the axon farther.

One way to lower the axon's internal resistance is to expand the axon's diameter; larger-diameter axons conduct axon potentials faster. In squid this is how the conduction speed needed to quickly contract muscles and avoid predators is achieved. The question is, How big would an axon's diameter have to be to achieve the speed required to communicate signals from a giraffe's brain to the motor neurons of the hind limbs? The answer is, Too big to fit all the needed axons into the spinal cord. Evolution had to solve this dilemma in another way before larger animals could thrive. Myelination held the key: Myelin wrapped around the axons of peripheral and central neurons increases membrane resistance. Currents, then, are shunted down the axon a greater distance. This means that action potentials do not have to be generated as often, and that they can be spread out along the axon at more distant intervals. Indeed, action potentials in myelinated axons need appear only at the nodes of Ranvier where myelination is interrupted. At the nodes, voltage-gated Na$^+$ channels can trigger action potentials that regenerate fast electrotonic currents that flow to the next node, where another action potential is generated. So the action potential appears to jump along the axons from node to node—hence, the name *saltatory conduction,* which means "to jump" (Figure 2.19). By such conduction, mammalian nerves can transmit at roughly 120 m/sec (the length of a football field in 1 second—quite fast!).

Synaptic Transmission

The ultimate act in neuronal signaling is for a neuron to communicate with other neurons or muscles. We must understand how neurons bridge the gap between neurons in order to transmit signals—an action called *synaptic transmission.*

The essentials of synaptic transmission have been understood for decades, but the details continue to be unraveled to the present. First, an action potential must arrive at the axon terminal where the synapse is located. This leads to the depolarization of the axon terminal, which initiates an influx of Ca^{2+} ions into the terminal region. As a result, small vesicles containing neurotransmitter fuse with the membrane at the synapse and release this transmitter into the synaptic cleft, the space

Figure 2.19 Saltatory conduction in a myelinated nerve. Action potentials in a myelinated nerve occur only at the nodes of Ranvier. The current generated at the nodes flows in the internode region under the constraints determined by the principles of electrotonic conduction. The distance between the nodes is determined by the length constant of the axon, which is affected by the myelination of the axon and the axon's diameter. Hence, the nodes are optimally spaced such that electrotonic currents from the action potential at the last node are still strong enough to depolarize the membrane to threshold at the present node, thus handing the signal down the axon.

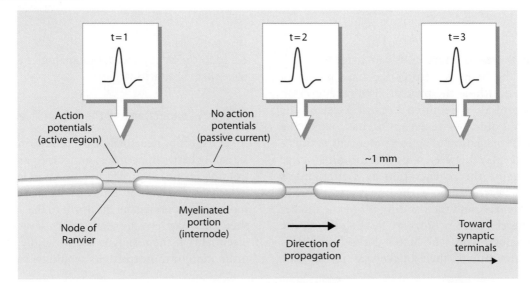

between the presynaptic and postsynaptic neuronal membranes. The transmitter diffuses across the cleft and, on reaching the postsynaptic membrane, binds with protein molecules (receptor molecules) embedded in the membrane (Figure 2.20).

The chemical interaction of the neurotransmitter and the postsynaptic receptor initiates events that lead to either depolarization (excitation) or hyperpolarization (inhibition) of the postsynaptic cell (Figure 2.21). If this cell is a neuron, then an excitatory postsynaptic potential (EPSP) can lead to the generation of action potentials in this neuron. In most neurons action potentials are initiated at the interface between the cell body and the axon (axon hillock). If the postsynaptic cell is a

Figure 2.20 Neurotransmitter release at the synapse. The synapse consists of various specializations where the presynaptic and postsynaptic membranes are in close apposition. When the action potential invades the axon terminals, it causes voltage-gated Ca^{2+} channels to open **(1)**, which triggers vesicles to bind to the presynaptic membrane **(2)**. Neurotransmitter is released into the synaptic cleft by exocytosis and diffuses across the cleft **(3)**. Binding of the neurotransmitter to receptor molecules in the postsynaptic membrane completes the process of transmission **(4)**. Adapted from Kandel et al. (1991).

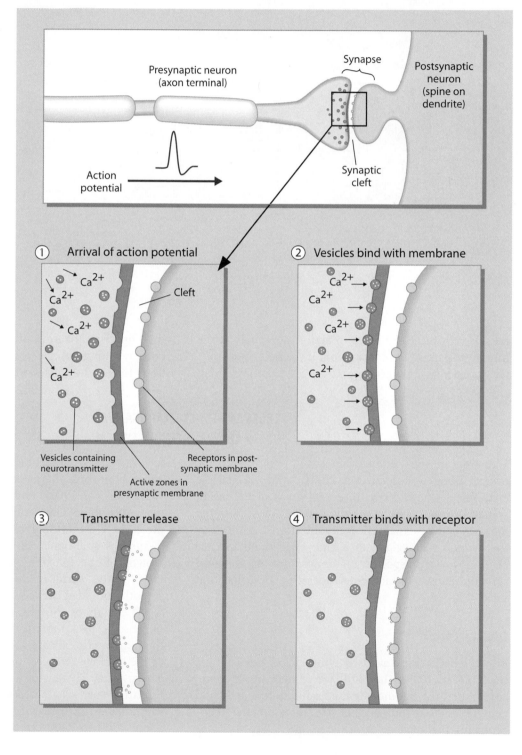

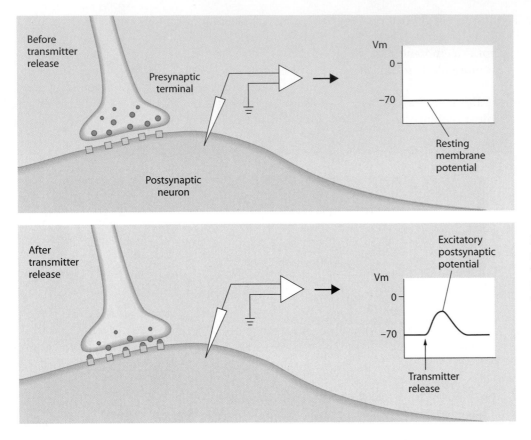

Figure 2.21 Neurotransmitter leading to postsynaptic potential. The result of neurotransmitter binding to the postsynaptic membrane receptors is to change the membrane potential. These postsynaptic potentials can be either excitatory as shown here (depolarize the membrane) or inhibitory (hyperpolarize the membrane).

muscle cell, the EPSP leads to action potentials in the muscle and muscular contraction. If the neurotransmitter has an inhibitory action on the postsynaptic neuron, then hyperpolarization of the membrane potential occurs, resulting in the postsynaptic neuron being less likely to generate an action potential.

GROSS AND FUNCTIONAL ANATOMY OF THE CENTRAL NERVOUS SYSTEM

Signaling in the nervous system occurs along well-defined pathways, and via specific anatomical relays to circumscribed areas of the brain, spinal cord, and peripheral musculature. A review of the nervous system's anatomical organization clarifies how this works. We begin with a global view and in later chapters focus on specific anatomical and physiological systems relevant to a mental operation or behavioral state.

Cerebral Cortex

The cerebral cortex has two symmetrical hemispheres that consist of large sheets of layered neurons. It covers core structures that include the limbic system and basal ganglia and surrounds the structures of the diencephalon that will be considered later: Together, the cerebral cortex, basal ganglia, and diencephalon form the *forebrain*. The term *cortex* means "bark," as in tree bark, and in higher mammals and humans it contains many infoldings or convolutions (Figure 2.22). The infoldings of the cortical sheet are further defined as sulci (the enfolded regions) and gyri (the crowns of the folded tissue that one observes when viewing the surface). Many mammal species have smooth, unfolded cortices and few sulci and gyri.

The folds of the human cortex serve a functional purpose: to pack more cortical surface into the skull. If the human cortex were smoothed out to resemble that of the rat, for example, humans would need to have gigantic heads. There is about a one-third savings in space when the cortex is folded as compared with unfolded. The total surface area of the human cerebral cortex is about 2200 to 2400 cm^2, but because of the folding, about two-thirds of this area is confined within the depths of the sulci. Although the cortex is composed of several cell layers, its thickness averages only 3 mm but ranges from 1.5 to 4.5 mm in different cortical regions. The cortex itself contains the cell bodies of neurons, their dendrites, and some of their axons. In addition, the cortex has axons and terminals of neurons projecting to the cortex from other brain regions such as the thalamus, and of course it also contains blood vessels. Be-

cause the cerebral cortex has such a high density of cell bodies, it appears a grayish brown in relation to underlying regions that are composed primarily of axons of neurons and appear slightly paler or even white. For this reason anatomists used the terms *gray matter* and *white matter* when referring to areas of cell bodies and axon tracts, respectively. The latter tracts represent the billions of axons that connect the neurons of the cerebral cortex to other locations in the brain. The whitish look

Figure 2.22   Lateral view of the left hemisphere **(a)** and dorsal view of the cerebral cortex **(b)** in humans. The major features of the cortex are indicated, including the four cortical lobes and various key gyri. Gyri (singular is *gyrus*) are separated by sulci (singular is *sulcus*) and result from the folding of the cerebral cortex that occurs during development of the nervous system, to achieve an economy of size.

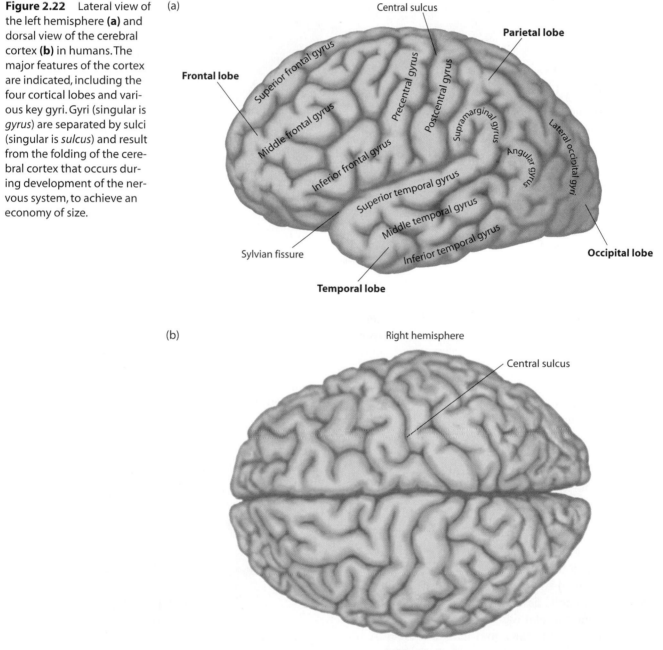

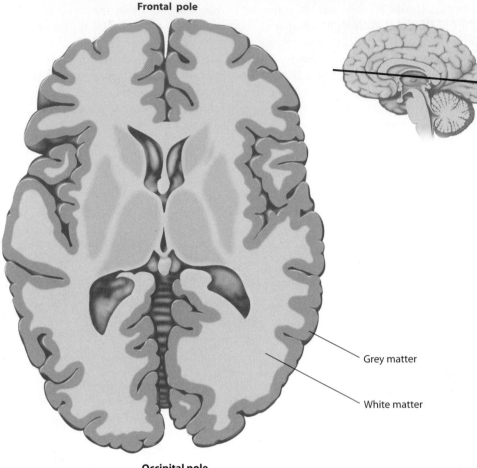

Frontal pole

Occipital pole

Grey matter

White matter

Figure 2.23 Horizontal section through the cerebral hemispheres at the level indicated. White matter is composed of myelinated axons and gray matter is composed primarily of neurons. From this diagram one can see that the gray matter on the surface of the cerebral hemispheres forms a continuous sheet that is heavily enfolded. Adapted from DeArmond et al. (1976).

of axon groups in the CNS and in the peripheral nerves is primarily caused by the myelin sheaths that surround the axons (Figure 2.23).

ANATOMICAL SUBDIVISIONS OF THE CEREBRAL CORTEX

The cerebral hemispheres have four main divisions or lobes. These regions have different functional properties and can be distinguished from one another by anatomical landmarks, principally sulci. The names of the brain areas were derived from names originally given to the overlying skull bones; for example, the temporal lobe lies underneath the temporal bone. The temporal bone derived its name from the graying of hair overlying the temporal bone—a sign of passing time if there ever was one.

The four lobes are the frontal, parietal, temporal, and occipital lobes (Figure 2.24). The central sulcus (singular of sulci) divides the frontal from the parietal lobes, and the lateral fissure separates the temporal from the frontal and parietal lobes. The occipital lobe is demarcated from the parietal and temporal lobes by the parieto-occipital sulcus on the brain's dorsal surface and

Figure 2.24 Four lobes of the cerebral cortex, in lateral view of the left hemisphere. See text for details.

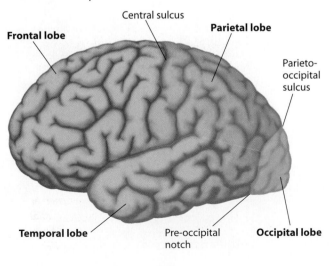

Central sulcus

Frontal lobe

Parietal lobe

Parieto-occipital sulcus

Temporal lobe

Pre-occipital notch

Occipital lobe

the preoccipital notch located on the ventral-lateral surface. The left and right cerebral hemispheres are separated by the interhemispheric fissure that runs from the rostral to the caudal end of the forebrain. Interconnections between the cerebral hemispheres are accomplished by axons from cortical neurons that travel through the corpus callosum, which represents the largest white-matter commissure in the nervous system (*commissure* is a special term for white matter tracts that cross from the left to the right side, or vice versa, of the CNS). The term *corpus callosum* means "hard body," so named because of its tough consistency. Indeed, early anatomists believed that the corpus callosum served a structural function in supporting the cerebral hemispheres because it prevented them from collapsing onto structures below; this is not correct. As we discuss later in the book, the corpus callosum carries out valuable integrative functions for the two hemispheres.

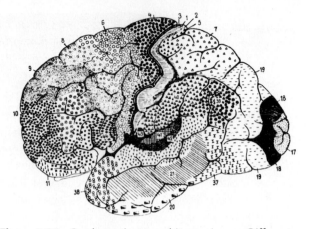

Figure 2.25 Brodmann's cytoarchitectonic map. Different regions of cortex have been demarcated by histological examination of the cellular microanatomy. Brodmann divided the cortex into about 50 areas.

CYTOARCHITECTURE OF CEREBRAL CORTEX

The cerebral cortex can be divided more finely than the four main lobes, in various ways. For example, it can be divided according to functional subdivisions of the cortex. But there are other, more purely anatomical criteria for subdividing the cortex: One is by the microanatomy of cell types and their organization. This is generally referred to as *cytoarchitectonics*—*cyto* means "cell" and *architectonics* means "architecture"—and has to do with how cells in a region appear morphologically and are arranged with respect to each other. Cytoarchitectonic investigations entail performing detailed histological analysis of the tissue from different regions of the cerebral cortex, and attempting to define the extent of regions wherein the cellular architecture looks similar, and therefore might signal a homogeneous region of cortex that represents a functional area. This work began in earnest with Korbinian Brodmann at the turn of this century.

Brodmann (1909) identified approximately fifty regions of the cerebral cortex. These areas, categorized according to differences in cellular morphology and organization, were numbered, and the numbers are still used today to describe cortical areas (Figure 2.25). Other anatomists further subdivided the cortex into almost 200 cytoarchitectonically defined areas, but many classified transition zones as separate areas when perhaps they should not be considered so. A combination of cytoarchitectonic and functional descriptions of the cortex is probably most effective in dividing the cerebral cortex into meaningful units; this type of work will likely continue into the foreseeable future because we are only beginning to learn the cerebral cortex's functional organization. In the sections that follow, we use Brodmann's numbering system to describe the cerebral cortex as well as anatomical names. The Brodmann system often seems unsystematic—indeed, the numbering has more to do with the order in which Brodmann sampled a region than with any meaningful relation between areas— nonetheless, in some regions the numbering system has a rough correspondence with the relations between areas that carry out similar functions, such as vision.

FUNCTIONAL DIVISIONS OF THE CEREBRAL CORTEX

The lobes of the cerebral cortex have a variety of functional roles in neural processing. Major identifiable systems can be localized within each lobe. These systems do not map one-to-one onto the lobe they primarily reside in, but in part the gross anatomical subdivisions of the cerebral cortex can be related to functionality. Because one of the goals of this book is to review what we know about the functional localization of higher cognitive and perceptual processes, what follows is a beginner's guide to the cortex's functional anatomy.

Motor Areas of the Frontal Lobe The frontal lobes play a major role in the planning and execution of movements. This includes the precentral gyrus, which is also called the motor strip (Brodmann's area 4), and is located just anterior to the central sulcus. The precentral gyrus represents the primary motor cortex (motor area 1, or MI). Anterior to this area are two more main motor areas of cortex (within Brodmann's area 6), the premotor cortex on the lateral surface of the hemisphere and the supplementary motor cortex that lies dorsal to the premotor area and extends around to the

Navigating in the Brain

Because the brain is a complex three-dimensional object with numerous structures and pathways that are difficult to imagine in two-dimensional pictures, it is important to utilize conventions for describing the relations of regions. In general, the terms we use were derived from those used by anatomists to describe similar relations in the body as a whole, and therefore the brain's orientation with respect to the body determines the coordinate frame of reference that is used to describe anatomical relationships in the brain. But some confusing aspects of the terminology arise from differences in how the head and body are arranged in animals that walk on four legs versus humans, who are upright. Consider a dog's body surfaces. The front end is the rostral end, meaning "nose." The opposite end of this is the caudal end, the "tail." The back is the dorsal surface and the bottom surface is the ventral body surface (Figure A). We can now refer to the dog's nervous system by using the same coordinates (Figure B). The part of the brain toward the front is the rostral end, toward the frontal lobes; the posterior end is the caudal end, toward the occipital lobe; and the top and bottom are the dorsal and ventral surfaces of the brain. This seems to be a reasonable set of conventions, or is it? Consider the human (Figure C).

Humans are atypical, and thus create confusing problems with respect to anatomical nomenclature. The reason is simple: Humans stand upright and therefore tilt their heads down in order to be parallel with the ground. Thus, the dorsal surface of the body and brain are now at right angles to each other. But the conventions still apply, though there may be some confusion unless we remember that humans have tilted their heads. Rostral still means toward the frontal pole, while caudal still means toward the occipital pole as long as we are referring to the brain; however, when we discuss the spinal cord, the coordinate systems shift with respect to one another, but not with respect to the local body axis. Thus, in the spinal cord, rostral means in the direction toward the brain, just as it does in the dog.

Some more definitions: The diagrams in this chapter are illustrated according to the plane of section that best shows the brain areas described. We can see from the figure that sagittal sections cut between the two hemispheres of the brain or spinal cord are perpendicular to the ground and thereby divide the nervous system left from right. Cross sections, or transverse sections, are slices that divide the nervous system in the rostral-caudal direction, and hence are at 90-degree angles through the rostral-caudal dimension. When in the brain, coronal sections are essentially cross sections with respect to the forebrain. Horizontal sections of the brain are those that are parallel with the floor when the subject is standing upright.

Definitions:

Rostral, anterior = toward the nose or front end

Caudal, posterior = toward the tail of an animal, or toward the feet in humans

Dorsal = the back of an animal walking on four legs, or the back in humans

Ventral = the belly side of animals upright or on four legs

Lateral = toward the outside and away from the midline of the human body

Medial = toward the midline and away from the periphery of the human body

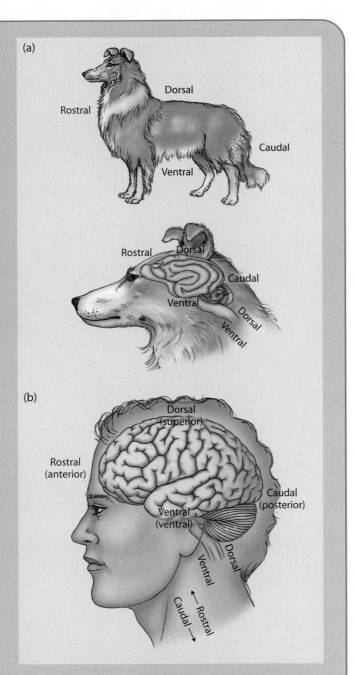

Anatomical terms for describing various views of anatomy and sections through brain and body. The relationship between a bipedal human and quadruped animal leads to some important considerations in describing the surfaces of the brain and spinal cord.

hemisphere's medial surface. These motor cortical areas contain motor neurons whose axons extend to the spinal cord and brainstem and synapse on motor neurons in the spinal cord. The motor neurons, located in the output layer 5 of the motor cortex, have fascinating specializations. In particular, layer 5 of the primary motor cortex contains large pyramidal neurons known as Betz's cells, named after Vladimir Aleksandrovich Betz who described them. They are the largest neurons in the cerebral cortex, reaching 60 to 80 microns in diameter at the cell body.

The most anterior region of the frontal lobe, the prefrontal cortex, takes part in the higher aspects of motor control and the planning and execution of behavior, tasks that require the integration of information over time. The prefrontal cortex has two main areas: the dorsolateral prefrontal cortex, which is found on the lateral surface of the frontal lobe anterior to the premotor regions, and the orbitofrontal cortex (Figure 2.26). The orbitofrontal cortex is located on the frontal lobe's anterior-ventral surface, and extends medially to limbic lobe structures, with which it maintains interconnectivity.

Somatosensory Areas of the Parietal Lobe The somatosensory cortex is in the postcentral gyrus and adjacent areas (Brodmann's areas 1, 2, and 3). These cortical regions receive inputs from the somatosensory relays of the thalamus and represent information about touch, pain, temperature sense, and limb proprioception (limb position). The primary somatosensory cortex (or SI) is immediately caudal to the central sulcus, and a secondary somatosensory cortex (SII), receiving information via projections primarily from SI, is located ventrally to SI. Somatosensory inputs projecting to the posterior parietal cortex arise from SI and SII. Somatosensory information coming into the thalamus and then to the primary somatosensory cortex traverses two main pathways: the anterolateral system for pain and temperature sense, and the dorsal column—medial lemniscal system for information about touch, proprioception, and movement (Figure 2.27). Receptor cells in the periphery transduce physical stimuli into neuronal impulses conducted to the spinal cord and toward the brain, making synaptic connections at relay sites along the ascending pathway. The two systems for somatosensory information take slightly different paths in the spinal cord, brainstem, and midbrain on their route to the thalamus, and thence the cortex.

Visual Processing Areas in the Occipital Lobe The primary visual cortex (also known as striate cortex or V1,

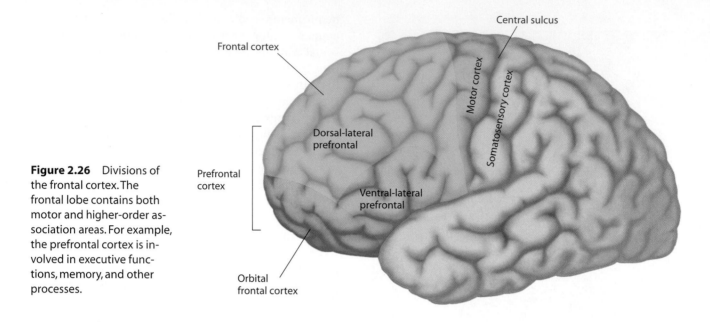

Figure 2.26 Divisions of the frontal cortex. The frontal lobe contains both motor and higher-order association areas. For example, the prefrontal cortex is involved in executive functions, memory, and other processes.

Figure 2.27 The somatosensory cortex is located in the postcentral gyrus. Inputs from peripheral receptors project via the thalamus (shown in cross section) to the primary somatosensory cortex (SI).

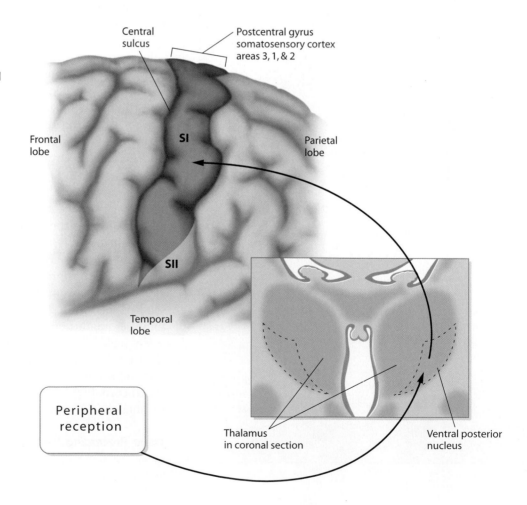

or Brodmann's area 17) receives visual inputs relayed from the lateral geniculate nucleus of the thalamus (Figure 2.28). In humans, the primary visual cortex is primarily on the medial surface of the cerebral hemispheres, extending only slightly onto the posterior hemispheric pole. Thus, most of the primary visual cortex is effectively hidden from view, between the two hemispheres. The cortex in this area has six layers; it is largely responsible for coding visual features like color, luminance, spatial frequency, orientation, and movement, but these properties are organized within the two main projection streams of visual processing. Visual information from the outside world is processed by the retina's cells and transmitted via the optic nerve to the lateral geniculate nucleus of the thalamus, and thence to V1, a pathway often referred to as the retino-geniculostriate, or primary visual pathway. Note that visual projections from the retina also reach other subcortical brain regions by way of secondary projection systems. The superior colliculus of the midbrain is the main target of the secondary pathway and participates in visuomotor functions.

Surrounding the striate cortex is a large visual cortical region called the *extrastriate* ("outside the striate") *visual cortex* (sometimes referred to as the prestriate cortex in monkeys, to signify that it is anatomically anterior to the striate cortex). The extrastriate cortex includes Brodmann's areas 18 and 19. From physiological recordings and anatomical studies in monkeys, it is now known that there are more than three dozen distinct visual areas in the primate extrastriate cortex. These visual areas contain partially redundant maps of the visual world, but each is specialized to analyze spe-

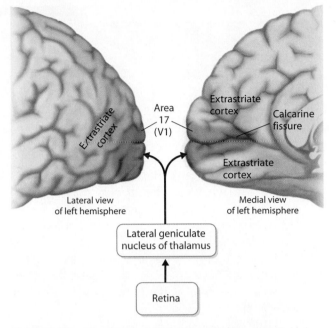

Figure 2.28 The visual cortex is located in the occipital lobe. Area 17 of Brodmann, also called the primary visual cortex (V1), is located at the occipital pole, and extends onto the medial surface of the hemisphere where it is largely buried within the calcarine fissure.

cific aspects of a scene, such as color, motion, location, and form. Two pathways from the striate cortex to extrastriate regions convey prominent streams of information (Figure 2.29). One pathway flows from V1 to the temporal lobe (ventral pathway or "what" pathway) and conveys analysis of stimulus features and their conjunctions, and ultimately the information is used to

Figure 2.29 Projections from the primary visual cortex (V1) to visual areas in the extrastriate cortex follow two main projection routes. A dorsal "where" pathway that codes motion and location, and a ventral "what" pathway that processes detailed stimulus features, form and object identity.

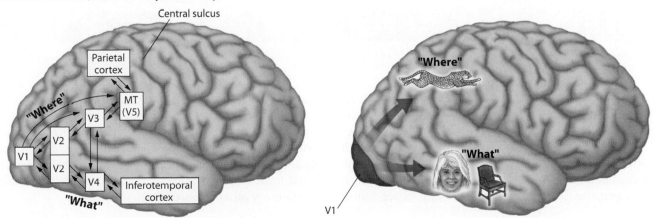

The Chambers of the Mind

We have understood for many decades that neurons in the brain are functional units, and that how they are interconnected yields specific circuits for the support of particular behaviors. Centuries ago, early anatomists, believing that the head contained the seat of behavior, examined the brain to see where the conscious self (soul, if you wish) was located. They found a likely candidate: some chambers in the brain that seem to be empty (except for some fluid) and thus possible containers for higher functions. These chambers are called *ventricles* (see Figure 2.23). What is the function of these chambers within the brain?

The brain weighs a considerable amount but has little or no structural support—there is no skeletal system for the brain. To overcome this potential difficulty, the brain is immersed in a fluid, called *cerebrospinal fluid* (CSF). This fluid allows the brain to float to help offset the pressure that would be present if the brain were merely sitting on the base of the skull. CSF also reduces shock to the brain and spinal cord during rapid acceler-

ations or decelerations, such as when we fall or are struck on the head.

The ventricles inside the brain are continuous with the CSF surrounding the brain. The largest of these chambers are the lateral ventricles, which are connected to the third ventricle in the brain's midline. The cerebral aqueduct joins the third to the fourth ventricle in the brainstem below the cerebellum. The CSF is produced in the lateral ventricles, and in the third ventricle by the choroid plexus, an outpouching of the ventricular wall by blood vessels. Hence, CSF is similar to blood, being formed by the transport of what resembles an ultrafiltrate of blood plasma; essentially CSF is a clear fluid containing proteins, glucose, and ions, especially potassium, sodium, and chloride. It slowly circulates from the lateral and third ventricles through the cerebral aqueduct to the fourth ventricle, and on to the subarachnoid space surrounding the brain, to be reabsorbed by the arachnoid villi in the sagittal sinus (the large venous system located between the two hemispheres on the dorsal surface).

carry out form discrimination and object identification. The other pathway projects from V1 toward the parietal lobe (dorsal or "where" pathway) and carries information about stimulus motion and localization within visual space. Each of the multiple extrastriate areas maintains strong neural interconnectivity with areas prior to it in the visual hierarchy (a reciprocal connectivity) and with other areas in the same processing stream. As well, many interconnections are between the dorsal and ventral visual processing streams. Indeed, interconnectivity of the visual cortex is complex but not random; that is, despite how it might appear on first look, not every area of visual cortex is connected with every other (Figure 2.30).

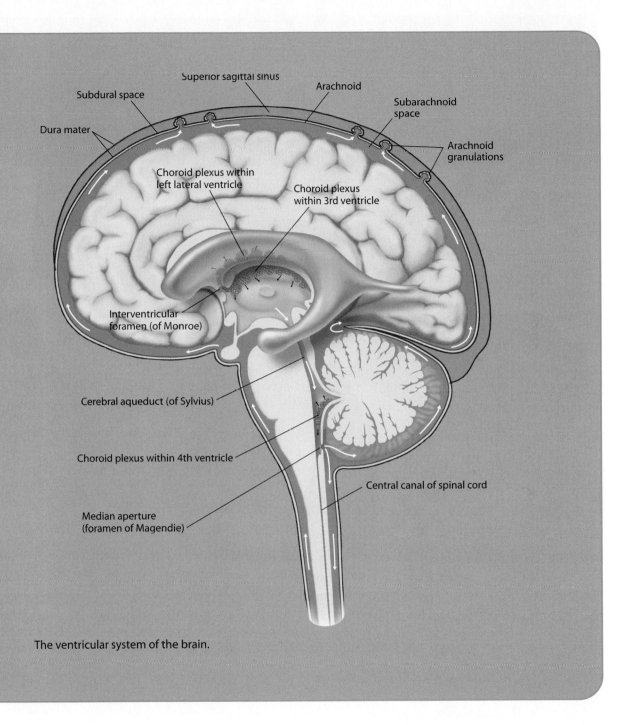

The ventricular system of the brain.

Auditory Processing Areas in the Temporal Lobe The auditory cortex lies in the superior part of the temporal lobe and is buried within the sylvian fissure (Figure 2.31). The projection from the cochlea, through the subcortical relays to the medial geniculate of the thalamus, then proceeds to the supratemporal cortex in a region known as *Heschl's gyri*. This region represents AI, the primary auditory cortex, and AII, the auditory association area surrounding it and posterior to the primary auditory cortex (Brodmann's areas 41 and 42). Area 22, which surrounds the auditory cortex, aids in the perception of auditory inputs; when this area is stimulated, sensations of sound are produced in humans. One can represent the sensory inputs to the auditory cortex using

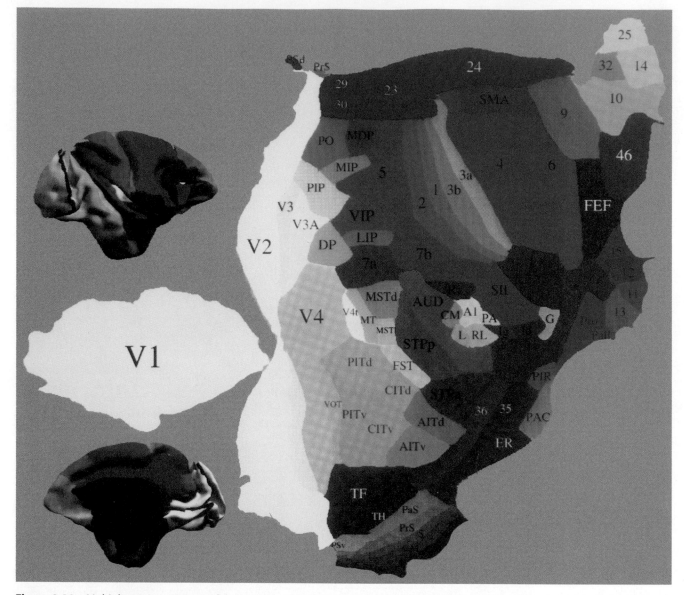

Figure 2.30 Multiple representations of the visual world exist in extrastriate visual areas. Somewhere between 30 and 35 of these visual areas have been identified in monkeys, using a combination of anatomical and physiological methods. Each contains neurons performing specialized processing of the visual inputs. This representation shows how the cortex of a macaque monkey looks in normal perspective and when the cortex is flattened to aid in viewing the relationships of the various cortical areas. This flattened representation produced by David Van Essen and his colleagues includes areas outside of visual cortex **(right)** as well as the visual areas **(left)**.

a tonotopic map; the orderly representation of sound frequency within the auditory cortex can be determined with several tonotopic maps.

Association Cortex The volume of cortex that is not sensory or motor has traditionally been termed the *association cortex*, which is composed of regions that receive inputs from one or more modalities. These regions have specific functional roles that are not exclusively sensory or motor. For example, take the visual association cortex. Though the primary visual cortex is necessary for the conscious sensation of vision, neither it nor the extrastriate cortex are the sole loci of visual perception. Regions of visual association cortex in the parietal and temporal lobes are important for correct perception of the visual world. As described below, portions of the

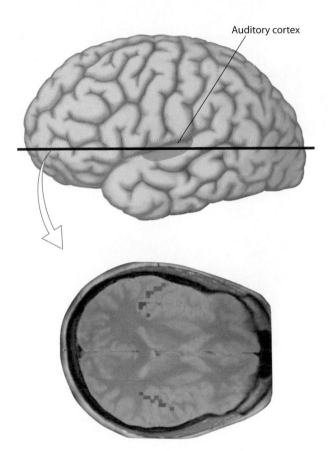

Auditory cortex

Figure 2.31 Primary auditory cortex is located in the superior temporal lobe **(top).** The primary auditory cortex and surrounding association auditory areas contain representations of auditory stimuli and show a tonotopic organization. The magnetic resonance image **(bottom)** shows areas of the superior temporal region in horizontal section that have been stimulated by tones of different frequency and which showed increased blood flow as a result of neuronal activity (Reprinted from Wessinger et al., 1997, Figure 2).

limbic lobe take part in emotional processes, and the frontal association cortex plans and calculates the long-term outcomes of a certain act. Finally, the association areas of the parietal-temporal-occipital junction have a prominent role in language processing. Thus, higher mental processes are the domain of the association cor-

tical areas, in interaction with sensory and motor areas of cortex.

LIMBIC SYSTEM

We now take a look at portions of the forebrain that are collectively known as the *limbic lobe* (Figure 2.32).

Figure 2.32 The limbic lobe. Medial view of right hemisphere indicating the structures that comprise the limbic system.

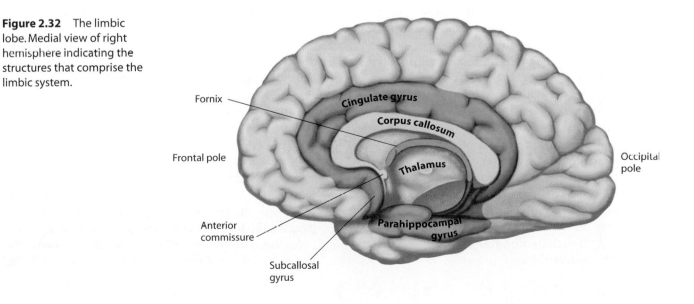

Fornix

Cingulate gyrus

Corpus callosum

Frontal pole

Thalamus

Occipital pole

Anterior commissure

Parahippocampal gyrus

Subcallosal gyrus

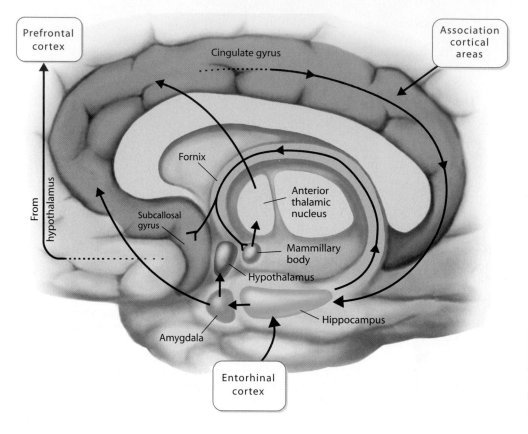

Prefrontal cortex

Association cortical areas

Cingulate gyrus

Fornix

From hypothalamus

Subcallosal gyrus

Anterior thalamic nucleus

Mammillary body

Hypothalamus

Hippocampus

Amygdala

Entorhinal cortex

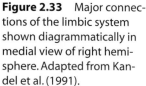

Figure 2.33 Major connections of the limbic system shown diagrammatically in medial view of right hemisphere. Adapted from Kandel et al. (1991).

These include several structures that form a border (Latin, *limbus*) around the brainstem, named the *grand lobe limbique* by Paul Broca. Above the corpus callosum, a band of cortex known as the *cingulate gyrus* reaches from anterior to posterior. Together with the parahippocampal gyrus, subcallosal gyrus, dentate gyrus, and the hippocampal formation, these structures constitute the limbic lobe (Figure 2.33).

Limbic structures interconnect with each other and with major subcortical structures (such as the amygdala, hypothalamus, thalamus, and basal ganglia) to form the limbic system. The limbic lobe comes from a more primitive type of cortex, not the six-layered neocortex like the rest of the cortical mantle. Limbic structures such as the cingulate gyrus have less than six visible cell layers, as well as other differences from the neocortex. Limbic lobe structures are also phylogenetically older than the surrounding neocortex and are more common in the brains of nonmammalian species; for example, reptiles have little neocortex, whereas the primate brain is composed mostly of neocortex. The limbic system participates in emotional processing, learning, and memory. With each passing year we discover new functions of this system.

THE BASAL GANGLIA

The basal ganglia are a collection of subcortical neuronal groups in the forebrain located beneath the anterior portion of the lateral ventricles (see below). The basal ganglia have a significant role in the control of movement, and the three main subdivisions of the basal ganglia are the globus pallidus, caudate nucleus, and putamen (Figure 2.34). The caudate and putamen are referred to together as the *neostriatum,* because they are phylogenetically the most recent of the basal ganglia to appear and are developmentally related. The neostriatum together with the globus pallidus (the *paleostriatum*) form the *corpus striatum.*

Some anatomists have considered the amygdaloid complex to be part of the basal ganglia, but this is not the convention agreed on by most neuroscientists today. Some say that both the subthalamic nucleus and the substantia nigra are part of the basal ganglia because of their similar neuronal structure and strong interconnectivity with the principal cell groups forming the basal ganglia. Yet the substantia nigra, at least, is generally considered part of the midbrain—actually located at the juncture of the midbrain and diencephalon—while the

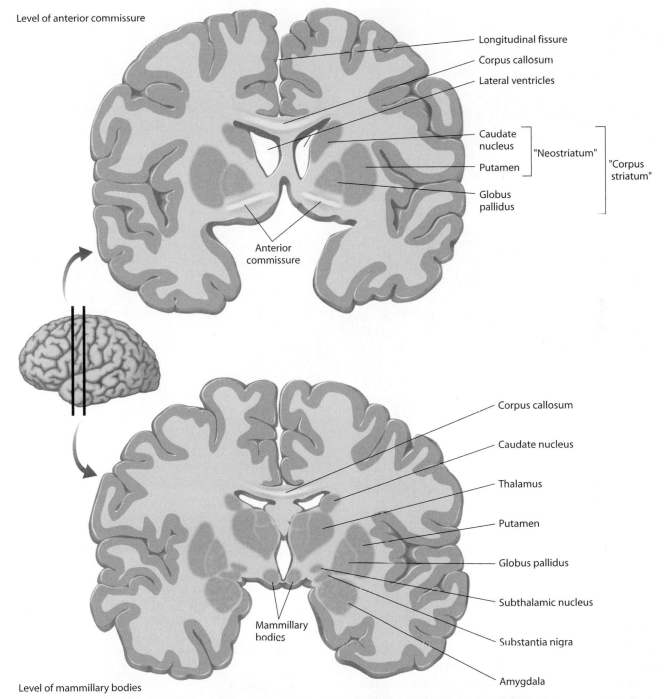

Level of anterior commissure

Longitudinal fissure
Corpus callosum
Lateral ventricles
Caudate nucleus
Putamen
Globus pallidus
"Neostriatum"
"Corpus striatum"
Anterior commissure

Corpus callosum
Caudate nucleus
Thalamus
Putamen
Globus pallidus
Subthalamic nucleus
Substantia nigra
Amygdala
Mammillary bodies

Level of mammillary bodies

Figure 2.34 Cross section through the brain showing the basal ganglia. Adapted from Carpenter (1976).

basal ganglia are in the forebrain. This gross anatomical distinction between the substantia nigra and the nuclear groups of the basal ganglia may not be as important as the microanatomical (cellular) and functional relationships. Perhaps then, deciding how to classify these structures anatomically is less important than understanding their functional relations, an observation with general application in neural anatomy and physiology.

The basal ganglia, subthalamic nucleus, and substantia nigra participate in circuits with the cortex and thalamus to mediate aspects of motor control (both somatic motor and oculomotor systems), as well as cognitive

Dancing to Death: Diseases of the Motor System

In 1982 Nancy Wexler and a team of scientists from the Huntington's Disease Foundation traveled to a small fishing village in Venezuela. There, Nancy observed a startling sight—a population full of people walking as though drunk, some with wildly swaying gaits, and grand hand gestures or simple repetitive movements of the body, limbs, and face. Many were unable to speak clearly, if at all. She recognized this disease because it had killed her mother, and it was her arch enemy—she too had a 50% chance of becoming like these people as did her siblings. The disease is known as *Huntington's chorea* or *Huntington's disease*. Huntington's chorea (*chorea* means "dance") was first described by Huntington in the 1870s. He was a physician in a rural area of Long Island, New York, and he and his father, also a physician, had observed the disease over generations in certain families. It typically has an onset after the age of 40 (but can be earlier, even in childhood), and includes both motor and cognitive symptoms leading finally to death after progressive decline over a 10- to 20-year period. These symptoms are caused by cell losses in the basal ganglia, and probably also in part from damage to cortical neurons as the result of the basal ganglia cell loss and subsequent deterioration in the cortical-striatal circuitry. There is no cure. Thanks to research on the population living in Venezuela, however, there is now a genetic marker for the disease. Using molecular genetic techniques, we can know whether a person carries the disease and will develop it in his or her lifetime. To date, although the Wexler family has dedicated itself to tracking down and curing this disease, none of the Wexler children has used the genetic techniques they helped to develop, to look into their own futures. Nancy Wexler remains healthy and continues her phenomenal personal struggle against this terrible disease.

functions such as the short-term memory processes of the dorsolateral prefrontal cortex, and some functions that can be called *executive functions* because they involve high-level control of behavior, something we discuss later in this book.

The primary circuits projecting to the basal ganglia include a "cortico-striatal" projection that includes direct projections from all major cortical regions onto neurons in the caudate and putamen, which are the input structures of the basal ganglia. In addition, motor areas of cortex can project to the basal ganglia via the cell groups in the thalamus, and the subthalamic nucleus. The major outputs of the basal ganglia project from the globus pallidus to thalamic nuclei and thence to cortex, primarily motor and premotor cortex, as well as prefrontal cortex (Figure 2.35). Thus, the basal ganglia are not in a projection pathway from motor cortical areas to the spinal cord, to control muscular activity directly, but instead are part of a cortical-subcortical motor loop that is thought to monitor aspects of how motor activity as well as nonmotoric functions are progressing (see Dancing to Death: Diseases of the Motor System, above).

Figure 2.35 Major inputs and outputs of basal ganglia. The basal ganglia form a cortical-subcortical motor loop that monitors motor behavior. Adapted from Kandel et al. (1991).

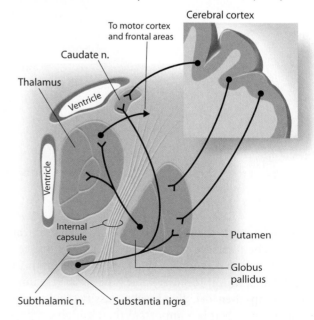

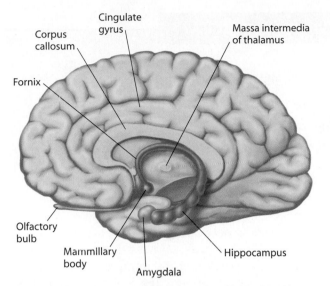

Figure 2.36 Anatomy of the hippocampal formation. The hippocampus is located in the inferior medial temporal lobe.

HIPPOCAMPAL FORMATION AND MEDIAL TEMPORAL LOBE

The region of the forebrain along the ventral medial surface of the temporal lobe contains the hippocampus, and the associated areas of the dentate gyrus, parahippocampal gyrus, and entorhinal cortex—the latter being the anterior portion of the parahippocampal gyrus (Brodmann's area 28) (Figure 2.36). The hippocampus and dentate gyrus are composed of a three-layer cortex, whereas entorhinal cortex and the parahippocampal gyrus is a form of six-layer cortex in humans.

The hippocampus has been subdivided into zones known as cornu ammonis (CA) 1, CA2, CA3, and CA4 based on differences in cellular morphology, connectivity, and development (Figure 2.37). The entorhinal cortex provides the main inputs to the dentate gyrus and hippocampus, via two projection pathways that terminate primarily on pyramidal neurons in the hippocampus. In turn, the entorhinal cortex receives inputs from the cingulate cortex, and thus a pathway to the hippocampus from the cingulate cortex appears to project via the entorhinal cortex. The hippocampal pyramidal neurons project out of the hippocampus via the fornix, a large white-matter tract. Some of these fibers cross to the opposite hemisphere, but the majority make an arching projection, first posteriorly and then anteriorly running below the corpus callosum. Finally, this projection pathway dives ventrally, and anterior to the thalamus, through the hypothalamus to make contacts with the mamillary bodies, with some regions of thalamus, and via a separate projection, to the medial septal area of cortex. The hippocampus has been implicated in emotional processing (because of its interconnections with cingulate and mamillary bodies) and memory.

DIENCEPHALON

The remaining portions of the forebrain to consider are the thalamus and hypothalamus, which together comprise the diencephalon. *Thalamus* is the Greek term for "inner chamber," even though it is not actually hollow. It lies at the most rostral end of the brainstem (Figure 2.38), in the dorsal part of the diencephalon, and is bordered dorsally by the third ventricle, fornix, and corpus callosum and laterally by the internal capsule—the projection fibers from the motor cortex to the brainstem and spinal cord—which separates the thalamus from the basal ganglia. The thalamus is a bilateral structure that is separated along the midline by the third ventricle. In some people, the two halves of the thalamus are connected by a bridge of gray matter called the *massa intermedia.*

The thalamus has been referred to as the "gateway to the cortex" because, with the exception of some olfactory inputs, all sensory modalities make synaptic relays

Figure 2.37 Histological slide of a cross section through the hippocampus. The dentate gyrus (DG), entorhinal cortex (EC), and subiculum (S) can be seen, as well as cells of CA fields. (Courtesy of David Amaral.)

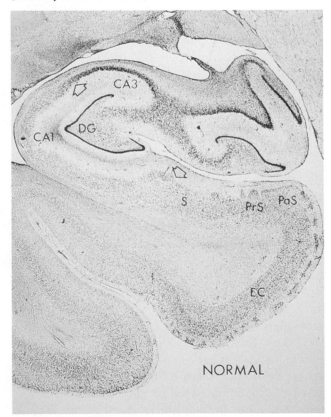

An Interview with David Amaral, Ph.D.

Dr. Amaral is a Professor of Psychiatry at the Center for Neuroscience, University of California, Davis, and the founding and current editor of the scientific journal Hippocampus.

Authors: You have done some of the pioneering work on the anatomy of the hippocampus and its function. How would you characterize how studying neuroanatomy informs our understanding of how the brain works?

DA: Understanding the intrinsic circuitry and the inputs and outputs of a brain region not only provides insight into how it functions, but also provides essential information on how it interacts with other brain regions. Understanding the unique neuroanatomical features of a brain region is particularly helpful in interpreting the unique neural computations that it is capable of carrying out.

Using the hippocampal formation as an example, we now know that virtually all of the sensory input that it receives arises from higher-order, multimodal cortical regions. This would indicate that whatever processing is done by the hippocampus in the service of forming long-term memories is accomplished with fairly abstract, gestalt-like representations of experience. It is also now clear that in addition to its subcortical connections, the hippocampal formation has massive return connections to the neocortex. This fits well with the emerging view that the hippocampal formation is not the final repository of long-term memories. Thus, a reasonable strategy for defining the storage sites would be to search the cortical areas that receive hippocampal inputs.

Authors: The intrinsic connections of the hippocampus have also been extensively studied. Why has this received so much attention?

DA: Well, the effects of hippocampal lesions on memory suggest the hippocampus ought to be a neural machine designed for forming associations. Indeed by studying the local connections, one can get a feel for how this structure goes about its business. It appears that by way of the extensive associational connections, hippocampal neurons can form essentially limitless networks to create representations of perceived experiences. We have learned that one of the cardinal features of the intrinsic anatomy of the hippocampal formation is the high degree of divergence and convergence of its stepwise connections. Unlike regions of primary sensory neocortex that demonstrate a point-to-point mapping of connections, connections originating in one portion of the hippocampal formation project to as much as half of the entire region of the next processing step. This is particularly true in the hippocampus proper where the vast majority of the inputs to a pyramidal cell in the area known as CA3 originate from other CA3 neurons. Thus, the neuroanatomical fact of high levels of associational connections predicts that individual neurons can be addressed by myriad inputs; that is, their response properties are not hard wired as a neuron in V1 might be.

Authors: Lesions to most cortical structures are never as dramatically devastating as are those to the hippocampus. There always seems to be some sparing of function with cortical lesions. Why is that?

DA: A unique feature about the intrinsic hippocampal circuitry is that the major intrinsic connections are all unidirectional. This neuroanatomical feature suggests that information processing in the hippocampal formation follows an obligatory sequence of steps at which different computations are carried out. The prac-

in the thalamus before continuing to the primary cortical sensory receiving areas. The thalamus is divided into several nuclei that act as specific relays for incoming sensory information. The lateral geniculate nucleus receives information from the ganglion cells of the retina, and sends axons to the primary visual cortex, area 17 (Figure 2.39). Similarly, the medial geniculate nucleus receives information from the inner ear, via other brainstem nuclei in the ascending auditory pathway, and sends axons to the primary auditory cortex (AI). Somatosensory information from ascending pathways synapses with Brodmann's areas 1, 2, and 3.

tical ramification of this unique circuitry is that damaging any link in the chain can have devastating effects on function. An example of this is the amnesic syndrome that is produced in human patients who have suffered an ischemic loss confined to the CA1 field. These patients show a severe, anterograde amnesic syndrome despite the fact that the remainder of the hippocampal formation is intact.

Authors: Actually, the hippocampus was once viewed as the essential brain region involved with establishing memories. Now that view has undergone a significant change. Why has there been this change?

DA: The hippocampal formation was implicated in memory function because it was sensitive to a variety of neurological pathologies which resulted both in damage to the hippocampus and in impairment of memory (see Chapter 7). But the capricious nature of neuropathology couldn't be relied on to define all of the memory-related brain regions. So, again, one can come to appreciate the value of careful neuroanatomical studies. Such studies can define the total system of brain structures involved in a particular cognitive function. By starting at the hippocampal formation and examining its inputs and outputs, neuroanatomists have provided a much more comprehensive understanding of brain regions involved in memory. In the last 10 years, for example, studies carried out in the monkey have determined that the largest contributor of sensory information to the hippocampal formation comes from two regions of neocortex, the perirhinal and parahippocampal cortices, that lie adjacent to the hippocampal formation in the primate temporal lobe. These brain regions were ignored for many years by behavioral neuroscientists interested in the medial temporal lobe substrate of memory, and their damage during lesions of the hippocampus or amygdala was considered to be inconsequential to observed behavioral deficits. Spurred on by the newer neuroanatomical findings, however, recent behavioral and electrophysiological studies have demonstrated that the perirhinal and parahippocampal cortices not only play an important role in contributing sensory information to the hippocampal formation but also subserve some forms of memory function on their own, that is, independent of the hippocampal formation. Thus, neuroanatomical studies can provide clues as to which regions to study by more functionally oriented methodologies.

Authors: And what about the role neuroanatomy plays for those interested in more molecular approaches to the nervous system?

DA: The neuroanatomy of the last twenty years has been heavily involved in defining the chemical identity of neurons and pathways in the brain. The neuroanatomical fact that one of the highest brain densities of N-methyl-D-aspartate (NMDA) receptors is found in the CA1 field of the hippocampus has heightened interest in the role of this glutamate receptor in memory function. Chemical neuroanatomy is essential in defining the functional valence (excitatory versus inhibitory) of defined brain pathways and for determining potential modulators of cognitive function. Again, confirmation of the neuroanatomical predictions must rely on functional analyses such as electrophysiology and neuropharmacology. All in all, neuroanatomy provides essential information on the components and organization of brain systems that carry out particular cognitive functions. It can provide insight into the kinds of inputs the system is using and unique features of the information processing within the system. All of this information constrains hypotheses as to how the system functions. While I have used examples from studies of the hippocampal formation and memory, similar examples could be generated from the visual cortex, striatum, or even the spinal cord. In each case, neuroanatomy provides essential clues that facilitate the design and interpretation of functionally oriented studies.

Not only is the thalamus involved in relaying primary sensory information; but it also receives inputs from the basal ganglia, cerebellum, cortex, and medial temporal lobe, and sends projections back to these structures to create circuits involved in many different functions. One important structure within the thalamus is the pulvinar nucleus, located at the posterior pole of the thalamus. The pulvinar nucleus has a series of reciprocal connections with posterior cortical areas including the parietal lobe and areas in the visual cortex. The pulvinar has several subdivisions that make different connections with the cortex and other subcortical areas.

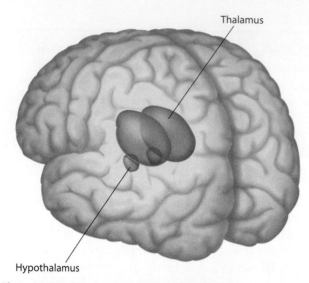

Figure 2.38 Gross anatomy of the thalamus. This diagram shows the thalami of the left and right hemispheres in a see-through brain. The thalamus is egg-shaped and serves as the gateway to cortex for the sensory systems.

sensory relay nuclei of the thalamus not only project axons to the cortex, but also receive heavy descending projections back from the same cortical area they contact. This descending cortico-thalamic projection terminates in a thin layer of cells that surrounds the thalamic nuclei, known as the *thalamic reticular nucleus.* Neurons in the thalamic reticular nucleus form a lateral inhibitory network of cells that may act in the modulation of thalamo-cortical outputs, perhaps to fine-tune sensory transmission, or partially gate the flow of information to cortex.

Below the thalamus is the hypothalamus, a small collection of nuclei that lie on the floor of the third ventricle (Figure 2.40). The hypothalamus is important for the autonomic nervous system and the endocrine system, and controls functions necessary for the maintenance of homeostasis (i.e., maintaining the normal state of the body). The hypothalamus is also involved in emotional processes. The hypothalamus contains many nuclei and fiber tracts and is involved in control of the pituitary gland, which is attached to the base of the hypothalamus.

Recent evidence implicated the pulvinar as a critical structure in attentional processing because of its heavy interconnectivity with regions of the cortex known to be involved with attentional control (posterior area of the parietal lobe) and the areas of visual cortex where feature analysis and object recognition are accomplished (ventral projection pathway). A final note is that the

The hormones produced by the hypothalamus control much of the endocrine system. For example, hypothalamic hormones stimulate the anterior pituitary gland to secrete its hormones vasopressin and oxytocin into the blood to regulate water retention in the kidneys and the production of milk and uterine contractility, respectively. The hypothalamus not only receives inputs

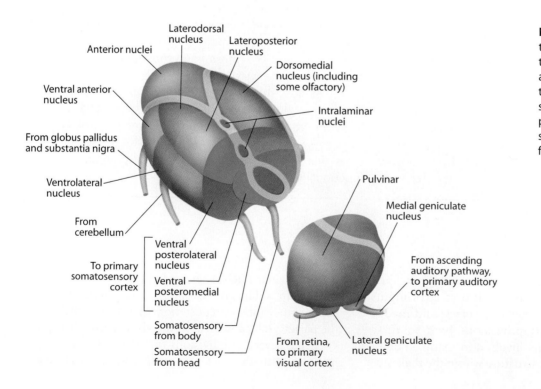

Figure 2.39 Diagram of the anterior and medial thalamus showing inputs and outputs. Subdivisions of the thalamus serve different sensory systems, and participate in various cortical-subcortical circuits. Adapted from Netter (1983).

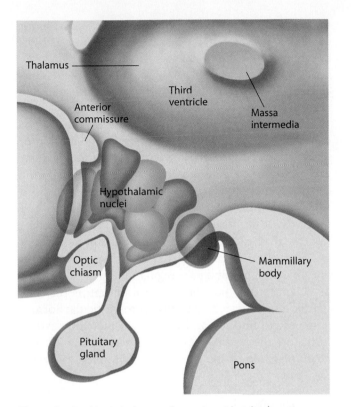

Figure 2.40 Hypothalamus shown in midsagittal section. Various nuclear groups are shown diagrammatically. The hypothalamus is the floor of the third ventricle, and as the name suggests, it sits below the thalamus. Adapted from Netter (1983).

primarily from the limbic cortex, but also receives inputs from other brain areas including the mesencephalic reticular formation, amygdala, and the retina to control circadian rhythms (light-dark cycles). Projections from the hypothalamus include a major projection to the prefrontal cortex, amygdala, and spinal cord. One of the most prominent projections is the one to the pituitary.

In addition to the direct neuronal projections of the hypothalamus, one important manner in which the hypothalamus influences the activity of other neurons is via neuromodulatory processes that involve the secretion of peptide hormones into the blood. These circulating peptide hormones can influence a wide range of behaviors by acting on distant sites through the bloodstream. In a similar fashion, the hypothalamus can be affected by hormones circulating in the blood, and thereby produce a neural response.

Brainstem

We usually think of the brainstem as having three main parts, the mesencephalon (midbrain), metencephalon (pons), and myelencephalon (medulla), which range from the level of the diencephalon to the spinal cord, respectively. Compared to the vast bulk of the forebrain, the brainstem is rather small (Figure 2.41). This region of the nervous system contains groups of motor and

Figure 2.41 Midsagittal section of the brain, brainstem, and spinal cord.

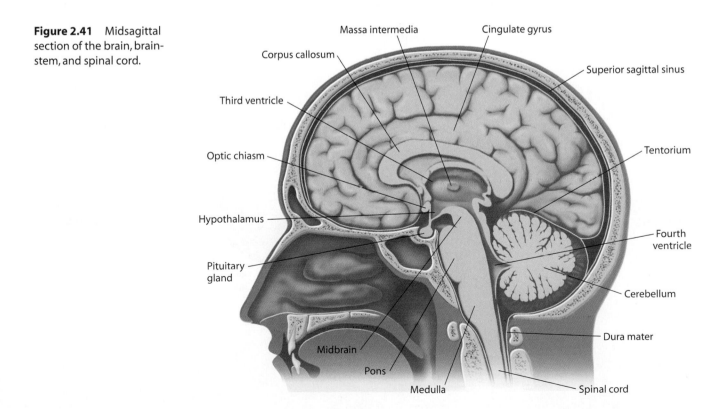

sensory nuclei, nuclei of widespread modulatory neuro-transmitter systems, and white matter tracts of ascending sensory information and descending motor signals. The organization becomes more complex as it proceeds from the spinal cord through the medulla, pons, and midbrain to the diencephalon and cerebral cortex. This neuronal complexity reflects the increasingly complex behaviors that these regions enable. However, this does not mean that the brainstem is unimportant or simplistic in its processing, nor does it signify that the brainstem's functions are ancillary. Indeed, damage to the brainstem is highly life-threatening, in part because of the brainstem's size—being small means that a small lesion encompasses a large percentage of the tissue—and also because brainstem nuclei control respiration and even states of consciousness such as sleep and wakefulness. Therefore, damage to the brainstem can often be fatal, while damage to the cerebral cortex may have (relatively) minor consequences, depending on where and how much cortex is damaged.

MIDBRAIN

The mesencephalon or midbrain lies caudal to the diencephalon and is bounded posteriorly by the pons. It surrounds the cerebral aqueduct and consists of the tectum (meaning "roof," and representing the dorsal portion of the mesencephalon), tegmentum (the main portion of the midbrain), and ventral regions occupied by large fiber tracts from the forebrain to the spinal cord (cortico-spinal tract), cerebellum, and brainstem (cortico-bulbar tract). The midbrain contains neurons

that participate in visuomotor functions (e.g., superior colliculus, oculomotor nucleus, trochlear nucleus), visual reflexes (e.g., pretectal region), auditory relays (inferior colliculus), and the mesencephalic tegmental nuclei involved in motor coordination (red nucleus) (Figure 2.42).

Much of the midbrain is occupied by the mesencephalic reticular formation, a rostral continuation of the pontine and medullary reticular formation. It is lateral and dorsal to the red nucleus, and ventral to the cerebral aqueduct (the connection between the third and fourth ventricles). The reticular formation is best seen as a set of nuclei in the brainstem that participate in arousal, respiration, cardiac modulations, modulation of reflex muscular activity at the segmental level (i.e., in the limbs), and pain regulation.

A final major portion of the midbrain is the substantia nigra, located ventrally to the reticular formation and red nucleus, and dorsally to the white matter tracts on the ventral surface. The connectivity and functional role of the substantia nigra were reviewed earlier.

PONS AND MEDULLA

The last areas of the brainstem to consider are the metencephalon (pons) and myelencephalon (medulla). Together they form the hindbrain. The pons includes the pontine tegmental regions on the floor of the fourth ventricle, and the pons itself, a vast system of fiber tracts interspersed with pontine nuclei. The fibers are continuations of the cortical projections to the spinal cord,

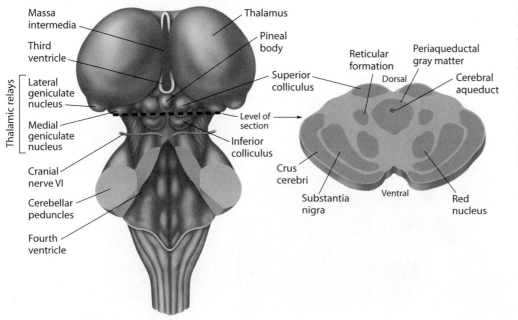

Figure 2.42 Anatomy of the midbrain. The dorsal surface of the brainstem is shown with the cerebral cortex and cerebellum removed. Cross section is through the midbrain at the level of the superior colliculus, the subcortical visuomotor nuclei. Adapted from Carpenter (1976).

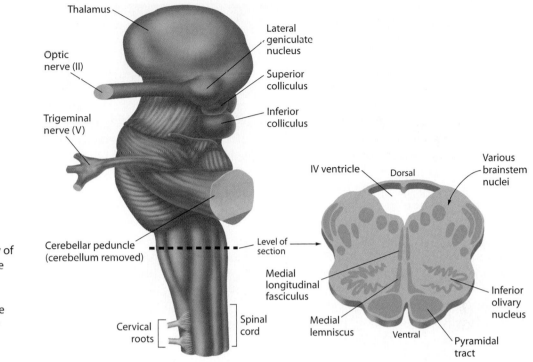

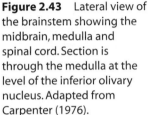

Figure 2.43 Lateral view of the brainstem showing the midbrain, medulla and spinal cord. Section is through the medulla at the level of the inferior olivary nucleus. Adapted from Carpenter (1976).

brainstem, and cerebellar regions (see Figure 2.42); they are compact fiber tracts on the ventral surface of the midbrain. At the pons, they explode into smaller tracts that continue to their final destinations as they course around the pontine nuclei, some terminating on neurons in this region.

The many nuclei at the pontine level have auditory and vestibular (balance) functions; primary CNS synapses of axons coming from the auditory and vestibular periphery are located in cell groups of the pontine tegmentum. As well, sensory and motor nuclei from the face and mouth are located here, as are visuomotor nuclei controlling some of the extraocular muscles. This level of the brainstem also contains a large portion of the reticular formation.

Finally, the brain's most caudal portion is the medulla, which is continuous with the spinal cord. Here, the fourth ventricle narrows and begins to shift more ventrally until at the level of the transition from the medulla to the spinal cord, it is a narrow tube running through the medulla to connect with the central canal of the spinal cord. The medulla has two prominent bilateral nuclear groups on the ventral surface (the gracile and cuneate nuclei) that are the primary relay nuclei for ascending somatosensory information entering the spinal cord. These projection systems continue through the brainstem to synapse in the thalamus en route to the

somatosensory cortex. On the ventral surface of the medulla the continuations of the cortico-spinal motor projections are grouped once again as tight bundles of nerve fibers into the pyramids, bilateral bumps on the ventral medulla. At the level of the medulla these motor axons to the spinal cord cross (pyramidal decussation) in order to project to the contralateral side of the spinal cord; that is, for example, the right-hemisphere motor systems control the left side of the body. At the rostral end of the medulla are large and characteristically formed nuclei of the olivary complex (inferior and medial accessory olivary nuclei). They appear in cross section as highly enfolded nuclei that are part of the cortical-cerebellar motor system (Figure 2.43). The olivary nuclei receive inputs from the cortex and red nucleus and project them to the cerebellum. Sensory nuclei that carry out vestibular processing (caudal portions of the vestibular nuclei) and some sensory inputs from the face, mouth, throat (including taste), and abdomen are in the medulla. There are also motor nuclei that innervate the heart and muscles of the neck, tongue, and throat.

In sum, the brainstem's neurons carry out numerous sensory and motor processes, especially visuomotor, auditory, and vestibular functions, and sensation and motor control of the face, mouth, throat, respiratory system, and heart. It houses fibers of passage that extend

Blood Supply and the Brain

Approximately 20% of the blood flowing from the heart is pumped to the brain. A constant flow of blood is necessary because the brain has no way of storing glucose or extracting energy without oxygen. Disruption in the flow of oxygenated blood to the brain lasting only a few minutes can produce unconsciousness, and finally death. Two sets of arteries bring blood to the brain: the vertebral artery, which supplies blood to the caudal portion of the brain, and the internal carotid artery, which supplies blood to the rostral portions. Although the major arteries sometimes join together and then seperate again, there is actually little mixing of blood from the rostral and caudal arterial supplies or from the right and left sides of the rostral portion of the brain. As a safety measure, in the event of a blockage or ischemic attack, blood should be re-routed to reduce the probability of loss of blood supply, but in practice this backup system is relatively poor.

The blood flow in the brain is tightly coupled with metabolic demand of the local neurons. Hence, increases in neuronal activity lead to a coupled increase in regional cerebral blood flow. The increased blood flow is not for increasing the delivery of oxygen and glucose to the active tissue, but rather to hasten the removal of the resultant metabolic byproducts of this increased blood flow. The precise mechanisms, however, remain hotly debated. These local changes in blood flow permit regional cerebral blood flow to be used as a measure of local changes in neuronal activity. This is the principle upon which some types of functional neuroimaging are based. Particular examples are positron emission tomography using methods such as the ^{15}O-water method, and functional magnetic resonance imaging, whic is sensitive to changes in the concentration of oxygenated versus deoxygenated blood in the region of active tissue.

from the cortex to the spinal cord and cerebellum, and sensory fibers from spinal levels to the thalamus and thence the cortex. Many neurochemical systems have nuclei in the brainstem that project widely to the cerebral cortex, limbic system, thalamus, and hypothalamus. Finally, inputs and outputs of the cerebellum traverse, or originate or terminate in the brainstem.

Cerebellum

The cerebellum (small cerebrum, or little brain) is actually a very large neuronal structure overlying the brainstem at the level of the pons (see Figure 2.41). It forms the roof of the fourth ventricle and sits on the cerebellar peduncles (meaning "feet"), which are massive input and output fiber tracts of the cerebellum (see Figure 2.43, top). The cerebellum has several gross subdivisions, including the cerebellar cortex, the four pairs of deep nuclei, and the internal white matter (Figure 2.44). In this way the cerebellum resembles the forebrain's cerebral hemispheres.

Figure 2.44 Gross anatomy of the cerebellum. Dorsal view of cerebellum shows underlying deep nuclei in a see-through projection. Adapted from Carpenter (1976).

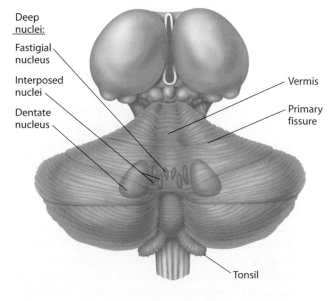

The inputs to the cerebellum come into the deep nuclei, but some projections extend directly to the cerebellar cortex. Most outputs of the cerebellum are via the deep nuclei. Inputs to the cerebellum come from the parts of the brain that participate in motor and sensory processing; hence, they convey information about motor outputs, and sensory inputs describing body position. Inputs from vestibular projections involved in balance, and auditory and visual inputs also project to the cerebellum from the brainstem. The cerebellum's output is to the thalamus and thence to the motor and premotor cortex. Cerebellar projections to the brainstem's nuclei ultimately influence descending projections to the spinal cord. The cerebellum is key to maintaining posture, walking, and performing coordinated movements. By itself, the cerebellum does not control movements directly; instead it integrates information about the body and motor commands and modifies motor outflow to effect smooth, coordinated movements. The cerebellum's role in motor control is given more attention in Chapter 10.

Spinal Cord

The last neural portion of the CNS to be reviewed is the spinal cord, which runs from the medulla to its termination in the cauda equina (meaning "horse's tail") at the base of the spine, where only nerve bundles remain. The spinal cord primarily projects the final motor signals to muscles, and takes in sensory information from the body's peripheral sensory receptors and relays it to the brain. In addition, at each level of the spinal cord, reflex pathways exist, as for example, that for the knee-jerk reflex. The gross anatomy of the spinal cord is simple: It consists of white matter tracts of ascending and descending, sensory and motor information, respectively (plus intraspinal projection fibers), and neuronal cell bodies organized in a more central gray matter (Figure 2.45). These include motor neurons, interneurons, and sensory neurons. The gray matter, when

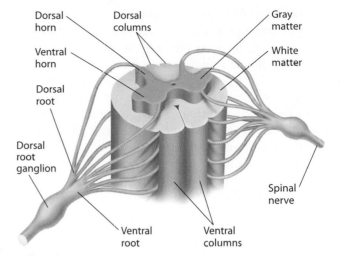

Figure 2.45 Cross section of the spinal cord showing the central butterfly-shaped gray matter, which contains neurons, and the surrounding white-matter tracts conveying information up and down the spinal cord from the brain to neurons in the cord, and to the brain from peripheral receptors. The dorsal and ventral nerve roots are shown exiting the cord—they fuse to form peripheral nerves.

viewed in cross section, resembles a butterfly, with two separate sections, or horns, called *dorsal* and *ventral horns*. The ventral horn contains the large motor neurons that project to muscles, while the dorsal horn contains sensory neurons and interneurons. The latter project to motor neurons on the same and opposite sides of the spinal cord to aid in coordination of limb movements.

The spinal cord is protected within the bone of the spine, but with the spine removed, one can view the bilateral pairs of spinal nerves that carry motor output (ventral root) and sensory information (dorsal root) into and out of the spinal cord. They pass through small gaps in the spinal cord to leave the spine.

SUMMARY

The nervous system is composed of cells—neurons—and their supportive counterparts, the glial cells. The neuron is the elementary unit of structure and function within the brain, spinal cord, and PNS. When it is at rest, the neuronal membrane has properties that allow it to pass some materials (primarily ions) dissolved in cellular fluids and extracellular space better than others. In addition, active processes pump ions across the membrane to separate different species of ions, thereby setting the stage for electrical potential differences inside and outside the neuron. This electrical difference is a form of energy that can be used to generate electrical currents, which can, via active conduction, travel great distances down axons that extend away from the neuron's cell body. When the action potential reaches an axon terminal, it prompts the release of chemical at a specialized region, the synapse, where the neuron contacts another neuron. The chemical (neurotransmitter) diffuses across the synaptic cleft between the neurons and contacts receptor molecules in the next (postsynaptic) neurons. This leads to the generation of currents in the postsynaptic neuron and the continuation of the signal through the system of neurons that comprise a neuronal circuit.

Neuronal circuits are organized in highly specific interconnections between groups of neurons in subdivisions of the CNS. Different neuronal groups have different functional roles. The functions may be localized within discrete regions that contain a few or many subdivisions, identifiable either anatomically or functionally, but usually by a combination of both. Brain areas are also interconnected to form higher-level circuits or systems that may be involved in complex behaviors such as motor control, visual perception, or cognitive processes such as memory, language, and attention.

SUGGESTED READINGS

KATZ, B. (1966). *Nerve, Muscle and Synapse.* New York: McGraw-Hill.

SHEPHERD, G.M. (1988). *Neurobiology,* 2nd edition. New York: Oxford University Press.

3

The Methods of Cognitive Neuroscience

The frontiers of scientific discovery are defined as much by the tools available for observation as by conceptual innovation. In the sixteenth century, the earth was considered the center of the solar system. Simple observation verified it: The sun rose each morning in the east and slowly moved across the sky to set in the west. But the invention of the telescope in 1608 changed astronomers' observational methods. With this new tool, astronomers suddenly found galactic entities that they could track as these entities moved across the night sky. These observations exposed geocentric theories as painfully wrong. Indeed, within 5 years, Galileo spoke out for a heliocentric universe—a heretical claim that even the powerful Roman Catholic Church could not suppress in the face of new technology.

Similar breakthroughs in theory can be linked in all scientific domains to the advent of new methods for observation. The invention of the bubble chamber allowed particle physicists to discover new and unexpected elementary particles such as mesons, discoveries that have totally transformed our understanding of the microscopic structure of matter. Gene cloning and sequencing techniques provided the tools for identifying new forms of proteins and for recognizing that these proteins formed previously unknown biological structures such as the neurotransmitter receptor that binds with tetrahydrocannabinol, the psychoactive ingredient in marijuana. Research in this area is now devoted to searching for endogenous substances that utilize these receptors rather than following the more traditional view that tetrahydrocannabinol produces its effects by binding to receptors linked to known transmitters.

The emergence of cognitive neuroscience has been similarly fueled by new methods, some of which utilize high-technology tools unavailable to scientists of previous generations (Sejnowski and Churchland, 1989). The positron emission tomography (PET) scanner, for instance, enables scientists to observe the brain's activity. Brain lesions can be localized with amazing precision

owing to methods such as magnetic resonance imaging (MRI). High-speed computers allow investigators to construct elaborate models to simulate patterns of connections and processing. Powerful electron microscopes bring previously unseen neural elements into view.

The real power of these tools, though, is still constrained by the types of problems one chooses to investigate. The dominant theory at any point in time defines the research paradigms and shapes the questions to be explored. The telescope helped Galileo to plot planets' positions with respect to the sun. But without an appreciation of the forces of gravity, he would have been at a loss to provide a causal account of planetary revolution. In an analogous manner, the problems investigated with the new tools of neuroscience are shaped by contemporary ideas of how the brain works in perception, thought, and action. Put simply, if well-formulated questions are not asked, even the most powerful tools will not provide a sensible answer.

In this chapter we examine the methods used in cognitive neuroscience, beginning with ones commonly used by neuroscientists, neurologists, cognitive psychologists, and computer modelers. While each of the areas represented by these professionals has blossomed in its own way, the interdisciplinary nature of cognitive neu-roscience has depended on the clever ways scientists have integrated paradigms across these areas. The chapter concludes with examples of this integration.

NEUROANATOMY

Neuroanatomy is the study of the nervous system's structure, concerned with identifying the parts of the nervous system and describing how the parts are connected. As with all of anatomy, descriptions can be made at many levels (Figure 3.1). For the neuroanatomist, investigations occur at one of two levels: gross neuroanatomy, in which the focus is on general structures and connections, and fine neuroanatomy, in which the main task is to describe components of individual neurons.

Histology is the study of tissue structure through dissection, and forms the core course of the first year of all medical programs. Histological methods are essential for anatomists to know. For a neuroanatomist, the challenge of extracting a human brain makes clear that evolution has devised specialized defenses to protect it. Not only is the brain enclosed within the skull's protective bony structure; but once this encasement is penetrated, the brain's soft tissue is surrounded by dura mater, dense layers of collagenous fibers.

Upon extraction, a superficial examination reveals many prominent structures (Figure 3.2). The gyri and primary sulci of the cerebrum, the gradual narrowing of the brainstem, and the elaborate folding of the cerebellar cortex can be identified without the aid of a microscope. Further dissections expose internal structures and reveal organizational principles. For example, by slicing through the brain, the dichotomy of gray and white matter is readily apparent: The gray matter forms a continuous cortical sheath enshrouding a seemingly homogeneous mass of white matter.

By simply looking at the brain in this superficial manner, we would not know that structures such as the white matter were neural elements rather than supportive tissues. To make this inference, neuroanatomists must probe for finer detail with high-power microscopes. For example, closer examination reveals that the white matter is composed of millions of individual fibers, each surrounded by myelin. It is the myelin that gives the fibers their white color. Cell bodies forming the cortical surface are devoid of myelin and appear gray when exposed in dissection.

A primary concern for neuroanatomy is to identify the patterns of connectivity in the nervous system, to lay out the highways that allow information to get from one place to another. This problem is made complex by the fact that neurons are not wired together in a simple,

(a)

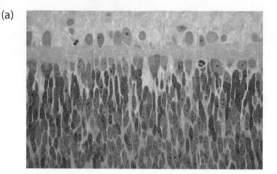

(b)

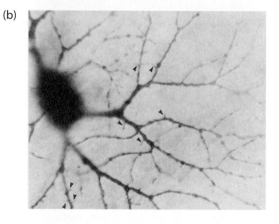

(c)

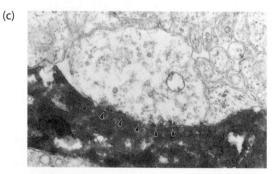

Figure 3.1 Neuroanatomical analysis occurs at different scales. **(a)** shows the retina from a young ferret, magnified by a light microscope. This section of the retina spans approximately 1.5 mm. In **(b)**, a ganglion cell from the cat retina has been injected with stain to highlight its dendritic aborization. The magnification by light microscopy here is much greater. The arrows highlight places where short dendritic extensions, or spines can be seen. Processes along one dendritic branch can be visualized with the electron microscope. **(c)** The dark region is one of the stained dendrites of the cell in (b). The light regions are axons forming synapses along the dendrite. At this magnification, it is possible to see the synaptic vesicles in the axons. These contain neurotransmitter.

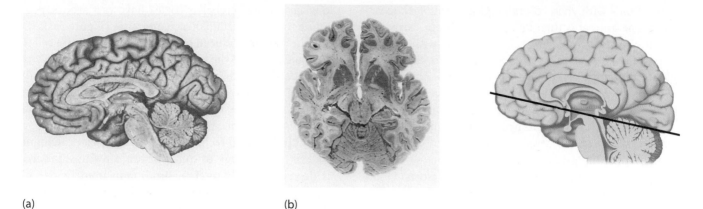

(a)   (b)

Figure 3.2   **(a)** A sagittal section through the human cerebral cortex highlights prominent features of the gross anatomy. The superficial aspects of the cortex are referred to as gyri, the enfolding regions, the sulci. **(b)** The gray and white matter are clearly seen in this horizontal section.

serial circuit. A single cortical neuron is likely to be innervated by many neurons, and the axons from these input neurons can originate in widely distributed regions. Most axons are short projections from neighboring cortical cells. Others can be quite long, having originated in more distant cortical regions and only reaching their target zone after descending below the cortical sheath into the white matter. Neighboring and distant connections between two cortical regions are referred to as *cortico-cortical connections,* following the convention that the first term identifies the source and the second term the target. Inputs that originate in subcortical structures such as the thalamus would be referred to as *thalamo-cortical connections.*

Much of the progress in neuroanatomy has been prompted by the development and refinement of new

stains, chemicals that are selectively absorbed by specific neural elements (see Chapter 1). One common technique involves horseradish peroxidase, or HRP. HRP is a retrograde tracer in that it is taken up by the axons at the site of injection and transported back to their soma. Thus, it provides a tool to visualize where the input to a particular neural region originates (Figure 3.3). Suppose that a researcher wants to know which subcortical structures project to the primary visual cortex; she could use HRP as a retrograde transport tool. She injects the visual cortex's input layers with HRP. HRP is absorbed through the same axonal channels that allow neural transduction via the inflow and outflow of sodium, potassium, and calcium ions. Once inside, the HRP diffuses up the axon to the cell body.

Over a few days, the HRP becomes oxidized, producing

Figure 3.3   Staining techniques reveal connections between distant neural structures. Horseradish peroxidase is a commonly used retrograde tracer. After being injected, the agent permeates axonal terminals and is transported back to the cell bodies. The animal is then killed and histological methods are used to identify the location of the stain. **(a)** Injection site in the lateral geniculate nucleus of the thalamus of a rat. **(b)** The retina under low-level magnification. The tracer is evident as the dark spots on the right side. **(c)** Under high magnification, the stain can be seen filling individual neurons.

(a)   (b)   (c)

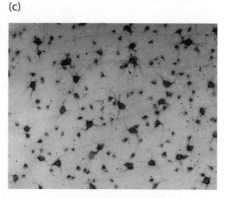

compounds with vivid colors ranging from black to orange. The animal is then killed and its brain extracted. Examining thin slices of brain tissue cut with a sharp knife called a *microtome,* the researcher can identify regions containing cell bodies labeled by HRP. As shown in Chapter 4, a primary projection to the visual cortex comes from the lateral geniculate nucleus, a result that could not have been known by looking at the white matter: The fibers are too dense and many connective highways become merged.

HRP is just one of many retrograde tracers. Other chemicals serve as anterograde tracers, in that they are absorbed at the dendrites or soma and then diffuse along the axons. In combination, retrograde and anterograde tracers allow researchers to identify the inputs to a specific region and determine where the axons from a particular region terminate. In this manner, the neuroanatomist can construct projection maps of the patterns of connectivity (Figure 3.4).

Neuroanatomists are also interested in describing the structure of neurons. We describe neurons as a homogeneous class of cells, each having a soma, axon, and dendritic branches. But on closer examination it is clear that despite these commonalities, neurons are heterogeneous, varying in size and shape (see Chapter 2). For some neurons such as the giant pyramidal cells in the cerebral cortex, the dendritic arbor is relatively small, allowing few synaptic connections. In contrast, the Purkinje cells of the cerebellar cortex have vast arbors, providing more than 200,000 synaptic sites (Figure 3.5).

The stain introduced by Golgi allows an entire cell to be visualized once the tissue is dehydrated. A mystery of this procedure is that only about 1% of the cells will absorb the stain. However, this selectivity is advantageous in that it becomes possible to visualize individual cells without interference from its anatomical neighbors.

With the Golgi technique a researcher can catalogue the cell morphology of different brain regions. Indeed, as described in Chapter 2, Brodmann used this technique to devise his cytoarchitectonic map of the brain. He methodically applied the Golgi technique to the entire surface of the cortex and obtained a picture of cell architecture. By doing so, he discerned two important principles of cortical structure. First, as shown in Figure 3.6, the laminar structure of the cortex becomes clear, reflecting the segregated apportionment of cell types. Second, the density of cell types varies as one moves across the cortical surface. Brodmann partitioned cortical areas according to these differences in density, introducing a numbering scheme that continues to be the most widely employed in the neurosciences (Figure 3.7). Other methods have verified that physiological correlates are associated with these anatomical differences. For example, a clear architectonic difference distinguishes the primary motor cortex and the somatosensory cortex.

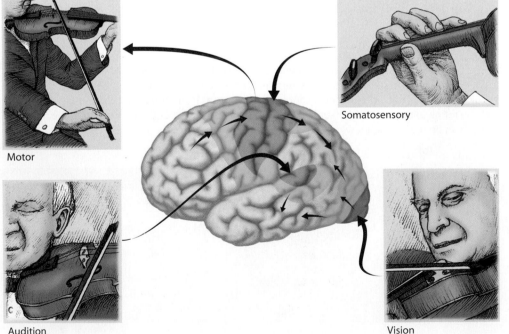

Motor

Somatosensory

Audition

Vision

Figure 3.4 A projection map of the cerebral cortex can be derived with anatomical tracing techniques. The blue regions show the primary projection areas of the sensory pathways and the primary output region to the spinal cord. The secondary sensory and motor areas are colored green. Anatomical projections overlap extensively in the tertiary areas (pink regions). Adapted from Kolb and Whishaw (1996).

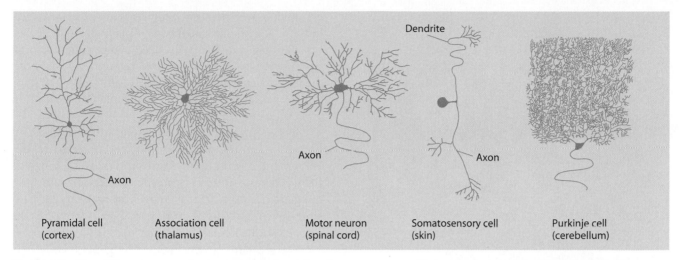

Figure 3.5 Five different neurons in the central and peripheral nervous systems. These neurons vary greatly in size (not drawn to scale): The axon of an association cell in the thalamus may extend less than 1 mm whereas the axon of the pyramidal cell may traverse the length of the spinal cord.

Neuroanatomists rely also on histochemical techniques, methods that examine the chemical content of neural tissue and identify neural elements sharing common characteristics. For example, neurotransmitters like dopamine and norepinephrine, called *catecholamines*, have similar molecular structures that are absent in other transmitters like serotonin and acetylcholine. When tissue with catecholamines is exposed to formaldehyde, under the right conditions and with a histofluorescent technique that locates transmitter systems, a fluorescent

Figure 3.6 The gray matter of the cerebral cortex is composed of unmyelinated cell bodies that give a layered appearance as a function of the different cell types. As shown in these examples from the macaque monkey, across different cortical areas, the density of the cell types varies. Brodmann used these variations in density to define the boundaries between different cortical areas. From McClelland and Rummelhart (1986).

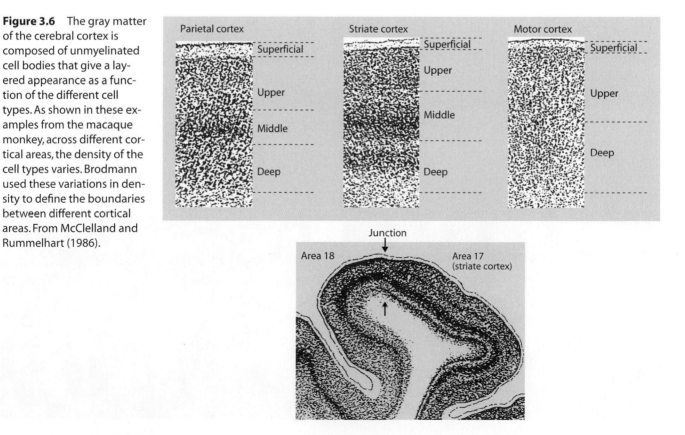

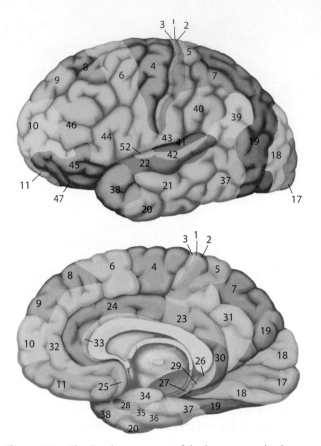

Figure 3.7 The Brodmann areas of the human cerebral cortex. In Brodmann's original cytoarchitectonic map, there were 52 areas. Over the years, the map has been modified and the standard version no longer includes Areas 12–16 and 48–51.

compound will be seen. Other assays of transmitters look for metabolites in the cerebrospinal fluid, an approach that may help in diagnosing neurochemical pathology. For example, the compound 5-hydroxyindoleacetic acid, a metabolite of serotonin related to serotonin levels in the brain, has been linked to depression and aggressive behavior.

Techniques for analyzing cell morphology have been essential for researchers interested in neural development. A prominent question is, How do synapses form? One possibility is that the connections are all in the genetic code. But this hypothesis appears implausible given the number of synapses (10^{15}) in the human adult. Researchers thus pose a less restrictive hypothesis; namely, that while the genetic code may constrain the target region for each precursor cell or neuroblast, the exact form and number of connections may be shaped by experience. To assess this, cellular neuroanatomists compare dendritic structure during development, as with dendritic arborization in cats, shown in Figure 3.8. The arborization is most complex early in development. In an adult cat, the number of branches has been considerably reduced. However, the remaining synapses may be more efficient, a hypothesis supported by the thicker dendrites.

Figure 3.8 Neural development entails a refinement of dendritic and axonal processes. **(a)** The dendritic arbor of a retinal neuron in the prenatal cat, eight days before birth. **(b)** The dendritic arbor of a neuron from this same structure in the adult cat. Many dendritic branches are eliminated during development. The remaining branches become thicker and thus more efficient for neurotransmission.

(a)

(b)

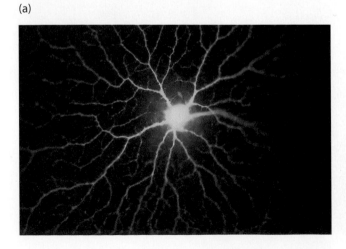

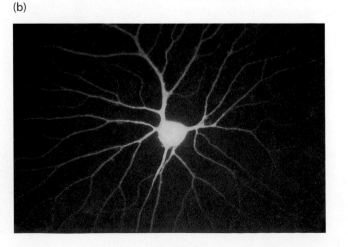

NEUROPHYSIOLOGY

Structure is tied to function; it is not possible to understand brain function from neuroanatomy alone. Because neural function depends on electrochemical processes, numerous techniques are used to measure and manipulate neuron activity. Some measure and record cell activity, either in passive or in active conditions. Others manipulate activity by applying electrical stimulation or chemical induction.

Electrical Stimulation

Early insights to human cortical organization were made possible by directly stimulating the cortex of awake humans undergoing brain surgery. In patients with severe chronic epilepsy, surgeons have sought to identify and remove regions of the cortex where seizures appear to originate. By resecting the epileptogenic tissue, the seizures either will be eliminated or will be controlled so the person can pursue normal activities. Pioneering work was carried out in the 1940s by Wilder Penfield and Herbert Jaspers at the Montreal Neurological Institute (Penfield and Jaspers, 1954). These surgeons took advantage of the fact that the cortex is exposed during a resection and explored the effects of small levels of electrical current applied to the cortical surface. Because no pain receptors inhabit the central nervous system (CNS), the patients do not experience any discomfort from stimulation. Thus, stimulation can be applied even when they are awake and fully conscious, thereby enabling the researchers to gather the patients' subjective experiences—an impossibility in animal studies.

For many years Penfield and his associates systematically explored the effects of brain stimulation over large areas of the cortical surface. Much of their early work concentrated on areas surrounding the central sulcus, the large fissure dividing the parietal and frontal lobes. Stimulation in the precentral gyrus, the most posterior region of the frontal lobe, produced movement. Moreover, the type of movement was directly related to the area being stimulated. Whereas stimulation on the medial portion of the gyrus and enfolded sulcus led to movements of the contralateral toes and foot, stimulation on the lateral surface evoked movements of the mouth, jaws, and hands. Systematic movement of the stimulating electrode across the precentral gyrus revealed a complete motor representation of the body. This type of representation is called a functional map since the organization of the map is defined according to behavior (Figure 3.9).

Figure 3.9 A functional map of the primary motor and somatosensory cortex. By plotting the movements and sensations that are evoked by electrical stimulation along the precentral and postcentral gyri, a representation, or homunculus of the body surface is revealed (bottom). From Ramachandran (1993).

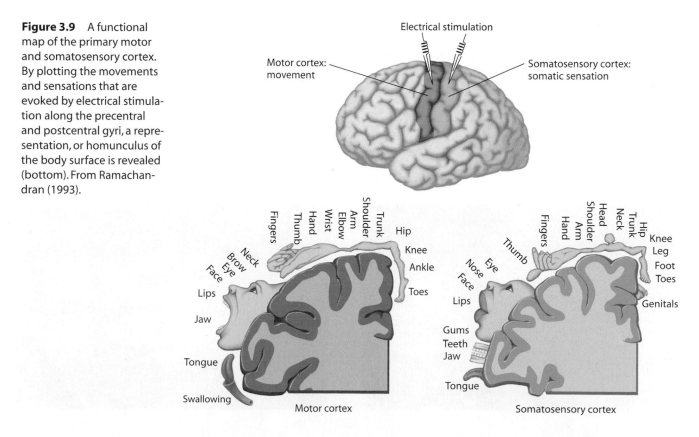

The correspondence between a cortical region and the body is sometimes referred to as a *homunculus*. The homunculus refers to the fact that there is an organized representation of the body across a given cortical area. Note that there is not a one-to-one relation between the actual size of body parts and the cortical representation of the body's parts. For example, areas within the motor homunculus that activate muscles in the fingers, mouth, and tongue encompass much larger areas than would be expected for proportional representation. The large cortical representation for the fingers and mouth allows for the fine coordination required when we manipulate objects or speak.

When stimulation is applied to the postcentral gyrus, the patient does not move. Rather, stimulating this surface leads to reports of distinct sensations such as a light touch, brush, or itch. As in the motor cortex, an orderly representation of the body can be easily discerned. Indeed, the sensory homunculus provides a close match to the motor homunculus. There is a corresponding disproportionate representation of areas that require finer perceptions. We can easily discriminate wooden and plastic surfaces with our fingers, but would find this task quite difficult if our explorations were restricted to the feet.

Electrical stimulation, however, is of limited value for understanding brain organization and function. A strong correspondence between brain area and function is seen only in the primary motor and sensory areas. For the rest of the cortex, the effects of electrical stimulation are much less clear. There have been many reports of specific memories being evoked after stimulation in the temporal lobes. Indeed, the experience has been likened to déjà vu. A person suddenly reports being transported in space and time to an earlier episode: a birthday party or a walk in the woods. But the experiences are rare and fleeting, and have sometimes been determined to be false memories. Restimulating the same location may elicit a different report. Moreover, electrical stimulation in many cortical regions elicits no phenomenal experience, or the experience is vague and poorly defined.

Electrical stimulation is still used in neurosurgery. Over 1000 temporal lobectomy operations are performed across North America each year. The treatment is extremely successful: The average patient experiences a reduction of seizure activity of about 90% or better. Few negative side effects occur with the surgery, especially when the patient's preoperative state is considered. It had been a concern that removing up to 6 cm of cortical tissue would have serious consequences on cognitive function. Yet this appears not to be so; in fact, many patients show improvements in their overall cognitive function after surgery. One reason is that the excised tissue was probably of little functional value given its high rate of seizure activity. Secondly, new methods continue to be developed that allow surgeons to carefully map the functional activity of the regions that are candidates for removal (Figure 3.10). When the electrode probe is used as a recording device, the neurosurgeon can identify the foci of seizure activity. When the probe is used as a stimulator, the neurosurgeon can assess the function of cortical regions. Of particular concern has been the delineation of cortical areas associated with language or

Figure 3.10 A subdural grid of electrodes can be used to measure epileptic activity in humans **(b)**. This method allows for chronic recordings across a large region of the cortical surface. Neurosurgeons use this information to identify the focus of seizure activity. The electrodes can also be used as stimulators to assess neural function. **(a)** shows the brain prior to grid placement.

(a)

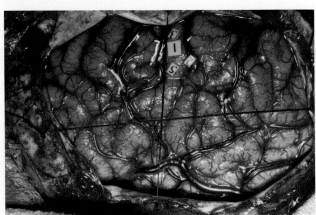

(b)

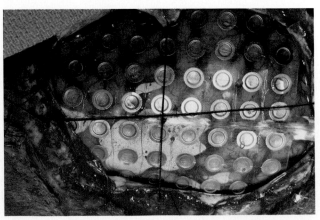

motor functions so these regions will be spared. If speech is arrested during the stimulation of an area, it will be left intact. In a similar sense, if language comprehension is disrupted during stimulation, the activated areas will be spared. In this way surgeons can ensure that they will not introduce severe cognitive deficits by removing functional tissue.

Single-Cell Recording

The most important technological advance in neurophysiology—perhaps all of neuroscience—has been the development of methods to record the activity of single neurons in laboratory animals. With this method, the understanding of neural activity jumped a quantum leap. No longer would the neuroscientist have to be content with describing nervous system action in terms of functional regions. Single-cell recording enabled researchers to describe response characteristics of individual elements.

In single-cell recording, a thin electrode is inserted into an animal's brain. If the electrode is in the vicinity of a neuronal membrane, electrical changes can be measured (see Chapter 2). Although the surest way to guarantee that the electrode records the activity of a single cell is to record intracellularly, this technique is difficult and penetrating the membrane frequently damages the cell. Thus, single-cell recording is typically done extracellularly. With this method, the electrode is situated on the outside of the neuron. The problem with this approach is that there is no guarantee that the changes in electrical potential at the electrode tip reflect the activity of a single neuron. More likely, the tip will record the activity of a small set of neurons. Computer algorithms are used to differentiate this pooled activity into the contributions from individual neurons.

Neurons are constantly active, even in the absence of stimulation or movement. This baseline activity varies widely from one brain area to another. For example, some cells within the basal ganglia have spontaneous firing rates of over 100 spikes/sec whereas the baseline rate for cells in another basal ganglia region are around 1 spike/sec. Moreover, these spontaneous firing levels fluctuate. The primary goal of single-cell recording experiments is to determine experimental manipulations that produce a consistent change in the response rate of an isolated cell. Does the cell increase its firing rate when the animal moves its arm? Is this specific to movements in a particular direction? When is the movement terminated by a particular stimulus (e.g., food)? As interesting, what makes the cell decrease its response rate? The

neurophysiologist is interested in what causes change in the synaptic activity of a neuron.

As such, single-cell recording is essentially a correlational approach. The experimenter seeks to determine the response characteristics of individual neurons by correlating their activity with a given stimulus pattern or behavior. The technique has been used in almost all regions of the brain in a wide range of nonhuman species. For sensory neurons, the experimenter might manipulate the type of stimulus presented to the animal. For motor neurons, recordings can be made as the animal performs a task or moves about the cage. Single-cell recordings have also been made in higher brain centers to examine changes in cellular activity related to emotion and learning.

In the typical neurophysiological experiment, recordings are obtained from a series of cells in a targeted area of interest. In this manner, a functional map can describe similarities and differences between neurons in a specified cortical region. One area where the single-cell method has been used extensively is in the study of the visual system of primates. In a typical experiment, the researcher will target the electrode for a cortical area that contains cells thought to respond to visual stimulation. Once a cell is identified, the researcher tries to characterize its response properties.

A single cell is not responsive to all visual stimuli. There are a number of stimulus parameters that might correlate with the variation in the cell's firing rate such as the shape of the stimulus, its color, and whether or not it is moving (see Chapter 4). An important factor is the location of the stimulus. As shown in Figure 3.11, all visually sensitive cells only respond to stimuli in a limited region of space. This region of space is referred to as that cell's *receptive field*. For example, some neurons will respond when the stimulus is located in the lower left portion of the visible field. For other neurons, the stimulus may have to be in the upper left region of the visible field. The size of the receptive fields of visual cells varies, with a general rule being that they are smallest in primary visual cortex and become larger toward association visual areas. Thus, a stimulus will only alter the response of a cell in primary visual cortex when it is positioned in a very restricted region of the visible world. If the stimulus is moved outside this region of space, the cell will return to its spontaneous level of activity. In contrast, displacing a stimulus over a large distance may produce a similar increase in the firing rate of visually sensitive cells in the temporal lobe.

Neighboring cells have at least partially overlapping receptive fields. As a region of visually responsive cells is traversed, there is an orderly relation between the

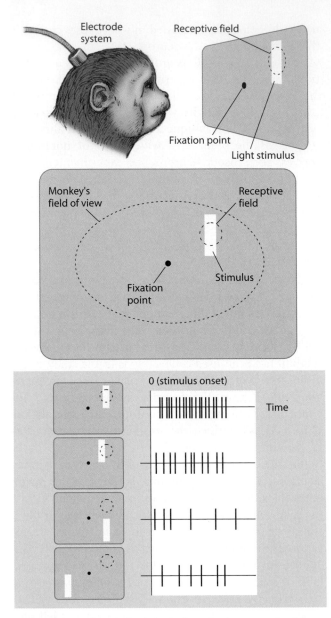

Figure 3.11 Electrophysiological methods are used to identify the response characteristics of cells in the visual cortex. While the activity of a single cell is monitored, the monkey is required to maintain fixation, and stimuli are presented at various positions in the visual field. (Lower panel) The vertical lines to the right of each stimulus correspond to individual action potentials. The cell fires vigorously when the stimulus is presented in the upper right quadrant, thus defining the receptive field for this cell.

receptive field properties of these cells and the external world. A representation of external space is reflected in a continuous manner across the cortical surface; neighboring cells have receptive fields of neighboring regions of external space (Figure 3.12). As such, cells form a topographic representation, an orderly mapping between an external dimension such as spatial location

and the neural representation of that dimension. In vision, topographic representations are frequently referred to as being *retinotopic*. The retina is composed of a continuous sheet of photoreceptors, neurons that respond to visible light passing through the lens of the eye (see Chapter 4). Visual cells in subcortical and cortical areas maintain retinotopic information. Thus, if light falls on one spot of the retina, cells with receptive fields spanning this area will be activated. If the stimulus moves and light falls on a different region of the retina, activity ceases in these cells and begins in other cells whose receptive fields encompass the new region of stimulation. In this manner, visual areas provide a representation of the location of the stimulus. Cell activity within a retinotopic map correlates with (i.e., predicts) the location of the stimulus.

There are other types of topographic maps. The motor and somatosensory maps (areas 4 and 3) described by Penfield and Jaspers are topographic representations of the body surface. In a similar sense, auditory areas in the subcortex and cortex contain tonotopic maps, in which the physical dimension reflected in neural organization is a stimulus's sound frequency. With a tonotopic map, some cells are maximally activated by a 1000-Hz tone, and others by a 5000-Hz tone. In addition, neighboring cells tend to be tuned to similar frequencies. As such, sound frequencies are reflected in cells that are activated upon the presentation of a sound. Tonotopic maps are sometimes referred to as *cochleotopic* because the cochlea, the sensory apparatus in the ear, contains hair cells tuned to distinct regions of the auditory spectrum.

Single-cell recordings have limitations. As with any correlational technique, it is hard to establish cause and effect. Suppose that we find two areas, areas X and Y, with visually responsive cells. We could consider three distinct possibilities: Cells in area X might be elaborating on information provided by cells in area Y, cells in area Y might be activated by cells in area X, or areas X and Y might reflect independent processing of input from other visual sensory cells.

Some problems can be overcome by combining physiological and neuroanatomical methods. If the anatomist can establish that the primary visual cortex is the main recipient of output from the thalamus's lateral geniculate nucleus, it is likely that what gets processed in the primary visual cortex is limited by what is provided by the lateral geniculate nucleus. Yet reciprocal connections happen between many brain regions: Area X is innervated by area Y and in turn sends axonal projections back to area Y. This makes it difficult to determine if one area is downstream of another, especially for cortical areas that are not part of the primary sensory zones.

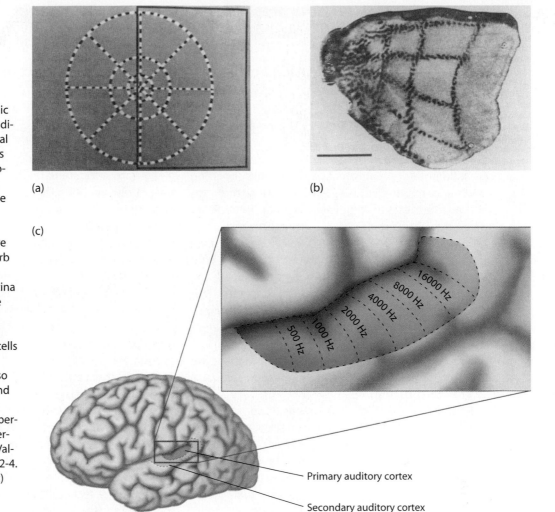

Figure 3.12 Topographic maps of the visual and auditory cortex. **(a)** In the visual cortex, the receptive fields of the cells define a retinotopic map. While viewing the stimulus shown on the left, the monkey was injected with a radioactive agent. Metabolically active cells in visual cortex absorb the agent, revealing how the topography of the retina is preserved across striate cortex (right). In auditory cortex **(b),** the frequency tuning properties of the cells define a tonotopic map. Topographic maps are also seen in somatosensory and motor cortex (see Figure 3.9). (a,b) Reprinted with permission from Tootell, Silverman, Switkes and R.L. DeValois, 1982a, *Science, 218,* 902-4. Copyright 1982, AAAS. (c) Adapted from Bear et al. (1996).

(a)

(b)

(c)

Primary auditory cortex

Secondary auditory cortex

Neurophysiologists' techniques provide better insight to potential cause-and-effect relations. One approach is to compare the time it takes two brain areas to respond to a common dimension. For motor control, cells in the primary motor cortex (area 4) and those in the cerebellum are activated prior to movement. Do cells in one area activate the other? From neuroanatomical studies, we know this may be a possibility since there are reciprocal connections between the two structures. Output from the cerebellum is projected to the motor cortex via the thalamus. Moreover, the motor cortex provides a large input to the cerebellum, either directly via collaterals from the cortico-spinal tract or indirectly via brainstem nuclei. Thus, the reciprocal pattern of connectivity makes cause-and-effect ambiguous. To overcome this, W.T. Thach (1975) of Washington

University in St. Louis recorded from cerebellar and motor cortex cells while monkeys performed a simple movement task. By making the monkey perform the task many times, he constructed histograms showing the distribution of cellular latencies in relation to the onset of movement. This analysis revealed two interesting results. First, the latency of cells in the lateral region of the cerebellum, the dentate nucleus, preceded the latency of cells in the motor cortex. It is unlikely, then, that cerebellar cells are activated by motor commands. More likely, they contribute to movement planning. Second, cells in the cerebellum's intermediate region became active after motor cortex cells fired, which suggests that these cells primarily regulate ongoing movement rather than contribute to motor planning.

When the single-cell method was first introduced,

The Ethics and Practice of Animal Research

Students on most university campuses are familiar with the annual protests during Animal Liberation Week of groups opposed to the use of animals for research purposes. These groups hand out inflammatory pamphlets graphically depicting how researchers callously exploit laboratory rats, cats, and especially monkeys in their pursuit of knowledge. While many of the protests are peaceful and law-abiding, there have been numerous incidents of violence against people and property: Windows have been smashed, equipment destroyed, animals kidnapped, and professors harassed at their homes. The protesters argue that university administrators have become dependent on the money generated by the public and private grants supporting "frivolous and unnecessary" research, and thus are forced to resort to more dramatic measures to raise the public's consciousness.

Scientists have taken the offense over the past decade, eager to educate the public about the importance of these forms of research. Almost all that we know about the structure and physiology of the nervous system has depended on invasive studies of animals. Human autopsies can only provide the crudest understanding of the anatomy of the nervous system. The fine structure that is revealed by sophisticated staining procedures is not possible unless the stains are injected into live animals and allowed to propagate along metabolically active tissue. All that we know about the operation of single neurons has been made possible only by the use of laboratory animals.

This basic research does not exist in a vacuum, sought after as part of an ephemeral quest for knowledge. Scientists and public policy makers have long recognized that advances in medicine depend on our ability to carry out both basic research and clinically inspired research. Human studies of brain metabolites may reveal that excessive dopamine levels are associated with schizophrenia, but animal research is essential for understanding where dopamine is produced and the metabolic processes that regulate the production and uptake of this transmitter. Only rarely have medical treatments been discovered in the absence of animal models. In most cases, new medical treatments only become available after years of careful experimental work with animals, first involving years of basic research, then followed by the careful development of clinical measures involving animal studies.

The scientific research community has served as a visible target for animal rights groups. One reason has been a few well-publicized cases in which videotapes or photographs were used to demonstrate the extreme experimental manipulations being practiced on laboratory animals. Two of the more well-known cases involved monkeys. In one case the animals were subjected to severe blows to the head as part of a study of head trauma in car accidents. In the other case, the animals were in poor health after undergoing fetal surgery to destroy sensory fibers. The latter case resulted in the only conviction recorded in this country of a scientist on animal cruelty charges.

While abuses most certainly exist, research with laboratory animals is closely regulated by both research institutions and federal agencies. All research protocols must be approved by institutional animal care and use committees that include not only scientific peers but also lay members of the community. Three basic principles must be met for any research project to be certified (Rowan and Rollin, 1983). First, the goals of the research must be clearly articulated, making clear that these are worthwhile studies that will advance our knowledge of the nervous system. Second, experiments must be conducted so as to minimize pain and distress through the use of anesthetics and analgesics. Any animals that show evidence of suffering must be humanely destroyed. Third, alternative methods that might yield similar knowledge must be considered.

The evidence suggests that these codes are strictly followed. One study involved a review of the psychological literature over a 5-year period and revealed that less than one-tenth of 1% involved studies in which animals were subjected to pain without anesthesia. The few studies that did not use anesthesia focused on the question of how the brain reacts to pain, an important problem faced by people recovering from surgery. Moreover, the argument that computer models can serve as realistic substitutes for animal research is specious. Current models can simulate only the simplest of neural functions, and even these models are only useful in terms of how well they converge with the results of studies on living organisms.

Nonetheless, it is important that the public debate the fundamental question regarding whether it is ethical for humans to exploit another species for their own benefit. A researcher in 1898 was quoted as saying, "Animals have no more rights than inanimate objects, and it is no worse from an ethical point of view to flay the forearm of an ape or lacerate the leg of a dog than to rip open the sleeve or rend a pair of pantaloons." It is clear that few would take this stance in our modern society. We must understand both the benefits and the costs of animal research in order to form educated opinions on these ethical matters.

The morality of using animals for research purposes has been debated for centuries. People on both sides of the debate have recognized the importance of engaging the public, a point underscored by the fact that the members of the United States Congress receive more letters on this issue than any other.

neuroscientists were optimistic that the mysteries of brain function would be solved. All they needed was a catalogue of different cells' contributions. Yet it soon became clear that, with neurons, the aggregate behavior of cells might be more than the sum of its parts. The function of an area might be better understood by identifying correlations in the firing patterns of groups of neurons rather than by identifying the response properties of each individual neuron. This has inspired single-cell physiologists to develop new techniques that allow recordings to be made in many neurons simultaneously. Bruce McNaughton at the University of Arizona studied how the rat hippocampus represents spatial information by simultaneously recording from 150 cells (Wilson and McNaughton, 1994)! Other researchers use multiple-cell recordings to ask whether temporal correlations between neurons might provide significant processing information. Multiple single-cell recording may bring about the next revolution in neurophysiology.

Lesions

The brain is a complicated structure, composed of many structures including subcortical nuclei and distinct cortical areas. It seems evident that any task a person performs requires the successful operation of the brain's components. A long-standing method of the neurophysiologist has been to study how behavior is altered by selectively removing one or more of these parts. The logic of this approach is straightforward. If a neural structure contributes to a task, then rendering structure dysfunctional should impair the performance of that task.

Humans obviously cannot be subjected to brain lesions to investigate their nervous system's function. Human neuropsychology requires patients with naturally occurring lesions. But animal researchers have not been constrained in this way. They share a long tradition of studying brain function by comparing the effects of different brain lesions. Around the turn of the twentieth century, the English physiologist Charles Sherrington employed the lesion method to investigate the importance of feedback in limb movement in the dog (see Chapter 10). By severing the nerve fibers carrying sensory information into the spinal cord, he observed that the animals stopped walking.

Lesioning a neural structure will eliminate that structure's contribution. But the lesion may also force the animal to change its normal behavior and alter the operation of intact structures. One cannot be confident that the effect of a lesion eliminates only the contribution of a single structure. An example is found in contemporary extensions of Sherrington's work.

Sherrington (1947) concluded from his lesion studies that sensory information was necessary for movement. Over a half century later, Edward Taub and his colleagues (1968) replicated Sherrington's work in studies with monkeys. Rather than lesion a single limb, these researchers performed bilateral dorsal root resections. The results were surprising. They had expected the monkeys to act as though both arms were paralyzed. Instead, they found that the animals used the deafferentated limbs—not only for quadrupedal locomotion but also for climbing about their cage or reaching for food. Sherrington's original studies had not, after all, shown the true requirements for movement. Rather, they indicated that, without feedback, an animal will avoid using the limb and rely on its intact one. If both limbs are deprived of feedback, the animal will have no choice but to use its deafferentated limbs. Movement is indeed possible without feedback.

So with this methodology we should remember that a lesion may do more than eliminate the function provided by the lesioned structure. Nonetheless, the method has been critical for neurophysiologists. Over the years, lesioning techniques have been refined, allowing for much greater precision. Most lesions were originally made by aspirating neural tissue. In aspiration experiments, a suction device is used to remove the targeted structures. Other methods for destroying tissue involved applying electrical charges strong enough to destroy tissue. One problem with these methods is the difficulty of being selective. Any tissue within range of the voltage generated by the electrode tip would be destroyed. For example, a researcher may want to observe the effects of a lesion to a certain cortical area, but if the electrolytic lesion extends into underlying white matter, these fibers will also be destroyed. This may render a distant structure dysfunctional because it will be deprived of some input.

Newer methods allow for more control over the extent of lesions. Most notable are neurochemical lesions. Sometimes a drug will selectively destroy cells that use a certain transmitter. For instance, systemic injection of 1-methyl-4-phenyl-1,2,3,6-tetrahydropyridine (MPTP) destroys dopaminergic cells in the substantia nigra, producing an animal version of Parkinson's disease (see Chapter 9). Other neurochemical lesions require applying the drug to the targeted region. Kainic acid is used in many studies because its toxic effects are limited to cell bodies. Application to an area will destroy the neurons whose cell bodies are near the site of the injection, but will spare any axonal fibers passing through this area. Other researchers choose to make reversible lesions using chemicals that produce a transient disruption in nerve conductivity. So long as the drug is active, the exposed neurons will not function. When the drug wears off, function gradually returns. The appeal of this method is that each animal can serve as its own control. Performance can be compared during the "lesion" and "nonlesion" periods. A different form of reversible lesion involves cooling neural tissue by injecting a chemical that induces a low temperature. When the tissue is cooled, metabolic activity is disrupted, thereby creating a temporary lesion. When the coolant is removed, metabolic activities resume and the tissue becomes functional again.

Pharmacological manipulations can also be used to produce transient functional lesions. For example, the acetylcholine antagonist scopolamine produces temporary amnesia such that the recipient fails to remember much of what he or she was doing during the period when the drug was active. Since there are no adverse consequences from the low doses required to produce the amnesia, scopolamine provides a tool with which researchers can study the kinds of memory problems that plague patients with hippocampal damage (Nissen et al., 1987). However, systemic administration of this drug produces widespread changes in brain function, and thus limits its utility as a model of hippocampal dysfunction.

NEUROLOGY

Human pathology has long provided key insights to the relation between brain and behavior. Observers of neurological dysfunction have certainly contributed much to our understanding of cognition—long before the advent of cognitive neuroscience. Discoveries concerning the contralateral wiring of sensory and motor systems were made by physicians in ancient societies attending to warriors with open head injuries. Postmortem studies by early neurologists, such as Broca and Wernicke, were instrumental in linking the left hemisphere with language functions (see Chapter 1). Many other disorders of cognition were described in the first decades of the twentieth century, when neurology became a specialty in medicine.

Even so, there is now an upsurge in testing neurological patients in order to elucidate issues related to normal and aberrant cognitive function. As with other subfields of cognitive neuroscience, this enthusiasm has been partly inspired by advances in the technologies for diagnosing neurological disorders. As important, studies of patients with brain damage have benefited from the use of experimental tasks derived from research with healthy people.

Examples of the merging of cognitive psychology and neurology are presented at the end of this chapter; in this section, we focus on causes of neurological disorders and the tools that neurologists use to localize neural pathology. We also take a brief look at treatments for ameliorating neurological disorders.

Basic research questions, such as those attempting to link cognitive processes to neural structures, can be best addressed by selecting patients with a single neurological disturbance whose pathology is well circumscribed.

Patients who have suffered trauma or infections will frequently have diffuse damage, rendering it difficult to associate a behavioral deficit with a structure. Nonetheless, extensive clinical and basic research studies have focused on patients with degenerative disorders such as Alzheimer's disease, both to understand the disease processes and to characterize abnormal cognitive function.

Structural Imaging of Neurological Damage

Brain damage can occur from vascular problems, tumors, degenerative disorders, and trauma. The first charge of the neurologist is to make the appropriate diagnosis. She needs to follow appropriate procedures, especially if a disorder is life-threatening, and to work toward stabilizing the patient's condition. While diagnosis can frequently be made on the basis of a clinical examination, most hospitals in the Western world are equipped with tools that help neurologists visualize brain structure.

Computed tomography (CT or CAT scanning) is the most common method for imaging the brains of living people. This method is an advanced version of the conventional x-ray study; whereas the conventional x-ray study compresses three-dimensional objects into two dimensions, CT allows for the reconstruction of three-dimensional space from the compressed two-dimensional images. Figure 3.13 depicts the method, showing how x-ray beams are passed through the head and a two-dimensional image is generated using sophisticated computer software.

To undergo CT, a patient lies supine in a scanning

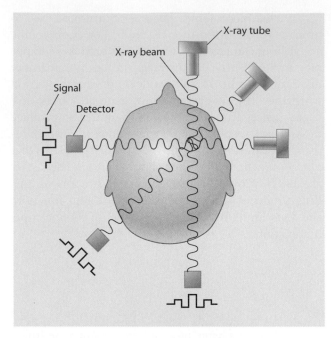

(a)

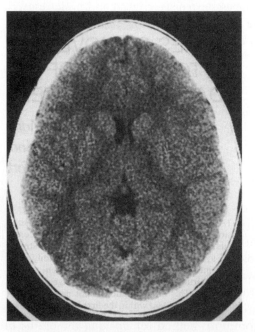

(b)

Figure 3.13 Computed tomography (CT) provides an important tool for imaging neurological pathology. **(a)** The CT process is based on the same principles as x-rays. An x-ray is projected through the head and the recorded image provides a measurement of the density of the intervening tissue. By projecting the x-ray from multiple angles and using computer algorithms, a 3-d image based on tissue density is obtained. **(b)** A transverse CT image. The dark regions along the midline are the ventricles, the reservoirs of cerebrospinal fluid.

machine. The machine has two main parts: an x-ray source and a set of radiation detectors. The source and detectors are located on opposite sides of the scanner. These sides can rotate, allowing the radiologist to project x-ray beams from all possible directions. Starting at one position, an x-ray beam passes through the head. Some radiation in the x-ray is absorbed by intervening tissue. The remainder passes through and is picked up by the radiation detectors located on the opposite side of the head. The x-ray source and detectors are then rotated and a new beam is projected. This process is repeated until x-rays have been projected over 180 degrees. At this point, recordings made by the detectors are fed into a computer that reconstructs the images.

The key principle underlying CT is that the density of biological material varies, and that the absorption of x-ray radiation is correlated with tissue density. High-density material such as bone will absorb a lot of radiation. Low-density material such as air or blood will absorb little radiation. The absorption capacity of neural tissue lies between these extremes. Thus, the software for making CT scans really provides an image of the differential absorption of intervening tissue. The reconstructed images are usually contrast reversed: High-density regions show up as light colored and low-density regions are dark colored.

The lower half of Figure 3.13 shows a CT scan from a healthy individual. Most of the cortex and white matter appear as homogeneous gray areas. The typical spatial resolution for CT scanners at most hospitals is approximately 0.5 to 1.0 cm in all directions. Each point on the image reflects an average density of that point and the surrounding 1.0 mm of tissue. Thus, it is not possible to discriminate two objects that are closer than approximately 5 mm. Since the cortex is only 4-mm thick, it is very difficult to see the boundary between white and gray matter on a CT scan. The white and gray matter are also of very similar density, further limiting the ability of this technique to distinguish them. But larger structures can be easily identified. The surrounding skull and eye sockets appear white because of the high density of bone. The ventricles are black owing to the cerebrospinal fluid's low density.

Resolution down to about 0.1 mm is made possible by MRI. In contrast to the x-rays used for CT, the MRI process exploits the magnetic properties of organic tissue. Certain atoms are especially sensitized to magnetic forces given the number of the protons and neurons in their nuclei. One such atom that is pervasive in the brain, and indeed in all organic tissue, is hydrogen. In their normal state, the orientation of hydrogen atoms is randomly distributed (Figure 3.14). When surrounded by a magnetic field, however, the hydrogen atoms become aligned in the direction parallel to the magnetic force. Radio waves are then passed through the magnetized regions, which makes the atoms rotate in a uniform fashion. When the radio waves are turned off, the atoms rebound toward the orientation of the magnetic field. This synchronized rebound produces a local magnetic field that is detected by energy detectors surrounding the head.

The reconstruction of MRI scans is similar to that used for CT scans. Computer software depicts differences in density. The increased spatial resolution is obvious when comparing the scans shown in Figure 3.14 with those in Figure 3.13. With MRI, it is easy to see the individual sulci and gyri. A sagittal section at the mid-

(a)

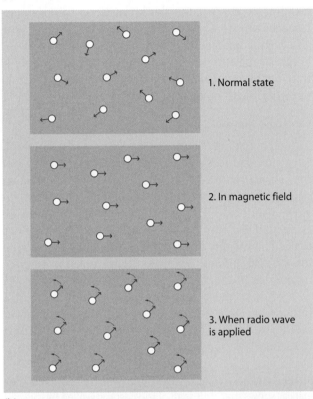

1. Normal state

2. In magnetic field

3. When radio wave is applied

Figure 3.14 Magnetic resonance imaging (MRI) exploits the fact that many organic elements such as hydrogen are magnetic **(a).** In their normal state, the orientation of these elements is random. When an external magnetic field is applied, the elements become aligned and can be perturbed in a systematic fashion by the introduction of radio waves. The MRI scanner measures the endogenous magnetic fields generated by these elements as they spin. The density of hydrogen atoms is different in white and gray matter, making it easy to visualize these regions. **(b)** Transverse, coronal, and sagittal MR images. The finer resolution offered by MRI can be seen by comparing the transverse slice in this figure with the CT image in the previous figure. Both are from about the same level.

(b)

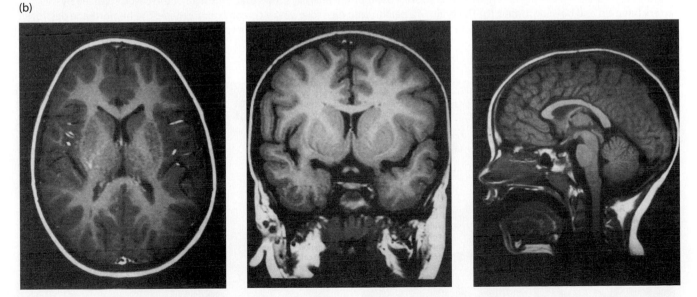

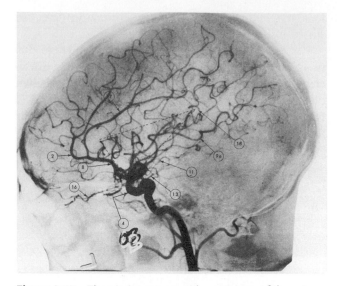

Figure 3.15 The angiogram provides an image of the arteries in the brain.

line reveals the impressive size of the corpus callosum. Even small structures such as the mamillary bodies or superior colliculus can be visualized with MRI.

An imaging method also commonly used in neurology is angiography. As shown in Figure 3.15, this method helps visualize the distribution of blood by highlighting major arteries and veins. A dye is injected into the vertebral or carotid artery and then the person undergoes an x-ray study. This method is particularly useful for diagnosing disorders related to vascular ab-

normalities. Some people are born with an arteriovenous malformation, an irregularity in the shape of an arterial branch or wall. Such a malformation can leak, causing an ischemic disorder, a temporary loss of blood, or hemorrhage, resulting in a massive disruption in blood flow.

Causes of Neurological Disorders

Nature has sought to ensure that the brain remains healthy. Structurally, the skull provides a thick, protective encasement. The distribution of arteries is extensive and even redundant for much of the brain. Even so, the brain is subject to numerous disorders, and their rapid treatment is frequently essential to avoid chronic, debilitating problems or death.

VASCULAR DISORDERS

As with all tissue, neurons need a steady supply of oxygen and glucose. These substances are essential for the cells to produce energy and make transmitters for neural communication. The brain uses 20% of all the oxygen we breathe, an extraordinary amount considering that it accounts for only 2% of the total body mass. The continuous supply of oxygen is essential: A loss of oxygen for as briefly as 10 minutes can result in neural death.

Oxygen and glucose are distributed to the brain from four primary arteries: the two internal carotid and two vertebral arteries. Each carotid artery

Figure 3.16 Strokes occur when the blood flow to the brain is disrupted. **(a)** The brain from a person who had an occlusion of the middle cerebral artery. The person survived this stroke. Post-mortem analysis shows that almost all of the tissue supplied by this artery has died and been absorbed. **(b)** The brain of a person who died following a cerebral hemorrhage. The hemorrhage destroyed the dorsomedial region of the left hemisphere. The effects of a cerebrovascular accident two years prior to death can be seen in the temporal region of the right hemisphere.

(a)

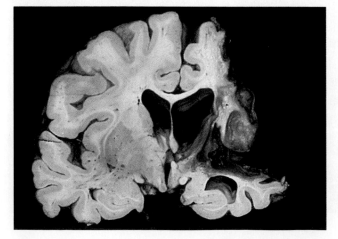

(b)

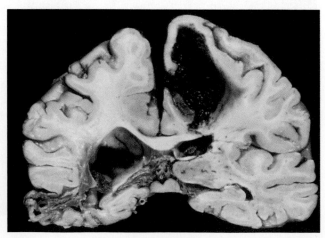

branches into two major arteries, the anterior cerebral artery and the middle cerebral artery, as well as several smaller ones. Together, these arteries act as a network to supply the anterior and middle portions of the cortex with blood. The vertebral arteries join together to form the basilar artery. Inferior branches from the basilar artery irrigate the cerebellum and posterior part of the brainstem. More superiorly, this system branches into two posterior cerebral arteries to provide blood to the occipital lobe and medial temporal lobe. The major cerebral arteries partially overlap in their distribution, in areas referred to as *borderzones* or *watershed areas.*

Cerebral vascular accidents, or strokes, occur when blood flow to the brain is suddenly disrupted. The most frequent cause of stroke is when a foreign substance occludes the normal passage of blood. Over years, arteriosclerosis, the buildup of fatty tissue, occurs in the heart. This tissue can break free, becoming an embolus that is carried off in the bloodstream. An embolism that enters the cranium may easily pass through the large carotid or vertebral arteries. But as the arteries and capillaries reach the end of their distribution, their size decreases. Eventually, the embolism becomes stuck, or infarcted, blocking the flow of blood and depriving all downstream tissue of oxygen and glucose. Within a short period of time, this tissue will become dysfunctional. If the blood flow is not rapidly restored, the cells will die (Figure 3.16).

The onset of stroke can be quite varied, depending on the afflicted area. Sometimes the person may lose consciousness and die within minutes. Here the infarct is usually in the vicinity of the brainstem. When the infarct is cortical, the presenting symptoms may be striking, such as the sudden loss of speech and comprehension. In other cases, the onset can be innocuous. The person reports a mild headache or finds himself or herself unable to use a hand in an appropriate manner. The vascular system is fairly consistent between individuals; thus, stroke of a particular artery will typically lead to destruction of tissue in a consistent anatomical location. For example, occlusion of the posterior cerebral artery will invariably lead to deficits in visual perception.

There are many other types of cerebral vascular disorders. Ischemia can be caused by partial occlusion of an artery or capillary due to an embolus, or it can arise from a sudden drop in blood pressure that prevents blood from reaching the brain. A sudden rise in blood pressure can lead to cerebral hemorrhage, or bleeding over a wide area of the brain due to the breakage of blood vessels. Spasms in the vessels can result in irregular blood flow and have been associated with migraine headaches.

Other disorders are due to problems in arterial structures. Cerebral arteriosclerosis is a chronic condition in which cerebral blood vessels become narrow due to the thickening and hardening of the arteries. This can result in persistent ischemia. More acute situations can arise if a vessel suddenly expands or bursts, a condition referred to as an *aneurysm.* While some aneurysms appear to develop spontaneously, others can develop in people born with an arteriovenous malformation. An arteriovenous malformation that has remained innocuous for many years may suddenly weaken.

Cerebral vascular accidents require immediate attention. Often a neurological examination and CT can reveal the problem. Arteriovenous malformations or aneurysms may require the more precise MRI or angiography. In these instances, surgery is frequently required to prevent further bleeding. Occlusive strokes, on the other hand, do not generally require surgery. Either the occluded tissue is already completely infarcted, the clot is too small to remove, or the embolus has been absorbed into the surrounding tissue by the time of surgery. Treatment here usually involves the administration of drugs to dissolve the clot and restore circulation prior to permanent tissue injury.

TUMORS

Brain lesions can also result from tumors. A tumor, or neoplasm, is a mass of tissue that grows abnormally and has no physiological function. Brain tumors are relatively common, with most originating in the glia and other supporting white-matter tissues. Tumors can also develop from gray matter or neurons, but these are much less common, particularly in adults. Tumors are classified as benign when they do not recur after removal and tend to remain in the area of their germination (although they can become quite large). Malignant, or cancerous, tumors are likely to recur after removal, and are often distributed over a number of different areas. With brain tumors, the first concern is not usually whether the tumor is benign or malignant, but rather its location and prognosis. Concern is greatest when the tumor threatens critical neural structures. Neurons can be destroyed by an infiltrating tumor or become dysfunctional due to displacement by the tumor (Figure 3.17).

Three major types of brain tumors are distinguished according to where they originate. Gliomas are brain tumors that begin with the abnormal reproduction of glial cells. The rate of growth of different subtypes of gliomas can vary widely: Some escape detection for years; others expand rapidly and are malignant, with a poor prognosis because a lot of tissue is quickly disturbed. The second type of tumor, the meningioma, originates in the

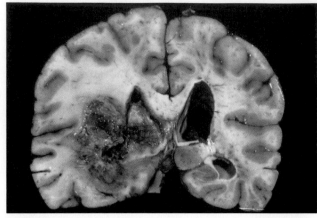

(a)

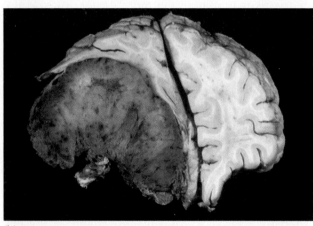

(b)

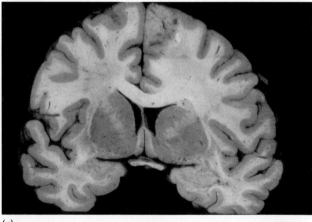

(c)

Figure 3.17 Post-mortem views of three types of brain tumors. **(a)** A malignant glioma has infiltrated the white matter of the parietal lobe in the right hemisphere. **(b)** A large meningioma led to massive compression of the right frontal lobe. This patient had been hospitalized at age 41 for psychotic behavior, quite likely due to the effects of this slow-growing tumor. The tumor was not detected until autopsy. **(c)** A metastatic tumor is seen in the dorsomedial tip of the left hemisphere. This woman died five years after undergoing a mastectomy for breast cancer.

meninges, the protective membrane that surrounds the brain. Although meningiomas do not invade the brain, they can create severe neurological problems by producing abnormal pressure. The third type are metastatic tumors. These tumors originate in a noncerebral structure such as the lungs, skin, and breasts. The malignant tissue invades the bloodstream or lymphatics and is ultimately carried to the brain. It is common for metastatic tumors to be widely distributed, affecting many structures.

DEGENERATIVE AND INFECTIOUS DISORDERS

Many neurological disorders result from progressive disease. Table 3.1 lists some of the more prominent degenerative and infectious disorders. In later chapters we review some of these disorders in detail, exploring the cognitive problems associated with them and how these problems relate to underlying neuropathologies. Here, we focus on the etiology and clinical diagnosis of degenerative disorders.

Table 3.1 Prominent Degenerative and Infectious Disorders of the Central Nervous System

Disorder	Type	Most Common Pathology
Alzheimer's disease	Degenerative	Tangles and plaques in limbic and temporal-parietal cortex
Parkinson's disease	Degenerative	Loss of dopaminergic neurons
Huntington's disease	Degenerate	Atrophy of interneurons in caudate and putamen nuclei of basal ganglia
Pick's disease	Degenerative	Frontal-temporal atrophy
Progressive supranuclear palsy (PSP)	Degenerative	Brainstem atrophy including colliculus
Multiple sclerosis	Possibly infectious	Demyelination, especially of fibers near ventricles
AIDS dementia	Viral infection	Diffuse white-matter lesions
Herpes simplex encephalitis	Viral infection	Destruction of neurons in temporal and limbic regions
Korsakoff's disease	Nutritional deficiency	Destruction of neurons in diencephalon and temporal lobes

Degenerative disorders have been associated with both genetic aberrations and environmental agents. A prime example of a degenerative disorder that is genetic in origin is Huntington's disease (see Chapter 10). The genetic link in degenerative disorders such as Parkinson's disease and Alzheimer's disease is weaker. Environmental factors are suspected to be important, perhaps in combination with genetic dispositions. The causes of Parkinson's disease are unknown, but it is suspected that the cell death in dopaminergic neurons may be accelerated by unknown toxins accumulating in the environment. Unlike many neurological disorders, there are no descriptions of people with parkinsonian symptoms in the pre–Industrial Age medical literature. The causes of Alzheimer's disease also remain a mystery, despite intense research efforts. About 5% of the cases are clearly linked to a genetic deficiency; in the rest, there is no identifiable genetic component. Many hypotheses have been proposed regarding the cause of Alzheimer's disease: The disorder has been linked to exposure to aluminum silicates (e.g., an active ingredient in most antacids) and to overactivity in cortical neurons. More recently, it was suggested that the production of amyloid, a ubiquitous protein in organic tissue, goes awry,

and leads to the characteristic plaques found in the brains of patients with Alzheimer's disease (Figure 3.18).

Progressive neurological disorders can be caused by a virus. The human immunodeficiency virus (HIV) that causes acquired immunodeficiency syndrome (AIDS)–related dementia has a tendency to lodge in subcortical regions of the brain, producing diffuse lesions of the white matter through the destruction of axonal fibers. The herpes simplex virus, on the other hand, destroys neurons in cortical and limbic structures if it migrates to the brain. Viral infection is also suspected in multiple sclerosis, although evidence for this is indirect, coming from epidemiological studies. For example, the incidence of multiple sclerosis is highest in temperate climates and a number of isolated tropical islands had not experienced multiple sclerosis until the population came in contact with Western visitors.

Degenerative and infectious disorders are usually characterized by a gradual onset of symptoms. Often the patient may not notice the deterioration of motor or cognitive abilities. Rather, the changes may be more apparent to a spouse or other family members. The neurological examination is especially critical for reliable diagnosis. The first signs of multiple sclerosis may be

Figure 3.18 Degenerative disorders of the brain. **(a)** On the left is a coronal section from an Alzheimer patient who died at age 67, eight years after the first reports of memory problems. There is severe cortical atrophy; at death, her brain weighed only 750 grams, less than half that of a normal brain. The right side shows the brain of a patient who died of Pick's disease. The atrophy here is limited to frontal and temporal lobe regions. **(b)** Transverse MRI scans from a patient with Alzheimer's disease. Atrophy has led to the enlargement of the sulci and ventricles.

(a)

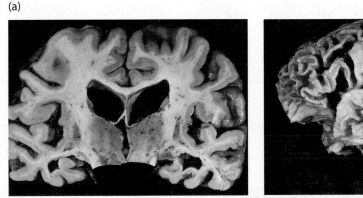

(b)

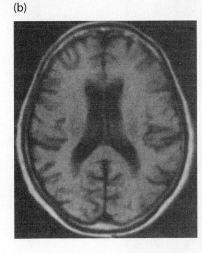
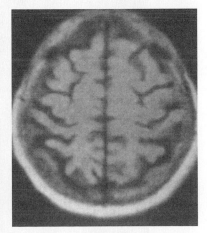

slight disturbances in sensation or double vision. The insidious onset of the memory problems associated with Alzheimer's disease may be difficult to detect given our expectations of cognitive changes in normal aging. A patient developing Parkinson's disease may first note difficulty standing up or initiating movement. The experienced clinician will recognize the implications of these signs. CT and MRI may confirm a diagnosis, but usually the scans do not reveal any pathology in the early phases of these disorders. As the diseases progress, evidence of neural atrophy or degeneration become obvious (see Figure 3.18).

The pace of deterioration varies enormously according to the degenerative disorder. Whereas Huntington's disease invariably results in progressive deterioration and death within 5 to 15 years, demyelinating disorders such as multiple sclerosis may go into remission for many years. Part of this variation is due to differences in the underlying mechanisms producing the neural pathology. For example, in multiple sclerosis, the disease process affects white matter, whereas Alzheimer's disease involves widespread atrophy of cell bodies. Another important factor affecting a patient's outcome is the use of medication to treat symptoms. Just 30 years ago, patients with Parkinson's disease were generally bedridden within a few years of diagnosis, and the disorder would be listed as the cause of death. With the introduction of

drugs categorized as dopamine agonists, the symptoms are greatly minimized for many patients.

TRAUMA

More than any natural cause such as stroke or tumor, most patients arrive on neurology wards after a traumatic event such as a car accident, a gunshot wound, or an ill-advised dive into a shallow swimming hole. The traumatic event can lead to a closed or an open head injury. In closed head injuries, the skull remains intact, but the brain is damaged by the mechanical forces generated by a blow to the head. The most common cause of closed head injury is a car accident in which a person's head slams against the windshield. The damage may be at the site of the blow, for example, just below the forehead—damage referred to as a *coup*. In addition, reactive forces may bounce the brain against the skull on the opposite side of the head, resulting in a *countercoup*. Occipital deficits are sometimes observed in car accident victims who suffer a countercoup. Certain regions are especially sensitive to the effects of coups and countercoups. The inside surface of the skull is markedly jagged above the eye sockets. As can be seen in Figure 3.19, this rough surface can produce extensive tearing of brain tissue in the orbitofrontal region. Open head injuries happen when the skull is penetrated by an object like a bullet or missile. With these injuries, tissue may be

Figure 3.19 Trauma can produce extensive destruction of neural tissue. Damage can arise from the collision of the brain with the solid internal surface of the skull, especially along the jagged surface over the orbital region. In addition, accelerative forces created by the impact can cause extensive shearing of dendritic arbors. **(a)** The brain of a 54-year-old man who had sustained a severe head injury 24 years prior to death. Tissue damage is evident in orbitofrontal regions, and were associated with intellectual deterioration subsequent to the injury. **(b)** The suspectibility of this region to trauma was made clear by A. Holbourn of Oxford in 1943 who filled a skull with jello and then violently rotated the skull. While most of the brain retains its smooth appearance, the orbitofrontal region has been chewed up.

(a)

(b)

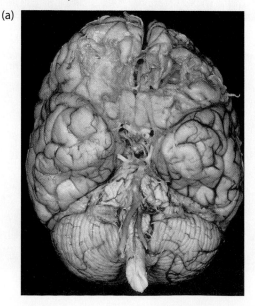
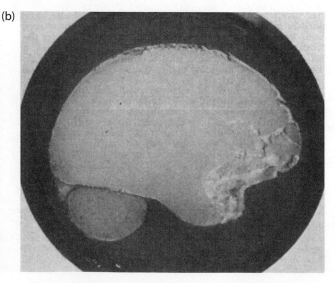

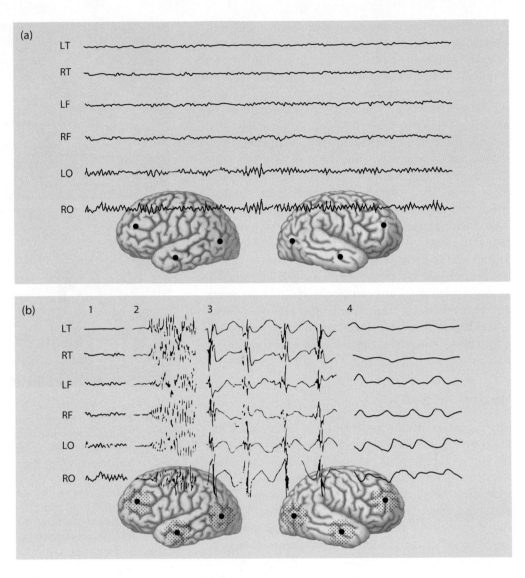

Figure 3.20 EEG recordings from six electrodes, positioned over the frontal, temporal, and occipital cortex on both the left and right sides. **(a)** Activity during normal cerebral activity. **(b)** Activity during a grand mal seizure. From Kolb and Whishaw (1996).

directly damaged by the penetrating object. The impact of the object can also be expected to create reactive forces producing coup and countercoup.

Additional damage may follow a traumatic event as a result of vascular problems and increased risk of infection. Trauma can disrupt blood flow by severing vessels or it can change intracranial pressure as a result of bleeding. Swelling after trauma may generate further brain damage, and seizures, common after trauma, can originate in scarred tissue.

Early work on localizing cognitive function often involved patients with traumatic injuries. The eminent British neurologist Sir Gordon Holmes (1919) provided some of the classic descriptions of cerebellar and occipital lobe function based on his observations of World War I soldiers who had received open head injuries. Indeed, prior to the invention of CT, open head injuries offered the best way to localize brain damage while the patient was still alive. Researchers now avoid studying trauma patients to see how brain regions relate to cognitive functions; such patients often have multiple neuropsychological problems, perhaps because neurological damage is generally extensive and diffuse.

EPILEPSIES

Epilepsy is a condition characterized by excessive and abnormally patterned activity in the brain. The cardinal symptom is a seizure, a transient loss of consciousness. The extent of other disturbances varies. Some epileptics will shake violently and lose their balance. For others, the seizure may be perceptible only to the most attentive friends and family. Seizures are confirmed by performing electroencephalography (EEG) to record the patient's brain waves (see Electrical Signals in the Brain, later in this chapter). During the seizure, the EEG profile is marked by large-amplitude oscillations (Figure 3.20).

The frequency of seizures is also variable. The most severely affected patients can have hundreds of seizures each day, with each seizure disrupting function for a few minutes. Other epileptics will suffer only an occasional seizure, but it may incapacitate the person for a couple of hours. Furthermore, simply having a seizure is not diagnostic of epilepsy. While 0.5% of the general population has epilepsy, it is estimated that one in twenty people will have a seizure at some point in their life. Often the seizure is triggered by an acute event such as trauma, exposure to toxic chemicals, or high fever. Approximately 50 to 70% of epileptics respond well when treated with antiseizure medication. For the remaining patients, surgery may be an option if the disorder is chronic and severely debilitating.

Neuropsychologists are generally not interested in the cognitive deficits associated with epilepsy as they relate to normal function. Since the seizures disrupt neural activity across large sections of the brain, it is difficult to link behavioral deficits with structural abnormalities.

Functional Neurosurgery

Surgical interventions for treating neurological disorders provide a unique opportunity to investigate the link between brain and behavior. The best example of this comes from research involving patients who have undergone surgical treatment for the control of intractable epilepsy. The extent of tissue removal is always well documented, enabling researchers to investigate correlations between lesion site and cognitive deficits. But caution must be exercised in attributing cognitive deficits to surgically induced lesions. It is possible that other, structurally intact tissue is dysfunctional owing to the chronic effects of epilepsy because the seizures spread beyond the epileptogenic tissue. One method used with epilepsy patients compares their performance before and after surgery. The researcher can differentiate changes associated with the surgery from those associated with the epilepsy.

An especially fruitful paradigm for cognitive neuroscience has involved the study of patients who have had the fibers of the corpus callosum severed (corpus callosotomy). In these patients, the two hemispheres have been disconnected—the so-called *split-brain procedure.* While few patients have had this procedure, they have been extensively studied. Indeed, over the past 10 years, 100 studies published in scientific journals have been based on just the five most tested patients from the Dartmouth group. Insights to the role of the two hemispheres on a wide range of cognitive tasks have been

Figure 3.21 A *Life* magazine cartoon from 1947 sketches the mechanisms underlying the supposed benefits of the frontal lobotomy. Freudian theory was in its heyday at the time, as reflected in the accompanying caption: "In agitated depression (top drawing), the superego becomes overbearing and unreasonable, unbalancing the whole mind ...The surgeon's blade, slicing through the connections between the prefrontal areas (the location of the superego) and the rest of the brain, frees the tortured mind from its tyrannical ruler (bottom drawing) ... Lobotomy, however, should be performed only on those patients whose intelligence is sufficient to take control of behavior when the moral authority is gone."

made possible by studying these patients. Split-brain patients also offer the opportunity to assess the unity of consciousness. We return to these issues in more detail in subsequent chapters.

The logic of lobectomy and corpus callosotomy stems from the idea that a surgeon's knife can reduce the number or frequency of seizures and thereby eliminate physiological abnormalities that interfere with normal function. This idea, that surgery can eliminate abnormal brain function, has a long and sometimes troubled history in neurology. This reasoning motivated the notorious frontal lobotomy operation. Though the procedure enjoyed widespread popularity in the middle of this century as a treatment for depression, schizophrenia, and other psychiatric disorders, its theoretical motivation was weak—perhaps best captured in the *Life* magazine cartoon shown in Figure 3.21. A hyperactive superego, localized in the frontal lobes, was assumed to exert excessive control over posterior brain regions. Slicing the white matter in the frontal cortex (with crude techniques such as inserting an ice pick behind the eye sockets!) was thought to restore balance by reducing the connections between frontal and posterior brain regions.

Whereas in the preceding examples neurosurgery was eliminative in nature, it has also been used as an attempt to restore normal function. One example that generates much excitement is the use of fetal brain transplants to treat Parkinson's disease. Patients with Parkinson's disease, as we know, have movement problems. They may find themselves unable to initiate movement or move with normal fluidity and speed (see Chapter 10). This disorder results from a loss of cells in the substantia nigra, a nucleus that is the source of dopaminergic inputs to the basal ganglia and frontal cortex. To restore function to the basal ganglia, cells from aborted fetuses are placed in structures that receive inputs from the nigra. The behavioral results from this procedure are encouraging. Patients' performance on motor tests improves substantially following surgery, and metabolic imaging reveals activity in the vicinity of the implants (Lindvall et al., 1990). The mechanism underlying these changes remains unclear. One hypothesis is that new cells stimulate old cells in the substantia nigra to produce more dopamine. Alternatively, transplanted tissue may heighten the sensitivity and responsiveness to whatever dopamine is produced by the nigra or may develop into dopamine-sensitive neurons.

Transplantation techniques offer a promising method for clinical neurology and open up areas of research for cognitive neuroscience. In animals, fetal grafts have been placed in the spinal cord to promote reconnectivity of descending motor fibers following spinal resection (see Chapter 12). Rather than simply focus on removing aberrant tissue, these procedures raise the possibility that neurosurgical techniques can improve function by restoring damaged tissue.

WHAT IS COGNITIVE PSYCHOLOGY?

It would be naive to suppose that people have only recently sought to relate behavior to brain function. What marks cognitive neuroscience as a new field for this endeavor are the paradigms developed in cognitive psychology, the study of mental activity as an information-processing problem. Cognitive psychology rests on the assumption that we do not directly perceive and act in the world. Rather, our perceptions, thoughts, and actions depend on internal transformations or computations. Information is obtained by sense organs, but our ability to comprehend the information, to recognize it as something we have experienced before, and to choose an appropriate response depends on a complex interplay of processes.

Mental Representations and Transformations

Two key concepts underlie the cognitive approach. The first idea, that information processing depends on internal representations, we usually take for granted. Consider the concept "ball." If we met someone from a planet composed of straight lines, we could try to convey what this concept means in many ways. We could draw a picture of a sphere, we could provide a verbal definition indicating that such a three-dimensional object is circular along any circumference, or we could write a mathematical definition. Each instance is an alternative form of representing the "circle" concept. Whether one form of representation is better than another depends on our visitor. To understand the picture, our visitor would need a visual system and the ability to comprehend the spatial arrangement of a curved drawing. To understand the mathematical definition, our visitor must comprehend geometrical and algebraic relations. Assuming our visitor has these capabilities, the task will help dictate which representational format is most useful. For example, if we want to show that the "ball" rolls down a hill, a pictorial representation is likely to be much more useful than an algebraic formula.

The second critical notion of cognitive psychology is that mental representations undergo transformations. The need to transform mental representations is most obvious when we consider how sensory signals are connected with stored knowledge in memory. Perceptual representations must be translated into action representations if we wish to achieve a goal. Moreover, information processing is not simply a sequential process from sensation to perception to memory to action. Memory may alter how we perceive something and the manner in which information is processed is subject to attentional constraints. Cognitive psychology is all about how we manipulate representations.

Consider the categorization experiment introduced by Michael Posner (1978) at the University of Oregon

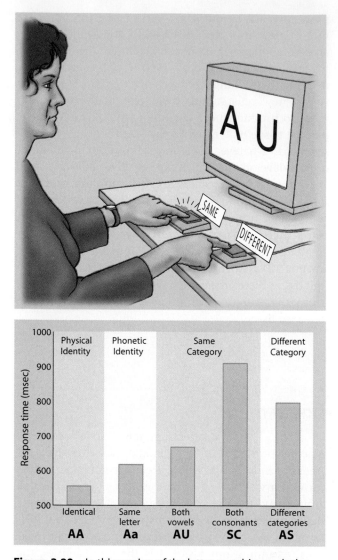

Figure 3.22 In this version of the letter matching task, the subject responds "SAME" when the letters are either both vowels or consonants and "DIFFERENT" when they are from different categories. The reaction times for different conditions are shown in the bottom panel. Bottom panel adapted from Posner (1986).

that is schematized in Figure 3.22. Two letters are simultaneously presented in each trial. The subject's task is to evaluate whether they are both vowels, both consonants, or one vowel and one consonant. If the letters are from the same category, the subject presses one button. If they are from different categories, then he or she should respond with the other button.

One version of this experiment includes five conditions. In the physical identity condition, the two letters are exactly the same. In the phonetic identity condition, the two letters have the same identity, but one letter is a capital and the other is lower case. There are two types

of same-category conditions, conditions in which the two letters are different members of the same category. In one, both letters are vowels; in the other, both letters are consonants. Finally, in the different condition, the two letters are from different categories and can be either of the same type size or of a different one. Note that the first four conditions, physical identity, phonetic identity, and the two same-category conditions, all require the same response. On all three types of trials, a correct response is "yes," the two letters are from the same category. Nonetheless, as shown in Figure 3.22, response latencies differ significantly. Subjects respond fastest to the physical identity condition, next fastest to the phonetic identity condition, and slowest to the same-category condition, especially when the two letters are both consonants.

The results of Posner's experiment suggest that we derive multiple representations of stimuli. One representation is based on the physical aspects of the stimulus. In this experiment, it is a visually derived representation of the shape presented on the screen. A second representation corresponds to the letter's identity. This representation proves that many stimuli can correspond to the same letter. For example, we can recognize that A, a, and a all represent the same letter. A third level of abstraction represents the category a letter belongs to. At this level, the letters A and E activate our internal representation of the category "vowel." Posner maintains that different response latencies reflect the degrees of processing required to do the letter-matching task. By this logic, we infer that physical representations are activated first, phonetic representations next, and category representations last.

This experiment provides a powerful demonstration that, even with simple stimuli, the mind derives multiple representations. Other manipulations with this task have explored how representations are transformed from one form to another. In a follow-up study, Posner and his colleagues used a sequential mode of presentation. Two letters were again presented, but a brief interval (referred to as the *stimulus-onset asynchrony*, the time between the two stimuli) separated the presentations for the letters. As shown in Figure 3.23, the difference between the physical identity and phonetic identity conditions was reduced as the stimulus-onset asynchrony became longer. Hence, the internal representation of the first letter is transformed during the interstimulus interval. The representation of the physical stimulus gives way to the more abstract representation of the letter's phonetic identity.

As you may have experienced personally, experiments such as these elicit as many questions as answers.

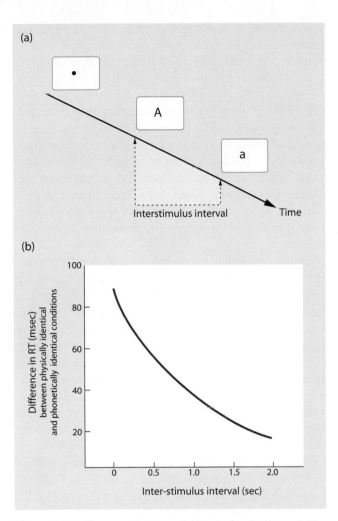

Figure 3.23 The same letter matching task as in Figure 3.22 except that an inter-stimulus interval separates the presentation of the two letters **(a).** As this interval is lengthened, the difference between the identical and same letter condition becomes reduced **(b),** suggesting a transformation of the representation into a more abstract code. Data from Posner (1986).

Why are subjects slower to judge that two letters are consonants in comparison to two letters that are vowels? Would the same advantage for identical stimuli exist if the letters were spoken? What about if one letter were visual and the other were auditory? Suppose that the task is to judge whether two letters are physically identical. Would manipulating the stimulus-onset asynchrony affect reaction times on this version? Cognitive psychologists address these questions and then devise methods for inferring the mind's machinery from observable behaviors.

In the preceding example, the primary dependent variable has always been reaction time, the speed with which the subjects make their judgments. Reaction time experiments utilize the chronometric methodology.

Chrono comes from the Greek word meaning "time," and *metric* for "measure." The chronometric study of mind is essential for cognitive psychologists because mental events occur rapidly and efficiently. If we only consider whether a person is correct or incorrect on a task, we miss subtle differences in performance. Measuring reaction time permits a finer analysis of internal processes. In addition to measuring processing time as a dependent variable, chronometric manipulations can be applied to independent variables, as with the letter-matching experiment in which the stimulus-onset asynchrony was varied.

Characterizing Mental Operations

Suppose you arrive at the grocery store and discover that you forgot to bring your shopping list. As you wander up and down the aisles, you gaze upon the thousands of items lining the shelves, hoping that they will help prompt your memory. You can cruise through the pet food section, but hesitate when you come to the dairy section: Was there a carton of eggs in the refrigerator? Was the milk supply low? Were there any cheeses not covered by a 6-month rind of mold?

This memory retrieval task draws on a number of cognitive capabilities. A fundamental goal of cognitive psychology is to identify the different mental operations that are required to perform tasks such as these. Not only are cognitive psychologists interested in describing human performance—the observable behavior of humans and other animals—but they also seek to identify the internal processing that underlies this performance. A basic assumption of cognitive psychology is that tasks are composed of a set of mental operations. Mental operations involve taking a representation as an input, performing some sort of process on the input, and then producing a new representation, or output. Thus, mental operations are processes that generate, elaborate upon, or manipulate mental representations. Cognitive psychologists design experiments to test hypotheses about mental operations.

Consider an experimental task introduced by Saul Sternberg (1975) when he was working at Bell Laboratories. The task bears some similarity to the problem faced by our absent-minded shopper, except that in Sternberg's task, the difficulty is not so much in terms of forgetting items in memory, but rather of how well people can compare sensory information with representations that are active in memory. On each trial, the subject is first presented with a set of numbers to memorize (Figure 3.24). The memory set could consist of one, two, or four numbers. Following this, a single number is presented and the subject has to decide if this number was

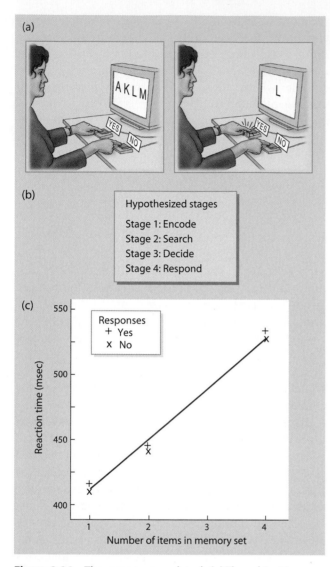

Figure 3.24 The memory search task. **(a)** The subject is shown a set of letters (either one, two, or four) and is asked to memorize them. After a delay, a single probe letter appears and the subject indicates whether it was a member of the memory set. **(b)** Hypothesized mental operations required to perform this task. **(c)** Reaction time increases with set size, indicating that the search through the memory set must be performed sequentially rather than in parallel. Adapted from Sternberg (1966).

part of the memorized set. One button is pressed if the subject thinks the target was part of the memory set ("yes" response) and a second button if the target was not part of the set ("no" response). The primary dependent variable is reaction time.

Sternberg postulated that, to respond on this task, the subject must engage in four primary mental operations. First, the target must be encoded. That is, the subject must identify the visible target. Second, the mental

representation of the target must be compared to the representations of the items in memory. Third, a decision must be made as to whether the target matches one of the memorized items. Finally, based on this decision, the appropriate response must be generated. Note that each of these operations—encode, compare, decide, and respond—is likely to be composed of additional operations. For example, responding might be further fractionated into processes involved in selecting the appropriate finger, and processes involved in activating the muscles that make the finger move. Nonetheless, by postulating a set of mental operations, experiments can be devised to explore the operation of putative mental operations.

A basic question for Sternberg was how to characterize the efficiency of recognition memory. Assuming that there are active representations of all of the items in the memory set, one could conceive of (at least) two different ways the recognition process might work. A highly efficient system might compare a representation of the target with all of the items in the memory set simultaneously. On the other hand, the recognition operation might be limited in terms of how much information it can handle at any point in time. For example, it might require that the input be compared successively to each item in memory. Sternberg realized that the reaction time data could distinguish between these two alternatives. If the comparison process could occur for all items simultaneously, what would be called a *parallel process*, then reaction time should be independent of the number of items in the memory set. But if the comparison process operates in a sequential or serial manner, then reaction time would be expected to slow down as the memory set became larger. It would take more time to compare an item with a large memory list than with a small memory list. Sternberg's results convincingly supported the serial hypothesis. In fact, reaction time increased in a constant, or linear, manner with set size. Moreover, the functions for the "yes" and "no" trials were essentially identical.

The parallel, linear functions allowed Sternberg to make two inferences about the mental operations associated with this task. First, the linear increase in reaction time as the set size increased implied that the memory comparison operation took a fixed amount of internal processing time. In the initial study, the slope of the function was approximately 40 msec/item, implying that it takes about 40 msec for each successive comparison of the target to the items in the memory set. This does not mean that this value represents a fixed property of memory comparison. It is likely to be affected by factors such as task difficulty (e.g., are the nontarget items in the memory set similar or dissimilar to the target item) or experience. Nonetheless, the experiment demonstrates how both qualitative and quantitative characterizations of mental operations can be made from simple behavioral tasks.

Second, the fact that the two functions were parallel implied that subjects compared all of the memory items to the target before making a response. If subjects had terminated the comparison as soon as a match was found, then the slope of the "no" function should have been twice as steep as the slope of the "yes" function. This follows because in "no" trials all of the items have to be checked. On average, with "yes" trials only half the items need to be checked before a match is found. The fact that the functions were parallel implies that comparisons were carried out on all items, and that comparison was serial and exhaustive (as opposed to serial and self-terminating). An exhaustive process seems illogical, though. Why continue to compare the target to the memory set once a match is detected? One possible answer is that it is easier to store the result of each comparison for later evaluation than to monitor "on-line" the results of successive comparisons.

While memory comparison appears to involve a serial process, many other tasks demonstrate cognitive operations that operate in parallel. A classic demonstration of this is the word superiority effect (Reicher, 1969). In this experiment, a stimulus is shown briefly and the subjects are asked which of two target letters (e.g., *A* or *E*) was present. The stimuli can be composed of either words, nonsense letter strings, or letter strings in which all of the letters are *X*'s except for the target letter (Figure 3.25). Brief presentation times are used so that errors will be observed, with the critical question centering on whether the context affects performance. The *word superiority effect* refers to the fact that subjects are most accurate when the stimuli are words. Somewhat counterintuitively, this suggests that we do not need to identify all of the letters of a word before we recognize the word. Rather, when processing the word lists, parallel activation occurs for representations corresponding to the individual letters and the entire word. Performance is facilitated because both representations can provide information as to whether the target letter is present. A word-level representation is not possible with nonsense words and letter strings, and thus judgments must be based solely on letter-level representation.

Constraints on Information Processing

In Sternberg's memory search experiment, information processing operates in a certain manner because the

Does the stimulus contain an "A" or "E"?

Condition	Stimulus	Accuracy
Word	**RACK**	90%
Nonsense string	**KARC**	80%
X's	**XAXX**	80%

Figure 3.25 The word superiority effect. Subjects are more accurate in identifying the target vowel when it is embedded in a word. This result suggests that both letter and word levels of representation are activated in parallel.

memory comparison process is limited. The subjects cannot simultaneously compare the target item to all of the items in the memory set. An important question is whether this limitation reflects properties that are specific to memory or a more general processing limitation. Perhaps there is a limitation to how much internal processing people can do at any one time, regardless of the task. An alternative explanation is that processing limitations are task-specific. Processing constraints are defined only by the particular set of mental operations associated with a particular task. For example, while the comparison of a probe item to the memory set might require a serial operation, encoding might occur in parallel such that it would not matter whether the probe was presented by itself or among a noisy array of competing stimuli.

Exploring the limitations in task performance is a central concern for cognitive psychologists. Consider a simple color-naming task that was devised in the early 1930s by an aspiring doctoral student, J.R. Stroop (1935; for a recent review, MacLeod, 1991), and that has become one of the most widely employed tasks in all of cognitive psychology. In this task, a list of words is presented and the subject is asked to name the color of each stimulus as fast as possible. As you can experience from Figure 3.26, it is much easier to do this task when the words do not spell the names of conflicting colors. The Stroop effect powerfully demonstrates the multiplicity of mental representations. The stimuli in this task appear to activate at least two separable representations. One representation corresponds to each stimulus's color; it is what allows the subject to perform the task.

Color matches word	Random colors	Color doesn't match word
RED	XXXXX	GREEN
GREEN	XXXXX	BLUE
RED	XXXXX	RED
BLUE	XXXXX	BLUE
BLUE	XXXXX	GREEN
GREEN	XXXXX	RED
BLUE	XXXXX	GREEN
RED	XXXXX	BLUE

Green, I mean red.

GREEN

Figure 3.26 The Stroop task. Time yourself as you work through each column, naming the color of the ink of each stimulus as fast as possible. Assuming you do not squint to blur the words, it should be easy to read the first and second columns, but quite difficult to read the third.

Yet a representation corresponding to the color concept associated with the words is also activated, despite the fact that this representation is irrelevant to the task and produces interference in the incongruent condition. The activation of a representation based on the words rather than the colors of the words appears to be automatic. The Stroop effect persists even after thousands of trials of practice, reflecting the fact that skilled readers have years of practice in analyzing letter strings for their symbolic meaning. On the other hand, the interference is markedly reduced if the response requires a speeded key press rather than a vocal response. Thus, the word-based representations are closely linked to the vocal response system and have little effect when the responses are produced manually.

A second method used to examine constraints on information processing involves dual tasks. For these studies, performance on a primary task alone is compared to performance on that task concurrently with a secondary task. The decrement in primary-task performance during the dual-task situation helps elucidate the limits in cognition. Sophisticated use of dual-task methodology can also identify the exact source of interference. For example, the Stroop effect is not reduced when the color-naming task is performed simultaneously with a secondary task in which the subject must judge the pitch of an auditory tone. However, if the auditory stimuli for the secondary task are a list of words and the subject must monitor this list for a particular target, the Stroop effect is attenuated. It appears that the verbal demands of the secondary task interfere with the automatic activation of the word-based representations in the Stroop task, thus leaving the color-based representations relatively free form interference.

The efficiency of our mental abilities and the way mental operations interact can, of course, change with experience. The beginning driver has her hands rigidly locked to the steering wheel; within a few months, she is unfazed to steer with her left hand while using the right hand to scan for a good radio station and maintain a conversation with the person in the passenger seat. Even more impressive is that, with extensive practice, people can become proficient in simultaneously performing two tasks that were originally quite incompatible. Elizabeth Spelke and her colleagues at Cornell University studied how well college students read for comprehension while taking dictation (Spelke et al., 1976). Prior to any training, their subjects could read about 400 words/min when faced with difficult reading material such as modern short stories of American and European writers. This rate fell to 280 words/min when the subjects were required to simultaneously take dictation at a rate of 1 word every 6 seconds, and their comprehension of the stories was also impaired. After 85 hours of training spread over a 17-week period, the students' reading rate and comprehension level were hardly disrupted during the dual task. The results offer an elixir for all college students. Imagine finishing the reading for an upcoming psychology examination while taking notes during a history lecture!

This dual-task study raises significant problems about what is meant by *processing resources*. For instance, it challenges notions of general processing limits.

If subjects initially cannot read and write at the same time because of a processing limit, we would have to hypothesize that practice improves this general resource. If this were so, then training should have improved the subjects' cognitive capabilities. But the effects of practice were limited to Spelke's pair of tasks. We might hypothesize, then, that it is difficult to read and write at the same time because both tasks require manipulating common verbally activated representations. With prac- tice, representations associated with auditory and visual inputs may become dissociated. On the other hand, it is likely that the subjects had little comprehension of the dictated words, suggesting that comprehension on both tasks requires similar representations. A student would probably be better off using a tape recorder for the history lecture if he or she really needs the time to prepare for the psychology examination.

COMPUTER MODELING

The computer is a powerful metaphor for cognitive neuroscience. Both the brain and the computer chip are impressive processing machines, capable of representing and transforming large amounts of information. While there are vast differences in how these machines process information, cognitive scientists use computers to simulate cognitive processes. *Simulation* means to imitate, to reproduce behavior in an alternative medium. The simulated cognitive processes are commonly referred to as *artificial intelligence*—artificial in the sense that they are artifacts, man-made creations, and intelligent in that the computers perform complex functions. Computer programs control robots on factory production lines, assist physicians in making differential diagnoses or in detecting breast cancer, and create models of the universe in the first nanoseconds after the "big bang."

Many commercial computer applications are developed without reference to how brains think. More relevant to our present concerns are the efforts of cognitive scientists to create models of cognition (Rummelhart and McClelland, 1986). In these investigations, simulations are designed to mimic behavior and the cognitive processes that support that behavior. The computer is given input and then must perform internal operations to create a behavior. By observing the behavior, the researcher can assess how well it matches behavior produced by a real mind. Of course to get the computer to succeed, the modeler must specify how information is represented and transformed within the program. To do this, concrete hypotheses regarding the "mental" operations needed for the machine must be generated. As such, computer simulations provide a useful tool for testing theories of cognition. Successes and failures of models give valuable insights to a theory's strengths and weaknesses.

In the chapters that follow, we make few references to work in computer modeling. For the most part, this work is still in its infancy and has focused on developing models that can simulate a task as a way of demonstrat- ing proof of a particular theoretical account of that task. We choose to focus on the experimental evidence from which these models are derived. Nonetheless, a brief overview is provided to serve as a reference guide for a growing methodology that has assumed a prominent position in the scientific journals of cognitive neuroscience.

Models Are Explicit

Computer models of cognition are useful because they can be analyzed in detail. In creating a simulation the researcher has to be completely explicit; the way the computer represents and processes information must be totally specified. This does not mean that a computer's operation is always completely predictable and that the outcome of a simulation is known in advance. Computer simulations can incorporate random events or be on such a large scale that analytic tools do not reveal the solution. But the internal operations, the way information is computed, must be specified. Computer simulations are especially helpful to cognitive neuroscientists in recognizing problems the brain must solve to produce coherent behavior.

Braitenberg (1984) gave elegant examples of how modeling brings insights to information processing. Imagine observing the two creatures shown in Figure 3.27, as they move about a minimalist world consisting of a single heat source such as a sun. From the outside, the creatures look identical: They both have two sensors and two wheels. Despite this similarity, their behavior is distinct. One creature moves away from the sun and the other homes in on it. Why the difference? As an outsider with no access to the internal operations of these creatures, we might conjecture that they have had different experiences and so the same input activates different representations. Perhaps one was burned at an early age and fears the sun, and maybe the other likes the warmth.

But, as can be seen from their internal wiring, the behavioral differences depend on how the creatures are

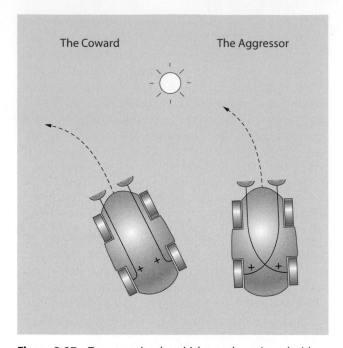

The Coward   **The Aggressor**

Figure 3.27 Two very simple vehicles, each equipped with two sensors that excite motors on the rear wheels. By simply changing the wiring scheme from uncrossed to crossed, the behavior of the vehicles is radically altered. The "coward" will always avoid the source whereas the "aggressor" will relentlessly pursue it. Adapted from Braitenberg (1984).

wired. The uncrossed connections make the creature on the left turn away from the sun; the crossed connections force the creature on the right to orient toward it. Thus, the two creatures' behavioral differences arise from a slight variation in how sensory information is mapped onto motor processes.

These creatures are exceedingly simple—and inflexible in their actions. At best, they offer only the crudest model of how an invertebrate might move in response to a phototropic sensor. The point of Braitenberg's example is not to model a behavior; rather, it represents how a single computational change—from crossed to uncrossed wiring—can yield a major behavioral change. When interpreting such a behavioral difference, we might postulate extensive internal operations and representations. However, when we look inside Braitenberg's models, we see that there is no difference in how the two models process information, only in their patterns of connectivity.

Cognitive psychologists are sometimes accused of creating models that attribute internal processes to homunculi. A list of internal operations may be postulated, but their control is unspecified or attributed to an internal executive controller. Computer models do not allow this. A programmer must be explicit about how information is represented and transformed. Moreover, since computer languages eventually translate into bi-

nary numbers, information transformation is a computational process. Not only do computer models have to describe internal processes, but also they must quantitatively elucidate their operation. Computer modeling forces the theorist to be precise.

Representations in Computer Models

Computer models differ widely in their representations. Symbolic models include, as we might expect, units that represent symbolic entities. A model for object recognition might have units that represent visual features like corners or volumetric shapes. Over the past decade or so, an alternative architecture has gained popularity: connectionism. In connectionist models, processing is distributed over innumerable units whose input and output can represent specific features. For example, they may indicate whether a stimulus contains a visual feature such as a vertical or horizontal line. Of critical importance in these models, however, is that so-called hidden units are connected with input and output units. Hidden units provide intermediate processing steps between the input and output units. They allow the model to extract the information that allows for the best mapping between the input and desired output by changing the strengths of connections between units. To do this, a modeler must specify a learning rule, a quantitative description of how processing within the model changes according to how well it performs. If the model performs poorly, the change is likely to be large. If the model performs well, the change is small.

Connectionist models are very powerful in solving complex problems. Simulations cover the gamut of cognitive processes including perception, memory, language, and motor control. One of the most appealing aspects of these models is that the architecture resembles, at least superficially, the nervous system. In connectionist models, processing is distributed across many units, similar to the way neural structures depend on the activity of many neurons. The contribution of any unit may be small in relation to the system's total output, but complex behaviors can be generated by the aggregate action of all units. Moreover, the computations in connectionist models are simulated to occur in parallel. The activation level of the units in the network are all updated simultaneously.

An appealing aspect of connectionist models, especially for those interested in cognitive neuroscience, is that "lesion" techniques demonstrate how a model's performance changes when its parts are altered. Unlike strictly serial computer models that collapse if a circuit is broken, connectionist models degrade gracefully. The model may continue to perform appropriately after some units are removed, because each unit plays only a small part in the processing. "Artificial lesioning" is thus a fascinating way to test a model's validity. At the first level, a model is constructed to see if it adequately simulates normal behavior. Then "lesions" are made to see if the breakdown in the model's performance resembles the behavioral deficits observed in neurological patients.

Models Lead to Testable Predictions

The contribution of computer modeling usually goes beyond the assessment of whether a model succeeds in mimicking a cognitive process. Models can generate novel predictions that can be tested with real brains. An example of the predictive power of computer modeling comes from the work of John Desmond and John Moore (1991) at the University of Massachusetts. One of the best-studied animal models of learning is the classic conditioning of a rabbit's nictitating membrane response. An unconditioned, aversive stimulus—a puff of air to the eye—is preceded by a tone. The rabbit blinks after the air puff, which is referred to as an *unconditioned response* because it does not have to be learned; the blink occurs spontaneously. With repeated pairings of the tone and air puff, the animal begins to blink in response to the tone, which is a *conditioned response* because the animal must learn that the tone predicts the air puff.

Rabbits are sensitive to the temporal relation between the tone and the air puff. The conditioned response is timed so it peaks prior to the air puff, which is what makes this type of learning adaptive. By timing the response appropriately, the animal can minimize the air puff's impact. Animals can learn to associate these two stimuli even when a silent interval separates the tone's offset and the air puff's onset. This is referred to as a trace learning task because the rabbit must learn to associate the air puff with a stimulus that no longer is present. Only a trace remains upon presentation of the air puff.

Desmond and Moore were interested in how animals timed their responses in a trace learning task. Two hypotheses appeared tenable. The conditioned response could be time locked either to the tone's onset or to its offset. If the former, we assume that the animal has a way to sustain a stimulus's activation beyond its actual duration. Alternatively, the offset of the tone might be the salient signal that triggers the response. Desmond and Moore simulated learning with either type of representation. And they also found that a model incorporating both representations not only simulated the behavior but also led to a novel prediction. Consider a condition in which the tone and trace interval last 200 and 200 msec, respectively. With these parameters, the rabbit learns to close its eye just short of 400 msec. Learning that is time locked to the tone's onset requires the animal to represent an interval of 400 msec; the tone's offset (or trace interval) requires only 200 msec.

These observations led Desmond and Moore to explore a series of simulations with a previously untested transfer task. After training a "model rabbit," the tone's duration was extended to 400 msec while the trace interval remained constant at 200 msec (Figure 3.28).

Figure 3.28 **(a)** Basic paradigm for eyeblink conditioning. A 200-msec tone is followed by a 50-msec air puff. Early in training, the animal blinks in response to the air puff. With repeated pairings, the animal makes a conditioned response to the tone, minimizing the aversive effects of the air puff. **(b)** In the transfer test, the duration of the tone is extended to 400 msec. Divergent predictions are derived from models in which the timing between the tone and air puff is triggered by either the onset or offset of the tone. The experimental results showed that the rabbits actually made two conditioned responses in the transfer phase, one linked to the tone onset and one linked to the tone offset.

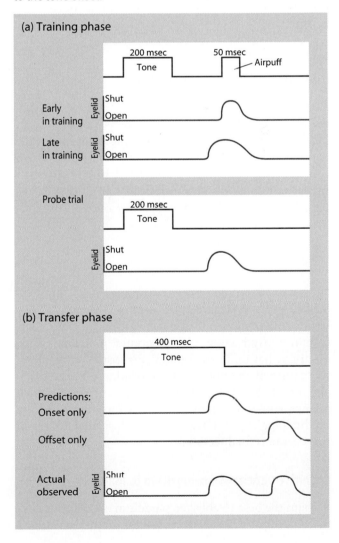

Models with either an onset or an offset representation yielded unsurprising predictions: When the response was time locked to the tone's offset, the response was delayed by 200 msec, resulting in an optimally timed behavior. When the response was time locked to the tone's onset, the latency of the response was unchanged, and it now preceded the air puff by 200 msec. The model that incorporated two timing mechanisms, on the other hand, revealed a surprising prediction: During transfer, this model produced two conditioned responses, one that was timed to the tone's onset and a second that was timed to the tone's offset. When researchers returned to real rabbits, they confirmed the prediction!

With hindsight, it may seem like Desmond and Moore did not need computer modeling to derive this prediction. The problem could have been revealed by a careful analysis of the information that rabbits must represent. But this analysis eluded researchers who had worked on this problem for many decades. The modeling work led Desmond and Moore to be explicit in deriving mechanisms for representing temporal information, and, with an explicit model, new predictions could be generated.

Limitations with Computer Models

Computer modeling is limited as a method for studying the operation of living nervous systems. For one thing, there are almost always radical simplifications in how the nervous system is modeled. While the units in a typical connectionist model bear some similarity to neurons—for example, nonlinear activation rules produce spikelike behavior—the models are limited in scope, usually consisting of just a few hundred or so elements, and it is not always clear whether the elements correspond to single neurons or ensembles of neurons. Second, some requirements and problems arise in modeling work, particularly on learning, and are at odds with what we know occurs in biological organisms. Many connectionist models require a homunculus-like teacher who "knows" the right answer and can be used to correct the behavior of the internal elements. And these models can suffer "catastrophic interference"—the loss of old information when new material is presented.

Third, most modeling efforts are restricted to relatively narrow problems such as demonstrating how the Stroop effect can be simulated by postulating separate word-name and word-color representations, under the control of a common attentional system. As such, they provide useful computational tests of the viability of a particular hypothesis, but are typically less useful in generating new predictions. Moreover, as some critics have argued, unlike experimental work which by its nature is cumulative, modeling research tends to occur in isolation. There may be lots of ways to model a particular phenomenon, but less effort has been devoted to devising critical tests that pit one theory against another.

These limitations are by no means insurmountable, and we should expect the contribution of computer simulations to continue to grow in the cognitive neurosciences. Indeed, the trend in the field is for modeling work to be more constrained by neuroscience, with researchers replacing generic processing units with elements that embody the biophysics of the brain. In a reciprocal manner, computer simulations provide a useful way to develop theory, which may then aid experimentalists in designing experiments and interpreting results.

CONVERGING METHODS

So far, we have taken a brief look at the basic methodologies in the neurosciences, neurology, cognitive psychology, and computer modeling. Each discipline has unique methodologies for learning about the nature of the mind and the relation between brain and mind. But the real strength of cognitive neuroscience comes from the way in which these diverse methodologies are integrated, which is the subject of this chapter's final section.

Cognitive Deficits Following Brain Damage

Perhaps the best-established paradigm of cognitive neuroscience involves the effects of brain injury on behavior. For many centuries lesions have been extensively studied in animals and humans, and, as noted earlier in this chapter, the lesion model has laid an empirical foundation for learning about brain organization. Fundamental concepts, such as the left hemisphere's dominant role in language or the dependence of visual functions on posterior cortical regions, were developed by observing the effects of brain injury.

For two reasons, research on neurological patients has been booming over the past two decades. First, with neuroimaging methods such as CT and MRI, we can precisely localize brain injury in vivo. Second, the paradigms of cognitive psychology have provided the tools for making more sophisticated analyses of the behavioral deficits observed after brain injury. Early neuropsychological work focused on localizing complex tasks: language, vision, executive control, motor programming. The essence of the cognitive revolution has been that these complex tasks require the integrative activity of many component operations. Cognitive neuropsychologists have extended this to research on brain-injured patients. Indeed, the excitement about neuropsychological research is not restricted to its potential to link mental activities to brain structures. Equally important, many researchers recognize that the study of dysfunctional behavior can help identify the component operations that underlie normal cognitive performance.

The logic of this approach is straightforward. If a behavior depends on processing within a certain brain structure, then damage to this structure should disrupt the behavior. As such, this approach assumes that brain injury is eliminative—that brain injury disturbs or eliminates the processing ability of the affected structure.

Consider the following example. Suppose that damage to brain region A results in impaired performance on task X. One conclusion is that region A contributes to the processing required for task X. For example, if task X is reading, we might conclude that region A is critical for reading. But from cognitive psychology we know that a complex task such as reading has many component operations: Fonts must be perceived; letters and letter strings activate representations of their corresponding meanings; and syntactic operations link individual words into a coherent stream. By merely testing reading ability, we will not know which component operation or operations are impaired when there are lesions to region A. What the cognitive neuropsychologist wants to do is design tasks that diagnose the function of specific operations. If a reading problem stems from a general perceptual problem, then comparable deficits should be seen on a range of tests of visual perception. If the problem reflects the loss of semantic knowledge, then the deficit should only be limited to tasks that require some form of object identification or recognition.

Associating neural structures with specific processing operations calls for appropriate control conditions. The most basic form of control is to compare the performance of a patient or group of patients with that of healthy subjects. Poorer performance by the patients might be taken as evidence that the affected brain regions are involved in the task. Thus, if we had a group of patients with lesions of the frontal cortex who showed impairment on our reading task, we might suppose that this region of the brain was critical for reading. However, it is important to keep in mind that brain injury can produce widespread changes in cognitive abilities. The frontal lobe patients not only may have trouble in reading, but also may demonstrate impairment on just about any task we give them such as problem solving, memory, or motor planning. Thus, the challenge for the cognitive neuroscientist is to determine whether the observed behavioral problem results from damage to a particular mental operation or whether it is secondary to a more general disturbance. For example, many patients are depressed after a neurological disturbance such as a stroke, and depression is known to affect performance on a wide range of tasks.

SINGLE AND DOUBLE DISSOCIATIONS

More typically, cognitive neuropsychologists design experiments that have at least two tasks, an experimental task and a control task. The best experiments are those in which two tasks are similar in most respects but differ in requiring one hypothetical mental operation. Suppose that a researcher is interested in the association between two aspects of memory. One aspect of memory is knowledge about when we learned a particular fact or piece of information. For example, people who were alive in 1963 can recall not only that President Kennedy was killed in Dallas, but also where they were when they first heard about the tragedy. A second aspect relates to the familiarity we have with that fact or piece of information. We recognize that our memory of Kennedy's death is not simply the result of that initial experience, but also due to the fact that the event has been recalled in countless news documentaries, books, and movies.

Our researcher hypothesizes that these two aspects of memory are separable. One way to test this hypothesis would be to examine patients with memory disorders. For example, if the researcher hypothesizes that familiarity is associated with the temporal lobe, then he might test patients with temporal lobe lesions on two memory tests, one designed to look at memory of when information was acquired and the second designed to look at familiarity. To test this, patients with memory problems would be required to perform two tasks. For each task, the stimuli would be identical—a series of abstract drawings in which some items are shown once, others twice, and others three times. To test how well the patients remember when they learned something, a temporal-order task would be used. The subjects are presented with a pair of drawings and judge which was presented first. To test for familiarity, a frequency-judgment task can be used. Here, the subjects would again be presented with a pair of drawings, but now they must decide which drawing was seen more often. If temporal lobe lesions disrupt familiarity, but not the ability to remember when something was learned, then the patients should demonstrate selective impairment on the frequency task. To detect the impairment, it would be necessary to include a control group such as people without any neurological problems.

Such a result would constitute a single dissociation (Figure 3.29). Two groups are tested on two tasks and a between-group difference is apparent in only one task. Two groups are necessary to compare the patients' performance with that of a control group. Two tasks are necessary to examine whether a deficit is specific to a particular task or reflects a more general impairment. Many conclusions in neuropsychology are based on single dissociations. When compared to control subjects, patients with hippocampal lesions cannot develop long-term memories despite their short-term memory being intact. Patients with Broca's aphasia have intact comprehension but struggle to speak fluently.

Single dissociations have unavoidable problems. In particular, the two tasks are assumed to be equally sensitive to differences between the control and experimental groups. However, often this is not the case. One task may be more sensitive than the other because of differences in task difficulty or sensitivity problems in how the measurements are obtained. For example, the frequency-judgment task might be more demanding than the temporal-order task, requiring a greater degree of concentration. If the brain injury produced a generalized problem in concentration, then the patients might have difficulty with this task, but the problem would not be due to a specific problem in memory for familiarity. As an analogy, consider a comparison between two six-cylinder cars, one with an engine in mint condition and a second that is running on only five cylinders. It might be difficult to tell the difference between the two cars when driving through the city because the speed must be kept low and frequent stops are necessary. However, when the cars are taken out on the highway, it would quickly become apparent that one car drives rougher than the other. However, we would not want to conclude that this car has a selective deficit in highway driving. Rather, our city driving test was not sufficiently sensitive to detect the persistent problem.

Double dissociations avoid these problems. As with single dissociations, double dissociations require two groups and two tasks. What defines double dissociation is that group 1 shows impairment on task X and group 2, impairment on task Y (see the bottom panel in Figure 3.29). The two groups' performance may be compared to each other. Or, each group's performance may be impaired with respect to a control group that shows no impairment. With a double dissociation, it is no longer reasonable to argue that a difference in performance merely results from the unequal sensitivity of the two tasks. In our memory example, the claim that temporal lobe patients have a selective problem with familiarity would be greatly strengthened if it were shown that a second group of patients (e.g., frontal lobe patients) showed selective impairment on the temporal-order task. Double dissociations offer the strongest neuropsychological evidence that a patient or patient group has a selective deficit in a certain cognitive operation.

The inferential power of double dissociations has been exploited in many settings beyond the neuropsychology laboratory. Lesion studies in animals have been most convincing when the conclusions were based on double dissociations. Cognitive research on healthy subjects has also benefited from the logic of double dissociations. Evidence of separable cognitive operations can be gained by demonstrating that one task is affected by one type of manipulation whereas a second task is selectively affected by a different manipulation. For example, it might be found in normal subjects that the rate at which the stimuli appear affects performance on the temporal-order task whereas the similarity between the stimuli affects familiarity performance. Here, the same subjects serve as their own controls. The double dissociation arises because the two manipulations—rate and similarity—differentially affect performance on the two

Figure 3.29 Hypothetical series of results conforming to either a single **(a)** or double **(b)** dissociation. With the single dissociation, the patient group shows impairment on one task and not on the other. With the double dissociation, one patient group shows impairment on one task and a second patient group shows impairment on the other task. Double dissociations provide much stronger evidence for a selective impairment.

(a) Single dissociation

Group	Tasks (% correct)	
	Recency memory	Familiarity memory
Temporal lobe damage	90%	70%
Controls	90%	95%

(b) Double dissociation

Group	Tasks (% correct)	
	Recency memory	Familiarity memory
Temporal lobe	90%	70%
Frontal lobe	60%	95%
Controls	90%	95%

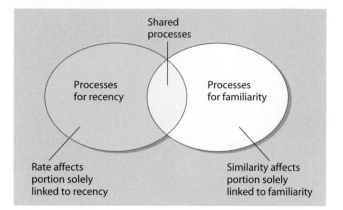

Figure 3.30 Identifying the mental operations required for a particular task can be accomplished by showing that different manipulations selectively influence different aspects of performance. In this example, recognition memory is hypothesized to depend on both recency and familiarity, and that these two processes can be influenced by separate manipulations.

tasks. Such a result would suggest that the two tasks involve nonoverlapping component operations (Figure 3.30).

GROUPS VERSUS INDIVIDUALS

In many neuropsychological studies, groups are defined according to whether patients received a common neurological diagnosis (e.g., Alzheimer's disease) or have pathology in a common neural region (e.g., frontal strokes). Group studies have been criticized as inappropriate for human neuropsychology because of the variability among patients assigned to the same groups. No two strokes or tumors are exactly alike. In a similar sense, neurological and cognitive deficits found in degenerative diseases such as Alzheimer's disease vary from patient to patient. Human neuropsychology will never approximate the type of control that is possible in animal research, where the experimenter can control the size and location of the lesion. Even powerful MRI machines provide a relatively crude resolution compared to the histological procedures available to researchers working with animals, and some types of lesions go undetected with either CT or MRI. Given this anatomical variability, the utility of lumping patients into a single group has been questioned, as we should expect a similar lack of correspondence at the behavioral level. Instead, it has been argued that insights to cognitive processes can best be achieved by comprehensively documenting the performance of individual patients and making comparisons across case studies (Caramazza, 1992).

In general, proponents of the case study approach want to use patient studies to develop models of cognitive architecture. Double dissociations are especially prominent. Individuals with unique deficits help to isolate the component operations for a task. Yet the case study approach is more limited for linking neural structures to cognition operations. Lesions from strokes or tumors encompass a wide area and affect several disparate structures. It is difficult to know which affected area correlates with a deficit. Group studies offer hope. Though the extent and location of damage may be heterogeneous, reconstruction software can identify regions of overlap, as shown in Figure 3.31. While individual differences may occur because lesions extend into nonidentical regions, one hopes that the common site of pathology produces a consistent pattern of deficits on a task being studied.

The group-versus-case study debate reflects the difference between the root words in cognitive neuro*science* and cognitive neuro*psychology*. The case study method affords powerful insights into the functional components of cognition. For example, case studies have been essential for demonstrating that brain lesions can selectively disrupt restricted semantic classes. One patient studied by Alfonzo Caramazza and his colleagues at Johns Hopkins University showed a peculiar *anomia*, an inability to name things (Hart et al., 1985). For this patient, the problem was restricted to certain classes of objects. He was unable to generate the names of fruits and vegetables. In contrast, he showed no impairment when asked to name objects such as tools or furniture. If a study had been conducted with a group of patients with anomia, this patient's selective problem might have been attributed to normal between-subject variability. When treated as an isolated case, the problem stood out and inspired researchers to look for patients with similar problems as well as patients with other category-specific anomias. This work has led to sophisticated models of the functional organization of semantic knowledge.

On the other hand, group studies have proved useful for relating cognitive processes to underlying brain structures (Robertson et al., 1993). If a brain structure is hypothesized to perform a particular mental operation, then lesions to this structure should be associated with deficits on tasks that depend on this putative operation. This does not mean that all patients will be similarly affected. For some patients, the pathology may not be as extensive or encroach upon the critical tissue. Moreover, as with healthy subjects, individuals will differ in how they perform a particular task or may have developed idiosyncratic strategies. Nonetheless, group studies allow the researcher to look for similarities across patients with related lesions as well as make systematic

Left Prefrontal

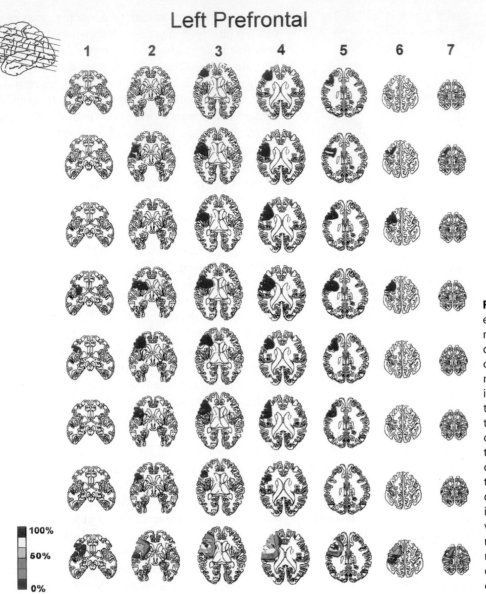

Figure 3.31 Drawing inferences from the study of humans with brain damage is difficult since naturally-occurring brain lesions are never identical. Group studies can facilitate the functional analysis of brain structures by identifying regions of lesion overlap. Sketches of the lesion extent in a series of patients with lesions in the left frontal cortex. The individual patients are shown in each row, with the transverse slices going from inferior to superior. The bottom row shows the extent of damage for the group in composite form.

comparisons between the effects of lesions centered in different brain structures.

Imaging the Healthy Brain

We already mentioned that patient research rests on the assumption that brain injury is an eliminative process: The lesion disrupts certain mental operations and has little or no impact on others. But this assumption need not be correct. The brain is massively interconnected, and damage in one area may have widespread consequences. Moreover, it is not always easy to analyze the function of a missing part by looking at the operation of

the remaining system. Allowing the spark plugs to decay or cutting the line distributing the gas to the pistons will cause an automobile to stop running. This does not mean that spark plugs and distributors do the same thing; rather, their removal has similar functional consequences.

Concerns such as these point to the need for methods that measure activity in the normal brain. Along this front have occurred remarkable technological breakthroughs during the past decade. Indeed, new tools and methods of analysis develop at such an astonishing pace that new journals and scientific organizations have been created to rapidly disseminate this information. In the following section, we review some of the technologies that allow researchers to observe the electrical and metabolic activity of the healthy human brain in vivo.

ELECTRICAL SIGNALS OF THE BRAIN

Neural activity is an electrochemical process. Although the electrical potential produced by a single neuron is minute, when large populations of neurons are active together, they produce electrical potentials large enough to be measured by placing electrodes on the scalp. These surface electrodes are much larger than those used for single-cell recordings, but involve the same principles: A change in voltage corresponding to the difference in potential between the signal at a recording electrode and that at a reference electrode is measured. This potential can be recorded at the scalp because the tissues of the brain, skull, and scalp passively conduct the electrical currents produced by synaptic activity. The record of the signals is referred to as the *electroencephalogram.*

Electroencephalography, or EEG, provides a continuous recording of overall brain activity, and has proved to have many important clinical applications. The reasons for this stem from the fact that there are predictable EEG signatures associated with different behavioral states (Figure 3.32). For example, in deep sleep, the EEG is characterized by slow, high-amplitude oscillations, presumably resulting from rhythmic changes in the activity states of large groups of neurons. In other phases of sleep and during various wakeful states, this pattern changes, but in a predictable manner.

Since the normal EEG patterns are well established and consistent among individuals, EEG recordings can detect abnormalities in brain function. As noted earlier, EEG provides valuable information in the assessment and treatment of epilepsy (see Figure 3.20). Of the many forms of epileptic seizures, generalized seizures have no known locus of origin and appear bilaterally symmetrical in the EEG record. Focal seizures, in contrast, begin in a restricted area and spread throughout the brain. Focal seizures frequently provide the first hint of a neurological abnormality. They can result from congenital abnormalities such as a vascular malformation or can develop as a result of a local infection, enlargement of a tumor, or residual damage from a stroke or traumatic event. Surface EEG can crudely localize focal seizures as some electrodes detect the onset earlier and with higher amplitude than other electrodes.

EEG is limited in providing insight to cognitive processes because the recording tends to reflect the brain's global electrical activity. A more powerful approach used by many cognitive neuroscientists focuses

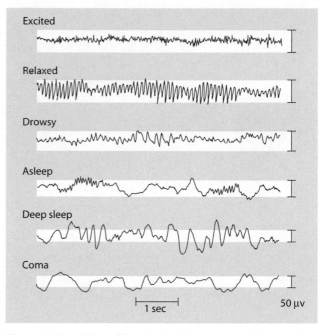

Figure 3.32 EEG profiles obtained during various states of consciousness. From Kolb and Whishaw (1986) after Penfield and Jaspers (1954).

on how brain activity is modulated in response to a particular task. The method requires extracting an evoked response from the global EEG signal.

The logic of this approach is straightforward. EEG traces from a series of trials are averaged together by aligning the records according to an external event, such as the onset of a stimulus or the onset of a response. This alignment washes out variations in the brain's electrical activity that are unrelated to the events of interest. The evoked response, or event-related potential (ERP), is a tiny signal embedded in the ongoing EEG. By averaging the traces, investigators can extract this signal, which reflects neural activity that is specifically related to sensory, motor, or cognitive events, hence, the name *event-related potential* (Figure 3.33). A significant feature of evoked responses is that they provide a precise temporal record of underlying neural activity. The evoked response gives a picture of how neural activity changes over time as information is being processed in the human brain.

ERPs have proved to be an important tool for both clinicians and researchers. Sensory evoked responses offer a useful window for identifying the level of disturbance in patients with neurological disorders. For example, the visual evoked potential can be very useful in the diagnosis of multiple sclerosis, a disorder that leads to

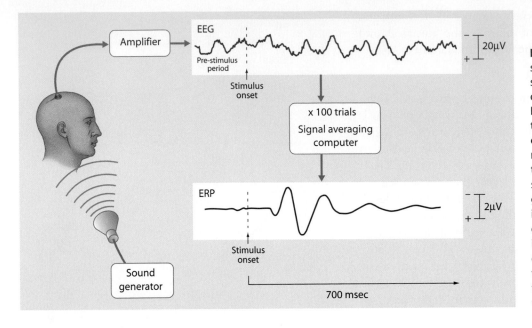

Figure 3.33 The relatively small electrical responses to specific events can only be observed by averaging the EEG traces over a series of trials. The large background oscillations of the EEG trace make it impossible to detect the evoked response to the sensory stimulus from a single trial. However, by averaging across tens or hundreds of trials, the background EEG is removed, leaving the event-related potential. Note the difference in scale between the EEG and ERP waveforms.

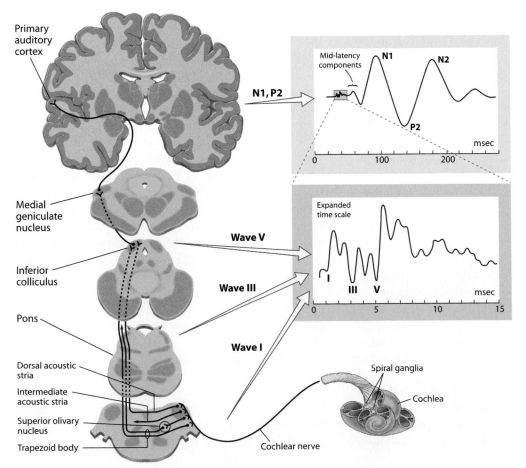

Figure 3.34 The evoked potential shows a series of positive and negative peaks at predictable points in time. In this auditory evoked response potential, the early peaks are invariant and have been linked to neural activity in specific brain structures. Later peaks are task dependent and localization of their source has been a subject of much investigation and debate.

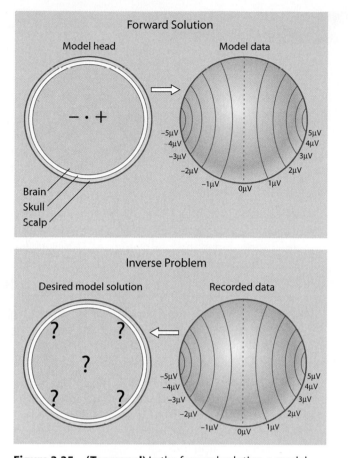

Figure 3.35 **(Top panel)** In the forward solution, a model head is created based on known conductivities of various tissues of the brain, skull, and scalp. The pattern results from the location and orientation of a single dipolar charge, used to simulate an active neuronal population. The dipolar charge creates electric currents that flow to the surface of the sphere creating a distinct pattern of electrical voltages in the surface—this is the forward solution. **(Bottom panel)** The inverse problem arises because a given pattern observed on the surface of the scalp can result from many possible locations of underlying neural generators.

demyelination. When demyelination occurs in the optic nerve, the early peaks of the visual evoked response are delayed in their time of appearance. Similarly, in the auditory system, tumors that compromise hearing by compressing or damaging auditory processing areas can be localized using auditory evoked potentials (AEPs) because characteristic peaks and troughs in the AEP are known to arise from neuronal activity in anatomically defined areas of the ascending auditory system. The earliest of these AEPs indexes activity in the auditory nerve, occurring within just a few milliseconds of the sound. Within the first 20 to 30 msec, there are a series of re-

sponses that index, in sequence, neural firing in the brainstem, midbrain, thalamus, and cortex (Figure 3.34). These stereotyped responses allow the neurologist to pinpoint the level at which the pathology has occurred. Thus, by looking at the sensory evoked responses in patients with hearing problems, the clinician can determine if the problem is due to poor sensory processing, and, if so, at what level the deficit becomes apparent.

In this example, we specified the neural structures associated with the early components of the ERP. It is important to note that these localization inferences are not derived by analyzing the electrical signals themselves. Rather, they are inferred from other studies that use direct recording techniques as well as considerations of the time required for peripheral pathways to transmit neural signals. This is not possible when we look at evoked responses generated by cortical structures. The auditory cortex relays its message to many cortical areas; all contribute to the measured evoked response. Thus, the problem of localization becomes much harder once we look at these latter components of the ERP.

For this reason, at present, ERPs are best suited for addressing questions about the time course of cognition rather than elucidating the brain structures that produce the electrical events. For example, as we will see in Chapter 6, evoked responses can tell us when attention affects how a stimulus is processed. ERPs also provide physiological indices of when a person decides to respond, or when an error is detected.

Nonetheless, much progress has been made in developing analytic tools to localize the sources of ERPs recorded at the scalp. This problem has a long history: In the late nineteenth century, the German physicist Herman von Helmholtz showed that an electrical event located within a spherical volume of homogeneously conducting material (approximated by the brain) produced one unique pattern of electrical activity on the surface of the sphere. This is called the *forward solution* (Figure 3.35). However, he also determined that given a particular pattern of electrical charge on the surface of the sphere, it was impossible to determine the distribution of charge within the sphere that caused it. This is called the *inverse problem*. The problem arises because an infinite number of possible charge distributions in the sphere could lead to the same pattern on the surface. ERP researchers unfortunately face the inverse problem, given that all of their measurements are made at the scalp. The challenge is to determine what areas of the brain must have been active to produce the recorded pattern. In other words, where are the generators of a particular event in the ERP?

An Interview with Robert T. Knight, M.D. Dr. Knight is associated with the Department of Neurology, University of California, Davis. His research provides an elegant demonstration of how measurements of evoked potentials in neurological patients can reveal interactions between different cortical regions.

Authors: Cognitive neuroscience is practiced by many people who are not medically trained. For those working on patients with lesions, what is it they should always know and keep in mind when they are considering their results?

RTK: The "golden rule" of lesion studies in cognitive neuroscience is that the neuroanatomy of the lesion, albeit structural (i.e., stroke or resection) or neurochemical (i.e., Parkinson's), drives interpretations of all results that make inferences about brain-behavior relationships. People often make the mistake that a large number of patients is by definition better than a smaller one. However, as in all experimental work, the variance of the group under investigation is paramount. Your interpretations are only as reliable as the variance in your group of interest. Confusion in this area has led to some of the divisive interactions in the literature over single-case versus group studies.

Variance raises its ugly head in many forms in experimental research employing clinical populations. For instance, medication effects in Parkinson's (i.e., How long since the last dopamine treatment were the data recorded in your Parkinson's patient?), seizure control in postlobectomy patients, and anatomy of damage in stroke or trauma patients are all major issues in data gathering and analysis. The nonmedical cognitive neuroscientist must rely on a collaborator to help address these issues. As in all forms of research, the more interactive the collaboration, the more likely fruitful results will emerge.

The tools (i.e., fMRI, PET, high-density EEG, and MEG) to address the issue of diaschisis or remote effects of le-

sions are also emerging for implementation in lesion, neuropsychological, and cognitive neuroscience research. In the future, clarification of the anatomy of a focal lesion may include the distributed cortical or subcortical network affected by the area of damage both in the resting and in the task conditions. This likely will have profound implications for brain-behavior theoretical formulations.

Authors: There are a growing number of instances where brain imaging studies using PET or fMRI (blood flow techniques) do not coincide with lesion data. Do you think this is a serious problem?

RTK: The divergence between PET and fMRI in comparison to lesion studies raises several interesting issues. One basic experimental design problem is the type of subjects studied by each method. Except for a few aging and lesion studies the metabolic techniques are limited to young, normal subjects. Conversely, lesion studies typically involve older populations who now have a superimposed brain lesion. Thus, you have a double confound of aging effects and postlesion brain reorganization when trying to compare metabolic physiological findings in young subjects to results in lesioned populations. Obviously the correct design is between fMRI and PET results in older normal controls in comparison to lesioned groups. Hopefully, this approach coupled with examination by PET and fMRI in lesioned populations will tease out true differences and convergences between blood flow and lesion approaches.

A more fundamental issue is determining exactly what blood flow techniques actually measure. The well-

To solve this problem, researchers have turned to sophisticated modeling techniques. This is done by simplifying assumptions about the physics of the brain and head tissues, as well as the electrical nature of the active neurons. Of critical importance is the assumption that neural generators can be modeled as electrical dipoles,

conductors with one positive end and one negative end, as shown in Figure 3.36. For example, the excitatory postsynaptic potential generated at the synapse of a cortical pyramidal cell can be viewed as a dipole.

Inverse dipole modeling is relatively straightforward. Using a high-speed computer, one creates a model

known coupling between blood flow, glucose utilization, and neuronal firing supports an important role of fMRI and PET techniques in cognitive research. However, it is not clear what a 2 to 10% change in blood flow translates into in terms of neural processing. Most likely, fMRI and PET are measuring the most robust aspects of neural processing in any given task, whereas electrophysiological techniques may be measuring more distributed activity in many situations.

One frequently cited example involves imaging studies using tasks that lesion studies have shown to involve mesial temporal structures such as the hippocampus. When healthy people perform these same tasks, PET and fMRI studies consistently fail to reveal activity in these regions, a classic example of "technique divergence". However, the problem may not be as serious as first glance would suggest. Electrophysiological recordings in humans reveal strong hippocampal activation in a range of memory tasks. However, different regions of the hippocampal formation are also activated during a variety of tasks which might serve as the control task in a blood flow memory experiment. The subtraction technique would show no net differential activation since mesial temporal structures are active in both the control and the memory tasks. Obviously, no technique is wrong or right; each has its own strengths and weaknesses. One should note, however, that only the lesion approach clearly documents the critical role of the hippocampal formation in memory. The subtraction approach of blood flow techniques shows no or minimal activation and EEG techniques show activation during many nonmemory tasks. Thus, neither would give an investigator an inkling about the paramount role of the hippocampus in memory. This strongly argues for the use of combined approaches in the field of cognitive neuroscience.

Authors: When doing developmental studies, is there a rule of thumb for when a cortical lesion most likely causes a reorganization of function? Is the pattern of deficits in a 6-year-old with a focal or diffuse brain lesion different from that in a 20-year-old with the same lesion?

RTK: Brain reorganization after central nervous system insult is a poorly understood phenomenon; the experimental data available are limited despite the great clinical and theoretical significance of the topic. As a practical rule, recovery of function is felt to decrease dramatically somewhere between the ages of 6 and 10 years. Support for this contention derives mainly from research in the field of neurolinguistics on aphasic children with focal lesions and children requiring hemispherectomy. Interestingly, "language plasticity" decreases at about the time the corpus callosum undergoes myelination connecting the two hemispheres, providing support for interhemispheric inhibition theories. However, even the evidence for this connection is largely indirect.

A more critical point may be the effects of age on the temporal parameters of reorganization of function. For instance, the notion that adults with aphasia do not recover substantial function over time is incorrect. What is true is that they may take a substantially longer time to recover than children. An example of this would be aphasia with a left-hemisphere lesion in a child at age 4, and aphasia with a lesion of comparable size and location in an adult at the age of 40 and in an adult at age 70. Major recovery might occur over 1 year in the child, over 10 years in the 40-year-old, and over the same 10 years in the 70-year-old. However, the 70-year-old is likely to be dead by age 75. Thus, the older adult would be noted to have limited recovery. Since the literature is biased toward deficits in older adults, it incorrectly concludes that recovery is weak or nonexistent in adults. However, the 40-year-old at age 50 might look as good language-wise as the 5-year-old 1 year after the insult. It appears that reorganization of function is available at all ages. A key issue may be understanding the influence of age on the time constant of recovery.

of a spherical head and places a dipole at some location within the sphere. The forward solution is then calculated to determine the distribution of voltages that this dipole would create on the surface of the sphere. This predicted pattern is then compared to the data actually recorded. If the difference between the predicted and obtained results is small, then the model is supported; if the difference is large, then the model is rejected and another solution is tested by shifting the location of the dipole. In this manner, the location of the dipole is moved about the inside of the sphere until the best match between predicted and actual results is obtained. In many

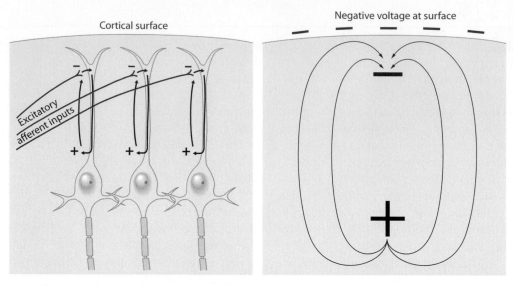

Figure 3.36 Inverse dipole modeling. At left are three cortical pyramidal cells oriented perpendicular to the cortical surface. Each is receiving an excitatory synaptic input at its apical dendrite. The postsynaptic potential that is created causes a current sink (–) at the apical dendrite, and a current source (+) near the cell body. This pattern is dipolar, which means that positive and negative electrical poles exist as shown. The dipolar fields of the population of pyramidal cells, represented by the three drawn, summate and can be represented by a single equivalent current dipole that is shown at the right. This equivalent current dipole is what is used in the inverse dipole model. To the extent that the actual neural activity corresponding to the evoked response that is being modeled is localized to a discrete set of neurons, this dipole assumption is valid.

cases, it is necessary to use more than one dipole to obtain a good match. But, this should not be surprising: It is likely that many ERPs are the result of processing in multiple brain areas!

Unfortunately, as more dipoles are added, it becomes harder to identify a unique solution—the inverse problem returns. Researchers are exploring two new ways to overcome this problem. First, by using anatomical MRI, investigators can study precise three-dimensional models of the head instead of generic spherical models. Second, results from anatomically based neuroimaging techniques such as PET can be used to constrain the locations of the dipoles.

A related technique to ERP is magnetoencephalography, or MEG. In addition to the electrical events associated with synaptic activity, active neurons also produce small magnetic fields (see Chapter 2). Just as with EEG, MEG traces can be averaged over a series of trials to obtain event-related fields (ERFs). MEG provides the same temporal resolution as with ERPs, and also has an advantage in terms of localizing the source of the signal. This stems from the fact that magnetic fields are not distorted as they pass through the brain, skull, and scalp. Thus, the generators can be identified without extensive modeling. There are, however, disadvantages with MEG, at least in its present form. First, it is only possible to detect sources producing fields oriented parallel to the surface of the skull (i.e., neurons in the sulci). Second, the cost of MEG machines is quite prohibitive compared to EEG. A "whole-head" machine consisting of 120 sensors can cost millions of dollars.

FUNCTIONAL IMAGING

The most exciting methodological advances for cognitive neuroscience have been provided by new imaging techniques that identify anatomical correlates of cognitive processes (Raichle, 1994). The two prominent methods are PET and functional MRI, or fMRI. These methods detect changes in metabolism or blood flow in the brain while the subject is engaged in cognitive tasks. As such, they enable researchers to identify brain regions that are activated during these tasks, and to test hypotheses about functional anatomy.

Unlike EEG and MEG, PET and fMRI do not directly measure neural events. Rather, they measure metabolic changes correlated with neural activity. Neurons are no different from other cells of the human body. They require energy in the form of oxygen and glucose, both to sustain their cellular integrity and to perform their specialized functions. As with all parts of the body, oxygen and glucose are distributed to the brain by the circulatory system. The brain is an extremely metabolically demanding organ. As noted previously, the central nervous system uses approximately

20% of all the oxygen we breathe. Yet the amount of blood supplied to the brain varies only a little between the time when the brain is most active and when it is quiet (perhaps because what we regard as active and quiet in relation to behavior does not correlate with active and quiet in the context of neural activity). Thus, the brain must regulate itself. When a brain area is active, more oxygen and glucose are made available by increased blood flow.

PET activation studies measure local variations in cerebral blood flow that are correlated with mental activity (Figure 3.37). To do this, a tracer must be introduced into the bloodstream. For PET, radioactive elements, or isotopes, are used as tracers. Owing to their unstable state, these isotopes rapidly decay by emitting a positron from their atomic nucleus. When a positron collides with an electron, two photons, or gamma rays are created. Not only do the two photons move at the speed of light, passing unimpeded through all tissue, but also they move in opposite directions from one another. The PET scanner—essentially a gamma ray detector—can determine where the collision took place. Because these tracers are in the blood, a reconstructed image can show the distribution of blood flow: Where there is more blood flow, there will be more radiation.

The most common isotope used in cognitive studies is ^{15}O, an unstable form of oxygen with a half-life of 123 seconds. This isotope, in the form of water (H_2O), is injected in the bloodstream while a person is engaged in a cognitive task. While all areas of the body will absorb some radioactive oxygen, the fundamental assumption of PET is that there will be increased blood flow to the brain regions that have heightened neural activity. Thus, PET activation studies do not measure absolute metabolic activity, but rather relative neural activity. In the typical PET experiment, the injection is administered at least twice: during a control condition and during an experimental condition. With the newest generation of high-resolution PET scanners, subjects may receive up to twelve injections, with each dose containing very low levels of radiation so that the total amount of exposure is equal to that received during a transcontinental jet ride or two chest x-ray studies.

Consider, for example, a PET study designed to identify brain areas involved in visual perception: In the experimental condition the subject views a circular checkerboard surrounding a small fixation point (to keep subjects from moving their eyes); in the control condition, only the fixation point is presented. With PET analysis, researchers subtract the radiation counts measured during the control condition from those measured during the experimental condition. Areas that

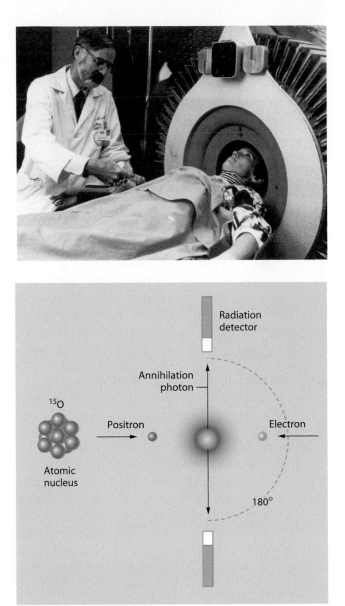

Figure 3.37 Positron emission tomography (PET) scanning allows metabolic activity to be measured in the human brain. In the most common form of PET, water labeled with radioactive oxygen, ^{15}O, is injected into the subject. As positrons break off from this unstable isotope, they collide with electrons. A byproduct of this collision is the generation of two gamma rays, or photons, that move in opposite directions. The PET scanner measures these photons and calculates their source. Regions of the brain that are most active will increase their demand for oxygen. From Posner and Raichle (1994).

were active when the subject was viewing the checkerboard stimulus will have higher counts, which reflects increased blood flow. This subtractive procedure ignores variations in absolute blood flow between the brain's areas. The difference image identifies areas that

An Interview with Marcus E. Raichle, M.D.   Dr. Raichle is in the Department of Neurology at Washington University School of Medicine. Dr. Raichle's PET group provided the seminal cognitive neuroscience imaging studies in the mid-1980s.

Authors: As one of the world's pioneers and authorities on brain imaging, and in particular PET, how would you characterize its short history? Are the kinds of problems you think about now the kinds you guessed you would be thinking about 10 years ago?

MER: The history of modern functional brain imaging, now exemplified by a combination of PET, fMRI, and ERPs, in my mind represents a remarkably successful merging of developments in imaging technology, neuroscience, and behavior. The pieces of the puzzle had developed quite separately until about 10 years ago, when cognitive science joined neuroscience in using the newly developed PET techniques to measure changes in brain blood flow in relation to changes in normal human behavior. The power of this combined approach became apparent almost immediately, although the learning curve remains steep.

I certainly didn't envision my current scientific agenda when I began working in the late sixties on issues of brain metabolism and blood flow. I was intrigued by the unique properties of positron-emitting radionuclides for measuring regional brain metabolism and blood flow in humans—little did I know at the time how regional and how unique. Luckily, I was in the right place at the right time, as events unfolded rather quickly with the introduction of x-ray CT in about 1972 and the invention of PET in our laboratory over the ensuing 2 years.

Authors: PET was initially built to deal with medical issues, perhaps looking at cerebral stroke per se or studying chemotherapeutic agents for brain tumor, or looking at neurotransmitters in psychiatric and degenerative diseases. PET today seems mostly committed to the study of functional correlates of cognitive function. Is this true, and if so, why?

MER: Actually, at its inception PET had a very varied agenda in the minds of the people who created it. The physics and engineering people who developed the

imaging devices themselves had what I would describe as a clinical nuclear medicine orientation. In my estimation, they saw PET as the means by which clinical nuclear medicine could maintain a position in the clinical area along with x-ray CT, which was clearly getting all of the attention at the time. Nuclear brain scans, which had been staples of the practice of nuclear medicine, were quickly replaced by x-ray CT. Imaging had clearly captured everyone's imagination.

With PET, we suddenly had a tool that could give us measures of blood flow, blood volume, oxygen consumption, glucose utilization, tissue pH, and receptor pharmacology, among other things. These measurements in the brain had never been a part of the clinical practice of medicine. We had to develop our existent methods to develop an understanding of how to use this new information. That process is still very much ongoing, and in many areas such as brain pharmacology, it is a slow and tedious process. I'm still optimistic that it will provide important information in a variety of areas ranging from movement disorders and psychiatric diseases to certain types of brain injury. PET is, however, "competing," so to speak, with many other approaches in these areas. These approaches range from cellular and molecular techniques to various animal models.

You're absolutely right that PET and, more recently, fMRI have established a preeminent position in the study of the functional anatomical correlates of cognitive function in humans. The wonderful relationship between blood flow and neuronal activity, and the accuracy and simplicity of the technique, allowed for the design of an elegant paradigm, and thanks to input from my good friend Mike Posner, functional imaging with PET was off and running. The final ingredient was, certainly, that the questions we could address were immensely interesting and important. This was not a technique in search of a question.

Authors: Could you elaborate on the principle of

image subtraction that is the standard in PET studies of cognition?

MER: The image subtraction methodology represents the wedding of objectives from the cognitive and imaging sciences. From an imaging perspective, the objective was to identify areas of the brain active during the performance of a particular task. Prior to the advent of the subtraction methodology, investigators using brain imaging techniques, as well as their predecessors who used simpler regional blood flow techniques, made a priori decisions about where in the brain they would look for changes. This was the so-called region-of-interest, or ROI, approach. The brain was arbitrarily divided, according to various schemes, into regions that would be analyzed for a change in blood flow or metabolism. This approach was particularly problematic when it came to the human cerebral cortex, where uncertainty was the rule, rather than the exception, in the areas much beyond primary motor and sensory cortices.

The subtraction methodology changed our perspective completely. In this approach, images obtained in two states (what we have come to refer to as a *task state* and a *control state*) are subtracted from one another to create a difference image. This image identifies for us those areas of the human brain that differ between the task and control states. There are no a priori assumptions about where such regions lie within the cerebral cortex or elsewhere. The subtraction images define the location and shape of the regions and also allow us to quantify the magnitude of the change. In one sense, this is a hypothesis-generating exercise—we're letting the human brain tell us how it is organized.

Authors: What concerns arise with the subtractive procedure? It has certainly had its critics.

MER: One of the most common criticisms is that the assumption of "pure insertion" is an incorrect assumption, and therefore, the subtraction methodology is invalid. The idea of pure insertion assumes that when a task state is compared to a control state, the difference represents the addition of processing components unique to the task state without affecting processing components in the control state. The issue is, How do we know this to be true? In imaging, we can also ask whether this is a serious concern.

Consider two scenarios. In the first, the control state

and the task state are different only by the addition of brain processing components unique to the task state. Everything used in the control state remains unchanged. A subtraction image, under such circumstances, will predictably reveal areas of increased brain activity unique to the task state without changes in the areas known to be used in the control state.

Now, let us consider a second scenario, in which the notion of pure insertion is violated. Under these circumstances, areas of the brain that are active in the control state are not active in the task state. Now the subtraction image reveals not only areas of increased activity relative to the task state, but also areas of decreased activity, reflecting areas that are used in the control state but not in the task state. Far from presenting us with a frustrating dilemma of interpretation, such data provide us with an even richer and less ambiguous understanding of human brain functional organization.

A second major criticism of the subtraction method has centered on the issue of averaging. Averaging, of course, is used to enhance the signal-to-noise properties of the images and is common to both PET and fMRI. Initially, the naysayers suggested, despite considerable empirical imaging data to the contrary, that subtraction-image averaging wouldn't work because of "obvious" individual differences among subjects. I'm just glad we didn't hear this criticism before we got started, or we might never have gotten into this work! If individual differences had been the methodological limitation portrayed by some, this entire enterprise would never have gotten off the ground.

So, does this mean that individual differences don't exist? Hardly. One has only to inspect individual human brains to appreciate that they do differ. However, general organizing principles emerge that transcend these differences. Such principles, coupled with our increasing ability to anatomically warp images to match one another anatomically in the averaging process, will further reduce the effect of individual differences. I find it amusing to reflect on the fact that our initial work was aided by the relative crude resolution of PET scanners. The blurring of data brought responses common across individuals together and allowed us to "see" them. Early on, even robust responses could be caused to "disappear" when one attempted to go to too high a resolution.

show changes in metabolic activity as a function of experimental manipulation (Figure 3.38).

The control condition need not be a simple resting, or fixation-only condition; it could include a second experimental task. The difference image would then show the areas that are more active during the first task in comparison to the second task, and also the areas that are more active during the second task. Moreover, some PET studies compare groups of subjects rather than experimental conditions, for example, how brain activity in schizophrenics compares with that in healthy individuals.

PET provides a powerful tool for localizing metabolic changes. Current methods allow for resolution of approximately 5 to 10 mm. While a volume of this size includes thousands of neurons, it is sufficient to identify cortical and subcortical areas, and can even show functional variation within a given cortical area. Panels b, c, and d in Figure 3.38 show a shift in activation within the visual cortex as the stimulus's location moves from being adjacent to the fixation point to more eccentric places.

As with PET, fMRI exploits the fact that local blood flow increases in active parts of the brain. The procedure is essentially identical to the one used in traditional MRI: Radio waves make atoms oscillate and a detector measures local magnetic fields when the atoms return to the orientation of an external magnetic field. With fMRI, however, imaging is focused on the magnetic properties of hemoglobin. Hemoglobin carries oxygen in the bloodstream, and when the oxygen is absorbed, the hemoglobin becomes deoxygenated. Deoxygenated hemoglobin is more sensitive, or paramagnetic than oxygenated hemoglobin. The fMRI detectors measure the ratio of oxygenated to deoxygenated hemoglobin. We might, intuitively, expect this ratio to become smaller in brain areas that are active as oxygen becomes consumed. Yet the reverse occurs. Although blood flow increases in active brain regions, neural tissue cannot absorb most of the oxygen. Thus, active brain regions

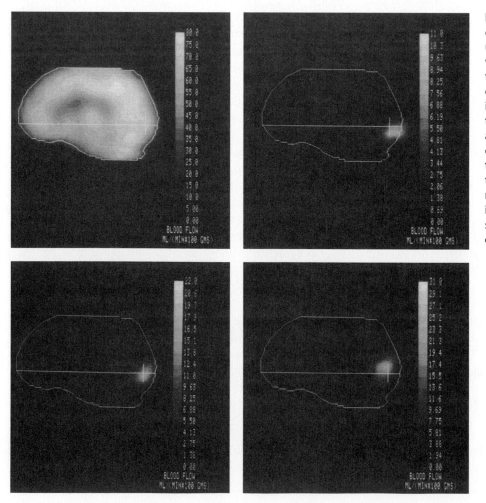

Figure 3.38 Measurements of cerebral blood flow using PET. The upper left panel shows blood flow when the subject fixated on a central spot. Activity in this baseline condition was subtracted from that in three other conditions in which the central spot was surrounded by a checkboard, either in the center of view **(top right),** more toward the periphery **(bottom left),** or in the far periphery **(bottom right).** A retinotopographic map can be identified, with central vision represented more inferiorly than peripheral vision.

have a higher ratio of oxygenated to deoxygenated hemoglobin; fMRI is sensitive to this change, and thus creates a map of changes in regional blood flow that are coupled to local neuronal activity.

The changes are quite small, generally less than 5% of the total fMRI signal. Nonetheless, by carefully selecting experimental and control conditions, researchers can vary the magnetic signal. One advantage of fMRI is that the two conditions can be tested in a continuous, alternating manner. For example, testing can alternate between periods of visual stimulation and those of no stimulation. The intensity of the signal measured from the visual cortex alternates in correspondence with this manipulation (Figure 3.39). In contrast, with PET, a break is almost always required between the experimental conditions in order to allow the radioactive tracer to wash out of the system.

fMRI has several potential advantages over PET. Whereas PET is expensive and exposes participants to low levels of radioactive tracers, fMRI is cheaper and does not involve any known risks. With minor modifications, scanning machines in place in most hospitals can be adapted for functional imaging studies. Second, the spatial resolution can be finer, especially if high-powered magnets (2–4 tesla) are substituted for standard, clinical magnets (typically 1.5 tesla). Third, because the experimental conditions can be repeated many times, one can do statistical analyses on data from a single subject. This is important, given the individual differences in brain anatomy; with PET, computer algorithms are used to average the data and superimpose them on a "standardized" brain. Finally, high-resolution anatomical images can be obtained with the same scanner used in fMRI studies without having to alter a subject's position, allowing precise localization of metabolic events. With PET, not only is anatomical precision compromised by averaging across individuals, but also the position of each person's head can vary from the PET scanner to the MRI machine.

The limitations of imaging techniques such as PET and fMRI must be borne in mind. Even if we discover that a brain area's metabolic activity correlates with an experimental variation, we still need to make inferences about the area's functional contribution. Correlation does not imply causation. For example, an area may be activated during a task without playing a critical role in the task's performance. It may simply be "listening" to other brain areas that provide the critical computations. In this respect, imaging studies are frequently guided by other methodologies. Single-cell recording studies in primates can be used to identify regions of interest in a PET study with humans. Or, imaging stud-

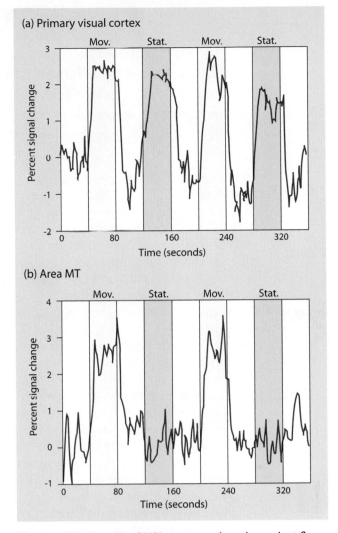

Figure 3.39 Functional MRI measures time-dependent fluctuations in oxygenation with excellent spatial resolution. The subject viewed a field of randomly positioned white dots on a black background. The dots would either remain stationary or move along the radial axis. The 40sec epochs of stimulation alternated with 40sec epochs during which the screen was blank. Measurements from primary visual cortex (V1) showed consistent increases during the stimulation epochs compared to the blank epochs. In area MT, a visual region associated with motion perception (see Chapter 4), the increase was only observed when the dots were moving.

ies may be designed to isolate a component operation that is thought to be linked to a particular brain region based on the performance of patients with injuries to that area. Obtaining converging evidence across methodologies enables us to make the strongest conclusions possible.

Another limitation of PET and fMRI is that they have poor temporal resolution. PET is constrained by

An Interview with Michael I. Posner, Ph.D. Dr. Posner is in the Department of Psychology at the University of Oregon. His research on attention has encompassed many of the major methodologies of cognitive neuroscience and has been extended to populations ranging from newborn infants to patients with schizophrenia.

Authors: Your work in cognitive psychology is singular and established a whole field of research. You then became interested in cognitive neuroscience and have employed a variety of new techniques to measure brain function, including PET and ERPs. Do you think the traditional behavioral methods of cognitive psychology are antiquated and no longer sufficient for studying how the brain enables mind?

MIP: By traditional methods, I assume you mean accuracy and reaction time including the many variants such as signal detection theory, additive factor theory, etc. In my view, an impressive aspect of the anatomical methods such as PET and fMRI is how much they have supported the view that cognitive measures can be used to suggest separate neural structures. One impressive example is the recent paper in the *Journal of Cognitive Neuroscience* by Stan Dehaene (1996). He applied additive factors theory to determine separate stages in simple numerical judgments. Additive factor theory assumes separate serial stages, and tests this by showing independence between the variables that influence the time for each stage. Dehaene found that each stage, as determined from an analysis of independence in reaction time, was generated by a separate brain area. Another example is the close correspondence we have found between the conditions required for executive function based on cognitive models and the conditions in which PET studies have found activation of the anterior cingulate. This is not to argue that cognitive and anatomical methods will always converge, but to support the importance of their joint contribution to understanding brain function.

Authors: Would it be fair to say your center has changed? By that we mean 10 to 15 years ago you read the cognitive psychology literature which dealt solely with behavioral measures and from those one inferred cognitive states. Do you now read mostly in the area of cognitive neuroscience?

MIP: Yes, it would be fair to say that my reading habits have changed, but I still like to read the cognitive literature to help understand the theoretical issues involved. In the end we have to interpret the anatomy and circuitry found in imaging studies in terms of the functions they serve. The methods of cognitive neuroscience have made the dream of a deep understanding of how the brain carries out thought seem so much closer now than 15 years ago. It is almost exactly 15 years ago that I began work with parietal patients in hopes of connecting the cellular studies with cognitive studies of normal human beings. Now most neuroimaging studies illustrate the

the decay rate of the radioactive agent. Even the fastest isotopes, such as ^{15}O, require measurements for 40 seconds to obtain stable radiation counts. While fMRI can operate much faster, it still lacks synchrony between stimulation changes and measured signal changes. This is because changes in blood flow do not happen immediately on stimulation, but take a few seconds. Thus, PET and fMRI cannot give a temporal picture of the "on-line" operation of mental operations. Even complex tasks such as deciding if the sum of the square roots of 16 and 25 is an even or odd number can be performed in seconds. Researchers have opted to combine the temporal resolution of evoked potentials with the spatial resolution of PET or fMRI for a better picture of the physiology and anatomy of cognition (see Chapter 6).

SUMMARY

Two goals guided this overview of the methods of cognitive neuroscience. The first was to provide a sense of the methodologies that come together to form an interdisciplinary field such as cognitive neu-

close connection between local neuronal activity on the one hand and cognitive operations on the other.

Authors: Suppose PET studies reveal the circuitry for a particular cognitive process. How do we then go on to seek an explanation of the mechanism of the process? Obviously this is a difficult, perhaps impossible question. But how are you beginning to think about the job of the next generation of scientists?

MIP: It's probably best to answer by example. In the 1970s Roger Shepard showed that reaction time to rotate something in your head was exquisitely related to the angle through which the rotation had to occur. Recent PET studies have provided a nice treatment of the anatomy involved in this act. More recently, Georgopoulos provided a neuronal model of how a changing population vector of cells could produce a rotation. The population vector orientation shifted during the reaction time in a way that fit with the idea of a rotation. Similar efforts to relate the cellular, anatomical, and cognitive level are now emerging in areas such as motion perception, visual search, and shifts of attention. Some of these areas involve accounts of the transmitters involved as well as the cellular activity. I don't necessarily want to claim that the population vector is a complete explanation of mental rotation, but just a few years ago it would have been hard to imagine even a good start in the direction of answering your question.

Authors: For new students wanting to study those lofty issues of cognition and indeed the very nature of consciousness itself, what do you recommend they do? Put differently, what does the research scientist of tomorrow working on these questions have to be trained in today?

MIP: A good background in cognition that might involve courses in cognitive psychology, linguistics/anthropology, and philosophy would be important. A strong background in computational methods involved in model building is also important. The neuroscience background should include studying systems and cellular levels, and a good knowledge of genetics is becoming important.

Authors: What do you expect a cognitive neuroscience lab, or conference, or journal will look like in 10 years?

MIP: Here is my idea of what the Table of Contents of an issue of the *Journal of Cognitive Neuroscience* in 2005 might look like:

- How communication between brain areas involved in first and second language comprehension changes with mastery of the new language
- At what age are genes coding for extroversion expressed?
- Laser images of neuronal activity in parietal cortex during mental rotation
- Function of monkey cortex homologous to the human visual word-form system
- A pharmacological study designed to reduce loss of brain plasticity with age
- Size of brain areas devoted to the semantic category "animal" as a function of expertise: A functional MRI study
- Change in blood flow and dopamine uptake in auditory areas following pharmacological treatment for auditory hallucinations in first break schizophrenics

roscience (Figure 3.40). The practitioners of the neurosciences, cognitive psychology, and neurology differ not only in the tools they use, but also in the questions they seek to answer. The neurologist may request a CT scan of an aged boxer to find out if the patient's confusional state is reflected in atrophy of the frontal lobes. The neuroscientist may want a blood sample from the patient to search for metabolic markers indicating a reduction in a transmitter system. The cognitive psychologist may design a reaction-time experiment to test whether a component of a decision-making model is selectively impaired. Cognitive neuroscience endeavors to answer these questions by taking advantage of the insights that each approach has to offer and using them together.

The second goal was to introduce methods encountered in subsequent chapters. These chapters focus on content domains such as perception, language, and memory, and on how the tools are being applied to understand the brain and behavior. Each chapter draws on research that uses the diverse methods of cognitive neuroscience. Often the convergence of results yielded by different methodologies offers the most complete theories. A single method cannot bring about a complete understanding of the complex processes of cognition that rely on numerous brain structures.

We have reviewed many methods, but the review is incomplete, in part because new methodologies for investigating the relation of the brain and behavior spring

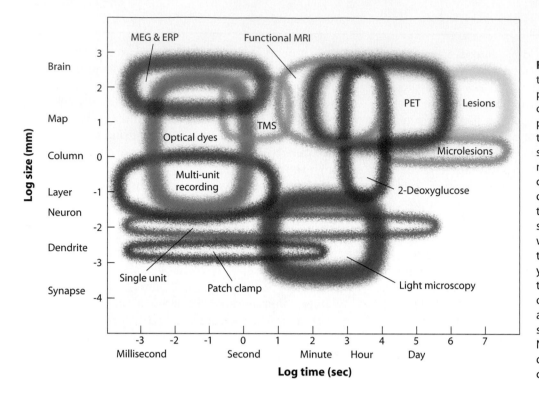

Figure 3.40 Spatial and temporal resolution of the prominent methods used in cognitive neuroscience. Temporal sensitivity, plotted on the x axis, refers to the time scale over which a particular measurement is obtained. It can range from the millisecond activity of single cells to the behavioral changes observed over years in patients who have had strokes. Spatial sensitivity, plotted on the y axis, refers to the localization capability of the methods. Light microscopy allows activity at individual synapses to be observed. Naturally occurring lesions damage large regions of the cortex.

to life each year. For example, an exciting development is the use of transcortical magnetic stimulation (TMS) to alter the activity of a targeted brain region. A magnetic field is applied to the external surface of the head and causes a massive discharge of underlying neural elements. If TMS is applied over the motor cortex, discrete movements can be elicited—similar to what happened when Penfield applied electrical current to an exposed cortex during neurosurgery (Pascual-Leone et al., 1994). With TMS, no surgery is necessary, so one can apply this technique with healthy subjects engaged in behavioral tasks. This method can create transient functional "lesions" in which participants experience cortical blindness, attentional deficits, and memory losses, but only

for the few milliseconds following magnetic stimulation. This method is only one example of new methodologies becoming available to cognitive neuroscientists.

We began this chapter by pointing out that paradigmatic changes in science are often fueled by technological developments. In a symbiotic way, the maturation of a scientific field such as cognitive neuroscience provides a tremendous impetus for the development of new methods. The questions we ask are constrained by the available tools, but new research tools are promoted by the questions we ask. It would be foolish to imagine that current methodologies will become the status quo for the field, which makes it an exciting time to study brain and behavior.

SUGGESTED READINGS

ADAMS, R.D., and VICTOR, M. (1993). *Principles of Neurology,* 5th edition. New York: McGraw-Hill.

CHURCHLAND, P.S. (1986). *Neurophilosophy: Toward a Unified Science of the Mind/Brain.* Cambridge, MA: MIT Press.

HILLYARD, S.Y. (1993). Electrical and magnetic brain recordings: Contributions to cognitive neuroscience. *Curr. Opin. Neurobiol.* 3:217–224.

KANDEL, E.R., SCHWARTZ, J.H., and Jessell, T.M. (1991). *Principles of Neural Science,* 3rd edition. New York: Elsevier Science.

KERTESZ, A. (1994). *Localization and Neuroimaging in Neuropsychology.* San Diego: Academic Press.

POSNER, M.I., and RAICHLE, M.E. (1994). *Images of Mind.* New York: W.H. Freeman.

4

Perception and Encoding

How does the brain convert sensory signals into a perception of a coherent world? Our phenomenal experience suggests that this is an effortless process: Without effort we absorb the familiar sights of the neighborhood, recognize the sounds of children playing at the nearby playground, and take delight in the smells of a backyard barbecue. When we consider the nervous system, it is quite amazing how easily we take in all of this information. Our sensory apparatus cannot take multisensory snapshots of the world; the receptors in our eyes respond to the photons of light in a manner clearly distinct from the fine filaments in the inner ear that sense changes in air pressure that correspond to sounds. Moreover, when we focus on a single sensory modality, we can appreciate the complexity of the information-processing task we face. The cars along the street are of different shapes and colors. Some are parked; some are moving. We not only hear the sounds about us, but also can rapidly pinpoint their location.

In the next few chapters, we explore the cognitive neuroscience of perception. In this chapter, the focus is on the initial stages of perception—how sensory information is represented and processed to form integrated percepts. In Chapter 5, we examine how we recognize these percepts as meaningful entities: objects that we can manipulate or navigate about, or other organisms like our friends and family. A full appreciation of perception also requires consideration of how we attend to certain stimuli at the expense of others, and how we connect this information to our stored knowledge of the world. Chapters 6 and 7 address the problems of attention and memory.

To begin, let us consider a person for whom perception has become a challenge. By studying the damaged brain, we can gain insight to the processes required for perceiving the world.

DISORDERS OF PERCEPTION: A CASE STUDY

Patient P.T. was presented at the Neurology Grand Rounds in Portland, Oregon. The Grand Rounds, a weekly event, is when staff neurologists, internists, and residents gather to review the most puzzling and unusual cases being treated on the ward.

The cause of P.T.'s neurological disorders was not a mystery; he had had a stroke. Four months previously, P.T. had awakened and experienced acute dizziness and weakness in his left hand and leg. On visiting his family physician that morning, he was told that he had probably had a cerebrovascular accident, a diagnosis based on his history of chronic hypertension. Indeed, P.T. had suffered a left-hemisphere stroke 6 years previously, and so the physician was confident in his diagnosis, especially since multiple strokes are not uncommon. P.T. was referred to the hospital, where the stroke, localized in the right hemisphere this time, was confirmed by computed tomography (CT).

What was unusual about P.T. was the collection of symptoms he continued to experience 4 months after the stroke occurred. The dizziness had ended by the second day after the stroke, and the left-sided weakness had mostly subsided during the first month. The only remaining sign of these initial symptoms was that P.T. continued to drag his left leg slightly, although he was not aware of it.

Yet P.T. experienced some problems as he tried to resume the daily routines required on his small family farm, his home for 66 years. He had particular difficulty recognizing places and objects. He would be working on a stretch of fence, look out over the hills, and suddenly realize that he did not know the landscape. It was hard for him to pick out individual dairy cows, a matter of concern lest he attempt to milk a bull! And, most troubling of all, P.T. no longer recognized the people around him including his wife. The woman who had served him breakfast each morning when he sat down at the table was a stranger. He had no trouble seeing her standing over the kitchen stove, he could describe her actions when she served his bacon and eggs, and he noticed when she walked. But, in simply looking at her, he failed to identify her as his wife. He knew that her parts—body, legs, arms, and head—formed a person. But P.T. failed to see these parts as belonging to a specific individual. His deficit was not limited to his wife; he had the same problem with other members of his family and friends from his small town.

A striking feature was that P.T.'s inability to recognize objects and people was limited to the visual modality. As soon as his wife spoke, he immediately recognized her voice. Indeed, he claimed that on hearing her voice, the visual percept of her would "fall into place." The shape in front of him would suddenly metamorphose into his wife. In a similar fashion he could recognize specific objects by touching them.

P.T. is not the first person to have difficulty visually recognizing objects and people. Indeed, neurologists have a term for this type of disorder, *agnosia*. Although agnosia is rare, patients such as P.T. have been described and studied extensively. In presenting the case during Grand Rounds, the chief neurologist assessed P.T.'s processing abilities to pinpoint the problems underlying his deficit.

During the examination, P.T. demonstrated a striking dissociation. He was shown two paintings, one by Monet depicting a subdued nineteenth-century countryman dressed in his Sunday suit, and the other by Picasso of a woman with a terrified expression (Figure 4.1). P.T. was asked to describe what he saw in each painting. When shown the Monet, he looked puzzled. He saw no definable forms, just an abstract blend of colors and shapes. His problem in interpreting the painting was consonant with the deficits he experienced at home. Yet he readily identified the figure in Picasso's painting and pointed out that it was a woman, or perhaps a young girl. This dissociation is even more compelling, as most would readily agree that the Monet is more realistic.

(a)

(b)

Figure 4.1 Two portraits: **(a)** Detail from "Luncheon on the Grass," painted in 1886 by the French Impressionist, Claude Monet; **(b)** Pablo Picasso's "Weeping Woman," painted in 1937 during his Cubist period.

The two paintings differ radically from each other. A psychoanalyst might choose to focus on the different emotional responses evoked by the images. Picasso's painting is clearly unsettling, and perhaps this stirring of emotions facilitates recognition. But this is an unlikely connection to P.T.'s problems at home, which are manifest across a range of objects. Moreover, he does not have difficulty recognizing objects through modalities other than vision.

In Grand Rounds, attention was paid to how the visual information in the two paintings differs. For example, facial features are well marked in the Picasso. The oval eyes are clearly demarcated by black contours encircling white irises. The teeth are individually drawn, as are the hairs of each eyebrow. In Monet's portrait, these features either are absent or slowly emerge from the background. A slight change of shading cues to the transition from forehead to eyebrows. In a similar way, the nose has only faint detailing. These differences in contours are matched by the level of contrast, or brightness, used by the two artists. Picasso, following his cubist tradition, used bold colors and sharp contrasts. Each part has a different color; even in the facial skin yellow switches rapidly to white, a transition emphasized by a black contour. Monet, in contrast, selected colors that are fairly equal in brightness. Using a variety of colors, he blended each region into the next.

This example demonstrates at least three prominent differences. Picasso painted the parts as separate units. He used sharp contrasts in brightness and vivid colors to highlight facial regions. Monet opted for a softer approach, in which parts are best seen in a continuous whole, with gradual changes in contrast and color. Can any of these factors account for P.T.'s performance in identifying the figures in Picasso and Monet? Do the differences explain his problems with recognizing familiar objects? Is his problem related to one of these factors or a combination of them? To answer these questions, we need to know more about how visual information is processed and represented. After considering these issues, we will return to P.T.'s deficits and formulate hypotheses about their cause.

OVERVIEW OF NEURAL PATHWAYS

Humans, like most diurnal creatures, depend on the sense of vision. While other senses such as hearing and touch are essential, visual information dominates our perceptions and frames the way we think. We use visually derived metaphors such as "I see" and "Your hypothesis is murky" to describe cognitive states.

Consider the vast amount of neuroanatomical tissue involved in visual perception. Not only are there millions of neurons in the eye, but these sensors project countless bits of data to the subcortex and cortex. Indeed, over 50% of the cortex in the macaque monkey is devoted to visual perception. Beware, though: Estimates such as these may be biased by researchers' reliance on visual stimulation. If auditory or somatosensory stimuli were used as readily, many brain regions might be found to be responsive to these modalities.

The Eye, Retina, and Receptors

One reason why vision is so important is that it enables us to perceive information at a distance, to engage in what is called *remote sensing* or *exteroceptive perception*. We need not be in immediate contact with a stimulus to process it. Contrast this ability with the sense of touch. For this sense, we must be in direct contact with the stimulus. The advantages to engaging in remote sensing are obvious. An organism surely can avoid a predator better when it can detect the predator at a distance. It is probably too late to flee once shark teeth pierce the skin.

Visual information is contained in the light reflected from objects. To perceive objects, we need sensory detectors that respond to the reflected light. These *photoreceptors* form the retina, the sheet of neurons located along the eye's inner surface (Figure 4.2). Each photoreceptor contains light-sensitive molecules, or *photopigments*. When exposed to light, the photopigments become unstable and split apart. Their decomposition alters the flow of the electrical current around the photoreceptors. This light-induced change triggers action potentials in downstream neurons. Thus, photoreceptors provide for translation from an external stimulus, light, into an internal neural signal, the detection of that stimulus.

The two types of photoreceptors are rods and cones. *Rods* are sensitive to low levels of stimulation. They are most useful at night when light energy is reduced. They will also respond to a bright light, but because replenishing the photopigment in rods takes time, they are of little use during daytime. *Cones* require more intense levels of light and use photopigments that can be generated rapidly. Thus, cones are most active during daytime

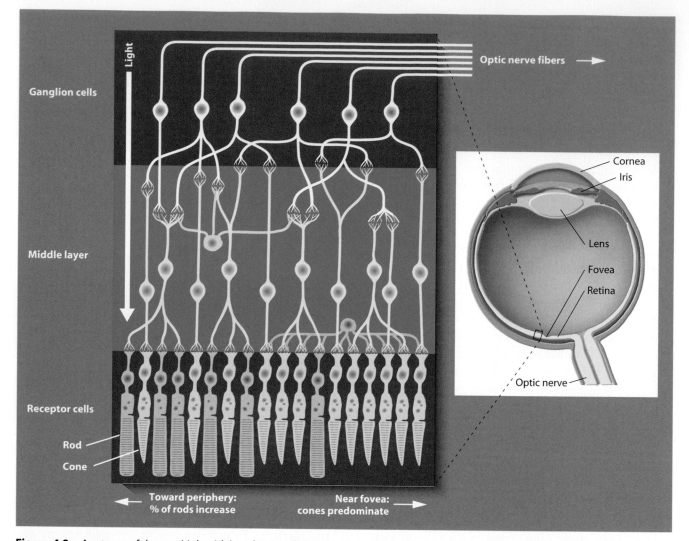

Figure 4.2 Anatomy of the eye (right side) and retina (left side). Light enters through the cornea and activates the receptor cells of the retina located along the rear surface. There are two types of receptor cells, rods and cones. The output of the receptor cells is processed in the middle layer of the retina and then relayed to the central nervous system via the optic nerve, the axons of the ganglion cells. Adapted from Sekuler and Blake (1990).

vision. Cones are essential for color vision, and we commonly speak of them as being one of three types: red, green, or blue. These names are somewhat misleading. Cones do not respond to colors per se; as shown in Figure 4.3, they differ in the sensitivity of their photopigments to different wavelengths of visible light.

Rods and cones are not distributed equally across the retina. Cones are densely packed near the center of the retina, in a region called the *fovea*. Few cones are in the more eccentric regions of the retina, whereas rods are distributed throughout the retina. An easy demonstration of the differential distribution of rods and cones can be made by having a friend slowly bring a colored marker into your view from one side of your head. Notice that you see the marker and its shape well before

you identify its color because of the sparse distribution of cones in the retina's peripheral regions.

From the Eye to the Central Nervous System

Extensive signal processing of visual information is performed within the eye. The output from the photoreceptors is projected to bipolar cells and from there to ganglion cells. Extensive convergence of information happens within these processing layers. Indeed, while humans have an estimated 260 million photoreceptors, there are only 2 million ganglion cells, the eye's sole output source. This compression of information suggests that higher-level visual centers should be efficient processors to recover the details of the visual world.

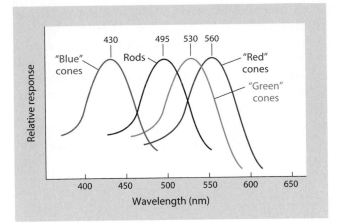

Figure 4.3 Spectral sensitivity functions for rods and the three types of cones. The short, or "blue" cones are maximally responsive to light with a wavelength of 430 nm. The peak sensitivities of the medium, "green," and long, "red" cones are shifted to longer wavelengths. White light such as daylight will activate all three receptors because it contains all wavelengths.

Axons of the ganglion cells form a bundle, the *optic nerve*. By way of this nerve, visual information is transmitted to the central nervous system.

Figure 4.4 diagrams how visual information is conveyed from the eyes to the central nervous system. Be-

fore entering the brain, each optic nerve splits into two parts. The temporal, or lateral, branch continues to traverse along the same side. The nasal, or medial, branch crosses over to project to the opposite side; this crossover place is called the *optic chiasm*. Given the eye's optics, the crossover of nasal fibers ensures that visual information from each side of external space will be projected to contralateral brain structures. For example, because of the retina's curvature, the temporal half of the right retina is stimulated by objects in the left visual field. In the same fashion the nasal hemiretina of the left eye is stimulated by this same region of external space. Since fibers from each nasal hemiretina cross, all information from the left visual field is projected to the right hemisphere and information from the right visual field is projected to the left hemisphere.

Once inside the brain, each optic nerve divides into pathways that differ with respect to where they terminate within the subcortex. Figure 4.4 focuses on the retino-geniculate pathway, the projection from the retina to the lateral geniculate nuclei (LGN) of the thalamus. This pathway contains more than 90% of the axons in the optic nerve and provides input to the cortex via the geniculo-cortical projections. The remaining 10% of the fibers innervate other subcortical structures

Figure 4.4 The primary projection pathways of the visual system. The optic fibers from the temporal half of the retina project ipsilaterally, while the nasal fibers cross over at the optic chiasm. In this way, the input from each visual field is projected to the primary visual cortex in the contralateral hemisphere after the fibers synapse in the lateral geniculate nucleus (geniculo-cortical pathway). A small percentage of visual fibers of the optic nerve terminate in the superior colliculus and pulvinar nucleus.

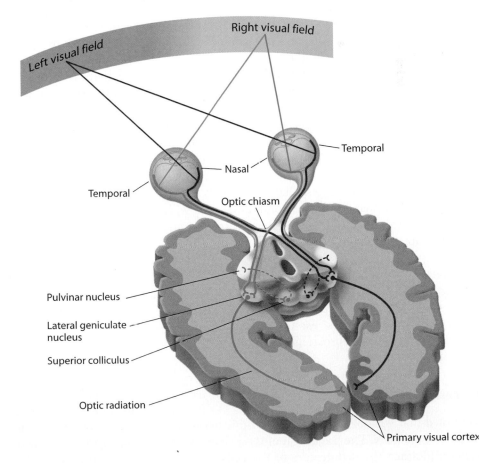

including the pulvinar nucleus of the thalamus and the superior colliculus of the midbrain. However, because these other receiving nuclei are innervated by only 10% of the fibers does not mean that these pathways are unimportant. The human optic nerve is so large that 10% of the optic nerve constitutes more fibers than are found in the entire auditory pathway. The superior colliculus and pulvinar nucleus play a big role in visual attention, and the retino-collicular pathway is sometimes viewed as a more primitive visual system.

We return to possible functions of this pathway later in this chapter.

The final projection to the visual cortex is via the geniculo-cortical pathway. This bundle of axons exits from the LGN and ascends to the cortex, with almost all of the fibers terminating in the primary visual area of the occipital lobe. Thus, visual information in the cortex has been processed by at least five distinct neurons: photoreceptors, bipolar cells, ganglion cells, LGN cells, and cortical cells.

PARALLEL PROCESSING IN THE VISUAL SYSTEM

We have described the pathways enabling the transmission of visual information from the eye to the cortex. We have focused on anatomical patterns of connectivity, the wiring that permits neural regions to communicate with other neural regions. What we also need is a description of the information carried in these tracts: What do neural signals in the visual pathway represent?

A central hypothesis in visual perception is that visual information is distributed across distinct subsystems. By this view, perception is analytic. Early processes are devoted to analyzing attributes of a stimulus: Some processes represent shape, other processes focus on color, and others provide information about the dynamics or movement in the visual scene.

In some ways, this hypothesis is counterintuitive. Our introspection is that objects are perceived as unified wholes. If a blue Volkswagon passes you on the highway, you do not have the impression that your final percept was produced in a piecemeal manner. For example, introspection would not suggest that the analysis of the Volkswagon-like shape and the color associated with that shape occurred separately. Rather, from the moment you are aware of the car, its color and shape appear as an integrated whole.

Nonetheless, converging evidence provides compelling support for the idea that perception operates in an analytic manner. Indeed, the feature-extraction hypothesis is one of the best examples of how different branches of cognitive neuroscience can provide complementary evidence.

Organization of the Lateral Geniculate Nucleus

We noted that 90% of the fibers in the optic nerve terminate in the LGN. The projection of these fibers is not random. Rather, the architecture of the LGN is highly organized, and this is manifest at several levels of analysis. At a macroscopic level, the LGN contains six well-defined layers (Figure 4.5). These layers should not be confused with the six-layered structure of the cerebral cortex. In the cortex, the layering reflects functional differences such as whether cells receive input from subcortical areas, project to subcortical areas, or are involved in intracortical processing. In contrast, each layer within the LGN receives inputs from axons of the optic tract and sends outputs that terminate in the cortex.

At a more microscopic level, additional organizational principles can be seen in the structure and connectivity of individual cells within the LGN. In particular, the LGN are characterized by three organizational properties. First, three of the layers receive input from one retina while the other three are innervated by the other retina. Ganglion cell axons from the right temporal hemiretina terminate in layers 2, 3, and 5 of the right LGN and ganglion cell axons from the left nasal hemiretina terminate in layers 1, 4, and 6. The opposite pattern is seen for the left LGN. It is important to keep in mind that the ipsilateral temporal hemiretina and contralateral nasal hemiretina are responsive to stimuli in the same visual field (see Figure 4.4). This ensures that visual information from a region in space is projected to the same LGN.

The second organizational principle pertains to the specificity of projections from the visual field to the LGN. Each layer of the LGN contains a topographic map of the retina (and thus of external space) that is in tight register. An object at a certain position in space will activate cells within each layer that fall along a line perpendicular to the LGN's surface.

Consider a stimulus located in the upper portion of the right visual field. This stimulus activates the nasal hemiretina in the right eye and the temporal hemiretina

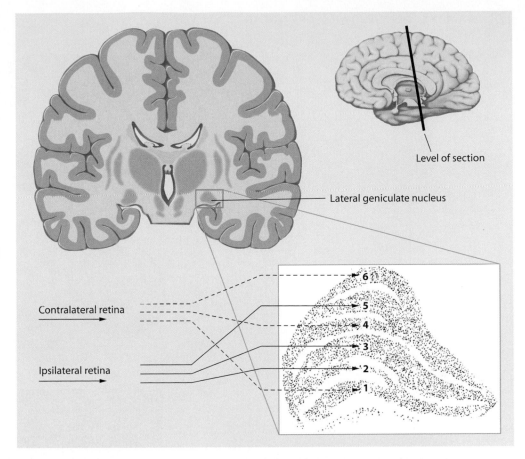

Figure 4.5 The lateral geniculate nucleus is located in the most lateral, inferior region of the thalamus. It is composed of six layers, with the ipsilateral eye projecting to layers 2, 3, and 5 and the contralateral eye projecting to layers 1, 4, and 6. Layers 3 through 6 contain the smaller neurons of the parvocellular system; layers 1 and 2 contain the larger neurons of the magnocellular system.

Level of section

Lateral geniculate nucleus

Contralateral retina

Ipsilateral retina

in the left eye. Ganglion cells with receptive fields that encompass this region of space activate cells in the left LGN. Activation occurs in all six layers, and the selected cells are all located at comparable positions within the LGN. So each LGN has six distinct retinotopic representations, one within each layer. The evidence for this relies not only on anatomical tracing techniques that detail the patterns of connectivity between the retina and LGN; cellular recordings from the LGN also verify the functional relevance of these connections. If a stimulus is presented at a location, cellular activity is found within each layer as the electrode successively penetrates the six layers.

The third organizational principle of the LGN shows that the multilayered system is not simply redundant. With regard to cytoarchitecture, the cell types of each layer have clear distinctions. As can be seen in Figure 4.6, the axons of the cells within the lower two layers are considerably larger in diameter than the cells of the upper four layers. This difference in size gives rise to the names that have become associated with the layers. Because of

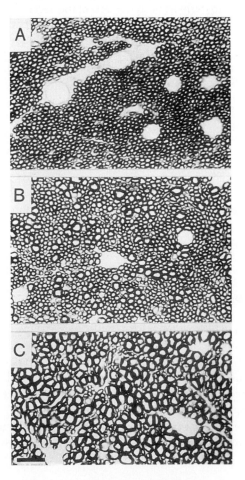

Figure 4.6 A cross section through the optic tract of the macaque shows the large-diameter fibers of the magnocellular layer and the small-diameter fibers of the parvocellular layer. The large white circles represent blood vessels. The three regions, A–C, are magnifications of different sections from dorsal to ventral.

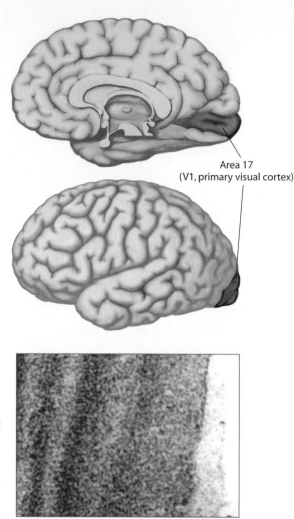

Area 17
(V1, primary visual cortex)

Figure 4.7 Brodmann's area 17 is the primary visual cortex. It extends to the most posterior pole of the occipital lobe and, in humans, extends along the medial surface. The bottom panel shows a magnification of the gray matter of the primary visual cortex in the macaque, highlighting the striated, or striped layers. This area is referred to as V1 by physiologists. Adapted from Bear et al. (1996).

their large size, the bottom two layers are referred to as the *magnocellular,* or *M,* system, while smaller cells in the upper four layers constitute the *parvocellular,* or *P,* system. In the macaque, 80% of the LGN neurons are part of the P system. We discuss functional differences between the M and P systems after we describe their cortical projections.

Multiple Pathways in the Cortex

The first cortical synapses for neurons carrying visual information are in the medial portion of the occipital lobe, area 17 in Brodmann's map. This receiving area is located medially and buried below the superficial surface of the cortex along the calcarine sulcus. The cytoarchitecture is quite regular and stippled, thus giving rise to the name *striate cortex.* Area 17 is also referred to as the *primary visual area,* and more commonly among

physiologists, as *V1* (Figure 4.7). This latter nomenclature refers to the hypothesis that this region is the first visual processing area in the cortex.

The segregation of M and P pathways is maintained in the cortex. Axons from both regions terminate in layer 4 of the striate cortex. But the terminal zones of the axons within this layer are offset from one another. And, within the striate cortex, the P pathway involves a second synapse. An interlaminar projection carries information in the P pathway from layer 4 to the more superficial layers 2 and 3 (Figure 4.8).

Even more striking anatomical evidence for multiple pathways within the visual stream comes from a new staining technique called the *cytochrome oxidase method,* which stains for the enzyme of the same name. Cytochrome oxidase is concentrated in areas of high metabolic activity. When applied to the surface of the primary visual cortex, this stain reveals a beautiful mosaic in which regions of low saturation surround regions

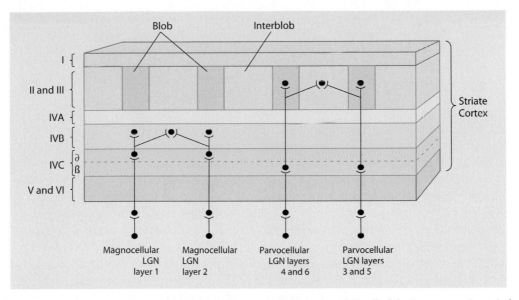

Figure 4.8   The terminal projections in area 17 of the geniculo-cortical pathway. While all of the inputs terminate in layer 4, the parvocellular inputs synapse on intracortical neurons that terminate in layers 2 and 3. Adapted from Bear et al. (1996).

of high saturation. In essence, the stain indicates that metabolic activity does not vary randomly across the surface but in a systematic way. Darker regions associated with high metabolic rates are referred to by the highly technical name *blobs;* lighter regions are called *interblobs.* Thus, data derived from the cytochrome oxidase method suggest that the P pathway has at least two branches (Figure 4.9).

Visual information is segregated into distinct pathways in the adjacent cortical area. This area is referred to as the *prestriate cortex* to indicate its location in front of the striate cortex; physiologists know it as *V2,* indicating that this is the second physiological visual area. When cytochrome oxidase is applied to the cortical surface of this visual region, the stain reveals three subregions: thick stripes, thin stripes, and interstripes, which tracing techniques show as the continuation of the M, P-blob, and P-interblob pathways, respectively.

Whether these pathways are completely independent of one another is arguable. Many researchers maintain that there is cross talk between the M and the two P pathways. More important, a lot of convergence and divergence takes place when we look past the first few synapses in the cortex.

Figure 4.9   Cytochrome oxidase stain reveals the blob/interblob regions in primary visual cortex (V1) of the macaque. The blob areas are metabolically more active and absorb more of the stain. **(a)** A section taken parallel to the cortical surface through layers 2 and 3 shows the islands of blobs. **(b)** A radial section through the cortex. The white circles are blood vessels.

(a)   (b)

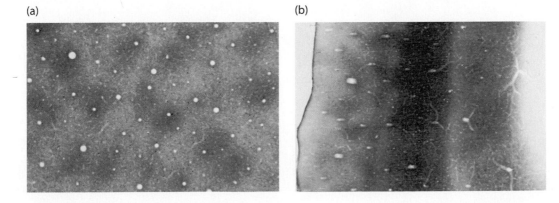

Pioneers in the Visual Cortex

Akin to the voyages of the fifteenth-century European explorers, the initial investigations of the cerebral cortex's neurophysiology required a willingness to sail in uncharted waters. The two admirals in this enterprise were David Hubel and Torsten Wiesel. Hubel and Wiesel arrived at Johns Hopkins University in the late 1950s, hoping to extend the pioneering work of Steve Kuffler. His research had elegantly described the receptive field organization of ganglion cells in the cat retina, laying out the mechanisms that allowed cells to detect edges that defined objects in the visual world. Rather than focus on the lateral geniculate nucleus (LGN), the next relay in the system, Hubel and Wiesel set their sights on the primary visual cortex (1977). Vernon Mountcastle, another Hopkins researcher, was just completing his seminal work in which he laid out the complex topographic organization of the somatosensory cortex. Hubel and Wiesel were inspired to look for similar principles in vision.

During the first few weeks of their recordings, the research duo was puzzled by what they observed. While they had little difficulty identifying individual cortical cells, the cells failed to respond to the kinds of stimuli that had proved so effective in Kuffler's studies—small spots of light positioned within a cell's receptive fields. Indeed, the lack of consistent responses made it difficult to determine where the receptive field was situated. Their breakthrough came when they switched to dark spots, created by placing an opaque disk on a glass slide. While the cell did not respond to the dark spot, Hubel and Wiesel noticed a burst in activity as the edge of the glass moved across part of the retina. After hours of playing with this stimulus, the first organizational principle of primary visual cortex neurons became clear: Unlike the circular receptive fields of ganglion cells, cortical neurons were responsive to edges.

Subsequent work revealed that LGN cells behaved similarly to ganglion cells, being maximally excited by small spots of light. Such cells are best characterized as exhibiting a concentric center-surround organization. Figure A shows the receptive field of an LGN cell. When the spot of light falls within the excitatory center re-

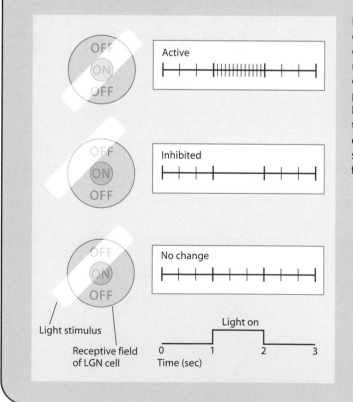

Light stimulus

Receptive field of LGN cell

Figure A Characteristic response of a lateral geniculate cell. Cells in the lateral geniculate nucleus (LGN) have concentric receptive fields with either an on center–off surround or off center–on surround organization. This on center–off surround cell fires rapidly when the light encompasses the center region **(top)** and is inhibited when the light is positioned over the surround **(middle).** A stimulus that spans both the center and the surround produces little change in activity **(bottom).** As such, LGN cells are ideal for signaling changes in illumination such as that which arise from stimulus edges.

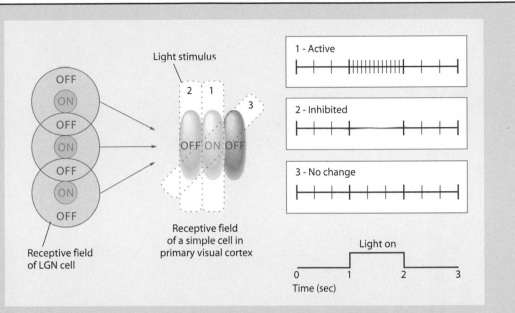

Figure B Simple cells in the primary visual cortex can be formed by linking the outputs from concentric LGN cells with adjacent receptive fields. In addition to signaling the presence of an edge, simple cells are selective for orientation. This simple cell is either excited or inhibited by an edge that follows its preferred orientation. It shows no change in activity to an edge at a perpendicular orientation.

gion, the cell is activated. If the same spot is moved into the surrounding region, the activity is inhibited. Moreover, a stimulus that encompasses both the center and the surrounding will fail to activate the cell, as the activity from the excitatory and inhibitory regions will cancel each other. This clarifies a fundamental principle of perception: The nervous system is most interested in change. We recognize an elephant not by the homogenous gray surface of its body, but by the contrast between the gray edge of its shape against the background.

In Figure B, outputs from three LGN cells with receptive fields centered at slightly different positions are linked to a single cortical neuron. This cortical neuron would continue to have a center-surround organization, but for this cell the optimal stimulus would have to be an edge. Moreover, the cell would be selective for edges in a certain orientation. As the same stimulus is rotated within the receptive field, the cell would cease to respond because the edge would now span excitatory and inhibitory regions of the cell. Hubel and Wiesel called these cells *simple cells,* to connote that fact that

their simple organization would extract a fundamental feature for shape perception: the border of an object. The same linking principle can yield more *complex cells,* cells with a receptive field organization that makes them sensitive to other features such as corners or edge terminations.

Orientation selectivity has proved to be a hallmark of neurons in the primary visual cortex. Across a 2 X 2-mm chunk of cortex, the receptive fields of neurons are centered on a similar region of space (Figure C). Within the chunk, the cells vary in terms of their preferred orientation, and alternate between columns that are responsive to inputs from the right and left eyes. A series of such chunks allows for the full representation of external space, which provides the visual system with a means for extracting the visible edges in a scene.

Hubel and Wiesel's studies established how a few organizational principles can serve as building blocks of perception derived from simple sensory neurons. The importance of their pioneering studies was acknowledged in 1981, when they shared the Nobel Prize in Physiology or Medicine.

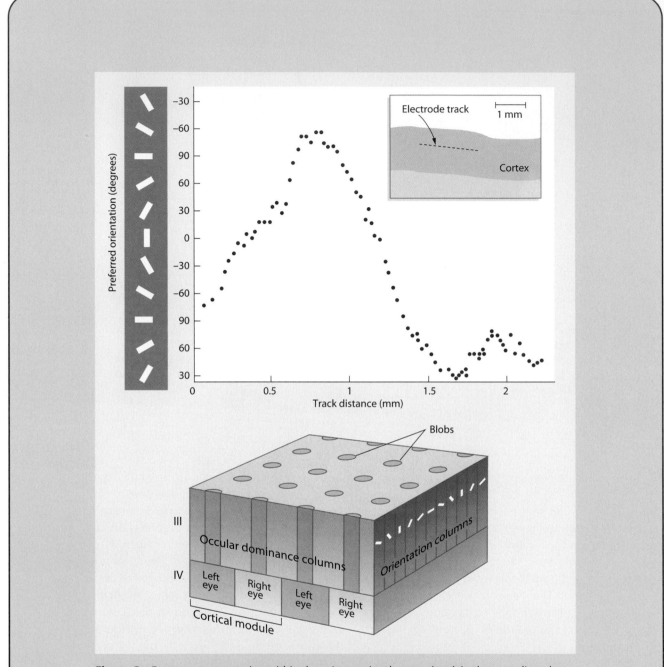

Figure C Feature representation within the primary visual cortex. **(top)** As the recording electrode is moved along the cortex, the preferred orientation of the cells varies in a continuous manner. The preferred orientation is plotted as a function of the location of the electrode. **(bottom)** The orientation columns are crossed with occular dominance columns to form a cortical module. Within a module, the cells have similar receptive fields (location sensitivity), but vary in terms of input source (left or right eye), orientation sensitivity, color sensitivity, and size sensitivity (not shown). This organization is repeated for each location. Adapted from Bear et al. (1996). Top panel after Hubel and Wiesel (1968).

CORTICAL VISUAL AREAS

Figure 4.10 shows a map of the visual areas of the cortex. Each box in the figure stands for a region of cortex that is purported to be a distinct region of visual processing. The number of visual areas stands at 32 as of 1993, an increase of almost 200% since a similar map was published in 1983. Some say that physiologists "discover" new visual areas faster than rabbits reproduce. Note that this figure follows the nomenclature developed by physiologists for functional maps. As we mentioned, striate cortex, or V1, is the initial projection region of geniculate axons. While other areas have names such as *V2*, *V3*, *V4*, and *V5*, this numbering scheme should not be taken to mean that the synapses proceed in a sequential manner from one area to the next. The lines connecting these *extrastriate* visual areas demonstrate extensive convergence and divergence across

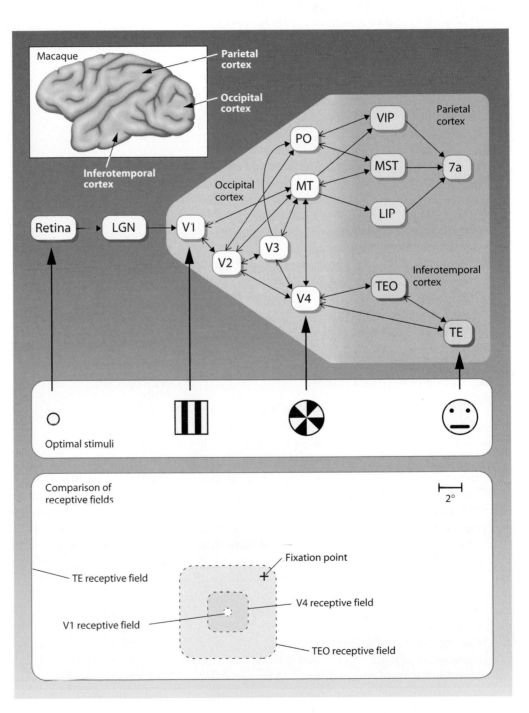

Figure 4.10 Summary of the prominent visual areas and the pattern of connectivity in the macaque. Whereas all cortical processing begins in V1, there are two processing streams that extend either dorsally to the parietal lobe or ventrally to the temporal lobe (see Chapter 5). The stimulus required to produce optimal activation of a cell becomes more complex along the ventral stream. In addition, the size of the receptive fields of these cells increases, ranging from the 0.5-degree span of a V1 cell to the 40-degree span of a cell in area TE. Adapted from art provided courtesy of Steven Luck.

visual areas; also, connections between many areas are reciprocal. Areas frequently receive input from an area to which they project.

How a visual area is defined depends on the criteria used. An obvious criterion is that cells within the area respond to visual stimuli; however, if this were the sole criterion, it would be difficult to tell where one visual area begins and another ends. Sometimes neuroanatomy might help. For example, the border between V1 and V2 corresponds to the boundary between Brodmann's areas 17 and 18. But boundaries often cannot be identified with anatomical methods. For the physiologist, area 19 has many distinct visual areas. Physiologists depend on criteria different from the ones used by anatomists.

A primary physiological method for establishing visual areas is to measure how spatial information is represented across a region of cortex. Each visual area has a topographic representation of external space in the contralateral hemifield, and the boundaries between anatomically adjacent visual areas are marked by topographic discontinuities (Figure 4.11). In the same way that each LGN has six representations of the retina, the cortex has at least as many retinotopic maps as visual areas. The replication of topography within the cortex does not result from independent inputs to each area. As one area projects to another, topography is preserved. Precise spatial information is preserved by these multiple retinotopic maps, at least in early visual areas, reflecting the fact that the system has to link features that emanate from a common location.

Cellular Correlates of Visual Features

Why would it be useful for the primate brain to have evolved so many visual areas? One possibility is that the areas form a hierarchy in which each area successively elaborates on the representation derived by processing in earlier areas, representing the stimulus in a specific way. The simple cells of the primary visual cortex calculate edges used by more complex cells to detect corners and edge terminations used by higher-order neurons to represent shapes. Successive elaboration culminates in formatting the representation of the stimulus so it matches (or not) information in memory. As shown in Figure 4.10 though, there is not a simple hierarchy; extensive patterns of convergence and divergence result in multiple pathways.

An alternative hypothesis relates to the idea of visual perception as an analytic process. Although each visual area provides a map of external space, the maps differ with regard to the type of information they represent.

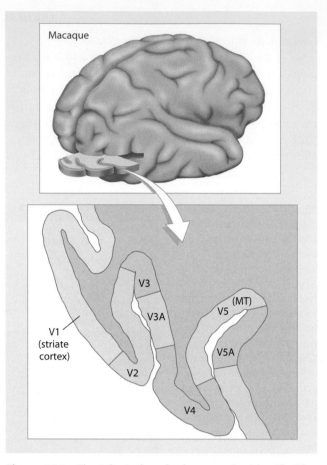

Figure 4.11 Physiological methods are used to identify different visual areas. An area is defined by a discontinuity in the retinotopic representation of the cells. Along this continuous ribbon of cortex, seven different visual areas can be identified. However, processing is not restricted to proceeding from one area to the next in a sequential order. For example, axons from V2 project to V3, V4, and V5. Adapted from Zeki (1993).

For instance, neurons in some areas are highly sensitive to color variation. In other areas, the neurons may be movement sensitive but color insensitive. By this hypothesis, neurons within an area not only code where an object is located in visual space but also provide information about the object's attributes. Visual perception is a divide-and-conquer strategy. Rather than have each visual area represent all attributes of an object, each area provides its own limited analysis. Processing is distributed and specialized. As we advance through the visual system, different areas elaborate on the initial information in V1 and begin to integrate this information across dimensions to form recognizable percepts.

Extensive physiological evidence supports the specialization hypothesis. For instance, single-cell recordings in the M pathway reveal that these neurons are not sensitive to variations in the color of the stimulus. Neurons in the magnocellular layer of the LGN (layer 4b of V1, the thick stripes of V2) and area MT, a visual area in the middle temporal region, will respond similarly to either a green or red circle on a white background. Even more striking, these neurons respond only slightly when presented with an alternating pattern of red and green stripes whose colors are of equal brightness.

In contrast, these neurons are quite sensitive to movement and direction, as shown in Figure 4.12 (Maunsell and Van Essen, 1983). The neuron shown in Figure 4.12 was located in area MT. The stimulus, a rectangular bar, was passed through the receptive field in varying directions. The cell's response was greatest when the stimulus was moved downward and left. In contrast, this cell was essentially silent when the stimulus was moved upward or to the right. Thus, the cell's activity correlates with two attributes of the stimulus. First, it is active only when the stimulus falls within its receptive field. Second, the response is greatest when the stimulus moves in a certain direction. This specificity is even more remarkable. Activity in MT cells also correlates with the speed of motion. The cell in Figure 4.12 responded maximally when the bar was moved rapidly. At slower speeds, the bar's movement in the same direction failed to raise the response rate above baseline.

Figure 4.12 Directional and speed tuning of an MT neuron. A rectangle was moved through the receptive field of this cell in various directions. The red traces beside the stimulus cartoons indicate the response of the cell to these stimuli. In the polar graph, the firing rates are plotted, with the angular direction of each point indicating the stimulus direction and the distance from the center indicating the firing rate as a percentage of the maximum firing rate. The polygon formed by connecting the points indicates that the cell was maximally responsive to stimuli moved down and to the left; the cell responded minimally when the stimulus moved in the opposite direction. The graph shows speed tuning for a cell in MT. In all conditions, the motion was in the optimal direction. This cell responded most vigorously when the stimulus moved at 64 degrees psec. Adapted from Maunsell and Van Essen (1983).

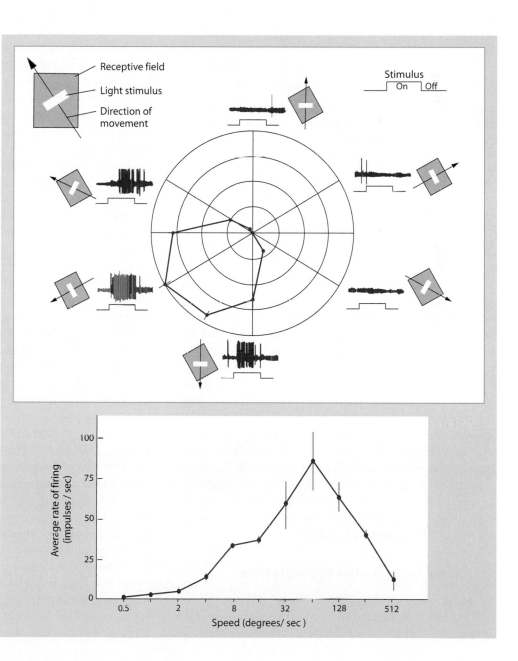

Parallel Pathways in Visual Perception			
Neural Structure	**Cell Types**		
Thalamus (LGN)	Magnocellular	Parvocellular	
Area 17 (VI)	Layer 4b	Blobs	Interblobs
Area 18 (V2)	Thick stripes	Thin stripes	Interstripes

Cellular Correlates			
Contrast (brightness)	high	low	low
Location	low	low	high
Motion	high	low	middle
Color	low	high	middle
Orientation	middle	low	high

Figure 4.13 Summary of the responsiveness of cells in the three pathways to different stimulus properties. Cells in the magnocellular pathway are very responsive to motion and are very sensitive to contrast (brightness) differences. Cells in the blob, thin-stripe regions of the parvocellular pathway also have high contrast sensitivity. While they show little sensitivity to motion, they are sharply tuned for wavelength, or color. Cells in the interblob, interstripe regions of the parvocellular pathway are sensitive to location and orientation, and show some variation in firing rates as motion and color parameters of a stimulus are varied.

Figure 4.13 summarizes stimulus variations used in neurophysiological studies to identify the representational characteristics of cells in the M, P-blob, and P-interblob pathways. As we noted, neurons in the M pathway are movement sensitive and color (or, more precisely, wavelength) insensitive. In contrast, neurons in the P-blob pathway are highly selective to color and are minimally responsive to movement or changes in orientation. A cell within the blobs of V1 that responds to a red stimulus will respond regardless of whether the stimulus is oriented vertically or horizontally. Orientation information, on the other hand, is well represented by cells in the P-interblob pathway and is poorly represented by neurons in the P-blob pathway and weakly represented by M pathway neurons.

Analysis and Representation of Visual Features

Anatomical and physiological results suggest that the visual system is characterized by multiple pathways, each with their individual specializations. Information is thus processed in such a way that analysis across the different pathways proceeds concurrently.

While single-cell recording methods can elucidate what makes a cell fire, it is often difficult to relate this cellular activity to behavior. Hundreds of millions of cells are in the striate cortex and extrastriate visual areas. At any time, thousands if not millions of these cells are active. Is it possible to know how percepts are related to this activity (Newsome et al., 1995)? More specific to visual perception, what are the behavioral consequences of having concurrent processing pathways?

VISUAL SEARCH

Cognitive psychologists have developed behavioral tests to explore the hypothesis that visual perception is an analytic process. Anne Treisman (1988), working at the University of British Columbia in the 1970s, introduced the visual search task as a model of the perceptual problems we may encounter in the world. Sherlock Holmes, for instance, describes looking for his red-headed friend at a train station in London by rapidly scanning the crowd and examining only the faces of people with red hair. Treisman asked if we are equally capable of searching by any arbitrary criteria, or whether certain targets are easier than others.

In the visual search task, subjects are presented with displays containing multidimensional objects. In Treisman and Gelade's seminal study (1980), each object was a colored letter. There were two conditions (Figure 4.14). In the feature-search condition, the target object differed from all of the distractor objects by a single dimension. Suppose that the distractor objects were either brown *T*'s or green *X*'s. A target in the feature-search condition might be either a brown *S* or a green *S*. Here the target's color is identical to half the distractors but its shape is different from that of all the distractors. Alternatively, the target in a feature search could be defined by a color difference. Here, the target might be a blue *T* or blue *X*.

In the conjunction-search condition, the target could not be identified from a single dimension such as color or shape; instead, the target was defined by the conjunction of information from two or more dimensions. For example, the search might be for a green *T* among brown *T*'s and green *X*'s. Conjunction targets such as the green *T* share color with half the distractors and shape with the other half.

Of particular interest in this task was the relation between the time required to make a response and the number of items in the display; see Chapter 3 for a similar logic applied in the study of memory search. The slope of this function is taken as a behavioral index of

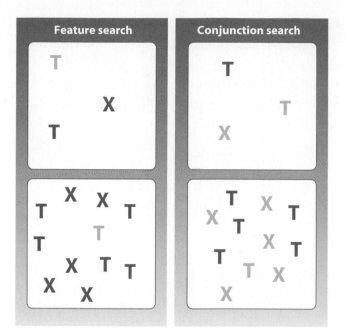

Figure 4.14 Sample displays in a visual search task. In each panel, find the target, the green T as quickly as possible. The target is readily apparent in both panels on the left (feature search) despite the variation in the number of distractors, because it is the only green object. In contrast, the target is harder to find in the conjunction search, especially when there are many distractors.

the processing demands to detect either simple features or conjunctions of features. To see this, Treisman and Gelade varied the number of distractors in the display, with the number ranging from 1 to 30. For target-present displays, one of these objects was the target. For target-absent displays, all objects were distractors. The subjects were asked to determine whether the display contained a target, and to decide as fast as possible. Reaction time might be expected, a priori, to be longer as the number of items increased. But the effect of display size might differ for the two types of search. The investigators reasoned that if the visual system processed features such as shape and color separately, then it ought to be easy to do a feature search—the slope of the search function should be shallow. Conjunction searches, though, might be difficult because they require processing to a stage where feature representations combine into multidimensional percepts. An indicator of this would be a positively sloped search function with a reaction time that increases as a function of the number of distractors.

The results in Figure 4.15 support these predictions. Conjunction search was greatly affected by how many distractors were in the display. Indeed, the shape of the conjunction function suggests that subjects must engage

Figure 4.15 Results obtained by Treisman and Gelade (1980) on the two types of visual search tasks. In the feature-search task, the time to detect the presence of a target was independent of display size. When the target was absent, reaction times increased because subjects adopted a cautious strategy of checking each item to confirm that it did not match the target. In the conjunction-search task, reaction times in both conditions increased as a function of display size. Moreover, the slope on target absent trials was twice as steep as that on target present trials, suggesting a serial, terminating search process.

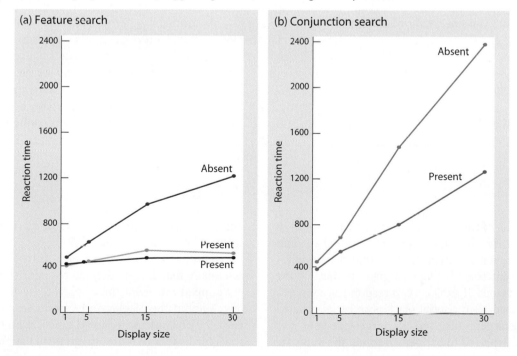

An Interview with Anne Treisman, Ph.D. Dr. Treisman is associated with the Department of Psychology at Princeton University. Based on behavioral methods, her work anticipated the neuroanatomical and neurophysiological work on the analytic aspects of visual perception.

Authors: How did you get on to the importance of studying features in your research on attention?

AT: I'm not sure I can accurately reconstruct the past, but certainly the distinction between parallel processing of simple physical features and limited attention to more complex items goes back to the development of the filter model of attention, and played a central role in the selective listening research on the "cocktail party problem." [The cocktail party problem refers to the problems that arise when we selectively attend to one input among a host of competing signals. At a cocktail party, we may wish to filter out the buzz from neighboring conversations to hone in on an intimate discussion. Alternatively, if we are conversing with a boring acquaintance, we may find ourselves picking up bits and pieces of chatter being shared across the room.] That was the subject of my Ph.D. dissertation. I was also influenced by research on discrimination learning in animals, particularly the thought that the more they learn about one property, the less they learn about others. My interest in applying the distinction to vision (rather than hearing) goes back to a paper I wrote in 1966, when I suggested that different properties are analyzed in parallel in separate modules, and that perhaps we could attend selectively either to one property, by switching out the analyzers for other properties, or to one object (or source of stimuli), by selecting which sensory inputs to gate before they reach certain analyzers. Looking at my flow diagrams with separate boxes for color, shape, motion, and so on started me wondering how the properties get reassembled, and whether we might sometimes make the wrong bundles and experience illusory conjunctions.

I remember sitting on the lawn with my children in the early 1970s, drawing displays of mixed red *X*'s and green *O*'s on scraps of paper, and asking them to find either a blue *O* or a red *O*. I noticed that they took much longer to find the conjunction targets. This led to the idea that focused attention to each element would be one way of solving what is now known as the *binding problem*. Either space or time can be used to individuate objects; these two fundamental attributes also provide media within which we can attend selectively to a subset of the features present in the field. A crucial test (which I put off for a while because I didn't really believe it would work) was to see whether illusory conjunctions (binding errors) actually would be experienced when attention was overloaded or directed elsewhere. One of the high points of my research was when my research assistant told me that, contrary to my firm impression, I was making many of those errors in reporting colored letters that I believed I was seeing quite clearly.

Authors: How does one decide what constitutes an elementary feature of visual perception?

AT: Defining what counts as a feature for the visual system is an empirical question. I suggested some criteria for finding out: parallel processing and pop out with divided attention, minimal interference when responding along one dimension from variations along other di-

in a serial search of the display, examining each object to determine if it has the right combination of shape and color. Evidence for this hypothesis is that the slope for the target-absent trials is twice as great as that for the target-present trials. If subjects can respond as soon as a target is detected, then a serial search can be terminated as soon as the target is detected. On target-present trials, this would be expected to happen after half the items are examined. On target-absent trials, all items must be checked before a response can be made.

In contrast, the functions for feature searches were essentially flat. Targets defined by color (blue) or shape *(S)* popped out from the display; there was no need to search about the display and examine each object individually. The positively sloped function on target-absent trials for feature searches suggests that subjects adopted

mensions, the occurrence of illusory recombinations of features or binding errors, selective adaptation. The hope was that these would converge on a limited num ber of candidates. I also found an interesting asymmetry on visual search tasks between many pairs of contrasting features, suggesting that one of the two counts (for the visual system) as the presence of something and one as its absence, just as the presence of a slash on the *Q* distinguishes it from an *O*, which lacks the slash. In all these pairs (*Q* versus *O*, tilted versus vertical line, curved versus straight line, gap versus closed curve, ellipse versus circle, converging versus parallel lines) the search for the first of the pair in a background of the second was much easier than the reverse. What is shared by all but the *Q/O* pair is that the second is a standard or reference value and the first can be thought of as a deviation from it. By analogy with the *Q/O* pair, it is as if the brain assumes the standard value and codes deviations from it as the presence of something to be signaled. This signal makes the target that has it pop out from a background of elements in which it is absent.

Authors: These are behavioral criteria, yet in your interpretation you make inferences about brain function. What evidence supports the idea that we can expect a convergence between what we define as a feature in tasks such as visual search and how the brain extracts information about the visual world?

AT: It would be tempting to look for single units coding the features that pop out in behavioral studies. While this might be illuminating, I suspect that the activity of a single unit will not always correspond directly to what the visual system as a whole is doing. It's more likely that some form of coarse coding is used—activities in different cell populations with overlapping sensitivities carry the relevant information. I recently generated illusory conjunctions of slightly tilted purple bars by presenting brief exposures of vertical blue bars

and more tilted red bars. Thus, the observer's perception can reflect a blending of the stimulus information rather than simply a miscombination of the available features. This blending is likely a result of the crude coding by individual neurons.

Some neural evidence supports the idea that the search for feature-defined targets differs from the search for targets defined only by conjunctions of features. By looking at the early P1 component event-related potential researchers have found attentional suppression at distractor locations in a visual search task only when participants needed to conjoin features and not when they were asked simply to detect the presence of particular features. PET studies have shown similar patterns of activation in the parietal lobes both when participants shift attention in space and when they search for a conjunction target, suggesting that the same spatial selection mechanisms are used in both. This is consistent with my account of the need for a serial scan with focused attention when features must be bound. Neurophysiologists have begun to look also at attention effects on single unit responses in V1, V2, and V4 in relation to the risk of binding errors: Attention effects were seen only when the monkey had to respond to one of two objects presented within the same receptive field, where presumably their features would otherwise risk being exchanged or pooled.

Exciting research is taking place to explore the possibility that synchronized firing is used as a temporal code to link the neural representations of the features from one object—an intriguing solution for how the brain might solve the binding problem. In this context, attention limits might reflect limits on the number of different synchronies that can be maintained at one time, and illusory conjunctions might reflect accidental synchronies that result when too many objects are coded at once.

a conservative response criterion. Although they could detect a feature target in parallel across the display, the heterogeneity of the displays led them to seek confirmation that none of the items matched the target.

Treisman proposed a model to account for differences in feature and conjunction searches as they pertain to the limits of concurrent processing (Figure 4.16). Her premise is that object perception begins with

the parallel analysis of its component features. Feature registration, she assumed, does not require attentional resources: The visual system automatically registers the colors and shapes from all visible stimuli. She postulated feature maps as representational structures that indicate the presence or absence of features. Feature maps correspond to visual dimensions like color or shape. Activation within the map would signal the

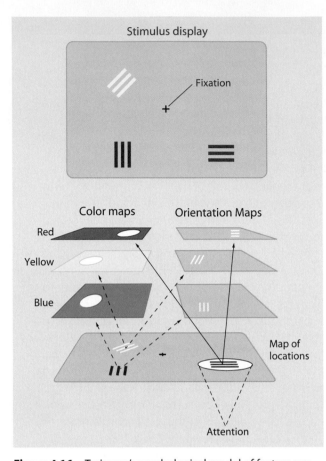

Figure 4.16 Treisman's psychological model of feature perception and integration. The dimensions of color and orientation are represented by a series of feature maps tuned to specific values (e.g., red, yellow, or blue for color maps). Stimuli automatically activate cells tuned to their features on these maps. Attention is directed to particular locations and allows the features at that location to be integrated. Adapted from Treisman (1988).

presence of a certain value on that dimension. For example, the brown and green distractors would activate detectors on the color feature map that are tuned to these colors. A blue target would similarly activate a detector tuned to blue. To perform a feature search based on color, the subject would simply have to determine whether the blue detector was active or not.

Conjunction searches cannot be performed by simply checking the activation of detectors on feature maps. Instead, conjunction search requires that activation on two different maps not only be checked but also be linked to a specific location. When searching for a green *T*, it is not enough to check for activity in green detectors or *T* detectors. The target is present only when both a green and *T* detector are simultaneously activated by an object at a single location.

The visual search task was originally developed to explore how object perception might be constrained by a display's complexity. It is now used as a diagnostic tool by cognitive psychologists. Targets that yield flat search functions are assumed to reflect visual primitives, the basic building blocks of perception. The dimensions that neurophysiologists use to describe activity in early visual areas generally correspond well with stimulus conditions that produce flat search functions. This correspondence holds not only for features that differ in shape and color, but also when the target moves in a different direction (Nakayama and Silverman, 1986) or at a significantly different speed from the distractors (Ivry and Cohen, 1992).

Flat search functions have also been found when the target differs in depth from the distractors or is uniquely illuminated, creating a distinct shadowing pattern for the target in comparison to the distractors (Figure 4.17). The effect of illumination is especially striking, as it depends on the orientation of the stimulus display. If the display in Figure 4.17b is rotated 90 degrees, the target becomes easier to find. Visual detectors can be sensitive to the direction of illumination and use this to extract depth information. Our visual system evolved in an environment where the primary source of illumination, the sun, projects from overhead and so illumination-sensitive detectors are limited.

Within a dimension, the search task can be used to explore critical factors that lead to flat search functions. The steepness of the slope on a visual search task and the similarity between the target and distractor features positively correlate. If the target is different from the distractor, the search function is flat. For example, a red target will pop out from green and blue distractors. As the target becomes more similar to the distractors, the search function rises steeply. Search will become slower if the red target is placed among orange and violet distractors. This dependency is in agreement with results of single-cell recording studies. As the value of a dimension like color is changed, the response of the cell changes in a smooth fashion from active to quiescent.

The visual search task enables us to ask questions about what makes a feature (Beck, 1982). Consider shape. As we just found, an *S* pops out from a display of *X*'s and *T*'s. Does this mean that each letter should be viewed as a primitive of visual perception? It is unlikely that specialized detectors would be tuned to letters since alphanumeric characters in the English language are arbitrary. Indeed, as can be seen in Figure 4.17c, the letter *L* does not pop out when embedded among a set of *T*'s. It is much easier to find the upright *L* among a display of tilted *L*'s than among upright *T*'s. So the critical feature

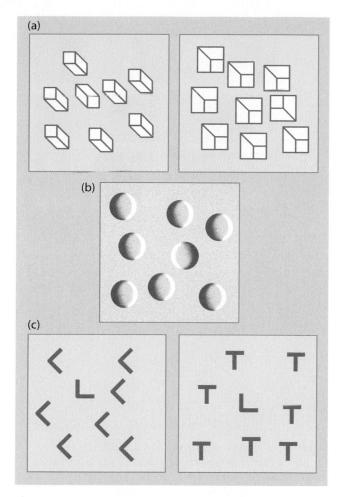

Figure 4.17 Does one object "pop out" in these displays? The ability to rapidly identify a unique stimulus property has been used as one defining criterion for identifying the basic building blocks of perception. **(a)** The deviant object is created by varying the end at which the arrowhead is placed. This difference is much easier to detect when this attribute changes the orientation of a three-dimensional box rather than a flat, abstract shape. **(b)** Variations in lightness can also provide a cue to depth. Turn your book sideways and examine **b** again. The deviant object will now pop out, literally! **(c)** Despite our familiarity with letters, it is easier to find the upright L among tilted L's than among the T's. The pop-out phenomenon here is likely due to the difference in orientation of the component parts of the letters rather than their overall shapes. Part a is adapted from Enns and Resnick (1990); b is from Ramachandran (1988); c is from Beck (1982).

is not the letter as a whole but its parts. When the target L is among tilted L's, the rapid search can be performed by detecting either the horizontal or the vertical line. When distractors are upright T's, the target's components are shared by all distractors. Again, this finding meshes nicely with the results of neurophysiology. Cells

at many levels within the P-interblob pathway are highly selective according to a stimulus's orientation.

ILLUSIONS AND FEATURE INDEPENDENCE

Examine the black and white drawing in Figure 4.18. Compare the length of the two horizontal lines. Is the upper line longer than the lower line? Or are they equal? Your ruler can confirm that the two lines are equal, yet this does not match our percept, at least not for the stimulus on the left. For this black-on-white stimulus, we have a striking illusion that the upper line is longer. This *Ponzo illusion* arises because the diagonal lines appear to recede in depth. While the two horizontal lines produce retinal images of equal size, the upper line looks father away, which leads us to perceive it to be much longer than the lower line.

Now consider the red-on-green versions of the illusion. Most people readily see the illusion in the left version. But, surprisingly, the illusion is reduced in the right version. To understand this discrepancy, we need to know how the borders between the background and the lines are created. For the black-on-white version, the

Figure 4.18 The Ponzo illusion. **(a)** Which horizontal line is longer, the one on the top or the one on the bottom? People almost always perceive the top line as longer, even when they are aware of the illusion. The diagonal lines give the impression of train tracks receding into the horizon and thus the top line is judged as farther away. **(b)** The Ponzo illusion is also effective with color (left) except when the stimulus is isoluminant with the background (right), and thus reduces the perception of depth.

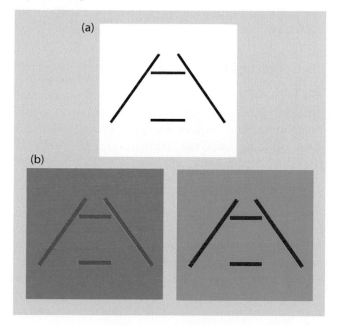

brightness between the white background and the black lines is quite different. This is not so for the red-on-green version shown on the right. Here, the intensities of the red lines and green background are identical or *isoluminant*. *Luminance* refers to the perceived brightness of a stimulus. For isoluminant stimuli, the brightness of each region is set so that each part is of equal brightness. Thus, for the stimulus on the left, brightness and color distinguish the lines from the background; for the stimulus on the right, color is the only cue.

The loss of the Ponzo illusion at isoluminance provides further evidence for a segregation of function within the visual pathways. In Figure 4.13, color-sensitive cells in the P-blob pathway are depth insensitive. Since only these cells are activated by the isoluminant stimulus, depth information is lost. Without the impression of depth, the two lines appear to be equidistant from the viewer and hence equal in length.

Isoluminant stimuli have been used in many other illusions to demonstrate the functional implications of the concurrent pathway architecture (Livingstone and Hubel, 1988). Especially dramatic is the loss of motion information with isoluminant stimuli. Figure 4.19 presents a computer-generated motion display in which a striped pattern is continuously shifted over time, which creates the impression of rightward motion. If the striped regions are isoluminant, though, the perceived speed of the moving display slows down. Indeed, one almost has the impression that the display is stopped. This percept is paradoxical. We can clearly tell that a region has moved from one location to another. With isoluminant stimuli, the perception of motion becomes inferential, as if we conclude that because something is not where it was, it must have moved. Yet the percept of the movement is attenuated.

Neurophysiological Evidence for Concurrent Processing

The behavioral evidence we have reviewed implies that, early in visual perception, perceived features such as form, color, and motion are concurrently processed. These findings dovetail with results of single-cell recording experiments, but remember that behavioral studies do not provide insight to brain mechanisms. We have no direct way of knowing that the distortion of motion at isoluminance is due to the poor response of M pathway neurons. It is difficult to make inferences about anatomy and physiology from behavioral responses such as button presses.

Positron emission tomography (PET) provides a way to link behavior to anatomy. Even though this method remains correlational, it does allow the re-

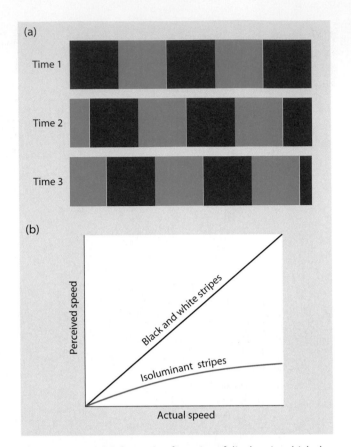

Figure 4.19 **(a)** Schematic of a series of displays in which the striped pattern moves across the page similar to a rotating barber pole. **(b)** The perceived speed of the stimulus is veridical when the striped regions are black and white. However, when the stripes are isoluminant, the perceived speed is much slower suggesting that color differences are, at best, weakly signaled in the motion system.

searcher to identify active brain regions while subjects perform tasks. In a recent study, Semir Zeki (1993) of the University College, London, and his colleagues at Hammersmith Hospital used PET to verify that different visual areas are activated when subjects are processing color or motion information.

Subtractive logic was used by factoring out the activation in a control condition from the activation in an experimental one. Consider first the color experiment. For the control condition, subjects passively viewed a collage of achromatic rectangles. Various shades of gray, spanning a wide range of luminances, were chosen. The control stimulus would be expected to activate neural regions with cells that are contrast sensitive (e.g., sensitive to differences in luminance).

For the experimental condition, the gray patches were replaced by a variety of colors (Figure 4.20). Each color patch was matched in luminance to its corresponding gray patch. Thus, neurons sensitive to luminance information should be equally activated in control and experimental conditions. However, the colored stimulus should produce more activity in neural regions sensitive to chromatic information. These regions should be detected if the metabolic activity recorded when subjects viewed the gray stimulus is subtracted from the one recorded when subjects viewed the colored stimulus.

The same logic was used to design the motion experiment. For this study, the control stimulus consisted of a complex black-and-white collage of squares. The

Figure 4.20 Schematic of the stimuli used in a PET experiment to identify regions involved in color and motion perception. **(a)** For the color experiment, the stimuli were composed of an arrangement of rectangles that were either shades of gray (control) or various colors (experimental). **(b)** For the motion experiment, a random pattern of black and white regions was either stationary (control) or moving (experimental). Adapted from Zeki (1993).

(a) Mondrian display

(b) Pattern of moving squares

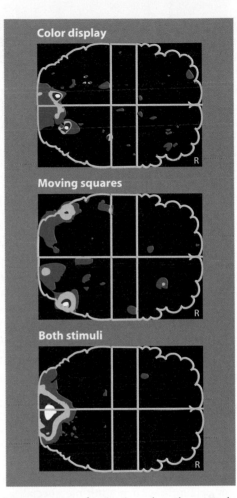

Figure 4.21 Regions of activation when the control conditions were subtracted from the experimental conditions. In the color condition, the prominent activation is medial, in areas corresponding to human V4. In the motion condition, the activation is more lateral, in areas corresponding to human V5, or MT. Both stimuli also produced significant activation in primary visual cortex when compared to a control condition in which there was no visual stimulation. Adapted from Zeki (1993).

same stimulus was used in the experimental condition, except that the squares were all set in motion. They would begin to move in one direction for 5 seconds and then the reverse direction for the next 5 seconds.

The results of the two studies provided clear evidence that the two tasks activated distinct brain regions (Figure 4.21). After subtracting activation during the viewing of the achromatic collage, investigators found numerous residual foci of activation when subjects viewed the colored collage. These were bilateral and located in the most anterior and inferior regions of the occipital lobe. Although the spatial resolution of PET is coarse, these areas were determined to be in front of the striate (V1) and prestriate cortex (V2). In contrast, after the appropriate subtraction in the motion experiment, the residual foci were bilateral, near the junction of temporal, parietal, and occipital cortices. These foci are more superior and much more lateral than the color foci. Zeki and his colleagues were so taken with this dissociation that they proposed that the nomenclature developed by primate researchers should be applied here. They labeled the area activated in the color foci as *human V4* and the area activated in the motion task as *human V5*. Of course, with PET data we cannot be sure that the foci of activation really consist of just one visual area.

DEFICITS IN FEATURE PERCEPTION

The research described in the last few sections has emerged over the past two decades. From these diverse sources, the evidence for concurrent processing is quite compelling. Within the realm of neurology, the idea of concurrent processing has a much longer and more tumultuous history. In 1888 a Swiss ophthalmologist, Louis Verrey (cited in Zeki, 1993), described a patient who had lost the ability to perceive colors in her right visual field. Verrey reported that the patient had problems with acuity within restricted portions of this right visual field. But the color deficit was uniform and complete. We can guess that this patient's world looked similar to the drawing in Figure 4.22: On one side of space, the world was multicolored; on the other, it was a montage of grays.

Verrey speculated that if a person could selectively lose color perception, then multiple specializations of function within the visual cortex should be presumed. The idea of a specialized color center, let alone multiple visual centers, met with great resistance over the next century. The anatomy of the cortex was just beginning to be known in detail, and so the focus was not on specializations within a domain. Rather, scientists were debating about which cortical regions were critical for visual perception. Researchers sought to find the "cortical retina." War victims provided compelling evidence that losing a retina led to total loss of vision in that eye. In a corresponding manner, lesions to the cortical retina were assumed to disrupt all aspects of vision. More recent studies of patients with neurological disorders provided convincing evidence that brain lesions can produce selective impairments.

Deficits in Color Perception

When we speak of someone who is color blind, we are usually describing a person who has inherited a gene that produces an abnormality in the photoreceptor system. *Dichromats,* or people with only two photopigments, can be classified as red-green color blind if they are missing the photopigment sensitive to either medium or long wavelengths, or blue-yellow color blind if they are missing the short-wavelength photopigment. *Anomalous trichromats,* in contrast, have all three photopigments but one has abnormal sensitivity. The incidence of these genetic disorders is high in males—about 8% of the population. The incidence rate is much lower in females: less than 1%.

Much rarer are disorders of color perception that arise from disturbances of the central nervous system. These disorders are called *achromatopsia,* taken from the prefix *a* or "without" and the stem *chroma* or "hue." As evident in Verrey's description, these patients see the world without color. J.C. Meadows (1974) of the National Hospital in London described one such patient as follows: "Everything looked black or grey. He had diffi-

Figure 4.22 In achromatopsia, the world is seen as devoid of color. Because color differences are usually correlated with brightness differences, the objects in a scene might be distinguishable and appear as different shades of gray. This figure shows how the world might appear to a person with hemi-achromatopsia. In most cases, there is some residual color perception, although the person cannot distinguish between subtle color variations.

culty distinguishing British postage stamps of different value which look alike, but are of different colors. He was a keen gardener, but found that he pruned live rather than dead vines. He had difficulty distinguishing certain foods on his plate where color was the distinguishing mark."

Patients with achromatopsia often report that colors have become a bland palate of "dirty shades of gray." The shading reflects variations in brightness rather than hue. Other aspects of vision like depth and texture perception also remain intact, enabling the achromatopsic to see and recognize objects in the world. Indeed, color is not a necessary cue for shape perception. Its subtlety is underscored when we consider how people often do not notice that movie classics like "The Wizard of Oz" or "Schindler's List" are in black and white, a subtlety sorely missed when lost forever.

In almost all published cases of achromatopsia, patients exhibit abnormalities in other areas of visual perception as well. What remains clear is that the deficit in color perception is markedly more severe.

Consider the performance of an achromatopsia patient on tests of hue discrimination and brightness discrimination (Heywood et al., 1987) While we think of colors as differing in hue, they also vary in brightness and saturation (i.e., purity). Special color charts were employed to study which subjective ratings equated with differences along these three dimensions (Figure 4.23). Thus, while there is no objective way to equate a difference in hue with a difference in brightness, we can determine the psychological equivalence of differences across the dimensions.

On each trial the subject viewed three color patches. Two patches were identical; the third varied in hue, brightness, or saturation. The subject was asked to identify the stimulus that was different. As evident in Figure 4.23, the task was much more difficult when stimuli varied in hue. Brightness differences, for example, were almost always correctly identified with a four-step difference. For hue differences, the patient still scored only 70% correct even with a ten-step difference, which corresponds to a transition from a yellowish green to a

Figure 4.23 **(a)** Psychological scaling techniques can be used with healthy individuals to create stimulus sets in which the similarity of all neighboring pairs is judged as equal. These techniques are used to create norms for the similarity across the different dimensions of a color (hue, saturation, and reflectance/brightness). **(b)** Pairs of color chips were presented and the achromatopsia patient was asked to judge whether they were the same or different. This patient's ability to make such judgments was severely impaired when the pairs differed in hue, even when the stimuli differed by 10 units. His ability to discriminate brightness, although not normal, was much better. Here, he almost always labeled the stimuli as different when they were separated by at least 4 units. Bottom panels from Heywood et al. (1987).

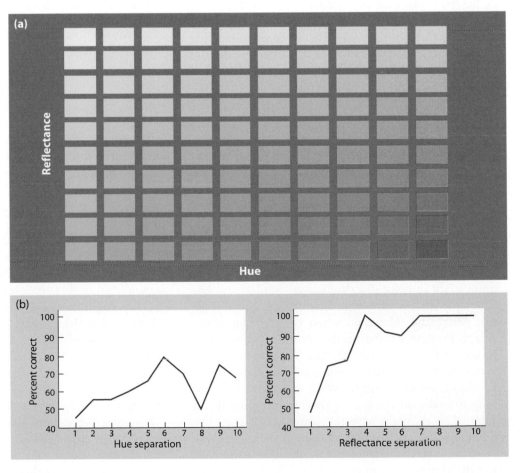

deep orange! Though this hue perception deficit is striking, the patient's performance on brightness differences was also impaired. Healthy subjects rarely make errors with a one-step difference on any of the dimensions. Moreover, this patient had lost visual acuity after his stroke. He could read, but only if the letters were in enlarged print.

For at least two reasons we should not be surprised that deficits in achromatopsia are not restricted to color perception. First, since the color-sensitive neurons of the P-blob pathway are also orientation sensitive, we would expect that losing these neurons would affect form perception. Second, neurological disorders such as strokes and tumors do not respect the borders of visual areas. Achromatopsia has consistently been associated with lesions that encompass human V4, but the lesions typically extend to neighboring extrastriate areas and compromise other aspects of visual perception.

A selective deficit of color perception is even less likely to occur if the lesion is in regions upstream to V4 such as the blobs of V1 or the thin stripes of V2. A vascular lesion or trauma that affects these areas would not be confined to cells in the P-blob pathway. Yet the puzzling case reported by Zeki of a patient with transient achromatopsia may reflect a temporary loss of function within these cells. Over several weeks, this patient experienced brief episodes when the world was suddenly drained of color. This occurred despite the fact that his vision remained intact and he could still identify objects. After a minute or so, color perception slowly returned. The disorder's transient nature suggests that blood flow to the brain temporarily diminishes. This decrease would be most disruptive to the most metabolically active cells. Cytochrome oxidase–sensitive cells within blobs and thin stripes are candidates for being disproportionately affected by reduced blood flow.

Animal lesions might provide the strongest clues that color perception depends on the P-blob pathway. Lesions of the parvocellular layers of the LGN produce a severe deficit in color discrimination (Schiller and Logothetis, 1990). As expected, these lesions also disturb form perception. However, when cortical lesions are made in primate V4, the results are more problematic. The lesions do not severely hamper hue discrimination; the monkeys can still discriminate colored regions from an isoluminant background. What is disturbed is their ability to maintain color constancy, to recognize that a region of space might have the same surface color but vary in how that surface reflects color to the eye because of variations in the light source or shadowing. Perhaps color discrimination can be sustained by hue-sensitive

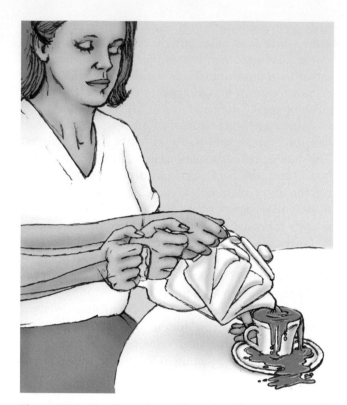

Figure 4.24 For the patient with motion blindness, the world appears as if viewed through a strobe light. Rather than see the liquid rise continuously in the teacup, the patient reports seeing the liquid jump from one level to the next.

neurons in upstream visual areas. V4 may be invaluable in constructing a representation of how colors help to define regions of visual space.

Deficits in Motion Perception

Researchers at the Max Planck Institute in Munich reported in 1983 a striking case of a woman who had incurred a selective loss of motion perception, or *akinetopsia* (Zihl et al., 1983). For this woman, whom we call M.P., perception was akin to viewing the world as snapshots. Rather than seeing things move continuously in space, moving objects would appear in one position and then another. When pouring a cup of tea, M.P. would see the liquid frozen in air, like a glacier. She would fail to notice the tea rising in her cup and would be surprised when the cup overflowed (Figure 4.24). The loss of motion perception also made M.P. hesitant about crossing the street. As she noted, "When I'm looking at the car first, it seems far away. But then when I want to cross the road, suddenly the car is very near."

Examination revealed M.P.'s color and form perception to be intact. Her ability to perceive briefly presented objects and letters, for example, was within the normal range. But she was severely impaired in judging the direction and speed of moving objects. This deficit was most apparent with stimuli moving at high speeds. At speeds faster than 20 degrees/sec, M.P. never reported detecting the motion. She could see that the dot's position had changed and hence could infer motion. But her percept was of two static images; there was no continuity from one image to the other. Even when presented with stimuli moving at lower speeds, M.P. was hesitant to report a clear impression of motion.

CT scans of M.P. revealed large, bilateral lesions that involved the temporoparietal cortices. On each side, the lesions included posterior and lateral portions of the middle temporal gyrus. These lesions roughly correspond to areas that participate in motion perception. Furthermore, the lesions are lateral and superior to human V4.

While this case has been widely cited for many years, the fact that similar patients have not been identified suggests that akinetopsia may result only from bilateral lesions. The receptive fields in primate area MT are huge and have cells that can be activated by stimuli presented in either visual field. Motion perception deficits in humans may be rare because the patient can perform such tasks so long as area MT is intact in at least one hemisphere. The lack of replication has led researchers to depend on animal studies to bolster the case for a functional specialization of motion perception. Lesions in the magnocellular layer of the LGN and in cortical area MT produce deficits in motion perception in primates. Further support for the hypothesis that the motion pathway is color blind is provided by the fact that these lesions cause no deficits in hue discrimination.

Deficits in Other Aspects of Visual Perception

Physiological evidence indicates that the strongest segregation of function is in motion and color perception. This hypothesis is supported by double dissociations found in the neurological literature. As with patient M.P., motion perception can be impaired without losing color perception. Conversely, deficits in color perception arise without losing the ability to perceive movement.

The case for specific deficits in other visual features is more contentious. A report from early in this century (Riddoch, 1917) described a patient to whom the world appeared essentially flat. This depth perception impairment was said to exist despite the patient's ability to perceive variations in color and shading. However, it is not possible to evaluate the selectivity of the deficit because careful assessments of other visual functions were not performed. In a similar manner, patients who have lost visual acuity after suffering cortical lesions generally have widespread problems in visual perception. Thus, there are no unambiguous reports of selective deficits in form or depth perception.

The visual system is likely to redundantly represent form and depth. Depth perception arises from a multitude of cues. One potent cue, binocular disparity, arises when each eye has a slightly different view of the world. Inputs from the two eyes project to the magnocellular and parvocellular layers of the LGN and converge on common cortical neurons. Cells in all three cortical streams are sensitive to depth.

Depth can also be inferred from motion. A moving object will obscure a more distant object or be hidden by a nearer object. In a similar sense, as we move, the change in the retinal image is greater for near objects than for ones far away. All these cues can be used in normal depth perception. This redundancy would be expected to help preserve depth perception even if certain modules were lesioned.

Form perception also stems from multiple sources of information. Indeed, form perception is an essential goal of vision, and all visual processing is devoted to determining what objects are in the visual field and where they are located. Motion perception may be important for a predator in anticipating the location of a moving prey. Nonetheless, movement can also help to identify prey, to separate it from the background, and to determine if its motion is characteristic of an animal worthy of pursuit. A hungry frog does not want to flick its tongue at any moving object. Rather, the frog can recognize a potential snack by its specific motion—for example, that produced by a fly. Color perception is important only in that it facilitates form perception. Colors do not exist without forms. It is a potent cue for discriminating an object or part of one from other regions of space.

Therefore, it is not surprising that we have no clinical reports of patients who are "form blind." The P-interblob pathway may have heightened sensitivity to features that correspond to shape in comparison to the M and P-blob pathways. But the latter two also contribute to form perception, and in ways that the P-interblob pathway cannot. Indeed, evolutionary theorists have proposed that color perception is a recent adaptation that refines the recognition capabilities of the visual system. It is reasonable to suppose that concurrent pathways provide multiple inputs to systems devoted to object recognition. In the next chapter we explore how these higher-level aspects of perception operate.

Tactile "Seeing" in the Visual Cortex

What happens in the visual cortex of people who are blind because of damage to the peripheral visual apparatus? Unlike patients with cortical lesions, the central nervous system is intact—there is no widespread loss of tissue and the cells continue to fire. But what causes cells in the visual cortex to respond under such conditions? Is it just noise, random firing that is unrelated to any external events? Or does the brain become reorganized and exploit this tissue in other functions?

This issue was explored in a recent PET study (Sadato et al., 1996). The results suggest a remarkable degree of functional reorganization, or what neuroscientists refer to as *cortical plasticity*. The subjects for this study included people with normal vision and people who were blind, either congenitally or from a young age (average age at onset of blindness less than 5 years). In the first experiment the subjects were scanned under two experimental conditions. In one condition the subjects were simply required to sweep their fingers back and forth over a rough surface covered with dots. In the second condition they were given tactile discrimination tasks such as deciding whether two grooves in the surface were the same or different. Blood flow in the visual cortex during each of these tasks was compared to that during a rest condition when the subjects were scanned while keeping their hands still.

Amazingly, changes in blood flow in the visual cortex were in opposite directions for the two groups of subjects. For the sighted subjects, a significant drop in blood flow was found in the primary visual cortex during the tactile discrimination tasks. Analogous decreases in the auditory or somatosensory cortex happened during visual tasks given to normal subjects; this means that as attention was directed to one modality, blood flow decreased in other sensory systems. In contrast, in blind subjects the blood flow increased—but only during discrimination tasks and not when they swept their fingers over the surface without having to use tactile information. As with normal subjects, blood flow changes were most apparent when the sensory information required a response. For blind subjects, the enhanced activity was seen in what would be the visual cortex of normal subjects.

The second experiment explored the same issue, but with a task of great importance to blind subjects: reading Braille. Here blind subjects explored strings of eight Braille letters and had to decide whether the strings formed a word or nonword. In accord with the results of the first study, blood flow in the primary and secondary visual cortex rose during Braille reading in comparison with the rest state. It is unlikely that this rise was associated with the motor demands of the experimental task. Subjects responded only on the nonword

INDEPENDENT OR CONVERGENT PATHWAYS

In this chapter we have emphasized that the visual system contains multiple pathways, each specialized to abstract specific information. Yet the outputs from these systems are designed to complement each other. This paradox has led to a lively debate concerning the independence of pathways. Advocates favoring a segregationist viewpoint have focused on anatomical, physiological, and behavioral data indicating that processing of features such as motion and color involves separable mechanisms from the first synapses in the central nervous system all the way to the extrastriate cortex. To these theorists, neurological dissociations are the crowning piece of evidence. On the other side are those who emphasize the lack of perfect segregation. Cells in the M and P-blob pathways exhibit some orientation selectivity. Color sensitivity is not the exclusive domain of the P-blob pathway; it is also in the P-interblob pathway's cells. Lesion studies of animals have brought into question the notion that processing features like depth, color, and orientation depend solely on a single pathway.

For these reasons we prefer the term *concurrent pro-*

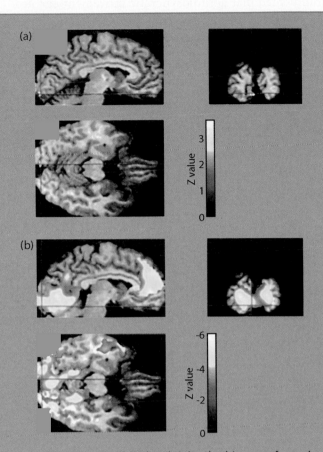

Activation loci when blind and sighted subjects performed a tactile discrimination task compared with control condition in which subjects simply rested. For the blind subjects **(a)**, activation increased in primary visual cortex during the discrimination task. For the sighted subjects **(b)**, activation decreased in primary visual cortex during this condition.

trials, which accounted for less than 10% of all trials.

At present, it is unclear how tactile information ends up activating visual cortex neurons in blind people. One possibility is that somatosensory projections to thalamic relays spread into the nearby LGN, exploiting the geniculo-striate pathway. But this hypothesis is unlikely since the blood flow changes in the blind subjects were bilateral. Somatosensory inputs to the thalamus are strictly lateralized. Because the subjects performed the tactile tasks with their right hand, the blood flow changes should have been restricted to the left hemisphere. A more viable hypothesis is that a massive reorganization of cortico-cortical connections follows peripheral blindness. The sensory-deprived visual cortex is taken over, perhaps through back projections originating in polymodal association cortical areas.

While this study provided a dramatic demonstration of cortical plasticity, the results also suggest a neurobiological mechanism for the greater nonvisual perceptual acuity exhibited by blind people. Indeed, Louis Braille's motivation to develop his tactile reading system was spurred by his belief that vision loss was offset by heightened sensitivity in the fingertips. One account of this compensation focuses on nonperceptual mechanisms. While the sensory representation of somatosensory information is similar for blind and sighted subjects, the former group is not distracted by vision (or visual imagery) and thus can use somatosensation more efficiently. These new PET data, though, suggest a perceptual-based mechanism. Sensitivity increases because more cortical tissue is devoted to representing nonvisual information.

cessing, coined by David Van Essen of Washington University in St. Louis (Van Essen and DeYoe, 1995). This phrase emphasizes the analytic characteristic of visual perception. There is strong and converging evidence that the visual system does not analyze the input as a unified whole but engages in a strategy of divide and conquer. It has evolved mechanisms that enable visual information to be distributed over specialized subsystems. Even with this strategy, though, there is a benefit to letting systems interact. Color information that partitions a face into components can be supplemented by information derived from contours and shading. Concurrent processing emphasizes the analytic nature of perception devoted to common goals.

With this in mind, we can reconsider the case of the Oregon farmer, P.T. For him, the most distressing symptom was his inability to recognize faces, especially his wife's. But the patient's deficit was not limited to face perception. He had difficulty discriminating among his cows and identifying the landscape around his farm. He demonstrated a puzzling dissociation in which he readily identified the portrait in Picasso's painting while failing to discern the face in Monet's.

We can see how difficult it is to make an unambiguous diagnosis. In his conclusion, the neurologist evaluating P.T. emphasized that the primary problem stemmed from a deficit in color perception. This hypothesis is in accord with one of the primary differences between the Monet and the Picasso. In the Monet painting, the boundaries between the face and the background are blended: Gradual variations in color demarcate the facial regions and separate them from the background landscape. A deficit in color perception provided a parsimonious account of the patient's problems in recognizing faces and landscapes. The rolling green hills of an Oregon farm can blur into a homogeneous mass if one cannot discern fine variations in color. In a similar way, each face has its characteristic coloration.

Yet it seems equally plausible that the problem may have stemmed from a deficit in contrast or contour perception. These features are salient in the Picasso and absent in the Monet. What is clear is that the patient's stroke primarily affected the cortical projections of the P pathways, the pathways essential for color and form perception. In contrast, the cortical projections of the M pathway were intact. The patient did not have any trouble recognizing his wife as she moved from the stove to the kitchen table; indeed, P.T.

commented that her idiosyncratic movement enabled him to recognize her.

Differentiating between a color-based hypothesis and a contour-based one requires more details than were offered at Grand Rounds. It would have been informative to test P.T. on Treisman's visual search tasks to compare his ability to detect features based on color and form differences. Given the neurologist's hypothesis, we would expect the patient to have difficulty when the target is defined by a unique color. For P.T., like other achromatopsia patients, the ability to find a red target among isoluminant green distractors might be similar to what a normal person experiences when searching for a red target among orange distractors. The critical question centers on whether P.T. would demonstrate difficulty with a visual search task that included shape differences such as a tilted line among vertical lines. The analytic tools of cognitive psychology could provide the key to making a much more precise diagnosis of P.T.'s deficits.

DISSOCIATIONS OF CORTICAL AND SUBCORTICAL VISUAL PATHWAYS

We know that the retino-geniculate-cortical tract contains 90% of the fibers in the optic tract, and we know how subdivisions of this pathway provide building blocks for form, color, and motion perception. From these building blocks, we can recognize and identify complex visual scenes.

The importance of this pathway is underscored by the dramatic deficits that develop when this pathway is damaged. While lesions of the LGN are rare, it is not uncommon to come across patients who have had a stroke that encompasses portions of the primary visual cortex. Such lesions are devastating for visual processing. The patients become blind to stimuli falling within the receptive fields of the affected area. This deficit, referred to as a *scotoma,* or field cut, renders patients incapable of detecting an object presented within the scotoma, let alone reporting the object's color or shape (Figure 4.25). When the entire visual cortex is lesioned, the patient is unable to see anything in the contralesional hemifield. When the lesion is more circumscribed, affecting merely a portion of the visual cortex, the scotoma is more limited. For instance, if a lesion is restricted to the lower bank of the calcarine fissure, the scotoma is limited to the upper quadrant of the contralesional hemifield. Correspondingly, a lesion in the upper bank produces a scotoma in the lower visual field on the side opposite the lesion.

Clinicians can easily map the extent of a scotoma. The standard technique, called *perimetry,* involves presenting a small spot of light in various places in the visual field and asking the patient to report whether she can detect the light. When this stimulus falls outside the scotoma, detection is immediate. Within the scotoma, the patient fails to see the stimulus. The patient is, in essence, cortically blind. While rods and cones continue to function in a normal manner, the cells fail to produce any sensation or percept.

The phenomenology of cortical blindness led neurologists to assume that visual processing in humans depends entirely on the geniculo-striate pathway. Anatomists could point out that numerous optic nerve fibers terminate in subcortical structures other than the LGN, but that the function of these pathways was vestigial—they had become dormant. This hypothesis has come into question owing to surprising findings in animal and human research.

"What" and "Where" Processing in the Hamster

Lesion studies in animals provided the first line of evidence. Many nongeniculate fibers terminate in the superior colliculus. This structure plays a critical role in producing eye movements. If this midbrain structure

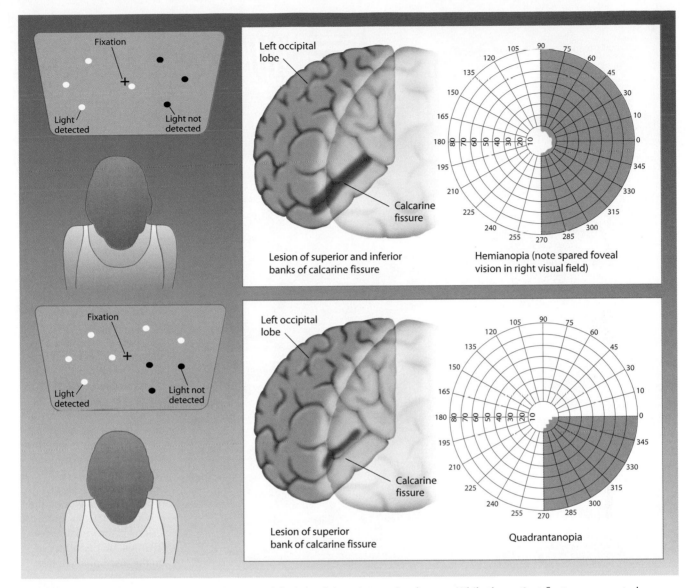

Figure 4.25 Plotting the scotoma in patients with lesions of the primary visual cortex. While the patient fixates on a central marker, a small light is flashed at various locations. The patient is asked to report when she sees the stimulus. If the lesion includes tissue on both the upper and lower banks of the calcarine fissure, the scotoma will include the entire contralesional hemifield. This is referred to as a *hemianopia*. If the lesion is restricted to the upper bank, the patient will have a *quadrantanopia*, referring to the fact that she only misses targets in one quadrant, the lower region of the contralesional hemifield. Although each eye is tested separately, the scotoma will be essentially identical because the lesions are in the cortex.

becomes atrophied, as with supranucleur palsy, the patient will lose the ability to generate eye movements. It is as if the eyes have become paralyzed. Stimulation studies in primates further demonstrate the role of the superior colliculus in eye movement. When this area is stimulated, the eyes move, and their direction depends on the stimulation site.

Gerald Schnieder (1969), working at the Massachusetts Institute of Technology (MIT), provided initial evidence of the importance of the colliculus in studies of

hamsters. These animals were trained to do the two tasks schematized in Figure 4.26. In one task, the hamsters were trained to turn their head in the direction of a sunflower seed held in an experimenter's hand. The task was easy for hamsters since they have a strong propensity to find sunflower seeds and put them in their cheek.

The second task presented more of a challenge. Here, the animals were trained to run down a two-arm maze and to enter the door behind which a sunflower seed was hidden. The task required the animals to make

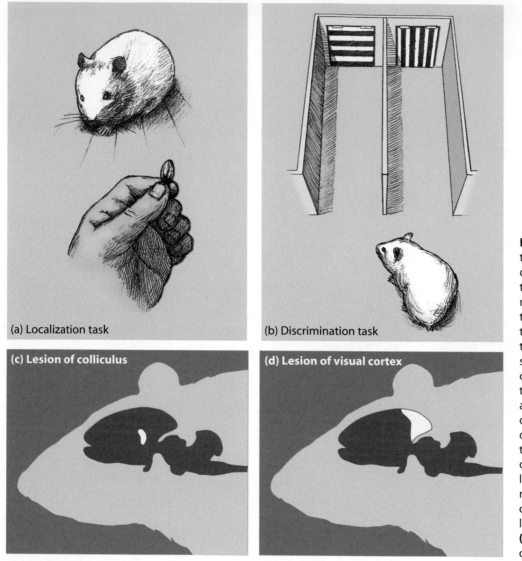

(a) Localization task

(b) Discrimination task

(c) Lesion of colliculus

(d) Lesion of visual cortex

Figure 4.26 Schneider's tests to demonstrate the double dissociation between lesions of the superior colliculus and visual cortex. **(a)** In the localization task, the animals were trained to collect sunflower seeds that were held at various positions in space. **(b)** In the discrimination task, the animals were trained to run down one of two alleys that differed in terms of whether the stripes were horizontal or vertical. Lesions of the colliculus **(c)** selectively disrupted performance on the orientation task. In contrast, lesions of the visual cortex **(d)** impaired performance on the discrimination task.

simple visual discriminations such as distinguish between black and white doors or doors with vertical or horizontal stripes. With normal hamsters, the discriminations are not taxing. Within a few trials, they became proficient in selecting the right door in almost all trials.

After training hamsters for both tasks, Schneider divided them into two experimental groups. One group received bilateral lesions of the visual cortex, including all of areas 17 and 18. For the second group, the superior colliculus was rendered dysfunctional by ablating all input fibers. This strategy was necessary because direct lesions to the colliculus were likely to kill the animals; the structure borders numerous brainstem nuclei essential for life.

The two lesions yielded a double dissociation. Cortical lesions severely impaired the animals' performance on visual discrimination tasks. The animals could run

down the maze and had sufficient motor capabilities to enter one of the doors, but they could not discriminate black from white or horizontal from vertical stripes. In contrast, the animals with functionally collicular lesions demonstrated no impairment.

The deficits were reversed on the sunflower localization task. Animals with cortical lesions were perfect at this task once they had recovered from the surgery. Yet animals with collicular lesions acted as though they were blind. They made no attempt to orient toward the seeds, and not because they were unmotivated or had a motor problem. If the seed brushed against a whisker, the animal rapidly turned in its direction and gobbled it up.

These data provide compelling evidence for dissociable functions of the hamsters' superior colliculus and visual cortex. The collicular lesions damaged their ability to locate a stimulus, while the cortical lesions disrupted visual acuity. For the hamster, one might think of this double dissociation as reflecting two systems: One devoted to "where is it?" problems and the other devoted to "what is it?" problems.

Blindsight: Evidence of Residual Visual Function Following Cortical Blindness

Collicular function in the hamster cannot be directly extrapolated to humans. It might be that when elaborate visual systems evolved in humans, cortical areas subsumed functions that had depended on subcortical areas in our ancestors. But residual visual function has now been documented in patients with cortical blindness.

The best-known case was reported by Lawrence Weiskrantz (1986) of Oxford University. Patient D.B. had experienced severe headaches since early childhood. The headaches became more frequent when he reached his twenties, when he noticed that he could not see anything in his left visual field. Though he could compensate by moving his eyes, he sought medical advice. An angiogram revealed an arteriovenous malformation in the right occipital lobe. After drug therapy proved ineffective, D.B. underwent corrective surgery in 1973, which involved excision of most of the striate cortex in his right hemisphere. As would be expected, the surgery rendered D.B. cortically blind. Perimetry testing 8 months after surgery revealed a scotoma covering almost all of the left visual field.

Inspired by Schneider's findings that cortically blind hamsters could still locate the sunflower seeds, Weiskrantz and his associates initiated experiments to determine whether D.B. could still detect the location of objects within his scotoma. Weiskrantz was not satisfied with the usual method of self-report to test for visual function. Rather, he designed a clever behavioral assay for residual function. After presenting a spot of light, the experimenters sounded a tone; D.B. was asked to move his eyes to the stimulus's location. This task was easy for D.B. when stimuli were presented in his intact right visual field. But when stimuli were presented within the scotoma, the task struck D.B. as utter nonsense. He could not understand how he should know where to move his eyes when he failed to see anything. Nonetheless, the experimenters encouraged D.B. to guess. On control trials, a tone was sounded, requiring D.B. to move his eyes, but it was not preceded by a light. D.B., of course, was not aware of this difference between the control and experimental trials. To him, all of the trials seemed bizarre in that he was being asked to look at stimuli that he had not been aware of (Figure 4.27).

The results could hardly have been more dramatic. As expected, D.B.'s eye movements on the phantom trials were random. But in the experimental trials, D.B. did much better than chance at localizing the stimuli. When the stimuli were within degrees of the fovea, D.B.'s eye movements were highly correlated with the position of the stimuli. Weiskrantz named this paradoxical phenomenon *blindsight*. The patient acts and feels as if he is blind, yet shows a residual ability to localize stimuli.

D.B.'s case is not an insular one. Many patients have residual visual function when tested for blindsight, even though they are unaware of seeing anything. But this phenomenon appears to be the exception and not the rule: Most patients with striate cortex lesions fail to demonstrate any residual function.

Is Blindsight due to Residual Cortical Function?

These results were controversial, and it would be premature to conclude that the blindsight phenomenon reflects processing along the subcortical, collicular pathway. Some researchers have argued that blindsight results from residual cortical function. One possibility is that information can reach extrastriate visual areas in the cortex, either through direct geniculate projections or via nongeniculate cortical pathways. A PET study demonstrated that extrastriate regions such as V5 can be metabolically activated by moving stimuli, even when the ipsilateral striate cortex is completely destroyed (Barbur et al., 1993).

A second possibility is that the lesions in the primary visual cortex are incomplete and that blindsight results from residual function in the spared tissue. Although residual function can be demonstrated in monkeys with complete lesions of the striate cortex, it is also true that many patients who exhibit blindsight have incomplete lesions. While D.B.'s operation removed a large portion of striate cortex, some tissue remained. As D.B. recovered from his surgery, the scotoma shrank, eventually encompassing only the lower quadrant of the left visual field. Moreover, even within this quadrant, D.B. maintained a residual patch in which he reported the presence of a stimulus. Perhaps other tissue within the scotoma was still functional; its output, though, was not enough to convince D.B. that he was truly seeing something. With stroke patients, the possibility of spared tissue is even greater because of the variable nature of the infarction pattern at the most distal points of the posterior cerebral artery.

Robert Fendrich and his colleagues (1992) at the University of California, Davis, maintain that blindsight reflects preserved islands of function within the striate

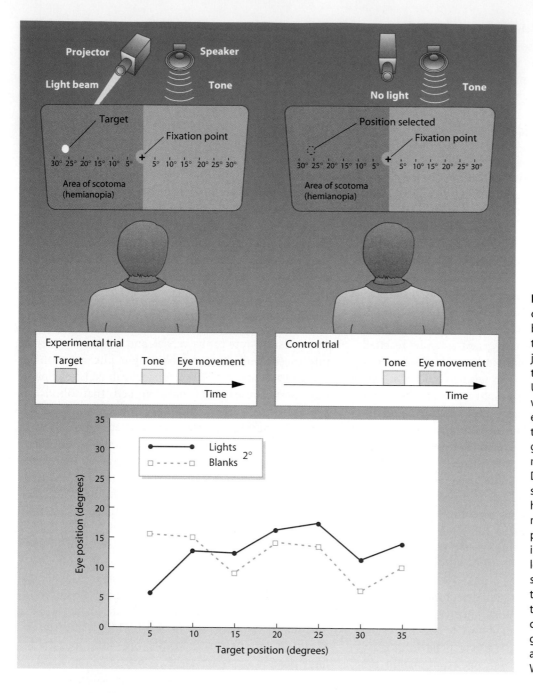

Figure 4.27 Experimental conditions to demonstrate blindsight. In the experimental trials, a light beam is projected at one of seven locations within D.B.'s scotoma. Upon hearing a tone, D.B. was required to move his eyes to the target location. In the control conditions, a target was selected but not illuminated prior to the tone. To D.B., the two conditions seemed identical, and he had to be encouraged to move his eyes since he reported not seeing anything in either condition. Nonetheless, D.B.'s eye movements showed a systematic relationship to the target position in the experimental condition, at least for the targets within 20 degrees of fixation. Adapted from Weiskrantz (1986).

cortex. They tested a patient who, according to standard perimetry, had a complete scotoma of the left visual field outside the foveal region. But when they used sophisticated perimetry in which an image is stabilized on the retina, they discovered certain regions within the scotoma where the patient could reliably report the presence of a stimulus (Figure 4.28). These islands were surrounded by regions where performance was at chance. These researchers argued that with most blind-sight studies, small eye movements could enable a stimulus to move within the islands.

Functions of the Retino-collicular Pathway in Humans

Resolving the debate over the source of blindsight requires more research. It may well turn out that different aspects of the blindsight phenomenon are attributable to different mechanisms. Some hemianopic

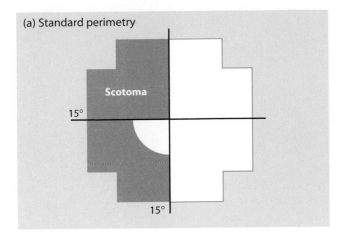

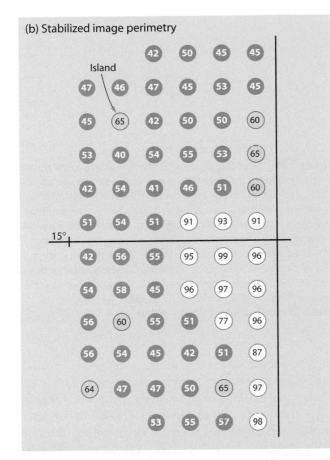

Figure 4.28 Blindsight in some patients may be due to spared "islands" of intact tissue. Standard perimetry indicated that this patient had a complete hemianopia outside the foveal region in the left visual field. However, by using a finer measurement tool, Fendrich and colleagues showed that the patient detected targets at above chance levels when he was presented within small, isolated regions. The numbers in the circles show the percent correct for different locations within the scotoma (chance is 50%). These islands suggest that the lesions in the visual cortex may not be complete.

patients perform better than chance when they are forced to make simple color and form discriminations concerning stimuli presented within their scotoma, and thus outside their awareness. These abilities most likely reflect residual function in striate or extrastriate cortical areas, as the nongeniculate visual pathways are not sensitive to color and have fairly uniform receptive fields.

Nonetheless, an important feature of many blind-sight studies is that patients can localize stimuli they are not aware of. This ability to identify where a stimulus is fits the known functions of the retino-collicular pathway. The superior and inferior colliculus receive input from visual and auditory pathways and use it to develop a representation of where objects are in space and to generate eye movements to attend to these objects. Subcortical visual systems may collaborate with cortical visual systems. As an object is detected on the periphery, the colliculus may help to generate an eye movement that would bring the object into the center of view so the cortical system can analyze and identify it. From this view, we might expect that stimuli falling within the scotoma would activate the collicular orienting system.

In a clever test of this hypothesis, Robert Rafal, also at the University of California, Davis, and colleagues (1990) measured how quickly patients with dense scotomas could look at stimuli presented in their intact visual field. Since the patients were conscious of the stimuli, the task seemed quite reasonable—unlike the traditional blindsight studies. The key manipulation, though, was that simultaneously with the stimulus's presentation, an irrelevant stimulus was presented in the scotoma (Figure 4.29). The patients, of course, did not report seeing it. Nonetheless, the irrelevant stimulus led to a significant boost in reaction time in comparison to a control condition where the irrelevant stimulus did not appear until after the response. Through this implicit measure of interference, then, we see evidence of residual processing within scotomas.

Rafal and colleagues argued that this interference arises because the irrelevant stimulus provides competing activation between the distractor and target in the intact retino-collicular pathway. This competition slows eye movement toward the target. Further evidence that this interference is related to the collicular system comes from a second experiment where subjects were asked to press a button after detecting the target rather than look at the target. Now the competing stimulus had no effect on reaction time. Thus, the interference was present

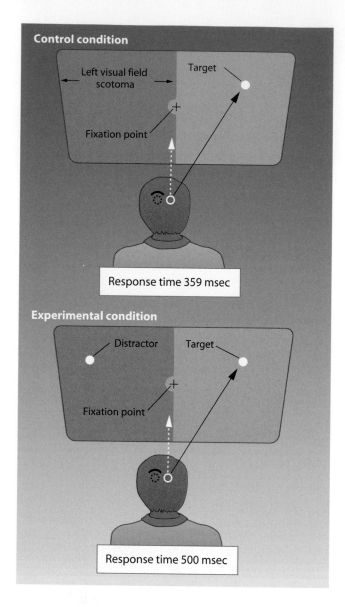

Figure 4.29 Subcortical pathways remain active in the presence of lesions of the primary visual cortex. Hemianopic patients were asked to look at targets in the ipsilesional (intact) hemifield as quickly as possible. In the experimental condition, the onset of the target was preceded by a distractor presented in the scotoma. Despite their lack of awareness of the distractors, the patients were slower to look at the targets in comparison to a control condition in which the distractor was not presented. The slower response times are attributed to competing eye movement signals being generated by the superior colliculus following the onset of the distractor.

only when the response required an eye movement, a result that meshes with the functions of the superior colliculus.

The design of this study admittedly was subtle and complicated. Yet it provided a beautiful example of the fertile interactions that can develop in cognitive neuroscience. Anatomical and physiological studies had implicated the colliculus in a rapid orienting system for preparing eye movements to new stimuli. From these considerations, Rafal and colleagues devised behavioral predictions based on chronometric methodologies. Their study findings do not rule out the possibility that other visual pathways continue to function in the presence of lesions to the primary visual cortex. But the study elegantly showed that, as with Schneider's hamsters, a collicular orienting system remains intact in hemianopic patients.

AUDITORY PERCEPTION

Compared to what we know about visual perception, our knowledge of the functional organization of other sensory systems is sparse. We have a clear understanding of the anatomy of the senses of audition, touch, position, olfaction, and taste. But the physiology and functional analysis of these systems have not been developed with the degree of sophistication applied to vision. In this section we present an organization scheme similar to the one for visual perception.

Overview of the Auditory Pathways

An overview of the auditory pathways is presented in Figure 4.30. The complex structures of the inner ear provide the mechanisms for transforming sounds, or variations in sound pressure, into neural signals. Sound waves arriving at the ear make the eardrum vibrate. These vibrations produce tiny waves within the inner ear's fluid that stimulate tiny *hair cells* located along the surface of the basilar membrane. Analogous to the eye's photoreceptors, hair cells are primary auditory receptors. Oscillations of the basilar membrane prompt hair cells to generate action potentials. In this way, a mechanical signal, the fluid oscillations, is converted to a neural signal—the output from hair cells.

The basilar membrane and hair cells are located within a spiral structure known as the *cochlea*. Even at this early stage of the auditory system, much information about the sound source can be discerned. Hair cells have receptive fields analogous to the retina's ganglion cells. While receptive fields of ganglion cells refer to a coding of locations in space, receptive fields of hair cells refer to a coding of sound frequency. Human auditory sensitivity ranges from a low of about 20 Hz to a high of 20,000 Hz. Hair cells at the thick end, or base of the cochlea are activated by high-frequency sounds; cells at the opposite end, or apex are activated by low-frequency sounds. These receptive fields have extensive overlap. Further, natural sounds like music or speech are made up of complex frequencies; thus, sounds activate a broad range of hair cells.

Important subcortical relays are in the auditory system. The output from the cochlea is projected to two midbrain structures, the cochlear nucleus and the inferior colliculus. From there, information is sent to the medial geniculate nucleus. As with vision, the geniculate nucleus serves as the final relay point to the auditory cortex. Area 41 is considered the primary auditory cortex in humans. Areas 42 and 43 are secondary cortical areas, although they too receive direct projections from the medial geniculate nucleus.

Figure 4.30 An overview of the auditory pathway. The hair cells of the cochlea are the primary receptors. The output from the cochlear nerve projects to the cochlear nuclei in the brainstem. Ascending fibers reach the auditory cortex following synapses in the inferior colliculus and medial geniculate nucleus. Adapted from Bear et al. (1996).

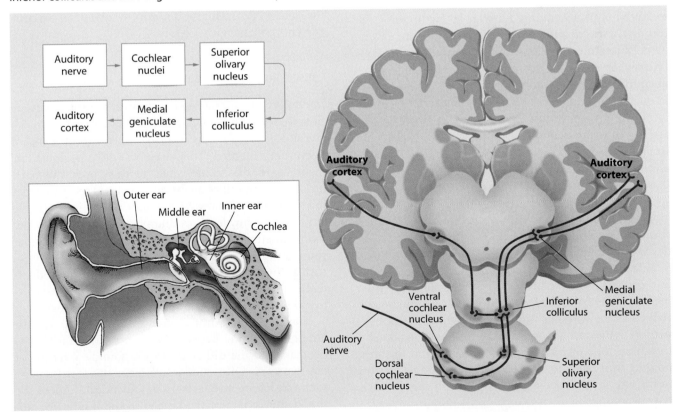

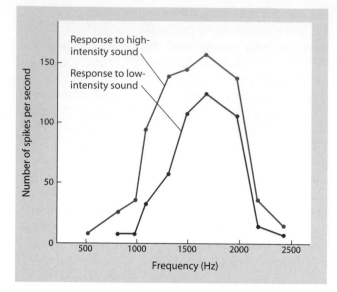

Response to high-intensity sound

Response to low-intensity sound

Figure 4.31 Tuning curves for a cell in the auditory nerve of the squirrel monkey. This cell is maximally sensitive to a sound of 1600 Hz, and the firing rate falls off rapidly for either lower or higher frequency sounds. The cell is also sensitive to intensity differences, although this does not cause a shift in its tuning profile. Other cells in the auditory nerve would be tuned for different frequencies. Adapted from Bear et al. (1996), after Rose et al. (1971).

Neurons throughout the auditory pathway continue to have frequency tuning. As seen in Figure 4.31, the tuning curves for auditory cells can be quite broad; single cells respond to sounds ranging over a couple of octaves, where an octave corresponds to a doubling in frequency. The fact that individual cells do not give precise frequency information but provide *coarse coding* indicates that our perception must depend on the integrated activity of many neurons. Such integration is probably facilitated by *tonotopic maps* found in most auditory areas; within such maps, there is an orderly correspondence between the location of the neurons and their specific frequency tuning. For example, cells in one region of an auditory area will respond to low-frequency stimuli; the cells in another region will respond to middle or high frequencies.

Electrophysiological studies of the cat reveal a second general principle of auditory processing. The tuning specificity of auditory receptive fields becomes more refined as the stimulus proceeds through the system. A neuron in the cochlear nucleus that responds maximally to a pure tone of 5000 Hz may also respond to tones ranging from 2000 to 10,000 Hz. A comparable neuron in the auditory cortex is likely to respond over a much narrower range.

Computational Goals in Audition

Frequency data are essential for deciphering a sound. Sound-producing objects have unique resonant properties that provide a characteristic signature. The same note played on a clarinet and a trumpet will sound different. Though they may share the same base frequency, the resonant properties of each instrument will produce great differences in the note's harmonic structure. In a similar way we produce our range of speech sounds by varying the resonant properties of the vocal tract. Movements of lips, tongue, and jaw change the frequency content of the acoustic stream produced during speech. Frequency variation is essential for a listener to identify words or music.

Auditory perception does not merely identify the content of an acoustic stimulus. A second important function of audition is to localize sounds in space. Consider a bat, which hunts by echo location. The echoes create an auditory image of an object, preferably a tasty moth. But knowing a moth is present will not lead to a successful hunt. The bat also has to determine the moth's precise location. As demonstrated in the comparison of collicular and cortical vision, vision researchers have intensively studied "what" (i.e., object recognition) and "where" (i.e., spatial cognition) problems. In contrast, the cognitive neuroscience of audition has primarily focused on "where" problems. In solving the "where" problem, the auditory system relies on concurrent processing.

Concurrent Processing for Sound Localization

In developing animal models to study auditory perception, we select an animal with well-developed hearing. A favorite species for this work has been the barn owl, a nocturnal creature. They have excellent *scotopia*, or night vision that guides them to their prey. But barn owls must also utilize an exquisitely tuned sense of hearing to locate their prey. Visual information is unreliable at night. The low levels of illumination provided by the moon fluctuate over the lunar cycle; this and stellar sources can be obscured by dense cloud cover. Sound, such as the patter of a mouse scurrying across a field, offers a more reliable stimulus. Indeed, barn owls have little trouble finding prey in a totally dark laboratory.

Barn owls rely on two cues to localize sounds: the difference in time between when a sound reaches the two ears and the difference in the sound's intensity at the two ears. Both cues result from the fact that the sound reaching two ears is not identical. Unless the sound source is directly parallel to the head's orientation, the sound will reach one ear before the other. Moreover, since the intensity of a sound wave becomes attenuated over time, the magnitude of the signal at the two ears will not be identical. The time and intensity differences are quite small in magnitude. For example, if the stimulus is located at a 45-degree angle to the line of sight, the interaural time difference will be approximately 1/10,000th of a second.

The intensity differences resulting from sound attenuation are even smaller—indistinguishable from variations due to noise. These small differences are amplified by a unique asymmetry of owl anatomy, however. The left ear is higher than eye level and points downward, while the right ear is lower than eye level and points upward. Because of this asymmetry, sounds coming from below are louder in the left ear than the right. Humans do not have this asymmetry, but the complex structure of the human outer ear, or *pinna* may amplify the intensity difference between a sound at the two ears.

Interaural time and intensity differences provide independent cues for sound localization. To show this, stimuli are presented over headphones and the owl is trained to turn its head in the sound's perceived direction. The headphones allow the experimenter to manipulate each cue separately. When amplitude is held constant, asynchronies in presentation times prompt the owl to shift its head in the horizontal plane. Variations in amplitude produce vertical head movements. Combining the two cues by way of binaural fusion provides the owl with a complete representation of three-dimensional space. If one ear is plugged, the owl's response indicates that a sound has been detected, but it cannot localize the source.

These two cues are processed by independent neural pathways. The auditory nerve synapses on the cochlear nucleus. Each cochlear nucleus is composed of two parts, the *magnocellular nucleus* and the *angular nucleus* (Figure 4.32). The auditory nerve fibers innervate the cochlear nucleus bifurcate, sending one axonal branch to the magnocellular nucleus and a second branch to the angular nucleus. This parallelism is maintained in the ascending projections to the midbrain lemniscal nuclei. The magnocellular and angular nuclei project to the anterior and posterior regions of the lemniscal nucleus, respectively.

Mark Konishi of the California Institute of Technology provided a well-specified neural model of how the brain codes interaural time and intensity differ-

Figure 4.32 Parallel pathways in the auditory system of the barn owl. The cochlear nucleus is actually composed of two parts, the magnocellular nucleus and the angular nucleus. The magnocellular pathway is specialized to compute interaural time differences, information essential for locating the lateral position of a stimulus. The angular pathway is specialized to compute intensity differences, information essential for locating the distance to a stimulus.

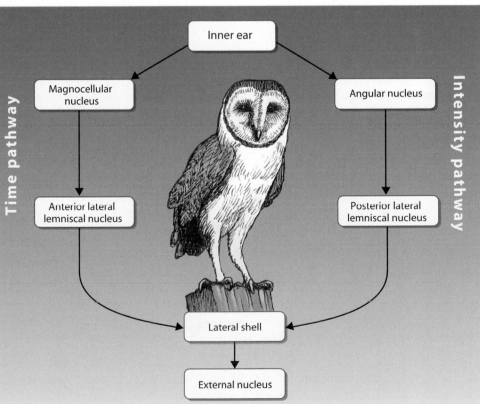

ences (Konishi, 1993). For detecting time differences, Konishi assumed that the first site of convergence from the two ears is in the anterior lemniscal neurons. These neurons operate as coincidence detectors. To activate an anterior lemniscal neuron, it must simultaneously receive an input from each ear. In computer science terms, these neurons act as AND operators. An input from either ear alone or in succession is not sufficient; they will fire only if an input is received at the same time from both ears. Simultaneous activation from a sound source is restricted to only some of these neurons because the magnocellular axons from each half of the brain converge from opposite directions on the coincidence detectors.

Figure 4.33 explains how this model works. In the left half of the figure, the sound source is directly in front of the animal. In this situation, the coincidence detector in the middle is activated because the stimulus is received at each ear at the same time. In the right half of the figure, the sound source is to the animal's right, which gives the magnocellular axon from the right ear a slight head start. Simultaneous activation now occurs in a coincidence detector to the left of center. This simple arrangement provides the owl with a complete representation of the sound source's horizontal position. Physiological studies have confirmed that neurons of the anterior lemniscal nucleus act as coincidence detectors.

A different coding scheme represents interaural intensities. The lemniscal nucleus's posterior region is again the first point of convergence. But the neural code for intensity is based on the input's firing rate. The louder the stimulus, the more action potentials come into play. Neurons in the posterior region use combined signals from both ears to pinpoint the source's vertical position.

Localization is incomplete at the level of the lemniscal nucleus; horizontal and vertical positions must be combined. Outputs from each region of the lemniscal nucleus converge on another brainstem nucleus, the *external nucleus*. Neurons within this nucleus are considered space-specific. They activate only when sound comes from a certain location.

Konishi and his colleagues provided an elegant account of how the barn owl can pinpoint a sound in three-dimensional space. The theory stands as an excellent example of the power of cognitive neuroscience. We know from an owl's behavior that they precisely localize sounds. In vision, neural representation of space is more straightforward. Sensory detectors in the retina provide a topographic map that is maintained throughout the processing system. In audition, though, sensors do not code spatial information. The location of a sound source must be computed by integrating signals received from two ears. Anatomy and physiology led Konishi and colleagues to realize that temporal and intensity information was independently processed. Computational models of co-

Figure 4.33 Slight asymmetries in the arrival times at the two ears can be used to locate the lateral position of a stimulus. **(a)** When the sound source is located directly in front of the owl, the stimulus will reach the two ears at the same time. As activation is transmitted across the delay lines, the coincidence detector representing the central location will be simultaneously activated from both ears. **(b)** When the sound source is located to the right, the sound reaches the right ear first. Now a coincidence detector offset to the opposite side receives simultaneous activation from the two ears. Adapted from Konishi (1993).

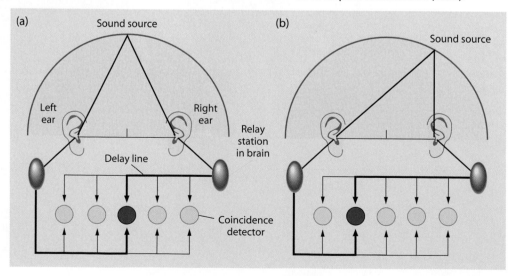

incidence detectors and neural summation then guided their search for the derivation of location information.

In Konishi's model, the barn owl solved the problem of sound localization at the level of the brainstem. To date, this theory has not explained higher stages of processing such as the auditory cortex. Perhaps cortical processing is essential for converting location information into action. The owl does not want to simply attack every sound; it must decide if the sound is generated by a potential prey. Another way of thinking about this is to reconsider the issues surrounding the computational goals of audition. Konishi's brainstem system provides the owl with a way to solve "where" problems but has not addressed the "what" question. The owl may need other auditory processing to discriminate whether a sound is the movement of a mouse or a deer.

SUMMARY

This chapter provided an overview of the organization of the pathways involved in visual and auditory perception. This review is not complete: Not only have we ignored the senses of somatosensation, taste, and smell, but we have also described only briefly the operation of peripheral mechanisms that transduce external information into neural signals.

A point emphasized in this chapter is that specialized mechanisms for solving different computational problems have evolved in the brain. In auditory and visual perception, there is a segregation between systems that focus on determining "where" something is and "what" it is. Moreover, within these two functional domains, the sensory systems apply an analytic strategy. The auditory system exploits two distinct cues contained in the sounds reaching the ears and uses this information to localize the source. With the visual system, specialized mechanisms are devoted to processing different attributes of a complex stimulus.

An account of how sensory information is processed provides only the initial building blocks of a theory of perception. A complete theory must take into account how this information is used: What are the ultimate goals of having sophisticated sensory machinery? To answer this question, we need to know how we recognize the information that reaches our eyes and ears, and how we select which information is relevant. The following chapters tackle these issues.

SUGGESTED READINGS

KONISHI, M. (1993). Listening with two ears. *Sci. Am.* 2681:66–73.

LIVINGSTONE, M., and HUBEL, D. (1988). Segregation of form, color, movement, and depth: Anatomy, physiology, and perception. *Science* 240:740–749.

TREISMAN, A. (1988). Features and objects: The Fourteenth Bartlett Memorial Lecture. *Q. J. Exp. Psychol. A* 40:201–237.

VAN ESSEN, D.C., and DEYOE, E.A. (1995). Concurrent Processing in the Primate Visual Cortex. In M.S. Gazzaniga (Ed.). *The Cognitive Neurosciences* (pp. 383–400). Cambridge, MA: MIT Press.

WEISKRANTZ, L. (1986). *Blindsight.* Oxford, UK: Clarendon Press.

ZEKI, S. (1993). *A Vision of the Brain.* Oxford, UK: Blackwell Scientific.

5

Higher Perceptual Functions

With analytic perception, visual and auditory systems use a "divide and conquer" strategy. Features like color, shape, and motion are processed along distinct neural pathways. But perception requires more than simply perceiving the features of objects. When looking at a bed of flowers, we do not have the impression of blurs of red, blue, yellow, and green, floating among a sea of petals and stems. We perceive unified objects: red roses, yellow gladiolas, blue pansies, and green stems.

What is more, perceptual capabilities are enormously flexible; perception does not change from one viewing position to another. The garden looks the same whether we view it with both eyes or with only the left or right eye. A change in position may reveal unseen flower beds and hedges, but we still recognize that we are looking at the same garden (Figure 5.1). The percept remains stable even if we stand on our head. The retinal image may be inverted, but we readily attribute this change to our inverted viewing position. We do not see the world as upside-down.

The product of perception is intimately interwoven with memory. Object recognition is more than linking features to form a coherent whole. That whole triggers memories. If the scene is a familiar one, like a garden, we may recognize it as our own or that of a neighbor. Even if we have never seen the garden before, there must be an interplay of perception and memory. Our first view of a garden might remind us of a friend's backyard. Or, the garden may be so unusual that we recognize it as such: a place unlike any other we have ever seen.

This chapter delves into the cognitive neuroscience of object recognition. We consider the problems inherent in a computational system that not only processes sensory information but also links this information to memory. To begin with, we describe a patient who lost the ability to recognize visually presented objects. Surprisingly, this deficit cannot be attributed to any sort of sensory problem. Patient P.T. retained all the fundamental capabilities for identifying shapes and colors. He was able to use this information to navigate through busy city streets, use silverware to feed himself, or copy complex drawings. But these abilities may obscure a severe limitation in P.T.'s use of visual information. He frequently failed to recognize the very objects that he was drawing! Moreover, P.T.'s performance on other visual tasks was not impaired. For example, he had no difficulty recognizing his friends. Paradoxes such as these raise many intriguing questions about how the brain represents and stores knowledge of the world. Are there separate representational systems for different types of information such as objects and faces? Do the sensory modalities have their own memory systems, or do they access a modality-independent knowledge base? At an even more fundamental level, the case of patient P.T. forces us to be precise when we use terms like *perceive* or *recognize*. Perception and recognition do not appear to be unitary phenomena but are manifest in many guises. This problem forms one of the core questions of cognitive neuroscience. Not only will it play a central role in this chapter, but it will also reappear when we turn to problems of attention, memory, and consciousness.

163

Figure 5.1 Our view of the world depends on our vantage point. These two photographs are taken of the same scene, but from two different positions. Each vantage point reveals new views of the scene, including objects that were obscured from the other vantage point. Despite this variability in the stimuli, we readily recognize that the photographs are both of the Manhattan skyline.

AGNOSIA: A CASE STUDY

Failures of perception can happen even when processes such as the analysis of color, shape, and motion are intact. This disorder is referred to as *agnosia*. The label was coined by Sigmund Freud and is derived from the Greek word *gnostic,* meaning "to know." To be agnosic means to experience a failure of knowledge, or recognition. When the disorder is limited to the visual modality, the syndrome is referred to as *visual agnosia.* Patient P.T. had one form of agnosia. He had had a stroke while still in his thirties. Though the stroke was initially life-threatening, he eventually recovered most of his cognitive functions. On examination a few years after the stroke occurred, his sensory abilities were intact. Language function was normal and there were no problems in coordination, yet P.T. had severe problems recognizing objects. When shown household objects such as a candle or a salad bowl, he was unable to name the objects. His deficits were even more marked when he viewed photographs of the objects.

P.T.'s problems did not seem to result from a loss of visual acuity. When presented with two lines, he had no difficulty judging which was longer. Indeed, he could describe the color and general shape of stimuli without hesitation. The candle was described as elongated, the salad bowl as curved. His deficit also did not reflect an inability to retrieve verbal labels of objects, as was demonstrated in two ways: First, if the experimenter asked P.T. the name of a round, wooden object in which lettuce, tomatoes, and cucumbers are mixed, he would respond "salad bowl"; second, P.T. could identify objects by using other senses such as touch or smell. When presented with a candle, he reported that it was a "long object." Upon touching it, he labeled it a crayon, but corrected himself after smelling it and came up with the correct answer of "candle." Thus, P.T.'s deficit was modality-specific. His agnosia was limited to the visual mode.

As with many neuropsychological labels, the term *visual agnosia* has been applied to a number of distinct disorders. As we see in this chapter, by focusing on these subtypes of agnosia, cognitive neuroscientists have been able to develop detailed models of the processes involved in object recognition. In some patients, the problem is one of developing a coherent percept; in others, the agnosia reflects an inability to access conceptual knowledge of perceived objects and using this knowledge to identify the object. P.T.'s problem seems to be more closely related to this latter type of agnosia. However, despite his relatively uniform difficulty in identifying visually presented objects, other aspects of his performance indicated that in some situations, this knowledge was being accessed.

Consider what happened when P.T. was shown a picture of a combination lock. At first, he failed to respond. He then noted the round shape but did not describe any of the details of the lock's face. When prompted by experimenters to make a guess, P.T. reported that the picture was of a telephone. Indeed, he remained adamant, insisting that the picture was of a telephone, even after the experimenter emphatically informed him that the picture did not contain a telephone. P.T.'s choice of a telephone was not random. He had perceived the numeric markings around the lock's circumference, and this was enough to make him believe that it was a telephone.

P.T.'s actions also indicated that his knowledge of the stimulus went beyond his erroneous report of a telephone. While viewing the picture, he kept twirling his fingers, pantomiming the actions one would make when opening a combination lock (Figure 5.2). When asked about this, P.T. reported that it was a nervous habit, something to do to keep his hands busy so he would not reach out and touch the picture. Finally, the experimenter asked P.T. if the picture was of a "telephone, lock, or radio." By this time, P.T. was convinced from the experimenter's responses that the picture was not of a telephone. After a moment's hesitation, he responded "clock." And then, after a look at his fingers, he proudly announced, "It's a lock, a combination lock." Truly a case where he had let his fingers do the talking!

A similar thing happened when he saw a picture of a clarinet. Partial retrieval was evident by his initial report that the picture was of a "flute." But again his actions indicated otherwise. Rather than adopt the posture for playing a flute, P.T. configured his hands as if he were playing a clarinet. When told that "flute" was incorrect, P.T. quickly changed his response to "clarinet." We return to this interesting dissociation of awareness and indirect measures of processing in later chapters; for now we focus on the role of the cortex in making sense of the visible world.

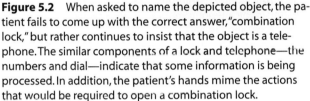

Figure 5.2 When asked to name the depicted object, the patient fails to come up with the correct answer, "combination lock," but rather continues to insist that the object is a telephone. The similar components of a lock and telephone—the numbers and dial—indicate that some information is being processed. In addition, the patient's hands mime the actions that would be required to open a combination lock.

CORTICAL PATHWAYS FOR HIGHER-LEVEL PROCESSING: THE "WHAT" AND "WHERE" SYSTEMS

The pathways carrying visual information from the retina to the first few synapses in the cortex provided a clear segregation into multiple processing streams. Early on there was the partitioning into magnocellular and parvocellular pathways, followed by their differential projection to blob and interblob zones in the primary visual cortex. But once past the initial cortical regions, convergence and divergence become the anatomical rules (see Figure 4.10). Higher-level areas such as the motion-processing center, MT, and color area, V4, receive inputs from many visual areas, and correspondingly send outputs to diverse regions. This complex wiring diagram presents a daunting challenge to theorists interested in functional organizational principles of visual perception. One hypothesis, though, is inspired by the fact that the output from the occipital lobe is primarily contained in two major fiber bundles, or *fasciculi*. As shown in Figure 5.3, the inferior longitudinal fasciculus follows a ventral route into the temporal lobe. The superior longitudinal fasciculus takes a more dorsal path, with most of its terminations in the posterior regions of the parietal lobe.

Two researchers at the National Institutes of Health in Washington, D.C., Leslie Ungerleider and Mortimer Mishkin (1982), proposed that processing along these two pathways is designed to extract fundamentally different types of information. The ventral or occipito-temporal pathway is specialized for object perception and recognition, for determining what it is we are looking at. The dorsal or occipito-parietal pathway is specialized for spatial perception, for determining where an object is, and for analyzing the spatial configuration between different objects in a scene. "What?" and "Where?" are the two basic questions to be answered in visual perception. Not only must we recognize what we are looking at, but

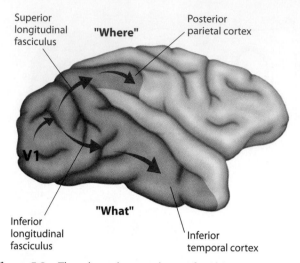

Superior longitudinal fasciculus

"Where"

Posterior parietal cortex

V1

Inferior longitudinal fasciculus

"What"

Inferior temporal cortex

Figure 5.3 The what-where pathways for object recognition. The outputs from the primary visual cortex (V1) follow two general pathways. The superior longitudinal fasciculus includes axons terminating in the posterior parietal cortex, a region associated with identifying the location of the object (where). The inferior longitudinal fasciculus contains axons terminating in the inferior temporal cortex, a region implicated in object recognition (what).

also we need to know where it is in order to respond appropriately.

Physiological Support for the What-Where Distinction

The physiological properties of neurons within the temporal and parietal lobes are quite distinct. Neurons in both lobes have large receptive fields. An interesting property of parietal neurons is that they may respond in a nonselective way (Robinson et al., 1978). For example, a parietal neuron, recorded in an awake monkey, might be activated when a stimulus such as a spot of light is restricted to a small region of space or when the stimulus is a large object that encompasses much of the hemifield (Figure 5.4). Moreover, many parietal neurons are responsive to stimuli presented in the more eccentric parts of the visual field. While 40% of these neurons have receptive fields near the central region of vision, the fovea, the remaining cells have receptive fields that exclude the foveal region.

These eccentrically tuned cells are ideally suited for detecting the presence of a stimulus, especially one that has just entered the field of view. Remember that in examining subcortical vision, we suggested a similar role for the superior colliculus. Chapter 6 reviews the important role of these two structures in visual attention.

The response of neurons in the temporal lobe is quite different (Ito et al., 1995). The receptive fields for these neurons always encompass the fovea, and the majority of these neurons can be activated by a stimulus that falls within either the left or the right visual field. The disproportionate representation of central vision appears to be ideal for a system devoted to object recognition. We usually look directly at things we wish to identify, thereby taking advantage of the greater acuity of foveal vision.

Cells within the visual areas of the temporal lobe have a diverse pattern of selectivity. Robert Desimone (1991), also working at the National Institutes of Health, studied these cells in detail. In one study, a wide range of stimuli were employed. Some stimuli were simple, involving edges or bars at orientations that varied in color or brightness. Others were complex and included

Figure 5.4 Single-cell recordings from a neuron in the posterior parietal cortex of the monkey. The receptive field of the cell was centered in the lower quadrant of the left visual field. While fixating, the animal was presented with either a large or a small stimulus. The cell responds to both stimuli, although the magnitude of activity is correlated with the size of the stimulus.

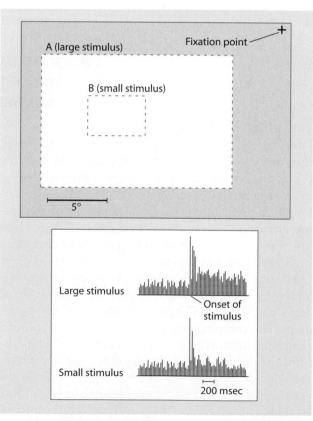

A (large stimulus)

Fixation point

B (small stimulus)

5°

Large stimulus

Onset of stimulus

Small stimulus

200 msec

photographs and three-dimensional models of objects like a human head, hand, apple, flower, and snake. Of the 151 cells sampled, 110 consistently responded to at least one of the stimuli. A large minority of these (41%) were similar to parietal neurons: They were activated by any of the stimuli, and their firing rates were similar across the set of stimuli. The remaining 59% of the cells exhibited some selectivity and responded more vigorously when presented with the complex stimuli.

An example of such a cell, located in the inferior temporal cortex, is given in Figure 5.5. This cell is most highly activated by a model of the human hand. The top row shows the response of the cell to views of a hand. Activity is high regardless of the hand's orientation and is only slightly reduced when the hand is considerably smaller. The last panel in this row shows that the response diminishes if the same shape lacks defining fingers.

Cells in the parvocellular layer of the striate cortex are highly responsive to edges with a specific orientation. From the top row in Figure 5.5, you might wonder if this inferior temporal cell is behaving similarly, preferring vertically aligned edges. But the response of the cell to other stimuli argues against this hypothesis. First, nonhand stimuli with multiple vertical lines (akin to the fingers) failed to activate the cell. Second, the cell also responds to a hand rotated 90 degrees.

It is tempting to conclude that this cell signals the presence of a hand, independent of its size or orientation. Other cells in the inferior temporal area respond preferentially to complex stimuli such as jagged contours or fuzzy textures. The latter might be useful for a monkey, to identify that an object has a fur-covered surface, perhaps the backside of another member of its group. Even more intriguing has been the discovery of cells in the inferior temporal gyrus and the floor of the superior temporal sulcus that are selectively activated by faces. The questions before us now, though, are inspired by neurophysiologists' explorations of the inferior temporal cortex: How specific is the responsiveness of individual cells, and does recognition depend on the specificity of a few neurons or the aggregate behavior of large groups of them?

Grandmother Cells and Ensemble Coding

The finding that cells selectively respond to complex stimuli agrees with hierarchical theories of object perception. According to these theories, cells in the cortical areas code elementary features such as line orientation and color. The outputs from these cells are then combined by detectors sensitive to higher-order features such as corners or intersections, an idea consistent with the findings of Hubel and Wiesel (see Pioneers in the Visual Cortex, in Chapter 4). The process is continued as

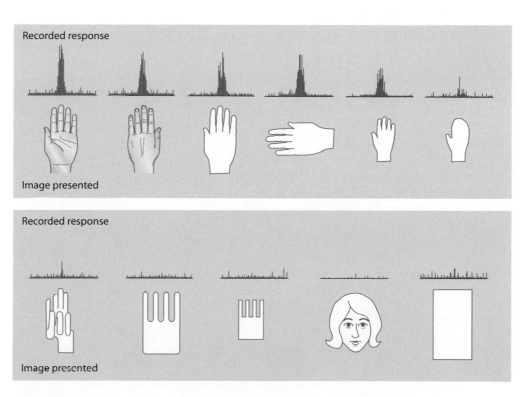

Figure 5.5 Single-cell recordings from a neuron in the inferior temporal cortex. These cells rarely respond to simple stimuli such as lines or spots of light. Rather, they respond to more complex objects such as the hand drawings shown in the top row. Note that the cell shows only a weak response to the mitten, indicating that its activity is not associated with the general shape of a hand. Moreover, this cell does not respond to the comblike objects that contain the series of parallel lines as in the hand stimuli. Adapted from Desimone et al. (1994).

Recorded response

Image presented

Recorded response

Image presented

each successive stage codes more complex combinations (Figure 5.6). At the top of the chain are inferior temporal neurons, selective for complex shapes like hands or faces. This type of neuron has been called a *gnostic unit,* which refers to cells that code for the presence of stimuli that an animal might encounter in the world. In a tongue-in-cheek manner, the term *grandmother cell* has been coined to refer to the notion that there might be gnostic cells that become excited only when one's grandmother comes into view. Other gnostic cells would be specialized to recognize grandpa, or a blue Volkswagen, or the Golden Gate Bridge.

The grandmother cell hypothesis presents three troubling problems. First, the theory requires numerous gnostic units, each coding a certain object in the world. Not only would we need to have grandmother cells that are activated when granny is in view, but we would require additional cells that enable us to recognize all the other people we know. Moreover, each person or object would require many gnostic units, as we recognize people and objects from many vantage points, even though the visible features can change dramatically. When we consider how many objects we can recognize, this idea

becomes suspect. Second, the idea of grandmother cells rests on the assumption that the final percepts of an object are driven by a single cell. Since cells are in a constant state of spontaneous firing and refractoriness, a coding scheme of this nature would be highly susceptible to error. If a gnostic unit were to die, we would expect to experience a sudden loss for an object. Third, the grandmother cell hypothesis cannot adequately account for the fact that we perceive novel objects, a perception whose mechanism is unexplained.

One alternative to the grandmother cell hypothesis is to regard object recognition as resulting from activation across complex feature detectors (Figure 5.7). Granny, then, is perceived when higher-order neurons are activated; some respond to her shape, others to the color of her hair, and still others to the markings on her face. With this population, or *ensemble hypothesis,* recognition is not due to one unit but to collective activation. Ensemble theories readily account for why we can confuse one visually similar object with another; both objects activate many of the same neurons. Losing some units might degrade our ability to recognize an object, but the remaining units might suffice. Ensemble theories also account

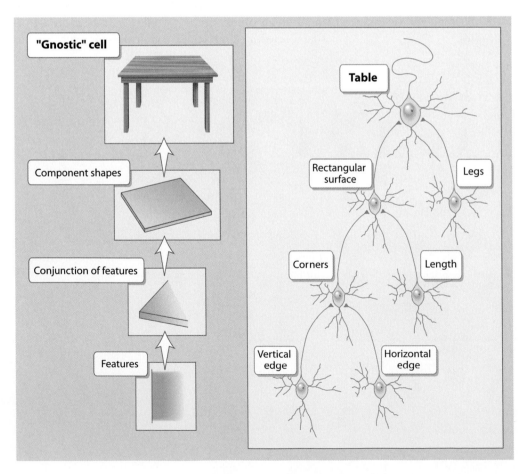

Figure 5.6 Hierarchical coding hypothesis in which elementary features are combined to create gnostic units that recognize complex objects. At the lowest level of the hierarchy are edge detectors, units that operate similar to the simple cells discussed in Pioneer in the Visual Cortex in Chapter 4. These feature units combine to form corner detectors which in turn are combined to create cells that respond to even more complex stimuli such as surfaces. The left side of the figure shows the hypothesized computational stages for hierarchical coding; the right side is a neural implementation based on the idea of grandmother cells.

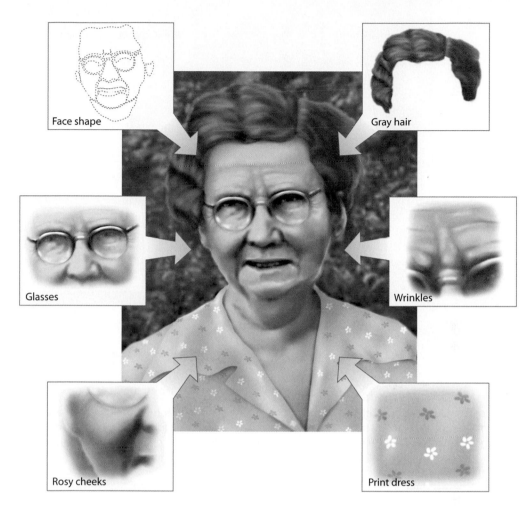

Figure 5.7 Ensemble coding hypothesis in which an object is defined by the simultaneous activation of a set of defining properties. "Granny" is recognized here by the co-occurrence of her glasses, facial shape, hair color and style and so on.

for our ability to recognize novel objects. Such objects bear a similarity to familiar things, and our percept results from activating units that represent their features.

The results of single-cell studies of temporal lobe neurons are in accord with ensemble theories of object recognition. While it is striking that some cells are selective for complex objects, the selectivity is almost always relative, not absolute. The cells in the inferior temporal cortex prefer certain stimuli over others, but they are also activated by visually similar stimuli. The cell in Figure 5.5, for instance, increases its activity when presented with a mitten-like stimulus. No cells respond to an individual's hand; the hand-selective cell responds equally to just about any hand. In contrast, our perceptual abilities demonstrate that we make much finer discriminations.

Functional Dissociations in Animal Research

Simple discrimination learning tasks have been used in primate research to demonstrate functional dissocia-

tions of the ventral and dorsal processing pathways. Walter Pohl (1973) of the University of Wisconsin trained rhesus monkeys to do two spatial learning tasks. The landmark discrimination task, the first of Pohl's tasks, was to retrieve food from two food wells, recessed into a tabletop. In this task, shown in Figure 5.8, the well located near a small red cylinder was always baited and the other was empty. The position of the cylinder was randomized: Sometimes it was next to the well on the right and sometimes next to the well on the left. Each day the animals were given thirty trials, a simple task for humans but difficult for other primates. The animals had a strong tendency to probe the well that contained the reward in preceding trials. Control monkeys averaged 150 errors over successive sessions before reaching a criterion of twenty-eight out of thirty correct responses.

Once the discrimination had been learned well enough to meet the criterion, the reward was reversed: The food was placed in the well farthest from the cylinder. Learning would then contain this new contingency until the animals reached criterion, at which point the

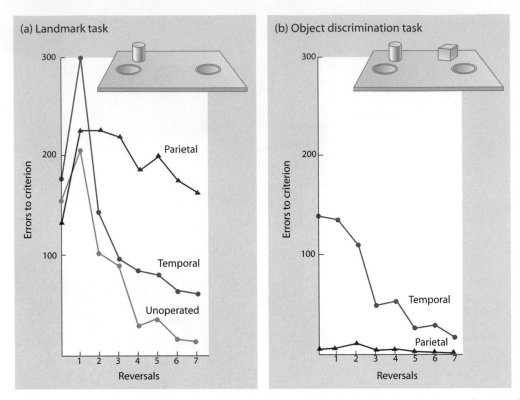

Figure 5.8 Double dissociation in support of the what-where dichotomy. **(a)** In the landmark task, the monkey initially finds a reward in the food well closest to the cylinder. Once this association is learned, the rule is reversed so that now the food is always placed in the well farthest from the cylinder. While all the animals have difficulty following the first few reversals, the control animals as well as those with bilateral temporal lobe lesions show significant improvements with subsequent reversals. Animals with bilateral parietal lobe lesions fail to improve. **(b)** In the object discrimination task, the location of the food is associated with one of the objects. Now the animals with temporal lobe damage show more impairment than those with parietal lobe lesions. Adapted from Pohl (1973).

contingency would reverse again. The experiment continued until the animal successfully completed seven reversals.

The second task, the object-discrimination task, was quite similar, with one critical difference. Rather than have a single object near one of the food wells, the displays now contained two objects, a cylinder and a cube. Each object was located near a food well, and the left-right position of the objects was randomly varied from trial to trial. Working with different animals, training began with the well near the cylinder being baited. After the animal reached criterion, the contingency was reversed. Thus, if the cube is not taken into consideration, the animals' training is essentially identical in the two tasks: First, they must learn to respond to the food well closest to the cylinder and then they must learn to respond to the food well farthest from the cylinder.

Despite such similarities, Pohl found a double dissociation between the effects of temporal lobe and parietal lobe lesions. Bilateral lesions of the parietal lobe selectively disrupted performance on the landmark discrimination task. The animals learned the initial contingency,

but failed to improve with each reversal. In contrast, monkeys with bilateral lesions of the temporal lobes demonstrated impairment on the object-discrimination task. They were slow to learn the initial contingency and took more trials than did the animals with parietal lobe lesions to switch once the contingency was reversed.

In Ungerleider and Mishkin's terminology, the temporal lobe lesions disrupted the "what" pathway. These animals had great difficulty discriminating between the cylinder and the cube. Recognizing "what" the object is, though, is not needed in the landmark discrimination task. Here the task depends on a "where" computation. The animal needs only to perceive the single object's position in the display and to respond on the basis of its position relative to the food wells. Animals with parietal lobe lesions could not learn the relative position contingencies: The "where" pathway was malfunctioning.

Subsequent lesion work confirmed the what-where dissociation between ventral and dorsal pathways. This research also showed that, at least for the ventral pathway, object discrimination deficits are restricted to the visual modality. Moreover, lesion studies indicated a dissociation between posterior and anterior regions of the temporal lobe. Whereas damage to the posterior region disrupts performance on visual discrimination tasks, damage to the anterior region impairs visual memory.

Bear in mind that deficits in these experiments are apparent only in the presence of bilateral lesions, especially ones in the temporal lobe. One explanation is that while information is segregated within each hemisphere, the monkeys scan the entire visual field; thus, stimuli fall within the left and right visual fields. Alternatively, cells in the temporal cortex can respond to stimuli in either visual field when it is near the fovea. Bilateral responsiveness happens because visual areas in the temporal lobe are innervated by ipsilateral projections from occipital areas such as V2 and V4, and by callosal projections from the contralateral hemisphere.

Experiments with combination lesions provided convincing evidence that the "what" pathway involves bilateral inputs. For example, animals were tested with an object-discrimination task after lesions were created in the right striate cortex and left inferior temporal cortex. The striate lesions rendered the animals cortically blind to any stimuli falling within the left visual field. Thus, the pathway providing intrahemispheric input to the right temporal lobe was silenced. With a lesioned left temporal lobe, these animals are deprived of all temporal lobe function if all the connections are intrahemispheric. But this combination lesion produced little or no deficit in performance. When the callosal fibers were cut, though, the animals' performance immediately fell to chance (Figure 5.9). After combined right striate–left temporal lobe lesions were made, the

Figure 5.9 Combination lesion studies indicate that connections over the corpus callosum are more important for transmitting information related to "what" processing. **(a)** Monkeys were given a primary visual cortex lesion on one side and a temporal lobe lesion on the other side. If each hemisphere only received input from the ipsilateral visual cortex, then the animal should demonstrate severe impairment on the object discrimination task since the intact temporal lobe would be deprived of all input. However, animals with this combination of lesions showed little deficit. Further evidence of the importance of callosal fibers for interhemispheric "what" processing is given by the fact that cutting the corpus callosum in these animals severely disrupts performance. **(b)** A combined parietal lobe and visual cortex lesion led to a severe deficit on the landmark task, suggesting that "where" processing is primarily intrahemispheric. Adapted from Ungerleider and Mishkin (1982).

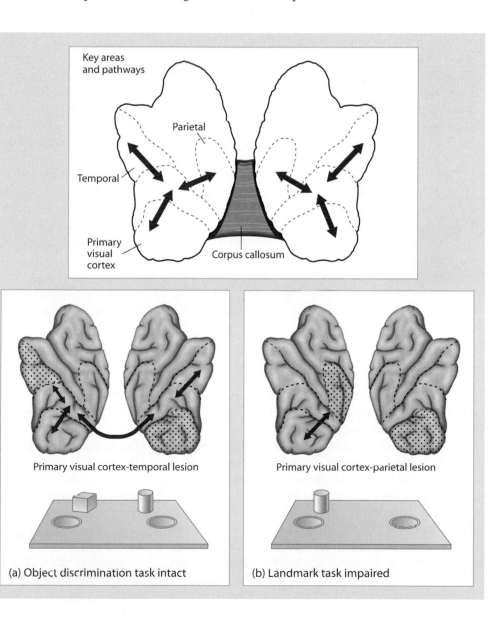

Key areas and pathways

Parietal

Temporal

Primary visual cortex

Corpus callosum

Primary visual cortex-temporal lesion

Primary visual cortex-parietal lesion

(a) Object discrimination task intact

(b) Landmark task impaired

An Interview with Horace Barlow, Ph.D. Dr. Barlow is affiliated with the Department of Physiology at Cambridge University. While neurophysiology has made great inroads in describing the activity of single cells, Dr. Barlow's theoretical discussions of "grandmother" cells have ensured that researchers in this field keep in mind the larger-scale problems faced by a system seeking to recognize objects.

Authors: Do you still believe in the grandmother cell?

HB: I don't believe in grandmother cells and never have, but there are several important associated ideas. I think grandmother cells are the elements of a mutually exclusive representation—a representation in which only a single element is active at any one time—of the whole sensory input. One good reason for not believing in them is the one usually advanced, namely, that you would require an impossibly large number of such elements. Another equally good reason is that it doesn't achieve the kind of representation one needs, namely, classifying similar things together: In a mutually exclusive representation you need a separate grandmother cell for each view of grandmother, for example.

Now, for some of the good ideas lurking behind grandmother cells, consider the softer idea, that of mother cells. These respond to any view of mother, and only to views of mother. Thus, they *generalize* in the appropriate way and are *selective* in the appropriate way; furthermore, mothers are behaviorally important not only for humans but also for our ancient ancestors. It makes sense to have cells that respond to all views of behaviorally important objects, and only to views of these objects.

I still think gnostic cells and their implied sparse representations are good ideas. *Gnostic cells* are representational elements that are infrequently active so they carry a lot of information when they do fire. Their firing corresponds to a complex feature or event in the sensory input. Thus a whole scene can be represented by a small number of them, and they can classify or categorize parts of the scene in sensible ways. Such cells might account for the "unreasonable effectiveness" or real perceptual mechanisms, compared with standard machine vision mechanisms.

Finally the idea of grandmother cells emphasized that individual neurons are the brain's computational elements. They are the only things we know of that can do the logical operations required for survival in a complex environment. The network can connect them to each other, but it is the elements themselves that must make the logical decisions underlying our behavior.

So although I don't believe in grandmother cells, I think we owe a lot to them.

Authors: Surely the neuron doctrine—that each neuronal element has an all-or-none character to its discharge—is not threatened by the idea that whole neuronal networks are the fundamental building

---

intact right temporal lobe processed information received from the contralateral right striate cortex. This input was blocked after the callosal resection.

Combination lesions of the dorsal pathway revealed a slightly different situation. Unilateral parietal lobe lesions produced only mild deficits in the landmark reversal task. When these lesions were followed by a second lesion in the contralateral striate cortex, performance was greatly disrupted. The animals relearned the task but needed extensive training. Sectioning the corpus callosum disrupted performance again, yet the deficit was not as marked as after striate lesions were made. Thus, while callosal fibers are essential for discriminating objects in

the setting of opposite-side striate and temporal lobe lesions, these fibers are less important in transmitting location information from the contralateral hemisphere—results that agree with physiological studies showing that the majority of parietal lobe neurons have unilateral receptive fields. Processing within the "where" pathway appears to be more segregated within each hemisphere.

Human Research on the What-Where Dichotomy

A positron emission tomography (PET) study investigated whether the what-where dichotomy pertains to normal processing (Haxby et al., 1994). Subjects were

blocks of object perception. Given that an object has a spatial component, a size component, an angular component, a color component, and so on, is it not mandated that a whole network is essential to its being perceived and acted on?

HB: You generally don't react to the whole of a sensory scene but just a part of it. If it contains mother, or hungry tiger, you have to ascertain that, and only then can you react appropriately. The trouble is that the mother or hungry tiger can occupy any parts of the sensory input, and it is only by detecting the pattern among these widely dispersed parts that you can decide whether either is present or which it is. You have to do some analysis, or computation, on the whole sensory input, and you will certainly need all the network's parts connected to your mother or tiger cells, which might be quite a large part of the whole network.

The tiger or mother cells, and those detecting more primitive features in the hierarchy, collect the information required to make efficient decisions at each level. The connectivity of the network is invaluable in this task, but only because the connections consolidate all the information so a decision can be made. Again, cells are the only elements we know of that can make these decisions. If you think you know other ways of making them, tell me!

Authors: OK, both of these ideas—sparse and coarse coding schemes—have been around for a long time. Lots of smart people have done clever experiments, both in physiology and in perception. Why aren't we any closer to resolving the dilemma now than we were 30 years ago? Or phrased another way, what do you think we need to distinguish the two extremes?

HB: Our perceptual system performs a horrendously difficult and complex task when it gives us knowledge of the world. It all seems so easy—we just look and see a world full of objects that we instantly know a lot about. But doing this implies that our visual system has accumulated extraordinarily deep knowledge of the associative structure of sensory stimuli we have received in the past, and that it continues to do so all the time.

I think the ideas we have been talking about *do* have the potential to explain how all this is done, but they are not like the glorious general laws of physics, which state absolute limits that cannot be broken in just a few words or even shorter mathematical expressions. Ideas such as sparse coding require fleshing out with a lot of detail. We do not know yet what these steps are, but we shall probably soon find out because machines that use images and other data effectively will have to perform analogous tasks.

It's the complexity of the task that has held things up, and although I would not be a bit surprised at new principles emerging over the next few years, I believe the ones we already have will take us quite a distance. The view I'm proposing is that perception performs tasks that are genuinely difficult, in the information-processing sense. When we adequately define these tasks we shall discover that single neurons perform them well, that is, well compared with the whole brain's performance, and well compared with current computer vision methods of doing the same task.

scanned while performing three tasks. For each trial of the object task, three faces were displayed within three squares arranged in the form of a triangle (Figure 5.10). Subjects pressed one of two keys to indicate whether the face in the square at the triangle's apex matched the face on the left or right. For the spatial localization task, the top square contained a dot and two lines. The lower two boxes also had a dot and two lines, but the figures were rotated so the dot and lines in one box had the same relative positions or had reversed ones. A control task presented three empty boxes to subjects who simply responded by alternating between the two keys.

Activation during the two tasks was subtracted from activation during the control task. Both tasks heightened activity in the occipital regions. More importantly, significant areas of activation during the face-matching task included regions within the inferior and medial temporal cortex. The line-dot matching task led to activation within the parietal cortex. Activation foci within the face task were in the left hemisphere; the line-dot foci were predominantly in the right hemisphere. It is unclear whether the laterality effects reflect asymmetries in perceptual processing or differences in the tasks' recognition demands.

Patient studies offer even more support for a dissociation of what-where processing, although there are discrepancies between humans and primates. The parietal

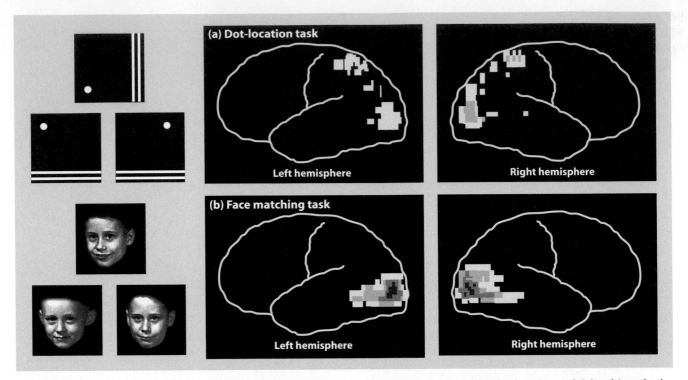

Figure 5.10 PET study to verify that the what-where dichotomy also applies to humans. In the dot-location task **(a)**, subjects had to judge which of the two lower figures was a rotated version of the upper figure. In the face-matching task **(b)**, subjects had to judge which faces were of the same individual. Compared to the control condition, activation in the dot-location task was dorsal to that observed in the face-matching task. Adapted from Haxby et al. (1994).

cortex is central to spatial attention. Lesions of this lobe can produce severe disturbances in representing the world's spatial layout and the spatial relations of objects in it. Lesions associated with agnosia do not have a clear pattern that maps onto animal results. The lesions often fall along the ventral pathway, especially in patients with impaired face perception, or prosopagnosia, but they frequently extend into parietal structures. Unlike examples from animal research, patients with severe deficits in object recognition can have unilateral lesions of either the right or the left hemisphere.

More revealing have been functional dissociations in the performance of patients with agnosia. Goodale and Milner (1992) at the University of Western Ontario described a 34-year-old patient, D.F., who suffered carbon monoxide intoxication due to a leaky propane gas heater. Although D.F.'s computed tomography (CT) scans appeared normal, magnetic resonance imaging (MRI) revealed bilateral lesions in the occipital lobes. D.F. had a severe disorder of object recognition. When asked to name household items, she made errors such as labeling a cup an ashtray or a fork a knife. She usually gave crude descriptions of a displayed object; for example, a screw-

driver was "long, black, and thin." Picture recognition was even more disrupted. When shown drawings of common objects, she could not identify a single one. Her deficit could not be attributed to *anomia*, a problem with names to objects; whenever an object was placed in her hand, she identified it. Sensory testing further indicated that D.F.'s agnosia could not be attributed to a loss of visual acuity. She could detect small gray targets displayed against a black background. While her ability to discriminate small differences in hue was abnormal, she correctly identified primary colors.

Most relevant to our concerns is the dissociation of her performance on two tasks designed to assess her ability to perceive the orientation of a three-dimensional object. For these tasks, D.F. was asked to view a circular block into which a slot had been cut. The orientation of the slot could be varied by rotating the block. In the recognition task, D.F. was given a card and asked to orient her hand so the card would fit into the slot. As can be seen in Figure 5.11, she failed miserably, orienting the card vertically even when the slot was horizontal. When asked to insert the card into the slot, D.F. quickly reached forward and inserted the card. Her performance on this visuomo-

(a) Perception condition

(b) Action condition

(c) Memory (recall)

Figure 5.11 A dissociation of perception linked to awareness and perception linked to action. **(a)** When asked to match the orientation of the card to that of the slot, the patient demonstrated severe impairment. **(b)** When instructed to insert the card in the slot, the patient produced the correct action without hesitation. **(c)** The patient also did not show any impairment in the memory condition, verifying that her knowledge of orientation was intact.

tor version did not depend on tactile feedback that would result when the card contacted the slot. She simply oriented her hand prior to touching the block.

D.F.'s performance shows that processing systems make use of different sources of perceptual information. From the first task, it was clear that D.F. could not recognize the orientation of a three-dimensional object. This deficit is indicative of her severe agnosia. Yet when D.F. was asked to insert the card, her performance clearly indicated that she had processed the orientation of the slot. This dissociation suggests that the "what" and "where" systems support different aspects of cognition. The "what" system is essential for determining the identity of an object. If the object is familiar, we will recognize it as such; if novel, we may compare the percept to stored representations of similarly shaped objects. The "where" system appears to be essential for more than determining the location of different objects; it is also critical for guiding interactions with these objects. D.F.'s performance provides another example of how information accessible to action systems can be dissociable from information accessible to knowledge and consciousness.

The opposite dissociation can be found in the clinical literature. Patients with *optic ataxia* can recognize objects yet cannot use visual information to guide their action. When reaching for an object, they fail to move directly toward it but grope about like a person trying to find a light switch in the dark. Their eye movements present a similar loss of spatial knowledge; *saccades,* or directed eye movements may be directed inappropriately and fail to bring the object within the fovea. Such patients have the inverse problem of D.F.'s: They can report the orientation of a visual slot even though they cannot use this information for moving their hand toward the slot. In accord with what we expect based on dorsal-ventral dichotomy, optic ataxia is observed in patients with lesions of the parietal cortex.

In sum, the what-where dichotomy offers a functional account of two computational goals for higher visual processing. This distinction is best viewed as a heuristic one rather than reflecting an absolute distinction. The dorsal and ventral pathways are not isolated from one another but communicate extensively. Processing within the parietal lobe, the termination of the "where" pathway, serves many purposes. We focused here on its guiding of action, and in the next chapter we see that the parietal lobe plays a critical role in selective attention, the enhancement of processing at some locations instead of others. Moreover, spatial information can also be useful for solving "what" problems. For example, depth cues help to segregate a complex scene into its component objects. The remainder of this chapter concentrates on object recognition: how the visual system has an assortment of strategies for perceiving and recognizing the world.

COMPUTATIONAL PROBLEMS
IN OBJECT RECOGNITION

Object perception depends primarily on the analysis of the shape and form of a visual stimulus although nonshape cues such as color, texture, and motion certainly contribute to normal perception. For example, when looking at the surf breaking on the shore, our acuity is not sufficient to see grains of sand; water is essentially amorphous, lacking any definable shape. Yet the surface texture of the sand and the water's edge, and their differences in color, enable us to distinguish between the two regions. The water's motion is important, too. But even if surface features like texture and color are absent or applied inappropriately, recognition is minimally affected: We can readily identify pink elephants, striped apples, and stick figure drawings in Figure 5.12. Here object recognition is derived from a perceptual ability to match an analysis of shape and form.

To account for shape-based recognition, consider two things. The first has to do with shape encoding. How is a shape internally represented? What salient features enable us to recognize differences between a triangle and a square or a monkey and a person? The second centers on how shape is processed when the perceiver's viewing position is rarely constant. We can recognize shapes from an infinity of positions and orientations, and our recognition system is not hampered by scale changes in the retinal image as we move close to or far away from an object.

Variability in Sensory Information

Questions about shape encoding and processing arise because our perceptual capabilities must be maintained in the face of a variable world. *Object constancy* refers to the amazing ability to recognize an object in countless situations. Figure 5.13 shows four drawings of an automobile, each having little in common with respect to sensory information reaching the eye. And yet we have no problem identifying the car in each picture and discerning that all four cars are the same model. Object constancy is thus essential for perception. Imagine how difficult life would be if we could not recognize familiar things or people unless we gazed at them from a specific point of view.

Variability in the visual information emanating from an object arises for several reasons. First, sensory information depends highly on viewing position. Changes in viewpoint not only arise as the perceiver moves about the world; objects also change their orientation. If we command a dog to roll over, our interpretation of the object remains the same despite the change in our perception. The retinal projection of shape, and even the visible components of an object, can change dramatically as the object's and viewer's positions alter. For instance, when a car is viewed from the front, the retinal projection of its width is larger than the projection of its length. Yet our percept does not reflect this distortion. We do not have the impression of a squashed car. Our perceptual system is adept at separating changes caused by shifts in viewpoint from those intrinsic to the objects themselves.

Changes in the illumination of an object introduce a second source of sensory variability (Figure 5.14). The visible parts of an object may differ depending on whether the object is illuminated from above or from the side. Variations in shadowing can also alter the illumination of an object's parts. Because so many visual

Figure 5.12 Despite the irregularities in how these objects are drawn, we have little problem in recognizing them. We may never have seen pink elephants or plaid apples, but our object recognition system can still discern the essential features.

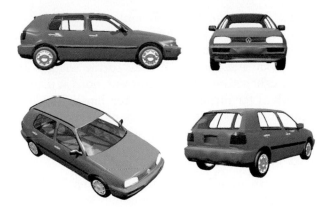

Figure 5.13 The image on the retina is vastly different for these four drawings of a car. Despite this sensory variability, our phenomenology is that we rapidly recognize that the drawings are of the same car.

cells are sensitive to brightness, we might expect them to have an impact on perception, but recognition is mainly insensitive to changes in illumination.

A third source of variability arises because objects are rarely seen in isolation. While cars can be drawn on a blank page, they are usually seen on streets with pedestrians, buildings, and traffic signs—and these other objects frequently occlude part of the car. We have no trouble separating other objects from a car; our perceptual system quickly partitions the scene into components.

While object recognition must overcome these three sources of variability, it must also accommodate the fact that changes in perceived shape can reflect changes in the object. Though we recognize that all the objects in Figure 5.13 are cars, we also detect the differences be-

Figure 5.14 Object constancy must be achieved in spite of the many sources of variation in the sensory input, including shadows (**left**) and occlusion (**right**).

tween them. Not only must object recognition be general enough to support object constancy, but also it must be specific enough to pick out slight differences between members of a category or class.

Object-Centered or Viewer-Centered Recognition?

A central debate in object recognition has to do with defining the frame of reference where recognition occurs (Perrett et al., 1994). Two general approaches have been proposed. In viewer-centered theories, perception is assumed to depend on recognizing an object from a certain viewpoint. According to this theory, perception proceeds from analyzing a viewpoint's information (Figure 5.15). When a bicycle is viewed from the side, we may recognize it by the shape of its frame, wheels, and seat. We may also recognize a bicycle when viewed from an aerial perspective, even though this vantage point obscures the wheels. Perhaps from this orientation the

Figure 5.15 Viewer-centered theories of object recognition posit that recognition processes are dependent on the vantage point. Recognizing that these drawings depict bicycles, one from a side view and the other from an aerial view, requires matching the distinct sensory inputs to view-dependent templates. For the side view, we may include the features of the seat, chain, and spokes to match the drawing with a stored template of a bicycle. For the aerial view, the template match would have to rely on the axis, seat, handlebars and pedals.

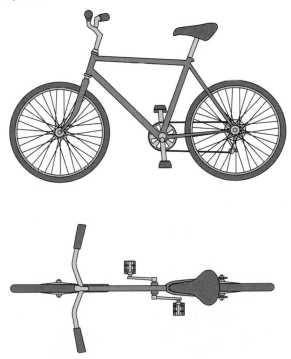

handlebars and elongated shape provide the defining components. Viewer-centered theories posit that we have a cornucopia of templates in memory and recognition; we simply need to match a stimulus to a stored template. The key idea is that the template for recognizing a bicycle from the side is different from the template for recognizing a bicycle from above. Hence, our ability to recognize that two stimuli are depicting the same object is assumed to arise at a later stage of processing.

One shortcoming of viewer-centered theories, one that we encountered when we discussed grandmother cells, is that they require an extremely large memory of templates. We would need to store memories of all the objects we recognize. More troubling, the perception of objects across a broad range of vantage points requires multiple templates of each object.

A more efficient scheme is to posit that recognition occurs in an object-centered frame of reference. With this approach, recognition does not happen by simply analyzing the stimulus information. Rather, sensory input defines basic properties; the object's other properties are defined with respect to these properties. David Marr of MIT, in his book titled *Vision* (1992), articulated a comprehensive and influential theory of recognition based on object-centered representations. In Marr's theory, a critical property for recognition is establishing the major and minor axes inherent to the object. The major axis of a bicycle runs along its length. The handlebars can be represented as two appendages arranged perpendicularly to the primary axis. These properties will generally hold across different vantage points. It is true that if viewed head on, the minor axis produces a larger retinal image than the foreshortened major axis. But Marr would consider this a degenerate case, one that may pose a challenge for our usual effortless recognition systems. In such situations, recognition may depend on an inferential process based on a few salient features.

Shape Encoding

Viewer- and object-centered theories of recognition propose that recognition depends on breaking a scene or object into its component parts. Earlier, we introduced the idea that recognition may involve hierarchical representations in which each successive stage adds more complexity. Features such as lines can be combined into edges, corners, and intersections to parse a visual array into component regions. These, in turn, are grouped in parts and the parts in objects. Recognition of a triangle entails perceiving three segments that join together to form three corners which define an enclosed region. Another object could be defined if these same features were combined differently, for example, an arrow derived from three lines connected at their endpoints. But there is only one point of intersection, and the lines do not enclose an area; so the triangle and arrow might activate similar representations at the lowest levels of the hierarchy. Yet the combination of these features produces distinct representations at higher levels of the processing hierarchy.

EXPLOITING SALIENT SOURCES OF INFORMATION

What information is coded at these higher levels? We might expect that the representations would include the most salient aspects of the stimulus. Each of the abstract shapes in Figure 5.16 is composed of a single, continuous curved line. In comparing the two shapes, however, it is apparent that some regions of curvature provide more information than do others. We are not sensitive to the slight differences in curvature along the right side, but the sharp inflection point along the bottom of one of the figures is very salient. We would describe the shape on top as having a flat bottom; the shape on the bottom resembles an object with two bases of support, or legs. We might use this information to guess that the figure on the right is more mobile than the object on the left.

Figure 5.16 Study these two drawings for 10 seconds and then attempt to draw them from memory. Your drawings are likely to reflect the fact that points of greatest curvature provide the most salient sources of information. The knob on the left edge of the top figure is more distinctive than the wavy edge on the right edge. Reproductions of the bottom figure will surely include the gap separating the two appendages.

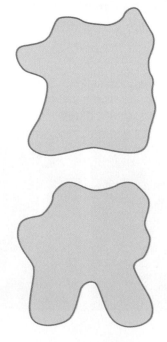

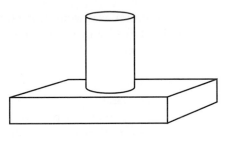

Figure 5.17 Certain perceptual cues are invariant across vantage points. The parallel edges of the rectangle will remain parallel when viewed from any position (given slight distortions due to depth). In contrast, the border between two objects is likely to depend on the viewpoint. In the top drawing, T-junctions are formed by the long edge of the rectangle and the sides of the cylinder. These junctions shift to the short edge of the rectangle when the objects are viewed from the end as in the lower drawing.

Sensory information can change from one viewpoint to another. Nonetheless, the world has regularities that the visual system exploits—sources of information that remain constant across vantage points. Theories of object recognition have emphasized the significance of these invariant properties. Apples can be red, green, or yellow, but they all share a basic shape. Moreover, invariant cues are often retained in the two-dimensional retinal projection of the three-dimensional world.

Consider the stimulus in the top panel of Figure 5.17. This percept completely depends on analyzing the objects' shapes: No color or texture distinguishes the two parts. Rather, the stimulus is simply the composition of lines at various orientations. Even so, from a glance we see that the scene is composed of two objects, a cylinder perched on a rectangle.

This reflects our ability to infer invariant properties on the basis of the depicted information. In this drawing, the simplest invariance has to do with the line segments themselves. In all viewing positions, straight edges on a three-dimensional object will appear as straight in a two-dimensional projection. In a similar manner, curved surfaces are seen as such over a wide range of viewpoints.

Other invariants like parallelism and symmetry bring into play comparisons of features in a stimulus. In Figure 5.17, parallelism is violated in the two-dimensional projection due to perspective. Even so, the visual system infers parallelism, which reflects the ubiquity of this feature in natural objects like trees and riverbanks and in human creations like streets and buildings. Indeed, psychologists take advantage of our bias to infer parallelism in creating compelling illusions (Figure 5.18).

More subtle invariant properties help to define the shapes of the two objects. At the corners of the rectangle the two or three lines intersect. The angles formed at the intersection vary greatly depending on the viewing position. Across all viewing positions, though, many invariant

Figure 5.18 The illusory Ames room exploits the fact that, given our knowledge of rooms, we expect the back wall to be parallel with the front wall and the ceiling to be at a constant height. Our perceptual system assumes the two people are at the same distance, and ends up interpreting the closer one as a giant.

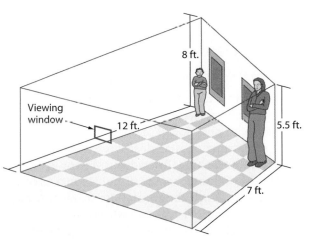

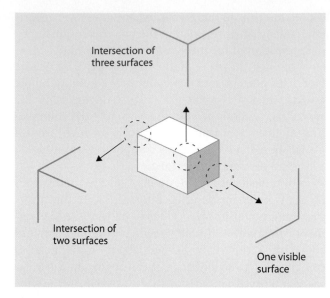

Intersection of
three surfaces

Intersection of
two surfaces

One visible
surface

Figure 5.19 Invariant cues to surface perception. The intersection of three visible surfaces creates a Y-junction. An arrow and shaft indicate the intersection of two visible surfaces whereas an arrow alone indicates the corner of one visible surface.

rules hold. If three lines come together, the intersection defines the corner of two visible surfaces. If two lines come together, then only one surface is visible and all other surfaces are occluded (Figure 5.19).

To recognize the cylinder and rectangle in Figure 5.17, it is necessary to resolve the ambiguity introduced at points where the two objects intersect. Our percept is that the cylinder sits on the square and occludes the rectangle's rear edge, an interpretation reflecting two cues. First, the fact that the upper borders of the two rear segments are collinear, forming a discontinuous line, is a powerful cue that these borders are part of the same object. Second, the edges of the rectangle and cylinder form a T junction. Such intersections almost always define two objects or two parts of a single object (such as the base and the top of a table). Again, these properties are invariant. The two-dimensional projection of collinearity and T intersections persists as an object is rotated.

RECOGNITION BY PARTS ANALYSIS

Certain properties remain invariant across vantage points—a central fact of object constancy. Recognizing an object need not depend on matching the percept to a stored representation that closely resembles the pattern of sensory information. Instead, the object can be recognized by determining that the stimulus contains component parts by which the objects are defined. A bicycle contains an elongated axis, two wheels, and handlebars. A third wheel and compression of the difference be-

tween the major and minor axes would correspond to a tricycle. Perhaps the difficulty in recognizing a bicycle from an aerial vantage point is that one of the critical features is obscured.

But what defines a part? Is it a list of higher-level features such as corners, parallelism, symmetry, enclosure—invariant properties that can be extracted from the two-dimensional projection of three-dimensional objects? Or, do we use these properties to build representations of defining parts?

Irv Biederman (1990) of the University of Southern California proposed a theory of object recognition that emphasizes a part-to-whole analysis. The central tenet of his theory is that any object can be described as a configuration of limited parts. Indeed, these parts form a perceptual alphabet, a set of simple geometric volumes referred to as *geons,* an acronym for geometric ions. In the way ions form the building blocks of chemical elements, visual geons are hypothesized to constitute fundamental shapes for object recognition. According to Biederman, twenty-four geons can be specified by viewpoint-invariant features (Figure 5.20). Three of these properties can be described by considering cross sections through the volume. First, is the cross section curved or straight? The cross section of a rectangle is straight; that of a cylinder is curved. The second property relates to size variation: Is the distance between the sides constant (parallel edges as in a rectangle or cylinder) or changing (as in a cone)? Symmetry constitutes a third property. A fourth property characterizes the axis running the length of the volume as curved or straight. Each geon thus combines attributes of these four properties.

Objects can be defined by a combination of geons. Figure 5.20 shows objects whose constituent geons are labeled. Note that two geons, the cylinder and the handle, are common to many of the objects. The telephone requires an extra geon. The cup and bucket are differentiated by the arrangement of the two geons. For the cup, the handle is attached along the side of the cylinder; for the bucket, the handle spans the cross section. According to Biederman, the combination of geons can be specified by relations such as "on top of" or "larger than."

It is surprising to think that all objects can be defined by a combination and arrangement of twenty-four primitive shapes. Yet 5760 unique objects could, in principle, be specified by two-geon objects if there were ten possible relations. If we add three-geon objects, the possibilities grow to 138,240. Biederman proposed that almost all objects can be identified so long as three geons are visible. Thus, the viewpoint-invariance aspect of the feature can be qualified. From some vantage points, cer-

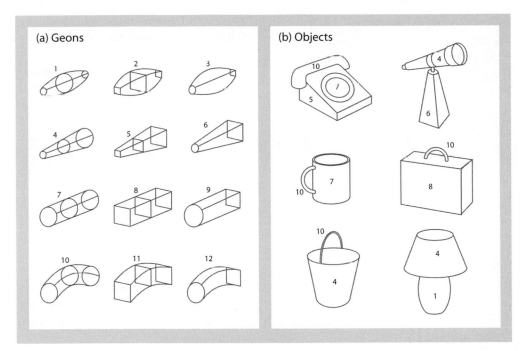

Figure 5.20   The geon theory posits that object recognition is based on identifying the defining geons, or geometrical "ions," that constitute an object. **(a)** Twelve geon shapes, formed by varying the shape of the cross section (e.g., circular for left column, straight for middle column), the constancy of the cross section (e.g., varying for the upper-right geons, constant for the lower-right geons), and parallelism (e.g., long axes parallel in horizontal direction for the upper-right geon, but not parallel in the vertical direction). **(b)** A set of common objects with their component geons marked. The numbers indicate the geons in the left panel. Adapted from Biedermann (1990).

tain geons will be obscured. But so long as some of the geons can be discerned, the object can be recognized.

Summary of Computational Issues

We have considered several computational issues that must be worked out before objects can be recognized. First, information must be represented on multiple scales. While early visual input can specify simple features, object perception involves intermediate stages of representation where features are assembled into parts. The appropriate characterization of a part-based representation remains a topic of dispute. Some theorists favor a feature-based representation and others, such as

Biederman, emphasize that these features are compiled in an alphabet of three-dimensional primitives.

Second, objects are not determined solely by their parts; they are defined by relations between parts. An arrow and a *Y* contain the same parts but differ in their arrangement. While parts may change (for example, we could extend the length of each segment), we continue to recognize the object if these relations are constant. Third, for object recognition to be flexible and robust, the perceived spatial relations among parts should not vary over viewing conditions. Object perception would be limited if we had a different representation for each point of view of an object.

FAILURES OF OBJECT RECOGNITION

Where does the syndrome of visual agnosia fit in with these considerations? To repeat, visual agnosia is when patients have difficulty recognizing visually presented objects. A key word here is *visual:* Many people who have incurred a traumatic neurological insult or who have a degenerative disease such as Alzheimer's disease may experience problems recognizing things. But

these problems will be generic: If the same object is placed in their hands or described verbally, patients with Alzheimer's disease will still have problems recognizing it. For visual agnosics, the deficit is restricted to the visual domain. Recognition can occur through other sensory modalities like touch or audition. They may fail to recognize the fork, but as soon as the object is placed

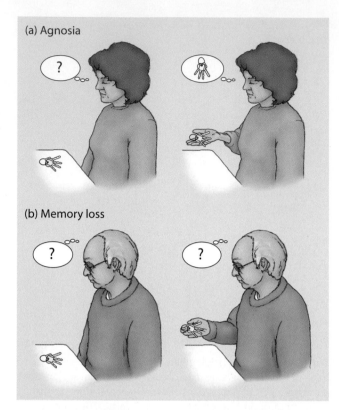

(a) Agnosia

(b) Memory loss

Figure 5.21 To diagnose an agnosic disorder, it is essential to rule out general memory problems. **(a)** The patient with agnosia is unable to recognize the keys by vision alone, but immediately recognizes the keys when she picks them up. **(b)** The patient with a memory disorder is unable to recognize the keys even when he picks them up.

in their hand, they will immediately recognize it (Figure 5.21). Indeed, after touching the object, an agnosia patient may now report that the object can be seen clearly. Because the patient can recognize the object through other modalities, and through vision with supplementary support, we know that the problem does not reflect a general loss of knowledge. Rather, it must reflect a loss of knowledge that is intimately linked to visual perception or an inability for the products of visual perception to access modality-independent knowledge stores.

Subtypes of Agnosia

Visual agnosia is differentiated from visual deficits caused by an impairment in sensory abilities. A patient who is completely blind will be unable to recognize a visually presented object. But a blind patient does not have a problem linking visual information to stored knowledge about the world; rather, a blind patient lacks the perceptual input needed to activate this internal knowledge. The label *visual agnosia* is restricted to cases

where object recognition problems occur despite the fact that visual information continues to be registered at the cortical level.

The nineteenth-century German neurologist H. Lissauer first suggested the existence of two types of visual agnosia. Lissauer (1890) distinguished between recognition deficits that were primarily sensory based and those that reflected an inability to visually access memory, a disorder that he melodramatically referred to as *Seelenblindheit*, or "soul blindness." In the current literature, the general distinction is made between apperceptive agnosia and associative agnosia. Apperceptive agnosia describes failures in object recognition linked to problems in perceptual processing. Associative agnosia, in contrast, is reserved for patients who derive normal visual representations but cannot use this information to recognize things. While research has led to more refined taxonomies, the distinction between apperceptive and associative agnosias continues to provide a useful classification scheme.

APPERCEPTIVE AGNOSIA

The inability to recognize objects can arise from a host of perceptual disorders. A severe case was apparent in a young man who had suffered carbon monoxide poisoning, an injury that produced widespread bilateral cortical damage. The poisoning had not produced any scotomas, and the patient could distinguish small differences in brightness and color. Yet his ability to discriminate between even the simplest shapes was essentially nonexistent. For example, he was unable to distinguish between two rectangles of equal area, even when they were oriented in opposite directions. He could not read letters, except for those composed of straight segments (e.g., *I*), nor could he copy drawings. Face perception was impossible for him. He even failed to recognize his own face in a mirror; he thought it might be his doctor's.

In patients with apperceptive agnosia, the perceptual problems are much more subtle. Indeed, a standard clinical evaluation may fail to reveal any visual problems, and the patient will have to insist that he or she is having difficulties in recognizing objects to receive a more detailed examination. The patient may perform normally on shape-discrimination tasks, yet make many mistakes when asked to recognize line drawings or photographs of objects. To demonstrate that the agnosia is truly of the apperceptive subtype and not an associative agnosia, it is necessary to devise refined tests of perceptual acuity. For example, tasks like the Gollin Picture Task and Incomplete Letters Task examine whether patients can recognize objects in a degraded format (Figure 5.22).

Auditory Agnosia

Other sensory modalities besides visual perception surely contribute to object recognition. Distinctive odors in a grocery store enable us to figure out which bunch of greens is thyme and which is basil. Touch can differentiate between a cheap polyester and a fine silk garment. And we depend on sounds, both natural and man-made, to cue our actions. A siren prompts us to search for a nearby police car or ambulance. Or an anxious parent immediately recognizes the cries of his or her infant and rushes to the baby's aid. Indeed, we often overlook our exquisite auditory capabilities for object recognition. Have a friend rap on a wooden tabletop, or metal filing cabinet, or glass window. You will easily distinguish between these objects.

Numerous studies have documented failures of object recognition in other sensory modalities. As with visual agnosia, a patient has to meet two criteria to be labeled agnosic. First, a deficit in object recognition cannot be secondary to a problem with perceptual processes. For example, to be classified as having auditory agnosia, patients must perform within normal limits on tests of tone detection: How loud must a sound be for the person to detect it? Second, the deficit in recognizing objects must be restricted to a single modality. A patient who cannot identify environmental sounds such as the ones made by flowing water or jet engines must be able to recognize a picture of a waterfall or an airplane.

Consider a patient, C.N., reported by Isabelle Peretz and her colleagues (1994) at the University of Montreal. C.N., a 35-year-old nurse, had suffered two aneurysms, one in the right middle cerebral artery and the other in the left middle cerebral artery, over a 3-month period. Both required surgery. Postoperatively, her ability to detect tones and comprehend and produce speech was not impaired. But she immediately complained that her perception of music was deranged. Her *amusia*, or impairment in music abilities was verified by tests. For example, she could not recognize melodies taken from her personal record collection, nor could she recall the names of 140 popular tunes including the Canadian national anthem. C.N.'s deficit could not be attributed to a problem with long-term memory. She also failed when asked to decide if two melodies were the same or different. That the problem was selective to auditory perception was evidenced by her excellent ability to identify these same songs when shown the lyrics. Or when given the title of a musical piece such as *The Four Seasons,* C.N. would respond that the composer was Vivaldi and even recalled when she had first heard the piece.

As interesting as C.N.'s amusia is her absence of problems with other auditory-recognition tests. C.N. understood speech, and she was able to identify environmental sounds such as animal cries, transportation noises, and human voices. Even within the musical domain, C.N. did not have a generalized problem with all aspects of music comprehension. She performed as well as normal subjects when asked to judge if two tone sequences had the same rhythm. But her performance fell to a level of near chance when she had to decide if the two sequences were the same melody. This dissociation makes it less surprising that, despite her inability to recognize songs, she still enjoyed dancing!

Other cases of domain-specific auditory agnosia have been reported. Many patients are impaired in their ability to recognize environmental sounds, and, as with amusia, this deficit is independent of language-comprehension problems. In contrast, patients with *pure word deafness* cannot recognize oral speech even though they exhibit normal auditory perception for other types of sounds and have normal reading abilities. Such category specificity suggests that auditory object recognition involves several distinct processing systems. Whether the operation of these processes should be defined by content—for example, verbal versus nonverbal input—or by computations—for example, words and melodies may vary with regard to the need for part versus whole analysis—remains to be seen … or, rather, heard.

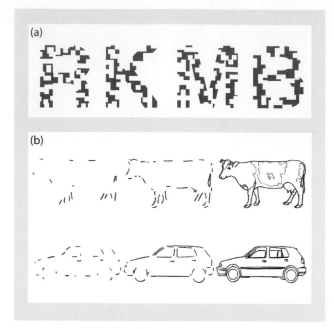

Figure 5.22 **(a)** Patients with agnosia following right-hemisphere lesions have more difficulty than patients with left-hemisphere lesions, despite the more severe language problems for the left-hemisphere group. **(b)** In the Gollin picture test, the subjects are presented with a series of drawings of an object, each successive drawing being more complete than the previous one. Patients with right-hemisphere lesions were found to require more complete drawings in order to correctly identify the objects. Adapted from Warrington (1985).

Working out of the National Hospital in London, Elizabeth Warrington (1985) has carefully investigated perceptual disabilities in patients over the past 20 years. One of her first studies included more than eighty patients with right- or left-hemisphere lesions. Inclusion was not dependent on whether the patients showed signs of agnosia; indeed, it is unlikely that many patients would have presented any clinical signs of object-recognition problems. Instead, the main criterion for inclusion was evidence of a unilateral cerebral lesion (stroke or tumor). In addition, the patients were all right-handed with normal visual acuity, either with or without glasses. This last criterion excluded patients with object-recognition deficits caused by obvious sensory problems.

In the Gollin Picture Task and the Incomplete Letters Task, patients with right-sided lesions performed more poorly than did either control subjects or patients with left-sided lesions. Left-sided damage had little effect on performance, a result made even more impressive by the fact that many of these patients had language problems. This laterality effect, with apperceptive ag-

nosia being more apparent after right-hemisphere damage, has been observed during a variety of object-recognition tasks. How are we to interpret these results? Do they implicate a primary role for the right hemisphere in object recognition? Or does the right hemisphere perform a special cognition operation essential for tasks like the Gollin Picture Task? Can we interpret this deficit within the framework of the computational problems described in the previous section?

Warrington maintained that such an analysis is possible and, indeed, provided a most cogent account of the deficit in patients with right parietal lesions. She contended that the problem is not one of contour discrimination. If patients with right parietal lesions are asked to make fine discriminations between the shapes of simple geometric figures, their performance is only slightly poorer than that of healthy subjects. The critical problem, then, is that perceptual categorization in these patients is impaired—the patient's ability to achieve object constancy is disrupted.

To test this hypothesis, Warrington devised an Unusual Views Object Test. For this test, photographs were taken of twenty objects, each from two distinct views, as shown in the example in Figure 5.23. For one view, the object was oriented so the photograph would depict a standard or prototypical view. For example, a cat was photographed with its head facing forward. In the other view, the photograph depicted an unusual or atypical view. For example, the cat was photographed from behind, without its face or feet in the picture.

Subjects were shown the photographs and asked to name them. While normal subjects made few, if any, errors, patients with right posterior lesions had difficulty identifying objects photographed from unusual orientations. But they could name the objects when photographed in the prototypical orientation, further confirming that their problem is not a deficit of lost visual knowledge.

A second task verified the claim that the pairs of photographs were not recognized as depicting the same object. Here pairs of photographs were presented in each trial, one from the prototypical set and one from the unusual set. The two photographs were either of the same or of different objects, and the subjects' task was to judge if the objects were the same. As expected, patients with right posterior lesions showed more impairment than did healthy subjects and patient control groups. Similar results were obtained from other photographic transformations that presumably tax the object-constancy mechanism. The patients had problems matching an object photographed from the exact same position but in two different lighting conditions.

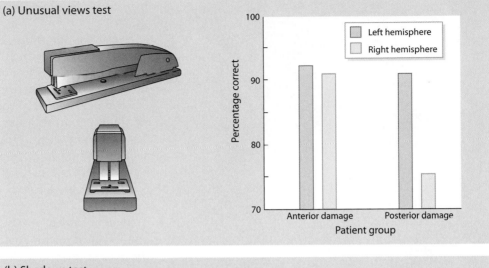

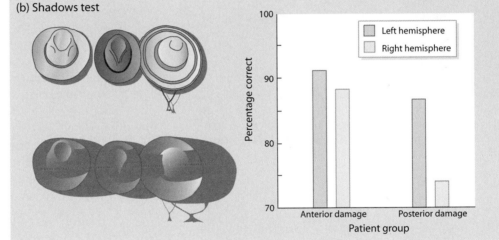

Figure 5.23 Tests used to identify apperceptive agnosia. **(a)** The unusual-views test. The subject must judge if the two pictures are of the same object. **(b)** The shadows test. Subjects must identify the object when seen under normal or shadowed illumination. In both tests, patients with right-hemisphere lesions, especially in the posterior area, performed much more poorly than did control subjects (not shown) or patients with left-hemisphere lesions. Adapted from Warrington (1982).

Warrington's analysis thus specified the critical deficit underlying apperceptive agnosia. Her evaluation did not simply restate the problem—that patients with right-hemisphere lesions have difficulty with object recognition because the right hemisphere is so prominent in object perception. Instead, she postulated a cognitive process associated with the posterior part of the right hemisphere, a principal player in perceptual categorization. People can normally recognize an object under nearly infinite orientations, distances, and illuminations. Although we see these percepts as distinct, we can identify the similarities. A cat will be identified whether it is sleeping on the couch, rolling on the floor, or prowling through the garden. This implies that we can readily achieve object constancy; from the infinity of percepts, we extract critical features to identify the object. Patients with right parietal lobe lesions are less able to recognize objects. When presented so the perceptual input highlights the most salient features, the object

can be recognized. If these features must be inferred or extracted from a limited perceptual input, apperceptive agnosics have difficulties.

ASSOCIATIVE AGNOSIA

Associative agnosia is, by definition, a failure of visual object recognition that cannot be attributed to perceptual abilities. These patients rarely perform normally on perceptual tests, but their perceptual deficiencies are not proportional to their recognition problems, a point emphasized in a case reported by McCarthy and Warrington (1986). The patient, F.R.A., awoke one morning and discovered that he could not read his newspaper, a condition known as *alexia,* or *acquired dyslexia.* When the problem did not subside, he visited his local hospital. A CT scan revealed an infarct of the left posterior cerebral artery. The lesioned area was primarily in the occipital region of the left hemisphere, although the damage probably extended into the posterior temporal cortex.

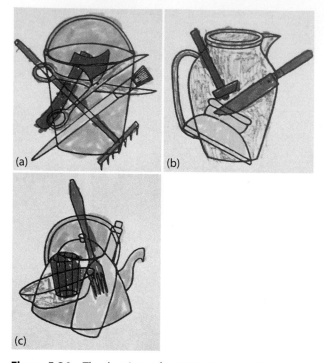

Figure 5.24 The drawings of patient F.R.A. Despite her inability to name visually presented objects, F.R.A. was quite successful in coloring in the components of these complex drawings. She clearly had succeeded in parsing the stimuli, but still was unable to identify the objects.

This patient's story is not atypical: Strokes often go unnoticed until the patient discovers an inability to perform a task.

After F.R.A.'s condition had stabilized, perceptual tests were administered. He copied geometric shapes with ease and could point to objects when they were named. Most impressive was his ability to segment a complex drawing into its parts (Figure 5.24). Apperceptive agnosia patients fail miserably when instructed to color each object differently. In contrast, F.R.A. performed the task effortlessly. Despite this ability, though, he could not name the objects he had colored.

Further testing revealed the extent of F.R.A.'s deficits. When shown line drawings of common objects, he could name or describe the function of only half of them. If he was given the name verbally, he could readily generate a verbal description. In a similar manner, when presented with pictures of two animals like a mouse and a dog and asked to point to the largest, his performance was barely above that which would occur by chance. If the two animal names were said aloud, F.R.A. could do the task perfectly. His problems were clearly restricted to the visual modality. The ability to recognize the mean-

ing of visually presented objects was compromised by the stroke.

This hypothesis was explored in another test used by Warrington in her group studies. Recall that in the Unusual Object Views Test, subjects were required to judge if two pictures depicted the same object from different orientations. This task requires that the subjects categorize information according to their perceptual qualities. In an alternative task, the Matching-by-Function test, subjects are shown three pictures and asked to point to the two that are functionally similar. In Figure 5.25, the correct response would be to match the closed umbrella to the open umbrella, even though the former is physically more similar to the cane. Thus, the Matching-by-Function test requires subjects to categorize stimuli on the basis of their semantic properties, that is, in relation to how they are used.

Patients with posterior lesions in either the right or the left hemisphere showed impairment on this task. Yet Warrington maintained that the problems in the two groups happen for different reasons. Patients with right-sided lesions cannot do the task because they fail to recognize many objects, especially those depicted in an unconventional manner, such as the closed umbrella. Patients with left-sided lesions can frequently recognize objects in isolation, but they cannot make the functional connection between the two visual percepts. They lack the semantic representations needed to link the functional association between the open and closed umbrella.

In summary, Warrington (1985) proposed an anatomical model of the cognitive operations required for object recognition (Figure 5.26). The central feature of the model is two categorical stages of object recognition. Initial visual processing is assumed to involve both occipital cortices. Subsequently the first categorical operation, perceptual categorization, is invoked. Perceptual inputs are matched with stored representations of visual objects, a stage of processing essential for dealing with the variability of sensory information. The visual system must distinguish between idiosyncratic sources of information such as shadowing patterns, and those that provide invariant sources of information. This stage, associated with processing in the right hemisphere, can be characterized as presemantic in the sense that we may recognize two pictures that depict the same object without being able to name the object or describe its function. To do this, a second categorization stage, semantic categorization, is needed, one that depends on the left hemisphere. Here, visual input is linked with knowledge in long-term memory concerning the name and functions of that input.

Figure 5.25 The matching by function test. The subject is asked to choose the two objects that are most similar in terms of function. In both examples, the correct match is with the object on the right despite the greater physical similarity of the objects on the left. Agnosic patients with left-hemisphere lesions demonstrate impairment on this task. Top is adapted from Warrington (1982); bottom is adapted from Warrington and Taylor (1978).

Category Specificity in Agnosia

In Warrington's view, associative agnosia usually results from the loss of semantic knowledge regarding the visual structure or properties of objects. Early perceptual analyses proceed normally, but the long-term knowledge of vi-

sual information is lost, and thus the object cannot be recognized. Further support for the idea of a loss of visual semantics comes from bizarre reports of patients whose object recognition deficit appears to be selective for specific categories of objects (Warrington and Shalliu, 1984).

Patient J.B.R. was diagnosed as having herpes simplex encephalitis in 1980. His illness left him with a complicated array of deficits including a dense *amnesia,* or memory loss, and word-finding difficulties. While his performance on tests of apperceptive agnosia was normal, J.B.R. had a severe associative agnosia. Most notable about his agnosia was that it was disproportionately worse for living objects than inanimate ones. For drawings of common objects such as scissors, clocks, and chairs, his success rate was about 90%. In contrast, he could correctly identify only 6% of the pictures of living things. A similar dissociation of agnosia for living and nonliving things has been reported for other patients (Satori and Job, 1988).

How are we to interpret such puzzling deficits? Warrington's visual semantics hypothesis provides an answer. If we assume that associative agnosia represents a loss of knowledge about visual properties, we might suppose

Figure 5.26 Warrington's two-stage model of object recognition. Visual analysis occurs in both hemispheres, at least when we look directly at an object. The first stage of object categorization is perceptual, the processes required to overcome the perceptual variability in the stimulus. This stage is dependent on the right hemisphere. The second stage involves semantic categorization in which the perceptual representation is linked to semantic knowledge. This stage is dependent on the left hemisphere.

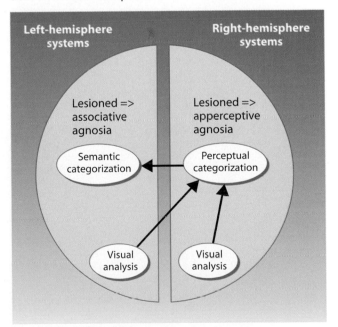

that a category-specific disorder results from the selective loss within this knowledge system. Semantic knowledge is structured: We recognize that birds, dogs, and dinosaurs are animals because they share common features. In a similar way, scissors, saws, and knives share characteristics. Some might be physical (e.g., they all have an elongated shape) and others functional (e.g., they all are used for cutting). Brain injuries that produce agnosia in humans do not completely destroy the connections to semantic knowledge. Even the most severely affected patient will recognize some objects. Because the damage is not total, it seems reasonable that circumscribed lesions might destroy tissue that is devoted to processing similar types of information. Category-specific deficits support

this form of organization. The lesions in such patients have affected regions associated with processing information about living things.

If this interpretation were valid, we might expect to find opposite results: patients whose recognition of non-living things is disproportionately impaired. Indeed, there have been a few; for example, one patient showed much more impairment in recognizing common objects than animals. Each trial consisted of presenting an array of five objects. A target, presented either visually or auditorily, was then given, and the subject's task was to choose the object in the array that was from the same category (Figure 5.27). For both modalities, the patient was much slower and made more errors with the objects.

Figure 5.27 Tests used to demonstrate category-specific agnosia. In each condition, the subject is asked to choose from the array of five drawings, the one that goes best with the probe item in the box. A patient with a selective deficit for common objects would perform poorly in the top example, but perform normally in the bottom example. The reverse would be expected in a patient with a category-specific deficit for living things. Adapted from Warrington and McCarthy (1994).

So we do have evidence of a double dissociation between agnosia for living things and for nonliving things. But we should be cautious: No studies have shown this double dissociation by using the exact same stimulus materials. In the study just reviewed, no patients showed the opposite pattern of results, nor were there any control data. It may be, then, that the nonliving-object trials were harder than the living-object trials for these stimuli. Given that reports of patients with selective deficits in recognizing nonliving objects are much rarer, we should consider alternative accounts for this pattern of category-specific agnosias.

One idea is that many nonliving things evoke representations not elicited by living things (Damasio, 1990). In particular, manufactured objects can be manipulated. As such, they are associated with kinesthetic and motoric representations. When viewing an object, we can activate a sense of how it feels or of the actions required to manipulate the object (Figure 5.28). Corresponding representations will not exist for living objects. While we may have a kinesthetic sense of how a cat's fur feels, few of us have ever stroked an elephant. And we certainly have no sense of what it feels like to pounce like a cat or fly like a bird.

According to this hypothesis, manufactured objects are easier to recognize because they activate additional forms of representation. While brain injury can produce a common processing deficit for all categories of stimuli, these extra representations may be sufficient to recognize nonliving objects. The viability of this hypothesis can be seen in the behavior of patient P.T., described at the beginning of this chapter. Remember that when shown the picture of the combination lock, his first response was to call it a telephone. But even when verbalizing "telephone," his hands began to move as if they were opening a combination lock. Indeed, he was able to name the object after he looked at his hands in wonder and realized what they were trying to tell him.

A less glamorous interpretation of category-specific agnosia for living things must also be considered. David Gaffan and Charles Heywood (1993) of Oxford University created 260 pictures, some of which depicted living things and the rest nonliving things. Healthy observers were able to name all the objects. To make the task more difficult, the pictures were presented for only 20 msec. This manipulation was highly effective: Error rates were higher than 35%, thereby creating a transient pseudoagnosia in the normal subjects. Of greatest interest, all five normal subjects made many more errors on pictures of living things than on those of nonliving things. In a second experiment, similar results were obtained with six monkeys.

To account for these findings, Gaffan and Heywood argued that living things are inherently more difficult to

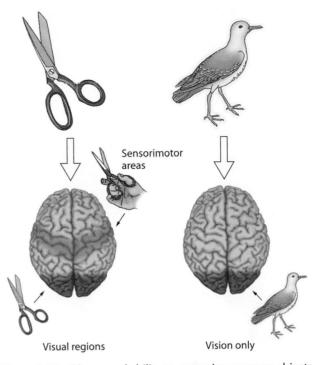

Figure 5.28 The spared ability to recognize common objects has been attributed to the fact that our visual knowledge is supplemented by kinesthetic codes developed through our interactions with these objects. When a picture of the scissors is presented, the visual code may not be sufficient for recognition. However, when supplemented with priming of kinesthetic codes, the person is able to name the object. Kinesthetic codes are unlikely to exist for most living things.

discriminate than are nonliving things. Members of categories such as mammals and fruits share more salient and distinctive features than do categories such as tools. For example, most of the animals in Figure 5.29 have appendages or legs; it is hard to identify a commonality across the nonliving objects. The greater similarity between the pictures of living things made it harder for normal subjects to determine the correct label under limited viewing conditions.

If this interpretation is correct, agnosia patients' selective deficit for living things may not reflect differences in the types of representations; it may simply reflect differences in object similarity. A fundamental tenet of testing brain-injured patients is that the more difficult a task is, the more apparent their deficits are. Agnosia patients may fail more often at recognizing living things simply because these objects are less discriminable than are nonliving things.

Integrating Parts into Wholes

Martha Farah and Jay McClelland (1991) used a series of computer simulations to integrate a number of these

Figure 5.29 Line drawings of objects used to compare recognition of living and nonliving things by normal subjects. Notice the greater similarity (and thus confusability) of the living things: they tend to have rounded bodies and appendages of some sort. There is little similarity among the set of nonliving things. Adapted from Snodgrass and Vanderwart (1980).

ideas. Their study was designed to contrast two ways of conceptualizing the organization of semantic memory (Figure 5.30). One hypothesis is that semantic memory is organized according to category membership. According to this hypothesis, there are distinct representational systems for living and nonliving things, and perhaps further subdivisions within these two broad categories. An alternative hypothesis is that semantic memory reflects an organization based on object properties. The idea that nonliving things are more likely to entail kinesthetic and motor representations is one variant of this view. The simulations were designed to demonstrate that category-specific deficits can result from lesions to a semantic memory system organized by object properties.

The architecture of their model involved a simple connectionist network, designed to simulate performance when people are asked to associate names for ob-

jects with visual representations of the objects. As with standard connectionist networks, information was distributed across a number of processing units. One set of units corresponded to peripheral input systems, divided into a verbal and visual system. Each of these was composed of 24 input units. The visual representation of an object involved a unique pattern of activation across the 24 visual units. Similarly, the name of an object involved a unique pattern of activation across the 24 verbal units. In the simulations, the model was presented with 20 unique patterns representing 20 objects, half of them living objects and the other half nonliving.

Each object was also linked to a unique pattern of activation across the second type of unit in the model, the semantic memory. Within the semantic system, there were two types of units, visual and functional. While these units did not correspond to specific types of information (e.g., colors or shapes), the idea here is that our semantic knowledge consist of at least two types of information. One type of sematic knowledge is visually based, akin to Warrington's visual semantics. For example, visual semantics would embody facts, such as a tiger has stripes or a chair has legs. The other type of semantic memory corresponds to our functional knowledge of objects. For example, functional semantics would include our knowledge that tigers are dangerous or that a chair is a type of office furniture.

The researchers imposed two constraints on the semantic memory system, intended to capture psycholog-

Figure 5.30   Top: Two hypotheses concerning the organization of semantic knowledge. A category-based hypothesis proposes that semantic knowledge is organized according to our categories of the world. For example, one prominent split would be between living and nonliving things. A property-based hypothesis is that semantic knowledge is organized according to the properties of objects. These properties may be visual or functional. **Bottom:** The architecture of Farah and McClelland's (1991) connectionist model of a property-based semantic system. The initial activation for each object is represented by a unique pattern of activation in two input systems and the semantic system. In this example, the darkened units would correspond to the pattern for one object. The final activation would be determined by the initial pattern and the connection weights between the units. There are no connections between the two input systems. The names and pictures are linked through the semantic system.

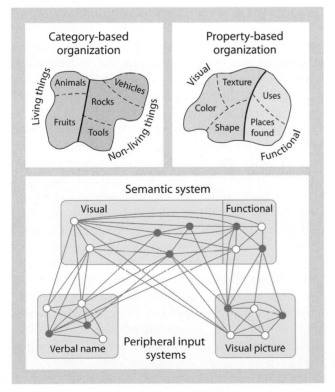

ical differences in how visual and semantic information might be stored. The first constraint was that, of the 80 semantic units, 60 were visual and 20 were semantic. This 3:1 ratio was based on a preliminary study in which human subjects were asked to read the dictionary definitions of living and nonliving objects and indicate whether a descriptor was visual or functional. On average, three times as many descriptors were classified as visual. Second, the preliminary study indicated that the ratio of visual to functional descriptors differed for the two classes of objects. For living objects, the ratio was 7.7:1; for nonliving objects this ratio dropped to 1.4:1. Thus, as discussed previously, our knowledge of living objects is much more dependent on visual information than is our knowledge of nonliving objects. This constraint was incorporated into the model by varying the number of visual and functional semantic units used for the living and nonliving objects.

The model was trained to link the verbal and visual representations of a set of 20 objects, half of them living and the other half nonliving. Note that the verbal and visual units were not directly linked, but can only interact by way of their connections with the semantic system. The strength of these connections was adjusted in a training procedure. This procedure was not intended to simulate how people acquire semantic knowledge. Rather, the experimenters would set all of the units, both input and semantic, to their values for a particular object and then allow the activation of each unit to change depending on both its initial activation and the input it received from other units. The connection weights were then adjusted to minimize the difference between the resulting pattern and the original pattern. The model's object-recognition capabilities can be tested by measuring the probability of correctly associating the names and pictures.

This model proved to be extremely adept. After 40 training trials, it was perfect when tested with both the living and nonliving stimuli. The key question centered on how well the model did after receiving "lesions" to its semantic memory, lesions assumed to correspond to what happens in patients with visual associative agnosia. Lesions in a model consist of deactivating a certain percentage of the semantic units. As can be seen in Figure 5.31, selective lesions in either the visual or the functional semantics system produced category-specific deficits. When the damage was restricted to visual semantic memory, the model had great difficulty in correctly associating the names and pictures for living objects. In contrast, when the damage was restricted to functional semantic memory, failures were limited to nonliving objects. Note that the resulting "deficit" is

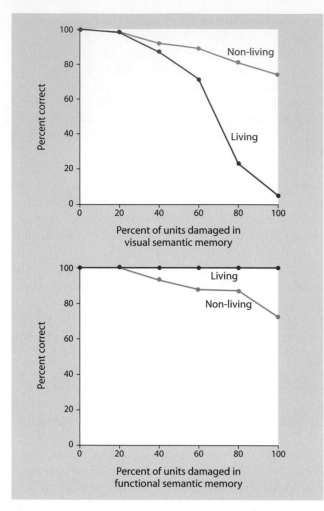

Figure 5.31 Lesions in the semantic units resulted in a double dissociation between the recognition of living and nonliving objects. After a percentage of the semantic units were eliminated, two measurements were made. In the picture-naming task, the visual input pattern for each object was activated and the resultant pattern on the verbal units was evaluated as either correct or incorrect. In the matching-to-sample test, the name pattern was activated and the resulting pattern on the picture units was evaluated. When the lesion was restricted to the visual semantic memory units, the model showed much more impairment in correctly associating the name and picture patterns for the living things. When the lesion was restricted to the functional semantic memory units, the model showed impairment only in associating the input patterns for non-living things. Adapted from Farah and McClelland (1991).

much more dramatic in the former simulation, the visual semantic lesion's effect on identifying living things. This result meshes nicely with reports in the neuropsychological literature of many more instances of patients with a category-specific agnosia for living things. Even when functional semantic memory is damaged, the model remains proficient in identifying the nonliving objects, presumably because knowledge of these objects is distributed across both the visual and the functional memory units.

These simulations demonstrated how category-specific deficits may reflect the organization of semantic knowledge. The modeling work makes the important point that we need not postulate that our knowledge of objects is organized along categories such as living and nonliving. The double dissociation between living and nonliving things has been taken to suggest that we have specialized systems sensitive to these categorical distinctions. In contrast, in Farah and McClelland's model, the same system is used to recognize both living and nonliving things. Rather than assume a partitioning of representational systems in terms of the type of object, they proposed that semantic memory is organized according to the properties that define the objects. Category-specific deficits are best viewed as an emergent property of the fact that different sources of information are needed to recognize living and nonliving objects. Our knowledge of living things is highly dependent on visual information, whereas this dependency is lessened for nonliving objects. While stripes are the defining property of a tiger, chairs come in all shapes and sizes, but have the consistent property that they are to be sat on.

The Warrington model is a simple look at how we go about recognizing objects. The model requires elaboration, though. First, neuropathological findings have not always proved a correspondence between associative agnosia and left-hemisphere lesions. More typically, these patients usually have bilateral lesions that affect occipital-temporal regions. In addition, unilateral right-hemisphere lesions restricted to this region can produce an agnosia more similar to the associative subtype than to the apperceptive subtype.

Detailed analysis of a few case studies also pointed to the need for more refined analysis at the cognitive level of what happens in perceptual categorization. Glyn Humphreys and Jane Riddoch and colleagues (1994) of the University of Birmingham in England described a patient, H.J.A., who suffered a stroke while undergoing an appendectomy. Although the CT scans were negative, the patient had a distributed pattern of scotoma in both visual fields, consistent with a bilateral loss of blood flow in the superior branch of the posterior cerebral arteries. Ten years of testing revealed extensive agnosia. When asked to name common household objects, H.J.A. succeeded in about 80% of the trials; his performance fell to 40% when line drawings were used as stimuli. As with all visual agnosics, his ability to identify objects tactilely was normal.

An assessment of H.J.A.'s performance on standard measures of agnosia led to a classification of associative agnosia. He had no problem with shape-matching tasks and was able to copy accurately. Moreover, he matched photographs of objects from unusual views, Warrington's test for a perceptual categorization deficit.

But it was apparent that H.J.A.'s perceptual abilities were quite abnormal. When presented with overlapping figures, his object-recognition ability failed completely; he recognized objects in isolation but had great problems when the contours of two objects overlapped. Further evidence of his limited capabilities was found in his drawings. His renditions were produced in a piecemeal, slavish fashion. He drew each segment individually, repeatedly examining the model before progressing to the next part.

Humphreys and Riddoch proposed that H.J.A. had difficulty in integrating the parts of an object into a coherent whole, a deficit they labeled *integrative agnosia*. He was unable to perceive an object "at a glance." Instead, his ability to identify objects depended on recognizing salient features or parts. For H.J.A. to recognize a dog, he must independently perceive each of the legs and the characteristic shape of the body and head. These part representations are then used to identify the whole. Such a strategy would run into problems with overlapping figures where it is necessary not only to identify the parts, but also to make the correct assignment of parts to objects.

Many tests can provide evidence that H.J.A. has a deficit in grouping and integrating features. Consider the task in Figure 5.32, where subjects must determine whether a display contains an upside-down T among distractors that are upright or tilted T's. This task can be considered a conjunction-search task: The upside-down target contains the same features of a horizontal with vertical lines as the upright distractors. Normal subjects are much faster when the distractors form a homogeneous set (e.g., all upright T's) than when they are drawn from a heterogeneous set (e.g., upright and tilted T's). It appears that we can rapidly group homogeneous elements and detect a deviation from this consistent texture. H.J.A., though, did not have this advantage with organized displays. His reaction times were comparable in organized and random conditions, which accords with the hypothesis that H.J.A. must treat each object as an independent entity, examining each pair of lines to determine whether the T is upright or upside-down. H.J.A. also failed to identify objects when contours were well structured as opposed to being fragmented.

H.J.A. does not represent a special case of integrative agnosia. Indeed, an inability to integrate features

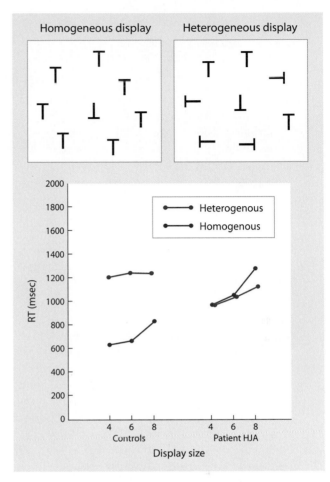

Figure 5.32 Patients with integrative agnosia have difficulty grouping common elements together. Normal subjects find the upside-down T much faster when all of the distractors are upright T's. When the distractors are heterogeneous, the patient's reaction times (RT) are much slower. The benefit is likely due to the fact that the distractor elements group together in the homogeneous condition. Patient H.J.A.'s reaction times are comparable in the two conditions, indicating a failure to group. Adapted from Humphreys et al. (1994).

into a coherent whole may be the hallmark of many agnosia patients. A telling example of this deficit is provided by the drawings of patient C.K., a young man who suffered a head injury in an automobile accident (Behrmann et al., 1994). C.K. was asked to draw three geometric shapes in a specific configuration. We might be impressed if we simply look at the final product of his drawing, shown in Figure 5.33. What is abnormal is the order in which he produced the segments. For example, after drawing the left-hand segments of the upper diamond, C.K. proceeded to draw the upper left-hand arc of the circle. Rather than continue with the circle, he branched off to draw the lower diamond before returning to complete the

Seeing in the Mind's Eye

Imagine walking along the beach at sunset. The glowing orange sun has kissed the water's edge and the cloud-streaked sky bursts into a palette of reds, violets, and blues. Screeching seagulls flutter over the remains of a fish washed up in the afternoon tide. The smell of the rotting carcass is pungent, adding to the saltiness of the ocean mist.

Our images can be vivid. Most likely our images are of a specific place where we once enjoyed an ocean sunset. Some details may be quite salient; others may require further reflection. Were any boats passing by on the horizon in the image? Was the surf calm or were the waves rolling in, perhaps topped by a couple of surfers trying to catch one last ride for the day?

The relation between perception and imagery has been a point of heated debate in psychology for more than two decades (Kosslyn, 1988). At the center of this debate has been the question of whether imagery uses the same neural machinery as is used in perception. When we imagine our beachside sunset, are we activating the same neural pathways and performing the same internal operations as when we gaze upon such a scene with our eyes?

Introspection provides few answers to this debate. If asked to imagine a ripe banana, we can easily describe the oblong shape, the bright yellow color, and perhaps the splotches of black where the fruit has been bruised. Have we really activated neurons in the shape and color regions of visual areas? Or is this image created from a knowledge of what bananas look like without having to "see with the mind's eye"?

Experimental psychologists have devised many ways to answer these questions. Several studies demonstrated similarities in how we process images and percepts. Roger Shepard of Stanford University developed several tasks to explore the dynamics of mental processing (Podgorny and Shepard, 1978). In one task, subjects view a grid of twenty-five squares that contains either a block letter or one that they are to imagine as a designated letter (Figure A). The display is then turned off, and after a short delay, the grid reappears, containing a dot in one of the squares. The subjects must decide if the dot falls on or off the previously seen or imagined letter. Responses are considerably slower when the dot is near an edge of the letter. Most importantly, this

effect is as strong in the imagery condition, as if the subjects must inspect their image in detail.

Neuropsychological research may provide the most compelling evidence of shared processing for imagery and perception. Martha Farah of the University of Pennsylvania (1988) carefully reviewed the literature, identifying cases in which brain lesions that cause perceptual deficits were also found to lead to corresponding deficits in imagery. For example, strokes may disrupt the connections of visual information to language areas, causing difficulty in both perception and imagery tasks. One patient was able to sort objects according to color, but when asked to name a color or point to a named color, her performance was impaired. With imagery, the patient could not answer questions about the colors of objects. She could say that a banana is a fruit that grows in southern climates, but could not name its color. Even more surprising, the patient answered metaphorical questions about colors. For example, she could answer the question, "What is the color of envy?" Questions like these cannot be answered through imagery.

Patients with higher-order visual deficits have related deficits in imagery. Consider two patients, one with bilateral lesions of the temporal cortex and left-sided occipital involvement and another with bilateral lesions of the parieto-occipital cortex. The patient with the more ventral, occipitotemporal lesions had difficulty imaging faces or animals. He described an elephant as having long legs and a neck that could reach the ground to pick things up, and Abraham Lincoln as having a short, round face. Despite these difficulties, this patient could readily draw a floor plan of his house and locate major cities on a map of the United States. In contrast, the patient with damage to the dorsal pathways produced vivid descriptions when asked to image objects, but he failed spatial imagery tasks. He described the elephant as being big, with a long nose, big floppy ears, a little tail, and four thick legs. Yet this patient was unable to describe how to get around his own neighborhood or provide knowledge of more extensive geographic regions. Chicago was described as being north of Boston. Together, these patients provide a dissociation in imagery of what-where processing that closely parallels that observed in perception.

Another source of neuropsychological evidence

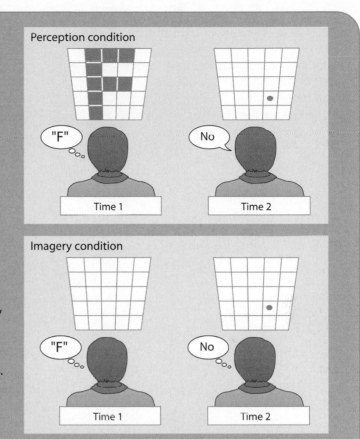

Figure A Recall processes appear to be similar when remembering either a seen or imaged object. Subjects are shown a grid that contains a letter **(left)** or upon which they are to imagine the letter. After a delay, a probe dot is presented and the subjects must judge whether the probe was on or off the seen or imagined letter. The time required to make these judgments is quite similar in the two conditions. For example, subjects are slower to respond "NO" in both conditions when the probe dot is close to the edge of the seen or imagined letter. Adapted from Podgorny and Shepard (1978).

comes from physiological studies of normal subjects. Farah measured evoked potentials while subjects read a list of words or read the words and simultaneously imaged their referents. The early evoked responses were identical for the two conditions. But in the imaging condition, the waveform increased over occipital electrodes. Although the stimuli were the same in both conditions, the imagery condition selectively enhanced activation in visual areas. Similar findings have been reported for cerebral metabolism (Kosslyn et al., 1993). In fact, the evidence suggests that imagery not only activates visual association areas, but also produces metabolic changes in the primary visual cortex.

The evidence provides a compelling case that imagery uses many of the same processes critical for perception. The sights in an image are likely to activate visual areas of the brain; the sounds, auditory areas; and the smells, olfactory areas. Indeed, the imagery results demonstrate that memory for perceptual information is not independent of perceptual processes. We need not think of perceptual processing and the memory of that processing as distinct neural entities. Perceptual

memory might simply reactivate perceptual pathways.

Despite the similarities between perception and imagery, it would be premature to conclude that the two are identical. Patients frequently have corresponding deficits in perception and imagery, but there are notable exceptions. Patients with no evidence of agnosia may have imagery deficits, being unable to recall whether animals have long or short tails, or whether the letter *P* has a curved segment. By contrast, intact imagery has been observed in patients with severe agnosia.

We can try to account for the dissociations between imagery and perception by supposing that while imagery and perception share forms of representation, they may achieve them in distinct ways. Consider two versions of a task that requires you to decide if a donkey's ears are pointed or floppy. In the imagery version, you must generate an internal representation. It is unlikely that you could do this by imaging the donkey's ears. Instead, an image of the entire animal will probably be created and the observer will zoom in for a closer examination of the head. Imagery as such requires that the parts be generated and arranged appropriately. Now consider the perceptual version where an observer is shown a donkey's picture and, as with imagery, is asked to identify parts and make comparisons. In perception, the parts need not be generated but must be extracted from the representation of the stimulus. The critical process is to partition the percept into its component parts—to segment the ears from the head.

Dissociations between imagery and perception have led to models in which access to visual knowledge can occur through multiple pathways. Consider again patient C.K., the patient with severe agnosia who had difficulty in extracting the parts of a complex object. C.K. had no problems with imagery tasks. When read the names of objects, C.K. produced excellent drawings (Figure B). When shown the same drawings during a subsequent visit, he failed to identify any of them. In a similar way, while C.K. had difficulty recognizing letters, he was successful at imagery tasks that required multiple transformations. He readily provided the answer to the question, "What letter do you get when you take the letter *L*, flip it from top to bottom and add a horizontal line in the middle." In these tasks, C.K. demonstrated that he can represent objects visually and has knowledge of visual attributes. His representations are not simply of whole objects: The letter transformation task demonstrated that he can generate and manipulate the parts. C.K. failed when he had to extract parts from the perceptual input. Without this capability, his object recognition capacity is limited.

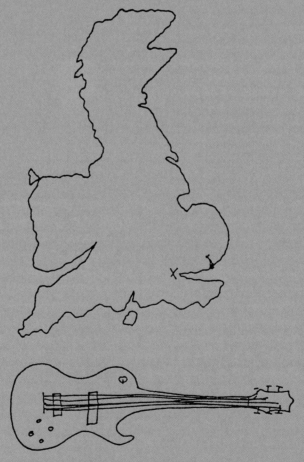

Figure B The ability to draw objects from memory may be spared in agnosia. Patient C.K.'s drawings of a map of the United Kingdom and an electric guitar. His ability to generate an internal visual representation would appear to be intact. However, C.K. was unable to recognize the objects in his own drawings on a subsequent visit.

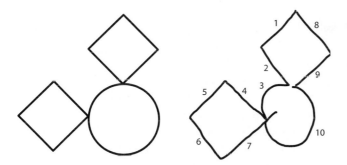

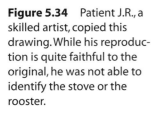

Figure 5.33 Patient C.K. was asked to copy the figure shown at the left. As can be seen at the right, his overall performance was quite good: One can readily identify the two diamonds and the circle. However, the numbers indicate the order in which he produced the segments. Unlike healthy subjects, C.K. did not draw each object in its entirety, but followed the outer boundary, even if this meant switching between objects. Adapted from Behrmann et al. (1994).

upper diamond and the rest of the circle. For C.K., each intersection defined the segments of different parts. He failed to link these parts in recognizable wholes.

Another dramatic case involved an artist who became agnosic after an occipital stroke. The patient retained a keen sense of drawing, as can be seen in his copy of a silk screen in Figure 5.34. Even after drawing the picture, though, he could not recognize the objects; he failed to identify the stove, and only after prodding was he willing to admit that the animal might be a "domestic bird."

Warrington's analysis of perceptual and semantic categorization fails to capture the integration problems faced by these patients, to synthesize parts into a coherent whole. An isolated part may provide the perceiver with a hypothesis about the identity of a stimulus, perhaps even proving sufficient with unique objects (e.g., the frame of a bicycle). But, in most situations, parts must be integrated into wholes. Patient P.T. was fixated on the belief that the depicted combination lock was a telephone because of the circular array of numbers, a salient feature on the rotary phones of his time. He was unable to integrate this part with the other components of the combination lock. Object perception is truly a situation where the whole is greater than the sum of its parts.

Figure 5.34 Patient J.R., a skilled artist, copied this drawing. While his reproduction is quite faithful to the original, he was not able to identify the stove or the rooster.

PROSOPAGNOSIA

It is hard to deny that the most important things we must recognize are faces. Though people may have characteristic physiques and mannerisms, their facial features provide the strongest distinctions of one person from another. Think about what you say when describing a new acquaintance to a friend. You may begin by providing information about the person's shape (e.g., large or small), but beyond that, most of the description will center on facial features: Does the person have a long or round face? Are the eyes spaced far apart or close together? Do the lips turn upright into a perpetual smile, or are they drawn down into a pout?

The importance of face perception is reflected in our extraordinary ability to remember faces. In browsing through an old yearbook, we readily recognize the faces of people we have not seen for over 30 years. Unfortunately, our other memory abilities are not as keen. While we may recall that the person in this photograph was a lab partner in biology, her name may remain elusive. Of course it does not take 30 years to experience this frustration. On a regular basis we run into an acquaintance whose face is familiar, but we cannot remember the name or where and when a previous encounter had taken place.

Given the importance of face perception, prosopagnosia is one of the most fascinating disorders of object recognition. *Prosopagnosia* is a deficit in the ability to recognize faces that cannot be directly attributed to a deterioration in intellectual function. As with all visual agnosias, prosopagnosia requires that the deficit be specific to the visual modality. Like the patient described in the beginning of Chapter 4, patients with prosopagnosia can recognize a person upon hearing that person's voice.

Prosopagnosiacs can have difficulty recognizing the faces of familiar and unfamiliar people. A patient with bilateral occipital lesions failed to identify not only his wife, but also an even more familiar person, himself (Pallis, 1955). As he reported, "At the club I saw someone strange staring at me, and asked the steward who it was. You'll laugh at me. I'd been looking at myself in the mirror." Not surprisingly, this patient was also unable to recognize pictures of famous individuals of his time including Churchill, Hitler, Stalin, Marilyn Monroe, and Groucho Marx. This inability was particularly striking in that the patient had an excellent memory, recognized common objects with no hesitation, and could read and recognize line drawings—all tests that agnosia patients often fail.

While this patient had "normal" object perception, most patients who have been studied in laboratories show abnormalities on other tests of visual perception. Nonetheless, it is clear that their recognition problems for faces are disproportionate to their ability to recognize other objects. For example, patients with severe prosopagnosia may perform perfectly on Warrington's standard perceptual categorization tasks (e.g., matching by unusual views), yet fail miserably when face stimuli are substituted for the objects. Results such as these suggest that prosopagnosia is not related in a simple way to problems with recognizing nonfacial stimuli.

Are Faces Special?

Face perception, some say, may not use the same processing mechanisms as the ones for object recognition, but this hypothesis is counterintuitive. It is more reasonable and certainly more parsimonious to assume a single, general-purpose system for recognizing all sorts of visual inputs. Why should faces be treated differently from other objects?

One argument in favor of a specialized face-processing module is based on evolutionary arguments. When we meet other individuals, we usually look at their faces rather than their bodies—a behavior that is not a newly acquired cultural convention. The tendency to focus on faces reflects behaviors deeply engraved in our evolutionary history. Across cultures, facial expressions provide the most salient cues regarding affective states. Facial gestures help to discriminate between pleasure and displeasure, friendship and antagonism, agreement and confusion.

While evolutionary arguments can motivate a hypothesis, it is essential to develop empirical tests. Three criteria can be useful in considering whether face and other forms of object perception utilize distinct processing systems. First, do the processes involve physically distinct mechanisms? Do face perception and other forms of object perception depend on different regions of the brain? Second, are the systems functionally independent? Can each operate without the other? The logic of this criterion is essentially the same as that underlying the idea of double dissociations. Third, do the two systems process information differently?

Neural Mechanisms for Face Perception

Some patients show impairment only on tests of face perception. More often, though, the patients' performance on other object-recognition tasks is below normal. This result is in itself inconclusive with regard to the existence of specialized brain mechanisms for face perception. Do not forget that brain injury in humans is an uncontrolled experiment! Prosopagnosia rarely occurs with single, well-circumscribed lesions. This syndrome is frequently associated with bilateral lesions caused by multiple strokes, head trauma, encephalitis, or poisoning. It is likely that even if there were a specialized face perception module, other visual areas would be affected.

Given this caveat, we can still evaluate whether patients with prosopagnosia have a common foci of lesions. In her comprehensive monograph, *Visual Agnosia: Disorders of Object Recognition and What They Tell Us about Normal Vision* (1990), Martha Farah identified 81 patients reported to be prosopagnosic. Table 5.1 summarizes the general location of the pathology in 71 of these patients. What is most notable is that the lesions were bilateral in 46 patients (65%). The number would probably increase if the brains were examined at autopsy, as CT and MRI frequently do not detect lesions, especially with head trauma. For the remaining 25 patients (35%) with unilateral lesions, the incidence was much higher for right-sided lesions than left-sided ones. For bilateral and unilateral situations, the lesions generally involved occipital and temporal cortices.

Knowing the messiness of human neuropsychology, researchers have turned to single-cell recordings in primates as an alternative methodology for testing the hypothesis that dedicated neural mechanisms act on face perception. The researchers have concentrated on the temporal cortex. Visual cells in the superior and inferior regions of the temporal lobe have huge receptive fields. A preferred stimulus can be placed almost anywhere in the field of view and the cell will respond. Intriguingly, many cells respond most strongly to faces. Their behavior closely resembles what would be expected of a grandmother cell in almost a literal sense, although no one has ever compared pictures of grandma and grandpa.

In one study, recordings were made from cells in the superior temporal sulcus while a monkey was presented with stimuli like the ones in Figure 5.35. Five of these stimuli were faces, either of other monkeys or, once, of an experimenter. The other five stimuli ranged in complexity but included the most prominent features in the facial stimuli. For example, the grating contains the symmetry of faces, and the circle has a shape similar to eyes. Some cells were highly selective: They responded only to the clear frontal profile of another monkey. Other cells raised their firing rate for all facial stimuli. Nonfacial stimuli hardly activated the cells. In fact, compared to spontaneous firing rates, activity decreased for some nonfacial stimuli.

Table 5.1	Summary of Lesion Foci in Patients Described as Prosopagnosic*	
Bilateral (n = 46)	65%	
Temporal		61%
Parietal		9%
Occipital		91%
Left only (n = 4)	6%	
Temporal		75%
Parietal		25%
Occipital		50%
Right only (n = 21)	29%	
Temporal		67%
Parietal		28%
Occipital		95%

*Within each subcategory, the percentages indicate how the lesions were distributed across the temporal, parietal, and occipital lobes. The sum of these percentages is greater than 100% because many of the lesions spanned more than one lobe. The majority of the patients had bilateral lesions. Adapted from Farah (1990).

We cannot conclude that cells like these respond only to faces. It is impossible to test all stimuli, and many cells in this cortical region are triggered by nonfacial stimuli. But two decades of research confirmed that many cells are activated by faces, though the studies failed to identify alternative features that explain the cells' face-selective properties, which produce little or no response to textures, gratings, or complex objects. Facial stimuli are not special because they evoke more emotional responses; the same cells are not activated by stimuli that produce a fear response in monkeys. In contrast, we find marked responses to real faces and to photographs of monkey or human faces.

Dissociations of Face and Object Perception

These provocative neurophysiological results support our first criterion, that face perception and object perception utilize distinct physical processing systems. In turning to the second criterion—whether face and object perception can be dissociated—keep in mind the problems with single dissociations. As we discovered, many case reports recount patients who have a selective disorder in face perception; they cannot recognize faces but have little problem recognizing objects. Even so this evidence does not mandate a specialized processor for faces. Perhaps the tests that assess face perception are more sensitive than the ones that evaluate object recognition.

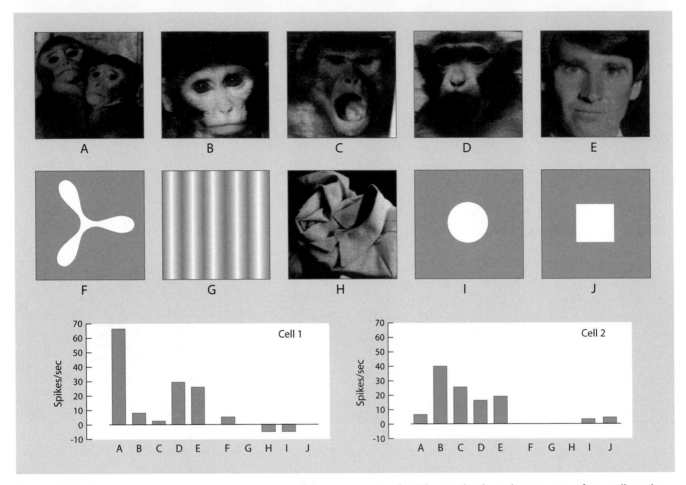

Figure 5.35 Face cells in the superior temporal sulcus of the macaque monkey. The graphs show the response of two cells to the ten stimuli (labeled A–J). Both cells responded vigorously to many of the facial stimuli. Either there was no change in activity when the animal looked at the objects, or in some cases, the cells were actually inhibited relative to baseline. The firing rate data are plotted as a change from baseline activity for that cell when no stimulus was presented. Bottom panel, adapted from Baylis et al. (1985).

One concern has been that face-perception tests are qualitatively different from the ones that test recognition of common objects. In particular, the stimuli for assessing face perception are all from the same category: faces. The subjects' task is to judge whether two faces are the same or different, or they are required to identify specific faces. When object perception is tested, the stimuli cover a much broader range. Here subjects are asked to discriminate chairs from tables, or identify common objects such as clocks and telephones. The category-specific agnosia for living things may simply reflect the fact that these objects are more similar to one another and thus harder to discriminate. Perhaps the same logic can account for a deficit in face perception. Face-recognition tasks call for identifying a specific face rather than a generic object.

This argument is probably not valid, though. In a clever study, McNeil and Warrington (1993) assessed a sheep farmer on two within-category identification tasks (Figure 5.36). In a face-perception task, the patient, who had suffered several strokes, responded at chance when asked to pick out the photograph of a famous face displayed along with photographs of two people unfamiliar to the subject. In contrast, the patient performed well on tests that required him to identify sheep from his own flock. A second experiment tested recognition memory for faces and sheep. He first viewed pictures of sheep or faces. After a short delay, these same stimuli were intermixed with new photographs and the patient had to judge if he had seen the animal or face before. For his own sheep and sheep from a different breed, the patient's performance was higher than that of other subjects, including some who were also sheep farmers! For faces, though, the patient's performance was at the level of chance while the control subjects' performances were close to perfect.

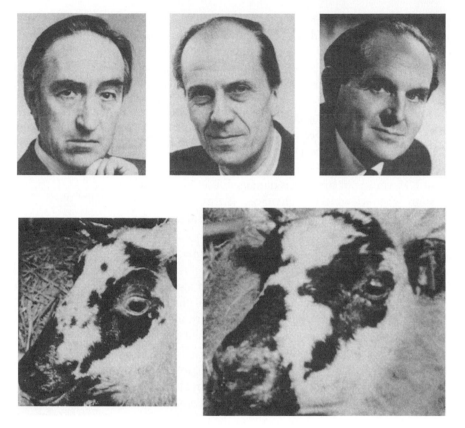

Figure 5.36 Face-specific recognition deficits cannot be attributed to the fact that faces represent a difficult within-category discrimination. A sheep farmer, W.J., with prosopagnosia demonstrated impairment in recognizing famous faces, yet was more accurate in recognizing both his own sheep and unfamiliar sheep in comparison to control subjects. In one of the face discrimination tasks, the subjects were shown three faces and asked to point to the one familiar face. In this example, the familiar face is Norman Tebbit, a well-known (to the British population) politician of the Thatcher era. The faces on the left and right were unfamiliar to the subjects. The sheep is from W.J.'s farm. One group of control subjects was selected based on W.J.'s previous work experience; the other was selected based on their experience in raising sheep. Reprinted with permission from McNeil and Warrington (1993).

Farah and her colleagues (1994) also argued that prosopagnosia cannot be attributed to the fact that face recognition entails a difficult within-category discrimination. Their experiments demonstrated that face perception does not involve the same processes and representations as object perception. A central figure in this work was a prosopagnosia patient, L.H., a person with diffuse brain damage resulting from a car accident. L.H. was tested with two recognition memory tests, one with face stimuli and the other with eyeglasses. Using only eyeglasses for the second set mitigates the criticism that nonfacial object recognition tests involve stimuli much more distinct from one another than facial stimuli. In the study phase, half the stimuli from each set were presented. Then, in the memory test, all the stimuli were presented and the patient had to judge if the stimulus was old or new. Control subjects correctly recognized 85% of the faces and 69% of the eyeglasses. L.H. scored only 64% correct with the faces in comparison to 63% with the eyeglasses. A patient with integrative agnosia had an opposite pattern of deficits: Performance with faces rose to 98% but fell to chance for eyeglasses.

Farah also exploited a well-established phenomenon in face perception: the face inversion effect. Look at the face in Figure 5.37. Try recognizing the face in its upside-down orientation and then turn your book upside-down. The effect is striking. Recognition is im-mediate when the stimulus is viewed in its proper orientation but difficult with inverted faces.

One interpretation of the inversion effect is that we no longer can use a specialized face-processing system but must revert to a more analytic, analysis-by-parts mode of processing for an upside-down face. These faces constitute the perfect control stimulus for assessing the

Figure 5.37 Who is this person? Is there anything unusual about the picture? Recognition can be quite difficult when faces are viewed upside down. Even more surprising, we fail to note a severe distortion created by inverting the eyes and mouth—something that would be immediately apparent when viewed right side up. The person is former British prime minister Margaret Thatcher, a face that would be widely recognized even in the United States in the late 1970's.

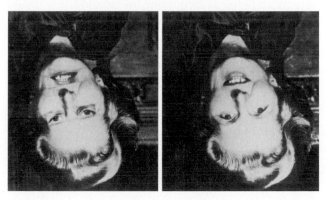

special status of face perception. While stimuli in the normal orientation and upside-down orientation contain identical information, only the normal condition should be disrupted in patients with prosopagnosia. This is exactly what was found. In fact, L.H. had the opposite of an inversion effect. For the upright and upside-down conditions, control subjects were correct on 94% and 82% of the trials, respectively. L.H.'s performance was better with upside-down faces (72%) in comparison with upright faces (58%). One surprising finding was that L.H. could not bypass his damaged face-recognition system when viewing upright faces. If this were so, he would have performed well with both stimuli. But he continued to utilize his face-recognition system, even though it failed to produce the representations required for the recognition memory task.

Research with healthy people reinforced the notion that face perception requires a representation that is not simply a concatenation of individual parts. In one study, subjects were asked to recognize line drawings of faces and houses. Each stimulus was constructed of limited parts. For faces, the parts were eyes, nose, and mouth; for houses, the parts were doors, living room windows, and bedroom windows. In a learning phase, subjects saw a name and either a face or a house (Figure 5.38). For the face, they were instructed to associate the name with the face. For example, Larry had round eyes, a pointed nose, and a narrow mouth. For the house, they were instructed to learn the name of the person who lived in the house. For example, Larry lived in a house with a three-paneled door, shuttered living room window, and rounded bedroom windows.

After learning, a recognition memory test was given. The critical manipulation was whether the probe item was presented in isolation or in context, embedded in the whole object. For example, when asked whether the stimulus matched Larry's nose, the nose was presented either by itself or in the context of Larry's eyes and mouth. As predicted, house perception did not depend on whether the test items were presented in isolation or as an entire object. But face perception did. The subjects were much better at identifying the person when shown a face containing all three features.

Two Systems for Object Recognition

If we accept that there is a specialized system for face perception, a natural question is whether other forms of object perception also entail specialized systems. To answer this question, Farah (1990) focused on another subtype of visual agnosia, *acquired alexia*. *Acquired alexia* refers to reading problems after a patient has had a stroke or head trauma. When these patients succeed in reading a word,

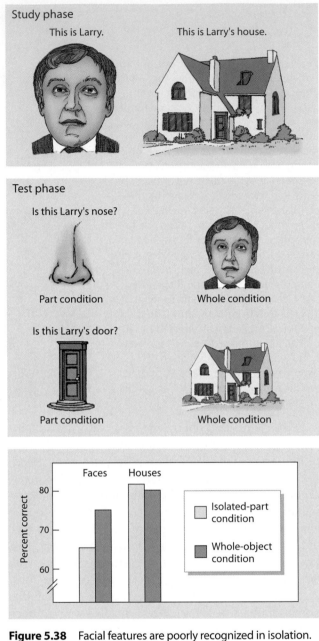

Figure 5.38 Facial features are poorly recognized in isolation. Subjects first learned the names that correspond with a set of faces and houses. During the recognition test, subjects were presented with either a face, a house, or a single feature from the faces or houses. They were asked if a particular feature belonged to an individual. When presented with the entire face subjects were much better in identifying the facial features. Recognition of the house features was the same in both conditions. Adapted from Farah (1994).

they painstakingly identify each letter. Errors usually reflect visual confusions. The word *ball* may be misread as *doll* or *snake* as *stale*. This syndrome brings up a few relevant points. First, alexia is typically associated with lesions of the left hemisphere, particularly lesions encompassing the angular gyrus in the posterior region of the parietal lobe. Thus, the anatomical focus is distinct from the temporal lobe regions associated with face-selective cells and prosopagnosia. Second, as with prosopagnosia, alexia is another example of a class-specific visual agnosia. Modality specificity is obvious because people with pure alexia do not have problems with comprehending language. They understand spoken speech and can speak without problems. Moreover, many patients retain the ability to write, a syndrome known as *alexia without agraphia*. Third, tasks that these patients fail, the analysis of printed words, are within-category deficits. Thus, alexia is similar to prosopagnosia in that the tasks for assessing this syndrome require one to discriminate between items that are a lot alike.

Another similarity to prosopagnosia is that alexia rarely occurs in isolation. Many of these patients have problems with other types of object recognition. Importantly, a double dissociation between prosopaganosia and acquired alexia becomes evident when we consider the patterns of correlation between three types of agnosia: agnosia for faces, agnosia for objects, and agnosia for words. Table 5.2 lists the pattern of co-occurrence reported by Farah in a thorough review of the literature on visual associative agnosia. She did not tally the number of patients with a selective deficit in reading because these are so numerous. She did find several patients who were impaired in recognizing all three types of materials. The lesions were probably extensive and affected multiple processes. More telling was the dissociation of face and word perception. Either deficit frequently occurred along with a disorder in object recognition. But, most critical, Farah could not find a single unequivocal

Table 5.2	Patterns of Co-occurrence of Prosopagnosia, Visual Agnosia, and Alexsia*
Deficits in all three.	21 patients
Selective deficits	
Face and objects	14 patients
Words and objects	15 patients
Faces and words	1 patient (possibly)
Faces alone	35 patients
Words alone	Many patients described in literature
Object only	1 patient (possibly)

*Note that there was only a single case in the literature reporting a patient who showed impairment in recognizing both faces and words, but not objects. Adapted from Farah (1990).

patient in whom face and word perception were impaired without a corresponding deficit in object perception. Thus, one could be prosopagnosic and agnosic without being alexic. Or, one could be agnosic and alexic without being prosopagnosic. This double dissociation suggests that face perception operates independently from the recognition of another class of visual objects: words.

A second significant result can be gleaned from Table 5.2. While alexia and prosopagnosia do not occur together, it is equally telling that agnosia for objects is always accompanied by a deficit in either word or face perception, or both. Because patients with deficits in object perception also have a problem with one of the other types of stimuli, we might be tempted to conclude that object recognition involves two independent processes. It would be unparsimonious to postulate three processing subsystems. If this were so, we would expect to find three sets of patients: those with deficits in word perception, those with face-perception deficits, and patients with object-perception deficits.

Given that the neuropsychological dissociations suggest two systems for object recognition, we can now examine the third criterion for evaluating whether face perception depends on a processing system distinct from the one for other forms of object perception. Do we process information in a unique way when attempting to recognize faces? To answer this question, we need to return to the computational issues surrounding the perception of facial and nonfacial stimuli. Are there differences in the way information is represented when we recognize faces in comparison to when we recognize common objects and words? Farah maintained that face perception is unique in one special way; whereas object recognition decomposes a stimulus into its parts, face perception is more holistic. We recognize an individual according to the facial configuration. A person is not recognized by his or her idiosyncratic nose or eyes or chin structure. The individual parts are not sufficient for face recognition; analyzing the structure and configuration of these features is what counts—hence, integrative agnosia and prosopagnosia represent two extremes. The patient with integrative agnosia cannot identify the critical parts that form an object. In contrast, the prosopagnosic patient may succeed in extracting these parts but cannot derive the holistic representation necessary for face perception.

In summary, face perception does depend on a specialized processing system. First, the neuroimaging of human lesions and single-cell recordings in primates implicate parts of the temporal lobe in face perception, with some cells responding only to facial

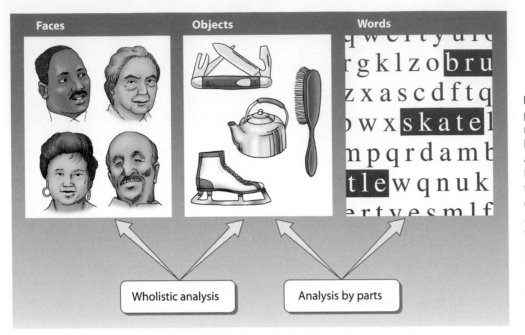

Figure 5.39 Farah's two-process model for object recognition. Recognition can be based on two forms of analysis, wholistic and part based. The contribution of these two systems varies for different classes of stimuli. Analysis by parts is essential for reading and is central for recognizing objects. A unique aspect of face recognition is its dependence on wholistic analysis. This process also contributes to object recognition.

stimuli. Second, deficits in face perception can be dissociated from other forms of agnosia, particularly agnosia for words. Third, information for face perception is represented differently from that for other objects. For object perception, decomposing the object into defining parts is emphasized. For faces, the critical information requires a more holistic representation to capture the configuration of the defining parts.

This is not to say that these two modes of object recognition operate exclusively of one another. Farah proposed that, in normal perception, both systems are activated. The relative contribution of the analysis-by-parts and holistic systems depends on the task (Figure 5.39). Words represent a special class of objects that must be successfully decomposed into their constituent parts. We benefit little from noting general features such as word length. We have to recognize the individual let-

ters in order to differentiate one word from another. But even here, phenomena such as the word superiority effect suggest that we represent both the individual letters and their combination into words.

Face perception is at the other extreme. For these stimuli, discerning the parts is of little importance. Think how hard it is to notice that a casual acquaintance has shaved his mustache. Rather, recognition requires that we perceive a familiar arrangement of the parts.

Object recognition falls somewhere between these two extremes. A telephone can be identified by defining features such as the number pad and receiver, but recognition can be facilitated when we perceive the shape of this familiar object. This hypothesis accounts for why agnosia for objects can occur with either alexia or prosopagnosia. With either disorder, object recognition depends on a single, intact system.

SUMMARY

This chapter provided an overview of the higher-level processes involved in visual perception. The first section focused on the what-where distinction. People, like most mammals, are visual creatures: Most of us rely on our eyes not only to identify what it is that we are looking at, but also to guide our actions. These processes are surely interactive. To accomplish a skilled behavior such as catching a thrown object, we have to

determine the object's size and shape and to track its path through space so we can anticipate where to place our hands.

We have also reviewed fundamental computational problems that must be solved for successful object recognition. In doing so, we have seen that object recognition can be achieved in a multiplicity of ways and involves many levels of representation. We must overcome the variability inherent in the sensory input by extracting the critical information that distinguishes one shape from another. Perceptual categorization solves only part of the recognition problem. For this information to be useful, the contents of current processing must be connected to our stored knowledge about visual objects. Semantic categorization allows us to see the similarities between percepts and recognize the unique features of objects. We do not see a meaningless array of shapes and forms: Rather, visual perception is an efficient avenue for recognizing and interacting with the world: what path to take across a cluttered room or which tools to make our actions more efficient.

Moreover, vision provides a salient means for one of the most essential goals of perception: recognizing conspecifics. One might suppose that the importance of face perception led to the evolution of an alternative form of representation, one that analyzed the global configuration of a stimulus rather than its parts. On the other hand, we may have evolved multiple forms of representation, and face perception may be highly dependent on the configural form of representation. As seen in Farah's model, the evidence leads us to regard the dichotomy between part-based and configural-based representations as absolute. In object recognition, these two forms of representation interact; their relative contribution varies according to the task and the objects being perceived.

The goals-oriented aspects of perception—that we use vision to guide our movements, to manipulate tools, or to recognize faces—also underscores the selective aspects of cognition. We are not passive processors of information. We can select from the dazzling array that impinges on our senses at any one time. Depending on our goals, the relative importance of different sources of information constantly changes.

SUGGESTED READINGS

BIEDERMAN, I. (1990). Higher-Level Vision. In D.N. Osherson, S.M. Kosslyn, and J.M. Hollberbach (Eds.), *Visual Cognition and Action: An Invitation to Cognitive Science,* Vol. 2, Cambridge, MA: MIT Press.

DESIMONE, R. (1991). Face-selective cells in the temporal cortex of monkeys. *J. Cogn. Neurosci.* 3:1–8.

FARAH, M.J. (1990). *Visual Agnosia: Disorders of Object Recognition and What They Tell Us about Normal Vision.* Cambridge, MA: MIT Press.

UNGERLEIDER, L.G., and Mishkin, M. (1982). Two Cortical Visual Systems. In D.J. Engle, M.A. Goodale, and R.J. Mansfield (Eds.), *Analysis of Visual Behavior,* Cambridge, MA: MIT Press.

WARRINGTON, E.K. (1985). Agnosia: The Impairment of Object Recognition. In P.J. Vinkin, G.W. Bruyn, and H.L. Klawans (Eds.), *Handbook of Clinical Neurology,* New York: Elsevier Science.

6

Attention and Selective Perception

How do we attend to the world around us? How much do our internal desires, beliefs, momentary necessities, and intent affect our perceptual experiences? How do external events in the world capture our attention, and how does this interact with our voluntary control? What brain systems and mechanisms underlie these attentional processes, and what syndromes and deficits occur when these systems are damaged or fail to develop normally?

How important is attention? Consider for a moment the perilous consequences of a lapse in attention. In 1987, a Northwest Airlines passenger jet (Flight 255) departing from Detroit crashed moments after takeoff, killing 154 passengers and crew and two persons on the ground. The team from the National Transportation Safety Board investigating the incident filed their summary report several months later: The crash could not be attributed to mechanical failures, sabotage, or the weather. The report suggested a simpler explanation: The wing flaps were not set in the proper position required for takeoff, hence the crash. The veteran pilots were, however, well aware that the position of the flaps was crucial for takeoff, yet the flaps were not properly set, the pilots began takeoff, and the jet crashed. The mystery deepens because the pilots apparently failed to notice cockpit warning indicators that should have alerted them to the improperly set flaps, including visual and auditory warnings. Another airline pilot who doubted that the flaps could have been overlooked said, "You don't get in a car and forget to close your door, and you don't get in your plane and forget to set your flaps." Offering an explanation for such a seemingly improbable event, the chair of the Federal Aviation Administration at that time suggested that perhaps the pilots had become complacent, saying, "You [become] so good at what you do that you do it routinely rather than with the attention and proficiency that it demands." [Quotes from the *New York Times*, August 21, 1987, Wilkerson, I. Apparent lapse on wing flaps shocks experts.]

The concept of "attention" is at once intuitive and enigmatic. You understand what it means to pay attention to something—be it the material of a lecture, the path you are navigating on your bicycle, or a bird flying overhead. At first pass it may appear that attention is identical to seeing or perceiving, but on deeper reflection it is clear that attention involves something more than sensation and perception, though it undoubtedly interacts with them. For example, one can attend to things other than sensory inputs. Attention can be directed to internal mental processes such as memories, or the performance of a complex task such as mental arithmetic. Much of the introspective flavor of attention was captured by early psychologists like William James (Figure 6.1), brother of Henry, the novelist and playwright.

> Everyone knows what attention is. It is the taking possession of the mind, in clear and vivid form, of one out of what seem several simultaneously possible objects or trains of thought. Focalization, concentration of consciousness are of its essence. It implies withdrawal from some things in order to deal effectively with others, and is a condition which has a real opposite in the confused, dazed, scatterbrain state. . . .
>
> William James (1890)

Figure 6.1 William James (1842–1910).

In this insightful quote, James captures characteristics of attentional phenomena that are under investigation today. For example, his statement that "it is the taking possession by the mind" comments on the voluntary aspects of attention; we can control the focus of our attention. And his mention of "one out of what seem several simultaneously possible objects or trains of thought" refers to the inability to attend to many things at once, and hence the selective aspects of attention. James reinforces the idea of limited capacity in attention by noting that "it implies withdrawal from some things in order to deal effectively with others. . . ."

As clear and articulate as James's writings were, very little of the computational mechanisms and virtually none of the neurophysiological implementation of these processes were understood during his lifetime. Even after more than 100 years of investigation, the study of attentional mechanisms continues to accelerate as we seek to understand the neural substrates of attention and selective perception.

The merging of neurobiology and psychology in the study of attention defines the cognitive neuroscience of attention. The reasons for such a combined research endeavor have been aptly summarized by the eminent cognitive psychologist Alan Allport (1993) of Oxford University, who noted that ". . . attentional functions are of very many different kinds, serving a great range of different computational purposes. There can be no simple *theory of attention,* any more than there can be a simple *theory of thought.* A humbler but more ambitious task for the next 25 years will be to characterize, in cognitive neurobiological terms, as much as possible of this great diversity of attentional functions." Many of these diverse aspects of attention and their known or hypothesized neural substrates are presented in this chapter.

Studies of the cognitive neuroscience of attention have three principal goals: (1) to understand how attention enables and influences the detection, perception, and encoding of stimulus events, as well as the generation of actions based on the stimuli; (2) to describe what computational algorithms enable these effects; and (3) to uncover how these algorithms are implemented in the human brain's neuronal circuits and neural systems. Understanding these processes will ultimately permit us to comprehend how damage or disease in these systems leads to attentional deficits and cognitive problems.

THEORETICAL MODELS OF ATTENTION

In 1894, Hermann von Helmholtz performed a fascinating experiment in visual perception (Figure 6.2). He constructed a screen on which letters were painted at various distances from the center of the screen. He hung the screen and then used an electrical spark to briefly illuminate it, essentially just a flash of light. Helmholtz wanted to investigate aspects of visual processing, but also came upon an interesting phenomenon. The screen was too large to view all of it without moving the eyes. But if Helmholtz held his eyes still in the center of the screen, he could decide in advance where he would pay attention; that is, he made use of

something we now refer to as *covert attention,* wherein the visual field location to which gaze is directed can be different from that to which one chooses to pay attention. In so doing he observed that during the brief period of illumination, he could perceive the letters located within the region of the screen to which he had directed his attention in advance (without moving his eyes) but could not discriminate the letters elsewhere on the screen. Helmholtz noted that, "These experiments demonstrated, so it seems to me, that by a voluntary kind of intention, even without eye movements, and without changes of accommodation,

Behavioral Arousal and Selective Attention

Attention has complex definitions. It involves consciousness, awareness, and attentiveness, not to mention related deficits. Scientists concentrated primarily on global states of attention prior to the beginnings of the information-processing revolution in the late 1950s and early 1960s. The emphasis then was on distinctions between conscious and unconscious states, such as sleep versus wakefulness. In the late 1940s, Giuseppi Moruzzi and Horace Magoun (1949) at the University of California at Los Angeles showed that stimulating a cat's brainstem changed its global behavioral state. In some regions of the brainstem, sleep was induced by stimulation, while in other regions wakefulness resulted.

These changes in global state or arousal can be related to specific neurons in the brain, and are reflected by changes in the electroencephalogram (EEG), the small voltage fluctuations that accompany neuronal activity in the brains of all animals. The EEG is a clear indicator of the state of global arousal and sleep in normal subjects; one can pinpoint the change from wakefulness to sleep and to different stages of sleep by viewing the EEG alone. Such changes must, however, be distinguished from the changes in brain activity that form the basis for selective attention and selective perception.

Attentive behaviors have a hierarchical structure. At the most global level are states of alertness such as sleep and wakefulness. Wakefulness includes more and less attentive states: drowsiness, alertness, and hyperalertness such as when a life-threatening situation arises. At a finer level of description are levels within each awake, global state of awareness; here we reach levels of description that are appropriate for considering selectivity, as with the cocktail party effect.

The cocktail party effect is not just a global change in behavioral arousal or attentive state, but a reflection of a *selective* attention because the listener's goal is to attend to one source of sound while simultaneously ignoring potentially distracting inputs. These effects may be covert because we may not become aware of them by observing the listener we think is listening to us. This distinction between selective processes and global state changes is essential for its implications in attention research—which is not to say that arousal, vigilance, and other global states are not interesting topics of research—and for the implications that nonselective behavioral changes can have for experimental design and the changes in neural activity correlated with different tasks. Showing that neurons are more active when an animal is excitedly performing a task, as compared with drowsily watching stimuli, might be an example only of a nonspecific state difference induced by the excitement of the task, and not evidence of neuronal mechanisms of selective processing. Nonspecific behavioral arousal might increase the activity of all sensory neurons and not merely those processing the attended stimuli. These design considerations plagued the interpretation of many early studies of selective attention as described in the text. The problems were overcome by controls that physiological psychologists used for studying auditory attention in humans. This victory is largely due to the appreciation of a theoretical framework in the psychological literature that distinguished between nonspecific global state changes and selective processes—just one example of how hard-fought theories fuel scientific advances.

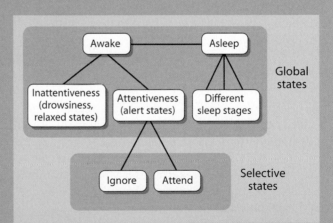

Hierarchical relationships between states of arousal, attentiveness, and selective attention.

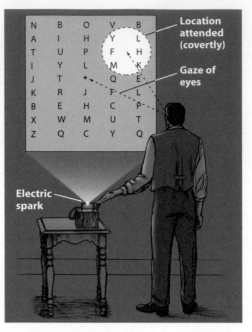

Figure 6.2 Hermann von Helmholtz (1821–1894). Experimental setup by Helmholtz to study visual attention. Helmholtz observed that while keeping his eyes fixated in the center of the screen, during a very brief illumination of the screen, he could "covertly" attend to any location on the screen and perceive the letters located within this region.

one can concentrate attention on the sensation from a particular part of our peripheral nervous system and at the same time exclude attention from all other parts."

From the work of James and Helmholtz, much of what we understood from introspective examination of attentional phenomena was laid out by the turn of the century. Not until the last half of this century, though, have psychologists been able to provide empirical support for any of the concepts put forth by either James or Helmholtz. In the 1950s, psychologists asked about the mechanisms of attention, and the scientific study of Helmholtz's covert attention began.

The Cocktail Party Effect

British psychologist E.C. Cherry (1953) examined the so-called cocktail party effect. How is it that in the noisy, confusing environment of a cocktail party, people can focus on a single conversation? Is the conversation more salient because of the speaker's and listener's proximity? No, this explanation is inadequate because our everyday experience indicates that the loudest inputs are not always the best perceived. Indeed, one goal of the listener at the cocktail party is to overcome the louder inputs of the environment (e.g., the music or nearby boisterous conversations) and to attend to the conversation of interest. Imagine that you have just met an alluring person at a party and you are desperately trying to hear what the person is saying so you can respond intelligently and with panache. The desired response to comments is not "Huh? . . . excuse me? . . . what did you say?" Rather, you want to reply with style, and so you pay close attention

to what is said and try to avoid interference from other inputs.

Selective auditory attention is the mechanism by which you achieve your goal—perception of a weak speech signal in a noisy environment—and avoid the necessity of cupping your ear, requesting the band to play more quietly, or insulting other party goers by telling them to pipe down. By selectively attending, you can perceive the signal of interest amidst the louder noise, and remain charming in a difficult social context. But if you think the person is boring, you may choose (or be unable to avoid) to attend to another conversation (Figure 6.3).

This cocktail party effect clearly demonstrates the kinds of phenomena that interest psychologists studying attention. Cherry analyzed the effect by providing competing speech inputs to the two ears of a normal subject through headphones (dichotic listening). In different conditions he asked people to attend to and verbally "shadow" (immediately repeat) a train of speech coming into one ear, while simultaneously ignoring similar inputs to the other ear.

Cherry discovered that when a different train of speech was played into each ear, and the subjects were asked to shadow what was played into only one ear at a time, they could not remember the details of the speech in the unattended ear (Figure 6.4). This led Cherry and others to propose that attention to one ear resulted in better encoding of the inputs to the attended ear.

British psychologist Donald Broadbent (1958) at Cambridge University proposed a model of attention to explain data from researchers like Cherry. He concep-

Figure 6.3 The cocktail party effect of Cherry (1953), illustrating how in the noisy confusing environment of the cocktail party, people are able to focus attention upon a single train of conversation.

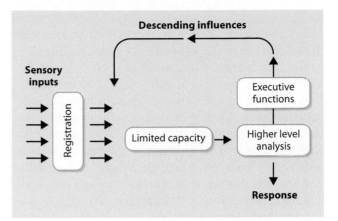

Figure 6.5 Broadbent's model of selective attention. In this model, a gating mechanism determines what limited information is passed on for higher analysis. Adapted from Broadbent (1958).

tualized the system as having a limited-capacity channel through which only a certain amount of information could pass (Figure 6.5). Hence, the many sensory inputs capable of entering higher levels of the brain for processing had to be screened to let the most important (attended) events through. Broadbent described this limited capacity system as a gate that could be opened for attended information and closed for ignored information.

Some features of Broadbent's model fit the data well, and explained the processing limitations revealed in experiments like those of Cherry; but not all data could be understood by a strict gating mechanism. Cherry and his

contemporaries such as Neville Moray (1959) also noted that, even though information coming into the unattended ear was not noticed in most circumstances, if it contained information of high enough priority to the subjects—for example, if their name was presented to the unattended channel of inputs—then they could discriminate and orient to the information. This concept of intrusion of unattended inputs led many to believe that all information was analyzed, regardless of whether it was attended or ignored later. This set the stage for a debate that has persisted to the present. The question is, Can we completely close the gate on a source of inputs and eliminate it from further processing? If so, where does this gate reside in the information-processing system, and does this affect all subsequent encoding and memory processes that might normally act on those inputs?

Early- Versus Late-Selection Theories

A central question raised by the cocktail party experiments has to do with the stage(s) of stimulus processing where incoming signals can be selected or rejected by internal attentional processes. This is the "early- versus late-selection" idea in which psychologists asked about the extent of processing that supposedly ignored signals might actually attain. That is, if we are unaware of ignored conversations, perhaps we simply close the gate on irrelevant inputs before they reach conscious awareness: But the key question is, How much before?

Early selection is the idea that a stimulus need not be completely perceptually analyzed and encoded as semantic or categorical information before it can be either selected for further processing or rejected as irrelevant. Using the observations of Helmholtz (see Figure 6.2),

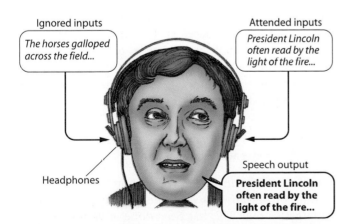

Figure 6.4 Cherry's shadowing experimental setup that presents auditory information to both ears of a subject. The subject is asked to report the auditory stimuli from one input.

we can describe early selection as the idea that, during visual processing, it may be possible to process only those letters from the to-be-attended spatial position by gating information from irrelevant positions prior to when they are encoded as letters (i.e., their nonperceptual, meaning representation) within the brain. In early-selection models, it may even be possible to select inputs prior to a full analysis of the stimuli's elementary features—before analysis of luminance, form, and color, to name a few examples. Thus, the concept of early selection suggests that this type of attention could potentially alter our perceptions by gating ignored inputs at an early point in visual processing.

Early-selection models can be contrasted with an alternative concept called *late selection*, which assumes that attended and ignored inputs are processed equivalently by the perceptual system and reach a stage of semantic (meaning) encoding and analysis. Thereafter, selection for additional processing and representation in conscious awareness takes place. This view implies that attentional processes cannot affect our perceptions of stimuli by changing the way they are processed by the sensory-perceptual processing system. Instead, all selection takes place at higher stages of information processing that involve decisions about whether the stimuli should gain complete access to awareness, be encoded in memory, or initiate a response—the term *decisions* in this context refers to nonconscious processes, not a conscious decision on the part of the observer. Differential stages of early versus late selection are presented in Figure 6.6.

The strict versions of early-selection models proposed by Broadbent did not permit semantic encoding or analysis of unattended information. Given that high-priority signals could break through from supposedly unattended sources of sensory input, this original view of Broadbent was in need of modification. This was because a simple gating mechanism which assumed that ignored information was lost could not accommodate the fact that sometimes unattended information was not perceived but at other times it was. Anne Treisman (1969) proposed that perhaps unattended channel information was not completely gated out of higher analysis but merely degraded or attenuated. Broadbent (1970) agreed with this view, and hence early versus late selection was modified to make room for the possibility that information on the unattended channel could pass the gate, but in a greatly attenuated fashion. Because such information could reach the level of semantic analysis, if it was important enough it might lead to an attentional switch (selection) at the level of semantic coding, and thereby reach awareness.

LIMITED-CAPACITY PROCESSES

One aspect of the early versus late debate is the concept of *limited capacity,* an idea that naturally flows from the observation that human performance suffers when overloaded by multiple inputs. The early- and late-selection views assume that the human (or animal) information-processing system cannot simultaneously process multiple inputs if there is a high information load, so the system must make hard "decisions" about what to process next—the core of selection. When a stage of processing has a lower capacity than its input stage, then a processing bottleneck occurs; this happens at key way stations during information processing. Presumably the information-processing system evolved selection mechanisms to control information flow at these bottlenecks and to establish priorities.

The difference between early- and late-selection theories has sometimes been framed by the following questions: Where does the bottleneck reside? And thus, Where must selection take place? Is it at an early perceptual level or at later encoding, decision, or response levels? Let us examine the evidence from normal subjects who were given detection and discrimination tasks that manipulated attention.

Figure 6.6 Diagram of early versus late selection of perceptual processing. This conceptualization is concerned with the extent of processing an input signal might attain before it can be selected or rejected by internal attentional processes.

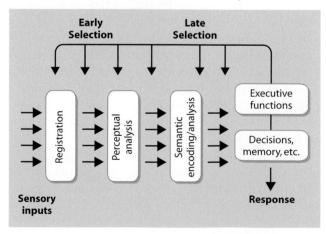

Quantifying Attention in Perception

One way of measuring the effect of attention on information processing is to examine how subjects respond to target stimuli. This has been done in various experiments, but one of the most fruitful approaches has been to measure the reaction time for detecting or discriminating a visual target when it appears at locations that are attended and unattended (visual spatial attention). Spatial attention can be manipulated by inducing subjects to believe that targets are more likely to be in one place versus another (voluntary attentional orienting) or by attracting visual attention to locations by using sensory stimuli (automatic attentional orienting). Attention is manipulated by an attention-directing cue, which is presented prior to the delivery of each target stimulus. The speed of responses to attended or unattended location events is an index of attention-related processing.

VOLUNTARY ORIENTING

In voluntary attention experiments, subjects are instructed that the most likely location for the next target is the one preceded by a cue such as an arrow pointing to a location. If the relation between cue and target is strong—that is, the cue usually predicts the target location—then subjects learn to use the cue to predict the next target's location. Sometimes, though, the target is presented to locations not indicated by the cue on that trial (Figure 6.7). The result is that subjects respond faster to the target stimulus when the cue cor-

rectly predicts the target's location, even when they do not move their eyes to the cued spot. That is, if the target appears where subjects expect it, they are faster to respond to it; they are also slower to respond to targets at unexpected locations (Figure 6.8).

Differences in reaction time as a function of expectancy have been called *benefits* (speeding of reaction time) and *costs* (slowing of reaction time) with respect to a neutral situation in which the subject does not expect the target at one location more than another. These effects have been attributed to the influence of covert attention on the efficiency of information processing. According to some theories, such effects result when the predictiveness of the cue induces the subjects to internally direct a mental "spotlight" of attention to the cued visual field location. The spotlight is merely a metaphor for changes in brain processes that accompany attending to a spatial location. Because subjects are typically required to keep their eyes on a central fixation spot on the viewing screen, this means that internal or covert mechanisms are at work. Michael Posner, of the University of Oregon, and others (1980) suggested that this spotlight may affect reaction times by influencing sensory and perceptual processing; hence, representations of attended-location stimuli

Figure 6.7 The spatial cuing paradigm of Posner and colleague. A subject sits in front of a computer screen and fixates on the central cross. An arrow cue indicates to which visual hemifield the subject is to covertly attend. The cue is then followed by a target in either the correctly or the incorrectly cued location.

Figure 6.8 Results of the study by Posner and colleagues, as shown by reaction times (RT) to unexpected, neutral, and expected targets for the right and left visual hemifields. Reaction times for expected locations are significantly faster than those for neutral or unexpected targets. Adapted from Posner et al. (1980).

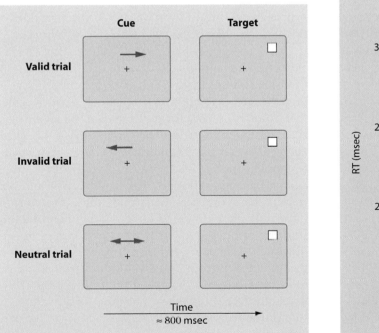

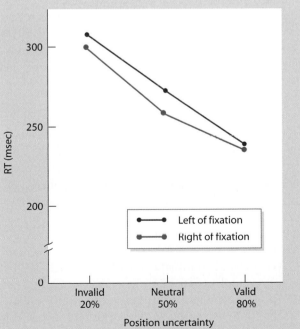

are enhanced with respect to unattended-location stimuli. This formulation, one early-selection model, proposes that changes in perceptual processing can happen when attending to a stimulus location.

AUTOMATIC ORIENTING

Introspection and experimental data converge to support the idea that attention can be directed voluntarily to locations or objects in the sensory world—and to internal mental events. In addition, things in the environment sometimes attract our attention without our cooperation, as any student sitting in the back of a classroom can attest. What happens when the lecturer leaves the door to the hallway open and, in the middle of lecture, someone walks down the hallway passing the open door? Heads turn toward the sounds and sights in the hall and then wag back to the lecturer a moment or two later. This sometimes happens before we can stop ourselves, and is a sign of the overt orientation of attention to external cues—"overt" because heads and eyes turn toward the event in the hallway. But even in the absence of overt signs of orienting, covert attention is also attracted to the sensory stimulus, which can be demonstrated experimentally by using a variant of cuing methods.

As with voluntary attention, reaction times can be shorter for targets presented to previously stimulated locations even when the observer's voluntary attention is not involved, that is, when automatic attention is invoked. One way to demonstrate this is to examine the effects of presenting a flash of light somewhere in the visual field and then measuring the speed of responses to subsequent task-relevant target stimuli. This is referred to as *exogenous cuing* because attention is controlled by external stimuli and not by internal voluntary control. The typical exogenous cuing design uses cues (light flashes) that do not predict the location of subsequent targets; nonetheless, performance is faster at the cued location, but only for a short time after the light flash (usually within about 50–250 msec). When more time passes between the cuing light flash and the target (> 300 msec), the effects are reversed: Subjects respond more slowly to these stimuli. This slowing of responses is called the *inhibitory aftereffect* or, more commonly, *inhibition of return* (IOR); as the name suggests, it means that the recently attended location becomes inhibited over time.

Why would automatic attentional orienting have such profound variations in its effect over time after a sensory cue? The answer is simple: If sensory events in the environment caused automatic orienting that lasted for many seconds or tens of seconds, it would be diffi-

cult to function normally in the world. We would be continually distracted by things happening around us. Imagine the potential disaster for someone driving a car. It is no surprise, then, that the automatic orienting system has built-in mechanisms to prevent this; so, over time (a few tens or a couple of hundred milliseconds) the automatic capturing of attention subsides and the likelihood that attention will be attracted back to that location is slightly reduced. If the event is important, we merely invoke our voluntary mechanisms to sustain attention longer. Thus, the nervous system has evolved clever methods to control attention so we can function in this hectic sensory world.

SEARCHING THE VISUAL SCENE

A natural aspect of everyday perception is the search for items in busy scenes. Imagine that you are at the airport and lose track of your companion in the crowded terminal. You begin a visual search of the scene to find him or her. Or, if you have misplaced your car keys in your home, you search the nooks and crannies of your abode to locate them. What happens during the visual search for a target (i.e., your companion or your keys) among distracters (i.e., the hundreds of people in the airport terminal, or the dozens of things in you home)? What role do attentional processes play in this search, and how does your knowledge of the appearance of the lost items affect the way you hunt for them? If your airport companion was last seen wearing a bright-red sweater, you may use the color information to constrain your search. This might prove an easy method of finding your friend if nobody else in the crowd is dressed in red. But if many people are wearing red, you have to use other information like their hair color, height, and facial features.

These mechanisms of visual search were investigated and modeled by Anne Treisman and her colleagues (Treisman and Gelade, 1980). They presented arrays of multiple simple stimuli (distracters) on a video screen that sometimes contained a target item requiring a speeded motor response. The complexity of the search task could be manipulated by having the target item differ from distracters by a unique feature (e.g., red target among blue stimuli) or by having the target and distracters share some features such that the target was defined only by a conjunction of two or more relevant stimulus features (e.g., red letter *O* as a target among distracters that could be green *O*'s or red *X*'s). In the former, simpler case, the target could be identified simply by color. These targets popped out of the visual scene; that is, they were immediately obvious to the observer as soon as the array was shown. Under these so-called popout conditions, the average time it took the observers to respond when the target was presented was not affected by how many distracter stimuli were included in the display. Some displays had two, four, eight, sixteen, thirty-two, and more distracters. Hence a plot, called a *search function,* of reaction time as a function of distracter number was flat (Figure 6.9).

In contrast, when the target was defined by a conjunction of features shared with distracters, the search functions had positive slopes. These slopes can be interpreted as evidence that the stimulus items are searched one at a time. This process occurs independently of eye movements; that is, if subjects are not permitted to move their eyes during the search, the results are still obtained, which means that the search is covert. Treisman defined this as an attentional mechanism that must move from item to item to identify individual stimuli, sort of an automatic spotlight that searches the visual scene.

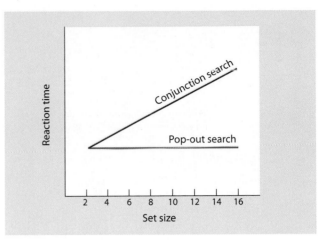

Figure 6.9 Pop-out versus conjunction-search time graphs. In pop-out searches, the subjects' reaction times do not increase as a function of set size as they do in conjunction searches.

NEURAL SYSTEMS IN ATTENTION AND SELECTIVE PERCEPTION

So far, we have focused on attention in visual perception, and on how we select some visual inputs for analysis while rejecting others. The methods we described are those of experimental and cognitive psychology. They are useful for investigating attentional mechanisms, but they fall short of fully describing these mechanisms because they do not inform us about neural substrates. For example, where in the human brain does attention influence signal processing? If we can respond more quickly to a target appearing at an attended location, is this because it was more efficiently processed in our visual cortex, or because motor systems in the frontal lobe were biased to generate fast responses to it?

The limitations in behavioral and psychophysical measures for elucidating neural mechanisms should not be taken to mean that they are inferior or uninformative—far from it. Rather, they have helped to describe attentional phenomena in terms of the observer's behavior. What remains are unanswered questions that require new approaches. In their search for answers, many investigators have turned to physiological methods in humans and animals to determine how intermediate neural events give rise to changes in perceptual and cognitive experience, and task performance during attention. Physiological studies and data from cases of neurological damage and disease provide a wealth of information about the neural mechanisms of attentional

processes. We now review studies that demonstrated how selective attention works in modulating sensory and perceptual processing.

Neurophysiology of Human Attention

To describe the mechanisms of attentional selection at the neural level in humans, researchers use several tools, including electrical and magnetic recordings of brain activity and neuroimaging techniques. Each provides measures of human brain activity that elucidate sensory, perceptual, cognitive, and motor processes, but the pictures of brain activity provided by each measure are different. Electrical and magnetic recordings (electroencephalography, event-related potentials, magnetoencephalography, and event-related magnetic fields) directly measure neuronal activity as millisecond-to-millisecond changes in electrical and magnetic fields. In humans, these small signals can be recorded noninvasively by placing electrodes and sensors on the head (and inside it in certain neurological procedures: See Human Brain Activity During Attention). How well the noninvasive electrical and magnetic recordings can localize a signal to a specific brain structure is limited, though. This is because it is difficult to infer where inside the head the signals are coming from. To facilitate localization, functional neuroimaging methods such as positron emission tomography (PET)

Human Brain Activity During Attention

On rare occasions it is necessary to record the human brain's electrical activity with electrodes located in the brain rather than on the scalp. This medical procedure is performed when physicians want to localize a defective region of brain tissue. Such is the case when neurologists and neurosurgeons wish to treat patients with intractable epilepsy, a condition in which the usual medications that control epilepsy are not working. The goal is to locate the spot in the brain where abnormal neural tissue touches off uncontrolled neural activity that spreads to otherwise normal tissue. When this happens, the patient is said to be having a seizure, which can be so severe it renders the victim unconscious. If a confined region of the brain is responsible for starting the epileptic seizures, it is possible to remove the neuronal tissue and perhaps alleviate the epileptic attacks.

One way to localize a seizure focus is to try to infer it from scalp EEGs, which show characteristic patterns of abnormal electrical waves during a seizure. If the seizure is local, scalp recordings often provide a strong enough clue for the surgeon to use to remove the abnormal tissue without excising healthy brain tissue. However, it is difficult to determine a seizure's anatomical location from scalp recordings, and sometimes it is necessary to implant electrodes in the brain. Often when this is done, the electrodes are in place for several days. Under these circumstances, if the patient permits, it may be possible to record from the electrodes while the patient performs psychological tasks such as selective attention.

Gregory McCarthy, Truet Allison, and their colleagues at Yale Medical School have been performing such experiments for years. These researchers asked patients with electrodes implanted via a posterior entry through the occipital cortex and into the medial temporal lobe to attend to some stimuli while ignoring others, just as with scalp recording in healthy volunteers. In this manner the researchers obtained event-related potentials directly from within the cerebral cortex of humans. The result was clear evidence for modulations of activity in the extrastriate cortex as a function of spatial- and color-selective attention. These dramatic medical circumstances support the idea that scalp-recorded activity generated in modality-specific cortical areas is amplitude modulated during selective attention.

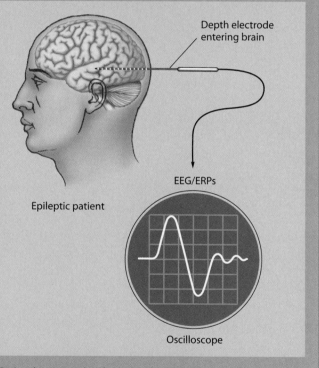

By implanting a depth electrode in some epileptic patients' occipital cortices, McCarthy and his colleagues recorded ERPs directly from the cortex and provided clear evidence of neuronal modulations during selective attention in humans.

and functional magnetic resonance imaging (fMRI) can capture changes in blood flow or metabolic activity related to neuronal activity with high three-dimensional resolution. Thus, when considered together, electromagnetic and neuroimaging methods can outline the time course and neuroanatomy of higher mental processes such as attention.

As we compare studies using electrical and magnetic methods to those using functional neuroimaging, we do so keeping in mind the theoretical context derived from cognitive experimental studies. From this integration, which is the core of cognitive neuroscience, we hope to identify the functional architecture of brain attention systems.

ELECTRICAL AND MAGNETIC RECORDINGS OF THE HUMAN BRAIN

In humans, attentional selection in the brain was first demonstrated electrophysiologically. This was actually first tried with animals but failed because of flawed experimental designs. Yet the history of the early neurophysiology of attention makes crystal clear some important aspects of the search for evidence of selective attention in the nervous system. For this reason, let us consider some research on cats that was performed more than four decades ago.

Auditory Selective Attention Raul Hernandez-Peon and his colleagues (1956) attempted to determine whether phenomena like the cocktail party effect might result from gating auditory inputs in the ascending sensory pathways. They tested their theory on cats by presenting sounds and recording from subcortical stages of the auditory pathway when the animals attended to (as opposed to ignored) the sounds. They reported modulations in the neuronal activity of the cochlear nucleus and auditory nerve; unfortunately these findings were later shown to result from the animals differentially orienting their ears with respect to the sound-emitting speaker. Anyone familiar with cats knows they can do this even without moving their head. Without moving any other part of their body, cats can rotate the external ear toward sounds of potential interest, such as the sound of an electric can opener (Figure 6.10).

Given these experimental failures, we may well ask, Why start a section on the neurophysiology of human attention with a negative result from animal work? The answer is that it points to a more fruitful approach and

Figure 6.10 Early work by Hernandez-Peon and colleagues attempted to relate single-cell recordings in cats to auditory attention. By recording from subcortical structures while the cat attended or ignored sounds, Hernandez-Peon and colleagues initially observed modulations at the subcortical level of processing. This was later shown to be due to differential orienting of the cat's ears rather than auditory attention.

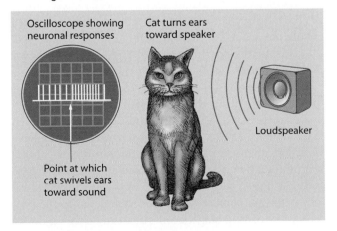

highlights significant controls germane to the physiological measurement of selective attention.

Hernandez-Peon and his colleagues' principal error related to the control over stimuli. The altered positions of a cat's external ear with respect to the loudspeaker led to varied amplitude signals reaching the eardrum in the attended versus ignored conditions—hence the differing activity levels recorded from the auditory structures. We already know that changes in stimulus amplitude at the eardrum will alter the firing rates of neurons. The question was whether such changes in neuronal firing could occur owing to selective internal neural control over sensory processing. One lesson that emerges from this work is that experimental controls must prevent any adjustment of the peripheral organs of sensory reception, a lesson that applies to all sensory modalities but especially to auditory and visual ones. The solution is rigorous monitoring of ear, head, and eye positions, and controls such as placing small headphones in the external ear canal, a method similar to the one which revealed that Hernandez-Peon's results were incorrect and why.

In the late 1960s and early 1970s, the first well-controlled experiments on the neurophysiology of attention were conducted on humans. These studies were made possible by the development of methods to perform signal averaging of the electroencephalogram (EEG), which revealed tiny brain waves directly related to the processing of a stimulus, but which in the absence of signal averaging were hidden in the larger EEG rhythms. These tiny brain waves are referred to as *event-related potentials* (ERPs), a term which stems from the fact that they are "potentials" in the electrical sense of the word and that they are related to some "event," namely the stimulus and its processing in the brain. By designing clever experiments that controlled the subject's global state of arousal, these experiments compared brain wave responses (i.e., ERPs) elicited by stimuli when they were attended as compared to when they were ignored.

These experiments were first performed by Steven Hillyard and his colleagues (1973) at the University of California at San Diego. They developed a selective listening method where scalp-recorded ERPs were obtained from humans in response to auditory stimuli. Streams of sounds that differed in pitch were presented to the two ears of volunteers wearing headphones. During one condition they were asked to attend to the sounds in one ear while ignoring those in the other (e.g., attend right-ear sounds and ignore left-ear sounds). Then in a second condition they were asked to pay attention to the stimuli in the other ear (e.g., attend left-ear sounds and ignore right-ear sounds). In this manner, they separately obtained auditory ERPs to stimuli entering one ear when that ear's input was attended and when it was ignored. The significant design feature of the experiment was that during the two conditions of attention, the subjects were always engaged in a difficult attention task: All that varied was the direction of attention, that is, which ear was attended. In addition, the researchers controlled the orientation of the subject's head with respect to the source of sound by using headphones to deliver the sounds. Thus, they controlled for the confounding factors that had led to failures in previous animal research.

Hillyard and his colleagues discovered that auditory ERPs were enlarged in amplitude when stimuli were attended as compared with when they were ignored. This effect in the ERPs appeared as a deflection in the ERP waveform known as the *auditory N1 potential* because it is the first of the large, negative polarity deflections in the signal-averaged waveform (Figure 6.11). The N1 component is believed to be a sensory-evoked wave with a latency of less than 90 msec to peak after stimulus onset, and thus provides evidence for early selection during sensory processing.

An important piece of information for interpreting the auditory N1 attention effect is to understand what brain regions generate the effects observed in the N1 component. Where does the N1 come from inside the brain? If this effect represents early selection of stimulus inputs—a sort of filtering of perceptual signals—what evidence eliminates the possibility that the N1 attention effects are not reflecting brain activity that occurs after semantic encoding and so are effects of late selection? One way to resolve these questions is to understand

where these attentional modulations in the auditory system are coming from. If we knew that the N1 effect was from the medial geniculate nucleus of the thalamus (the auditory thalamic relay) or the primary auditory cortex in Heschl's gyrus, then we might rely on animal studies to elucidate the functional properties of early analysis stages and argue that semantic encoding had not yet occurred. How can we learn this from humans?

Additional methods come to our rescue. The magnetic counterpart of the EEG is called the *magnetoencephalogram* (MEG), which can be signal averaged to derive event-related magnetic fields (ERFs). By combining ERP recordings in selective listening paradigms with recordings of magnetic field fluxes generated by active neurons, we know where these auditory attention effects are generated and what they might mean for information processing.

From Marty Woldorff and Steven Hillyard's (1993) combination of ERPs and ERFs, we now know that the earliest effects of selective listening happen prior to the N1 component, in the latency range of the auditory potentials between 20 and 50 msec after stimulus onset. In this so-called mid-latency time span, attending to one ear versus ignoring that ear's inputs leads to amplitude modulations of ERPs and ERFs. Attention-related magnetic field fluxes can be coregistered with magnetic resonance images (MRIs) of each subjects' brain to locate the specific brain structure affected by the attentional manipulation. Such modeling indicates that the earliest modulations of auditory inputs take place in the auditory cortex in Heschl's gyri (Figure 6.12). Attention, therefore, can affect stimulus processing in the auditory cortex, but we do not know whether in humans this represents modulations in the primary auditory cortex or in the secondary auditory areas. Even so, attention clearly affects sensory-specific stages of auditory analysis at latencies that strongly indicate that auditory sensory analysis has not been completed. At this level of processing, the auditory system cannot select information based on higher-order aspects of auditory inputs such as speech cues; rather, the ear of entry is the cue for selection. Longer latency changes in an ERP or ERF waveform reflect attentional selection involving the stimuli's higher-order properties such as a speaker's voice or semantic meaning.

Could the attention effects at the auditory cortex be the result of gating that happened earlier in auditory processing, such as in the thalamus, brainstem, or even the cochlea? For the auditory system we certainly have sufficient anatomical evidence that top-down control over auditory inputs can take place at the earliest processing stages. Each neural relay in the ascending auditory pathway sends return axons back down to the preceding processing stage, even out to the cochlea in the

Figure 6.11 Event-related potentials (ERPs) in a dichotic listening task. The solid line represents the average voltage response to an attended input over time, and the dashed line to an unattended input. Hillyard and colleagues found that the amplitude of the N1 component was enhanced with attention as compared to when ignored. Adapted from Hillyard et al. (1973).

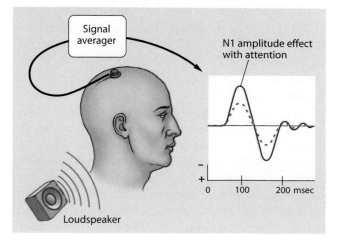

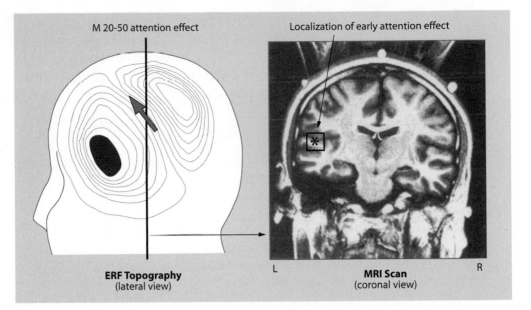

Figure 6.12 Topographic map of attention effects and MRI scan localizing the early auditory attention effect, seen here in the primary auditory cortex in the supratemporal plane in Heschl's gyri. Adapted from Woldorff et al. (1993).

form of the olivocochlear bundle. Electrical recordings of human auditory processing measure sensory activity as early as the brainstem relays, and even the compound action potential of the auditory nerve itself. The auditory brainstem response (ABR) is composed of voltage deflections in the auditory ERPs with latencies of 1 to 10 msec. Can these components be modulated by selective attention? The answer is that voluntary selective attention in the auditory system does not appear to involve modulations of subcortical auditory neurons, but this issue is not yet resolved. Suffice it to state that modulation of subcortical auditory inputs, if present, is not a robust phenomenon.

Visual Selective Attention   Similar investigations have been made of neural mechanisms of visual selective at-

tention. As with auditory studies, visual studies using ERPs directly measure the electrical activity generated by visually responsive neurons in the brain to indicate stages of processing that can be affected by selective attention. The first investigations, made in 1969 by psychologist Robert Eason and his colleagues, found that during visual-spatial attention (selection by location), certain visual ERPs showed changes in their amplitudes. Many studies replicated this effect and showed that such modulation can begin about 70 msec after the onset of the visual stimulus.

The pattern of attention effects in the visual system is now well established. Directing voluntary covert attention toward rather than away from a stimulus (Figure 6.13) leads to amplitude modulations in ERPs as early as 70 to 90 msec after stimulus onset. These effects

Figure 6.13 Stimulus display used to investigate sustained, spatial selective attention. For periods of seconds to minutes the subject fixates the eyes on the central cross-hairs (+), while stimuli are flashed in random order to the left and right field locations. During some blocks the subject is instructed to covertly attend left stimuli in order to detect infrequent targets. During other blocks they are instructed to attend to the right location.

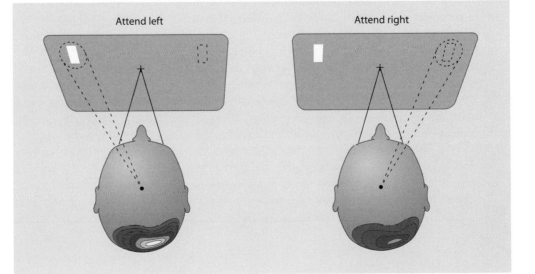

An Interview with Steven A. Hillyard, Ph.D.
Dr. Hillyard is a professor of Neuroscience at the University of California School of Medicine at San Diego. He is widely recognized as the attention researcher that unequivocally demonstrated selective attention physiologically.

Authors: You began studying the electrophysiology of sensory processing during attention some 25 years ago. Why did you choose to work with humans rather than animals?

SAH: At that time people were excited about studies in animals and humans showing that evoked potentials from sensory pathways became enlarged when attention was paid to the evoking stimuli. These findings offered the first real possibility of identifying specific levels of the sensory pathways where attended signals are enhanced and unattended inputs are suppressed. At the same time, a lively controversy was brewing about whether these electrophysiological changes were associated with selective sensory processing or with changes in general arousal or alertness.

We chose to study the neural bases of attention in humans rather than in animals for several reasons. First, computer technology enabled us to make noninvasive scalp recordings of evoked activity in a person's sensory pathways as he or she performed a demanding attentional task. Since humans can be trained to carry out complex sensory discrimination and decision tasks much more rapidly than any animal, we could implement rigorous experimental designs that revealed brain activity specifically related to selective attention rather than to general arousal states. Second, we wanted to test a hypothesis about attention—that is, early versus late levels of selection—that had emerged from the psychological literature and for which experimental designs had already been well established in humans. Third, we didn't really know to what extent studies in animals, including those in our fellow primates, could serve as valid models for human attention. Of course, we still don't know this.

The intellectual repertoire of humans is so much more elaborate than our nearest relatives' it would be presumptuous to assume that all the rich manifestations of human attention have their equivalents in animals. Perhaps animal models may be suitable for studying simpler aspects of attention, but the ability to attend to language, for example, has evidently been evolving separately in humans for tens if not hundreds of thousands of years. Thus, if we are ever to understand the full range of human attentional abilities and the neural bases thereof, I believe it is necessary to direct a major research effort toward humans, despite the limitations inherent in noninvasive studies.

Authors: What have these noninvasive studies revealed about attention mechanisms in humans?

SAH: For auditory attention we examined evoked potentials to rapidly presented sounds coming from speakers in a cocktail party situation; this was designed to rule out nonspecific arousal and alertness effects. We found that short-latency evoked potentials, beginning at 50 to 60 msec after stimulus onset, became markedly enlarged in response to attended sounds in one ear versus unattended sounds in the other ear. In follow-up studies by Marty Woldorff—my colleague who is a professor at the University of Texas, San Antonio—using neuromagnetic recordings in conjunction with MRI-based source localization, evoked sensory activity was enhanced by attention as early as 20 to 50 msec after stimulus onset in the primary auditory cortex. These results strongly confirm early selection theories of attention, which assert that attended sensory inputs are boosted and unattended inputs are suppressed at an early stage of processing, before more complex features of the stimuli are analyzed in higher cortical areas.

Authors: What about visual attention?

SAH: Analogous effects were demonstrated in visual attention, most notably in spatial attention tasks where a subject was cued to attend to stimuli at one location in the visual fields while ignoring stimuli at others. In this situation, evoked potentials in the visual cortex were enlarged for attended versus unattended stimuli starting at 70 to 80 msec after stimulus onset. By combining techniques for localizing the sources of this attention-related activity, including parallel experiments using PET, Hans-Jochen Heinze and one of the authors of this text, George R. Mangun, my colleagues of many years, determined that sensory transmission is modulated by attention primarily in extrastriate visual areas throughout the interval 80 to 200 msec. In contrast, earlier activity evoked in the primary visual cortex in the 50- to 80-msec range was not altered by attention in spatial attention tasks. From electrophysiological and neurometabolic imaging studies we concluded that a principal mechanism of visual attention is the amplification of attended sensory signals in the extrastriate cortical areas that encode those signals.

Authors: Tell me more about this amplification mechanism. For example, what does it mean when a brain potential—or for that matter a PET signal or single-unit discharge—is enlarged in response to an attended signal? What is the behavioral significance of a bigger evoked response and how has this link been established?

SAH: What you're asking about is the nature of the neural codes for sensory/perceptual information. There is a general assumption that more activity—greater firing rates, etc.—within a nerve cell population means that more information is being represented or processed by those cells. Conversely, a suppressed response reflects diminished processing. But you're right, this is something that needs to be established in each case rather than taken for granted.

In simple, low-level sensory signals, greater physical stimulus energy produces systematic increases in neural response amplitudes that are paralleled by elevations in the perceived stimulus magnitude. Also, signal detection experiments in humans and monkeys have shown that moment-to-moment fluctuations in neural response amplitudes can predict precisely whether the person or animal detects a faint signal. Thus, for low to moderately intense sensory inputs, there is good evidence that heightened neural responses often represent enhanced perceptual information. This relationship has also been observed in attention experiments which showed that increased evoked potential amplitudes to stimuli at attended locations were associated with improved accuracy at discriminating the features of those stimuli. It's unlikely, though, that such simple relationships would hold in general. The neural codes for representing complex perceptual or cognitive events undoubtedly involve elaborate patterns of excitation and inhibition in neuronal populations that cannot be simply characterized by increases or decreases in response amplitude.

Authors: Very well, you have identified evoked responses that vary with attention. What about animal studies of detailed anatomical circuits and cellular-level events?

SAH: I think we need a combined approach that brings together human and animal studies in common conceptual and experimental frameworks. Invasive animal studies are certainly necessary to reveal the fine-grained neurophysiology of the brain's attentional systems, and also the neurotransmitters and microcircuitry involved. Numerous monkey experiments demonstrated attentional modulation of single-cell activity patterns in several well-defined cortical areas. With few exceptions, however, these monkey experiments used attention tasks that differed from the ones employed in behavioral and physiological studies of humans. It is usually difficult to know whether the attentional phenomena were truly equivalent or homologous to those displayed by humans, but that hasn't stopped researchers such as my colleague Steve Luck, now at the University of Iowa, or our colleague, neuroscientist Robert Desimone at NIMH, and others. Their promising studies have great potential for bridging the gap between the human and animal literature.

I think the most effective research strategy would be to carry out animal and human experiments in parallel and to use equivalent or identical experimental tasks. Then let the results in one species guide the experiments in the other. For example, with current technologies, noninvasive human studies can reveal the brain areas activated by a task with a resolution of about 1 cm or better (using PET and fMRI) and the timing of neural population dynamics with a millisecond level of resolution (using ERPs and MEG). These macrolevel activity patterns can be studied in relation to precisely defined cognitive processes in humans and can point the way to brain systems that should be explored in parallel with animal experiments. Moreover, if similar macrolevel brain activity patterns were observed in humans and monkeys performing equivalent tasks, this would greatly strengthen the validity of the animal model for the cognitive process under investigation, which can then be investigated further by using invasive techniques to get at the microlevel structure of the underlying neural events. Unless we have such interplay between human and animal studies, we are whistling in the dark with regard to the applicability of animal findings to human selective attention.

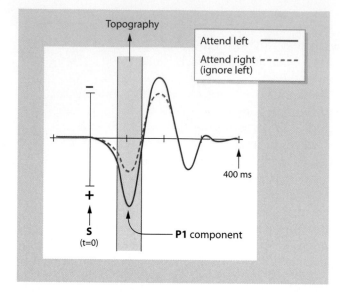

Figure 6.14 EEG recordings during visual spatial–selective attention tasks show that attended stimuli have greater amplitudes than unattended stimuli. The topography on the left shows the right lateral occipital area that is maximally activated in the P1 component range. The shaded area on the ERP on the right shows the difference in amplitude between attended and unattended events.

are first observed in an ERP wave known as the *P1* (first major positive wave), which can be recorded over lateral occipital regions of the scalp. When a visual stimulus appears at a location a subject is attending the P1 is larger in amplitude (Figure 6.14). Such a pattern is therefore consistent with filtering mechanisms like the one for auditory processing.

These so-called P1 attention effects have been obtained only during spatial attention, not during selection based on other stimulus features like color, spatial frequency, orientation, or conjunctions of these features. As well, selection of visual inputs based on higher-order properties such as what object it is—attend to chairs but ignore tables—does not lead to P1 attention effects; rather, attention effects for these more complex tasks appear later in the ERPs (> 200-msec latency).

We can ask the same question about spatial attention effects as we did about auditory ones: Do attention-related modulations of visual ERPs during spatial attention reflect processing in cortical or subcortical stages? And can we say whether they reflect selection occurring before or after semantic encoding? The answers to these questions are remarkably similar to those for the auditory system.

Spatial selective attention occurs in part via the modulation of sensory processes in the visual cortex. These effects happen primarily in extrastriate cortical areas, but may involve mechanisms in the striate cortex.

We know this because the early P1 spatial attention effect has properties indicative of a visual sensory stage of processing. For example, the P1 effect has a scalp topography that follows a retinotopic pattern (Figure 6.15). That is, initially the P1 attention effect is maximal over the contralateral occipital region of the scalp, as would

Figure 6.15 Topographic maps showing the scalp distribution of brain responses to stimuli presented in each of the four quadrants of a computer screen while subjects had their eyes fixated on the cross in the middle. The topographies represent the difference in activity between the attended and unattended stimulus responses in the P1 time range. Adapted from Mangun et al. (1993).

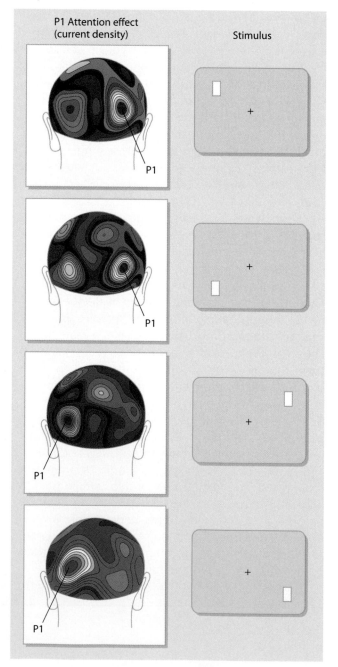

be expected from the contralateral projection of the visual pathways. Moreover, its latency (onset of 70 msec) is consistent with neuronal firing latencies in early extrastriate areas, as we know from research on monkeys.

To what extent can we assume that spatial attention effects in ERPs might be reflections of the neural processes underlying the behavioral effects of spatial attention? Can we conclude, for example, that better performance in spatial cuing paradigms was brought about by processing changes in the extrastriate visual cortex? ERP methods have also been applied to this question by recording ERPs in the same paradigms used by prior cognitive studies (see Figure 6.7). If the improved performance—faster response time and more accurate responses—that was observed for targets presented to precued locations was due to better processing in the visual cortex, this should be reflected in the ERPs to the targets. Indeed, the target stimuli flashed to precued locations elicited larger sensory ERPs than when presented to uncued locations (Figure 6.16).

Figure 6.16 Grand-averaged ERP waveforms over 14 persons show the contralateral P1 and N1 visual attention effects between valid and invalid trials at lateral occipital scalp sites. Adapted from Mangun & Hillyard (1991).

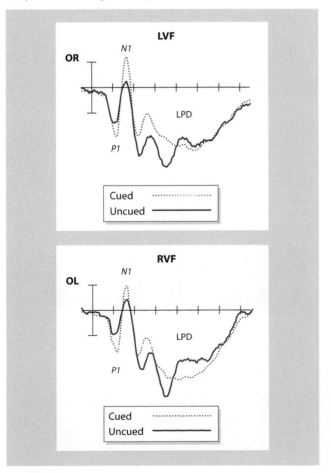

Now that we know that voluntarily focusing attention on a location in response to verbal instructions or visual precues enhances visual ERPs, we might ask whether similar neural mechanisms participate when attention is attracted to locations automatically. That is, when our attention is automatically attracted to a location in the visual field, does this heighten neural processing in the visual cortex? The answer is yes. Remember that automatic cuing happens when a sensory event immediately precedes a target at the same location. Under such conditions, response times are faster at the cued location than at the uncued location, but only when the time between the cuing and target stimuli is short (< 300 msec); with longer periods, this effect reverses. When ERPs to the targets are recorded, the result is that the early occipital P1 wave is enlarged for targets that quickly follow a sensory cue at the same location, but as the time after cuing grows longer, this effect reverses and the P1 response is inhibited (Figure 6.17). Therefore, these data indicate that automatic and voluntary attention to locations involves a common mechanism with regard to the effect on cortical stimulus processing.

The idea has emerged that attention is a focal spotlight that can be voluntarily or automatically focused on a discrete spatial location. Presumably this spotlight is similar to the one that moves through the array of stimuli during visual search for a target among multiple distracters. This hypothesis was investigated electrophysiologically by presenting subjects with arrays of targets and distracters in a conjunction-search paradigm (see Figure 6.18). At brief time intervals after the search array was presented, a solitary probe stimulus was flashed on the screen to elicit a visual ERP. The probe elicited larger early visual responses (i.e., P1) at the location of a conjunction target rather than in regions where nothing other than distracters were present. Hence, the idea that focal spatial attention is required to analyze multifeature targets found electrophysiological support.

To summarize what we now know, human electrophysiological and neuromagnetic recordings prove the concept of early selection and extend it with evidence on the neural stages of perceptual processing that are likely involved. The general model supported by these data is that incoming sensory signals may be altered within the sensory-specific cortex when stimuli having relevant physical features are encountered. The earliest form of this selection can be defined by location in auditory and visual systems. The implication of these data is that descending projections from attentional control systems affect the excitability of neurons coding the features of the to-be-attended or ignored stimuli. These data inform us about the site where attention effects are

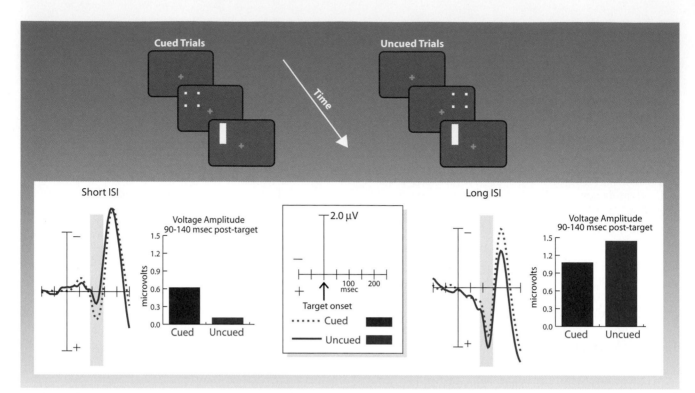

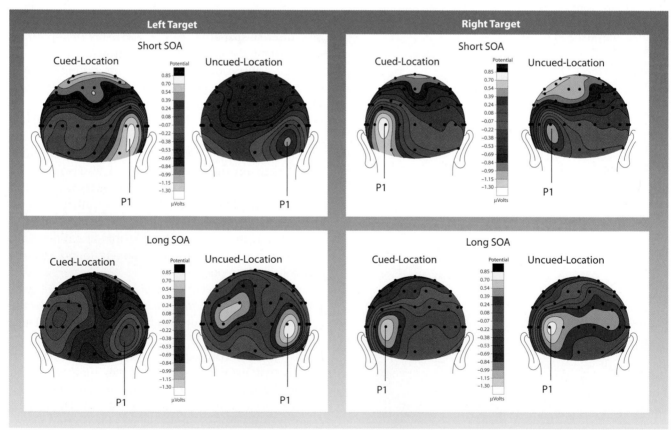

Figure 6.17 When attention is attracted to a location by the occurrence of an abrupt visual stimulus onset, the same extrastriate cortical responses that are affected by voluntary spatial attention are enhanced (dotted versus solid lines). This enhancement is replaced within a few hundred milliseconds by a relative inhibition of the response. This physiological finding parallels that observed with reaction time and provides a neuronal mechanism for the behavioral findings. These physiological effects are summarized in the bar graph at the right. After Hopfinger and Mangun (1998).

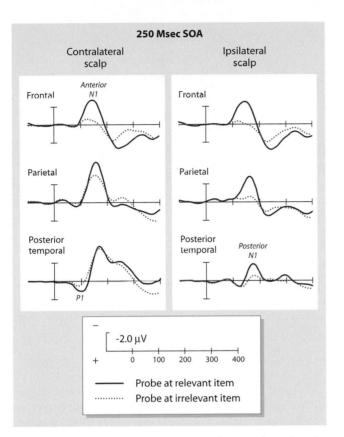

250 Msec SOA

Contralateral scalp

Ipsilateral scalp

Frontal — *Anterior N1*
Frontal

Parietal
Parietal

Posterior temporal
Posterior temporal — *Posterior N1*

P1

-2.0 µV

+ 0 100 200 300 400

——— Probe at relevant item

············ Probe at irrelevant item

Figure 6.18 Grand-averaged ERP waveforms at frontal, parietal, and posterior temporal scalp sites compare the response to probes at relevant and irrelevant items in the array 250 msec after the onset of the search array. The probe elicited a larger P1 when it occurred at the location of a conjunction target than when it was presented to regions of the array where no target was present, supporting the idea that focal spatial attention is required in order to conjoin features of targets. Adapted from Luck et al. (1993).

manifest during perceptual processing. In addition, we also want to know which brain structures and mechanisms are active in controlling these perceptual modulations. That is, what are the sources of the top-down neural signals that modulate perceptual analyses during attention? This question can be investigated in healthy humans by using functional neuroimaging methods.

FUNCTIONAL NEUROIMAGING IN HUMAN ATTENTION

Modern tools that measure human brain activity in vivo provide a powerful means for investigating the anatomy of higher mental functions. In neuroimaging, as in electromagnetic recording, the effects of experimental manipulations are observed as differences in the images of brain conductivity obtained as volunteers perform different attention tasks. This is visualized by contrasting or subtracting images made during one condition from those made during another, which can be done for im-

ages of regional cerebral blood flow (rCBF) obtained with PET. Such approaches were refined by Mike Posner, Steven Petersen, Maurizio Corbetta, Marcus Raichle, and their colleagues at Washington University in St. Louis.

In the PET studies of Corbetta and colleagues (1991), it was found that attention to stimulus features like color, form, and movement leads to characteristic increases in rCBF (also referred to as *activation*) in the extrastriate visual cortex. While blood flow in the brain was monitored by using radioactive water as a tracer, the volunteers were shown pairs of visual displays that had arrays of stimulus elements. The first display of each trial was a reference stimulus; the second was a test stimulus. The subjects' task was to view the first array and compare it with a second array to detect changes in prespecified aspects of the stimulus. In different selective-attention blocks (groups of test trials), the subjects were required to discriminate whether the arrays differed in color, shape, or motion. In other blocks, subjects were required to detect changes in any of the features (divided attention) or to passively view the stimuli or only a fixation point. Separate PET scans were made during each type of experimental block. To uncover which brain areas were activated during selective attention to color versus shape or motion, PET scans corresponding to each condition were subtracted from one another, thereby showing only the regions that differed between the conditions.

Selective attention to color, form, or motion activated distinct, largely nonoverlapping regions of extrastriate cortex (Figure 6.19). Extrastriate cortical regions specialized for processing color, form, or motion were modulated during visual attention to the individual stimulus features. This provides additional support for the idea that selective attention in modality-specific cortical areas alters the perceptual processing of inputs prior to completing feature analysis. Similar results for spatial selective attention were found by neurologist Hans-Jochen Heinze (1994) of the University of Magdeburg, Germany and one of the authors (G.R.M.), who also performed PET studies. They found that spatial attention led to activations in extrastriate cortex in the hemisphere contralateral to the stimulus, and they related this activity to ERP attention effects recorded from the same volunteers (Figure 6.19). Thus, in addition to localizing the effects of spatial attention, they could tell when the activity occurred—something not possible with PET alone.

In addition to determining the activation of sensory-specific cortical areas, PET studies of selective attention revealed high rCBF in several brain areas: the thalamus (probably exclusively the pulvinar nucleus), the basal ganglia, the insular cortex, the frontal cortex,

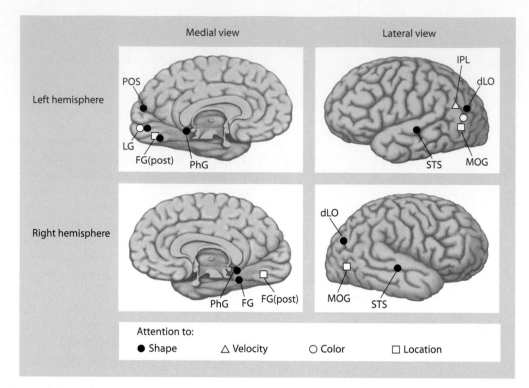

Figure 6.19 PET study by Corbetta and colleagues illustrates that regions of extrastriate cortex specialized for the processing of color, form, or motion are selectively modulated during visual attention to these stimulus features. Selective attention to color activated areas in bilateral extrastriate cortex, but the activations were generally larger for left-hemisphere structures. Attention to shape led to bilateral activations in the fusiform gyrus and parahippocampal gyri, collateral sulcus of the left hemisphere, right superior temporal sulcus, and a region between the calcarine sulcus and parieto-occipital sulcus in the right hemisphere. Selective attention to the motion of the stimuli activated the left parahippocampal gyrus and the right superior temporal sulcus (in a region different from that activated for attention to shape). PET study by Heinze and colleagues showed that attention to spatial location produced activations in the posterior fusiform and middle occipital gyri. Adapted from Corbetta et al. (1991) and Heinze et al. (1994).

the anterior cingulate nucleus, and the posterior parietal cortex. Some regions are involved in directing attention according to a task's requirements (frontal cortex, parietal cortex, and pulvinar nucleus). For instance, Corbetta and colleagues (1993, 1995) showed that the superior parietal cortex is activated when attention is switched from one location to another to detect a target (Figure 6.20); it is interesting that this occurs whether attention is voluntarily switched in a controlled manner to expected target locations, or moves through a field of potential targets in a visual search task. This suggests that movements of attention during visual search are subserved by the same neuronal machinery as are voluntary movements in response to cues.

How do activations in nonsensory brain regions and in the pulvinar nucleus of the thalamus explain the modulations in extrastriate visual areas observed in PET and ERP studies? Somehow axons from control areas project to neurons in sensory-specific cortical areas in order to alter their excitability. Therefore, when a stimulus excites those neurons, the response is enlarged. A

network including the pulvinar nucleus of the thalamus, the posterior parietal cortex, and the dorsolateral prefrontal cortex may mediate cortical excitability in the extrastriate cortex as a function of selective attention (Figure 6.21). The pulvinar nucleus is not part of the projection pathway from the retina to the primary visual cortex; instead, it maintains reciprocal connections with cortical and subcortical areas. Hence, the pulvinar nucleus is ideally suited to afford the frontal and parietal cortices a way to influence extrastriate visual cortical processing. In doing so, it presumably uses information from location maps in the parietal cortex. In the next section, on single neuronal responses during attention in animals, we consider converging evidence about brain attention mechanisms.

Animal Studies of Attentional Mechanisms

Neurophysiological studies of humans that employ electrical, magnetic, and functional imaging techniques have revealed some of the inner workings of attentional

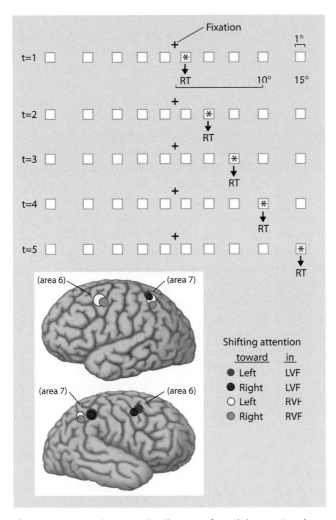

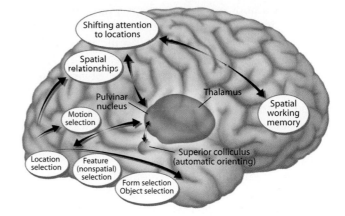

Figure 6.21 Model of executive control systems and the way in which extrastriate cortex processing is affected by a network of brain areas.

Figure 6.20 Corbetta and colleagues found that regional cerebral blood flow in the posterior parietal cortex increased when attention was switched from one location to another, in order to detect a relevant target. This same area was activated when attention was moved through the visual field during visual search. Adapted from Corbetta et al. (1993).

selection and control. We now see that complex interactions take place within neuronal circuits to achieve selective processing. What are the underlying cellular-level events, and what can we learn from animal studies that confirm, amplify, or perhaps contradict what we have found in humans?

We expressed earlier that animal studies preceded neurophysiological recording in humans (see Figure 6.10), but the first experiments were flawed and provided few real answers about whether selective sensory-level gating of inputs occurred during attention. The first well-controlled studies that demonstrated such effects involved recordings of ERPs in humans (see Figure 6.11). Nevertheless, single-cell recording methods provide details on the attentional mechanisms at the synaptic, cel-

lular, and circuit levels—a difficult thing to do in humans (but see Human Brain Activity During Attention).

Activity in the visual pathways of monkeys has been investigated during selective attention. A microelectrode is lowered into a candidate structure in the visual pathways, and the extracellular activity of cortical or subcortical neurons is measured in different conditions of attention. In principle, the methods are similar to those for recording human ERPs or ERFs, except that individual neuronal responses are obtained rather than ensemble responses of tens or thousands of activated neurons as is the case of ERPs or ERFs.

Single neurons in area V4 of a monkey's extrastriate cortex lie in the ventral, or "what" pathway from the primary visual cortex to the inferior temporal cortex, the pathway that carries out feature analysis and object discrimination (see Chapters 4 and 5). It is plausible, then, that the firing of neurons in this cortical stream of visual processing might be modulated during spatial attention, thereby providing a way to gate relevant feature information for perception. Indeed, Jeff Moran and Robert Desimone (1985) of the National Institute of Mental Health found that the firing rates of neurons in V4 are significantly modulated during selective spatial attention. When a stimulus is attended, it elicits a stronger response than when it is ignored; yet this effect manifests itself differently from what was seen in the ERP studies described earlier. With V4 neurons, attentional modulation of neuronal firing happens only when attended and ignored locations are located within the V4 neuron's receptive field.

In these studies, Moran and Desimone first identified the V4 neuron's classic receptive field and then determined which stimulus was good for exciting a response from the neuron (e.g., perhaps a vertical red bar) and which was a poor one (e.g., perhaps a horizontal green bar); that is, the red one makes the cell fire whereas the green one might not. Both stimuli could fit simultaneously within the neuron's receptive field, which for V4 neurons may extend over several degrees of visual angle. The task involved attending covertly to a cued visual field location, and thus, prior to each testing block, the monkey was cued to the location where a discrimination task would be required—similar to what is done with humans in spatial cuing paradigms.

At the beginning of each stimulus trial, the monkey viewed a sample stimulus and then simultaneously the pair of target stimuli, one within the attended location and one at another location, but both within the large V4 receptive field. If the target stimulus at the attended location matched the sample stimulus, the monkey had to make a motor response, for which a food or drink reward was given. When the optimal stimulus for eliciting responses from the V4 neuron was within the attended location, the responses were enhanced in comparison to when the optimal stimulus fell within the receptive field but outside the attended region. The changes in neuronal firing were related to the location of attention and not to the stimulus features (Figure 6.22). A fascinating

aspect of this neuronal attention effect was that it directed attention to or away from stimuli that were inside the cell's receptive field. In V4 neurons, when attention was directed to locations outside the receptive field, modulations of responses to the optimal stimuli presented in the receptive field were not found.

The pattern for V4 neurons is markedly different from that of neurons in subsequent stages of visual analysis in the ventral pathway. In the inferior temporal cortex, attention can modulate neural activity even when the to-be-ignored stimulus is far from the to-be-attended stimulus. This happens partly because the receptive fields of inferior temporal neurons are huge, encompassing the entire central visual field. Processing in visual areas prior to V4 appears to be less successful in modulating cortical visual processing even when proper controls are utilized, like when the conditions are equally well matched for arousal. Thus, spatial attention effects of the type evident in V4 and inferior temporal cortex have been difficult to obtain, for example, in V1, which led to the idea that perhaps attentional modulations happen only in extrastriate cortical areas—a conclusion supported by studies of humans. But changes in V1 firing rates may occur with attention when percep-

Figure 6.22 Desimone and associates studied the effect of selective attention on the responses of a neuron in area V4 of macaque monkeys. The areas that are circled indicate the attended locations. Bars in blue are effective sensory stimuli and bars without color are ineffective sensory stimuli. When the animal attended to effective sensory stimuli, the V4 neuron gave a good response, whereas a poor response was generated when the animal attended to the ineffective sensory stimuli. Adapted from Moran and Desimone (1985).

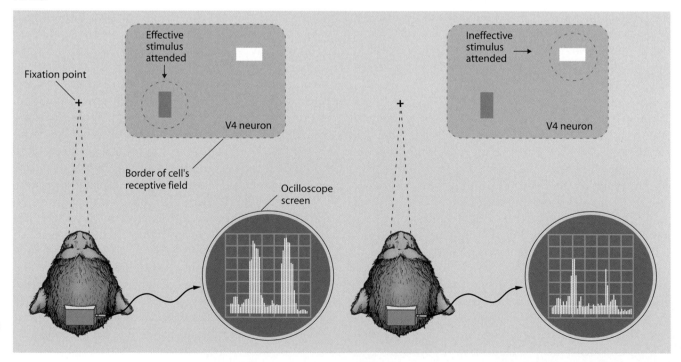

tual demands require filtering of sensory inputs on a spatial scale appropriate for the size of the V1 receptive fields, which are very small (< 1 degree of visual angle at the fovea). What might this mean about where attention can modulate visual inputs?

If there are attentional modulations of the primary visual cortex, could they reflect gating earlier in the thalamus, or even in the retina? Unlike the cochlea, no efferent projection to the retinas of humans could serve as a substrate for modulating retinal activity. But in primates massive neuronal projections extend from the visual cortex back to the thalamus. These projections synapse on neurons in what is known as the *reticular nucleus of the thalamus* or, more specifically for the visual system, on the *perigeniculate nucleus,* which is the portion of the reticular nucleus that surrounds the lateral geniculate nucleus (Figure 6.23).

These neurons maintain complex interconnections with neurons in the thalamic relays and could, in principle, gate information flow from the thalamus to the cortex. Indeed, this can happen during intermodal (visual-auditory) attention, as demonstrated in cats by Charles Yingling and James Skinner in 1976. Such a mechanism might also select the visual field location for the current spotlight of attention in perception according to theories by Nobel Laureate Francis Crick (1992). But these effects do not appear to participate in selection for locations during voluntary visual attention. Therefore, we can say with confidence that modulations of retinal processing with spatial attention do not occur, but must leave open the possibility that the thalamus or primary visual cortex (V1) might be gated during some forms of visual attention. Within the extrastriate visual cortex, though, robust changes in neuronal firing rates are involved in selective attention for spatial locations (see Cell-to-Cell Firing in the Visual System).

Figure 6.23 Diagram of the thalamus, perigeniculate nucleus, and projections to and from the thalamus and visual cortex.

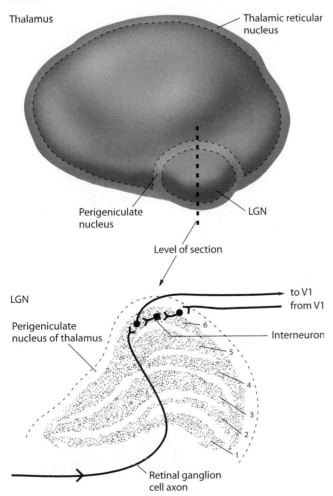

ATTENTIONAL MODULATIONS IN SUBCORTICAL STRUCTURES AND PARIETAL CORTEX

In the early 1970s, Robert Wurtz and his colleagues at the National Eye Institute began to investigate the superior colliculus in the midbrain for its role in attentional processes. They discovered visually responsive neurons that were affected by how monkeys responded to stimuli. When a monkey's eyes made a rapid movement from one location to another (saccadic eye movement) where a target stimulus was presented, the firing rates of the cells whose receptive fields included this region increased. Eye movement did not enhance cell firing, because without sensory stimuli, eye movements would not elicit neuronal responses (Figure 6.24). Eye movements to other locations also did not enhance responses to the stimulus. These cells responded as though they were involved in attentional mechanisms having to do with the stimulus. In subsequent experiments, these investigators found that when the stimulus was task relevant but not the target for saccadic eye movement, the cell did not become more responsive. These neurons, then, were facilitated not just by attending to the stimulus's location, as were inferior temporal neurons; they also needed the eyes to move to the target. The conclusion was that cells in the superior colliculus do not participate in visual selective attention per se, but are part of an eye movement system.

Scientists have demonstrated more recently that local deactivation of superior colliculus neurons lowers performance in discriminating targets when more than one is present in the visual field (one inside and another outside the neuron's receptive field). When there is no distracter stimulus, there is no decline in performance

Cell-to-Cell Firing in the Visual System

f attentional selectivity leads to changes in the firing rates of neurons in extrastriate cortical maps, what happens at the neuronal level? We do not really know. Neurons can be modulated by numerous hypothetical mechanisms, but at present it remains unknown which mechanism might produce the effects observed in monkeys. Robert Desimone and his colleagues (1990) at the National Institute of Mental Health described two possible ways that attention might affect neuronal firing rates in a visual area like V4.

One is the input-gating model, where the receptive fields of hypothesized intermediate neurons correspond to the attended or ignored regions of the visual field. The primary purpose of these neurons is to provide an inhibitory signal to V4 neurons for any regions of the V4 cell's receptive field to which attention is not currently directed. Although in this case it is the V4 neurons that show attention-related modulations of firing, the site of action of the attention effect is on the inputs to V4, not the V4 neurons themselves. The main alternative is a neuron-gating model; the effect here is hypothesized to be on the actual V4 neurons showing enhancement and suppression with attention. At present, too little is known about cellular-level interactions that produce attention effects in extrastriate neurons, such as those in V4, to choose between the competing models. Nor can we be certain what the source of the attention-related command may be. In principle, it is possible to obtain the information necessary to precisely specify the neuronal mechanisms underlying selective attention, but it is technically very challenging. There is little doubt, however, that in the not-too-distant future, these mechanisms will be revealed.

Two models for how attentional gating of extrastriate neurons is represented at the neuronal level. **(a)** In the "input-gating" model, intermediate neurons provide an inhibitory signal to regions that are outside of the to-be-attended location. **(b)** In the "neuron-gating" model, the V4 neurons of interest show both enhancement and suppression with attention.

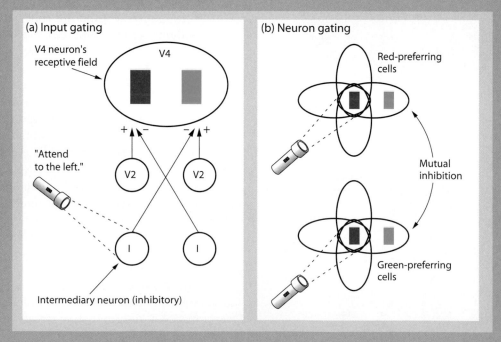

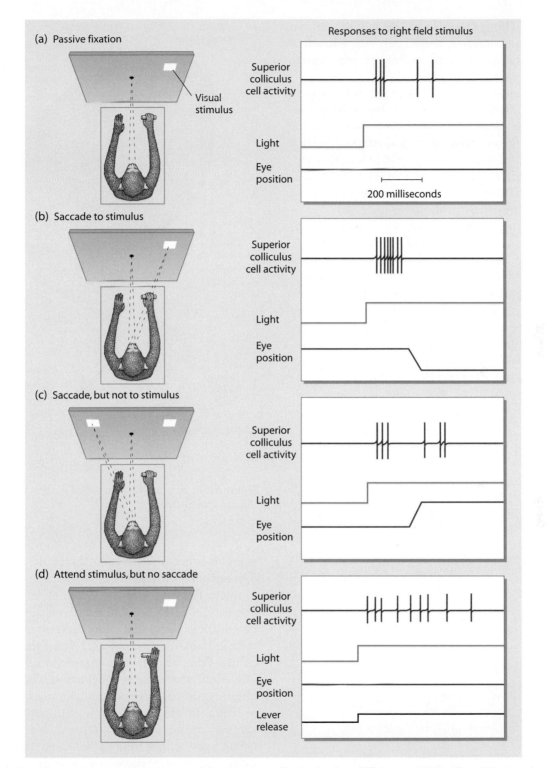

Figure 6.24 Experimental setup and responses of the superior colliculus for four different conditions from Wurtz and colleagues. **(a)** The monkey kept its eyes fixated on the central point and ignored the stimulus that was flashed in the right visual field. A few bursts of activity were found in the superior colliculus. **(b)** The monkey made a rapid saccadic eye movement to the location of a nonfoveal stimulus, and the firing rates of the cells with receptive fields coding that area of space greatly increased. **(c)** The monkey moved its eyes to a location outside the cell's receptive field and the cells in the superior colliculus did not respond. **(d)** The monkey attended to the location in the field but did not make a saccadic eye movement, and a few bursts of activity were found. Adapted from Wurtz, Goldberg and Robinson (1982).

(Figure 6.25). This pattern led to the speculation that the superior colliculus may indeed participate in attentional processes that do not involve eye movements, though we do not yet know how.

Another major subcortical structure that has been implicated in attentional processes is the pulvinar nucleus of the thalamus (Figure 6.26). We know that the pulvinar nucleus is activated during attentional filtering tasks, and later we will consider human lesions that suggest an orienting role for this nucleus. Here we discuss what has been learned from animal studies about the pulvinar's role in visual attention.

The pulvinar nucleus has visually responsive neurons that show color, motion, and orientation selectivity. In addition, it has subdivisions containing retinotopic maps of the visual world and interconnections with frontal, parietal, occipital, and temporal cortical areas. Recordings in awake monkeys have demonstrated longer response latencies in neurons in the dorsal medial region of the lateral pulvinar (Pdm), than in neurons in other regions of the pulvinar nucleus. In addition, responses in these neurons are enhanced when the

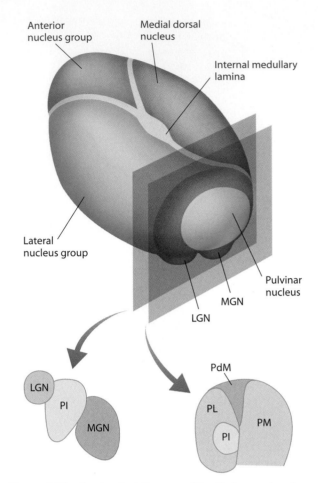

Figure 6.26 Anatomical diagram of the thalamus showing the pulvinar nucleus.

Figure 6.25 Experimental setup and effects of deactivation of a site in the superior colliculus on the discrimination of a target in the same hemifield. From Desimone et al. (1990).

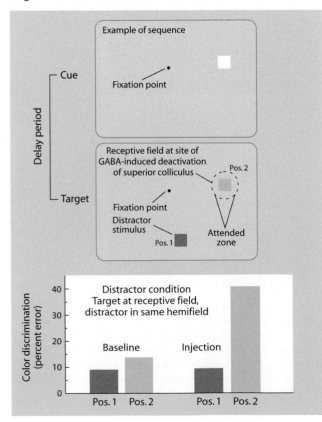

stimulus either is the target of a saccadic eye movement or is attended without eye movements to the target.

Steve Petersen, David Lee Robinson, and their colleagues (1987, 1992) examined effects of unilateral Pdm deactivations on spatial cuing tasks similar to the ones used in humans. They injected drugs that inhibited or excited Pdm neurons and examined how these drugs influenced the monkey's behavior. The drugs either mimic (agonists) or oppose (antagonists) the actions of neurotransmitters such as the inhibitory transmitter gamma-aminobutyric acid (GABA). When muscimol, a GABA agonist that inhibits neuronal activity, was injected, the monkey could not easily focus on targets in the contralateral visual field. In contrast, when a GABA antagonist, which prevents the normal inhibition caused by GABA, was administered, the monkey readily directed its attention to contralesional targets. Hence the pulvinar is central to covert spatial attention (Figure 6.27).

The pulvinar may also filter distracting information.

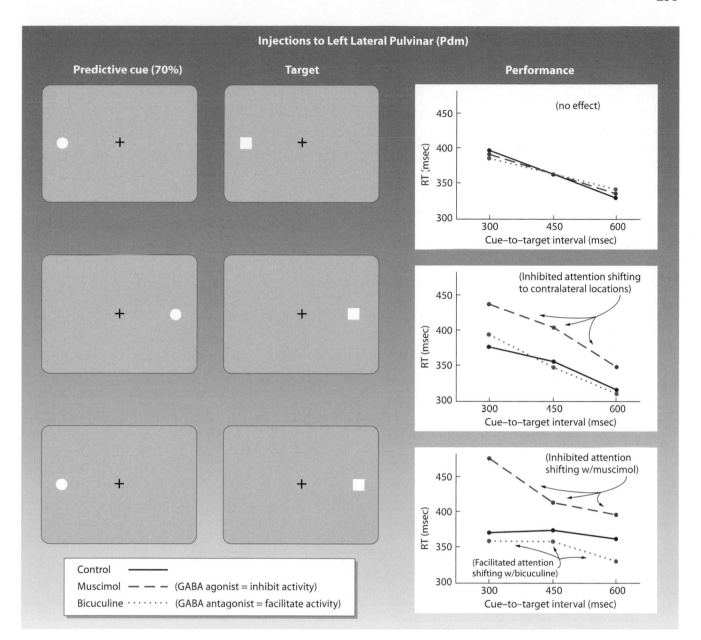

Figure 6.27 Effects on behavior when the pulvinar nucleus is injected with GABA agonists and antagonists. Adapted from Robinson and Petersen (1992).

Injections of muscimol led to deficits in color or form discrimination when competing distracter stimuli were in the visual field. This is similar to findings by University of California at Irvine psychologist David LaBerge (1990) in humans. He employed a task in which filtering of distracter stimuli was required to succeed at the task, and found PET activations in the pulvinar.

The parietal cortex figures into attentional control, as we know from its activation in PET studies, and it participates in the representation of spatial relationships. It maintains connection with subcortical areas like the pulvinar as well as the frontal cortex. Indeed,

most early research on attention in the primate brain was performed in the parietal cortex. Attention creates significant increases and decreases in the activity of parietal cortical neurons.

Vernon Mountcastle (1976) of The Johns Hopkins University discovered that attentive fixation to visual stimuli led to higher firing rates in parietal neurons. The main question is how these neuronal enhancements occur. The firing rates in neurons of the parietal cortex increase in response to a target stimulus when an animal is using the stimulus as a target for a saccade or when covertly discriminating its features. But if a monkey is merely waiting attentively for the next trial in a sequence of trials, the parietal neurons do not usually have enhanced responses to visual stimuli in their receptive fields (Figure 6.28).

The parietal cortex's response pattern is different from that of the superior colliculus in that parietal neurons become enhanced when stimuli either are the target for saccade or are covertly attended. These neurons are participants in visual selective attention—but how? What is the parietal cortex's role? To answer the question, we must remember that parietal lesions in monkeys cause deficits in tasks that require them to discern spatial relations between objects. Also, the parietal cortex is activated when covert attention shifts from location to location, and when subjects have to analyze the spatial relations between targets, as found in PET studies. Finally,

damage to the human parietal cortex leads to deficits in attention, which are described later. Thus, the parietal lobe appears to function both to represent spatial locations and to control voluntary orienting to locations.

In summary, single-unit recordings and lesions studies in animals have shown that subcortical and cortical brain areas are involved in various aspects of attentive behavior and orienting. However, concerning selective attention, the evidence that gating in the subcortical relays to the visual cortex plays a role is weak. The first clear evidence for gating or filtering of inputs occurs in the cortex, and perhaps not until the extrastriate cortex. Neurons in other cortical areas such as the parietal cortex are also sensitive to attentional processes, and appear to play a role in coding the locations of behaviorally relevant stimuli. Together with evidence from neuroimag-

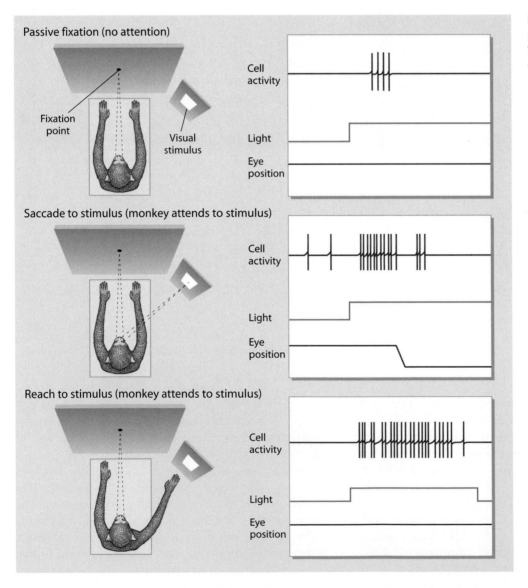

Figure 6.28 Properties of parietal neurons in visual attention. Adapted from Wurtz et al. (1982).

When Attention Is Lost

Patient N.R. is a 61-year-old man who had a stroke in the right parietal lobe 1 week prior to a neurological examination. He experienced weakness, clumsiness, and some loss of sensation in his left hand and leg. His speech was fine, and he comprehended what was said to him. But when approached by his neurologist from the left side, N.R. was unaware of her presence. This is called *neglect* because the patient appears not to notice or pay attention to some stimuli. Yet when the neurologist spoke, the patient moved his upper torso and head toward her and greeted her, showing surprise to find her there. This did not happen when N.R. was approached from the right side; he detected and recognized the physician normally. When the neurologist showed N.R. visual stimuli in the left and right field, he detected and responded to them if presented one at a time. Therefore, N.R. was not blind in any portion of the visual field.

When stimuli were presented simultaneously in the left and right visual fields, the patient reported seeing only the one in the right visual field. This effect is called *extinction* because the presence of the stimulus in the right field leads to the stimulus on the left being extinguished from awareness. When asked how he felt, N.R. complained of being ill, but when describing his problems he did not mention any difficulty in noticing things on his left side. MRI of his brain verified that much of the inferior parietal lobe in the right hemisphere had been damaged. There is no treatment for the symptoms of the neglect syndrome, and the patient partially recovers over time. Six months after the incident, N.R. was vastly improved and rarely failed to notice when someone approached from the left; yet for weak stimuli, he still manifested some extinction and was slower to respond to stimuli on the left side of visual and body-centered space.

Neurologist testing patient with right parietal lesion for signs of extinction. When confronted with simultaneous stimuli in the left and right visual fields, the patient only responds to the one in his unaffected (right) visual field, extinguishing the stimulus in the contralesional (left) visual field.

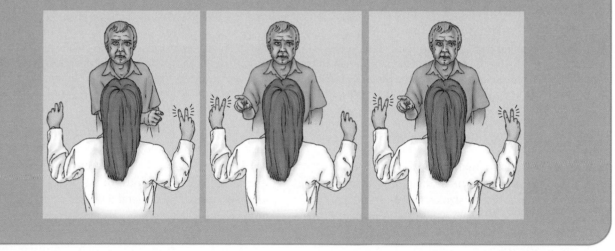

ing, the take-home message is that the parietal cortex and subcortical structures like the pulvinar nucleus are key parts of a system for orienting attention to relevant locations. The consequence of this attentional orienting during perception is seen in the visual cortex, where analyses of stimulus features and form are carried out. Convergent evidence for the role of the parietal and subcortical structures in orienting comes from observations of what happens to these abilities in humans with neurological damage, and is reviewed in the next section.

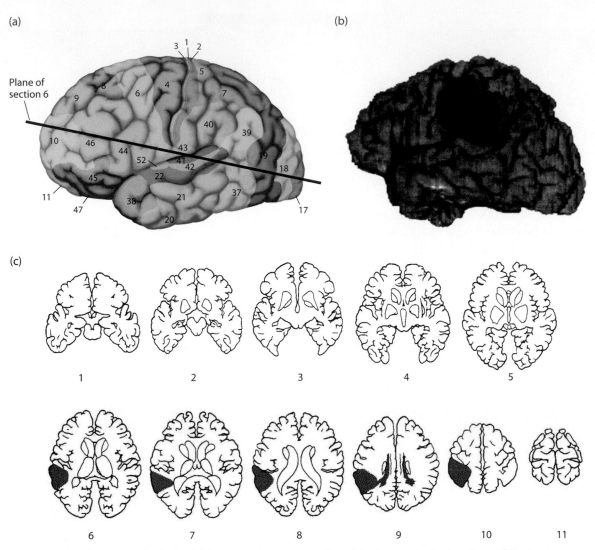

Figure 6.29 Imaging damage to the brain. **(a)** Brodmann's representation of the human brain showing architectonic areas. **(b)** Three dimensional reconstruction of brain of patient with cortical lesion. The lesion was produced by an infarct of parietal and temporal cortex caused by occlusion of the posterior trunk of the middle cerebral artery. The patient has a conduction aphasia. **(c)** The lesion of this patient traced onto templates of horizontal brain sections through lower (top left) and upper (lower right) regions of the brain. Courtesy of Dr. Robert T. Knight.

Neurological Damage and Attention

One of our most informative sources of data on brain attention systems is also one of the oldest: data from the human brain damaged by stroke, tumor, trauma, or progressive disease. Early neurologists appreciated that brain damage led to characteristic deficits, including problems in attention and orienting. We now investigate these deficits from the perspective of cognitive neuroscience theory and use cognitive experimental approaches; further, we can now more precisely describe damage in an individual. Anatomical neuroimaging such as computed tomography (CT) and MRI enables us to look with high anatomical resolution at intracranial damage associated with an external behavioral symptom

(Figure 6.29). A new era of cognitive neurobiological investigation of neurological patients has begun.

In neurological patients, attention deficits can result from damage to various brain regions. One type of damage, unilateral parietal damage, often leads to symptoms of the *neglect syndrome,* wherein patients fail to acknowledge that objects or events exist in the hemispace opposite their lesion. A prominent feature of the neglect syndrome is *extinction,* the failure to perceive or respond to a stimulus contralateral to the lesion (contralesional) when presented with a simultaneous stimulus ipsilateral to the lesion (ipsilesional). Neglect of contralesional space can be diagnosed by neuropsychological tests such as line cancellation. Patients suffering from neglect are given a sheet of paper containing many hori-

Two Brains Are Better Than One

The human visual system is remarkably adept at searching for target items in complex scenes. But when a target differs from other items by a conjunction of simple features like brightness and shape, search time grows linearly with the number of distracters. What is happening, then, is a serial process in which a unitary focus of attention searches the representation of the visual scene in the normal brain. But how would a unitary process such as this function after the cerebral hemispheres in split-brain patients are disconnected by surgically sectioning the corpus callosum? Or can it?

Because split-brain patients have had their corpus callosum cut to treat epilepsy, there is little or no perceptual or cognitive interaction between the hemispheres. And so, specializations of the two halves of the brain can be investigated separately. From studying visual search, we know that split-brain patients, unlike normal subjects, can search at twice the rate when items are split evenly between hemifields rather than concentrated within a single field. It is clear that each disconnected hemisphere possesses its own attentional scanning mechanism. So the old adage that two brains are better than one has real meaning for mental processes in split-brain patients.

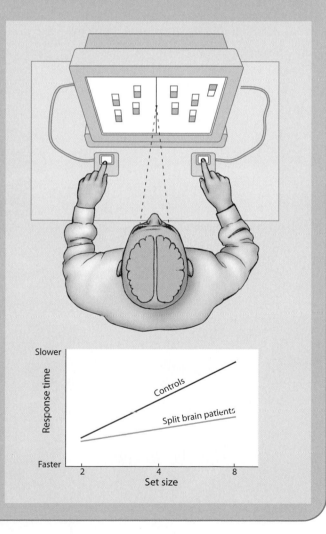

A split-brain patient seated in front of a computer monitor and performing a visual search task for conjunction targets (top). Graphs of the patient's reaction times in comparison to healthy control subjects for bilateral stimulus arrays of various set sizes (bottom). Control subjects take longer to perform the task (red line) than does the split-brain patient (green line) as set size increases. The split-brain patient has a search rate that is twice as fast, indicating that he is searching the array for the target separately with each hemisphere.

zontal lines and are asked under free-viewing conditions to bisect the lines precisely in the middle by placing a vertical line. Patients with lesions of the right hemisphere tend to bisect the lines to the right of the midline. They may also miss lines altogether in the direction opposite the lesioned hemisphere (Figure 6.30).

The syndrome of neglect is unfortunate for those afflicted, and yet fascinating to contemplate. What would it mean to have a deficit that makes part of the world inaccessible to us, and we did not know it? A graphic example comes from paintings by the late German artist Anton Raederscheidt. The artist had a severe stroke that left him with neglect; the pictures in Figure 6.31 are self-portraits done at progressive time points after the stroke occurred and during his partial recovery. They show his failure to represent a portion of contralateral space, including, remarkably, portions of his own body!

We might speculate that neglect patients have disorders of sensation and perception, but this is not really so; neglect happens even in the absence of damage to the visual system and can have nonvisual components such as motor and representational problems—like the

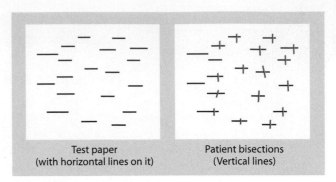

Figure 6.30 Patients suffering from neglect are given a sheet of paper containing many horizontal lines and asked under free-viewing conditions to bisect the lines precisely in the middle with a vertical line. They tend to bisect the lines to the right (for a right-hemisphere lesion) of midline due to neglect for contralesional space.

ones in Raederscheidt's self-portraits. To relate the clinical syndrome of neglect to attention in normal volunteers, researchers have tried to determine which components of normal attentional orienting and selection are lost or damaged after parietal damage.

Figure 6.31 The late German artist Anton Raederscheidt's self-portraits painted at different times following a severe stroke, which left him with neglect to contralesional space.

Michael Posner, Robert Rafal, and their colleagues (1984) studied patients with unilateral lesions of the parietal cortex in a trial-by-trial cuing design like the one shown in Figure 6.7. Even though under normal conditions these patients may neglect contralesional stimuli, neurologists have noted that they can often be instructed to attend to the neglected field. Indeed, in the cuing paradigm, when they were cued to attend to locations in the contralesional hemifield, they responded quickly to target stimuli there. But if they were cued to expect the target stimulus in the ipsilesional field—for example, the right visual field for a right parietal lesion—they were unusually slow to respond to the target when it unexpectedly appeared in the contralesional field. These reaction times to uncued contralesional targets were much slower even than those to uncued trials presented to the field ipsilesional to the lesion (Figure 6.32). This reaction time pattern has been described as an "extinction-like reaction time pattern" to indicate its similarity to the clinical finding of extinction in bedside neurological testing of these patients (see also Two Brains Are Better Than One).

These results were interpreted according to a hypothetical three-stage model of attention and orienting: (1) disengagement of attention from its current focus, (2) movement or shifting of attention to a new location or object, and (3) engagement of attention on the new location or object to facilitate perceptual processing of the stimuli. If parietal patients had exceptionally long reaction times when the cue was in the ipsilesional field and the target was in the contralateral field, it signified a deficit in the disengage operation. One role for the parietal lobe, then, was to disengage attention from its spatial location. Disengagement probably causes the deficit, as subjects can shift attention to contralesional space and engage targets if cued there, but they show particular impairment when their attention is first attracted somewhere else in the visual field and then moves toward the contralesional hemispace.

In patients having lesions in other brain regions, Rafal and colleagues (1987) suggested that the move-and-engage operations are associated with subcortical structures. They targeted the thalamic area, perhaps the pulvinar nucleus, as being in the hypothetical engage operation. Patients' reaction times were slowed for validly cued and invalidly cued targets that appeared in the contralesional space, but they demonstrated only a minor disengage pattern. In contrast, patients with lesions of the midbrain resulting from a neurological disease, progressive supranuclear palsy (PSP), had a different pattern of reaction times in the task. They were slowed in responding to cued targets in the direction of their orienting deficit, and thus displayed a deficit in the hypothetical move operation. These patterns of reaction times are consistent with the three-stage model of attention (Figure 6.33).

Figure 6.32 Extinction-like reaction time pattern in patients with unilateral lesions of the parietal cortex. Reaction times to precued (valid) targets contralateral to the lesion were almost "normal"; that is, while being slower than control times, they were not much slower than those for targets that occurred in the ipsilesional hemifield when that field was cued. When the patients were cued to expect the target stimulus in the field ipsilateral to the lesion (e.g., right visual field for a right parietal lesion), they were unusually slow to respond to the target when it occurred in the opposite field (invalid trials). Adapted from Posner et al. (1984).

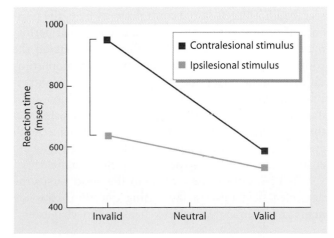

Figure 6.33 The three-stage model of attention of Posner and colleagues (1984).

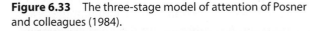
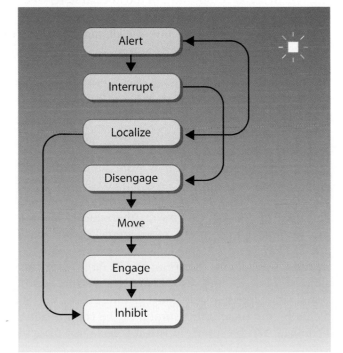

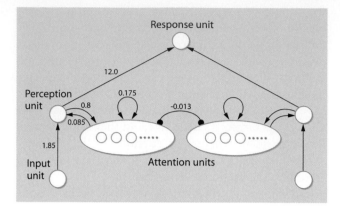

Figure 6.34 The attentional model of Cohen and colleagues. This model represents various processing stages as nodes in a computer connectionist network. Biases that were intended to simulate the damage in neglect were imposed on certain nodes by altering their weighting such that they contributed more or less to activity in the entire network. Adapted from Cohen et al. (1994).

An alternative model to explain reaction time and behavioral patterns in neglect patients is based on how systems in a spatial localization and attention network might interact when components are damaged. One such model, shown in Figure 6.34, predicts the behavioral performance of normal subjects and patients with lesions to the parietal lobe without having to identify a mechanism for disengaging attention. This is a competitive interaction model where excitatory and inhibitory interactions between modules in the attentional orienting system are in equilibrium in the normal state; when part of the system is damaged, various behavioral manifestations can arise—including the disengage pattern. Computer simulations are quite useful for investigating alternative models.

The idea from either the disengage or competitive interaction models is still that attention to the intact visual hemifield causes poorer performance for items presented to the damaged hemifield; thus, items in the intact field affect processing in the contralesional field. Support for this notion comes from studies of visual search in patients with unilateral parietal lesions. When visual search arrays were presented to only the contralesional or ipsilesional hemifields, the patients did not perform differently in the two hemifields. But when search arrays were presented to both hemifields simultaneously, the patients' performance in target detection differed between the two hemifields (Figure 6.35). Search for targets in the intact hemifield was not affected by the presence of stimuli in the contralesional hemifield. Yet the reverse was not true: When patients

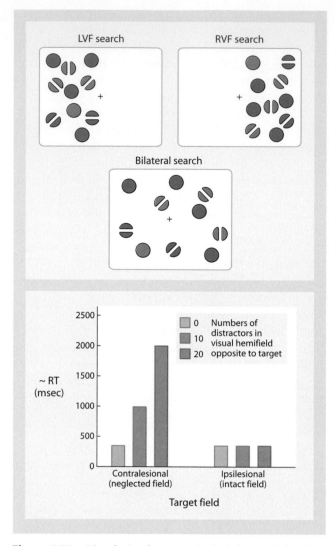

Figure 6.35. Visual stimulus arrays in the left or right hemifield and arrays spanning both hemifields. The graph summarizes the changes in reaction times for targets as a function of the field in which the targets appear. Adapted from Eglin et al. (1989).

searched for targets in the contralesional field, the presence of stimuli in the intact field did affect their performance. They were slower at finding the targets on the contralesional side, and this worsened when more stimuli were on the intact side. Thus, in spatial cuing and visual search paradigms, patients with unilateral lesions of the parietal lobe perform poorly at target detection on the contralesional side, and this worsens when stimuli are presented to the ipsilesional side, or when they are cued to expect a target to be in the ipsilesional field.

This pattern of interference in the good versus the neglected field raises a fascinating question: How are items processed in the neglected field, and to what extent?

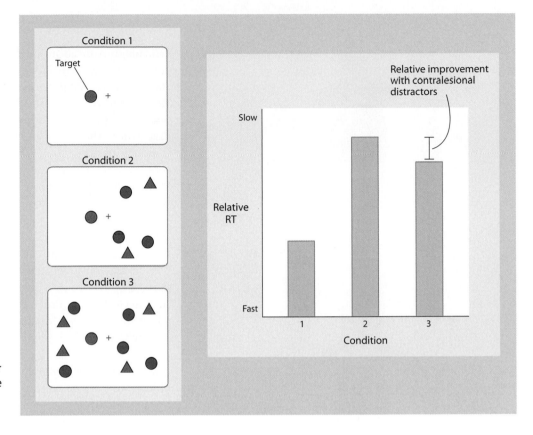

Figure 6.36 The bias toward the field ipsilateral to the lesion in unilateral neglect patients can be reduced by the presentation of target or distracter items in the neglected hemifield. This is indicated by the improvement in the detection of the target near the midline (i.e., in the direction of the neglected field) in the good hemifield. The logic for this effect is described in the text. Adapted from Grabowecky et al. (1993).

Is information in the neglected field not available because it is neglected behaviorally? Bruce Volpe and one of the authors (M.S.G.), and their colleagues (1979) demonstrated that neglect patients could make accurate same-different judgments between items in the intact versus the neglected field, even when they could not identify items on the neglected side of visual hemispace. These provocative data suggest that information on the neglected side can be processed, even though it may not be accessible to awareness.

Information processed in the neglected field can sometimes affect the processing of stimuli. In search tasks, the presence of distracter stimuli in the peripheral regions of the neglected, contralesional hemifield actually helps improve the detection of targets closer to the vertical midline but still in the neglected field (Figure 6.36): This was observed as a reduction in deficits induced by the presence of distracters ipsilateral to the lesion. The logic is that normally the patients are biased toward the right (for right-hemisphere lesions) and neglect the left. But if distracter stimuli are presented bilaterally, the stimuli contralateral to the lesion partially attract attention to that field or, rather, reduce the asymmetrical contralateral-ipsilateral attentional bias caused by the unilateral parietal. Targets near the visual field's midline are now more likely to be quickly detected even

when located in the neglected field. The reason for this is that even though the targets are in the neglected field, the center of mass of the stimulus array has shifted to the direction contralateral to the lesion and this helped patients direct attention leftward.

To what level is information in the neglected field processed? Patients may display extinction for simultaneous bilateral stimulus presentation when the stimuli are similar. For example, in testing visual extinction, when a physician holds up two items, one in each visual field, and they are different objects, the extinction is less than when the two items are the same, like two coins versus a coin and a paper clip. Therefore, patients process information in the neglected field to the extent that they can detect its difference from information in the intact field, just as Volpe and his colleagues showed. In one study, colored letters were presented to both fields. The letters were either different but of the same color, the same but of a different color, or different with a different color. Patients were required to say where the stimulus occurred, and what letter or color it was. If the color was the same when it was the relevant dimension to be reported, then extinction was greater. But when in the color trials the letters were the same on the left and the right, there was no effect on extinction. Hence, interactions between neglected and intact fields manifest

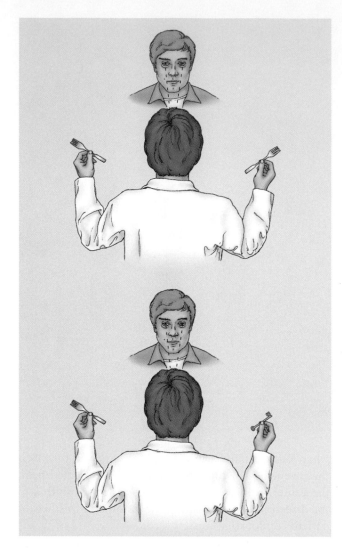

Figure 6.37 Extinction test. **(Top)** A neurologist holding up two identical items in two hemifields (and getting extinction). **(Bottom)** A neurologist holding up different items in the two fields (resulting in less extinction).

normal extraction of visual feature information; moreover, a difference signal can be calculated between contralesional and ipsilesional visual fields. So, patients exhibit greater extinction for similar items in the two fields and can make same-different judgments even without knowing what was in the neglected field (Figure 6.37).

The general idea that information in the neglected field is processed to a high level has been extended to include the meanings of items. Words presented in the neglected field are processed to a semantic level even when patients are unaware of the stimuli because of their neglect. Thus, the word *doctor* in the neglected field primes the subsequent presentation of the word *nurse* in the good field such that patients are faster to decide whether *nurse* is a real word versus a nonword in a lexical decision task.

COORDINATE SYSTEMS OF ATTENTION AND NEGLECT

One major issue about neglect was illustrated in a clever study by Eduordo Bisiach and Claudio Luzzatti (1978) in Italy. They studied patients with neglect who had lived in the same town for most of their lives and were familiar with the city's major landmarks, especially the central piazza where there is a church, restaurants, shops, and buildings of note. They asked patients to imagine themselves on the church steps and to describe the piazza. In their description from memory, they neglected things on the side of the piazza contralateral to their lesion. But when they asked them to imagine themselves standing at the other end of the piazza, facing the other way toward the church, they reported items they had previously neglected and now neglected the side of the piazza they previously reported! Thus, in this striking demonstration, neglect was not merely for items in the external sensory world but also for items in visual memory during remembrance of a known scene (Figure 6.38). The key point is that the piazza was well known to the patients prior to the damage; thus, their neglect of buildings and objects on the side contralateral to the lesion could not be attributed to not having memories of neglected scenes, but rather reflected that attention to parts of the recalled images was biased by parietal damage.

Patients with lesions of the parietal cortex sometimes have disturbed attention in object-based coordinates and not merely eye-, head-, or body-centered coordinates. For example, in tests of line bisections, patients neglect the left half of the page, and each object (each line) on the page. Such effects are still spatial since the side of each object (the line or the page) contralateral to the lesion was neglected. But these results show that object-based coordinates for neglect can exist even when the objects themselves are not in the neglected field. When dumbbell-shaped stimuli have targets flashed within the confines of the two circular ends, parietal lesion patients manifest a deficit in responding to the side contralateral to the lesion (Figure 6.39). When the dumbbell rotates around the center of the visual field, the targets presented on the end of the dumbbell that was first on the neglected side continue to be neglected even when the end is rotated in the ipsilesional field. These data demonstrate that neglect can be distributed within objects; neglect can then follow the object's movements and be represented in its new coordinate frame of reference.

That attention can be object based is supported by a remarkable condition known as *Balint's syndrome.* Patients with this malady have less ability to attend to multiple objects. The typical lesion in a Balint's syndrome patient is *bilateral,* posterior parietal and lateral occipi-

Figure 6.38   Diagram of a person recollecting visual memory from two ends of a piazza and neglecting the contralesional side. From Bisiach and Luzzatti (1978).

tal damage; this is unlike the hemispatial neglect lesion, which is unilateral (Figure 6.40).

Patients with Balint's syndrome can perceive objects but only one at a time. Their visual systems correctly identify objects but have difficulty relating objects to one another. For example, when shown two or more objects such as a comb, brush, and pen, they may report

Figure 6.39   Behrmann and Tipper's rotating dumbbell experiment showing that neglect can be object based. After Behrmann and Tipper (1994).

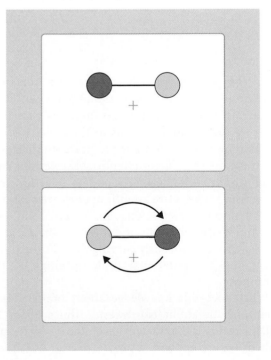

Figure 6.40   Diagrams showing unilateral parietal lesions **(top)** and bilateral parietal/parieto-occipital lesions **(bottom)** of Balint's syndrome.

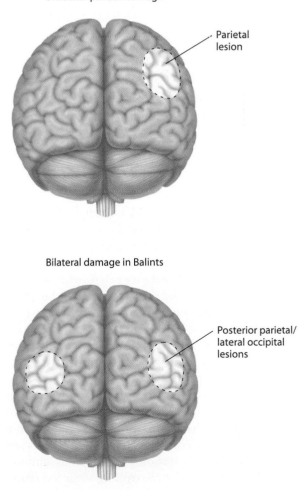

Unilateral parietal damage

Parietal lesion

Bilateral damage in Balints

Posterior parietal/ lateral occipital lesions

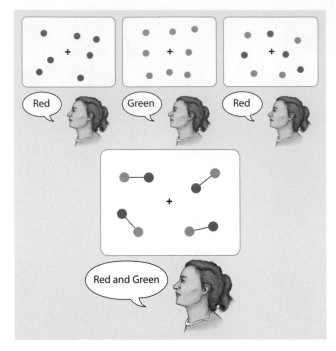

Figure 6.41 Stimuli used to test object attention in Balint's patients. Colored circles were presented in two conditions: with and without connecting lines. After Humphreys and Riddoch (1992).

seeing only one of the objects. Even when the objects are close together or overlapping, they may still report only one of the objects. Which object is perceived may vary over time, and the patients cannot control their attention to the objects. For example, patients shown a person wearing glasses may report the face, or glasses, but not a person wearing glasses. The patient's attention is drawn to one object to the exclusion of others.

These clinical observations of Balint's syndrome patients were supported by a study by Glyn Humphreys and Jane Riddoch (1992) that asked the patients to report what colors were presented in an array of colored circles. The circles were all green, or all red, or half were green and half were red circles (Figure 6.41). The patients were not very good at saying they saw red and green in the two-color arrays, presumably because they would perceive only one object at a time, and each object was either red or green. But when the red and green circles were connected by lines, the patients improved markedly, saying that two colors existed. This happened because connecting the circles of colors formed a single object (a dumbbell) that the patients could see in its entirety, and therefore could perceive the two colors.

Research on patients with lesions in the lateral temporal lobe is rarer than that in regions of the parietal lobe, yet we know that damage or ablation of the lateral temporal lobe is associated with deficits in visual object attention and perception. Here lesions reduce a patient's ability to recognize objects' features in their totality and diminish the recognition of known objects. Effects that dissociate the parietal or "where" deficit, such as spatial neglect, and those that highlight more ventral or "what" deficits, such as object processing, are highly consistent with PET findings. Attention to spatial relations between parts of visual objects activated the dorsal stream; attention to the objects' form activated the ventral stream in PET studies in healthy persons.

SUMMARY

We now know that animal and human studies which address theoretical issues about the brain's attention systems have been contemplated for more than 100 years. If Helmholtz were alive today, he would marvel at how much physiological data we can provide to answer his questions about selective attention. Although we have not addressed the whole of attention—it is too great a task—we have looked at selective aspects of perception that result from attention, and we have examined the executive systems that engender selection within the sensory pathways.

The picture we have formed is of distributed brain systems participating in attentional control. These systems' roles and limits in attention are becoming more clearly defined as we combine attention theory, experimental and cognitive psychological methods, and neurophysiology. Systems for controlling attention require the parietal lobe in concert with subcortical structures—the *source* of attentional selection. The result, in visual processing for example, is that in the cortex we see the modulations in the activity of neurons as they analyze and encode perceptual information; these are the *sites* of attentional selection. We no longer wonder whether early or late selection is the mechanism for selective attention; both are part of the act. Attentional phenomena are diverse and entail many brain computations and mechanisms. Cognitive neuroscience is vigorously carving away at the physiological and computational underpinnings of these phenomena.

What does this knowledge about brain attention systems tell us about Northwest Airlines Flight 255? Well, the reality is that we will never know why the plane crashed. We are left with a puzzle, part of which is the possibility that after forgetting to extend the flaps for takeoff, the pilots then failed to take note of the fact, even though warnings may have flashed and buzzed. If this monumental failure in attention is the root of the explanation, we can speculate what might have happened, because after decades of investigation we now understand that signals that impinge on the retina or cochlea may not be expressed in our conscious awareness, either when they occur or later via our recollections. The implications for human error are obvious yet difficult to resolve. Even so, we now understand that what we see, perceive, remember, and act on may depend on our intentions and momentary necessities, as well as on pressures from the sensory world that manipulate our awareness.

SUGGESTED READINGS

ALLPORT, A. (1993). Attention and Control: Have We Been Asking the Wrong Questions? A Critical Review of 25 Years. In D. Meyer and S. Kornblum (Eds.), *Attention and Performance XIV: A Silver Jubilee* (pp. 183–218). Cambridge, MA: MIT Press.

CORBETTA, M., MIEZIN, F., DOBMEYER, S., SHULMAN, G., and PETERSEN, S. (1991). Selective and divided attention during visual discriminations of shape, color, speed: Functional anatomy by positron emission tomography. *J. Neurosci.,* 11:2383–2402.

EGLIN, M., ROBERTSON, L.C., and KNIGHT, R.T. (1989). Visual search performance in the neglect syndrome. *J. Cogn. Neurosci.* 1:377–385.

GRABOWECKY, M., ROBERTSON, L.C., and TREISMAN, A. (1993). Preattentive processes guide visual search. *J. Cogn. Neurosci.* 5:288–302.

MANGUN, G.R., and HILLYARD, S.A. (1991). Modulations of sensory-evoked brain potentials indicate changes in perceptual processing during visual-spatial priming. *J. Exp. Psychol. Hum. Percept. Perform.* 17:1057–1074.

POSNER, M.I., WALKER, J.A., FRIEDRICH, F.J., and RAFAL, B.D. (1984). Effects of parietal injury on covert orienting of attention. *J. Neurosci.* 4:1863–1874.

7

Memory Systems

Fundamental among cognitive processes is the ability to acquire and retain information about the world around us and our experiences in it—we learn and remember. Amazingly, we remember millions of pieces of vital and trivial information, sometimes with ease and sometimes with tremendous effort. Most people have no difficulty remembering a birthday party during their youth. What may stand out vividly are the taste and color of the cake, the friends who attended, and some gifts. If we pick a salient event such as a birthday party, we will be amazed by how much we can recall about that special day. But what about the birthday party from the year before or the year after? Or what we did the next day?

Memory has the peculiar quality of being incomplete, and yet the totality of life's accumulated experiences is immense. Despite the information we already possess, everyday we acquire new information and form new memories. How is it possible that we can recall the first day of school, the hair color of our best friend in first grade, or the smell of our grandmother's apple strudel as we entered her home for one of those memorable weekend visits?

Memory is a fantastic faculty with many faces. A dominant trend in the cognitive neuroscience of memory has been to appreciate that multiple memory systems exist and to search in earnest for their properties and substrates in the brain. Today scientists ask questions such as: Are all memories the same? Is learning and remembering how to ride a bicycle the same as learning and remembering the relationship between the sides of a right triangle, or an episode in our lives?

We search for neural correlates of learning and memory in many ways: by developing animal models of memory in simple systems (invertebrates) and complex ones (nonhuman primates); through the study of what is and is not lost in amnesia; and with brain imaging to investigate normal encoding, retrieval, and recall in healthy humans. In this chapter we explore learning and memory on psychological and biological levels.

COGNITIVE THEORIES OF MEMORY

Before we delve into the biological bases of memory, we need to explore a bit about cognitive studies on learning and memory. A simple definition is handy, and this is from Larry Squire (1987) of the University of California at San Diego, who wrote, "Learning is the process of acquiring new information, while memory refers to the persistence of learning in a state that can be revealed at a later time." Learning, then, has an outcome—memory, which can be affected by training. With continued exposure to information, or extended practice at a task, behavior should change. Thus, learning happens when memory is strengthened by repetition. This need not involve the conscious attempt to learn. Performance can improve simply from more exposure to information or to a task. We remember the details of a person's face better by seeing it more, without having to memorize facial features.

This general description is accompanied by hypo-

Flashbulb Memories

What were you doing when you heard the news of the Challenger shuttle explosion? Questions like this are typically asked when citing examples of "flashbulb" memories, the vivid memories of the circumstances surrounding shocking or emotionally charged news. Chances are that you can recall the details of your whereabouts, the source of the news, and the companions with you at the time. Since the term was first coined by Roger Brown and James Kulik in 1977, *flashbulb memories* have been the topic of debate for many psychologists. The concept is much older, however. In the last century, the renowned psychologist William James wrote that "an impression may be so exciting emotionally as almost to leave a scar upon the cerebral tissues." This view has some similarity to Brown and Kulik's "Now Print!" mechanism as a possible basis of flashbulb memories. Under this proposed explanation, the mechanism for such vivid recollection is neurophysiological in nature. Researchers into this fascinating instance of long-term memory have asked, How do these memories compare to other recollections? Is there a special mechanism for flashbulb memories? Are flashbulb memories especially accurate or long-lasting?

The Challenger shuttle explosion in 1986 presented a unique opportunity to study flashbulb memories over a range of persons' ages, and at various periods of time after the event. This has provided interesting insights. Ulric Neisser and Nicole Harsch (1992) queried students at Emory University about hearing the news of the Challenger explosion at various times after the incident. They began as early as 24 hours after the occurrence, and then followed up 2½ years later.

Two and a half years after the incident, one student wrote: "When I first heard about the explosion I was sitting in my freshman dorm room with my roommate and we were watching TV. It came on a news flash and we were both totally shocked. I was really upset and I went upstairs to talk to a friend of mine and then I called my parents."

Along with this recollection, the student gave the highest score possible in confidence ratings on the accuracy of the memory. How close was this recollection to his previous report? Two and a half years earlier, 24 hours after the explosion, he had written: "I was in religion class and people walked in and started talking about it. I didn't know any details except that it had exploded and the schoolteacher's students had all been watching, which I thought was so sad. Then after class I went to my room and watched a TV program about it and I got all the details."

Like this student, over 40% of the participants were quite inconsistent in their descriptions of the incident; nonetheless, they gave high confidence ratings to their later recollections. How sure are you now of your answers to the question?

Alternative explanations for flashbulb-like memories have been offered by Neisser (1982) and others who postulated that ordinary aspects of memory can explain the phenomena of flashbulbs and apparent "phantom flashbulbs." So, are there flashbulb memories? The answer is that emotionally charged events have vivid "tags" in memory; therefore, confidence in the recollection, even years later, is high. However, flashbulb memories are no more accurate than other memories of everyday experiences.

---

thetical stages of memory: encoding, storage, and retrieval. *Encoding* refers to processing incoming information to be stored. The encoding stage has two separate steps: *acquisition* and *consolidation*. Acquisition registers inputs in sensory buffers and sensory analysis stages, while consolidation creates a stronger representation over time. *Storage*, the result of acquisition and consolidation, creates and maintains a permanent record. Finally, *retrieval* utilizes stored information to create a conscious representation or to execute a learned behavior like a motor act.

Immediate and Short-Term Memory

One way to characterize memory is to subdivide memory processes by the duration of memory retention. The distinctions between *sensory memory, immediate* or *short-term memory*, and *long-term memory* are based on how long information is retained. Sensory memory has a lifetime measurable in milliseconds to seconds, as when we recover what was said to us while we were not paying close attention to the speaker. Immediate or short-term memory is associated with retention over seconds to minutes. This may include retaining a phone number provided by a telephone operator, which we try to remember as we frantically dial it. Long-term memories are measured in days or years—events from childhood or last week. Let us review how these concepts shaped the language of memory in the 1950s and 1960s.

FORGETTING OVER THE COURSE OF SECONDS

In the late 1950s, an experimental paradigm was developed by Petersen and Petersen (1959) and others to measure how long it takes to forget information. Volunteers were presented with three-letter strings (consonants) and after varying intervals of time, a light would cue the person to recall and say the letters aloud. In the interval, which lasted from 3 to 18 seconds, the subjects were distracted from rehearsing the letters by being asked to perform mental arithmetic such as backward subtraction (Figure 7.1a). The effect of distraction on recalling the letter strings was clear; by 18 seconds the

percentage of correct responses dropped below 10%. The curve that describes the retention of the original letter string is shown in Figure 7.1b.

These data from short-term forgetting experiments were surprising. Think about whether you could remember the letter string XTR for 18 seconds; of course you could, but the key is that you would not be able to do so if you were presented a distracting task. If a friend asks who you are calling while you try to hold a phone number in memory long enough to dial it, you might forget the number and have to look it up again. Most prior work on forgetting had been done by using long-term memory tasks. Contemporary thought about forgetting things from long-term memory held that new information interfered with older memories (interference models). This explanation was, however, inconsistent with the data from the short-term forgetting experiments which showed that forgetting could happen when no new information was being learned, and therefore interference

Figure 7.1 **(a)** To test a person's short-term retention of verbal items, an experimenter presents the subject with a string of three consonants such as *XCJ*, and then a number such as *309*. The subject listens to the consonant string and then starts counting backwards by threes from the number given by the experimenter. After 3 to 18 seconds, a red light signals the subject to recall and repeat aloud the consonant string. **(b)** Correct recalls as a function of retention delay. In the study of Petersen and Petersen, by 18 seconds the subjects could recall the consonant string less than 10% of the time. Adapted from Petersen and Petersen (1959).

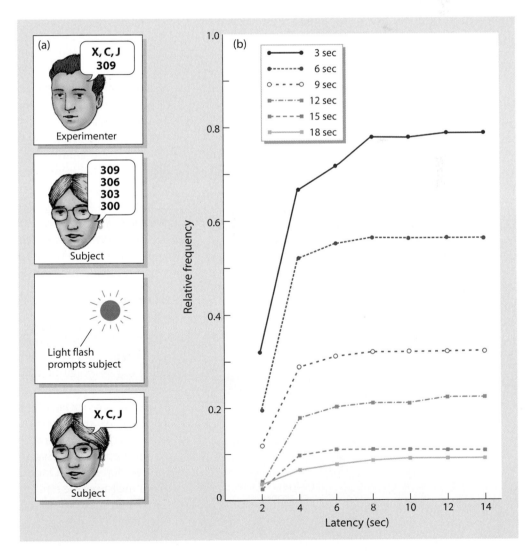

from newly learned information could not have caused the forgetting. Rather, the contention that information could merely decay over time was supported by *decay models*. The interpretation of the short-term forgetting data was that the distracting task of backwards subtraction caused a real interference of its own that led to the memory loss, and thus, it was not a simple decay of information. Thus, much of memory research during this period focused on whether losses of information (forgetting) from memory were the result of information merely fading away over time (decaying), versus the idea that it was actively displaced (interfered with) by newly learned information.

Decay versus interference in forgetting was also investigated using a new method developed in the 1960s by Donald Norman and his colleagues (Waugh and Norman, 1965) and a different conclusion was reached. They presented subjects with strings of random numbers up to sixteen digits long. Each digit was present once in the list except for the last or "probe" digit, which was a repeat of one of the prior digits (Figure 7.2). The probe signaled that the subject should report the number that had followed the *original* presentation of the probe digit. Because the probe digit might previously have been in any position, this method manipulated the time between the initial presentation of the information and the point of attempted recall. In addition, during different conditions, the presentation rate of the digits in the string was either one or four digits per second. Hence, two factors were being manipulated: the number

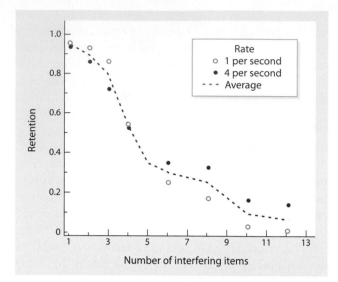

Figure 7.3 Waugh and Norman found that subjects' retention performance declined as the number of intervening items between the two presentations of the probe digit increased. The rate of presentation did not affect forgetting. This means that interference, and not decay, is causing forgetting from short-term memory. Adapted from Waugh and Norman (1965).

of intervening items, which should be a factor if interference is relevant to forgetting, and the time between presentation and recall, which would be most important if decay caused forgetting from short-term memory.

Data were analyzed by comparing the accuracy of recall as a function of intervening items for the two presentation rates. This experiment clearly showed that the memory loss functions were virtually the same for the two rates, which indicated that the number of intervening items was affecting recall (Figure 7.3). The conclusion is that interference from subsequent items causes loss of information from short-term memory.

IMPORTANCE OF ORDER IN MEMORY

When we make a shopping list but forget to take the list to the market, we often remember some items better than others. The pattern for what we typically remember is called the *serial position effect*. We are better at recalling items at the beginning and end of a list, known as *primacy* and *recency* effects, respectively. Figure 7.4 shows the serial position effect, a u-shaped curve when accuracy of recall is plotted against the item's position on the list.

Two separate mechanisms are proposed for primacy and recency effects. One model of the primacy effects is that it measures the efficiency of transferring items from short-term memory to long-term storage. The logic of this view is as follows. At the beginning of the list, the memory system has enough space to successfully trans-

Figure 7.2 The probe method used by Waugh and Norman to investigate the effect of interference on forgetting. Strings of random numbers were presented, each once except for a probe digit that was presented at a random position in the list and then again as the last digit. The subjects were asked to report the number that followed the initial presentation of the probe digit.

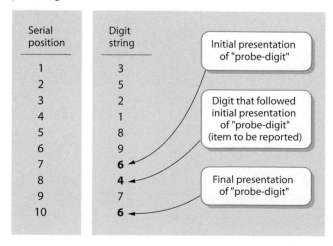

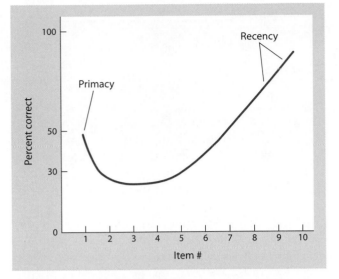

Figure 7.4 Serial position effect. The percentage of items recalled is plotted as a function of the item's position in the list. Primacy and recency effects can be seen by the better recall of items presented toward the beginning and end of the list.

fer from short- to long-term memory by rehearsing the items. (Remember that when rehearsal was prevented in Figure 7.1b, the items were rapidly forgotten.) In contrast, the recency effect happens because items at the end of the list are available in short-term memory, having recently been seen.

Studies supporting these mechanisms for primacy and recency employed a distracting task after a list of items was presented. The distracting task eliminated the recency effect, as one would predict if recency effects represented storage in short-term memory. The primacy effect was however, unchanged by adding a distracting task at the end of the list.

In contrast, the primacy effect could be eliminated if the list items were presented more quickly, a manipulation that did not affect the recency effect. Presumably, the primacy effect was reduced at faster rates because the rehearsal of early items was hindered by the large information load generated by rapid presentation of list items, and rehearsal was needed for successful transfer to long-term memory. The tests, then, supported the idea that primacy and recency effects resulted from separate memory characteristics. The primacy effect reflects transfer from short- to long-term memory through rehearsal, but the recency effect reflects retention in short-term memory. These distinctions between primacy and recency effects highlight the distinction between short- and long-term storage, and emphasize the concept of *transfer* from short-term memory to long-term memory.

SHORT-TERM MEMORY CAPACITY

Precisely how much information a healthy individual can retain in short-term memory varies among individuals (see The Memorist). However, experiments have demonstrated an interesting characteristic of human memory. In the 1950s, George Miller (reviewed by Miller, 1994) investigated how much information individuals can process. Although the initial work centered on perception, the research was extended to memory for the retention of items.

Volunteers were presented with items to be remembered, in groups of varying size. The results were quite amazing: Regardless of the information in the items (e.g., digits versus words), the number of items that were retained typically proved to be around seven. When more than seven items were presented, volunteers were less successful at recalling all the items. This should come as no surprise, again, think about phone numbers. Miller referred to this characteristic feature of human memory as the *span of immediate memory*.

The memory limits discovered in these studies turned out to be defined by the number of items, not the information content of each item. This distinction has sometimes been cast as the difference between a bit of information and a chunk—a *bit* being the elementary piece of information and a *chunk* being a unit composed of bits. The use of words allows individual letters to be chunked. The word *cerebellum* is either ten letters, or one word. If ten letters have to be remembered, this taxes the short-term memory system, but if the letters can be chunked as one word (*cerebellum*) then about seven of these (words) can be remembered. The consequence of this chunking is that during recall of the material, the chunked information can be essentially unpacked (unchunked) to yield more bits of information than could normally be retained. That is, if we can retain seven words of ten letters each in memory, we can unpack this into seventy bits of information by using knowledge about word spelling. This evidence points to the ability of humans to recode information in manageable packets, packets that can be handled within the constraints of short-term memory.

SENSORY MEMORY

How do limitations in memory affect perception? That is, what is the relationship between our short-term memory capacity and perception? If we can only hold seven (plus or minus two) items in short-term memory, does this imply that only seven or so items can be perceived in a brief instant of, say, visual perception? The answer is that we can "see" much more than we can remember. As George Sperling (1960) wrote a few decades

The Memorist

Do you think that you have a pretty good memory for numbers? Can you remember your license plate number? Social security number? Telephone numbers of friends? How about the digits of *pi*? What was that again, 3.1415...? How good can people be at remembering numbers?

Rajan Mahadevan recalled being very good as a child in memorizing license plates—lots of them. To test the extent of his memory for numbers, he spent a few months of his adult life memorizing the digits of pi, and won his place in the *Guinness Book of World Records* in 1981 for reciting the first 31,811 digits. Not bad considering there is nothing too meaningful in strings and strings of numbers. Rajan is considered a "memorist,"

one with an extraordinary skill for learning and reciting information—most commonly, a genius for memorizing numbers, as contrasted with "prodigious savants" who are mentally and often physically impaired, but have one phenomenal talent. Unlike the character played by Dustin Hoffman in the movie *Rain Man*, Rajan is a perfectly normal individual of above-average intelligence.

How is it that Rajan memorized over 30,000 digits? According to Rajan, he uses a method of pairing matrix locations with individual digits, as in the table below, which consists of a matrix of ten columns by N rows, each place holding a ten-digit number sequence.

Amazingly, Rajan now knows the first 5000 digits of *pi* so well that when given a location number (counting

pi = 3. +

1415926535	8979323846	2643383279	5028841971	6939937510	5820974944	5923078164	0628620899	8628034825	3421170679
8214808651	3282306647	0938446095	5058223172	5359408128	4811174502	8410270193	8521105559	6446229489	5493038196
4428810975	6659334461	2847564823	3786783165	2712019091	4564856692	3460348610	4543266482	1339360726	249141273...

ago, "When stimuli consisting of a number of items are shown briefly to an observer, only a limited number of the items can be correctly reported. The fact that observers commonly assert that they can see more than they can report suggests that memory sets a limit on a process that is otherwise rich in information."

Using the method of *partial report*, investigators can assess how much is picked up by sensory systems immediately after a stimulus is briefly presented. This information cannot be readily indexed by merely asking the observer to state what she saw, because of the limits in short-term memory. The partial report procedure is shown in Figure 7.5.

Observers actually perceive two to three times more information than they can report in a traditional verbal report test in which no cues are used. However, this information is only present for a few hundred milliseconds and is then rapidly forgotten such that at some point it no longer surpasses the memory limits of seven items. This decay time is about 1 second, but most of it occurs by 300 to 500 msec in the visual system, indicat-

ing that by as short a time as 500 msec the visual sensory trace is gone.

This short-term form of information is a type of visual persistence known as the *iconic visual store*. *Iconic* refers to a "picture" available as a sensory image. A similar system operates in other sensory modalities; in the auditory system, an *echoic store* represents a sensory memory for auditory inputs. Some estimates of the time course of the echoic trace have been as long as 20 seconds, thus indicating a fundamental difference in the physiological processes underlying the visual and auditory sensory registers (see Physiological Evidence for the Decay of Sensory Memory). In general, these sensory registers or traces are not considered to be directly accessible to conscious awareness, although information can be read out of these stores and analyzed. Hence, the key features of the sensory memory traces are that they decay swiftly, have a large capacity compared to immediate and short-term memory, and store a sensory representation of information as opposed to a semantic or meaning-based representation.

from left to right and top to bottom in the matrix), he can tell the digit in that location, or he can fill in the remaining five digits within a few seconds of being read the first five digits of any ten-digit sequence.

Throughout the years, many memorists have been written about. The most famous was Shereshevskii, who was studied for 30 years by Alexander Luria, the great Russian neuropsychologist (1968). Instead of the location-digit matching used by Rajan, Shereshevskii claimed that he used rich visual images akin to photographic memories to reproduce number matrices and mathematical formulas. Memorists have varied in their specific abilities of memorization; Rajan's specialty is restricted to digit strings. If you are feeling like your memory is not quite up to par, you may be encouraged to know that he can perform no better than control subjects on tests of spatial memory and word lists.

Three general principles for skilled memory have been proposed: (1) meaningful encoding, the use of preexisting knowledge as a tool in storing new information in memory; (2) retrieval structure, the attachment of cues to new material for later retrieval of in-

formation; and (3) speed-up, the effect of practice on the ability to learn material. According to some experts on this phenomenon, anyone can demonstrate the skills of memorists such as Rajan if they follow these general principles. Yet, Rajan does not follow the first principle, as he does not relate the numbers to anything significant and already known, as some memorist have done. The memorist Arnould substituted consonants for numbers and made sentences to aid in memorization. Based on extensive comparisons between Rajan and control subjects, Rajan's ability is now attributed to a combination of practice and some underlying biological component. The idea of a genetic explanation for his unusual skill is interesting in light of the fact that he is named after a distant cousin, one of the most famous mathematicians in India, Srinivasa Ramanujan, who claimed that "every number was a personal friend."

How has Rajan's place as a world record holder withstood the test of time? In 1987, Hideaki Tomoyori claimed Rajan's place in the Guinness Book of World Records by reciting the first 40,000 digits of pi from memory.

Figure 7.5 Partial report experiment of sensory memory. Subjects are presented with brief (50-msec) glimpses of stimuli like letter arrays that consist of three rows of four letters each. If asked to report as many items as possible, they would show the typical limitation in short-term memory and report about seven (plus or minus two) items. In the partial report method, they see the entire array briefly and then report on only a subset of the array. Which subset to report is indicated by an auditory cue presented after the visual array (e.g., high frequency tone indicates top row). The cue can tell the subjects to report the first, second, or third rows of letters; the key here is that the subjects do not know prior to the stimulus which row of letters they will be asked to report. Nonetheless, the subjects are accurate at reporting the four letters from any row cued. This makes sense because the four letters in the row to be reported are well within the limits of the span of immediate memory. This is interesting because the subjects do not know in advance which letters to retain in memory. This means that for some period after the presentation of the visual stimulus, all twelve letters are retained, and so the letters in any row can be reported.

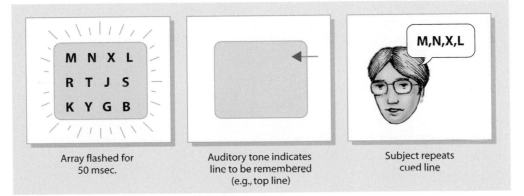

Physiological Evidence for the Decay of Sensory Memory

Experimental psychologists have attempted to determine the duration of sensory memory by varying the time between the presentation of a stimulus and the perceptual signal (typically a mask) that presumably erases the contents of the sensory register. In the visual system, this iconic store lasts only a few hundred milliseconds. But the auditory system takes longer for the echoic memory trace to decay, perhaps a few seconds, and maybe as long as 20 seconds! This is consistent with the hypothesized uses of a sensory memory store in audition. In speech perception, integrating information takes more time: It may take many seconds for a speaker to articulate a complex sentence.

Physiological approaches have been employed to investigate the time course of auditory sensory memory. The persistence of the human auditory sensory memory trace was studied by recording a human brain response known as the *electrical mismatch negativity* (MMN) or *magnetic mismatch field* (MMF). This brain response is elicited by a deviant stimulus such as a high tone presented within a sequence of identical stimuli of a different pitch. The MMN is a negative polarity component in the event-related potential elicited by the deviant tone. The MMF is the magnetic counterpart to this, and is recorded in a magnetoencephalographic (MEG) device that is sensitive to the minute magnetic fields produced by active neurons. It occurs with a latency of about 150 to 200 msec after stimulus onset and is generated in the auditory cortex. These mismatch responses have been interpreted as representing sensory memory processes that hold recent auditory experience in echoic memory for comparison to new inputs. When these inputs differ, the MMF is generated. This implies that the amplitude of the MMF could measure how long the echoic memory trace persists. Mikko Sams and his colleagues (1993) at the Helsinki University of Technology in Finland varied the interstimulus intervals between standard and deviant tones and found that the MMF could still be elicited by the deviant tone at interstimulus intervals of 9 to 10 seconds. After about 10 seconds the amplitude of the MMF declined to the point where it could no longer be distinguished reliably from noise. Behavioral results yielded a similar 10 seconds for the echoic trace. Thus, the idea that the auditory sensory memory trace lasts up to 10 seconds provides a convincing physiological measure of the duration of auditory sensory memory in humans.

The magnetic response known as the *mismatch field* (MMF) elicited by deviant tones. The amplitude of the MMF declines over time between the preceding standard tone and the deviant tone. This can be interpreted as evidence for an automatic process in sensory memory.

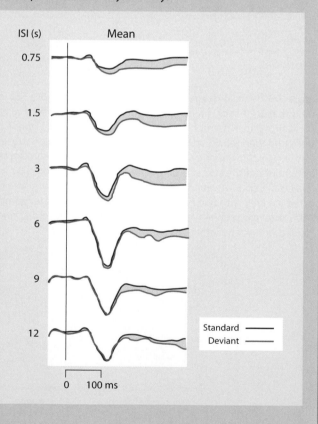

Models of Short-Term Memory

These early data on short-term memory led to some influential models that proposed discrete stages of information processing during learning and memory. One model, the *modal model,* represents a way of viewing data generated by studies on sensory, immediate, and short-term memory.

Richard Atkinson (the current president of the University of California) and Richard Shiffrin (1968) at Indiana University elaborated the details of the modal model (Figure 7.6). Information is first stored in sensory memory. Items selected by attentional processes can move into short-term storage. Once in short-term memory, if the item is rehearsed, it can be moved into long-term memory. At each stage, information is lost by decay, interference, or a combination of both.

LEVELS OF PROCESSING MODELS

New formulations about memory mechanisms developed partly from challenges to the modal model in Figure 7.6. For example, other factors besides simply holding information in short-term memory seemed to influence long-term memory. One notion was that the "deeper" an item was processed, the more it was consolidated and stored in long-term memory, known as the *levels of processing model.*

Let us consider experiments by Fergus Craik and Robert Lockhart (1972). Written words were presented to subjects in three conditions. In one condition, the subjects were told to identify whether the words were

Figure 7.6 The Atkinson and Shiffrin "modal" box model of memory. Sensory information enters the information-processing system and is first stored in a sensory register. Items that are selected via attentional processes are then moved into short-term storage. With rehearsal, the item can move from short-term to long-term storage. Adapted from Atkinson and Shiffrin (1968).

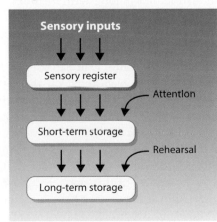

composed of uppercase or lowercase letters—considered a superficial processing task. In a second condition, the subjects were asked to determine whether a word rhymed with another word—an intermediate level of processing. In a final condition, the subjects were asked to make a judgment about the meaning of a word (e.g., does it fly?)—a deep, semantic level of processing. Subjects showed better subsequent memory for items more deeply processed during learning; thus, how information is processed affects how it is remembered.

Deep or elaborate rehearsal and encoding create meaning-based codes that relate information directly to previously acquired knowledge. The result is better learning compared to when information is merely repeated and stored as simple visual or phonological codes. This feature of memory is inconsistent with the concept of a short-term store because it distinguishes between merely holding information in short-term memory long enough to get it into long-term storage and the type (superficial or deep) of encoding used.

WORKING MEMORY MODELS

The concept of *working memory* was developed to address various shortcomings of the short-term store concept. Working memory represents a limited-capacity store for performing mental operations. The contents of working memory might originate from sensory inputs by way of sensory memory, or by retrieval from long-term memory. In either case, working memory contains information that can be acted on and processed.

In their original formulation of working memory in the 1970s, Allan Baddeley and his colleagues (1974) proposed that a unitary short-term memory was insufficient to explain the processing and maintenance of information over short periods. They constructed a three-part working memory system: a central executive controlling two subordinate systems, the phonological loop and the visuospatial sketchpad. What do these hypothesized subsystems do, and what evidence supported this formulation?

The central executive is a command-and-control center that presides over the interactions between the subordinate systems (the phonological loop and the visuospatial sketchpad) and long-term memory. It is a modality nonspecific cognitive system that coordinates processes in working memory and controls actions. This concept of a central executive was thought of as a supervisory attentional system (SAS) by Donald Norman and Tim Shallice (1980). The SAS overrides routine execution of learned behaviors when novel circumstances require modified actions, and it also coordinates and plans activities.

The phonological loop is a hypothesized mechanism

for acoustically coding information in working memory. The evidence for this came first from studies that asked subjects to recall letter stings composed of consonant letters. The letters were presented visually, but the pattern of recall errors indicated that perhaps the letters were not coded visually over the short term. The subjects were apparently using an acoustic code because during recall they were more likely to replace a presented letter with an erroneous letter having a similar sound (e.g., *T* for *G*) rather than similar in form (e.g., *Q* for *G*). The idea is that *tee* and *gee* are acoustically more similar that *kyoo* and *gee,* even though the round-shaped letter *Q* is more similar to *G* in appearance. This was the first insight that an acoustic code might participate in rehearsal. Immediate recall of lists of words also is poorer when many words on the list sound similar compared to when they sound dissimilar, even when the latter are semantically related. This indicates that an acoustic but not a semantic code is used in working memory, because words that sound similar interfere with one another, while words related by meaning do not.

The phonological loop may have two parts: a short-lived acoustic store for sound inputs and an articulatory component that plays a part in the subvocal rehearsal of items to be remembered over the short term. This latter part would also code visually presented information in working memory.

Evidence for a visually based short-term representation parallels the phonological loop and permits information storage in either purely visual or visuospatial codes. Evidence for this system came from dissociations between verbal and visuospatial codes. The idea is that if two codes are separate, they should not interfere with one another in working memory. If some information is coded acoustically, the introduction of a secondary visuospatial task during retention should not disrupt performance. Indeed, acoustic and visuospatial codes are separated; what emerges is a working memory with a central executive and two independent subsystems (Figure 7.7).

The advantage of the working memory conceptualization over the short-term memory idea represented in the modal model is that it fills in details about the relation between short-term and long-term memory. Further, the working memory concept does not assume a unitary short-term store. Instead, it accounts for short-term forgetting and for processing new information in a context that describes the codes used.

Long-Term Memory

Information maintained for a significant time is referred to as *long-term memory.* We have already re-

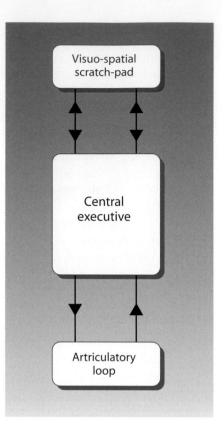

Figure 7.7 Simplified representation of the working memory model by Baddeley and Hitch. This three-part working memory system has a central executive that controls two subordinate systems, the phonological loop by which information can be acoustically coded in working memory, and the visuospatial sketchpad by which information is visually coded in working memory. Adapted from Baddeley (1995).

viewed evidence for the behavior of short-term and working memory, and set the stage for the idea that memory can be divided into at least two systems based partly on retention time. Now we discuss data and concepts about distinctions in long-term memory.

Much of memory research has dwelt upon distinctions in long-term memory. Theorists have split long-term memory into two major divisions. Endel Tulving of the University of Toronto, Dan Schacter of Harvard (1990), and others have elaborated on the distinction between *explicit* and *implicit* forms of memory. In a similar way, Larry Squire (1987), Neal Cohen (1993), and their colleagues have used the terms *declarative* and *nondeclarative* memory.

Both theoretical views signal the fact that not all knowledge is the same. For this chapter *explicit* and *declarative* mean knowledge that we have conscious access to; that is, knowledge we usually know we have, including personal and world knowledge. In contrast, we use *implicit* or *nondeclarative* memory to refer to knowledge we have no conscious access to, such as procedural knowledge (e.g., bike riding), perceptual priming, and simple learned behaviors that derive from conditioning, habituation, or sensitization. The essential relations between these forms of long-term memory are summarized in Figure 7.8. There remains uncertainty in memory research as to whether semantic knowledge (facts or world knowledge) is or is not supported by the same memory system that supports explicit (declarative) knowledge. Some evidence suggests that it is, while other evidence dissociates episodic from semantic memory, as in amnesia.

EXPLICIT MEMORY

We can distinguish between things that we recall about our own lives and knowledge about the world that does not relate to events in our lives. This is the distinction between episodic and semantic memory, first proposed by Endel Tulving (1989). Examples of episodic memory are those that represent episodes in our personal history, such as meeting a friend for the first time, our eighteenth birthday party, or the time we fell from a bicycle and skinned an elbow. Episodic memory involves conscious awareness of past events; it is one's personal, biographical memory.

Semantic memory, in contrast, reflects knowing things such as how to tell time, who the twenty-first president was, how to cook an omelet, how to subtract two numbers, how to use a telephone, and other similar forms of knowledge. Semantic memory is world knowl-

edge that one remembers in the absence of any circumstances about learning it; that is, no episodic memory is associated with the semantic information. Semantic and episodic memory of an event might overlap in that we remember the episode of learning who the twenty-first president was, but generally the distinction holds: World knowledge is separate from our recollection of events in our life.

Some models place semantic memory under declarative memory because it is knowledge that we know we know and can bring into conscious awareness as facts we can declare. Yet because we have evidence that episodic and semantic memory may be differentially affected in amnesia, other scientists, notably Tulving who defined these terms, consider semantic memory a form of implicit memory. This is because people with some kinds of amnesia completely lose their ability to form new episodic memories, while the ability to acquire new semantic knowledge may be partially preserved, as we find later.

IMPLICIT MEMORY

One of the most exciting areas of memory research in the past decade or so is *implicit memory,* a term coined by Daniel Schacter (1987). This memory is revealed when previous experiences facilitate performance on a task that does not require intentional recollection of the experiences.

Implicit memory encompasses several forms of knowledge that we can observe on a day-to-day basis, and that can be revealed with appropriately designed

Figure 7.8 A generalized diagram of the relationships with long-term memory. This composite scheme combines concepts from Tulving (1995) and from Squire and Knowlton (1995). Later, these memory systems will be related to brain structures.

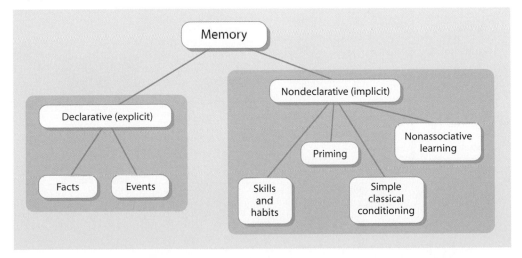

experimental testing. In Figure 7.8, which presents a taxonomy of memory, implicit memory includes all nondeclarative memory. Memory that can be subsumed under implicit memory includes nondeclarative knowledge that is learned and retained even when explicit memory for that knowledge does not exist (e.g., procedural knowledge, conditioning, and habituation). Here we concentrate on implicit memory that acts within the perceptual system, but we return to other forms of implicit, nondeclarative memory when investigating amnesia.

Perceptual Representation System Priming tasks have been extensively used to demonstrate implicit memory. Implicit memories obtained in this way are associated with activity in a perceptual representation system (PRS). Priming is the improvement in identifying or processing a stimulus as the result of its having been previously observed. For example, subjects can be presented with lists of words and then in a test phase, their memory of them can be evaluated using either an explicit or an implicit test. In explicit memory tests, subjects consciously attempt to recognize previously seen material. To achieve this, subjects are presented with a second word list (after a delay of hours or days) composed of new words plus ones in the previous list (old words). The subjects are asked to identify words that they had been shown in the initial presentation. In contrast, an implicit memory test might use a word-fragment completion task. Here, during the later test phase, subjects view only some letters; for example,

t_ou_h_s for *thoughts*. The fragments can be from either new words or old words. The task is to complete the fragment. Subjects are not told that some words could have been in the initial list; thus, there is no attempt to recall whether the words were part of the initial list, and anyway it is not relevant to the task.

These priming experiments found first, that in fragment-completion tests (implicit memory test), subjects are significantly better at correctly completing fragments for words presented in the initial list (Figure 7.9). Subjects benefit from having seen the words before, even if they are not told that the words were in the previous list! Priming for fragment completion does not lessen over time (hours versus days). In contrast, performance in the recognition task (explicit test) does decrease over time.

The evidence we have that priming effects do not depend on explicit memory is simple: There is not a relation between the ability to recognize old words (e.g., "Did we show you this word before?") and to complete fragments of those same words. This pattern, termed *stochastic independence,* implies that better recognition of a word as old will not help in fragment-completion tests (Figure 7.10). That is, stochastic independence would be predicted if the tasks tapped into two separate memory systems (explicit and implicit). Stochastic independence is important because it demonstrates that subjects benefit from previously seeing a word even though they have no conscious recollection of having done so.

Explicit and implicit memory are apparently sepa-

Figure 7.9 A typical word-priming study. Subjects are shown lists of words and then wait varying amounts of time to perform a fragment-completion task. Tulving and Schacter (1990) showed that subjects are better at completing fragments of words that were previously shown to them.

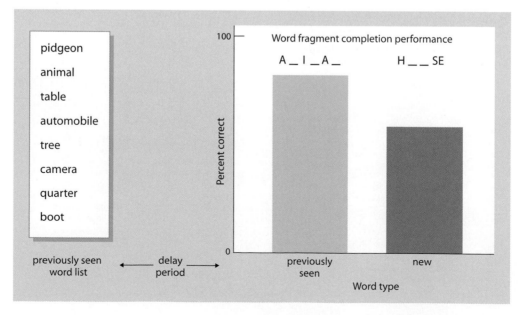

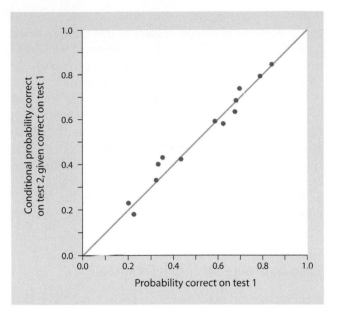

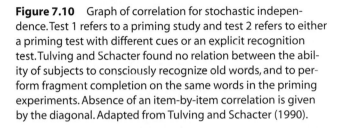

Figure 7.10 Graph of correlation for stochastic independence. Test 1 refers to a priming study and test 2 refers to either a priming test with different cues or an explicit recognition test. Tulving and Schacter found no relation between the ability of subjects to consciously recognize old words, and to perform fragment completion on the same words in the priming experiments. Absence of an item-by-item correlation is given by the diagonal. Adapted from Tulving and Schacter (1990).

rate as shown by stochastic independence. However, are they independent in all ways? Information is remembered better on recall or recognition tests if it is processed more deeply during encoding; however, this was found not to be true for tests of implicit memory performance such as fragment-completion priming. Subjects are not more likely to complete a fragment of a word if it was previously viewed under conditions requiring deep versus shallow encoding. Thus, explicit memory is independent from implicit memory regardless of how this is assessed.

When subjects complete fragments of words and perform better with words previously viewed even without explicitly recognizing them, does this reflect anything more than perceptual-level priming for the writ-

ten word? That is, is there implicit learning of the word's meaning or not? The answers to these questions can be determined in many ways. One method is to present the initial words auditorily and then perform the implicit tests visually. When this is done, priming from auditory to visual is reduced for the implicit tests, which suggests that perceptual information drives the priming phenomenon. Implicit memory in priming reflects a PRS that subserves structural, visual, and auditory word form representations.

Additional evidence that priming involves a PRS comes from studies of nonverbal stimuli like pictures, shapes, and faces. Subjects viewed drawings of objects that were either possible forms or impossible forms (Figure 7.11). Impossible forms are those that cannot

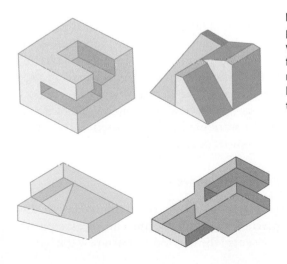

Figure 7.11 Possible and impossible objects used in experiments on object priming. During tests, the subjects were asked to make decisions about whether the stimuli were possible (top figures) or impossible objects (bottom figures). Schacter, Cooper, and Delaney (1990) found that subjects were better making the decision for possible objects that were previously viewed if they had been instructed to pay attention to the global form of the stimulus at the time of encoding.

Figure 7.12 Drawing by artist M.C. Escher that shows water circulating endlessly through waterwheels and troughs by apparently flowing downhill.

exist in three-dimensional space, as in drawings by M.C. Escher (Figure 7.12).

In later tests, subjects had to decide whether stimuli were possible or impossible objects. They showed priming for object forms; that is, they were better at deciding on objects previously viewed. But this occurred only for possible objects, and only when subjects were instructed to pay attention to the global form of the stimulus at the time of encoding. This effect did not improve when subjects elaborated during encoding by trying to match the object with a real world object from memory.

In summary, the PRS apparently mediates word and nonword forms of priming and so implicit memory of this type is not based on conceptual systems. Additional evidence suggests that the PRS develops early in life and is preferentially maintained during aging. Further, it is insensitive to drug manipulations that affect explicit memory. As we will see, implicit memory can also be dissociated from explicit memory in patients with amnesia.

Summary of Cognitive Theories of Memory

Memory theories make two main distinctions about how we learn and retain knowledge. The first is that memory can be defined by retention time. Thus, sensory memory, short-term/working memory, and long-term memory have been identified. The second main concept is the idea that long-term memory consists of several subtypes. The main distinction is the explicit (declarative) versus implicit (nondeclarative) dichotomy. Knowledge is sometimes in the form of explicit memories about events from our lives or even world knowledge that we have conscious access to and can make declarations about. Other forms of knowledge, such as implicit or nondeclarative knowledge (how to ride a bike: procedural knowledge), perceptual priming, and conditioned responses, are out of the reach of our conscious awareness. In the next section we look at properties of memory that stem from brain damage leading to amnesia.

MEMORY AND BRAIN

The cognitive and experimental psychology of memory is rich with theory and data, and has produced a consistent set of concepts about the organization of human memory. What emerges is a group of memory systems that process and store different types of knowledge. What are the biological underpinnings of these systems? Do multiple memory systems indicate partially or wholly segregated anatomical structures? What has investigation into the biological bases of memory done to clarify the functional view of memory that emerged from cognitive experiments? The answer is that much of our conceptualizations of memory systems is derived from knowledge of dissociations in memory processes observed in patients with brain in-

jury that led to memory impairment. Also, studies of animals with lesions and direct measurements of brain processes during memory performance by using electrophysiological and neuroimaging approaches in humans have helped investigate memory systems. Let us now review how biological studies of memory have contributed to our theoretical conceptualizations of knowledge storage.

Human Memory and Amnesia

Deficits in memory as a function of brain damage, disease, or psychological trauma are known as *amnesia*. Amnesia may entail the inability to learn new things or a

Eye Witness Testimony

Every prosecutor in a criminal case knows that an eye witness account is among the most compelling evidence for establishing guilt. But is this type of testimony to be trusted? Elizabeth Loftus and her colleagues (1978, 1980) illustrated the difficulty of relying on witness's recall by showing subjects color slides detailing the time of an accident and asking people what they saw in a later test session. One of the slides showed a car at an intersection before it turned and hit a pedestrian. Half the subjects viewed a red stop sign and half a red yield sign. Subjects then answered questions about the slides: Half were presented with questions referring to the correct sign and half with the incorrect sign. For example, if a subject had been shown a yield sign, she might have been asked, "When the car came to the stop sign, did the driver stop?" During subsequent recognition tests for whether a certain slide was what they had previously seen, 75% of the subjects correctly recognized a previously seen slide if the correct sign had also been mentioned in the questioning session. But when subjects had previously been questioned with the wrong sign being mentioned, only 41% had correct recognition for the slides. This indicates that recollections of an event can be influenced by misleading statements made to them during questioning.

Misinformation about things as obvious as hair color and the presence of a mustache can lead subjects to wrongly identify people they had seen previously. What does this say about witness's suggestibility and the influence of misinformation on recall? Do witnesses really know the correct information but later fail to distinguish between their own memories and information supplied by another person? One line of thinking is that perhaps the information was not encoded initially, and when forced to guess, the subject provides the information given by someone else.

Not just adults are eye witnesses in court cases. Children are often asked to testify as witnesses. Since adults with fully developed memories have difficulty recalling what they have seen, how do young children with potentially underdeveloped memory systems behave under the pressures of authorities and courtrooms? This is a controversial issue because of situations where children are eyewitnesses to crimes against themselves, such as child abuse or sexual abuse in which they may be the only witness.

The question of how well children remember and report things they have experienced is of special concern when the events may be traumatic. One way to effectively study such conditions is to use events traumatic for children, and involving contact between them and others that can be verified. Physicians sometimes must perform genital examinations on children, which may include painful medical procedures. The children's memories of these events can be systematically examined. In one study, half of seventy-two girls between the ages of 5 and 7 years were given a genital examination as part of necessary medical care and half were not. Children who received the examination were unlikely to report anything about the event during free recall or when using anatomically detailed dolls. Only when asked leading questions did they reveal that they had been examined. No false reports were made by the control group during free recall or with the dolls, but with leading questions, three children made false reports. Psychologist Gail Goodman and her colleagues (1994) at the University of California at Davis emphasize that one of the most important predictors of accurate memory performance is age. Memory performance for traumatic events is significantly worse in children 3 to 5 years old than in older children. Dr. Goodman also notes, however, that other factors influence memory accuracy in children. These include how well the traumatic episode is actually understood, the degree of parental emotional support and communication, and the children's emotional (positive versus negative) feelings. The goal of this research is to determine the validity of children's reports on events—including negative ones such as abuse—that may have happened to them, and how they might invent stories. Of special interest is whether children can be induced by leading questions to fabricate testimony. We need to know this when interpreting their testimony that involves other persons such as therapists or members of the legal system.

loss of previous knowledge. In each case, losses may differ for short-term and long-term memory including semantic knowledge, episodic knowledge, priming, and procedural knowledge. Thus, by examining amnesia in conjunction with cognitive theories derived from experiments on normal subjects, we can understand the organization of memory at a functional and a neurobiological level. Much compelling information about the organization of human memory during amnesia was first derived from medical treatments that left patients amnesic.

In the late 1940s and early 1950s, surgeons carried out many attempts to treat neurological and psychiatric disease. These included the prefrontal lobotomy (removing or disconnecting the prefrontal lobe), corpus callosotomy (surgically sectioning the corpus callosum), amygdalotomies (removing the amygdala), temporal lobe resection (removal), and various other surgeries. These surgeries opened a new window on human brain function as they revealed, often quite by accident, fundamentally important principles of the organization of human cognition. One surgical procedure relevant to memory was removal of the medial portion of the temporal lobe, including the hippocampal formation.

In 1953 at a medical conference, the neurosurgeon William Beecher Scoville from the Montreal Neurological Institute reported on bilateral removal of the medial temporal lobe in one epileptic and several schizophrenic patients. Shortly thereafter he wrote:

> Bilateral resection of the uncus, and amygdalum alone, or in conjunction with the entire pyriform amygdaloid hippocampal complex, has resulted in no marked physiologic or behavioral changes with the one exception of a very grave, recent memory loss, so severe as to prevent the patient from remembering the locations of the rooms in which he lives, the names of his close associates, or even the way to the toilet... (Scoville, 1954)

At the time, prefrontal lobotomy or orbitofrontal undercutting—a less radical method of treating severe mental disorders—might have been useful in treating severely psychotic patients without causing more disruption. Because of the links between the orbitofrontal cortex and the medial temporal lobe, physicians thought that further resections of the medial temporal lobe might ameliorate certain mental illnesses. However, the one epileptic patient treated by Scoville underwent similar surgery (without the orbitofrontal undercutting), removal of the abnormal brain tissue to control epilepsy.

When Scoville introduced his patients to a young psychologist, Brenda Milner, the neuropsychological examination of these patients began in earnest. The findings in ten patients were reported in 1957; two of them were reported in Scoville's earlier publication. Patients manifested memory impairment in relation to how much of the medial temporal lobe was removed. The farther posterior the resection was, the worse the amnesia was. Moreover, only bilateral resection of the hippocampus resulted in severe amnesia. In one patient whose entire right hippocampus and hippocampal gyrus were removed, no residual memory deficit was found.

THE STORY OF PATIENT H.M.

Patients who underwent bilateral medial temporal lobe resection developed dense amnesia. The worst case was the famous H.M., whose medial temporal lobes were removed bilaterally. The case of H.M. holds a prominent position in the history of memory research because although he has epilepsy, he is of normal intelligence, has no psychological or mental illness, but developed a severe and permanent inability to acquire new information after the surgery (Scoville and Milner, 1957; Milner et al., 1968).

H.M., an epileptic in his late twenties at the time of the surgery, had seizures that progressed in severity from the age of 10. He had major and minor seizures, but finished high school and worked in a factory winding electrical motors. He was treated with anticonvulsant medications, but they were largely ineffective. Over time his seizures worsened until he could no longer work. To control his seizures, which often originated in the medial temporal lobe (thereupon spreading to other cortical regions), his physicians decided to perform bilateral medial temporal lobectomy. Despite scant evidence in H.M. for localized epileptogenic activity from scalp-recorded electroencephalograms (EEGs) or from cortical surface recordings made during surgery, bilateral medial temporal lobectomy was performed. The epilepsy was remediated enough to reduce his anticonvulsant medication, and the frequency and severity of seizures diminished. However, he permanently lost his ability to form new long-term memories.

Twenty months after the surgery, psychologists evaluated H.M. Upon questioning, his memory deficit was obvious. He reported the date as March 1955, and his age to be 27; the date was April 1955, he was 29; his surgery was performed in September 1953. When specialists interviewed H.M. and then left the room for a few minutes, H.M. could not recall having met them before, or that anyone had spoken to him. His recollections were often only of distant memories, including childhood events.

Neuropsychological testing revealed that H.M.'s intelligence was above normal after the surgery (IQ of 112 on

Temporary Losses of Memory

A common theme in novels and movies is temporary loss of memory after a bump on the head or psychological trauma. Such things do happen outside of Hollywood and may have many causes including head injury or epilepsy. However, sometimes temporary memory loss occurs for other reasons, and one such syndrome is known as *transient global amnesia,* or TGA. Most clinicians consider TGA to be distinct from temporary memory loss caused by head injury, epileptic activity, or stroke. Vascular effects are suspected as the main cause of TGA, but this is limited to transient ischemia (reduced blood flow to a brain area) that does not lead to cerebral infarct (permanent damage to brain tissue). The tissue recovers, and so does the patient's memory. The prime candidates for the brain areas affected are the medial temporal lobe and diencephalic areas. The patients have symptoms similar to that of persons, such as H.M., with permanent damage to the medial temporal lobe.

A simple scenario common for TGA is the following. An otherwise healthy person over 50 years old is brought (or goes) to the hospital after experiencing some problems with memory. During questioning by a physician, the person is not sure why he is there, and may not be sure how he got there or where he is. He does know his name, birth date, job, and perhaps address, but has retrograde amnesia pertaining to a period of weeks or months—perhaps even years. Thus, if he had recently moved, he would supply his past address and circumstances. He has normal short-term memory, and thus can repeat lists of words told to him. But his ability to form new episodic memories is impaired, and when told to remember a list of words, he forgets it within a couple of minutes if he is prevented from rehearsing it. He will continually ask who the physician is, and why he is there. He does show an awareness that he should know the answer to some questions, but he just doesn't, which worries him. He performs normally on most neuropsychological tests,

except for the ones indexing memory. He manifests a loss of time sense, and so responds incorrectly to questions asking how long he has been in the hospital. He may also have reduced verbal fluency, and shows impairment in generating words that begin with a certain letter, like *a,* when asked to do so. He does not, though, have deficits in producing category names, for example, general names for fruits. This latter pattern is typical of frontal lobe problems.

Over the hours after the amnesia-inducing event occurred, distant memories return, and his anterograde memory deficit resolves. Within 24 to 48 hours he is essentially back to normal, although mild deficits may persist for days or even weeks.

Persons having one such attack are more likely to have TGA again, but it does not usually occur often. Some people may never have another episode. The recurrence rate is about 18% within a 20-year period. Men are more likely to experience TGA.

The physiological cause is thought to be an ischemia due to disruption of normal blood flow in the vertebral-basilar artery system, which supplies blood to the medial temporal lobe and diencephalon. TGA is most often triggered by physical exertion. Unlike patient R.B. described in the text, who had such a severe ischemic attack that it caused neurons in his hippocampus to die, TGA patients only suffer from a transient deficit in the medial temporal lobe or thalamic functioning. PET and single-photon emission computed tomography studies in a few patients have demonstrated this transient deficit: Blood flow in the medial temporal lobe decreases during a TGA attack, but later returns to normal. So far, we do not know whether these patients have normal implicit learning or memory, in part because their impairment does not last long enough for researchers to adequately index things like procedural learning. This would be informative in understanding human memory and learning more about an amnesia that could happen to any of us later in life.

the Wechsler-Bellevue Intelligence Scale)—presurgically it was 104. The slight postsurgical improvement probably reflected the reduction in his anticonvulsant medication. His perceptual skills and reasoning ability were normal; H.M. was cooperative and motivated. In line with his memory problems, though, his scores on standardized

memory tests (Wechsler Memory Scale) were below normal. He completely lost his memory for events subsequent to the surgery, and partially lost it for events in the years immediately prior to the surgery. The bilateral removal of H.M.'s medial temporal lobe left him profoundly amnesic.

Taken together, the evidence from patient H.M. implicates the medial temporal lobe in memory, but only certain aspects of memory. H.M.'s deficit, called *anterograde amnesia* (forward-going) because the ability to form new memories was disrupted, does not mean that he remembered nothing. He was able to recall his personal past and world knowledge that he acquired about 3 years before the surgery but could not acquire new memories. Damage to the hippocampus affects the ability to acquire new long-term memories, not information already in long-term memory stores—at least not all of it.

H.M. did, though, have *retrograde amnesia* extending backward from his surgery for about 3 years. Long-term memories from his recent past were lost, but the loss was limited in time.

H.M. had normal short-term memory (sensory registers and primary-immediate memory). Like many other amnesics (Figure 7.13), H.M. had normal digit span abilities. He did well at holding strings of digits in short-term memory, but, unlike normal subjects, he performed poorly on digit span tests that required the acquisition of new long-term memories—his digit span ability hardly improved with practice. What was disrupted was the transfer of information from short-term to long-term stores.

AMNESIA AND THE MEDIAL TEMPORAL LOBE

For the past 40 years, investigators of H.M. used reports of his lesions to guide theories of amnesia, memory, and the brain. Original reports by Scoville, who performed the surgery, indicated that all of H.M.'s hippocampus in each hemisphere had been removed. Scoville indicated that this amounted to removal of about 8 cm of tissue, measuring from the anterior tip of the hippocampus toward the posterior portions of the medial temporal lobe (Figure 7.14a). New evidence, however, suggests that less was removed than was previously thought.

With high-resolution neuroimaging methods such as magnetic resonance imaging (MRI), H.M.'s brain and the surgical lesions were re-evaluated with improved accuracy. For many years H.M. could not be scanned by MRI because of the metal clips placed in his brain to prevent major vessels from bleeding during surgery—a normal procedure. MRI cannot be performed in persons with some types of metal in their brains because the intense magnetic field of the scanner can cause any indwelling objects to move, which could lead to injury. This restriction applies only to ferromagnetic items affected by magnetic fields; many metals are not. With H.M. the problem was not knowing whether his clips were ferromagnetic. His surgery was performed long before MRI had been developed for imaging the human brain, and clips developed for surgery during that time might or might not have been ferromagnetic. Thus, it was possible that MRI scanning would endanger H.M.

In an unusual detective story, Sue Corkin of MIT and journalist and author Philip Hilts (1995), tracked the history of H.M.'s surgery. They determined that the clips in H.M. were not ferromagnetic, and that it would be safe to scan him using MRI. Hence, more than 30 years after his surgery, H.M.'s surgical lesion was investigated using neuroimaging techniques (Figure 7.14b).

Data gathered by Corkin and her colleagues were analyzed by neuroanatomist David Amaral of the University of California at Davis (1997). This analysis, shown in Figure 7.14c, revealed remarkable scientific and historical revisionism. In contrast to Scoville's reports, approximately half of the posterior region of H.M.'s hippocampus was intact. And 5 cm, not 8 cm, of the medial temporal lobe was removed. The remaining portion of H.M.'s hippocampi was, however, atrophied, probably because of the loss of inputs from the surrounding perihippocampal cortex that had been removed. Thus, despite the original error in our knowledge about H.M.'s lesion, it may be that no functional hippocampal tissue actually remained. Bear in mind that in addition to the hippocampus, some of H.M.'s surrounding cortex was removed.

Is damage to the hippocampus sufficient to block new long-term memories? Consider another patient, R.B., who lost his memory after an ischemic episode during bypass surgery. R.B. developed dense anterograde amnesia similar to H.M.'s: He could not form new long-term memories. He also had retrograde amnesia that extended back about 1 to 2 years, slightly less severe than H.M.'s retrograde loss. R.B. was a remarkable person with a highly circumscribed lesion to his hippocampus. He died a few years after surgery, but because he was being tested until his death, much was known about his memory capacities. And upon his death, his brain was donated to verify how much brain damage might have been related to his memory impairments.

On gross examination of the medial temporal lobe of R.B., the hippocampus appeared to be intact (Figure 7.15). But he had a specific lesion restricted to the CA1 pyramidal cells of the hippocampus bilaterally. This supports the idea that the hippocampus is crucial in forming new memories. More recent evidence by Rempel-Clower and colleagues (1996) supports the finding in R.B., and shows that damage that includes areas outside the CA1 field but still restricted to the hippocampus produces even more severe anterograde amnesia. R.B.'s case also supports the distinction between

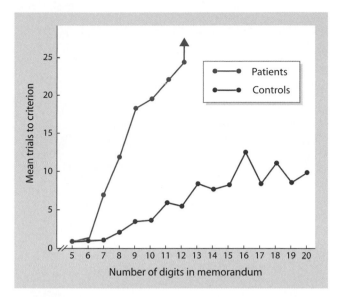

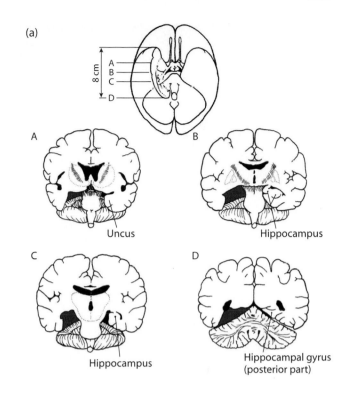

Figure 7.13 Digit span for amnesic and control subjects. A sequence of five digits was read to the subjects, who were then asked to repeat the digits back to the experimenter. If the digits were repeated correctly, one more digit was added to the next sequence presented. If the digits in a sequence were reported incorrectly, that sequence was repeated until the subject reported it correctly. Amnesic patients had normal digit spans, but required more trials to learn strings of digits. Adapted from Drachman and Arbit (1966).

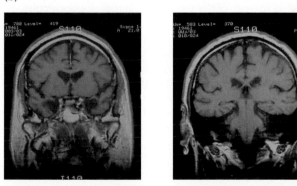

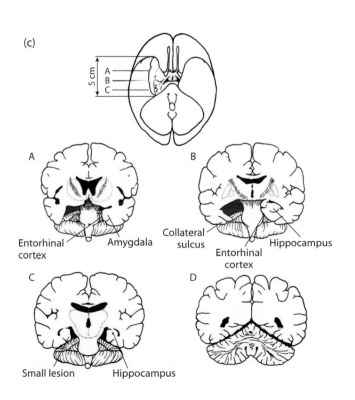

Figure 7.14 **(a)** Anatomy of the medial temporal lobe and areas believed removed from H.M. (resection is shown on one side only for diagrammatic reasons). **(b)** MRIs of H.M.'s brain. On the left, the scan shows a more anterior slice in which the medial temporal lobe is removed bilaterally. On the right, however, a more posterior slice is shown. Here, the intact hippocampus can be seen in both hemispheres. **(c)** Modern reconstruction by Amaral and colleagues showing that portions of H.M.'s posterior hippocampus were not removed during surgery. This tissue does, however, show signs of atrophy, and may no longer be functioning normally. Adapted from Corkin et al. (1997).

(a)

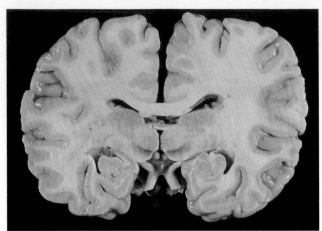

(b)

(c)

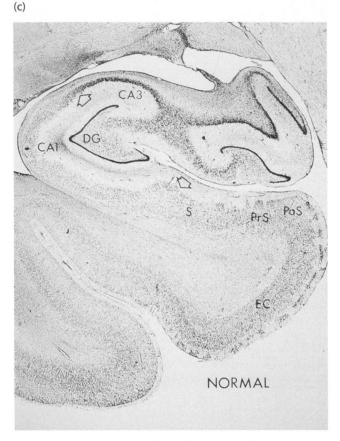

Figure 7.15 **(a)** Section of brain from patient R.B. following his death. In contrast to MRI sections from H.M. in Figure 7.14b, showing absence of the anterior and middle hippocampus, R.B.'s medial temporal lobe appeared intact on gross examination. **(b)** However, upon careful histological examination, it was clear that cells in the CA1 region of the hippocampus were absent (see arrow top left corner). This occurred as the result of an ischemic episode following surgery. Cells of the CA1 region are particularly sensitive to transient ischemia (temporary loss of blood supply to a brain region). **(c)** Histological section from brain of a normal subject showing an intact CA1 region. Courtesy of David Amaral.

areas that store long-term memories and the hippocampus's role in forming new memories. Even though retrograde amnesia is associated with medial temporal lobe damage, it is temporally limited and does not affect long-term memories of events that happened more than a few years prior to the amnesia-inducing event.

MEMORY CONSOLIDATION AND THE HIPPOCAMPUS

Because damage to the medial temporal lobe does not wipe out most of the episodic and semantic memories formed over a lifetime, we know that the hippocampus is not the repository of stored explicit knowledge. The medial temporal lobe is central in forming new memories; that is, the hippocampal region is critical for transfer of short-term memories into long-term ones, but it must take place over the long haul, not just minutes, such as when rehearsing words helps to convert short-term or working memory items into long-term stores, but over a longer time. The strongest evidence is the fact that amnesics have retrograde amnesia for memories from one to a few years prior to the damage to the medial temporal lobe or diencephalon. A significant time course is evident in this pattern.

Long-term memories are solidified in long-term

stores over days, weeks, months, and years, and this is referred to as *consolidation,* an old concept that refers to how long-term memory develops after learning. This concept was developed to explain the behavioral consequences of interference effects from newly learned items on previously learned items as a function of their temporal proximity. From a cognitive neuroscience perspective, consolidation is conceived of as biological changes that underlie the retention of learned information.

What might consolidation entail at the neural level? One idea is that consolidation strengthens the associations between multiple stimulus inputs and activations of previously stored information. The hippocampus coordinates this strengthening, but the effects take place in the neocortex, and do not then require the hippocampus (or perhaps any medial temporal lobe or diencephalic memory system) for storage or retrieval, which implies that memories are stored in the neocortex.

Interesting evidence for temporal consolidation comes from patients who have undergone electroconvulsive therapy to treat psychological disturbances. Electroconvulsive therapy involves passing an electrical current through the brain by electrodes placed on the scalp, a useful treatment for conditions such as severe depression. In patients so treated, a retrograde amnesia is more likely to affect items that were learned near the time of the treatment (Figure 7.16). A similar pattern happens with severe head trauma. Retrograde amnesia is more likely for recent events, and even as the amnesia remits over time, the recent events are affected longest, and sometimes permanently.

TEMPORAL LOBES AND MEMORY STORES

Amnesia can also be caused by damage to other regions of the neocortex, especially the temporal neocortex outside the medial temporal lobe. Lesions that damage the lateral cortex of the anterior temporal lobe, near the anterior pole, lead to a dense amnesia that includes severe retrograde amnesia: The entorhinal cortex and perihippocampal cortex are involved. The retrograde amnesia

may be severe, extending back many decades before the amnesia occurred, or may encompass the patient's entire life. Various forms of damage can lead to this condition: progressive neurological diseases like Alzheimer's, or herpes simplex encephalitis involving viral infection of the brain.

Some patients with dense retrograde amnesia might still form new long-term memories. This type of amnesia is called *isolated retrograde amnesia.* It is particularly related to damage of the anterior temporal lobe. This portion of the temporal lobe is important for memory storage but not for acquiring new information, and it is not the only region where new information can be stored in long-term memory. If this were the sole repository of all episodic and semantic memories, we would not find patients like these who lost all previously acquired memories but still acquired new ones.

Korsakoff's Syndrome and Diencephalic Amnesia

The medial temporal lobe is not the only area of interest in human memory. Amnesia emerges from brain damage in other regions too. For example, damage to midline structures of the diencephalon of the brain causes amnesia. The prime structures are the dorsomedial nucleus of the thalamus and the mamillary bodies. Damage to these midline subcortical regions can be caused by stroke, tumors, and metabolic problems like those brought on by chronic alcoholism as well as by trauma.

In the last half of the nineteenth century, the Russian psychiatrist Sergei Korsakoff reported an anterograde and retrograde amnesia associated with alcoholism. Long-term alcohol abuse can lead to vitamin deficiencies that cause brain damage. Patients suffering from alcoholic Korsakoff's syndrome have degenerated diencephalons, especially the dorsomedial nucleus of the thalamus and the mamillary bodies (Figure 7.17).

Controversy has arisen as to whether the dorsomedial thalamic nucleus, the mamillary bodies, or both were necessary for the patients' amnesia. Nonetheless, damage to the diencephalon can produce amnesia. The

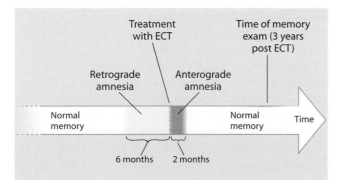

Figure 7.16 Effects of electroconvulsive therapy effect on memory performance. Memory apparently changes for a long time after initial learning, with some material being forgotten and the material that remains becoming more resistant to disruption. Adapted from Squire and Slater (1983).

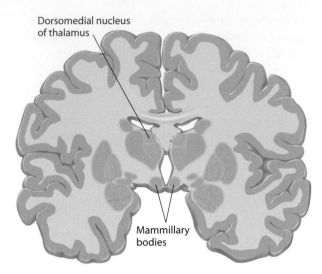

Figure 7.17 A section of the brain through the anterior nucleus of the thalamus, mamillo-thalamic tract, and the rostral portion of the crus cerebri. The diagrammed dorsomedial nucleus of the thalamus (DMNu) and mamillary bodies (MB) are damaged in Korsakoff's syndrome.

symptoms of amnesia resulting from Korsakoff's syndrome resemble those that accompany damage to the medial temporal lobe. Both types of amnesics lose explicit memory and preserve implicit (nondeclarative) memory. Since patients with Korsakoff's syndrome have no damage to the medial temporal lobe, this region cannot be solely responsible for forming explicit memory. Rather, both regions (medial temporal lobe and midline diencephalon) participate in this memory formation.

WHAT CAN THE AMNESIC LEARN?

The insights derived from H.M. and other amnesic patients with medial temporal lobe or diencephalic damage indicate that a core problem with this amnesia is the inability to learn and retain new information. Thus, medial temporal lobe damage is generally associated with the inability to learn new information, as opposed to loss of memories obtained prior to the damage (except for a time-limited retrograde amnesia). The inability to learn new information was often equally true for episodic, semantic, and procedural information. Here we consider whether new learning of semantic information (world knowledge) can take place in amnesia patients even though the forming of new episodic memories is lost.

H.M. had severe anterograde amnesia; nonetheless, he was still able to learn some verbal information. Indeed, amnesics can retain new information, albeit to varying extents. Amnesics' learning of new information includes semantic knowledge, such as details related to other people, target words in sentences, new vocabulary for technical terms, and novel, one-word descriptions of

ambiguous circumstances. This acquisition of new knowledge typically happens in amnesics who do not remember the source of the knowledge; that is, they do not know about the episode in which the information was learned, a condition termed *source amnesia*. Tulving and his colleagues (1991) examined this phenomenon in one very interesting amnesic patient, K.C.

Patient K.C. developed amnesia following a motorcycle accident at the age of 30. He suffered severe head injury, and a subdural hematoma (a pool of blood under the sheath covering his brain) was surgically removed. Following a long convalescence and rehabilitation, K.C. exhibited several residual neurological complications. MRI revealed damage in several brain areas, including the medial temporal lobe and the frontal, parietal, and occipital cortices. The damage was greater in the left hemisphere. Nonetheless, neuropsychological testing revealed normal intelligence (IQ was 94 on the Weschsler Adult Intelligence Scale–Revised), with some deficits on tests of frontal lobe function and verbal fluency. He had normal short-term memory, showing retention of eight or nine digits in memory span tests. But, as expected with amnesics, K.C.'s score on the Wechsler Memory Scale was below normal for delayed recall. Of particular note is that K.C. had severe anterograde and retrograde amnesia. Curiously, his retrograde amnesia involved episodic information from his entire life! He did not remember a single event, although he knew things that pertained to his life.

Despite K.C.'s dense source amnesia, he had an intact semantic memory for general world knowledge acquired prior to his accident. K.C. had not forgotten how to use implements common to daily life or knowledge about the structure of the world around him. K.C. was able to learn new information, but could not remember how he acquired it. For example, in tests of K.C.'s memory skills, he was presented with three-word sentences together with a related picture (Figure 7.18). In each sentence the final words were the critical ones that he was to be tested on later.

During the subsequent test he was presented with word fragments (perceptual cues) or conceptually based cues consisting of the two other words of the sentences or the associated picture. These latter cues are conceptual because they do not provide any perceptual information about the target word to be remembered, that is, any of its letters, or length, and so on. K.C. demonstrated perceptual priming effects with the word fragments that lasted up to twelve months. He also displayed a greater likelihood of generating the target word when he saw the associated words or picture. Although the learned semantic information took longer to acquire, once it was learned, forgetting it occurred at the same

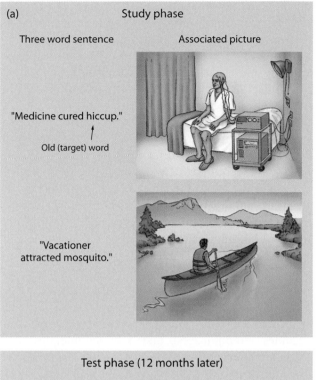

(a) Study phase

Three word sentence | Associated picture

"Medicine cured hiccup."

↑
Old (target) word

"Vacationer attracted mosquito."

Test phase (12 months later)

Perceptual cue: e.g.,   _ i c _ _ p

Conceptual cues: e.g.,   "Medicine cured _____"

Figure 7.18 **(a)** To test K.C.'s memory skills, Tulving and colleagues presented him with three-word sentences together with a related picture. In each sentence, the final word was the critical word tested for later. During subsequent test sessions, K.C. was presented with word fragments (perceptual cues), or conceptually based cues consisting of the other two words of the sentences or the associated picture. K.C. showed priming effects with the word fragments, and these effects remained twelve months later. K.C.'s lesions are shown in **(b)**. Adapted from Tulving et al. (1991).

rate in K.C. as it would for normal subjects—and, again, K.C. had no inkling of how this information was acquired. Thus, amnesics can learn semantic information, even though it might be more difficult to acquire, but such learning is not possible for episodic memories.

Psychologists Neal Kroll and Andrew Yonelinas and their colleagues at the University of California at Davis believe this ability for some amnesics to learn new information can be conceptualized as a preservation of their ability to recognize prior events based on a kind of strength signal. In their studies of amnesics who had damage in the left medial temporal lobe following stroke, they quantified, using theories borrowed from perceptual science, the patients' ability to recognize words they had heard previously. A strength score was assigned and indicated how well the amnesics could distinguish a true signal (the words presented to them an hour before) from noise (distractor words not presented previously). The amnesics reliably indicated that they had heard a word before, even though they had no episodic memory for its prior presentation (Figure 7.19). Similar approaches are difficult to apply

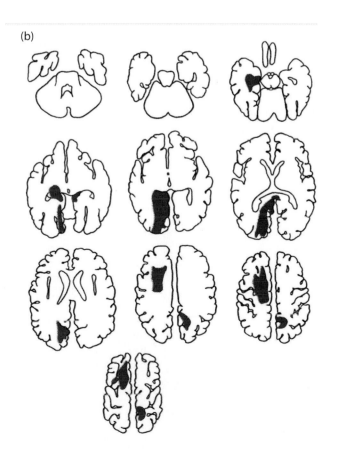

(b)

Figure 7.19 Investigators read lists of words to amnesic patients. Then 1 hour later, the words were read again together with new words that were not in the previous reading. The patients were asked to indicate their confidence that the words had been presented previously. Their answers were used to compute quantitative metrics of their memory ability using signal-detection theory, a method borrowed from perceptual sciences and adapted to studies of memory.

in persons with normal memory because the memory for items is aided by their intact explicit episodic knowledge of the prior events.

Procedural Learning in Amnesia Studies of amnesia have revealed that fundamental distinctions between long- and short-term memory have biological correlates, and that episodic and semantic memory can also be distinguished by their relative sensitivity to brain damage. However, learning with amnesia is not limited to semantic knowledge. Amnesics learn other implicit (nondeclarative) knowledge such as that for procedures (see Figure 7.8).

One test of procedural learning is the serial reaction time task. Subjects press buttons that correspond to locations of stimuli. For example, if four buttons are located under each of the fingers on one hand and are connected to four lights, the task would be to press the button with the finger that maps the location illuminated (Figure 7.20). The lights are presented in a pseudorandom order; they seem to be random to the participant but have a complex repetitive sequence. Over time, in normal subjects the speed of response to the repeating sequence, as compared with a totally random sequence, increases. Thus, learning the sequence can be characterized by improved performance. When subjects are questioned about such sequences, they have no knowledge that any pattern existed (if the sequence is constructed properly). Yet they learn the skill, which is procedural learning requiring no explicit knowledge about what was learned.

Some have challenged the idea that normal subjects learn in the absence of any explicit knowledge of what was learned. Sometimes one can ask them about the sequences and show that they can in fact explicitly describe the learned material. Given this result in normal subjects, if we do not find evidence for explicit knowledge during skill acquisition, how can we be sure it is not there? Perhaps the subject merely failed to demonstrate it.

Studies of procedural learning in amnesics like H.M. with anterograde amnesia have helped to resolve this controversy. The logic is that if amnesics cannot form new episodic memories for newly learned material but can learn in these procedural tasks, then explicit knowledge is not required for acquiring procedural knowledge. What was found was that amnesics with dense anterograde amnesia (with loss of episodic learning) can improve their performance by repeating the task. Therefore, procedural learning can proceed independently of the brain systems required for explicit memory. This type of dissociation of explicit and implicit learning and memory for procedural learning also happens in patients with diencephalic amnesia such as Korsakoff's syndrome. Normal subjects taking drugs like benzodiazepines (tranquilizers) and scopolamine, an anticholinergic agent that acts on the muscarinic acetylcholine receptor, can also show this dissociation. These drugs cause deficits in explicit memory but do not affect implicit learning.

Implicit Learning of Concepts Implicit memory encompasses more than procedural learning and processes like priming. The learning of more abstract knowledge, such as artificial grammar, also exemplifies an implicit (nondeclarative) form of learning and memory.

Artificial grammar represents rules that govern how groups of letter strings can be formed. In artificial grammar tasks, subjects see groups of letter strings that

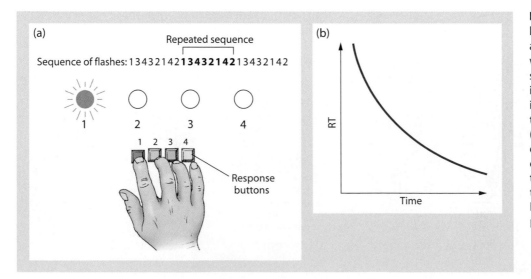

Figure 7.20 (a) Sequence learning paradigm. Subjects are asked to push buttons with their fingers corresponding to flashes of lights in a complex sequence that is repeated. **(b)** Over time, the subject's reaction time (RT) to the repeating sequence becomes faster as compared to a sequence that is totally random, although they apparently have no knowledge that any pattern exists.

(a)

Repeated sequence

Sequence of flashes: 1 3 4 3 2 1 4 2 **1 3 4 3 2 1 4 2** 1 3 4 3 2 1 4 2

1   2   3   4

1 2 3 4

Response buttons

(b)

RT

Time

follow the grammatical rules of an artificial system devised by the investigators, and about which the subjects have no knowledge. After studying the strings, the subject is presented new letter strings and asked to judge whether they follow the same rules as the original strings. Amazingly, healthy subjects demonstrate above-chance performance even when they report that they cannot describe the rule system. The argument is that they have implicitly learned the artificial grammar.

As with implicit sequence learning, a lingering concern about acquiring artificial grammar is that the normal subjects may have deduced the rule and have explicit knowledge about it but are not confident in reporting it. This can be ruled out in amnesic patients because they also learn the rules of the artificial grammar. Again, because amnesics with damaged medial temporal lobe–diencephalic structures have no ability to learn explicit information, but still acquire implicit knowledge, there is a clear split between explicit memory and the implicit learning of artificial grammar. Implicit learning, then, encompasses more than motor skills that can be acquired by amnesic patients who have lost their episodic memory.

DEFICITS IN IMPLICIT LEARNING AND MEMORY

Amnesic patients provide evidence for a dissociation between explicit and implicit memory. One strong interpretation of this finding is that preserving implicit but not explicit memory in amnesia proves separate explicit and implicit memory systems.

One alternative interpretation might have to do with the differential demands that explicit versus implicit memory place on the psychological-neural memory system. If such were true, a single memory system might subserve explicit and implicit memory, but deficits are more obvious for the more demanding type of memory. Here the argument would be that explicit memory is more demanding, and thus is first affected by partial damage to a hypothesized unitary memory system. An analogy might be useful in conveying the point. Take locomotion, and consider the effects of a knee injury on walking versus running. One would not conclude that walking and running were subserved by different anatomical systems merely because damage to the knee caused severe impairments in running, but left walking intact. Rather, walking and running rely on the same anatomical systems, but running is more demanding on the now weakened locomotor system.

As introduced in Chapter 3, double dissociations are the strongest evidence for demonstrating that two systems are separate. Patients like H.M. demonstrate only a single dissociation—preserved implicit but damaged explicit memory. To provide a double dissociation, it would be necessary to demonstrate that it is possible to have a loss in implicit memory while preserving explicit memory.

John Gabrieli and his colleagues (1995) at Stanford University tested a patient, M.S., who had a right occipital lobe lesion, and they compared him to amnesics. M.S. was an epileptic who had undergone surgery at the age of 14 to treat intractable seizures. The surgery removed most of areas 18 and 19 of his right occipital lobe, leaving him blind in the left visual field (Figure 7.21). M.S. has above-average intelligence and memory. Tests of explicit memory (recognition and cued recall) and implicit memory (perceptual priming) were administered to other amnesics and to M.S. The test materials were words presented briefly and then read aloud. During the implicit memory test, the words were presented and then masked with rows of X's. The duration of presentation increased from 16 msec to a time when the subject could read the word. Any reductions in duration required to read the word when the word was previously seen would be evidence for implicit perceptual priming.

Figure 7.21 A reconstruction of the brain lesion of patient M.S. studied by Gabrieli and colleagues. Most of areas 18 and 19 (extrastriate cortex) of the right hemisphere were removed surgically to treat epilepsy. Patient M.S. showed intact explicit memory, but had a deficit in perceptual priming, and implicit memory process. Adapted from Gabrieli et al. (1995).

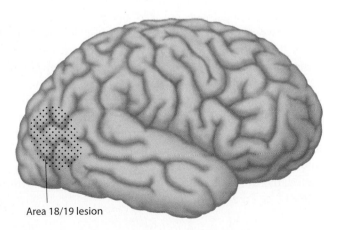

Area 18/19 lesion

In a separate explicit recognition test, subjects saw old and new words and had to judge whether they had seen them before.

The amnesic patients displayed the expected impairments of explicit word recognition, but they did not show impairment in implicit perceptual priming. In contrast, M.S. had the novel pattern of normal performance on explicit recognition, but impairment in the implicit perceptual priming test! This deficit was not due to his partial blindness because his explicit memory for word recognition and recall indicated that he perceived them normally by using the intact portions of his visual field.

M.S. showed a pattern opposite to that typical of amnesics like H.M. These data show that perceptual priming can be damaged in the absence of impairments in explicit memory, thereby completing a double dissociation for explicit and implicit memory systems. The anatomical data indicate that perceptual priming depends on the perceptual system because M.S. had lesions to the visual cortex leading to deficits in perceptual priming. It is likely that this right occipital memory system is not specific to words but is more generally involved in priming of visual forms. This is supported by evidence that other patients with similar lesions show impairment in priming for nonword stimuli like fragmented pictures. The key point is that explicit and implicit memory systems can be doubly dissociated by brain lesions; hence, separate areas mediate learning explicit and implicit knowledge.

SHORT-TERM MEMORY AND AMNESIA

Brain damage can also cause losses in the ability to hold information in short-term memory. One reason why the working memory concept was deemed important during its formulation was precisely because amnesics appeared to have selective losses of short-term memory. In 1969, neuropsychologists Tim Shallice and Elizabeth Warrington of Great Britain reported a patient whose left perisylvian damage reduced his digit span ability (about two items), and created a deficit in his ability to recall lists of items. Most interestingly, this patient retained the ability to form new long-term memories. This pattern argued against the idea that memory was a unitary process, just as did evidence from patients like H.M. who had preserved short-term memory. Further, the loss of short-term memory meant that the short-term system was not necessary for entering information into long-term memory in the simplified manner suggested by the stage model of Atkinson and Shiffrin (1968) (see Figure 7.6).

Deficits in short-term memory are believed to result from damage to subcomponents of the working memory system. Remember that the working memory model of Baddeley and colleagues consisted of three parts: a central executive (attentional) system and two slave systems, the phonological loop and the visuospatial sketchpad (see Figure 7.7). Each system can be selectively damaged by brain lesions. Lesions of the left supramarginal gyrus (Brodmann's area 40) lead to deficits in phonological short-term memory. Patients with lesions to this area have reduced auditory-verbal memory spans; they cannot hold strings of words in short-term memory. The rehearsal process of the phonological loop includes a region in the left premotor region (area 44). Thus, a left-hemisphere network consisting of the lateral frontal and inferior parietal lobes subserves phonological short-term memory. These deficits in short-term memory for auditory-verbal material (digits, letters, words) were not associated with deficits in speech perception or production. The distinction between aphasia and deficits in auditory-verbal short-term memory is quite important.

The visuospatial sketchpad is associated with damage in the parieto-occipital region of both hemispheres, but damage to the right hemisphere produces more severe deficits in visuospatial short-term memory. Patients with lesions in the right parieto-occipital region have difficulty with nonverbal visuospatial working memory tasks like retaining and repeating the sequence of blocks touched by the investigator. For example, if an investigator touched blocks on a table in sequences that had to be repeated by the patient, and gradually increased the number of blocks touched, patients with parieto-occipital lesions would be deficient in this task. Similar lesions in the left hemisphere can lead to impairments in short-term memory for visually presented linguistic material.

Short-term memory impairments, then, are associated with discrete brain lesions in areas that are distinct from those that correlate with anterograde memory deficits (medial temporal lobe and diencephalic structures) or dense, isolated retrograde amnesia (lateral and anterior temporal lobe, and entorhinal and perihippocampal cortex). But patients with short-term memory deficits can learn new episodic and semantic information, and so studies of amnesics have demonstrated double dissociations of symptoms for short-term and long-term memory.

SUMMARY OF AMNESIA AND MEMORY SYSTEMS

The special cases we have reviewed have implicated specific brain regions in memory loss. The learning and retention of new information about one's autobiographi-

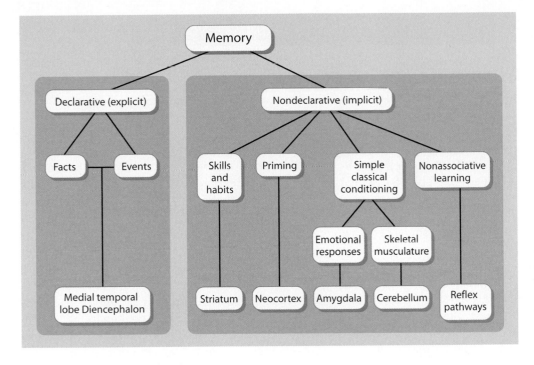

Figure 7.22 A generalized diagram of the relationships of long-term memory systems to the underlying brain systems. This figure is an elaboration on Figure 7.8 including candidate brain areas.

cal history are supported by medial temporal lobe structures and the midline diencephalon; damage to these areas impedes the formation of new explicit memories. Damage to these areas also leads to difficulties in remembering events in the years immediately prior to the injury, but leaves intact most previous episodic and semantic memories acquired during life. These structures are not storage sites of information in long-term memory. In contrast, damage to regions of the temporal lobe outside the hippocampus can cause losses of episodic memories, even while the ability to acquire new ones may be intact. Brain damage leading to impairments in implicit learning and memory has affected some patients, even when explicit memory is intact; this involves regions outside the medial temporal lobe and midline diencephalon, and so explicit and implicit memory processes rely on separate brain systems. Short-term memory deficits can be related to brain regions different from those supporting long-term memory. The area of left supramarginal gyrus and left premotor cortex relates to the phonological loop of the working memory system, while the visuospatial sketchpad is localized in the posterior parieto-occipital regions—lateralized to the right for visuospatial and to the left for visuoverbal short-term memory. Data from patients with amnesia demonstrate that important theoretical distinctions in the cognitive psychology of memory have been supported and elaborated by deficits in memory suffered following brain damage. Figure 7.8 outlined the concep-

tual relations between memory systems. Figure 7.22 is a modification of Figure 7.8, to include brain regions that are hypothesized to subserve the various memory processes.

Animal Models of Memory

Studies in monkeys with lesions to the hippocampus and surrounding cortex have been invaluable in learning about the contributions of the medial temporal lobe to primate memory systems. The goal of such research is to develop animal models of human memory and amnesia. Through research, such models could provide major advances on relations between specific memory and brain structures. Several animal species, ranging from invertebrates to monkeys, have been investigated for clues to human memory and its functional neuroanatomy; it is likely that monkeys will contribute the most directly applicable knowledge about human processes. We must always keep in mind, however, that the gross organization and functional capabilities of the brains of monkeys and humans differ significantly. Thus, animal models of cognitive processes like memory are perhaps most informative when linked with studies in humans.

One of the key questions in memory research was how much the hippocampus alone, as compared with surrounding structures in the medial temporal lobe, participated in the memory deficits of patients like

An Interview with Endel Tulving, Ph.D.   Dr. Tulving is an emeritus professor of Psychology at the University of Toronto. He is considered the world's foremost authority on cognitive theories of memory.

Authors: When beginning to think about the problem of human memory, what are some of the essential principles a student should know?

ET: The same that apply to all similar endeavors: What exactly is it that you want to study, or know about? There are as many ways (infinite ways?) of thinking about human memory as there are ways of sightseeing in, say, Europe. Therefore, the most essential principle is to make sure that you go for the essence of what you want to think about, rather than some peripheral matter that happens to fit under the rubric.

Authors: Well, what we are after is making the distinction between observations about memory as opposed to how memory works, why there are things like episodic memory, which are different from semantic memory, and so on. How does one go past merely describing the simple observations about a phenomenon, to actually elucidating the mechanisms of the phenomenon?

ET: That is a tough question that has no simple answer. At the present time we are far away from the specification of "mechanisms" of memory phenomena. We are still trying hard to figure out what exactly the phenomena are that need explanations.

Getting from observations to mechanisms, or from data to theory, is an arduous process involving many steps. The key point is that memory phenomena can be analyzed at a number of different levels, and this levels problem—how to connect one level of analysis to another—has so far remained largely unsolved. An absolutely necessary condition for delineating the mechanism of a phenomenon is to know what it is and how to decompose it into its constituent elements at the level of analysis at which the description of the mechanism is sought.

People have different ideas about what it means to explain or to understand phenomena of memory, and specifying its mechanisms is only one of them. One can take a simple phenomenon, such as the fact that under certain conditions an animal will come to respond to a conditioned stimulus in a way similar to how it originally responded to an unconditioned stimulus, and one

H.M. In other words, what structures of the medial temporal lobe system act in episodic memory? For example, does the amygdala influence memory deficits in amnesics (Figure 7.23)? Data from amnesics indicate that the amygdala is not part of the brain's episodic memory system.

To verify this, surgical lesions were created in the medial temporal lobe and amygdala of monkeys, to cause memory impairment. In classic work by Mortimer Mishkin (1978) at the National Institute of Mental Health (NIMH), the hippocampus, amygdala, or both hippocampus and amygdala of monkeys were removed surgically. He found that the amount of impairment, as measured on tests, varied according to what was lesioned.

The brain-lesioned monkeys were tested with a popular behavioral task known as the *delayed nonmatching to sample task* developed by Mishkin. A monkey is placed in a box with a retractable door in the front

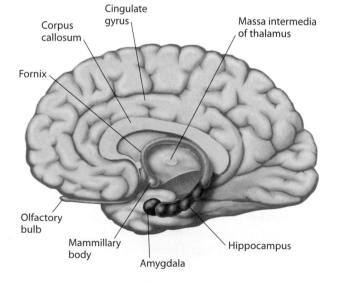

Figure 7.23 Medial temporal lobe structures including the hippocampus and amygdala (shown in red).

can specify the mechanism at the level of, say, neuronal connectivity. One can also take a more complex phenomenon, such as a person re-experiencing something from an earlier time and place, and no amount of tracing of the neuronal circuitry will provide you with a mechanism of such conscious recollection. It is essential that we not freeze our thinking about the nasty problems, hoping to get to them down the road somewhere. Rather, we must address the hard problems, and thus clear the bush for building the next stretch of the road.

Authors: In building the next stretch, what kind of equipment would you invest in? One might think enough has been learned already about how focal brain lesions produce one or another memory deficit. Now we need to understand why. Shouldn't we abandon behavioral measures and move on to physiology?

ET: I would not give up on brain lesions, and I would not focus on memory deficits. We want to understand memory, and studying deficits does help. There is still a lot of gold left in the lesion mines, because so far the progress in understanding what is really going on has been slow. Those of us who are interested in human brains necessarily have to rely on Nature to do interpretable experiments for us, and she is in no hurry. Lesion work with animals gives experimenters better control over what happens, but it cannot tell us everything we want to know about humans. This is why those who have access to the new toys are placing their bets on

functional neuroimaging techniques, all of which are promising and some of which are downright exciting.

The good news for researchers young or old, however, is that the single most critical piece of equipment is still the researcher's own brain. All the equipment in the world will not help us if we do not know how to use it properly, which requires more than merely knowing how to operate it. Aristotle would not necessarily have been more profound had he owned a laptop and known how to program. What is badly needed now, with all those scanners whirring away, is an understanding of exactly what we are observing, and seeing, and measuring, and wondering about. If we record from a single cell that responds to physical stimuli, we can, at least in principle, bifurcate the whole world into those things or their features that the cell is interested in and those that it is not. But there are no memory cells in the brain, and even if there were, most of the time we would not know how to ask the cell to do the bifurcating for us because we are still largely ignorant about how to carve memory at its joints, and therefore do not know how to put the questions to a cell. And when it comes to recording the activity of millions of cells, subgroups of which have different interests in the world, these being variably satisfied by the whole brain's mission under the scanner, the interpretive problem becomes the major obstacle to progress. Thinking about scanning memory is much harder than scanning memory.

(Figure 7.24). When the door is closed, the monkey cannot see out. With the door closed, a food reward is placed under an object. The door is opened and the monkey is allowed to pick up the object to get the food. The door is closed again and the same object plus a new object are put in position. The new object now covers the food reward, and the monkey must pick it up to get the reward. If the monkey picks up the old object, there is no reward. With training, the monkey picks the new, or nonmatching, object—hence learning and memory are measured.

In his early work, Mishkin found that in the monkey, memory was impaired only if the lesion included the hippocampus and amygdala. This led to the idea that the amygdala was a key structure in memory. The idea does not fit well with data from amnesics like R.B., who had anterograde amnesia caused by a lesion restricted to CA1 neurons of the hippocampus, and no damage to the amygdala.

This dilemma was investigated by Stuart Zola and his colleagues (1993) at the University of California at San Diego. They performed more selective lesions of the brains of monkeys by distinguishing between the amygdala and hippocampus, and the surrounding cortex near each structure. They surgically created lesions of the amygdala, the entorhinal cortex, or the surrounding neocortex of the parahippocampal gyrus and the perirhinal cortex (Brodmann's areas 35 and 36) (Figure 7.25). They wanted to extend Mishkin's work, which always involved lesions of the neocortex surrounding the amygdala or hippocampus owing to the way the surgery was performed.

They found that lesions of the hippocampus and amygdala produced the most severe memory deficits only when the cortex surrounding the amygdala was also lesioned. When lesions of the hippocampus and amygdala were made but the surrounding cortex was spared, the presence or absence of the amygdala lesion

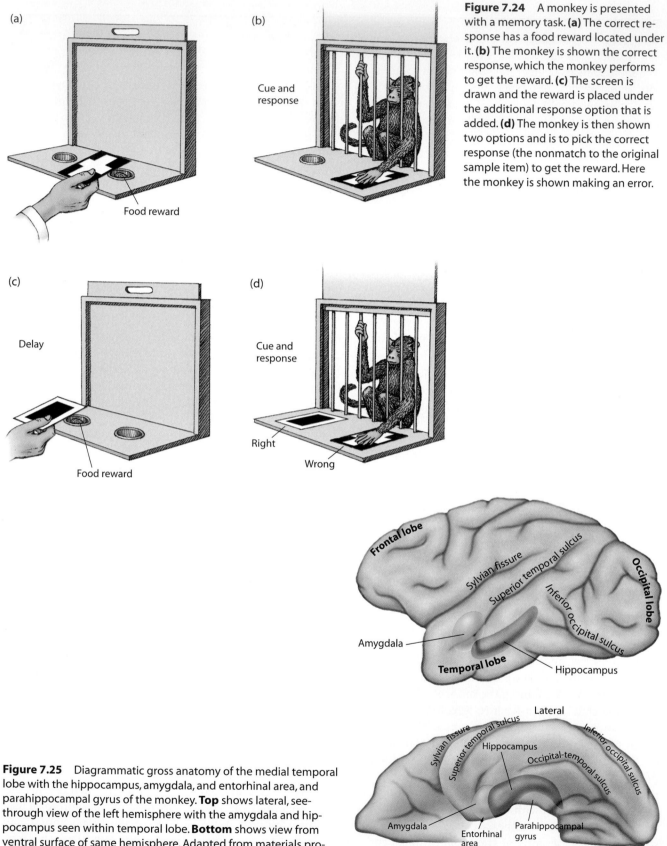

(a)

Food reward

(b)

Cue and response

Figure 7.24 A monkey is presented with a memory task. **(a)** The correct response has a food reward located under it. **(b)** The monkey is shown the correct response, which the monkey performs to get the reward. **(c)** The screen is drawn and the reward is placed under the additional response option that is added. **(d)** The monkey is then shown two options and is to pick the correct response (the nonmatch to the original sample item) to get the reward. Here the monkey is shown making an error.

(c)

Delay

Food reward

(d)

Cue and response

Right

Wrong

Frontal lobe
Sylvian fissure
Superior temporal sulcus
Occipital lobe
Inferior occipital sulcus
Amygdala
Temporal lobe
Hippocampus

Lateral
Sylvian fissure
Superior temporal sulcus
Hippocampus
Inferior occipital sulcus
Occipital-temporal sulcus
Amygdala
Entorhinal area
Parahippocampal gyrus

Medial

Figure 7.25 Diagrammatic gross anatomy of the medial temporal lobe with the hippocampus, amygdala, and entorhinal area, and parahippocampal gyrus of the monkey. **Top** shows lateral, see-through view of the left hemisphere with the amygdala and hippocampus seen within temporal lobe. **Bottom** shows view from ventral surface of same hemisphere. Adapted from materials provided by David Amaral.

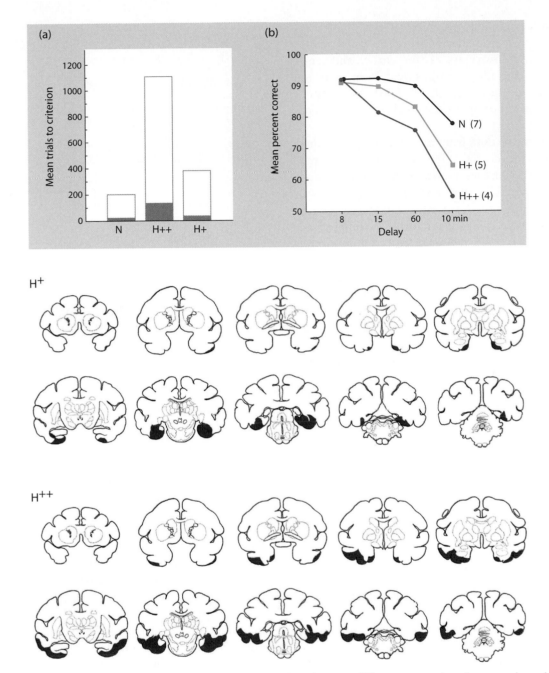

Figure 7.26 Performance on the delayed nonmatching to sample task at two different test sessions for normal monkeys (N); monkeys with lesions of the hippocampal formation, parahippocampal cortex, and perirhinal cortex (H++); and monkeys with lesions of the hippocampal formation and the parahippocampal cortex (H+). **(a)** Initial learning of the task with a delay of 8 seconds: Open bars = test 1, Filled bars = test 2. **(b)** Performance across delays for the same groups: Lesions (red) in H+ **(top)** and H++ **(bottom)** shown in coronal sections. Adapted from Zola-Morgan et al. (1993).

did not affect the monkey's memory. The amygdala, then, could not be part of the system that supported the acquisition of long-term memory.

In subsequent investigations, Zola and his colleagues selectively created lesions of the surrounding cortex in the perirhinal, entorhinal, and parahippocampal regions. This worsened memory performance in delayed nonmatching to sample tests (Figure 7.26). Follow-up work showed that lesions of only the parahippocampal and perirhinal cortices also produced significant memory deficits.

How does this make sense in relation to R.B.'s profound anterograde amnesia with damage limited to the hippocampus and not the surrounding parahippocampal or perirhinal cortex? The parahippocampal and perirhinal areas receive information from the visual, auditory, and somatosensory association cortex, and send these inputs to the hippocampus, and from there to other cortical regions (Figure 7.27). The hippocampus cannot function properly if these vital connections are damaged.

In summary, the data from animals are highly consistent with evidence from human amnesic patients such as R.B. and H.M. that implicates the medial temporal lobe hippocampal system and associated cortex as critical for forming long-term memories by interacting with the neocortex. Lesions that damage the hippocampus directly, or damage the input-output relations of the hippocampus with the neocortex, will produce severe memory impairments. The amygdala is not a crucial part of the system. Moreover, the animal data match perfectly with those for amnesics with regard to the preservation of short-term memory processes after the medial temporal lobe has been damaged; the monkeys' memory deficits in the delay nonmatching to sample task became more pronounced as the interval between the sample and test increased. The medial temporal lobe, then, is not essential for short-term or working memory processes. As we noted earlier, the medial temporal lobe memory system is not the locus of long-term storage because retrograde amnesia is not total after damage; rather, the medial temporal lobe is a key component in consolidating long-term memory that is permanently stored in the neocortex.

Neuroimaging of Human Brain and Memory

The work described so far has dealt with evidence from humans and animals with brain damage. These data are consistent with regard to the role of the medial temporal lobe in memory. Adding to this research are studies of normal subjects using brain imaging methods. The results are quite provocative.

IMPLICIT VERSUS EXPLICIT LEARNING OF MOTOR SEQUENCES

Earlier we discovered that amnesics demonstrate implicit learning of motor sequences even when they cannot form explicit memories about the stimulus sequence (see Figure 7.20). Amnesics provide powerful evidence that implicit learning of sequences need not be mediated by explicit knowledge of them.

Scott Grafton, Eliot Hazeltine, and one of the authors (R.B.I.) (1995) investigated the brain basis of implicit sequence learning in normal subjects. They com-

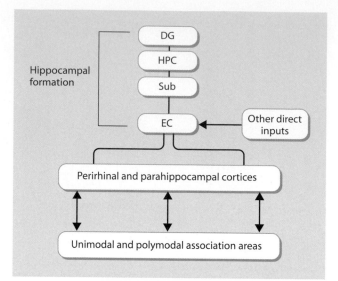

Figure 7.27 Diagrammatic flow of information between the cortex and the hippocampal system. From Cohen and Eichenbaum (1993).

pared conditions in which the subjects learn motor sequences implicitly during dual-task conditions, which helps prevent subjects from explicitly learning the sequence. Here the subjects respond to stimulus sequences with button pushes, while monitoring a sequence of tones and counting those of lower frequency. The investigators compared this to the condition where subjects only perform the sequence learning task and thus might become explicitly aware of the sequence.

Positron emission tomography (PET) conducted during the dual-task condition demonstrated activation of the motor cortex and the supplementary motor area of the left hemisphere (they responded with their right hands), and bilaterally the putamen. Also activated were the rostral prefrontal cortex and parietal cortex. Therefore, when subjects were implicitly learning the task, brain areas that control limb movements were activated. When the distracting auditory task was removed, the right dorsolateral prefrontal cortex, right premotor cortex, right putamen, and parieto-occipital cortex bilaterally were activated (Figure 7.28). Under these conditions, seven of the twelve subjects became aware of the sequence. The differences in activations for the seven aware and five unaware subjects are presented in Figure 7.28. These differences called for recruiting activity in the right temporal lobe, left and right inferior parietal cortex, right premotor cortex, and anterior cingulate cortex.

These PET data, and convergent evidence from transcranial magnetic stimulation and animal work, indicate that the motor cortex is critical for implicit procedural

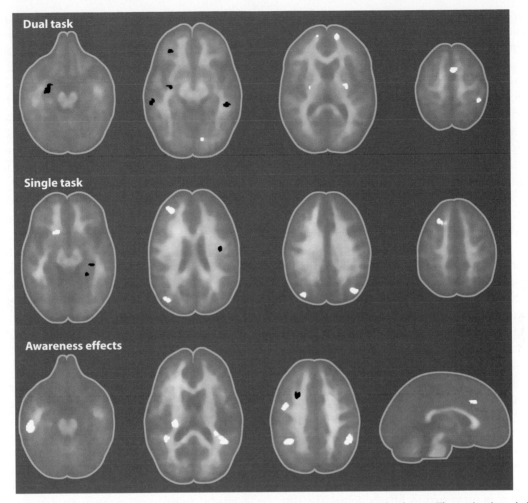

Figure 7.28   Activations corresponding to implicit learning of motor sequences in normal subjects. The activations (white areas) are overlaid onto MRI. Different brain areas were activated when subjects performed the task under dual-task conditions designed to emphasize implicit learning **(top row)** and single-task conditions where the subject might develop explicit awareness **(middle row).** The differences between the subjects who reported awareness of the sequence (N = 7) and those who did not (N = 5) in the single-task condition are shown at the bottom. From Grafton, Hazeltine, and Ivry (1995).

learning of movement patterns. Activations in the putamen would be expected given that patients with Huntington's disease (disease of the basal ganglia) have deficits in sequence learning tasks. Because the supplementary motor cortex was also activated during implicit learning, it may be part of a network of subcortical and cortical areas collectively known as the *cortical-subcortical motor loop,* which regulates voluntary movements. Explicit learning and awareness of the sequences required more activations in the right premotor cortex, the dorsolateral prefrontal cortex associated with working memory, the anterior cingulate, areas in the parietal cortex concerned with voluntary attention, and the lateral temporal cortical areas that store explicit memories. Demonstrated here are clear dissociations between brain systems in-

volved in explicit and implicit learning and memory in healthy humans.

What about the role of the medial temporal lobe? If the hippocampus helps to acquire new explicit memories, we would expect to see it become more active when subjects are explicitly learning sequences. However, activity actually decreases in the right hippocampus for implicit and explicit learning conditions. It is not clear how to interpret this since the task requires motor sequence learning. Therefore, let us examine neuroimaging data from more direct investigations of the hippocampus.

HIPPOCAMPAL ACTIVATION AND RETRIEVAL

PET has been used to investigate the participation of the hippocampus in memory. In experiments by Larry

Squire and his colleagues (1992), normal volunteer subjects were first asked to study a list of words. The subjects were then tested while their brains were scanned. The tests had two conditions: The implicit test included stem-completion priming with blocks where no test words were on the prior study list, and blocks where half the words had been on the study list; the explicit test included recall words using the word stems as aids. It was then possible to compare these conditions for changes in local brain activity. Activations occurred in the right hippocampus and the right prefrontal cortex (Figure 7.29). Activation in the right hippocampus was greater during the explicit memory test but still significant during the implicit conditions. This activation during implicit retrieval is hard to reconcile with evidence from amnesics whose implicit priming is intact while explicit learning and memory are impaired.

The conclusion was that the right hippocampus retrieved information from memory. That it was the right and not the left hippocampus may have been due to which task was required. Because the retrieval cues were word stems—and thus implicit cues that required perceptual priming systems—perhaps during recall the subjects relied more on visual-perceptual representations and less on linguistic coding, which would presumably rely on the left hemisphere. The left hippocampus, then, is activated only for certain tasks.

In another study, the left hippocampus, and not the right, was activated. In this task, subjects were shown word lists that contained two to fifteen items. The lists were repeated three times. The left hippocampus as well as the right and left prefrontal cortices were activated. The results of these two PET studies together would be consistent with a bias in which the hippocampus is activated according to the task: verbal ones for the left hippocampus, and perceptual ones for the right hippocampus. One mystery is the difference between evidence from amnesia patients and PET activations. The conclusion from amnesia is that the hippocampus neither stores nor retrieves long-term memories; instead, it encodes and consolidates knowledge in long-term memory. Why, then, was the hippocampus activated during retrieval? Squire and colleagues argued that the activations reflect retrieval of recently acquired information from memory. The emphasis on "recent" memory grew out of comparing PET activations with data from amnesics. The idea was that retrieving recently acquired information still depends on the hippocampus, which is consistent with the time-limited retrograde amnesia observed with damage to the medial temporal lobe.

HIPPOCAMPAL ACTIVATION AND ENCODING

Evidence supporting hemispheric differences in hippocampal memory also comes from studies of face encoding and recognition. Again, the issue is whether the hippocampus is active when encoding new information. James Haxby, Leslie Ungerleider, and their colleagues (1996) at the NIMH presented subjects with pictures of either faces or nonsense patterns and, using PET, investigated memory performance. Subjects were required to remember (encode) the face, recognize the face, and perceptually analyze the face by comparing two faces (Figure 7.30).

The right hippocampus was activated only for encoding, not recognition (Figure 7.31). Unlike the preceding studies, investigators discovered that the hippocampus encodes but does not retrieve, which is more consistent in patients whose medial temporal lobe damage created deficits in anterograde amnesia but preserved distant retrograde memories. Encoding activated the left prefrontal cortex, whereas recognition activated the right prefrontal cortex. Thus, we have more support for the hippocampus's role in memory, as well as possible hemispheric asymmetries in memory.

HIPPOCAMPAL ACTIVATION AND IMPLICIT AND EXPLICIT MEMORY

Squire and his colleagues did not explicitly address one of the most common distinctions in memory in their study: that amnesia caused by temporal lobe damage

Figure 7.29 PET showing activations of the right hippocampus, from the study of Squire and colleagues (1992) (Courtesy of Larry Squire).

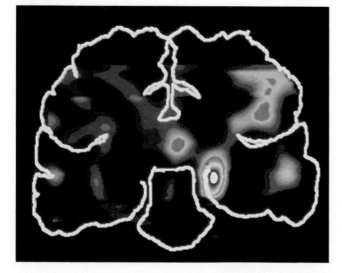

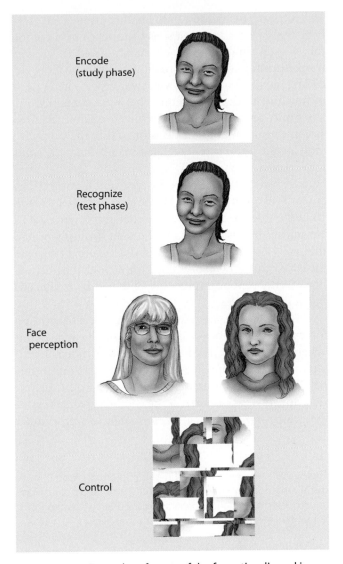

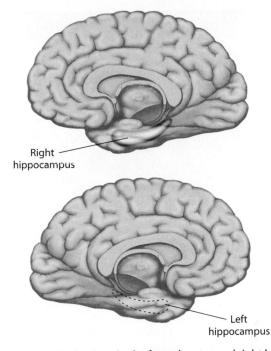

Figure 7.31 Activations in the frontal cortex and right hippocampus during encoding and retrieval of information. The hippocampus was only activated during encoding of information. Presumably the right hippocampus was more activated because the task was not linguistically based, and because face-specific processes are lateralized to the right hemisphere.

Figure 7.30 Examples of some of the face stimuli used in a PET study of encoding and retrieval of face information. During a face-encoding task, the subjects tried to memorize the faces for a later test. During a face recognition task, they were required to determine whether the face had been previously seen. During a face perception control task, they were supposed to match the two faces. Finally during a sensorimotor control task, nonsense patterns were presented and the subjects pressed a button.

affects explicit but not implicit memory. The reason this explicit-implicit distinction was downplayed is because they found hippocampal activation during both explicit and implicit memory tasks. Either these data reflect a new finding from neuroimaging that wholly or partially refutes the evidence from amnesia patients, or interpretations of PET data should be reconsidered. Daniel Schacter and his colleagues (1996) at Harvard

University suggested a new interpretation of the PET data in which the hippocampus is activated during the recollection of an event; the premise is that previous implicit tests may have been contaminated by occasional explicit recollections of the target item. They argued that the hippocampus should not be activated in implicit memory tasks when explicit processes are eliminated.

To eliminate the possibility that subjects would have later explicit recollections of seeing a list of test words, Schacter and colleagues showed them the words but required the subjects to process them only for surface perceptual features (the number of T junctions—any perpendicular lines that intersect in the shape of a T—in the letters of the word). They were assigned an implicit stem-completing task in which some blocks had stems from previously presented words, and other blocks had stems of new words. Scanning was performed only during testing. Subjects manifested implicit priming behaviorally; they completed more stems when they were from words previously seen. No activations or deactivations were noted in the hippocampus, but blood flow in the bilateral occipital cortex (area 19) decreased. The

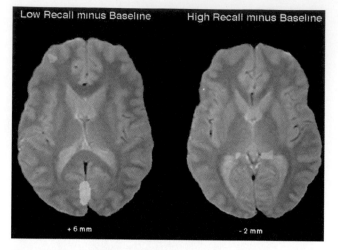

Figure 7.32 Activations from PET scans overlaid onto averaged MRI scans. Subtraction of scans taken during baseline minus priming yielded no activations in the hippocampus, but there were decreases in the occipital cortex. Low recall minus baseline caused activations in the left prefrontal cortex and area 18 of the occipital lobe (left). High recall minus baseline showed bilateral activations in the hippocampus (right). Adapted from Schacter et al. (1996). (Courtesy of Daniel Schacter).

hippocampus was not activated, then, even though implicit perceptual priming was obtained (Figure 7.32).

In a separate experiment, encoding was manipulated to produce high recall during one test (words shown four times for semantic judgments) versus low recall during another test (one presentation of words and judgment about perceptual qualities—T-junction detection). The idea was that when the words were recalled, more explicit recollections would happen for the list studied more deeply (i.e., the high recall condition). Subjects did have better recall, and significant activations took place bilaterally in the hippocampus.

The conclusions from this and other studies are that implicit and explicit retrieval of information is subserved by separate brain systems. Schacter's study indicated that the hippocampus will most likely be activated when explicit retrieval includes significant experiences, not merely an attempt to retrieve information. Together with the face encoding data from Haxby and colleagues using PET (see Figure 7.31), and animal and human lesion data, a reasonable conclusion is that the hippocampus encodes new information and retrieves recent information when explicit recollection is involved.

HEMISPHERIC CORTICAL ASYMMETRIES IN ENCODING AND RETRIEVAL

How much does the cortex figure into encoding and retrieving? Tulving and colleagues investigated encoding

and retrieval of episodic information using PET (Nyberg et al., 1996). In a first study, the depth of encoding for episodic information was manipulated in various ways. Encoding was either shallow or deep. Shallow encoding required subjects to view words presented one at a time and to decide whether the word contained the letter *a*. A second, "deep" encoding condition required animate versus inanimate decisions about the words. To evaluate the brain activity related to encoding, the scans for each were compared. Deeper encoding led to greater blood flow in the left inferior prefrontal cortex. The anatomical areas were Brodmann's areas 45, 46, 47, and 10 in the inferior and middle frontal gyri (Figure 7.33). No activation was observed in the right hemisphere, and thus it is clear that encoding episodic memories involves the left frontal lobe. It is curious, though, that no activations of the hippocampus were obtained in the encoding in these studies.

When subjects are asked to perform a retrieval task for episodic memories, the right, not the left, hemisphere is activated. In these PET studies, normal subjects were given sentences in a learning session on one day. The sentences were sentence frames—short definitions for a word presented at the end (e.g., recreation for the jumpy—*trampoline*). These sentences were similar

Figure 7.33 A comparison of regional cerebral blood flow in the left inferior frontal regions in a deep processing condition as compared to a shallow processing condition. Adapted from Kapur et al. (1994).

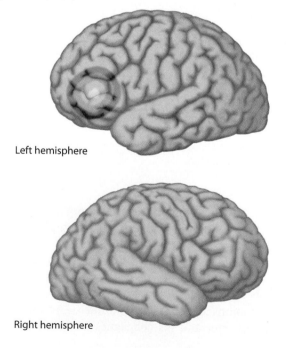

Left hemisphere

Right hemisphere

to ones used for new semantic learning in patient K.C.; however, normal subjects can readily remember the episode of learning new definitions, whereas K.C. learned them without any episodic memory of the learning experience.

On the day of study, 120 of the definitions were presented to the normal volunteer subjects. Then on the next day, when scanning was performed, these 120 plus a novel 120 definitions were included. During some scanning sessions, new and old definitions were given in such a way that mostly old definitions were presented; during others, mostly new ones were presented. Blood flow was compared for when subjects heard mostly new versus mostly old definitions. The subjects' performance was better than 95% in identifying old versus new items; they correctly recognized the definitions they had heard before. In conjunction with this, cerebral blood flow rose in the right dorsolateral prefrontal cortex. Some activation occurred in the left dorsolateral prefrontal cortex, but not in areas symmetrical to those in the right, and to a lesser degree. In addition, activation was found in the parietal lobe (Figure 7.34).

Encoding and retrieval processes were lateralized in the left and right hemispheres, respectively, giving rise to a model with the acronym of HERA, which stands for hemispheric encoding retrieval asymmetry. It represents the idea that encoding is more in the left hemisphere and retrieval is more in the right. Both processes occur predominantly in the dorsolateral prefrontal cortex. In encoding and retrieving information from long-term memory, cortical areas, not the hippocampus, are most active. Indeed, the medial temporal lobe is not activated, as we find for encoding faces or explicit retrieval. Despite the lack of consistency in hippocampal activations, the activations of the frontal cortex during encoding and retrieval are supported by data from PET experi-

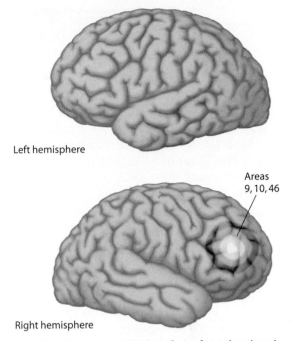

Left hemisphere

Areas 9, 10, 46

Right hemisphere

Figure 7.34 Activations of right inferior frontal regions involved in memory retrieval. Adapted from Kapur et al. (1994).

ments. Any model of brain and long-term memory must consider how the medial temporal and frontal cortex interact during encoding and retrieval.

In summary, neuroimaging studies demonstrated patterns of neuronal activation that are consistent with memory systems derived from cognitive research, studies in human amnesics, and animal models. Neuroimaging also provided some notable findings in the cognitive neuroscience of memory, including, for example, the hemispheric asymmetries in encoding and retrieval. Functional neuroimaging clearly will continue to provide invaluable information about human memory and its neural substrates in the healthy human.

CELLULAR BASIS OF MEMORY

In dwelling on the big picture of memory research, we may have lost sight of the fact that memory entails changes in neurons that facilitate storage of new information. Memory is the result of changes in the strength of synaptic influences among neurons in neuronal networks that process and store information.

Long-Term Potentiation and the Hippocampus

Because of the hippocampal formation's role in memory, it has long been hypothesized that neurons in the hippocampus must be plastic, that is, able to change their synaptic interactions. Since the late 1960s researchers have sought the mechanisms behind this type of plasticity in learning and memory storage. Although it is now clear that storage itself is not in the hippocampus, this was not understood when work on hippocampal cell physiology first began. This fact does not invalidate the hippocampal models we examine, because the same cellular mechanisms can operate in various cortical and subcortical areas.

First, let us quickly review the three major excitatory

Monitoring Recollection Using Human Brain Electrophysiology

An invaluable criterion for ascertaining whether explicit and implicit processes are subserved by separate brain systems is to show that they are independent. What one wants to show is that performance on implicit tests is not correlated with explicit recollections about test items. One problem in memory research has been the difficulty of revealing how much recollective experience patients may have for previously viewed information, even when they are not asked to do so. It would be tremendously helpful to distinguish between normal subjects who do have and those who do not have recollective experiences. Recently, Ken Paller, Marta Kutas, and their colleagues (1995) provided a means of doing this through electrical recordings (event-related potentials, or ERPs) of brain activity in healthy persons.

They used a method in which they varied the depth of encoding words by having subjects generate a mental image corresponding to the word or merely indicate whether the word contained more than one syllable. Later, the subjects were asked to make a lexical decision (is it a word?) about a list of words and nonword letter strings. The words were a mixture of those from the prior image task list, those from the prior syllable task list, or new words that they had not seen. In a second experiment, the researchers asked subjects to perform the lexical decision task and give a recognition judgment about whether they had seen the words before. In each experiment, the researchers performed separate recognition post-tests to assess the extent to which subjects could recollect the words.

The behavioral measures revealed priming in the lexical decision task (previously seen words were classified as words faster than were new words). Priming was not affected by whether subjects had studied the words in the image versus the syllable condition. Recognition scores from the posttest, though, differed significantly according to the study task—subjects were better at recognizing previously seen words if at the time of the study they had generated an image corresponding to the word. Thus, the behavioral data differed in how the task affected implicit (lexical decision) versus explicit (recognition) processes. Were there any electrophysiological signs of recollection? Yes, the voltage of ERPs elicited by words was more positive 500 to 900 msec after onset of words that had been seen previously in the image condition as compared with the ones in the syllable condition. Because this ERP mirrored the effect of the study task on recognition performance, it is a physiological sign of recollection. This is especially true since recollection was not necessary for the implicit memory test. The researchers noted that the ERPs permitted a view of human subjective experience that was not contaminated by introspective reports, which are notoriously unreliable.

ERPs from two experiments by Paller, Kutas, and McIsaac (1995) showing responses for words on the test that had been previously seen in one of two conditions: when the words were used to generate images **(solid line)** and when the subjects decided how many syllables were present in the word **(dashed line).** At bottom, the difference between these two conditions is plotted as the subtraction waveform (image minus syllable condition). Words that had been encoded during the image task elicited more positivity between latencies of 500 to 900 msec, and this effect was larger when on the test the subjects were required to include recognition judgments.

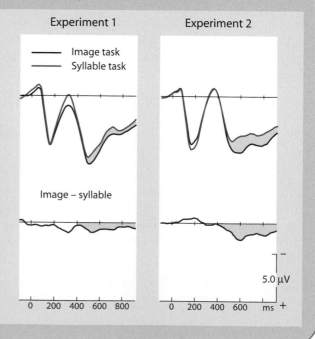

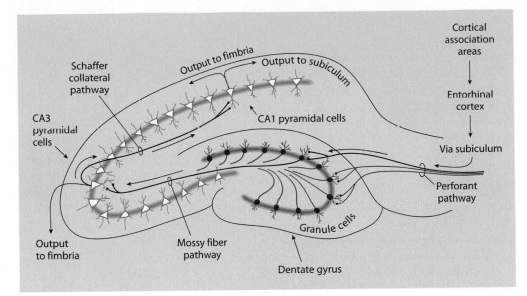

Figure 7.35 Diagram of the synaptic organization of the rat hippocampus.

synaptic pathways in the hippocampus (Figure 7.35): (1) the perforant pathway that forms excitatory connections between the parahippocampal cortex and the granule cells of the dentate gyrus, (2) the mossy fibers that connect the granule cells of the dentate gyrus to the CA3 pyramidal cells (on dendritic spines), and (3) the Schaffer collaterals that connect the CA3 pyramidal cells to the CA1 pyramidal cells. This system provides an opportunity for researchers to examine synaptic plasticity as the mechanism of learning at the cellular level.

In studies by Bliss and Lømo (1973) stimulation of axons of the perforant pathway of the rabbit resulted in a long-term increase in the magnitude of excitatory postsynaptic potentials (EPSPs). That is, the stimulation led to greater synaptic strength in the perforant pathway such that later stimulation created larger postsynaptic responses in the granule cells of the dentate gyrus. This phenomenon, named *long-term potentiation* (LTP) (*potentiate* means "to strengthen or make more potent"), was later extended to the other two excitatory pathways of the hippocampus. The changes could last for hours in isolated slices of hippocampal tissue placed in dishes, where recording was easier. LTPs can even last for days or weeks in living animals. It has since been found that the LTPs in the three pathways vary; nonetheless, Hebb's (1949) law is confirmed physiologically by the discovery of LTP: The law states that if a synapse is active when a postsynaptic neuron is active, the synapse will be strengthened.

One way that LTPs can be recorded is by placing a stimulating electrode on the perforant pathway and a recording electrode in a granule cell of the dentate gyrus (Figure 7.36). First, a single pulse is presented, and the resulting EPSP is measured. The size of this first recording is the strength of the connection before the

LTP is induced. Then the perforant pathway is stimulated with a burst of pulses; early studies used approximately 100 pulses per sec but more recent ones use as few as five pulses per sec. After LTP is induced, a single pulse is sent again, and the magnitude of the EPSP in

Figure 7.36 Stimulus and recording setup for the study of long-term potentiation (LTP) in perforant pathways. **(a)** The pattern of responses before and after inducing LTP is shown (microvolts). **(b)** The pattern of response in long-term depression (LTD) is shown.

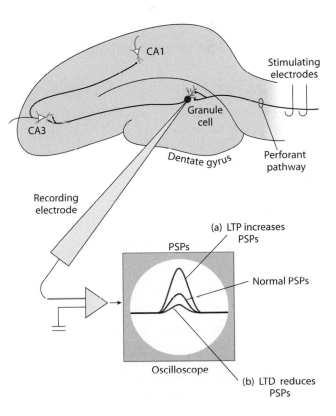

the postsynaptic cell is measured. The magnitude of the EPSP grows after LTP is induced, signaling the greater strength of the synaptic effect (Figure 7.36a). A fascinating finding is that when the pulses are presented at a slow rate, the opposite effect, long-term depression (LTD), develops (Figure 7.36b).

HEBBIAN LEARNING

Associative LTP is an extension of Hebb's law and asserts that if a weak and a strong input act on a cell at the same time, the weak synapse becomes stronger. This has been tested directly by manipulating LTP in the CA1 neurons of the hippocampus. When two weak inputs (W1 and W2) and one strong input (S1) are given to the same cell, and when W1 and S1 are active together, W1 is strengthened whereas W2 is not. Subsequently, if W2 and S1 are active together, W1 is not affected by the LTP induced from W2 and S1. From this finding, three rules for associative LTP can be stated: More than one input must be active at the same time (cooperativity), weak inputs are potentiated when co-occurring with stronger inputs (associativity), and only the stimulated synapse shows potentiation (specificity).

For LTP to be produced, the postsynaptic cells must be depolarized in addition to receiving excitatory inputs; in fact, LTP is reduced by inhibitory inputs to postsynaptic cells. As well, when postsynaptic cells are hyperpolarized, LTP is prevented. Conversely, when postsynaptic inhibition is prevented, LTP is facilitated. If an input that is normally not strong enough to induce LTP is paired with a depolarizing current to the postsynaptic cell, LTP can be induced.

THE NMDA RECEPTOR

That an excitatory input and postsynaptic depolarization are needed to produce LTP is explained by the properties of the doubly gated N-methyl-D-aspartate (NMDA) receptor located on the dendritic spines of postsynaptic neurons that show LTP. Glutamate is the major excitatory transmitter in the hippocampus, and it can bind with NMDA and non-NMDA receptors. When 2-amino-5-phosphonopentanoate (AP5) is introduced to CA1 neurons, NMDA receptors are chemically blocked and LTP induction is prevented. But the AP5 treatment does not produce any effect on previously established LTP in these cells. Therefore, NMDA receptors are central to producing LTP but not maintaining it. It turns out that maintenance of LTP may depend on the non-NMDA receptors.

What is the cellular mechanism that permits LTP to develop via the NMDA receptors, and why does blocking them with AP5 prevent LTP? NMDA receptors are normally blocked by magnesium ions (Mg^{2+}). The Mg^{2+} ions can be ejected from the NMDA receptors only when the neurotransmitter glutamate binds to the receptors and when the membrane is depolarized; that is, the NMDA receptors are transmitter and voltage dependent (gated). When these two conditions are met, Mg^{2+} is ejected and calcium (Ca^{2+}) can enter the cell (Figure 7.37).

The effect of Ca^{2+} influx via the NMDA receptor is critical in forming LTP. Ca^{2+} acts as an intracellular messenger conveying the signal which changes enzyme activities that influence synaptic strength. Despite rapid advances in understanding the mechanisms of LTP at physiological and biochemical levels, the molecular mechanisms of synaptic strengthening in LTP are still subject to extensive debate.

The synaptic changes that create a stronger synapse after LTP induction likely include presynaptic and postsynaptic mechanisms. One hypothesis is that LTP raises the sensitivity of postsynaptic non-NMDA glutamate receptors and prompts more glutamate to be released presynaptically. Or perhaps changes in the physical characteristics of the dendritic spines transmit EPSPs more effectively to the dendrites. Finally, via a postsynaptic to presynaptic cell message, the efficiency of presynaptic neurotransmitter release is increased.

LONG-TERM POTENTIATION AND MEMORY PERFORMANCE

Having identified a candidate cellular mechanism for long-term plastic changes in synaptic strength, it should be possible to produce deficits in learning and memory by eliminating LTP. Chemically blocking LTP in the hippocampus of normal mice impairs their ability to demonstrate normal place learning; thus, blocking LTP prevents normal spatial memory. In a similar way, genetic manipulations that block the cascade of molecular triggers for LTP also impair spatial learning. These experiments provided strong evidence of impairing spatial memory by blocking NMDA receptors and preventing LTP.

Studies with different results cast doubt on the role of LTP in learning and memory, however (Bannerman et al., 1995) (Saucier and Cain, 1995). Both experiments found that pharmacological NMDA receptor blockers did not stop rodents from learning how to navigate in a water maze; the animals were able to develop a new spatial map even when LTP was prevented. Unlike previous studies, these studies pretrained the rodents to swim to a platform, which prevented the impairment of new spatial learning when the NMDA receptors were blocked. When mice were pretrained by either a water maze task or a nonspatial task, the introduction of AP5 (the NMDA receptor blocker) in the hippocampus pre-

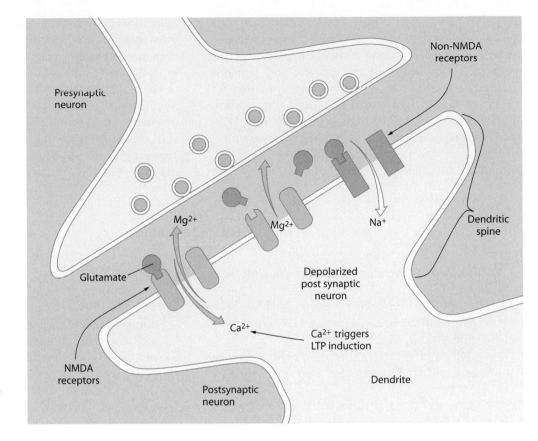

Figure 7.37 The role of Mg²⁺ and Ca²⁺ in the functioning of the NMDA receptor.

vented new learning in mice pretrained for the nonspatial task, but it did not affect mice pretrained for the spatial task. The conclusion is that NMDA receptors may be needed to learn a spatial strategy but not to encode a new map. Another experiment also reported that blocking LTP did not affect behavior, but the pattern was slightly different. When mice were pretrained with a nonspatial task, spatial memory was not interrupted by introducing an NMDA antagonist. The conclusion is that the pretraining merely allowed the motor-related side effects of NMDA receptor blockage to be avoided. Although these two studies did not exclude the possibility that new spatial learning involves NMDA receptors, they do point to the possibility that at least two memory

systems could utilize NMDA receptors. These systems participate in the water maze task but could possibly be consolidated by pretraining.

The role of LTP in memory on the cellular and behavioral levels is still being unraveled. There is great debate over whether the maintenance of LTP is located presynaptically or postsynaptically and even whether LTP is necessary for spatial memory. Two points of agreement are that LTP does exist at the cellular level and that NMDA receptors play a crucial role in LTP induction in many pathways of the brain. Because LTP is also in brain areas outside the hippocampal system, the possibility that LTP forms the basis for long-term modification within synaptic networks remains promising.

SUMMARY

The ability to acquire new information and retain it over time defines learning and memory. Cognitive theory and neuroscientific evidence argue that memory is supported by multiple cognitive and neural systems. These systems support different aspects of memory, and their distinctions in quality can be identified. Sensory registration, perceptual presentation,

working memory, semantic memory, and episodic memory, as well as memory for skills and procedures, all represent systems or subsystems for learning and memory. The brain structures that support various memory processes differ depending on the type of information to be retained.

The biological memory system includes the medial

temporal lobe, which forms and consolidates new episodic and perhaps semantic memories; the prefrontal cortex, which encodes and retrieves information; the temporal cortex, which stores episodic and semantic knowledge; and the association and sensory cortices for aspects of implicit perceptual memory. Other cortical and subcortical structures participate in learning skills and habits, especially those with implicit motor learning.

The brain is not equipotential in the storage of information, and although widespread brain areas coop- erate in learning and memory, the individual structures form systems that support and enable rather specific memory processes. At the cellular level, changes in the synaptic strengths between neurons in neural networks in the medial temporal lobe, neocortex, and elsewhere are the most likely mechanisms for learning and memory, including LTP and LTD. We are rapidly developing a very clear understanding of molecular processes that support synaptic plasticity, and thus learning and memory in the brain.

SUGGESTED READINGS

BADDELEY, A. (1986). *Working Memory.* Oxford, UK: Clarendon Press/Oxford University Press.

BADDELEY, A. (1995). Working Memory. In *The Cognitive Neurosciences* M.S. Gazzaniga (Ed.), (pp. 755–764). Cambridge, MA: MIT Press.

COHEN, N.J., and EICHENBAUM, H. (1993). *Memory, Amnesia and the Hippocampal System.* Cambridge, MA: MIT Press.

COLLINGRIDGE, G.L., and BLISS, T.V.P. (1995). Memories of NMDA receptors and LTP. *Trends Neurosci.* 18:54–56.

ERICSSON, K., and CHASE, W. (1982). Exceptional memory. *Am. Sci.* 70:607–615.

GABRIELI, J., FLEISCHMAN, D., KEANE, M., REMINGER, S., and MORELL, F. (1995). Double dissociation between memory systems underlying explicit and implicit memory in the human brain. *Psychol. Sci.* 6:76–82.

HILTS, P.J. (1995). Memories ghost: the strange tale of Mr. M. and the nature of memory. New York: Simon and Schuster.

LARKMAN, A.U., and JACK, J.B. (1995). Synaptic plasticity: Hippocampal LTP. *Curr. Opin. Neurobiol.* 5:324–334.

MCCLOSKEY, M., WIBLE, C., and COHEN, N. (1988). Is there a special flashbulb-memory mechanism? *J. Exp. Psychol. Gen.* 117:171–181.

MILLER, G. (1994). The magical number seven, plus or minus two: Some limits on our capacity for processing information. *Psychol. Rev.* 101:343–352.

PALLER, K., KUTAS, M., and MCISAAC, H. (1995). Monitoring conscious recollection via the electrical activity of the brain. *Psychol. Sci.* 6:107–111.

SCHACTER, D., ALPERT, N., SAVAGE, C., RAUCH, S., et al. (1996). Conscious recollection and the human hippocampal formation—Evidence from positron emission tomography. *Proc. Nat. Acad. Sci. U.S.A.* 93:321–325.

SQUIRE, L.R., and ZOLA-MORGAN, S. (1991). The medial temporal lobe memory system. *Science* 253:1380–1386.

THOMPSON, C., COWAN, T., and FRIEMAN, J. (1993). *Memory Search by a Memorist.* Hillsdale, NJ: Lawrence Erlbaum Associates.

TULVING, E., and SHACTER, D.L. (1990). Priming and human memory systems. *Science* 247:301–306

8

Language and the Brain

Communication and brain complexity took a monumental leap from the most intelligent of the non-human primates to humans, for whom communication includes language. Speech and language, uniquely human, mark a dramatic shift between monkey brains and human brains. It has been surprisingly difficult, though, to identify human brain systems and specializations that support language. Some brain regions are critical for normal speech and comprehension, but these 100-year-old clues from medicine have provided only modest insights into the neural organization of language. Yet, a growing body of work on the brain and language processes, guided by careful psycholinguistic models and aided by modern tools, is providing fantastic new data for cognitive neuroscientists to ponder. This chapter introduces a cognitive neuroscience perspective on the human language system, arguably the most complex of the human brain's feats of wonder.

PSYCHOLINGUISTIC THEORIES OF LANGUAGE

How does our brain cope with spoken and written input? To begin to answer this question we have to know how words are represented in the brain. For now, let us describe this from the perspective of theoretical-experimental models rather than neurophysiological data. The implicit message, though, is that something similar must reside in the brain's neural networks.

The Mental Lexicon

Of central importance in word representation is the concept of the *mental lexicon*—a mental store of information about words that includes *semantic information* (what is the word's meaning?) and *syntactic information* (how are the words combined to form a sentence?), and the details of *word forms* (how are they spelled and what

is their sound pattern?). Most psycholinguistic theories agree on the central role for a mental lexicon in language. But some theories propose one mental lexicon for both language comprehension and production, whereas other models distinguish between input and output lexica. In addition, the representation of orthographic (vision-based) and phonological (sound-based) forms has distinctions. The principal concept, though, is that a store or stores of information about words exist in the brain and we have some idea how it must be organized.

A normal adult speaker has passive knowledge of about 50,000 words, and yet we can recognize and produce about three words per second without any difficulty. Given this speed and the size of the database, the mental lexicon must be organized very efficiently. It cannot be merely the equivalent of a dictionary. If, for example, the mental lexicon were organized in simple alphabetical order, it might take longer to find words in the middle of the alphabet, such as the ones starting with *K, L, O,* or *U,* than to find a word starting with an *A* or *Z.* Fortunately, this is not the case.

The mental lexicon differs in other respects from the dictionary on our shelves. For one thing, it has no fixed content: Words can be forgotten and new words can be learned—when was the last time you picked up a dictionary to see that new words had miraculously appeared? Another significant difference is that in the mental lexicon, more frequently used words are accessed more quickly; for instance, the word *table* is more readily available than the word *snail.*

The mental lexicon is quite dissimilar to the average college dictionary. The mental lexicon is thought to be organized as information-specific networks. For example, Collins and Loftus (1975) proposed that word meanings are represented in a *semantic network* in which words, represented by conceptual nodes, are connected with each other. An example of a semantic network is presented in Figure 8.1. The strength of the connection and the distance between the nodes are determined by the semantic relations or associative relations between the words. For example, the node that represents the word *car* will be close to and have a strong connection with the node that represents the word *truck.* A major component of this model is the assumption that activation spreads from one conceptual node to others, and ones closer together will benefit more from this spreading activation than will distant nodes. If

we hear the word *car,* then the node that represents *car* in the semantic network will be activated. In addition, words like *truck* and *bus* that are closely related to the meaning of *car* and are therefore nearby and well connected in the semantic network, will receive a considerable amount of activation. In contrast, a word like *tulip* will most likely not receive any activation at all upon hearing "car." This model would predict that hearing the word *car* should facilitate recognition of the word *truck* but not *tulip.*

Support for the idea of a semantic network in the brain comes from semantic priming studies that entail a lexical (word) decision task. Subjects are presented with pairs of words. The first member of the pair, the prime, is a word, while the second member, the target, can be either a real word, a nonword (like *sfhsi*), or a pseudo-word (like *fisch*). If the target is a word, it can be related or unrelated in meaning to the prime. In a lexical decision task, the subjects must decide as fast and as accurately as possible whether the target is a word and press a button indicating the decision. Subjects are faster and more accurate at word decisions when the target is preceded by a related prime (e.g., *car–truck*) than an unrelated prime (e.g., *tulip–truck*). Other evidence is found when the subject is asked to pronounce the target, which is always a word. Here, naming latencies are faster for related words than for unrelated ones.

Over many years of research on priming with lexical decision tasks, it has become clear that priming can result from an automatic spread of activation in a word network. But other mechanisms contribute to this

Figure 8.1 An example of a semantic network. Note that words that have strong associative or semantic relations are closer together in the network (e.g., CAR–TRUCK) than are words that have no such relation (e.g., CAR–CLOUDS). Related words are colored similarly in the figure.

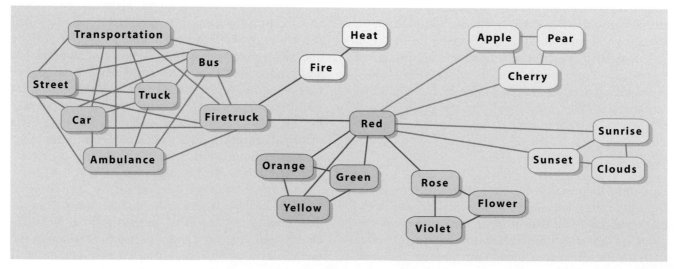

priming effect. These effects are postlexical; they happen after representations in the mental lexicon have been accessed. For example, expectancy-induced priming might occur if the time between the presentation of primes and targets is long and the proportion of related pairs in a list is large. Subject will then expect the possible target words after hearing the prime. If the target word matches one of the words in the expectancy set, then reaction times to this word will be facilitated. *Semantic matching* happens when subjects actively try to match the meaning of the target word with the meaning of the prime. In a lexical decision task this leads to faster "yes" responses to words that match than to words that do not match in meaning with the preceding context word. Therefore, apparently word priming effects do not always result from implicit or automatic types of processes.

Not all psycholinguistic models agree that the meanings of words are part of a separate mental store for linguistic information. Some maintain that word meanings are part of a larger conceptual network outside of the mental lexicon. And it is still a matter of dispute as to how word meanings are organized. One proposal, the semantic network model, directly relates concepts and words.

Other models propose that concepts are represented by their semantic features or semantic properties. For example, the word *dog* has several semantic features, such as "is animate," "has four legs," and "barks," and they are assumed to be represented in the conceptual network. Such models are confronted with the problem of activation: How many features have to be activated in order for a person to recognize a dog? For example, it is possible to train our dogs not to bark, yet we can recognize a dog even when it does not bark, and we can identify a barking dog that we cannot see. Furthermore, it is not exactly clear how many features would have to be stored. For example, a table could be made of wood or glass, and in both cases we would recognize it as a table. Does this mean that we have to store the features "is of wood/glass" with the "table" concept? In addition, some words are more "prototypical" examples of a semantic category than others, as reflected in our recognition and production of these words. When we are asked to generate bird names, for example, the word *robin* will come to mind as one of the first examples, while a word like *ostrich* might not come up at all, depending on where you grew up.

In sum, it is a matter of debate how word meanings are represented. No matter how they are represented, everyone agrees that a mental store of word meanings is crucial to normal language comprehension and production. Evidence from brain-lesioned patients, and from functional brain imaging studies, is revealing how the mental lexicon is organized.

BIOLOGICAL EVIDENCE ABOUT THE MENTAL LEXICON

Through observations of deficits in patients' language, we can infer some things about the functional organization of the mental lexicon. Different types of neurological problems create deficits in understanding and producing the appropriate meaning of a word or concept. Patients with *Wernicke's aphasia* (a language deficit usually due to brain lesions in the posterior parts of the left hemisphere, we will discuss aphasia in detail later) make errors in speech production that are known as *semantic paraphasias*. They could for example use the word *horse* when they mean *cow*. Similar errors in reading are made by patients with *deep dyslexia*: They might read the word *horse* where "*cow*" is written (see From Written Text to Sound: Reading Aloud, p. 292). Patients with *progressive semantic dementia* initially show impairments in the conceptual system, while other mental abilities are spared. These patients have difficulty assigning objects to a semantic category. In addition, they often name a category when asked to name a picture; when viewing a picture of a horse, they will say "animal," and a picture of a robin will prompt "bird." This neurological evidence provides support for the semantic network idea because related meanings are substituted, confused, or lumped together, as we could predict from the degrading of a system interconnected by nodes that specify information.

Semantic problems can also be specifically localized to certain semantic categories, such as animals versus objects. Warrington and McCarthy (1983, 1987) reported patients who have great difficulties pointing to pictures of food or living things when presented with a word, whereas their performance with man-made objects like tools is much better. These difficulties are also found when the patients are asked to name foods or living things when presented with a picture, whereas their naming of man-made things is spared. The reverse pattern is also found in other patients: preserved identification of foods and living things, but impaired performance on man-made objects.

Warrington and her colleagues suggested that the patients' problems are indicative of the types of information stored with different words in the mental lexicon. Whereas the biological categories (fruits, foods, animals) rely more on physical properties or visual features (for example, what is the color of an apple?),

From Written Text to Sound: Reading Aloud

Languages such as English pose difficulties in translating letters (graphemes) to sounds (phonemes), called *grapheme-to-phoneme conversion.* For example, the combination *ph* is pronounced differently in *physiology* and in *uphill,* and the *c* is pronounced differently in *cop* and *cerebellum.* So, how do we know how to pronounce *physiology* when we read it? We might be relying on rules based on the language's regularities; the combination *mb* signals separate pronunciation of the *m* and the *b* when it is in the middle of a word *(ambulance)* but not when it is at the end *(bomb).* But it is difficult to come up with rules that will predict all combinations of letters and sounds. Consider *bomber* and *bombard;* a rule-based system alone will not do the job for us. There must be a direct route from reading text to pronunciation: from the whole-word orthographic input to representations in the mental lexicon. Getting from written text to sounds might be accomplished in two ways, or dual routes: grapheme-to-phoneme translation, or written input directly to the mental lexicon.

Evidence for a dual route comes from patients with acquired dyslexia. These patients' reading problems are due to brain damage. The deficit is modality-specific; that is, the patients can comprehend spoken language, and they may even be able to produce written language (alexia without agraphia). Two types of acquired dyslexia have been found. Patients with deep or phonological dyslexia are unable to read aloud pseudowords like *grimp,* but they do not have any problem with reading irregular words like *broad* or difficult ones like *chrysanthemum.* Thus, they cannot read aloud words that do not have a representation in the mental lexicon but have no difficulties with words that are in their lexicons. In addition, the patients also make semantic errors *(rose* for *iris).* Such problems cannot be explained as a loss of phonological representations because patients with deep dyslexia usually perform well on a rhyming task if the stimuli are presented auditorily. Instead, the patients rely exclusively on the direct lexical route when reading. In contrast, patients with surface dyslexia rely only on regularity rules; they overregularize the pronunciation of irregular words (for example, they will read "heed" for *head*) and thereby show a propensity for a direct translation from the letter to the sound representations. These forms of dyslexia provide a powerful double dissociation that tells us that there must be two routes by which text we read can be converted into verbal output.

---

man-made objects are identified by their functional properties (for example, how do we use a hammer?). Hence, we have more evidence for a conceptually organized mental lexicon.

Positron emission tomography (PET) reveals how intriguing dissociations in neurological patients can be identified in neurologically normal brains. When subjects are asked to name pictures of animals or tools, their ventral temporal lobes are bilaterally activated. But naming of animals also activates a brain area associated with the early stages of visual processing, namely, the left medial occipital lobe. In contrast, naming tools is associated with the left premotor area activated by imagining hand movements. Conceptual representations of living things versus man-made tools in our brain rely on neuronal circuits engaged in processing perceptual and functional information.

Powerful evidence for category-specific deficits comes from Hannah Damasio and her colleagues (1996) at the University of Iowa, who investigated a large population of patients with brain lesions. These patients had to perform a naming task in three conditions: naming famous faces, naming animals, and naming tools. To dissociate conceptual problems from problems at the level of word retrieval, the following procedure was used: If a subject was able to describe many of the features of the picture but was unable to name it, then that was scored as a naming error. For example, when the subject was asked to name the picture of a skunk, the following answer showed that the subject recognized it but could not name it: "Oh, that animal makes a terrible smell if you get too close to it; it is black and white, and gets squashed on the road by cars sometimes." But if they were unspecified in their description of the picture,

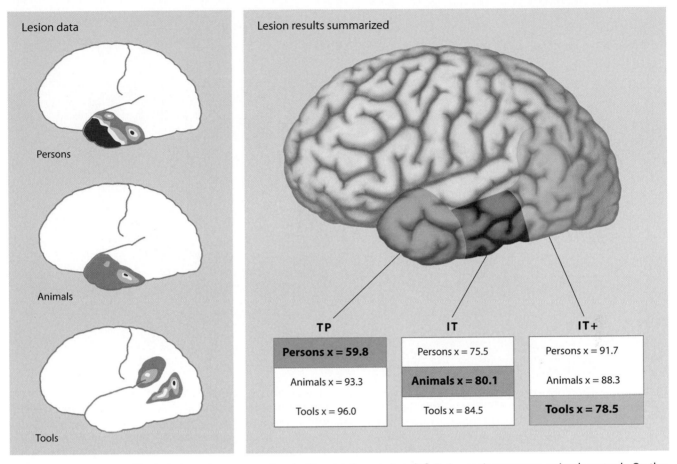

Figure 8.2 Locations of brain lesions that are correlated with selective naming deficits in naming persons, animals, or tools. On the left, the actual averaged lesion data are displayed for patients that had person-naming **(top)**, animal-naming **(middle)**, or tool-naming **(bottom)** deficits. The colors indicate the percentage of patients with a given deficit whose lesion is located in the indicated area. Red indicates that most patients had a lesion in that area, whereas purple indicates that few had a lesion in that area. On the right, the lesion results are summarized. The blue area corresponds to the temporal pole (TP), the red area to the inferotemporal region (IT), and the green area to the posterior part of the inferotemporal lobe extending to the anterior part of the lateral occipital region (IT+). Scores at the bottom of the right side of the figure indicate the percentage of recognized items that were correctly named. Patients with TP lesions scored lowest on naming persons (59.8%), patients with IT lesions scored lowest on naming animals (80.1%), and patients with IT+ lesions scored lowest on naming tools (78.5%). Adapted from Damasio et al. (1996).

the answer was not included in the naming score (for example, "Some kind of animal; I don't know what... just an animal.").

A naming response was scored correct when it was the same as that of normal subjects. Thirty patients, twenty-nine of whom had a lesion in the left hemisphere, showed impairment on this task. The naming deficit could be very selective: Seven of the patients demonstrated impairment in naming faces; five patients, in naming animals; and seven, in naming tools. The remaining eleven patients had a combination of problems in word retrieval for faces/animals/tools, faces/animals, animals/tools, but never for faces/tools. When the researchers examined where the patients had their brain lesions, they found that they could correlate naming deficits with specific regions (Figure 8.2).

Damasio discovered that brain damage in the left temporal pole (TP) correlated with problems in retrieving the names of persons, the anterior part of the left inferior temporal (IT) lobe correlated with problems in naming animals, and the posterolateral part of the left inferior temporal lobe, along with the lateral temporo-occipito-parietal junction (IT+), correlated with problems in retrieving the names of tools. In a coordinated study with neurologically unimpaired subjects that used PET, these same areas were activated when subjects are engaged in naming persons (TP), animals (IT), and tools (IT+), as illustrated in Figure 8.3.

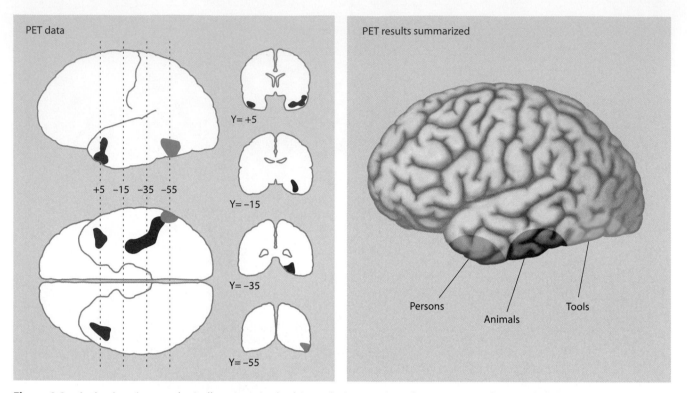

Figure 8.3　Activations in neurologically unimpaired subjects during naming of persons, animals, or tools as determined by positron emission tomography (PET). The left side shows the PET activations in lateral and ventral views, and in four coronal sections at the levels indicated by the dashed lines. The values correspond to millimeters in anterior and posterior directions from a zero point in the brain defined by a stereotactic coordinate system. The right side shows the summarized PET results. Naming persons mostly activated the temporal pole, naming animals mostly activated the middle portion of the inferior temporal gyri, and naming tools mostly activated the posterior portions of the inferior temporal gyrus. Adapted from Damasio et al. (1996).

Damasio and her colleagues concluded that, since they made sure that patients with problems retrieving the names of words could still activate many of the conceptual properties relevant to the word, the correlated brain areas that were lesioned in these patients must play a role in word retrieval. This indicates that the brain has three levels of representation for word knowledge, as illustrated in Figure 8.4. These representational levels were predicted by cognitive models for word production.

The top level in Figure 8.4 represents the conceptual level, a preverbal level that contains the semantic information about words (beak, feathers, wings). At the lexical level the word form that matches the concept is represented (bird). Finally, at the phonological level the sound information that corresponds to the word is represented. Damasio and her colleagues proposed that the brain's conceptual network brings into play several neuronal structures in the left and the right hemisphere. These conceptual networks are connected to the lexical networks in the left temporal lobe, and, as with the temporal lobe areas, might contain specialized information for persons, animals, or tools. These areas in turn acti-

vate the phonological network that touches off the sound patterns needed to pronounce the word.

The Linguistic Input

Any model of normal language comprehension has to deal with the problem of how words are represented. The next step is to identify what leads to understanding the linguistic input; Figure 8.5 represents the components in language comprehension.

PERCEPTUAL ANALYSES

The first task that faces a listener or reader is to identify individual words in a spoken utterance or in a text. One has to perceptually analyze input, which is a prelexical process that does not involve the mental lexicon. Perceptual analyses required for spoken and written input are, not surprisingly, quite different.

A main difference between the visual and auditory modalities essential to comprehension is how much they are segmented. In written language, physical boundaries divide words and sentences; these boundaries are mostly absent in speech. As you read this text,

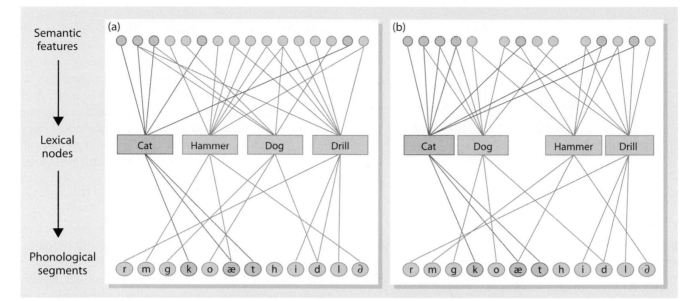

Figure 8.4 Three levels of representation that are needed in speech production: semantic features, lexical nodes, and phonological segments. **(a)** The semantic features of the word *cat* (four legs, furry) activate the lexical node of the word *cat*, which in turn activates the phonological segments of that word. **(b)** A model that fits the data of Damasio and colleagues shown in Figures 8.2 and 8.3. The information at the lexical level is organized according to specific semantic categories (e.g., animals versus tools). Adapted from Caramazza (1996).

you see each word separated by a blank space, and each sentence ended by a period. These physical cues help you to discriminate between words and sentences. By contrast, the word boundaries of speech are murky, as illustrated in Figure 8.6, where the speech waveform of the word *captain* looks as though the signal represents two words because of a "silence" within the word.

Figure 8.5 Schematic representation of the components that are involved in spoken and written language comprehension. Inputs can enter via either auditory (speech) or visual (written) modalities.

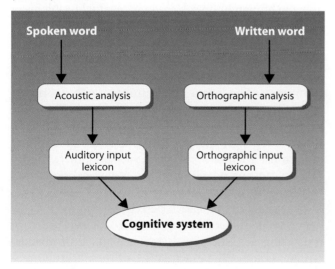

Figure 8.6 Speech waveform for the word *captain*. Note the silence within the word. Time progresses from left to right, and amplitude is registered in the vertical dimension. Courtesy of Tamara Swaab.

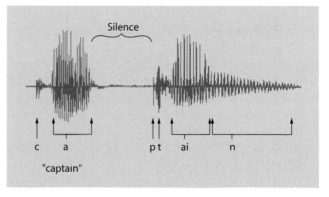

In addition to silences within words, spoken sentences usually lack a clear silence between words because they become coarticulated. Their ends and beginnings are united, as in "I dunno" instead of "I don't know." As shown in Figure 8.7, no clear boundaries fall between the words "do you mean" when they are uttered at normal conversational speed (i.e., connected speech).

Spoken input fortunately has other clues as to how to divide the speech stream into meaningful segments, namely, through prosodic information, which is what the listener derives from the speech rhythm and the

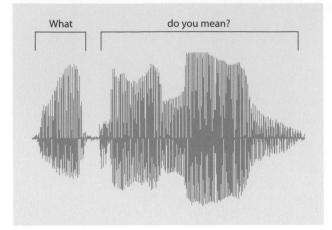

Figure 8.7 Speech waveform for the sentence "What do you mean." Note that the words *do you mean* are not physically separated. Even though the physical signal provides little cues to where the spoken words begin and end, the language system is able to parse them into the individual words for comprehension. Courtesy of Tamara Swaab.

pitch of the speaker's voice. The speech rhythm is introduced by varying the duration of words and by placing pauses between words. Prosody is apparent in all spoken utterances but is clearly illustrated when a speaker asks a question or emphasizes something: When asking a question, the voice of a speaker will rise toward the end of a sentence, and when emphasizing a part of speech, a speaker does this by raising his or her voice and including a pause after the critical part of the sentence. Other cues that segment the continuous speech stream can be derived from the speech signal itself. Psycholinguistic research on English listeners revealed that syllables help to establish word boundaries. For example, a word like *lettuce* is usually heard as a single word and not as two words ("let us"). In contrast, words such as *invests* are usually heard as two words ("in vests") and not as one word (although we know it is).

Prosodic cues are absent when one reads a text, which sometimes can present problems when reading something for the first time. For example, read this: "Because the boy left the room seemed empty." This sentence can be understood properly only if "mental prosody" is added to it by inserting a comma after the word *left*.

Written Input   For written input, readers must recognize a visual pattern. To do so, they have to analyze primitive features, or the shape of the letters: horizontal lines, vertical lines, closed curves, open curves, intersections, and others. A model for letter recognition, the pandemonium model proposed by O.G. Selfridge in 1959, is displayed in Figure 8.8.

In this model, the sensory input ("R") is temporarily stored as an iconic memory by the so-called image demon. The term "demon" was used to refer to a discrete stage or substage of information processing by Selfridge. Then twenty-eight feature demons sensitive to features like curves, horizontal lines, and so forth start to decode features in the iconic representation of the sensory input. Figure 8.8 indicates as black dots where all the feature demons are located. In the next step, all the representations of letters with these features are activated by cognitive demons. Finally, the representation that best matches the input is selected by the decision demon.

As we know from earlier chapters, the brain is well equipped for pattern recognition, so let us fill in lower-order demons in the pandemonium model with physiological models. Single-cell recording techniques, for example, have enlightened us about some of the basics of visual feature analysis. We know how edges, curves, and so on are analyzed by the brain. But unresolved questions remain because letter and word recognition are not really understood at the cellular level. Recordings in monkeys are not likely to enlighten us about letter and word recognition in humans. However, PET studies by Petersen and colleagues (1990) revealed areas in the human extrastriate visual cortex that "light up" when the cortex processes visual word forms; there appears to be a highly specialized brain module for recognition and processing of the visual word forms in our native languages. The so-called word form area is located in the early stages of processing visual information and is lateralized to the language-dominant left hemisphere (Figure 8.9). Lesions of this area can give rise to "pure alexia" in which patients cannot read words even though other aspects of language are normal. This convergent neurological and neuroimaging evidence gives clues to how the human brain solves the perceptual problems of letter and word recognition.

Spoken Input   Unlike written text, speech carries very different perceptual information, being auditory and continuous. The listener is confronted with enormous variability in input: the rate of speech, the dialect of the speaker, and the sex of the speaker, to name a few. In spoken language, the perceptual analysis of auditory input must account for all these variables; there cannot be a one-to-one relation between a physical signal and representations in memory.

Most theories of speech perception assume that the first step in understanding spoken language calls for translating acoustic signals into a pattern of abstract representations. The exact nature of these featural representations is not clear. Some researchers assume that

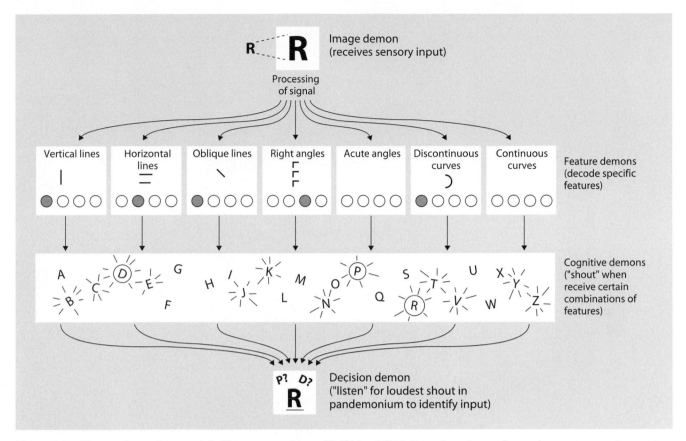

Figure 8.8 The pandemonium model of letter recognition of Selfridge (1959). For written input, the reader must recognize a pattern that starts with the analysis of the sensory input. The sensory input is temporarily stored in iconic memory by the *image demon,* and a set of 28 *feature demons* decode the iconic representations. The *cognitive demons* are activated by the representations of letters with these features, and the representation that best matches the input is then selected by the *decision demon.* Adapted from Coren et al. (1994).

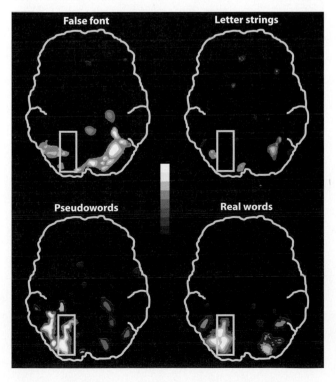

Figure 8.9 Activations of the human extrastriate visual cortex (the "word-form area") during processing of visual word-forms as determined by PET. Adapted from Petersen et al., 1990.

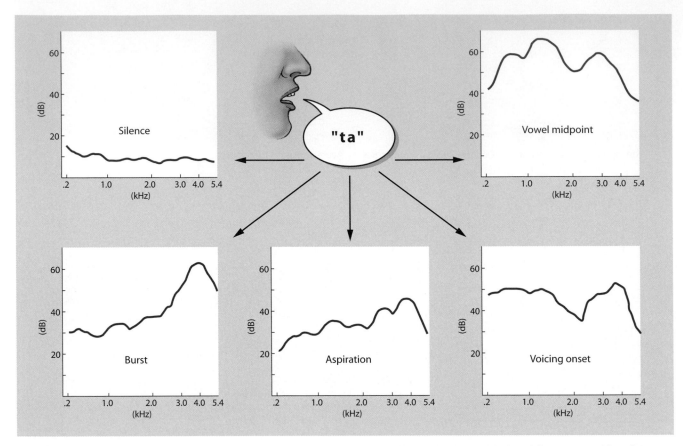

Figure 8.10 Spectral properties vary according to sounds. The sound *ta* can be analyzed to yield five different critical-band spectra. Each critical band has a particular frequency content. For example, the "burst" portions of the sound have a lot of higher-frequency content, with power in the 4- to 5-kHz range. Adapted from Klatt (1989).

the representations are built on spectral properties of the incoming signal. These spectral properties vary according to different sounds, as shown in Figure 8.10. The features derived from spectral analysis form a phonetic representation, and this may be the access code to phonological representations. As with the coding of written words shown in Figure 8.9, PET has been used to analyze processing of single spoken words. The left temporoparietal cortex and anterior superior temporal regions were activated for real words presented auditorily (Figure 8.11). Lesions of the nearby angular and supramarginal gyri lead to a deficit in phonological processing, and thus the activation in the temporoparietal area demonstrated by PET may well represent where phonological coding takes place in spoken language processing.

The Processing of Words

Word or lexical processing is a well-investigated phenomenon in psycholinguistics. Most agree on its components: lexical access, lexical selection, lexical integration. The output of perceptual analysis is probably projected on to word form representations in the mental lexicon. Labeled *lexical access*, this results when representations are activated and spread to semantic and syntactic attributes of the word forms.

Lexical access clearly differs for visual and auditory modalities. As noted earlier, the continuity of the speech signal in spoken input is different from the clear boundaries in written input. A listener is challenged to seg-

Figure 8.11 Activations in neurologically normal subjects for auditorily presented real words as determined by PET. Adapted from Petersen and Fiez (1993).

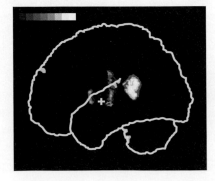

ment speech and to control the speed of its input. When we read a text in a book, we can go back and re-read it. But when we are trying to understand what someone is saying, we can lose track of the conversational flow. Spoken language, then, has a temporal dimension that should be factored into any model of spoken language comprehension.

An influential model in this respect is the cohort model of British psychologist William Marslen-Wilson (Marslen-Wilson and Tyler, 1980). This model assumes that processing in speech starts with the very first sound or phoneme that the listener has identified as the onset of a word. It is clear that initially, when not all the perceptual information is yet available, more than one representation will be activated because more than one representation will fit the first part of the output of the perceptual system. This means that of the activated word form representations, the one that best matches the sensory input has to be selected—a process labeled *lexical selection.* Here is an example of how lexical selection plays a role in understanding words: The word initial sound "ca" of the word *captain* fits *captain,* but also fits words like *cap, capital, capitalist, caption,* and *capitol.* When we hear "ca," all the word forms that match this sound will become activated in what is called a *word initial cohort.* When more perceptual information becomes available, the number of activated representations narrows to the element that best matches the input, resulting in selection of the word *captain,* and deactivation of the other nonmatching word forms. In this model, selecting the appropriate word form depends on the incoming sensory information and the number of competitors in the word initial cohort. A word is selected at its uniqueness point, the time when a word is uniquely distinguishable from all its competitors.

Usually words are not processed in isolation but in the context of other words (sentences, stories, etc.). To understand words in their context we have to integrate syntactic and semantic properties of the recognized word into a representation of the whole utterance.

THE ROLE OF CONTEXT IN WORD RECOGNITION

One question that puzzles psycholinguistic researchers is at what point during language comprehension does linguistic context influence word processing. More specifically, does context influence word processing before or after lexical access and selection are complete?

Two types of representations play a role in word processing in the context of other words: lower-level representations, constructed from sensory input, and higher-level representations, constructed from the context preceding the word to be processed. Contextual representations are crucial to determine in what sense or what grammatical form a word should be used. But without sensory analyses, no message representation would result in the first place. The information has to interact sometime. When this occurs depends on the models used.

Models of Word Recognition   In general, three types of models explain word comprehension. *Modular models* (also called autonomous models) claim that normal language comprehension is executed within separate and independent modules. Thus, higher-level representations cannot influence lower-level ones, and therefore the flow is strictly data driven or "bottom up." In modular models the representation of the context information cannot affect lexical access and lexical selection processes.

In contrast, *interactive models* maintain that all types of information can participate in word recognition. In these models, context can have its influence even before the sensory information is available, by changing the activational status of the word form representations in the mental lexicon.

Between these two extreme views is the notion that lexical access is autonomous and not influenced by higher-level information but that lexical selection can be influenced by sensory and higher-level context information. In these *hybrid models* information about word forms that are possible given the preceding context is provided, thereby reducing the number of activated candidates. We do not yet know which type of model fits word comprehension the best, but there is growing evidence that at least lexical selection is influenced by higher-level context information.

INTEGRATION OF WORDS IN SENTENCES

So far, we have examined processes dedicated to recognizing a word in the linguistic input. But normal language comprehension requires more than just recognizing individual words. To understand the message conveyed by a speaker or a writer, we have to integrate the syntactic and semantic properties of the recognized word into a representation of the whole sentence or utterance. For example, consider the following sentence. "The tall man planted a tree on the bank." Why do we read *bank* to mean "side of the river" instead of "place to put money"? We do so because the rest of the sentence has created a context that is compatible with one meaning and not the other. Let us consider another example. "The pianist rose to the applause of the audience." Once again, there is more than one way to interpret the sentence, and via integration processes, we interpret *rose* as a verb ("to stand") and not a noun ("a flower"). This integration process has to be executed in real time—as soon as we are confronted with the linguistic input. So if we come upon a word like *bank* in a sentence, we are usually not aware that this word has an alternative meaning because the appropriate meaning of this word has been rapidly integrated into the context.

Understanding a word with respect to the higher-order representation of sentence meaning involves semantic and syntactic integration processes. Higher-order semantic processing is important to determine the right sense or meaning of words in the context of a sentence, as with ambiguous words such as *bank,* which have the same form but more than one meaning. Semantic analysis is also needed for making sense of non-ambiguous words such as *piano,* whose meanings can be emphasized in different contexts (as in "the piano is a heavy instrument" versus "the piano is a beautiful instrument").

For a full interpretation of linguistic input, though, we also have to assign a grammatical structure to the input. Semantic information in words alone is not enough to understand the message, as is clear from the following sentence. "The little old lady bites the gigantic dog." Syntactic analysis of this sentence reveals its structure: Who was the actor, what was the theme, and what was the subject? The syntax of the sentence demands that we imagine an implausible situation where an old lady is biting and not being bitten.

Syntactic analysis goes on even in the absence of real meaning. Experimental subjects are faster at detecting a target word in a sentence when it does not make any sense but is grammatically intact, than when the grammar is locally disrupted. Typically, subjects listen to sentences in different conditions, and are asked to press a button as soon as they hear a target word such as *kitchen.* In a baseline condition, they would be presented with normal sentences. A normal sentence might be, "The maid was carefully peeling the potatoes in the garden because during the summer the very hot kitchen is unbearable to work in." In this baseline condition, subjects will take about 300 msec to press a button (from the onset of the target word *kitchen*). These reaction times can be compared to sentences that are semantically absurd but grammatically normal, such as, "An orange dream was loudly watching the house during smelly nights because within these signs a very slow kitchen snored with crashing leaves." Here the subjects' response to the target word would be slowed by about 60 msec. Yet when the syntax of the sentence is also disrupted, the response times would be even slower (by another 45 msec). For example, "An orange dream was loudly watching the house during smelly nights because within these signs a slow very kitchen snored with crashing leaves" is a sentence where the word order of

the phrase *a slow very kitchen* is grammatically incorrect. These types of findings inform us that syntactic analysis proceeds, even when sentences are meaningless.

Syntactic processing is crucial to language understanding, which becomes strikingly clear when we confront deficits in the ability to process syntactic information. These deficits are apparent in so-called agrammatic aphasic patients, who generally produce two- or three-word sentences that consist exclusively of content words and hardly any function words (the ones that we use to mark a phrase such as *and then*), or grammatical or morphological markers and inflections (such as *was pushing*). An example of such an impoverished sentence would be: "Son... university" instead of "My son is at the university."

In language comprehension, agrammatic aphasic patients often have great difficulties understanding complex syntactic structures. So when they hear the sentence, "The gigantic dog was bitten by the little old lady," they would most likely understand this sentence to mean that the little old lady was bitten by the gigantic dog. This problem in assigning syntactic structures to sentences has traditionally been associated with lesions that include Broca's area of the left hemisphere, a region we will describe later, but a lot of variability has been found.

A very influential theory on how syntactic analysis takes place is the garden-path model, proposed by Lynn Frazier (1987) and others. The essence of the model is that sentences have a preferred interpretation. This could lead to garden-path effects, which means being led to believe something that seems correct at first but is not. To understand this model, we must introduce the idea of sentence structure.

A sentence consists of a linear arrangement of phrases and words, which can be represented by a hierarchical tree that reflects the sentence's structure. An example of a hierarchical tree for the sentence "The spy saw the cop with binoculars" is presented in Figure 8.12, where the sentence consists of two large phrases, a noun phrase and a verb phrase. The noun phrase has an article (*the*) and a noun (*spy*). The verb phrase is divided into the main verb (*saw*), a noun phrase (*the cop*), which has an article (*the*) and a noun (*cop*), and a prepositional phrase (*with binoculars*), which has a preposition (*with*) and a noun (*binoculars*). Mental representations of the tree's components are labeled *syntactic nodes.*

The formation of constituent structures plays a central role in the garden-path model. According to this model, syntactic analysis or parsing is initially based on structural information only; it is not influenced by other linguistic processes. Hence, syntactic processing is autonomous. Other interactive models assume that se-

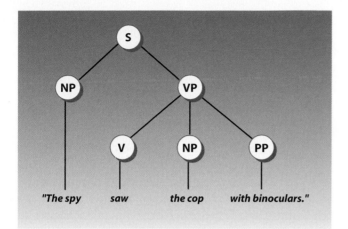

Figure 8.12 Constituent structure of a sentence. As explained in the text, this structure is based on the principles of *minimal attachment*.

mantic information can immediately interact with syntactic information in sentence comprehension.

The garden-path model assumes that we process syntactic information in a way that minimizes what we have to do to meet the demanding time pressure of normal comprehension. Two mechanisms that would help this economy principle are postulated: *minimal attachment* and *late closure*. The minimal attachment mechanism makes sure that syntactic analysis is done in such a way that the minimum number of additional syntactic nodes must be computed. The late closure mechanism tries to assign incoming words to the syntactic phrase or clause currently being processed.

Let us consider the same version of the example sentence represented by the hierarchical tree shown in Figure 8.12. In the example in Figure 8.13, the meaning of the sentence is changed because a different syntactic structure is assigned. This tree leads to the interpretation that the cop rather than the spy was equipped with binoculars. The reason why the interpretation in the tree in Figure 8.12 is preferred over that in Figure 8.13 is because it has fewer and less complex nodes. The minimal attachment and late closure principles were proposed for reasons of economy. Since the language processor must work under an enormous time pressure, the less time required for syntactic analysis, the better. Sometimes the minimal attachment principle leads to mistakes, as for example in "Albert loves Holland and his mother enjoyed her trip to Amsterdam." This is a garden-path sentence whose preferred interpretation leads to a wrong solution and hence must be reanalyzed.

Speech Production

We have mainly focused on language comprehension, and now we turn our attention to language production.

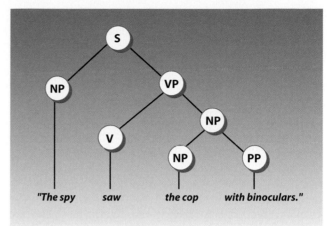

Figure 8.13 Constituent structure of the same sentence as in Figure 8.12. The hierarchical tree in the present figure presents an example of *nonminimal attachment*. See the text for a further explanation.

We will concentrate on one influential model for language production proposed by Willem Levelt (1989) of the Max-Planck Institute for Psycholinguistics in Holland. Figure 8.14 illustrates this model.

A seemingly trivial, but nonetheless important

Figure 8.14 The model of speech production developed by Willem Levelt. In this figure, the processing components in language production are schematically displayed. Adapted from Levelt (1993).

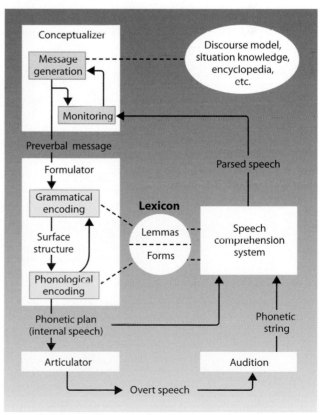

difference between comprehension and production is our starting point. Whereas language comprehension starts with spoken or written input that has to be transformed into a concept, in language production we start with a concept for which we have to find the appropriate words. Yet, input for comprehension does not have to come from an external source. A lot of internal "speech" goes on in our minds, and we have to make sense of our own messages.

The first step in speech production is to prepare the message. Levelt maintains that there are two crucial aspects to message preparation: macroplanning and microplanning. The speaker must determine what she wants to express in her message to the listener. The formulation of the message will be different when we direct someone to our home than when we want someone to close the door. This communicative intention is planned in goals and subgoals expressed in an order that best serves the communicative plan. This aspect of message planning is macroplanning. Microplanning, in contrast, proposes how the information is expressed, which means taking perspective. If we describe a situation where there is a house and a park, we must decide whether to say that "the park is next to the house" or "the house is next to the park." The microplan determines word choice and the grammatical role the words play (e.g., subject, object, theme).

The output of the macroplanning and microplanning is a conceptual message that constitutes the input for the formulator, which puts the message in a grammatically and phonologically correct form. During grammatical encoding, a message's surface structure is computed—its syntactic but not the conceptual representation, including information such as "is subject of," "is object of," the grammatically correct word order, and so on. The lowest-level elements of surface structure are the lemmas. These are stored in the mental lexicon and contain information about a word's syntactic properties (for example, whether the word is a noun or a verb, gender information, and other grammatical features) and its semantic specifications, or the conceptual conditions where it is appropriate to use a certain word. Lemmas in the mental lexicon are organized in a network that links them by meaning, as in Figure 8.15, which is a fragment of a lexical network.

Imagine that a subject is presented with a picture of a sheep, and her task is to name the picture. This is what will happen according to Levelt's model. First, the con-

Figure 8.15 A fragment of a lexical network according to the Levelt model. See the text for a description. Adapted from Levelt (1994).

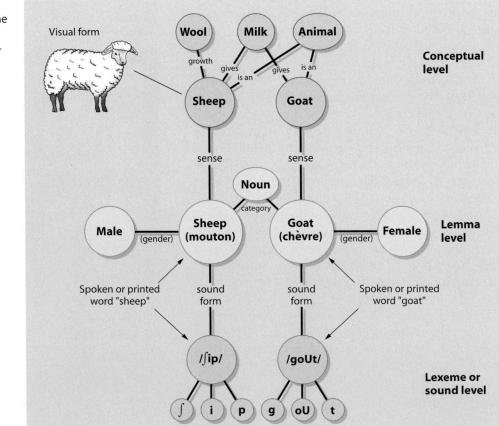

cept that represents sheep is activated, but also concepts related to the meaning of *sheep* are activated: goat, wool, milk. Evidence for the idea that related concepts are activated on seeing the picture of a word like *sheep* comes from the picture-word interference paradigm, where subjects are asked to name pictures as fast and as accurately as they can. Soon after the picture is presented, an interfering auditory word is shown. The naming latency for the word *sheep* will increase if the interfering stimulus is the word *goat,* but not when the interfering stimulus is the word *house.*

Activated concepts in turn activate nodes at the lemma level to access syntactic information. At this point, the lemma appropriate to the presented picture must be retrieved, which is called lexical selection in word production. The selected lemma activates the lexeme, or the sound form of words in the mental lexicon during phonological encoding. Sometimes we cannot activate this sound form: the "tip of the tongue" (TOT) state. You most likely have had a TOT state: You know a lot about the word, you can say it has four legs and white curly hair, you reject other words that do not match the concept *(goat),* and if someone tells you the word's first letter you probably say, "Oh yes, 'sheep.'"

In addition to mental blocking on a word, speech errors might also happen during the transition from the lemma level to the lexeme level. Sometimes we mix up speech sounds or exchange words in a sentence. But if all goes well, the appropriate word form is selected and phonetic and articulatory programs are matched. In the last phase of speech production, we plan our articulation: The word's syllables are mapped onto motor patterns that move the tongue, mouth, and vocal apparatus to generate the word. At this stage, we can repair any errors in our speech, for example, by saying "um" and gaining more time to generate the appropriate term.

Not only do production errors happen in normal speech, but also brain damage can affect each of the processing stages. Some anomic patients (deficit in naming) are afflicted with an extreme TOT state. When asked to name a picture, they can often give you a fairly accurate description but cannot name the word. Their problem is not one of articulation because they can readily repeat the word aloud; these patients' problems are on the lexeme level. Patients with Wernicke's aphasia produce semantic paraphasias; they produce words related in meaning to the intended word. This problem can be one of inappropriate selection of concepts or lemmas or lexemes. Patients with Wernicke's aphasia might also make errors at the phoneme level by incorrectly substituting one sound for another. Finally, Broca's aphasia is often accompanied by *dysarthria,* which hinders articulation and results in effortful speech, because the muscles that articulate the utterance cannot be controlled.

To summarize, language processing involves representing, comprehending, and communicating. During reading and listening, the most important issues are how the meanings of words are stored in the brain and how they are accessed by visual or auditory inputs. Specializations in the brain code language inputs and produce outputs, but the richness of linguistic capacity escapes simple analysis of language's organization. The most significant features are its amazingly rapid time course and vast store. Where is language hiding in the vast uncharted reaches of the human brain? To get some answers, let us examine how language processes are localized within the complex cortical networks that enable language's comprehension and production.

LANGUAGE AND BRAIN

Investigators of brain function have struggled with the concept of localization, as we noted at the beginning of this book. The opportunity for research on brain structure-function relations that arises in brain-damaged or brain-diseased subjects has provided numerous insights to perception, attention, and memory, and the same holds for language. The language system's complexity, however, hampers the elucidation of its structure and neural mechanisms, and so the struggle to clarify the mechanisms of language remains one of the great scientific adventures (Figure 8.16).

We are unable to describe how the detailed psycholinguistically defined functions of the language system map directly onto the brain's complex anatomical structures. However, we do have clues to the language-brain puzzle, many coming from patients with aphasia. We begin, then, by reviewing the contributions of aphasia research to our knowledge of language and the brain. We start with the history of aphasia and brain-language research. After considering classic models, we ponder the view emerging from current studies of aphasia, brain, and language.

Aphasia

Brain injury can lead to language disorders called *aphasia,* which refers to the collective deficits in language comprehension and production that accompany

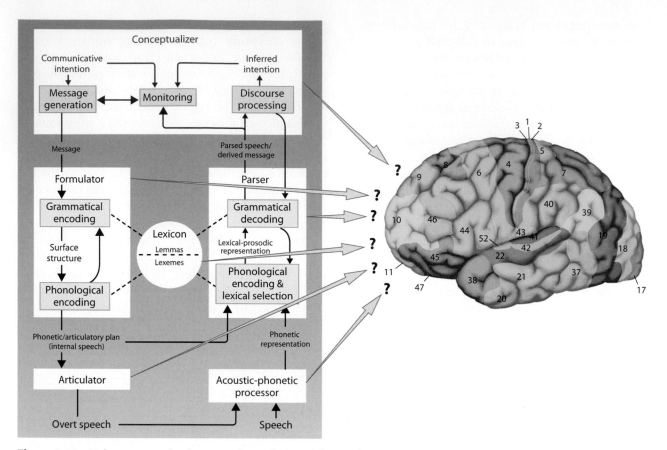

Figure 8.16 Unknown mapping between theoretical models onto brain structures. As of now, there is no clear mapping between the processing components of comprehension and production and their neural substrates in the brain. Research in language and brain is striving to create a comprehensive understanding of the neural bases of human language.

neurological damage. Aphasia is extremely common. Approximately 40% of all strokes produce some aphasia, at least in the acute period during the first few months after the stroke occurred. However, in many patients the aphasic symptoms persist, and they are confronted with lasting problems in understanding or producing spoken and written language. Primary and secondary aphasic impairments are distinct: The former are due to problems with the language-processing mechanisms themselves. Aphasic problems can also result from memory impairments, attention disorders, or perceptual problems, and these are called *secondary aphasias*. Some investigators only classify patients as aphasic when their problems are caused by impairment to the language system.

HISTORICAL FINDINGS IN APHASIA

The most useful way to understand classification schemes of aphasia is to review the history of brain and language with respect to aphasia.

Nineteenth-century phrenologists held that local-

ized brain lesions should lead to specific functional losses. One such phrenologist, the Frenchman Jean-Baptiste Bouillaud, collected evidence from several hundred brain-injured patients who displayed language problems. Based on the side (left or right hemisphere) and position of the damage, he concluded that language resided in the frontal lobe. This line of thinking was dominant during the period when Paul Broca began his observations of language and brain.

Broca treated a patient with a leg infection. The patient was an epileptic who for many years had been unable to utter anything but the nonsense word *tan* ("Tan tan tan, tan tan, tan tan tan...") . The patient died only a few days after being treated for his leg infection. Upon autopsy, Broca observed that the patient had a brain lesion in the posterior portion of the left inferior frontal gyrus. This region, which includes the subdivisions of the inferior frontal gyrus known as the *pars triangularis* and *pars opercularis,* is referred to as *Broca's area* (Figure 8.17). During the autopsy, only a superficial anatomical analysis was performed, and the brain was not sectioned

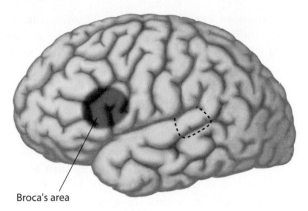

Figure 8.17 Area in the left hemisphere known as Broca's area (in red). The dotted lines indicate the location of Wernicke's area.

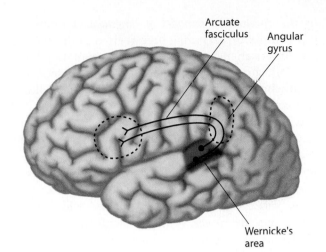

Figure 8.18 Lateral view of Wernicke's area. The arcuate fasciculus is the bundle of axons that connect Wernicke's and Broca's areas. It originates in Wernicke's area, goes through the angular gyrus, and terminates on neurons in Broca's area.

or studied with microanatomical techniques. The patient's brain tissue was, however, tested for signs of softening, a clue to damage. Broca found softening from the frontal lobe, where the lesion was noticeable on visual inspection, to the parietal operculum, which included the most inferior portions of the precentral gyrus and adjoining regions.

After this patient, Broca studied other patients with language deficits associated with brain damage. They generally had right hemiparesis (weakness of the right arm and leg) in conjunction with language disorders. Since these persons were right-handed, he concluded that brain areas that produce speech were localized in the inferior frontal lobe of the left hemisphere. This deduction was based on the fact that damage to the right hemisphere led to the most severe deficits in sensation and motor control for the left side of the body, and vice versa. Thus, if the right side is hemiparetic, the left hemisphere is damaged. If language disorders are present, they must also result from left-hemisphere damage.

A second brain region involved in language was found in posterior areas, as opposed to the frontal region described by Broca. In Germany in the 1870s, another physician, Carl Wernicke, described two patients who had problems understanding spoken language after having a stroke. Unlike the aphasics described by Broca, these patients had fluent speech but spoke nonsensical sounds, words, and sentences. Later, Wernicke performed an autopsy on one patient's brain and discovered damage in the posterior regions of the superior temporal gyrus. Since the auditory area was in the superior temporal region of Heschl's gyrus, Wernicke assumed that this more posterior region participated in the auditory storage for words, that is, as an auditory memory area for words. This area later became known

as *Wernicke's area* (Figure 8.18). According to Wernicke, damage to this area produced poor language comprehension because it had lost word-related memories, whereas nonsense speech resulted from patients' inability to monitor their own output.

Wernicke's discovery was the second key piece of information derived from observing language deficits following brain injury. It constituted the dominant view of brain and language for almost 100 years: Damage to Broca's area of the inferior-lateral left frontal lobe created difficulties in producing speech (expressive aphasia), and damage to the posterior inferior-lateral left parietal and supratemporal areas (including the supramarginal gyrus, angular gyrus, and posterior regions of the superior temporal gyrus) hampered the comprehension of language (receptive aphasia). During Broca's time, most emphasis was on word-level analysis; little consideration was given to processing losses at the sentence level. This was reflected in the prevailing view of language where word memory was the key. Broca's area concentrated on the motor memory for words; Wernicke's area was the region concerned with the sensory memory for words. These ideas led to a view of language in which three brain centers interacted as the foundations of language: a production area, a comprehension area, and a conceptual area.

A Simple Model of Language Organization Wernicke, Broca, and their contemporaries fueled the idea that language was localized in structures interconnected anatomically to create the brain's total language system. Sometimes referred to as the *classic localizationist view* or the *connectionist model of language,* it dominated through the 1970s, having been revived in the 1960s by the American neuropsychologist Norman Geschwind (1967). Figure 8.19 presents a version first described by Lichtheim in 1885. Three main centers for auditory–oral language processing in this model are labeled *A, B,* and *M*. Wernicke's area, *A,* represents the phonological lexicon—the area that stored permanent information about word sounds. Broca's area is labeled *M;* it is the speech planning and programming area. Concepts are marked *B* in Figure 8.19. The nineteenth-century language models had concepts distributed widely in the brain, but the newer Wernicke-Lichtheim-Geschwind model localizes concepts in more discrete areas. As an example, in this model the region containing the supra-marginal gyrus and angular gyrus is the region where incoming sensory properties (auditory, visual, and tactile) or features of words are thought to be processed.

This connectionist model of language represents linguistic information localized to discrete brain regions interconnected by white matter tracts. Language processing activates these linguistic representations and their transfer between language areas. The idea is sim-

Figure 8.19 Lichtheim's classic model of language processing. "A" represents the area that stores permanent information about word sounds. "M" is the speech planning and programming area. Conceptual information is stored in "B". The arrows indicate in which direction the information flows. From this model it was predicted that lesions in the three main area's or in the connections between the areas could account for seven main aphasic syndromes. The locations of possible lesions are indicated by the line segments transecting the connections between A, B, and M. Adapted from Caplan (1994).

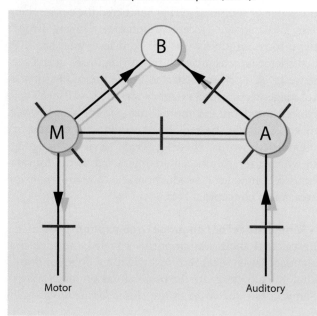

ple. In auditory language the flow of information is as follows. Auditory inputs are transduced in the auditory sensory system that passes the information to the parieto-temporo-occipital association cortex (angular gyrus), and then to Wernicke's area, where representations of words can be accessed from phonological information. From Wernicke's area, information flows through the arcuate fasciculus to Broca's area, where the grammatical properties are stored, and phrase structure can be assigned. Word representations in turn activate related concepts in the concept centers and, voilà, auditory comprehension occurs. In speech production, a similar thing happens when concepts activated in the concept areas generate phonological representations of words in Wernicke's area and are sent to Broca's area to program motor actions for speech articulation.

In Figure 8.19, lines connecting *A, B,* and *M* are transected. These lines represent white matter fibers in the brain that interconnect Wernicke's area, Broca's area, and the conceptual centers; they are sites where lesions might disconnect the areas. Lesions in centers A, B, and M themselves would reflect damage to specific language areas. Thus, if the Wernicke-Lichtheim-Geschwind model were correct, we would expect forms of language deficit from brain damage that had symptoms and signs corresponding to the ones predicted by the model. Indeed, various aphasias correspond to what would be predicted by the model.

Lichtheim observed predicted aphasias in pure form, but it remains unclear how distinct they really are. Some extant data support the basic tenets of the Wernicke-Lichtheim-Geschwind model, yet the model still has significant shortcomings. For one thing, prior to the advent of neuroimaging with computed tomography (CT) and magnetic resonance imaging (MRI), lesion localization was poor and relied on sometimes inaccessible autopsy information, or guesses based on co-occurrence of other more well-defined symptoms (e.g., hemiparesis). Second, there is great variability in how lesions are defined in autopsy as well as neuroimaging data. And third, there is great variability in the lesions themselves; as an example, sometimes anterior lesions produce Wernicke's aphasia! Finally, when classified, patients often fall into more than one diagnostic syndrome category. Broca's aphasia has several components, for instance. It is now worth reviewing major aphasic syndromes and considering interpretational difficulties in the literature on brain and language. The goal is to provide insights to aphasic syndromes and their relation to brain structures in classic models and more recent views. Prior to reviewing the syndromes, though, we should briefly consider how aphasia is diagnosed and classified in the clinic.

CLASSIFICATION OF APHASIA

Speech pathologists and aphasiologists have elaborate criteria for diagnosing and characterizing language disorders such as aphasia. Diagnostic classifications may exclude neuropathologies that may be treatable or require special management, care, and rehabilitation of aphasic patients. The schemes also vary in their ability to distinguish language deficits. This is partly because a brain lesion in one patient rarely, if ever, has the same pattern as that in another patient. Nonetheless, the classification of aphasic patients into subtypes is successful within certain limitations. The three main test parameters for language disorders are spontaneous speech, auditory comprehension, and verbal repetition. The patients' performance permits a trained person to classify aphasics into general groups, as presented in Figure 8.20.

Broca's Aphasia   Broca's aphasia is the oldest and perhaps most well-studied form of aphasia. Characterized by speech difficulties, it includes a wide range of symptoms. In the most severe forms of Broca's aphasia, single utterance patterns of speech such as that of Broca's original patient are often observed. But the variability is large and may include unintelligible mutterings, single syllables or words ("tan," "yes," "no"), short simple phrases or sentences that mostly lack function words or grammatical markers, or idioms such as "fit as a fiddle and ready for love...." Sometimes the ability to sing normally is undisturbed, as might be the ability to recite phrases and prose, or to count.

The speech of Broca's aphasics is often telegraphic and very effortful, coming in bursts. The ability to find the appropriate word or combination of words and to execute pronunciation is compromised in Broca's aphasics. Some problems are derived from speech deficits such as dysarthria (loss of control over articulatory muscles) and speech apraxia (deficits in the ability to program articulations).

The extent to which Broca's aphasia is limited to language production, especially spoken language, depends on the extent of any comprehension deficits that may also be present. These deficits are easiest to observe when the meaning of a sentence requires precise interpretation of its grammatical structure and cannot be derived simply from the sentence's individual words. Consider the following examples: "The boy ate the cookie" and "The boy kicked the girl." The second sentence might be misunderstood except that grammatical rules determine who kicked whom, whereas grammatical rules are not needed for the aphasic to understand that the boy ate the cookie and not vice versa (the cookie ate the boy). The notion that Broca's aphasics have only an

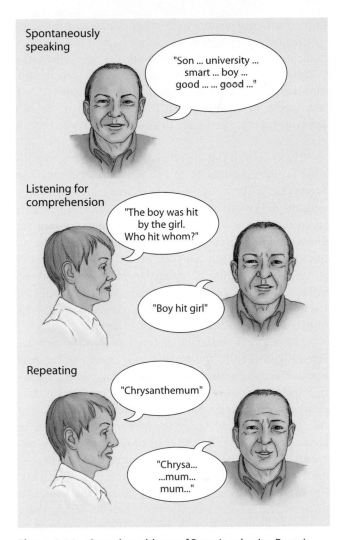

Figure 8.20   Speech problems of Broca's aphasics. Broca's aphasics can have various problems when they speak, or try to comprehend or repeat the linguistic input provided by the clinician (woman at left). The speech output of this patient is slow and effortful, and it lacks function words: It resembles a telegram **(top)**. Broca's aphasics also may have a hard time understanding reversible sentences, where a full understanding of the sentence depends on correct syntactic assignment of the thematic roles (who hit whom?) **(middle).** Finally, these patients will sometimes have problems with speech articulation because of deficits in the regulation of the articulatory apparatus (e.g., muscles of the tongue) **(bottom).**

expressive disorder is not correct; they also have comprehension deficits. Broca's aphasics are not devoid of grammatical knowledge, though; rather, they have deficits in processing grammatical aspects of language, as described by the term *agrammatism.*

Broca's Area   Several components of Broca's aphasia include problems with comprehension. When Broca first described the disorder, he called it *aphemia* and related it to damage in Broca's area (see Figure 8.17). He limited his conclusions to cortical damage in the inferior frontal lobe regions, which he claimed was a participant in language production, but as we described, the symptoms may encompass comprehension deficits too, especially those related to grammar. Unfortunately, we are unable to correlate well the symptoms of Broca's aphasia with the classically defined structures in Broca's area.

Challenges to the idea that Broca's area was responsible for speech deficits in aphasia were laid down in Broca's time. Some reports noted damage to Broca's area without deficits in speech; others noted speech deficits when damage was limited to more posterior brain regions, outside Broca's area. Researchers continue to question the relation between Broca's area and Broca's aphasia. For example, aphasiologist Nina Dronkers (1996) at University of California at Davis reported twenty-two patients with lesions in Broca's area, with only ten having Broca's aphasia.

The regions classically defined as Broca's area are generally limited to the cortical gray matter of the pars opercularis and pars triangularis in the posterior inferior frontal gyrus of the left hemisphere. The involvement of underlying white matter, cortex, and subcortical structures may clarify the role of Broca's area in language disorders. By the turn of the last century, scientists were proposing that structures deep to Broca's area were responsible for the deficits of Broca's aphasia. Brain areas including the insular cortex, the lenticular nucleus of the basal ganglia, and fibers of passage have been implicated in Broca's aphasia. Recent research by Dronkers found that all patients with Broca's aphasia, including those studied by autopsy or neuroimaging, have damaged insulae.

This was the case even for Broca's original patient. His brain is now housed in a French museum, and recent CT scans showed that he had lesions that extended into regions underlying the superficial cortical zone of Broca's area, and thus included the insular cortex and portions of the basal ganglia. Damage to the classic regions of the frontal cortex known as Broca's area is not solely responsible for the deficits of Broca's aphasics.

Wernicke's Aphasia
Wernicke's aphasia, we know, is primarily a disorder of language comprehension. Patients with this syndrome have problems understanding spoken or written language, and sometimes cannot understand at all. They are cut off from communication with others by their comprehension problems, and they cannot speak meaningful sentences. Patients can produce fluent-sounding speech, in contrast to the broken speech patterns of Broca's aphasics, but the speech is meaningless. To provide insight to what it means for a person to be fluent and to have Wernicke's aphasia, imagine you are listening to someone speaking a language you do not know. You would probably not detect any deficits. And as might be expected, the speech of Wernicke's patients sounds fine but is composed of meaningless strings of words, sounds, and jargon. Figure 8.21 shows the speech of two patients with Wernicke's aphasia, one in English and the other in Dutch. Unless you speak Dutch, it is unlikely that you can discriminate this passage from that of normal Dutch prose.

Wernicke's Area
The syndrome known as *Wernicke's aphasia* was first related to Wernicke's area in the classic studies of the last century. Wernicke's area includes the posterior third of the superior temporal gyrus. However, language comprehension deficits also arise from damage to the junction between the parietal and temporal lobes, including the supramarginal and angular gyri. How well do language comprehension deficits relate to Wernicke's area, and how much can be attributed to damage in the surrounding cortex and white matter?

As with Broca's aphasia and Broca's areas, sometimes lesions that spare Wernicke's area lead to comprehension deficits. In one study of seventy patients with

Figure 8.21 Wernicke's aphasics can speak fluently. If one is not a native speaker of a language, one might not detect that there was anything wrong with the speech of a patient with Wernicke's aphasia. For example, to most people in the United States, the message in Dutch in the lower part of the figure might sound perfectly normal (unless you speak Dutch), because it flows smoothly. However, as the English translation at the top indicates, the speech output of Wernicke's aphasics is often meaningless. They will also make semantic errors, for example, television for telephone.

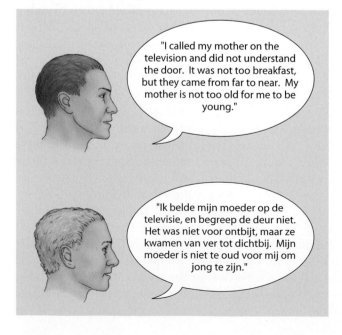

HOW THE BRAIN WORKS

The Man Without Nouns

Damage to Wernicke's area or surrounding cortex can sometimes produce a disorder called *anomia*, the inability to name things in the world. Patients with anomia have difficulty finding the words that label objects. This disorder can sometimes be strikingly discrete; the language deficit is limited to the inability to name objects, but comprehension is intact and speech unaffected. One such patient is H.W., an intelligent businessman who headed his own company. He was studied by cognitive neuroscientist Dr. Kathleen Baynes of the University of California at Davis. After suffering a stroke in his left hemisphere, H.W. was left with anomia and almost no other deficits of note except a slight right-side hemiparesis (actually quite minor; he's a physically robust individual) and a slight deficit in face recognition. But his anomia was extraordinary. Here is a passage of H.W.'s speech as he described the contents of a picture of a boy falling off a stool while reaching for cookies in a jar on the shelf and handing one to his sister:

> First of all this is falling down, just about, and is gonna fall down and they're both getting something to eat... but the trouble is this is gonna let go and they're both gonna fall down... I can't see well enough but I believe that either she will have some food that's not good for you and she's to get some for her, too... and that you get it there because they shouldn't go up there and get it unless you tell them that they could have it. And so this is falling down and for sure there's one they're going to have for food and, and this didn't come out right, the, uh, the stuff that's uh, good for, it's not good for you but it, but you love, um mum mum [H.W. intentionally smacks lips]... and so they've... see that, I can't see whether it's in there or not... I think she's saying, I want two or three, I want one, I think, I think so, and so, so she's gonna get this one for sure it's gonna fall down there or whatever, she's gonna get that one and, and there, he's gonna get one himself or more, it all depends with this when they fall down... and

when it falls down there's no problem, all they got to do is fix it and go right back up and get some more.

H.W. was able to describe aspects of the scene, but without the ability to say nouns, the information was minimal. Nonetheless, H.W. used proper grammatical structures, such a noun phrases; they simply missed a noun. For example, H.W. would say "this" instead of "the chair." He substituted generic nouns such as "food" for "cookie" although he knew it was a cookie, that it tasted good, and that adults consider this food bad for children. The location of his lesion is enlightening and disappointing: He had a large left-hemisphere lesion that included large regions of the posterior language areas. Yet his functional deficit was discrete—he had no nouns.

Picture similar to that shown to H.W. by psychologist Dr. Kathleen Baynes. The patient's description of this scene is provided in the text.

Wernicke's aphasia, about 10% had damage confined to regions outside of Wernicke's area. In contrast, some patients who have Wernicke's aphasia with damage in Wernicke's area may be able to comprehend more as their aphasia improves over time, leaving a milder aphasia or

even only an anomic syndrome (see The Man Without Nouns).

Recent studies support this picture. Dense and persistent Wernicke's aphasia is assured only if there is damage in Wernicke's area and in the cortex of the posterior temporal lobe—or damage to the underlying white matter that connects temporal lobe language areas to other brain areas. Thus, Wernicke's area remains in the center of a posterior region of the brain whose functioning is required for normal comprehension. Lesions confined to Wernicke's area lead to only temporary Wernicke's aphasia because the damage to this area does not actually cause the syndrome; instead, secondary damage due to tissue swelling contributes to the most severe problems. When swelling around the lesioned cortex goes away, comprehension improves. Some researchers such as Dronkers suggest that the white matter underlying Wernicke's area may hold the key. Cortical damage that temporarily compromises white matter tracts below the cortex may explain much of the "here and gone again" characteristics of Wernicke's aphasia. More functional analyses are clearly needed.

DAMAGE TO CONNECTIONS BETWEEN LANGUAGE AREAS

In describing the Wernicke-Lichtheim-Geschwind model, we alluded to strong links between anterior and posterior regions of the brain involved in speech production and comprehension, respectively. In the context of the model, as presented in Figure 8.19, systematic syndromes were implied to result from damage to these white matter tracts. Wernicke predicted that a certain type of aphasia should result from damage to fibers projecting from Wernicke's to Broca's areas. Indeed, a disconnection syndrome, now know as *conduction aphasia*, can occur when the arcuate fasciculus, the pathway from Wernicke's to Broca's area, is damaged. Conduction aphasics have problems producing spontaneous speech as well as repeating speech, and sometimes they use words incorrectly. They can understand words that they hear or see and can hear their own speech errors, but they cannot repair them. Hence, conduction aphasias arise from damage to connections between posterior and anterior language areas. But similar symptoms happen with lesions to the insula and portions of the auditory cortex. One explanation for this similarity may be that damage to other passage fibers is not visualized, or that connections between Wernicke's area and Broca's area are not as strong as connections between the more widely spread anterior and posterior language areas. The emphasis should not be on Broca's or Wernicke's area but on regions better correlated with the syndromes of Broca's and Wernicke's aphasia. Considered in this way, a lesion to the area surrounding the insula could disconnect comprehension from production areas.

The Wernicke-Lichtheim-Geschwind model also predicts that damage to the connections between conceptual representation areas (B of Figure 8.19, perhaps

in the supramarginal and angular gyri) and Wernicke's area harms the ability to comprehend spoken inputs but not the ability to repeat what was heard (transcortical sensory aphasia). Patients with lesions in the supramarginal and angular gyri regions display such problems. Further, they have the unique ability to repeat what they heard and to correct grammatical errors in what they heard when they repeat it. This is strong evidence that this aphasia comes from losing the ability to access semantic information without losing syntactic or phonological abilities.

In major aphasic syndromes and ones associated with damaged brain areas, the picture is not unlike the one in the Wernicke-Lichtheim-Geschwind model, but with notable extensions, mostly concerning the location of language deficits. The anterior regions in and around the classically defined Broca's area, program and execute speech. The posterior superior temporal cortex, Wernicke's area, is involved in comprehending spoken language, but lesions to this area alone do not result in permanent Wernicke's aphasia. Rather, as with Broca's area, Wernicke's aphasia only occurs when damage extends into the white matter or the surrounding temporal cortex. Areas at the junction of the parietal and occipital and temporal lobes, in the supramarginal and angular gyri, are needed for processing conceptual information, but do not store information about grammar. With these modifications to our definitions of the anterior production area and the posterior comprehension areas, a more complete model of language organization in the human brain is being achieved. Yet these models alone are merely elaborations on 100 years of neurology; they do not constitute a cognitive neuroscience model of language. As with Hannah Damasio's work, areas of the temporal lobe not implicated in aphasia turn out to be central to representing aspects of language (see Figures 8.2 and 8.3).

THE NATURE OF APHASIC DEFICITS

We have reviewed numerous problems associated with major classes of aphasia and noted that these must represent problems in language faculties. But what form does this take? Is the deficit the result of losses of parts of the language system, like selective damage to the second gear in an automobile transmission while the other gears are intact? Or is the problem in aphasia more like losing the ability to use the linguistic information properly, like having a perfectly good set of gears but a burned-out clutch?

These questions represent a pivotal concern in aphasia: Do comprehension deficits in aphasic patients result from losses of stored linguistic information, or from disruption of computational language processes that act

Does the Right Hemisphere Understand Language?

Although the left hemisphere is dominant for language processing, this does not mean that the right hemisphere is completely without language function or is unable to understand language. One bit of evidence that the right hemisphere has some ability to understand language comes from patients with surgically isolated hemispheres. These split-brain patients have had a resection of the fiber tracts that connect the right and the left hemisphere (the corpus callosum), to relieve severe epilepsy. In other words, the right and the left hemisphere can no longer communicate to each other at the cortical level; therefore, when visual information is presented to the left visual hemifield, it goes exclusively to the right hemisphere. This opens the possibility to study the language capabilities of the isolated right hemisphere because there can be no transfer of information from the perceptual areas of the right hemisphere to the language areas in the left.

Split-brain patients with a disconnected right hemisphere can make simple semantic judgments and can read. However, only grammatically simple sentences can be managed well by the isolated right hemisphere; thus, such patients can misunderstand sentences like "The boy that was hit by the girl cried."

Other evidence for the right hemisphere's role in linguistic processing comes from patients with lesions in the right hemisphere. Although these patients are generally nonaphasic, they do have subtle language deficits. Hagoort and his colleagues (1996) found that patients with right-hemisphere lesions have normal priming effects for words that are associatively related (cottage cheese). In contrast, these patients do not show priming effects for words that are not associatively related but from the same semantic category (dog-horse). This could mean that the left hemisphere is not very good at processing distant semantic relations but that the right hemisphere is—an idea supported by experimental research. Chiarello (1991) found a left-visual-

field/right-hemisphere advantage for the processing of words that come from the same semantic category, but that have no associative relation like, for example, *dog-horse*. In short, the right hemisphere does have language abilities that might play an important role in the processing of meaning.

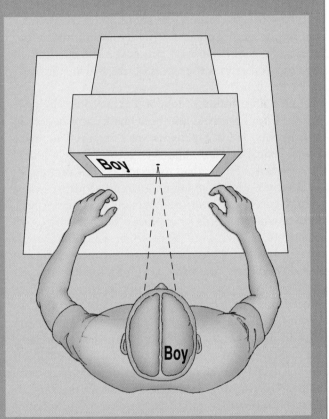

Words presented to the disconnected right hemisphere of a split-brain patient. Stimuli entering the left visual field are transmitted to the right hemisphere. In split-brain patients, the absence of the corpus callosum means that the information *(boy)* does not get to the language-dominant left hemisphere. This permits the language capacity of the right hemisphere to be investigated.

on linguistic inputs? Aphasic deficits have classically been attributed to losses of semantic or syntactic knowledge structures. In recent years, however, many deficits in aphasia are thought of as processing impairments rather than true losses of knowledge. Two results are central to this change in perspective.

Broca's aphasics with severe problems in syntactic understanding were tested in a sentence-picture matching task. They often were unable to point to a picture that matched the meaning of the sentence they had to read, especially when more complex sentence constructions were used. For example, Broca's aphasics might not understand who is kicking whom in the sentence "The boy was kicked by the girl." If they have to choose from two pictures, one picture where a girl is kicking a boy and one where a boy is kicking a girl, they often select the wrong picture. But in one seminal study, Broca's aphasics performed normally when they had to distinguish syntactically well-formed sentences from incorrect ones in a grammar judgment task, even when they had to cope with numerous syntactic structures.

The task that one uses, then, directly influences the aphasic patient's performance; moreover, sometimes Broca's aphasics can also access and exploit structural knowledge. Variable performance across linguistic tasks supports the notion that agrammatic comprehension results from a processing deficit rather than a representational one; patients still have syntactic knowledge but sometimes they cannot use it while at other times they can.

The classic notion of loss of semantic knowledge in Wernicke's aphasics has also been challenged. In certain experiments, aphasic patients were required to make speedy lexical decisions about target words. In a lexical decision task, aphasics had to decide as quickly as possible whether a letter string or a sound sequence was a word. Neurologically normal persons made faster lexical decisions on words primed by a semantically or associatively related word than when preceding words were unrelated. Wernicke's aphasics consistently displayed the normal pattern of priming for semantically or associatively related word pairs in this task. They showed this effect even though they demonstrated severe impairment when asked to make judgments on word meaning. Thus, despite problems in comprehension, when lexical-semantic processing is tested in an implicit test (such as in the lexical decision task), patients do not show impairment. This means that lexical-semantic knowledge might be preserved but aphasics sometimes cannot access or exploit it to achieve normal comprehension.

In general, these intertask variations demonstrate that not all aphasic comprehension deficits are due to losses of stored linguistic information. Instead, in patients that show this variability in performance, it is more likely that their deficit is related to an impairment in real-time processes that act on linguistic information. These patients' brains cannot keep up with the time pressure of language comprehension or production because accessing and exploiting stored linguistic information no longer operates at normal speeds.

One central question about the processing impairment model of comprehension deficits in aphasics is, when is the impairment manifested during language processing? Two suggestions have been put forward: One is that the dynamics of lexical access are affected in aphasic comprehenders (usually referred to as Broca's aphasics); an alternative proposal is that automatic lexical access might be largely intact but problems arise later, during lexical integration.

The claim for impaired lexical access has been derived, for example, from word priming experiments. Some studies found that Broca's aphasics lack semantic priming in lexical decision tasks, even though normal control subjects and Wernicke's aphasics do show faster reaction times to words related to the prime. Yet support for this claim is not decisive, for two reasons. First, in other semantic priming studies, Broca's aphasics actually do demonstrate an effect of semantic priming. Second, to make claims about automatic access, the time between prime onset and target onset (stimulus-onset asynchrony, or SOA) should be short (approximately 200 msec). This is because in normal subjects, semantic priming at long SOAs does not result only from automatic lexical activation but may also include other postlexical processes. In line with this, studies using long SOAs between prime and target words in aphasics failed to find priming, whereas those using shorter SOAs did reveal semantic priming.

What emerges is more compatible with the idea that in these patients lexical integration rather than lexical access is impaired. The idea is that the patients have difficulty integrating the meaning of words into the current context established by the preceding word in the sentence; that is, they cannot use the context information to select the appropriate meaning of a word quickly enough for normal comprehension. Thus, in the sentence "The man planted a tree on the bank," under normal conditions the context tells us that *bank* refers to the side of a river and not a monetary institution. One can readily appreciate the comprehension problems that would ensue if such processes were disrupted as with aphasia (see Aphasia and Electrophysiology, p. 318).

NEUROPHYSIOLOGY OF LANGUAGE

The neuropsychological lesion approach epitomized by research on aphasia and language disorders represents only one way to investigate the biological bases of language. In this section, we briefly review evidence from functional neuroimaging by PET, stimulation of the human cortex during neurosurgical procedures, and recordings of language-related brain potentials (event-related potentials, or ERPs) from healthy and aphasic persons. These approaches yield information about the normal language system that may not be obvious from observations of the performance of damaged brains alone. Further, the neurophysiological approach can provide measures of brain activity and functional processing in persons with language disorders, that are not possible to infer from behavior or anatomical imaging.

Functional Neuroimaging of Language

PET can be applied to study language organization in two main ways. First, it can be used passively to investigate the metabolic correlates of language disorders such as Broca's aphasia during rest. The goal is to investigate which areas of the brain might have a lower metabolism after a stroke. The ^{18}F-deoxyglucose method measures neuronal metabolism by using radioactively labeled glucose analogues that are taken up by active cells and trapped within them. The radioactivity can then be imaged. Its advantage is that one can learn about the effects of lesions that extend beyond the obviously damaged region. Anatomical imaging with CT or MRI cannot detect many forms of functional lesions (i.e., regions of lowered metabolism or hypometabolism). First we consider the metabolic correlates of aphasia, and then return to blood flow activation studies in healthy volunteers.

METABOLIC CORRELATES OF APHASIA

Research on resting brain metabolism has revealed a complex picture of the effects of aphasia. Focal brain lesions from stroke can lead to widespread changes in metabolism; that is, the effects of stroke extend to brain regions outside the lesioned areas (Figure 8.22). Remote metabolic changes are typically observed in stroke victims who have observable symptoms, but not when the patient has no neurological symptoms.

In aphasic patients, resting PET measures revealed hypometabolism (lower glucose utilization) in the temporoparietal region in 100% of the patients, regardless of the type of aphasia. Of these, 97% had metabolic changes in the angular gyrus and 89% in the supramarginal gyrus; 87% showed hypometabolism in the superior temporal gyrus. These PET-defined hypometabolic regions were then compared to the anatomically defined lesions. Such comparisons showed that 67% of patients had parietal lesions, 67% had damage in Wernicke's area, and 58% had damage in the posterior middle temporal region. Even when the anatomically defined damage did not include the supramarginal and angular gyri, these brain areas had reduced resting neuronal metabolism. The lesson here is that correlating the behavioral

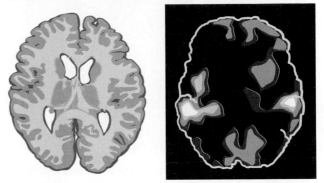

(a) Real tissue   (b) 18-FDG PET

Figure 8.22 PET scan showing regions of lowered metabolism in the brain of a stroke patient. The regions showing decreased metabolic activity include those that were damaged by the stroke and have cell loss, and the regions connected to the damaged areas experience changes in activity and hence possible function, but are not themselves damaged by the stroke. These areas can be thought of as functionally lesioned, and may contribute to deficits seen in the patients, thereby making it difficult to infer a structure-function correlation from computed tomography or magnetic resonance imaging that only reveal the areas of physical damage.

deficits in aphasia with only the visible anatomical lesions may not provide a complete picture, and may even lead to confusion.

Some researchers maintain that correlations between aphasic symptoms and metabolism as defined by PET are better than those with anatomical lesion data. Broca's aphasics, with anatomical damage to Broca's area and perhaps surrounding tissue, have marked hypometabolism in the prefrontal cortex. This effect is reduced in Wernicke's aphasia and even further diminished in conduction aphasia—but half of these patients display hypometabolism in Broca's areas.

Anatomically defined correlates of aphasia, therefore, may not capture the physiological brain changes that accompany the aphasic syndrome. These findings remind us of how limited the anatomical correlation method is in determining the brain's language functions. One certainty is the need for data from multiple methods in trying to pin down the organization of language.

ACTIVATION OF BROCA'S AREA AS MEASURED BY PET

During speech production, areas in and around Broca's area are activated. In addition to Broca's area, speech production also activates the motor cortex area representing the mouth and lips, and the supplementary motor area, which supports the idea that Broca's area is active in at least the motoric aspects of speech production (Figure 8.23).

Broca's area is activated by other language-related

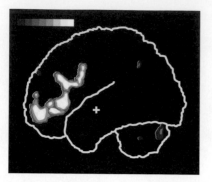

Figure 8.23 PET activations in and around Broca's area during speech production. Adapted from Petersen and Fiez (1993).

tasks such as making decisions about whether two non-sense syllables end in the same consonant, listening to words or stories in a native versus an unknown language, and understanding syntactically complex sentences. This indicates a role for Broca's area in grammatical processes, as had been proposed for aphasic patients.

This evidence for a role of the classically defined Broca's area in grammatical processing is not unequivocal. In particular, a role for Broca's area in working memory may be a better explanation for the activation of Broca's area during these tasks. One idea is that Broca's area may participate in the phonological loop (Chapter 7) in which linguistic information is held in a short-term buffer as part of the working memory sys-

tem. Such a role fits well with the articulatory role proposed for Broca's area. Hence, a plausible role for Broca's area need not be grammatical processing.

If Broca's area is not involved in grammatical processing, we should expect to find another brain area activated during such tasks—and there is one. A candidate for grammatical processing has been identified by PET as being in the anterior portions of the superior temporal gyrus, in the vicinity of area 22 (Figure 8.24a). Dronkers also implicated this area in aphasics' grammatical processing deficits (Figure 8.24b). So we have yet another new candidate brain region associated with language processing, especially grammatical processing, not included in the classic models: the anterior superior temporal lobe (see Figure 8.19).

ACTIVATION OF WERNICKE'S AREA AS MEASURED BY PET

Attempts to activate the posterior language areas with PET have been surprisingly difficult in normal subjects. Several investigators found activations of the posterior superior temporal gyrus during tasks that require the discrimination of words while listening to speech, which means that posterior regions of the superior temporal gyrus may participate in perceptual analyses of auditory speech. When the task required more complex grammatical or semantic analysis, as with comprehension, PET revealed activations generally in the posterior temporal lobe outside the superior temporal area or in the anterior portion of the superior temporal gyrus. Though lesions to the temporoparietal area are associ-

(a)

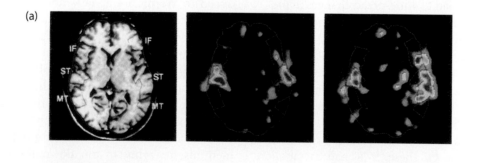

(b)

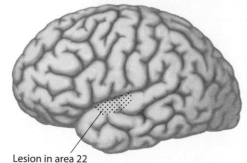

Lesion in area 22

Figure 8.24 **(a)** PET activations in the anterior portion of the superior temporal gyrus related to grammatical processing. Adapted from Mazoyer et al. (1993). **(b)** Summary of lesions in the anterior superior temporal cortex that lead to deficits in grammatical processing.

ated with aphasic symptoms, PET activations in normal subjects provide scant evidence for the participation of these areas in language. This striking dichotomy between the PET and aphasia findings has perplexed language researchers.

In summary, PET studies paint a slightly different picture of the brain's role in language processing from the one we have based on neurological lesion methods alone. The evidence from functional neuroimaging in normal subjects points to new areas that should be investigated for their role in human language. This work is underway, as evidenced by the PET studies mentioned earlier in this chapter. As neuroimaging progresses, we will be able to outline the functional architecture of human language with increasing accuracy.

Electrophysiology of Language

In previous chapters we reviewed the ERP method and described how ERPs are obtained for different stimuli and mental processes. ERPs also can be used to investigate human language. For many reasons, they provide a powerful tool to study language comprehension. To appreciate this, let us look at two brain waves or *ERP components* that index aspects of semantic and syntactic processing during language comprehension.

SEMANTIC PROCESSING AND THE N400 WAVE

The N400 is a brain wave related to linguistic processes. It was named *N400* because it is a negative polarity volt-

age peak in brain waves for words that usually reach maximum amplitude around 400 msec after onset of the word stimulus. This brain wave is especially sensitive to semantic aspects of linguistic input.

Marta Kutas and Steven Hillyard (1980) discovered the N400 wave. They compared the processing of the last word of sentences in three conditions: normal sentences that ended with a word congruent with the preceding context, like "It was his first day at work"; sentences that ended with a word anomalous to the preceding context, like "He spread the warm bread with socks"; and sentences that ended with a word semantically congruent with the preceding context but physically deviant, like "She put on her high-heeled SHOES." The sentences were presented on a computer screen, one word at a time. The subjects were to read the sentences attentively, knowing that questions about the sentences would be asked at the end of the experiment. The electroencephalograms (EEGs) were averaged for the sentences in each condition, and the ERPs were extracted by averaging data for the last word of the sentences separately for each sentence type.

The amplitude of the N400 to the anomalous words ending the sentence was increased when compared to that of the N400 to congruent words (Figure 8.25). This difference in the amplitude of the N400 is called the *N400 effect.* In contrast, words that were semantically congruent with the sentence but were merely physically deviant (larger letters, etc.) elicited a positive potential rather than an N400. Subsequent experiments showed

Figure 8.25 Event related potential (ERP) waveforms differentiate between congruent words *(work)* at the end of sentences and anomalous last words that do not fit the semantic specifications of the preceding context *(socks).* The anomalous words elicit a large negative deflection in the ERP called the N400. Words that fit into the context but are printed with a larger font *(shoes)* elicit a positive wave (P560) and not the N400, indicating that the N400 is not generated only by surprises at the end of the sentence. Adapted from Kutas and Hillyard (1980).

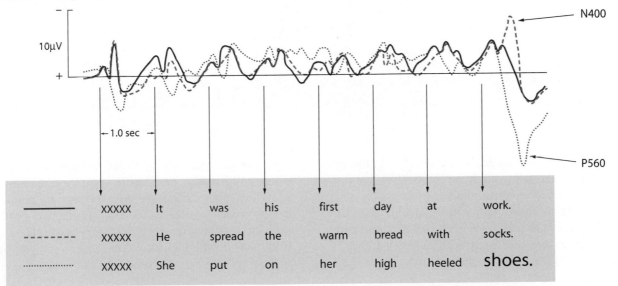

Stimulation Mapping of the Human Brain

The scene is out of a Walt Disney or Steven Spielberg film. A young man lies on a table covered with clean light-green sheets. He is lying on his side and is awake. His head is partially covered by a sheet of cloth, so we can see his face if we wish. On the other side of the cloth is a woman wearing a surgical gown and mask. The man is a patient; the woman is his surgeon. His skull has been cut through and his left hemisphere is exposed. Yes, he is awake; no, this is not another time or another place. This is here and now at the University of Washington Medical School where Dr. George Ojemann and his colleagues (1989) have been using direct cortical stimulation and recording methods to map the brain's language areas.

The patient suffers from epilepsy and is about to undergo a surgical procedure to remove the epileptic tissue. But first, because this epileptic focus is in the left language dominant hemisphere, it is essential to find where language processes are localized in the patient's brain. This can be done by electrical stimulation mapping. Electrodes are used to pass a small electrical current through the cortex, momentarily disrupting activity; thus, electrical stimulation can probe where a language process is localized. The patient has to be awake for this test. Language-related areas vary among patients and so these areas must be mapped carefully. During surgery, it is essential to leave the critical language areas intact.

One benefit of this work is that we can learn more about the organization of the human language system. Patients are shown line drawings of everyday objects and are asked to name those objects. During naming, regions of the left perisylvian cortex are stimulated with low amounts of electricity. When the patient makes an error in naming or is unable to name the object, the deficit is correlated with the region being stimulated during that trial, and so that area of cortex is assumed to be critical for language production and comprehension.

Stimulation of between 100 and 200 patients revealed that aspects of language representation in the brain are organized in mosaic-like areas of 1 to 2 cm^2. These mosaics usually include regions in the frontal and posterior temporal areas. However, in some patients, only frontal or posterior areas were observed. The correlation between these effects in either Broca's or Wernicke's areas was weak; some patients had naming disruption in the classic areas and others did not. Perhaps the single most intriguing fact is how much the anatomical localizations vary across patients, a point that has implications for how across-subject averaging methods, such as PET activation studies, reveal significant effects.

that nonsemantic deviations like musical or grammatical violations also fail to elicit the N400 effect. Thus, the N400 is specific to semantic analysis.

N400 effects are modality independent. They happen when subjects read sentences, but they also occur when subjects are presented with auditory input, including languages like English, Dutch, French, and Japanese (for speakers of those languages), and even when congenitally deaf subjects are presented with American Sign Language. With respect to linguistic-neural processing, the N400 reflects primarily postlexical processes involved in lexical integration. Hence, an N400 effect will happen when lexical integration is hampered by a mismatch between semantic specifica-

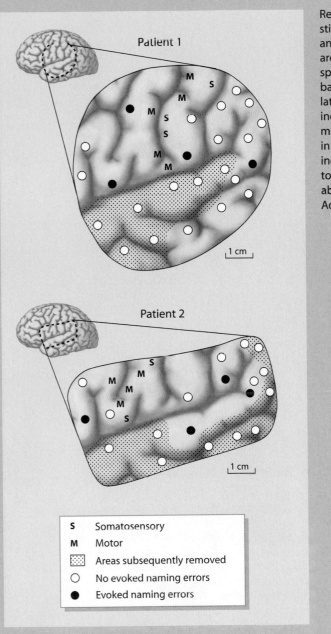

Patient 1

Patient 2

S	Somatosensory
M	Motor
▦	Areas subsequently removed
○	No evoked naming errors
●	Evoked naming errors

Regions of the brain of two patients studied with cortical stimulation mapping. During surgery, with the patient awake and lightly anesthetized, the somatosensory and motor areas are mapped by stimulating the cortex and observing the responses. Then patients are shown pictures and asked to verbally name them. Discrete regions of the cortex are stimulated with electrical current during the task. Areas that induce errors in naming when they are stimulated are mapped, and those regions are implicated as being involved in language. The surgeon uses this mapping to avoid removing any brain tissue associated with language. The surgery is to treat brain tumors or epilepsy, but also enlightens us about the cortical organization of language functions. Adapted from Ojeman et al. (1989).

tions of a word and semantic specifications of its preceding word or sentence context.

SYNTACTIC PROCESSING AND EVENT-RELATED POTENTIALS

In comparison with the N400, much less work has been done on electrophysiological correlates of other aspects of linguistic analysis such as syntax. One ERP component that has shown up is the syntactic positive shift (SPS), a large positive component elicited by words after a syntactic violation. Dutch psychologists Peter Hagoort, Colin Brown, and their colleagues (1993) asked subjects to silently read sentences presented one word at a time on a video monitor. Brain responses to normal sentences were compared with those to sentences containing a

Aphasia and Electrophysiology

Since investigators have been struggling with the question of whether aphasic symptoms reflect processing versus representational losses, interest in on-line measures of language processing has grown. Such measures include the ERPs elicited by language processing. The idea is to investigate the processing of spoken language and observe how the patient's brain responds to linguistic inputs and to compare these responses to those in healthy control subjects. One study used the N400 component of the ERP to investigate spoken-sentence understanding in Broca's and Wernicke's aphasics. Tamara Swaab, Colin Brown, and Peter Hagoort at the Max-Planck Institute for Psycholinguistics in Holland (1997) tried to determine whether spoken-sentence comprehension might be hampered by a deficit in the on-line integration of lexical information.

The patients listened to sentences spoken at a normal rate. In half of the sentences, the meaning of the final word of the sentence matched the semantic meaning building up from the sentence context. In the other half of the sentences, the final word was anomalous with respect to the preceding context. As in Kutas and Hillyard's study (1980), the N400 amplitude should be larger to the final words that are anomalous than to those that are congruent. This result was obtained for normal age-matched control subjects. In comparison to the controls, nonaphasic brain-damaged patients (right hemisphere–damaged controls) and aphasic patients with a light comprehension deficit (high comprehenders) had an N400 effect comparable to that of neurologically unimpaired subjects. In aphasics with moderate to severe comprehension deficits (low comprehenders), the N400 effect was reduced and delayed. The results are compatible with the idea that aphasics with moderate to severe comprehension problems have an impaired ability to integrate lexical information into a higher-order representation of the sentence context because the N400 component indexes the process of lexical integration. The incorporation of electrical recordings into studies of neurological patients with behavioral deficits such as aphasia permits scientists to track the processing of information in real time as it occurs in the brain. This can be combined with analysis using traditional approaches such as using reaction time measures in, for example, lexical decision tasks. But importantly, ERPs can also provide measures of processing in patients whose neurobehavioral

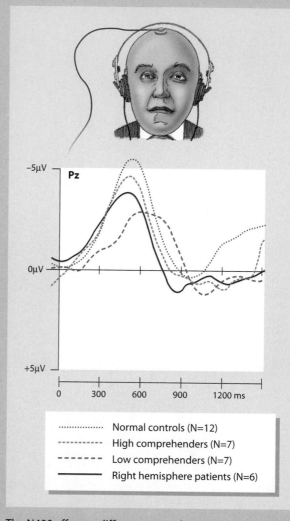

The N400 effect to different anomalous words at the end of a sentence in different groups of patients and healthy control subjects. The recording is from a single electrode located over centroparietal scalp regions in the elderly healthy control subjects, aphasics with high comprehension scores, and patients with right-hemisphere lesions (control patients). The waveform for the low comprehenders is clearly delayed and somewhat reduced compared to that for the other groups. The waveforms for the normal control subjects, the high comprehenders, and the patients with right-hemisphere lesions are comparable in size and do not differ in latency. This pattern implies a delay in time course of language processing in the patients with low comprehension. Adapted from Swaab, Brown, and Hagoort (1997).

deficit is too severe to use behavior alone because their comprehension is too low to understand the task instructions.

grammatical violation. The results are shown in Figure 8.26. Syntactic processing is also reflected in other types of brain waves. A negative wave over the left frontal areas of the brain, described by neurologist Thomas Münte and colleagues (1993), is compared to the N400 wave in Figure 8.27.

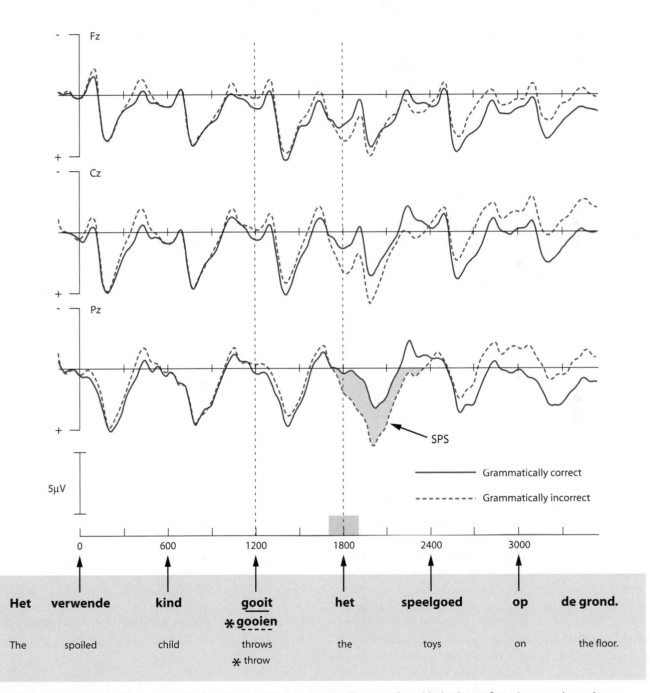

Figure 8.26 ERPs elicited to each word of sentences that are syntactically anomalous (dashed waveforms) versus those that are syntactically correct (solid waveforms). In the violated sentence a positive shift emerges in the ERP waveform at about 600 msec after the syntactic violation (shaded). It is called the syntactic positive shift (SPS). Adapted from Hagoort, Brown, and Groothusen (1993).

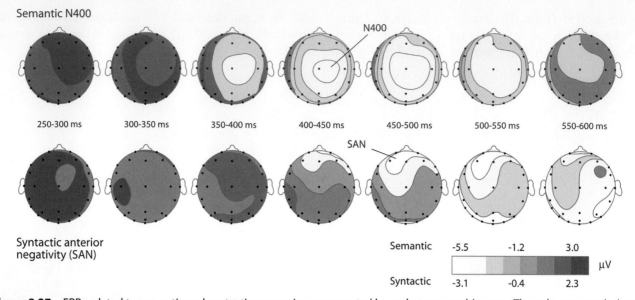

Figure 8.27 ERPs related to semantic and syntactic processing represented by scalp topographic maps. The voltage recorded at multiple locations on the scalp at specific time periods can be displayed as a topographic voltage map. These maps show views of the topographies of the N400 to semantic violations (see Figure 8.25 for equivalent waveforms), and syntactic anterior negativity (SAN) to syntactic violations. The maps are read in a similar manner as are elevation maps of mountain ranges, except here the topography shows "mountains" and "valleys" of voltage. The N400 and SAN have different scalp topographies, which implies that they are generated in different neural structures in the brain. Adapted from Münte et al. (1993).

One issue that has long intrigued psycholinguistic researchers is whether semantic and syntactic processes are modular or interactive. The distinct electrophysiological signatures of these processes enable us to address this question physiologically. As well, now that clearly defined electrical activity has been linked to things like semantic and syntactic processing, these waves can be used as tools to probe human language in persons with deficits due to neurological disease and damage (see Aphasia and Electrophysiology, p. 318). Such approaches for looking into the human language system are powerful tools for understanding language structure.

SUMMARY

Language is unique among mental functions in that only humans possess a true language system. Where is language localized in the human brain, and what can this functional-anatomical organization tell us about the cognitive architecture of the language system? We have known for more than a century that regions around the sylvian fissure of the dominant left hemisphere participate in language comprehension and production. However, classic models are insufficient for understanding the computations that support language.

We are continually modifying our view of the computational and brain organization by new analyses of patients with brain lesions who have language disorders, and by neuroimaging, electromagnetic brain recordings, and intracranial stimulation (see Stimulation Mapping of the Human Brain, p. 316). The future of language research is promising as psycholinguistic models combine with neuroscience to elucidate the neural code for this human mental function.

SUGGESTED READINGS

AITCHISON, J. (1987). *Words in the mind: An Introduction to the Mental Lexicon.* Oxford, UK: Blackwell.

CAPLAN, D. (1994). Language and the brain. In M.A. Gernsbacher (Ed.), *Handbook of Psycholinguistics.* (pp. 1023–1053). San Diego: Academic Press.

CAPLAN, D. (1992). *Language: Structure, Processing, and Disorders.* Cambridge, MA: MIT Press.

CARAMAZZA, A. (1996). The brain's dictionary. *Nature* 380:485–486.

DAMASIO, H., GRABOWSKI, T.J., TRANEL, D., HICHWA, R.D., and DAMASIO, A.R. (1996). A neural basis for lexical retrieval. *Nature* 380:499–505.

DRONKERS, N.F., and PINKER, S. (In press). Language and the Aphasias. In E.R. Kandel, J. Schwartz, and T. Jessel (Eds.), *Principles in Neural Science* (4th ed.). New York: Elsevier North Holland.

GAZZANIGA, M.S. (1983). Right hemisphere function following brain bisection: A 20 year perspective. *Am. Psychol.* 38:525–549.

KUTAS, M., and HILLYARD, S.A. (1980). Reading senseless sentences: Brain potentials reflect semantic incongruity. *Science* 207:203–205.

LEVELT, W.J.M. (1989). *Speaking: From Intention to Articulation.* Cambridge, MA: MIT Press.

LEVELT, W.J.M. (1993). The Architecture of Normal Spoken Language Use. In G. Blanken, J. Dittman, H. Grimm, J.C. Marshall, and C-W. Wallesh (Eds.), *Linguistic Disorders and Pathologies: An International Handbook.* Berlin: Walter de Gruyter.

MARSLEN-WILSON, W., and TYLER, L.K. (1980). The temporal structure of spoken language understanding. *Cognition* 8:1–71.

MARTIN, A., HAXBY, J.V., LALONDE, F.M., WIGGS, C.L., and UNGERLEIDER, L.G. (1995). Discrete cortical regions associated with knowledge of color and knowledge of action. *Science* 270:102–105.

MILBERG, W., and BLUMSTEIN, S.E. (1981). Lexical decision and aphasia: Evidence for semantic processing. *Brain Lang.* 14:371–385.

OJEMANN, G., OJEMANN, J., LETTICH, E., and BERGER, M. (1989). Cortical language localization in left, dominant hemisphere. *J. Neurosurg.* 71:316–326.

OSTERHOUT, L., and HOLCOMB, P.J. (1992). Event-related brain potentials elicited by syntactic anomaly. *Journal of Memory and Language* 31:785-806

OSTERHOUT, L., and HOLCOMB, P.J. (1995). Event related potentials and language comprehension. In M.D. Rugg and M.G.H. Coles (Eds.), *Electrophysiology of mind: Event-related brain potentials and cognition* (Oxford psychology series, No. 25). Oxford, Oxford University Press, p 171-215.

PETERSEN, S.E., FOX, P.T., SNYDER, A.Z., and RAICHLE, M.E. (1990). Activation of extrastriate and frontal cortical areas by visual words and word-like stimuli. *Science* 249:1041–1044.

PINKER, S. (1994). *The Language Instinct.* New York: William Morrow, & Co, Inc.

SIGNORET, J-L., CASTAINE, P., LEHRMITTE, F., ABELANET, R. and LAVOREL, P. (1984). Rediscovery of Leborgne's brain: Anatomical description with CT scan. *Brain Lang.* 22:303–319.

9

Cerebral Lateralization and Specialization

We live in a society that treasures the individual. Unique twists and interpretations of life's events are a marvel, and friends who offer other ways of looking at the world are a delight. So imagine how intriguing the world might be if our brain's two hemispheres were disconnected. Surgeons have done so, mainly in an effort to limit epilepsy, and their patients have been studied extensively. Each hemisphere is evaluated as to whether it and only it possesses specific functions. The big question is, Could each half of the brain provide a different view of the world?

W.J. was the first patient to have his brain split in recent years. A charismatic war veteran, W.J. appeared perfectly normal, possessed a sharp sense of humor, and always charmed all those whom he met in life. Following his surgery in 1961, his delightful personality remained unchanged but a most remarkable phenomenon happened. He was able to name and describe visual information presented to his left dominant hemisphere, but when the same information was presented to the right hemisphere, W.J. claimed he saw nothing. How could that be?

Such questions gave birth to human split-brain research. The phenomenon seen in W.J. has been observed repeatedly in other patients. Even so, much of the split-brain story was revealed in this one study. What was so remarkable was that this patient's right hemisphere could do things the left could not do. For example, there were striking differences between the performance of the two hemispheres on the block design task shown in Figure 9.1. Previously he could write dictated sentences, could carry out any kind of command such as making a fist or drawing geometrical shapes, or whatever, with his right hand. But after surgery, with his right hand he could not arrange four simple red and white blocks in a simple pattern. The surgery had disconnected specialized systems in the right hemisphere from motor apparatus in the left

hemisphere, which in turn controls the right hand. Even though W.J. was given as much time as needed, he was unable to perform tasks with his right hand because motor commands specific to the tasks could not be communicated from the isolated left hemisphere.

At the same time W.J.'s right hemisphere was a whiz. When blocks were presented to his left hand, he quickly and adeptly arranged them into the correct pattern. This

Figure 9.1 The pattern in red to the right is the shape that the patient is trying to create with the blocks given to her. **(a)** With her right hand (left hemisphere), she is unable to duplicate the pattern, whereas **(b)** with her left hand (right hemisphere), she is able to perform the task correctly.

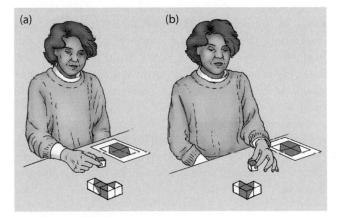

simple observation gave birth to the idea that Mind Left did different things from Mind Right, supporting the idea that the central nervous system is laterally specialized. The two cerebral hemispheres each have processes the other does not have—hence W.J.'s unique perspective on the world.

After the first testing session revealed this so clearly, investigators arranged to film W.J. carrying out tasks. The scientists knew a young fashion photographer, Baron Wolman, who dabbled in film making; he was invited to come to a session during which the whole test was carried out again. Wolman, who later founded *Rolling Stone* magazine, could not believe his eyes. When he was filming, W.J.'s right hand attempted to arrange the blocks and his left hand kept trying to intervene.

Mind Right saw the problem, knew the solution, and tried to help out just like a good friend. W.J. had to sit on his left hand so the inadequate but dominant right hand could at least try.

It was all to no avail. For the film's final scene, everyone decided to see what would happen if both hands were allowed to arrange the blocks. Here we witnessed the beginning of the idea that Mind Left can have its own view of the world with its own desires and aspirations and Mind Right can have another view. As soon as Mind Right, working through the left hand, began to arrange the blocks correctly, Mind Left would undo the good work. The hands were in competition. The specializations of each hemisphere were different, and growing out of that were the behaviors of each half of the brain.

DIVIDING THE MIND

From the perspective of natural selection, by which organisms acquire specific adaptations, one would imagine that the two hemispheres do not function identically. After all, one does not need two speech production systems or two places to store the memory of faces. Once a brain region has evolved a functional specialization, there would seem to be no need to duplicate it in a second region. Be that as it may, the cerebral cortex's organization suggests that duplication, rather than unilateral specialization, is the rule. The two hemispheres are much more similar to one another in function; differences surface at a more subtle level of analysis. Each hemisphere's visual areas are devoted to representing the shapes and colors of objects, and their primary specialization relates to the objects' position: Is the object on the left side of space or the right side? What is more, the motor cortices are roughly mirror images of one another, both in structure and in function. While each has a motor homunculus of the body, it is dominated by fibers that project to muscles on the opposite side of the body.

Evolution could have utilized the available cerebral space in a completely different way. Visual functions could have been isolated in the left hemisphere, and motor projections to both limbs could have originated in the right hemisphere. Yet selective pressures appear to have favored a cerebral organization that reflects structural properties of the world and the organism. The world's spatial structure is reflected in our biology.

Hemispheric specializations are best conceived as superimposed on this fundamental symmetry. In some instances, specializations may have evolved because there was an advantage in having a single system devoted to a certain process. For example, one hypothesis postulates that speech production became strongly lateralized because of the need to communicate at rapid rates. Transcortical processing and integration take time and might slow down complicated articulatory gestures. Indeed, lateralization may underlie stuttering because of the two parallel systems that compete for control of speech output.

Others argue that hemispheric specializations evolved because of the inherent advantages in having nonidentical forms of representation. Homologous visual areas perform related operations, but differently enough that the resultant nonidentical representations are imbued with unique advantages in performing certain tasks. This does not mean that these tasks are strictly localized—that language functions are restricted to the left hemisphere or that spatial behavior emanates from the right hemisphere. Not only does the normal performance of these tasks require distributed operations that might span both hemispheres, but also usually both hemispheres contain the essential machinery for performing the task. This helps explain why patients with large unilateral lesions that damage 25% of the cortical tissue on one side still have an amazing capacity for recovery. Even more dramatic evidence comes from patients with isolated cerebral hemispheres, a condition that arises after a split-brain operation. Because this radical operation remarkably preserves function, such patients are invaluable for giving us clues to subtle functional asymmetries and basic capabilities of each cerebral hemisphere.

This chapter examines the differences between the right and left cerebral hemispheres. Research on the human brain has revealed marked differences between the two halves. We begin at the beginning: the anatomy and physiology of the two halves and their interconnections.

PRINCIPLES OF CEREBRAL ORGANIZATION

The two cerebral cortices of the human brain are of equal size and surface area. The major lobes (the occipital, the parietal, the temporal, and the frontal) appear, at least superficially, to be symmetrical. Nonetheless, for centuries the effects of unilateral brain damage have revealed major functional differences. Most dramatic has been the effect of left-hemisphere damage on language functions. The dominant role of the left hemisphere in language has been confirmed by various behavioral methods in normal humans using stimulation techniques in which the input is directed to one hemisphere or the other and with injections of amobarbital, a fast-acting barbiturate that can produce a transient anesthesia in one half of the brain or the other (Figure 9.2).

Anatomical Correlates of Hemispheric Specialization

The dominant role of the left hemisphere in language is not strongly correlated with handedness. Approximately 50% of all left-handers also have left-hemisphere dominance for language, despite the fact that they comprise only 7 to 8% of the total population. Thus, taken together, over 96% of humans have left-hemisphere specialization for language. Given this dramatic functional asymmetry, most anatomical studies of hemispheric specialization have looked for structural asymmetries in regions of the brain associated with language functions.

Anatomists in the nineteenth century could see that the lateral fissure—the large sulcus that defines the superior border of the temporal lobe—has a more prominent upward curl in the right hemisphere in comparison to the left hemisphere (Figure 9.3). In more recent times, the 1960s, Norman Geschwind of the Harvard Medical School followed this up by examining brains obtained from 100 people known to be right-handed (Geschwind and Levitsky, 1968). After slicing through the lateral fissure, they measured the temporal lobe's surface area and discovered that the *planum temporale,*

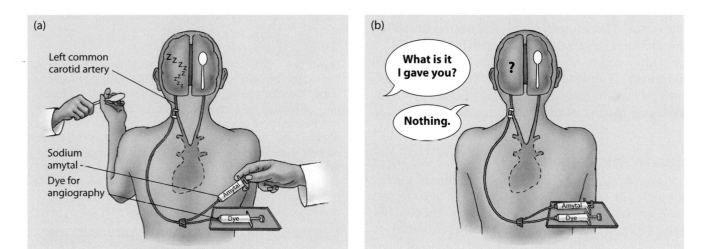

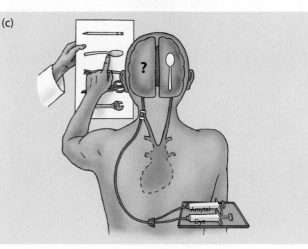

Figure 9.2 The methods used in amytal testing. **(a)** Subsequent to angiography, amytal is administered into the left hemisphere, anesthetizing the language and speech systems. A spoon is placed in the left hand, and the right hemisphere takes note. **(b)** When the left hemisphere regains consciousness, the subject is asked what was placed in his left hand, and he responds, "nothing." **(c)** When a board with a variety of objects pinned to it is held up, it is discovered that the patient can easily point to the appropriate object due to the right hemisphere directing the left hand during the matching-to-sample task.

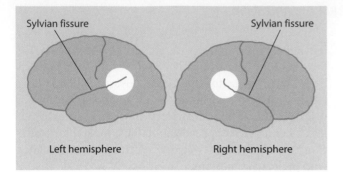

Figure 9.3 Geschwind and Galaburda examined brains obtained from 100 people known to be right-handed and measured the temporal lobe's surface area. They discovered that the planum temporale was generally larger in the left hemisphere and that the asymmetry in this region of the temporal lobe also extended to subcortical structures that are connected to these areas.

which encompasses Wernicke's area, was larger in the left hemisphere, a pattern found in 65% of the brains. Of the remaining brains, 11% had a larger surface area in the right hemisphere and 24% had no asymmetry. The asymmetry in this region of the temporal lobe also extends to subcortical structures that are connected to these areas. For example, the lateral posterior nucleus of the thalamus also tends to be larger on the left.

Other investigations have explored whether this asymmetry is absent in people with developmental language disorders. Magnetic resonance imaging (MRI) reveals that the area of the planum temporale is approximately symmetrical in children with dyslexia, a clue that their language difficulties may stem from the lack of a specialized left hemisphere.

The planum temporal's asymmetry is one of the few examples in which an anatomical index is correlated with a well-defined functional asymmetry. The complex functions of language comprehension presumably require more cortical surface. However, a number of questions remain concerning both the validity and the explanatory power of this asymmetry. First, while the left-hemisphere planum temporale is larger in 65% of right-handers, functional measures indicate that at least 95% of right-handers show left-hemisphere language dominance. Second, recent work suggested that the apparent asymmetries in the planum temporale result from the techniques and criteria used to identify this region. When new three-dimensional imaging techniques—ones that take into account differences in curvature patterns in the superior temporal lobe—are applied, hemispheric asymmetries become negligible (Figure 9.4). If this new view is correct, then the anatomical basis for left-hemisphere dominance in lan-

guage may not be reflected in gross morphology; instead it would require analysis of the microcircuitry.

Microanatomical Investigations of Anatomical Asymmetries

The cellular basis of hemispheric specialization is an exciting new field of investigation. Although many investigators have examined gross size differences between the two hemispheres, relatively few have questioned whether differences in neural connectivity or organization underlie hemispheric asymmetries. One possibility is that specific organizational characteristics, such as the number of local synaptic connections, may be responsible for the unique functions of different coritcal areas. Current knowledge of local cortical organization is quite limited, mainly because it is based mostly on studies of the visual cortex.

With language, cortical differences between the hemispheres exist in both Wernicke's region and Broca's region. The cortex can be pictured as a sheet of tightly spaced columns, each of which comprises a circuit of cells that is repeated over and over across the cortical surface. These columns not only are wider in the left

Figure 9.4 Three-dimensional computer reconstructions such as this one can be used to model the cortical surface as a folded mesh composed of many small polygons. These models, which are derived from magnetic resonance images, permit measurement of specific regions of the cortex such as the planum temporale located on the dorsal surface of the temporal lobe. Measurements in both hemispheres can be used to assess left-right anatomical asymmetry in living subjects. Investigations of the planum temporale based on these models have revealed that it may not be as asymmetric as was previously thought.

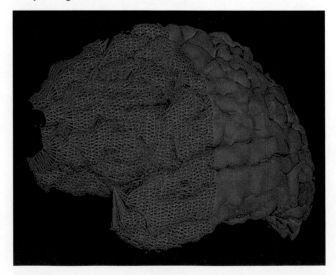

temporal lobe but also are spaced farther from each other. Cells within a column of the left primary auditory cortex have a tangential dendritic spread that is commensurate with the greater distance between these cell columns; secondary auditory areas do not have an increase in dendritic spread in the left temporal lobe and thus contact fewer cell columns than do those in the right. The columnar organization itself also varies between the left and right posterior temporal areas. The left hemisphere is organized into clear columnar units; columns in the right hemisphere are much less distinct. Examination of a small sample of pyramidal cells from layers II and III—the cells that project to other regions within the cortex—reveals that the total dendritic length of left-hemisphere cells is greater than that of right-hemisphere cells—an asymmetry that may decrease with age. Structural differences have also been documented in the anterior speech regions in Broca's area. Asymmetries include cell size differences between the hemispheres such as those shown in Figure 9.5, and a possible difference between the fine dendritic structure of each hemisphere.

Most of these comparisons between the hemispheres focus on the gross appearance of individual cells or their position within the cortex. Little effort has been expended on subgroups of cortical cells that can be identified by their neurotransmitters and related chemicals. Chemical assays have documented higher levels of choline acetyltransferase in the left hemisphere. This substance resides in axons and cell bodies and is responsible for assembling acetylcholine, a major excitatory neurotransmitter within the central nervous system. Acetylcholine-containing axons and their postsynaptic targets are similar in both hemispheres.

In comparison with the vast literature on aphasic deficits following cortical damage and putative size differences between the hemispheres, few investigators have honed in on the question of whether the hemispheres' microanatomical circuitry contributes to the specialized functions of cortical regions. And even fewer have addressed this question from the standpoint of examining subgroups of cells within the cortex by using modern microanatomical labeling techniques.

A thorough understanding of the anatomy and

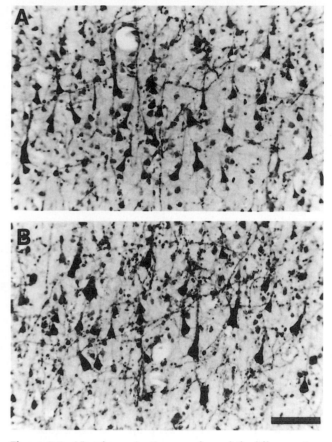

Figure 9.5 Visual examination reveals a subtle difference in the sizes of the largest subgroups of layer III pyramidal cells in the left hemisphere (pyramidal cells stained with acetylthiocholinesterase).

physiology of language-associated cortices could shed considerable light on the cortical mechanisms that facilitate linguistic analysis and production. Since cortical areas have a basic similar organization, documenting cortical locations involved in certain functions should distinguish between the form and variety of neural structures common to all regions and the structures that are critical for a region to carry out particular cognitive functions. These questions hold importance not only for the greater understanding of a species-specific adaptation such as language, but also for understanding how evolution might build functional specialization into the framework of cortical organization.

HOW THE TWO HEMISPHERES COMMUNICATE

The two cerebral cortices are interconnected by the largest fiber system in the brain, the corpus callosum. In humans, this bundle of white matter includes more than 200 million axons. As shown in Figure 9.6, many of the callosal projections link together homotopic areas, areas in corresponding

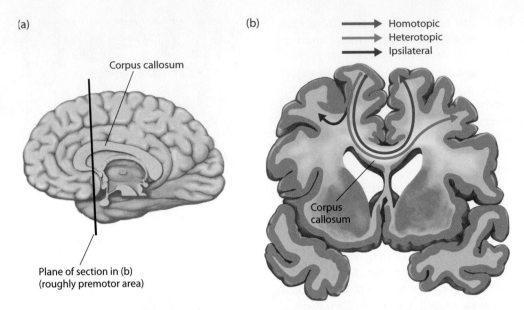

Figure 9.6 **(a)** Mid-sagital view of the right cerebral hemisphere with the large corpus callosum labeled. **(b)** The caudal surface of a coronal section of brain roughly through the premotor cortical area. Homotopic callosal fibers (blue) connect corresponding sections of the two hemispheres via the corpus callosum, whereas, heterotopic connections (green) link different areas of the two hemispheres of the brain. In primates, both types of contralateral connections (blue and green) as well as ipsilateral (red) connections start and finish at the same layer of neocortex. Adapted from Gazzaniga and LeDoux (1978).

locations in the two hemispheres. For example, regions in the left prefrontal cortex project to homotopic regions in the right prefrontal cortex. Although this pattern holds for most areas of the association cortex, it is not always seen in primary cortices. Few callosal projections from the visual cortex represent the most eccentric regions of space, and homotopic callosal projections are sparse in the primary motor and the somatosensory cortices.

Callosal fibers also project to heterotopic areas. These projections generally mirror the ones found within a hemisphere. A prefrontal area sending projections to premotor areas in the same hemisphere is also likely to send projections to the same premotor area in the contralateral hemisphere. Yet, heterotopic projections are usually less extensive than comparable projections within the same hemisphere.

The functional role of callosal projections remains unclear. Some researchers point out that in the visual association cortex, receptive fields can span both visual fields. Communication across the callosum enables information from both visual fields to contribute to the activity of these cells. Indeed, the callosal connections could play a role in synchronizing oscillatory activity in cortical neurons as an object passes through these receptive fields (Figure 9.7). In this view, callosal connections facilitate processing by pooling together diverse inputs. Other researchers take a more competitive view

of callosal function. If the callosal fibers are inhibitory, then they would provide a means for each hemisphere to compete for control of current processing. For example, multiple movements might be activated, all geared to a common goal; later processing selects one of these candidate movements (see Chapter 10). Inhibitory connections across the corpus callosum might be one contributor to this selection.

In developing animals, callosal projections are diffuse, being more evenly distributed across the cortical surface. Cats and monkeys lose approximately 70% of their callosal axons during development; some of these transient projections are between areas (portions of the primary sensory cortex) that in adults are not connected by the callosum. Yet, this loss of axons does not produce cell death in each cortical hemisphere. Recall that a single cell body can send out more than one axon terminal, one to cortical areas on the same side of the brain and one to the other side of the brain. Thus, loss of a callosal axon may well leave its cell body alive with its secondary collateral connection to the same hemisphere intact. The refinement of connections is a hallmark of callosal development, just as such refinement characterizes intrahemispheric development (see Chapter 12).

In general terms, hemispheric specialization must have been influenced and constrained by callosal evolution. The appearance of new cortical areas might be expected to require more connections across the callosum (expansion). In contrast, lateralization might have been facilitated by a lack of callosal connections. The resultant isolation would promote divergence among the functional capabilities of homotopic regions.

As with the cerebral hemispheres, researchers have investigated functional correlates of anatomical differences in the corpus callosum. Usually investigators measure gross aspects like the cross-sectional area of the callosum. Variations in this measure are linked to gender, handedness, mental retardation, autism, and schizophrenia. Interpretation of these data is complicated by methodological disagreements and by contradictory results. The underlying logic of measuring the corpus callosum's cross-sectional area relies on the relation of area to structural organization. Callosal size could be related to the number and diameter of axons, the proportion of myelinated axons, the thickness of myelin sheaths, and measures of nonneural structures such as the size of blood vessels or the volume of extracellular space. With large samples of callosal measures from aged-matched control subjects, sex-based differences are seen in the shape of the callosum but not in the size. Handedness may be associated with the size of the callosum's subregions, but geometric parsing of the callosum is artificial, at best. The interpretation of a smaller callosum, such as that found in autistic patients, remains unknown.

Cortical Disconnection

Because the corpus callosum is the primary means of communication between the two cerebral hemispheres, we learn a lot when we sever the fibers. This approach was most successfully used in the pioneering animal studies of Ronald Myers and Roger Sperry (Gazzaniga and Sperry, 1967) at the California Institute of Technology. They showed how crucial the corpus callosum is for unified cortical function. For example, Myers and Sperry demonstrated that visual discrimination learned by one hemisphere did not transfer to the other. For example, cats were trained to choose a "plus" stimulus versus a "circle" stimulus that were randomly alternated between two doors. If the cats chose correctly, they were rewarded with food. Myers and Sperry made the startling discovery that such visual discriminations trained to one half of the brain were not known to the other half when the callosum and anterior commissure was sectioned.

This important research laid the groundwork for comparable human studies initiated by Sperry and Michael Gazzaniga in the 1960s (Sperry et al., 1969). Unlike lesion studies, the split-brain operation does not destroy any cortical tissue; instead, it eliminates the connections between the two hemispheres. With split-brain

Figure 9.7 **(a)** When receptive fields (1 and 2) on either side of fixation are stimulated by two separate light bars moving in different directions, the firing rates of the two cells are not correlated. **(b)** In animals with an intact corpus callosum, cells with spatially separate receptive fields fire synchronously when stimulated by a common object, such as a long light bar spanning both fields. **(c)** In animals whose corpus callosa have been severed, synchrony is rarely observed. Adapted from Engel et al. (1991) and Gray et al. (1989).

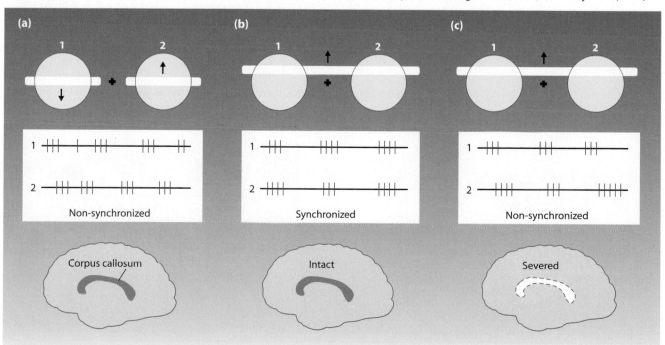

patients, functional inferences need not be based on how behavior might change after the cortical areas are eliminated. Rather, it becomes possible to see how the two hemispheres operate in relative isolation.

Patients who undergo split-brain surgery suffer from intractable epilepsy. As with all forms of neurosurgery, the procedure is applied only when other forms of treatment, such as medication, fail. By severing the transcortical connections, surgeons think that the epileptogenic activity is held in check. Indeed, the operation is almost always successful. Seizures generally subside immediately, even in patients who prior to the operation experienced up to fifteen seizures per day. The operation enables them to resume a normal life with no obvious side effects.

Many methodological issues arise when evaluating the performance of split-brain patients. First, we must bear in mind that these patients were not normal prior to the operation: They were all chronic epileptics. Therefore, it is reasonable to ask whether they provide an appropriate barometer of normal hemispheric function after the operation. But there is no easy answer to this question. Several patients do display abnormal performance on neuropsychological assessments, and they may even be mentally retarded. But in some patients the cognitive impairments are negligible; these are the patients studied in closest detail.

Second, it is important to consider whether the transcortical connections were completely sectioned or whether some fibers remain intact. In the original California operations, one had to rely on surgical notes to determine the completeness of the surgical sections. In recent years, MRIs, such as in Figure 9.8, and electrical brain mapping techniques have provided a more accurate representation of the extent of surgical sections. Accurate documentation of a callosal section is crucial for learning about the organization of the cerebral commissure.

The main methods of testing the perceptual and cognitive functions of each hemisphere have changed little over the past 30 years. Researchers mainly use visual stimulation, not only because of the preeminent status of this modality for humans, but also because the visual system is more strictly lateralized than other sensory systems such as the auditory and olfactory systems. The visual stimulus is restricted to a single hemisphere by quickly flashing the stimulus in one visual field or the other (Figure 9.9). Prior to stimulation, the patient is required to fixate on a point in space. The brevity of stimulation is necessary to prevent eye movements, which would redirect the information into the unwanted hemisphere. Eye movements take roughly 200 msec, and so if the stimulus is presented for a briefer period of time, the experimenter can be confident that the stimulus was lateralized. More recent image stabilization tools—ones that move in correspondence with the subject's eye movements—allow a more prolonged, naturalistic form of stimulation. This technological development has opened the way for new discoveries in the neurological and psychological aspects of hemisphere disconnection.

Functional Consequences of the Split-Brain Procedure

Reports on the California patients dealt with several fundamental issues concerning the psychological properties of separated cerebral hemispheres, as well as basic aspects of neurological organization. In many respects,

Figure 9.8 **(a)** The sagital view of the human brain. The corpus callosum is the large fiber tract that is sectioned by a neurosurgeon seeking to control otherwise intractable epilepsy. **(b)** MRI of a corpus callosum that has been entirely sectioned, resulting in no transfer of information between the cerebral hemispheres.

(a)

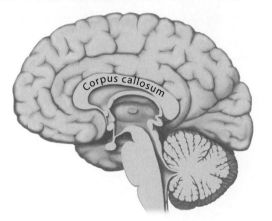

(b)

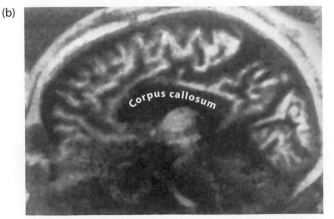

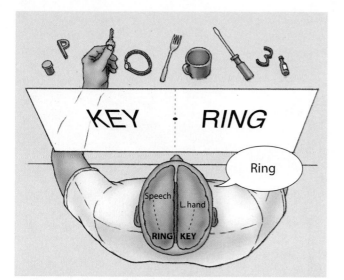

Figure 9.9 The split-brain patient reports through the speaking hemisphere only the items flashed to the right half of the screen and denies seeing left-field stimuli or recognizing objects presented to the left hand. The left hand correctly retrieves objects presented in the left visual field for which the subject verbally denies having any knowledge.

the issues raised in the original studies still drive current research efforts, so let us review the neurological consequences of callosum sectioning before we investigate the separate psychological properties of the two cerebral hemispheres.

Humans were studied in the context of new animal evidence that a division of the cerebral commissure produces a profound deficit in the interhemispheric transfer of sensory and motor information. After operations on cats, monkeys, and chimpanzees that followed the midline sectioning of the corpus callosum and anterior commissure, researchers discovered that visual and tactile information that was lateralized to one hemisphere did not transfer to the opposite hemisphere—hence, the split-brain animal. This startling discovery was completely contrary to earlier reports on the effects of human commissure section reported by A.J. Akelaitis (1941) of the University of Rochester. He claimed that no significant neurological and psychological effects were seen after the callosum was sectioned.

Careful testing with the California patients, however, revealed behavioral changes similar to those seen in split-brain primates. Visual information presented to one half of the brain was not available to the other half. The same principle applied to touch. Patients were able to name and describe objects placed in the right hand but not objects presented in the left hand. Sensory in-

formation restricted to one hemisphere was not available to accurately guide movements with the ipsilateral hand. For example, when a picture of a hand portraying the "ok sign" was presented to the left hemisphere, the patient was able to make the gesture with the right hand, which gains its control from the left half of the brain. However, the patient was unable to make the same gesture with the left hand, which gains its control from the disconnected right hemisphere.

From a cognitive point of view, these initial studies confirmed long-standing neurological knowledge about the nature of the two cerebral hemispheres. The left hemisphere is dominant for language, speech, and major problem solving, while the right one appears specialized for visuospatial tasks such as drawing cubes and other three-dimensional patterns. This means that split-brain patients cannot name or describe visual and tactile stimuli presented to the right hemisphere because the sensory information is disconnected from the dominant left (speech) hemisphere. But this does not mean that knowledge about the stimuli is absent in the right hemisphere. Nonverbal response techniques are required to demonstrate the competence of the right hemisphere. For example, the left hand can be used to point to named objects or to demonstrate the function of depicted objects presented in the left visual field.

Specificity of Callosal Function

When the corpus callosum is fully sectioned, little or no perceptual or cognitive interaction occurs between the hemispheres. Surgical cases where callosal section is limited or part of the callosum is inadvertently spared have enabled investigators to examine specific functions of the callosum by region. For example, when the *splenial region*, the posterior area of the callosum that interconnects the occipital lobe, is spared, visual information is transferred normally between the two cerebral hemispheres (Figure 9.10). In these instances, pattern, color, and linguistic information presented anywhere in either visual field can be matched with information presented to the other half of the brain. Even so, the patients show no evidence of interhemispheric transfer of tactile information from felt objects. These observations are consistent with other human and animal data showing that major callosum subdivisions are organized into functional zones whose posterior regions are more concerned with visual information and whose anterior regions transfer auditory and tactile information.

The anterior part of the callosum is involved in higher-order transfer of semantic information. Surgeons sometimes prefer to perform the split-brain procedure

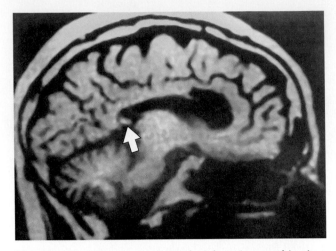

Figure 9.10 MRI scan showing splenial sparing, resulting in the ability of visual information to be transferred between the cerebral hemispheres.

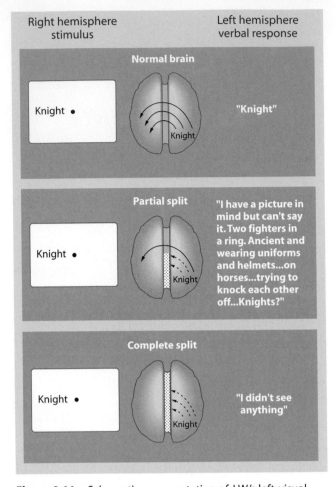

Figure 9.11 Schematic representation of J.W.'s left-visual field naming ability at each operative stage. Adapted from Sidtis et al. (1981).

in stages, restricting the initial operation to the front (anterior) or back (posterior) half of the callosum. The remaining fibers are only sectioned in a second operation if the seizures continue to persist. This two-stage procedure offers a unique glimpse into what the anterior callosal regions transfer between the cerebral hemisphere. When the posterior half of the callosum is sectioned, transfer of visual, tactile, and auditory sensory information is severely disrupted. Yet the remaining intact anterior region of the callosum is able to transfer higher-order information. For example, one patient was able to name stimuli presented in the left visual field following a resection limited to the posterior callosal region. Close examination revealed that the left hemisphere was receiving higher-order cues about the stimulus without having access to the sensory information about the stimulus itself (Figure 9.11). In short, the anterior part of the callosum transfers semantic information about the stimulus but not the stimulus itself. After the anterior callosal region was sectioned in this patient, this capacity ceased.

HEMISPHERIC SPECIALIZATION

One of the cardinal features of behavioral studies of human and animal brains has been the realization that specific brain areas appear to be involved with specific perceptual and cognitive functions. The split-brain approach to this issue has been straightforward. By testing each disconnected hemisphere, one can assess the different capacities each might possess. While some claims are exaggerated, there are marked differences between the two halves of the brain. The most prominent lateralized function in the human brain is the left hemisphere's capacity for language and speech.

Language and Speech

A useful dichotomy when trying to understand the neural bases of language is the distinction between grammatical and lexical functions. The grammar-lexicon distinction is different from the more traditional syntax-semantic distinction commonly invoked to understand differential effects of brain lesions on language processes (see Chapter 8). In general terms, grammar is the rule-based system humans have for ordering words to facilitate communication. The *lexicon,* by contrast, is the mind's dictionary where words are associated with specific meanings. The reason for the distinction is that it takes into account such factors as memory in the sense that, with memory, word strings as idioms can be learned by rote. For example, the cliche "you can't teach an old dog new tricks" is most likely a single lexical entry. Though it is clear that the lexicon cannot encompass most phrases and sentences—there are endless unique sentences, such as the one you are now reading—memory does play a role in many short phrases. When uttered, such word strings do not reflect an underlying interaction of syntax and semantic systems; they are, instead, essentially an entry from the lexicon. A modern view would predict that there ought to be brain areas wholly responsible for grammar, whereas the lexicon's location ought to be more elusive since it reflects learned information and thus is part of the brain's general memory-knowledge systems. The grammar system, then, ought to be discrete and hence localizable, and the lexicon should be distributed and hence more difficult to completely damage.

Language and speech processes are rarely present in both hemispheres. While the separated left hemisphere normally comprehends all aspects of language, the right hemisphere is not always devoid of linguistic capabilities. Indeed, out of dozens of split-brain patients who have been carefully examined, only six showed clear evidence of residual linguistic functions in the right hemisphere. However, even in these patients, the extent of right-hemisphere language functions is severely limited and restricted to the lexical aspects of comprehension.

The left and the right lexicon of these special patients can be near equal in their capacity but are organized quite differently. For example, both hemispheres show a phenomenon called the *word superiority effect* (WSE) (see Chapter 3). Normal readers are better able to identify letters (e.g., *L*) in the context of real English words (e.g., *BELT*) than when the same letters appear in pseudowords (e.g., *KELT*) or nonsense letter strings (e.g., *KTLE*). Since pseudowords and nonwords do not have lexical entries, letters occurring in such strings do not receive the additional processing benefit bestowed on words. Thus, the WSE emerges.

The WSE may be a useful measure of the integrity of the visual lexicon. When these effects are assessed for each hemisphere, the patients with right-hemisphere language exhibit a visual lexicon, as evidenced by a WSE. Yet it may be that each hemisphere accesses this lexicon in a different way. To resolve this issue, investigators evaluated the possibility by using a letter priming task. The task was simply to indicate whether a briefly flashed uppercase letter was an *H* or a *T.* On each trial the uppercase letter was preceded by a lowercase letter that was either an *h* or a *t.* Normally subjects are significantly faster, or primed, when an uppercase *H* is preceded by a lowercase *h* than when it is preceded by a lowercase *t.*

The difference between response latency on compatible (*h-H*) versus incompatible (*t-H*) trials is taken to be a measure of letter priming. Patient J.W. performed a lateralized version of this task in which the prime was exposed for 100 msec to either the right or the left visual field, and 400 msec later the target letter appeared in either the right or the left visual field. The results, shown in Figure 9.12, provide no evidence of letter priming for left visual field trials but clear evidence of priming for right visual field trials. Thus, the lack of a priming phenomena in the disconnected right hemisphere suggests a deficit in letter recognition, prohibiting access to parallel processing mechanisms. There were a variety of other deficiencies in J.W.'s right-hemisphere functions. For example, he was unable to judge whether one word was superordinate to another (e.g., *furniture-chair*), or whether two words were antonyms (e.g., *love-hate*).

In sum, there can be two lexicons, one in each hemisphere—but this lexical organization is rare. When present, the right hemisphere's lexicon seems organized differently from the left hemisphere's lexicon, or at least is accessed in different ways. These observations are consistent with the view that lexicons reflect

Figure 9.12 Letter priming as a function of visual field for split-brain patients. The graph shows the latency for compatible and incompatible words in the right and left visual fields. The latency for both types of words are much longer for the left visual field-right hemisphere words.

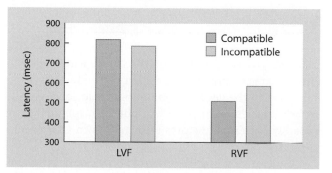

MILESTONES IN COGNITIVE NEUROSCIENCE

An Interview with Michael Corballis, Ph.D. Dr. Corballis is associated with the Psychology Department at the University of Auckland, New Zealand. His writings have provided an important evolutionary perspective to the study of hemispheric specialization.

Authors: The human brain is full of lateralized functions. Are we the only species with such cerebral organization?

MC: There is of course growing evidence for cerebral asymmetries in other species, but I have yet to be convinced that they are of the same degree and consistency as our own. The most conspicuous asymmetries of the human brain, moreover, seem to apply to functions that are themselves characteristically human, namely, language and manual praxis, in which I include such things as writing, accurate throwing, manufacture of tools, carving, painting, etc. I think these activities themselves constitute something of a discontinuity in primate evolution, although I don't want to adopt an extreme chomskian stance about language, or to deny the considerable manual dexterity seen in the gorilla, for example. I rather like Marian Annett's idea of a laterality gene, specific to humans, that imposed a left-hemispheric dominance for language and manual praxis. I think it may have been imposed on a structure that was already lateralized to some extent, specifically with respect to spatial and emotional functions, but it gave humans a distinctive lopsidedness.

Authors: But cognitive functions, save perhaps for grammar systems, are not wholly lateralized in humans. Disconnected left and right hemispheres each can process facial information although the right hemisphere is much better. Children, injured during development, can learn grammar with their nondominant right hemisphere and so on. How do you think of these phenomenon in the context of the laterality gene?

MC: I think that the laterality gene may control growth gradients. There is evidence for a spurt of left-hemispheric growth between the ages of about 2 and 4, and this coincides with the development of grammar. If this is disrupted, then grammar may be acquired by the right hemisphere in a later growth spurt, though at the expense of the usual right-hemisphere functions. For this mechanism to work, you need to postulate some sort of interhemispheric inhibition, so that if grammar is acquired in normal fashion in the left hemisphere, the right hemisphere does not acquire it during its later growth phase. All of this is fairly hypothetical, of course, but may go some distance toward explaining the equipotentiality (or near-equipotentiality) of the two hemispheres for grammar. I should point out that equipotentiality is not the same as equality—the right hemisphere does appear to have a potential for grammar, but is normally denied the opportunity to exploit it, so there must be some kind of inhibitory process.

I think that growth gradients provide an elegant explanation for hemispheric asymmetries—much simpler than supposing that the brain was somehow rewired in the course of evolution, yet powerful because they allow the environment to do much of the work. The other conspicuous feature of the human brain is the long postnatal period of growth, which maximizes environmental influences while the brain is at its most plastic. If you suppose that growth is programmed to occur asymmetrically during this period, then I think you have a recipe for much that is unique about the human mind.

To get back to the question of right-hemisphere language, I think that language can be quite sophisticated in the absence of grammar (and perhaps phonol-

learning processes and as such are more widely distributed in the cerebral cortex. Still, it would be folly to ignore that in the general population the lexicon appears to be in the left hemisphere. A right-hemisphere lexicon is rarely present and stores information in a more random fashion.

Generative syntax is present in only one hemisphere. While the right hemisphere of some patients clearly has a lexicon, the hemispheres perform erratically on other aspects of language such as understanding verbs, pluralizations, the possessive, or active-passive differences. In patients that possess some language, the right hemisphere also fails to use word order to disambiguate stimuli for correct meaning. Yet these right hemispheres can indicate when a sentence ends with a semantically odd word! What is more, right hemispheres with language

ogy). However, grammarless language can't be stretched to generative, propositional speech, but may be able to get by on cliches and learned phrases. (The speech of L.B., the split-brain man well known in the literature, is most of the time like a long-playing record of cliches, endlessly repeated—I have often wondered if his right hemisphere plays a role in this.) I must say I am quite impressed by the apparent ability of the disconnected right hemisphere to follow verbal instructions, although I am not sure how general this is among the split-brain population. I am nevertheless still enough of a chomskian to think that there is something special about normal, human left-hemispheric language, and that grammar is the key.

Authors: The general rule seems to be that only one hemisphere has a grammar but both can have a lexicon which would include cliches and phrases. But more generally, do you feel all specialized systems as revealed through brain damage to adults occur or crystallize sometime during development? Are you saying the blueprint for the brain is symmetrical until some process stamps out the lateralization pattern?

MC: I think that most specialized systems are crystallized during development, and that some become lateralized in the process. Of course, we can obtain specialized knowledge in adulthood, but this is not a "system" in the way that grammar, face recognition, etc., are. By the way, I have yet to discover evidence for a right-hemispheric specialization that is anywhere near as pronounced as the left-hemispheric specialization for grammar and propositional language. I still think that much of what is called right-hemispheric specialization is really so by default—a slight weakness due to the presence of left-hemispheric functions rather than a programmed specialization. I think that goes for face recognition, but I may be wrong.

Is the blueprint for the brain symmetrical? Depends what you mean by "blueprint," I suppose. I think that there may be programmed gradients that are asymmetrical, and to the extent that these are part of

the blueprint, the answer is "No." But I do think that millions of years of evolution have selected for symmetry, largely on the grounds that, in the absence of consistent asymmetry in the natural environment, locomotion is best accomplished by a symmetrical system. Symmetry of sensory systems would naturally follow, since to a freely moving organism there is no systematic sensory bias. Asymmetry could be a disadvantage—as Martin Gardner once put it, a predator "could sneak up on the right." However, once you get to a level of sophistication beyond mere sensorimotor function, toward a "computational brain," then there could be advantages to asymmetry. I like to distinguish between actions that are reactions to the environment, which are by and large symmetrical, and operations on the environment, which are much more likely to be asymmetrical. Skilled cricketers can usually catch equally well with either hand, but can only throw accurately with one.

Authors: What is the future for research on cerebral lateralization? Where is it going?

MC: I have thought for years that it was coming to an end, but it never seems to. Nevertheless, I think we should all remember that there was a good deal of fanciful speculation about cerebral lateralization in the late nineteenth century, but it pretty well dried up in the early twentieth. It may well happen again as we cross into the twenty-first. I don't think we are getting any further in the search for some "fundamental" dichotomy that characterizes the difference between the hemispheres, and I'm not sure either that a multicomponent view is very satisfying, although it may be nearer the truth. My guess is that further insights are likely to come from a more evolutionary approach, rather than yet more dichotic-listening and visual-hemifield studies, although imaging techniques may provide new information. It would be really great if we could discover the gene or genes that control cerebral lateralization. If such a gene exists, its discovery should not be too far away.

capacities can make grammar judgments. For some peculiar reason, they cannot use syntax to disambiguate stimuli, but they can judge that one set of utterances is grammatical while another set is not. This startling finding suggests that patterns of speech are learned by rote. Yet, recognizing the pattern of acceptable utterances does not mean a neural system can use this to understand word strings (Figure 9.13).

One of the hallmarks of most split-brain patients is that their speech production is from the left hemisphere and not the right. This observation, consistent with the literature and with amobarbital studies, shows that the left hemisphere is the dominant hemisphere for speech production. Nonetheless, there are now a handful of documented cases of split-brain patients who can produce speech from both hemispheres. While speech is

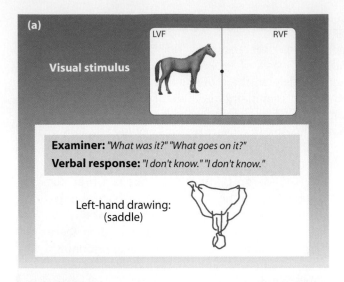

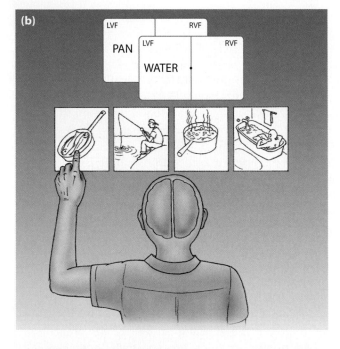

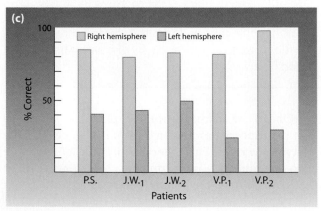

Figure 9.13 **(a)** The right hemisphere is capable of understanding language but not syntax. When presented with a horse stimulus to the left visual field-right hemisphere, the subjects maintain through the left hemisphere that they saw nothing. When asked to draw what goes on the object, the left hand-right hemisphere is able to draw a saddle. **(b)** The capacity of the right hemisphere to make inferences is extremely limited. Two words are presented in serial order, and the right hemisphere is simply required to point to a picture that best depicts what happens when the words are causally related. The left hemisphere finds these tasks trivial while the right cannot perform the task. **(c)** Data from three cases show how the right hemisphere is more accurate than the left in recognizing unfamiliar faces. Gazzaniga and Smylie (1984).

restricted to the left hemisphere following callosal bisection, in these rare patients the capacity to make one-word utterances from the disconnected right hemisphere has emerged over time.

This intriguing development raises the question of whether information is somehow transferring to the dominant hemisphere for speech output or whether the right hemisphere itself is capable of developing speech production. After extensive testing it became apparent that the latter hypothesis is correct. For example, the patients were able to name an object presented in the left field and in the right field but were not able to judge whether they were the same objects! Or when words like *father* were presented such that the fixation point fell between the *t* and the *h*, the patients said either "fat" or "her," depending on in which hemisphere speech production dominated. These findings illustrate that an extraordinary plasticity lasts sometimes as long as 10 years after callosal surgery. In fact in one patient, the right hemisphere had no speech production capability for approximately 13 years before it "spoke."

Visuospatial Processing

The second primary task domain that has been studied in split-brain patients is visuospatial processing. As shown in Figure 9.1, the isolated right hemisphere is frequently found to be superior on neuropsychological tests such as the block design task, a subtest of the Wechsler Adult Intelligence Scale. Here, the simple task of arranging some red and white blocks to match those of a given pattern can find the left hemisphere performing poorly while the right triumphs. However, asymmetries with tasks such as these have proved to be inconsistent. In some patients, performance is impaired with either hand; in still others, the left hemisphere is quite adept on this task.

This inconsistency is, at least in part, due to the fact that the component operations required for the block design task have not been identified. Patients who demonstrate a right-hemisphere superiority for this task can evince no superiority on the perceptual aspects of the task. If a picture of the block design pattern is lateralized, either hemisphere can easily find the match from a series of pictures. And since each hand is sufficiently dexterous, the crucial link must be in the mapping of the sensory message onto the capable motor system.

It is also true that monitoring and producing facial expressions are managed by different hemispheres. In the perceptual domain, it appears that the right hemisphere has special processes devoted to the efficient detection of upright faces. Although the left hemisphere can also perceive and recognize faces and can reveal superior capacities when the faces are familiar, the right hemisphere appears specialized for unfamiliar facial stimuli. This pattern of asymmetry has also been shown for the rhesus monkey.

As the right hemisphere is superior for perception of faces, it would be reasonable to suppose it is also specialized for the management of facial expressions. Recent evidence however, shows that while both hemispheres can generate spontaneous facial expressions, only the dominant left hemisphere can generate voluntary facial expressions.

Attention and Perception

The attentional and perceptual abilities of split-brain patients have been extensively explored. Visual perception is the easiest to study. After cortical disconnection, perceptual information does not interact between the two cerebral hemispheres, but the supporting cognitive processes of attentional mechanisms do sometimes interact.

Split-brain patients cannot cross-integrate visual information between the two visual fields. When visual information is lateralized to either the left or the right disconnected hemisphere, the unstimulated hemisphere cannot use the information for perceptual analysis. This is also true for stereognostic information presented to each hand. Although touching any part of the body is noted by either hemisphere, patterned somatosensory information is lateralized. Thus, when a split-brain patient is holding an object in the left hand, he is unable to find an identical object with the right hand. Although some investigators argue that higher-order perceptual information is integrated by way of subcortical structures, these results have not been replicated by others.

For example, in one study, split-brain patients sometimes drew pictures that combine word information presented to the two hemispheres (e.g., *ten + clock* = a picture of a clock set at 10). Although this outcome initially seemed to imply the subcortical transfer of higher-order information between the hemispheres, subsequent observations (Kingstone and Gazzaniga, 1995) suggested that it actually reflects dual hemispheric control of the drawing hand (with control biased to the left hemisphere). Conceptually ambiguous word pairs, such as *hot dog*, were always depicted literally (e.g., a dog panting in the heat) and never as emergent objects (e.g.,

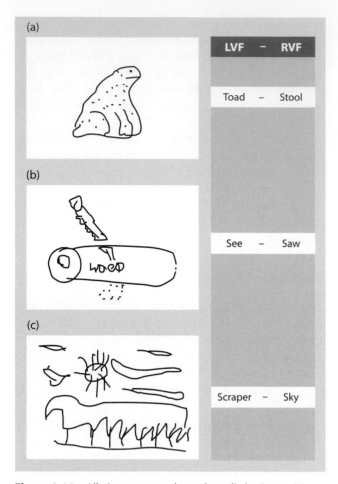

LVF	–	RVF
Toad	–	Stool
See	–	Saw
Scraper	–	Sky

Figure 9.14 All pictures were drawn by split-brain participant J.W.'s left hand. **(a)** Drawing of the left visual field word TOAD (ipsilateral to the drawing hand). **(b)** Drawing of the right visual field word SAW (contralateral to the drawing hand). **(c)** Drawing combines both words SCRAPER and SKY (ipsilateral + contralateral).

a frankfurter). Moreover, right- and left-hand drawings often depicted only the words presented to the left hemisphere (Figure 9.14).

Whereas the previous work showed that object identification processes work in isolation in the split-brain patient, the evidence does suggest that crude information concerning spatial locations can be cross-integrated. In one set of experiments, a four-point grid was presented to each visual field. On a given trial, one of the positions on the grid was highlighted and one condition of the task required the subject to move her eyes to the highlighted point within the visual field stimulated (Figure 9.15). In the second condition, the subject was required to move her eyes to the relative point in the opposite visual field. Split-brain subjects did this easily, which raised the possibility of crude cross-integration of spatial

information. This was true even when the grid was randomly positioned in the test field.

The finding that some type of spatial information remains integrated between the two halves of the brain raises the question, Are the attentional processes associated with spatial information affected by cortical disconnection? Surprisingly, split-brain patients can use either hemisphere to direct attention to positions in either the left or the right visual field. This conclusion was based on studies using a modified version of the spatial cuing task (see Chapter 6). To review, in this task, subjects respond as quickly as possible upon detecting a target that appears at one of several possible locations. The target is preceded by a cue, either at the target location

Figure 9.15 The upper example depicts the spatial tests. **(a)** On within-field trials, the eye moved to the stimulus that was surrounded by the probe. **(b)** On between-field trials, the eye moved to the corresponding stimulus in the other hemifield. The lower example depicts the perceptual tests. **(c)** On within-field trials, the probe appeared centered in one of the arrays, and the eye moved to the corresponding stimulus in the field in which the probe appeared. **(d)** On between-field trials, the eye moved to the corresponding stimulus in the opposite field.

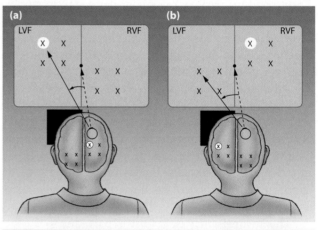

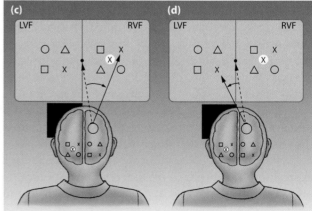

(i.e., a valid cue) or at another location (i.e., an invalid cue). Responses are faster on valid trials, indicating spatial orienting to the cued location. In split-brain patients, as with normal subjects, a cue to direct attention to a particular point in the visual field was honored no matter which half of the brain was presented with the critical stimulus. These results suggest that the two hemispheres rely on a common orienting system to maintain a single focus of attention.

The discovery that spatial attention can be directed with ease to either visual field raised the question of whether each separate cognitive system in the split-brain patient can, if instructed to do so, independently direct attention to a part of its own visual field. Can the right hemisphere direct attention to a point in the left visual field, while the left one simultaneously attends to a point in the right visual field? Normal subjects cannot so divide their attention. Perhaps the split-brain operation frees the two hemispheres from this constraint.

Alas, the split-brain patient cannot divide spatial attention between the two halves. There appears to be only one integrated spatial attention system that remains intact following cortical disconnection. Thus, like neurologically intact observers, the attentional system of split-brain patients is unifocal. They are unable to prepare for events in two spatially disparate locations.

The dramatic effects of disconnecting the cerebral hemispheres on perception and cognition might suggest that each half has its own attentional resources (Kinsbourne, 1982). If true, the cognitive operations of one half, no matter what the difficulty, would have scant influence on the cognitive activities of the other. The competing view is that the brain has limited resources that manage such processes; if they are being applied to task A, fewer are available for task B. According to this model, the harder hemisphere A worked on a task, the worse hemisphere B would do on a task of constant complexity.

Many have studied this phenomenon and all confirmed that the central resources are limited. Consider the following experiment, diagrammed in Figure 9.16. In what was called the *mixed* or *hard condition,* two series of three different geometric shapes were displayed concurrently to the left and right of central fixation and thus were lateralized to the right and left hemispheres, respectively. In the redundant or *easy* condition, the three geometric shapes were presented to only one hemisphere while three identical geometric shapes were presented to the other. To test recognition memory, a single shape was then presented in either the left or the right visual field. The observer indicated with a forced-

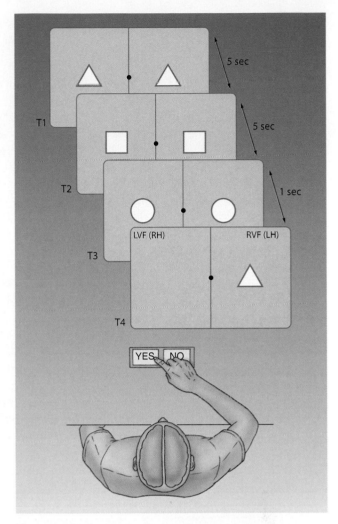

Figure 9.16 Sequence of events for a redundant three-condition trial. Stimuli were selected from a set of seven geometric forms. Each stimulus appeared for 150 msec. A delay followed the presentation of the last stimulus, and the unilateral probe stimulus was presented for 150 msec. The subject then made a decision as to whether or not the stimulus had been previously viewed in the corresponding visual field. Adapted from Holtzman and Gazzaniga (1984).

choice key press whether this probe matched any of the shapes that had been presented in the same hemifield. When the shapes had all been identical in the other hemifield (redundant condition), performance was better than when three different shapes had been presented in the other hemifield (mixed condition). Indeed, in the mixed condition, where six distinct shapes had been presented, performance was poor with either hemisphere.

This concept of resources should be distinguished from other properties of sensory systems associated

Interhemispheric Communication: Cooperation or Competition?

Theories of callosal function have generally focused on the idea that this massive bundle of axonal fibers provides the primary pathway for interhemispheric transfer. For example, in Chapter 5 we discussed Warrington's model of object recognition. In her view, the right hemisphere performs a specialized operation essential for perceptual categorization. This is followed by a left-hemisphere operation for semantic categorization. Interhemispheric communication is essential in this model for shuttling the information through these two processing stages. Even in less serially oriented models, interhemispheric transfer is frequently assumed to allow each hemisphere to have access to the information that might have initially been lateralized.

On the other hand, interhemispheric communication need not be conceptualized as a cooperative process. Connections across the corpus callosum may actually underlie a competition between the hemispheres. Indeed, the primary mode of callosal communication may be inhibitory rather than excitatory. As activation builds in a region within a hemisphere, the homologous, corresponding region in the other hemisphere would be inhibited. By this view, we need not assume that interhemispheric communication is designed to share information processing within the two hemispheres to facilitate concurrent, and roughly identical activity in homologous regions. Similar to the way in which split-brain behavior is assumed to reflect the

independent operation of the two hemispheres, behavior produced by intact brains may also reflect the (fluctuating) dominance of one or the other hemisphere.

Why might the brain have evolved such that the two hemispheres act as competitors rather than cooperators? One challenge for a cooperative system is that there must be a means to ensure that the two hemispheres are operating on roughly the same information. Such coordination might be difficult given that the perceptual input as well as the focus of our attention are constantly changing. While computers can perform their operations at lightening speed, neural activity is a relatively slow process. The processing delays inherent in transcallosal communication may limit the extent to which the two hemispheres can cooperate.

There are a number of factors limiting the rate of neural activity. First, to generate an action potential, activity within the receiving, dendritic branches must integrate tiny inputs across both space and time in order to reach threshold. Second, the rate at which individual neurons can fire is limited, owing to intrinsic differences in membrane properties, tonic sources of excitation and inhibition, as well as refractory periods between each spike-generating event. Third, and most important, neural signals need to be propagated along axons. These conduction times can be quite substantial, especially for the relatively long fibers of the corpus callosum.

James Ringo and his colleagues (1994) at the University of Rochester provided an interesting analysis of

with information processing. The limits to information processing captured by the concept of resource limitations are more general than the limits and mechanisms now studied in such phenomena as searching a visual scene for information. For example, while the overall resources a brain commits to a task appear constant, the method by which they are deployed can vary. The time to detect a complex object increases as more items are

added to the display. For example, normal control subjects require about an extra 70 msec to detect the target when two extra items are added to the display, and another 70 msec for each additional pair of items. In split-brain patients, when the items are distributed across the midline of the visual field, as opposed to all being in one visual field, the reaction time to added stimuli is cut almost in half.

this problem. They began by calculating estimates of transcallosal conduction delays. Two essential numbers were needed: the distance to be traveled and the speed at which the signal will be transmitted. If the distances were direct, the average distance of the callosal fibers would be short. However, most axons follow a circuitous route. Taking this into consideration, a value of 175 mm was used as representative of the average length of a callosal fiber in humans. The speed at which myelinated neural impulses travel is a function of the diameter of the fibers. Using the limited data available from humans in combination with more thorough measures in the monkey, an estimate of the average conduction speed was calculated to be around 6.5 m/sec. Thus, to travel a distance of 175 mm would take almost 30 msec. Single-cell studies in primates have confirmed that interhemispheric processing entails relatively substantial delays.

Ringo used a neural network to demonstrate the consequences of slow interhemispheric conduction times. The network consisted of two identical sets of processing modules, each representing a cerebral hemisphere. It included both intrahemispheric and interhemispheric connections, with the latter much more sparse to reflect the known anatomy of the human brain. This network was trained to perform a pattern-recognition task. After it had learned to classify all of the patterns correctly, the interhemispheric connections were disconnected. Thus, performance could now be assessed when each hemisphere had to operate in isolation. The critical comparison was between networks in which the interhemispheric conduction times during learning had been either slow or fast. The results showed that for the network trained with fast interhemispheric connections, the disconnection procedure led to a substantial deterioration in performance. Thus, object recognition was dependent on cooperative processing for the network with fast interhemispheric connections. In contrast, for the network trained with slow interhemispheric connections, performance was minimally affected by the disconnection procedure. For this network, recognition was essentially dependent only on intrahemispheric processing. These results led Ringo to conclude that a system with slow interhemispheric conduction delays, for example, the human brain, ends up with each hemisphere operating in a relatively independent manner.

Interestingly, these delays could be reduced if the callosal fibers were larger, as this would increase conduction speed. However, this would require a corresponding increase in brain volume. For example, to reduce the conduction delay by a factor of two would lead to a 50% increase in brain volume. Such an increase would, of course, have severe consequences, in terms of metabolic demands and for childbirth. The brain appears to have evolved such that each hemisphere can have rapid access to information from either side of space, but with limited capability for tasks that would require extensive communication back and forth across the corpus callosum. The delays associated with transcallosal communication not only may limit the degree of cooperation between two hemispheres, but also may have provided an impetus for the development of hemispheric specialization. Independent processing systems would be more likely to evolve nonidentical computational capabilities.

This finding was recently qualified; the strategy differed in how each hemisphere examined the contents of its visual field. The left dominant hemisphere utilized a "guided" or "smart" strategy and the right hemisphere did not. Hence, the left hemisphere adopts a helpful cognitive strategy in problem solving but the right hemisphere does not have extra cognitive skills.

The concept of resources in many ways refers to processes engaged when attention to an information-processing task is voluntarily allocated. Searching a visual scene, however, calls upon more automatic processes that may well be built-in properties of the visual system itself. That these systems are distinct is reflected in the discovery that splitting brains has a different effect on the processes.

CONVERGING EVIDENCE OF
HEMISPHERIC SPECIALIZATION

Studies on split-brain patients have given us the most dramatic evidence of hemispheric specialization (Gazzaniga, 1995). Many cognitive neuroscientists concentrate on identifying the capabilities of the two hemispheres when forced to act in isolation: Can the right hemisphere produce speech? Do the two hemispheres share common attentional resources? Can information be integrated at the subcortical level?

Functional Asymmetries in Patients with Unilateral Cortical Lesions

Research on hemispheric specialization has not been limited to split-brains. Two other prominent methodologies come into play. First, continuing the tradition initiated by Broca, many researchers have examined the performance of patients with unilateral, focal brain lesions. The basic idea has been to compare how patients perform when their lesions are restricted to either the right or the left hemisphere. An appealing feature of this approach is that there is no need to lateralize the stimuli to one side or the other: Stimuli can be presented without restriction. Laterality effects are assumed to arise because of the unilateral lesions. If lesions to the left hemisphere result in more disruption in reading tasks, the deficit is attributed to the hemisphere's specialization in reading processes.

In many of these studies, especially in work prior to the 1980s, investigators were not very concerned about the lesions' precise location: Patients were simply lumped together in relation to the side on which the lesion existed. Despite this crude parcellation, numerous laterality effects have been identified. Rather than infer general "left-hemisphere" and "right-hemisphere" syndromes, we think these results reflect the fact that strokes encompass substantial amounts of neural tissue. Thus, in large-scale group studies, there is probably substantial anatomical overlap of damaged tissue. Researchers now seek more than differences between the two hemispheres; they want to specify where the asymmetries arise.

Functional Asymmetries in the Normal Brain

The second important alternative methodology tests people with intact brains. Here the emphasis is on designing experiments that differentially require processing in either the right or the left hemisphere—similar to the procedures used in split-brain studies. In the visual domain, comparisons are made between when stimuli are presented in the left or the right visual field. While this procedure ensures that information will be initially projected to the contralateral hemisphere, the potential for rapid transcortical transfer is high. Even so, we find consistent differences from various sides of stimulation. For example, subjects are more adept at recognizing whether a briefly presented string of letters forms a word when the stimulus is shown in the right visual field than in the left visual field. Results like these lead to the conclusion that transfer is of limited functional utility, or that the information becomes degraded during the transfer. Thus, we assume that performance is dominated by the contralateral hemisphere with peripheral visual input.

Studies of auditory perception similarly attempt to isolate the input to one hemisphere. Analogous to the vision work, the stimuli can be presented monaurally, that is, restricted to one ear. But because auditory pathways are not as strictly lateralized as visual ones, an alternative methodology for isolating the input is the dichotic listening task shown in Figure 9.17. In this task, two competing messages are presented simultaneously, one to each ear, and the subject tries to report both messages. The ipsilateral projections from each ear are presumably suppressed when a message comes over the contralateral pathway from the other ear.

The dichotic listening task was introduced in the early 1970s by Doreen Kimura (1973) while she was at the Montreal Neurological Institute. In a typical study, subjects heard a series of dichotically presented words. When asked to repeat as many words as possible, they consistently gave words that were presented to the right ear, an effect dubbed *the right-ear advantage*. Results like these mesh well with expectations that the left hemisphere is dominant for language.

In vision and audition, performance asymmetries with lateralized stimuli generated great excitement. Here at last was a simple method for learning about hemispheric specialization in neurologically healthy people! It is not surprising that thousands of laterality studies on healthy subjects have been conducted using almost any imaginable stimulus manipulations.

The limitations of this kind of laterality research should be kept in mind (Efron, 1990):

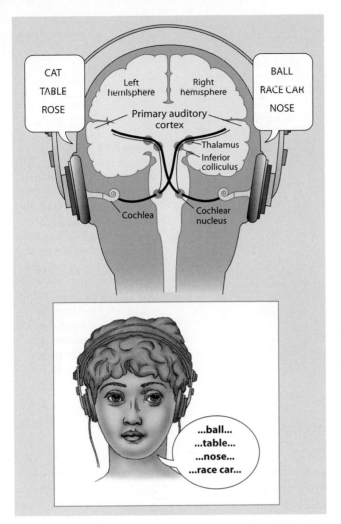

Figure 9.17 The dichotic listening task is used to compare hemispheric specialization in auditory perception. **(Top)** Competing messages are presented, one to the left ear and one to the right ear. Auditory information is projected bilaterally. Although the majority of ascending fibers from the cochlear nucleus project to the contralateral thalamus, some fibers ascend on the ipsilateral side. **(Bottom)** The subject is asked either to report the stimuli or to judge whether a probe stimulus was part of the dichotic message. Comparisons focus on whether the reported information had been heard in the right or left ear, with the assumption that the predominant processing occurred in the contralateral hemisphere. With linguistic stimuli, subjects are more accurate in reporting the information presented to the right ear. Top adapted from Kimura (1973).

- The effects are small and inconsistent, perhaps because healthy people have two functioning hemispheres connected by an intact corpus callosum.
- There is a bias in the scientific review process to publish papers that find significant differences over papers that report no differences. It is much more exciting to report asymmetries in the way we remember lateralized pictures of faces than to report that effects are similar for right and left visual field presentations.
- There is the problem of interpretation. What can be inferred from an observed asymmetry in performance with lateralized stimuli? In the preceding examples, the right visual field and right-ear advantages were assumed to reflect the fact that these inputs had better access to the language processes of the left hemisphere. But perhaps people are just better at identifying information in the right visual field.

To rule out this last possibility, one must identify tasks that produce a left-ear or left visual field advantage. For example, shortly after Kimura's initial work, scientists discovered that people are better at recognizing the left-ear member of dichotic melody pairs; indeed, a double dissociation happens when subjects are presented with dichotic pairs of sung melodies (Bartholomeus, 1974). We find a right-ear advantage for the song's words but a left-ear advantage for its melodies (Figure 9.18).

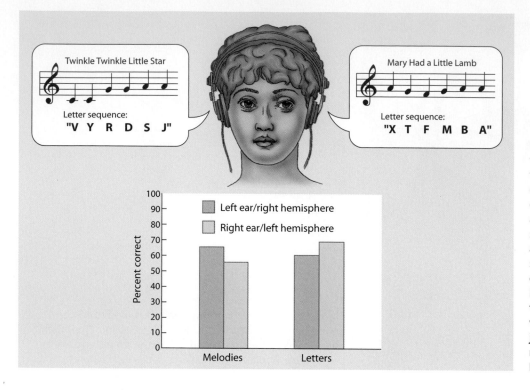

Figure 9.18 A right-ear advantage is not found on all tasks. Subjects listened to a dichotic message in which each ear was presented with a series of letters sung to short melodies. When given a recognition memory test, subjects were more accurate on the letter task for stimuli heard in the right ear. In contrast, a left-ear advantage was observed when the subjects were tested on the melodies. Adapted from Bartholomeus (1974).

WHAT IS LATERALIZED?

Laterality researchers continually grapple with appropriate ways to describe asymmetries in the function of the two hemispheres (Allen, 1983; Bradshaw and Nettleton, 1981; and Bryden, 1982). Early hypotheses fixed on the stimuli's properties and the tasks employed. For example, the left hemisphere was described as verbal and the right hemisphere as spatial. By this view, one might suppose that the left hemisphere has sole province over all language functions. In the dichotic listening task, words presented to the left ear are recognized only when they succeed in being transferred to the left hemisphere. But, as seen in split-brain and stroke research, such absolutes are rare. Many tasks can be successfully performed by either hemisphere, although they may differ in efficiency.

An alternative approach for characterizing hemispheric specialization is to look for differences in processing style. Here, the left hemisphere has been described as analytic and sequential, whereas the right hemisphere is viewed as holistic and parallel. The popular press has promoted such descriptions, triggering industries devoted to helping people learn to "think" with the right hemisphere or improve the "power" of the left hemisphere (Figure 9.19).

Hypotheses about modes of processing are not restricted to specific task domains—they describe general processing styles. Hemispheric specializations may emerge because certain tasks benefit from one style or another. Language, for example, is seen as sequential: We hear speech as a continuous stream that requires rapid analysis of its component parts; an accurate representation of space calls for not just perceiving the component parts but seeing them as a coherent whole.

A problem here is knowing whether a task requires analytic or holistic processing. The theoretical interpretation frequently disintegrates into a circular redescription of results. Though a right-ear advantage exists in perceiving consonants, no asymmetry is found for vowels; consonants require the sequential, analytic processors of the left hemisphere, while vowel perception entails a more holistic form of processing.

With verbal-spatial and analytic-holistic hypotheses, we assume that a single fundamental dichotomy can characterize the differences in function between the two hemispheres. The appeal of "dichotomania" is one of parsimony: The simplest account of hemispheric specialization rests on a single difference. Current dichotomies all have their limitations, but perhaps a new one will capture a unitary distinction.

Yet it is also reasonable to suppose that the fundamental dichotomy is a fiction. Hemispheric asymme-

Figure 9.19 Pop psychology books have tended to trivialize the differences between the two cerebral hemispheres. The right hemisphere has been suggested to be the creative, intuitive side, the left hemisphere the analytic, logical side.

Left hemisphere painting

Right hemisphere painting

tries have been observed in many task domains: language, motor control, attention, object recognition. It may be that specializations are specific to particular task domains. There need not be a causal connection between hemispheric specialization in motor control (e.g., why people are right- or left-handed) and why the hemispheres differ in representing language or visuospatial information. Maybe the commonality across task domains is their evolution: As the two hemispheres became segregated, there was a common impetus for the evolution of systems that were nonidentical. Asymmetry in how information is processed, represented, and responded to may be a more efficient and flexible design principle than redundancy.

The idea of asymmetrical processing also underscores an important point in modern conceptualizations of hemispheric specialization; namely, the two hemispheres may work in concert to perform a task, even though their contributions may vary. There is no need to suppose some sort of master director who decides which hemisphere is needed for a task. Language is not the exclusive domain of the left hemisphere. The right hemisphere may also contribute, although the types of representations it derives may not be efficient for certain tasks. And the left hemisphere does not defer to the right hemisphere on visuospatial tasks, but processes this information in a different way. Seen this way, we begin to realize that much of what we learn from clinical tests of hemispheric specialization tell us more about our tasks rather than the computations performed by each hemisphere. This point is also evident in split-brain research. With the notable exception of speech production, each hemisphere has competence in every cognitive domain.

Asymmetries in Perceptual Representations

Objects that are attended to are rarely restricted to a single visual field. If we notice a fast car approaching from the left, we quickly shift our gaze to its direction. Given that foveal input is projected bilaterally, coupled with small eye movements, a stimulus is projected to both hemispheres. But this does not mean that the two hemispheres will derive identical representations from a common input. Indeed, the two hemispheres will amplify different sources of information, which in turn vary in importance for operations devoted to identifying a stimulus and deciding whether it requires a response.

A MODEL TASK FOR THE PERCEPTION OF HIERARCHICAL STIMULI

Consider the stimulus in Figure 9.20. If asked to describe the stimulus, your first response might be to say it is a house. When prodded for more description, you would note the intricate detailing in the front door, the windows running across the front facade, and the roof made of asphalt shingles. In recounting the picture, you would have provided a hierarchical description. The house can be described on multiple levels: In terms of its shape and distinction, it is a house. But it is also a specific house, with a certain configuration of doors, windows, and materials. This description is hierarchical in that the finer levels of description are embedded in the higher levels. The house's shape evolves from the configuration of its component parts, an idea developed in Chapter 5.

David Navon (1977) of the University of Haifa introduced a model task for studying hierarchical structure.

Figure 9.20 We represent information at multiple scales. At its most global scale, this drawing is of a house. We can also recognize and focus on the component parts of the house.

He created stimuli that could be identified on one of two levels, an example of which is given in Figure 9.21. At each level, the stimulus contains an identifiable letter. The critical feature is that the letter defined by the global shape is composed of smaller letters. In Figure 9.21a, the global *H* is composed of *F*'s.

Navon was interested in how we perceive hierarchical stimuli. He initially found that the perceptual system first extracted the global shape. Not only were reaction times slower when subjects had to identify local elements, but considerable interference happened when the global shape and local elements were discordant. The interference was not symmetrical. The time required to identify the global letter was independent of the identity of the constituent elements. Subsequent research qualified these conclusions, though. Global precedence is not always found but depends on factors like object size and number of local elements. Although Navon had assumed that a single system processes hierarchical stimuli, the lack of invariance suggested otherwise. Perhaps different processing systems were essential for representing local and global information.

Inspired by laterality dichotomies in analytic-holistic processing, Justine Sergent (1982) of the Montreal Neurological Institute modified the task to look for hemispheric asymmetries. On each trial, a hierarchical pattern was presented for 150 msec in either the left or the right visual field (or at a central viewing location, a condition we will not consider here). As with split-brain studies, brief exposures ensured that subjects could not move their eyes and look directly at the peripheral stimuli, thus allowing the information to be projected to both hemispheres. The subjects were asked to press one button if the stimulus contained an *H* or *L,* and the other button if neither of these targets was present. The target could be either at the local and global level (one *H* and one *L*), at one level only, or on neither level. The letters *F* and *T* were shown at levels that did not contain a target.

Figure 9.22 shows the intriguing interaction between the target level and the side of presentation. When both the global and local levels contained a target, subjects were faster to respond when the stimulus was presented in the left visual field. Even though this might reflect heightened arousal for the right hemisphere or a generalized advantage on visual tasks, the local-only results suggest otherwise; reaction times were fastest when the stimulus was in the right visual field. The asymmetries between the two target conditions were tied to the type of analysis required. The left hemisphere was more adept at representing local information and the right hemisphere was better with global information.

Figure 9.21 Local-global stimuli used to investigate hierarchical representation. Each stimulus is composed of a series of identical letters whose global arrangement forms a larger letter. The subjects' task is to indicate whether the stimulus contained an *H* or *L*. When the stimulus set included competing targets at both levels **(b)**, the subjects would be instructed to respond either only to local targets or only to global targets. Neither target is present in **(e)**.

(a)	(b)	(c)
F F	L L	H H
F F	L L	H H
F F F	L L L	H H H
F F	L L	H H
F F	L L	H H

(d)	(e)
H H H H	T T T T
H	T
H H H H	T T T T
H	T
H	T

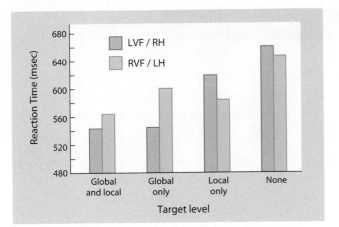

Figure 9.22 Reaction times to hierarchical letter stimuli, presented in either the left or the right visual field. Subjects judged whether the stimulus contained (at least) one of two letters, H or L. Reaction times were faster for left-visual-field/right-hemisphere stimuli when the target was defined at the global level or at both levels. In contrast, reaction times were faster for the right-visual-field/left-hemisphere stimuli when the target was defined at the local level. Adapted from Sergent (1982).

Similar experiments with neurologically impaired patients confirmed that this interaction stems from the asymmetrical functions of the hemispheres. Local and global stimuli were presented to the center of view (the critical laterality factor was the side of the lesion). Patients with left-sided lesions were slow to identify local targets, and patients with right-sided lesions were slow with global targets.

By carefully determining the focus of patients' lesions, Lynn Robertson and her colleagues (1988) at the Veteran's Administration Medical Center in Martinez, California, discovered that interaction arises when the damage encompasses the border of the temporal and parietal lobes; frontal or superior parietal lobe lesions do not affect performance. These findings agree with others that identified the tempoparietal junction as important in visual object recognition.

Even though this view is consistent with the processing mode hypothesis—the left hemisphere as an analytic processor and the right hemisphere as a holistic processor—it is important to keep in mind that both hemispheres can abstract either level of representation. How they differ is in the efficiency with which they represent local or global information. Thus, patients with left-hemisphere lesions are still able to analyze the local structure of a hierarchical stimulus. But they must rely on an intact right hemisphere, and this hemisphere is inefficient in abstracting local information. Further confirmation of this idea comes from local-global stud-

ies with split-brain patients (Robertson et al., 1993). Here, too, patients generally identify targets at either level regardless of the side of presentation. But, as with normal subjects and patients with unilateral lesions, split-brain patients are faster to identify local targets presented to the right visual field and global targets presented to the left visual field.

In extreme cases, the hemispheric biases for one level of representation can completely override other levels. In the case study at the beginning of this chapter, W.J. was unable to manipulate blocks into their global configuration when restricted to using his right hand. Similar dramatic things happen with stroke victims. Figure 9.23 displays drawings made by patients who recently had strokes in either the right or the left

Figure 9.23 Extreme failures of hierarchical processing following brain damage. Two patients were asked to draw the two figures shown in the left column. The patient with right-hemisphere damage was quite accurate in producing the local element, the "z" or the square, but failed to arrange these elements into the correct global configuration. The patient with left-hemisphere damage drew the overall shapes, but left out all of the local elements. Note that the drawings for both patients were quite consistent for both the linguistic and nonlinguistic stimuli, suggesting a task-independent representational deficit. Adapted from Delis et al., 1986.

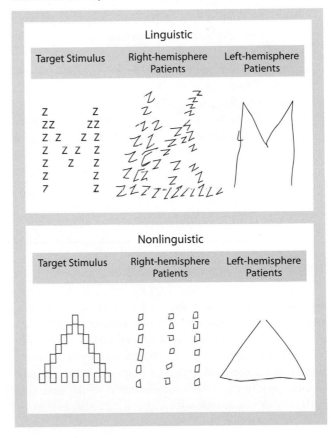

An Interview with Stephen M. Kosslyn, Ph.D.
Dr. Kosslyn is affiliated with the Department of Psychology at Harvard University. In addition to his study of hemispheric specialization, Dr. Kosslyn has used a variety of behavioral and imaging methods to examine the relationship between perception and imagery.

Authors: How do you think the two hemispheres of the human brain are different?

SMK: As a first stab, consider the possibility that the hemispheres differ in three ways. First, there are neuroanatomical differences. For example, the visual cortex is larger in the right hemisphere. I presume these differences have implications for function, but it isn't entirely clear yet what the implications are. Second, the hemispheres differ in how efficiently they can perform specific "elementary" operations, such as specifying an object's location in space, iterating through a mental list, or detecting basic geometric properties in a shape. In my view, relatively simple, mechanical functions are implemented in local regions of cortex, and any complex task requires combinations of such basic functions. Local cerebral activation detected using positron emission tomography, say, indicates that such an operation is used, and patterns of activation reflect combinations of operations that are used to carry out a task. Third, combinations of basic operations correspond to a specific "strategy." The hemispheres may differ in the types of strategies they use best. For example, perhaps the left hemisphere is better at analyzing things into basic units (shapes into parts, stories into phases, etc.), as some researchers have suggested, whereas the right is better at using overall patterns (global shape, general theme, etc.). Such strategy differences may arise in part because of differences in the relative efficiency of specific operations, but may also reflect "strategy biases" that arise for other reasons.

Authors: What are the implications of your approach?

SMK: If you want to know whether to slice through the left or right hemisphere to remove a subcortical tumor, it would be nice to know what the two sides are doing. If the patient is an architect, I would recommend avoiding regions that deal with spatial relations, whereas that might not be quite so important if the patient is an English teacher.

Authors: We will keep this in mind next time we need neurosurgery. But are there deeper implications of this approach for our understanding of "human nature"?

SMK: The basic idea is that people are different, but not in boring ways; rather than trying to sort people into categories—such as "analyzers" versus "synthesizers," or "visuals" versus "audiles"—we need to think about the efficiency of different processing systems, and how these differences in efficiency can have widespread consequences. People are not going to be pigeon-holed very easily.

Authors: What about cerebral lateralization more specifically?

SMK: This is an area where dichotomies have run amuck. The hemispheres have been characterized in terms of many sorts of dichotomies, such as verbal versus perceptual, analytic versus holistic, logical versus intuitive, cooked versus raw, and so on. On my view, such dichotomies won't get us very far. For some tasks in some contexts, a particular dichotomy might help summarize the performance of the parts of systems that are more efficient in one or the other hemisphere. But these dichotomies are basically descriptive, and when

hemisphere. They were shown a hierarchical stimulus and asked to reproduce it from memory. Drawings from patients with left-hemisphere lesions faithfully followed the contour, but without any hints of local elements. In contrast, patients with right-hemisphere lesions produced only local elements. Note that this pattern was consistent with either linguistic and non-linguistic stimuli; hence the representational deficits were not restricted to certain stimuli.

COMPUTATIONAL BASIS OF LOCAL AND GLOBAL ASYMMETRIES

What defines the local and global structure of a stimulus? An obvious answer is that they differ in size: Global structure is larger than local structure. But how does the

we look at brain function more closely—for example, as revealed by current brain-scanning techniques—we see many and varied patterns of activation in each half-brain. In my view, we won't understand the functions of the hemispheres unless we think about the whole brain; the two halves work together, after all, and only by considering how they function in a single system will we be able to work out what each contributes.

Authors: But how does this "mechanical" view you have espoused tell us about mental life?

SMK: Well, depending on what question you ask, different things count as answers. I am interested in mental functions, such as memory, perception, language, imagery, and so on. This approach seems appropriate for answering questions about how such functions operate. Now, if you ask me why they are as they are, or why they are used in specific circumstances, this approach is less useful. These questions get us into talking about how specific types of information, specific contents ("meanings") engage the system. But even for these kinds of questions, knowing that the structure of the system is a certain way will—at the least—help one to couch the question better and will give one a framework for formulating answers.

Authors: It is now widely agreed that most complex perceptual and cognitive skills such as language or the detection of upright faces are specific adaptations that have been established through natural selection. That such adaptations would be lateralized makes sense since there isn't an obvious reason why these circuits should be laid down twice. Any comments?

SMK: Hmmm, seems to me that the same argument would also apply to lungs, kidneys, and so forth . . . which are, of course, duplicated. Nothing like a little redundancy to increase survival value; in contemplating the possibility of a stroke, I rather like the idea of having all my cognitive functions duplicated in different parts of the brain. In general, it seems clear that the structure

of the brain is dictated by the genes, and hence is a product of evolution (not just natural selection, but the entire process), but it is not clear to me that any particular kind of "content" has been built into the brain by such mechanisms.

Authors: Do I detect a trace of "environmentalist" sentiment in that last remark?

SMK: Yes, indeed. I am impressed as much by the variability in human cognition and behavior as by the constancy. It is true that some of the variability could be due to noise around the mean (and evolutionary processes definitely produce such variation), but at least some of it is probably a consequence of one's interactions with the environment. My own view is that the genes program some parts of the brain precisely, but most of it is rather loosely prespecified—and these parts are subsequently configured by one's interaction with the environment. The fact that so many "extra" connections are present at birth, and then "pruned" away after the animal has some interaction with the environment, is consistent with this view. Indeed, I spent a good chunk of time developing computer simulation models of how interaction with the environment could cause different patterns of laterality.

Authors: But research with split-brain patients has not revealed such variability. Perhaps the work with normal subjects has nothing to do with laterality, but instead reflects attentional variations or something like that.

SMK: Perhaps. But recall that one doesn't get to be a split-brain patient for no reason. Those people are very sick people before the surgery. So they aren't exactly a random, representative sample; maybe their epilepsy forces a greater consistency than would otherwise exist. In addition, there is a pretty small number of such patients, which again argues for caution in generalizing from them to the population at large. Finally, I believe that there is considerable variability even among split-brain patients, if one chooses to focus on it.

visual system process differences in size? To answer this, consider the receptive field properties of neurons involved in the analysis of shape.

A notable feature of visual receptive fields is that they are tuned to detect changes in contrast, or lightness. Most visual neurons respond weakly to a uniform field of light. Instead, as we saw in Chapter 4 (see Pioneers in the Visual Cortex, p. 130), they are most sensitive to changes in lightness because the neurons have a center-surround structure in which one region is excited by light and flanking regions are inhibited by it. In an on-off cell, the center region is excited by light; in an off-on cell, the center is inhibited by it (Figure 9.24). Moreover, the sizes of the center-surround regions vary. Such

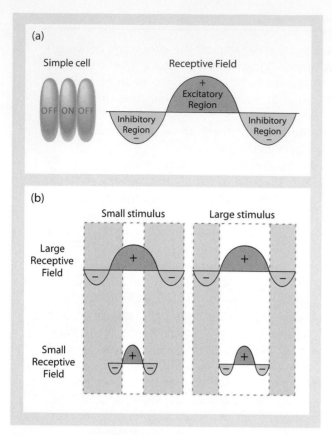

Figure 9.24 Stimulus size is encoded by the spatial extent of a neuron's receptive field. **(a)** Striate cortex neurons not only have a preferred orientation, but are also sensitive to the size of a stimulus. Size sensitivity is determined by the width of the excitatory and inhibitory regions of the cell's receptive field. An on-off cell responds when a light stimulus falls in the excitatory region and a dark stimulus falls in the inhibitory region. **(b)** A narrow stimulus produces a high response rate in the neuron with the smaller receptive field. This stimulus produces little activity in the neuron with the large receptive field because the excitatory center region is also stimulated by the dark background. The opposite occurs with the large stimulus. The larger receptive field is maximally responsive to this stimulus. The smaller receptive field does not respond because the stimulus spans both the excitatory and inhibitory regions.

a computational device is sensitive to an object's size. The narrow receptive field fails to respond to the large bar because the bar spans the excitatory and inhibitory regions; this yields a net effect in which the excitation is canceled by the inhibition. In contrast, the same receptive field is maximally activated by the narrow bar.

The center-surround structure has led some theorists to conceptualize visual neurons as *spatial frequency filters*, which refers to how the brightness of a visual pattern varies as a function of space. Consider the simple

patterns in Figure 9.25 in which brightness varies in a sinusoidal manner along the horizontal axis. In the top pattern, the variation is slow. The transition from light to dark and back to light again spans most of the page. The variation is much faster in the bottom pattern; hence, there is more rapid transition between the contrasting stripes. The transition rate can be described by its periodicity with respect to a unit of space. For example, the top pattern has a frequency of 2 cycles/page and the bottom one has a frequency of 8 cycles/page. In visual perception, units are expressed as cycles per degree, where the unit corresponds to 1 degree of visual angle (about the size subtended by a thumb held at arm's length).

Figure 9.25 Three sinusoidal gratings. Intensity varies in a sinusoidal manner across the horizontal dimension. The frequency of the sinusoids varies, being lowest for the stimulus on top and highest for the stimulus on bottom. The firing rate of a visual cortex neuron to these stimuli will vary, depending on the width of the neuron's receptive field. In this way, visual neurons operate as spatial frequency filters.

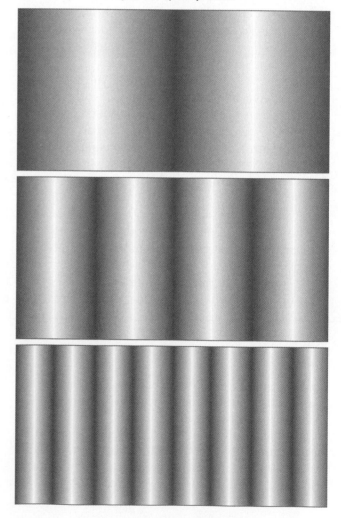

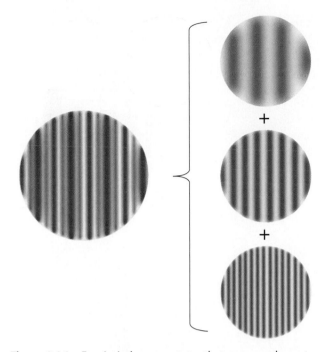

Figure 9.26 Fourier's theorem states that any complex pattern can be described as the composite of sinusoids that vary in power and phase (starting position). The grating pattern on the left is created by combining the three sinusoids on the right. For each position along the horizontal axis, the brightness in the compound grating is determined by averaging the brightness at the corresponding points in the sinusoids. In an identical manner, any complex pattern could be decomposed into a set of sinusoids. The set would have to include a large range of component frequencies that are oriented in all possible directions.

A cell with narrow center-surround regions operates like a high-frequency spatial filter that responds vigorously to high-frequency patterns. A cell with a wide center-surround region operates as a low-frequency filter and responds only to low-frequency patterns.

An appealing feature of the spatial frequency hypothesis is that any complex pattern can be described by its component spatial frequencies (Figure 9.26). This relation was established by Charles Fourier, one of the great French mathematicians of the nineteenth century, and scientists have proposed that the visual system analyzes shape by performing a Fourier analysis of the stimulus. In essence, this is another manifestation of a divide-and-conquer strategy. An array of neurons, tuned to a range of spatial frequencies, gives a complete representation of a stimulus. We can see this by using computer algorithms in which a stimulus is filtered to eliminate low- or high-frequency information.

Sergent (1982) conjectured that the spatial frequency hypothesis is a computational basis for hemispheric asymmetries in visual perception. She pro-

posed that the left hemisphere is more adept at representing high spatial frequency information and that the right hemisphere is better with low-frequency information. Sergent assumed that the local structure of a hierarchical pattern would be carried in higher frequencies than the global structure. In Figure 9.27,

Figure 9.27 A hierarchical letter stimulus, before and after low- and high-pass frequency filtering. **(a)** the unfiltered stimulus. **(b)** The same stimulus after all of the high frequencies have been removed (low pass). Neurons sensitive only to these low frequencies would not be able to represent the local elements. **(c)** The stimulus after all of the low frequencies have been removed (high pass). High frequencies can still support local and global identification. However, the contrast of the stimulus is reduced.

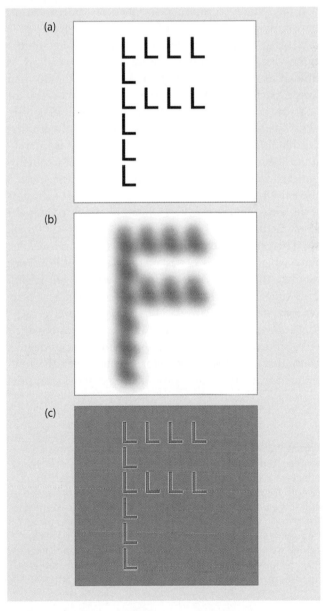

computer algorithms were used to recreate a hierarchical stimulus after either the high- or the low-frequency information was removed. In a low-pass stimulus, the identity of local elements cannot be distinguished even though the global shape persists. In a high-pass stimulus, both levels can be identified, but much of the contrast is absent. The advantage of identifying global targets is abolished with high-pass filtered patterns, presumably because the same units—such as receptive fields with narrow center-surround regions—are required for both kinds of stimuli.

More direct support for the spatial frequency hypothesis comes from Fred Kitterle and his colleagues (1990) at the University of Toledo. They used sinusoidal gratings rather than hierarchical patterns. An advantage with sinusoids is their simplicity: Any complex pattern will have many component frequencies, but sinusoids have only one. Sinusoids of either 1 cycle/degree or 3 cycles/degree were presented in either the left or the right visual field. Subjects were asked to respond as quickly as possible, pressing one key if the stimulus had "wide" stripes (1 cycle/degree) and the other key for "narrow" stripes (3 cycles/degree). While subjects were always faster when responding to the wide pattern, the results also showed the predicted side-by-size interaction. The reaction times for wide-striped, low-frequency patterns were faster when the stimulus was presented to the left visual field; narrow-striped, high-frequency patterns were identified fastest when presented to the right visual field (Figure 9.28).

This study yielded two other significant results. First, when subjects were asked to detect stimuli and not identify them, no visual field differences were found. This suggests that laterality effects do not arise at early sensory stages but emerge during higher-level perceptual analysis. Second, the same interaction was obtained with sinusoids of 3 cycles/degree and 9 cycles/degree. With this pair, the 3 cycles/degree becomes the low-frequency member, and now there is a left visual field

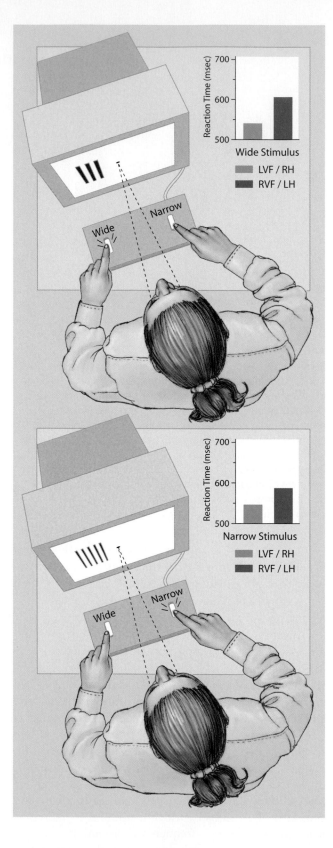

Figure 9.28 Asymmetries in how frequency information is represented in the two hemispheres may account for laterality effects in visual perception. A low-frequency (1 cycle/degree) or high-frequency (3 cycles/degree) stimulus was presented in either the left or the right visual field. Subjects judged whether the pattern was "Wide" or "Narrow." Reaction times to the low frequency stimuli presented in the left visual field/right hemisphere were much faster. This side also showed an advantage for the high-frequency stimulus, but the magnitude of the asymmetry was reduced. Adapted from Kitterle et al. (1990).

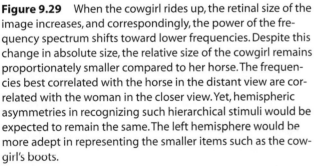

Figure 9.29 When the cowgirl rides up, the retinal size of the image increases, and correspondingly, the power of the frequency spectrum shifts toward lower frequencies. Despite this change in absolute size, the relative size of the cowgirl remains proportionately smaller compared to her horse. The frequencies best correlated with the horse in the distant view are correlated with the woman in the closer view. Yet, hemispheric asymmetries in recognizing such hierarchical stimuli would be expected to remain the same. The left hemisphere would be more adept in representing the smaller items such as the cowgirl's boots.

advantage for the stimulus. Again, we find that the laterality effect is not tied to how spatial frequency filters differ within the two hemispheres. Rather, laterality effects are based on relative frequency (Figure 9.29). Within the range of task-relevant information, the left hemisphere is biased to represent high-frequency information and the right hemisphere represents low-frequency information. This fits our view that local-global asymmetries are generally invariant with respect to a hierarchical pattern's size. Irrespective of size, local structure is conveyed by higher spatial frequencies rather than global structure (Christman and Kitterle, 1991).

APPLYING THE FREQUENCY HYPOTHESIS

The frequency hypothesis offers a powerful account of hemispheric asymmetries in visual perception. Rather than emphasize dichotomies that may be hard to define a priori because of stimulus characteristics (e.g., local-global) or processing modes (e.g., analytic-holistic), the hypothesis centers on an explicit source of information in the stimulus. Moreover, the hypothesis is grounded in a well-developed computational theory of how the visual system operates. An extension to laterality research builds on the idea that the visual system is composed of spatial frequency filters used in an asymmetrical manner by the two hemispheres (Ivry and Robertson, in press).

The frequency hypothesis has been applied to assess perceptual asymmetries across a range of tasks. For example, it can account for the fact that numerous manipulations lead to greater impairments in the perception of stimuli presented to the right visual field in comparison to the left visual field. Blurring the stimulus, reducing its contrast, and restricting the exposure time reduce the fidelity of high-frequency content more than low-frequency content. As such, this should disproportionately interfere with left-hemisphere representations that amplify the high frequencies.

The frequency hypothesis offers a parsimonious interpretation of experiments that show reversals in visual field advantages even when stimuli remain unchanged. Sergent (1985) presented sixteen photographs of familiar faces, with each face shown in either the left or the right visual field. In one condition, subjects judged whether the person was male or female. In another condition, subjects had to identify the person shown in the photographs. Performance on the male-female task revealed a left visual field advantage and that on the identification task showed a right visual field advantage. Sergent maintained that this reversal reflected the fact that the critical information for performing each task was contained in different portions of the frequency spectrum. Determining whether a person is male or female could be done with low spatial frequency information. Identifying a specific person, however, requires the more detailed information in higher spatial frequencies. This hypothesis was tested in a second experiment, using the same photographs, but with the high-frequency information removed (Figure 9.30). This manipulation had little effect on the male-female task but was very disruptive to the identification task. A processing mode hypothesis would have to account for this by assuming that the two tasks required subjects to shift between analytic

Figure 9.30 Tasks vary in terms of which spectral cues are most informative. When shown pictures of faces that contain the full spectrum of frequency information, subjects can state whether the person is male or female and, if familiar, the person's identity. Gender can still be determined when only the low frequencies are left intact **(right)**, but the person's identity has been obscured.

and holistic processing modes. The frequency hypothesis assumes that the processing remains unchanged. The laterality effects reverse simply because the critical information is different for the two tasks.

A similar asymmetry may hold in auditory perception, but here the distinction is based on sound frequencies rather than spatial frequencies (Ivry and Lebby, 1993). While there is no obvious connection between spatial and sound frequencies—one refers to variations in contrast over space, the other to changes in sound pressure over time—this hypothesis does provide new insight to puzzling laterality effects in music and speech perception.

Diana Deutsch (1975) of the University of California, San Diego, observed a powerful grouping illusion when subjects were presented with dichotic melodies. In her experiment, two scales were presented, one descending in pitch and the other ascending in pitch. But the notes in each scale were presented to alternate ears. Thus, the stimulus at the right ear alternated high and low notes, and the reverse happened at the left ear. Deutsch maintained that people do not hear this alternating cacophony but, instead, segregate the sounds by pitch in order to hear the two coherent scales. The percept in one ear is of a scale that first descends and then ascends, and the opposite is heard in the other ear (Figure 9.31). The assignment of scales to ears is not arbitrary. Subjects consistently reported hearing the lower-pitched scale in the left ear and the higher-pitched scale in the right ear. This bias fit with the idea that the left hemisphere is biased to perceive higher-frequency sounds compared to the right hemisphere.

Even more intriguing is an extension of the sound frequency hypothesis to speech perception, for which the left hemisphere is clearly dominant (Ivry and Robertson, in press). For instance, patients with left-hemisphere lesions may be unable to discriminate simple consonant contrasts such as *BA* and *DA*; the problem is rare in patients with right-hemisphere lesions.

Figure 9.31 The scale illusion. For this dichotic stimulus, notes to each ear alternate between high and low pitch, or base frequency. Rather than report hearing pogo-like sounds, people group the sounds so that two scales are heard. The scale composed of the higher-pitch sequence is usually reported to be heard in the right ear while the scale composed of the lower-pitch sequence is localized to the left ear. The frequency hypothesis does not explain the grouping phenomenon, but can account for the way the scales are assigned to ears. Adapted from Deutsch (1985).

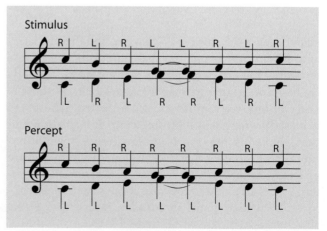

But the right hemisphere has been linked to one aspect of speech perception, *prosody*. Prosody refers to the connotative aspects of oral language, the way we vary articulation to convey affect or intonation. The statement "We need to talk" can be perceived either as an encouraging solicitation or as a stern warning, depending on intonation. The response "We should talk now" is perceived as a confirmation or a question, depending on how the sentence is spoken.

Prosodic information is primarily carried by fluctuations in the low-frequency portion of the speech signal, the fundamental frequency. For example, we usually produce a slight rise in the pitch, or fundamental frequency of our voice at the end of a sentence when asking a question; for declarative sentences, the intonation contour is flat or drops at the end (Figure 9.32). The importance of low-frequency information is evident from the way people can still make prosodic judgments even when high sound frequencies are eliminated. For example, consider an overheard conversation from the office next door. While we may fail to recognize the words because the walls effectively filter out the relatively high frequencies, the low-frequency information is sufficient to alert us when the voices have taken on an angry tone.

Lesions of the right hemisphere disrupt prosody much more than do lesions of the left hemisphere (Ley and Bryden, 1982; Blonders et al., 1991). A task-based account of laterality must assume that the left hemisphere is activated for linguistic tasks and the right is for paralinguistic tasks such as prosody. A frequency hypothesis assumes that the speech signal is projected to both hemispheres, but that the two hemispheres produce representations that amplify different frequency regions of the stimulus. Identifying words requires an analysis of the signal's high-frequency portion. Prosodic analysis can be performed on low-frequency portions of speech.

Asymmetries in Representing Spatial Relations

In the preceding section, we focused on hemispheric differences in how stimuli are identified. The central message is that different sources of information identify the attributes of a stimulus. In vision, high-frequency information is critical for identifying the local structure, or details; low-frequency information is more efficient for abstracting the global structure or shape. In a similar fashion, if we extend the model to sound and speech, lexical analysis depends on the higher sound frequency components of the speech signal—prosodic information is carried in lower frequencies.

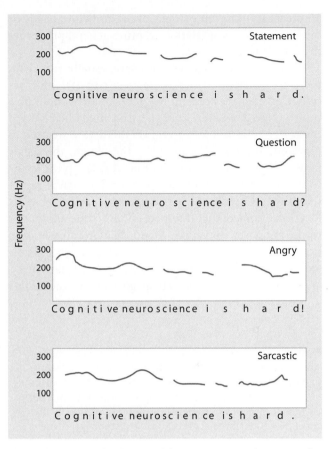

Figure 9.32 The fundamental frequency, or pitch contour, for four different ways of saying the sentence, "Cognitive neuroscience is hard." Prosodic cues allow very different meanings to be extracted from the same set of words.

In Chapter 5 we noted an important distinction between cortical pathways involved in identification and those involved in localization (the what-where distinction). Studies of hemispheric asymmetries have not been limited to "what" problems, but have also been applied to "where" problems.

CATEGORICAL AND COORDINATE REPRESENTATIONS IN MEMORY

Stephen Kosslyn (1987) of Harvard University contended that a distinction can be made between two types of spatial representations. One type is essential for specifying the positions of objects or parts of objects. For example, when a guest begins to search through the kitchen drawers to locate the silverware, the host might instruct her to "look to the left" or "just under that drawer." Here the emphasis is on the relative spatial position between two objects—the drawer being searched and the drawer containing the silverware. Kosslyn termed this *categorical* because it assigns the relation to a broad equivalence class. With respect to some referent, an object is to the left or right, above or below, inside or outside. Categorical relations capture general properties in abstract terms.

Though categorical relations are usually sufficient, there are times when one needs precise spatial information. Consider the scene in Figure 9.33. We would know where to go if we were told to sit on the couch behind the coffee table, but to accomplish this action we need to represent the exact locations of the couch, the coffee table, and any other obstacles that clutter up the living room. So we need coordinate, or metrical spatial representations. *Coordinate representations* specify the exact location of objects, with respect either to one another or to the perceiver's position. A coordinate representation not only gives the relative position of the couch and coffee table but also specifies the couch's exact location.

Kosslyn maintained that categorical and coordinate

Figure 9.33 Spatial information can be represented in abstract, categorical terms, or in a precise coordinate manner. Categorical representations capture basic relational information such as the relative position of two objects from a particular point of view. Coordinate representations specify the exact positions of the objects and the distances between the objects.

Categorical representation

Rocking chair LEFT of couch

Wine glass on TOP of table, candy INSIDE candy dish

Coordinate representation

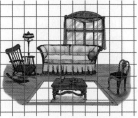

Rocking chair is CLOSER than the dining chair to the couch

representations have distinct purposes. A primary purpose of categorical representation is in using spatial information to classify objects. For example, the letters *b*, *d*, *q*, *p*, and *P* have the same component parts (or geons—see Chapter 5), but differ in terms of the relative position of the line and circle. Within a wide range of sizes and handwriting styles, we can make the appropriate classification once we learn the invariant categorical relations: for example, that the circle is to the left and at the base of the line for *d*. In this respect there is no strict segregation of "what" and "where." Spatial relations provide valuable cues to an object's identity.

Coordinate relations, by contrast, are essential for action. We need to know the exact location of a wine glass on the coffee table in order to pick it up. We do not just grope about, knowing the categorical relation that it is on top of the table. When navigating across a rocky beach, we have to estimate the exact distance between two rocks to decide if our step can span the distance.

Kosslyn hypothesized that the two hemispheres might differ in their contribution to categorical and coordinate representations. He proposed that the left hemisphere forms categorical spatial representations and the right hemisphere forms coordinate representations. This hypothesis is motivated by consideration of the similarity between categorical representations and language. The general equivalences given by categorical relations are captured by linguistic terms (e.g., *up*, *down*, *inside*), and categorical encoding is a prominent feature of language. For example, despite the many variations in how a word can be articulated, the cardinal feature of speech perception is that the surface attributes of an utterance are stripped away to identify the phonemes that form the word. In a similar sense the precise specification of an object's location might rely on, or underlie, the dominant role of the right hemisphere in perceiving spatial information.

To test this hypothesis, Kosslyn and his associates devised tasks that require judgments based on either categorical or coordinate spatial relations (Kosslyn et al., 1989). In one study, the stimulus consisted of a bar and a dot, presented to either the left or the right visual field. In the categorical condition, the subjects had to decide whether the dot was located above or below the line. In the coordinate condition, the judgment required metrical information: Here, the subject was required to judge the distance between the line and the dot, discriminating between distances that were near and those that were far. The clever twist in this experiment is that the same set of stimuli were used in both conditions. However, the assignment of stimuli to response categories differed as a function of the instruction (Figure 9.34).

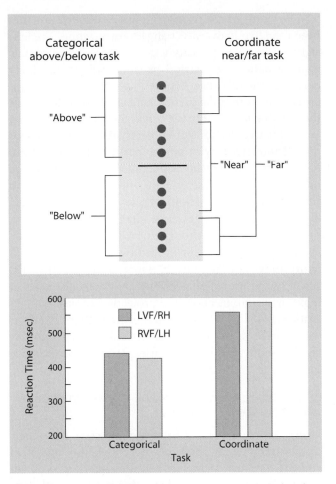

Figure 9.34 Hemispheric asymmetries on categorical and coordinate spatial judgments. **(Top)** On each trial, the stimulus consisted of the bar and one of the twelve dots. For the categorical task, subjects judged whether the dot was "above" or "below" the bar. For the coordinate task, subjects judged whether the dot was "near" or "far" from the bar. **(Bottom)** The reaction time data show a task by visual field interaction. Categorical judgments were faster when the stimuli were shown in the right visual field/left hemisphere. Coordinate judgments were faster when the stimuli were shown in the left visual field/right hemisphere. Adapted from Kosslyn et al. (1989).

Responses on the near-far task were faster when stimuli were presented to the left visual field, a result consistent with the hypothesis that the right hemisphere is more adept in making metrical judgments. The opposite trend was found for the above-below task. These categorical judgments were made more rapidly when the stimuli were presented in the right visual field.

These results call for a few caveats. First, as with many laterality studies, there have been problems with replication. Tasks such as the line-dot task appear to be especially problematic. Even in the original study, the effects disappeared after a few blocks of practice. Kosslyn

suggested that subjects quickly form new categories that can be applied in the near-far task since the stimulus set is relatively small.

Second, it is important to ask whether the observed differences can be accounted for by alternative hypotheses such as the spatial frequency hypothesis. It turns out that there may be differences in the critical frequencies required for the two tasks. As shown in the low-pass filtered image in Figure 9.35, low-frequency information may be insufficient for determining whether dots at the closest locations are above or below the line. Thus, the above-below task may depend on the left hemisphere—

Figure 9.35 Frequency-based interpretation of the categorical-coordinate dissociation. **(a)** Two of the stimuli. **(b)** Low-pass-filtered representation of the stimuli. **(c)** High-pass-filtered representation of the stimuli. The categorical, above-below task distinction is difficult to make from the low-frequency information alone. This suggests an alternative reason for the left hemisphere advantage on this task. Adapted from Ivry and Robertson (1998).

(a) Actual stimulus

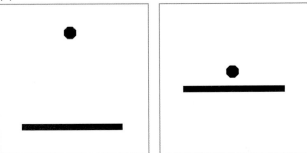

(b) Low-pass filtered image

(c) High-pass filtered image

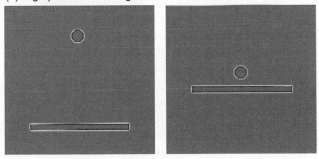

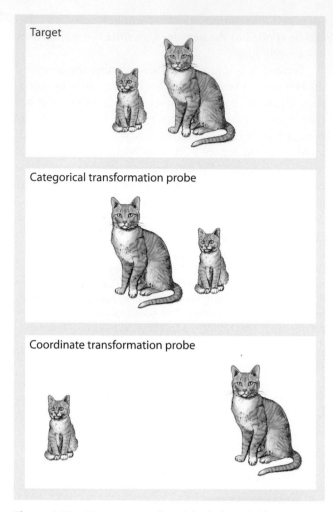

Target

Categorical transformation probe

Coordinate transformation probe

Figure 9.36 Memory test of spatial relations. Subjects were presented with a target stimulus consisting of a pair of objects such as the two cats. After a 5-second delay, a probe stimulus appeared and the subjects judged whether it was the same as the target. In these two examples, the correct answer would be "no." The left-right reversal alters categorical relations; increasing the distance between the cats constitutes a coordinate transformation. Adapted from Laeng (1994).

not because of the categorical nature of the judgment but because of the need for examining high-frequency information.

These problems alert us to seek converging evidence. Bruno Laeng (1994) of the University of Michigan reported results of a study of neurologically impaired patients that support the categorical-coordinate dichotomy. At the beginning of each trial, the patients were shown a drawing of a pair of items such as two cats. After a 5-second delay, a pair of drawings were shown, one that matched the original drawing and one that was a transformed version of the original. The transformations were of two types, as shown in Figure

9.36. In categorical transformations, the relation between the two items was changed; for example, the left-right position of the cats was reversed. In coordinate transformations, a metrical property was changed; for example, the distance between the two cats was increased. In both tasks participants were asked to choose the drawing identical to the original drawing.

Compared to control subjects, the patient groups made more errors with both types of transformations. For patients with left-hemisphere impairment, however, most errors involved selecting a drawing that required a categorical transformation. The reverse was found for the patients with right-hemisphere lesions. For them, the errors involved coordinate transformations.

This experiment emphasized two advantages of patient studies in laterality research. First, because the stimuli were presented centrally, one does not need to make assumptions about the projection of visual information to the contralateral hemisphere. Second, effects that may be small and transient with normal subjects are frequently amplified when explored in people with neurological disorders.

GENERALIZING CATEGORICAL AND COORDINATE DISTINCTIONS TO OTHER PROCESSING DOMAINS

Laeng's task represents an interesting intersection of perception and memory. Subjects first encoded a target item and, after a short delay, were asked to match it to one of two probe items. The tendency for patients with left-hemisphere lesions to select probes in which categorical relations were transformed may reflect an encoding problem—an inability to represent the information—or a memory problem—an inability to retain the information. And the difficulty patients with right-hemisphere lesions have with coordinate relations could be attributed to either an encoding or a memory problem.

While the parietal lobes are critical for abstracting spatial relations, the inferior part of the temporal lobe is the neural locus for memories of visual representations of shape. The format of the representations appears to differ for the two hemispheres: Whereas left-hemisphere memories appear to be abstract or categorical, right-hemisphere representations retain the specific metrics of the stimulus.

Think about what a dog looks like. Your image might be of a small animal with four legs, covered with shaggy fur, floppy ears, and a long, wagging tail. Of course this picture does not describe all dogs. It might be apt for an English sheep dog, but a German shepard has short fur and pointed ears (Figure 9.37). The initial image was not necessarily of a particular species; rather, it reflected a *prototype*, a composite melded by combin-

Figure 9.37 Knowledge may be represented in an exemplar or prototype format. Exemplars would correspond to particular dogs such as the English sheepdog or Irish setter. The prototypical dog is a composite blend, the "average" dog.

ing features from lots of dogs. The dogs you are familiar with are *exemplars,* or specific examples of dogs. A long and contentious debate rages as to whether memory contains prototypes or exemplars. Results of recent laterality studies suggest that both views may be correct. The left hemisphere may rely on prototypes, or representations that categorize information into general equivalence classes. The right hemisphere may use an exemplar representational format.

This distinction is made clear in two studies conducted by Chad Marsolek of the University of Minnesota (Marsolek et al., 1992; Marsolek, 1995). In the first experiment, eight sets of abstract line drawings were created by shifting the components of an initial set of eight prototypes (Figure 9.38). During a training phase, subjects viewed a subset of the drawings and were trained to categorize them using the labels 1 through 8. After training, the subjects were given a speeded classification task in which they categorized the drawings as quickly as possible. In this test phase, the stimuli were presented in either the left or the right visual field. When judging the studied subset, the subjects were faster when the stimuli were presented in the left visual field. In contrast, when judging the previously unseen prototypes, the subjects were faster when the stimuli were presented in the right visual field.

The second experiment used a priming procedure that is widely employed in implicit memory studies. The primary test is a stem-completion task in which subjects are shown three letters and asked to generate a word that completes the stem (e.g., *WHI: whistle, whittle,* or *whiskey*). Prior to the task, subjects study a list of words, but with instructions designed to avoid alerting the subjects that the stimuli will be of relevance to the subsequent priming experiment. This list contains items that could complete the stems, although the subjects are not aware of the connection between the two tasks. Nonetheless, this procedure produces a priming effect in that people tend to use words from the study list in the stem-completion task.

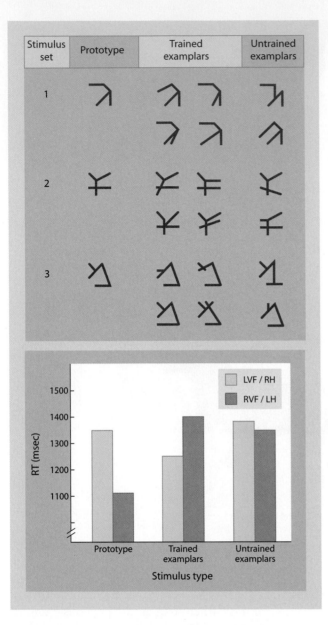

Figure 9.38 Hemispheric asymmetries in exemplar and prototype memory tasks. **(Top panel)** Stimulus sets were constructed by distorting a prototype pattern to create six exemplars. During the study phase, subjects were presented with a subset of the exemplars and learned to categorize them, using the arbitrary numbers assigned to each set. At the test, they performed the categorization task with the prototype, the trained exemplars, and the untrained exemplars. **(Bottom panel)** Classification of the prototype was faster when presented in the right visual field, supporting the idea that this form of representation is characteristic or left hemisphere processing. The trained exemplars, in contrast, were more rapidly classified when presented in the left visual field. Adapted from Marsolek (1995).

Marsolek's study had two novel features. First, the presentation of the stems was lateralized. Second, the case of the stems was either identical to that used during the study phase or it was changed; for example, if the study list has *WHISKEY*, the prime might be presented in upper case (*WHI*) or lower case (*whi*). Priming was observed for both visual fields. Of note, though, is that case manipulation affected performance only in the left visual field. The right hemisphere was much more primed when the initial letters of the study items were identical to the stems—indicative of an exemplar memory trace. The left hemisphere was equally primed by either stem, proof that some of the surface features of the study words were not part of the representation.

Kosslyn used the metaphor of a rolling snowball to account for the generalization of the categorical-coordinate distinction to multiple task domains. In his view, a fundamental asymmetry appears as a specialization to solve a problem. But this asymmetry then cascades into secondary specializations that build on the initial functional difference. While it is difficult to trace the evolutionary development of hemispheric specialization, Kosslyn conjectured that the key event was the establishment of a left-hemisphere specialization for language production. Unlike manual gestures that can be performed by one hand or the other, speech production requires the bilateral coordination of the muscles required for articulation. This created a pressure to localize control in a single foci since interhemispheric communication requires time and might limit how fast we can vocalize. A left-hemisphere specialization for language followed since this hemisphere had primary access to the speech production system. As we noted, language is categorical in nature, with its emphasis on mapping percepts to broad semantic classes. The tendency for the left hemisphere to categorize is now found in many processing systems including language, perception, and memory.

VARIATIONS IN HEMISPHERIC SPECIALIZATION

In this chapter we have reviewed general principles of hemispheric asymmetry in humans. The research showing asymmetries in how perceptual information is processed or in how spatial relations are represented has focused on differences that characterize the typical person. Most of us are right-handed and rely on the left hemisphere for speech production, but a significant percentage of the population is left-handed and may have a different organization of hemispheric specialization. Even within the right-handed population, there are significant individual differences in lateralization profiles. A complete understanding of hemispheric specialization must account for these differences as well as the prototypical organization.

The Relation Between Handedness and Left-Hemisphere Language Dominance

An ongoing debate in the laterality literature centers on whether there is a causal relationship between the predominance of right-handedness and left-hemisphere specialization for language. Some theorists point to the need for a single motor center as the critical factor. Though there may be benefits to perceiving information in parallel, our response to these stimuli must be unified. We cannot allow the left hemisphere to choose one course of action while the right hemisphere opts for another. Our brains may have two halves, but we have only one body. By localizing action planning in one hemisphere, the brain can achieve unification.

One hypothesis is that the left hemisphere is specialized for the production of sequential movements. Speech is obviously dependent on such movements. Our ability to produce speech is the result of many evolutionary changes in the shape of the vocal tract and articulatory apparatus. These adaptations make it possible for us to communicate at phenomenally high rates—the official record is 637 words/min, set on the British TV show *Motor Mouth*. Such competence requires an exquisite control of the sequential gestures of the vocal cords, jaw, tongue, and other articulators.

Similarly, the left hemisphere has been linked to sequential movements in nonlinguistic domains. Left-hemisphere lesions are more likely to produce *apraxia*, a disorder in producing coherent actions that cannot be attributed to weakness or a problem in controlling the muscles (see Chapter 10). This deficit may manifest in movements with either hand. Oral movements also have a left-hemisphere dominance, regardless of whether the movements create speech sounds or nonverbal facial gestures. In both domains, the gestures are more pronounced on the face's right side and activation of the right facial muscles is quicker than that of the corresponding muscles on the left. Hence, the left hemisphere may have a specialized role in the control of sequential actions and this may underlie hemispheric asymmetries in both language and motor functions.

In his book *The Lopsided Ape: Evolution of the Generative Mind*, Michael Corballis of the University of Auckland eloquently articulates this hypothesis. He takes an evolutionary perspective to account for the emergence of language and handedness. To Corballis, the main characteristic of human cognition is that we act and think in a *generative* manner. Thousands of human languages are based on a limited set of phonemes, or basic articulatory gestures. From these sixteen to forty-four elements (the number of basic speech sounds varies across languages), we have created vocabularies of over a million words, and can combine these words to generate an infinity of sentences expressing perceptions, intentions, and desires. Corballis believes that the left hemisphere is uniquely equipped with a generative assembling device (GAD), a device that generates complex representations from a small vocabulary of primitive units (Figure 9.39).

Corballis assumes that the processing capabilities of the GAD are available to other left-hemisphere functions, including control of the right hand. With bipedal-

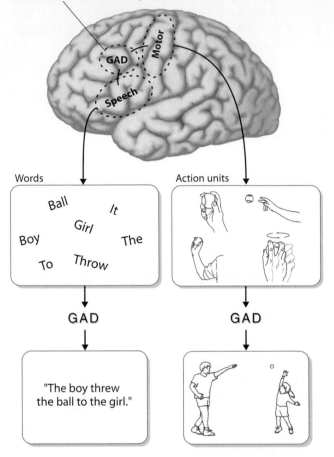

GAD: Generative Assembly Device

Figure 9.39 Corballis hypothesizes that the left hemisphere has evolved a generative assembly device (GAD). This mechanism underlies the production of an infinite set of sequences from a relatively small set of units such as words or gestures.

ism, the hands became free to operate independently. In quadrupeds, the forelimbs and hindlimbs are primarily used for locomotion. Symmetry is favored here: The animal moves along a linear trajectory. If the limbs on one side of the body were longer than the other, an animal would circle about. As our ancestors adopted an upright posture, however, no longer were the hands required to move symmetrically. One hand could hold a carcass while the other reached inside to extract morsels of meat.

The generative aspects of an emerging communication system could have been applied to the way hands manipulated objects, and the lateralization of GAD would have favored the right hand. This would be most evident in tool use. While nonhuman primates and birds can fashion primitive tools to gain access to foods that are out of reach or encased in hard shells, humans manufacture tools generatively. We not only design tools to solve an immediate problem, but also can recombine the parts to create new tools. The wheel, an efficient component of devices for transportation, can be used to extract energy from a flowing river or record informa-

tion in a compact, easily accessible format. Handedness, then, is most apparent in our use of tools. As an example, right-handers differ only slightly in their ability to use both hands to block balls thrown at them. But when they are asked to catch or throw the balls, the dominant hand has a clear advantage.

In Corballis's scheme, specialization in language became accessible to nonlinguistic functions: As the left-hemisphere GAD allowed language to take on its generative quality, it also imbued the right hand with a functional advantage for skilled actions. Alternatively, the left hemisphere's dominance in language may be a consequence of a specialization in motor control. The asymmetrical use of hands to perform complex actions, including those associated with tool use, may have promoted the development of language. For example, as our ancestors' use of tools became more advanced, a communication system to disseminate that knowledge was needed. From comparative studies of language we believe that most sentence forms convey actions. Not only will an infant first order commands such as "come" or "eat" before using adjectives ("hungry"), but this order is preserved in phylogeny. The earliest forms of communication centered on action commands such as "look" or "throw." If the right hand was being used for many of these actions, there may have been a selective pressure for the left hemisphere to be more proficient in establishing these symbolic representations.

It is also possible that the mechanisms producing hemispheric specialization in language and motor performance are unrelated. There is not a perfect correlation between these two cardinal signs of hemispheric asymmetry. Not only do a small percentage of right-handers exhibit either left-hemisphere language or bilateral language, but also in at least half of the left-handed population the left hemisphere is dominant for language.

These differences may reflect the fact that handedness is at least partly affected by environmental factors. Children may be encouraged to use one hand over the other, perhaps owing to cultural biases or to parental pressure. Yet it is possible that handedness and language dominance may reflect different factors. Fred Previc (1991), a researcher with the United States Air Force, proposed an intriguing hypothesis along these lines. According to Previc, the left-hemisphere dominance for language is primarily related to a subtle asymmetry in the skull's structure. In most individuals, the orofacial bones on the left side of the face are slightly larger, an enlargement that encroaches on middle-ear function and could limit the sensitivity to certain sound frequencies. Previc maintained that this enlargement has a dele-

terious effect on the projection of auditory information to the right hemisphere, especially in the frequency region that carries most of the critical information for speech. As such, the left hemisphere is favored for phonemic analysis and develops a specialization for language.

In contrast to this anatomical asymmetry, Previc argued that handedness is determined by the position of the fetus during gestation (Figure 9.40). Most fetuses are oriented with the head downward and the right ear facing toward the mother's front. This orientation leads to greater in vitro stimulation of the left utricle, part of the *vestibular* apparatus in the inner ear that is critical for balance. This asymmetrical stimulation will lead to a more developed vestibular system in the right side of the brain, causing babies to be born with a bias to use the left side of the body for balance and the maintenance of posture. This frees the right side of the body for more exploratory movement, resulting in right-handedness.

According to Previc's theory, then, different factors determine language asymmetries and handedness. At present, the data are too scant for evaluating either of the mechanisms. Previc's own research concerns the demographics of the entire population, not whether language dominance or handedness can be predicted in any one person by orofacial asymmetries or fetal position. Nonetheless, it does raise the interesting possibility that there may be numerous and unrelated factors that determine patterns of hemispheric specialization.

Figure 9.40 Functional asymmetries in manual coordination have been attributed to the prenatal environment of the fetus. The position of the fetus in the uterus influences prenatal vestibular experience. Most fetuses are oriented with the right ear facing outward which results in a larger vestibular signal in the right hemisphere. At birth, the left side of the body is more stable, freeing the right hand for exploration. Adapted from Previc (1991).

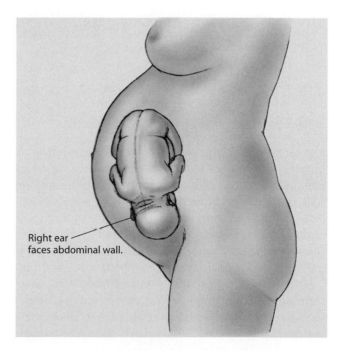

Right ear faces abdominal wall.

To Approach or Withdraw: The Cerebral Tug-of-War

It is Friday night and you are heading to a party at the apartment of a friend of a friend's. You arrive and look about: Loud music and swirling bodies move about the living room, and a throng has gathered in the kitchen, around the counter laid out with chips and dips. Unfortunately, your friend is nowhere to be seen and you have yet to recognize a single person among the crowd.

Your reaction will depend on a number of factors—how comfortable you feel mingling with strangers, how lively you are feeling tonight, whether a host approaches and introduces you to a few of the guests. Unless you have the flair for flamboyance, it is unlikely you will head to the dance floor. A more likely response is to head for the kitchen and find yourself a soda or beer.

Richard Davidson (1995) of the University of Wisconsin proposed that the fundamental tension for any mobile organism is between approach and withdrawal. Is a stimulus a potential food source to be approached and gobbled up? Or a potential predator that must be avoided? Even the most primitive organisms display at least a rudimentary distinction between approach and withdrawal behaviors. The evolution of more complex nervous systems has provided mechanisms to modulate the tension between these two behavioral poles—we might overcome our initial reaction to flee from the party, knowing that in the end, we are likely to have made a few new friends and had a few good laughs.

According to Davidson, this tension involves a delicate interplay between processing within the medial regions of the prefrontal cortex in the right and left cerebral hemispheres. The prefrontal cortex is a major point of convergence in the central nervous system, for information not only from other cortical regions, but also from subcortical regions, especially those involved in emotional processing (see Chapters 11 and 13). In Davidson's theory, these inputs are processed asymmetrically. Left-hemisphere processing is biased to promote approach behaviors; in contrast, right-hemisphere processing is biased to promote withdrawal behaviors.

This theory has provided an organizing principle to evaluate the changes in behavior that follow neurological damage. For example, damage to the left frontal lobe can result in severe depression, a state in which the primary symptom is withdrawal and inactivity. While we might expect depression to be a normal response to brain injury, the opposite profile has been reported in patients with right frontal damage. These patients may appear manic. Damage to the right-hemisphere "withdrawal" system biases the patient to be socially engaging, even when such behaviors are no longer appropriate.

More compelling evidence comes from physiological studies that have looked at the brain's response to

Gender Differences in Hemispheric Specialization

The differences in the behavior of men and women are obvious. The sources are likely to be manifold, reflecting cultural pressures and environmental constraints, as well as biological differences. It remains a major challenge for the behavioral sciences to sort out the contributions of these factors. Notwithstanding these concerns, some behavioral differences have major implications for theories of hemispheric specialization.

Numerous studies (Inglis and Lawson, 1982; MacCoby and Jacklin, 1974) consistently found gender differences in the two domains most studied in laterality research: language and visuospatial skills. On average,

girls begin to acquire language about 1 month prior to boys, and by age 11, they consistently perform better on tests of verbal abilities, with the gender gap growing at least until adulthood. Female superiority is seen on tests of both receptive and productive language, and on more complex tasks such as making analogies and creative writing. The gender difference is not large, with extensive overlap between the two groups. But it is consistent. For example, girls are much better than boys at generating sentences when given the initial letter of each word (Figure 9.41).

Males have an advantage in visuospatial reasoning. The bottom panel in Figure 9.41 demonstrates a gender difference. Males are more adept at performing the in-

affective, or emotional stimuli (Gur et al., 1994). By their very nature, positive stimuli are likely to elicit approach while negative stimuli will elicit withdrawal or avoidance. Thus, an affective stimulus is likely to differentially engage the two hemispheres depending on its valence. Davidson (1995) tested this idea by taking electroencephalographic (EEG) measurements while subjects viewed short video clips, chosen to evoke either positive (e.g., a puppy playing with flowers) or negative (e.g., a leg being amputated) emotional reactions. The EEG activity to these stimuli was compared to that during a baseline condition in which the subjects watched a neutral video segment. As predicted, more neural activity was observed over the left frontal lobe when the subjects watched the positive videos in comparison to the negative videos. In contrast, there was a huge increase in activity over the right frontal lobe while subjects viewed the disgusting video.

Similar results have been found in a variety of related experiments. For example, in one study, subjects were required to make rapid responses, either to acquire financial rewards or to avoid financial penalties. Left-hemisphere activation was greater during the reward trials and right-hemisphere activation was greater during the penalty trials, even when the analysis was restricted to the time period prior to the onset of the stimulus. At this point, the subjects had not experienced the reward or punishment; rather they anticipated its consequences (see Chapter 11).

There are, of course, individual differences in this cerebral tug-of-war between approach and withdrawal.

Depression has been linked to an abnormal imbalance favoring neural activity in the right hemisphere. Whether the imbalance preceded or followed the depression remains unclear. More provocative, EEG asymmetries in 3-year-old children are correlated with how well the kids tolerate being separated from their mothers. Children showing higher basal EEG activity in the right hemisphere are more inhibited, staying next to their mother, even when surrounded by an array of new toys. Children with higher basal EEG activity in the left hemisphere are quite content to leave their mother to play with the toys.

The study of hemispheric asymmetries in emotion is in its infancy. Prior to the past decade, physiological studies of emotion generally focused on interactions between subcortical limbic systems and the cortex. In developing his account of cortical differences, Davidson started from a consideration of a marked behavioral dichotomy. What remains to be explored are the computations that might lead to one type of behavior over another, and whether these computations are related to those uncovered in the study of hemispheric specialization in other cognititve domains.

But in the interim, we might cull from this work one strategy to test the next time we find ourselves alone at a party: Start talking to someone, if just to get the left hemisphere active! Perhaps there is a reason why the left hemisphere appears specialized to promote approach behavior and is dominant in that most social of all behaviors, language.

ternal spatial transformations required by this task. Similar results crop up in a wide range of tasks, including tests of shape recall, geometry, maze learning, and map reading. The male advantage in spatial reasoning may be one reason why they score higher on math tests and why most chess masters are men. Cultural factors surely contribute. In some cultures, male infants are given more freedom for exploration; female babies tend to be restricted in their movements. Environmental differences such as these could well underlie the behavioral asymmetries.

Attempts to link behavioral asymmetries to differential patterns of hemispheric specialization have been difficult. One explanation might be that females are left-hemisphere dominant and males are right-hemisphere dominant. If anything, the neuropsychological literature argues against this simplistic account. In comparison to men, women have fewer aphasic disorders after suffering left-hemisphere lesions: In one study, the lesions caused language disorders in 77% of the women and 89% of the men. Moreover, after reviewing several studies, M.P. Bryden (1982) of the University of Waterloo contended that right-handed men are more likely to have left-hemisphere language dominance (95%) than are women (79%). Finally, despite numerous attempts, investigators using dichotic listening studies rarely found gender differences.

An alternative hypothesis is that cerebral asymmetry

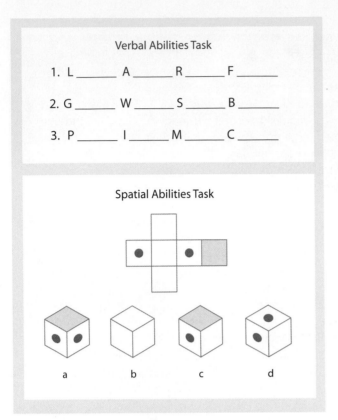

Figure 9.41 Functional differences between the two sexes are observed on some verbal and visuospatial tests. Females perform better than males in generating sentences, using the given letters as the first letter for each word. In contrast, males are more adept on spatial tests. In the mental rotation task, subjects must judge which pattern can be created by folding the two-dimensional picture on top. From Kolb and Whishaw (1996).

is more marked in males than in females. In one study, patients with unilateral brain damage were given the Wechsler Adult Intelligence Scale, a test that provides global measures of verbal and spatial performance abilities. As can be seen in Figure 9.42, males followed the expected pattern: The performance of men with left-hemisphere lesions was most impaired on verbal tests whereas that of men with right-hemisphere lesions was most impaired on spatial measures (performance tests). Most surprising were the results for women. Left-hemisphere lesions for these patients resulted in equally depressed scores on verbal and spatial tests. Women with right-hemisphere lesions did not perform the same as did control subjects on both tests.

One would certainly not want to conclude from this study that women do not use the right hemisphere. The results may reflect gender differences in hemispheric specialization, but they also could be due to strategies used in performing the tasks. Women may, for exam-

ple, be more likely to use a verbal strategy when performing a spatial transformation rather than using visual imagery.

Nonetheless, the asymmetries observed in normal and neuropsychological populations suggest significant gender differences in hemispheric specialization. While much of the early work focused on establishing the reality of gender differences, more recent investigations strived to identify causal mechanisms. One approach has been genetic. Individual differences in spatial abilities have an inherited component. Some researchers hypothesized that the responsible gene is recessive on the X or female chromosome, which makes it more probable that the gene will be expressed in males.

Another promising path concerns the role of hormones in cognition. Studies with birds and mammals showed that testosterone is critical for the appearance of *dimorphic* or sex-based anatomical asymmetries in brain structures as well as the gonads. Even though the effects are most critical during the early stages of development, hormones continue to affect behavior at all stages of life, inspiring researchers to assess whether gender differences in cognition tasks may be related to hormonal differences. For example, in both humans and rodents, high levels of estrogen in females are associated with poorer performance on spatial learning tasks. Sim-

Figure 9.42 Hemispheric asymmetries may be less marked in females compared to males. Verbal and performance IQ scores following brain injury (normal score = 100). Left-hemisphere lesions in men produce a severe impairment on the verbal subtest. Right-hemisphere lesions are only associated with an impairment on the performance subtest. Left-hemisphere lesions in women disrupt performance on both tests, while no deficits are observed in women with right-hemisphere lesions. Adapted from Kolb and Whishaw (1996).

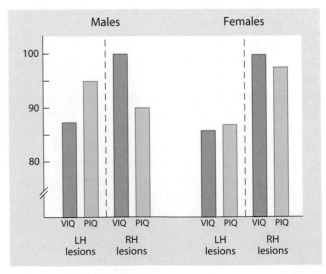

ilarly, fluctuations in spatial abilities and testosterone levels have been found in men. One provocative study involved elderly men who received testosterone supplements through scrotal patches, to regulate bone and mineral metabolism. Compared to a placebo control group, the experimental group performed significantly better on the block design test (Janowsky et al., 1994). Notably, the effect of the hormone was not ubiquitous: No changes were observed on tests of motor dexterity, verbal memory, and cognitive flexibility.

Finally, ecological considerations of the behavior of nonhuman species may shed light on gender differences in spatial abilities. In many species, the activities of males span a much larger province than those of females. For example, in the meadow vole, the females have a narrow home, defending their nests from competitors and predators as they raise the young. Males, on the other hand, roam over a large territory in their quest for potential mates. When tested on spatial tasks like maze learning, male meadow voles outperformed their female counterparts, perhaps reflecting the fact that their behavioral repertoire demands an accurate representation of relatively vast areas of space (Sherry et al., 1992). Male meadow voles also have larger hippocampi in comparison to females, providing an anatomical correlate of this cognitive difference. Could similar evolutionary pressures had led to gender differences in humans on spatial cognition tasks? Similar to the meadow vole, ancestral male humans may have ranged over a larger territory than females.

Hemispheric Specialization in Nonhumans

Because of the central role of language in hemispheric specialization, laterality research has focused on humans. It is possible that asymmetries between the left and right cerebral hemispheres arose only after the evolutionary divergence of the line leading to *Homo sapiens*. But the evolutionary pressures that underlie hemispheric specialization—the need for unified action, rapid communication, reduced costs associated with interhemispheric processing—can be applied to other species. It is now clear that hemispheric specialization is not a unique human feature (Bradshaw and Rogers, 1993).

Anatomical considerations might lead us to expect to find even greater specialization in some nonhuman species such as birds. In birds, almost all of the optic fibers cross at the optic chiasm, ensuring that all of the visual input from each eye projects to the contralateral hemisphere. The lack of crossed and uncrossed fibers probably reflects the fact that there is little overlap in the

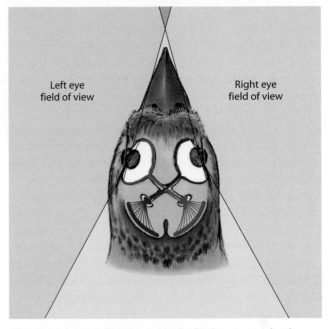

Figure 9.43 Visual pathways in the birds are completely crossed. This organization reflects the fact that there is little overlap in the regions of space seen by each eye, and thus, the visual input to the left hemisphere is independent of the visual input to the right hemisphere. This anatomical segregation would be expected to favor the emergence of hemispheric asymmetries.

visual fields of birds, owing to the lateral placement of the eyes (Figure 9.43). Moreover, birds do not have a corpus callosum. This limits the communication between the visual systems within each hemisphere and might lead to functional asymmetries.

Several asymmetries are known. Chickens and pigeons are better at categorizing stimuli viewed in their right eye. For example, they are more proficient in discriminating food from nonfood items when stimuli are presented to the right eye. In contrast, the left eye appears more adept when chickens are trained to respond to unique properties like color, size, and shape, or when the task requires that they learn the exact location of a food source. Thus, the difference between prototype- and exemplar-based representations that account for human memory asymmetries might apply to birds.

According to Kosslyn's snowball hypothesis, the seed asymmetry for the categorical-coordinate distinction in memory was the evolution of a language system that exploited categorical representations. That is, the primary impetus for hemispheric specialization came from language, eventually being exploited by other processing domains such as perception and memory. If we assume that the categorical nature of human language is unique to our species, the same evolutionary story could not be applied to birds. The similar memory asymmetries in humans and birds may well be fortuitous. This may well be plausible. If asymmetries such as the exemplar-prototype distinction independently arise in two evolutionary lines, half the time one would expect, by chance, a similar pattern of hemispheric organization.

Yet almost all birds have a communication system: They vocalize to scare away enemies, mark territory, and lure mates. In many species, the mechanisms of song production depend on structures in the left hemisphere. The seminal finding here was by Fernando Nottebohm of Rockefeller University in the early 1970s (Nottebohm, 1980). He discovered that sectioning the canary's hypoglossal nerve in its left hemisphere severely disrupted song production. Right-hemisphere lesions had little effect. This happens in other species, although in some the lesions to either hemisphere can interfere with song production.

Nonhuman primates also have differences in hemispheric structure or function. In anatomical studies of Old World monkeys and apes, we find similar asymmetries as with humans. For example, the sylvian fissure shows a greater upward slope in the right hemisphere and there is a similar forward skewedness of the right hemisphere.

Whether these anatomical asymmetries are associated with behavioral specializations remains unclear; the case for hemispheric specialization in nonhuman primates is not compelling. Unlike humans, nonhuman primates do not show a predominance of right-handedness. Individual animals may show a preference for one hand or the other, but there is no consistent trend for the right hand to be favored over the left hand, both when making manual gestures and when using tools.

Perceptual studies provide more provocative indications of parallel asymmetrical functions in humans and nonhuman primates. Rhesus monkeys are superior in making tactile discriminations of shape when using the left hand, similar to that in humans. What is more impressive, split-brain monkeys show hemispheric interactions comparable to what is seen with humans on visual perception tasks. In a face recognition task, the monkeys have a right-hemisphere advantage; in a line orientation task, the monkeys have a left-hemisphere advantage. Also, left-hemisphere lesions in the Japanese macaque can impair the animals' ability to comprehend the vocalizations of conspecifics. But unlike the effects on some aphasic patients, this deficit is relatively mild and transient.

In summary, nonhuman species exhibit differences in the function of the two hemispheres. Hemispheric specialization is surely not a unique human characteristic. How should we interpret these findings? Does the left hemisphere, which specializes in bird song and human language, reflect a common evolutionary antecedent? If so, this adaptation has an ancient history because humans and birds have not shared a common ancestor since before the dinosaurs. But the fact that hemispheric specialization occurs in many species may reflect a general design principle for brain function. Specialized function between hemispheres may reflect similar advantages gained by specialization in each hemisphere. The auditory and visual cortices are each uniquely designed to solve problems. Hemispheric asymmetries may provide a similar benefit.

SUMMARY

Research on laterality has provided extensive insights into the organization of the human brain. The surgical disconnection of the cerebral hemispheres has produced an extraordinary opportunity to study which perceptual and cognitive processes are cortical in nature and which are subcortical. We have seen how visual perceptual information, for example, remains strictly lateralized to one hemisphere following callosal section. Tactile-patterned information remains lateralized. Attentional mechanisms, however, can involve subcortical systems. Taken together, cortical disconnection produces two independent sensory information-processing systems that call upon a common attentional resource system in the carrying out of perceptual tasks.

Split-brain studies have also revealed the complex mosaic of mental processes that go into human cognition. The two hemispheres do not represent information in an identical manner, as evidenced by the fact that each hemisphere has developed its own set of specialized capacities. In the vast majority of individuals, the left hemisphere is clearly dominant for language and speech, and seems to possess a uniquely human capacity to interpret behavior and to construct theories about the relationship between perceived events and feelings.

Right-hemisphere superiority, on the other hand, can be seen in tasks such as facial recognition and attentional monitoring. Both hemispheres are likely to be involved in the performance of any complex task, but with each contributing in their specialized manner.

Complementary studies on patients with focal brain lesions and on normal subjects tested with lateralized stimuli, and even comparative approaches have underlined not only the presence but also the importance of lateralized processes active in cognition and perception. Recent work, such as the spatial frequency hypothesis, has moved laterality research toward a more computational account of hemispheric specialization, seeking to explicate the mechanisms underlying many lateralized perceptual phenomena. These theoretical advances are taking the field away from the pop interpretations of cognitive style and providing a scientific basis for these robust processes.

SUGGESTED READINGS

BROWN, H., and KOSSLYN, S. (1993). Cerebral lateralization. *Curr. Opin. Neurobiol.* 3: 183–186.

CORBALLIS, M.C. (1991). *The Lopsided Ape: Evolution of the Generative Mind.* New York: Oxford University Press.

GAZZANIGA, M.S. (1995). Principles of human brain organization derived from split-brain studies. *Neuron* 14: 217–228.

HELLIGE, J.B. (1993). *Hemispheric Asymmetry: What's Right and What's Left.* Cambridge, MA: Harvard University Press.

10

Motor Control

In July 1982, the physicians in the emergency room at hospitals in the San Jose, California area were puzzled. Working in emergency rooms requires physicians to have uncommon skills. Not only do they encounter the carnage from cars and guns, but also they are generally the first point of contact for people who have suffered a neurological disturbance such as a stroke or severe discomfort, perhaps from exposure to a toxic substance. Life and death decisions hinge on these doctors' ability to make an accurate diagnosis, frequently on the basis of scant information—especially when the patient is too injured or sick to provide a sufficient history. Years of medical training and experience usually provide the best guidance. But this time, none of the attending physicians could recall any precedent for what they had seen over the past few days. Four adults, ranging in age from 26 to 42 years, showed symptoms that did not resemble any known disease. While still conscious, the patients were essentially immobile, were unable to speak, had frozen facial expressions, and showed extreme rigidity in their arms. It was as if they had encountered an evil fairy who had cast a spell on them, rendering them stone statues. The physicians knew they had to act fast, but they could not figure out what to do.

Interviews with the patients' friends and family uncovered a few clues. Even more puzzling was the fact that, while two of the patients were brothers, they did not know the other two. This pointed toward exposure to a toxic agent. More questions revealed an important commonality among the cases: All were heroin users.

The symptoms, however, bore little resemblance to those of a heroin overdose. While this narcotic is a powerful central nervous system (CNS) depressant, these patients did not exhibit the typical flaccidity of a person under the influence of heroin. On the contrary, their rigidity was the opposite of what one expects from a powerful dose. No one could recall seeing a case of heroin overdose that produced these effects, nor did the symptoms resemble those of other street narcotics. A new substance was at work here. A few friends who had taken smaller doses confirmed this suspicion. When injected, this heroin had unexpectedly produced a burn-

ing sensation at the site of injection, rapidly followed by a blurring of vision, a metallic taste in the mouth, and, most troubling, an almost immediate jerking of the limbs.

It was a few days before a breakthrough in this case occurred. Computed tomography (CT) and magnetic resonance imaging (MRI) revealed no structural abnormalities either in the brains of the patients, who were still rigid, or in the brains of those who had been lucky enough to have been injected with only a small dose. A neurologist at Stanford University, Dr. William Langston (1984), provided the first insight. When examining the patients, he was struck by how similar their symptoms were to those of a patient with advanced Parkinson's disease. This disorder, a common malady affecting approximately 0.5% of the population, is marked by muscular rigidity and disorders of posture and volitional movement, or *akinesia,* the inability to produce volitional

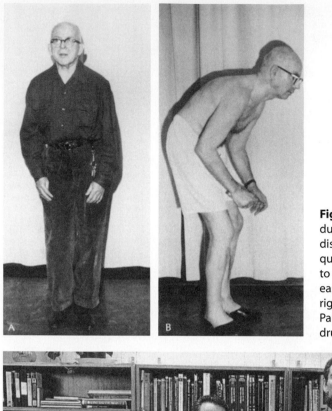

Figure 10.1 Parkinson's disease not only disrupts the production and flexibility of voluntary movement, but can also distort posture. Facial expression, including blinking, is frequently absent giving the person the appearance of seeming to be frozen. The person to the left has had Parkinson's disease for many years and is no longer able to maintain an upright posture. The people below developed symptoms of Parkinson's disease in their 20's and 30's after ingesting the drug MPTP.

movement (Figure 10.1). Everything about the patients' conditions matched this disorder. The biggest puzzles, though, were the age and history of the patients. The onset of Parkinson's disease is gradual and rarely becomes clinically evident until a person is over the age of 45. The heroin users had developed full-blown symptoms of advanced Parkinson's disease within days. Langston suspected that the drug users had come to inject a new synthetic drug being sold as heroin, and that this drug had triggered the acute onset of Parkinson's disease.

This diagnosis proved to be correct. Parkinson's disease results from cell death in the *substantia nigra*, a brainstem nucleus that is part of the *basal ganglia*. These cells are the primary source of the neurotransmitter dopamine. Although Langston could not see any structural damage on CT and MRI scans, subsequent positron emission tomography (PET) studies confirmed hypometabolism of dopamine in the people who injected the toxic heroin, regardless of whether they developed Parkinson's disease. Of more immediate concern was how to treat the drug users. For this, Langston adopted the universal treatment applied in Parkinson's disease: He prescribed high doses of L-dopa, a synthetic cousin that is highly effective in compensating for the attrition of the endogenous source of dopamine. When Langston administered this medication to the drug abusers, they immediately showed a positive response. Their muscles relaxed and they could move, albeit in a limited form.

While this episode was tragic for the patients, the incident signified a breakthrough in research on Parkinson's disease. Researchers tracked down the tainted drug and performed a chemical analysis; it turned out to be a previously unknown synthetic substance, bearing little resemblance to heroin but similar in structure to meperidine, a synthetic opioid that creates the sensations of heroin. Based on its chemical structure, it was given the name *MPTP*. Laboratory tests demonstrating that MPTP is selectively toxic for dopaminergic cells led to great leaps forward in medical research on the basal ganglia and on treatments for Parkinson's disease. Prior to the drug's discovery, it had been difficult to induce parkinsonism in nonhuman species. Primates do not develop Parkinson's disease naturally, perhaps because their life expectancy is short. Moreover, it is difficult to access the substantia nigra with traditional lesion methods because of its proximity to vital brainstem nuclei. By

administering MPTP, researchers can now destroy the substantia nigra and create a parkinsonian animal.

Two treatment methods directly tie into work with MPTP. In one, parkinsonian animals are given brain grafts with fetal tissue in the hope of regenerating dopaminergic cells (Lindvall et al., 1990). This method has met with some success, not only in MPTP-treated animals but also in experimental clinical trials with humans who have true Parkinson's disease (see Chapter 12). A second radical treatment method is based on the complex inhibitory and excitatory connections of the basal ganglia. As a result of dopamine depletion, the output from the basal ganglia ends up inhibiting movement. Researchers have explored surgical methods that might reduce this inhibition (Bergman et al., 1990). In one study on MPTP-treated monkeys, the neurotoxin ibotenic acid was injected into the unilateral lesions of the subthalamic nucleus. Within a minute of injection, the animals moved their contralateral extremities, purposeful movements revived, and soon they were grooming and feeding themselves.

While this surgical procedure has been restricted to primate studies, the MPTP story exemplifies how neurological aberrations can elucidate the complicated patterns of connectivity in the motor structures of the CNS. Let us review how these structures enable us to interact with the environment.

MOTOR STRUCTURES

We might say that the complexity of our nervous system is designed for one purpose: to improve the efficiency of our actions. We are not passive processing machines but organisms built for interacting in the world. For organisms with simple nervous systems, we can readily see how sensory information is designed to promote efficient action. In the well-studied sea snail, the aplysia, the sensory neurons regulate the function of motor neurons with little intermediary processing. As we examine more complex nervous systems, the connections between sensation and action become more distant, and we may be fooled into thinking that we can study perception, attention, and memory in isolation. But we would be missing the forest for the trees. Elaborate sensory and memory capabilities are of use to an organism only in improving how it interacts with the world. No purpose is served by the capability of perceiving color unless this information imparts an advantage in how the organism responds to this stimulus. In a similar sense, learning and memory functions are of use only in enabling an animal to draw on its history to

modify its future actions. Effective action is the ultimate goal for all internal processing.

With these considerations, it is not surprising that so much of the CNS is implicated in controlling action; so let us take a look at the main structures associated with this control. We initially focus on anatomy: the essential components of the motor system and how they are connected. Later we develop a more detailed picture from a cognitive neuroscience perspective, when we consider what mental operations are performed by our action systems.

Muscles, Motor Neurons, and the Spinal Cord

A part of the body that can move is referred to as an *effector*. For most actions, we think of *distal* effectors, those far from the body center, such as the arms, hands, and legs. But we can also produce movements with more *proximal* or centrally located effectors, such as the waist, neck, and head. The jaw, tongue, and vocal tract are essential effectors for producing speech, and vision is highly dependent on eye movements.

All forms of movement result from changes in the state of muscles that control an effector or group of effectors. *Muscles* are composed of elastic fibers, tissue that can change their length and tension. As shown in Figure 10.2, these fibers are attached to the skeleton at joints and are usually arranged in antagonist pairs, which enable the effector either to flex or to extend. For example, the biceps and triceps from an antagonist pair that regulates the position of the forearm. Activating the biceps makes the muscle contract or shorten, hence flexing the forearm about the elbow. If the muscle is relaxed, or if the triceps is contracted, the forearm becomes extended.

The primary interaction of muscles and the nervous system comes about through *alpha motor neurons,* so-called because of their large size. Alpha motor neurons originate in the spinal cord, exit through the ventral root, and terminate in the muscle fibers. As with other neurons, an action potential in an alpha motor neuron releases a neurotransmitter; here the transmitter is acetylcholine. The release of transmitter does not modify downstream neurons, however. Instead, it makes the muscle fibers contract. Thus, alpha motor neurons provide a physical basis for translating nerve signals into mechanical actions. Movement happens when the alpha motor neurons change the length and tension of muscles.

Input to the alpha motor neurons has a variety of sources. At the lowest level, alpha motor neurons receive input from sensory fibers located in the muscles themselves. When a muscle is unexpectedly stretched, a sensory signal is generated in the joints and muscle fibers and enters the dorsal roots of the spinal cord before synapsing directly on corresponding alpha motor neurons. This signal rapidly increases the output of the alpha motor neurons, a process that returns the muscle to its original length. Figure 10.3 shows the chain of reflexes that occur when the family physician raps just below the knee cap. This test assesses the integrity of rapid spinal reflexes.

Alpha motor neurons also receive input from the descending fibers of the spinal cord and the interneurons within the spinal segment. The descending fibers originate in several subcortical and cortical structures.

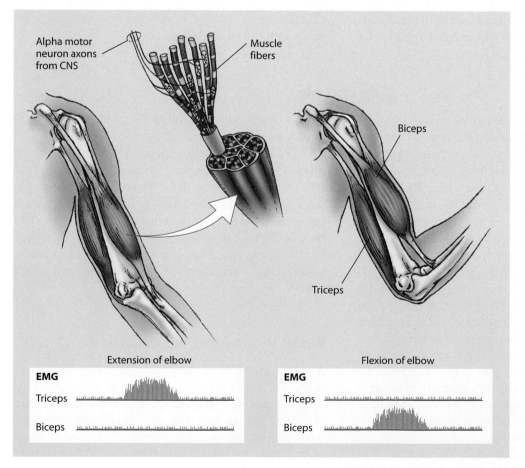

Figure 10.2 Muscles are activated by the alpha motor neurons. Electrodes placed on the skin over the muscle can measure this electrical activity, producing an electromyogram (EMG). The input from the alpha motor neurons causes the muscle fibers to contract. Antagonist pairs of muscles span many of our joints. Activation of the triceps produces extension of the elbow; activation of the biceps produces flexion of the elbow.

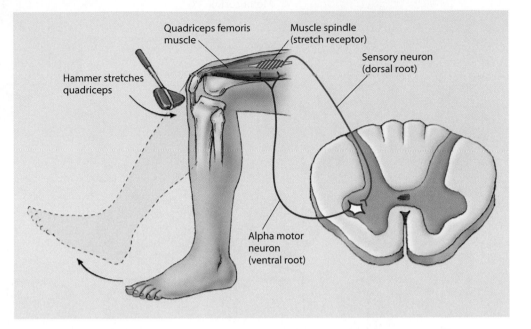

Figure 10.3 The stretch reflex. When the doctor raps your knee, the quadriceps is extended. This stretch triggers receptors in the muscle spindle to fire. The sensory signal is transmitted through the dorsal root of the spinal cord and directly activates an alpha motor neuron to contract the quadriceps. In this manner, the stretch reflex helps to maintain the stability of the limbs following unexpected pertubations.

These signals can be either excitatory or inhibitory, and are the basis for voluntary movements. For example, a central command for elbow flexion will require excitation of the biceps. This event by itself results in a passive stretch of the triceps. If unchecked, it would trigger, via a stretch reflex, excitation of the triceps and the limb would return to its original position. Excitatory signals to one muscle, the agonist, are accompanied by inhibitory signals to the antagonist muscle via interneurons. In this way, the stretch reflex that efficiently stabilizes unexpected perturbations can be overcome to permit volitional movement.

A third source of input to the alpha motor neurons comes from the descending fibers of the spinal cord. These fibers are a means for central commands to produce movement, for the results of central processing to be translated into action. The source of these fibers originates in several subcortical and cortical structures.

Subcortical Motor Structures

Many neural structures of the motor system are in the brainstem, which contains the twelve cranial nerves essential for critical reflexes involving breathing, eating, eye movements, and facial expressions. In addition, many nuclei within the brainstem send direct projections down the spinal cord. These tracts are referred to collectively as the *extrapyramidal tracts,* indicating that they do not originate in the pyramidal neurons of the motor cortex (Figure 10.4). Extrapyramidal tracts are a primary source of control over spinal activity; they receive input from subcortical and cortical structures.

Figure 10.5 shows the location of two prominent subcortical structures that play a key role in motor control: the cerebellum and basal ganglia. The *cerebellum* is a massive structure that receives extensive sensory inputs, including information from somatosensory, vestibular, visual, and auditory channels. It also receives input from many association areas of the cortex. This input is primarily projected to the cerebellar cortex, perhaps the most densely packed neural region in the brain; indeed, more cells are in the cerebellum than in all the rest of the nervous system. The cerebellar cortex, though, does not send direct output to the brain. Rather, the cortex relays information to nuclei buried within the midst of the cerebellar enfolding; all cerebellar output comes from these nuclei. Within the cerebellum, there is a partitioning with respect to whether the output provides descending or ascending neural signals. Axons from more medial nuclei can synapse directly on spinal interneurons, but the majority terminate on the nuclei of the extrapyramidal tracts. In contrast, output from lateral regions influences motor and frontal cortical regions by way of relays in the thalamus. An interesting feature of cerebellar anatomy is that outputs cross to contralateral subcortical and thalamic targets. Thus, each half of the cerebellum regulates effectors on the body's ipsilateral side.

The *basal ganglia* are a collection of five nuclei. Taken as a whole, the organization of the basal ganglia bears a similarity to that of the cerebellum. Input is

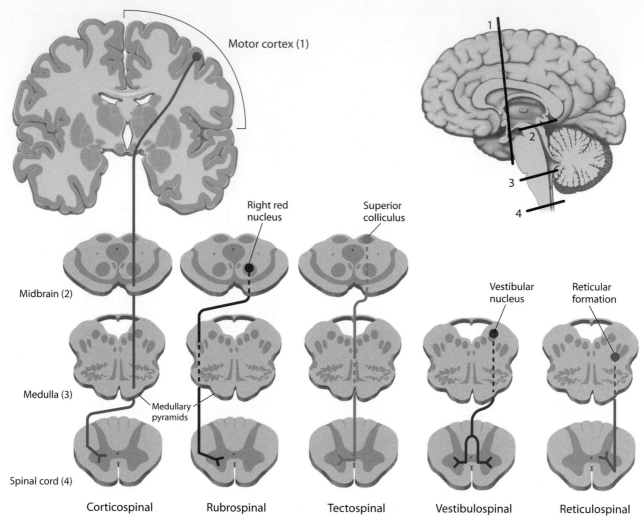

Figure 10.4 The brain innervates the spinal cord via the pyramidal and extrapyramidal tracts. The pyramidal, or cortico-spinal tract originates in the cortex, and almost all of the fibers cross over to the contralateral side at the pyramids. Extrapyramidal tracts originate in various subcortical nuclei, and terminate in both contralateral and ipsilateral regions of the spinal cord. Adapted from Bear et al. (1996).

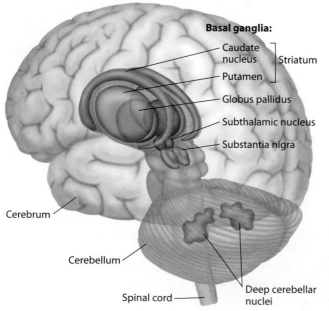

Figure 10.5 The basal ganglia and cerebellum are two prominent subcortical components of the motor pathways. The basal ganglia proper includes the caudate, putamen, and globus pallidus, three nuclei that surround the thalamus. Functionally, the subthalamic nuclei and substantia nigra are also considered part of the basal ganglia. The cerebellum sits below the posterior portion of the cerebral cortex. All cerebellar output originates in the deep cerebellar nuclei.

mainly restricted to the two nuclei forming the striatum—the caudate and the putamen. Output is almost exclusively by way of the internal segment of the globus pallidus and part of the substantia nigra. The remaining components (the rest of the substantia nigra, subthalamic nucleus, and external segment of the globus pallidus) are in a position to modulate the output of the globus pallidus. As with the lateral cerebellum, basal ganglia output is primarily ascending. Axons of the globus pallidus terminate in the thalamus, which in turn projects to motor and frontal regions of the cerebral cortex. Basal ganglia provide scant input to the brainstem nuclei forming the extrapyramidal tracts. Instead, motor control is cortically mediated by thalamic projections.

Cortical Regions Involved in Motor Control

The cerebral cortex can regulate the activity of spinal neurons in direct and indirect ways. Direct connections are provided by the cortico-spinal tract. As its name implies, this tract is composed of neurons that originate in the cortex and terminate directly or monosynaptically on alpha motor neurons or spinal interneurons. Thus, single axons of the cortico-spinal tract can stretch for more than 3 feet. The cortico-spinal tract is frequently referred to as the *pyramidal tract* because it was once believed that the sole origin of these fibers was the giant pyramidal cells of the cortex. Now we know that cortico-spinal axons can arise from cells of different sizes in layer 5 of the cortex.

Cortico-spinal fibers originate from many parts of the cerebral cortex (Figure 10.6). The most prominent of these is the primary motor cortex, or area 4. This area is anterior to the central sulcus, the anatomical division separating the frontal and parietal cortex. Other sources of cortico-spinal fibers include area 6, the premotor cortex, and portions of the parietal cortex, especially somatosensory areas 1, 2, and 3. Because the somatosensory cortex contains many direct projections to the spinal cord, it is clear that the brain is not divided into sensory, motor, and association areas; the processes must work in concert to produce coherent action.

While the cerebral cortex has direct access to spinal mechanisms via the cortico-spinal tract, it can also influence movement in four other prominent ways. First, the motor cortex and premotor areas receive input from most regions of the cortex by way of cortico-cortical connections. Second, many cortical axons terminate on brainstem nuclei, thus cortically influencing the extrapyramidal tracts. Third, the cortex sends massive

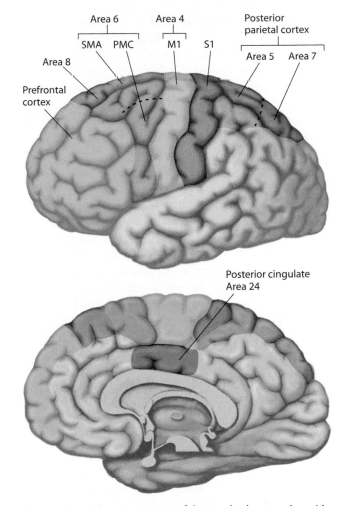

Figure 10.6 The motor areas of the cerebral cortex. Area 4 is the primary motor cortex. Area 6 on the medial surface is referred to as the supplementary motor area and on the lateral surface as the premotor cortex. Area 8 includes the frontal eye fields. Lesions in many posterior areas can also produce severe problems in coordination.

projections to the basal ganglia and cerebellum. Fourth, the cortico-bulbar tract is composed of cortical fibers that terminate on the cranial nerves.

The Organization of Motor Areas

The anatomical organization of the motor areas follows two principles. First, within each motor structure is an organized, somatotopic representation of the body, a concept introduced in Chapter 3 (see Figure 3.9). In the motor cortex, this somatotopy is particularly clear. For example, an electrical stimulus applied to the medial wall of the precentral gyrus will create movement in the foot; the same stimulus applied at a ventral lateral site will elicit tongue movement. Representation of the effectors does not correspond to their actual size. Rather, the cortical area devoted to a certain effector reflects the importance of that effector for movement and the level of control required for manipulating the effector. For this reason, the fingers span a large portion of the human motor cortex because of the significance of manual dexterity.

The somatotopic representation, particularly for distal effectors, is restricted to one side of the body. As with sensory systems, each cerebral hemisphere is devoted primarily to controlling behavior on the opposite side of the body. For cortico-spinal tracts, this contralateral organization occurs because almost all of these fibers cross, or *decussate*, at the junction of the medulla and spinal cord. Most extrapyramidal fibers also decussate so each side controls movements on the body's opposite side. The one exception to this crossed arrangement is the cerebellum. Fibers from the cerebellum cross as soon as they exit this structure; they project to either the contralateral cerebral hemisphere via the thalamus or the contralateral brainstem nuclei. The result is an ipsilateral organization of the cerebellum; the right side is associated with movements on the right side of the body and the left side with movements on the left side of the body.

The second general principle refers to the relation between motor areas. The components form a hierarchy with multiple levels of control. As can be seen in Figure 10.7, the lowest level of the hierarchy is the spinal cord. Not only do spinal mechanisms provide a point of contact between the nervous system and muscles, but also simple reflexive movements can be controlled at this level. At the highest level are premotor and association areas. Processing within these regions is critical for planning an action based on present perceptual information, past experience, and future goals. The motor cortex and brainstem structures, with the assistance of the cerebellum and basal ganglia, translate this action goal into a movement.

Viewing the motor system as a hierarchy enables us to recognize that motor control is a distributed process. The highest levels might not be concerned with the details of a movement, but they may allow lower-level mechanisms to translate motor commands into movements. Hierarchical organization also can be viewed from a phylogenetic perspective. Movement in organisms with primitive motor structures is primarily based on simple reflexive actions. An unexpected blast of water against the abdominal cavity of the sea slug auto-

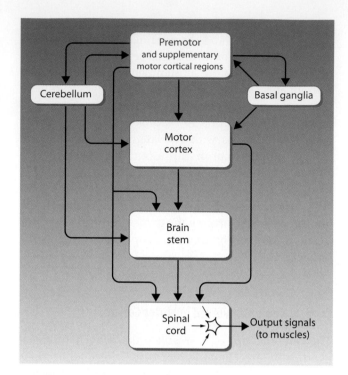

Figure 10.7 The motor hierarchy. All connections to the arms and legs originate in the spinal cord. The spinal signals are influenced by inputs from the brainstem and various cortical regions, whose activity in turn is modulated by the cerebellum and basal ganglia. Control is thus distributed across various levels of the hierarchy.

matically elicits a withdrawal response. Additional layers of control enable these reflexes to be modified, perhaps being expressed only in certain conditions. For example, a brainstem structure can inhibit spinal neurons so a change in a muscle does not automatically trigger a stretch reflex.

In an analogous fashion, the cortex can provide additional means for regulating the actions of the lower levels of the motor hierarchy. This ability offers an organism greater flexibility in its actions. We can generate any number of movements in response to a sensory signal. A tennis player can choose to hit a cross-court forehand, go for a drop shot, or pop a defensive lob. Cortical mechanisms also enable us to generate actions that are minimally dependent on external cues. We can sing aloud, wave our hands, or pantomime a gesture. Reflecting this greater flexibility, the cortico-spinal tract is one of the latest evolutionary adaptations, appearing only in mammals. It affords a new pathway over which the cerebral hemispheres can activate ancient motor structures.

COMPUTATIONAL ISSUES IN
MOTOR CONTROL

We have seen the panoramic view of the motor system: how muscles are activated and how this activity can be influenced by spinal, subcortical, and cortical signals. Though we identified the major anatomical components, we have yet to consider the structures' functional roles. But it is useful first to examine certain behavioral phenomena to understand the information processing that must take place in the motor systems. This section elucidates computational issues in motor control and sets the stage for the final sections in which physiological and neurological evidence is assessed in developing a cognitive neuroscience of action.

Peripheral Control of Movement and the Role of Feedback

The notion of hierarchical control implies that higher-level systems can modulate the activity of lower-level mechanisms. One implication of this view is that lower levels can produce movement. The stretch reflex is one such example. Some spinal mechanisms can maintain postural stability even in the absence of higher-level processing.

Are spinal mechanisms a simple means for generating more complicated movements? At the end of the nineteenth century, Charles Sherrington, a Nobel Laureate British neurophysiologist, developed a procedure in which he severed the spinal cord in cats and dogs to disconnect peripheral motor structures such as alpha motor neurons and spinal interneurons from the cortex and subcortex (Sherrington, 1947). This procedure allowed Sherrington to observe whether the animals could produce any movement in the absence of higher-level commands. As expected, stretch reflexes remained intact; in fact, these reflexes were exaggerated due to the removal of inhibitory influences from the brain. More surprisingly, Sherrington observed that these animals could alternate the movements of their hind limbs. With the appropriate stimulus, one leg flexed while the other extended, and then the first leg extended while the other flexed. In other words, without any signals from the brain, the animal displayed movements that resembled walking. Sherrington subsequently observed that these movements depended on intact sensory processes. When the sensory signal to a limb was eliminated by cutting the dorsal root of the spinal cord, the animal ceased using that limb.

Sherrington concluded that the spinal reflex arc provided the essential components for movement. The alpha motor neurons could trigger movement, but the normal maintenance of efferent motor commands required a continual sensory signal from the periphery concerning the consequences of these commands. More complicated movements might utilize a similar process in which sensory signals and motor outputs were joined in a stream of gestures. Each movement would change the sensory signal, and this new sensory signal could trigger movement; hence, complex movements could be seen as the successive chaining of stimuli and responses via reflex processes.

Sherrington was only partly correct. While movement does not require signals from the brain, it also does not need sensory signals, a phenomenon that was first demonstrated by T.G. Brown in 1911. When Brown sectioned the spinal cord and dorsal roots, he discovered that the animal still generated rhythmic walking movements (Figure 10.8). Hence, neurons in the spinal cord can generate an entire sequence of actions without any external feedback signal.

These neurons have come to be called *central pattern generators*, and they underscore two major features of motor control. First, they offer a powerful mechanism for the hierarchical control of movement. Consider, for instance, how the nervous system might initiate walking. Brain structures would not have to specify patterns of muscle activity. Rather, they would simply activate the appropriate pattern generators in the spinal cord, which in turn trigger muscle commands. The system is truly hierarchical in that the highest levels need be concerned only with issuing commands to achieve an action, while lower-level mechanisms translate the commands into a movement.

We cannot expect there to be central pattern generators for a wide range of movements. Locomotion probably represents a special situation, an action for which specialized mechanisms have evolved. But more arbitrary movements could exploit central pattern generators. When we reach to pick up an object, for example, low-level mechanisms could make the necessary postural adjustments to keep our body from tipping over as our center of gravity shifts.

The second important insight yielded by Brown's work is the observation that movements are not entirely dependent on peripheral feedback. As such, they imply internal representations of movement patterns. This

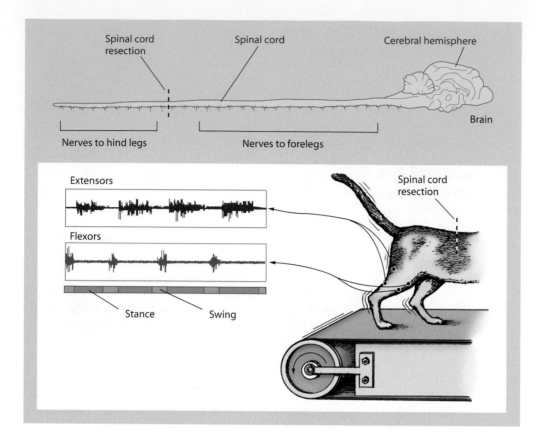

Figure 10.8 Movement is still possible following a resection of the spinal cord. In Brown's classic experiment, the spinal cord was severed so that the nerves to the hind legs were isolated from the brain. The cats were still able to produce stereotypic, rhythmic movements with the hindlegs when walking on a moving treadmill. Since all inputs from the brain were eliminated, the motor commands must have originated in the lower portion of the spinal cord. Adapted from Kandel et al. (1991).

hypothesis has been supported by a myriad of evidence over the past 50 years. One influential study demonstrating the central control of movement comes from an experiment on a colony of monkeys that lived in a large, enclosed environment (Taub and Berman, 1968). Their dorsal roots were cut; in other words, the animals were deafferented, deprived of all sensory, or deafferent, feedback from the affected limb. In this study, the deafferentation procedure was conducted in two stages. In the first stage, the operation was restricted to a single arm. Following this surgery, the animals showed little evidence that they could still use the limb. They hung the limb by their side and never engaged in activities like climbing, which requires coordinated actions of the two forelimbs. In the second stage, the researchers severed the dorsal root in the remaining intact limb. Paradoxically, the animals now began to use both limbs (Figure 10.9). Indeed, an outside observer would be hard-

Figure 10.9 Movement without feedback. If the dorsal root on one side of the body is sectioned, the animal does not use the limb; it hangs limply by the animal's side. In a second operation, the dorsal root on the other side is sectioned. Now the brain does not receive sensory information from either upper limb. Paradoxically, the monkeys now begin to use the limbs, moving about on all fours, climbing fences, and using their hands to pick up objects.

pressed to notice any abnormalities in the behavior of these animals. They would move about their cages in a quadrupedal gait and could be coaxed into climbing the sides of their cages to fetch a reward. These results demonstrate that sensory signals are not essential for movement, although, as we might expect, an animal prefers to use a limb that has intact sensory signals.

This same sort of phenomenon has been observed in humans with severe sensory deficits, or *neuropathies.* In some patients, the peripheral sensory fibers are destroyed or become nonfunctional for unknown reasons; however, the motor fibers are relatively spared, perhaps due to their smaller size and reduced metabolic demands. Careful clinical examinations are required to document that there is no residual perception of joint position, touch, or vibration in the distal extremities. One patient was reported to be oblivious to pinprick or even electrical stimulation of moderate intensity (Rothwell et al., 1982). Nonetheless, despite their severe sensory problems, these patients can still make complicated movements. Figure 10.10 shows the tracings of one patient who was asked to draw geometric shapes in midair. In each case, the shape is drawn correctly and consistently, even though the gestures require the coordinated interplay of many muscles.

The fact that they can make the movements emphasizes that movements can be centrally generated without feedback. This is not to say that feedback is unimportant, however. Errors accumulate quickly in its absence, and even in the initial tracings, the movements are not as precise as those of subjects who have intact sensation. Moreover, feedback is essential for learning and keeping the motor system calibrated. The dart thrower is constantly using the results of his last toss to make subtle adjustments.

The Representation of Movement Plans

Research on central pattern generators and movement without feedback highlights the importance of representations in controlling movement. Patients who are functionally deafferented must have an internal representation of the expected consequences of a motor command. For example, to trace a circle or figure eight, they must have learned the required series of motor commands, commands that can be accessed without requiring any sort of feedback signal. A central issue is how to characterize properties of these representations and how they translate into actions (Keele, 1986).

THE CONTENT OF MOTOR PLANS

Consider a simple motor task. A light is presented at a certain location, and after it is turned off the subject

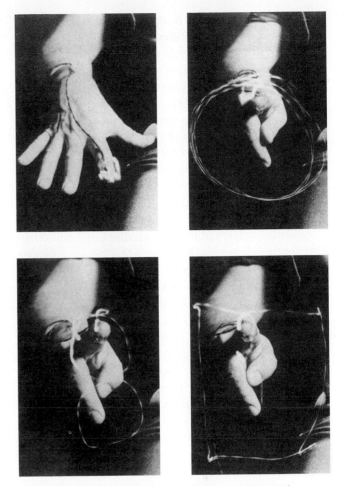

Figure 10.10 Movements produced by a patient with a severe sensory neuropathy. Time-lapse photography was used to record the patient's tracings of a circle, a figure 8, and a square. All of the movements were made in the dark. Despite the absence of proprioceptive, kinesthetic, and visual feedback, the shapes are readily identified.

must move her arm to the position of the light. With practice, she can improve on the task, even if visual feedback from the moving limb is precluded. For example, she might complete the movement more rapidly and with less error. This improvement implies that the representation of the movement has changed. But how? Two possibilities can be considered. Either she developed a distance-based representation of the desired movement—she might have learned that a certain pattern of muscular activity will displace the limb a desired distance—or she developed a location-based representation of the final position. By this latter hypothesis, practice might improve the representation of an endpoint configuration for the limb that matches the target location.

Emilio Bizzi and his colleagues at MIT (1984) provided evidence in favor of the hypothesis that the central representation is primarily based on a location code.

In their experiments, deafferented monkeys were trained in a simple pointing experiment. On each trial, a light appeared at one of several locations. After the light was turned off, the animal was required to rotate its elbow to bring its arm to the target location.

The critical manipulation included trials in which an opposing torque force was applied just when movement started. These forces were designed to keep the limb at the starting position for a short time. Since the room was dark and the animals were deafferented, they were unaware that their movements were counteracted by an opposing force. The critical question centered on where the movement ended once the torque force was removed. If the animal has learned that a muscular burst will transport its limb a certain distance, applying an opposing force should result in a movement that falls short of the target. But if the animal generates a motor command specifying the desired position, it should achieve this goal once the opposing force is removed. As shown in Figure 10.11, the results clearly favor the location hypothesis. When the torque motor was on, the limb stayed at the starting location. As soon as it was turned off, the limb rapidly moved to the correct location.

An even more dramatic demonstration of endpoint planning occurred in a follow-up experiment. Here the torque motor was used to transport the limb from the starting position to the final position just as the target location was illuminated. Because of the surgery, the animals were unaware of this passive displacement. Thus, the question centered on what would happen at the beginning of the movement. If the animal is programming muscular events that will result in movement of a desired distance, then the arm should be propelled well past the target. Yet if the animal is programming a desired final location, there should be no movement—the arm has already been moved to the target location. Neither of these predictions was confirmed. When the torque was removed, the limb moved toward the original location, followed by a reversal after a few hundred milliseconds toward the final location. Indeed, a similar return toward the starting position is also seen when this manipulation is done in the monkey with intact feedback mechanisms. These results provide even more compelling support for the location hypothesis and reveal insights into the dynamics of location-based representations. At the time the target was illuminated, the monkey was still generating a motor command corresponding to the initial location (Figure 10.12). Thus, the arm began to drift toward this position once the torque force was removed. When the target's location is identified, the representation of action commands corresponding to this location are instantiated and the arm

Figure 10.11 Endpoint planning. **(a)** Deafferented monkeys were trained to point in the dark to a target indicated by the brief illumination of a light. The top trace shows the position of the arm as it goes from an initial position to the target location. The bottom trace shows the EMG activity in the biceps. In the control condition, the animals were able to accurately make the pointing movements despite the absence of all sources of feedback. **(b)** An opposing force is applied at the onset of the movement, preventing the arm from moving (bar under the arm position trace). Once this force is removed, the limb rapidly moves to the correct target location. Since the animal could not sense the opposing force, it must have generated a motor command corresponding to the target location. Adapted from Bizzi et al. (1984).

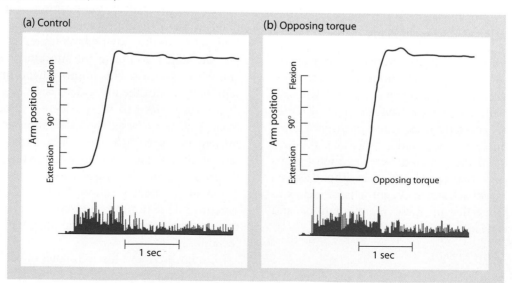

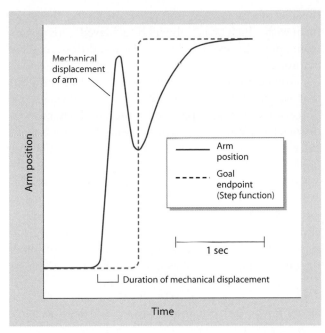

Figure 10.12 Pointing movements from a displaced starting location. Prior to the onset of EMG activity, the monkey's limb (solid line) was mechanically displaced to the target location. When this external force was removed, the limb began to move back to the initial location, and then reversed direction to move to the target location. The central commands (dotted line) can be viewed as a step function from one posture to another, initially specifying the starting location and then abruptly shifting to the target location. Adapted from Bizzi et al. (1984).

moves toward the target location. The experiment demonstrated how movement can be viewed as a shift from one postural state to another.

Location planning is computationally appealing when considered from a hierarchical perspective. By this perspective, the highest level of the planning system is concerned with achieving a final configuration, a movement that reaches a goal. The way the plan is executed can be assigned to lower levels of the motor hierarchy. Consider how this might apply to a simple reaching task like moving a hand from a computer keyboard to grasp a coffee cup at one side. The action can be achieved in many ways—we can glance at the cup to guide our hand movements, grope about as we remain engrossed in our text, or rotate about the waist so the cup is directly in front of us. This redundancy arises because we have multiple joints (elbow, shoulder, waist) that provide great flexibility; yet this redundancy can increase the complexity for a control system. According to the location hypothesis, the highest level of the hierarchy need represent only the ultimate goal—the elbow and hand assume a position where the cup can be grasped with

minimal effort. How this goal is met does not have to be included in this representation. Lower levels of the motor hierarchy are concerned with translating a final goal into a certain trajectory.

While Bizzi and his colleagues provided impressive evidence in favor of location planning, it is also clear that we can represent other parameters of movement such as distance. For example, we can reproduce a movement to a fixed distance, even when the reproduced distance is to a novel location. Moreover, when movements are made to successive locations, errors that arise in the initial movements are manifest in the final movements. If the sequence is represented as independent locations, we should not expect to observe this persistence.

We can also control the form with which a movement is executed. For example, in reaching for the coffee cup, we can choose to extend only the arm or can bend forward by rotating about the waist. We can also vary how fast we execute the movement. Indeed, in many tasks, the trajectory is as important as the final goal. When a skilled figure skater performs an aerial maneuver, it is essential that she land properly to maintain her balance. But it is just as important that the jump follow a certain trajectory to achieve the desired number of rotations in the most graceful manner. Viewed in this way, we can argue that endpoint control reveals the fundamental capabilities of the motor control system; the distance and trajectory planning demonstrate additional flexibility in the control processes.

Consider one other possibility. To this point, we have emphasized the hierarchical nature of the motor system. For example, at the highest level, the representation is in terms of locations and goals, with lower levels transforming this plan into a movement. An alternative conceptualization is that location and distance planning represent two independent forms of representation (Figure 10.13). This hypothesis provides an interpretation for why pointing movements generally have two phases: a rapid, ballistic phase when the arm is transported to the vicinity of the target followed by a secondary phase when the target location is achieved. Although the second phase has been interpreted as showing the activation of feedback processes, it could reflect a transition from a representation based on distance to one based on location.

Some suggestive results favor the hypothesis of separate forms of representation. Richard Abrams and his colleagues (1994) at Washington University in St. Louis ran an experiment in which a dot was displaced across the computer screen, either by 4 or 7 degrees of visual angle. In separate blocks of trials, subjects were asked

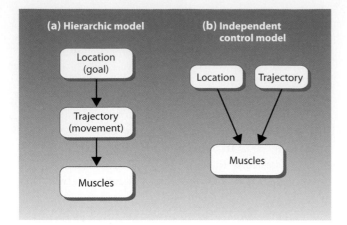

Figure 10.13 Location and trajectory planning of motor commands. In the hierarchical model, goals are initially specified as target locations. A translation process is then required to determine the trajectory and corresponding muscle activity required to move a limb to the goal. An alternative hypothesis is that location and trajectory planning provide two different representations for determining muscle activity.

either to reproduce the distance that the dot had moved or to move to the final position of the dot. The critical manipulation was that on half the trials, background elements on the computer display moved in the opposite direction. This opposing motion creates a powerful illusion, amplifying the perceived motion of the dot (Figure 10.14). The effect of this illusion was obvious in the subjects' performance in the distance condition. They overestimated the distance the dot had moved relative to conditions where the background moved in the same direction as the target dot. But the background motion had minimal effect on their performance in the location condition. If responses in the two conditions were based on a single representational system, one would expect the illusion to affect both conditions similarly. The fact that the illusion produced differential effects in the two conditions indicates that the movements were guided by different representations.

In the Abrams study, only the distance-based representation was susceptible to the effects of the illusion. The location-based code appeared to be immune to these perceptual distortions. Results such as these suggest the provocative hypothesis that the human brain might have evolved two separate modes for planning movements. Perhaps location planning represents a more ancient and primitive system, one in which the representation is simply to specify the goal, or target location of an action. This system could produce movements that reach a final target location, but without much flexibility. In contrast, a second system might be

capable of distance planning, of specifying the exact form with which an action will be achieved. This system would provide flexibility but with the additional costs of planning.

Other evidence is also consistent with the hypothesis that location planning might be isolated from cognitive processes, and that aspects of motor performance are dissociated from consciousness (see Chapter 7). Consider a particularly diabolic experiment in which the target changes position just as the person begins to reach for it (Castiello et al., 1991). Subjects were required to respond to the change in two ways. To assess motor adjustments, subjects were required to continue with the movement until they had grasped the target at its new target location. To assess conscious perception of the displacement, the subjects were asked to say "tah" as

Figure 10.14 Dissociation of location and distance planning. **(a)** A dot was moved to the right, traversing a distance of either 4 or 7 degrees. In half of the trials, the frame moved to the right; in the other half, the frame moved to the left. Subjects were asked to move a lever, indicating in separate conditions the distance the target dot moved or the final location of the dot. **(b)** Distance judgments were more susceptible to the motion of the frame than were the location judgments. Adapted from Abrams and Landgraf (1990).

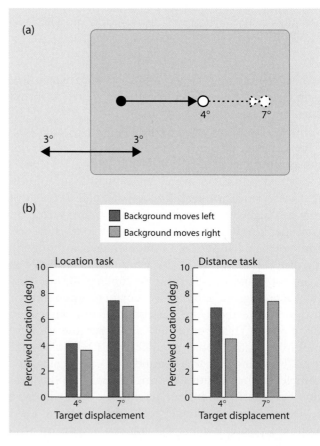

Where Is It? Assessing Location Through Perception and Action

To demonstrate that spatial information can be represented differently in systems involved in conscious perception and those associated with guiding action, try the experiment outlined in the figure. While standing in an open area, have a friend place an object between 6 and 12 meters from you. Then, have your friend move along the perpendicular direction and stop him or her when you perceive that you are both equidistant from the object. Measure your accuracy. Now, have your friend place the object in a new location, again between 6 and 12 meters away. When ready, close your eyes and walk forward, attempting to stop right over the object. Measure your accuracy.

Assuming that your performance matches that of the average person, you will notice a striking dissociation (Loomis et al., 1992). You would have been quite in-accurate on the first task, underestimating the distance from you to the object. Yet on the second task you should be very accurate. This dissociation between two forms of judgment, one perceptual and the other motoric, is similar to that found in the Abrams experiment. In both situations, the results suggest that separate representational systems underlie judgments of location and distance. While location judgments are veridical, the representation of distance is subject to perceptual distortions. Our perception of distance is highly compressed—things almost always are farther away than they appear (perhaps a "safety" mechanism to ensure that we ready ourselves for an approaching predator?). But as this experiment demonstrates, our action systems are not similarly fooled. There is little, if any, compression of distance when we move to a target location.

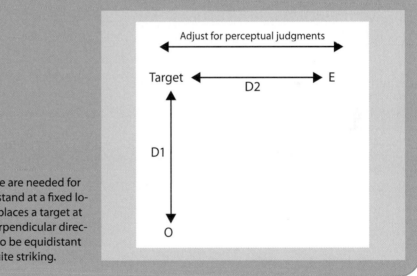

Perceptual judgment of distance. Two people are needed for this demonstration. The observer, O, should stand at a fixed location in an open area. The experimenter, E, places a target at some point in the area. E walks along the perpendicular direction and stops when O judges each person to be equidistant to the target (D1 = D2). The results will be quite striking.

soon as they detected the change. While changes in the movement trajectory were evident within 107 msec of the displacement, vocal responses had a latency of more than 400 msec. Control experiments convincingly showed that this effect could not be attributed to differences in the response times of the two response modalities. Instead, the motor corrections were issued well in advance of when subjects became aware of the change in stimulus location. Rather than action resulting from cognition, this experiment suggests that cognition followed action.

HIERARCHICAL REPRESENTATION OF ACTION SEQUENCES

In the preceding actions, the movements entailed simple gestures such as pointing to a location in space. Most of our actions are more complex, however, and involve a sequence of movements. In serving a tennis ball, we have to toss the ball with our nondominant hand, and swing the racquet so it strikes the ball just after the apex of rotation. In playing the piano, we must strike a sequence of keys with appropriate timing and force. Are these actions simply constructed by linking

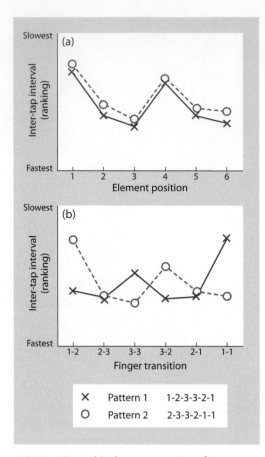

Figure 10.15 Hierarchical representation of movement sequences. The intervals between the successive responses can be plotted in two ways: as a function of element position **(a)** or as a function of the finger transition **(b)**. The functions are essentially identical in terms of element position and very different in terms of finger transitions. For both sequences, the transition times reflect the fact that the sequences are broken into chunks of three, with a longer time required to shift from one chunk to the other. Adapted from Povel and Collard (1982).

independent movements? Or are they guided by hierarchical representational structures that govern the entire sequence?

Consider a task that requires tapping two sequences with three fingers. The first sequence is 1-2-3-3-2-1 where 1, 2, and 3 correspond to the index, middle, and ring fingers, respectively. The second sequence is 2-3-3-2-1-1. Practice the first sequence, cycling through the six-element sequence repeatedly. Now practice the second sequence in the same manner. When we measure the intervals between each tap, we discover that two transitions are slower than the other four (Figure 10.15). These would correspond to the transitions that mark the beginning of each cycle and the transition between the third and fourth tap. This pattern is evident for both sequences.

When we take a closer look at the two sequences, we see that, when repeated cyclically, the two sequences involve the exact same finger transitions. The second sequence is identical to the first with only one change: The first element (i.e., the 1 or first index-finger tap) has been moved to the end of the sequence. And yet the two intertap interval profiles reveal that despite this similarity with regard to motor demands, the reproductions of the sequences are quite different (Povel and Collard, 1982). For example, in the first sequence a long pause happens between the two 3's; in the second sequence this intertap interval is one of the shortest.

The reason for these differences is that the production of the sequences is guided by distinct hierarchical representations. We do not simply produce the sequences as a chain of six cyclical movements. Rather, we group the elements into chunks. Chunking provides a mechanism for building hierarchical structures—a way of decomposing a large representation into constituent parts. Chunking is an efficient way to represent large amounts of information. Phone numbers in the United States are not remembered as a list of ten numbers but as two chunks of three numbers and one chunk of four numbers. Similarly, the six-element tapping sequences are chunked into two subcomponents of three elements each. The top level of the hierarchy can represent the overall structure—the number of elements and the order in which they are to be produced. Details within a particular chunk are part of a lower level.

Figure 10.16 presents a model developed by Donald MacKay (1987) of the University of California to show how the ideas of hierarchical representation can be applied to motor control. The top of the hierarchy, the conceptual level, corresponds to a representation of the goal of the action. In this example, the man intends to accept the woman's invitation to dance. At the next level, this goal has to be translated into a system. He could make a physical gesture such as offer his hand or start tapping his foot. Or he could verbally respond to the invitation, selecting one sentence from a large repertoire of appropriate responses: "Yes, that would be nice," "Yes, I've been dying to get out there and shake my booty," or "Yes, the music is really hot." MacKay referred to this as the *lexical level* to indicate that a common concept can be conveyed through a distinct set of actions. Lower levels of the hierarchy will then translate these units into patterns of muscular activation. For example, a verbal response will entail a pattern of activity across the speech articulators or the extension of the hand will require movements of the arm and fingers.

The hierarchical properties of this model are explicit. Each level corresponds to a different form for rep-

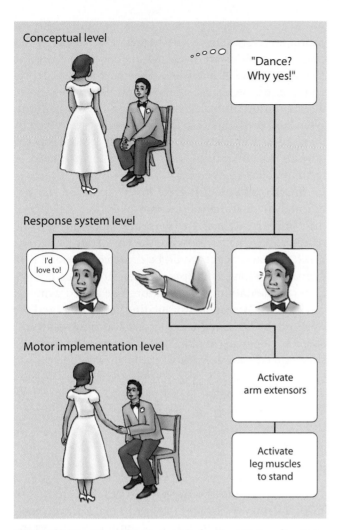

Figure 10.16 Hierarchical control of action. Motor planning and learning can occur at multiple levels. At the lowest level are the actual commands to implement a particular action. At the highest level are abstract representations of the goal for the action. There are usually multiple actions that can achieve the same goal. Learning occurs at all levels. If the motor commands (lowest level) are well established, then motor learning will be limited to strengthening the more abstract representations rather than involving the muscles themselves.

resenting the action. Actions can be described in relation to the goals to be achieved, and this level need not be tied to a specific form of implementation. Whether our gentleman responds physically or vocally, the two forms of responding share a common level of representation. In a similar fashion, when we convey a linguistic message by speaking or by writing, a common level of representation is on both the conceptual and the lexical level. Higher levels in the hierarchy need not represent all of the information.

MacKay's model has also proved useful in explaining the learning of new motor patterns. People frequently attribute motor learning to low levels of the hierarchy. We speak of our muscles having learned how to respond: how to maintain our balance on a bike, or how to throw a dart with fine precision. The fact that we have great difficulty verbalizing how to perform these skills reinforces the notion that the learning is noncognitive. The Olympic gymnast Peter Vidman expressed this sentiment when he said, "As I approach the apparatus... the only thing I am thinking about is... the first trick.... Then, my body takes over and hopefully everything becomes automatic...." (Schmidt, 1987.)

But, upon closer study, we find that some aspects of motor learning are independent of the muscular system used to perform the actions. Demonstrate this to yourself by taking a piece of paper and signing your name. Having done this, repeat the action but use your nondominant hand. Now do it again, holding the pen between your teeth. If you feel especially adventurous, you can take off your shoes and socks and hold the pen between your toes.

While the atypical productions are not as smooth as your standard signature, the more dramatic result of this demonstration is the high degree of similarity across all of the productions. An example from one such demonstration is given in Figure 10.17. This high-level

Figure 10.17 Motor representations are not linked to particular effector systems. These five productions of "cognitive neuroscience" were produced by moving a pen with **(a)** the right hand, **(b)** the right wrist, **(c)** the left hand, **(d)** the mouth, and **(e)** the right foot. There is a degree of similarity in the productions despite the vast differences in practice writing with these five limbs.

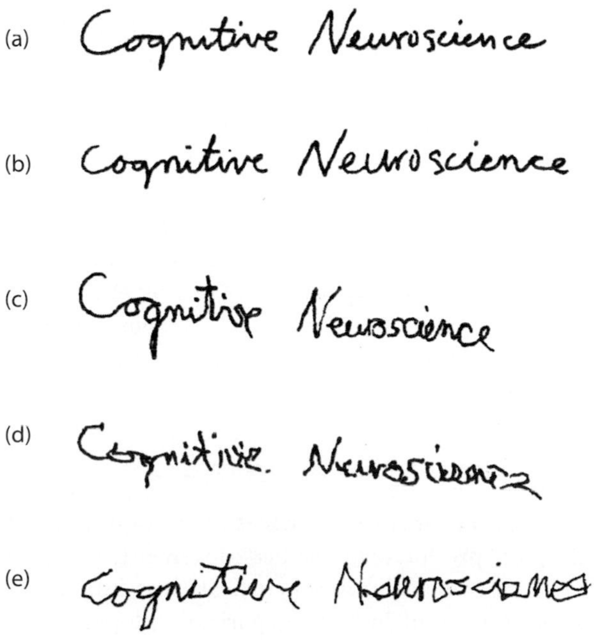

(a) *Cognitive Neuroscience*

(b) *Cognitive Neuroscience*

(c) *Cognitive Neuroscience*

(d) *Cognitive Neuroscience*

(e) *Cognitive Neuroscience*

representation of the action is independent of any particular muscle group. The differences in the final product reflect the fact that some muscle groups have more experience in translating an abstract representation into a concrete action.

Viewed in this way, we can see that motor learning can take place at multiple levels. When a learned action is produced by a new set of effectors, learning is greatest at the lower level. In contrast, if we are acquiring a new action, the effects of learning are likely to be at more conceptual levels of the action hierarchy. To show this, MacKay recruited a group of subjects who were fluent in English and German. These subjects were asked to produce novel sentences such as "This morning, I got out of bed eleven times." The subjects would repeat the sentence in English several times, and as expected, they became faster with practice. Then he would have them repeat the same sentence, but for this transfer test, they were required to speak the sentence in German. Even though they had never said the sentence in this language, the subjects showed perfect transfer on this task: They were just as fast as when they practiced the sentence in English.

MacKay argued that the effects of practice in this situation are restricted to the highest abstract level. Because the subjects are bilingual, the lower levels of the hierarchy are well established. They have a strong representation of the lexical items in both languages and of the translation of these items into articulatory patterns. What is learned, then, are the new concepts conveyed by these novel sentences. Since this level is abstract, the learning benefits can be seen in either the practiced or the unpracticed language.

Sports psychologists have long recognized the significance of hierarchical control of action. As part of their training, athletes are frequently taught to mentally rehearse movements. As with MacKay's transfer experiment, mental practice would be expected to benefit performance, so long as the practice can strengthen higher-level representations of the action. The skilled gymnast can improve by mentally simulating her routine, and the weekend golfer can benefit from watching a professional's videotape. Long hours of practice help to strengthen the lower levels of the hierarchy.

PHYSIOLOGICAL ANALYSIS OF MOTOR PATHWAYS

So far in this chapter we have stressed two critical points on movement: First, as with all complex domains, motor control depends on several distributed anatomical structures. Second, these distributed structures operate in a hierarchical fashion. We have seen that the concept of hierarchical organization also applies at the behavioral level of analysis. The highest levels of planning are best described by how an action achieves an objective; the lower levels of the motor hierarchy are dedicated to translating a goal into a movement. We now turn to the problem of relating structure to behavior: How can we best characterize the functional role of the different components of the motor system? In this section we take a closer look at the neurophysiology of motor control. In the following section, we address this same issue from the perspective of neurology.

The Neural Representation of Movement

The primary motor cortex provides the most important signal for the production of skilled movement. This area receives input from almost all cortical areas implicated in motor control, including the parietal, the premotor, and the frontal cortices, and from subcortical structures such as the basal ganglia and cerebellum. In turn, the motor cortex's output constitutes the largest signal in the cortico-spinal tract—not to mention its indirect influence on spinal mechanisms by way of projections to the extrapyramidal pathway. The significance of this area is strongly attested to by the motor problems that develop when this area is lesioned. If the primary motor cortex is destroyed by stroke, volitional movement will disappear on the side contralateral to the lesion.

DIRECTIONAL TUNING OF MOTOR CELLS

Neurophysiologists have long puzzled over how best to describe cellular activity in the primary motor cortex. Direct stimulation can produce discrete movements about single joints and has been useful for mapping the somatotopic organization of the motor cortex. But this method does not provide insight to the activity of single neurons, nor can it be used to study how and when cells become active during volitional movement. To address these issues, we have to record the activity of single cells and ask what parameters of movement are coded by that activity. For example, is cellular activity in the primary

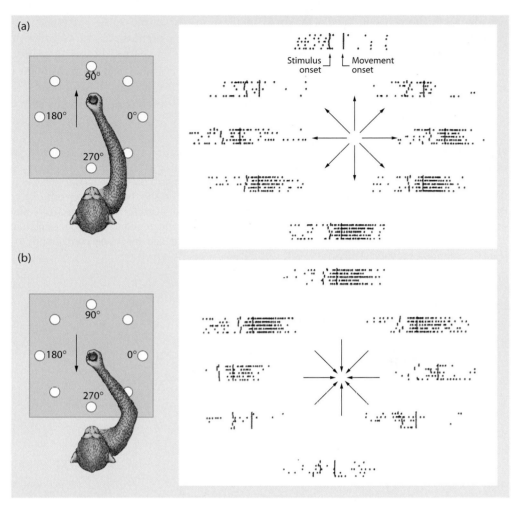

Figure 10.18 Motor cortex activity is correlated with movement direction. **(a)** The animal was trained to move a lever from the center location to one of eight locations. The activity of a motor cortex neuron is plotted next to each target location. Each row represents a single movement and the dots correspond to action potentials. **(b)** Movements originated at the eight peripheral locations and always terminated at the center location. The activity for the neuron is now plotted next to the starting locations. The neuron is most active for movements in the downward direction, regardless of starting and final location. Adapted from Georgopoulos (1990).

motor cortex correlated with movement direction or movement location?

Apostolos Georgopoulos (1995) of the Veteran's Administration Medical Center in Minneapolis studied this question by recording from cells in the motor cortex of rhesus monkeys. The monkeys were trained with the apparatus shown in Figure 10.18, moving a lever to one of several targets. The animal initiates the trial by moving the lever to a designated starting position. After a brief hold period, a light comes on at a target position and the animal moves the lever to this position to obtain a food reward. This movement is similar to a reaching action and usually involves rotating two joints, the shoulder and the elbow.

The results of these studies convincingly demonstrate that movement direction provides a far superior correlate of motor cortex activity than does final location. The middle panel of Figure 10.18 shows a neuron's activity when movements were initiated from a center location to eight radial locations. This cell was most strongly activated when the movement was toward the

animal. The bottom panel of the figure shows results from the same cell when movements were initiated at radial locations and always ended at the center position. In this condition, the cell was most active for movements initiated from the most distant position; movement was again toward the animal.

From such data, one could argue that motor cortex cells code movement direction and that movement in a certain direction requires activating appropriate cells. Indeed, cells within a cortical column have a common directional tuning, with that direction changing in a systematic manner across the cortex. As indicated in Figure 10.18, though, the cells' directional tuning is broad—there is significantly more activity in four of the eight directions.

Since the tuning is so broad, we should consider an alternative coding scheme. A command to move in a direction is distributed across all cells devoted to a certain limb. The response of each cell is a function of how closely the target direction corresponds to its preferred direction. If the target and preferred direction are identical, the cell will have a maximal increase in responsiveness. If the target and preferred direction are in opposite directions, the cell will have a maximal decrease. When the two axes are not parallel, the responsiveness is a function of their difference.

This coding scheme—the summed activity over all of the cells—turns out to be the best predictor of movement direction. Georgopoulos and his colleagues called it the *population vector* because it is a way to see how a global event, a movement in a certain direction, can result from the summed activity of many small elements, each contributing its own vote (Figure 10.19). The pop-

Figure 10.19   The population vector provides a cortical representation of movement. The activity of a single neuron in the motor cortex is measured for each of the eight movements **(a)** and plotted as a tuning profile **(b)**. The preferred direction for this neuron is 180 degrees, the leftward movement. **(c)** Each neuron's contribution to a particular movement can be plotted as a vector. The direction of the vector is always plotted as the neuron's preferred direction and the length corresponds to its firing rate for the target direction. The population vector (dotted line) is the sum of the individual vectors. **(d)** For each direction, the solid lines are the individual vectors for each of 241 motor cortex neurons; the dotted line is the population vector calculated over the entire set of neurons. While many neurons are active during each movement, the summed activity closely corresponds to the actual movements. Adapted from Georgopoulos (1990).

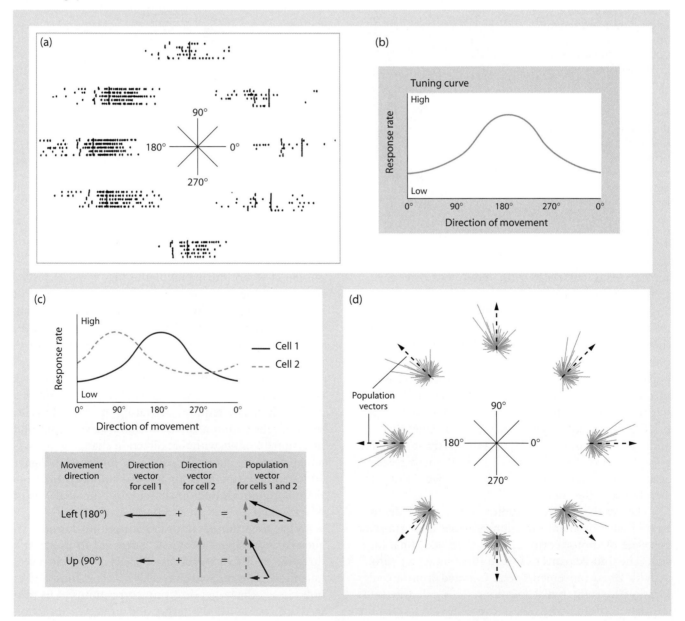

ulation vector is powerful for analyzing motor neurophysiology. For example, once an experimenter has plotted the tuning curves for cells, the population vector for any movement closely agrees with the trajectory adopted by the animal—an analysis that holds for movement in three-dimensional space.

It is essential to factor time into the directional representation of movement. In the motor cortex, the population vector shifts in the direction of the upcoming movement before the movement is produced. This indicates that the cells help to plan the movement rather than simply reflect changes during a movement. To dissociate movement planning and movement execution, Georgopolous provided two signals on each trial: The first indicated the movement's target direction; the second served as a "go" signal indicating that the movement could now be initiated. Thus, the animals were trained to prepare the movement in advance so that they could initiate their responses as fast as possible. Figure 10.20 shows that, expressed as a population vector, cells in the motor cortex coded the intended direction well in advance of the "go" signal. The movement's direction could be precisely predicted when the popula-

tion vector was recorded more than 300 msec prior to the movement. Such results clearly indicate that the motor cortex plans movement, and they also demonstrate that cellular activity in this area does not automatically lead to movement. Some downstream process must regulate when the activity translates into motor commands.

We have viewed the population vector in the context of how it corresponds to the direction of movement. Bear in mind that an alternative way of considering these representations is in relation to specific muscles; that is, movements to the right from the center position occur because the monkey is extending the elbow and rotating the shoulder. The population vector could represent a pattern of activation for the muscles participating in these joint actions. After all, the population vector is not abstract but linked to specific joints. Consider two ways a wrist rotation could achieve a new position. If the arm is in its natural position facing inward, the movement requires wrist extension. When the wrist is rotated, the same direction of movement requires wrist flexion. No cells code direction abstractly—that is, independently of the muscles that make the movement. Cells with a high level of activity in the former situation will generally have a low level of activity in the latter. Moreover, if movement along a direction is made from different starting positions, the preferred direction of single cells rotates in a manner consistent with a representation of the muscle activity (Caminiti et al., 1991). Cellular activity cannot be directly mapped onto muscle activity because, as we noted, population vector transformations arise well in advance of muscle activation.

GOAL-BASED REPRESENTATION IN MOTOR STRUCTURES

Population analyses have been performed in other neural regions including the basal ganglia, cerebellum, premotor cortex, and posterior parietal cortex (Alexander and Crutcher, 1990). As with the motor cortex, the population vector indicates the movement's direction, as might be expected since all these areas contain topographic maps of the body surface and effectors; yet the fact that a common basis of representation is coded across large areas of the cortex and subcortex is puzzling. From a hierarchical viewpoint, we might expect the areas to contribute to movement in distinct ways. There might, for example, be an initial representation of the final target location; this location code would be transformed into a directional code. To date, though, all of the areas show only directional tuning. It remains to be seen if location-based coding will be found in association areas of the cortex that feed into motor and premotor areas.

Figure 10.20 The direction of the population vector predicts the direction of a forthcoming movement. At the cue, one of the eight targets is illuminated, indicating the direction for a subsequent movement. The animal must refrain from moving until the "go" signal. The population vector was calculated every 20 msec. The population vector is oriented in the direction for the planned movement even though EMG activity is silent in the muscles. Adapted from Georgopoulos (1990).

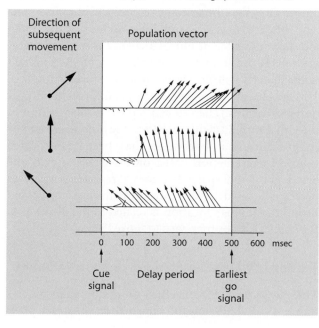

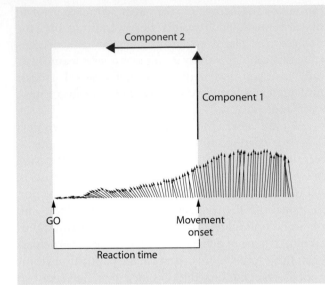

Figure 10.21 The population vector for a two-step movement. The forthcoming movement is shown by the two arrows. The initial direction of the population vector is toward the final component of the movement. It gradually changes so that by the start of movement, it corresponds to the direction of the first component. Adapted from Ashe et al. (1993).

One neurophysiological study showed how important the final location is in the cellular activity of single cells (Ashe et al., 1993). In this experiment, monkeys were trained to make a two-step movement by pushing a lever forward and then to the left (Figure 10.21). When the population vector was analyzed prior to the onset of movement, the initial shift was, surprisingly, to the second component. Only afterward did it point in the direction of the first component. It appears, then, that the motor plan unfolded in the reverse order of the actual movements—the initial representation was based on the final location.

Goal-based representations have also proved useful in analyzing single unit activity in the premotor cortex. Although cells in this area may still code the movement's direction, they are not uniformly activated in movements requiring similar muscular events. Rather, the cells prefer certain motor acts. Giacomo Rizzolatti of the University of Parma, Italy, proposed that these neurons form a basic vocabulary of motor acts (Rizzolatti et al., 1988). Some cells are preferentially activated when the animal reaches for an object with its hand; others become active when the animal makes the same gesture to hold the object, and still others when the animal attempts to tear the object, a behavior that might find its roots in the wild where monkeys break off tree leaves. Therefore, cellular activity in this area reflects not only the trajectories of a movement but also the context in which the movement occurs.

These contextual considerations remind us that motor gestures are not made in an abstract space. Most actions are designed to manipulate an object in space; that is, motor systems are powerful for interacting with the environment, for avoiding obstacles, and for obtaining rewarding stimuli. Such actions require that motor systems be constantly informed about the environment's layout to anticipate an action's consequences. Goal-based action depends on synthesizing sensory and motor information. Our skill in reaching for a desired object requires that we integrate perceptual information with what we know about the current state of the motor system.

Many cells in motor areas represent sensory and motor information. This is true not only for neurons in the parietal cortex but also for neurons in motor areas of the frontal cortex and in subcortical structures such as the basal ganglia, cerebellum, and superior colliculus. For example, cells in area 6 of the premotor cortex respond to visual stimuli. As with cells in visual areas of the cortex, these neurons have a receptive field: They respond to a visual stimulus only when it is presented in a certain region of space.

Receptive fields are dynamic, however. They depend on how the animal has positioned its arm in space and how the limb might interact with a seen object (Graziano and Gross, 1994). Consider the cell's behavior depicted in Figure 10.22. The receptive field shifts with the position of the arm. When the limb is placed in front of the animal, this cell will become active when a visual stimulus is presented in the vicinity of the hand. If the limb is moved to the side, the receptive field shifts to this new location. A visual stimulus presented at the initial location no longer produces a change in the activity of the cell. If the limb is positioned out of the animal's sight, the cell will not respond to any visual stimulus. This enables the animal to use visual information to coordinate actions. The cell can represent the position of the visual stimulus with respect to the limb's current position. Perceptual knowledge has been transformed from a representation based on external space to one based on internal space. The animal represents where an object is located in the three-dimensional world and how the stimulus's location is related to the position of the animal's limbs that have to move there.

The Flow of Information Processing in Motor Pathways

The hierarchical organization of motor pathways requires a coherent flow of information. Abstract plans

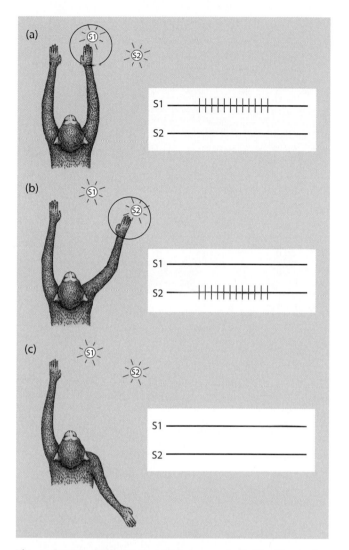

Figure 10.22 The activity of this neuron in the basal ganglia is dependent on the position of the hand. This neuron will respond to a visual stimulus falling within the circled region. When the hand is out of sight, the neuron does not respond to visual stimuli. Activity in this cell dynamically shifts as a function of hand position, and would be useful for coordinating visually guided movements. Adapted from Graziano and Gross (1994).

should be formed on the highest levels, transformed into movements at intermediate levels, and then implemented by way of the lowest levels of the hierarchy. In a crude sense, this pattern occurs. Cellular activity in prefrontal and premotor areas precedes activation of the primary motor cortex and neurons in the spinal cord. In a similar way, cerebellar neurons that project to the motor cortex become active prior to neurons in the motor cortex, while cerebellar regions that influence descending pathways become active after the motor cortex.

Yet it is clear from the neurophysiological record that stages of processing are not sequential. As diagrammed in Figure 10.23, processing in one area is not completed prior to the onset of activity in downstream areas. Rather, motor structures are recruited in a continuous manner, with only slight differences in their onset times. Indeed, serial models in which motor implementation

Figure 10.23 Response latencies in three regions of the motor pathway. Each function shows the distribution of onset latencies of cells in the motor cortex and two of the deep cerebellar nuclei, the dentate and the interpositus. The dentate is innervated by lateral regions of the cerebellar cortex; activity here precedes activity in motor cortex. The interpositus is innervated by medial regions of the cerebellum. Activity here generally begins after motor cortex activity. There is extensive overlap in the three distributions, suggesting that motor planning does not involve a series of strict, sequential steps. Adapted from Thach (1975).

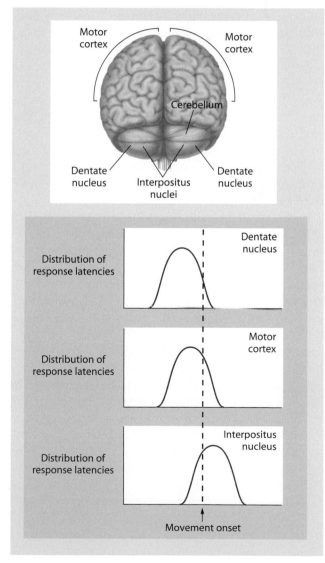

begins only after motor planning is completed are unlikely to reflect the normal flow of information processing. Planning can be expected to continue even as an action unfolds. We can vary a movement, either because
our goals change or because of information received
during the movement. A basketball player can adjust his
shot when an unseen defender suddenly looms ahead.
We quickly tighten our grip when a glass is slipperier
than expected. Given the similar coding of movement direction and the extensive overlap in the timing of activation across motor structures, other research strategies
have been exploited to identify functional differences in
how these structures contribute to movement.

Comparison of Motor Planning and Execution

Per Roland and his colleagues at the Karolinska Hospital
in Stockholm, Sweden (1993), used the single-photon
emission computed tomography (SPECT) methodology
to explore the functional organization of the motor
pathways. SPECT is sometimes labeled the "poor man's
PET" in that detection of radioactive decay is limited to
a single two-dimensional field. Construction of the
three-dimensional pattern of regional cerebral blood
flow (rCBF) requires multiple scans, usually acquired at
the expense of spatial resolution. Nonetheless, this
method is useful when the areas are large.

Figure 10.24 summarizes areas of activation during
a variety of motor tasks. When subjects repeatedly
flexed their index fingers, significant increases in rCBF
were restricted to the primary motor and somatosensory cortices in the contralateral hemisphere. These foci
of activation were similarly present when the task required a complex sequence of finger movements. In addition, the sequencing task also led to greater blood flow
in the contralateral premotor, supplementary motor,
and prefrontal cortices and basal ganglia, as well as the
ipsilateral cerebellum. Somewhat surprisingly, metabolic increases in the supplementary motor and prefrontal cortices were not restricted to the contralateral
hemisphere, which projects to the moving fingers; these
areas were also activated in the ipsilateral hemisphere. In
the final condition, subjects imagined the sequencing
task but did not produce any real movement (or muscle
activation). For this task, activation increases were restricted to the supplementary motor area, and again this
activation was bilateral. There was no reliable change in
rCBF over the motor cortex.

Taken together, these results are in accord with a hierarchical control system. Simple movements require
minimal processing, and, as such, changes in rCBF are
limited to primary motor and sensory areas. With

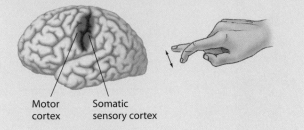

Simple flexion performed with right index finger

Motor cortex   Somatic sensory cortex

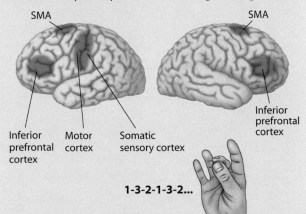

Movement sequence performed with fingers of right hand

SMA   SMA

Inferior prefrontal cortex

Inferior prefrontal cortex   Motor cortex   Somatic sensory cortex

1-3-2-1-3-2...

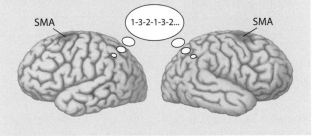

Movement sequence imagined with fingers of right hand

SMA   1-3-2-1-3-2...   SMA

Figure 10.24 Areas of metabolic activity associated with a
variety of motor tasks. Blood flow increases were restricted to
primary motor and somatic sensory cortical regions in the
contralateral hemisphere during simple flexion and extension
of the index finger on the right hand. When the subjects were
asked to perform a complicated series of sequential finger
movements with the right hand, blood flow increases were
also observed bilaterally in the supplementary motor area and
the prefrontal regions. The supplementary motor area was also
active, bilaterally, when the sequence was mentally rehearsed.
During this imagery condition, no increases were present in
the primary motor cortex. Adapted from Roland (1993).

greater complexity, cortical areas anterior to the primary motor area become activated. In addition, activation in these anterior areas occurs over both hemispheres. This bilateral activation can be interpreted in
several ways. It might correspond to the activation of an
abstract motor plan—one not tied to a specific effector.

Or the bilateral distribution could reflect many potential motor plans, each viable candidates for achieving a common goal. For example, we could reach for a water glass with either the left or the right hand. With either of these hypotheses, the unilateral activation in the basal ganglia and motor cortex can be interpreted as the transformation of higher-level plans into a movement linked to specific effectors. The transition of bilateral activation over premotor areas to unilateral activation over the motor cortex is also seen in measurements of evoked potentials (Figure 10.25).

INTERNAL VERSUS EXTERNAL GUIDANCE OF MOVEMENT

We have stressed that as a movement becomes more complex, structures beyond the primary motor cortex are activated. But how can we characterize the contribution of these areas? Is it just a matter of complexity, or are these additional contributions tied to certain tasks?

Based on blood flow studies, Roland suggested that the supplementary motor area is critical in controlling movement sequences. This was the only area where blood flow increased when the movement sequence was either produced or simply imagined. Nonetheless, we need to consider the computational demands in this finger-tapping task. Perhaps other types of sequential actions require different types of processing. For example, to return a tennis shot, a player adjusts her posture and swings according to the velocity and angle of the ball and her opponent's position. Here the action sequence for a successful return requires rapid integration of external cues.

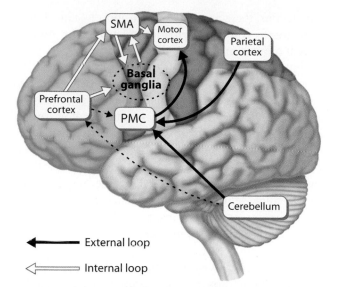

Figure 10.26 Movements may vary in terms of the contribution of internal and external sources of information. The external loop, including the cerebellum, parietal lobe, and lateral premotor cortex, dominates during visually guided movements. The internal loop, including the basal ganglia and supplementary motor area dominate during self-guided, well-learned movements.

Some neuroscientists propose that the control of movement sequences depends on area 6, but that it varies as a function of whether the action is internally or externally guided. The medial portion, the supplementary motor area, will dominate when the task is internally guided, as in Roland's finger sequencing task. In contrast, the lateral portion, the premotor area, becomes more relevant when the task depends on external cues. This area is activated when people are asked to perform movements under the guidance of visual, auditory, or somatosensory feedback. It can also be activated when extrapersonal sources of feedback are removed, but the action is performed with respect to an external frame of reference such as when tracing a path through a maze with the eyes closed. Even though the eyes are closed during the scanning sessions, visual feedback comes into play in the training session, and it is likely that the subjects use imagery.

Figure 10.26 provides an overview of the anatomical basis for the internal-external control hypothesis (Goldberg, 1985). The premotor area is extensively innervated by the parietal cortex and the cerebellum, two areas linked not only to visuomotor function, but also with rich representations extracted from other sensory channels like audition and touch. The supplementary motor area, by contrast, receives extensive projections from the prefrontal cortex and basal ganglia. Due to their anatomical

Figure 10.25 Evoked potentials recorded over the motor cortex before the right index finger presses a button. Following stimulus onset, the potential shows increased negativity, the Bereitschaft potential. This potential is observed bilaterally. Over the last 300 msec of the reaction time period, the potential becomes larger over the contralateral hemisphere.

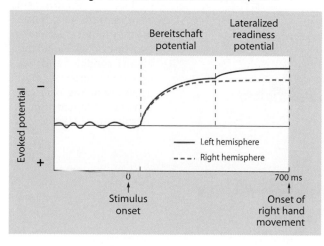

connections, these areas are in a position to allow limbic structures to convey information related to the animal's current motivational state and internal goals.

Physiological data in primate research support the hypothesized link of externally and internally directed actions to premotor and supplementary motor areas, respectively. Lesions of the supplementary motor area severely disrupt monkeys' ability to perform learned gestures without visual guidance. Lesions of the premotor cortex have no effect on performance. In contrast, the reverse pattern is observed when the monkeys are trained to move in the direction signaled by an external cue. Here, premotor lesions produce an impairment while ablation of the supplementary motor area has no effect.

To compare the roles of the supplementary motor area and the premotor cortex, monkeys were trained to generate a sequence of button presses according to two sets of instructions (Figure 10.27). In the external-guidance condition, the buttons were illuminated in succession and the animal pressed each one in turn. In the internal-guidance condition, the animal learned a sequence of button presses and then reproduced the sequence after hearing an auditory "go" signal. Physiological recordings were made in the supplementary motor area and the premotor cortex.

This study produced two critical results. First, in both areas, some neural activity could not be linked to specific movements but depended on the entire sequence of movements; hence, cellular activity corre-

lated with the direction of movement but only when that gesture was embedded in a certain sequence. When the same gesture was embedded in a different sequence, the activity of these cells showed only a slight increase compared to their baseline firing rate. This sequence specificity supports the hypothesis of a higher form of control for area 6. The other critical result is that supplementary motor area neurons were disproportionately active during internally guided movements while premotor neurons were more active during externally guided sequences.

This dissociation was not absolute, however. Many cells were active in both conditions. And some supplementary motor area cells were more active in the external condition than in the internal condition, while the reverse held for some premotor neurons. Although these results might raise doubts about a strict dichotomy, it is also likely that movements in both conditions depend on external and internal cues. Consider the tennis player again. The decision to return a shot with a deep lob or a short dropshot depends not only on the location and velocity of the arriving ball but also on knowing the opponent's skills. If the opponent moves slowly, the dropshot might be preferred.

SHIFT IN CONTROL WITH LEARNING

Learning plays a critical role in producing purposeful actions. We can describe the processes required to serve a tennis ball, but this description is likely to be different for the novice and skilled performer. The novice may

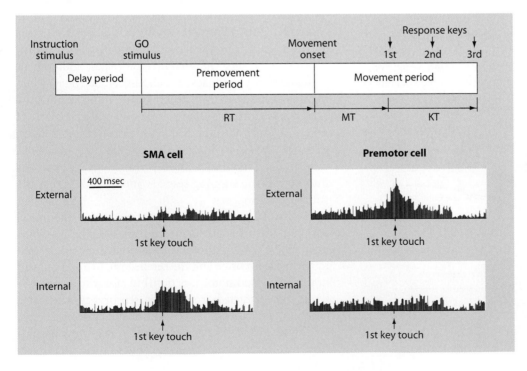

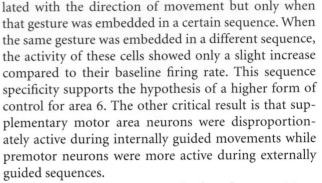

Figure 10.27 Monkeys were trained to make sequential button presses, either to a series of illuminated targets (external condition) or from memory (internal condition). Despite the fact that the movements were identical, the supplementary motor area neuron was most active during the internal condition and the premotor neuron was most active during the external condition. Adapted from Mushiake et al. (1991).

verbalize each movement as a monk chants his mantra: "Toss the ball straight up, swing the racquet in an arc, make contact as the ball begins to descend, follow through." Through years of practice, the production of this sequence appears effortless to the expert. She ponders the finer aspects of the serve. Is her top-spin serve working today? Should she serve to her opponent's forehand or backhand?

Feedback after the service is treated differently by the novice and expert. After impact, the novice may have little idea of where the ball is heading—in the service box, he hopes, but more likely into the net. Feedback from observing his shot helps in modifying the next service. While the expert is also concerned with the consequences of her actions, she uses feedback obtained during the course of the service to make fine adjustments. If the arm is moving too fast, the wrist can be flexed earlier to ensure an appropriate trajectory. Whereas a novice essentially uses feedback to make changes in subsequent actions, an expert uses feedback to make on-line changes in performance.

Motor systems invoked in the action of serving a tennis ball clearly differ for the novice and the expert. Indeed, learning considerations have led to an alternative conceptualization of the functional difference between the lateral and the medial premotor areas. Rather than thinking these differences reflect whether a task is performed in extrapersonal or interpersonal space, we could consider that learning involves a transition toward greater reliance on more medial motor structures. During the early stages of learning, the lateral premotor area, with its extensive connections to the parietal cortex, would be optimal for integrating external information with a motor plan—an essential job for developing any new skill. If we learn the mapping between the movements we produce and the effects they produce, we can anticipate the consequences of our actions and may tie into the functions of the more medial motor system.

A recent PET study explored metabolic changes associated with skill learning through trial and error (Jenkins et al., 1994). After hearing a tone, the subjects pressed one of four buttons. Correct responses were signaled by a high-pitched tone; incorrect ones were followed by silence. The subjects' task was to learn an eight-element pattern that was repeated cyclically. In the initial stages of training, the subjects simply had to guess the sequence. After six cycles, the subjects were averaging only one error per cycle. After one sequence was learned, the process was repeated with a new sequence. In this way, comparisons could be made between performance on new and performance on learned sequences without confounding the order of the scans

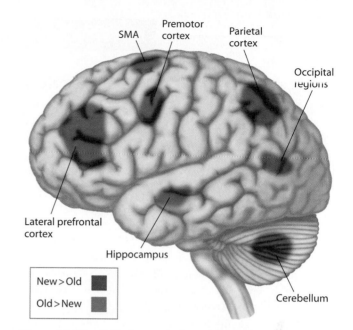

Figure 10.28 Shifts in metabolic activity during motor learning. Positron emission tomography (PET) scans were obtained under two conditions: while subjects performed a well-learned movement sequence (OLD) and during the course of learning of a movement sequence (NEW). Learning was associated with blood flow increases in lateral premotor and prefrontal areas; in contrast, performance of previously learned sequences was correlated with blood flow increases in the supplementary motor area and hippocampus. Adapted from Jenkins et al. (1994).

with skill level. If only one sequence had been used, the earlier scan would always reflect initial learning.

The metabolic results, shown in Figure 10.28, indicate that as learning progressed, activation shifted within area 6. The lateral premotor area was more activated during the acquisition of a new sequence in comparison to when an old sequence was being performed skillfully. In contrast, the supplementary motor area was more active during the skilled phase. Indeed, when the subjects began to learn a new sequence, activity declined in the supplementary motor area.

This study further revealed that the lateral and medial regions are embedded in distinct circuits related to skill acquisition. Higher metabolism in the lateral premotor cortex was correlated with increases in the superior parietal lobe and cerebellum. Changes in supplementary motor area activity were associated with changes in the temporal lobe and limbic structures.

Remember that there is usually a high degree of correspondence between the level of learning and the extent to which a behavior depends on external cues. If prompted to serve when blindfolded, the expert tennis

An Interview with Steven Keele, Ph.D. Dr. Keele is associated with the Psychology Department at the University of Oregon. His research helped bring the study of motor control into the mainstream of cognitive psychology.

Authors: The topic of motor control doesn't even get discussed in many textbooks on cognitive psychology. Why do you think this is so? Do the problems of motor control only become interesting when we consider the brain?

SK: It is not entirely clear why motor control has been so neglected, not only in textbooks of psychology, but even by psychologists themselves. The omission was noted by the famous learning theorist E.R. Guthrie in 1935, when he commented that psychology leaves an organism stranded in thought, unable to engage in action.

The basic neglect may derive from implicit but faulty assumptions that psychologists have had about motor control. They often think that motor control is an add-on, something beyond cognition itself. They often think as though the problems of motor control are simply problems of stringing together a series of motor actions, actions being defined in terms of movements and the muscles that power them. This prejudice reveals itself in many ways. Some scientists view the learning or control of a series of actions as being relatively primitive compared to such notable human achievements as declarative memory, the ability to reason, or language. This has led some to look for the engrams of motor learning in brain regions purely outside the cortex—in the basal ganglia or in the cerebellum—or within motor cortex. Indeed, this tendency has been reinforced by a belief that those brain systems are for motor control and motor control only, although the belief is beginning to come into serious question.

Authors: What do you see as a fundamental question for researchers in motor control in terms of cognitive function? For example, how does the study of coordination lend insights into other cognitive domains?

SK: Almost 50 years ago, the great neuropsychologist Karl Lashley pointed out a remarkable fact about human skill that should disabuse one of the notion that motor control and motor skill are less "human" than other remarkable capacities of our species. Humans speak, they type, they sign, they write—each an intricate motor skill. In the domain of music, people play the fiddle, they dance to it, and they may sing or hum along. People build cabinets, knit, and blow fine glassware. These diverse motor activities are beyond the realm of other animals, and suggest that motor capabilities are related to other intellectual capabilities.

Indeed, some psychologists, such as Jerome Bruner, have suggested that even human language capability is an outgrowth of capacities evolved to create new motor sequences. Consider this thought exercise. Imagine a person born deaf and dumb and totally without language. Could such a person learn to select boards, measure and saw each to size, nail them together to build a rafter, and attach the rafter to a house? Given this, might it be possible for the same person, given a capacity to hear and to speak, to attach symbols—that is words—to each component of the action and substrate—a board, a saw, sawing, a hammer, a nail, nailing. Might it be possible for the words to be assembled in some manner approximating the action order itself? From this perspective, it might well be imagined that expressions

player will most likely succeed on a high percentage of serves. The novice would be lucky to make contact with the ball. In a similar sense, we can see a shift in the reliance on external cues and feedback in just about any skill domain. Children have to carefully assess the outcome of each stroke as they learn to write their signature. With skill, handwriting suffers little when visual feedback is removed.

In summary, physiological studies using both single-cell recordings with primates and brain imaging techniques with humans have provided a window into how the brain produces action. We have seen that, at the neural level, motor structures represent the direction of a movement, although this coding may be constrained

of language are themselves parasitic on more fundamental achievements in humans, the ability to creatively arrange actions into new skills.

Authors: Are you saying that there is a general-purpose sequencing module that is used in both language and action? How does this mesh with the belief that language involves a highly modular system?

SK: Yes, the general idea is that brain mechanisms responsible for action sequencing also participate in language—in a sense, a general-purpose module. This kind of argument has been forcefully stated by Patricia Greenfield (1991), who argues that brain areas around Broca's region are not only responsible for aspects of sequence in speech and language but in sequences of action in general. She points at the parallel development of hierarchical organization during infancy both in language and in action and at instances of brain injury in which lesions produce a loss in both domains. She points out that apes show the same progression of sophistication in language and in action, both peaking substantially below the capability of humans.

Greenfield's hypothesis contrasts with a more classic view of modularity in which a complex system, such as the speech perception system, makes use of a set of modules, with each module supplying a particular function. In this classic view, the modules operate in a very limited domain. In contrast, the view I'm discussing suggests that many functions are shareable among a variety of tasks. Paul Rozin developed this idea some 20 years ago, suggesting that the ability of new tasks to draw on computations that had evolved for other task domains was at the heart of human intelligence.

Authors: What about the unique aspects of high-level skills such as those exhibited by Michael Jordan on the basketball court or Issac Stern in the concert hall? Do you see the unique gifts shown by these individuals as reflecting general cognitive principles or are these people born with a special gift? For example, if we want to understand what makes Michael Jordan so special, should we study his muscles and physiology or does his expertise in basketball have something to tell us about learning at the cognitive level?

SK: Especially for sporting skills, it is unlikely that the highest levels of performance can be achieved without having special physical gifts that allow extraordinary bursts of speed or jumping ability. But at the same time, certain "cognitive" capabilities also are likely to underlie the development of extraordinary skill. Extensive evidence suggests that knowledge acquired as a result of extensive practice—thousands of hours of highly dedicated practice—is the key factor separating the most successful people in various motor and nonmotor skill domains from the rest of us. This perspective grew initially out of analyses of chess expertise, but also has been found to apply to musical performance and basketball.

I'm not familiar with Michael Jordan's history of practice and knowledge, but some years ago I read a marvelous biography of Bill Russell, one of the most gifted basketball centers of all time and a defensive wizard. I recall three stories he told that helped me realize that the most talented of skilled performers often are so because of acquired knowledge and "cognitive" analysis. First, he and his college teammate, K.C. Jones, learned to steal the ball by working as a tandem, one distracting an opponent while the other would come in from the blind side to steal the ball. Second, he analyzed the geometry of ball flight and his own jumping and reaching to determine how best to block shots. Third, by imaging the moves of an opponent, he could learn to anticipate these moves during a game.

The surprising idea that stands out in the expertise literature is that the extraordinary motor capabilities of humans are best understood as an extension of their extraordinary cognitive capabilities.

---

by the goals of an action. Activation patterns across these motor structures argue against a strict serial flow of information processing. Nonetheless, processing in premotor and subcortical regions may converge on the motor cortex, and parallel circuits may be involved in motor planning. One circuit, including the parietal lobe, lateral premotor, and cerebellar pathways, is essential for producing spatially directed or guided movements. These movements are likely to dominate during the early stages of skill acquisition. A second circuit, associated with the prefrontal, supplementary motor area, basal ganglia, and perhaps the temporal lobe, becomes more dominant as the skill is well learned and driven by an internal representation of the desired action.

FUNCTIONAL ANALYSIS OF THE MOTOR
SYSTEM AND MOVEMENT DISORDERS

So far we have emphasized how motor areas might contribute to motor control according to the demands of the task. If an action requires the coordination of sensory and motor codes, the lateral, premotor loop will dominate. If sensory requirements are reduced, either by varying instructions or by practice, control shifts toward the medial, supplementary motor area loop.

What is lacking in this task-based analysis is an explanation of the computations performed by the different motor areas. For example, the neurophysiological work on population coding is an elegant tool for describing how neurons represent forthcoming actions. But several cortical and subcortical areas share this form of representation. One might consider this homogeneity and conclude that motor systems should be viewed as distributed networks having little specialization.

Such a hypothesis would be dismissed as utter foolishness by the neurologist. An hour in a movement disorders clinic would make it clear that the motor system is extensively specialized. Breakdowns in coordination can happen in many ways; such patterns of deficits afford clues to the contributions of the components of the motor pathways. Lesions' characteristic signatures enable neurologists to pinpoint the site and cause of pathology even in the absence of high-resolution MRI.

Before turning to motor disorders, consider the computations required to perform a skilled action such as playing a difficult piano passage from Beethoven's *Ninth Symphony* (Figure 10.29). For one thing, the pianist must figure out the mapping between notes and fingers. A single finger might suffice for the simplest melody line, but a skillful production requires all ten fingers. And as the context changes, the same note can be played by different fingers. Moreover, the notes must be linked in proper sequence. The popular nursery tunes, "Go Tell Aunt Rhody" and "Lightly Row" share identical notes, but the sequencing of notes creates distinct tunes. Finally, for a piece to sound musical, the notes must be played with the proper timing and intensity.

Hypothetical components such as selection, sequencing, timing, and force can serve as useful heuristics for analyzing disorders of the motor system. For example, if motor timing and motor selection are independent operations, then we might expect to find dissociations in the clinical problems of patients with motor disorders. A patient might select the appropriate fingers to play the notes of "Go Tell Aunt Rhody," but fail to provide the appropriate timing. Or the timing might be correct, but the notes out of order. In either case, we would fail to recognize this familiar tune. But the loss of coordination would reflect deficits in different component operations. In this way, we can develop a functional analysis of the cognitive neuroscience of motor control.

Cortical Areas

Some brain theorists would consider the entire cortex anterior to the central sulcus to be part of the brain's motor centers. And yet, many animals without a cerebral cortex are capable of complex actions. The fly can land with near-perfect precision or the lizard can flick its tongue at the precise moment required to snare its evening meal. Has evolution rendered a massive reorganization of the motor pathways? Or, should we consider the cortex as an additional piece of neural machinery superimposed on a more primitive apparatus?

HEMIPLEGIA

The preeminent status of the motor cortex is underscored by the fact that lesions to this area usually result in *hemiplegia,* the loss of voluntary movements on the contralateral side of the body. Hemiplegia most frequently results from a hemorrhage in the middle cerebral artery. It is perhaps the most telling symptom that a person has experienced a stroke. A person might wake up with a severe headache or experience a sudden loss of consciousness, and notice a complete loss of control in one limb. It is not a matter of will or awareness. The hemiplegic patient may exert great effort, but his limbs will not move. The loss of movement is most evident in the distal effectors.

Reflexes are absent immediately after a stroke that produces hemiplegia; within a couple of weeks the reflexes return and even become hyperactive. The hemiplegic patient presents a greater than normal reflexive response when a muscle is passively stretched. The muscles may even become spastic, reflecting the increased tone, or responsiveness, of the muscles. The spasticity is most pronounced in muscles that counteract the forces of gravity when we stand up or sit upright, leaving the patient with a contorted posture where the arm is maintained in a flexed position at the elbow with the fingers tightly curled into the palm. The legs become hyperextended, like pillars holding up the trunk.

Hyperactive reflexes and spasticity can be understood within a hierarchical framework. Muscular activ-

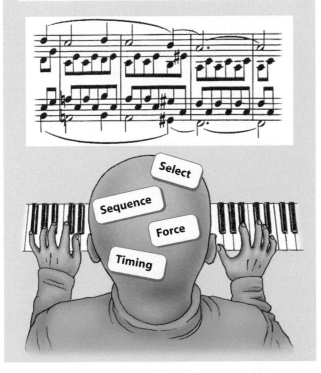

Possible mental operations/computations	Example: playing piano
1. Select	Match fingers to keys, notes.
2. Sequence	Group notes into a phrase.
3. Force	Strike accented notes with greater force.
4. Timing	Establish rhythm.

Figure 10.29 Hypothesized mental operations that must be completed in order to perform a complicated action such as playing the piano.

ity offsetting gravitational forces and reflexes comes from a simple form of motor control, a mechanism for ensuring postural stability. The cortex provides a way to inhibit these mechanisms. By inhibiting a tendency to maintain stability we can willfully impose an action. We can move our arm without having the stretch reflex counteract the gesture. When the cortical influence is removed, primitive reflexive mechanisms become manifest again.

Recovery from hemiplegia is minimal. When the motor cortex has been damaged, the patient does not recover the use of the limbs on the contralateral side. Movement is possible, but only when carried out by gross movements that do not require the independent control and coordination of different joints. If a leg is affected, the patient may be able to walk again, but in a far from normal manner, perhaps by rotating the entire leg about the pelvis. The patient cannot coordinate flexion and extension about the knee and ankle. Arm movements would also be quite limited—any persisting control would be left to proximal joints like the shoulder and perhaps the elbow. It is unlikely that extensive rehabilitation training would help the patient to recover use of the fingers. At best, rehabilitation could reduce spasticity and thereby maximize the effectiveness of whatever volitional control the patient has retained.

Lesions of the motor cortex affect the cortico-spinal and extrapyramidal tracts. The loss of control over individual joints and distal extremities is attributed to damage in the cortico-spinal tract. Localized lesions to the *internal capsule,* the white matter region containing the descending fibers, indicate that the loss of reflexes is also caused by damage to the cortico-spinal tract. Spasticity and hyperreflexivity are attributed to changes in the extrapyramidal system. When the cortical influence is removed, these more ancient systems become dominant, exerting their prominent role in maintaining postural stability. The hemiplegic patient no longer has the flexibility to generate an action based on internal goals and desires.

APRAXIA

Many cortical lesions result in coordination deficits that cannot be attributed to hemiplegia, motoric problems of weakness, sensory loss, or motivation. This syndrome is called *apraxia* (Keretsz and Hooper, 1982). While the term *apraxia* technically means "no action," it is used in a more general sense to describe a loss of motor skill. For example, a patient with bilateral lesions of the parietal lobes was unable to continue her work as a fish filleter. When attempting to perform a routine that she had completed thousands of times, she correctly inserted the knife point into the head of the fish, began the first stroke, but then stopped. She claimed to know how the action should be completed but could not execute it. At home, she found herself putting the sugar bowl in the refrigerator or the coffee pot in the oven. In each case, she retained the ability to move her muscles but could no longer link gestures to a coherent act or recognize the appropriate use of an object.

Several standard tests for apraxia have been developed over the past two decades. These tests generally involve asking patients to produce goal-directed gestures. These gestures may consist of arbitrary behavioral acts such as saluting or following a sequence of arm gestures.

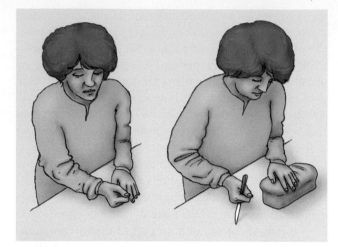

Figure 10.30 Apraxic patients are unable to produce coordinated actions, even though their strength is intact and they can move their limbs. The deficits are most pronounced when asked to pantomime actions. If given the object, they may succeed in producing the action, although with some clumsiness or inappropriate gestures.

Or they may be actions where the patient manipulates an external object such as lighting a pipe or slicing a loaf of bread. Apraxic patients are most impaired when trying to pantomime an action (Figure 10.30). For example, when requested to slice a loaf of bread, the patient may ball his hand in a fist and pound the table. If he is given a knife and a loaf of bread, his performance generally improves. Now the tool can be held appropriately, even if slicing is abnormal.

The literature on apraxia is difficult to disentangle. Part of the problem has been that the diagnosis is mainly based on exclusionary grounds: A patient is said to have apraxia if he or she has a coordination problem that cannot be linked to a deficit in controlling the muscles themselves. Moreover, it is not always clear that the problems are specific to the motor system; they may reflect a general problem in comprehension. Apraxia is much more frequently observed in patients with lesions to the left hemisphere. Perhaps the motor problems of apraxia represent a failure to understand instructions or a general loss of semantic knowledge. If we forget that sugar is best stored at room temperature, it is not so surprising that, when cleaning up after a meal, a person might put the sugar bowl in the refrigerator.

The correlation between aphasia and apraxia was made clear in a large-scale study of patients with left-hemisphere lesions (Figure 10.31). For example, all patients rated as severely apraxic were also severely aphasic. A corresponding fact is that patients who were not apraxic tended to have mild aphasia. As with all correla-

tions, though, we must be cautious in inferring cause and effect. A common mechanism may be responsible for some aspects of aphasia and apraxia. Yet the lesions are likely to have been largest in the patients who demonstrated impairment on both tests, perhaps resulting in damage to independent mechanisms associated with language and motor control. Evidence suggestive of this is that someone can be severely aphasic without showing any sign of apraxia. Failing to comprehend language does not imply that a person will fail on tests of praxis.

Attempts to pinpoint the neuroanatomical focus of apraxia have also been problematic. Apraxia has been observed in epileptic patients who have undergone lobectomy in either the frontal or the parietal cortex. The frontal lobectomies were centered on the prefrontal cortex, although sometimes the surgery included tissue in the lateral premotor cortex; yet apraxia is also seen in patients with lesions limited to the supplementary motor area. It should not be surprising that lesions in many areas can lead to apraxia, especially if we consider the flow of processing for generating an action. Disruption at any point in the complex motor circuit can interfere with the normal preparation of a movement.

Efforts have been made to create a taxonomy of subtypes of apraxia, some focused on the fact that apraxia can be limited to certain task domains. For example, frontal lesions are more likely to impair orofacial movements while parietal lesions disrupt arm movements. Other researchers have also fixed on an anterior-posterior distinction but with an emphasis on the hierarchical organization of motor systems. In this view,

Figure 10.31 The correlation between aphasia and apraxia. Patients with left-hemisphere lesions were rated on measures of aphasia and apraxia, and the frequency of each combination is shown in this table. Although severe aphasia can exist without any signs of apraxia, the overall correlation is quite high. For example, all of the patients who were rated as severely apraxic were also rated as severely aphasic. Adapted from Keretsz and Hooper (1982).

		Apraxia rating			
		None	Mild	Moderate	Severe
Aphasia rating	None	26	0	0	0
	Mild	104	16	4	0
	Moderate	19	28	8	0
	Severe	6	16	28	40

apraxia resulting from anterior lesions is said to result from deficits in implementing an action plan, while apraxia resulting from posterior lesions is linked to problems in retrieving and storing these plans.

At the beginning of the twentieth century, one of Wernicke's students, Hugo Liepmann, made two key observations regarding apraxia: The disorder was generally associated with lesions of the left hemisphere and was most frequently observed when the lesions included the parietal cortex (see Heilman et al., 1982). Liepmann proposed that this area is the critical region for the control of complex movement (Figure 10.32). In his view, the representation of a desired action would originate in area 40 of the left parietal cortex. Output from this area would be projected to the frontal cortex and, through various cortico-cortical connections, would activate area 4. If the desired movement were executed with the contralateral right hand, the processing would remain within the left hemisphere. And if the desired movement were executed with the ipsilateral left hand, Liepmann proposed that information would transfer to the right hemisphere through frontal connections over the corpus callosum. In this manner, unilateral lesions of the left parietal region would be associated with bilateral deficits.

In support of this model, Kenneth Heilman and his colleagues (1982) at the University of Florida reasoned that if the left parietal cortex contains the memory of actions, then damage to this area would impair performance on tests of either the production or the perception of gestures. That is, if representations of learned actions are destroyed, patients would find it difficult to produce movements and to recognize these movements when made by healthy individuals. To test this, two groups of apraxic patients were identified: those with anterior lesions and those with posterior lesions. On standard tests of apraxia, the two groups were indistinguishable. Patients in both groups made frequent errors when asked to mime gestures such as opening a door with a key or flipping a coin.

For the perception tests, the patients were shown short film segments in which an actor mimed these gestures. In one test, the actor performed three actions and the patient was asked to identify a target gesture;

Figure 10.32 Liepmann's model of the neural regions associated with the production of skilled actions. The premotor areas of the contralateral hemisphere are essential for skilled movements of limbs. These areas receive input from the parietal lobe of the left hemisphere, an area assumed to store the representations of the actions. Thus, a lesion in this posterior region will lead to apraxic movements with both contralesional and ipsilesional limbs.

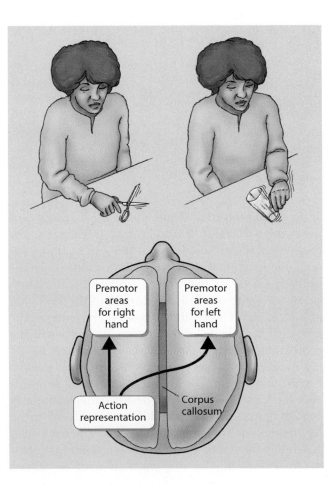

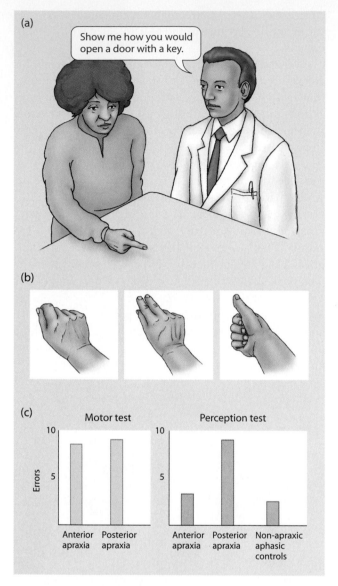

Figure 10.33 Patients with apraxia may also be unable to recognize skilled movements. **(a)** In the motor test, the patient is asked to pantomime a gesture such as using a key to open a door. **(b)** In the perception test, the patient views an actor pantomiming an action in three different ways, only one of which is appropriate. The patient must choose which action is correct. **(c)** Patients with either anterior or posterior lesions who produced apraxic gestures on the motor task were selected. Only the patients with posterior lesions showed impairment on the perception test. The apraxic patients with anterior lesions performed as well as nonapraxic, aphasic control subjects. Adapted from Heilman et al. (1982).

an example is given in Figure 10.33. For a second test, the actor performed the same task three times, but only one of the productions was well executed. In both tests, the patients with posterior lesions made significantly more errors than the patients with anterior lesions. The perceptual deficit for the posterior-lesion group could not be attributed to a general comprehension deficit. Patients with posterior lesions producing comparable aphasic problems but without apraxia did not have a problem on gesture comprehension tests.

To sum up, this recent work has provided new support for Liepmann's model. The left parietal lobe may contain representations of skilled movements. When the representations are damaged, the patient has difficulty generating these actions or recognizing them when produced by others. The implementation of an action,

however, requires that the representations be transformed into specific motor plans. This involves additional processing by premotor and prefrontal areas involved in motor control. Damage to these areas can also produce apraxia but will not disrupt the ability to perceive such actions when produced by another individual. Viewed in this way, the parietal cortex is the highest level of the motor hierarchy; frontal areas are a means for translating an action memory into a pattern of muscular commands.

THE CORTEX AND THE SELECTION OF MOVEMENT

We can hypothesize that cortical processing for motor control is primarily concerned with selecting appropriate effectors for performing a movement. In planning an action, the initial representation is abstract—a goal of what the person hopes to achieve. For example, your goal might be to drink some coffee or ask a friend to join you at the movies—goals that can be achieved in many ways. Your right or left hand could be used to reach for the coffee cup or a pencil on which to write your friend a memo. In picking up these objects, you might grasp them with all your fingers or use a prehensile pinch of the thumb and index finger.

Translating a goal into movement might be best envisioned as a competitive process, an idea captured in Figure 10.34. The goal activates all movements that could produce the desired action. These candidates then compete over which movement will be selected (Rosenbaum et al., 1991). The competition can be driven by many sources, some of which reflect our internal states and past experience. For example, activating movements with the dominant hand may be achieved more efficiently than activating movements with the nondominant hand. Other sources can be external ones. Preference may be given to the hand closer to the cup or pencil because this movement requires less effort. Or, in an experiment, the task instructions might ask the subject to use one hand or the other. The motor cortex can be viewed as the final tallying point of the competitive process, given that it provides the primary motor signal from the cortex. As such, it represents a movement chosen to achieve the desired goal. If the motor cortex is lesioned, the selected movement cannot be implemented to activate the effectors.

The cortical selection hypothesis agrees with evidence that motor planning is a distributed process involving many neural regions. These regions use a common representational code, the population vector corresponding to the direction of a forthcoming movement. This common code reflects the fact that each area has a topographic representation of the motor effectors. These areas, then, all promote movement, but with their relative contribution varying as a function of the task demands. The supplementary motor area reflects the contribution of internal sources of activation—goals and motivational states—whereas the lateral premotor area is more strongly driven by external sources such as the position of the effectors and objects that might be manipulated. A task is likely to encompass both sources—we should not expect only one area to be activated. The differences will be quantitative rather than qualitative.

Neurological lesions can disturb the balance between different inputs. In the acute stage after a stroke, patients with lesions of the supplementary motor area reach out and grasp objects with the affected arm, even when they have not been instructed to do so or have

Figure 10.34 Response selection involves a competitive process between potential responses. The writer wishes to take a swig from his coffee cup. This goal can be achieved by reaching with the left or right hand, either from the current position or by rotating the trunk. Various sources of information—the location of the cup, what the hands are currently doing, experience—help resolve the competition.

been told to refrain from moving. This *alien hand syndrome* reflects a dominance of externally guided lateral premotor pathways. The sight of an object within reaching distance evokes a motor plan to grasp the object. We can usually inhibit movement if instructed to do so, or if the movement is inappropriate. But when internal control sources are removed, the movement can be triggered by the appropriate external stimulus. The normal balance underlying movement selection is distorted.

If we view the process as competitive, we can understand why, under certain conditions, competing motor plans get activated. Consider an experiment by Steven Wise of the National Institute of Mental Health. Monkeys were trained to move a handle within one of two conditions: a compatible one and an incompatible one (Wise et al., 1996). In both conditions, a stimulus would appear at one of eight positions on a circle. For the compatible condition, the monkeys were trained to move the handle to the location of the stimulus; for the incompatible condition, the required movement was in the opposite direction of the stimulus. Population vectors were recorded in the lateral premotor cortex. In the compatible condition, the vector immediately pointed toward the forthcoming movement; in the incompatible one, though, the vector pointed first toward the stimulus—that is, the direction away from the forthcoming movement—and with more processing time, the vector shifted toward the movement (Figure 10.35). This shift comes from two competing movement plans.

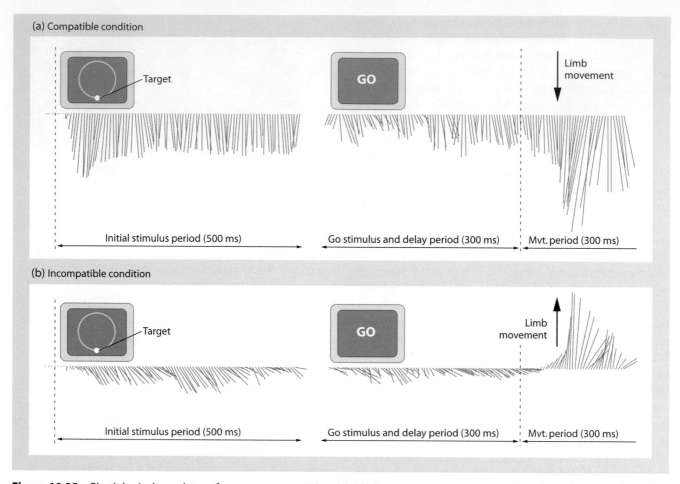

Figure 10.35 Physiological correlates of response competition. **(a)** A light comes on at a target position along the circumference of the circle. After a delay period, a "go" signal indicates that the monkey should move a lever to the target location. The population vectors indicate the movement direction, becoming manifest during the delay period. **(b)** In the incompatible condition, the animal must move to the location opposite that signaled by the light. During the delay period, the population vector corresponds to a movement planned toward the light. The magnitude of this vector is less than that in the compatible condition, reflecting the simultaneous activation of the opposite movement. After the onset of the "go" signal, the population vector orients in the direction of the (correct) movement. Adapted from Wise et al. (1996).

Because we usually move to a stimulus's location, a target's onset automatically activates a motor plan toward that location. Because of their training, though, the monkeys learned that they must move in the opposite direction. As input from this internal set became dominant, the population vector's direction shifted.

The hypothesis of widespread competition among motor plans fits in with the activation patterns observed in premotor and motor cortices. As noted, blood flow and evoked potentials indicate that premotor activation is generally bilateral—a paradox because in most studies all movements are performed with a single hand. While it is possible that these areas represent both sides of the body, the bilateral activation may reflect the planning of all possible movements that could achieve an abstract goal. Activation eventually becomes lateralized over the contralateral motor cortex—the presumed outcome of a competition for one hand over the other.

The supplementary motor area can play a critical role in the decision. While the primary source of output for the supplementary motor area is the ipsilateral motor cortex, this area also has callosal projections to the contralateral supplementary motor area and motor cortex. Another unusual symptom following lesions of the supplementary motor area is that patients produce mirror movements. When asked to reach for an object with the hand contralateral to the lesion, the ipsilateral hand will make a similar gesture, as if the patients cannot select a movement plan from multiple candidates that are bilaterally activated.

Apraxia is a disruption in the cortical selection of a movement plan. Patients with frontal apraxia may represent an action's abstract goal but fail in specifying the effectors required to achieve the plan. Rather than extending their fingers when saluting, patients may bring fingers curled into a fist to their forehead. Or they may mime lighting a pipe before striking a match. Performance improves with props because they aid the selection process by providing a salient source of stimulation. Patients with posterior apraxia, however, are especially handicapped; they cannot comprehend the goals and thus there is no activation of movement patterns that might achieve the required action.

Motor learning of complex actions may reflect the fact that, with practice, each movement helps to select subsequent elements in the sequence. Apraxic deficits are most pronounced in tasks that require executing a sequence of actions rather than a single gesture. This dissociation can be viewed as a breakdown in the hierarchical structure underlying complex, sequential actions. In one study, apraxic and nonapraxic patients were tested on two types of sequences, each composed of the gestures for pushing, poking, or clenching. For homogeneous sequences, a single gesture was repeated successively; for heterogeneous ones, all three gestures were performed in a specified order. Apraxic patients' reaction and movement times were disproportionately impaired in heterogeneous sequences: They treated each element as an independent gesture rather than organized them into a hierarchical pattern. For the apraxic patients, the selection process must begin anew for each element in the sequence.

Subcortical Areas: The Cerebellum and Basal Ganglia

In the preceding section we focused on how cortical motor areas select movement plans. The cortex is a vast processing network where input converges and helps an animal choose the action that achieves a goal. As such, the cortex is evolution's way of creating a flexible system. The animal need not slavishly respond to a stimulus but can modify its actions to meet current goals.

From this perspective, we can expect subcortical areas to participate less in selecting motor plans. Their role may be limited to ensuring that selected movements are executed efficiently. When the areas are lesioned, we would not expect representational disorders such as the ones observed in apraxia, a disorder that generates a wrong response. Instead, we would expect the response to be poorly executed.

This hypothesis accurately describes the motor disorders observed with subcortical lesions. In this section, then, we review the motor deficits of the primary subcortical structures associated with motor control: the cerebellum and basal ganglia. In examining these disorders, we develop functional hypotheses about how the structures contribute to the coordination of skilled action.

THE CEREBELLUM

Lesions of the cerebellum disrupt coordination in a variety of ways—a heterogeneity reflecting the distinct regions of the cerebellum. Figure 10.36 shows the three parts of the cerebellum: the vestibulocerebellum, the spinocerebellum, and the neocerebellum. This tripartite

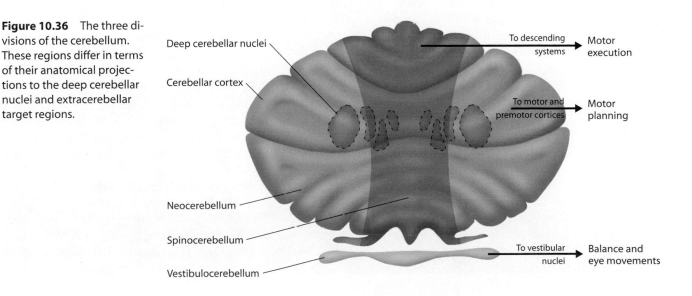

Figure 10.36 The three divisions of the cerebellum. These regions differ in terms of their anatomical projections to the deep cerebellar nuclei and extracerebellar target regions.

Deep cerebellar nuclei

Cerebellar cortex

Neocerebellum

Spinocerebellum

Vestibulocerebellum

To descending systems → Motor execution

To motor and premotor cortices → Motor planning

To vestibular nuclei → Balance and eye movements

Patting your Head While Rubbing your Stomach

Many actions call for coordinating both hands. Tying shoes, using a fork and knife, serving a tennis ball—all require the two hands to integrate their movement. How does the brain coordinate activity across the two cerebral hemispheres to control the actions?

There is little evidence that any part of the cerebral cortex is especially designed for bimanual movements. Some areas are activated during contralateral and ipsilateral movements. But, as we noted, bilateral activation can be attributed to multiple, independent movement plans that compete for selection. Indeed, a consequence of this competition is that we have great difficulty in generating bilateral movements that are spatially incompatible.

When we were children, we were all amused by our inability to pat the head while rubbing the stomach. It is nearly impossible to generate the conflicting spatial trajectories, having one hand move in an up-down fashion while the other produces a circular movement. The two movements compete. We fail to map one direction for one hand and the other direction for the opposite hand. Eventually, one of the movements dominates and we end up rubbing the head or patting the stomach. Within the selection hypothesis outlined in this chapter, we can think of this bimanual conflict as competition between two movement plans. Each task activates both hemispheres and we cannot keep the cross talk from these activation patterns from interfering with one another.

If this hypothesis is correct, spatial interference should be eliminated when each movement plan is restricted to a single hemisphere and the pathways connecting the two hemispheres are severed. To test this idea, Elizabeth Franz and her colleagues (1996) at the University of California, Berkeley tested a patient who had undergone resection of the corpus callosum. The stimuli for their bimanual movement study are a pair of three-sided figures, with the sides following either a common axis or perpendicular axes. The stimuli were projected briefly, with one stimulus presented in the left visual field and the other in the right visual field. After viewing the stimuli, the subjects were instructed to produce the two patterns simultaneously, using the left hand for the pattern projected in the left visual field and the right hand for the pattern in the right vi-

sual field. The brief presentation was used to ensure that each stimulus was isolated to a single hemisphere in the split-brain patient. In control subjects, rapid transfer of information should occur via the corpus callosum.

Control subjects had little difficulty producing bilateral movements when the segments of the squares followed a common axis of movement. Yet when the segments required movements along perpendicular axes, their performance dramatically deteriorated, with long pauses before each segment and trajectories frequently deviating from the target—something you can demonstrate to yourself by trying this task. Indeed, the control subjects would often add an extra segment at the end of one pattern, an extra movement that followed the same axis as the last movement in the other hand.

In contrast, the split-brain patient did not significantly differ between the two movements. He initiated and completed movements in the two conditions with comparable speed, and the movements were accurate in both. Indeed, in a second experiment, this patient simultaneously drew a square with the left hand and a circle with the right hand. Each hemisphere produced the pattern without any signs of interference from demands presented to the opposite hemisphere.

These results indicate that the callosotomy procedure yields a spatial uncoupling in bimanual movements. As striking, it was also apparent that, even for the split-brain patient, the actions of the two hands were not independent of one another. As with the control subjects, the two hands moved in synchrony. The segments of the squares were initiated and terminated at approximately the same time. This temporal coupling was seen more clearly when subjects were asked to produce oscillatory movements, with each hand moving along a single axis. Regardless of whether the two hands followed a common axis (e.g., both horizontal or both vertical) or perpendicular axes (e.g., one horizontal and the other vertical), the two hands reversed direction at the same time.

This study provided valuable insights to the neural structures underlying bimanual coordination. First, spatial aspects of bimanual movements are coordinated via processing across the corpus callosum. When a task requires conflicting directions of movement, interference is extensive, presumably because selection is taxed by movement plans that follow perpendicular directions. Second, callosal connections are not necessary for temporal coupling of movement. It may be that a single hemisphere regulates when movements are initiated or that the initiation is regulated by subcortical mechanisms. Third, the dissociation of spatial and temporal coupling emphasizes a distributed view of how the motor system's neural structures contribute to coordination. Even though the structures may rely on a common representational code such as movement direction, they likely contribute in distinct ways. The neural structures that integrate movement plans appear to be independent of those involved in movement initiation.

Bimanual movements following resection of the corpus callosum. While looking at a central fixation point, subjects were briefly shown the two patterns. They were instructed to simultaneously draw the pattern on the left with the left hand and the one on the right with the right hand. Normal subjects **(left)** were able to draw the mirror symmetrical patterns, but had severe difficulty when the orientation of the two figures differed by 90 degrees. The split-brain patient **(right)** performed equally well in both conditions. Adapted from Franz et al. (1996).

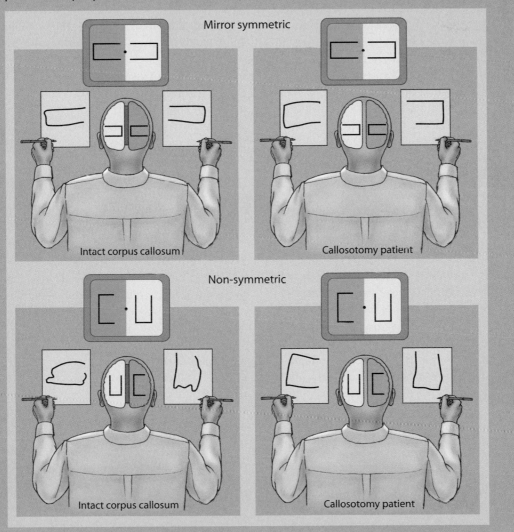

organization is reflected in their unique anatomical projections as well as by the fact that lesions within each area project distinct clinical symptoms. Moreover, the three regions appear to have followed different courses in phylogeny. As the name implies, the neocerebellum has emerged most recently, coming after the development of the spinocerebellum and the more ancient vestibulocerebellum.

Anatomical and Functional Divisions of the Cerebellum

The *vestibulocerebellum* is separated from the bulk of the cerebellum by the posterolateral fissure. This cerebellar region, the first to evolve, is innervated by the brainstem vestibular nuclei, and output is projected back to the same region. The vestibular system is essential for controlling balance and coordinating eye movements with body movements. Lesions of this area can affect the reflexes essential for maintaining equilibrium and stability. For example, the vestibulo-ocular reflex (VOR) ensures that the eyes remain fixed on an object despite movements of the head or body. This is essential for an organism that interacts with the environment: If the eyes were displaced with each movement, it would be difficult to monitor another organism or keep track of the location of a stimulus. Lesions of the vestibulocerebellum disrupt reflex functions and contribute to postural instability. Patients frequently experience nausea, as if they were on a ship sailing a stormy sea.

The main part of the cerebellum is divided into three regions: vermis, intermediate zone, and lateral zone. The vermis is separated by a small fissure running the vertical length of the cerebellum. No anatomical marker separates the intermediate and lateral zones. Based on the patterns of anatomical projections and physiology, however, the intermediate zone is functionally linked with the vermis. Together, they are referred to as the *spinocerebellum* because these two areas receive extensive sensory information from the periphery via the spinal cord. In addition, cells in this area respond to auditory and visual stimuli providing a basis for polysensory integration. This region developed later in vertebrate phylogeny than the vestibulocerebellum. The emergence of the spinocerebellum was thought to correspond to the need for more precise and flexible control of the limbs used for locomotion. Output of the spinocerebellum is projected through the medial cerebellar nuclei. In nonhuman primates these consist of the fastigial and interpositus nuclei; in humans, the interpositus has divided into two nuclei, the globose and the emboliform. These medial cerebellar nuclei innervate the spinal cord and nuclei of the extrapyramidal system. In addition, the interpositus sends some projections to the motor cortex via the thalamus.

Lesions of the spinocerebellum create problems for the smooth control of movement. For the most part, lesions to the vermis affect the postural muscles and lead to a breakdown in the coordination across axial muscles, which control the body's trunk. Chronic alcohol abuse destroys cells in the anterior portion of the vermis. These patients have difficulty walking and adopt a wide stance to compensate for their instability. Indeed, the cerebellum is especially sensitive to alcohol; tests used by police on suspected drunk drivers essentially record cerebellar function.

The effects of lesions on the intermediate zone are most apparent in the control of movements of the arms and legs. Such patients produce an appropriate action and initiate it in a normal manner, but their gestures will be clumsy, irregular, and erratic. Rapid pointing movements frequently extend beyond the target, a symptom referred to as *hypermetria*. Moreover, the patient cannot smoothly terminate the movement. Rather, as they approach the target, the effector goes into a series of oscillations (Hore et al., 1991).

The lateral zones of the cerebellar hemispheres constitute the *neocerebellum*. This area does not receive input from the spinal cord but is heavily innervated by cortical projections from sensory and motor areas. Output from this region is via the dentate nucleus. While some afferents from this nucleus terminate on nuclei of the extrapyramidal system, much of the information ascends to the cortex via projections to nuclei in the contralateral thalamus. Thalamic projections terminate in the primary motor cortex, lateral premotor cortex, and prefrontal cortical areas. As such, the neocerebellum contributes to the control of voluntary movements. This area has undergone tremendous expansion in primate evolution, reflecting the flexible and precise manner in which primates use their extremities. Indeed, in humans, the dentate nucleus contains over 90% of all neurons in the cerebellar nuclei.

Lesions of the neocerebellum produce symptoms similar to the ones in the intermediate cerebellum. Movements are clumsy (ataxic) and can be hypermetric, especially when an action consists of a sequence of gestures. Patients cannot smoothly switch from one gesture to another, and they end up producing irregular movements. In addition, the initiation of movement is prolonged in the presence of lesions to the neocerebellum. This region, then, is involved in the planning of movement while the intermediate cerebellum is essential in regulating the actual performance.

Interpreting Cerebellar Function

Exactly how the cerebellum does these things remains unclear. One hypothesis is that the cerebellum has a special role in timing movement. While cortical areas primarily select the effectors needed to perform a task, the cerebellum provides the precise timing needed for activating these effectors. As such, cerebellar neurons would also code movement direction because the timing is part of planning a specific trajectory.

Consider how the timing hypothesis can account for the cerebellar symptom of hypermetria. As shown in Figure 10.37, rapid movements require both agonist and antagonist activity. While agonist activity is clearly needed to displace the limb, antagonist activity is, at least superficially, counterproductive. Why produce a force that counteracts a desired action? One argument for the biphasic pattern is that it enables a person to move at fast speeds that are not reliant on sensory feedback. An initial agonist burst propels the effector rapidly in the correct direction with little opposing resistance. Then the antagonist brakes the movement. This anticipatory mode of control has a cost: The timing of the agonist and antagonist must be precise. In this view, the cerebellum's contribution to rapid movements establishes a temporal pattern across the muscles. The cerebellum can predict when the antagonist should be acti-

vated to terminate movement at the right location. If the cerebellum is lesioned, the agonist burst is sufficient to initiate the movement, but the animal cannot anticipate when the brake is needed. Other signals, such as feedback from the moving limb, may now be required to trigger the antagonist. Given delays in neural transmission, it is likely that the antagonist will be delayed and the animal will overshoot the target.

The timing hypothesis offers a novel slant on the role of the cerebellum in motor learning. Cerebellar lesions are most disruptive to highly practiced movements, which present the greatest need for precise timing. The novice tennis player may be pleased if he can simply get the ball over the net, and not care if his racquet strikes the ball a little early or a little late. But for the expert, it is essential that all gestures be exquisitely timed so the ball lands in a certain place on the court.

This point is highlighted in an experiment on one of the simplest learned movements, the pavlovian response (see Chapter 3). When a neutral stimulus like a tone is paired with an aversive stimulus like a puff of air to the eye, the air puff prompts a reflexive blink to minimize eye damage. With practice, an animal blinks in response

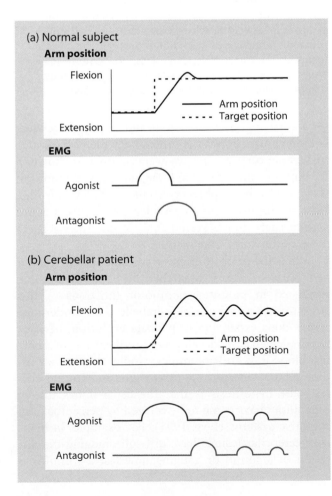

Figure 10.37 Arm movements and associated EMG activity during rapid elbow movements. **(a)** During rapid elbow flexion, the agonist, biceps muscle produces a burst to propel the limb. This movement is braked by the activation of the antagonist triceps. **(b)** The fine timing between the agonist-antagonist activity is disrupted in patients with cerebellar lesions. When the onset of the antagonist is delayed, the movement ends up overshooting the target because of the loss of the braking force. The oscillations seen at the end of pointing movements results from the alternation of agonist and antagonist activity.

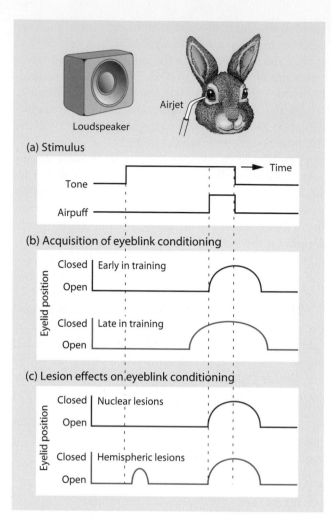

(a) Stimulus

(b) Acquisition of eyeblink conditioning

(c) Lesion effects on eyeblink conditioning

Figure 10.38 Lesions of the cerebellum disrupt the learned response in eye-blink conditioning. **(a)** A neutral tone precedes and coterminates with an aversive air puff to the eye. **(b)** Early in training, the air puff causes the animal to blink. Late in training, the animal blinks in response to the tone, thus reducing the impact of the air puff. **(c)** Lesions of the deep cerebellar nuclei abolish the learned response. The fact that the animal continues to reflexively blink in response to the air puff indicates that the lesion has produced a learning deficit and not a motor deficit. The anticipatory, learned responses are still present following lesions of the cerebellar cortex. However, they are inappropriately timed and, thus, no longer adaptive.

to the tone (Figure 10.38). This acquired response is adaptive: By blinking at the tone, the animal's eye closes before the air puff. This conditioned response is timed to reach maximal amplitude at the air puff's onset.

Unlike lesions of the cerebral cortex or hippocampus, cerebellar lesions disrupt the acquisition and retention of a conditioned blinking response. The problem is not one of an impaired motor system, as the unconditioned response is minimally affected by cerebellar lesions. One interpretation of the selective disruption of the conditioned response would be that it reflects a motor learning deficit, an idea in accord with the view that the cerebellum is essential for motor memory. On the other hand, the timing hypothesis provides an alternative computational account, emphasizing that the cerebellum is essential for eye blink conditioning because of the unique requirements in this task. Specifically, the essential information for the animal to learn is that the tone predicts exactly when the air puff will occur, to establish a representation of the temporal relations between the two stimuli. Without the cerebellum,

the animal might learn that tone and air puff are related, but the information is not functionally useful if the animal cannot correlate the two events in time. As shown in the bottom panel of Figure 10.38, rabbits with lesions in the cerebellar hemispheres continue to blink to the tone, but the response is no longer adaptive because it is not appropriately timed (Perrett et al., 1993). The eye is exposed at the time of the air puff.

While the cerebellum has traditionally been viewed as a motor structure, researchers have recently become interested in potential nonmotor functions of this structure. As noted, the neocerebellum has undergone tremendous expansion in primate evolution, perhaps in parallel with the development of the prefrontal cortex. Blood flow and anatomical studies have shown intimate links between the cerebellum and frontal cortex. One hypothesis is that the cerebellum's timing capabilities have come to be utilized by perceptual and cognitive systems (Ivry, 1993). For example, humans with cerebellar lesions have difficulty judging the duration of a sound or gauging how fast a stimulus is moving. The patients showed no impairment on control tasks that assessed general perceptual function. By this account, then, the cerebellum continues to perform a restricted computation—representing temporal information—but the computation is now available to other systems that require this information.

Whether or not this hypothesis is correct, it reveals a major feature of cognitive neuroscience's approach to brain function. Traditional neuroscience and neurology generally rely on task-based taxonomies such as motor or sensory systems. For the cognitive neuroscientist, the prime goal is to understand a neural structure's computational role, which can begin in a narrow domain but may also generalize to tasks that utilize a mental operation (Figure 10.39).

THE BASAL GANGLIA

The other major subcortical motor structure is the *basal ganglia,* composed of five nuclei: caudate, putamen, globus pallidus, subthalamic nucleus, and substantia nigra (see Figure 10.5). These nuclei do not form a single anatomical entity; rather, they are a functional structure whose interconnected network of inputs and outputs is restricted. Moreover, lesions in any part of the basal ganglia interfere with coordinated movement.

Before analyzing these disorders, we need to appreciate the complicated neuroanatomy of the basal ganglia, shown in Figure 10.40. All afferent fibers to the basal ganglia terminate in the caudate and putamen. Together, these nuclei are referred to as the *striatum.* The dominant input to the striatum is via the cortico-striate projection, fibers that originate from the entire cerebral cortex including sensory, motor, and association cortices. The motor cortex also influences striatal processing through indirect thalamic projections.

Efferent fibers from the basal ganglia are also restricted. Output from the basal ganglia originates in the internal segment of the globus pallidus (GPi) and the pars reticulata of the substantia nigra (SNr). SNr axons terminate in the superior colliculus and provide a crucial

Figure 10.39 Contrasting approaches for linking structure and function. **(a)** The traditional view has been to consider the task domain of a particular structure. For example, the cerebellum is viewed as one part of the motor system with an important contribution to the control of skilled movements. **(b)** The cognitive neuroscience view emphasizes the unique computational characteristics of a structure. In this approach, emphasis would be on the special role of the cerebellum in the representation of temporal information. Tasks that require precise timing will utilize the cerebellum, regardless of whether they are motoric or not.

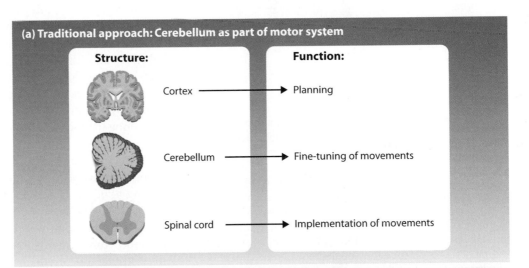

(a) Traditional approach: Cerebellum as part of motor system

Structure: Function:

Cortex → Planning

Cerebellum → Fine-tuning of movements

Spinal cord → Implementation of movements

(b) Cognitive neuroscience approach: Cerebellum representing temporal information

To cortex:

Planning temporal aspects of movement

Perceiving short time intervals

Judging velocity of moving objects

To spinal cord and subcortex:

Regulating temporal patterns of muscle activity including distal, proximal, and speech movements

Learning temporal relationships between stimuli in order to make precisely timed adaptive responses

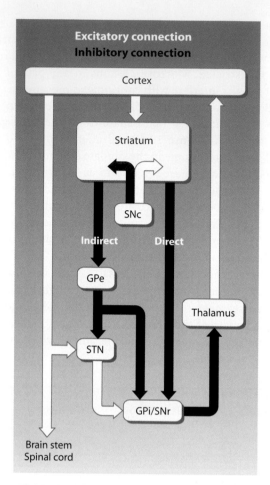

Figure 10.40 Wiring of the basal ganglia. Inputs from the cortex primarily project to the striatum. From here, processing flows along two pathways. The direct pathway goes to the output nuclei, the internal segment of the globus pallidus (GPi) and pars reticulata of the substantia nigra (SNr). The indirect pathway includes a circuit through the external segment of the globus pallidus (GPe), the subthalamic nucleus (STN), and then to the output nuclei. The output projections to the thalamus are relayed to the cortex, frequently terminating close to the initial source of input. The dopaminergic projections of the pars compacta of the substantia nigra (SNc) modulate striatal activity by facilitating the direct pathway via the D_1 receptors and inhibiting the indirect pathway via the D_2 receptors. Adapted from Wichmann and DeLong (1996).

signal for the initiation of eye movements. GPi axons, on the other hand, terminate in thalamic nuclei which in turn project to the supplementary motor area and prefrontal cortex.

Two important principles are critical for understanding basal ganglia function. Anatomically, most of the cortical areas projecting to the basal ganglia are reinnervated by fibers exiting the basal ganglia. Thus, the cortex and basal ganglia form a series of parallel circuits. Physiologically, the output from the basal ganglia is inhibitory. Neurons in the GPi and SNr have high

baseline firing rates that inhibit target neurons in the superior colliculus and thalamus. As a motor plan develops, this inhibition signal is decreased in selected neurons. It is as though the motor system is held in check by the basal ganglia until the inhibitory signal is removed (Figure 10.41).

Processing within the basal ganglia is complex. Mahlon DeLong (1990) of Emory University distinguished between direct and indirect pathways: The direct pathway consists of direct inhibitory projections from the striatum to the GPi and SNr; the indirect pathway also connects the striatum to these output nuclei, but only through intervening processing stages involving the external segment of the globus pallidus and the subthalamic nucleus. The final pathway of note is the projection from the pars compacta of the substantia nigra to the striatum. Interestingly, this pathway has opposite effects on the direct and indirect pathways despite a common transmitter, dopamine. The nigra excites the direct pathway by acting on one type of dopamine receptor (D_1) and inhibits the indirect pathway by acting on a different type of dopamine receptor (D_2).

The functional consequences of this organization can be understood by tracing what happens when cortical fibers activate the striatum. Via the direct pathway, target neurons in the output nuclei of the basal ganglia are inhibited, leading to excitation of the thalamus and cortical motor areas. On the other hand, striatal activation along the indirect pathway results in increased excitation of the output nuclei leading to increased inhibition of the cortex. It appears, then, that the direct and indirect pathways are at odds with one another; if processing along the indirect pathway is slower, however, the basal ganglia can act as a gatekeeper of cortical activity—less inhibition from the direct pathway is followed by more inhibition from the indirect pathway. The nigrostriatal fibers enhance the direct pathway while they reduce the effects of the indirect pathway. As such, this pathway is essential for promoting movement.

Disorders of the Basal Ganglia Several neurological disorders affect the basal ganglia; in these we see a breakdown in the delicate balance between postural stability and movement. We will concentrate on two, Huntington's disease and Parkinson's disease, since they best demonstrate how movement is disrupted by basal ganglia dysfunction. While psychiatric conditions such as Tourette's syndrome and obsessive compulsive disorder have been linked to the basal ganglia, the neuroanatomical picture is murkier.

Huntington's disease is a progressive degenerative disorder that appears in the fourth or fifth decade of life. The onset is subtle, usually a gradual change in mental

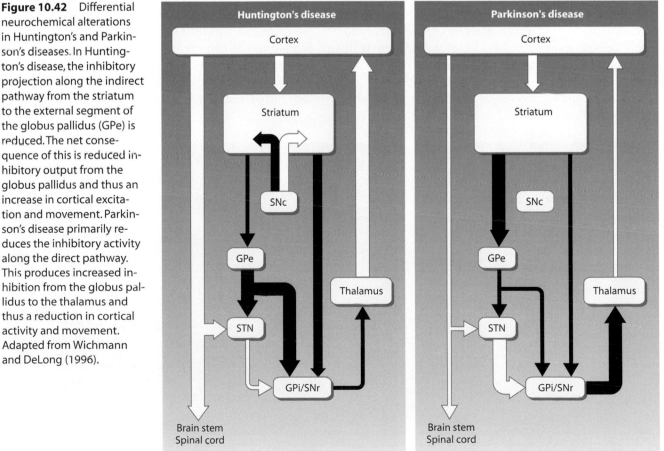

Figure 10.41 The basal ganglia play a critical role in movement initiation. Potential responses are held in check until a triggering response is provided by the basal ganglia.

attitude where the patient is irritable, is absentminded, and loses interest in normal activities. Within a year movement abnormalities are noticed: clumsiness, balance problems, and a general restlessness. These involuntary movements, or *chorea,* gradually dominate normal motor function. The patient may adopt contorted postures, with the arms, legs, trunk, and head in con-

stant motion. Movement ceases to be goal oriented and gestures lack any consistent pattern or regularity. Indeed, during the seventeenth century, on at least two continents, Huntington's disease patients were executed for witchcraft because their chorea made them appear possessed by an evil spirit (Figure 10.42).

Neurological deficits in Huntington's disease are not

Figure 10.42 Differential neurochemical alterations in Huntington's and Parkinson's diseases. In Huntington's disease, the inhibitory projection along the indirect pathway from the striatum to the external segment of the globus pallidus (GPe) is reduced. The net consequence of this is reduced inhibitory output from the globus pallidus and thus an increase in cortical excitation and movement. Parkinson's disease primarily reduces the inhibitory activity along the direct pathway. This produces increased inhibition from the globus pallidus to the thalamus and thus a reduction in cortical activity and movement. Adapted from Wichmann and DeLong (1996).

restricted to motor function. As motor problems worsen, patients develop dementia of a subcortical type, unaccompanied by apraxia, aphasia, or agnosia—common signs of a cortical dementia such as Alzheimer's disease. Even so, the patients have impaired memory, especially in acquiring novel motor skills, and become easily confused on problem-solving tasks. The disorder is also accompanied by emotional and personality changes, although it is hard to know whether these are due to the disease itself or are a reaction to the onset of such a debilitating disease.

The genetic origin of Huntington's disease is reviewed in Chapter 2. Despite such advances on its cause, there is no known cure; patients usually die within 12 years of its onset. At autopsy, the brain of a Huntington's disease patient typically reveals widespread pathology in cortical and subcortical areas. Atrophy is most prominent in the basal ganglia, and the cell death rate is as high as 90% in the striatum. These changes are also evident from imaging studies performed as the disease unfolds.

It has been difficult to make inferences about normal motor function from studying patients with Huntington's disease. They frequently cannot complete experimental tasks, or do so with only the most labored movements. Even these are masked by involuntary movements. As such, selective deficits are hard to observe: The disease affects all measures of coordination. The excessive movements, or *hyperkinesia*, seen with Huntington's disease can be understood by considering how the pathology affects information flow through the basal ganglia. In the early stages, striatal changes are primarily in inhibitory neurons forming the indirect pathway. As shown in the left panel of Figure 10.43, this leads to a reduced output from the basal ganglia, and thus greater excitation of thalamic neurons. A second hyperkinetic disorder, *hemiballism,* is also associated with lesions of the indirect pathway, but here the lesion is centered in the subthalamic nucleus. Patients with these lesions produce violent and uncontrollable movements. These problems may persist for many years, requiring special precautions to ensure that the patients do not hurt themselves or those who come within reach.

Parkinson's disease is the most common and well-known disorder affecting the basal ganglia. The disorder is characterized by positive and negative symptoms; that is, motor disorders that heighten muscular activity and disorders that diminish it. Positive symptoms include resting tremor and rigidity. The former, which refers to the rapid shaking evident in distal effectors, is a tremor that becomes quieter, if not entirely quiescent, once the patient initiates a volitional movement. Rigidity results when agonist and antagonist muscles are simultaneously activated. When the limb is passively displaced, the neurologist can feel alternations between resistance and relaxation, a phenomenon known as *cogwheeling.*

Negative symptoms of Parkinson's disease include disorders of posture and locomotion, hypokinesia, and bradykinesia. Parkinsonian patients often lose their equilibrium. When the patient is sitting, the head may droop forward, or when standing, the forces of gravity will gradually pull the person forward until balance is lost. *Hypokinesia* refers to an absence or reduction in

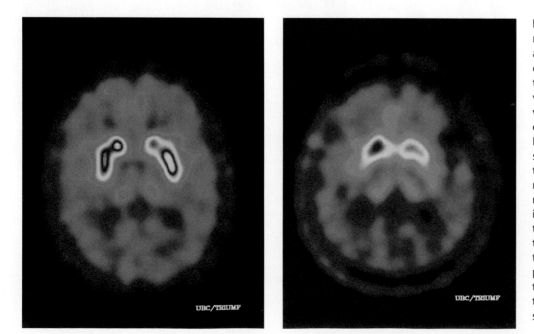

UBC/TRIUMF   UBC/TRIUMF

Figure 10.43 New neuroimaging techniques are able to label the distribution of specific transmitter systems. This procedure provides a new opportunity to visualize reduced dopaminergic activity in patients with Parkinson's disease. Healthy subjects and Parkinson patients were injected with a radioactive tracer, fluorodopa. This agent is visible in the striatum, reflecting the dopaminergic projections to this structure from the substantia nigra. Compare the reduced uptake in the patients' scan (**right**) to the scan from the healthy subjects (**left**).

voluntary movement. Parkinson's disease patients act as if they are stuck in a posture and cannot change it. This problem is especially evident when patients try to initiate a new movement. Many patients develop small tricks to help them overcome the hypokinesia. For example, one patient walked with a cane, not because he needed help in maintaining his balance, but because it provided him a visual target to give him a jump start. When he wanted to walk, he placed the cane in front of his right foot and kicked it—which caused him to overcome inertia and commence his walking. Once started, the movements may appear normal, although they are frequently slow, or *bradykinetic*. The parkinsonian patient can use his hand to reach for an object, though the entire sequence is in slow motion.

As noted at the beginning of this chapter, Parkinson's disease can develop following encephalitis or drug abuse. In most patients, however, the disease is *idiopathic*, a catch-all term used by neurologists when the cause is unknown. There is some evidence for a genetic origin, although the recent rise in early-onset Parkinson's disease has led researchers to suspect a rise in an environmental toxin. In all patients, the prominent pathology is a loss of dopaminergic nigrostriatal fibers. As with most brain tissue, these neurons gradually atrophy with age. If the percentage of lost neurons becomes too great, resulting in reduced dopamine levels of about 90%, Parkinson's symptoms will become obvious.

The role of dopamine in Parkinson's disease is incontrovertible. The first evidence came in the late 1950s when postmortem examinations correlated the disease with low dopamine levels. (The observations were the first time a brain disease was linked to a neurotransmitter deficiency.) Treatment programs were quickly developed in which patients were provided with synthetic precursors of dopamine, L-dopa, a therapy that is of great benefit to most Parkinson's disease patients. Many can function with little evidence of the disease, and Parkinson's disease is no longer considered a life-threatening condition. The drug's efficacy is far from perfect, though. Over the course of a day some patients experience rapid fluctuations in the severity of their symptoms. Over time, many patients develop hyperkinesias.

We noted earlier that input from the substantia nigra to the striatum can promote movement, both by its excitation of the direct pathway and by its inhibition of the indirect pathway. When the dopaminergic neurons are depleted, the parkinsonian patient has great difficulty in initiating a movement, as shown in the right panel in Figure 10.44. The patient looks frozen in place. The cortex may continue to select a movement plan, but the basal ganglia are needed to link that plan with commands to the motor effectors.

Parkinson's disease patients also show reduced flexibility in their volitional movements. For example, they may not be able to vary the force used to produce a movement. Normal subjects typically produce movements of different amplitude by scaling the magnitude of the initial agonist burst. A strong burst creates a larger force and enables one to move farther with minimal increase in the time required to complete the movement. In contrast, Parkinson's disease patients have to produce a series of small bursts to move a longer distance (Figure 10.44). Thus, the basal ganglia are significant not only in initiating movement, but also in adjusting an action's force. Both problems relate to properly energizing a movement plan. For the initiation deficit, the releasing signal is absent, preventing the muscles from becoming active; for the force deficit, the plan is implemented but in a fixed manner.

Movement deficits in Parkinson's disease patients are most evident when action is guided by internal cues. This observation fits with the anatomical picture developed earlier in that the output from the basal ganglia is primarily directed to medial regions of the premotor cortex. Indeed, the patients' problems can be virtually eliminated when their movements are guided by external cues. For example, parkinsonian patients are much poorer than control subjects in tracking a moving target when the target moves in a predictable, oscillatory pattern. If the target's motion is random, the patients perform as well as the control subjects. In the latter condition, movements must be visually guided since the target's future location is unknown. When the target oscillates, subjects anticipate its future location. Parkinson's patients, however, cannot take advantage of this information; in both conditions, their movements rely on external cues. They have difficulty selecting a movement pattern according to their own expectations. The patient who used a cane as a cue to initiate walking demonstrated his reliance on external cues. While he knew that he wanted to move from one location to another, he could not will it; he needed an external visual cue to activate his legs.

Basal Ganglia Contributions to Learning and Cognition Whether or not basal ganglia are central to generating movement sequences is a debatable issue. The slow movements in Parkinson's disease patients are most pronounced for the final elements of a movement pattern, and errors increase when the sequence is composed of heterogeneous gestures. Animal studies also point to the basal ganglia's role in generating movement sequences. In rats, lesions of the striatum disrupt their stereotyped grooming behavior, whereas this innate sequence is minimally affected by lesions of the cerebral cortex or cerebellum (Berridge et al., 1992). It is not clear whether this is a specific problem in sequencing. The difficulty in producing learned or innate movement sequences may also reflect an inability to energize movement plans or use internal cues to generate actions. For example, rats with striatal lesions do not produce random grooming patterns but fail to complete the sequence from start to finish.

A controversial topic in the literature on Parkinson's disease concerns whether symptoms are restricted to motor deficits, or whether the disease is accompanied by cognitive deficits. Neuropsychological testing clarifies that, at least for patients who have been afflicted for many years, cognitive performance is below that observed with age-matched control subjects. Some maintain that these cognitive problems are secondary to the disease and are attributed to depression—a frequent condition in people with chronic neurological problems—or to the effects of L-dopa therapy. Or, the deficits may not implicate a direct role for the basal ganglia in cognition but come from changes in cortical function caused by abnormal basal ganglia modulation.

Others have sought to elucidate the function of the basal ganglia in cognition by asking how the motor problems seen in parkinsonian patients might manifest on nonmotor tasks. One idea is that the basal ganglia perform an operation critical for shifting set. In the motor domain, a problem in energizing movements can be viewed as a deficit in set shifting. The parkinsonian patient gets stuck in one position, or posture, and cannot shift to a new one. Perhaps these patients' cognitive

problems can be linked to shifting from one mental set to another.

To test this idea, Steven Keele and his students at the University of Oregon (Hayes et al., in press) developed two tasks that required a shifting operation (Figure 10.45). In the motor task, the patients were taught two short movement sequences of three elements each. After this training phase, the patients were required to produce a six-element sequence composed of either the two sequences in succession or two repetitions of one of the sequences. As predicted, the responses for the parkinsonian patients were especially slow at the switching point, the transition from the third to the fourth element, in the shifting condition. Note that in both the repetition and the shifting condition, the fourth element requires the same response—a finger press with the index finger. The difference between the two conditions results from the hierarchical coding of these sequences. In the shifting condition, this response is part of a different subsequence.

For the cognitive task, the patients were trained on two choice reaction time tasks, one involving color discrimination and the other shape discrimination. After training on each dimension, pairs of trials were introduced in which the two responses were either along the same dimension (e.g., color-color) or required a shift from one dimension to the other (e.g., shape-color). As in the motor task, the parkinsonian patients were significantly slower when they had to shift dimensional set. This problem cannot be attributed to a motor problem

Figure 10.44 EMG amplitude is not scaled appropriately in Parkinson's disease. **(a)** In healthy people, the magnitude of EMG activity increases to produce larger movements. **(b)** The EMG profiles of Parkinson's disease patients tend to be more invariant. To move the limb over a large distance, a series of EMG bursts have to be generated.

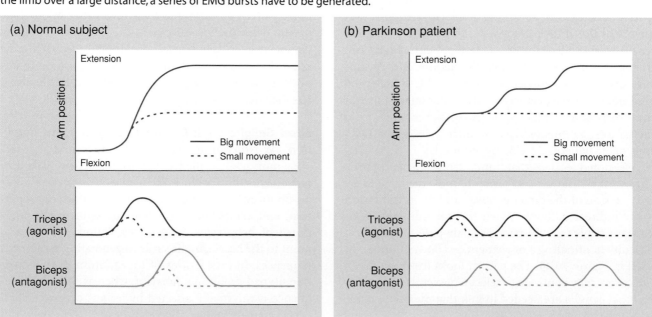

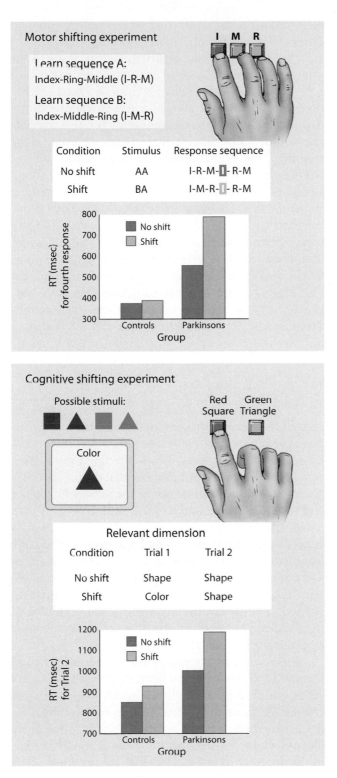

Figure 10.45   Motor and cognitive tests of set shifting. In the motor task, subjects performed two successive sequences that were either identical or different. Although the movement at the transition point was the same in both the no-shift and shift conditions, Parkinson's disease patients were much slower in the latter condition. In the cognitive task, subjects had to respond to either the color or the shape of a stimulus. Trials were paired such that the second response was along either the same dimension (no shift) or the other dimension (shift). As in the motor task, Parkinson's disease patients were especially slow when they had to shift.

as the responses on the second trial were identical in all conditions (e.g., decide whether the stimulus color was red or blue).

The shifting hypothesis offers a unified framework for understanding basal ganglia function in both action and cognition. The basal ganglia are in a position to monitor activation across wide regions of the cortex, allowing a shift between different actions and mental sets by removing an inhibitory influence in selected neurons. Indeed, recent neurophysiological studies have emphasized that the shifting operation is neither strictly motoric nor cognitive; rather, it is a necessary link between mental set and action (Brotchie et al., 1991). In this work, monkeys were trained to make a pair of movements, with a variable delay between the first and second movements. A burst in pallidal neurons observed at the end of this delay period was interpreted as a releasing signal for the cortex to switch from one plan to another.

This shifting hypothesis may also hold the key to the basal ganglia's role in learning. Dopamine is known to play a critical role in the reward systems of the brain, providing the organism with a neurochemical marker of the reinforcement contingencies that exist for different responses in the context of the current environment. Learning involves a change in behavior—either acquiring the appropriate response in an unfamiliar context or breaking a habitual response when contingencies change in a familiar context. For a rat in the wild, this might mean being sensitive to a change in the availability of food at a foraging site. For a human, it might mean recognizing that a demanding problem cannot be solved by conventional means.

Viewed this way, the ability to shift is required for producing novel behavior or for combining patterns of behavior into novel sequences. We can now see a link between basal ganglia dysfunction and psychiatric disorders such as Tourette's syndrome and obsessive compulsive disorder. A cardinal feature in each syndrome is the repetitive production of stereotyped movement patterns. For the patient with Tourette's syndrome, this might be a simple tic, a flick of the shoulder, or a hand brushing across the face. For someone with obsessive compulsive disorder, an entire behavioral sequence such as hand washing can be performed over and over again. A failure to shift may result in an absence of movement, the problem of the Parkinson's disease patient, or in the repeated production of a single pattern. In either case, basal ganglia dysfunction makes it difficult to select new actions that arise when sensory input or internal goals change.

SUMMARY

Cognitive neuroscience has had a major impact on our conceptualization of how the brain produces skilled action. Consider the two halves of Figure 10.46. The top panel, first introduced in 1974, shows the critical circuits of the motor pathway, emphasizing patterns of anatomical connectivity with a crude partitioning of function into motor planning, movement preparation, and movement execution. The bottom panel retains the basic circuitry, but offers a functional decomposition of the processes involved in planning and programming.

As can be seen in this figure, the control of action involves a number of distributed systems. Nonetheless, we need not conclude that this distributed pattern suggests that all of the systems operate in a similar manner. As with other processing domains such as attention and memory, the different motor structures have their unique specializations. The cortical pathways for movement selection are biased to provide particular sources of information. The subcortical loops through the basal ganglia and cerebellum are essential for movement preparation, but in quite different ways.

By specifying a functional role for these structures, we can appreciate the limitations of brain theories that focus on the task rather than the internal computations. For example, the loss of fine coordination and erratic movements seen in patients with cerebellar lesions has led to a view that this structure is essential for skilled movement, that somehow the representation of an action shifts from one neural locus to another with practice. But when viewed as a structure that is specialized to represent the temporal properties of a movement, we can see that the loss of skilled movements is a consequence of a breakdown in the fine timing. This computation would not be as essential during the early phases of skill acquisition when the person builds the representations that underlie the skill. Moreover, this functional analysis has made clear that the boundaries between perception and action are murky. In the same way that the parietal lobe is essential for both perceiving and acting in space, the timing functions of the cerebellum or shifting functions of the basal ganglia are not restricted to motor control. As noted at the beginning of this chapter, perceptual information is only useful to the extent that it facilitates behavior.

We are not simply robots that respond in a fixed manner to the information being delivered by our perceptual apparatus. Flexibility provides one metric for comparing the sophistication of the cognitive capabilities across species. Is the animal's behavior completely dictated by the environment? Or can it modify its behavior in order to attain goals that require more complex planning? In the next chapter, we continue with our emphasis on the goal-oriented aspects of behavior. This will take us to the highest level of abstraction in the hierarchical representations of actions, the level at which we form the plans that guide our most complex behaviors. To do so, we must consider the functions of the prefrontal cortex.

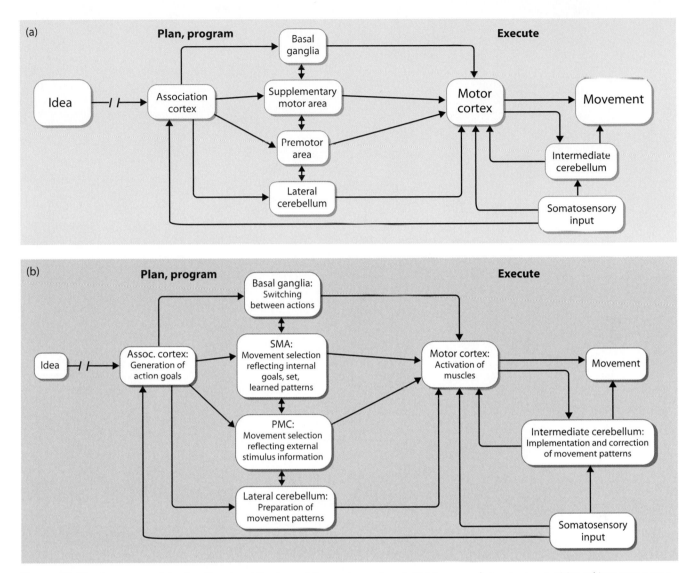

Figure 10.46 Summary of the functional architecture of the motor system. **(a)** Major neural structures, partitioned into areas associated with the planning and execution of movement. **(b)** Functional hypotheses regarding how these different structures contribute to actions.

SUGGESTED READINGS

DELONG, M.R. (1990). Primate models of movement disorders of basal ganglia origin. *Trends Neurosci.* 13:281–285.

GEORGOPOULOS, A.P. (1995). Motor Cortex and Cognitive Processing. In M.S. Gazzaniga (Ed.), *The Cognitive Neurosciences* (pp. 507–517). Cambridge, MA: MIT Press.

GOLDBERG, G. (1985). Supplementary motor area structure and function: Review and hypothesis. *Behav. Brain Sci.* 8:567–616.

IVRY, R. (1993). Cerebellar involvement in the explicit representation of temporal information. Ann. N.Y. Acad. Sci. 682: 214–230.

KEELE, S. (1986). Motor Control. In J.K. Boff, L. Kaufman, and J.P. Thomas (Eds.), *Handbook of Human Perception and Performance.* Vol. II (pp. 1–60) New York: Wiley & Sons.

ROLAND, P.E. (1993). *Brain Activation.* New York: Wiley-Liss.

11

Executive Functions and Frontal Lobes

In the late summer of 1848, Phineas Gage woke in his campsite near the Vermont hamlet of Cavendish, ready for another demanding day of work building the extension of the Rutland & Burlington Railroad. Gage was proud to be participating in expanding America's vast transportation system through uneven and rocky terrain, the remnants of unrelenting glaciers that had shaped northern New England. Laying track required blasting the rock so graders could smooth the surface for the rail lines. Gage was foreman of the construction crew, a position of responsibility that reflected his years of experience and his expertise with a risky task: setting dynamite charges.

Though the job was straightforward, great care had to be taken to ensure that each step was done properly. A hole was drilled in the rock, filled with explosive powder, and then a fuse was placed on top of the powder. To ensure that the explosion impacted the rock itself, the powder had to be covered with a dense layer of sand and tamped down with an iron rod. Over the years, Gage had given much thought to how these blasts could be made most efficient; he even had a tamping iron manufactured to his specifications.

Many blasts had been set that day, and the men were encouraged by their progress through the rugged landscape. As the afternoon heat waned, their thoughts turned to dinner and perhaps a cooling swim in the creek. Around 4:30, Gage set another charge. As he waited for his assistant to pour in the sand, however, he was distracted and failed to check whether the powder was covered. When he thrust down his tamping iron, the consequences were disastrous. The iron set off a spark and the explosion ripped through the worksite.

The work crew turned to find Gage sprawled on the ground. They gasped in horror, shocked by the blood seeping from two large holes, one where his left cheek had been and the other from an opening in the top of his head. The iron rod lay nearby, having careened

through the tissue and bone of Gage's brain and skull.

Equally shocking was the fact that their boss had not been killed. Though stunned, Gage was conscious! At first his body twitched convulsively, but within a few minutes he sat up and spoke to the men as they fetched a cart to take him to Cavendish for medical assistance. In town, he greeted the doctor in a most understated fashion, "Doctor, here is business enough for you." The physician, Dr. John Harlow, stopped the bleeding and sutured the wounds, liberally administering disinfectants to diminish the chances of infection. Within 2 months Gage was declared to be cured. As Harlow later wrote, "I dressed him, God healed him."

Unfortunately, the cure was only superficial. As soon as the injury's acute effects had subsided, it became apparent to all who knew Gage that his personality had undergone a radical transformation. Before the accident, Gage had been an exemplary citizen, hard working and energetic, a clear thinker who was a shrewd manager of his personal and financial affairs. Afterward, he grew impatient and rude, given to outbursts of anger and rage. He brushed off well-intended advice of friends and medical advisors with shocking profanity. He could not follow a coherent plan of action; instead, he reeled off a constant stream of ideas that were discarded al-

423

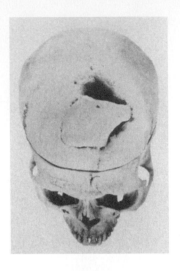

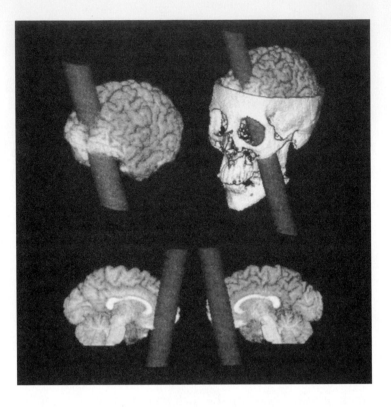

Figure 11.1 Phineas Gage's skull and computer reconstructions showing how the tamping iron passed through his brain. The iron entered just below the left eye and exited from the top. It destroyed much of the medial region of prefrontal cortex.

most as soon as they were vocalized. His employers with the railroad soon discharged him.

The new Gage embarked on a picaresque journey including stints with Barnum's freak show in New York, roping horses in South America, and laboring in California towns at the height of the Gold Rush. Fortune would never come his way because he was content with a transient lifestyle. The end came in 1861, when Gage died at age 38, a victim of violent epileptic seizures that resurfaced as remnants of the neurological trauma he had suffered 13 years previously. Gage was buried, with the tamping iron placed alongside his body.

Five years after Gage's death, Dr. Harlow had the body exhumed from its burial site in California and brought the skull and iron back East, where it made its way to the museum of the Harvard Medical School. Hanna Damasio and her colleagues (1994) at the University of Iowa recently used modern brain imaging techniques to reconstruct Gage's lesion. They carefully measured the skull and used computer simulations to create a brain that best fit the skull. Then, as shown in Figure 11.1, they observed which parts of the brain would be impacted by the iron's blow. While the rod had passed through the frontal cortex, the motor and premotor cortices were spared, accounting for reports that Gage had no obvious motor problems. Instead, the iron had destroyed the ventromedial aspects of the most anterior portions of the frontal cortex in the left and right hemispheres.

The sad tale of Phineas Gage forces us to think about the essence of what makes a person act the way he or she does. We recognize that every individual has a unique personality, a consistent manner of thinking and acting in a social world. This personality reflects our innate characteristics and how these dispositions are shaped by the experiences and social forces we encounter. We all have aspirations—the desire to be loved, to succeed, to procreate—and recognize that our actions as individuals cannot be generated with sole regard for their impact on us, but also with regard for how these actions will affect those around us. While we recognize that these aspirations and choices reflect the brain's operation, it is difficult to attribute our uniqueness to a physical substance. It is this dilemma that led Descartes to postulate a duality of mind and soul.

Experimenters in psychology and the neurosciences shy away from such issues, content to leave them to the domain of philosophy. But cases such as Phineas Gage bring these problems to the forefront. It is not sufficient to establish a cognitive neuroscience of how we perceive information, how this information is stored, and how we move. We need to know what motivates our actions and how they interact with our choice of a coherent action. Gage represents a situation in which a neurological event produced a dramatic change in personality. As one of his peers commented, "Gage was no longer Gage." When we turn to the question of what constitutes the self, we must consider the role of the enigmatic prefrontal cortex.

SUBDIVISIONS OF THE FRONTAL LOBES

The frontal lobes comprise about a third of the cerebral cortex in humans (Figure 11.2). The posterior border with the parietal lobe is marked by the central sulcus, the only sulcus to extend the entire length of the brain's lateral surface and down along the medial surface. The frontal and temporal lobes are separated by the lateral fissure. Though the frontal cortex is present in all mammalian species, it has undergone tremendous expansion in human evolution, especially in the most anterior aspects. Since the development of functional capabilities parallels phylogenetic trends, the frontal lobe's expansion is related to the emergence of capabilities associated with cognition.

Each frontal lobe is generally divided into three components (Passingham, 1993). First, the motor cortex (area 4) occupies the most posterior portion, the gyrus just in front of the central sulcus. Second, anterior to the motor cortex are the secondary motor zones including the lateral premotor cortex and supplementary motor area (area 6), the frontal eye field (area 8), Broca's area (area 44, perhaps area 45), and the posterior portion of the cingulate cortex. Third, the remainder of the frontal lobe is termed the *prefrontal cortex,* which includes half of the entire frontal cortex in humans. The ratio is considerably smaller for subhuman species (Figure 11.3).

A prominent feature of all three subregions is that they are part of a massive network that links the brain's motor, perceptual, and limbic regions (Goldman-Rakic, 1995). There are extensive projections to the prefrontal cortex from almost all regions of the parietal and temporal cortices, and even some projections from prestriate regions of the occipital cortex. Subcortical structures including the basal ganglia, cerebellum, and various brainstem nuclei project indirectly to the prefrontal cortex via thalaric connections. Indeed, almost all cortical and subcortical areas influence the prefrontal cortex either directly or within a few synapses. The prefrontal

Figure 11.2 The areas of the frontal lobe. The prefrontal cortex includes all of the areas in front of the primary and secondary motor regions. The three major subdivisions of prefrontal cortex are the lateral prefrontal, ventromedial prefrontal, and the anterior cingulate cortex.

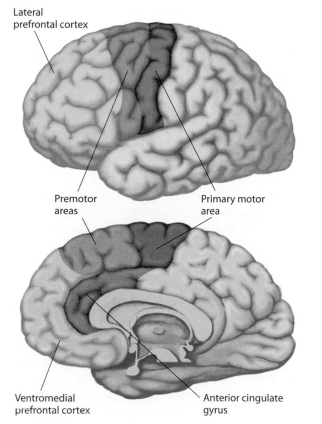

Lateral prefrontal cortex

Premotor areas

Primary motor area

Ventromedial prefrontal cortex

Anterior cingulate gyrus

Figure 11.3 The shaded areas show the extent of prefrontal cortex in six species. Note how small this region is in the cat, dog, and squirrel monkey. It is greatly enlarged in humans. The brains are not drawn to scale. Adapted from Fuster (1989).

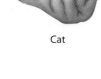

Squirrel monkey

Cat

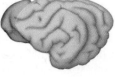

Rhesus monkey

Dog

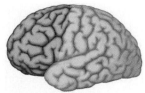

Chimpanzee

Man

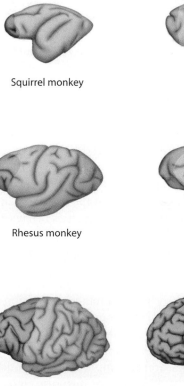

cortex also sends reciprocal connections to most areas that project to it, and to premotor and motor areas. The prefrontal cortex has many projections to the contralateral hemisphere—not only projections to homologous prefrontal areas via the corpus callosum but also bilateral projections to premotor and subcortical regions. From these neuroanatomical considerations we can assume that the prefrontal cortex is in an excellent position to coordinate processing across wide regions of the central nervous system (CNS).

In this chapter, we emphasize a tripartite view of the prefrontal cortex. The largest subregion includes the lateral prefrontal cortex, the lateral aspects of areas 9 to 12, all of areas 45 and 46, and the superior portions of area 47. The second subregion, the *ventromedial zone,* involves the inferior portions of area 47 and the medial parts of areas 9 to 12. The third subregion is the *anterior cingulate,* including areas 24, 25, and 32. Note that the cingulate is not always included in considerations of prefrontal function, perhaps because of its older, phylogenetic history and because it lacks the granular, six-layer structure of other cortical areas. Yet the cingulate plays a major role in executive functions. Moreover, granularity appears to be a questionable criterion since only primates have a granular prefrontal cortex. For all other mammals, prefrontal and cingulate regions have an agranular structure, an architecture quite distinct from more posterior cortical zones.

THE LATERAL PREFRONTAL CORTEX AND WORKING MEMORY

Patients with frontal lobe lesions present a paradox. In their everyday behavior, it is frequently difficult to detect a neurological disorder. They do not display obvious disorders in any of their perceptual abilities, and their speech is fluent and coherent. On conventional neuropsychological tests of intelligence, the patients perform normally. For example, when matched for education and age, patients with frontal lobe lesions score within the normal range on IQ tests such as the Wechsler Adult Intelligence Scale and most subtests of the Wechsler Memory Scale. Results such as these may contribute to the perpetuation of myths claiming that we fail to use vast portions of our cerebral capabilities. How else can we claim that lesions which destroy millions of cells fail to produce behavioral problems?

With more sensitive and specific tests, though, it becomes clear that frontal lesions disrupt normal cognition and produce a host of problems in memory function. Over the past three decades, investigators have catalogued memory disorders associated with frontal lesions. This work has had a major impact on our conceptualization of how knowledge is stored in the brain and, more importantly, how the knowledge influences behavior.

Distinguishing Between Stored Knowledge and Activated Information

We need to distinguish between memory functions associated with the long-term storage of information and its activation when it is relevant for on-line processing. The initial impetus for this work grew out of cognitive psychology when researchers emphasized a distinction between long-term and short-term memory. Here, too, we face a paradox. There are many dramatic demonstrations of the unbounded capacity of humans and animals to remember even the most minute details of past experiences. We can recall our first-grade classroom or recognize the face of a person only briefly encountered at a party. In contrast, sometimes when we are introduced to a person or given a new phone number, within seconds this information slips away—in one ear and out the other. (As mentioned in Chapter 7, studies of implicit learning convincingly demonstrate that the information often is not lost but is buried in the cortical abyss.) Short-term memory studies have shown that our ability to keep information active is severely limited—we can keep track of only a few pieces of information at a time.

Short-term memory and long-term memory depend on dissociable systems. Cognitive studies indicate that the way we represent information may shift over time. For example, when people are asked to immediately recall a visually presented list of words, memory failures are much more frequent when the list contains phonologically similar words (e.g., *man, mat, cap*) than when the list contains semantically similar words. But if the recall is delayed, the pattern of errors reverses. Now, performance is poorer for lists whose words are similar in meaning. Hence, we translate verbal information into an acoustic code immediately after its presentation, although long-term storage may be in a network that represents semantic properties.

Patient research supplements the cognitive evidence for the neural system's dissociation in short- and long-term memory. Many amnesic patients have severe deficits in their ability to develop new long-term memories while showing little impairment on tests of short-term memory. Although rarer, the reverse situation occurs. For example, a patient who is unable to remember lists of more than two digits may have normal long-term learning.

Early work on memory dichotomies emphasized that the critical function of short-term memory was to assist in the translation of newly acquired information into a format for longer-term storage. More recent work reconceptualized the functional role of short-term memory. The emphasis is now on how the system influences and constrains processing. We do not process information simply for putting it to use at a later time, a view that would be oriented only toward future behavior. Rather, representations are activated to shape behavior in the present. Reflecting this, the concept of a *working-memory* system has surfaced as an apt characterization of processes that represent the current contents of cognition.

Working Memory and On-line Processing

Our actions are not purely reflexive. What is immediately in front of us will surely influence our behavior, but we are not automata. We can hold off eating until all the guests are sitting about the table. We can resist jumping on the city bus that pulls over to the curb as we walk down the street. This capacity reflects the fact that, in addition to reacting to stimuli that currently dominate our perceptual pathways, we can also represent information that is not immediately evident. We can mind our dinner manners or choose to respond to some stimuli while ignoring other stimuli. This process requires integrating current perceptual information with stored knowledge, which may be from the distant past or from something recently experienced but no longer in view.

ANIMALS' WORKING MEMORY

The lateral prefrontal cortex is the primary repository for this type of interaction, or activity of working memory. A classic demonstration comes from delayed-response tasks. In the simplest version, sketched in Figure 11.4, a monkey is situated within reach of two food wells. At the start of a trial, the monkey observes the experimenter placing a food morsel in one of the two wells. Then the two wells are covered and a curtain is lowered to prevent the monkey from reaching toward either well. After a delay period, the curtain is raised and the monkey is allowed to choose one of the two wells and recover the food. While this appears to be a simple task, it demands one critical cognitive capability: The animal must continue to represent the location of the unseen food during

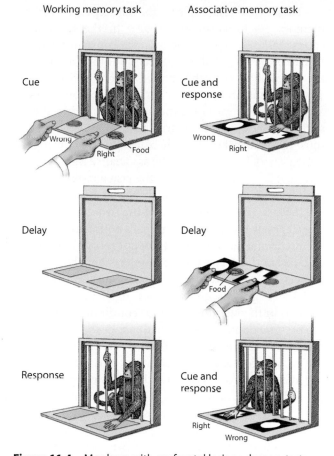

Figure 11.4 Monkeys with prefrontal lesions demonstrate selective impairment on the working-memory delayed-response task. **(Left)** In the working-memory task, the monkey sees one well baited with food. After a delay period, the animal retrieves the food. The location of the food is randomly determined. **(Right)** In the associative-memory task, the food reward is always associated with one of the two visual cues. The location of the cues (and food) is randomly determined. Working memory is required in the first task because, at the time the animal responds, there are no external cues indicating the location of the food. Long-term memory is required in the second task since the animal must remember which visual cue is associated with the reward. Adapted from Goldman-Rakic (1992).

the delay period. Monkeys with lesions of the lateral prefrontal cortex do poorly on the task.

This inability does not imply a general deficit in forming associations. In an experiment to test associative memory, the food wells are covered with distinctive visual cues: One cue is associated with the food location and the other with the position of the empty well. In this condition, the food morsel's location may be shifted during the delay period, but the visual cue will also be relocated so it continues to cover the food. Prefrontal lesions do not disrupt performance in this task.

These two tasks clarify the concept of working memory (Goldman-Rakic, 1992). In the delayed-response task, no explicit cue remains constant from one trial to the next. In half of the trials, the food is placed in the left well; in the other half, the right well is baited. Thus, there is no bias for either side to become associated with the reward over the long term. Rather, the associations fluctuate from trial to trial and the animal must remember the currently baited location during the delay period. In contrast, in the associative learning condition, it is necessary only that the visual cue reactivate a long-term association of which cue is associated with the reward. The reappearance of the two visual cues can trigger recall and guide the animal's performance.

Prefrontal lesions do not disrupt recognition memory. In another experiment, monkeys are shown three objects and allowed to select one. A curtain is lowered and the display is quickly rearranged by the experimenter. In the working-memory condition, two objects are presented, one of which had just been selected. The monkey is rewarded for choosing the other object. In the recognition-memory condition, the previously selected object is again presented, but now it is paired with a novel object. The animal is rewarded for choosing the novel object. In both conditions, then, the animal is rewarded for picking a previously unselected object.

Despite this similarity, animals with lesions that encompassed areas 46 and 9 of the dorsolateral prefrontal cortex had selectively impaired working memories. As a group, their performance was barely above the level of chance. In the recognition-memory task, this group performed as well as control subjects. Here, it was sufficient to recognize that one object was novel—or that the other was familiar. In the working-memory condition, both objects were familiar and the animal had to keep track of which had been previously selected. An important control in this study was the inclusion of animals who received frontal lesions in the vicinity of areas 6 and 8. These animals performed as well as the control animals on both versions of the task.

HUMAN STUDIES OF WORKING MEMORY

Humans also display frontal involvement in working memory. Adele Diamond of the University of Pennsylvania (1990) pointed out that a common marker of conceptual intelligence, Piaget's Object Permanence Test, is logically similar to the delayed-response task. In this task, a child observes the experimenter hiding a reward in one of two locations. After a delay of a few seconds, the child is encouraged to find the reward. Children younger than 1 year are unable to accomplish this task. At this age, the frontal lobes are still maturing. Diamond maintained that the ability to succeed in tasks such as the Object Permanence Test parallels the development of the frontal lobes. Prior to this development, the child acts as though "out of sight, out of mind." As the frontal lobes mature, the child can be guided by representations of objects and no longer depends on their presence.

Tasks similar to the ones used with animals do not sufficiently elicit deficits in adult human subjects. To challenge adults, a variant of the delayed-response task, the delayed-alternation task, is used. Here, a correct response requires the subject to choose the location opposite that of the previously reinforced one. Patients with frontal lesions have difficulty with this task, especially if the lesions are bilateral.

Errors in this task imply that the patients tend to perseverate, that is, return to the same location on successive trials. Perseveration is one of the most common symptoms of the frontal lobe syndrome. This tendency is exploited in one of the most widely accepted tests of frontal disorders, the Wisconsin Card Sorting Task, which involves cards containing objects that vary along three dimensions: shape, color, and numerosity (Figure

Figure 11.5 Patients with damage in the lateral prefrontal cortex have difficulty on the Wisconsin Card Sorting Task. On each trial, the subjects place the top card of the deck under one of the four target cards. The experimenter indicates whether the response is correct or incorrect, allowing the subject to learn the sorting rule by trial and error. The sorting rule changes whenever the subject makes ten consecutive correct responses.

11.5). The cards are presented one at a time and the subject is instructed to sort the cards according to an experimenter-defined sorting rule. The task has two catches. First, the subject is not informed of the sorting rule but must discover it through trial and error; the experimenter simply says correct or incorrect after each card is played. Second, and especially devilish, once the subject has learned to sort by one dimension, the experimenter changes the rule without informing the subject. So the subject not only must seek the appropriate sorting rule but also must be flexible enough to discard a previously reinforced hypothesis and begin the discovery anew. Patients with frontal lobe lesions perseverate, applying the initial rule over and over again after the switch, despite the experimenter's continued admonishment that the responses are incorrect.

There are obvious differences between the demands imposed by delayed-response tasks and the Wisconsin Card Sorting Task, but one essential feature is common:

Recognition of the stimulus by itself is insufficient to guide subjects to the correct response but must be integrated with how that information was relevant on previous trials. The subject's working memory must retain knowledge about the relevance of certain features in their previous responses.

Neuroimaging studies have provided new evidence that the lateral prefrontal cortex is essential for working memory. In a functional magnetic resonance imaging (MRI) study, subjects viewed fourteen to fifteen abstract shapes that were either white or red (McCarthy et al., 1994). The shapes could appear in one of twenty locations and were presented one at a time at a rate of one every 1.5 seconds. In the working-memory task, subjects were instructed to raise an index finger whenever a shape appeared in a location that had been occupied by another stimulus; thus, the subjects had to continually update a record of all the stimulus locations (Figure 11.6). For the control task, the same stimuli were used,

Figure 11.6   Lateral prefrontal activation revealed by functional magnetic resonance imaging (fMRI) in humans during a working-memory task. **(Top)** Subjects viewed a series of colored, abstract shapes, appearing one at a time at various locations on the screen. In the spatial working-memory condition, responses were required whenever a stimulus appeared at a location that had been used previously. In the control, color task, responses were required to all of the red objects. **(Bottom left)** During the spatial working-memory task, there was a pronounced increase in MR activity in lateral prefrontal cortex. This scan, obtained from a single subject shows a prominent focus in right prefrontal cortex (right hemisphere is on left). **(Bottom right)** The fMRI signal increased in right prefrontal cortex during the 8 second stimulus period for both tasks. Most notable, the percentage increase in this area relative to the baseline was more pronounced during the spatial working-memory task. Adapted from McCarthy et al. (1994).

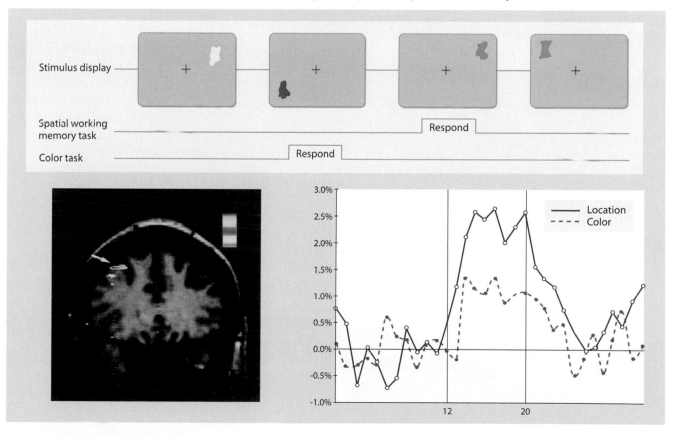

but the memory demands were eliminated: The subjects responded whenever a red shape appeared. These two tasks were compared to a baseline condition in which the subjects were instructed to relax with their eyes open. In this way, the stimuli were identical for the two experimental tasks and, assuming that the subjects correctly responded in all the trials, the total number of responses was equated. Yet oxygen delivery increased in the prefrontal cortex during the memory task, and the center of activation was in area 46. While this activation was bilateral, the effect was greatest in the right hemisphere. Similar asymmetries in other memory tasks have led to the hypothesis that the right prefrontal cortex may have a special role in memory retrieval.

CELLULAR MECHANISMS OF WORKING MEMORY

How is information activated and maintained in working memory? In Chapter 7 we mentioned the hypothesis that the hippocampus plays a critical role in forming long-term memories. The idea was that the hippocampus operated as a consolidation device, strengthening connections between conceptual and perceptual processing centers so further experiences with similar stimuli would produce more efficient activation and thus facilitate recognition. In the working-memory tasks just described, it is not enough for a stimulus to be recognized; we need to retain a record of its relevance, regardless of whether it pertained to the task at hand.

Two conditions are sufficient for a working-memory system: First, it should have a mechanism to access stored information; second, there should be a way to keep the information active. The prefrontal cortex can perform both operations. Clues to the neural basis for working memory have been provided by single-cell recordings in the lateral prefrontal cortex. Recall that in the delayed-response task, the animal is first shown a cue, the placing of a food morsel in one of two food wells. This is followed by a delay when the animal is prevented from viewing the food wells. The occluding blind is then removed and the animal tries to retrieve the morsel. Cells in the prefrontal cortex such as the ones in Figure 11.7 become active during this task and have sustained activity throughout the delay period (Fuster, 1989). Indeed, for some cells activation does not commence until after the delay begins and can be maintained up to 1 minute. These cells, then, provide a neural correlate for keeping active a representation after the triggering stimulus is no longer visible. The cells provide a continuous record of the response required for the animal to obtain the reward.

One could argue that this activity should not be interpreted as a mnemonic device but rather as a mechanism for maintaining a motor response. It is difficult to distinguish between remembering an event and anticipating a response triggered by that event. Having a record of recent processing can facilitate an upcoming action. Yet these cells are more closely linked to memory than to motor processes because their activity is modified by past experience. Fewer sustained responses are observed in untrained animals despite the fact that these animals will respond on every trial. As the animal becomes skilled in using the cue to guide performance, the activity during the delay period becomes more pronounced.

Sustained activity cannot be attributed to arousal. Some cells are activated after one cue; others fire more after the other cue appears. In the spatial delayed-response task, cues and responses are confounded; for instance, a cue on the left directs the animal to respond

Figure 11.7 Prefrontal neurons can show sustained activity during delayed-response tasks. Each line represents a single trial. The cue indicated the location for a forthcoming response. The monkey was trained to withhold the response until a "GO" signal (arrows) appeared. Each vertical tick represents action potential. This cell did not respond during the cue interval. Rather, its activity increased when the cue was turned off, and persisted until the response. Adapted from Fuster (1989).

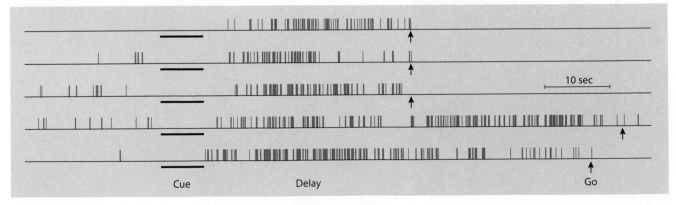

Cue   Delay   Go   10 sec

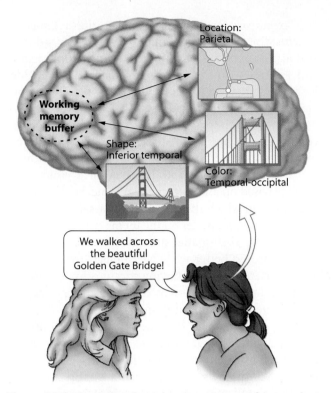

Figure 11.8 Lateral prefrontal cortex may provide a transient buffer for sustaining information stored in other cortical regions. In this example, the person is telling a friend about her walk across the Golden Gate Bridge during a visit to San Francisco. Long-term knowledge is reactivated and temporarily maintained through the reciprocal connections between the prefrontal cortex and the more posterior regions of the cortex. Note that the long-term memories of the Golden Gate Bridge are stored in dimensions-specific cortical regions.

to the left. But creatures can unconfound the factors; cellular activity need not be related to the forthcoming movement.

Cellular responses like these could indicate that long-term representations are stored in the prefrontal cortex and the cues activate them. By this hypothesis, the prefrontal cortex not only plays a role in working memory but also is implicated in the long-term storage of knowledge. While this idea is in accord with the single-cell results, it cannot account for the fact that prefrontal lesions have little effect on long-term memory.

Figure 11.8 presents an alternative view: Prefrontal areas are a temporary repository for representations accessed from other neural sites. Information is not permanently stored in the prefrontal cortex but is maintained there while it is relevant for performing a task. This hypothesis jibes nicely with the fact that the prefrontal cortex is intimately connected with postsensory regions of the temporal and parietal cortices. When a stimulus is perceived, a temporary representation is in-

stantiated in the prefrontal cortex via these connections to posterior brain regions. The sustained activation of prefrontal cells probably requires continuous reverberation across this network.

This hypothesis is supported by a metabolic imaging method with excellent spatial resolution (Friedman and Goldman-Rakic, 1994). Animals were trained to perform either working-memory tasks or control tasks that relied on associative memory. Prior to performing the task in the experimental session, the animals were injected with a slow radioactive tracer (^{14}C-2-deoxyglucose). A unique feature of this tracer is that it gets trapped in metabolizing brain tissue and thus can be measured with a photographic technique that highlights the radioactive agent. Glucose utilization was higher in prefrontal area 46 and in parietal area 7 in the working-memory group compared to the control groups (Figure 11.9). Glucose utilization in temporal cortical regions related to auditory perception was comparable for the two groups, which demonstrated that the memory groups did not simply have more active brains.

Two other results are noteworthy. First, glucose utilization in the parietal cortex was correlated with task

Figure 11.9 A radioactive tracer can reveal correlated activity in the prefrontal and inferior parietal cortex during a spatial working-memory task. After being injected with the tracer, the animal performed the memory task. Upon completion, the animal was killed. Histological analysis revealed how the slow-decaying tracer was trapped in different brain regions. The results are color-coded in units of local cerebral glucose utilization (LCGU). PS in the top panel refers to principal sulcus of prefrontal cortex. Area 7 refer to regions of parietal lobe. LS is the lateral sulcus, the division of parietal and temporal lobes. Embedded within this sulcus is the auditory cortex area measured for control purposes.

Prefrontal Cortex

Inferior Parietal Cortex

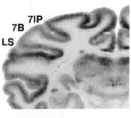

performance. Animals that performed well had higher rates of metabolism in the parietal cortex. In contrast, the degree of prefrontal metabolism depended on task difficulty, regardless of how well it was performed. This highlights the fact that memory tasks require that prefrontal areas devoted to memory functions interact with posterior areas that support long-term representations. More parietal activation reflects improved fidelity of the representations in working memory and thus more accurate performance. Prefrontal areas engage more when the task's memory demands increase.

Multiple Working Memories?

Working memory is conceptualized as a temporary network to sustain the current contents of processing. An open question is whether the prefrontal cortex contributes in a generic fashion, as a unitary working-memory system, or whether the activated regions depend on the type of information being processed. Cognitive and physiological studies favor the latter, but how the pie should be divided remains unclear.

Alan Baddeley of the Applied Psychology Unit in Cambridge, England (1995), promoted one influential view. His model is summarized in Figure 11.10: It consists of two subsystems that compete for access to a cen-

Figure 11.10 Baddeley's model of working memory. Working memory entails three critical components: a central executive and two "slave" systems, one for sustaining visual-spatial representations and the other for sustaining verbal representations in a phonological format.

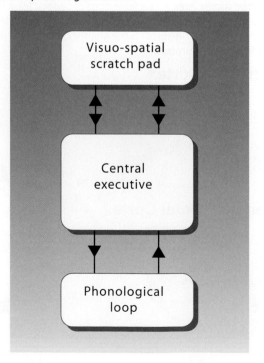

tral executive. One system, labeled the *visuospatial sketchpad,* activates representations of objects and their spatial positions. The other system is linguistic in nature and, referred to as the *phonological loop,* reflects Baddeley's belief that we maintain linguistic representations via covert articulatory rehearsal (i.e., subvocal speech). A key motivation for postulating two working-memory components comes from studies of subjects who were instructed to remember a list of words by using either a verbal strategy such as rote rehearsal or a visuospatial strategy based on an imagery mnemonic. Under control conditions in which the memory rehearsal was the only task, subjects were better on the memory test when they had used the visuospatial strategy. However, the verbal strategy proved better when the subjects were required to concurrently track a moving stimulus by operating a stylus during the retention interval. This reversal cannot be explained by assuming a unitary memory system.

One expectation is that the phonological loop and visuospatial sketchpad correspond to working-memory functions of the left and right hemispheres, respectively, an idea consistent with the general picture of hemispheric specialization. As noted, right-hemisphere activation was more prominent according to the functional MRI study of spatial working memory. One could argue that a role for the prefrontal cortex in language tasks requiring working memory is supported by positron emission tomography (PET) findings; for instance, when subjects are asked to generate a verb associated with a target noun, working memory is required to sort the possibilities (see Cortical-Subcortical Interactions in Executive Functions). When presented with the word *ball,* several semantic associates are automatically activated and the subject must decide which provides the most appropriate response given the target word and task demands. PET studies of phonological memory also reveal asymmetrical activation in the left hemisphere, although the frontal foci are restricted to more inferior aspects of the prefrontal cortex as well as the premotor cortex and Broca's area (Paulesu et al., 1993).

There are alternative dichotomies for hemispheric asymmetries in working memory. Ed Smith and John Jonides of the University of Michigan (1994) devised two PET studies to identify neural areas involved in working memory for either spatial locations or object identification (Figure 11.11). In one study, subjects viewed a display containing three dots and, after a 3-second delay, had to judge whether a probe circle encompassed one of the locations previously occupied by a dot. Here, the emphasis was on spatial working memory; prefrontal activation was significant only in the right hemisphere. In another study, subjects were asked to judge if a centrally presented shape matched one of

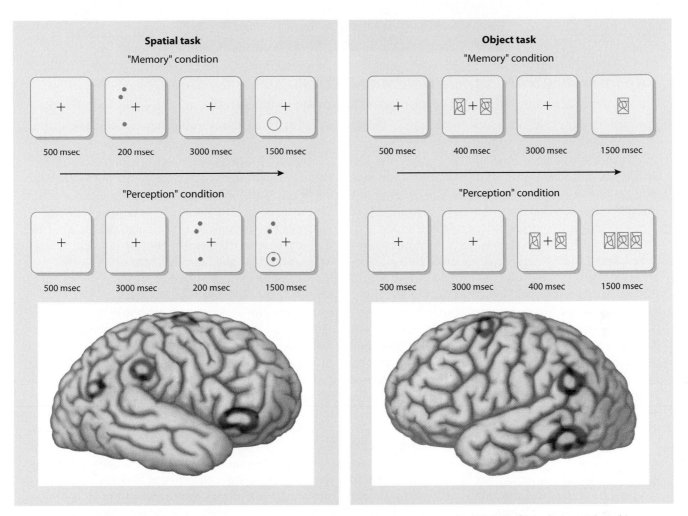

Figure 11.11 Subregions of working memory revealed by positron emission tomography (PET). **(Left)** In the spatial working-memory task, three dots appear. After a 3-second delay period, subjects judge whether a circle encompassed one of the dot's locations. The dots remain visible in the control, perception condition. **(Right)** In the object working-memory task, two abstract shapes are presented on each side of fixation. After the delay period, subjects judge whether a central object matches either of the previously seen stimuli. All three shapes are visible in the control condition. Activation foci during the memory conditions, after subtracting their respective perception conditions, suggested task-specific regions for working memory processes. Foci for the spatial task were in the RH including right prefrontal cortex. Activations during the object task were primarily in the LH.

two previously presented shapes. Location was not important; what counted was analyzing abstract shapes. The prefrontal activation shifted to the left hemisphere, which led to the proposal of a distinction between spatial memory (right hemisphere) and object working memory (left hemisphere).

Hemispheric dissociations are only the crudest cut of the pie. Electrophysiological studies of primates also suggested that distinct neural populations within a hemisphere may be associated with spatial and object working memory (Wilson et al., 1993). Cells in the more superior regions of the lateral prefrontal cortex were activated during the spatial task, whereas activation foci were more inferior during the object task. This superior-inferior distinction was confirmed in a human PET study where learned movements were based on either spatial location or the stimulus's color. Moreover, the posterior regions that were coactivated with the frontal foci provide further evidence that this compartmentalization of working memory systems may mirror the what-where distinction described in Chapter 5. Contrary to what one would predict based on the work of Smith and Jonides, the activation in both the spatial and object property tasks was most pronounced in the right hemisphere, suggesting a dominant role for this hemisphere in memory retrieval.

In summary, the notion that a unitary working-memory system maintains long-term representations does not appear tenable. Rather, the prefrontal cortex is linked to posterior memory systems in an ordered

An Interview with Patricia Goldman-Rakic Ph.D.

Dr. Goldman-Rakic is affiliated with the Department of Neurobiology at Yale University. She has studied prefrontal cortex at many levels, including the precise anatomy of its projections to the rest of the brain as well as its function, through neuroimaging research.

Authors: You have studied the frontal lobes for many years. At a time when most neurobiologists were examining the visual system in detail, you dove into the most complex cortical zone in the brain. How did your decision to study complex processes come about?

PG-R: I began my studies on the frontal cortex when Hubel and Wiesel were conducting their pioneering and celebrated work on the cat and monkey visual cortex. As interesting and influential as the visual system research was, I was never attracted to it. I was captivated by the opportunity to study the unexplored frontal lobe and was especially intrigued by the challenge of understanding its relation to higher cortical functions. It never occurred to me to be concerned with the complexity of the frontal lobes—I never thought of it as an obstacle; rather, it's an attractive feature of the subject.

Authors: When approaching a cognitive capacity in the setting of brain research, it is important to have a good test of that capacity. That is sometimes hard to do. How do you go about zeroing in on what tests you will use when studying how the frontal lobes enable this or that cognitive function?

PG-R: When I started in primate research, I used delayed-response tasks to assay functional involvement without fully appreciating their significance. At the time, the tests had a host of interpretations: They were considered tests of spatial memory, spatial discrimination, tests of attention, of motor preparation or kinesthetic discrimination, response perseveration, and tests of immediate memory. Bolstered in part by comparative research in humans and monkeys, I realized that delayed-response tests tap into a component of the working memory. Once I understood this connection, it reinforced the functional significance of delayed-response tests vis-à-vis human cognition and convinced me that the attempt to weave cellular and behavioral levels together would elucidate human brain and behavior. Once you take a process view of cognition, test design becomes theoretically driven rather than strictly empirical and descriptive.

Anyway, delayed response is an example of an "oldie but goodie"; this old test, devised by Walter Hunter in 1913, has achieved growing significance. These paradigms are used widely in studies of rodent learning and memory, in lesion and single-cell analysis of primate cortical function, and in human neuroimaging research. A common set of paradigms is what allows information from experiments in different laboratories to be cross-validated and built upon. But it's also productive to design new tasks when guided by a process theory of cognition. The most useful tests of brain and cognition research are those that comport with anatomical, physiological, and behavioral-clinical data bases and have cross-species validity.

Authors: Since the prefrontal cortex is so important for human cognition, how can we meaningfully study it in monkeys, where it represents such a small fraction of total cortical processes?

PG-R: Yes, the human cortex is larger than the monkey cortex. So the issue is whether one or more areas of a monkey's prefrontal cortex can be used for understanding the remaining areas of the macaque's prefrontal cortex and for understanding functional areas in the human prefrontal cortex not shared with the monkey. I believe that they can, and recent studies support that view. For example, the rhesus monkey has one area dedicated to visuospatial processing and a distinctly different area dedicated to processing the features of objects. PET and functional MRI studies in humans are showing this general compartmentalization of information processing to also be relevant when considering the functional role of different areas of prefrontal cortex in humans. The human obviously has additional modules for semantic processing that the monkey does not share. Yet, understanding how Baddeley's visuospatial sketchpad works (in monkeys) is likely to shed light on the workings of the phonological loop. We may also be able to approach the nature and organization of the central executive given the assumption that the functional architecture of the prefrontal cortex is conserved across species and that what is added in evolution are new or refined information-processing systems but not necessarily new principles of their organization and function.

manner, and regions that participate in working memory vary as a function of stimulus characteristics and task demands. Thus, as with many other brain systems, the mode of operation within a brain structure is consistent, but the areas activated within this system differ according to the tasks. For the prefrontal cortex, this operation temporarily activates the memory traces required to choose the appropriate action.

THE PREFRONTAL CORTEX PARTICIPATES IN OTHER MEMORY DOMAINS

The prefrontal cortex has also been implicated in many other memory tasks. In this section, we see how lesions in this area disrupt performance on these tasks. We then consider whether these problems reflect a common processing deficit, or whether they suggest a heterogeneity of function within the prefrontal cortex.

The Frontal Lobes and the Temporal Organization of Memory

Memory fades with time. It is impossible to remember all the details of our lives. We have a few memories of our childhood, perhaps a special birthday party, or a cross-country trip, or our first-grade classroom. But the details of most experiences become difficult to reconstruct as time passes. This information is not necessarily lost—it is absorbed into new experiences. We remember how to play Monopoly or how to bake a favorite cake, not by recalling our initial attempts but by repeating the activities. Practice makes perfect. By measuring and sifting flour, salt, and baking powder, by blending egg yolks and sugar, and by folding this mixture into the dry ingredients, we remember how to prepare the cake. The sequence for these actions must be executed in proper order for the cake to come out as planned. Something does not taste right if the sugar is added to the flour mix without first having been stirred with the eggs.

Even when it is unnecessary to remember a sequence of actions, memory is a temporal tagging process. Think about what you did yesterday. Perhaps the events have not yet faded from memory. Most likely, you can recall waking up and what you ate for breakfast, which classes you attended, where you ate lunch, and how you spent the evening, perhaps pouring over books in preparation for an exam or relaxing with friends. While no one required that the events be recalled in order, you probably used temporal cues to organize the information. Time continually moves forward, and our reconstruction of the past obeys this principle.

People with frontal lobe lesions may be impaired in their ability to organize and segregate events in memory (Milner, 1995). A *recency discrimination task* has been used to study temporal memory. In this task, the subjects are presented with study cards, each having two stimuli such as a pair of pictures. The subjects are instructed to study the pictures. Every so often, a probe card is presented with a question mark in addition to two pictures (Figure 11.12). The subject must decide which of the two pictures was seen most recently. For example, one of the pictures might have been on a study card presented four trials previously, whereas the other picture was on a study card shown thirty-two trials ago. For a control task, the procedure is modified: The probe card contains two pictures and the question mark, but only one of the two pictures was presented previously. Following the same instructions, the subject should choose that picture since, by definition, it is the one seen most recently. Note, though, that the task is really one of recognition memory. There is no need to evaluate the temporal position of the two choices.

Frontal lobe lesions were associated with a selective deficit in recency judgments. Patients performed as well as control subjects on the recognition-memory task, with both groups scoring above 90% correct. The recency task proved considerably more difficult, and, most importantly, this effect was even more marked in patients with frontal lobe lesions, which provided a single dissociation. Temporal lobe lesions did not affect performance on either task.

All the patients had undergone a unilateral brain operation for the treatment of severe, focal epilepsy. With this procedure, the extent of the surgically induced lesion can be limited and is precisely known. Hence one can distinguish between patients in whom the lesion encompassed dorsolateral prefrontal regions (area 46) from those in whom this area was spared. This analysis revealed that deficits in the recency task were restricted to patients in the dorsolateral group. Thus, the same area implicated in working-memory tasks, such as delayed response, is associated with the memory for temporal order. Moreover, a laterality effect was a function of stimuli. With word stimuli, the deficit was most evident in patients with left-hemisphere lesions, whereas right-hemisphere lobectomies were associated with impaired

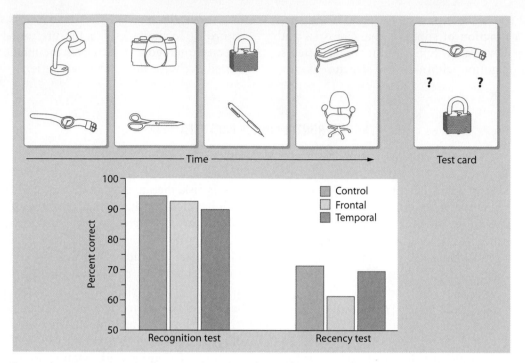

Figure 11.12 Recency memory is impaired in patients with prefrontal lesions. **(Top)** Subjects are presented with a series of cards, each one showing a pair of objects. The objects are flanked by question marks on test cards, and the subject must indicate which object was seen most recently. In the recency test, both objects on the test cards had been seen previously. In the item recognition test, only one object had appeared previously. **(Bottom)** The results revealed a single dissociation. Patients who had had a frontal lobectomy performed more poorly on the recency task compared to both control subjects and patients who had had a temporal lobectomy. The frontal group was not impaired on the item recognition task. Adapted from Milner, B., Corsi, P., and Leonard, G. (1991).

performance when drawings of common objects or abstract paintings were substituted for words.

A variant of the recency discrimination task is the self-ordered pointing task. Here, a series of n cards is presented, each with the same set of n objects (with n ranging from 6 to 12). The positions of the objects are shuffled about from card to card. The subject must point to a new object on each card. Thus, successful performance requires that the subject keep track of which items had been responded to on previous cards. As in the recency discrimination tasks, patients with frontal lesions make more errors than do control subjects and the deficit becomes more pronounced as the number of items per card increases.

The breakdown in the temporal structure of memory may account for more bizarre aspects of frontal lobe syndrome. For example, in a classic report of frontal lobe dysfunction, Wilder Penfield described a patient who was troubled by her inability to prepare her family's evening meal. This patient could remember the ingredients for dishes, but she could not organize her actions into a proper temporal sequence. Her behavior was haphazard. She might assemble all of the ingredients but become flustered and switch her preparation from one dish to the other, or mix up which items belonged to-

gether. No longer could she generate a temporal plan to achieve a coherent goal (Jasper, 1995).

Source Memory

Remembering when we learned a fact is a part of episodic memory. Our knowledge is not limited solely to content but includes the context in which learning took place. In essence, to remember a learning episode is to remember details about time and place, and the episode itself: who was present, what they wore, what kind of day it was. Sometimes source information is essential. The alert private detective has to recognize a face and recall the context in which that person was encountered. At other times these details may be irrelevant. It is not obvious what benefit there is in remembering that the professor who lectured on Freud and his theory of dream interpretation was wearing a bright-green suit. Are these details simply information cluttering up our cranial warehouse? Or can they facilitate memory? These obscure details are actually useful retrieval cues (Figure 11.13).

Source memory depends on the integrity of the frontal lobes. To show this, Larry Squire and his col-

Figure 11.13 *Source memory* refers to knowledge concerning the source of information or the context in which the information was learned. This student recalls the specific episode in which she learned about Freud's theory of the unconscious.

leagues (Janowsky et al., 1989) at the VA Medical Center in San Diego had control subjects and frontal lobe patients learn facts such as "The name of the dog on the Cracker Jacks box is Bingo" or "The body of water between Russia and Iran is the Caspian Sea." After a 6- to 8-day retention interval, the subjects were tested on these statements plus new ones with equally obscure facts or easy questions. Whenever subjects correctly answered a question, they were asked to recollect how they had learned the information. Subjects could answer that they had learned it during the previous testing session, or they could attribute it to something they learned in school or read in the paper. There was a dissociation between recall and source memory tasks. Patients performed as well as control subjects on the recall task but made more errors on the source task.

Healthy subjects also provided novel evidence linking the frontal lobes to source memory (Glisky et al., 1995). Although the patients never had a neurological disorder, they were given neuropsychological tests. According to their performance on tests designed to assess frontal lobe function, they were divided into groups based on "high" and "low" frontal function (the "low" group still performed higher than patients who had incurred a neurological insult in the frontal lobes). A similar division was based on their performance on tests designed to assess temporal lobe function. The two tests had minimal correlation. Subjects who scored well on

the frontal test did not necessarily score well on the temporal lobe test.

In the primary experiment, subjects were tested on item and source memory. During the study phase, the participants heard sixty sentences expressing common events (e.g., "The boy went to the store to buy some apples and oranges"). Half of the sentences were read by a woman and the other half by a man. Item memory was tested by pairing a study sentence with a novel sentence and asking subjects to choose the sentence they heard in the study phase. Source memory was tested by having the subjects hear the same sentence read by both speakers and then judge which voice matched the original presentation.

The results, presented in Figure 11.14, reveal a double dissociation. High temporal lobe function was associated

Figure 11.14 Double dissocation on tests of item and source memory in healthy elderly adults who were rated as having "high" or "low" function on tests of frontal and temporal lobe function. Low frontal lobe function was associated with poor performance on the source-memory test. Low temporal lobe function was associated with relatively poor performance on the item-memory test. Adapted from Glisky et al. (1995).

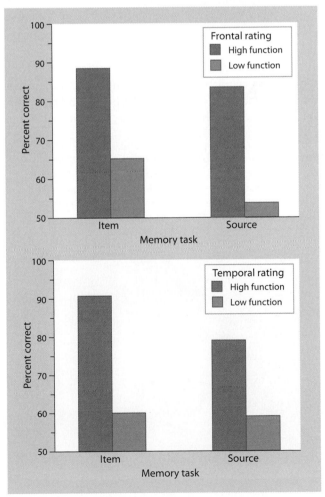

with good performance on the item-memory test, whereas the two frontal lobe groups did not differ significantly. In contrast, only the frontal lobe groups differed on the source-memory task. Participants rated as having low frontal function performed barely above chance,

whereas those whose function was rated high did considerably better. Thus, healthy people dissociate item and source memory, and the two tasks correlate with differences in temporal and frontal lobe function.

PROCESSING DEFICITS FOLLOWING FRONTAL LOBE DAMAGE

It is not clear whether deficits associated with frontal lobe dysfunction can be linked to a common processing deficit. One theme emphasized by theorists is that frontal lobes are essential for organizing a task's temporal aspects. Temporal processing, explicitly tested in recency discrimination tasks, indicates that the frontal lobes play a role in temporally tagging information (Figure 11.15). Not only do we encode the content of a stimulus, but also an automatic marker linked to this memory indicates when it developed. In many memory tasks, it is not essential to retrieve these time markers, and thus frontal lobe patients will not show any impairments. For example, in recognition-memory tasks, a decision can be made without having any knowledge of when the familiar stimulus was seen previously. It is sufficient to recognize that one stimulus is familiar and the other is novel.

But temporal tagging does not sufficiently explain other memory problems tied to frontal lobe lesions. For example, in delayed-response tasks, baited and empty locations are within the animal's view; it has to remember

which location has the reward. During a session the animal has associated both locations with many stimuli; successful performance involves referring to a temporal record to determine which location has the most recent temporal tag. But this temporal processing is different from what is found in recency judgments where the comparison is between the time of two events. Moreover, the frontal deficit in remembering context is not limited to the temporal dimension. Source problems appeared when subjects judged which speaker had uttered sentences rather than when they judged recency.

Heterogeneity of Function or Common Processing Mode?

An alternative view is to consider that the prefrontal cortex involves a heterogenous collection of processing systems (Petrides, 1994). The prefrontal cortex is expansive and encompasses many cytoarchitectonic areas, the numbered regions in Broadmann's map. A consistent feature in other cortical regions, such as the occipital and parietal cortex, is specialization: the cortical areas perform specific operations which support certain tasks. Doesn't it make sense to assume that the prefrontal cortex will similarly entail a modular organization? One area might be for temporal tagging, and other regions may be essential for working-memory functions like the sustained activation of recently encountered stimuli.

This hypothesis certainly has merit, but it is equally valuable to look for parsimonious theories of frontal lobe function that can tie together these disparate hypotheses. If we simply list tasks without analyzing their operations, we could end up with a catalogue of which brain areas are associated with which tasks, without understanding what goes on within the areas. Moreover, we frequently see that a neural structure performs a common operation across a variety of task domains. For example, in Chapter 9, we reviewed the hypothesis that the categorical-coordinate distinction could account for laterality effects in both perception and memory and in

Figure 11.15 It has been hypothesized that prefrontal cortex provides a temporal tag to each item that enters working memory. These tags are essential for making recency judgments and can also be used to retrieve the source of the information.

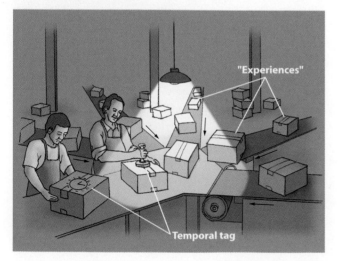

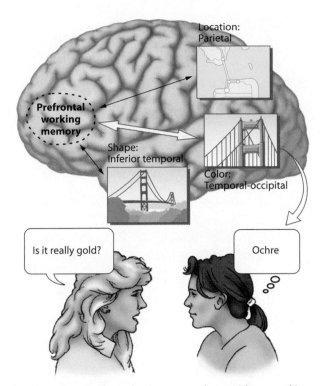

Figure 11.16 Prefrontal cortex not only provides a working-memory buffer, but may also use an inhibitory mechanism to highlight the information that is most relevant to the current task demands. When the subject is asked about the color of the Golden Gate Bridge, information regarding the location and shape of the bridge is inhibited.

Chapter 10, the idea that the cerebellum operates as an internal timing system for action and perception. Despite this commonality in terms of an area's computational contribution, the exact location within that neural structure can be expected to depend on the stimulus and task demands. In other words, inputs and outputs may project to different subregions of the structure, but the information may be operated upon in a consistent manner. In the working-memory discussion, we found that one function—sustaining representations during a delay period—was carried out by distinct subregions within the lateral prefrontal cortex. Can a common operation be identified to account for working memory, source memory, and recency memory?

Building on the model in Figure 11.16, Art Shimamura of the University of California (1995) proposed that a common processing requirement for tasks associated with the prefrontal cortex is to allocate attentional resources. Consider a task where the subject is presented with a stimulus and must remember its location. Assume that the stimulus activates features corresponding to color, shape, position, and perhaps a temporal record of when it was recently encountered. In the working-

memory model, a transient file is established whose contents can be sustained.

The task requires that some information be made more salient than others. In a spatial delayed-response task, the critical information is the object's location. In an object version of this task, the critical information is the stimulus's shape. Shimamura maintained that the frontal lobe not only establishes and maintains the transient record, but also ensures that the correct information is appropriately amplified. Viewed in this way, the prefrontal cortex can be conceptualized as a dynamic filtering mechanism. The frontal cortex is a repository of representations and selects information most relevant for meeting the task's demands. Working memory is more than the passive sustaining of representations; it requires an attentional component in which the subject's goals modify the salience of sources of information.

Can a deficit in attention account for problems in source-memory tasks? Perhaps, if we consider that memory for context is generally secondary to memory for content. We rarely need to recall where we learned something; it is usually sufficient to remember the information itself. We can successfully bake a cake by remembering how to combine the ingredients without recalling that we first learned to make this recipe in the *Joy of Cooking*. (But when we forget a step, it is useful to know where the information can be obtained.) What with the asymmetry between memory for content and memory for context, it is reasonable to suppose that source memory requires disproportionate attention. Content representations can be expected to be more salient and thus less sensitive to a loss of attention. Greater resources are required when we must ignore content and attempt to retrieve context. When we read a sentence, we derive its meaning while paying little attention to superficial aspects such as what font it is printed in or where it is in the text. We can recall this surface information, but only when we make an effort to encode it.

The hypothesis that the frontal lobes play a critical role in selecting task-relevant information can account for frontal lobe patients' problems with the Wisconsin Card Sorting Task, in which subjects sort multidimensional stimuli. They learn by trial and error; they hypothesize which information is relevant and which is not. Subjects, then, must learn to attend to the correct dimension while filtering the other two dimensions. Frontal lobe patients have difficulty with this. They are especially prone to perseverative errors—continuing to sort by an old rule even when told it is no longer appropriate. This tendency can be viewed as a failure in selection. After learning to attend to one dimension, a person with frontal lobe damage continues to focus on it.

Cortical-Subcortical Interactions in Executive Functions

Frontal lobes in executive functions do not exist in isolation; other regions have been linked to them. For example, the parietal lobe participates in spatial attention, ensuring that we focus on the most important stimuli. And the hippocampus can be conceived of as an executive coordinating system for linking representations across cortical areas.

The relation of the frontal lobes and the basal ganglia and cerebellum has attracted extensive interest. Researchers question traditional views that limit these two subcortical structures to motor control, contributing to the preparation, implementation, and monitoring of movements. Rather, the basal ganglia and cerebellum may form an integrated network with the prefrontal cortex subserving the executive functions of higher cognition.

The evidence for a more cognitive role for the basal ganglia and cerebellum comes from three directions. First, using a retrograde labeling technique, Peter Strick of the Veteran's Administration Hospital in Syracuse, New York, explored subcortical projections to the monkey's dorsolateral prefrontal cortex (Middleton and Strick, 1994). The method works transynaptically; thus, we can confirm that areas within the basal ganglia and cerebellum innervate the dorsolateral cortex via their projections to the thalamus. Second, PET studies consistently show activation in the basal ganglia, and especially the cerebellum, even when the experimental and control tasks require the same amount of overt movement. Activation is greater in the cerebellum when subjects generate a semantic associate to a word (e.g., *eat* to *apple*) in comparison to a control condition where subjects simply repeat the target word (e.g., *apple*). Third, patients with Parkinson's disease and cerebellar disorders perform poorly on neuropsychological assessment tests of frontal lobe function.

The contributions of the subcortical components of cortico–basal ganglia and cortico-cerebellar networks remain unclear. One possibility is that the frontal-like problems in patients with basal ganglia or cerebellar pathology are indirect. Hypometabolism has been observed in the frontal lobe following such pathology. Thus, the deficits may not reflect abnormal processing within the basal ganglia or cerebellum; rather, they may come from secondary alterations in frontal lobe activity.

A second possibility is that the basal ganglia and cerebellum contribute in a direct way to the executive functions of the frontal lobe. Here the analytic tools of cognitive neuroscience are promising. Neuropsychological tests such as the Wisconsin Card Sorting Task only provide crude comparisons of functional deficits. The problem is that the task is quite complex. Subjects must evaluate multidimensional stimuli, keep an internal record of their most recent responses, generate rule-sorting hypotheses, and be flexible about altering hypotheses based on feedback provided after each response. Problems with this task could arise from an inability to perform the operations. More sensitive, theoretically motivated tasks are required to isolate the component operations.

Adrian Owen and his colleagues (1993) at Cambridge University identified one intriguing dissociation between frontal and parkinsonian patients by using the two tasks in Figure A. In both tasks, the Wisconsin Card Sorting Task was preserved: Subjects were required to discover that the sorting rule changed from one dimension to another. The key modification in this experiment was that stimuli did not simultaneously vary in all dimensions. For instance, during the early trials, the target dimension might be shape, the irrelevant dimension color, and the constant might be the size. The conditions differed in how the dimensions were manipulated when the sorting rule changed. In the perseveration condition, size would become the target dimension and shape the irrelevant dimension. Thus, the subjects could continue to erroneously respond on the basis of shape. In the learned irrelevance condition, the target would become color and the irrelevant dimension would be the size. With this condition, it would not be possible to perseverate since shape is now constant. Rather, errors could be due to either an inability to respond to a previously irrelevant dimension or a bias to respond on the basis of the novel dimension.

In comparison to control subjects, patients with frontal lesions were selectively impaired on the perseveration condition. After the shift, they continued to respond on the basis of the dimension that had been the

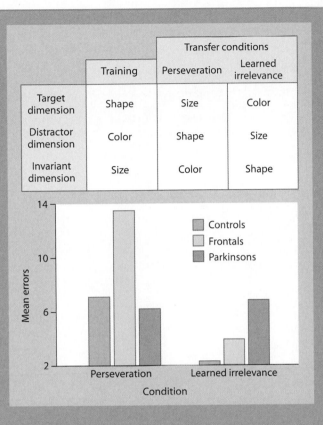

| | Training | Transfer conditions | |
		Perseveration	Learned irrelevance
Target dimension	Shape	Size	Color
Distractor dimension	Color	Shape	Size
Invariant dimension	Size	Color	Shape

Dissociation of the contributions of the frontal lobe and basal ganglia to set shifting. Both tasks are variants of the Wisconsin Card Sorting Task. Subjects must learn the correct sorting rule through trial and error. On each trial, they are shown a card with two stimuli that vary on two of the three dimensions; shape, color, and size. The value on the third dimension is fixed for a given condition. After they complete training, they are tested on two transfer conditions. In the perseveration condition, the target dimension becomes the irrelevant dimension after the shift. The new target dimension was not varied prior to the shift. In the learned irrelevance condition, the target dimension had been the irrelevant dimension prior to the shift. The new irrelevant dimension had not been varied prior to the shift. Frontal patients show selective impairment on the perseveration condition. Patients with Parkinson's disease show selective impairment on the learned irrelevance condition. Adapted from Owen et al. (1993).

target, perhaps reflecting an inability to inhibit recently activated and task-relevant information. These patients were not impaired on the learned irrelevance condition. In contrast, parkinsonian patients receiving L-dopa medication exhibited the opposite profile. They made few perseverative errors but had difficulty in responding to a previously irrelevant dimension. Whether this reflects excessive inhibition of this dimension or a bias to respond to the novel dimension requires further study. Nonetheless, this study elegantly demonstrates how superficial similarities on standard neuropsychological tests might arise from deficits in dissociable component operations.

A similar strategy is being pursued to tease apart the relation between the prefrontal cortex and the cerebellum (Fiez et al., 1996). Julie Fiez of Washington University in St. Louis noted that, based on several PET studies, tasks that require verbal rehearsal are associated with higher blood flow in inferior regions of lateral prefrontal cortex (areas 44 and 45) and the right cerebellum. Fiez proposed that this network might constitute part of the phonological loop of Baddeley's work-ing-memory model. A processing model of the phonological loop sketched in Figure B consists of three operations: A phonological store that contains phonological representations of words, an articulatory process that refreshes these representations through internal rehearsal, and for visual stimuli, a recoding process that translates written letter strings into phonological representations. So, with a visual list of words to remember, we recode stimuli into phonological representations and silently articulate the list as a means of keeping the words active in working memory. If stimuli are presented auditorally, there is no need for recoding; the stimuli activate representations sustained through internal rehearsal.

We can now ask whether neural structures are associated with these component operations of verbal working memory. Previous work had suggested a parietal locus for the phonological store. Fiez explored functional dissociations between the prefrontal cortex and cerebellum. In particular, she proposed that areas 44 and 45 in the left hemisphere are essential for phonological recoding. In support of this, these areas

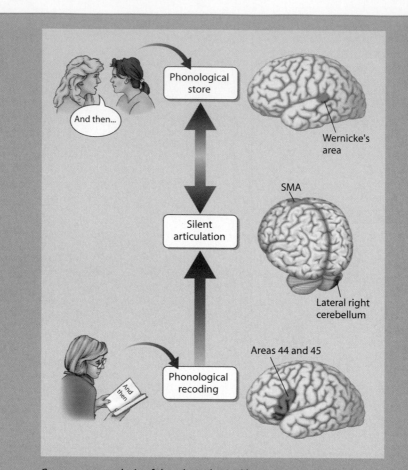

Component analysis of the phonological loop system of working memory. For the task of remembering a list of read words, the phonological loop is hypothesized to be composed of (at least) three components associated with the premotor/prefrontal cortex, cerebellum, and posterior region of the left hemisphere. The recoding process would not be required if the stimuli were presented auditorally.

are active, not only in working-memory tasks that may depend on internal rehearsal, but also on tasks that require a phonological judgment (e.g., is the *e* pronounced as a long or short vowel in the word *held*). In contrast, the cerebellum's role may be restricted to rehearsal. Numerous PET studies revealed that similar structures are active during overt and covert (or imagined) movement. Thus, the cerebellum may be activated during silent articulation in a manner similar to its contribution to overt speech.

This analysis can account for the cerebellum's being activated in many PET studies of working memory, even when the amount of overt movement is equated in experimental and control tasks. What remains to be seen is whether the cerebellum's role in this aspect of working memory is essential, or simply part of a network for internal speech. If the latter, the cerebellum's role would still remain closely linked to its motor functions. Yet it may be that the capability to sustain phonological representations depends on internal rehearsal. As such, we might expect that patients with cerebellar lesions are impaired on phonological analyses.

These questions await further study. For now, we can appreciate how cognitive neuroscience has opened new frontiers for exploring how the brain supports complex behaviors. Executive functions do not reside in a single structure but result from the interplay of diverse cortical and subcortical neural systems.

The filtering hypothesis also offers a way to appreciate the role of the frontal lobe in tasks where memory demands are minimal. Frontal lobe patients display heightened interference on the Stroop task. For the Stroop task, subjects are shown a list of colored words; the words spell color names such as *red, green,* or *blue.* In the congruent condition, the colors of the words correspond to their names; in the incongruent one, the word names and colors do not correspond (see Figure 3.26). With years of reading experience, we have a strong urge to read words even when the task requires us to ignore them in favor of color; thus, everyone is slower in responding to incongruent stimuli in comparison with congruent stimuli. This difference is even greater in patients with frontal lobe lesions.

Filtering as an Inhibitory Process

Dynamic filtering can influence the contents of information processing in at least two distinct ways. One is to accentuate the attended information. For example, when we attend to a location, our sensitivity to detect a stimulus at that location is enhanced. Or, we can selectively attend by excluding irrelevant information. Stroop interference can be eliminated by squinting one's eyes so the words are no longer legible. As seen in times of budgetary crises, the hypotheses are not mutually exclusive. If we have fixed resources, allocating resources to one thing places a limit on what is available for others.

In behavioral tasks, it is often difficult to distinguish between facilitatory and inhibitory modes of control. But electrophysiological studies indicate that losing inhibitory control may be a more appropriate descriptor of frontal lobe dysfunction. Robert Knight of the University of California recorded the evoked potentials in groups of patients with localized neurological disorders (Knight and Grabowsky, 1995). In the simplest experiment, subjects were presented with tones, and no response was required. As might be expected, the evoked responses were attenuated in patients with lesions in the temporo-parietal cortex in comparison to control subjects. This difference was apparent about 30 msec after stimulus onset, the time when stimuli would be expected to reach the primary auditory cortex. The attenuation presumably reflects tissue loss in the region that generates the evoked signal. A more curious aspect is in Figure 11.17: Patients with frontal lobe lesions have enhanced evoked responses. This enhancement was not seen in the evoked responses at subcortical levels; the effect did not reflect a generalized increase in sensory responsivity but was limited to the cortex.

The failure to inhibit irrelevant information was more apparent when the subjects were instructed to attend to auditory signals in one ear and ignore similar sounds in the opposite ear, with the attended ear varied between blocks. In this way, one can assess the evoked response to identical stimuli under different attentional sets (e.g., response to left-ear sounds when they are attended to or ignored). With normal subjects, these responses, diverge at about 100 msec; the evoked response to the attended signal becomes greater. This difference is absent in patients with prefrontal lesions, especially for stimuli presented to the ear contralateral to the lesion. What happens is that the unattended stimulus receives a heightened response, which accords with the notion that frontal lobes modulate the salience of perceptual signals by inhibiting unattended information. We are bombarded with stimuli: Our ability to respond appropriately requires that we select information relevant to the task.

In the study just described, we can see inhibition operating to minimize the impact of irrelevant perceptual information. This same mechanism can be applied to memory tasks for which information must be internally maintained. Again, consider the monkey attempting to perform the delayed-response task. The monkey views the target being placed in one of the food wells, and then the blind is closed during the delay period. The monkey's mind does not just shut down; it sees and hears the blind being drawn, looks about the room during the delay interval, and perhaps contemplates its hunger. All such intervening events can distract the animal and cause it to lose track of which location is baited. To succeed, it must ignore the distractions and sustain the representation of its forthcoming response. We have all experienced failures in similar situations. A friend gives us her telephone number, but we forget it. The problem is not a failure to encode the number. Something else captures our attention. We fail to block out the distraction. This point is underscored by the fact that primates with prefrontal lesions perform better on delayed-response tasks when the room is darkened during the delay (Malmo, 1942) or when given drugs that decrease distractibility.

Failure of inhibition also can account for the dissociation between recognition and recency memory. Subjects must remember all stimuli since they do not know which will be tested in probe trials. As we encode each stimulus, we pay attention to it, with one cost being the inhibition of previous stimuli. The degree of activation of a representation is inversely related to how long ago the stimulus was presented. As shown in Figure 11.18, recency judgments can be made by comparing the

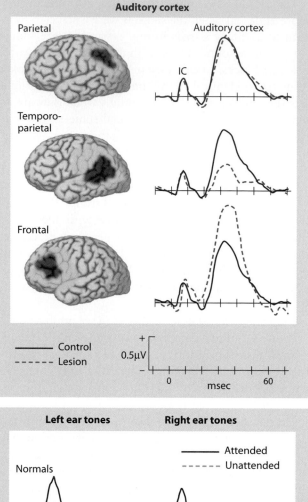

Figure 11.17 Evoked potentials reveal filtering deficits in patients with lesions in the lateral prefrontal cortex. **(Top)** Evoked responses to auditory clicks in three groups of neurological patients. The subjects were not required to respond to the clicks. The first positive peak occurs at about 8 msec and reflects neural activity in the inferior colliculus. The second positive peak occurs around 30 msec, the P30, reflecting neural responses in the primary auditory cortex. Both responses are normal in patients with parietal damage. The second peak is reduced in patients with temporo-parietal damage, reflecting the loss of neurons in the primary auditory cortex. The auditory cortex response is amplified in patients with frontal damage, suggesting a loss of inhibition from frontal lobe to temporal lobe. Note that the evoked response for control subjects is repeated in each panel. **(Bottom)** Difference waves for attended and unattended auditory signals. Subjects were instructed to monitor tones in either the left or right ear. The evoked response to the unattended tones is subtracted from the evoked response to the attended tones. In healthy individuals, the effects of attention are seen at approximately 100 msec, marked by a larger negativity (N100). Patients with right prefrontal lesions show no attention effect for contralesional tones presented in the left ear but show a normal effect for ipsilesional tones. Patients with left prefrontal lesions show reduced attention effects for both contralateral and ipsilateral tones. Adapted from Knight and Grabowecky (1995).

magnitude of the two target items. Whichever item has the strongest residual activation would be judged most recent. For normal subjects, inhibition could quickly lower the activation of distinct items. But for frontal lobe patients, the loss of inhibition would result in lingering activations and render such judgments difficult. A paradox is that they would not have a problem with recognition because their memory is so high.

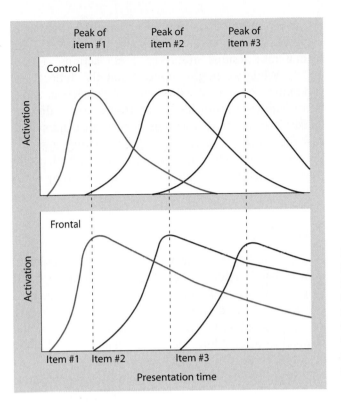

Peak of item #1   Peak of item #2   Peak of item #3

Control

Activation

Frontal

Activation

Item #1   Item #2   Item #3

Presentation time

Figure 11.18 When a subject is presented with a series of items, activation for each item decays. A loss of inhibitory mechanisms following frontal lobe damage will lead to a slower decay process. Judgments on a recency-memory task may be based on a comparison of the residual activation of the series of stimuli. In healthy people, the rapid decay of activation allows the temporal tag for each item to be distinct. In frontal lobe patients, the sustained activation leads to errors due to the similar activation states associated with successive items.

ACTION IN THE SOCIAL DOMAIN

Choosing how to act does not simply require discriminating between incoming stimuli. It is also essential to integrate them with current goals. Consider the daily commuter as she chugs along the highway during the evening rush hour. Certain actions will be dictated by familiar visual signs along the route. The golden arches of the neighborhood McDonald's, the Main Street sign, and the arrows signaling the exit near her home indicate that she must move to the right lane and begin to decelerate. These are familiar stimuli and her actions are habitual. She may not even be aware of her preparation for taking the exit as she tunes in to the latest news report on the radio. Habitual actions are carried out in conjunction with the appearance of each familiar landmark.

Even in this routine it is essential to maintain flexibility for alternative actions. Sometimes an external cue provides the critical trigger. Our commuter scans ahead and notices that the traffic is at a standstill as emergency vehicles drive along the shoulder lane. An accident must have happened—this is sure to add at least 40 minutes to the normal commute. Figuring that the surface road traffic will be moving, she quickly moves to the right to take the Central Avenue exit. Or, flexibility may be necessary because of a change in internal goals. It's Wednes-

day evening, her kids' time for soccer practice. She must drive past her usual exit to reach the playing fields down the road. If there is a particularly interesting news report, she may suddenly find herself turning off the highway at her familiar exit, not remembering the atypical goal required this evening.

Internal goals reflect personal desires and aspirations, and also can be socially mediated (Figure 11.19). The commuter is eager to get home. On an evening when her last meeting ran an hour too long, she considers using the lane reserved for carpools. But after mulling it over, she stays in the slow lanes filled with single drivers. She dreads the $250 ticket that she might get if she is caught by a cop, not to mention the scorn from fellow drivers for this socially inappropriate action.

Failures of Inhibition in the Social Domain

Frontal lobes play a critical role in how we select among a multitude of information. In an experimental situation such as the Wisconsin Card Sorting Task, the selection is choosing among the visual dimensions of the playing cards. Here, selection requires filtering irrelevant visual information. In other situations, selection is based on evaluating external cues within a social

Figure 11.19 Our behavior reflects the combined influences of our personal desires and social constraints. The driver is tempted to take the carpool lane to get home on time, but is restrained by her fear of the potential fine as well as the scorn of the other drivers.

context. Again, we find that lesions of the frontal lobes impair this ability.

Many anecdotes demonstrate how the behavior of frontal lobe patients can be dominated by perceptual information. F. Lhermitte of the Hôpital de la Salpêtrière in Paris demonstrated a black humor for exploiting this tendency (Lhermitte, 1983; Lhermitte et al., 1986). He would invite a patient to a meeting and place a hammer, nail, and picture on a table in the entryway. When encountered by this array of objects, a frontal lobe patient might pick up the hammer and nail and hang the picture on the wall. In another instance, Lhermitte put a hypodermic needle on his desk, dropped his trousers, and turned his back to the patient. While most would consider filing ethical charges in this situation, the patient was unfazed. He simply picked up the needle and gave his doctor a healthy jab in the buttocks!

Lhermitte coined the term *utilization behavior* to describe the fact that the patients demonstrated an exaggerated dependency on environmental cues in guiding their behavior. Their gestures indicate intact knowledge of the uses of the objects such as the hammer or needle. What is lacking is an ability to evaluate the social context and determine if the action is appropriate. Further evidence of this reliance on external cues is that frontal lobe patients are prone to *imitative behaviors*. In one study, Lhermitte sat opposite a patient and, without explanation, produced gestures. Some were innocuous: folding paper, combing his hair, or tapping his leg. Oth-

ers were socially inappropriate: thumbing his nose, chewing paper, or kneeling in prayer. The patients with frontal lobe lesions mimicked these actions (Figure 11.20). While we might suppose that this reflects the reverential status of doctors, control subjects and patients with lesions outside the prefrontal cortex did not engage in such imitative actions. Indeed, we can imagine that the control subjects were contemplating engaging the services of a new physician. Frontal lobe patients, in comparison, did not question or seem puzzled by Lhermitte's violation of social conventions.

The Social Mediation of Behavior

Recognizing that many behaviors are socially mediated affords new insights to the adjustment problems faced by patients such as Phineas Gage. Gage's frequent outbursts of anger and profanity, coupled with his inability to recognize these behaviors, eventually turned public sympathies against him. He could not sustain a plan for how to function in a social world, impervious to his plight as he descended into a transient state of existence.

A modern Phineas Gage also lost his ability to make decisions within a social context (Damasio, 1994). Elliot had a brain tumor that bilaterally invaded his brain's *orbital surface,* the cortical region just above the orbits of the eyes. After surgery, he demonstrated superior intellectual abilities, performing above-normal on long-term-memory and working-memory tasks. He even outperformed most age-matched control subjects on the Wisconsin Card Sorting Task. Nonetheless, Elliot could not perform the routines necessary to survive in today's world. He needed prompting to get up and go to work. He lost all sense of a schedule, and his fellow workers found him immersed in a mundane task for hours on end. After losing his job, he initiated risky ventures, against the advice of friends and family; he eventually went bankrupt. As striking as Elliot's lost sense of social norms was his personal detachment from his problems. He had no difficulty recounting the minutest details of his many failings, but spoke of them as if he were a dispassionate observer—a striking dissociation between decision making in the abstract and decision making about personal and social involvement.

A similar loss of social guidance of behavior can be observed in primates after they have suffered lesions to their prefrontal cortex. While social stratification is implicit in human society, animals like the rhesus monkeys live in a highly structured social setting. Each animal has an assigned place in the social hierarchy, a position mainly inherited at birth. Social position determines many behaviors such as access to food and

(a)

(b)

(c)

(d)
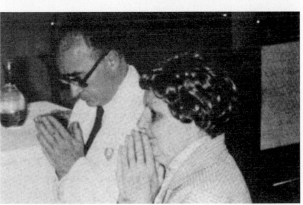

(e)

(f)

(g)

Figure 11.20   Imitative and utilization behaviors are two signs of prefrontal damage, usually associated with lesions in the ventromedial region. **(a–d)** Imitative behaviors. The patient mimicks the physician making a threatening gesture (a), putting on spectacles (b), smelling a flower (c), and praying (d). **(e–g)** Utilization behaviors. When objects are placed in front of him, the patient puts on three pairs of glasses (e) or proceeds to use the makeshift urinal (f–g).

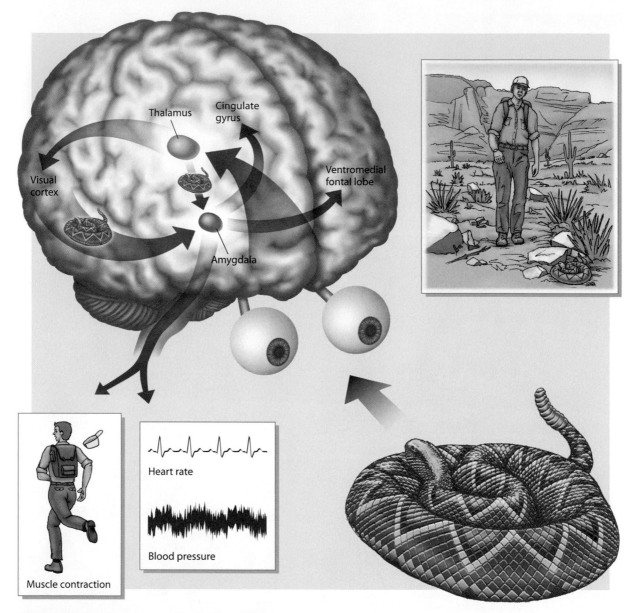

Figure 11.21 Emotional processing in the amygdala projects to the ventromedial prefrontal cortex and the anterior cingulate. When the hiker chances upon the rattlesnake, the visual information activates affective memories through the projections to the amygdala. These memories not only produce autonomic changes such as an increase in heart rate and blood pressure, but also can influence subsequent actions through the projections to the prefrontal cortex. The hiker will use this emotion-laden information in choosing his next action: Turn and run? Or slowly move around the snake? Adapted from Ledoux, J.E. (1994).

sexual partners—critical factors considering that morbidity rates are high in natural settings. The social status of animals that receive lesions of the orbitofrontal cortex plummets immediately (Myers et al., 1973). They are treated as outcasts by the group, incurring aggression and being forced to withdraw to a solitary existence. It is not clear what cues the healthy animals use to

reject the lesioned animals so quickly. Aberrant behaviors can be seen after surgery. The animals demonstrate restlessness, aimless pacing, occasional displays of aggression, and a failure to groom themselves. It is likely that, following frontal surgery, the lesioned animals cannot act in a manner appropriate for their position and therefore pose a threat to the social order.

DAMASIO'S SOMATIC MARKER HYPOTHESIS

Antonio Damasio of the University of Iowa (1994) articulated a theory of how social interactions can influence responses. Our everyday actions do not occur in an abstract, impersonal state; we know that they have personal and social consequences. We evaluate information not only with respect to logic but also with respect to how it helps to achieve personal goals. Yet personal achievement does not exist in a social vacuum. Acquiring wealth or academic honors is desired for its effect on our social position; a wealthy person can be admired and envied in our materialistic society or an honored professor esteemed by colleagues.

Damasio's theory is motivated by the fact that the frontal lobes, particularly the ventromedial region, is strongly interconnected with limbic structures tied to the emotions (Figure 11.21). Damasio dismissed the belief that reasoning and emotion are separate cognitive domains. He maintained that reasoning is guided by the emotional evaluation of an action's consequences, an idea captured by the main title to his book, *Descartes' Error*. Descartes argued for a duality of the mind and the body: The mind is a conscious entity of pure reasoning and thinking and the body is limited by its striving to satisfy physical needs. For Damasio, such a segregation is a myth. The mind is an adaptation designed to better our chances of satisfying physical and psychological needs. To do so, it must be informed by neural structures that process affective responses to stimuli and memories.

Consider this scenario. It is Friday night in late April of the year 2000 and you have planned to take three friends to the last Chicago Bulls game of the year, the game that Michael Jordan has announced will be his absolute last. You were lucky to be one of the 5000 fans who was selected in the lottery to purchase four tickets, and everyone you meet has been green with envy. No matter that your tickets are up in the nosebleed section, while the less fortunate will be sitting in the comfort of their living rooms and watching the game on television. You have the opportunity to see the action live, to be part of the excitement, and to know that this event will be talked about for years, a tale to relate to your progeny. As the evening approaches, though, a freak late-winter storm sweeps off Lake Michigan and covers the streets with ice. What do you do (Figure 11.22)?

Radio newscasters report severe traffic jams and warn everyone to stay home. Having experienced many midwestern storms, you can anticipate what the drive will be like. Not only will it be a challenge to avoid skidding on the ice, but there will be the terror of dodging cars sent spinning by drivers overeager to apply their brakes. But this is The Game. You have waited 5 weeks for this event. And there is the social pressure, the immediate one and the one with future consequences. How can you call your friends and tell them that you were too nervous to drive the car? They know that you didn't hesitate to drive through a blizzard last winter to get to Colorado for skiing (ignoring the fact that this decision led to a large dent in your front fender). And

Figure 11.22 Choosing an action can be characterized as an internal tug of war.

"Make the wise choice, my son. Think of the dangerous roads! You can stay home and watch the game on TV in comfort, have a pizza, enjoy yourself. Call your friends. Tell them you don't want to drive. Be honest. Do the right thing. It's not worth the risk. Remember the last time you went out on a night like this? If you go out tonight I'm sure something even worse will happen! It's ok to stay in tonight. I'm sure your friends will understand. Be a good boy, etc., etc...

"C'mon, don't be a wimp! What'sa matter with you? You can make it, what's a little ice and snow? Are you going to let your friends down? Here's your chance to be a real hero. Not only do you have tickets to the game but you can brave the worst storm in years to get there! Watch the game on TV? What a joke! What are people going to think? They're gonna laugh, that's what! You can't back out now. C'mon show some guts! Just get in the car and go. It's not that bad outside. Just do it! Etc., etc....

think about the embarrassment that you'll feel tomorrow when all the friends you've been taunting all week about your good fortune hear that you missed the game.

The situation requires rational decision making, an analysis of the costs and benefits of your options, which are played out in working memory. While you have to consider the future, you also have to base your decision on knowledge accumulated from the past. You can anticipate the excitement at the coliseum because you have watched many games in the past. You can imagine the challenges of the drive because you have driven in similar conditions. You can predict the whining pleas of your fearless friend who will taunt you for being chicken. A rational economist might perform a cost-benefit analysis of the possible scenarios. You have to compare the thrill of being at the game with the fear of being in an accident. You reason through the choices and decide.

Damasio argued that the ideal of a rational decision maker is not appropriate for an organism that continually faces choices. The choices may not be as dramatic or stressful as in this example, but we constantly decide between courses of action. And these decisions frequently must be made quickly. We need a mechanism that will help sort through the options, a mechanism that provides a common metric for evaluating options with respect to their potential benefit.

Damasio referred to this mechanism as the *somatic marker*. Somatic events are bodily sensations; thus, a somatic marker implies a link to a visceral experience. For Damasio, the phrase *gut feeling* is almost literal. When we watch a horror movie, our reaction is not detached and purely intellectual; it invokes a physical reaction. Our hands may become sweaty or we might experience a tightening in the muscles of our face and stomach. In a

similar way, our memories of these events reactivate these visceral reactions, or at least our memories of these visceral reactions. An upcoming decision calls for activating representations of similar events experienced in the past: Imagine sitting in the stands or driving on an icy road. But these memories are not generated as abstract entities. Rather, they are imbued with emotional associations. How did similar events make us feel in the past, and what were the affective consequences of our prior experiences? Whereas common wisdom tells us not to let our emotions get "in the way," Damasio argued that affective memories are essential for decisions. They allow us to sift through options, alert us to plans linked to negative feelings, and bias us toward ones connected with positive feelings. Somatic markers rapidly narrow the options by automatically anticipating the affective consequences of each action. They may not enable us to make an unambiguous choice, but they constrain the playing field. Working memory is a limited resource. We cannot consciously mull over the multitude of options that any situation offers. Somatic markers focus on restricted possibilities (Figure 11.23).

The intimate connections between the ventromedial frontal cortex and the limbic system are the pathway through which somatic markers mediate decision. The hippocampus and amygdala have been linked to memory formation. The hippocampus is a general-purpose device for forming associations between stimuli: A red traffic light is linked to cars stopping. The amygdala, though, has a narrower memory function. This limbic structure may not be essential for forming associations, but provides an emotional tag to go with the associations. When a representation is activated by stimuli, connections between the limbic and frontal systems ac-

Options:
1. Accept her invitation
2. Gracefully decline with excuse of back pain
3. Decline but ask her to sit down for a drink
4. Tell her "No way, you're a terrible dancer!"
5. Run away

Dance?

The rational approach

Costs   Benefits

Somatic markers

Most viable

Least viable

Figure 11.23 Somatic markers facilitate decision making by influencing candidate responses based on their affective value. The rational economist might assess the benefits and costs of each option, and then choose the one with the highest value. Limitations in information processing coupled with the need for expediency favor a faster system that can quickly eliminate actions associated with unpleasant consequences, while boosting those that experience has shown to be rewarding.

tivate somatic markers. The representation is not abstract—it is connected to affective experience. With little thought we stop at a red traffic signal, not because we have learned to but because we associate running red lights with bloody traffic accidents.

The somatic marker hypothesis is a fresh slant on the paradoxical behavior of patients with lesions of the ventromedial frontal cortex. When this region is damaged, the representations required to guide and produce a behavior are brought into working memory, but they are stripped of emotional content. A patient may still mull over problems, albeit in an impersonal manner. He may be aware of the death of a close relative and understand the finality of it, but he is divested of the emotional pain that accompanies the loss.

Emotional associations do not simply reflect idiosyncratic personal experiences; the moral standards of society come into play. Elliot was aware of his failings—he could see that his inability to keep a job caused pain and suffering for his family. But this awareness was not sufficient to induce him to take actions that would overcome the problems. He was forever trapped in a whirlpool of possible actions, unaided by somatic markers to help him prioritize matters at hand. While this failure to respond in a socially appropriate way can be shocking, it reflects a dissociation of the content of memory from affective associations that we assume are part and parcel of that content. Indeed, patients may even demonstrate a meta-awareness of this dissociation. Elliot reported that he was aware of his lack of emotionality, both his positive feelings (such as the joys of improving his family situation) and his negative ones (like the sorrows that accompanied his diminished social situation).

EMOTIONAL PROCESSING AND DECISION MAKING

Damasio and his colleagues demonstrated that frontal lesions can disrupt emotional processing. Their work initially focused on an autonomic response, the *galvanic skin response* (GSR). A current applied to the hands is conducted more efficiently when the skin is dampened by sweat, a physiological effect that underlies the polygraph, or lie detector test. Lying causes sweating, and the polygraph measures these changes as an increase in the GSR. The GSR presumably reflects heightened reactivity, a reflection of greater alertness or readiness to respond.

The mechanism generating this response is intact in frontal lobe patients. If a bright light or loud sound is presented, patients with frontal lobe lesions display a normal startle response, an element of which is increased GSR. Where patients differ from control subjects is when GSR changes are evoked by affective stim-

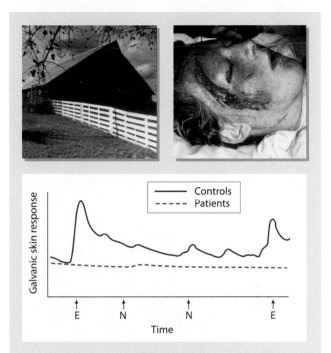

Figure 11.24 Patients with ventromedial cortical damage fail to show autonomic, emotional responses to arousing stimuli. Subjects were shown a series of stimuli while measurements were made of their galvanic skin response, a measure of emotional responsivity. Some of the stimuli were affectively neutral (N) such as photographs of the Iowa countryside. Others were expected to evoke strong emotional responses (E). The control subjects showed a large GSR to the emotional stimuli whereas the prefrontal lesion patients had a "flat" GSR. Bottom panel is adapted from Damasio (1994).

uli. In one experiment the stimuli were slides of mostly neutral images: scenery from the Iowa countryside or abstract paintings. Other slides were of disturbing or socially taboo images such as disaster scenes, mutilations, or nudity. When subjects viewed the latter images, the GSR record for control subjects had a consistent spike in comparison to the response to neutral images. As can be seen in Figure 11.24, the GSR record was flat for the frontal lobe patients. Again, patients showed a dissociation between the content of their memories and the emotional reaction to them. They could recall in detail the disturbing images and use words that convey emotional experience (e.g., "It was a disgusting image of a mutilated body"), but their lack of an affective response meant that their words reflected semantic associations, not emotional ones.

The lack of emotionality is obvious when patients view affect-laden stimuli. But an important question remains: Do emotional responses moderate decision making, as Damasio proposed? To explore this, a risk-taking

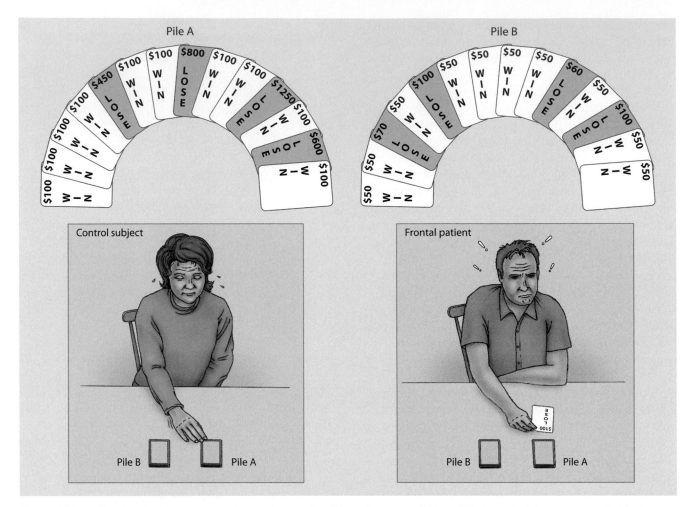

Figure 11.25 Emotional responses occur in reaction to stimuli, but also are useful in guiding our decision processes. Subjects were required to choose cards from one pile or the other, with each card specifying an amount won or lost. Through trial and error, the subjects could learn that pile A was riskier than pile B. Control subjects not only tended to avoid the high-risk pile, but also showed a large GSR when considering choosing a card from this pile. The patients with prefrontal lesions failed to show these anticipatory GSRs. Interestingly, they did show a large GSR upon turning over a card and discovering they had lost $1000 (of play money).

task was devised where (pretend) monetary rewards and penalties were associated with stimuli. Subjects were free to select from piles of cards and learned through trial and error the payoffs connected with each deck. You can try this yourself by covering the two columns in Figure 11.25. On each trial, choose one pile and unveil the top item on that pile. The goal is to maximize your total amount of money.

The cards in two decks usually provide large payoffs ($100) but can demand hefty payments ($1250). For other decks, rewards and penalties are milder (win $50 and lose $100). Control subjects gradually come to choose from the latter decks. Frontal lesion patients, though, favor riskier decks, perhaps because they are attracted to the frequent $100 payments even though they would eventually be offset by a severe penalty.

Most intriguing were the GSR responses for the two groups. On turning over a card, both groups displayed transient increases in GSR, hence an autonomic response to the rewards and penalties. Over time, though, these changes became anticipatory for the control subjects; that is, when the subjects were contemplating choosing a card from the risky decks, their GSRs would skyrocket. For frontal lobe patients, GSRs remained reactive and failed to show anticipatory changes. Thus, no physiological evidence proved that their decision was mediated by emotion.

The idea that memories have emotional associations is not controversial. What is less clear is whether evoking the associated affect depends on reactivating visceral responses. What we face is a problem of inferring causation from correlation. Are emotional responses absent because patients do not evaluate the affective content of stimuli? Or, do they make inappropriate decisions because they fail to generate somatic markers? Although this question remains, Damasio's hypothesis raises the provocative idea that emotion plays a central role in guiding cognition. This modulation is achieved when the limbic system and the working-memory systems of the frontal lobe interact.

PLANNING AND THE COORDINATION OF COMPLEX BEHAVIOR

So far we have emphasized how important the prefrontal cortex is in maintaining information and selecting an action. The lateral prefrontal regions are especially essential for sustaining transient representations, even when stimuli related to them are no longer present. The ventromedial prefrontal regions link information with past experience, especially with affective associations. When the prefrontal cortex is damaged, behavior becomes tightly coupled to stimuli in the present, and the patient's reactions are detached from personal experience.

In a sense, the frontal lobe syndrome results in a loss of flexibility. As Lhermitte wrote, "Some of the functions of the frontal lobe allow the subject to remain aloof from the outside world and to ensure his independence by modulating and inhibiting the activities" of more posterior brain regions. Loss of flexibility is unlikely to present a severe problem in experiments. Subjects' options are limited, which provides a controlled situation for isolating selective deficits. But the tasks fail to capture the complexities of behaving in the real world. The debilitating consequences of the frontal lobe syndrome can be best appreciated when viewed in a more ecologically valid context.

Goal-Oriented Behavior

Our actions are not aimless, nor are they entirely dictated by events and stimuli immediately at hand. We choose to act because we want to accomplish goals, to gratify personal needs. Goal-driven behavior can be as mundane as turning on a computer to play a game, or as complex as attending lectures, reviewing notes, and reading to learn. Goals dwell within a hierarchy. We can describe the immediate goal of an action—to learn—but also recognize that this is really a subgoal for a larger plan. Learning subjects is necessary for admission to graduate or professional school, and these institutions can be a ticket to fame, fortune, and personal satisfaction.

The ability to form a coherent plan of action is compromised after damage to the prefrontal lobe. Patients like Phineas Gage and Elliot are plagued by this problem, unable to resurrect a normal life long after the acute symptoms of their illness have passed. It is difficult to attribute the problem to a lack of knowledge or motivation. They are aware of their deteriorating social situation and have the intellectual capabilities to generate ideas that may alleviate their condition. Gage engaged in many lines of work, some designed to exploit his unusual medical condition. Elliot embarked on new business ventures that drew on his accounting skills. But these efforts were tragic failures. These two men could not sustain a plan of action and meet their goals.

Tim Shallice at the National Hospital in London (Shallice and Burgess, 1991) documented this problem in three patients who suffered frontal lesions from head traumas. On many neuropsychological assessment procedures, the patients demonstrated intact, perhaps even superior, cognitive abilities. Not only did they all score at least one standard deviation above average on an IQ test, but they had few problems on standard tests of frontal lobe function, including the Wisconsin Card Sorting Task. To examine their ability to engage in goal-oriented behavior, the experimenters designed tasks that mimicked the errands a person might have to run on a Saturday morning. Patients were asked to go to a shopping center and purchase items (a loaf of bread, a packet of throat lozenges), keep an appointment at a certain time, and collect four pieces of information such as the price of a pound of tomatoes or the exchange rate of the rupee. The task was not designed to tap memory. The patients were given a list of the errands and instructions to follow, such as spend as little money as possible.

Despite their superior intellectual abilities, all three patients had difficulty executing this assignment. One patient failed to purchase soap because the store she visited did not carry her favorite brand; another wandered outside the designated shopping center in pursuit of an item that could be found within the designated region. Others became embroiled in social complications. One succeeded in obtaining the newspaper but was pursued by the merchant for failing to pay! In a related experiment, patients were asked to work on three tasks for 15 minutes. Whereas control subjects successfully juggled their schedule to ensure that they made enough progress

Psychiatric Disorders and the Frontal Lobes

Psychiatric disorders such as schizophrenia and depression represent a widespread breakdown in mental function. Problems faced by patients affect almost all aspects of their behavior. It is unlikely that their problems are linked to a simple physiological mechanism. Rather, the disorders arise from a delicate interplay of physiological mechanism that reflect endogenous dispositions and a person's idiosyncratic experiences.

One of the most promising aspects of cognitive neuroscience is that it may offer new insights concerning the functional deficits associated with severe psychiatric disorders. Simple neuropsychological descriptions do not adequately account for these disorders. Schizophrenia cannot be thought of as a temporal lobe or frontal lobe problem; it arises as a disturbance in cognitive systems that span cortical and subcortical systems. Though schizophrenia has been linked to abnormal dopamine levels, we still need to know how this neurotransmitter affects cognition if we want to understand the functional consequences of this debilitating disorder.

As integrators of all cortical regions, the frontal lobes are, unsurprisingly, abnormal in psychiatric patients. One source of evidence is the comparative blood flow patterns in psychiatric patients and in control subjects (Drevets and Raichle, 1995). These results are, at best, weak predictors of dysfunction, perhaps because psychiatric labels encompass heterogeneous disorders and perhaps because patients are almost always under a cornucopia of medications. Yet we can tease out intriguing dissociations in metabolic profiles of schizophrenics and depressives: Schizophrenia is often tied to hypometabolism of the prefrontal cortex, and depression is linked to hypermetabolism in the same region (Figure A).

The first reports of hypofrontality, or reduced blood flow in the frontal cortex, in schizophrenia came when patients were scanned while at rest. With the distribution of blood flow in normal subjects used as a baseline, patients with schizophrenia had less prefrontal blood flow in comparison to posterior blood flow. Also, the degree of hypofrontality was correlated with the severity of the patients' symptoms. Studies now focus on blood flow changes during activities associated with frontal lobe function. For example, Daniel Weinberger at the National Institute of Mental Health (1988) scanned patients and controls during rest and in two behavioral conditions: First, when patients performed the Wisconsin Card Sorting Test; second, when the task had a number-matching rule that excluded working memory but controlled visual processing and motor response. Unlike earlier reports, blood flow in the two groups did not differ during the rest condition or the nonfrontal behavioral condition. During the Wisconsin Card Sorting Test, though, blood flow in the groups sharply diverged. Frontal patients had less blood flow in the dorsolateral prefrontal cortex than did the controls.

In a follow-up study the Wisconsin Card Sorting Test was performed twice, once after the patients had been given a placebo and once after administration of apomorphine, a morphine derivative with antipsychotic properties. For each patient, blood flow in the dorsolateral prefrontal cortex increased when they received drugs; hence, reducing dopamine levels heightens activity in the prefrontal cortex.

The chemical basis of depression is even more mysterious. Even so, patients have hypermetabolic prefrontal cortices during depressions in contrast to when they are asymptomatic. Hypermetabolism is widespread, encompassing much of the prefrontal cortex and the anterior cingulate and amygdala. Normal subjects also evince hypermetabolism in prefrontal regions when asked to think sad thoughts while being scanned.

It would be premature to definitively interpret these divergent metabolic profiles. Even so, we can make intriguing connections to themes in this chapter. Schizophrenics have an underactive frontal cortex, especially in lateral regions. Losing their working-memory and inhibitory capabilities renders them more reliant on activity in the posterior cortex. They may be easier to distract, and hence fail to inhibit irrelevant representations such as the ones related to persistent hallucinations.

Depressed patients exhibit a profile of overactivity in prefrontal regions associated with working memory and in areas linked to the generation of affective memories. With these people, representations persist for a

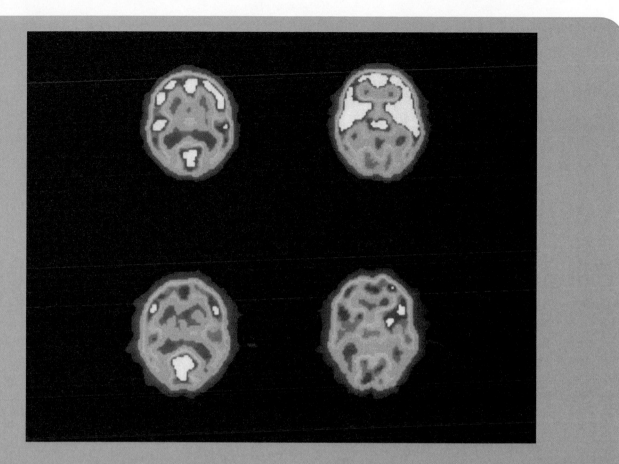

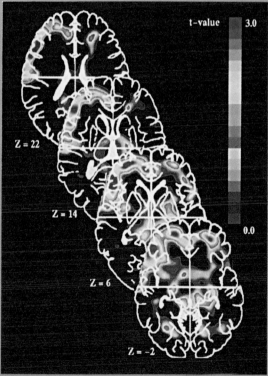

PET reveals abnormal patterns of blood flow in patients with psychiatric disorders. **(Top)** Schizophrenic patients show hypometabolism in the prefrontal cortex. This abnormality is especially marked during tasks that produce increased blood flow in this area in healthy subjects. In this study, subjects were involved in a continuous auditory-discrimination task. Compared to the control subjects (top slices), uptake of the tracer is much lower in schizophrenic patients (lower slices). **(Left)** Blood flow at rest was measured in control subjects and patients with depression. Colored areas indicate regions of increased blood flow in the depressed patients, and are centered in the lateral prefrontal cortex in the left hemisphere.

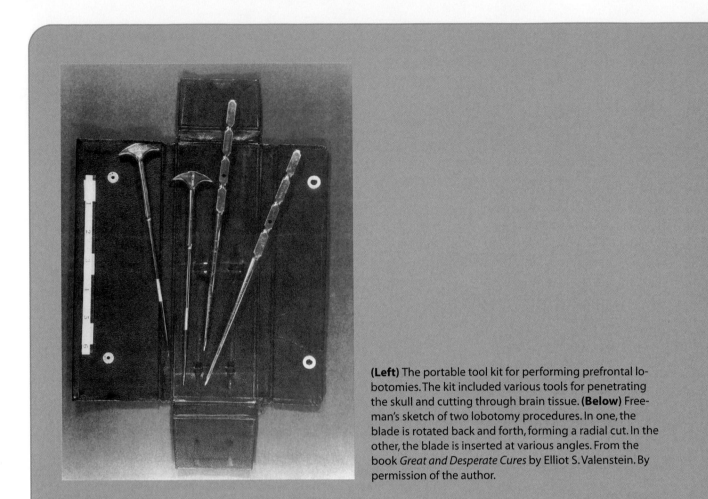

(Left) The portable tool kit for performing prefrontal lobotomies. The kit included various tools for penetrating the skull and cutting through brain tissue. **(Below)** Freeman's sketch of two lobotomy procedures. In one, the blade is rotated back and forth, forming a radial cut. In the other, the blade is inserted at various angles. From the book *Great and Desperate Cures* by Elliot S. Valenstein. By permission of the author.

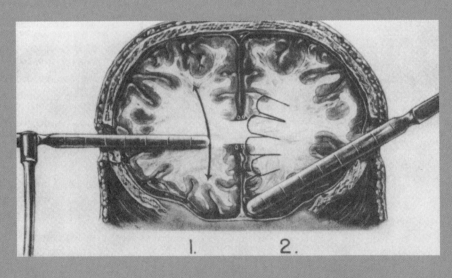

long time and are imbued with heightened affect. A situation that a normal person might find neutral, or at most mildly aggravating, becomes amplified and takes on onerous overtones. The depressed patient cannot let a situation go; the representation of a thought or obsession persists, sustained by input from inappropriate somatic markers.

With a cognitive neuroscience perspective, we can make sense of the outcome of one of the great debacles of neurosurgery: frontal lobotomies for treating psychiatric disorders (Valenstein, 1986). Prior to the implementation of drug therapies in the 1950s and 1960s, mental institutions were overflowing with desperate patients and doctors, eager to try any procedure that promised relief. In the 1930s, Dr. Egas Moniz, a renowned Portuguese neurologist who had developed cerebral angiography in 1927, introduced a psychosurgical procedure for treating patients with severe schizophrenia and obsessive-compulsive disorder.

Moniz's inspiration came from an international scientific conference where two American researchers reported the effects of frontal lobectomy in chimpanzees. One animal appeared to have undergone a personality change. Before the operation, the chimp was uncooperative and would throw temper tantrums. After the removal of most of her frontal lobes, the animal was cheerful and participated in experimental tests without hesitation. Moniz reasoned that the procedure might bring relief to severely agitated patients, a well-intended thought given the paucity of alternatives.

Removing large amounts of tissue from the frontal lobes seemed excessive. Instead, Moniz decided to isolate the prefrontal cortex from the rest of the brain by severing the white matter's connecting fibers. In his early efforts he applied toxic levels of alcohol through holes in the skull's lateral surface. He later switched to a procedure in which a leukotome, a plunger with an extractable blade, could be lowered into the brain to sever fibers in targeted regions.

This procedure was refined by Dr. Walter Freeman at Georgetown University, who developed a simple procedure that did not require a surgeon. The patient was first given an anesthetic consisting of a severe electrical shock. While the patient was unconscious for 15 minutes, the lobotomy was performed by jabbing an ice pick through the bone above each eye and wiggling it back and forth. Freeman assembled a portable kit containing his electroshock apparatus, ice picks, and a small hammer, and set off on a barnstorming trip to promote the benefits of this miracle cure (Figure B). The public and scientific community were welcoming. Thousands of procedures were performed over the next few decades, and Moniz received the Nobel Prize in Physiology and Medicine in 1949.

With the advantage of hindsight, we now recognize the abject failings of the lobotomy craze. There were few outcome studies, and those few revealed that the discharge rate from mental institutions was no greater for lobotomy patients than it was for controls. Scant concern was given to the patients selected; the procedure had minimal effect on schizophrenics but drastically altered patients with affective disorders like depression or severe neurosis, who felt much less anxious, impulsive, and depressed. But these feelings brought new problems that rendered them incapable of functioning outside the institutional setting. They were now withdrawn and underactive, lacking in affect or responsiveness. The benefits, if any, were experienced by attendants who rejoiced that the patients were docile and easy to manage. As with Phineas Gage, the patients' souls had been transformed.

These differential outcomes make sense in light of metabolic studies. Lobotomies targeted the prefrontal cortex, a region already underactive in schizophrenia. As such, we might expect little effect on schizophrenics, or maybe new problems for those with an excessive dominance of posterior brain function. For affective disorders, though, lobotomies isolated an overactive region. Moreover, the primary foci were on medial regions, which may have eliminated behaviors associated with exaggerated emotionality but turned patients into affectless zombies.

on each task, the patients got bogged down on one or two tasks.

Planning and Selecting an Action

In preparing for an exam, a good student develops an action plan such as the one in Figure 11.26. This plan can be represented as a hierarchy of subgoals, each requiring actions to achieve the goal. At the top is the goal of doing well on the exam. To do so, subgoals are designed: Reading must be completed, lecture notes reviewed, and material integrated to identify themes and facts. Perhaps the student will generate essay questions and practice writing answers. A timeline might include when the subgoals will be completed and how to devote the day before the exam to study.

Three components are essential for successfully executing an action plan (Duncan, 1995). First, one must identify the goal and develop subgoals. Perhaps the student has noticed that the professor often includes readings on exams, and so a subgoal might be to maximize the effort devoted to reading. Second, in choosing among goals, consequences must be anticipated. Will the information be remembered better if the student sets aside 1 hour a day for study during the week preced-

ing the exam, or is it better to cram intensively the night before? Third, what is required to achieve the subgoals? A place must be identified for study. The coffee supply must be adequately stocked. A pen must be available for marking critical passages. It is easy to see that these components are not entirely separate. Purchasing coffee can be an action *and* a goal.

When viewed this way, it is easy to see that failure to achieve a goal can happen in many ways. If reading is not completed, the student may lack knowledge essential for an exam. If a friend arrives unannounced to celebrate his birthday the weekend before the exam, critical study time can be lost. If coffee is not handy, the student may lack the stamina to stay awake for the final all-nighter.

The failures of goal-oriented behavior in patients with prefrontal lesions can be traced to many potential sources. Problems can arise because of deficits in working memory or with linking these memories to their affective consequences. Developing an action plan means a simultaneous consideration of subgoals. Without a sense of how these actions affect our personal aspirations and social position, we are impeded from evaluating plans of attack and establishing sensible goals.

Shallice, together with Donald Norman of the University of California (Norman and Shallice, 1986), developed the model in Figure 11.27 to account for goal-oriented behavior. This model conceptualizes the selection of an action as a competitive process. At the heart of the model is the notion of *schema control units* or representations of responses (a term used in a generic sense here). These schemas can correspond to explicit movements or to the activation of long-term representations that lead to purposeful behaviors. For example, when we see a word printed on paper, an action schema could be the articulatory gestures required to pronounce the word. Or, in reading the word, its semantic meaning and associated representations may be activated.

Schema control units receive input from many sources. Norman and Shallice emphasized perceptual inputs and their link to these control units. The strength of the connections, however, reflects the effects of learning. If we have had experience in restaurant dining, walking into a restaurant will activate behaviors associated with waiting for the hostess or looking at the menu. Moreover, walking into the restaurant can elicit varied affective responses—which is how somatic markers influence schema control units. A restaurant setting is often associated with pleasant memories of fine meals and good company. For some, though, it may reawaken painful thoughts of washing dishes or waiting for grown-ups to end dull conversations.

Figure 11.26 An action hierarchy. Successfully achieving a complex goal such as doing well on an exam requires planning and organization at multiple levels of behavior.

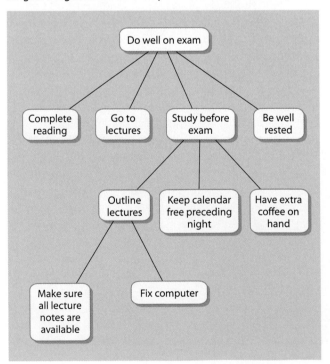

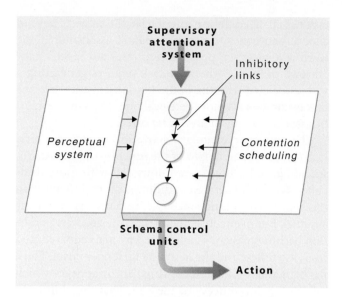

Figure 11.27 Norman and Shallice's model of response selection. Actions are linked to schema control units. The perceptual system produces input to these control units. However, selection of these units can be biased by the contention scheduling units and the supervisory attentional system (SAS). The SAS provides flexibility in the response selection system. Adapted from Shallice et al. (1989).

External inputs can be sufficient to trigger schema control units. For example, it is hard not to track a moving object by moving one's eyes. But in most situations our actions are not dictated solely by the input; many schema control units can be simultaneously activated, and a control process is needed to ensure that the appropriate control units are selected. Norman and Shallice postulated two types of selection. One type, which is rather passive, is what they call *contention scheduling*. Schemas not only are driven by perceptual inputs but also compete with one another, especially when two control units are mutually exclusive. We cannot look at two places at the same time, or move the same hand to simultaneously pick up a glass and a fork. By having inhibitory connections between schemas, the model accounts for why we act coherently. Only one schema (or nonoverlapping schemas) can win the competition. If competition does not resolve the conflict, the result is no action. None of the schemas is activated enough to trigger a response.

The second means for selection comes by way of the *supervisory attentional system* (SAS). The SAS is essential for ensuring that behavior is flexible. It is a mechanism for favoring certain schema control units, perhaps to reflect the demands of the situation or to emphasize some goals over others. We can postulate types of situations where selection would benefit from an SAS:

1. When the situation requires planning or decision making
2. When the situation requires error correction or troubleshooting
3. When links between the input and schema control units are novel or not well learned
4. When the situation is difficult or dangerous
5. When the situation requires a response that competes with a strong, habitual response

It is reasonable to summarize these five conditions as two: One for situations where an incorrect response is likely to occur through normal contention scheduling (situations 2, 3, and 5), and the other for when we lack a routine procedure for creating an appropriate response (situations 1, 3, and 4).

The Anterior Cingulate as a Supervisory Attentional System

In the last decade we have witnessed burgeoning interest in possible executive functions of the anterior cingulate cortex. Buried in the depths of the frontal lobes and characterized by a primitive cytoarchitecture, this structure was assumed to be a component of the limbic system, helping to modulate autonomic responses during painful or threatening situations. Whereas functional roles for most cortical regions have been inspired by behavioral problems associated with neurological disorders, interest in the anterior cingulate has been inspired by serendipitous activations found in this region during PET studies. For example, metabolic activity in the anterior cingulate increases when people generate semantic associates to words, a result that did not appear to jibe with the neurological literature showing that lesions of the cingulate were not associated with language disorders.

These findings have led to a reconceptualization of this area as part of an attentional hierarchy. In this view, the anterior cingulate occupies an upper rung on the hierarchy, playing a critical role in coordinating activity across attentional systems (Figure 11.28). Consider a PET study of visual attention in which subjects must selectively attend to a visual feature (color, motion, shape) or monitor changes in all three features simultaneously, a condition in which attentional resources must be divided (Corbetta et al., 1991). Compared to control conditions where stimuli are viewed passively, the selective attention conditions were associated with enhanced activity in feature-specific regions of visual association areas. For example, attending to motion was correlated with greater blood flow in the lateral prestriate cortex,

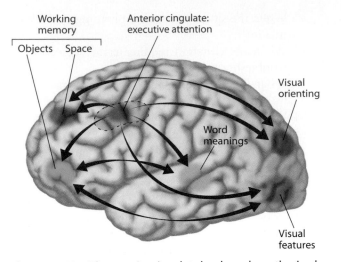

Figure 11.28 The anterior cingulate has been hypothesized to operate as an executive attention system. This system serves to ensure that processing in other brain regions is most efficient given the current task demands. Interactions with the prefrontal cortex may select working-memory buffers; interactions with the posterior cortex can serve to amplify activity in one perceptual module over others. The interactions with the posterior cortex may be direct or they may be mediated by connections with the prefrontal cortex. Adapted from Posner and Raichle (1994).

task has changed. In the initial trial, the subjects have to choose between alternative semantic associates. If the word is *apple,* then possible responses are "peel," "eat," "throw," or "type" when the task requires generating a verb associated with the noun. On subsequent trials, the task becomes a memory retrieval one. The same semantic associate is almost always reported.

The anterior cingulate activation during the first trial can be related to two of the functions of an SAS: responding under novel conditions and with more difficult tasks. The generate condition is more difficult than the repeat condition since the response is not constrained. But over subsequent trials, the generate condition becomes easier (as evidenced by markedly reduced response times) and the items are no longer novel. Thus, the higher blood flow in the cingulate disappears, which reflects a reduced need for the SAS. That this shift indicates the loss of novelty rather than a general decrease in cingulate activity with practice is shown by the fact that when a new list of nouns is used, the cingulate activation returns.

The poor temporal resolution of PET makes it difficult to distinguish between functions associated with activations in the cingulate, lateral prefrontal cortex,

whereas attending to color stimulated blood flow in more medial regions. In contrast, during the divided-attention task the most prominent activation was in the anterior cingulate cortex. This suggests that selective attention causes local changes in regions specialized to process certain features. The divided-attention condition, in contrast, requires a higher-level attentional system, one that simultaneously monitors information across these specialized modules. This function conforms to what one would attribute to an SAS. Indeed, the anterior cingulate is implicated in all five situations outlined by Norman and Shallice (Figure 11.29) (Posner, 1994).

Consider two conditions from an experiment that has been used in PET studies of language: repeating a stimulus word and generating a semantic associate. When activation in the repeat condition is subtracted from that observed during the generate condition, greater blood flow consistently occurs in the dorsolateral prefrontal cortex and anterior cingulate (Petersen et al., 1988). Moreover, when the rate of stimulus presentation is not too rapid, a third focus appears in more posterior regions near Wernicke's area. If the generate task is repeated, though, the pattern changes. Now the primary activation is within interior regions of the temporal lobe, the *insular cortex.* (Raichle et al., 1994). The

Figure 11.29 Five functions of an SAS. Evidence for a role of the cingulate in each function is listed on the right. (See text for details.)

Required function of the SAS	Evidence indicating function related to anterior cingulate
Novel situations	Blood flow increases during word generation task in comparison to word repeat task
Error correction	Evoked potential studies
Overcoming habitual responses	Blood flow increase during incongruent Stroop trial in comparison to congruent Stroop trials
Difficult situations	Blood flow increase during divided attention studies in comparison to focused attention studies
Decision making	Blood flow increase when movements are produced at "will" in comparison to when response is specified by the stimulus

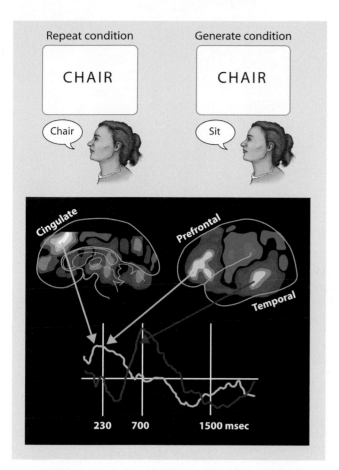

Figure 11.30 Neural generators associated with each peak in the difference waveform between generate and repeat tasks. **(Top)** Subjects hear a noun. In the repeat condition, they simply repeat the word; in the generate condition, they name a word that is a verb associate. To avoid including motor activity in the evoked potentials, subjects were instructed to withhold their responses until a "go" signal appeared, about 1500 msec after the stimulus. **(Bottom)** The difference waveform is obtained by subtracting the evoked potential in the repeat condition from the evoked potential in the generate condition. Dipole modeling techniques were used to identify the neural regions associated with each peak. Adapted from Snyder et al. (1995).

and posterior foci. An event-related potential (ERP) study sheds some light here (Snyder, 1995). The same subtractive logic was applied, but the difference was between ERP waveforms obtained during the generate and repeat conditions (Figure 11.30). Using ERP localization methods, researchers sought to identify the source of the differences and their time course. The PET foci constrained how the generators were modeled. The first difference was observed about 180 msec after the onset of the target noun and was attributed to a single generator in the anterior cingulate. About 30 msec later, a second

generator was required to model the data. This generator was localized to the lateral prefrontal cortex in the left hemisphere. Finally, around 620 msec after stimulus onset, a third generator was linked to the posterior cortex in the left hemisphere.

The time course fits well with the general picture developed in this chapter. We can hypothesize that the initial cingulate activity reflects the allocation of attentional resources to these novel stimuli. The cingulate may establish a node in the working-memory system of the lateral prefrontal cortex to hold representations retrieved from the longer-term semantic representations of word meanings in the posterior cortex. As processing spreads among the semantic network in the posterior cortex, the working-memory system will inhibit representations of irrelevant associates (e.g., "red" or "round") and allow a task-relevant associate to become sufficiently activated (e.g., "eat"). In this way, the SAS allows the task's goal—to generate a verb associated with the noun—to influence interactions between working and long-term memory. This study elegantly demonstrated the analytic power of combining the spatial resolution of PET and the temporal resolution of evoked potentials. PET had identified three foci of activity during the generative task. The ERP study revealed the time course of processing across these three areas.

The Stroop task reveals cingulate involvement in overcoming habitual responses. Recall that in this task, a subject is given a list of words that spell out the names of colors that are either congruent or incongruent with the ink color. In either case, the subject must name the color of the words, inhibiting the natural tendency to read the word names themselves. In the congruent condition (e.g., saying "blue" when seeing the word *blue* written in blue ink), there is no conflict; while the subject may focus on the color, the schema control unit activated by the words also promotes the same response. In the incongruent condition (e.g., saying "blue" when seeing the word *red* written in blue ink), the two schema control units are in conflict. Here, the subject must overcome the inclination to read the words and focus on the ink color. As would be expected by Norman and Shallice's model, the anterior cingulate is more active in this condition.

A role for the anterior cingulate in error detection comes primarily from work using evoked potentials. Figure 11.31 shows that when people make an incorrect response, a large evoked response sweeps over the prefrontal cortex just after the movement is initiated; this response has been localized to the anterior cingulate (Dehaene et al., 1994). This response, interestingly enough, is absent when the subject is unaware that the

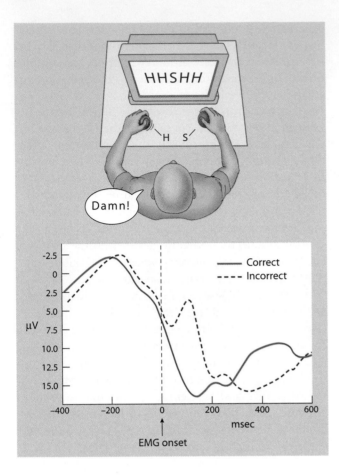

Figure 11.31 Subjects were tested on a two-choice letter discrimination task in which they made speeded responses with either the right or left hand. Errors were obtained by emphasizing speed and by flanking the targets with irrelevant distractors. Evoked potentials for incorrect responses deviated from those obtained on trials with correct responses just after the onset of peripheral motor activity. This error detection signal is maximal over a central electrode positioned over the prefrontal cortex, and has been hypothesized to originate in the anterior cingulate. The zero position on the x axis indicates the onset of electromyographic activity. Actual movement would be observed about 50 to 100 msec later. Adapted from Gehring et al. (1993).

response is erroneous, and its magnitude is correlated with the intensity of the incorrect response (Gehring et al., 1993). One might suppose that the SAS detects an incorrect schema control unit being fired and attempts to negate the response. Usually it is too late to inhibit it. Skilled typists experience this phenomenon with troubling frequency. In completing the word *with*, the middle finger on the left hand may move toward the letter *e*, reflecting the thousands of times that the word *the* has been typed. The schema for *the* may have been falsely activated by the final keystrokes *th*, and the error detection system is forced to play catch-up.

The contribution of the anterior cingulate to planning and decision making is harder to evaluate since these processes participate in all cognitive activities. A relevant study (Frith et al., 1991) comes from a paper, provocatively titled "Willed Action and the Prefrontal Cortex in Man: A Study with PET." Here somatosensory stimuli were applied randomly to either the first or the second finger of the right hand. In two control conditions, the stimuli dictated the subjects' responses: In one condition, they moved the stimulated finger; in the other, they moved the nonstimulated finger. In the "free-will" condition, the stimuli were applied as before, but

now the subjects were instructed to select which finger to respond with in a random fashion. In comparison to both control conditions, a significant increase in activation was observed in the anterior cingulate cortex for the free-will condition.

In addition to cingulate activation, blood flow increased in the lateral prefrontal cortex during the free-will condition. This makes sense when we consider the working-memory requirements for the different conditions. In control conditions, the subjects had to identify the stimulus's location and apply the appropriate response rule. In the free-will condition, the subjects not only had to decide which response to make on each trial, but also had to keep track of their responses on previous trials to ensure that they did not follow a pattern. It takes a lot of effort to be random!

Viewing the anterior cingulate as an SAS is, at present, speculative. It is quite possible that the SAS does not constitute a unified system; rather, its functions may be distributed among several brain structures or involve the interaction of these structures. Caution is warranted because lesions confined to the anterior cingulate do not produce lasting deficits in supervisory functions. Although one hears reports of neglect in patients with cin-

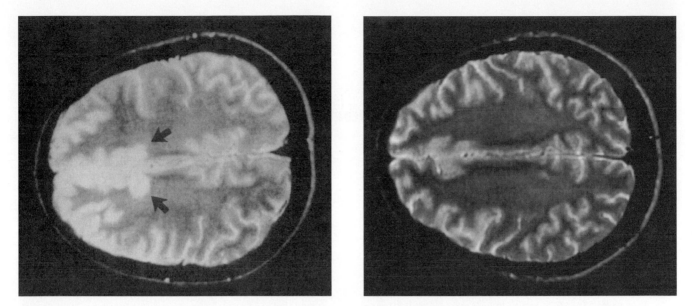

Figure 11.32 Complete resection of the anterior cingulate in both hemispheres is revealed by postsurgery MRI **(left)**. Normal brain is shown on the right for comparison.

gulate lesions that leads to *akinetic mutism,* the complete loss of all volitional behavior, the effects are generally temporary. A patient who underwent a bilateral anterior cingulotomy for the treatment of severe depression had problems with word generation and Stroop tasks when tested 2 weeks after her operation (Janer and Pardo, 1991). But the deficits were absent 8 months later, despite the fact that the operation removed almost the entire anterior cingulate (Figure 11.32). Moreover, her clinical picture did not reveal any change in cognitive function—although her psychiatric condition was much improved. It is not clear how recovery was possible if this region is the primary center of a higher-level attentional system.

SUMMARY

In this chapter, we described the crucial role played by the prefrontal cortex in complex behavior. Three primary functional systems have been reviewed. The lateral prefrontal cortex is conceptualized as a working-memory system devoted to sustaining representations of information stored in the cortex's more posterior regions. The ventromedial prefrontal cortex and the anterior cingulate are systems which ensure that these representations facilitate goal-oriented behavior. The ventromedial system is the link between cognition and emotion, perhaps for improving the efficiency with which we decide among alternative actions. The anterior cingulate is a higher-level attentional system, required to ensure that our behavior is efficient and flexible.

While we paid the most attention to a tripartite division of the prefrontal function, it is clear that the dorsolateral, ventromedial, and cingulate systems form a complex network. As emphasized in this chapter and the preceding one, the control of action has a hierarchical nature. Just as control in the motor system is delegated across many functional systems, an analogous organization characterizes prefrontal function. With control distributed in this manner, the need for an all-powerful executive, a *homunculus,* is minimized. The prefrontal cortex can be a reservoir of the current contents of processing by linking up to stored representations in the cortex's more posterior regions—representations that help to select actions. But these representations, the content of ongoing processing, are embedded in a context that reflects the history and current goals of the actor. By recognizing the intimate connection between the distinct functions of the prefrontal cortex, we can appreciate how a mind emerges from the common architecture shared in the human brain.

SUGGESTED READINGS

BADDELEY, A. (1995). *Working Memory.* In M.S. Gazzaniga (Ed.), *The Cognitive Neurosciences* (pp. 755–764). Cambridge, MA: MIT Press.

DAMASIO, A.R. (1994). *Descartes' Error: Emotion, Reason, and the Human Brain.* New York: G.P. Putnam.

FUSTER, J.M. (1989). *The Prefrontal Cortex: Anatomy, Physiology, and Neuropsychology of the Frontal Lobe,* 2nd edition. New York: Raven Press.

GOLDMAN-RAKIC, P.S. (1995). Architecture of the Prefrontal Cortex and the Central Executive. In J. Grafman, K.J. Holyoak, and F. Boller (Eds.), *Structure and Functions of the Human Prefrontal Cortex* (pp. 71–83). New York: The New York Academy of Sciences.

SHIMAMURA, A.P. (1995). Memory and Frontal Lobe Function. In M.S. Gazzaniga (Ed.), *The Cognitive Neurosciences* (pp. 803–813). Cambridge, MA: MIT Press.

12

Development and Plasticity

The fertilization of a single egg leads to the creation of an entire human being—think about it. Then think about it again! This is really quite fantastic and involves many mysteries yet to be solved. How do the cells produced by numerous mitotic divisions differentiate into the myriad cell types in the adult? How do they segregate into the isolated structures of the body? How is the nervous system, with its intricate wiring, constructed? How indeed?

Once the human organism is constructed by developmental processes, it is not a finished product. During growth and maturation the young human changes significantly, and perhaps the most impressive changes are those related to cognition. Learning and memory lead the child to develop amazing new abilities at an astounding rate. But once we reach adulthood, we are not done with change. We can still learn and remember, and this means changes occurring in the brain. Much of cognitive neuroscience is devoted to understanding these changes, which involve processes at the neuronal level such as long-term potentiation (LTP). But learning and memory are not the only signs of the plastic nature of the brain. Consider an experiment performed by Professor Vilayanur Ramachandran at the University of California at San Diego (Figure 12.1).

Ramachandran (1993) and his colleagues studied a healthy young man. While the man had his eyes closed, Ramachandran touched parts of his body with a Q-tip swab and asked the man to say where he was being touched. Ramachandran touched him and the young man said, "Left finger." He touched him again and the response was "left thumb." In response to additional touches, the young man reported sensations in various areas of the left hand and arm. What is so interesting about these reported sensations is that the man had no left arm—it was lost in an accident. What is more

Figure 12.1 An example of mapping sensation. Professor Ramachandran of the University of California, San Diego has tested the ability of persons to discriminate sensory stimuli. He performs these tests using a simple stroke of a cotton swab and asks the person to report where he feels the touch. During strokes to the cheek of one man who had his eyes closed, the man reported the sensation of being touched on the arm.

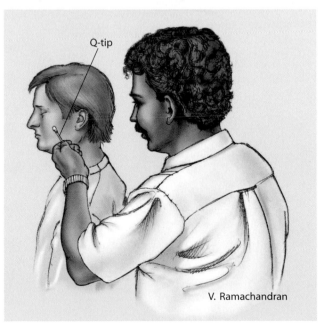

Q-tip

V. Ramachandran

amazing is that Ramachandran had been stroking parts of the young amputee's check! When his face was stroked by the Q-tip, the young man responded that he felt sensation in parts of his amputated left arm and hand (Figure 12.2)! With this patient Ramachandran demonstrated a remarkable example of plasticity in the human somato-sensory system. The precise mechanisms and the details of this story are presented later in this chapter. For now, we provide a hint for solving Ramachandran's mysterious findings. Consider the mapping of body regions onto the somatosensory cortex in the human shown in Figure 12.3—the answer lies here. Think "plastic"! Before we return to the topic of neuronal plasticity, we will review cognitive and neural development.

How will knowledge of normal cognitive and neural development enhance our understanding of the mechanisms underlying the adult mind? One way is by correlating cognitive function with a stage of neural development. If a behavior like complex reasoning appears at a certain postnatal time, brain structures that become functional (e.g., by way of myelination of input and output axons) at that same time are implicated in the behavior. The analysis of development and plasticity enlightens us about relations between specific brain circuits, structures and systems, and cognitive processes. By looking at the time course of neural and cognitive development, one can infer significant causal relations. This approach is being applied to perception, attention, memory, language, and motor skills, and also higher mental processes like reasoning.

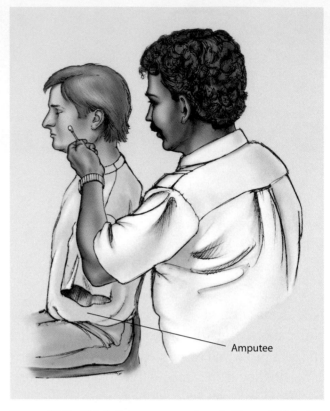

Figure 12.2 This is the same scenario as in Figure 12.1, but with a surprising twist. Stroking his cheek led the man to report sensation in his arm. However the man lost his arm in an accident some time earlier. This amazing demonstration is one that involves phantom limb sensation and yet something else as well. Why would touching the man's cheek lead him to feel touch to his missing arm?

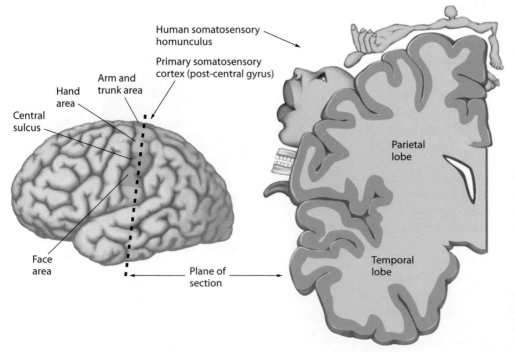

Figure 12.3 A human somatosensory homunculus. The representation of the body surface is mapped in a somatotopic fashion onto the somatosensory cortex of the parietal lobe. At the right is a coronal view of the right hemisphere showing the approximate location and relative cortical area (as indicated by distorted sizes of various body parts) dedicated to body parts. The anterior-posterior plane of the coronal section is indicated at the left. Of special note for the story told in Figures 12.1 and 12.2 is that the face representation and the hand representation are located in adjacent cortical areas of somatosensory cortex. Adapted from Kandel et al. (1991).

COGNITIVE DEVELOPMENT

The difference between the capabilities of newborns and those of adults are apparent to anyone taking the time to look. Newborns do not walk, hold objects, speak, or understand us when we speak to them. These differences could be explained in at least two ways. Newborns might have all the capabilities of adults but have not yet attained—via experience—the abilities of adults. In contrast, newborns may indeed differ radically from adults in neural or cognitive capabilities, or both. The former view amounts to newborns being merely small inexperienced adults, whereas the latter suggests that newborns do not yet possess neural and cognitive structures necessary to perform as adults do. This latter view has dominated based on both neural and psychological evidence. One classic view that newborns differ significantly from adults comes from the Swiss scientist Jean Piaget (Figure 12.4). Let us review Piaget's theory and then continue with the emerging view of development that has significantly modified the piagetian perspective.

A Theory of Cognitive Development

Jean Piaget is considered by many to be the father of modern developmental psychology. Piaget believed, and developed experiments to test, that human infants and children perceive and comprehend the world differently than adults do. He characterized the cognitive development of humans in a four-stage model (Table 12.1). Piaget conceived of the newborn as a work in progress. He held that the newborn experienced a disconnected welter of ill-formed sensory percepts and generated random motor acts. Thus, according to Piaget, in this first *sensory-motor intelligence stage,* the developing nervous system aims to achieve sensory-motor integration and cross-modality sensory integration. Piaget also believed that the newborn could not form a concept of self that could distinguish between it and the outside world, and thus the development of a self-identity begins during this period. These ideas were based on a biological view of development, and thus differed from prior behaviorally based theories.

The sensory-motor intelligence period, Piaget proposed, is also characterized by the development of sensory-motor schemas in infants. They learn to relate sensory inputs with motor acts and thus can purposively grasp objects they are looking at. During this stage, infants have poor concepts of objects in the world. Even when they are old enough to interact with objects, they do not exhibit object permanence, according to Piaget. *Object permanence* is the ability to know that an object does not cease to exist merely because it is out of view. Obscuring an object from an infant during this period will at first lead the infant to ignore it. Later the infant may learn to look for it but fail to integrate new information about where it might be. For example, in

Figure 12.4 Photo of Jean Piaget, the famous Swiss developmental psychologist.

| Table 12.1 | The Divisions of Cognitive Development in Humans as Formulated by Piaget |

Stage	Age	Characteristics
Sensory-motor intelligence	0–2 years	Unconnected sensations, representational thought
Preoperational period	2–7 years	Conservation of quantity and number, egocentrism
Concrete operations	7–11 years	Concrete concepts/no abstract thinking
Formal operations	11 years and older	Development of abstract thought

repeated trials, if an investigator hides a toy from a child in her plain view, she will explore the hiding place to retrieve the toy. If the same hiding place is used over consecutive trials but then a new hiding place is used, the child may look at the new hiding place while still exploring the old location for the toy (Figure 12.5). As the child ages, this perseverative behavior diminishes.

Figure 12.5 Testing a child's knowledge of the world— Object Permanence. A baby of two years of age or less is playing ball with an investigator **(a)**. Psychologist Adele Diamond (1991) has shown that if the investigator takes the ball and places it behind a screen in full view of the baby, a young infant might ignore it. As the infant ages, however, he will eventually come to understand that the ball is still there, but is merely occluded, and may reach for it at the hidden location. This is the concept of object permanence. However, if the baby is shown the ball being hidden in the same location over repeated trials, but is then shown the ball being hidden at a new location **(b)** during this period, the baby may look at the new location, but continue to reach to the old hiding place. This perseverative reaching behavior changes as the infant ages, and is replaced by normal looking and reaching to the new hiding place.

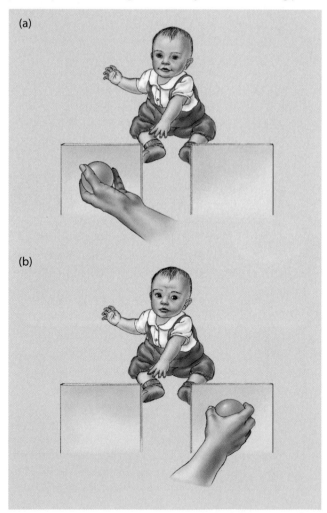

(a)

(b)

Finally, according to piagetian theory, the last cognitive process to develop in the sensory-motor intelligence stage is the ability to represent objects and events internally; that is, infants develop internal mental representations of objects and acts in their absence. For example, when object permanence is complete, the infant no longer has difficulty conceptualizing the presence of an unseen object, and indeed is peeved if expectations developed by direct observation are not met—like when the investigator tricks the infant about an object's location.

Many investigators have challenged Piaget's concept of the limited nature of a newborn's capabilities in the realms of cross-modal integration and object perception. These critics have argued that the newborn has some form of integration of sensory experiences across modalities of sight, sound, and touch. Infants' viewing preferences reveal that films of people speaking with the soundtrack in proper synchronization are more attractive to infants at only a few months of age than are identical films with the speakers' voices out of synch with mouth movements. This suggests a well-developed skill at cross-modal visual and auditory integration.

Young infants also evince knowledge of real world objects. We know that they normally perceive partially occluded objects and also can represent the relation between objects in three-dimensional space. This was demonstrated by showing infants an object and then placing it behind a vertical panel that occluded their view. The panel was then dropped under two conditions. In one condition the panel dropped and hit the object placed behind it, as would be expected. In the other condition the panel dropped, but the object had been secretly removed, so the panel fell flat to the table surface. In the second condition the infants showed more surprise than in the first condition (Figure 12.6).

If infants have well-developed object permanence, even at an early age, how can we explain the perseverative behavior when investigators hide the object (see Figure 12.5)? One interpretation has to do with properties of the frontal cortex. It is well known that adults suffering from frontal lobe damage cannot switch their motor set—they persevere with a previous response. In infants' perseverative motor behavior, they behave as though they were frontal lobe lesion patients. This can be interpreted in a surprisingly simple and gratifying way: Infants do not have complete myelination of projections to and from the prefrontal cortex, and thus their frontal cortex is not yet fully functional.

In the piagetian model three stages follow the sensory-motor intelligence stage. The first, from 2 to 7 years old, is the *preoperational stage* during which representational thought and object permanence are hypoth-

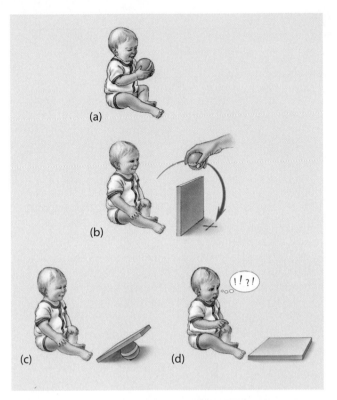

Figure 12.6 Physical reasoning in infants. Psychologist René Baillargeon (1991) tested infants knowledge about the relationships between physical objects in the world. Babies 4½ to 6½ months old were tested using the "time-of-looking" measure—babies look longer at surprising events. To test babies' knowledge of physical objects, they were shown an object placed behind an occluding screen **(b)**. Then the screen was allowed to fall onto the location the object was placed. In one condition, the screen strikes the hidden object **(c)**, in a second condition the object was secretly removed, and the screen falls to the floor **(d)**. Babies look longer at and are perplexed by the condition that violates the physical laws they believe to be correct. That is, the screen should have hit the object and stopped. This shows that babies have object permanence, and the ability to compute the size and relative locations of objects in the world, even when some are out of sight.

esized to be well established but other conceptual processes are not yet evident. Children in this stage cannot conserve quantity or numbers; that is, they cannot appreciate that two differently shaped glasses of liquid contain the same volume, even though they see them being filled by the same source. Thus, the visual appearance of a taller, thinner glass versus a shorter, fatter glass dominates the child's decisions about quantity. A similar effect happens with numbers of objects. By the end of this stage, however, at about 7 years old, children learn these abstract concepts and are rarely fooled if given all the information needed to make the correct decision.

From 7 to 11 years old, children become capable of some forms of quantitative conceptual thinking. Piaget argued that during this period they can initially perform these operations only on concrete items or events. They fail to make abstract inferences. Piaget called this period the stage of *concrete operations*. Then from 11 years onward, children learn to make abstract representations of relationships, something Piaget called *formal operations*. Children at this age can generalize mathematical relationships and manifest hypothetical-deductive thought—the ability to generate and test hypotheses about the world.

Piaget's contribution was to chart the timeline of cognitive development and to attempt to show when infants and children are able to perform complex cognitive operations. The fact that the precise age when a particular process is manifest may be earlier than what Piaget proposed, or that the discrete stages of Piaget may be more gradual than what is suggested in Table 12.1, does not significantly detract from his concept of cognitive development. Indeed, it is the job of science to modify theories with new concepts based on fresh data. In cognitive development, recent findings suggest a greater cognitive faculty in newborns and young infants than Piaget had proposed. Still, a timeline of cognitive maturation is, with proper modification, useful, because one goal of cognitive neuroscience is to relate the timeline of cognitive development to neural development in order to elucidate the biological bases of cognition.

The effort to relate this timeline to neural development is sometimes successful, as we learn later with respect to studies of the development of visual attention. But it can also be quite difficult, as with human language, when the neural substrates remain poorly defined. Yet there is another way that investigations of cognitive development can enlighten us about biological mechanisms, as for example when asking whether a cognitive ability is acquired by learning or is biologically predetermined (innate). This type of question probes the biology of cognitive processes but does not necessarily directly elucidate the neural circuitry involved. Nonetheless, whether an ability such as language is learned by a general-purpose cognitive-brain system, or is instead part of neural circuitry predestined for communication, is a fundamental question about cognition that can be addressed by consideration of cognitive development. In the next section we investigate the cognitive development of language from the perspective of whether language, as suggested by MIT psycholinguist Steve Pinker, is an instinct.

Language Acquisition During Development

Language is unique to humans, as most of us would agree. Whether it is an innate or acquired ability is a question that scientists have struggled with for decades. Humans

Gestural Communication in Infants Before Speech

Babies do not talk until between the ages of 1½ and 2 years, and so they cannot communicate, right? Wrong! You do not need to talk to communicate, and neither do babies. Researchers have known for some time that gesturing is an important form of communication between the baby and the parents. In a comprehensive study, Linda Acredolo of the University of California at Davis and Susan Goodwyn of California State University at Stanislaus investigated preverbal communication in babies in a sample of 140 families. The babies were studied for 3 years beginning at the age of 11 months. One-third of the families were encouraged to try to teach their babies baby signs, and the rest were not.

From tests on these children, the researchers discovered that babies who were encouraged to sign outperformed the other babies in many comparisons of communication skills, including the verbal ones that all babies come to develop naturally. Much of the reason for this can be attributed to the positive effects that preverbal communication has on the parent-child relationship. Babies and parents who sign communicate more and have more interactions. What are baby signs? The following is a story from the research files of the baby sign team:

Even though she is too young to say more than a few words, 13-month old Jennifer loves books. As her dad, Mark, settles on the couch after dinner she toddles over. Holding her palms together face up, she opens and closes them. Mark's immediate, "Oh, OK. Let's get a book to read," satisfies her and she soon returns with her favorite animal book, cuddles up close, and begins turning the pages. With delight she looks at a picture, scrapes her fingers across her chest, and looks up with a broad smile at Mark. "You're right. That's a zebra!" (Acredolo and Goodwyn, 1996).

The scene continues with Jennifer identifying animals and what the animals are doing without uttering a word. What has occurred? According to Acredolo and Goodwyn, Jennifer has just told her father what was in the book and he understood. Jennifer was using simple nonverbal gestures, or baby signs.

Infant children signing before they can verbally communicate their needs. (Courtesy of Linda Acredolo).

are not born with the ability to speak and understand a language; they must learn it through exposure—which means that language is a learned talent. But this does not provide the complete answer; we must still ask whether there is a learning mechanism for language, which is itself innate. We cannot say until we establish criteria for what qualifies as an innate ability.

Innate abilities should be present in all normal individuals in a population. The development of abilities should follow a common course among different individuals, and they should develop without overt training of one individual by another. Perhaps by definition, there should be a genetic component to innate behaviors; thus, language-related diseases might be inherited.

We might add other criteria, but the foregoing require the fewest assumptions. If the brain has a modular organization for cognition and sensation, and if this gross organization is similar across individuals, then an innate ability might be expressed in specific brain areas that are the same across individuals. But this characteristic is less crucial to the definition of innateness than the others. Overall, these defining characteristics of innate behavior are useful in evaluating behaviors of normal humans.

Is swimming, for instance, innate or learned? It appears to be innate for dogs (they swim the first time you place them in water) and other animals. Humans do not do a good job when they are thrown into water without prior experience with swimming, which usually requires some instruction. What about walking? This is slightly more difficult to intuit. Didn't our parents teach us to walk? They probably taught us a bit, but even without any instruction humans eventually stand and walk—a normal characteristic that occurs at a certain stage of development. And walking has dedicated neural structures within all individuals of a population. Walking is an innate ability in humans and swimming is probably not. So what about language?

COMMONALITY OF LANGUAGE IN HUMANS

How common is language as a behavior on this planet? Wide varieties of distinct languages are recognized. If each separate language represented different acquired knowledge and skills, then we would not want to argue that language is innate. It could be that we have innate predispositions to learning the language of our cultural heritage. If this were so, we would have to modify the characteristics that define an innate ability such that the word *population* did not refer to the entire species but merely the local genetic line in a region that spoke a certain language. It is not necessary to resort to such extreme positions because the data are unambiguous: Humans can acquire any language they are confronted with during childhood. Children of parents born in Beijing and raised speaking a Chinese language can acquire English without difficulty if raised in the United States speaking English. Indeed, if they are raised by native English speakers and only English is spoken, their language skills will be indistinguishable from those of Americans of English descent raised learning English. There is no mystery here; language is a system for communication and representation of events, items, and ideas that have universal qualities. It satisfies one defining characteristic of innate behavior in that it is shared by all members of the population.

This fact has been long understood by linguists who search for the universal features of language. Some, like Noam Chomsky, argued that all human languages are similar to one another. One such view is that a universal grammar is common to all languages and built into each person's language system. What differs from one language to the next are merely local characteristics of the grammar—how it is implemented in a specific language.

LANGUAGE ACQUISITION IS SIMILAR IN EVERYONE

The innateness of language ability can also be assessed by examining whether all individuals of the population express or acquire the ability in a similar fashion. Do children acquire language over a similar time period and by similar stages, or is there no norm? The answer is easy: All normal individuals acquire language in a similar way.

By their first birthday, children usually speak their first real words. Then over the next half year or so, they slowly gain about fifty more words. These first words usually refer to single objects in the world such as parents, food items, toys, pets, and so on. They also acquire verbs such as *eat* and words for interactions with others such as *hello*. Over the next few years of life, their acquisition of new words speeds up tremendously, the normal range being seven to nine new words a day.

The use of words in combination soon begins. First come two-word combinations, then three words and more, until sometime between the ages of 3 and 4, they start speaking complete sentences. If you studied a foreign language in high school or college, you know that it is difficult or impossible to achieve that rate of acquisition of a new language with such ease. A unique biological miracle happens to all of us in early life; we acquire language.

Language is more than strings of words, and children not only must acquire tags for items and actions, but also must learn the rules for putting the words together into grammatically correct sentences—not, as

Pinker (1994) put it, "the prescriptive grammar of school marms and style manuals, which list differences between standard and nonstandard dialects of English, and lay down conventions of written prose . . . ," but the mental grammar that describes how "words can be combined into bigger words, phrases, and sentences by rules that give a precise meaning to every combination." Children must learn morphology (combining words and fragments of words into larger words), syntax (combining words and phrases into sentences), and phonology (combining sounds into legitimate patterns appropriate for the language). English speakers have to differentiate between "man bites dog" and "dog bites man," and other, more complex formulations.

Children begin to acquire the mental grammar of a language early, and they learn these rules at similar ages. For example, children learning English have a highly similar order of acquiring grammatical morphemes, auxiliary verbs, and complex constructions such as negations or passive constructions. Their errors are also strikingly similar because they overgeneralize rules or apply them when exceptions exist, as with plurals like *mouses* instead of *mice*.

Acquiring categories for words begins early, when children learn to categorize words as verbs or nouns, and they probably learn this by experience. By combining cues, infants learn which category a word belongs to; for example, semantic cues and correlational cues tip infants to a word's syntactic category. Pinker proposed that semantic bootstrapping permits children to learn the differences between nouns and verbs. The idea is that the brain comes equipped to know that objects, actions, and attributes are different; we need only observe and infer the syntactic category of words. But this presents a paradox: How can we learn syntax if we have to know it before being exposed to it? Put another way, recognizing and becoming facile with knowing a noun from a verb requires that we are already born with that knowledge! How can we test this?

One way to test the idea that linguistic knowledge is innate rather than acquired is to examine situations where language errors predict whether a general rule is being applied. Take the relation between lexical and auxiliary verbs. A lexical verb is the prototypical verb (e.g., *eat, run, jump*), whereas an auxiliary or "helping verb" is one that varies tense, voice, or mood, or modifies aspects of another verb (e.g., *may* in "I may leave tonight"). Lexical and auxiliary verbs are quite similar in meaning and syntax, and in their lexical form; so a person learning these might confuse them and make predictable errors. Consider the lexical and auxiliary forms of *have*: "He has courses in psychology" (lexical) versus "He has taken courses in psychology" (auxiliary).

These two forms must be used properly or many types of incorrect sentences will be constructed. Linguists predict that children's speech errors might include things like incorrect order of lexical and auxiliary verbs ("She have should eaten"). This does not occur.

Children learn auxiliary verbs rapidly and accurately. One might argue that learning the correct use of auxiliary verbs results from parental feedback, correction, and instruction. But interactions between children and parents demonstrate that parents usually correct their children's speech mostly when errors are made in meaning, not grammar. If you have had experience with infants and young children, you may have noticed that you try to adopt their manner of speaking rather than correct their speech. Humans therefore have an innate, linguistic knowledge that enables them to employ syntactic structures of language, and thus develop complex forms of linguistic representation such as the use of auxiliary verbs. Humans do not have an innate ability to distinguish between lexical and auxiliary verbs per se; instead, the brain can apparently distinguish between lexical and functional categories. So we have at least one form of innate linguistic knowledge, which is part of the human brain's specialization for language. In summary, language has many characteristics of an innate property: as Pinker insisted, "Language is an instinct." The brain is predisposed to manifest the complex cognitive processes that comprise language.

Development of the Human Attention System

Language is a fascinating cognitive system. But what about other cognitive skills like attention? Can't babies, infants, and children orient to an event in the world with equivalent ease? OK, so babies are not good at this—it is sometimes hard to get their attention when they are lounging about in the crib. But what about infants? Research on visual perception, orienting, and attention has provided intriguing ideas about the attention system's development.

Primate visual systems have been extensively investigated over the past 40 years. We now know more about the visual system than perhaps any other part of the brain. Although much remains unknown about how the brain handles visual information, we have a clear picture of the mechanisms that control visuomotor processes. The structures and systems of relevance to the oculomotor system are well mapped; thus, observing how oculomotor behavior develops can enlighten us about the neural substrates of attentional orienting processes in humans.

The idea is simple, as Mark Johnson (1993) of

Carnegie-Mellon University clearly articulated it. The circuits in visuomotor behaviors become functional at varying postnatal times. An overt oculomotor behavior that develops at the same time as a specific circuit must be subserved by that circuit. Let us first review the time course of visual system development.

MATURATION OF SUBCORTICAL VISUAL CIRCUITS

The human retina's foveal region is immature at birth, whereas the peripheral retina is more developed. Hence, newborn vision is predominantly driven by peripheral inputs. In a similar way, the optic nerve is not completely myelinated in the newborn; however, myelination in the optic nerve occurs rapidly during the first 4 months of life, and reaches adult patterns at about the age of 2 years. The lateral geniculate nucleus of the thalamus—the main relay from the retina to the cortex—also experiences a rapid growth in the first 6 months after birth, almost doubling in volume. The time of maturation of the primary visual cortex varies with respect to different cortical layers. The cortex's deep layers, which project to the superior colliculus, develop earlier than the superficial layers. The superior colliculus is the primary subcortical target of retinal ganglion cells, and is the structure involved in saccadic eye movements and involuntary oculomotor movements toward salient events in the environment. The superior colliculus has a virtually normal pattern of neuronal lamination even before birth, and

the fibers of the retino-collicular projection are already partially myelinated prenatally, and are completely myelinated by 3 months postnatally. Thus, the first system to develop and to undergo myelination is the subcortical projection of the retina to the superior colliculus oculomotor system (Figure 12.7a).

The visuomotor behaviors of newborns and infants have been well characterized and have the following patterns: Newborns track moving objects but do not yet have smooth pursuit (smooth eye movement when tracking a moving object); rather, they use a saccadic pattern (small jumps in fixation from point to point) to follow a slowly moving object. Stimuli presented to their temporal visual field (stimuli on the right for the right eye, and stimuli on the left for the left eye) are more likely to elicit overt orienting of the head and eyes. Stimuli in the temporal hemifields impinge on portions of the retina that project more strongly to the superior colliculus and thus are more likely to induce oculomotor orienting (Figure 12.7b). Newborns also tend to ignore the internal features of complex stimuli. One view of these patterns is that in newborns the subcortical visuomotor system determines behavior.

When infants reach the age of 1 month, they often manifest obligatory attention, during which they fixate objects for long periods. Coincident with this in the striate cortex is the development of projections to subcortical structures that may inhibit activity in the supe-

Figure 12.7 **(a)** Diagram of the visual system showing the separate retino-geniculostriate pathway that carries visual information to cortical visual processing areas, and the retino-collicular pathway that projects from retina to the midbrain superior colliculus, part of the visuomotor system. Infants show a greater tendency to orient to stimuli in the temporal (peripheral) visual field of each eye. **(b)** This may be the result of a preferential projection of retinal ganglion cells from the nasal hemiretina to the superior colliculus. Ganglion cells in the nasal hemiretina are stimulated by stimuli location in the temporal hemifield.

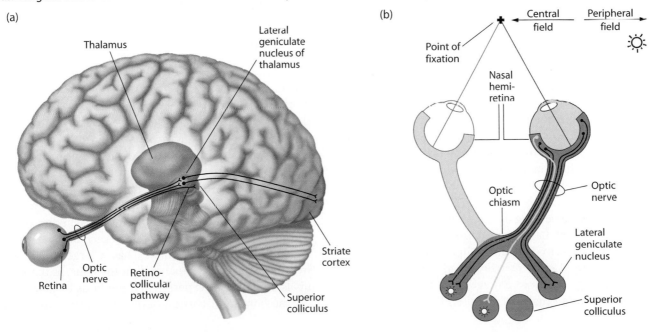

rior colliculus. The state where peripheral stimuli could trigger automatic overt orienting would be replaced by one in which the superior colliculus is less able to make saccadic eye movements, and hence 1-month-old infants fixate and become locked onto a stimulus event.

By 2 months, infants develop smooth pursuit tracking and orient to stimuli presented in the visual field. They also begin to attend to the internal features of complex stimuli. These patterns may result from coincident development and maturation of the striate cortex projection to the middle temporal (MT) motion areas of the extrastriate cortex. The MT pathway is essential for smooth pursuit. As well, ignoring internal features of complex scenes declines, which may relate to the improved acuity within the visual field's central regions.

Between the ages of 3 and 6 months, infants begin to make anticipatory eye movements. This is likely the result of maturation of the projection from upper layers of striate cortex to the frontal eye fields, which are the last to develop. The frontal eye fields participate in voluntary eye movements; therefore, frontal eye field maturation fits closely in time with the onset of more controlled oculomotor programs. In summarizing his data, Mark Johnson made three proposals about visuomotor behaviors.

1. The behavioral and neural sequence described above holds for a normal infant.
2. Specific neural events coincide with or precede observed behavioral changes.
3. The main limitation to the development of visuomotor behaviors is in the primary visual cortex (striate cortex).

What is the relation between overt signs of visuomotor behavior and covert attention? Michael Posner and Mary Rothbart (1980) proposed that covert attention should parallel the development of overt attention; they hypothesized that covert attention is involved in overt eye movements to locations in the visual field. Covert attention is thought to precede eye movements and may help to program the oculomotor system to make the correct eye movement.

Summary of Cognitive Development

In summary, cognitive development takes place over many years from birth to adulthood, but some cognitive functions mature earlier than others. This is not to say that the human infant is not capable of significant processing at a very early age. Indeed, the classic view of Piaget has been challenged and continues to be modified as researchers demonstrate that even young infants may have knowledge about objects around them, and that at an early age they develop sophisticated representations for the things they encounter. The evidence argues for a nervous system that acquires knowledge quickly by selecting from preconstructed neural circuits as soon as they physically come on-line. The result is that perception, action, and reasoning develop early and in parallel, and not in a simple progression from sensation to higher cognition. What are the substrates of this fantastic development, and how might they account for the timeline of cognitive development? In the next section we review the biological story of how the nervous system, especially the cortex, comes to be.

DEVELOPMENT OF THE NERVOUS SYSTEM

So far in this chapter we described aspects of cognitive development and how postnatal maturation can be correlated with aspects of behavior. By the time of birth, though, the fetal brain is well developed and shows cortical layers, neuronal connectivity, and myelination; in short, it is already extremely complex. To find out how this complex brain develops prenatally, let us examine the development of the human nervous system, with special reference to the neocortex, to learn about the rules governing development.

One rule that has emerged from the vast data on brain and behavior is that the brain is not an equipotential mass of randomly interconnected neurons. Indeed, this knowledge began to emerge from the work of the great anatomists Cajal and Golgi and their colleagues.

Today we know much more about the intricacies of the nervous system's neuronal circuits. These precise and complex circuits arise from a careful developmental plan that, if disrupted, may lead to disastrous consequences for the organism. The bulk of the brain consists of cortex, and, without minimizing the role of subcortical circuits, we can state that most cognitive activity involves cortical circuits and systems.

Animal models, such as the rhesus monkey, have permitted a close look at how neurons in the cortex achieve their final connectivity with each other and subcortical systems. The monkey has a large cortex and well-developed perceptual and motor skills. In these animals one can use experimental methods to determine the mechanism of cortical development that would not be possible by observing only humans. In the past decades a wealth of information has been derived on cellular, biochemical, and hormonal influences on the genesis of the cerebral cortex. New and sophisticated methods permit us to do more than merely observe the changes in the developing brain. They provide us with the chance to manipulate the course of development in ways that inform us about the underlying processes. For example, in addition to anatomical studies that observe the microanatomical organization of brain tissue at various developmental stages, investigators now also use advanced genetic techniques to learn about the formation of brains.

Overview of Gross Development

Before we discuss development at the cellular level, recall that from a single fertilized egg, an organism of billions of cells with specialized functions will arise. The peak of this complexity is clearly in the nervous system. Figure 12.8 depicts a primate's developmental path from fertilization to birth.

Recall that following fertilization, events lead to the multicellular *blastula* that has already begun to specialize. The blastula contains three main types of cell lines: the ectoderm, from which neural ectoderm will form;

the mesoderm; and the endoderm. In a broad sense, these respectively form (1) the nervous system and the outer skin, lens of the eye, inner ear, and hair; (2) the skeletal system and voluntary muscle; and (3) the gut and digestive organs. The blastula undergoes further development during *gastrulation,* when invagination and cell migration prompt the ectoderm to surround the entire embryo. The embryo now has mesoderm and endoderm layers segregated dorsally and ventrally, and thence undergoes *neurulation,* as shown in Figure 12.9. During this stage, the ectodermal cells on the dorsal surface form what is called the *neural plate.*

The development of the nervous system continues as the neural plate invaginates via neural folds being pushed up at its border. At this point there is already an axis of symmetry where the neural folds form a groove, the *neural groove.* As this groove deepens, the cells of the neural fold region eventually meet and fuse, forming the neural tube that runs anteriorly and posteriorly along the embryo. The adjacent nonneural ectoderm then reunites to seal the neural tube within an ectodermal covering that surrounds the embryo. At both ends of the neural tube are openings (the anterior and the posterior neuropore) that eventually close. When the anterior neuropore is sealed, this cavity forms the primitive brain consisting of three spaces or ventricles

Figure 12.8 Photographic sequence of a developing human fetus. **(a)** 7 weeks, **(b)** 9 weeks, **(c)** 7 months.

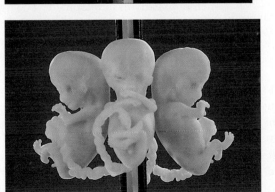

(a)

(b)

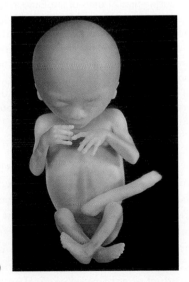

(c)

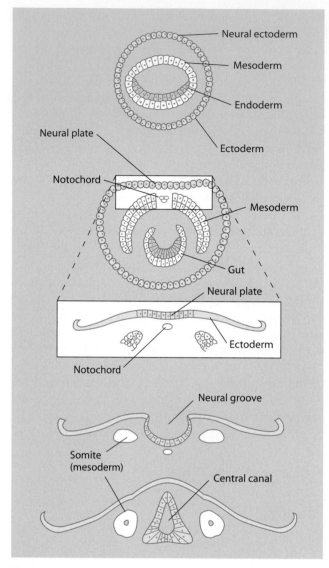

Figure 12.9 Development of the vertebrate nervous system. Cross sections through blastula and embryo at various developmental stages during first 21 days of life. Early in embryogenesis, the multicellular blastula (top) contains cells destined to form various body tissues. Migration and specialization of different cell lines leads to the primitive nervous system formed around the neural groove and neural tube on the dorsal surface of the embryo. The brain is located at the anterior end of the embryo and is not shown in these more posterior sections which are taken at the level of the spinal cord. Adapted from Carpenter (1976); Goldsby (1976); and Kandel et al. (1991).

(Figure 12.10). From this stage on, the brain's gross features are formed by growth and flexion (bending) of the neural tube's anterior portions, as described in Figure 12.10a. The result is a cerebral cortex that envelops the subcortical and brainstem structures that started out in line with the cortex along the neural tube. The final three-dimensional relations of the brain's structures are the product of continued cortical enlargement

and folding. One interesting feature of the flexions during fetal development is that at these early stages there is a striking similarity between fetuses of humans and those of other mammals (Figure 12.10b).

Genesis of the Cerebral Cortex

In the preceding section we briefly reviewed the development of the brain's gross anatomical features. Many details were omitted; you might refer to more complete sources in the Suggested Readings. We now consider mechanisms underlying the brain's growth and connectional specificity: neuronal proliferation, cell migration, cell determination and differentiation, and synaptogenesis.

NEURONAL PROLIFERATION

The first question about the brain's development is, When in the course of prenatal and postnatal development are neurons in the brain "born"? Examination of the brains of newborn monkeys or humans reveals that virtually the entire adult pattern of gross and cellular anatomical features is present at birth. With the exception of complete myelination of axons in the brain, the newborn has a well-developed cortex that includes the cortical layers and areas characterized in adults. Area 17 (the primary visual cortex) can be distinguished from the motor cortex by cytoarchitectonic analysis of neuronal makeup. Indeed, in primates there is no additional generation of neurons after birth, or apparently at any time during their decades of life. Thus, all neurons are generated prenatally. Again, the question remains, When are specific groups of neurons generated?

The timeline of neuronal development in nonhuman primates has been tracked by clever cell-labeling methods. The classic anatomical methods are unable to provide this information; by merely staining sections of cortex and observing the neurons present during embryogenesis, we cannot tell accurately which neurons arose first. The method developed, known as ^{3}H-thymidine labeling, involves injecting radioactively labeled thymidine into an embryo early in development. The thymidine is taken up by neurons and used to form DNA in cells undergoing cell division. Because the thymidine is labeled with a radioactive tag, the DNA of only the cells undergoing division at the time of injection will contain the radioactive label; hence, the label's distribution can localize the final fate of the neurons born at that time (Figure 12.11). Determining the distribution is done by the autoradiographic method. Sections of brain tissue are placed against photosensitive film and the radiation develops the film. The result is a picture showing the distribution within the brain section that contains the radiolabel.

Based on these cell-labeling studies on embryos dur-

(a)

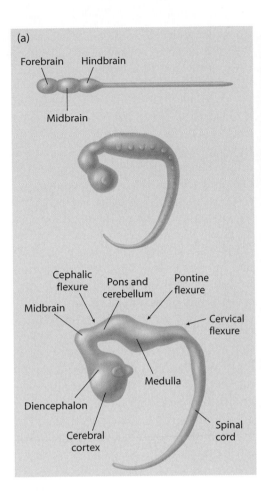

(b)

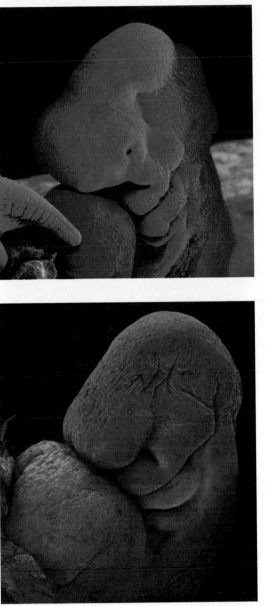

Figure 12.10 **(a)** Diagram of a developing embryo. The developing embryo goes through a series of folds, or flexures during development. These alterations in the gross structure of the nervous system give rise to the compact organization of the adult brain and brainstem in which the cerebral cortex overlays the diencephalon and midbrain within the human skull. Adapted from Carpenter, (1976). **(b)** There is significant similarity between the gross features of the developing fetuses of mammals, as shown by this comparison of human (top) and pig fetuses.

ing gestation, a clear view of the timing of cortical genesis is formed. The beginning of cortical genesis in primates is during the first quarter of gestation. All neurons in the primate cortex are derived within 1 to 2 months after the process begins, depending on which cortical region is under investigation. For example, production of the neurons of area 17 (striate cortex) is not finished until long after the neurons in the other brain areas have been born. Nevertheless, in primates the middle third of the gestational period accounts for the pro-

duction of all cortical neurons. This is untrue for other mammalian species, whose cortical neuronal genesis may continue until after birth or during a different circumscribed period in gestation. For example, in mice and rats, all cortical neurons arise during 1 week of the last third of gestation.

NEURONAL MIGRATION

Neurons that form the cortex arise from a layer of cells located adjacent to the ventricles of the developing

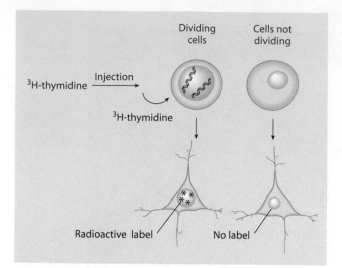

Figure 12.11 Diagramatic flow chart of the 3H-thymidine method to determine the fate of neurons that arise at a particular time in prenatal development. 3H-thymidine is incorporated into dividing cells, and remains within the cell body. The radioactive label can be viewed in the mature neurons and, because the investigator knows when the injection was made, can be used to trace when the neurons arose during development.

brain. This layer, known as the *ventricular zone,* has cells that divide to form cortical neurons. Figure 12.12 shows a cross section through the cortex and the precursor cell layers at various times during gestation. Precursor cells for both neurons and glial cells are in this ventricular zone. After these cells undergo mitosis, they migrate outward from the ventricular zone by moving along a peculiar cell known as the *radial glia,* which stretches

from the ventricular zone to the surface of the developing cortex. This unusual glial cell, first described by Cajal at the end of the nineteenth century, transforms into astrocytes in the adult brain.

The migrating neuron remains in contact with the framework provided by the radial glia cell via interactions of cell-surface molecules that keep the two cells intimately associated. The movement of the migrating cells is believed to result from contractions of skeletal-like intracellular molecules initiated by signals conducted across the membrane via ion channels.

Once the migrating neurons approach the surface of the developing cortex—a point known as the *cortical plate*—they stop short of the surface. Then neurons that migrate later pass the earlier neurons and end up in more superficial positions. Thus, it is said that the cortex is built from the inside out, because the first neurons to migrate lie in the deepest cortical layers, whereas the last to migrate move farthest out toward the cortical surface. This timeline of cortical cell genesis has been demonstrated with the thymidine-labeling method, as in Figure 12.13. Early in corticogenesis, injection of radioactive thymidine leads to labeling of neurons in the cortex's deepest layers, V and VI, and the underlying white matter. As noted earlier, the timeline of cortical neural genesis differs across cortical cytoarchitectonic areas (e.g., area 17 versus area 24), but the inside-out pattern is the same for all cortical areas. Because the timeline of cortical neurogenesis determines the ultimate pattern of cortical lamination, anything that affects the genesis of cortical neurons will lead to an ill-constructed cortex. Such events may underlie

Figure 12.12 Histogenesis of the cerebral cortex. Cross sectional views of developing cerebral cortex at early **(left)** and late **(right)** times during histogenesis. The cortex of mammals develops from the inside out as cells in the ventricular zone divide, and some of the cells migrate to the appropriate layer in the cortex. Radial glial cells form a superhighway along which the migrating cells travel enroute to the cortex. Adapted from Rakic, 1995.

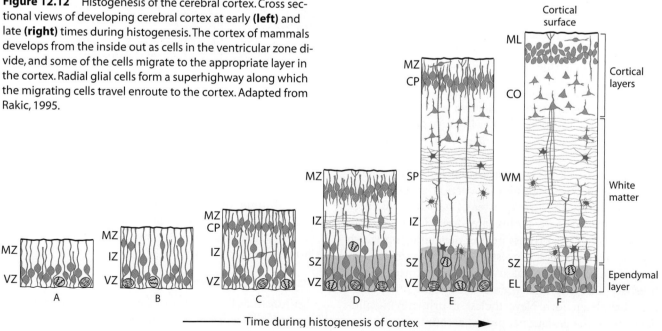

Time during histogenesis of cortex

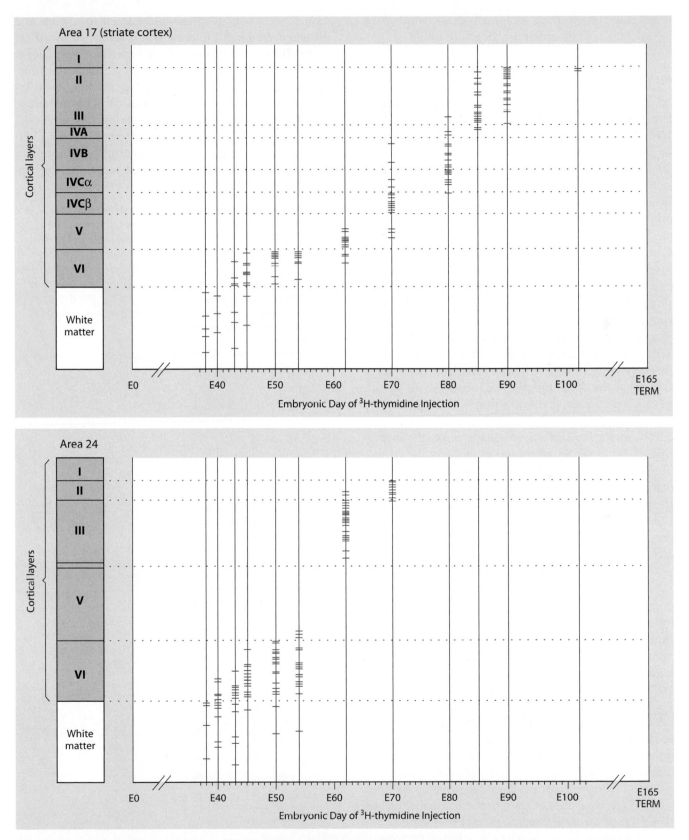

Figure 12.13 Birth ages of cortical neurons. Radio-labeled thymidine was used to label cells at different embryonic days in two cortical areas, Brodmann's area 17 and 24. The cortical layers present at birth are shown on the axis at the left with the cortical surface at the top of each plot. Cells with birth dates later in gestation are found in more superficial cortical layers, but the time course of this development differs for different cortical regions. Adapted from Rakic (1995).

many human disorders, such as dyslexia, which damages the brain's information-processing ability.

DETERMINATION OF NEURONAL TYPES IN THE CORTEX

So far we have regarded the cells in the ventricular zone as a single population. But how does this population of virtually identical precursor cells give rise to the variety of neurons in the adult cortex? Moreover, where do the glial cells come from? The answer is known: All cortical cells, including neuronal subtypes and glial cells, arise from precursor cells of the ventricular zone through cell division and differentiation.

For the first 5 to 6 weeks of gestation, the cells in the ventricular zone divide in a symmetrical fashion. The result is an exponential growth in the number of precursor cells. After this time, though, asymmetrical division begins and one of the two cells present after division becomes a migratory cell. The other remains in the ventricular zone and continues to undergo cell division. This subsequent division is also asymmetrical, yielding one remaining and one migratory cell. This process contributes to the cells migrating to cortical layers. In later gestational periods, the proportion of cells that migrate increases until eventually the final state yields a laminar cortex, with an epithelial layer that becomes the ependymal cell lining of the ventricles.

Which type of neuron a migratory neuron will become is determined at the point of cell division. Once the cell has been fated to migrate, the type of cell it will become and in which cortical layer it will reside are determined. This determination correlates with the time of its creation during gestation. Neurons that were supposed to migrate but were prevented from doing so by experimental intervention, such as exposure to x-rays, eventually develop patterns of connectivity that would be expected from neurons arising at the same gestational stage. Even though these neurons might remain in the ventricular zone, they display interconnections with other neurons that would be normal had they migrated to the cortical layers.

Similar evidence comes from transplanting cells from one animal to another. If embryonic cells from the ventricular region are removed at a certain stage of gestation and transplanted to the cortex of newborn host animals, such as ferrets, these transplanted neurons migrate to the proper cortical layer expected for their gestational age, regardless of the gestational period the host tissue is in at the time it receives the graft (Figure 12.14). Even if the host cortex is past the stage when neurons migrate to layers V and VI—for example, when the neurons in the host are migrating past these layers to form layers II and III—a transplanted neuron whose gesta-

tional age dictated that it should migrate to layers V and VI will indeed move to these layers. What is more, these transplanted neurons take on the morphological form (i.e., stellate cell, pyramidal cell, etc.) and the connectional pattern predicted by their age; that is, they are predetermined to be a certain neuronal type. The alternative would have been to have the properties (morphology, connectivity, biochemistry, etc.) of each cortical neuron determined by the neuronal environment where they reside, as with cells that form the neuronal

Figure 12.14 Determination of neuronal types in cortex. Transplants of fetal cells from one animal to another has demonstrated that neurons migrate to the region of cortex that is specified by the developmental stage at which they arose. Thus, neurons born at the same age migrate to their prespecified cortical layer regardless of whether they remain in the donor animal **(bottom left)**, or are transplanted to a host animal's brain that is actually older than the neurons being transplanted into it **(bottom right).**

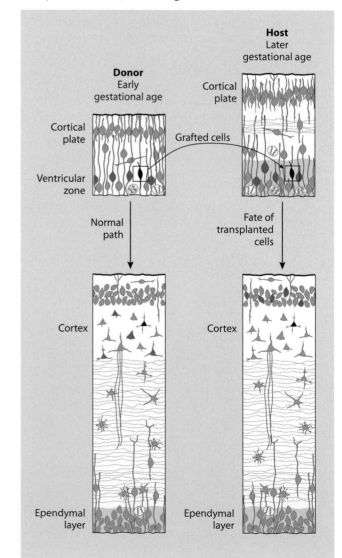

and glial cells of the peripheral sensory systems and the autonomic nervous system. The evidence is strong that, for mammalian cortical neurons, a prespecification of neuronal properties takes place long before the migrating neuron reaches its destination in the cortex.

THE RADIAL UNIT HYPOTHESIS

We now have a picture of how cortical neurons are born and how they migrate radially from the ventricular zone toward the surface of the developing cortex. The migration is along the radial glial cells that form a pathway for neurons. Because the radial glial highway is organized in a straight line from the ventricular zone to the cortical surface, there is a topographic relation between precursor and proliferating neurons in the ventricular area, and the cortical neurons they yield in the adult. Hence cells born next to each other in the ventricular zone end up near each other (in the plane perpendicular to the surface of cortex) in the cortex. As well, cells derived from precursor cells distant from one another will ultimately be distant in the cortex.

This concept, termed the *radial unit hypothesis* by Yale neuroscientist Pasko Rakic (1995a), is the idea that the columnar organization in the adult cortex is derived during development from cells that divide in the ventricular region (Figure 12.15). The cortical column is

Figure 12.15 Diagram of radial unit hypothesis. Radial glial cells in the ventricular zone project their processes in an orderly map through the various corical layers, thus maintaining the organizational structure specified in the ventricular layer. Adapted from Rakic (1995).

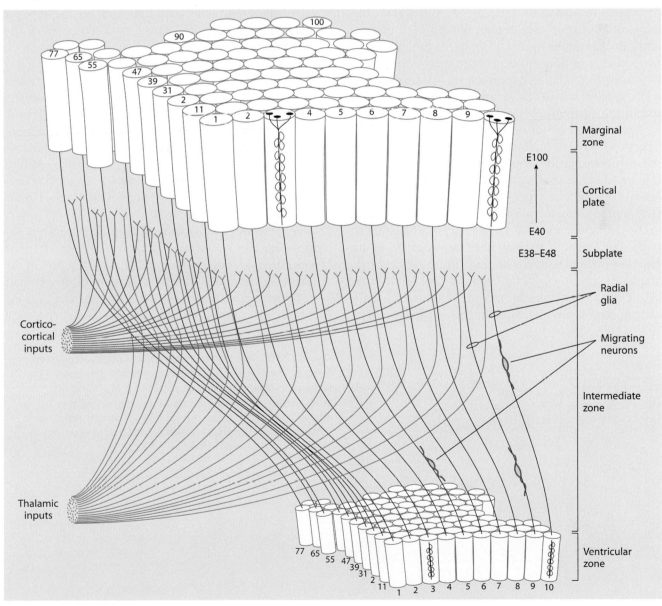

thus a principal unit of organization that has functional consequences and a developmental history. The radial unit hypothesis also provides a method for the evolutionary expansion of cortical size; the idea is that rather than enlarging each unit, the number of units is increased. The radial unit and the cortical columns that arise from these groupings have functional-anatomical consequences in the adult. For example, the intracortical interconnectivity among local neurons appears to be well suited to the size of cortical columns, which vary in adults from about 100 microns to 1 mm on a side, depending on the species and cortical area.

CYTOARCHITECTONIC VARIATION ACROSS CORTICAL AREAS

We discovered in Chapter 2 that distinctive variations appear in the cellular organization of the cortical regions. These cytoarchitectonic differences segregate the cortex into distinct areas. Thus, area 17 varies at the histological level from area 4, even though each of these cortical areas shares a general laminar organization and the positions of different neurons in each cytoarchitectonic area are similar. A question from the developmental perspective is how this variation occurs. What factors specify the differences between cortical areas?

One influential model posits that prespecified instructions inherent in developing neurons interact with signals derived from inputs by subcortical brain areas (Figure 12.16). According to this view, known as the *protomap hypothesis* of cytoarchitectonic diversity, genetic factors predetermine the organization. Neurons located in the ventricular zone will establish a protomap that attracts the thalamic afferent fibers appropriate to the function that the region is destined to perform. For example, the protomap in the region of the adult visual cortex will attract axons of neurons in the lateral geniculate nucleus of the thalamus, the thalamic relay that receives ascending projections from the retina. As well, the region of the protomap that becomes the primary auditory cortex attracts thalamo-cortical projections from the medial geniculate of the thalamus—the auditory relay nucleus.

Several lines of experimental evidence converge to support the view that the visual cortex in mammals can develop normal cellular makeup, intracortical synaptic organization, and neurotransmitter expression in the absence of activity from the retina, as do animals born without eyes or whose eyes were removed prenatally. The loss of visual input does affect the size and aspects of functional organization, however. For example, removal of one eye changes the pattern of ocular dominance columns in the cortex.

In cases of eye removal, the thalamic inputs still project axons to the visual cortex. But these aspects of cortical organization only partly depend on the type of thalamo-cortical inputs. In mice, cortical regions can be transplanted prenatally by microsurgical techniques. For example, we can transplant cells from the somatosensory cortex to another region of the cortex and then allow the fetus to develop. The transplant survives and makes connections with the thalamus. Genetic markers in the adult can tell us about the expression of genes in the transplanted tissue. With this procedure, we can see that although the transplanted cortex received nonsomatosensory afferents from the thalamus, the cortical neurons still express genes typical of the ones in the normal somatosensory cortex.

All features of the transplanted tissue are not expressed as they would be if the tissue had been left in the somatosensory cortex. Indeed, the final structure of the cortex is determined by the interactions of the intrinsic neuronal signals that are genetically specified, and the pattern of connections the neurons form with each

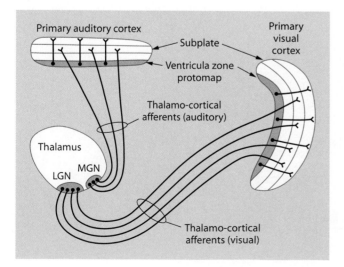

Figure 12.16 The protomap hypothesis of cytoarchitectonic diversity. The protomap model proposes that the neurons in the ventricular layer form a protomap that attracts the axons of neurons in the subcortical projection structure in a modality-specific manner. Thus, auditory fibers are attracted to auditory cortex, and visual fibers are attracted to visual cortex during embryogenesis (After Rakic, 1995).

THE COGNITIVE NEUROSCIENTIST'S TOOLKIT

Mutant Mice and Determination of Cortical Neuron Phenotypes

The reeler mouse has a genetic mutation that undermines the development of its cerebral cortex. This animal's cortex contains all classes of neurons, but they vary in position compared to normal mice, and the percentages of neuronal classes are altered—some are reduced from normal. The result is implied by the name "reeler"; these mice have severe problems with motor control: ataxic gait (clumsy walking), dystonic posture (improper muscle tone when standing), and tremors (shaking). These mice may also have a smaller cerebellum. All these problems are caused by an autosomal recessive gene.

The reeler mouse brain has another, more striking feature of its genetic failure. The radial glial cells in the reeler cortex are present during development but are oriented at unusual angles, rather than vertically as in the normal brain. Despite this strange alignment of the radial glia, the migrating neurons in the reeler still crawl along the glia, indicating that the cell-cell molecular interactions in normal mice are also present in the reeler mouse. The migratory process is relatively normal in the reeler; the neurons migrate as they should, outward along the radial glia toward the cortical surface. Yet the final positions of the neurons are not correct. In adults, the laminar organization of neurons is inverted in the reeler cortex. Large pyramidal cells are in deeper cortical layers, while smaller polymorphic neurons are located more superficially—the opposite of the normal mouse. The final positions of migratory neurons in the cortex are determined during a postmigratory stage. Once again, cellular morphology and patterns of connectivity are related to the time of cell birth at the ventricular zone, and not by the final position in the cortex, which in the reeler is incorrect.

Normal and reeler mouse cerebellar cortical layers. Adapted from Caviness and Rakic, 1978.

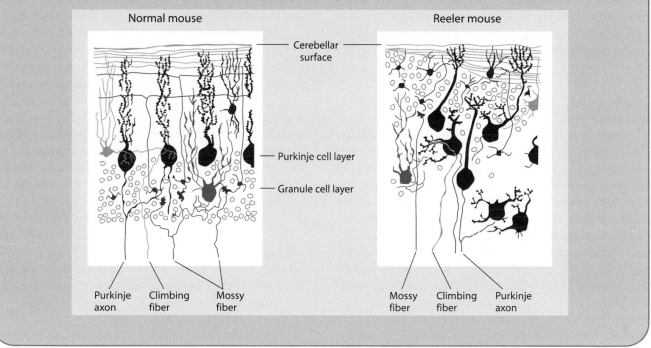

other and thalamic afferents. The studies of transplantations of embryonic cortex from the mouse visual cortex to the somatosensory cortex, and vice versa, uncovered enlightening facts about how much environmental factors alter the organization expressed by cortical neurons

(Figure 12.17). These studies used the barrel fields of the somatosensory cortex—characteristic circular arrangements (barrels) that are groups of neurons which receive input from a rodent's single whisker. Regions outside the somatosensory cortex do not have these

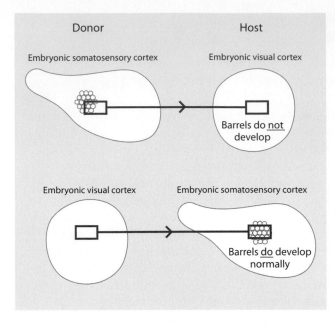

Figure 12.17 Transplanted tissue interacts with host neurons. The mouse whisker zones, barrels, in somatosensory cortex are characteristically identifiable anatomical structures. If portions of barrel cortex in fetal somatosensory cortex are transplanted to the visual cortex before the barrels arise, this tissue does not form the characteristic barrels. Similarly, visual cortical neurons can be induced to form barrels if transplanted from visual to somatosensory cortex.

anatomical features. When the somatosensory cortex is transplanted into the developing visual cortex, barrel fields do not develop. In contrast, visual cortex grafts placed in the somatosensory cortex do develop the barrel field organization typical in this cortical area. In both instances, the transplanted tissue is innervated by axons from the thalamus that are appropriate for the area where the transplant is placed, not by those appropriate for the region where the transplant was taken.

Summary of Cortical Development

The cortex's structure is controlled by complex interplay between intrinsic genetic factors that prespecify the fate of neurons and glia during gestation. Precursor cells in the ventricular zone of the mammalian cortex give rise to all the neurons and glia (except microglia) in the adult cortex, but different cell lines propagate only one of the neuronal subpopulations found in adults. The details of the organization of cortical connectivity are influenced by extrinsic properties of the afferent fibers that innervate the cortex. Inputs can affect the patterns

of organization in an area. Yet extrinsic influences do not have total control over a neuron's final state, in that genetic and biochemical properties of neurons may well be prespecified, although the extent is influenced by the environment.

Precursor cells in the ventricular zones of rodents are maleable to properties the cell line ultimately expresses biochemically, but this depends on gestational age. Early in gestation, precursor cells can be influenced to express, or not express, membrane proteins characteristic of the local population as defined by the cortical area. Later these neurons adopt rigid biochemical properties and express only specific proteins, unaffected by external influences. Thus, the concept of the protomap is supported, but with modifications to account for the precursor cell lines being influenced by extrinsic factors if it happens early enough in gestation. This cutoff time relates to the cells' mitotic cycle; premitotic cells can be affected by environment, but once they leave the cell cycle and become migratory neurons during asymmetrical division, they are fated to be a cell type, with the biochemistry, morphology, gross anatomy, and connectivity appropriate for that type.

PLASTICITY IN THE NERVOUS SYSTEM

It is obvious from the dramatic cellular events that go on during gestation that the nervous system is tremendously plastic during development; it can change its form, including the type and location of cells and how they are interconnected with one another. But this developmental plasticity stands in stark contrast to the apparent rigidity of the adult brain. Throughout development, however, nonplasticity is also a hallmark of the brain. For example, early in gestation undifferentiated precur-

Innovations in Cellular Labeling in the Study of Development

The developing cortex carries in its genetic make-up intrinsic instructions for controlling the differentiation of precursor neurons into mature cortical neurons of various types: astroglia, pyramidal cells, stellate cells, and so on. Investigating this differentiation calls for powerful biochemical and molecular techniques. These methods permit scientists to track the differentiation of neurons back to the first stages of development when different cell lines can be distinguished.

Cell-surface molecules such as proteins can be targets (antigens) for antibodies, proteins produced by the body for protection against infection. Antibodies can be harvested by researchers and labeled to be used as probes for specific proteins on cell surfaces. One simply adds a label (tag), either fluorescent or radioactive, to antibodies so they can be seen through a microscope. Visualization of the reaction of a tagged antibody with cell-surface proteins expressed by a subpopulation of cells is an ideal method for identifying those cells in the brain.

Using the antibody label specific to an adult cell, investigators found that cell-surface proteins in adult cells of animals' brains are sometimes expressed quite early in development. Monkeys' radial glia cells contain a protein called *glial fibrillary acidic protein* (GFAP). Using an antibody to GFAP, scientists showed that only some neurons in the ventricular zone had this protein—key support for the idea that a separate, prespecified group of precursor cells in the ventricular zone gives rise to radial glia and astrocytes.

Another powerful tool for investigating the lineages of neurons and glia derives from the use of certain viruses (retroviruses) to label the genetic material of neurons. The retrovirus is modified to prevent it from replicating, and to yield a protein that can be visualized later by using chemical reactions in histological slices. The retrovirus is injected locally and allowed to infect cells in the developing brain. (*Infection* means that the retrovirus inserts itself into the cell's DNA, effectively becoming part of the cell's genetic structure.) Careful quantitative methods ensure that the virus infects only a single precursor cell. When the cell divides to form two daughter cells, they also contain the retrovirus label, as will all descendants of the infected cell. With this approach, one can search later in development for neurons that contain this retrovirus marker. We have discovered that a precursor cell gives rise to either glia or neurons, but not both. Further, neurons that descend from the single infected cell are all of the same morphological type. It is curious that the timeline of generating descendant cells is unimportant. A single precursor cell can give rise to neurons that later appear in various cell layers, which means that they were born at different gestational times. Although the time when a neuron is born determines where it will reside, this alone does not indicate that it was derived from a certain precursor cell, because a cell line may produce migrating neurons at various gestational times and contribute to different cortical layers, but all these will be of the same cell types such as the pyramidal neuron.

---

sor cells become fated to express the characteristics of the brain region where they migrate to and remain. Thus, both plasticity and nonplasticity occur during prenatal development.

During postnatal development the brain still changes. In some notable instances, such as the orientation columns of the visual cortex, factors concerned with normal activity via afferent inputs rearrange the functional connectivity within the cortex. But postnatal plasticity is limited: Cells are not free to migrate to new areas, or to make large changes in long-distance connectivity. In contrast, local cortical connectivity can be affected during sensitive periods when extrinsic influences can alter brain organization.

Once these sensitive periods have passed, the central nervous system can be characterized by its marked lack of plasticity. Thus, damage to the central nervous system in the adult leads to irreversible damage; neurons do not regenerate damaged connections, nor does the brain replace lost neurons (see An Abundance of Neurons, p. 486).

This may be an adaptive strategy to prevent the wiring of the nervous system from changing too much during life. In contrast to the central nervous system, the peripheral nervous system does regenerate severed axons. A severed nerve in the arm will, if no obstructions are present, regenerate many millimeters in order to reinnervate a denervated target, like a skeletal muscle.

An Abundance of Neurons

The developmental events that lead to the adult brain include a fascinating wonder that is now a fundamental principle of corticogenesis: The developing brain produces more neurons and connections than will be used, and the numbers decline from this initial developmental explosion to the adult level. Between 30 and 60% more neurons are in the primate fetus than in the adult brain. More axons are present in the fetal and newborn primate than in the adult. Examinations of brain commissures (white matter tracts that connect the left and right hemispheres) reveal that the corpus callosum has 400% more axons in the prenatal monkey than in the 3-month-old infant or the adult. Peak numbers are found at birth. Axon loss occurs only after the cortex has reached its final connectional pattern, and thus axon loss does not reflect large-scale cortical reorganization. Rather, local circuits are primarily affected.

An exhuberance of synaptic connectivity does not correlate with axon numbers in the developing brain. The initial overproduction of synapses happens when axons are reducing in number. Unlike neuronal and axonal overproduction, synaptic overproduction occurs just prior to and after birth; the number of synapses declines through puberty (in macaque monkeys at about ages 3–4). Studies of the primate visual system showed that competition between inputs to a neuron leads to the strengthening of one contact and the weakening of others, which are subsequently eliminated. This competition is driven by activity in the afferent inputs, which appears to modify gene transcription in the neurons. The details of the mechanism are not fully understood, but we find a paradoxical pattern: The earlier in the cell development, the more numerous the neurons, axons, and synapses in the brain. This coincides with periods of minimal motor, perceptual, and cognitive skills in the developing primate, and with a time of greatest plasticity in the brain, as in the ability to learn. Thus, as with most things, more is not better in the brain.

This growth can be as fast as 1 mm/day. But this does not happen in the central nervous system, in part due to the interfering effects of glial cells that form impenetrable scars after brain damage (Figure 12.18). Neither the central nor the peripheral nervous system appear to produce new neurons after development is complete.

There is definitely plasticity in the adult brain. After all, we learn, don't we? Learning appears to involve changes in the synaptic weights between neurons in brain circuitry, as for example in long-term potentiation. So there must be some plastic change in the adult brain given the fantastic behavioral plasticity that adults display. The questions are, How great is this change, and To what extent might this reflect cortical reorganization in the adult brain? Fascinating experiments hold the answers.

Cortical Maps and Experience

An amazing revolution in neuroscience has taken place since the mid-1980s. It has grown out of the work of Michael Merzenich at the University of California, San Francisco, and John Kaas (1995) at Vanderbilt University (Merzenich et al., 1988; Merzenich and Jenkins, 1995). They and their colleagues launched a research program on how sensory and motor maps in the cortex can be modified with experience. To understand the story, we need details about cortical organization.

The body's sensory surface and our external auditory and visual worlds are represented in cortical maps. Part of our cerebral cortex, for example, is where neurons respond to stimulation of points on our body—the somatosensory cortex. When we analyze how all the neurons respond, we discover maps in the cortex that provide a point-for-point re-representation of the body's surface. There is a map for the hand, the face, the trunk, the legs, the genitals and so on. It is also true that the more sensitive a sensory surface is, the more neurons there are to represent that area. The neurons that respond to fingertips are greater in number and more densely packed than the neurons that respond to the back of the hand. This relation corresponds to sensitivity—fingertips are more sensitive than the back of the hand; this is known as the *cortical magnification factor*.

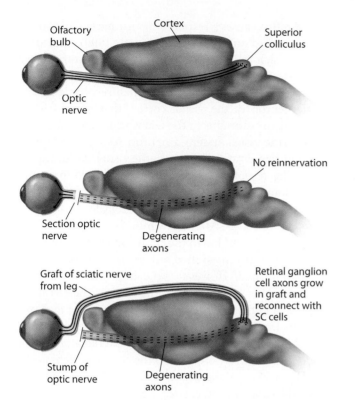

Figure 12.18 Inducing regeneration in the central nervous system (CNS). Neurons in the CNS **(top)** do not regenerate their connection with their target cells following damage **(middle)**, in part because glia cells interfere with regrowth. However, researchers have demonstrated that the neurons in the CNS can regenerate their axons and can reinnervate their old targets if a proper pathway is provided. Grafts of the sciatic nerve from the leg of rats can provide such a pathway, permitting regrowth, in this example, of retinal ganglion cells innervating the superior colliculus.

Body maps are also nicely organized such that the index finger is coded by neurons that are next to middle-finger neurons, which are next to ring-finger neurons, which in turn are next to the neurons coding inputs from the little finger. This is known as *somatotopy*, and these cortical areas are somatotopic maps. The maps are present in adult animals and humans and appear to be the basis for the ordering of our perceptions; they reflect the receptive field properties of the cortical neurons. It is not obvious why these maps exist the way they do. There is no inherent necessity for the organization. They are simply there—perhaps as a parsimonious organizational feature or perhaps as a means of coding relative relations as a place code—and because of this, fascinating phenomena have been discovered.

Merzenich's and Kaas's seminal observation was that

these maps change by manipulating peripheral receptors and nerves. This can be done by cutting the nerves innervating a portion of a limb, by tampering with the normal relations between adjacent regions of the limbs (e.g., by sewing together the fingers of one hand), or by altering the demands on the somatosensory system by increased use. They found, for example, that when a finger of a monkey is denervated, the relevant part of the cortex no longer responds to the touch of that finger (Figure 12.19). This is perhaps no big surprise—after all, the cortex is no longer receiving input from that finger. But here comes the strange part: The area of the cortex that formerly represented the denervated finger soon becomes active again and responds to stimulation of the finger *adjacent* to the amputated finger. The surrounding cortical area fills in the silent area and takes it over.

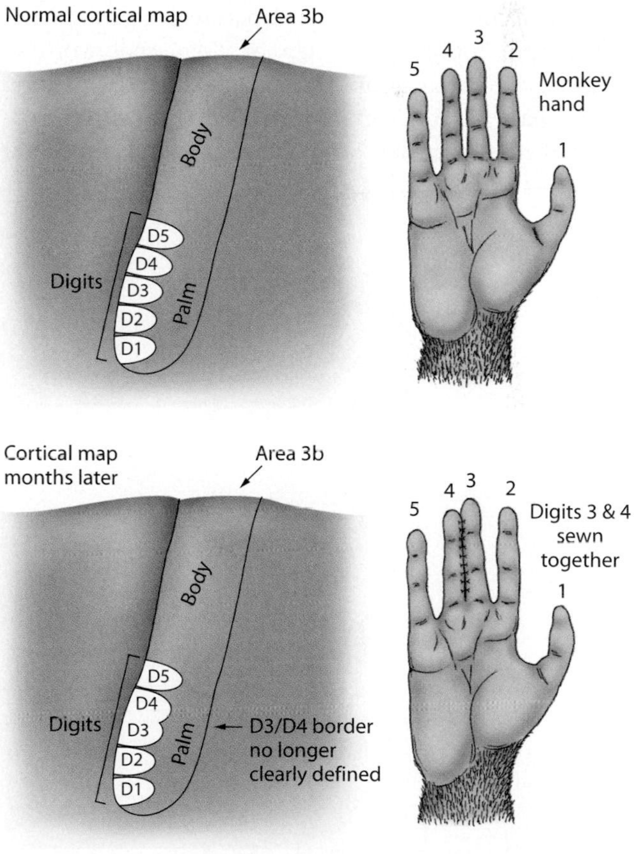

Figure 12.19 Reorganization of sensory maps in the primate cortex. Top left shows a mapping of the somatosensory hand area in a normal monkey cortex. The individual digit representations can be revealed using single unit recording. If the two fingers of one hand are sewn together, months later the cortical maps change such that the sharp border once present between the sewn fingers, is now blurred. Adapted from Kandel et al. (1991).

This *functional plasticity* suggests that the adult cortex is a dynamic place where changes can still happen. Such phenomena demonstrate a remarkable plasticity.

This cortical plasticity is not limited to the somatosensory system. It can also be observed in the auditory system. Gregg Recanzone at the University of California at Davis and Michael Merzenich trained owl monkeys to perform a tone-discrimination task for certain frequencies (Recanzone et al., 1993). They examined the tonotopic organization of the auditory cortex in the trained monkeys and compared it to control monkeys. The monkeys who had been performing the tone-discrimination task increased the cortical representation for those relevant frequencies in the auditory cortex (Figure 12.20). Thus, as in the somatosensory cortex, the auditory cortex has functional plasticity.

The visual system can also have such changes, as demonstrated by Charles Gilbert and Torsten Wiesel. The visual cortex, just like the somatosensory cortex, has a beautiful topographic map of the visual world—retinotopic organization. Stimulation of one point on the retina leads to a certain group of neurons responding in the visual cortex. Stimulation at an adjacent point on the retina causes a response in an adjacent area in the cortex, and so on. Gilbert and Wiesel (1990) created lesions in each retina to see what happened to the visual maps based on new recordings from the visual cortex. It is important to understand that when recording from a single neuron in the visual cortex, that neuron is responding to a stimulus in the real world. Remember that early in the visual system a neuron responds only to a certain narrowly defined area in the visual world, a space called the receptive field of that neuron. Gilbert and Wiesel found that almost instantly the size of the receptive fields changed for neurons adjacent to the lesioned area (Figure 12.21). After a few months, the cortical area that became silent due to the retinal lesions began to respond when the unlesioned but adjacent retinal regions were stimulated. However, note one crucial point of anatomy: After creation of a retinal lesion, there is also a silent area in the lateral geniculate nucleus, the thalamic relay to the striate cortex. Gilbert and Wiesel showed that this region of the lateral geniculate remained silent even after changes were seen in the cortex, which means all the changes at the higher-level cortex were accomplished by plasticity in cortical neurons.

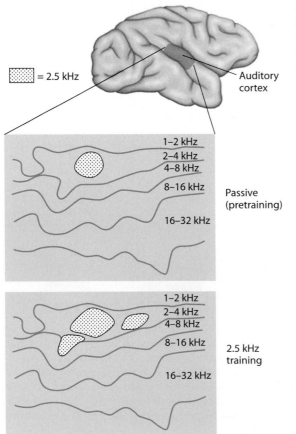

Figure 12.20 Changes in auditory frequency mapping following training. Gregg Recanzone and colleagues (1993) showed that training animals to discriminate specific tone frequencies leads to an enlargement of the cortical regions mapping the trained frequency.

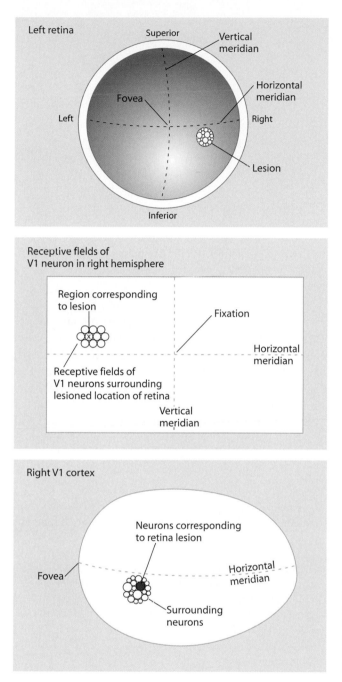

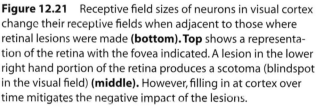

Figure 12.21 Receptive field sizes of neurons in visual cortex change their receptive fields when adjacent to those where retinal lesions were made **(bottom). Top** shows a representation of the retina with the fovea indicated. A lesion in the lower right hand portion of the retina produces a scotoma (blindspot in the visual field) **(middle).** However, filling in at cortex over time mitigates the negative impact of the lesions.

Reorganization in Human Cortex

Are phenomena of cortical functional plasticity limited to animals? How would one determine the answer to such a difficult question? Remember Professor Vilayanur S. Ramachandran who was introduced at the beginning of this chapter? His studies of amputees brought these dramatic animal results into the realm of human phenomena. Were you able to figure out the reason for the findings he obtained from his patients? Humans have maps of the body surface just like the experimental animals. When the whole map is considered, strange juxtapositions emerge. Consider the cortex's surface. Starting at one point in the somatosensory cortex, the pharynx is represented, then the face, with the sensitive lips having a huge representation, and next to the face are the fingers and hand, followed by the arm and leg (Figure 12.22).

Ramachandran reasoned that a cortical rearrangement ought to take place if an arm is amputated, just as Merzenich, Kaas, Recanzone, and their colleagues found.

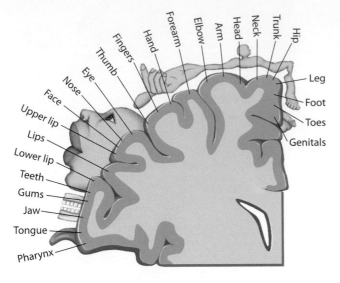

Figure 12.22 Diagrammatic map of a human humunculus in somatosensory cortex.

Such a rearrangement might be expected to create bizarre patterns of perception. Remember that the face area is next to the hand and arm area—an important point for understanding this story. Suppose there was no lower arm or hand to send sensory signals to the brain. According to animal research, the region coding for the arm that had been amputated might become functionally innervated by the surrounding cortex. That is exactly what happened in several spectacular cases like the one we described earlier. Here is the whole story.

Ramachandran studied a young man who had recently had his arm amputated just above the elbow. About 4 weeks after the amputation he was tested, and when a light Q-tip was brushed against his face, he reported feeling his amputated hand being touched! Feelings of sensation in missing limbs are the well-known phenomenon of *phantom limb sensation:* however, this case is different because the sensation was introduced by stimulating the face (Figure 12.23).

Indeed, with careful examination a map of his hand could be demonstrated on his face! Ramachandran goes on to report another case, which is too good not to quote verbatim:

> A neuroscience graduate student wrote to us that soon after her left lower leg was amputated she found that sen-

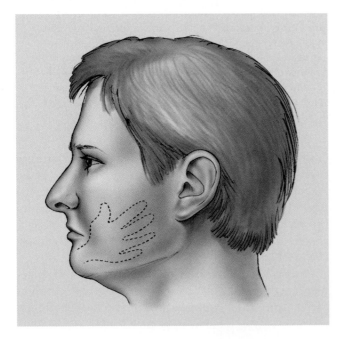

Figure 12.23 The drawing shows the hand representation drawn on the face of the amputee studied by Professor Ramachandran. The hand map on the face was obtained as described in Figures 12.1 and 12.2. Do you now have an idea as to why this might occur?

Plasticity in Fetal Tissues

Parkinson's disease affects approximately 500,000 Americans and is characterized by resting muscle tremors, rigidity of the limbs, difficulty in movement initiation, and slowness of movement execution. This neurodegenerative disease is most common in the elderly, but similar syndromes have also been induced by drugs in younger persons—street drugs are not pure, which can create catastrophic problems when impurities poison neurons in the brain.

Limb and body movements are controlled by the frontal cortex and the motor circuits of the basal ganglia. From the substantia nigra, dopaminergic neurons connect to the putamen, caudate, and globus pallidus of the basal ganglia (the *nigrostriatal bundle*). These areas also receive connections from the primary motor cortex and send neuronal connections back to the primary motor cortex and substantia nigra. Dopamine is synthesized in the nerve endings of the dopaminergic neurons whose cell bodies rest in the substantia nigra. Approximately 80% of the dopamine is in the basal ganglia, which comprises less than 0.5% of the total brain weight.

With Parkinson's disease, the dopaminergic pathway from the substantia nigra to the basal ganglia is disrupted. Up to 90% of the dopaminergic neurons in the substantia nigra degenerate and there is a reduction in the synthesis of dopamine. L-Dopa (L-3, 4-hydroxyphenylalanine), the amino acid precursor of dopamine, can be injected in parkinsonian patients to alleviate the disease's symptoms, but this leads to negative side effects, and its effectiveness diminishes with time.

Medical science has long searched for a way to protect or replace the damaged neurons of the parkinsonian patient's substantia nigra, or at least to mimic their function by other means. One way is by fetal tissue transplantation. The object of fetal transplantation is to introduce dopamine-producing cells, which have not fully differentiated, into brain areas where the cells can proliferate, form extensive neural connections, and release the deficient neurotransmitter.

Since the ban on fetal tissue transplants was lifted in 1992, approximately 200 operations worldwide have been performed. During the transplantation, fetal mesencephalon cells rich in dopaminergic neurons are ectopically grafted to key areas in the motor circuit of the basal ganglia, namely the caudate and putamen. Although success has varied, which makes generalizations difficult, the results look promising.

Widner and colleagues (1993) transplanted fetal tissue from six to eight fetuses 6 to 8 weeks old; the tissue was placed bilaterally into the caudate and putamen of two patients with MPTP (1-methyl-4-phenyl-1,2,3,6-tetrahydropyramidine) neurotoxin–induced Parkinson's disease. Positron emission tomography scans showed the uptake of radioactive L-dopa in the basal ganglia before transplantation (March 1988) and at two times after surgery (January and October 1990). The increased uptake of L-dopa indicated that the transplanted fetal cells successfully converted L-dopa to dopamine.

Parkinson's disease and its physical manifestations are not the only ailments treatable by transplanting fetal tissue. Cognitive abilities in rats with deficits induced by lesions and alcohol ingestion were restored almost to the levels of control animals, by grafting cholinergically rich fetal cells into the neocortex or hippocampus. The central nervous system's inability to regenerate after damage may be reversed by an increasing array of alternative therapies. We can predict a bright future for regeneration therapies.

---

sation in her phantom foot was enhanced in certain situations—especially during sexual intercourse and defecation. Similarly an engineer in Florida reported a heightening of sensation in his phantom (left) lower limb during orgasm and that his experience . . . actually spread all the way down into the [phantom] foot instead of remaining confined to the genitals: so that the orgasm was much bigger than it used to be . . . .

Together, these studies indicate that a significant degree of functional plasticity exists in the human cerebral cortex. The term *functional plasticity* is used because the effects are not caused by physical reorganization in cortical neuronal circuitry. Rather, in the normal case, the receptive fields of neurons overlap more than what is apparent from recordings from single neurons. Most of

An Interview with Helen J. Neville, Ph.D.   Dr. Neville is a professor of Psychology at the University of Oregon and a leading authority in developmental cognitive neurosciences.

Authors: You have studied deaf people by using event-related potentials (ERPs) and have discovered that their brains have a different organization than that of normal subjects. Could you tell us what this amazing finding entails?

HJN: Yes, we've been studying the role of experience on the development of neural systems important to aspects of cognition, and the people in our research are individuals who were born bilaterally deaf due to a genetic failure in the development of the cochlea. We have tested the idea that the lack of auditory input might lead to a reorganization of cortical areas that normally process auditory information. It appeared plausible that visual processing might spread into the "abandoned" auditory cortex, and we've studied how much this happens, the time that it might occur, and the mechanisms that might mediate such a change. Our deaf subjects also had a very different language experience: None learned an aural-oral language, but all learned a visuomanual language, American Sign Language (ASL). We examined the effects of this language on the development of the brain's language systems. One way we separately assess the effects of auditory deprivation from the effects of acquiring a visuospatial language is to study hearing people who were born to deaf parents. These people haven't had any auditory deprivation, but all learned ASL as a first language, just as our deaf subjects. Any effects from auditory deprivation shouldn't be evident in the hearing person born of deaf parents, but effects due to the acquisition of ASL should appear in this group as well as the deaf subjects. We have used ERPs extensively to study these issues, and also functional magnetic resonance imaging (fMRI) techniques. The former provide excellent temporal resolution, and the latter great spatial resolution. So they are highly complementary techniques.

Authors: Does the brain reorganize itself as a result of the loss of auditory input?

HJN: Our studies of visual processing in the deaf have indicated that there are indeed alterations in visual processing following auditory deprivation. Visual ERPs are several times larger in deaf than in hearing subjects. These effects are absent in the hearing subjects born of deaf parents. And the changes were specific: They were found in response to peripheral visual stimuli but not stimuli presented foveally. Such changes happen in visual sensory paradigms and visual attention tasks.

the time this overlapping connectivity produces no sensory effects, but when the main input to a cortical region is removed, the secondary inputs from nearby parts of the sensory map appear to become functional. This effect leads to changes in the observed shapes of the cortical maps.

SUMMARY

The development and plasticity story is complex, beginning with fantastic plastic changes as the brain and body form during embryogenesis and concluding with a much more rigid and nonplastic nervous system in the adult. In-between, during early development, important plastic changes can occur, and these take place in correspondence with sensitive periods during maturation. Thus, permanent changes in human brain organization can occur by the loss or alteration of sensory inputs during these sensitive periods of early life.

Even in the adult, however, plastic changes occur, as we are still capable of learning throughout life. Plastic changes can also occur in the sensory cortical areas, as with animals or humans with lost or denervated limbs and as the result of training. The story is not one of a completely plastic brain, but of a controlled development and maturation that lead to the marvelous complexity in the adult brain, a brain that we now know shows various forms of plasticity. Throughout development and maturation, the rise of cognition is a steady march toward language, literature, reason, and culture—the province of the human brain.

Authors: Yes, but do these physiological changes reflect any behavioral change?

HJN: You bet! The physiological effects have functional consequences: Deaf subjects are faster and more accurate at detecting moving targets in the peripheral visual fields. Anatomical investigations suggest that the periphery of visual space is largely represented along the dorsal visual pathway that projects from the striate cortex to the parietal cortex that includes motion-sensitive areas. By contrast, central visual space is represented mainly along the ventral pathway that projects from V1 to anterior temporal cortex. It's important for high-resolution form discrimination and color discrimination. We tested the ideas that big alterations in visual processing secondary to auditory deprivation happen along the dorsal pathway, and more generally that it displays more developmental plasticity than does the ventral visual pathway. We presented stimuli designed to stimulate the magnocellular and parvocellular pathways that project to the dorsal and ventral pathways. ERPs from deaf and hearing subjects are similar in response to the parvocellular stimuli (colored, high spatial frequency gratings, flickering at low rates), but responses from deaf subjects are several times larger than those from hearing subjects in response to the magnocellular stimuli (moving, black and white, low spatial frequency gratings, flickering at high rates).

Authors: How do the ERPs become larger in the deaf? Are there more neurons involved or the same ones yielding a more intense response?

HJN: Current density maps of the electrical pattern across the scalp of these groups suggest that extra generators within the temporal cortex in deaf subjects are involved in the response to these stimuli. We are now examining these issues by using fMRI to determine where within the temporal lobe these changes occur. Knowing the location of changes raises hypotheses about how visual processing might be enhanced after auditory deprivation. A likely area for change is the superior temporal polysensory area that normally receives auditory and visual input. In the absence of auditory input, visual afferents may take over what would normally be auditory cells and enhance visual responsiveness. Animal research shows changes within multimodal areas after congenital visual deprivation.

Authors: But couldn't the change reflect an unmasking of preexisting circuits?

HJN: Yes. There may be, in the immature human brain as in other animals, a transient redundancy of connections between sensory areas that is normally competitively displaced (anatomically or functionally) with normal sensory experience during development. In deaf subjects it may be that visual afferents projecting to auditory areas become stabilized in the absence of competition from normal auditory inputs. We are investigating this by studying deaf and hearing infants in the first few years of life to see whether auditory and visual systems differentiate more along a timeline that parallels the sensitive period when auditory deprivation leads to these changes in the visual system.

SUGGESTED READINGS

BAILLARGEON, R. (1995). Physical Reasoning in Infancy. In M. Gazzaniga (Ed.), *The Cognitive Neurosciences* (pp. 181–204). Cambridge, MA: MIT Press.

GAZZANIGA, M.S. (Ed.), *The Cognitive Neurosciences* (pp. 219–234). Cambridge, MA: MIT Press.

GOLDMAN-RAKIC, P.S. (1987). Development of cortical circuitry and cognitive function. *Child Dev.* 58:601–622.

JOHNSON, M.H., POSNER, M.I., and ROTHBART, M.K. (1994). Facilitation of saccades toward a covertly attended location in early infancy. *Psychol. Sci.* 5:90–93.

MANDLER, J.M. (1992). How to build a baby: II. Conceptual primitives. *Psychol. Rev.* 4:587–604.

NEVILLE, H. (1995). Developmental Specificity in Neurocognitive Development in Humans. In M. Gazzaniga (Ed.), *The Cognitive Neurosciences* (pp. 219–234). Cambridge, MA: MIT Press.

RAKIC, P. (1995a). Corticogenesis in Humans and Nonhuman Primates. In M. Gazzaniga (Ed.), *The Cognitive Neurosciences* (pp. 127–146). Cambridge, MA: MIT Press.

RECANZONE, G., SCHREINER, C.E., and MERZENICH, M. (1993). Plasticity in the frequency representation of primary auditory cortex following discrimination training in adult owl monkeys. *J. Neurosci.* 13:87–103.

SPELKE, E.S., VISHTON, P., and VON HOFSTEN, D. (1995). Object Perception, Object-Directed Action, and Physical Knowledge in Infancy. In M.S. Gazzaniga (Ed.), *The Cognitive Neurosciences* (pp. 165–180). Cambridge, MA: MIT Press.

13

Evolutionary Perspectives

One night a few years ago, my wife and I (M.S.G.) boarded the subway in the 13th Arrondisement in Paris. That section of Paris is wonderful for immigrants, and we had come from New York to do some research there. The minute we got on the subway I spotted four huge young men gazing solemnly at us. I immediately positioned myself between them and my wife and waited for the tussle that would surely occur. Their ominous presence led me to feel that I might be performing my last act of chivalry. Being an experienced New York subway rider, I knew the scene and was nervous.

As the train pulled into the station we wanted, I readied myself for defense. The largest male of the group approached me. I tensed. Then his pleasant voice rang, "Pardon, Monsieur, aprez-vous," as he invited my wife and me to exit the subway car before he and his friends followed suit.

Many things that bother us in our modern culture are represented by that event. New York statistics might support the idea that four men staring at a couple in a subway late at night with few people around means trouble. It means trouble because in New York the statistics for crime on the subway are high, especially at night in little-used subway cars. It means that young males disenfranchised by society have a high probability of being aggressive. Or, it means I was paranoid and misinterpreted the situation.

Violence in American inner cities is no illusion. How do we explain more than 1,700 homicides in New York every year? One explanation might be that there are plenty of guns in New York. That must be it. No. There are six homicides in Switzerland every year and every male in Switzerland under the age of 55 has a machine gun at home because they are in the military reserves. Another explanation might be that the criminals are black. No. East Los Angeles has similar statistics and the criminals are Mexican. Maybe homicides occur when

minorities are living in a white culture. No. Violence also exists in the inner cities of Scotland! Scotland's homicide rate is second to America's homicide rate. Well, then, it must be because the criminals are poor and want a better life.

Enter neuroscience. The brain team says, look, it must be brain chemicals that make people aggressive. Perhaps dominance and seeking dominance are products of an overactive serotonin system, even though being dominant is what most males seek. However, the opposite could be true—serotonin levels could be high because the person is the dominant male. One must always remember correlation does not mean causation.

The one brain mechanism–one symptom view is slowly giving way to more interesting views of how and why brains were built. It does not take a very active imagination to begin to see how the foregoing approach leads nowhere. Pick a normal point for serotonin levels. Then measure the level in athletes, in schizophrenics, in homosexuals, in ping-pong players, in stockbrokers, in whomever. Trying to sort out the role of serotonin in aggression in this light is a tough game. Everyone has a serotonin mechanism, which means anyone can become highly dominant (aggressive) or not. The factors that can lead to changing the level are complex. They can be self-generated by a change in philosophy of life, or they

An Interview with Steven Pinker, Ph.D.
Steven Pinker is a professor of Brain and Cognitive Science at MIT. He has worked on problems in vision, attention, development of language, and evolution.

Authors: Why is it important for students of the mind to understand the principles of evolution?

SP: The brain is a highly organized, nonrandom system, and it can't be understood without knowing the forces that gave rise to that organization. We know the brain did not fall out of the sky; like other parts of the body its functional complexity—the fact that it can do interesting things like see, think, and act—is a product of evolutionary forces, particularly natural selection.

Authors: OK, let's get down and dirty. Suppose a student is interested in the problem of memory or attention or even morality. These issues can be studied without mentioning natural selection. How does natural selection inform them about their chosen topic?

SP: These issues cannot be understood without natural selection. Natural selection is the rationale for reverse-engineering the brain—figuring out what it was designed to accomplish. Why do we remember recent and frequent items best? Is it some inherent property of the stickiness and softness of neural tissue? Or could evolution have built a brain that remembers everything equally well, but steps in that direction were selected against? When you compare the computer information retrieval system at the library, which spills hundreds of useless titles in your lap, to a human expert, who homes in on the five or six most appropriate ones, you appreciate that human memory might be close to optimal in trading off likelihood of finding the needed information against the costs in time of considering unneeded information. Since organisms operate in real time, this is not a trivial trade-off. John Anderson has shown that retrieving frequent and recent items is the optimal strategy for any information access system, so the explanation for the human case is quite likely to be that the brain is specially organized to be frequency and recency sensitive because of the selective advantages it brought, not that calcium channels or whatever make it inevitable. As for morality, the necessity of evolutionary thinking is even stronger. Evolutionary game theory has made very strong predictions of what kinds of algorithms have to be in the mind of an organism that can engage in moral behavior. Many commonsense notions prevalent among academics (e.g., that morality evolved for group cohesion, or that there is an instinct for aggression) are literally unevolvable.

can be artificially manipulated by antidepressants like Prozac (fluoxetine hydrochloride), which increases serotonin levels. Michael Raleigh and Michael McGuire and colleagues at the University of California (1984), Los Angeles, showed that when Prozac is given to a random male monkey in a colony, after the dominant male had been removed, the Prozac-laden monkey becomes the dominant male. Some suggest that American Corporations ought to beware of depressed middle managers who have been advised to take Prozac!

It is awareness of the fact that our brains were built by natural selection that allows us to think about such complex behaviors as violence. Indeed, what are our brains built for? Why do they do what they do? Consider the elegant characterization by John Tooby and Leda Cosmides (1995).

> . . . understanding the neural organization of the brain depends on understanding the functional organization of its cognitive devices. The brain originally came into existence, and accumulated its particular set of design features only because these features functionally contributed to the organisms propagation. This contribution, that is, the evolutionary function of the brain, is obviously the adaptive regulation of behavior and physiology on the basis of information derived from the body and from the environment. The brain performs no significant mechanical, metabolic, or chemical service for the organism; its function is purely informational, computational, and regulatory in nature. Because the function of the brain is informational in nature, its precise functional organization can be described accurately only in a language that is capable of expressing its informational functions that is, in cognitive terms, rather than in cellular, anatomical, or chemical terms. Cognitive investigations are not some soft, optional activity that goes on only until the real neural analysis can be performed. Instead, the mapping of the computational adaptations of the brain is an unavoidable and indispensable step in the neuroscience research

Authors: Unevolvable? Come at that point one more time.

SP: One might think a group of indiscriminate altruists, all helping each other out, would do better than a group of selfish creatures who refuse to sacrifice for the benefit of all. But the problem is getting the altruistic group to begin with. A mutant with a tendency toward selfishness would enjoy all the benefits of his altruistic buddies without paying the costs. Nothing could stop it from proliferating through the group, given that individuals reproduce faster than whole groups. As for aggression, again the text of other organisms has to be taken into account. A bully mutant would do fine at first, but after a bunch of generations everyone will be a bully, and the advantage is gone. It's not that altruism and aggression can't evolve; it's just that they can only evolve in conjunction with information-processing mechanisms that strategically assess how and when to deploy them.

Authors: Finally, with the new awareness of the importance of evolutionary thinking for understanding mental processes, how might experiments be executed in the future? If, for example, one hypothesized human memory systems were built to aid in finding food sources scattered about a home base, might one reject using word-pair associates as a way of understanding human memory? Instead wouldn't one want to study the efficiency of memory with and without a lot of spatial cues?

SP: Certainly, it would do everyone good to pay more attention to the ecological validity of the stimulus materials and the task used in experiments. It also is important to think of the brain as a family of systems engineered to solve the kinds of problems the organism faced in its evolutionary history (foraging, mating, language or other forms of communication, etc.) rather than hoping to explain intelligence exclusively with very crude general mechanisms like forming associative bonds. And attention to phylogeny and speciation would correct the lamentable tendency to treat all animals as half-baked humans we can cut up, rather than as cohesively functioning species that are well adapted to their own niches.

But ultimately, evolutionary thinking isn't a specific theory that one goes out and tests like a hypothesis about shape recognition. A cognitive neuroscientist should understand evolution for the same reason a biologist should understand chemistry or a chemist should understand physics. The chemist doesn't ask, "How will knowing physics help me to design my next experiment?" He or she had better know physics because *everything* done in chemistry ultimately has to make sense in the light of physics. Similarly, cognitive science and neuroscience are studying the products of specific causal processes (natural selection and other evolutionary forces) and ultimately nothing in those fields makes sense—no explanation, no experiment, no choice of an organism to study—until it is made consistent with what we know about those processes.

enterprise; it must proceed in tandem with neural investigations, and indeed will provide one of the primary frameworks necessary for organizing the body of neuroscience results.

There will come a time when the subject matter of this chapter will be presented in the first chapter of a text on cognitive neuroscience. The reason for its current position in the flow of information is that most practitioners of cognitive science and neuroscience do not yet fully appreciate the insights offered by an evolutionary perspective. In part, this has to do with the very history of neuroscience and psychology. Both fields have been dominated by an attitude, a belief that associationism is how we learn and remember what we know, and that most brains can learn anything. It can learn to be violent; it can learn to be nonviolent. Simple chemicals control such learning, and if we understand them, we will understand the social problems of violence. The past 100 years of research do not support this view. To learn why, we must examine the current cognitive neuroscience enterprise from an evolutionary perspective. What are brains for, why were they built the way they are, and, in a mechanistic sense, how should we view the relation between neuroscientific data and behavior?

Evolutionary theory, brought to this world by Charles Darwin (1859), is so powerful and so pervasive in modern knowledge that everyone thinks they understand it. After all, isn't the idea of natural selection that only the fittest survive? Doesn't it have something to do with our evolution from lower animals? It turns out that when most people are asked about the significance of evolution, a hodgepodge of ideas bubbles up to consciousness, unstructured and diffuse. If we are to thoroughly understand its importance, we must learn a few basic principles of evolutionary theory (Williams, 1966).

Darwin's Big Idea

Charles Darwin was a genius by any measure. He provided humankind with the key idea about our origins, the idea of natural selection. He was the first one who brought together extensive data that the idea of natural selection had sustaining value in understanding human origins. He summarized his idea in two long sentences, as recently recounted by Daniel Dennett in his fascinating book, *Darwin's Dangerous Idea* (1995). Here is that idea.

If during the long course of ages and under varying conditions of life, organic beings vary at all in the several parts of their organization, and I think this cannot be disputed; if there bye, owing to the high geometric powers of increase of each species, at some age, season, or year, a severe struggle for life, and this certainly cannot be disputed; then considering the infinite complexity of the relations of all organic beings to each other and to their conditions of existence, causing an infinite diversity in structure, constitution, and habits, to be advantageous to them, I think it would be a most extraordinary fact if not variation ever had occurred useful to each be-

ings own welfare, in the same way as so many variations have occurred useful to man. But if variations useful to any organic being do occur, assuredly individuals thus characterized will have the best chance of being preserved in the struggle for life; and from the strong principle of inheritance they will tend to produce offspring similarly characterized. This principle of preservation, I have called, for the sake of brevity, Natural Selection.

Now, while Darwin could have used an editor, he did condense the most powerful idea in biology into two sentences. And yet, as Dennett pointed out in his book, his brilliant idea was not born from whole cloth. David Hume, the great philosopher, in his *Dialogues* had three characters carry out a fictional debate about whether the world exists as a result of a design; that is, any complex entity must have a designer and in this case it is God. Cleanthes, the Greek philosopher, defended the Argument for Design.

Look round the world: Contemplate the whole and every part of it: You will find it to be nothing but one

FIRST PRINCIPLES

From the evolutionary perspective, organisms are described as self-reproducing machines, and, as Tooby and Cosmides (1995) put it, ". . . the defining property of life is the presence of a system of devices or organization that cause the system to construct new and similarly reproducing systems. From this defining property of self-reproduction, the entire deductive structure of modern darwinism logically follows." That observation is not only unbelievable, it has, as Henry Kissinger used to say, the added benefit of being true.

Right off the bat, things begin to happen. The reproductive process does not go on without error. Mutations, or spontaneous changes in genetic material, occur at a low frequency. When they happen, they can affect the offspring in a positive or a negative way. If they produce a negative effect, they are weeded out because changes that interrupt the complex developmental events result-

ing in a successfully reproducing organism will not survive. Thus, if the mutation prevented birth, or changed development in a significant way, or caused dysfunctions, or interfered with the ability to reproduce, the species mutation would not survive. Hence, most random mutations have no measurable effect on an organism. Natural selection gets rid of them.

One might ask why horrible diseases like Alzheimer's or even schizophrenia survive in the population. A disease like Alzheimer's appears late in life and past the years of reproduction. Thus, the genes responsible for unleashing the neuropathological state of this disease might be selected for because they play a positive role early in life and promote reproduction. That the same gene is responsible for bad things later in life is a cost to be paid. Even the genes for schizophrenia, which must be deeply embedded in the genome as it is so widely distrib-

Charles Darwin.

great machine, subdivided into an infinite number of lesser machines, which again admit of subdivisions to a degree beyond what human senses and faculties can trace and explain. All these various machines, and even their most minute parts, are adjusted to each other with an accuracy which ravished into admiration all men who have ever contemplated them. The curious adapting of means to ends, throughout all nature, resembles, exactly, though it much exceeds, the productions of human contrivance of human design, thought, wisdom, and intelligence. Since therefore the effects resemble each other, we are led to infer, by all the rules of analogy, that the causes also resemble, and that the Author of Nature is somewhat similar to the mind of man, though possessed of much larger faculties, proportioned to the grandeur of the work which he has executed. By this argument a posteriori, and by this argument alone, do we prove at once the existence of a Deity and his similarity to human mind and intelligence.

Translate "Deity" for "Natural Selection" and a tangible mechanism has been articulated, which was Darwin's genius. And yet, the idea was in the air 80 years before he wrote about it.

uted throughout all of humankind, most likely have a positive role as well. The families of those suffering from the disease are often highly creative. One study claimed that the participants of a famous writers' workshop had a high incidence of schizophrenia in their family.

It is what happens to the mutations that produce an improved method of reproduction that has startling and profound consequences. Since the method is better, the individuals who possess it gradually reproduce more and eventually take over as the representatives of the species. As a consequence—and here is the important implication—the new organism has replaced the old one and has taken a step toward greater functional organization for reproduction. This spontaneous feedback—natural selection—is the only known process by which functional organization emerges naturally in the world, without intelligent design and intervention. Consequently, and here is the fundamental point for cognitive neuroscience, all naturally occurring functional organi-

zation in organisms must be ascribed to natural selection and must be consistent with its principles.

It also follows that other inherited traits must, by definition, enhance the organism's reproductive capacity. The accumulation of adaptations, then, is linked together synergistically to create a more powerful organism. This reproductive fitness is the ultimate functional product of all evolved cognitive devices.

Even though Charles Darwin did not know about genes per se, he postulated that reproductive success varies because of hereditary differences among animals within a population. Modern theories of evolution maintain the following: While all animals have genes, there is also a source of genetic variation within a species since genes for certain traits can differ. Variations of genes, called *alleles*, allow for individual differences within a species (Figure 13.1).

We know that populations are limited and cannot grow forever. Food supplies and other factors limit the

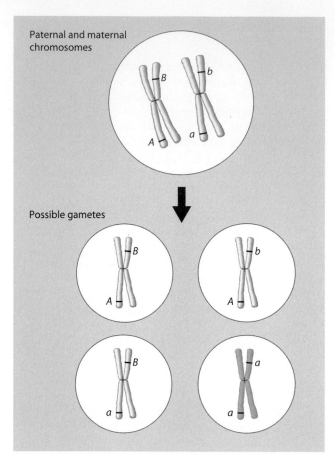

Paternal and maternal chromosomes

Possible gametes

Figure 13.1   The first stages of meiosis, the process by which haploid gametes (ova, sperm) arise from the normally diploid cell. It is a major point in development when new gene combinations are generated that give rise to the variations seen in any given species.

populations' size. The result is competition among the alleles in a gene pool. Survival of one allele inherently ensures the demise of other alleles. Animals that express the alleles have a survival advantage that is passed on through the generations. These individuals confer phenotypic or outwardly expressed traits regulated by genes, and since these traits help the species to survive, they do the same for the genes. What a beautiful mechanism.

At the level of the organism, adaptations, which refer to an organism's abilities to survive and reproduce, evolve and, by definition, increase the species's fitness for the environment. Since changes in a species's gene structures—and hence anatomical structures like the brain—are built to solve problems, it follows that brain structures reflect selective pressures because they confer an advantage to the species. To figure out how brain structures enable functions, we have to understand each structure's purpose and when it is used. Neuroscientists rarely do this, and frequently reach ill-advised conclusions.

Preuss (1985) presented an example of such a mistake. A few years ago, the visual system of some primates was discovered to have blobs, patches, or areas that reacted to a cellular stain called *cytochrome oxidase*. The blobs studied in Old and New World monkeys had a higher incidence of color-sensitive cells than did the surrounding cortex. Are blobs a special color-processing channel? Blobs were also found in nocturnal primates such as the gallagos and owl monkey. These animals have poor color vision because they are active in the dark and do not need color vision. On closer examination, blobs also contain cells sensitive to brightness and motion; hence, they might be part of a perceptual brightness constancy system (Figure 13.2).

Preuss's conclusion was that since nocturnal primates represent the ancestral condition, it is far more likely that color vision may have evolved from using these structures, which originally subserved other aspects of vision. This general idea underlines an important truth about evolution. It is common for new structures to be modifications of old ones; accordingly, it is risky to assign an absolute function without knowing relative environmental pressures.

Another telling example comes from understanding

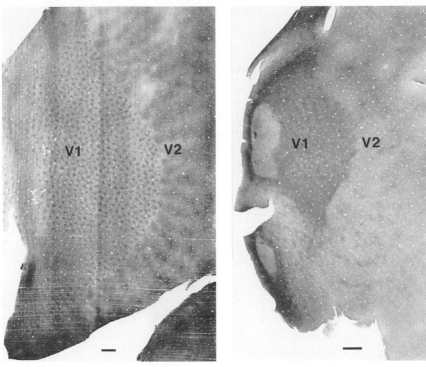

(a) (b)

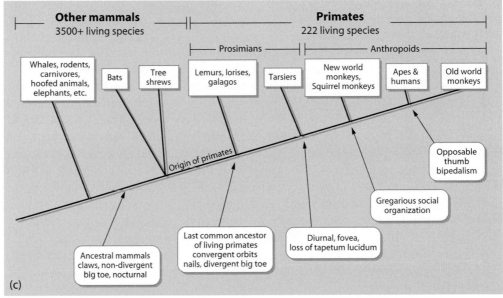

(c)

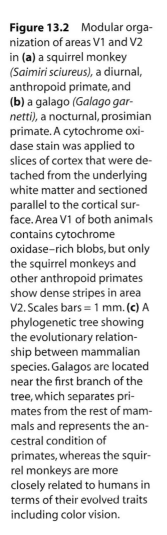

Figure 13.2 Modular organization of areas V1 and V2 in **(a)** a squirrel monkey *(Saimiri sciureus),* a diurnal, anthropoid primate, and **(b)** a galago *(Galago garnetti),* a nocturnal, prosimian primate. A cytochrome oxidase stain was applied to slices of cortex that were detached from the underlying white matter and sectioned parallel to the cortical surface. Area V1 of both animals contains cytochrome oxidase–rich blobs, but only the squirrel monkeys and other anthropoid primates show dense stripes in area V2. Scales bars = 1 mm. **(c)** A phylogenetic tree showing the evolutionary relationship between mammalian species. Galagos are located near the first branch of the tree, which separates primates from the rest of mammals and represents the ancestral condition of primates, whereas the squirrel monkeys are more closely related to humans in terms of their evolved traits including color vision.

how wings evolved. An assumption for years had been that they had evolved for flight because being aerial had its advantages. However, brilliant experimental work showed that a little wing, which is the piecemeal way in which adaptations must occur, conferred no advantage for flight but a big advantage for thermoregulation. It was only when the wings became big that flight was possible. This reality was called *exaptation* by Stephen Jay Gould (Gould and Vrba, 1981). A structure exists and is selected for because of one crucial function it subserves, but then takes over and supplies yet another crucial function. Thus, it may be difficult to identify the evolutionary history of a mechanism by focusing on its current utility.

ADAPTATION AND THE BRAIN

Evolutionists think that the modern human brain was adapted to deal with the world as it was in Pleistocene hunter-gatherer societies 100,000 years ago. This period was picked because of the slowness of new adaptations. Our auditory system, for instance, is not adapted to sensory events such as loud rock and roll music. This is why hard-rock musicians and their audiences wear earplugs, raising the question as to why they play their music that loud to begin with. Or, consider social structures. In hunter-gatherer times, groups were rarely larger than fifty. With today's vast cities and social structures like government bureaucracies, our brains are severely challenged to cope. So, when we think about the functions of the modern brain and what it does and does not do well, we should take into account what the early hunter-gatherers had to solve.

Natural selection has many nefarious ways. By chance, a useless trait could be inserted into an animal's architecture. So long as the trait did not interfere with its reproductive success, it could remain and coexist in the animal. This rarely happens; nonetheless it is a property of biological systems. What is clear is that such chance occurrences cannot explain the presence of sophisticated architectures like our visual system and language faculty.

One of the reasons so much stress abounds in contemporary society is that our brains are not built to cope with the social and physical inventions that have been thrown in our path of life. Our brains were built for a simpler life, the life of the Stone Age human. Back then, we had to be ready to defend ourselves, detect cheaters, read other people's facial emotions, forage, avoid incest, recognize kin, and read other people's minds and their intentions. Our mind does not instinctively share common goals with others. Have you ever been to a meeting that sets policies? It takes luck, persuasion, and brute force to get a group of independently minded people to agree on anything.

According to evolutionary thinking, these special capacities grow from separate and individual adaptations. The cognitive system that evolved is not a unified system that can work by applying special solutions to individual problems. This fundamental point is at the heart of the evolutionary perspective, and concurs with a vast amount of neuropsychological research. Localized brain lesions can lead to a loss of some capacity, say facial recognition, but local brain lesions can also have a maddening, mild effect on specific functions. This latter truth most likely reflects the observer's inability to present the right challenge to the patient. That is, the patient probably does possess deficits but the examiner's tests are either incorrect or not sensitive enough to detect the disorder. Alternatively, the failure to find a deficit may mean that devices built into the brain for other functions can solve other challenges. Just as a screwdriver can unscrew screws, it can also open paint cans.

The adaptations built in our brains are the physical, or neural, structural devices we should try to understand when trying to figure out how the brain works. An important rule to remember, one commonly overlooked, is to focus on the adaptation, not on the ancillary events associated with an adaptation. Bones are an adaptation, but their whiteness is a by-product of the calcium that gives bones their strength. Calcium was available in the environment and was used to build the bones' rigid structures. If we want to study bones and how they came to be, it would be a mistake to delve into the fact that they are white. We should simply distinguish between what are *proximate factors* versus *ultimate* ones when we consider why something evolved. Proximate factors are those at hand, and part of a structure. But their presence may not be why the structure evolved.

This principle of always considering the adaptation instead of the side effects illustrates the fallacy of our opening example. All members of our species have the capacity to be violent, to be aggressive. It is built into us. When we carry out this act, a by-product event occurs: Our serotonin levels change. Does this mean that serotonin levels guide our capacity to be violent? Certainly not.

ADAPTATIONS AT MULTIPLE BRAIN LEVELS

It is easy to see how adaptations gradually developed in primates; they occurred with primary sensorial systems like our visual and auditory systems. Furthermore, we have adaptations for more complex behaviors like our capacity to have a theory of mind about someone else. We look at another human and quickly theorize about their intentions toward us and how we should respond. At these levels evolutionary processes operate—and deserve comment.

At the simpler level of understanding vision, today's researcher may have insights that are consonant with the realities of the Pleistocene landscape. After all, the physical world of light and object has not changed all that much. Our visual system is built to take a two-dimensional retinal image and turn it into a real world representation of the visual scene. David Marr of MIT first articulated the true problems associated with understanding how vision must work. As Marr put it, "Trying to understand perception by studying only neurons is like trying to understand bird flight by studying only feathers: It just cannot be done. To understand bird flight, we have to understand aerodynamics; only then do the structure of feathers and the different shapes of birds; wings make sense." (Marr, 1982)

Marr is widely recognized as a genius, and the field was devastated when he died a young man. He was pursuing a computational analysis of what he was interested in understanding. In general terms, he liked three levels of description for any information-processing device, whether it be a cash register or a brain. In brief, he based his ideas on the following logic: First, information-processing devices are designed to solve problems. Second, they solve problems by virtue of their structure. And, third, they explain a device's structure when one knows what problem it was designed to solve, and why it was designed for that problem and not another one.

These issues were partly illuminated when researchers in artificial intelligence tried to build a device that could analyze a visual scene just as a human does. Marr first realized that the evolutionary function of vision is scene analysis: The brain must reconstruct a model of real world conditions from a two-dimensional visual array—the information on the retina.

The first discovery was that scene analysis is far more complicated than had been imagined. A simple object sitting on the horizon in the morning light looks completely different when the sun reaches high noon and then falls over the opposite horizon. An intricately specialized system must have been built into the primary visual system that allows for this natural progression and enables us to see the object as constant. Second, investigators discovered that our visual system apprehends far more information about a scene than can any artifact. It has many adaptations built in for this, all specific to vision. Finally—and this is the tricky part—our evolved visual system must have a cognitive, built-in component that has deduced that objects in the world have regularities which allow for the proper computations. This is what developmentalists mean by biologically prepared implicit knowledge in infants and children.

As we move up the scale to more complex adaptations like those associated with problem solving, social exchange, and the like, the insights we might gain by looking around us in our present world are probably not as helpful. Most studies do not take into account the sort of ways that Stone Age humans dealt with social problems. In many of today's attempts to understand human rational processes, subjects are presented with artificial thought problems developed in the laboratory. Yet our brains are adapted for only real world problems. For instance, many logic tests on issues of social exchange stump college sophomores because they are posed in the abstract. Does their failure mean that sophomores are illogical? No, because when the same logic problem is based on a real life story about obtaining beer or food, their logic systems work just fine.

Leda Cosmides (1984) worked out a telling example of this fact. She built on a test first developed by Peter Wagon who showed how poorly educated people can perform a simple logical task. Try it yourself: Each card has a number on one side and a letter on the other. Examine the following four cards:

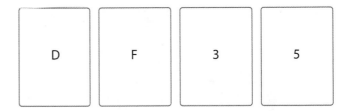

The task is simple. You are to determine if the following rule has any exceptions: If a card has a *D* on one side, it has a *3* on the other side. Which cards do you need to turn over to discover if this is true? Feel your mind rattling? But now consider the following problem: You are a bouncer at a bar and your job is to make sure no one under 21 drinks beer at the bar. The cards below have information about age on one side and what the patron is drinking on the other. Again, which cards do you need to turn over?

The mind springs to action on this task. It is obviously the first and last card, just like in the more abstract example earlier. Why? Cosmides and Tooby maintained that we have a built-in cheater detector system that has

Lessons from a Frog

Wonderful examples illustrate how evolutionary theory has led to great insights to brain function. Perhaps the most famous example is the work of Jerome Lettvin, one of the fathers of modern neuroscience and an extremely lively intellect. Many years ago, he wrote a famous paper with colleagues in 1959 titled, "What the Frog's Eye Tells the Frog's Brain." Lettvin broke with his predecessors and asked questions about the visual system based on his understanding of how a frog views the world.

Prior to Lettvin's work, the eye was regarded as an organ that translated an image into electrical impulses, and then the brain sorted out and interpreted this retinal information. The great American physiologist, H.K. Hartline, gave support to this idea in 1938 by studying the retina with simple points of light and dark. Using these abstract stimuli, Hartline and his colleagues be-lieved the frog's retina passed on information to the brain about the tone of various objects. They concluded that the retina's ganglion cells had but one function, and that was it.

Lettvin changed this interpretation. While recording from the frog's ganglion cells and stimulating the frog's visual system with bugs, twigs, and other ecologically relevant material, he and his colleagues discovered several types of ganglion cells: five, to be exact. In simple terms, Lettvin showed how much information is weeded out by biological systems like the retina. Evolution has seen to it that the frog's brain does not detect things about the visual environment that it does not need in order to function and survive. Hence, the male frog's brain does not spend energy on noticing the actor Melanie Griffith, but does detect the movement of female frogs.

Table 13.1 Types of Detectors

1. *Sustained-edge detectors* (SEDs): These showed the greatest response when a small, moving edge entered and remained in their receptive field. Immobile or long edges did not evoke a response.
2. *Convex-edge detectors* (CEDs): These were stimulated mainly by small, dark objects with a convex outline like beetles and other bugs.
3. *Moving-edge detectors* (MEDs): These were most responsive to edges moving in and out of their receptive fields.
4. *Dimming detectors* (DDs): These responded most to decreases in light intensity such as a shadow cast suddenly over the frog.
5. *Light-intensity detectors* (LIDs): These cells responded inversely proportional to light intensity, being most responsive in dim light.

SOURCE: Adapted from Alcock (1979).

been a necessary part of our brains ever since we as a species began to exist in social groups. The moment survival becomes conditional on what a group does as opposed to what an individual does; there must be a way to make sure the collective idea works as it is supposed to. In other words, we have the beginnings of a social contract.

The argument here is that social exchange can be expressed by a conditional statement such as, If you take the benefit, then you must pay the cost. For example, If you play on the hotel's golf course, then you must be a guest at the hotel. A cheater is someone who takes a benefit without paying the cost. People are quite good at detecting potential violations of these kinds of conditional rules (i.e., catching potential cheaters), whereas they cannot detect potential violations of purely descriptive rules. An example of the latter being, If a man wears a tuxedo, then he must wear a bow tie. In studies of undergraduates in the United States and Germany, 75 to 90% of people reason correctly about social exchange,

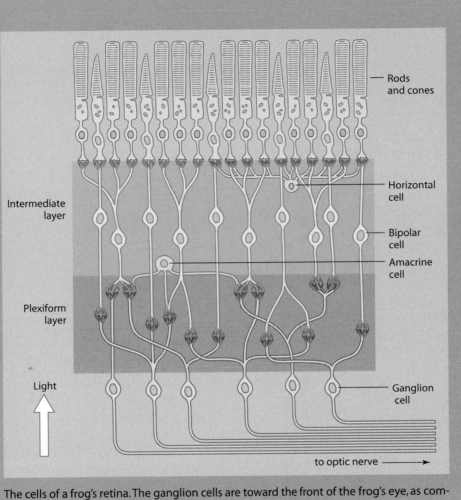

Intermediate
layer

Plexiform
layer

Light

Rods
and cones

Horizontal
cell

Bipolar
cell

Amacrine
cell

Ganglion
cell

to optic nerve ⟶

The cells of a frog's retina. The ganglion cells are toward the front of the frog's eye, as compared to the photoreceptors which are furthest away from the source of light but through which light must travel before processing in the ganglion cells takes place.

compared with 4 to 25% of people reasoning correctly about abstract or descriptive rules. Detecting potential cheaters is an important evolutionary problem—those who could not detect cheaters got ripped off more often and those people did not end up to be our ancestors.

This intriguing new work has built on the insight of Robert Trivers (1971). Many years ago Trivers, now at Rutgers University, showed that the elements of social exchange are based on the evolution of reciprocal altruism. Reciprocity amounts to roughly equal amounts of give and take in social relationships. The associated cognitive, psychological, and emotional systems allow us to develop and maintain friendships with nonkin. Kids implicitly recognize the reciprocal nature of friendships and socially reject kids who do not reciprocate.

Social exchanges and titrating of reciprocity give rise to many emotions. Indeed, Trivers argued that many emotional reactions regulate social exchange. If we give more than we take in a social relationship, we get angry; if we take more than we give, we feel guilty.

Guilt motivates returning the favor while anger motivates one to break off relationships with people who cheat, who do not reciprocate.

The foregoing adaptationist view contrasts with the *phylogenetic view* of evolution, an idea supported by many neuroscientists. Phylogenetic evolution maintains that because humans have a special capacity like language, chimpanzees, which are of the same biological phylum, ought to possess the ability. Being humans' closest relative implies shared homologous structures and capabilities. This idea, rampant in neuroscience, is dead wrong. It is a popular idea because scientists spending their lives working on a structure in, say, rats or monkeys or even chimpanzees deeply believe it has significance for understanding the same structure in humans. And yet, as the adaptationists argue, although it is true that apes do not have language, it is because they have not had the same selective pressures as humans; their niches are different. Hence, the phylogeneticists foolishly look at homologous structures for origins of the capacity.

SEXUAL SELECTION AND EVOLUTIONARY PRESSURES ON A BEHAVIOR

Sex has realities that are at once clear and puzzling. Darwin knew natural selection was at work, but he was bothered by why males and females differ so much, given their mutual goal of trying to survive in the same niche. It is easy to understand why genitalia are different, but why such big differences in behavior and bodily structure?

Some dispute whether sexual selection should be distinguished from natural selection, but leading researchers such as Steven Gaulin at the University of Pittsburgh (1995) argued that it should be. Gaulin, who has puzzled over the problem of sexual selection for years, maintained that a distinction between sexual selection and natural selection explains how ecologically useless characteristics such as antlers on a deer evolved and have survived. While not necessary for functions such as food gathering, these characteristics are important in enhancing sexual contact. An analogy would be that one can get around town in a Honda, but a red Corvette conveys a different message.

The sexual life of the deer readily illustrates how selection starts the two sexes down diverging paths. Once a female deer has mated and conceived her maximum litter, she has no need for further sexual contact. The male, though, can maximize his reproductive success by continuing to impregnate as many females as he can. Thus, any somatic event that would enhance a male's reproductive fitness would be selected for, while a similar change for the female would not. The female would not gain because her reproductive limit has been met (Figure 13.3).

This pattern for mammals has exceptions, and it is the exceptions that bring strength to the idea that sexual selection is distinct from natural selection. First, male mammals have small and many sex cells, whereas females have large cells. In other animals, the fast or quickly reproducing sex is the female, and the male stays home with the young. In some shorebirds, the male stays in the nest to incubate the egg. The female, right after laying the egg, leaves the nest and seeks other males, so she can lay yet more eggs for them to incubate. In this turnabout of roles, the fast-sexed females are larger, more brightly colored, and aggressive. It is clear, then, that the flamboyant characteristics of most males and of the less common fast-sex females enhance their capacity for a higher reproductive rate—which is not to say that there are no monogamous species. Over 90% of foxes and birds are deeply committed to each other because both must participate in child rearing if their species is to survive.

Another significant difference between mammals and birds is that mammals have an internal gestation period. This means that female mammals are making a larger commitment to offspring, which may underscore

Figure 13.3 The typical morphology of **(a)** a female doe that invests her energy into raising her offspring and that of **(b)** a polygamous male elk with its large investment of energy into the massive set of antlers, which aid his ability to attract mates and fight off competitors.

the known difference in how much the male and female invest in their offspring as compared with spending time on mating. For birds and many fish species, exter-nal gestation creates the potential for females to force parental care onto males, a more difficult trick with mammals.

SEXUAL ABILITIES AND SPATIAL ABILITIES

Too many jokes to recount here are made about the spatial skills of women versus men. While once good-humored, they now take on a social significance that becomes lost in current social values. Still, some facts are intriguing. Spatial abilities do vary according to sex—and they do so because of selective pressures. These spatial skills differ in humans and ani-mals of all kinds, which suggests that brains manage spatial skills differently in males and females.

Natural selection sees to it that males and females have basic navigational skills. Both meet the same challenges for reward and risk in food gathering and other life-perpetuating activities. Where sexual selection might start to mold differences is when males of a species are polygamous. Here the males might need better spatial skills to find available females for sex and yet return home. This phenomenon pertains to polygamous rather than monogamous mammals (Figure 13.4).

In trying to test the hypothesis that polygamous males would have greater spatial skills as compared to females, we run into a problem: Over 95% of mammalian species are polygamous. In fact, verifiable sex differences in spatial skills have been discovered in rats, mice, and people. To truly test the hypothesis, we would need a species with monogamous and polygamous strains, to evaluate each group's spatial skills.

Studies of wild voles have elucidated these issues. These rodents were chosen because we have a myriad of well-developed spatial tests for them. Yet the sizes of the ranges of the two monogamous pine and prairie voles did not differ (Figure 13.5). At the same time, the free-wheeling, polygamous meadow vole demonstrated huge differences in range sizes between females and

Figure 13.4 Typical home-range patterns for polygamous versus monogamous mammals. For many polygamous species, male home ranges overlap with numerous, smaller female ranges. Females and males in monogamous species where parenting by both sexes is necessary for the raising of young tend to have smaller, isomorphic home ranges.

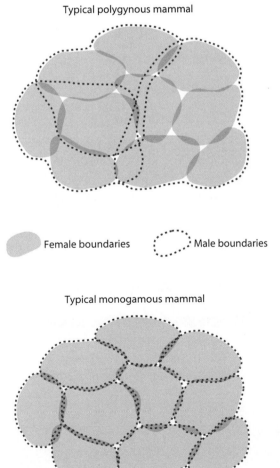

Typical polygynous mammal

Female boundaries   Male boundaries

Typical monogamous mammal

Figure 13.5 Thirty-day average range area of monogamous prairie voles and polygamous meadow voles. Adapted from Gaulin and Fitzgerald (1986, 1989).

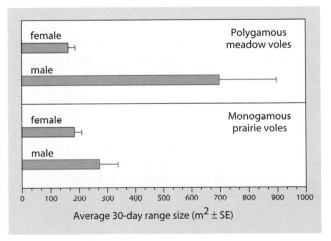

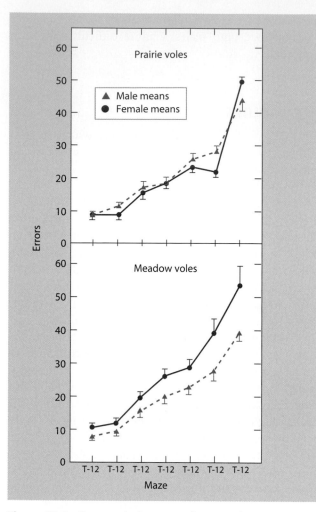

Figure 13.6 Symmetrical maze performance by monogamous prairie voles and polygamous meadow voles. Adapted from Gaulin and Fitzgerald (1989).

males. Gaulin and his colleagues confirmed these spatial skills by testing the same species in a laboratory. Males with larger range sizes had better spatial skills (Figure 13.6).

With the spatial abilities of the two sexes clearly established, researchers became eager to establish whether brain structures for spatial abilities varied. Over the years, many investigators discovered that the hippocampus is crucial to spatial memory tasks. Birds such as titmouses, nuthatches, and loud-mouth jays all cache their food over a large spatial area. Because they must have superb spatial skill to retrieve their food, one might expect their hippocampus to be larger, corrected for whole brain volume, when compared to birds which do not store food in this manner (Figure 13.7). This is exactly what occurs.

Lucy Jacobs and colleagues at the University of California at Berkeley (1990) asked similar questions of

kangaroo rats. In two species of kangaroo rats, she found that the hippocampus is larger in males that, during their breeding season, range more widely than do females. Just as fascinating is the cowbird, a species whose females sneak their eggs into the nests of other species. The cowbird's timing has to be just right, and she has to search a wide area to find the unsuspecting host nest. Sure enough, a female cowbird's hippocampus is much larger compared to a male cowbird's hippocampus. Males do none of these wide-ranging activities; they are the avian equivalent of couch potatoes.

Hormones play a fascinating role in the development of spatial abilities (Dawson et al., 1973). Investigators showed that sex-typical patterns of maze performance can be reversed by the early administration of appropriate hormones. How, we might ask, can hormones affect the genetic blueprint for sex differences such as spatial skills?

Figure 13.7 Comparison of hippocampal volume for monogamous pine voles and polygamous meadow voles. Adapted from Jacobs et al. (1990).

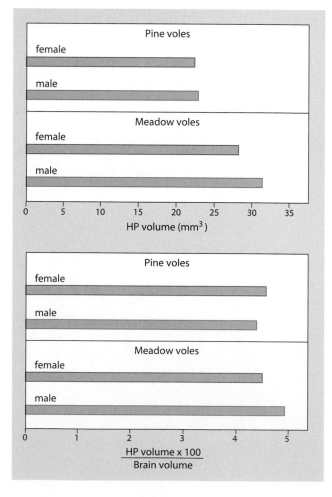

HOW THE BRAIN WORKS

Sexual Selection and Mathematics

The perennial topic of sex-related differences in mathematical abilities has been exhaustively studied by David Geary at Columbia University (1995). He observed that there are no sex-related differences in biological primary mathematical skills, even in nonhuman primates. This is true for all cultures. Yet there are sex-related differences in secondary mathematical skills, the kinds of math taught in schools in the industrialized world. Males consistently outperform females in word and geometry problems. Geary suggested this capacity builds on the sort of male superiority in spatial skills seen in many species, such as the ones described in this chapter. In short, it is a secondary benefit to males arising out of the sexual selection process we have described.

Geary went on to show that sex hormones, which are the proximate mechanisms associated with sexual selection, appear to indirectly influence mathematical ability. He argued that sexual selection resulted in greater elaboration of the neurocognitive systems that support navigation in three-dimensional space in males than in females. These navigational systems have evolved in the three-dimensional physical world, and so some information about the structure of the physical world is built into these systems. It appears that features of euclidean geometry are a mathematical representation of the organization of the physical world, and thus, an implicit understanding of aspects of geometry is built into the spatial system. Males do better in geometry than do females because evolution has provided males with more built-in knowledge of geometry. These same spatial skills can solve other types of math problems, such as word problems. This is because solving word problems is much easier if important information in the problems is diagrammed or spatially represented.

This same study also observed that many sex differences are in social styles and interests; these play into the superior math skills. Because of these differences, males are more likely to engage in mathematical problems, which further enhances their superiority. There is also clearly a practice effect. How do you get to Carnegie Hall? Practice, practice, practice.

The expression of sexual differences involves ontogenetic forces, which are the forces at work during an organism's development—in this case, in the fetal stage. The true genetic differences between males and females are slight, and they are expressed by factors such as the local hormone environment. For example, in humans who have Turner's syndrome, a neuroendocrine genetic disorder, the gonads remain undifferentiated. As a result, a phenotypic female who was deprived of androgen and estrogen during development has spatial disabilities significantly below her verbal skills. The same is true for males who experience low androgen levels during development, such as in Klinefelter's syndrome, another genetically based neuroendocrine disorder. They, too, exhibit depressed spatial skills.

EVOLUTION AND PHYSIOLOGY

By now, it should be clear that natural selection is crucial in shaping each species's brain (Gazzaniga, 1992). Special devices built into each brain enhance the species's capacity to reproduce and to promulgate itself; the devices vary tremendously, as each species has different niches and predators. Since no two species utilize the exact same kind of resources, and since no two species have the exact same predators, each species also has special isolating reproduction mechanisms. This is important to understand, as each species has unique traits to pass on, and thus sensory receptors and brain decoders in each species are rather idiosyncratic. This recurring theme is a fundamental one for students of the nervous system. Even though nerve cells may share similarities and nervous systems may be universally composed of certain nerve cells, each nervous system varies from one species to another in ecologically appropriate ways (Bullock, 1993).

An Interview with Leah Krubitzer, Ph.D.

Dr. Krubitzer is an assistant professor of Neuroscience and Psychology at University of California, Davis. She has studied the cortical organization of dozens of different and exotic species.

Authors: You have studied strange and wonderous species, trying to find clues about the nature of cortical organization. Why?

LK: Our major goal is to understand how evolution builds a complex brain. We can begin to answer this question by looking at the differences in cortical organization in a variety of lineages to determine if there is some common plan of cortical organization. Once this is established, we can then describe how this plan has been modified in different species, and how these modifications relate to increases in behavioral and cognitive complexity. Because independent changes have occurred in all mammalian branches of evolution, all mammals have derived or specialized features of organization, and even homologous cortical areas may not be analogous. In short, there is no normal or standard brain from which others deviate. Thus, your question regarding "strange and wondrous" species would include traditional mammals of study such as rats, cats, and nonhuman primates as well as humans. The nature of the beast is relative to the perspective of the observer.

Related to this issue are the mechanisms underlying cortical evolution. Do changes or additions to the plan of organization, although independently evolved, follow a particular set of rules? Are these rules or developmental programs highly conserved in all lineages? If so, what are the constraints imposed on cortical field evolution by existing methods of brain construction?

Finally, it is important to appreciate the dynamic nature of the neocortex both within the life of an individual and within a species over time. In any given experiment in any species, we are looking at a frozen moment; one snapshot of a continuing process. If we appreciate the mechanisms that generate the brains of extant mammals, we can begin to reconstruct that process, and understand how retained patterns of cortical activation incorporate additional components, how these changes alter the function of existing cortical areas, and generate new functions and behaviors.

Authors: That is a large order. Can you give an example of how a retained pattern was modified and how that contributed to a particular function?

LK: Because the neocortex is characterized by an array of individual fields, intricately interconnected with other fields, thalamic nuclei, and subcortical structures, the exact relationship between an individual cortical field and a specific function is difficult to nail down. However, I can give some examples of how the retained plan, or pattern of activation upon the cortical sheet, has been modified, and how those modifications loosely relate to changes in function. One of the consistent changes observed in cortical fields across mammals is the addition of modules (structural, anatomical, and physiological discontinuities within the limits of a cortical field) to an existing field. In the primary somatosensory area (SI) in a number of mammals, such discontinuities have been identified. For instance, in the platypus, cytochrome oxidase light and dark regions in SI are related to the segregation of mechanosensory and electrosensory inputs from the bill. Such segregation may be a developmental compromise for thalamic afferents to map close to like thalamic afferents (correlated in time, e.g., stimulus preference), thereby reducing the length and configuration of intrinsic connections between functionally similar submodalities, and also to map close to spatially similar afferents (e.g., on the same portion of the bill), which could enhance spatial resolution and aid in making discriminations regarding the direction of the stimulus. The ability of the platypus to detect the direction of a stimulus has been demonstrated behaviorally.

There are a number of similar examples in a variety of different mammals. The existence of modular specializations indicates that similar structural and anatomical changes to the cortex occur independently in different lineages. While these types of changes may not always be directly related to a particular function, it is likely that such changes to the existing network will alter how the network processes inputs from the periphery.

Another type of modification is the addition of cortical fields to the existing network. An example of this is the visual cortex of primates in which multiple fields have been identified. The function of these fields is not known, but we do know that the visual processing capacity and abilities of primates far exceed those of species with fewer visual areas, such as the hedgehog or mouse.

Given these observations, we can argue that such changes inevitably result in changes in processing abilities, and hence changes in function.

I believe these examples demonstrate the nonlinearity of neocortical evolution and the dynamic nature of the cortex, and also emphasize the futility of making strict one-to-one area-function correlations.

Authors: Thank you.

There is a wonderful example of how biological structures coevolve, each trying to adapt to meet its own needs. In a predator-prey relation, as the predator develops an edge by evolving toward better fitness, the prey responds by evolving a mutated member that counters the new predator's skill and subsequently enhances reproduction—much as the bat and the moth it eats.

As contrasted with the visual system we predominantly use to navigate, bats maneuver through their environments by emitting high-frequency sound waves and detecting their weak echoes off surfaces. The bat's nervous system has evolved sophisticated adaptations that enable the bat to be sensitive to these weak echoes. As a bat approaches an object like a moth, it emits more sound waves to gain exact information on the object's direction and distance. By nature of their mode of transportation, flying insects give more clues to the bat. As an insect moves its wings for flight, rhythmic reflections of the bat's sound waves striking the upper and lower surfaces of the insect's wings return to the bat. The bat uses these to distinguish between moths and tree leaves. With such an accurate detection system, it is hard to believe bats' prey could stand a chance of survival.

But prey, such as the noctuid moth, have evolved antipredator adaptations to prevent them from becoming the next meal of a strong hunter like the bat. The noctuid moth has two ears, each with only two receptors, the A1 and A2 receptors, with which to perceive an approaching bat (Figure 13.8). The A1 receptor responds to low-intensity sounds such as the ones from a bat from 10 to 100 feet away. The moth's ears work as ours do to locate a sound source; the moth relies on its knowledge that whichever receptor is closer to the sound will be activated slightly before the receptor that is farther from it. In this way, the moth can tell if the bat is to its left or right. Because the beating of the moth's wings makes small interruptions in the reception of the bat's signal, the moth can determine whether the bat is above or below it (Figure 13.9). If the bat approaches within 10 feet, the moth's A2 receptors, which are sensitive to high-intensity sounds, start firing, and the moth responds by beating its wings irregularly, thereby throwing off the bat's detection strategy and prompting the moth to dive for safety (Figure 13.10). This simplistic system of the noctuid moth, consisting of a mere four receptors, has coevolved with the bat's more sophisticated sensory system. The result is a balanced coexistence of these two species.

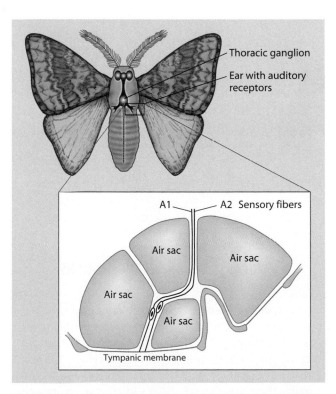

Figure 13.8 The noctuid moth's *(Agrotis ypsilaon)* ear and location of receptors. When sounds are of a sufficient frequency, the auditory receptors stimulate the tympanic membrane, which in turn induces the auditory neurons to fire.

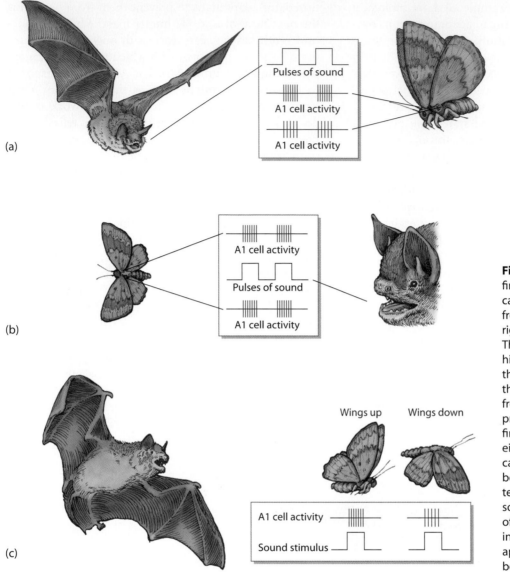

Figure 13.9 **(a)** Differential firing of the bilaterally located A1 receptors indicates from which direction, left or right, a bat is approaching. The receptor that fires with a higher frequency is closer to the source of the sound and thus indicates the direction from which the bat approaches. **(b)** Symmetrical firing of the A1 receptors on either side of the moth indicates that the bat is directly behind the moth. **(c)** The interruption of the bat's sounds due to the location of the moth's beating wings indicates whether the bat approaches from above or below.

NATURAL SELECTION AND THE EMOTIONS

No subject or phenomenon is more in need of an evolutionary perspective than the nature of emotions. When emotions go awry, the cost is large: mental disorders such as depression, anxiety, and stress disorders. These affect up to 20% of our population. How are emotions to be thought of and why does the brain sometimes make them overreact? Just as with our example of aggression, we have to think of these issues in relation to a continuum, and the key concepts that put this problem in perspective are inherent in the evolutionary context for emotions.

George Williams of the State University of Stony Brook, perhaps the world's leading evolutionary biologist, and Randolph Nesse, a psychiatrist at the University of Michigan, wrote a compelling book, *Why We Get Sick* (1996), in which they outline what they call the framework for darwinian medicine. Going back to the first

Figure 13.10 **(a)** The simplistic A1 and A2 receptors work together to process information about sounds of different intensities and frequencies. When the bat is further away, sounds of lower intensity effect the A1 receptor but not the A2 receptor. As the intensity increases, the A2 receptor starts firing to give the moth more detailed information about the location of the sound source. **(b)** The A1 receptor reacts strongly to high-frequency sounds that are detected in pulses. If the stimulus is a steady sound of the same frequency and intensity, the A1 receptor will cease firing after a short while. This prevents the moth from being overly sensitive to persistent, irrelevant sounds in its environment and reserves the functioning of these receptors for ecologically important situations such as detecting a hunting bat.

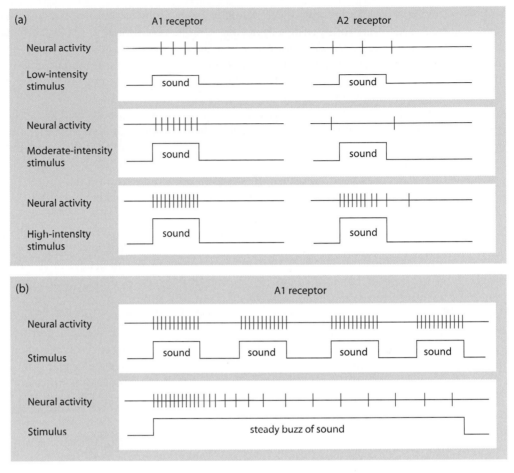

principles of natural selection, they realized that many body-mind functions are built into the body to help survival. Their concern is that these mechanisms are routinely interfered with by medical practitioners; they wonder about the consequences for the health and survival of our species.

A concrete somatic example deals with how the body controls fever. Fever may be an adaptive host response to infection. It is seen throughout the animal kingdom. Cold-blooded lizards, for example, seek a warm spot in the sun when they become infected. The sun raises their body heat a few degrees and wards off infection. When they cannot find the warm spot, they often die. Baby rabbits also cannot generate a fever. When they become infected, they, too, seek a warm place to raise their body temperature. Adult rabbits, though, have fever mechanisms, and if they are given a fever-lowering drug, they die when they have an infection.

These adaptive mechanisms were confirmed in a classic study at the turn of the century. Julius Wagner-Jauregg won the Nobel Prize in 1927 for showing that the survival rate in syphilis patients infected with malaria jumped 30%. The resulting fever assisted the body in its management of the syphilis.

This same basic insight can be applied to the emotions. Nesse and Williams argued that unpleasant emotions can be viewed as a defense against costly events. Just as vomiting gets rid of unwanted pathogens, or fatigue avoids overexertion, an emotion like sadness can change behavior in a way that may stop additional losses. In addition, when emotions are considered as products of natural selection, they become regarded as tractable subunits of the mind that can be studied.

When emotions are viewed as adaptations, it is clear that some must have been shaped by things such as attacks from predators or threats of exclusion from social groups. In this light, a sudden sense of anxiety could well signal someone not to behave in such a way that increases the likelihood of being excluded from a group. Or a sudden rush of anxiety in a potentially dangerous situation might find one waiting for a policeman to walk by before leaving a dark restaurant or bar at night. In short, a lot of emotions are indispensible to normal life.

This kind of view tempers any notion that normal life should be free of negative emotions. The great evolutionary biologist E.O. Wilson (1994) observed, "Love, joins hate; aggression, fear; expansiveness, withdrawal; and so on; in blends designed not to promote the happiness and survival of the individual, but to favor the maximum transmission of the controlling genes."

But how can mental states such as sadness and depression be adaptable? Suicide among teenagers is growing. Depressed people are not pleasant to be around and can barely function. Nesse and Williams reviewed the problem and argued that sadness and depression are on a continuum—that depression somehow arises from a dysfunction of a normal mechanism. Sadness can be triggered by the loss of something: money, power, a mate. The adaptive value is that it signals to the person that he is manifesting maladaptive behavior and should review his behavior. Sadness also replaces the normal person's chronic optimism. Humans are forever overestimating their abilities and effectiveness. Sadness triggers reappraisal mechanisms.

It has been suggested that depression is common in people who have intellect and mental skills superior to those they work for. In this context, the best protection for someone is to underestimate his skills and believe this is so; the outcome is low self-esteem but it reduces the risk that one will be too assertive around the boss and risk losing his job.

The Brain and Emotions

While the evolutionary perspective places emotion in a dynamic context, it still remains important to understand how the brain affects emotions. The evolutionary mechanisms of natural selection built the mechanism in the brain. How does this work?

The emotion seized on by most researchers is conditioned fear. This emotion has physiological manifestations, like high blood pressure, that are fairly uniform across species. It occurs quickly, is extinguished slowly, and is a normal reaction to threatening events. Fear conditioning is defined as the sensation occurring during the interval between when a stimulus has elicited it and the onset of the anticipated adverse stimulus.

To gain a sense of the process, one must distinguish three levels of analysis. Studies go on at the molecular, the cellular, and the behavioral level. At the molecular level, scientists use biochemical probes to identify sites where emotional information is processed. Once the site is identified, then cellular analysis is done to determine

which neurons and synaptic connections mediate the emotion. Finally, at the behavioral level, populations of neurons and specialized circuits are linked to see how the whole brain participates in the behavior.

The amygdala, and more specifically the central nucleus of the amygdala, has been linked to the management of the conditioned fear response. Lesions to this structure interrupt the fear response. Figure 13.11 outlines the major areas of the brain affected in fear conditioning.

Fear is one of many stressful emotions. Stress activates autonomic and neuroendocrine responses that evolved to enable vertebrates to adapt and survive while either fleeing from predators or fighting members of its own species for food, mates, or territory. Bruce McEwen at Rockefeller University (1995) investigated this for years and believed that humans face more than flight or fight options, which compounds our natural bodily response to stress. In addition, and quite importantly, there are huge individual differences in how people respond to stress. Genetic, developmental, and experiential differences among people help to produce varying responses to similar conditions. Figure 13.12 outlines possible steps in processing stressful situations and the behavioral responses.

Universal Emotions

Cultural anthropologists have always argued for the environment's power in dictating how we respond to life's events. Margaret Mead, the famed anthropologist, promoted the idea that Samoans have no human passions. They do not experience love or hate, fear or guilt, revenge or jealousy, or any other common emotions. This finding was widely reported and gave rise to a good deal of cultural relativism. The only problem with the claim is that it is simply not true. Dozens of anthropologists have since studied the Samoans and have found them full of emotions, as one would expect if the basics of our emotional life are built into all members of our species.

Charles Darwin suspected this and wrote eloquently about it in 1871. Darwin circulated a questionnaire about human emotions to people who interacted with primitive tribes. He asked them to describe how their facial muscles behave when they are upset or happy or whatever. He concluded that all people have the same emotions.

It would seem that back in the Pleistocene period, our capacity to register intentionally was beginning to occur. Since one's intention can easily be read in one's facial expression, just as Darwin noted, the capacity to mask one's intentions might well have evolutionary advantages. It turns out that humans are uniquely equipped

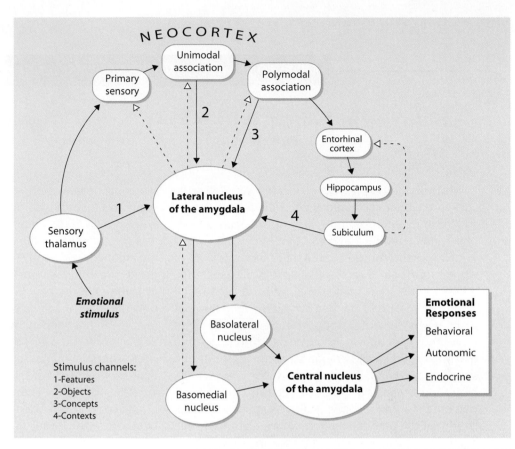

Figure 13.11 Amygdala pathways and fear conditioning. Adapted from Le Doux (1995).

Stimulus channels:
1-Features
2-Objects
3-Concepts
4-Contexts

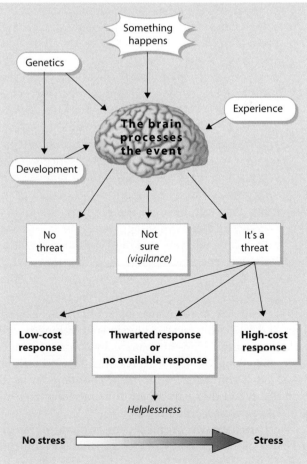

Figure 13.12 Different factors interact to determine how a person processes situations. The different personal characteristics for each individual influence the perception of stressful stimuli and the output of a coping response. Adapted from McEwen (1995).

An Interview with Joseph Le Doux, Ph.D.   Dr. Le Doux is a professor at New York University. He is the leading expert on the emotional brain.

Authors: You started out your career working on issues in brain laterality and then switched and are responsible for energizing the field of the neurobiology of emotion. How did that come about?

JL: A chance observation, a bit of luck, and a lot of work. It started with a study of split-brain patient P.S. When we put emotional stimuli into the right hemisphere, the left had no idea what the right saw, but could tell us how it felt about the stimulus, whether it represented something good or bad. This suggested that the cognitive and emotional representations of a stimulus are handled by different pathways in the brain. And since this patient had a corpus callosum section but his anterior commissure was intact, we speculated that the emotional information might be traveling from one amygdala to the other through this set of connections. The idea that cognition and emotion have somewhat different neural systems intrigued me, and I've been trying to figure out how it works ever since. That was the observation. The lucky part was that I was able to redirect my career in a way that would let me pursue the questions through animal research, since that was and still is the only way to get down to the nitty gritty of how the brain does something. Over the past 15 or so years, I have been working on the rat. It is interesting how hostile the neuroscience community was to this kind of thing 15 years ago. When I wrote my first grant to study emotion in the brain I proposed using classical fear conditioning as the behavioral model. The grant was disapproved, the lowest possible rating. The reviewers said that I was investigating con-

ditioning, not emotion, and that I should rewrite the grant and focus on learning and memory. I did and it was funded, which had two implications. One was that I was able to use learning and memory as the front for my emotion work, and the other was that I got interested in learning and memory and now regard myself as involved in the neurobiology of memory *and* emotion. I see the two as sort of the same. Most emotions involve memory, and many memories involve emotion. So that's why I do what I do today.

Authors: Animal research is essential. At the same time how does one study the subtle human states of emotion, like sorrow, in a rat?

JL: I think most scientists work somewhere in between what they want to do and what they can do. In my case, I realized pretty early on that if I want to get at the nuts and bolts of emotion, I would have to pick an approach that would let me study emotion in the animal brain. It took me a little longer to realize that my approach, which is to use conditioned fear in the rat, might not tell us about how emotion works so much as about how fear works. Many emotions—enough to make this a meaningful statement—involve phylogenetically old brain systems that evolved to control the body behaviorally and physiologically in response to environmental challenges. These systems take care of things like defense against danger, sexual behavior, maternal behavior, eating, and other things like this. These are the kinds of emotional systems we can study in the animal brain. There are two points to make about this. One is that these emotions need to be studied one at a

with a brain system for managing spontaneous expressions and for setting facial expressions by voluntary and conscious control. The chimpanzee, by contrast, is incapable of making voluntary expressions. David Premack showed that chimpanzees can make spontaneous facial expressions and thus have a hard time masking their intentions (personal communication).

Humans have two neural systems for controlling facial expressions (Figure 13.13). The system that controls voluntary expression is managed from the left hemi-

sphere (Gazzaniga and Smylie, 1990). It sends its messages to the contralateral VII nucleus, which in turn innervates the right facial muscles. At the same time, the left hemisphere sends a command over the corpus callosum to the right half of the brain. The right half sends the message down to the left facial nucleus, which in turn innervates the left half of the face. The result is that one can make a symmetrical facial response such as a smile or frown.

Spontaneous facial expression is managed by a dif-

NATURAL SELECTION AND THE EMOTIONS ● 517

time because they evolved for different reasons to do different things and to have different brain systems controlling them. The other is that these systems evolved before consciousness; the conscious feelings we know our emotions by are not the reason they evolved. Brains were nonconscious and nonverbal long before they were conscious and verbal, but we use the human state (conscious and verbal), especially the negation of the human state (nonconscious and nonverbal). When we consider emotion in animals, we are thinking of human negations that may not exist, and even if they do, they're going to be difficult to pin down. It's important to take the similarity of emotional behavior in animals and humans at face value. It tells us that when, for example, rats and people are in danger, they freeze and their blood pressure goes up and they release stress hormones. These similarities don't tell us that rats and humans experience fear. For that you need to be aware of the state you are in, and it's not clear that rats are. Yet there is an awful lot we can learn about emotion systems from studying animal brains, and this information can be useful for understanding conditions that humans experience as well. But we've got to be careful and not generalize too freely from one emotion to another. There is no unitary emotion system; lots of systems take care of things we call emotions. Some subtle human emotions may not be easily studied through animal experiments, but there are still plenty that can.

Authors: Emotions like fear cue one to the nature of a situation. The brain decides that a situation is dangerous. Why couldn't the brain have evolved in a way that allows for such decisions but in the absence of the emotion of the decision?

JL: The brain did evolve in a way that allows for decisions about danger and perhaps other challenging situations to be dealt with in the absence of emotion. A fruitfly or a snail, to use two common examples from neurobiology, defend themselves from danger by using cues in their environment. And both can learn that novel cues are signals for danger. They use the same conditioning processes we do: The time overlap of a neutral stimulus and an arousing one can modify how the brain copes with the previously neutral one. When the stimulus occurs, the organism (snail, rat, person) reacts the way its species normally responds to danger. No conscious awareness is needed in the snail or the human. These are just responses. And what evolved to evaluate stimuli and produce responses is the system that we have to understand to see where our emotional reactions originate. The difference between a rat and a person is not so much the system that produces the responses but instead is the cognitive layering above the more basic systems. Along with understanding emotional reactions we also need to understand emotional actions. That's where cognition and consciousness come into play and make a difference. These systems provide more flexibility to deal with reactions. We react to emotional situations unconsciously, but we then figure out what to do, make plans, use strategies, and so on. From the point of view of brain research, we are much farther along in understanding emotional reaction than emotion action, but now that we have a sense of how reactions occur, we can begin to look at action.

So I think that the brain did evolve to deal with danger and other so-called emotional situations without cognition and consciousness. After all, when evolution was putting defense response networks together in invertebrates, she didn't know that she would later make vertebrates and consciousness. I'm taking a chance and assuming that invertebrates are not consciously aware of their emotional reactions, but I'm willing to take that chance.

ferent neural pathway. First, unlike voluntary expressions, which only the left hemisphere can trigger, spontaneous expressions can be managed by either half of the brain. When either half triggers a spontaneous response, the pathways that activate the brainstem nuclei are signaled through another pathway, one that does not course through the cortex. Each hemisphere sends signals straight down through the midbrain and out to the brainstem nuclei. Clinical neurologists know of the distinction between these two ways of controlling facial muscles. For example, a patient with a lesion in the part of the right hemisphere that participates in voluntary expressions will be unable to move the left half of the face when told to smile. At the same time, the very same patient can easily move the left half of the face when spontaneously smiling because those pathways are unaffected by right-hemisphere damage. Also with Parkinson's disease, the pathways supporting spontaneous facial expressions do not work, whereas the pathways that support voluntary expressions do work. Such patients

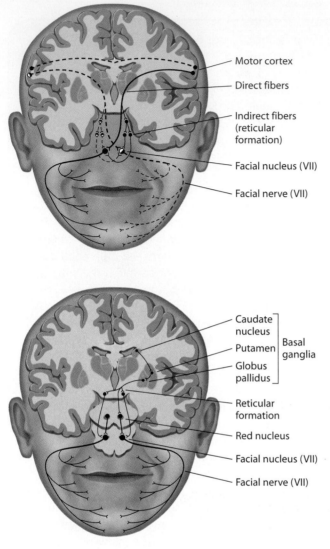

Motor cortex

Direct fibers

Indirect fibers
(reticular
formation)

Facial nucleus (VII)

Facial nerve (VII)

Caudate
nucleus

Putamen] Basal
ganglia

Globus
pallidus

Reticular
formation

Red nucleus

Facial nucleus (VII)

Facial nerve (VII)

Figure 13.13 The neural pathways that control voluntary and spontaneous facial expression are different. Voluntary expressions that can signal intention have their own new cortical networks in humans **(top).** The neural networks for spontaneous expressions **(bottom)** involve older brain circuits and appear to be the same as those seen in chimpanzees.

can lose their masked-face appearance when told to smile (Figure 13.14).

Spontaneous facial expressions are clearly another window on our emotional life. Paul Ekman at the University of California at San Francisco (1971, 1984) studied facial expressions across many cultures. He photographed people in one culture with the facial expression that depicted happiness, anger, fear, sadness, or disgust and showed them to people of another culture. He even went into the back country of New Guinea to find cultural groups (Figure 13.15). The result was always the same: Each culture readily identified the emotional state of another. Facial expressions of the emotions are universal.

It also appears that humans have a special neural circuit for overriding spontaneous expressions, for masking feelings. Once this mechanism is in place and becomes functionally active, we face what has been described as the *cognitive arms race.* How clever can we become at masking our intentions?

Robert Trivers (1971) presented a fascinating account of this topic. Trivers was taken with the way humans deceive themselves. He reasoned as follows: If caveman Jones is making voluntary expressions to fool caveman Smith, Smith should become more sensitive (over evolutionary time) to the difference between real and fake expressions. Smith should be able to detect any twitch, blush, quiver, pupil dilation, eye divergence, facial tension, or any other sign, no matter how slight, that indicates that Jones is lying. So what Jones must do (again, over evolutionary time) is convince himself that what he says is actually true. That way, there is no duplicity, and the tension between voluntary and involuntary processes disappears. By having in our brain a system that enables us to believe what we express and do, there is no leaking out of affect, leaks that caveman Smith

Figure 13.14 Facial expressions of two kinds of patients. **(Top)** The patient suffered brain damage to the right hemisphere; the lesion interfered with voluntary facial expression. **(Bottom)** A parkinsonian patient with a typical masked face. Since Parkinson's disease involves the part of the brain that controls spontaneous facial expression, the faces of these patients, when told to smile, lighted up, since the other pathway was still intact.

Figure 13.15 New Guinea tribesman making facial expressions that turn out to be easily identifiable to western evaluators. **(a)** Your friend has come and you are happy. **(b)** Your child has died. **(c)** You are angry and about to fight. **(d)** You see a dead pig that has been lying there for a long time. © Paul Ekman, 1972.

(a)   (b)

(c)   (d)

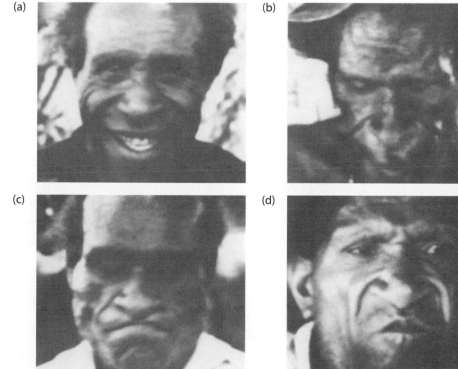

could discern. Thus, there could be times when it might be adaptive to keep embarrassing truths from ourselves!

Are such psychodynamic processes going on in humans? Surely they are, and they are most likely rampant. They result from the simple introduction of a special ability: to make voluntary expressions, which in turn allows for deception and the hiding of intentions. This capacity can quickly compound and create complex psychological states. From this viewpoint, natural selection gives us a rich way of thinking about how we have developed the psychological processes we commonly use.

ADAPTIVE SPECIALIZATIONS AND LEARNING MECHANISMS

In cognitive neuroscience there is no greater point of contact between evolutionary theory and the mind than on the question of the nature of learning. The recent history of the mind and brain sciences has emphasized the view that the brains of animals and humans have a learning system. The idea is that a general-purpose capacity in the brain acquires information during any and all kinds of learning tasks. The idea of simple associationism was prevalent and, in early American experimental hands, became known as *stimulus response* or *SR psychology*. With the right reinforcement contingencies and the right brain state, learning could proceed with ease.

This dominant view has changed over the past few years. Leading the charge has been Randy Gallistel at University of California, Los Angeles (1995). He argued for the idea that there are many learning mechanisms, each computationally specialized for solving problems. He took the strong view that the association formation mechanisms so ubiquitously touted by psychologists are not even responsible for classic and instrumental conditioning. To support his ideas, Gallistel recounted how migratory thrushes must learn the center of rotation of the night sky when they are mere nestlings. This knowledge, gained as a young bird, is called upon only when they grow up and use their knowledge of the night sky's celestial pole to maintain their southerly route during their first migratory flight (Figure 13.16). A simple associationism could never explain this behavioral capacity. The knowledge gained as a young nestling is not used at this stage of its life. There are no contingencies; the knowledge is called on only at a later time.

We have no shortage of examples of what is called *nonassociative learning*. The field of *ethology*—the study of animal behavior in the real world as opposed to the world of the laboratory rat maze—has many rich examples. An often-cited example has to do with the capacity of insects to learn dead reckoning, which is the capacity of all kinds of animals, including the lowly insect, to find their way home after they have been out foraging. When the ant leaves its home base, it computes and stores information on how to get back home. As Gallistel put it, "Like all learning mechanisms, it computes and stores the value(s) of variables. In this case, the mechanisms compute the values of the variables that represent the animal's position relative to

Figure 13.16 Two of the most prominent circumpolar constellations are the Big and Little Dippers. Here, the Big and Little Dippers are seen as they would appear at 9:00 P.M. and 4:00 A.M. from temperate latitudes in the northern hemisphere in the Spring. The migratory birds learn the directions North and South by observing the rotation of the circumpolar stars around the celestial pole (near Polaris now). Adapted from Gallistel (1995).

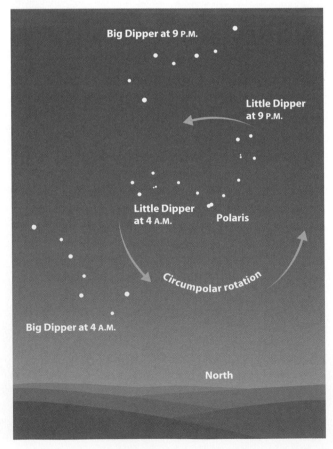

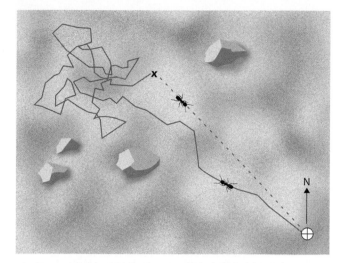

Figure 13.17 A foraging ant's path. The solid line represents the outward, searching journey until food was found at X. After making numerous turns in all directions, the ant is able to make a direct route (dead reckoning) home, as designated by the dashed line. Adapted from Harkness and Maroudas (1985) and Gallistel (1995).

its nest or home base. The computation is equivalent to integrating velocity with respect to time" (Figure 13.17).

These sorts of examples have led several ethologists to the view that an animal has a constellation of specialized learning mechanisms. The learning capacity exhibited in one situation works only in that situation and no other. Peter Marler at University of California at Davis (1991) and others called these examples of *problem-specific learning mechanisms*. The importance of this to issues in cognitive neuroscience is that when one is trying to understand how the brain enables learning, one must realize that there may be several mechanisms, not just one. We saw in Chapter 10 another example of this: the idea that the cerebellum is essential for representing

the temporal relation between a tone and a forthcoming air puff in order to respond at the right time.

Gallistel argued that although there are many different learning mechanisms, there may still be some commonalities. The basic computational operations may be the same. As he put it:

> In computer terms, they may all use the same basic instruction set. (Of course, they may not. At a time when we cannot specify the instruction set underlying any computation of any substantial complexity, we are in no position to say whether different complex computations use the same elementary computational operations.)
>
> The other thing that all learning mechanisms must do is store and retrieve the values of variables. The bird has to store values that represent the center of rotation of the night sky and retrieve them when it determines what orientation to adopt with respect to whatever constellation of circumpolar stars it can see at the moment. The foraging bee must store the distance and direction of the food source and retrieve that information when it gives the dance that transmits the values to other foragers. The dead-reckoning mechanism must store the values that represent the animal's current position and then add to them whenever the animal moves, because dead reckoning amounts to keeping a running sum of displacements.

As we ascend into the human brain, we can see from an evolutionary perspective how humans must possess special devices for learning. William James stated that the human has more instincts than animals, not fewer. It is in this setting that Noam Chomsky and Steven Pinker argued for the view that there is a special learning module for human language. It has specific features and capacities and most likely a definite neural organization. In short, the work on animals, where specialized systems are easily identified, raises provocative notions about the human brain's organization and cognitive powers.

EVOLUTIONARY INSIGHTS TO HUMAN BRAIN ORGANIZATION

A major assumption in neuroscience is being challenged: the idea that a larger brain with more cells is responsible for the greater computational capacity of the human being. Consider Passingham's (1982) main conclusion to his fascinating book, *The Human Primate:*

> Simple changes in the genetic control of growth can have far-reaching effects on form. The human brain differs from the chimpanzee brain in its extreme development of cortical structures, in particular the cerebellar cortex and the association areas of the neocortex. The proportions of these areas are predictable from rules governing the construction of primate brains of differing size. Furthermore, there appears to be a uniformity in the number and type of cells used in building neocortical areas; the human brain follows the general pattern for mammals. Even with two speech areas we believe we can detect regions in the monkey brain that are alike in cellular organization. The evolution of the human brain is characterized more by expansion of areas than by radical reconstructions.

The uniqueness of the human brain, it is commonly believed, can be traced to its larger size. It has more neurons and more cortical columns, and in that truth lies (somewhere) the secret to human experience. This is entirely consistent with many other observations of humans and animals. The disproportionately large cortical representation of some sensory and motor regions of the cortex in animals and humans is well established. The recognized correlation between the large inferior colliculus for echo-locating bats and dolphins and the enlarged optic lobes for visual fish is well known. In short, the idea that a larger brain structure reflects an increase in function is ubiquitous.

Even Charles Darwin promoted the idea that big brains explained the uniqueness of the human condition. In *The Descent of Man and Selection in Relation to Sex,* he wrote that there is no fundamental difference in the mental faculties of humans and the higher mammals. He went on to add that the difference in mind between humans and the higher animals, great as it is, is certainly one of degree and not of kind. He did not want to be part of any thinking that there may be critical qualitative differences between the subhuman primate and humans. Darwin left the actual anatomy to his colleague Thomas Henry Huxley. At that time, Richard Owen, another anatomist, maintained that there was a special structure in the human brain, the *hippocampus minor.* Yet Huxley proved that this structure was in other primates, thereby undercutting the idea that the human brain was qualitatively different from the primate brain. So, here we had Darwin, the genius who articulated natural selection and diversity, arguing for a straight-line evolution between primates and humans. Organisms, the product of selection pressures, displayed rich diversity in the evolution of species. But when it came to brain and mind, Darwin thought the human brain to be a blown-up monkey brain, a nervous system that had a monotonic relation to its closest ancestor.

Nonetheless, a lot of evidence shows that the human brain's unique capacities do not rely on cell number so much as the appearance of specialized circuits. That the human brain has more cells does not explain greater capacities. Evolutionary perspectives would find the human brain adapted to its own biological niche, and one would predict differences in brain organization from other animals. After millions of years of natural selection, we have accumulated circuits that enable us to carry out specific aspects of human cognition. In short, just as comparative neurobiologists have demonstrated the presence of specialized circuitry in lower animals that reflect adaptations to niches, similar demonstrations can be made in humans.

Let us look at more evidence for specialized circuits. Consider the human brain's two halves, left and right. We know the left cortex is specialized for language and speech, and the right has specializations of its own. Each half is the same size and has roughly the same number of nerve cells. The cortices are connected by the corpus callosum. The total, linked cortical mass contributes to our unique human intelligence. What would happen to intelligence if the halves were disconnected, leaving the left operating independently of the right and vice versa? Would split-brain patients lose half of their cognitive capacity because the left talking hemisphere would now operate with only half of the total brain cortex?

A cardinal feature of split-brain research is that after cerebral hemispheres are disconnected, the patient's verbal IQ remains intact, and the problem-solving capacity of the left hemisphere, such as hypothesis formation, remains unchanged. While there can be deficits in recall capacity and in other performance measures, the total capacity for problem solving remains unaffected. Isolating essentially half of the cortex from the dominant left hemisphere, then, causes no major change in cognitive functions. Following surgery, the integrated 1200- to 1300-gm brain becomes two isolated 600- to 650-gm brains, each about the size of a chimpanzee's brain. The capacity of the left half remains unchanged from its preoperative level, while the largely disconnected, equally sized right hemisphere is seriously hampered from performing tasks. Although the largely isolated right hemisphere remains superior to the isolated left hemisphere for things like recognizing upright faces, attentional skills, and perhaps emotions, it is poor at problem solving and many other mental activities. A brain system (the right hemisphere) with roughly the same number of neurons as one that easily cognates (the left hemisphere) is incapable of higher-order cognition—strong evidence that cortical cell numbers do not fully account for human intelligence.

Perhaps the most influential and dominant idea that more cortical area means higher-level function came from Norman Geschwind and Walter Levitsky (1968). Over the past 25 years, their report that the left hemisphere has a larger planum temporale solidified the belief that more brain area meant higher-level function. They concluded in their classic paper by stating, "Our data show that this area is significantly larger on the left side, and the differences observed are easily of sufficient magnitude to be compatible with the known functional asymmetries." In other words, the belief was that the greater brain area in this language zone was what was responsible for language.

Because this classic finding makes a strong case for a

relation between cortical area and function, the issue of whether the left planum temporale is larger than the right planum has been re-examined. With three-dimensional reconstructions of normal brains, magnetic resonance imaging of the posterior temporal region was carefully measured using the same methods Geschwind used; approximately the same percentage of brains had apparent asymmetry, with the left side being larger. But this measurement is not a true three-dimensional reconstruction since it does not take into account the natural curvature of the cortical surface from one coronal slice to another (see Figure 9.4, p 326). When a true three-dimensional reconstruction algorithm is applied to this region, its cortical surface area is not reliably asymmetrical. In a sample of ten brains, as many had a larger cortical surface area in the right as in the left hemisphere.

Many lines of anatomical and physiological research suggest that cortical areas within a species contain variable proportions of morphologically and neurochemically defined cell types. For example, primary and secondary visual, somatosensory, and auditory cortices express varying distributions of specific nerve fibers, and the density of certain nerve cells, called *chandelier cells,* differs between prefrontal and visual cortical regions (Lewis and Lund, 1990).

Cortical connectivity varies among species, which may reflect the organism's niche. The squirrel monkey and bush baby have differing connections of the interblob region in their visual cortices. In the bush baby, layer IIIB nonblobs receive input from lamina IV alpha, while in the squirrel monkey this layer receives input from lamina IV beta. The effect is altered inputs to lamina IIIB from magnocellular pathways in the bush baby and altered inputs to parvocellular pathways in the squirrel monkey (Lachica et al., 1993).

Blob regions in these two species are connected almost identically. The significance of the species' difference in the nonblob regions of visual cortex is likely related to their activity patterns (Livingstone and Hubel, 1984): Bush babies are nocturnal and squirrel monkeys are diurnal. Bush baby layer IIIB receives input from layer IV alpha (the magnocellular stream), while squirrel monkey layer IIIB receives input from layer IV beta (the parvocellular stream).

Fascinating clues have emerged from work on human brain tissue. For example, the physiological properties of dendritic spines in the human might differ from those in other animals. Gordon Shepherd and his colleagues (1989) at Yale University studied presumed normal cortical tissue removed from epileptic patients. Comparing the membrane and synaptic properties of human and rodent dentate granule cells, they noticed important varia-

tions. First, humans had less spike-frequency adaptation in comparison with rodents; second, feedback was inhibited in human tissue while rodent tissue showed feedforward and feedback inhibition—consistent with Shepherd's neuronal modeling. This work suggests that by simply adding a few calcium channels to the dendritic spine, vastly complex computational capacities can result in the spines and lead to more information-processing capability. These study results, though suggestive, are exciting and may point to new ways of thinking about variations in neuronal physiology among species (Williamson et al., 1993).

Nonhuman primate and human visual systems also have different organizational properties. When comparing, for example, the anterior commissure between humans and other primates, it is easy to see how the species differ in neural organization. The anterior commissure is one of the neural connections between the two halves of the brain. It is the smaller of the two cortical connections, second in size to the huge corpus callosum. In monkeys, when this structure is left intact but its corpus callosum is sectioned, visual information easily transfers in monkeys but not humans. Thus, species vary considerably in how they transfer visual information between hemispheres.

What is more, lesions to the human primary visual cortex render patients blind, whereas monkeys with similar lesions are capable of residual vision. When residual vision is discovered in a human, as with blindsight, it likely reflects incomplete damage to the primary visual cortex. When a monkey has residual vision, it reflects capacities of other secondary visual system processes.

Examples abound of system-level variations between primates and other lower animals, but less attention is paid to those between nonhuman primates and humans. Yet the preceding observations evince major differences in anatomical organization, even though the monkey's visual system and the human's visual system have virtually identical sensory capacities. Careful psychophysical measurement of acuity, color, and other parameters reveals identical sensitivities. In addition, at the level of anatomical processes, both have approximately 1.2 million retinal ganglion cells. Even though the gray matter volume of the human primary visual cortex, area striata, is three times larger than it is in the *Macaca mulatta* and five times larger than that in owl monkeys, Aotus V1 has the same number of cells in the rhesus monkey and the human brain.

In grasping the differences between monkey and human behavior, one has to consider the variations between the neuronal organization of each visual system. Can these differences be understood in relation to the connectivity of major processing areas or to the level of synaptic function? We do not know.

Arguing about similarities between species has been criticized by many. Take the problem of intelligence. It is naive anthropomorphism to compare the concept of human intelligence and apply it to the behavior of animals. It is simply a fact that each species has developed behavioral capabilities that are advantageous to its own survival and each member of that species would possess these capacities. There have been many attempts to raise the intelligence of a rat by selective breeding. All failed. A rat that might run a maze better turns out to be lousy at discrimination learning. Our human brains are larger because they have more devices for solving problems and the devices are shared by all members of the species. It is not likely that the variations seen in our own species's capacity to solve problems will vary with brain size; recent direct measures have shown there is no correlation.

Even though brain size cannot explain the unique capacities of the human, Noam Chomsky (1957) favored the view that although language is deeply biological in nature, it is not a product of natural selection. Chomsky left open the possibility that language is the result, the concomitant, of massive interactions of millions of neurons. So, in the heart of the great Chomsky, the one who argued deeply for the biological basis of language, there lingers the idea that bigger is better.

Steven Pinker (1997a) challenged this bit of back sliding by Chomsky. Cranking up his unusually insightful and lively style, Pinker chided his colleague: "If Chomsky maintains that grammar shows signs of complex design, but is skeptical that natural selection manufactured it, what alternative does he have in mind? What he repeatedly mentions is physical law. Just as the flying fish is compelled to return to the water and calcium-filled bones are compelled to be white, human brains might, for all we know, be compelled to contain circuits for Universal Grammar."

Chomsky wrote (see Pinker, 1994):

> These skills [e.g., learning a grammar] may well have arisen as a concomitant of structural properties of the brain that developed for other reasons. Suppose that there was selection for bigger brains, more cortical surface, hemispheric specialization for analytic processing, or many other structural properties that can be imagined. The brain that evolved might well have all sorts of special properties that are not individually selected; there would be no miracle in this—only the normal workings of evolution. We have no idea, at present, how physical laws apply when 1010 neurons are placed in an object the size of a basketball, under the special conditions that arose during human evolution. We may have no idea—just as we do not know how physical laws apply under the special conditions of hurricanes sweeping through junkyards—but it seems unlikely that an undiscovered corollary of the laws of physics causes human-size and -shaped brains to develop the circuitry for Universal Grammar.

Neuroscientists have had a hard time accepting the view that big brains may be a by-product of other processes for establishing the uniqueness of each species's nervous system. Yet biologists have known for years how specialized circuits define differences between fish and reptile, reptile and mammal, snail and octopus, worm and jellyfish. It is only logical that this information would help to define the neural processes supporting unique human capacities, especially language, and that big brains (corrected for body size) may get bigger because they collect more specialized circuits.

SUMMARY

The lesson of this chapter is simple. Complex capacities like language and social behavior are not constructs that arise out of our brain simply because it is bigger than a chimpanzee's brain. No, these capacities reflect specialized devices that natural selection built into our brains through blind trial and error. Mutations create variations in capacities. If the variations produce a slightly unique state of affairs that helps our brains make better decisions about enhancing reproductive success, the new capacities will survive. Variations that further enhance the capacity in question will also survive. An eye was not built in a day. Something that worked a little bit is better than something that did not work at all. As it evolved, the visual system became the finely tuned device it is now. So, too, with language and other mental abilities. The positive feedback mechanism of natural selection—not experience—builds complexity into organisms.

This notion is in direct contrast to the view that the mental complexity of humans is the result of a larger brain with more numerous neurons, which somehow allows for a greater computational skill. The idea that bigger is better—that more neurons allow for more associations that allow for more mental complexity—is simply not likely. Evolution through natural selection builds specific devices in our brain to handle specific challenges.

Even the inventive notion of exaptation has its limits. The strong form of this argument is that the human brain suddenly became large for some reason and that upon that big brain landscape, local solutions were painted. The human brain, because of its greater computational capacity, could now solve a multitude of problems. The larger brain could be exapted for new duties. This view of the biological process was proposed as a countermeasure to the view that all human psychological behavior was borne out of specific adaptations.

Our present knowledge of these matters suggests that the human brain is a collection of a vast number of instincts, as William James argued, and that these instincts, built into our brains for one purpose, can help out for another. Yet this in no way undermines the basic truth that the brain is a collection of processing devices.

Finally, a multitude of commonalities connect all species and lend strength to much of biological research. At the same time, species exhibit crucial differences, such as those reviewed here, and human brain research has uncovered unique aspects of human behavior that may be supported by specialized neural circuitry.

SUGGESTED READINGS

GEARY, D.C. (1995). Reflections of evolution and culture in children's cognition. *American Psychologist* 50:24–37.

GAULIN, S.J.C., and FITZGERALD, R.W. (1989). Sexual selection for spatial-learning ability. *Animal Behavior* 37:332–331.

JERNE N. (1968). Antibodies and learning: Selection versus instruction. In G. Quarton, T. Melnechuck, and F.O. Schmidt, eds. *The Neurosciences: A Study Program.* Vol 1. New York: Rockefeller University Press.

LE DOUX, JOSEPH E. (1995). Emotion: Clues from the brain. *Annual Review of Psychology* 46:209–235.

PINKER, STEVEN (1997). *How the Mind Works.* New York: W.W. Norton.

SHEPARD, R.N. (1994). Perceptual-cognitive universals as reflections of the world. *Psychonomic Bulletin & Review* 1:2–28.

14

The Problem of Consciousness

It was a boiling hot day in southern California in the early 1960s. One of us (M.S.G.) was playing horseshoes in the backyard of patient W.J.'s home. He was the first human in recent times to have his brain split in order to control his otherwise intractable epilepsy.

In those years the race was on to study the effects of disconnecting the two halves of the brain of animals. Research on cats, monkeys, and even chimpanzees showed that when one half of the brain was trained on visual or tactile discrimination problems, the other half remained ignorant of the training. It was as if someone had trained you such that every time you picked up an apple (and not an orange) with your left hand, you got five dollars, but if you used your right hand, you would not know to pick up the apple. It seemed too much to believe. Maybe animals were somehow different. But humans? No way.

The surgical idea was that by cutting the fibers that connect the two halves of the brain, an epileptic seizure starting in one hemisphere would not spread to the other. In such an instance while one half of the body might seize, the other would remain seizure free, and so the patients would not lose consciousness. W.J. was tested prior to his split-brain surgery and showed no disconnection effects. When an apple was placed in his left hand, he could name it, he could find the same apple with his right hand, he could name visual stimuli presented to either half of the brain, and so on. In short, he was normal with respect to sensory, motor, perceptual, and cognitive processes.

After his split-brain surgery, W.J. named and described information presented to his left (speaking) hemisphere. What was surprising was his apparent lack of response to stimuli presented to his surgically isolated right hemisphere. It was as if he was blind to visual stim-

uli presented to the left of where his eyes were fixated. Yet it became obvious that while the left (talking) hemisphere could not report on stimuli presented to the right hemisphere, the right hemisphere could easily react to a simple visual stimulus via its ability to control the manual responses of the left hand.

An early conclusion about these phenomena suggested dividing the hemispheres in order to control intractable epilepsy, leaving each half of the brain behaving independently of the other. Information experienced by one side seemed unavailable to the other. Moreover, each half appeared to be specialized for certain mental activities. The left was superior for language while the right was more adept at carrying out visuo-spatial tasks. The surgeon had separated structures with specific and complex functions.

The capacities demonstrated by the left hemisphere were no surprise. But when the first patients were able to read (but not speak) from the right hemisphere and were able to take that information and choose between test alternatives, the case for a dual, and now independent, conscious system appeared to be strong. After human cerebral hemispheres were separated, each half functioned outside the conscious realm of the other. Each could learn, remember, emote, and carry out planned activities.

Back to the story. As the game of horseshoes wore on, W.J. suddenly paused. He had been playing with his right hand, which meant his left (dominant) hemisphere—the hemisphere that talks and thinks and generally runs our mental life—had been in charge. W.J. had been losing the game and outwardly seemed nonchalant about it. He walked over to the side of his yard, picked up an ax with his left hand, gripped it firmly, and swung it around a couple of times, all the while smiling.

The left hand gains its major control from the silent, generally intellectually limited right hemisphere. Was it annoyed with its status in the game? Was it an independent conscious entity, different from the left mind? If it attacked, which half of the brain would be prosecuted and charged with the crime? In short, had surgical divisions of the cerebral connections between the two halves produced a person with two conscious systems?

Conscious experience is a wonderful thing. We all have it, we all talk about it, and we pity people who do not have it. Watching a trauma patient in a coma is grim. As his eyes stare off into space, even though the heart beats strongly and the muscles remain firm, we quickly realize that consciousness is the most precious jewel of our existence. When conscious experience begins to fade, as in Alzheimer's disease, the sight is stressful for everyone. The patient is awake, even alert, but out of touch with what is happening around her, even unsure about her own identity.

In normal activity, we speak of raising people's consciousness. That is what education is all about. It is one thing to be able to read the comic strip. It is another to understand the nature of gravity and to appreciate where planet earth is located in the universe. Having such knowledge affects one's conscious awareness.

Yet no one has been able to define consciousness to anyone's satisfaction. Consciousness is the key concept of mind-brain research, and over the years it has stayed on the sidelines. Some say that the origin of consciousness is so complex that the human brain cannot grasp it. For humans to understand consciousness would be like a flatworm trying to fathom a monkey.

People certainly do not try to understand what is meant by consciousness. In the last 10 years more than 15,000 articles have been published on the topic. Yet headway is limited, at best. The last 15,000 articles in molecular biology produced great advances in our appreciation of the molecular nature of biological processes. In some instances this made a real difference in understanding diseases or gene identification. But on the subject of consciousness, the publications appear to be only words and statements about viewpoints on the topic.

Some of the leading philosophers of our time, such as University of California's John Searle, maintained that science will never understand the nature of subjective experience. Searle (1992) claimed that subjectivity is beyond the descriptive resources of objective science as we now conceive it. It follows from this that we can never have an adequate theory of consciousness unless we treat irreducibly subjective concepts such as feelings as basic objects or explanatory constructs just like atoms or ions or force fields are used in the physical sciences.

But most scientists are not swayed by this argument. The quickness with which our ignorance evaporates is exemplified by merely noting what a leading academician said about the creation of the world a mere 145 years ago. As Robert J. Wenke (1980) pointed out in his fascinating book on prehistory, "Indeed, in the 1850s the eminent Dr. Lightfoot of Cambridge University, on the basis of his study of the Book of Genesis, proclaimed that the world had been created on October 23, 4004 B.C., at the civilized hour of 9:00 A.M."

We have come a long way in a short time, and other leading philosophers such as Patricia Churchland (1986) at the University of California, San Diego, raised the hope that we are dealing with a tractable problem. She related the truth that most knowledge we now receive from our cultural history was once held out as impossible to know. The mysteries of evolution, of genetics, of cellular mechanisms, and of vision were stupefying only a few dozen years ago. Now explanations abound for all these processes. Why, she asked, can the same not follow for the problems of consciousness?

Other naysayers asked how can we study a problem that does not yet have an agreed-on definition? On the surface, such complaints seem plausible. Yet, time and time again in science, people work on poorly defined problems, and as they stumble through the darkness, precision comes to their observations and to the definitions that motivate their initial reasons for doing experiments. The argument that we cannot learn about something because we do not know enough about it is an oxymoron. A much more productive posture is to study consciousness from every angle possible and come up with definitions and new methods for studying the mind.

PHILOSOPHICAL PERSPECTIVES

The problem of consciousness has been called the mind-brain problem or the ontological problem. It encompasses many questions: What is the real nature of mental states and processes? In what medium do they take place? How are they related to the physical world? Does consciousness survive death? Can a purely physical system construct conscious intelligence?

Two philosophies attempt to give direction to this problem—dualism and materialism. Dualism takes the stand that mind and brain are two distinct phenomena whereas materialism asserts that mind and body are both biological mediums. Within each of these philosophies, views differ on the specifics. Paul Churchland, at University of California, San Diego (1988), neatly outlined the distinctions.

All forms of dualism have a common premise: Conscious experience is nonphysical and beyond the scope of the physical sciences. The pure form of this view comes from Descartes, who believed the mind and the body are two completely separate entities. Descartes was not too clear on how these two entities interacted: When the mind decided to move a hand, the hand moved.

Another form of dualism is referred to as *popular dualism;* the idea is that people are ghosts in the machine (brain) and the spatial properties of the ghost interact with the spatial properties of the brain. This idea moves from the contention that matter is merely a manifestation of energy. The problem is that we have no evidence for a nonmaterial thinking substance that survives death.

A more interesting form of dualism is called *property dualism.* In this view there is no substance beyond the physical brain, but it has unique nonphysical properties possessed by no other physical object. Over the years this view gradually changed. The idea was first referred to as *epiphenomenalism,* which meant that mental phenomena are not part of the physical phenomena in the brain but rather ride above the fray. Mental phenomena are caused by various brain activities but do not have any causal effects on the brain itself.

Epiphenomenalism has given away to what Churchland called *interactionist property dualism.* This view suggests that mental phenomena can affect the brain and thereby behavior. As such, mental properties are emergent ones that do not appear until ordinary physical matter has managed to organize itself through evolution into complex systems. Also, mental properties are irreducible. They are not just organizational features of physical matter; they are novel properties of the brain. Examples include the concept of something being painful or fragrant or colorful. These mental states emerge from the brain's physical processes and can, once triggered, turn back on the brain and guide lower information processing. Roger Sperry, the great psychobiologist, in his later years pushed for this view.

With advances in cognitive neuroscience, most philosophers and scientists do not champion the dualists' idea in any of its forms. More typically they are *materialists.* Science has proved how parts of the brain have specific roles in our mental life. Lesioned parts and a person's emotional state can change. Change another part, and the patient loses the ability to recognize faces. While these findings do not completely rule out dualism, they do suggest that the brain enables mind. And, just as with dualism, there are many forms of materialism.

Philosophical behaviorism is one form of materialism. Here the view is that one cannot talk about inner experience at all. Rather, one simply talks about a person's capabilities and dispositions because these can be measured. This simplistic approach to the problem of the nature of conscious experience has been abandoned in recent years. After all, we do have inner experience, mental imagery, thoughts that are never expressed, and so forth.

According to *reductive materialism,* on the other hand, mental states are physical states of the brain and each type of mental state or process is numerically identical with some physical state or process in the brain. While most brain scientists believe this, it has been difficult to tie the myriad of mental processes to specific brain locations. Although we can catalogue the large-scale systems in mental activities such as language, we are not sure where mental states like ennui are managed.

Perhaps the most favored theory of mind and brain and the phenomena of consciousness is that of *functionalism.* This theory is widely adopted by psychologists, philosophers, and the artificial intelligence community. Its biggest proponent is Daniel C. Dennett (1991), one of the leading philosophers of the twentieth century. Functionalism differs from behaviorism in an important way. The behaviorist believes defining environmental input and behavioral output will be sufficient for understanding mind; the functionalist does not. For the functionalist any one mental state makes ineliminable reference to other mental states. In trying to understand a mental state with this view, there could be no possible explanation in solely behavioral terms.

Functionalists also believe anything that looks like it feels pain or sees red or thinks appropriately is functionally equivalent to the human brain. Thus, an artifact, such as the one being built at MIT by Rodney Strong, can become an equivalent human. Cog, as the robot at MIT is dubbed, is being built in an attempt to construct an entity that does all things human conscious agents do. If the developers succeed, they believe the system will be equivalent to a human mind and should receive all due rights and honors.

But the functionalist approach is challenged by many because it ignores subjective experience, or *qualia* as it is sometimes called. When this issue is put to leading proponents of functionalism, such as Daniel

An Interview with Daniel C. Dennett, Ph.D.

Professor Dennett is a leading philosopher of consciousness and the mind-brain problem. He is Director for the Center for Cognitive Studies at Tufts University.

Authors: Many scientists like to use the term *qualia* when discussing consciousness. It seems to refer to phenomenal awareness, raw feelings, that sort of thing. Can we get out on the table what you mean by *qualia*?

DD: I thought you'd never ask. *Qualia* are the souls of experiences. Now do you believe that each human experience has its own special and inviolable soul?

Authors: What are you getting at? What on earth does that even mean?

DD: That's just my wake-up call for people who think they know what qualia are. It's frustrating to learn that in spite of my strenuous efforts, people keep using the term *qualia* as if it were innocent. Consider a parallel: According to Descartes (and many churches) the difference between us and animals is that animals have no souls. Now when Darwin showed that we are a species of hominid, did he show that there really aren't any people after all—just animals? If Darwin is saying we're just animals, he must be denying we have souls! So he must be saying that people aren't really people after all!

In spite of tradition, the very real and important differences between people and (other) animals are not well described in terms of the presence or absence of souls fastened to their brains. At least I would hope most of your readers would agree with me about that. Similarly, the differences between some mental processes and others are not well described in terms of the presence or absence of qualia—for what are they? Not only is there no agreed-upon definition among philosophers; controversies rage. Until they get settled, outsiders would be wise to avert their gaze, and use some other term or terms—some genuinely neutral terms—to talk about properties of subjective experience. In fact the term *qualia,* which is, after all, a term of philosophical jargon, not anything established in either common parlance or science, has always had a variety of extremely dubious connotations among philosophers. Denying there are qualia is more like denying there are souls than denying that people are much smarter than animals. If that makes qualia sound like a term one would be wise to avoid, good!

To put it bluntly, nobody outside of philosophy should take a stand on the reality of qualia under the assumption that they know what they're saying. You might as well express your conviction that trees are alive by saying they are infused with elan vital. So when Francis Crick, for instance, says that he believes in qualia, or when Gerald Edelman contrasts his view with mine because his view, unlike mine, allows for qualia, these pronouncements should be taken with more than a grain of salt. I'd be very surprised if either Crick or Edelman—to take two egregious examples—believes in what the philosophical fans of qualia believe in. If they do, they have a major task ahead of them: sorting out and justifying their claims against a mountain of objections they've never even considered. I would think they'd be wise to sidestep the mess.

I fear I'm losing the battle over the term *qualia,* however. It seems to be becoming the standard term, a presumably theory-neutral way of referring to whatever tastes and smells and subjective colors and pains are. If that's how it goes, I'll have to go along with the gang, but that will just make it harder to sort out the issues, since it means that all the controversies will have to be aired every time anybody wants to ensure that others know what is being asserted or denied. Too bad. Don't say I didn't warn you.

Authors: Well, OK. Qualia is doomed to mean the feeling about the specialized perceptual and cognitive capacities we humans enjoy. Put directly, should we not distinguish between the task of characterizing the cog-

Dennett, they maintain that we are worried over nothing. When the cognitive neuroscience of intelligence, language, feelings, memory, attention, and perception are explained, qualia will come along free. It, too, will be understood.

As the battle of theories rages on, we are left with trying to explain how the brain enables mind. Dualism tends to ignore biological findings and materialism overlooks the reality of subjective experience. As we move forward in our understanding of conscious

nitive operations of the human mind and the, here we go, the qualia we have about them?

DD: Certainly we should divide and conquer. So we should distinguish between the task of characterizing some of the cognitive operations of the human mind, and the rest (which we conveniently set aside till later); but if we call the latter *qualia* and think that they are somehow altogether different from the cognitive operations we are studying now, we prejudge a major question.

Take experience of color, every philosopher's favorite example of a qualia. Suppose what interests you as a cognitive scientist are the differences in people's responses to particular colors (Munsell color chips will do for standard stimuli, at least for this imaginary example). But instead of looking at such familiar measures of difference as size of JNDs, or latency of naming, or choice of color words (where does each subject's pure red lie on the spectrum, etc.), or galvanic skin response, or an ERP [evoked-response potential] difference, suppose you looked at variations in such hard-to-measure factors as differences in evoked memories, attitude, mood, cooperativity, boredom, appetite, willingness to engage in theological discussion—you name it. Until you've exhausted all these imponderable effects, you haven't covered all the cognitive or disposition-affecting factors in subjective color experience, so there will be features of color experience, features of what it is like for each individual, that you are leaving out of your investigation. Obviously. But if you then call these unexamined residues qualia and declare (or just assume) that these leftovers are somehow beyond the reach of cognitive science, not just now but forever, you are committing a sort of fallacy of subtraction. There need be nothing remarkable about the leftovers beyond their being leftovers (so far). When some qualia freak steps up and says, "Well, you've got a nifty account of the cognitive side of color vision, but you still have a mystery: the ineffable what-it-is-likeness of color QUALIA," you needn't concur; you are entitled to demand specifics.

To cut to the chase, I once got Tom Nagel in discussion to admit that given what he meant by qualia, there could be two identical twins whose scores on every test of color discrimination, color preference, color memory, effects of color on mood, etc., etc., came out the same, and there would still be a wide-open question of whether the twins had the same color qualia when they looked into a particular can of paint! (By Nagel's lights, neither twin would have any grounds at all for supposing that now he knew that he and his twin brother had the same color qualia.) Nagel's position is an available metaphysical position, I guess, but I hope it is obvious that it doesn't derive any plausibility from anything we have discovered about the nature of color experience, and hence no cognitive neuroscientist needs to be shackled by any such doctrine of qualia.

There are obviously large families of differences and similarities in experience that are best ignored at this stage of inquiry—no one can get a good scientific handle on them yet. One can admit that there is a lot more to color experience, or any other domain of subjectivity, than we have yet accounted for without thereby endorsing the dubious doctrine that qualia are properties that elude objective science forever. But that doctrine is the standard destination of all the qualia arguments among philosophers.

Authors: So what is the task of the future student of the problem of consciousness? What should be the content of their research? Is it to solve the brain mechanisms enabling, say, problem solving, and along with that will come some deeper understanding of the ole ineffable qualia?

DD: That's roughly right, in my opinion. Here is one place—not the only one, of course—where cognitive neuroscientists could take a hint from AI [artificial intelligence]. The people in AI have almost never worried about consciousness as such, since it seemed obvious to them that if and when you ever got a system—an embodied robot, in the triumphal case—that actually could do all the things a person can do (it can reflect on its reflections about its recollections of its anticipations of its decisions, and so forth), the residual questions about consciousness would have fairly obvious answers. I have always thought they were right.

process, we will be best served by collecting new data and observations.

Steven Pinker of MIT pulled together a framework for thinking about the problem of consciousness from the perspective of cognitive neuroscience. In his new book, *How the Mind Works* (1997), Pinker reviewed the work of the linguist Ray Jackendoff of Brandeis University and the philosopher Ned Block at New York University. These mind scientists observed how people who write on the topic are guilty of using the term *consciousness* in so many ways that it becomes impossible to ascertain what each is talking about. The proposal for ending this confusion consists of breaking the problem of consciousness into three issues. Pinker summarized and embellished the view as follows:

- Sentience: Sentience refers to subjective experience, phenomenal awareness, raw feelings, first-person tense, what it is like to be or do something. If you have to ask, you will never know.
- Access to information: This is the ability to report on the content of mental experience without the capacity to report on how the content was built up by the nervous system. Information processing in the nervous system falls into two pools: One pool, which includes the products of vision and the contents of short-term memory, can be accessed by the systems underlying verbal reports, rational thought, and deliberate decision making. The other, which includes autonomic (gut-level) responses, the internal operations of vision, language, and motor control, and repressed desires or memories (if there are any), cannot be accessed.
- Self-knowledge: Among the people and objects that an intelligent being can have accurate information about is the being itself. As Pinker said, "I cannot only feel pain and see red, but think to myself, 'Hey, here I am, Steve Pinker, feeling pain and seeing red!'"

These three categories enable us to bring present cognitive neuroscience knowledge to bear on the topic of consciousness. Right from the start we can say that science has little to say about sentience. We are clueless on how the brain creates sentience. Dennett would not worry about this, but other scientists still believe it is an issue to be understood in scientific terms.

At the same time, cognitive neuroscience has much to say about access and self-knowledge. It does so because the cognitive neuroscience approach to the problem is not driven by a philosophical viewpoint. Cognitive neuroscience data and observations on the topic are used with great enthusiasm by philosophers. But the day-to-day work studying patients with broken brains or studying normal brains with brain imaging technologies goes on in the simple spirit of learning more about human brain organization and how it enables mind. In what follows, we present many studies that have implications, direct and indirect, for the problem of access and self-knowledge. We examine observations that most assuredly deal with conscious experience.

CONSCIOUS VERSUS UNCONSCIOUS PROCESSING

The insights gained from evolutionary theory are vast. It is essential to remember how many domain-specific specialized systems we have in our brains because they all interact in unique ways that produce our sensation of conscious experience. At the same time, the vast majority of mental processes that control and contribute to our conscious experience happen outside our conscious awareness. We really have little or no insight into what prepares us to throw a baseball, to see a colorful flower, or to speak a grammatical sentence. The staging of this behavior is not part of our conscious life. We do not have access to how the brain does those things.

A vast amount of research in cognitive science clearly shows we are conscious only of the content of our mental life, not what generates the content. It is the products of mnemonic processing, of perceptual processing of imaging, that we are aware of—not what produced the products. Sometimes people report on what they think were the processes, but they are reporting after the fact on what they thought they did to produce the content of their consciousness.

Richard Nisbett and colleagues (1980) at the University of Michigan made this point most clearly. The work is all cleverly done with the tried-but-true technique of learning word pairs. He first exposed subjects to word associations like *ocean-moon*. His idea is that subjects might subsequently say "Tide" when asked to free associate the word *detergent*. That is exactly what they do, but they do not know why. When asked, they might say, "Oh, my mother always used Tide to do the laundry."

Now any student will commonly and quickly declare that he is fully aware of how he solves a problem even when he really does not know. The famous Tower of Hanoi (Figure 14.1) problem is solved all the time. And when researchers listen to the running discourse of students articulating what they are doing and why they are doing it, the result can be used to write a computer program to solve the problem. But the subject calls on facts known from short- and long-term memory. These

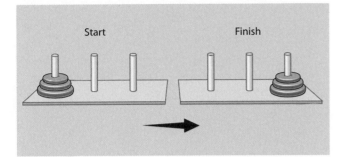

Figure 14.1 The Tower of Hanoi problem. The task is to rebuild the rings on another tower without ever putting a larger ring on top of a smaller ring. It can be done in seven steps and after much practice, students learn the task. After they have solved it, however, their explanations for how they solved it can be quite bizarre.

Figure 14.2 One technique for testing subliminal perception. A subject is quickly presented a picture of a boy, as viewed in either picture A1 or A2, in such a way that they do not have conscious awareness as to the content of the picture. The subject is then shown a neutral picture (B) and asked to judge the character of the boy. These judgments of the boy's character have been found to be biased by the previous subthreshold presentation.

events are accessible to consciousness and can be used to build a theory for their action. Yet no one is aware of how the events became established in short- or long-term memory.

Cognitive psychologists have also examined the extent and kind of information that can be processed unconsciously. Freud staked out the most complex range where the unconscious was hot and wet. Deep emotional conflicts are fought and their resolution slowly makes its way to conscious experience. Other psychologists placed more stringent constraints on what can be processed. Many researchers maintain that only low-level stimuli—like the lines forming the letter of a word, not the word itself—can be unconsciously processed. Over the last century these matters have been examined time and again; only recently has unconscious processing been examined in a cognitive neuroscience setting.

The classic approach was to use the technique of subliminal perception. Here a picture of a boy either throwing a cake at someone or simply presenting the cake in a friendly manner is quickly flashed. A neutral picture of the boy is subsequently presented, and the subject proves to be biased in judging the boy's personality as a function of the subliminal exposures he received (Figure 14.2). Hundreds of such demonstrations have been recounted, although they are not easy to replicate. Many psychologists maintain that elements of the picture are captured subconsciously and that this is sufficient to bias judgment.

In recent years cognitive psychologists have tried to reaffirm the role of unconscious processing yet again by using new experimental paradigms. A leader in this effort has been Tony Marcel of Cambridge University (1983a, b). Marcel used a masking paradigm in which

the brief presentation of either a blank screen or a word was quickly followed by a masking stimulus of a cross patch of letters (Figure 14.3). One of two tasks followed presentation of the masking stimulus. In a detection task, subjects merely had to choose whether a word had been presented. On this task, subjects responded at chance. They simply could not tell whether or not a word had been presented. If the task became a lexical decision task, however, the subliminally presented stimulus had effects. Here, following the masking stimulus, a string of letters was presented and subjects had to specify whether the string formed a word. Marcel cleverly manipulated the subthreshold words in such a way that

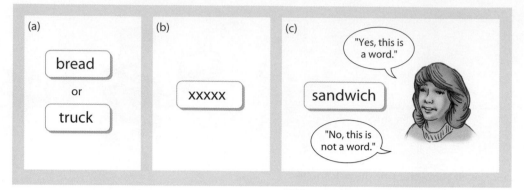

Figure 14.3 To test subliminal processing of words, Tony Marcel presented a word such as *bread* at a subthreshold level **(a)**. This word was quickly replaced by a cross patch of letters **(b)**. Then, in a lexical decision task, the subject was presented with a string of letters and asked if the letters formed a word or not. Presentation of subthreshold words influenced the response times to related words but had no effect on the response to unrelated words. Adapted from Marcel (1983).

some were related to the word string and some were not. If there had been at least lexical processing of the sub-threshold word, related words should elicit faster response times, and this is exactly what Marcel found.

As further work was done on the phenomenon, it became clear that the phenomenon was elusive. We now know that obtaining evidence of subliminal perception depends on whether subjective or objective criteria set the threshold. When the criteria are subjective, which is to say by introspective reports from each subject, priming effects are evident. When criteria are objectively set by requiring a forced choice as to whether a subject saw any visual information, no priming effects are seen. Among other things, these studies point out the gray area between conscious and unconscious. Thresholds clearly vary with the criteria.

Pinker presented an enticing analysis on how evolutionary pressures gave rise to access-consciousness. The general insight has to do with the fact that information has costs and benefits. He argued that at least three dimensions must be considered: cost of space, cost of time, and cost of resources. Regarding space, while the human cortex has exploded in size, it is not contributing simply because of its size. The brain is built by accumulating special processors that solve problems only when an answer must be calculated. As Pinker pointed out, a simple chess game has between 30 and 35 moves for each turn; and each game has about 40 moves, which yields 10^{120} different moves. (Only 10^{70} particles are in the visible universe.) In short, the brain must be built so specialized processes do calculations as needed. As for the cost of time, information processing takes time, and if all decisions were the products of rational conscious consideration, there would not be enough time in one's life to carry out what we do freely and easily in an hour. And finally, thinking is expensive. It takes energy in the form of oxygen and glucose, and the evolutionary pressure would reluctantly add to that resource.

The point is that any complex organism that is an information processor working in real time must have, as Pinker said, restrictions on the information it accesses. Only information relevant to the problem at hand should be allowed, which seems to be how the brain is organized.

Access-consciousness has four obvious features that Pinker recounted. First is the rich field of sensation we all live in. Second is the capacity to move information into and out of our awareness, into and out of short-term memory but turning our attentional spotlight on it. Third, such information always comes with salience, some kind of emotional coloring. Finally is the "I" that calls the shots on what to do with the information as it comes into the field of awareness.

Jackendoff (1987) argued that for perception, access is limited to the intermediate stages of information processing. We do not ponder the elements that go into a percept, only the output. Consider the patient described in Chapter 5 who could not see objects but could see faces, indicating he was a face processor. When this patient was shown a picture that deployed pieces of fruit arranged in such a way as to make them look like a face, the patient immediately said he saw the face but was totally unable to state that the eyes were tomatoes and the nose a banana. He only had access to output of the module.

Concerning attention and its role in access, the work of Anne Treisman (1991) at Princeton University reveals that unconscious parallel processing can only go so far.

Treisman proposed a candidate for the border between conscious and unconscious processes. In her famous pop-out experiments, a subject picks a prespecified object from a field of others. The notion is that each point in the visual field is processed for color, shape, and motion, outside of conscious awareness. The attention system then picks up elements and puts them together with other elements to make the desired percept. Treisman showed, for example, that when we are attending to a point in space and processing the color and form of that location, elements at unattended points seem to be floating. We can tell the color and shape, but make mistakes about what color goes with what shape. The illusory conjunctions of stimulus features are prime facie evidence for how the attentional system combines elements into whole percepts.

The other senses of access outlined by Pinker, the notion of salience and executive controller, have been touched on elsewhere. His notion of self-knowledge and its role in conscious experience and our own personal narrative are addressed at the end of the chapter.

The cognitive neuroscience approach also has revealed some evidence on sentience. When Block originally drew distinctions between sentience and access, he suggested that the phenomenon of blindsight provided a possible paradigm. *Blindsight,* a term coined by Larry Weiskrantz at Oxford University (1986), refers to the phenomenon that patients suffering a lesion in their visual cortex can respond to visual stimuli presented in the blind part of their visual field (Figure 14.4). Most interestingly, these activities happen outside the realm of consciousness. Patients will deny that they can do a task,

Figure 14.4 Weiskrantz and colleagues reported the first case of blindsight in a patient with a lesion in the visual cortex. The hatched areas indicate preserved areas of vision for the left and right eyes for patient D.B. Adapted from Weiskrantz et al. (1974).

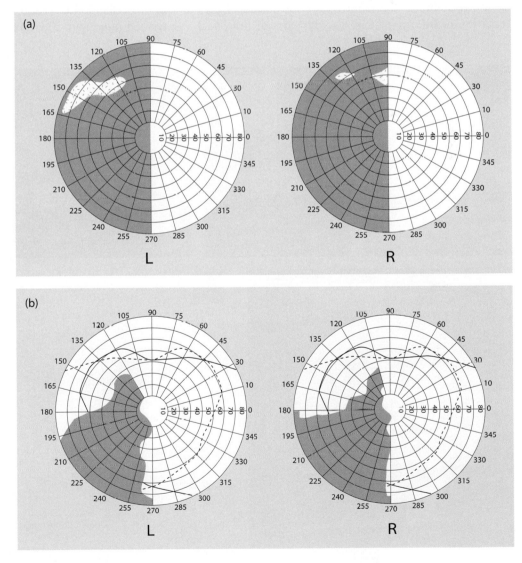

yet their performance is clearly above that of chance. Such patients have access to information but do not experience it.

Weiskrantz believed that subcortical and parallel pathways and centers could now be studied in the human brain; a vast primate literature had developed on the subject. Monkeys with occipital lesions not only can localize objects in space, but also make color, luminance, orientation, and pattern discriminations.

In the light of reports of blindsight and of the cortical lesion work, it hardly seemed surprising that subjects could use visually presented information not accessible to consciousness. Subcortical networks with interhemispheric connections provided a plausible anatomy on which the behavioral results could rest. It would be difficult to argue against the concept that perceptual decisions or cognitive activities routinely result from processes outside of conscious awareness.

A Purkinje eye tracker was recently augmented with an image stabilizer that allowed for the sustained presentation of information in discrete parts of the visual field (Figure 14.5). In one study, C.L.T., a robust 55-year-old outdoorsman, suffered a right occipital stroke 6 years prior to his examination. Magnetic resonance imaging (MRI) reconstructions revealed a lesion that damaged the calcarine cortex. But MRI also demonstrated some spared tissue in the region of the calcarine fissure and also an intact colliculus.

Standard perimetry indicated that C.L.T. had a left homonymous hemianopia with lower-quadrant macular sparing. Yet the eye tracker found small regions of residual vision (Figure 14.6). C.L.T.'s scotoma was carefully explored by using high-contrast, retinally stabilized stimuli and an interval, two-alternative, forced-choice procedure. The two-alternative procedure requires that a subject respond as to whether or not a stimulus had appeared in one of two intervals. Investigators found an isolated island of vision about 1 degree in diameter in the upper left quadrant of C.L.T.'s left visual field. Because C.L.T. reported no awareness of stimuli presented to this island, his vision at this location is properly termed *blindsight*. The retinal regions surrounding this

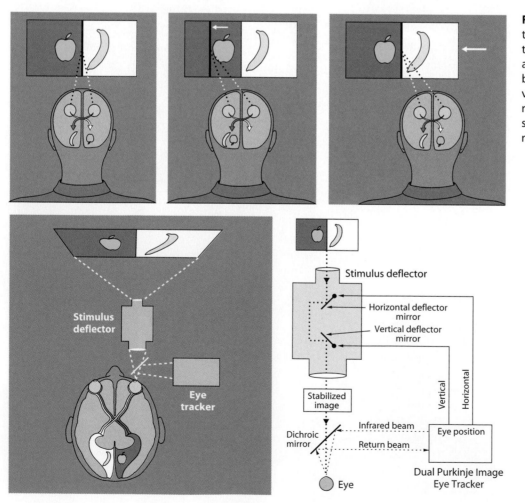

Figure 14.5 Schematic of the Purkinje image eye tracker that compensates for a subject's eye movements by moving the image in the visual field in the same direction as the eyes, and thus stabilizing the image on the retina.

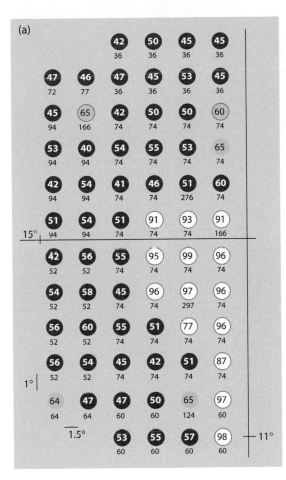

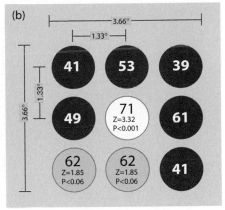

Figure 14.6 **(a)** Results of stabilized image perimetry in C.L.T.'s left visual hemifield. The large numbers in the circles represent the percentages for correct detection. The total number of trials to each location are indicated under the circles. The white circles indicate unimpaired detection, the green circles with black borders indicate impaired detection that was still above the level of chance with Bonferroni's correction, and the green circles without borders show detection that was better than chance without Bonferroni's correction. **(b)** Further detail of the retinal area containing C.L.T.'s island of preserved visual function. The large numbers in circles represent percentages for detection out of sixty-six trials. At the center position, detection was above the level of chance regardless of Bonferroni's correction for nine tests. The green areas indicate elevated but statistically insignificant detection rates.

island were totally blind. Since this residual vision is restricted to a small retinal region, the likely explanation is a corresponding remnant of spared striate cortex rather than a more general secondary visual system.

Before we can assert that blindsight is due to subcortical or extrastriate structures, we first must be extremely careful to rule out the possibility of spared striate cortex. With careful perimetric mapping, we can discover regions of vision within a scotoma that would certainly go undetected with conventional perimetry.

Blindsight demonstrates vision outside the realm of conscious awareness. This point has been taken as support for the view that perception happens in the absence of sensation, as sensations are presumed to be our experiences of impinging stimuli. Because the primary visual cortex processes sensory inputs, advocates of this view have found it useful to attribute blindsight to alternative visual processing pathways.

It is commonplace to design demanding perceptual tasks on which nonneurological subjects routinely report low confidence values for tasks they perform at a level above chance. Yet it is unnecessary to propose sec-

ondary visual systems to account for such data, since the primary visual system is intact and fully functional. For example, patients with unilateral neglect as a result of brain damage, usually to the right hemisphere, are unable to name stimuli entering their left visual field. The conscious brain cannot access this information. But when asked to judge whether two lateralized visual stimuli, one in each visual field, are the same or different (Figure 14.7), these same patients can do so. When they are questioned on the nature of the stimuli after a trial, they easily name the stimulus in the right visual field but deny having seen the stimulus in the neglected left field. In short, patients with parietal lobe damage but spared visual cortex can make perceptual judgments outside of conscious awareness. Their failure to consciously access information for comparing the stimuli should not be attributed to processing within a secondary visual system because their geniculo-striate pathway is still intact.

A variety of reports extended these initial observations that information presented in the extinguished visual field can be used for decision making. A central question is how sophisticated the processing can be

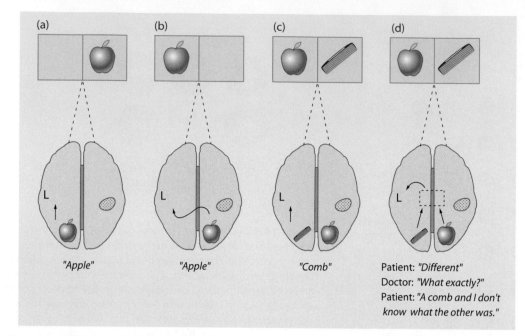

Figure 14.7 The same-different paradigm presented to patients with neglect. **(a)** The patient is presented an image to one hemifield. **(b)** The patient is subsequently presented an image to the other hemifield and asked to judge if the images are the same or different, a task that they are able to perform. **(c)** When the images are presented simultaneously to both hemifields, the patient with unilateral neglect is able to determine whether the images are the same or different but is unable to verbalize what image was seen in the extinguished hemifield that enabled them to make their correct comparison and decision **(d)**.

outside of conscious awareness. Recent work showed that quite complex information can be processed (Figure 14.8). In one study, a picture of a fruit or animal was quickly presented to the right visual field. Subsequently, a picture of the same item or of an item in the same category was presented to the left visual field. In another condition of the experiment, the pictures presented in each field had nothing to do with each other. All patients in the study denied a stimulus had been presented in the left visual field. But when the two pictures were related,

patients responded faster than they did when the pictures were different. The reaction time to the unrelated pictures did not increase. In short, high-level information was being exchanged between processing systems outside the realm of conscious awareness.

The vast staging for our mental activities happens largely without our monitoring. This can be identified in many experimental venues. The study of blindsight and neglect provides important insights. First, it underlines a general feature of human cognition: Many perceptual

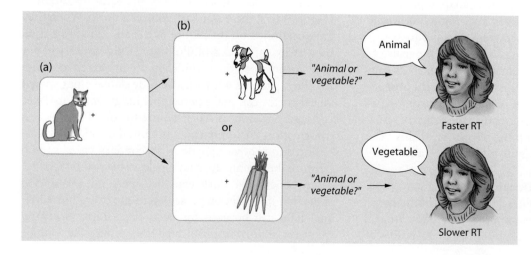

Figure 14.8 **(a)** A picture of an item such as a cat was flashed to the left visual field. **(b)** A picture of the same item or a related item such as a dog was presented to the right visual field and the subject was to discriminate the category to which the second item belonged. If the items were related by category, the time needed for the categorization of the second word was facilitated.

and cognitive activities can and do go on outside of the realm of conscious awareness. We can access information that we are not sentient about. Further, this feature need not depend on subcortical or secondary processing systems; it is more than likely that unconscious processes related to cognitive, perceptual, and sensory-motor activities happen at the level of the cortex.

NEURONS, NEURONAL GROUPS, AND CONSCIOUS EXPERIENCE

Neuroscientists interested in higher cognitive functions have been extraordinarily innovative in analyzing how the nervous system enables perceptual activities. Recording from single neurons in the visual system, they not only have tracked the flow of visual information and how it becomes encoded and decoded during a perceptual activity, but also have directly manipulated the information and influenced an animal's decision processes. One of the leaders in this approach to understanding the mind is William Newsome at Stanford University. He recorded information, stimulated small neuronal groups, and showed how this influences the decision an animal makes.

Newsome studied how neural events in area MT of the monkey cortex, which is quite involved in motion detection, correlate with the actual perceptual event. One of his first findings was striking. The animal's psychophysical performance capacity to make a motion discrimination was predictable by the neuronal response pattern of a single neuron (Figure 14.9). In other words, a single neuron in area MT was as sensitive to changes in the visual display as was the monkey!

This finding stirred the research community because it raised a fundamental question about how the brain does its job. Newsome's observation challenged the common view that the signal averaging that surely goes on in the nervous system eliminated the noise carried by individual neurons. Thus, the capacity of pooled neurons making a decision should be superior to the sensitivity of single neurons. And yet Newsome did not side with those who believe that a single neuron is the source for any one behavioral act. Since it is well known that killing a single neuron, or even hundreds of them, will not impair an animal's ability to perform a task, a single neuron's behavior is clearly redundant. Researchers are now building models of how many neurons would be needed to mimic an animal's performance.

An even more tantalizing finding of particular interest to the study of conscious experience is that careful microstimulation of these same neurons, which altered their response rates, can tilt the animal toward making the right decision on a perceptual task. The maximum effects are seen during the interval the animal is thinking

Figure 14.9 **(a)** The experimental design for Newsome and Pare (1988). The stimuli consisted of random patterns of dots that were briefly illuminated and then replaced by a dot at another location on the screen. If the successive replacement dots are slightly offset from the previously illuminated dot in time and location (far right), then the dots appear to move coherently, much like consecutive frames in a movie result in apparent motion. If the replacement dots are repositioned randomly on the screen (far left), then no motion is seen. By adjusting the number of dots carrying this motion signal, and thus manipulating how much motion is apparent in the stimulus, the threshold for motion direction discrimination in humans, monkeys, or single cells in the monkeys' brains can be determined experimentally. **(b)** The stimuli were presented, with varying levels of coherent motion, to rhesus monkeys trained in a motion-direction discrimination task. The monkey's decision regarding the direction of apparent motion, and the responses of single MT cells (which are selective for direction of motion) were recorded and compared to the stimulus coherence on each trial. Remarkably, on average, individual cells in MT were as sensitive as the entire monkey. Further, in subsequent work the firing rate of single cells actually predicted (albeit weakly) the choice of the monkey on a trial-by-trial basis. Adapted from Newsome and Pare (1988).

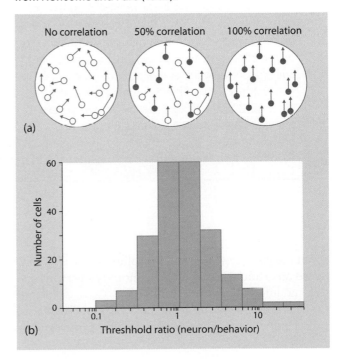

An Interview with David Premack, Ph.D.
Professor Premack, who now lives in Paris, is noted for his work in learning and motivation, and chimpanzee language and social development.

Authors: Over the years you have devised clever tests to examine complex issues in the area of motivation and language. It is that cleverness that has unlocked truths about the nature of organisms. When it comes to the issue of consciousness, can clever experimental questions be asked? Take an aspect of conscious experience, morality. Can such abstract issues be studied in the laboratory?

DP: Abstract, morality, consciousness—too many issues. Let's push consciousness aside for the moment, not for entirely inconsequential reasons. Some factors important for morality may owe little to consciousness. Further, if the word *consciousness* leads you to contemplate subjective states—of a kind you might grant apes but would deny earthworms—I'm not sure we're in experimental territory; I don't know how to do tests on subjective states. But abstract and morality shouldn't scare off experimentalists.

Authors: Are you saying the experimentalist can begin to pursue the content of conscious experience, like moral reasoning, and look to its roots and mechanisms? As an example of the content of conscious experience, that seems both rich but horridly complex. How do you break the problem down?

DP: Developmental psychology argues that infants divide the world into two basic domains, physical objects on the one hand and intentional or psychological objects on the other. Twenty years of work by Spelke, Carey, Leslie, Baillergeon, Gelman, and a host of other gifted people suggests that infants have definite expectations concerning physical objects. For example, they don't expect them to move unless caused to move by the action of another object. And they expect them to move continuously in space and time, not to appear at one location, disappear, and then reappear at another location. And not to come apart. And if two of them touch, not to stick together like drops of water. How do you know that that's what they expect? Looking-time experiments. When infants are shown objects that deviate from these properties—objects that move discontinuously or that come apart, etc.—they show increased looking time. But let's put physical objects aside, and move to the infants' other module, the one for psychological or intentional objects. That's what my wife Ann and I have been looking at.

Authors: What have you found?

DP: We've mainly been working on a model, though we've made a few tests of it. The model assumes that infants deal with intentionality in terms of two basic concepts: goal directedness and value, positive or negative. Infants younger than about 2 years of age don't appear to have a theory of mind. They don't attribute mental states perceive, want, belief. They understand psychological objects in a far simpler way. But lets make it official Here are the four basic assumptions of the model.

1. A physical object moves only when caused to move by another object; however, a psychological object starts and stops its own motion; it appears to be self-propelled.
2. Psychological objects display goal-directed action.
3. An infant who perceives an object that is both self-propelled and goal directed interprets the object as intentional and assigns unique properties to it.
4. Infants attribute value (either positive or negative) to the appropriate interaction between intentional objects.

---

about the task. Newsome and his colleagues, in effect, inserted an artificial signal into the monkey's nervous system and influenced how it thinks.

This discovery immediately raises the issue of whether one should consider the site of the microstimu-lation as the place where the decision is made. Researchers are not convinced that this is the way to think about the problem. Instead, they believe they have tapped into part of a neural loop involved with this particular perceptual discrimination. They argue that stim-

Incidentally, it's the motion of objects—and not their properties—that activates the modules. Motion is the key to activating the infants' modules in both the physical and psychological domains. That's our argument.

Authors: What do you mean by goal? What does an infant think a goal is?

DP: According to the model, they use four properties: trajectory, target, greater than default values, and satisfaction—but lets skip the middle two. Trajectory is the direction in which an object moves. Because a self-propelled object can move in many directions, its consistent movement in only one direction is significant. Consider the parallel between the trajectory of an object and that of both gazing and pointing. Infants follow the mother's gaze; rather than look at her they look where she is looking. They react in the same manner to pointing; rather than look at the end of the finger (as many species do), they look where the finger is pointing. We argue that infants react in the same manner to the trajectories of gazing, pointing, or object movement, i.e., by anticipating the target, whether it is a target being looked at, pointed to, or moved toward. Two simple experiments would bear that out. Change the location of the target toward which the object has been heading; if the object doesn't change its trajectory to accommodate this change, the infant should be surprised—show increased looking time. Or show the infant a trajectory that, in effect, has no target; that too should surprise the infant. When shown a trajectory—be it that of a finger, eye, or self-propelled object—infants expect a target—that's the heart of the matter. Satisfaction refers to those conditions that bring goal-directed action to an end. The infant who understands goal as a satisfiable state expects certain conditions to terminate goal-directed action, and would be surprised if, for example, an object that succeeded in escaping reinstated its confinement.

Authors: Aside from movement and goals, what's the main difference infants see between physical and intentional objects?

DP: In a word, value positive or negative. Infants not only expect intentional objects to interact, they assign value positive or negative to the interaction. They do not assign value positive or negative to interactions between intentional and physical objects. The model claims that the infant uses two criteria in distinguishing between positive and negative value. The simpler criterion is based on intensity. The hard action of hitting is coded negative; the soft action of caressing positive. The second criterion is the functional equivalent of helping and hindering. When one object is engaged in goal-directed action—for example, seeking to escape confinement—a second object can be seen as helping or hindering the first object achieve its goal. Helping is coded positive, hindering negative.

Authors: How do you prove those claims?

DP: By using Ann's animations in a standard habituation-dishabituation design. For example, habituate infants on each of the four cases—caress, hit, help, hinder—then transfer all of them to the same, say, negative condition—a new case of hit. Infants shifted from negative to negative should show little dishabituation, whereas those shifted from positive to negative should show far more; that's what the model predicts and that's what we found.

Authors: What has all this to do with morality and consciousness? You remember that's what we were going to talk about—but we're out of time.

DP: We argue that the infants' positive and negative, the value positive or negative that it automatically assigns to the interactions between intentional objects, are the moral primitives, the concepts that cultures transform into good and bad. A good thing we've run out of time, for it's exceedingly hard to give even an approximate account of the cultural transformation of biological primitives—almost as hard as explaining the brain!

ulation at different sites in the loop creates different subjective experiences. For example, let us say that the stimulus was moving upward and the response was as if the stimulus was moving downward. If this was your brain, you might think you saw downward motion if the stimulation occurred early in the loop. But if the stimulation occurred late in the loop and merely found you choosing the downward response instead of the upward one, your sensation would be quite different. Why, you might ask yourself, did I do that?

An Interview with William T. Newsome, Ph.D.   Dr. Newsome is a professor of Neuroscience at Stanford University. His neurophysiological studies on the monkey visual system have led to new insights on how the brain processes information.

Authors: What are the limitations of the single-neuron analysis? One might think assessing the behavior of one neuron at a time would severely limit the kind of analysis you could do.

WTN: The most obvious limitation of the single-unit approach is that we cannot analyze effectively neural representations that involve patterns of activity existing simultaneously at multiple locations in the brain. This limitation is, of course, rather severe since even simple sensory stimuli or motor acts evoke complex patterns of neural activity. A second limitation, which receives somewhat less attention, is that the single-unit approach provides little information about the relative timing of neural events at different locations in the brain. Simultaneous measurement of the onset and offset of neural activity in different brain structures can provide critical information about cause-and-effect relationships between those structures as cognitive operations unfold. A final limitation is that single-unit recording in the central nervous system virtually precludes precise analysis of input-output transfer functions. For any given neuron, we have only the most general notion of what its inputs might be, such notions being based largely on population studies of anatomical connections and physiological properties. The strongest statements that single-unit studies permit concerning transfer functions are usually of the following form: This type of response selectivity has not been observed at prior levels of the pathway, and is probably synthesized from simpler inputs for [some specific computational or behavioral purpose].

Having criticized the single-unit approach, let me hasten to add that we have not yet begun to exhaust its usefulness. Single-unit analyses are still employed profitably in conjunction with anatomical techniques to identify basic processing modules in different brain structures—what Hubel and Wiesel termed *functional architecture.* I suspect that this enterprise will continue to be productive, especially if molecular techniques can provide increasingly precise anatomical markers for neural circuits. Even more exciting to me is the recent trend toward applying the single-unit approach in behaving animals to identify neural correlates of simple cognitive operations. A growing number of laboratories are employing clever behavioral paradigms (frequently adapted from the experimental traditions of psychophysics and behavioral psychology) to investigate neural substrates of perception, attention, learning, memory, and motor planning, to name but a few. A wealth of new insight is emerging from these efforts, and I believe we have only scratched the surface of what can be learned with this approach.

THE EMERGENCE OF THE BRAIN INTERPRETER IN THE HUMAN SPECIES

Even with the exciting advances in systems neuroscience and with the insight that many of our cognitive capacities, so heavily a part of our conscious experience, appear to be built-in domain-specific operations, we think that we are a unified conscious agent with a past, a present, and a future. The domain-specific or modular systems are fully capable of producing behaviors, mood changes, and cognitive activity. With all of this apparent independent activity, what allows for the sense of conscious unity we possess?

A private narrative appears to take place inside us all the time, and it partly consists of the effort to tie together into a coherent whole the diverse activities of thousands of specialized systems we have inherited to handle challenges. The great American writer John Updike mused on the subject in his 1989 book *Self Consciousness:*

"Consciousness is a disease," Unamuno says. Religion would relieve the symptoms. Religion construed broadly, not only in the form of the world's barbaric and even atrocious religious orthodoxies but in the form of any private system, be it adoration of Elvis Presley or hatred of nuclear weapons, be it fetishism of politics or popular culture, that submerges in a transcendent concern the grimly finite facts of our individual human case. How remarkably fertile the religious imagination is, how fervid the appetite for significance; it sets gods to growing on every bush and rock. Astrology, UFOs, resurrections, mental metal-bending, visions in space, and voodoo flourish in the weekly tabloids we buy at the cash register along with our groceries. Falling in love—its mythologization of the beloved and everything that touches her or him is an invented religion, and religious also is our persistence, against all the powerful post-Copernican, post-Darwinian evidence that we are insignificant accidents within a vast uncaused churning, in feeling that our life is a story, with a pattern and a moral and an inevitability—that as Emerson said, "a thread runs through all things: all worlds are strung on it, as beads: and men, and events, and life come to us, only because of that thread." That our subjectivity, in other words, dominates, through secret channels, outer reality, and the universe has a personal structure.

Indeed. And what is it in our brains that provides for that thread? What is the system that takes the vast output of our thousands upon thousands of specialized systems and ties them into our subjectivity through secret channels to render a personal story for each of us? It turns out that we humans have a specialized system to carry out this interpretive synthesis, and it is located in the brain's left hemisphere. The interpreter is a system that seeks explanations for internal and external events in order to produce appropriate behaviors in response. We know it to be only in the left hemisphere, and it appears to be tied to our capacity to see how contiguous events relate to one another. The interpreter, a built-in specialization in its own right, operates on other adaptations built into our brains. The adaptations are most likely cortically based, but they work largely outside of conscious awareness, as do the vast majority of our mental activities. It is the consequences of their activity that are interpreted and that provide the thread for our personal story.

The interpreter was discovered by using a simultaneous concept test (Figure 14.10). A split-brain patient was shown two pictures, one exclusively to the left hemisphere and one exclusively to the right, and was asked to choose from an array of pictures placed in full view in front of him the ones associated with the pictures lateralized to the left and right sides of the brain. In one example of this test, a picture of a chicken claw was flashed to the left hemisphere and a picture of a snow scene to

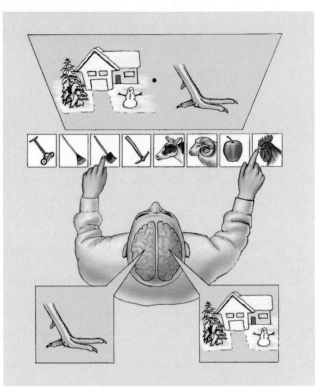

Figure 14.10 Method for presenting different cognitive tasks simultaneously to each hemisphere. In the split-brain patient, the right hemisphere processes the information in the left visual field, in this case the snow scene, and the left hemisphere processes the information in the right visual field, the chicken claw. Using each hemisphere, the patient is asked to associate the presented image with one of several choices. The patient verbalizes through the language-dominated left hemisphere that he sees a chicken claw, and thus creates reasons based on this knowledge as to why he picked the item that related to the image presented to the right hemisphere.

the right hemisphere. Of the array of pictures placed in front of the subject, the obviously correct association is a chicken for the chicken claw and a shovel for the snow scene. Split-brain subject P.S. responded by choosing the shovel with the left hand and the chicken with the right. When asked why he chose these items, he (his left hemisphere) replied, "Oh, that's simple. The chicken claw goes with the chicken, and you need a shovel to clean out the chicken shed." Here the left side of the brain, observing the left hand's response, interprets that response into a context consistent with its sphere of knowledge—one that does not include information about the left-hemifield snow scene.

Another example of this phenomenon of the left hemisphere interpreting actions produced by the disconnected right one involves lateralizing a written command, such as laugh, to the right hemisphere by

An Interview with Simon Baron-Cohen, Ph.D.
Professor Baron-Cohen has led the way in describing how brain pathologies disrupt the capacity to have a theory of mind.

Authors: David Premack introduced the concept of theory of mind when he asked the question about whether or not the chimp possessed such a thing. You have taken this same issue into the clinical setting by examining autistic children. You have also studied the emergence of such a module in children. Could you tell us a little about this fascinating work?

SB-C: I had just spent a fascinating year as a teacher of children with autism, in a small unit north of London, and had concluded that they were un-self-conscious. They did as they pleased, not in an antisocial way, but simply oblivious of how they might appear to others. They seemed totally unconcerned by what others might be thinking (about them, or about anything else, for that matter). The idea occurred to me that as well as being unaware of other people's thoughts, they might also be unaware of their own thoughts or mental lives.

Moving to the Cognitive Development Unit in London after that year, I began my Ph.D. on this topic. With Alan Leslie and Uta Frith, we sharpened the question to, Does the autistic child have a theory of mind? The wording of this question (the title of our first paper too) was intended to exactly mirror the wording from Premack and Woodruff (1978), about the chimpanzee. Even down to the scare quotes around the phrase *theory of mind*. This was because we realized the importance of situating the autism research in an evolutionary context. A theory of mind was so central to human social behavior, that in all likelihood it had evolved to support social be-havior—and its potential impairment in autism might be just the strand of neurological evidence to allow this evolutionary question to become tractable.

But my interest in this topic was never solely on this basic science. It was also to try to see how a new understanding of autism might lead to new ways of intervening. And the basic and applied sides to my research continue to intertwine.

Authors: But if an autistic child is the product of pathology, why does it make sense to place it in evolutionary framework?

SB-C: Autism as a form of neuropathology seems to be highly specific: an impairment in the brain system's underlying theory of mind. The value of considering this in an evolutionary framework is that since theory of mind seems to be a universal human ability—as pervasive as language, for example—autism may provide a strong clue about where in the brain our theory of mind is located, or which brain systems we employ during this cognitive activity. This is of interest in terms of tracing the origins of such brain systems, both phylogenetically and ontogenetically.

If one doubts whether theory of mind is indeed universal, consider Fodor's thought experiment: Try imagining a culture in which people did not use belief-desire reasoning. It seems impossible. And so far, the anthropological evidence suggests no such human cultures exist.

Authors: Well, what has the neuroscientific litera-

---

tachistoscopically presenting it to the left visual field (Figure 14.11). After the stimulus is presented, the patient laughs and, when asked why says, "You guys come up and test us every month. What a way to make a living!" In still another example, if the command "Walk" is flashed to the right hemisphere, the patient typically stands up from the chair and begins to take leave from the testing van. When asked where she is going, she (the left side of the brain) says, "I'm going into the house to get a Coke." However this type of test is manipulated, it always yields the same result.

There are many ways to influence the left-hemisphere interpreter. As we just mentioned, we wanted to know whether the emotional response to stimuli presented to one half of the brain would affect the other half. In this study, we presented, by lateralized stimulus procedures, film vignettes that included either violent or calm sequences. The emotional valence of the stimulus clearly crossed over from the right to the left hemisphere. The left hemisphere remained unaware of the content that produced the emotional change, but it interpreted and experienced the emotion.

The brain's modular organization has now been well established. The functioning modules do have some kind of physical instantiation, but the brain sciences cannot yet specify the nature of the neural networks.

ture taught us about the location of theory of mind (TOM) module? Couldn't it be that an adaptive specialization like the TOM module was represented by a highly distributed system which had specific function?

SB-C: At the moment it's too early to say much about the neuroscientific literature on theory of mind, because there are too few studies. One SPECT [single-photon emission computed tomography] study implicates right orbitofrontal cortex, another PET [positron emission tomography] study (using a different task) implicates left medial frontal cortex, and our model assumes theory of mind is highly likely to be distributed in that it makes use of emotion processing (amygdala?) and aspects of face processing (superior temporal sulcus?). But this is a new model that needs a lot more empirical investigation. Evidence from acquired brain damage might also help elucidate its brain basis, though so far nothing has been published concerning such cases.

Authors: Doesn't that suggest the TOM module could come perilously close to being the whole brain? Put differently, what are the studies that suggest it is an added chip into the human brain as opposed to an emergent property of a big brain?

SB-C: TOM could be a high-level emergent property of the whole brain—this is not yet ruled out in any definitive way. But then a new puzzle would need solving: Why are children with autism able to solve some tasks which appear to involve high-level reasoning and even forms of meta-representation (such as understanding nonmentalistic forms of representation), and yet they have such basic deficits in understanding mental representation? For example, they can understand that photos or drawings or maps or models can all represent the world (or misrepresent the world), and yet they fail to understand beliefs as representations (and misrepresentations) of the world. And in their reasoning, they can perform well on analogies and syllogisms, and yet fail on tests of psychological reasoning. Such neuropsychological dislocation strongly suggests TOM is not just an emergent property of the whole brain, but rather is subserved by highly specific neural systems which are open to selective deficit.

Authors: Finally, is there any evidence for a TOM module in nonhuman primates?

SB-C: That's an interesting question. Daniel Povinelli has carried out the most work on nonhuman primates in relation to TOM, and so far concludes that they have only rudimentary aspects of TOM, if at all. For example, a range of animals show sensitivity to when they are being looked at, though few seem to show any awareness of the importance of perception in communication, or as a source of knowledge. As for evidence of awareness of epistemic states (beliefs), there are no persuasive grounds yet for concluding that this is within nonhuman primate ability. There is some evidence (from Premack) that chimpanzees might be sensitive to intentions (goal states), though. So the answer to the question could be summarized as follows: Some nonhuman animals may be aware of the volitional and perceptual mental states; but none appear aware of the informational or epistemic ones.

I would end by pointing out that some people think that if other animals had a TOM, we should change our moral stance towards them: Accord them human rights. This is an interesting example of the relation between morality and science. Personally I wouldn't eat a primate whether it had a TOM or not.

What is clear is that they operate mainly outside the realm of awareness and announce their computational products to executive systems that result in behavior or cognitive states. Catching up with all of this parallel and constant activity appears to be the responsibility of the left hemisphere's interpreter module. The interpreter is a system of primary importance to the human brain: It allows for the formation of beliefs that in turn are mental constructs which free us from simply responding to stimulus-response aspects of everyday life. In many ways it is the system that provides the story line or narrative of our lives.

The problem of consciousness, like the problems of language, sexual selection, and visual motion, should always be considered from an evolutionary perspective. Then certain truths emerge that the core of human consciousness is a feeling—a felt sense about specialized capacities.

Looking at the past decades of split-brain research, we find one unalterable fact. Disconnecting the two cerebral hemispheres, an event that finds one half of the cortex no longer interacting in a direct way with the other half, does not typically disrupt the cognitive-verbal intelligence of these patients. The left dominant hemisphere remains the major force in our conscious experience and that force is sustained, it would appear, not by

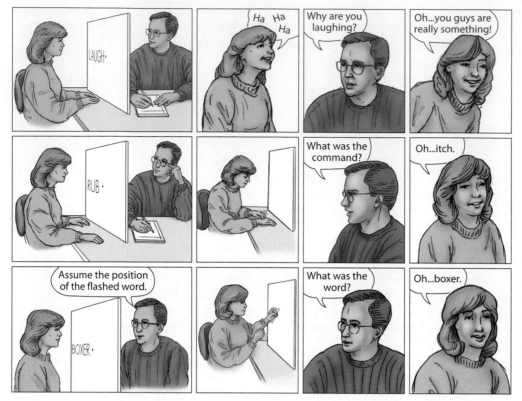

Figure 14.11 When the nonverbal right hemisphere is given a command, the person carries it out without specific knowledge as to why she is doing so. After performing the activity, the person is quickly able to generate a reason for this activity.

the whole cortex but by specialized circuits within the left hemisphere. In short, the inordinately large human brain does not render its unique contributions by simply being a bigger brain.

With the realization that the accumulation of specialized circuits accounts for the unique human experience, consciousness can be viewed from two perspectives, one that comes from realizing that the brain is a constellation of specialized circuits and the other from understanding that beyond early childhood our sense of being conscious never changes. When these views are taken together, it becomes evident that what we mean by consciousness is how we feel about our specialized capacities. We have feelings about objects we see, hear, and feel. We have feelings about our capacity to think, to use language, to apprehend faces. Hence, consciousness is not another system. It reflects the affective component of specialized systems that have evolved to enable human cognitive processes. With an inferential system in place, we have a system empowering all sorts of mental activity. And again, our consciousness of those mental activities is related to our capacity to assign feelings to them, which is what distinguishes us from the electronic artifacts surrounding us.

Given our capacity for consciousness and our biological similarity to other primates, it is not surprising that the question of nonhuman primate consciousness has been debated for years. If our conscious state has evolved as a product of our brain's biology, is it possible that our closest relatives might also possess this mental attribute or a developing state of our ability? The term *theory of mind* was coined by David Premack and refers to the ability to represent and infer unobservable mental states such as desires, intentions, and beliefs from the self and others.

If theory of mind is a biologically based human cognition, it follows that there should be corresponding neural components. From this reasoning, perhaps the best way to tackle the question of nonhuman primate consciousness would be to compare different species' brains to those of humans. Comparing the species on a neurological basis has proved to be difficult, however, except for the fact that the human prefrontal cortex is much larger in area than that of other primates. Another approach to interspecies comparative biology has been taken by comparative psychologists who study nonhuman primate theory of mind. Instead of comparing pure biological elements, their strategy is to focus on the behavioral manifestation of the brain. This approach parallels that of developmental psychologists who study the development of the theory of mind in children.

Two studies that explore a primate theory of mind have drawn from the idea that children develop abilities which outwardly indicate conscious awareness of themselves and their environment. For example, once children understand the concept of a false belief or the

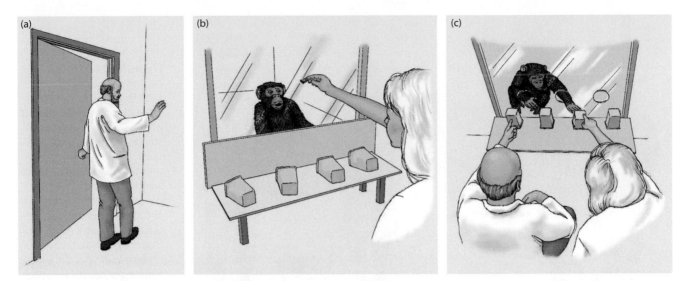

Figure 14.12 **(a)** One experimenter leaves the room (the guesser). **(b)** One experimenter hides food under one cup (the knower). **(c)** Both experimenters then point to different cups. Chimpanzees initially randomly choose which cup the food is under. In time, their performance improves, suggesting that they solve the task by making associations with the roles of the experimenters as opposed to inferring the seeing and knowing connection. By comparison, 4-year-olds perform correctly from the onset, whereas 3-year-olds respond randomly.

mind's ability to incorrectly represent the world, they realize that beliefs are mental representations and hence can distinguish between the mind and the world. This comprehension often happens between the ages of 3 and 5 years.

This awareness has been tested in nonhuman primates and stems from the assumption that along with comprehending the difference between mind and world comes an understanding of the sources of knowledge and the representation of beliefs by others. Children learn that direct contact with a situation can give an individual a privileged state of knowledge such as when a child sees a person looking into a box. A 4-year-old child can grasp that this person now knows what the box contains, whereas a younger child may not.

Povinelli and colleagues (1994) studied this perception relationship, or the connection between seeing and knowing, in chimpanzees (Figure 14.12). Another test of chimpanzees' conscious abilities concerns the emergence of conceptual knowledge of the self and others, which in children occurs at 18 to 24 months. Baldwin and her colleagues studied infants' understanding of the notion that when another person looks or points at an object or event, that person becomes connected to it subjectively through the mental state of attention.

That chimpanzees are capable of self-recognition, as seen when a mirror is present, and can follow a person's gaze might suggest that they have an understanding, as children do, of how the eyes and internal states of attention are connected (Figure 14.13). Drawing

Figure 14.13 **(a, b)** When initially presented with a mirror, chimpanzees react to it as if they are confronting another animal. After 5 to 30 minutes, however, chimpanzees will engage in self-exploratory behaviors, indicating that they know they are indeed viewing themselves. **(c)** Chimpanzees are also able to follow the gaze of an experimenter, which indicates that they might know that eyes direct attention.

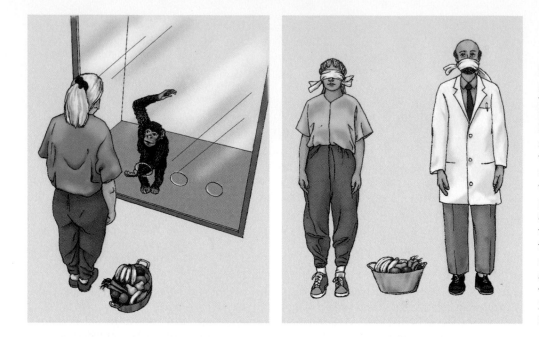

Figure 14.14 **(a)** Chimpanzees can learn to request food from an experimenter by reaching through the left hole when an experimenter stands on the left, and vice versa. **(b)** When two experimenters are present, one wearing a blindfold, chimpanzees respond randomly as to which hole to gesture through for food, suggesting that they do not have a firm understanding of the eyes as a means of communicating visual attention, as children 2½ years old indicate in similar tests.

from chimpanzees' awareness of eyes, Povinelli studied chimpanzees understanding of the eyes as portals through which the mental state of attention emanates (Figure 14.14).

Nonhuman primates demonstrate in countless ways their intelligence and ability to crudely communicate with humans; hence, it is not surprising that most people would like to believe that these relatives of ours also possess some form of consciousness like ours. But the two aforementioned studies indicate that contrary to popular hope, our closest relatives do not demonstrate conscious abilities as do growing children—at least in the paradigms set up to test assumptions about the expression of conscious awareness that emerges in children.

LEFT- AND RIGHT-HEMISPHERE CONSCIOUSNESS

When consciousness is viewed as a feeling about specialized abilities, one would expect the quality of consciousness emanating from each hemisphere to differ radically. While left-hemisphere consciousness would reflect what we mean by normal conscious experience, right-hemisphere consciousness would vary as a function of the specialized circuits that half brains possess. Mind left, with its complex cognitive machinery, can distinguish between sorrow and pity and appreciates the feelings associated with each state. The right hemisphere does not have the cognitive apparatus for such distinctions and consequently has a narrower state of awareness. Consider the following examples of reduced capacity in the right hemisphere and the implications this has for consciousness.

Split-brain patients without right-hemisphere language have a limited capacity for responding to patterned stimuli that ranges from none to the ability to make simple matching judgments above the level of chance. Patients with the capacity to make perceptual judgments not involving language were unable to make a simple same-difference judgment within the right brain when both the sample and the match were lateralized simultaneously. Thus, when a judgment of sameness was required for two simultaneously presented figures, the right hemisphere failed.

This minimal profile of capacity stands in marked contrast to patients with right-hemisphere language. One patient, J.W., who understood language and who had a rich right-hemisphere lexicon as assessed by the Peabody Picture Vocabulary Tests and other special tests could not, until recently, access speech from the right hemisphere. Patients V.P. and P.S. could understand language and speak from each half of the brain. Would this extra skill lend a greater capacity to the right hemisphere's ability to think, to interpret the events of the world?

It turns out that the right hemispheres of both patient groups are poor at making simple inferences.

When shown two pictures, one after the other (e.g., a picture of a match and a picture of a wood pile), the patients (or the right hemisphere) cannot combine the two elements into a causal relation and choose the proper result (i.e., a picture of a burning woodpile as opposed to a picture of a woodpile and a set of matches). In other testing, simple words are presented serially to the right side of the brain. The task is to infer the causal relation between the two lexical elements and pick the answer from six possible answers in full view of the subject. A typical trial consists of words like *pin* and *finger* being flashed to the right hemisphere, with the correct answer being *bleed*. Even though the patient (right hemisphere) can always find a close lexical associate of the words used, he cannot make the inference that *pin* and *finger* should lead to *bleed*.

In this light, it is hard to imagine that the left and right hemispheres have similar conscious experiences. The right cannot make inferences; consequently, it is extremely limited in what it can have feelings about. It deals mainly with raw experience in an unembellished way. The left hemisphere, though, is constantly, almost reflexively labeling experiences, making inferences as to cause and carrying out a host of other cognitive activities. The left hemisphere is busy differentiating the world whereas the right is simply monitoring the world.

Again as John Updike (1989) put it:

Perhaps there are two kinds of people: those for whom nothingness is no problem, and those for whom it is an insuperable problem, an outrageous cancellation rendering every other concern, from mismatching socks to nuclear holocaust, negligible. Tenacious of this terror, this adamant essence as crucial to us as our sexuality we resist those kindly stoic consolers who assure us that we will outwear the fright, that we will grow numb and accepting and, as it were, religiously impotent. As Unamuno says, with the rhythms of a stubborn child, "I do not want to die—no: I neither want to die nor do I want to want to die; I want to live forever and ever and ever. I want this 'I' to live this poor 'I' that I am and that I feel myself to be here and now."

SUMMARY

The problem of explaining how the brain enables human conscious experience remains a great mystery of human knowledge. Scientists are gaining vast knowledge of how parts of the brain are responsible for mental and perceptual activities. Though great advances are happening in the study of the content of conscious experience, our understanding of its subjective qualities is scant.

The philosopher Colin McGinn (1991) believed that if the mind is a biological device, there is no guarantee that it can conceive of the answer to every problem it can pose for itself. We are organisms, not angels, so some answers may not be thinkable by our limited brains. Just as a rat could never learn a maze in which it had to turn left at all the prime-number arms—a rat brain cannot entertain the notion "prime number"—people may never figure out why some kinds of information processing in the brain throw off sentient experience instead of just input and output. The rat might think that the food in the maze was placed by God, and might invent all kinds of cockamamie theories as to why it gets there—all because it does not have the kind of brain that thinks in terms of prime numbers. In a similar way, humans invent religion and philosophy, and go round and round pontificating about these questions for thousands of years, with no progress. Of course, McGinn cheerfully admitted that his view is not easily falsifiable, but then almost everything we say about sentience is nonfalsifiable at this point in human knowledge.

We believe there are a myriad of problems embedded in what we generally mean by the problem of consciousness. Issues of access, of self-knowledge, of attention, of perception, of salience, of history, are all addressable—and current research is illuminating these issues. The study of conscious experience is central to understanding the mind.

SUGGESTED READINGS

CHURCHLAND, P. (1993). Matter and Consciousness. Book Review: *Consciousness Explained.* 1988, Cambridge, MA: MIT Press. *The Journal of Philosophy* 90:181–193.

DENNETT, DANIEL C. (1991). *Consciousness Explained.* Boston: Little Brown.

FENDRICH, R., WESSINGER, C.M. and GAZZANIGA, M.S. (1992). Residual vision in a scotoma: Implications for blindsight. *Science* 258: 1489–1491.

JACKENDOFF, RAY S. (1987). *Consciousness and the Computational Mind.* Cambridge, MA: MIT Press.

GAZZANIGA, M.S. (1995). Consciousness and the Cerebral Hemispheres. In: M.S. Gazzaniga (Ed.), *The Cognitive Neurosciences* (pp. 1391–1399). Cambridge, MA: MIT Press.

GAZZANIGA, M.S. (1998). *The Mind's Past.* Berkeley, CA: University of California Press.

PREMACK, D. and WOODRUFF, G. (1978). Does the chimpanzee have a theory of mind? *Behavioral & Brain Sciences* 1:515–526.

WEISKRANTZ, L. (1986). *Blindsight: A Case Study and Implications.* New York: Oxford University Press.

REFERENCES

ABRAMS, R.A., AND LANDGRAF, J.Z. (1990). Differential use of distance and location information for spatial localization. *Perception and Psychophysics* 47:349–359.

ABRAMS, R.A., VAN DILLEN, L., AND STEMMONS, V. (1994). Multiple Sources of Spatial Information for Aimed Limb Movements. In C. Umilta and M. Moscovitch (Eds.), *Attention and Performance. Vol. 15: Conscious and Nonconscious Information Processing* (pp. 267–290). Cambridge, MA: MIT Press.

ACREDOLO, L., AND GOODWYN, S. (1996). *Baby Signs: How To Talk with Your Baby Before Your Baby Can Talk.* Chicago: Contemporary Books.

AKELAITIS, A.J. (1941). Studies on the corpus callosum: Higher visual functions in each homonymous visual field following complete section of corpus callosum. *Arch. Neurol. Psychiatry* 45:788.

ALCOCK, J. (1979). *Animal Behavior: An Evolutionary Approach,* 2nd edition. Sunderland, MA: Sinauer Assoc.

ALEXANDER, G.E., AND CRUTCHER, M.D. (1990). Preparation for movement: Neural representations of intended direction in three motor areas of the monkey. *J. Neurophysiol.* 64:133–150.

ALLEN, M. (1983). Models of hemisphere specialization. *Psychol. Bull.* 93:73–104.

ARVANITAKI, A. (1939). Recherches sur la résponse oscillatoire locale de l'axone géant isolé de 'Sepia.' *Arch. Int. Physiol.* 49:209–256.

ASHE, J., TAIRA, M., SMYRNIS, N., PELLIZZER, G., GERORAKOPOULOS, T., LURITO, J.T., AND GEORGOPOULOS, A.P. (1993). Motor cortical activity preceding a memorized movement trajectory with an orthogonal bend. *Exp. Brain Res.* 95:118–130.

ATKINSON, R.C., AND SHIFFRIN, R.M. (1968). Human Memory: A Proposed System and Its Control Processes. In K.W. Spence and J.T. Spence (Eds.), *The Psychology of Learning and Motivation,* Vol. 2 (pp. 89–195). New York: Academic Press.

BADDELEY, A. (1995). Working Memory. In M.S. Gazzaniga (Ed.), *The Cognitive Neurosciences* (pp. 755–764). Cambridge, MA: MIT Press.

BADDELEY, A., AND HITCH, G. (1974). Working Memory. In G.H. Bower (Ed.), *The Psychology of Learning and Motivation,* Vol. 8 (pp. 47–89). New York: Academic Press.

BAILLARGEON, R. (1991). Reasoning about the height and location of a hidden object in 4½ and 6½ month old infants. *Cognition* 38:13–42.

BALDWIN, D.A., AND MOSES, L. (1994). Early Understanding of Referential Intent and Attentional Focus: Evidence from Language and Emotion. In C. Lewis and P. Mitchell (Eds.), *Children's Early Understanding of Mind: Origins and Development* (pp. 133–156). London: Lawrence Erlbaum Associates.

BANNERMAN, D.M., GOOD, M.A., BUTCHER, S.P., RAMSAY, M., AND MORRIS, R.G.M. (1995). Distinct components of spatial learning revealed by prior training and NMDA receptor blockade. *Nature* 378:182–186.

BARBUR, J.L., WATSON, J.D.G., FRACKOWIAK, R.S.J., AND ZEKI, S. (1993). Conscious visual perception without V1. *Brain* 116:1293–1302.

BARTHOLOMEUS, B. (1974). Effects of task requirements on ear superiority for sung speech. *Cortex* 10:215–223.

BAYLIS, G.C., ROLLS, E.T., AND LEONARD, C.M. (1985). Selectivity between faces in the responses of a population of neurons in the cortex in the superior temporal sulcus of the monkey. *Brain Res.* 342:91–102.

BEAR, M.F., CONNORS, B.W., AND PARADISO, M.A. (1996). *Neuroscience: Exploring the Brain.* Baltimore: Williams & Wilkins.

BECK, J. (1982). Textural Segmentation. In J. Beck (Ed.), *Organization and Representation in Perception* (pp. 285–317). Hillsdale, NJ: Lawrence Erlbaum Associates.

BEHRMANN, M., AND TIPPER, S.P. (1994). Object-Based Attentional Mechanisms: Evidence from Patients with Unilateral Neglect. In C. Umilta and M. Moscovitch (Eds.), *Attention and Performance 15: Conscious and Nonconscious Information Processing* (pp. 351–375). Attention and performance series. Cambridge, MA: MIT Press.

BEHRMANN, M., MOSCOVITCH, M., AND WINOCUR, G. (1994).

Intact visual imagery and impaired visual perception in a patient with visual agnosia. *J. Exp. Psychol.* 20:1068–1087.

BERENT, S., GIORDANI, B., LEHTINEN, S., MARKEL, D., PENNEY, J.B., BUCHTEL, H.A., STAROSTA-RUBENSTEIN, S., HICHWA, R., AND YOUNG, A.B. (1988). Positron emission tomographic scan investigation of Huntington's disease: Cerebral metabolic correlates of cognitive function. *Ann. Neurol.* 23:541–546.

BERGMAN, H., WICHMANN, T., AND DELONG, M.R. (1990). Reversal of experimental parkinsonism by lesions of the subthalamic nucleus. *Science* 249:1436–1438.

BERRIDGE, K.C., AND WHISHAW, I.Q. (1992). Cortex, striatum and cerebellum: control of serial order in a grooming sequence. *Exp. Brain Res.* 61:275–290.

BIEDERMAN, I. (1990). Higher-Level Vision. In D.N. Osherson, S.M. Kosslyn, and J.M. Hollberbach (Eds.), *Visual Cognition and Action: An Invitation to Cognitive Science,* Vol. 2 (pp. 41–63). Cambridge, MA: MIT Press.

BISIACH, E., AND LUZZATTI, C. (1978). Unilateral neglect of representational space. *Cortex* 14:129–133.

BIZZI, E., ACCORNERO, N., CHAPPLEL, W., AND HOGAN, N. (1984). Posture control and trajectory formation during arm movement. *J. Neurosci.* 4:2738–2744.

BLISS, T.V.P., AND LØMO, T. (1973). Long-lasting potentiation of synaptic transmission in the dentate area of the anaesthetized rabbit following stimulation of the perforant pathway. *J. Physiol.* 232:331–356.

BLONDERS, L.X., BOWERS, D., AND HEILMAN, K.M. (1991). The role of the right hemisphere in emotional communication. *Brain* 114:1115–1127.

BRADSHAW, J., AND ROGERS, L. (1993). *The Evolution of Lateral Asymmetries, Language, Tool Use, and Intellect.* San Diego: Academic Press.

BRADSHAW, J.L., AND NETTLETON, N.C. (1981). The nature of hemispheric specialization in man. *Behav. Brain Sci.* 4:51–91.

BRAITENBERG, V. (1984). *Vehicles: Experiments in Synthetic Psychology.* Cambridge, MA: MIT Press.

BRITTEN, K.H., SHALDEN, M.N., NEWSOME, W.T., AND MOVSHON, J.A. (1992). The analysis of visual motion: A comparison of neuronal and psychophysical performance. *J. Neurosci.* 12:4745–4765.

BROADBENT, D.A. (1958). *Perception and Communication.* New York: Pergamon.

BROADBENT, D.A. (1970). Stimulus Set and Response Set: Two Kinds of Selective Attention. In D.I. Motofsky (Ed.), *Attention: Contemporary Theory and Analysis* (pp. 51–60). New York: Appleton-Century-Crofts.

BRODMANN, K. (1909). *Vergleichende Lokalisationslehre der Grosshirnrinde in ihren Prinzipien dargestellt auf Grund des Zellenbaues.* Leipzig: J.A. Barth. In G. von Bonin, *Some Papers on the Cerebral Cortex.* Translated as, *"On the Comparative Localization of the Cortex."* Springfield, IL: Charles C. Thomas, 1960. pp. 201–230.

BROTCHIE, P., IANSEK, R., AND HORNE, M.K. (1991). Motor function of the monkey globus pallidus. *Brain* 114:1685–1702.

BROWN, R., AND KULIK, J. (1977). Flashbulb memories. *Cognition* 5:73–99.

BROWN, T. (1911). The intrinsic factors in the act of progression in the mammal. *Proc. Royal Soc. London,* Series B 84:308–319.

BRYDEN, M.P. (1982). *Laterality: Functional Asymmetry in the Intact Human Brain.* New York: Academic Press.

BULLOCK, T.H. (1993). How are more complex brains different? One view and an agenda for comparative neurobiology. *Brain Behav. Evol.* 41:88–96.

CAMINITI, R., JOHNSON, P.B., GALLI, C., FERRAINA, S., AND BURNOD, Y. (1991). Making arm movements within different parts of space: The premotor and motor cortical representation of a coordinate system for reaching visual targets. *J. Neurosci.* 11:1182–1197.

CAPLAN, D. (1994). Language and the brain. In M.A. Gernsbacher (Ed.), *Handbook of Psycholinguistics* (pp. 1023–1053). San Diego: Academic Press.

CARAMAZZA, A. (1992). Is cognitive neuropsychology possible? *J. Cogn. Neurosci.* 4:80–95.

CARAMAZZA, A. (1996). The brain's dictionary. *Nature* 380:485–486.

CARPENTER, M. (1976). *Human Neuroanatomy,* 7th edition. Baltimore: Williams & Wilkins.

CASTIELLO, U., PAULIGNAN, Y., AND JEANNEROD, M. (1991). Temporal dissociation of motor responses and subjective awareness. *Brain* 114:2639–2655.

CAVINESS, V.S., Jr., AND RAKIC, P. (1978). Mechanisms of cortical development: A view from mutations in mice. *Ann. Rev. Neurosci.* 1:297–326.

CHERRY, E.C. (1953). Some experiments on the recognition of speech, with one and two ears. *J. Acoustic Soc. Am.* 25:975–979.

CHIARELLO, C. (1991). Interpretation of Word Meanings by the Cerebral Hemispheres: One Is Not Enough. In P.J. Schwanenflugel (Ed.), *The Psychology of Word Meanings.* Hillsdale, NJ: Lawrence Erlbaum Associates.

CHOMSKY, N. (1957). *Syntactic Structures.* The Hague: Mouton.

CHRISTMAN, S., AND KITTERLE, F.L. (1991). Hemispheric asymmetry in the processing of absolute versus relative spatial frequency. *Brain Cogn.* 16:62–73.

CHURCHLAND, P.S. (1986). *Neurophilosophy: Towards a Unified Science of the Mind/Brain.* Cambridge, MA: MIT Press.

CHURCHLAND, P. (1988). *Matter and Consciousness.* Cambridge, MA: MIT Press.

COHEN, J.D., ROMERO, R.D., SERVAN-SCHREIBER, D., AND FARAH, M.J. (1994). Mechanisms of spatial attention: The relation of macrostructure to microstucture in parietal neglect. *J. Cogn. Neurosci.* 6:377–387.

COHEN, N.J., AND EICHENBAUM, H. (1993). *Memory, Amnesia and the Hippocampal System.* Cambridge, MA: MIT Press.

COHEN, R.M., SEMPLE, W.E., GROSS, M., AND NORDHAL, T.E. (1988). From syndrome to illness: Delineating the pathophysiology of schizophrenia with PET. *Schizophrenia Bull.* 14:169–176.

COLLINS, A.M., AND LOFTUS, E.F. (1975). A spreading-activation theory of semantic processing. *Psychol. Rev.* 82:407–428.

CORBALLIS, M.C. (1991). *The Lopsided Ape: Evolution of the Generative Mind.* New York: Oxford University Press.

CORBETTA, M., MIEZIN, F.M., DOBMEYER, S., SHULMAN, G.L., AND PETERSEN, S.E. (1991). Selective and divided attention during visual discriminations of shape, color and speed: Functional anatomy by positron emission tomography. *J. Neurosci.* 11:2383–2402.

CORBETTA, M., MIEZIN, F.M., SHULMAN, G.L., AND PETERSEN, S.E. (1993). A PET study of visuospatial attention. *J. Neurosci.* 13:1202–1226.

CORBETTA, M., SHULMAN, G., MIEZIN, F., AND PETERSEN, S. (1995). Superior parietal cortex activation during spatial attention shifts and visual feature conjunction. *Science* 270:802–805.

COREN, S., WARD, L.M., AND ENNS, J.T. (1994). *Sensation and Perception,* 4th edition. Ft. Worth, TX: Harcourt Brace College Publishers.

CORKIN, S. (1984). Lasting consequences of bilateral medial temporal lobectomy: Clinical course and experimental findings in HM. *Semin. Neurol.* 4:249–259.

CORKIN, S., AMARAL, D., GONZALEZ, R., JOHNSON, K., et al.

(1997). H.M.'s medial temporal lobe lesion: Findings from magnetic resonance imaging. *J. Neurosci.* 17:3964–3979.

COSMIDES, L. (1984). The Logic of Social Exchange: Has Natural Selection Shaped How Humans Reason? Studies With the Wason Selection Task. *Cognition* 31:187–276.

COSMIDES, L., AND TOOBY, J. (1992). Cognitive Adaptations for Social Exchange. In J.H. Barkow, L. Cosmides, and J. Tooby (Eds.), *The Adapted Mind.* New York: Oxford University Press.

COWEY, A., AND STOERIG, P. (1991). The neurobiology of blindsight. *Trends Neurosci.* 14:140–145.

CRAIK, F.I.M., AND LOCKHART, R.S. (1972). Levels of processing: A framework for memory research. *J. Verbal Learn. Verbal Behav.* 11:671–684.

CRICK, F. (1992). Function of the Thalamic Reticular Complex: The Searchlight Hypothesis. In S.M. Kosslyn and R.A. Andersen (Eds.), *Frontiers in Cognitive Neuroscience* (pp. 366–372). Cambridge, MA: MIT Press.

DAMASIO, A.R. (1990). Category-related recognition defects as a clue to the neural substrates of knowledge. *Trends Neurosci.* 13:95–98.

DAMASIO, A.R. (1994). *Descartes' Error: Emotion, Reason, and the Human Brain.* New York: G.P. Putnam.

DAMASIO, H., GRABOWSKI, T., FRANK, R., GALABURDA, A.M., AND DAMASIO, A.R. (1994). The return of Phineas Gage: The skull of a famous patient yields clues about the brain. *Science* 264:1102–1105.

DAMASIO, H., GRABOWSKI, T.J., TRANEL, D., HICHWA, R.D., AND DAMASIO, A.R. (1996). A neural basis for lexical retrieval. *Nature* 380:499–505.

DARWIN, C. (1859). *On the Origin of Species.* London: J. Murray; reprinted. Cambridge, MA: Harvard University Press.

DARWIN, C. (1871). *The Descent of Man and Selection in Relation to Sex.* London: J. Murray.

DAVIDSON, R.J. (1995). Cerebral Asymmetry, Emotion, and Affective Style. In R.J. Davidson and K. Hugdahl (Eds.), *Brain Asymmetry* (pp. 361–387). Cambridge, MA: MIT Press.

DAVIDSON, R.J., MEDNICK, D., MOSS, E., SARON, C., AND SCHAFFER, C.E. (1987). Ratings of emotions in faces are influenced by the visual field to which stimuli are presented. *Brain Cogn.* 6:403–411.

DAWSON, J.L.M., CHEUNG, Y.M., AND LAU, R.T.S. (1973). Effects of neonatal sex hormones on sex-based cognitive abilities in the white rat. *Psychologia* 16:17–24.

DEARMOND, S., FUSCO, M., AND DEWEY, M. (1976). *A Photographic Atlas: Structure of the Human Brain,* 2nd edition. New York: Oxford University Press.

DEARMOND, S.J., FUSCO, M.M., AND DEWEY, M.M. (1989). *The Structure of the Human Brain: A Photographic Atlas,* 3rd edition. New York: Oxford University Press.

DEHAENE, S. (1996). The organization of brain activations in number comparison: Event-related potentials and the additive-factors method. *J. Cogn. Neurosci.* 8:47–68.

DEHAENE, S., POSNER, M.I., AND TUCKER, D.M. (1994). Localization of a neural system for error detection and compensation. *Psychol. Sci.* 5:303–305.

DEJONG, R.N. (1979). *The Neurologic Examination,* 4th edition. New York: Harper & Row.

DELBRÜCK, M. (1986). *Mind from Matter?* London: Blackwell Scientific.

DELIS, D., ROBERTSON, L., AND EFRON, R. (1986). Hemispheric specialization of memory for visual hierarchical stimuli. *Neuropsychologia* 24:205–214.

DELONG, M.R. (1990). Primate models of movement disorders of basal ganglia origin. *Trends Neurosci.* 13:281–285.

DENNETT, D. (1995). *Darwin's Dangerous Idea.* New York: Simon and Schuster.

DENNETT, D. C. (1981). *Consciousness Explained.* Boston: Little Brown and Co.

DESIMONE, R. (1991). Face-selective cells in the temporal cortex of monkeys. *J. Cogn. Neurosci.* 3:1–8.

DESIMONE, R., ALBRIGHT, T.D., GROSS, C.G., AND BRUCE, C. (1984). Stimulus-selective properties of inferior temporal neurons in the macaque. *J. Neurosci.* 4:2051–2062.

DESIMONE, R., WESSINGER, M., THOMAS, L., AND SCHNEIDER, W. (1990). Attentional control of visual perception: Cortical and subcortical mechanisms. *Cold Spring Harb. Symp. Quant. Biol.* 55:963–971.

DESMOND, J.E., AND MOORE, J.W. (1991). Altering the synchrony of stimulus trace processes: Tests of a neural-network model. *Biol. Cybern.* 65:161–169.

DEUTSCH, D. (1975). Musical illusions. *Sci. Am.* 233:92–104.

DEUTSCH, D. (1985). Dichotic listening to melodic patterns and its relationship to hemispheric specialization of function. *Music Percep.* 3:127–154.

DIAMOND, A. (1990). The Development and Neural Bases of Memory Functions as Indexed by the A(not)B and Delayed Response Tasks in Human Infants and Infant Monkeys. In A. Diamond (Ed.), *The Development and Neural Bases of Higher Cognitive Functions* (pp. 267–317). New York: New York Academy of Sciences.

DIAMOND, A. (1991). Neuropsychological insights into the meaning of object concept development. In S. Carey and R. Gelman (Eds.), *The Epigenesis of Mind: Essays on Biology and Cognition.* Hillsdale, NJ: Erlbaum.

DRACHMAN, D.A., AND ARBIT, J. (1966). Memory and the hippocampal complex. II. Is memory a multiple process? *Arch. Neurol.* 15:52–61.

DREVETS, W.C., AND RAICHLE, M.E. (1995). Positron Emission Tomographic Imaging Studies of Human Emotional Disorders. In M.S. Gazzaniga (Ed.), *The Cognitive Neurosciences* (pp. 1153–1164). Cambridge, MA: MIT Press.

DRONKERS, N. (1996). A new brain region for coordinating speech articulation. *Nature* 384:159–161.

DRONKERS, N.F., AND PINKER, S. (In Press). Language and the Aphasias. In E.R. Kandel, J. Schwartz, and T. Jessel (Eds.), *Principles in Neural Science,* 4th edition. New York: Elsevier.

DUNCAN, J. (1995). Attention, Intelligence, and the Frontal Lobes. In M.S. Gazzaniga (Ed.), *The Cognitive Neurosciences* (pp. 721–733). Cambridge, MA: MIT Press.

EASON, R., HARTER, M., AND WHITE, C. (1969). Effects of attention and arousal on visually evoked cortical potentials and reaction time in man. *Physiol. Behav.* 4:283–289.

EFRON, R. (1990). *The Decline and Fall of Hemispheric Specialization.* Hillsdale, NJ: Lawrence Erlbaum Associates.

EGLIN, M., ROBERTSON, L.C., AND KNIGHT, R.T. (1989). Visual search performance in the neglect syndrome. *J. Cogn. Neurosci.* 1:372–385.

EKMAN, P. (1971). Universals and Cultural Differences in Facial Expression. In J.K. Cole (Ed.), *Nebraska Symposium and Motivation* (pp. 207–284). Lincoln, NE: University of Nebraska Press.

EKMAN, P. (1984). Expression and the Nature of Emotion. In P. Ekman and K. Scherer (Eds.), *Approaches to Emotion* (pp. 319–343). Hillsdale, NJ: Lawrence Erlbaum Associates.

ENNS, J.T., AND RENSINK, R.A. (1990). Sensitivity to three-dimensional orientation in visual search. *Psychol. Sci.* 1:323–326.

FARAH, M.J. (1988). Is visual imagery really visual? Overlooked evidence from neuropsychology. *Psychol. Rev.* 95:307–317.

FARAH, M.J. (1990). *Visual Agnosia: Disorders of Object Recognition and What They Tell Us about Normal Vision*. Cambridge, MA: MIT Press.

FARAH, M.J. (1994). Specialization Within Visual Object Recognition: Clues from Prosopagnosia and Alexia. In M.J. Farah and G. Ratcliff (Eds.), *The Neuropsychology of High-Level Vision: Collected Tutorial Essays* (pp. 133–146). Hillsdale, NJ: Lawrence Erlbaum Associates.

FARAH, M.J., AND MCCLELLAND, J.L. (1991). A computational model of semantic memory impairment: Modality specificity and emergent category specificity. *J. Exp. Psychol. Gen.* 120:339–357.

FENDRICH, R., WESSINGER, C.M., AND GAZZANIGA, M.S. (1992). Residual vision in a scotoma: Implications for blindsight. *Science* 258:1489–1491.

FIEZ, J.A., RAIFE, E.A., BALOTA, D.A., SCHWARZ, J.P., RAICHLE, M.E., AND PETERSEN, S.E. (1996). A positron emission tomography study of short-term maintenance of verbal information. *J. Neurosci.* 16:808–822.

FINGER, S. (1994). *Origins of Neuroscience*. New York: Oxford University Press.

FLOURENS, M.-J.P. (1824). Recherches Expérimentales sur les proprieties et les functiones du Systeme Nerveux dans le Animaux Vertébrés. Paris: J.B. Ballière.

FOX, P.T., MIEZIN, F.M., ALLMAN, J.M., VAN ESSEN, D.C., AND RAICHLE, M.E. (1987). Retinotopic organization of human visual cortex mapped with positron-emission tomography. *J. Neurosci.* 7:913–922.

FRANZ, E., ELIASSEN, J., IVRY, R., AND GAZZANIGA, M. (1996). Dissociation of Spatial and Temporal Coupling in the Bimanual Movements of Callosotomy Patients. *Psychol. Sci.* 7:306–310.

FRIEDMAN, H.R., AND GOLDMAN-RAKIC, P.S. (1994). Coactivation of prefrontal cortex and inferior parietal cortex in working memory tasks revealed by 2DG functional mapping in the rhesus monkey. *J. Neurosci.* 14:2775–2788.

FRITH, C.D., FRISTON, K., LIDDLE, P.F., AND FRACKOWIAK, R.S.J. (1991). Willed action and the prefrontal cortex in man: A study with PET. *Proc. R. Soc. of Lond., Biol. Sci.* 244:241–246.

FUSTER, J.M. (1989). *The Prefrontal Cortex: Anatomy, Physiology, and Neuropsychology of the Frontal Lobe*, 2nd edition. New York: Raven Press.

GABRIELI, J., FLEISCHMAN, D., KEANE, M., REMINGER, S., AND MORELL, F. (1995). Double dissociation between memory systems underlying explicit and implicit memory in the human brain. *Psychol. Sci.* 6:76–82.

GAFFAN, D., AND HEYWOOD, C.A. (1993). A spurious category-specific visual agnosia for living things in normal human and nonhuman primates. *J. Cogn. Neurosci.* 5:118–128.

GALL, F.J., AND SPURZHEIM, J. (1810–1819). *Anatomie et Physiologie du Systè me Nerveux en Gèneral, et der Cerveauen Particulier*. Paris: F. Schoell.

GALLISTEL, C.R. (1995). The Replacement of General-Purpose Theories with Adaptive Specializations. In M.S. Gazzaniga (Ed.), *The Cognitive Neurosciences* (pp. 1255–1267). Cambridge, MA: MIT Press.

GAULIN, S.J.C. (1995). Does Evolutionary Theory Predict Sex Differences in the Brain? In M.S. Gazzaniga (Ed.), *The Cognitive Neurosciences* (pp. 1211–1225). Cambridge, MA: MIT Press.

GAULIN, S.J.C., AND FITZGERALD, R.W. (1989). Sexual selection for spatial-learning ability. *Anim. Behav.* 37:322–331.

GAZZANIGA, M.S. (1983). Right hemisphere language following brain bisection: A twenty year perspective. *Am. Psychol.* 38:525–547.

GAZZANIGA, M.S. (1992). *Nature's Mind: The Biological Roots of Thinking, Emotions, Sexuality, Language, and Intelligence*. New York: Basic Books.

GAZZANIGA, M.S. (1995). Principles of human brain organization derived from split-brain studies. *Neuron* 14:217–228.

GAZZANIGA, M.S. (Ed.). (1995). *The Cognitive Neurosciences*. Cambridge, MA: MIT Press.

GAZZANIGA, M.S., AND SMYLIE, C.S. (1990). Hemispheric mechanisms controlling voluntary and spontaneous facial expressions. *J. Cog. Neurosci.* 2:239–245.

GAZZANIGA, M.S., AND SPERRY, R.W. (1967). Language after section of the cerebral commissures. *Brain* 90:131–148.

GAZZANIGA, M.S., HOLTZMAN, J.D., AND SMYLIE, C.S. (1987). Speech without conscious awareness. *Neurology* 35:682–685.

GEARY, D.C. (1995). Reflections of evolution and culture in children's cognition. Implications for mathematical development and instruction. *Amer. Psychologist* 50:24–37.

GEHRING, W.J., GOSS, B., COLES, M.G.H., MEYER, D.E., AND DONCHIN, E. (1993). A neural system for error detection and compensation. *Psychol. Sci.* 4:385–390.

GEORGOPOULOS, A.P. (1990). Neurophysiology of Reaching. In M. Jeannerod (Ed.), *Attention and Performance XIII: Motor Representation and Control* (pp. 227–263). Hillsdale, NJ: Lawrence Erlbaum Associates.

GEORGOPOULOS, A.P. (1995). Motor Cortex and Cognitive Processing. In M.S. Gazzaniga (Ed.), *The Cognitive Neurosciences* (pp. 507–517). Cambridge, MA: MIT Press.

GESCHWIND, N. (1967). The varieties of naming errors. *Cortex* 3:97–112.

GESCHWIND, N., AND GALABURDA, A.M. (1987). *Cerebral Lateralization: Biological Mechanisms, Associations, and Pathology*. Cambridge, MA: MIT Press.

GESCHWIND, N., AND LEVITSKY, W. (1968). Human brain: Left-right asymmetries in temporal speech region. *Science* 161:186–187.

GILBERT, C.D., AND WIESEL, T.N. (1990). The influence of contextual stimuli on the orientation selectivity of cells in primary visual cortex. *Vision Res.* 30:1689–1701.

GLISKY, E.L., POLSTER, M.R., AND ROUTHUIEAUX, B.C. (1995). Double dissociation between item and source memory. *Neuropsychology* 9:229–235.

GOLDBERG, G. (1985). Supplementary motor area structure and function: Review and hypothesis. *Behav. Brain Sci.* 8:567–616.

GOLDMAN-RAKIC, P.S. (1992). Working memory and the mind. *Sci. Am.* 267:111–117.

GOLDMAN-RAKIC, P.S. (1995). Architecture of the Prefrontal Cortex and the Central Executive. In J. Grafman, K.J. Holyoak, and F. Boller (Eds.), *Structure and Functions of the Human Prefrontal Cortex* (pp. 71–83). New York: The New York Academy of Sciences.

GOLDSBY, R.A. (1976). *Basic Biology*. New York: Harper and Row Publishers. (pp. 282–297).

GOODALE, M.A., AND MILNER, A.D. (1992). Separate visual pathways for perception and action. *Trends Neurosci.* 15:22–25.

GOODMAN, G., QUAS, J., BATTERMAN-FAUNEE, J., RIDDLESBERGER, M., et al. (1994). Predictors of accurate and inaccurate memories of traumatic events experienced in childhood. *Consciousness and Cognition* 3:269–294.

GOULD, S.J., AND VRBA, E. (1981). Exaptation: A missing term in the science of form. *Paleobiol.* 8:4–15.

GRABOWECKY, M., ROBERTSON, L.C., AND TREISMAN, A. (1993). Preattentive processes guide visual search. *J. Cogn. Neurosci.* 5:288–302.

GRAFTON, S., HAZELTINE, E., AND IVRY, R. (1995). Functional mapping of sequence learning in normal humans. *J. Cogn. Neurosci.* 7:497–510.

GRAHAM, J., CARLSON, G.R., AND GERARD, R.W. (1942). Membrane and injury potentials of single muscle fibers. *Fed. Proc.* 1:31.

GRAZIANO, M.S.A., AND GROSS, C.G. (1994). Mapping space with neurons. *Curr. Direct. Psychol. Sci.* 3:164–167.

GREENBERG, J.O. (1995). *Neuroimaging: A Companion to Adams and Victor's Principles of Neurology.* New York: McGraw-Hill, Inc.

GREENFIELD, P.M. (1991). Language, tools and brain: The ontogeny and phylogeny of hierarchically organized sequential behavior. *Behav. Brain Sci.* 14:531–595.

GUR, R.C., SKOLNICK, B.E., AND GUR, R.E. (1994). Effects of emotional discrimination tasks on cerebral blood flow: Regional activation and its relation to performance. *Brain Cogn.* 25:271–286.

HAGOORT, P., BROWN, C., AND GROOTHUSEN, J. (1993). The syntactic positive shift (SPS) as an ERP measure of syntactic processing. Special Issue: Event-related brain potentials in the study of language. *Lang. Cogn. Processes.* 8:439–483.

HAGOORT, P., BROWN, C., AND SWAAB, T. (1996). Lexical semantic event-related potential effects in patients with left hemisphere lesions and aphasia, and patients with right hemisphere lesions without aphasia. *Brain* 119:627–649.

HARKNESS, R.D., AND MAROUDAS, N.G. (1985). Central place foraging by an ant (Cataglyphis bicolor Fab.). A model of searching. *Anim. Behav.* 33:916–928.

HART, J., BERNDT, R.S., AND CARAMAZZA, A. (1985). Category-specific naming deficit following cerebral infarction. *Nature* 316:439–440.

HARTLINE, H.K. (1938). The response of single optic nerve fibers of the vertebrate eye to illumination of the retina. *Am. J. Physiol.* 121:400–415.

HAXBY, J., UNGERLEIDER, L., HORWITZ, B., MAISOG, J., ROPOPORT, S., AND GRADY, C. (1996). Face encoding and recognition in the human brain. *Proc. Natl. Acad. Sci. U.S.A.* 93:922–927.

HAXBY J.V., HORWITZ B., UNGERLEIDER, L.G., MAISOG, J.M., PIETRINI, P., AND GRADY, C.L. (1994). The functional organization of human extrastriate cortex: A PET-rCBF study of selective attention to faces and locations. *J. Neurosci.* 14:6336–6353.

HAYES, A., DAVIDSON, M., KEELE, S.W., AND RAFAL, R. (in press). Toward a functional analysis of the basal ganglia. *J. Cogn. Neurosci.*

HEBB, D. (1949). *The Organization of Behavior: A Neuropsychological Theory.* New York: John Wiley and Sons.

HEILMAN, K.M., ROTHI, L.J., AND VALENSTEIN, E. (1982). Two forms of ideomotor apraxia. *Neurology* 32:342–346.

HEINZE, H.J., MANGUN, G.R., BURCHERT, W., HINRICHS, H., SCHOLZ, M., MÜNTE, T.F., GÖS, A., SCHERG, M., JOHANNES, S., HUNDESHAGEN, H., GAZZANIGA, M.S., AND HILLYARD, S.A. (1994). Combined spatial and temporal imaging of brain activity during visual selective attention in humans. *Nature* 372:543–546.

HELLIGE, J.B. (1993). *Hemispheric Asymmetry: What's Right and What's Left.* Cambridge, MA: Harvard University Press.

HENDERSON, L. (1982). *Orthography and Word Recognition in Reading.* London: Academic Press.

HERNANDEZ-PEON, R., SCHERRER, H., AND JOUVET, M. (1956). Modification of electrical activity in cochlear nucleus during attention in unanesthetized cats. *Science* 123:331–332.

HEYWOOD, C.A., WILSON, B., AND COWEY, A. (1987). A case study of cortical colour "blindness" with relatively intact achromatic discrimination. *J. Neurol. Neurosurg. Psychiatry* 50:22–29.

HILLYARD, S.A., HINK, R.F., SCHWENT, V.L., AND PICTON, T.W. (1973). Electrical signs of selective attention in the human brain. *Science* 182:177–180.

HOLBOURN, A.H.S. (1943). Mechanics of head injury. *The Lancet* 2:438–441.

HOLMES, G. (1919). Disturbances of visual orientation. *British J. of Ophthalmol.* 2:449–468.

HOLTZMAN, J.D. (1984). Interactions between cortical and subcortical visual areas: Evidence from human commissurotomy patients. *Vision Res.* 24:801–813.

HOPFINGER, J., AND G.R. MANGUN, (1998). Reflexive attention modulates visual processing in human extrastriate cortex. *Psychological Science* 9.

HORE, J., WILD, B., AND DIENER, H. (1991). Cerebellar dysmetria at the elbow, wrist, and fingers. *J. Neurophysiol.* 65:563–571.

HUBEL, D., AND WIESEL, T. (1968). Receptive fields and functional architecture of monkey striate cortex. *J. of Physiol. (London)* 195:215–243.

HUBEL, D.H., AND WIESEL, T.N. (1977). The Ferrier Lecture: Functional architecture of macaque monkey visual cortex. *Proc. R. Acad. London, Series B* 198:1–59.

HUMPHREYS, G.W., AND RIDDOCH, M.J. (1992). Interactions Between Objects and Space-Vision Revealed Through Neuropsychology. In D.E. Meyers and S. Kornblum (Eds.), *Attention and Performance XIV* (pp. 143–162). Hillsdale, NJ: Lawrence Erlbaum Associates.

HUMPHREYS, G.W., RIDDOCH, M.J., DONNELLY, N., FREEMAN, T., BOUCART, M., AND MULLER, H.M. (1994). Intermediate Visual Processing and Visual Agnosia. In M.J. Farah and G. Ratcliff (Eds.), *The Neuropsychology of High-Level Vision: Collected Tutorial Essays* (pp. 63–102). Hillsdale, NJ: Lawrence Erlbaum Associates.

HYDE, I.H. (1921). A micro-electrode and unicellular stimulation. *Biol. Bull.* 40:130–133.

INGLIS, J., AND LAWSON, J.S. (1982). A meta-analysis of sex differences in the effects of unilateral brain damage on intelligence test results. *Can. J. Psychol.* 36:670–683.

ITO, M., TAMURA, H., FUJITA, I., AND TANAKA, K. (1995). Size and position invariance of neuronal responses in monkey inferotemporal cortex. *J. Neurophysiol.* 73:218–226.

IVRY, R. (1993). Cerebellar involvement in the explicit representation of temporal information. *Ann. NY Acad. Sci.* 682: 214–230.

IVRY, R.B., AND COHEN, A. (1992). Asymmetry in visual search for targets defined by differences in movement speed. *J. Exp. Psychol. Hum. Percept. Perform.* 18:1045–1057.

IVRY, R.B., AND LEBBY, P.C. (1993). Hemispheric differences in auditory perception are similar to those found in visual perception. *Psychol. Sci.* 4:41–45.

IVRY, R.B., AND ROBERTSON, L.C. (in press). The Two Sides of Perception. Cambridge, MA: MIT Press.

JACKENDOFF, R.S. (1987). *Consciousness and the computational mind.* Cambridge, MA: MIT Press.

JACOBS, L.F., GAULIN, S.J.C., SHERRY, D.F., AND HOFFMAN, G.E. (1990). Evolution of spatial cognition: Sex-specific patterns of spatial behavior predict hippocampal size. *Proc. Natl. Acad. Sci. U.S.A.* 87:6349–6352.

JAMES, W. (1890). *Principles of Psychology.* New York: H. Holt.

JANER, K.W., AND PARDO, J.V. (1991). Deficits in selective attention following bilateral anterior cingulotomy. *J. Cogn. Neurosci.* 3:231–241.

JANOWSKY, J.S., OVIATT, S.K., AND ORWOLL, E.S. (1994). Testosterone influences spatial cognition in older men. *Behav. Neurosci.* 108:325–332.

JANOWSKY, J.S., SHIMAMURA, A.P., AND SQUIRE, L.R. (1989). Source memory impairment in patients with frontal lobe lesions. *Neuropsychologia* 27:1043–1056.

JASPER, H.H. (1995). A historical perspective: The rise and fall of prefrontal lobotomy. *Adv. Neurol.* 66:97–114.

JENKINS, I.H., BROOKS, D.J., NIXON, P.D., FRACKOWIAK, R.S.J., AND PASSINGHAM, R.E. (1994). Motor sequence learning: A study with positron emission tomography. *J. Neurosci.* 14:3775–3790.

JOHNSON, M.H. (Ed.) (1993). *Brain Development and Cognition: A Reader.* Cambridge, MA: Blackwell.

KAAS, J. (1995). The Reorganization of Sensory and Motor Maps in Adult Mammals. In M.S. Gazzaniga (Ed.), *The Cognitive Neurosciences* (pp. 51–71). Cambridge, MA: MIT Press.

KANDEL, E., SCHWARTZ, J., AND JESSELL, T. (Eds.) (1991). *Principles of Neural Science,* 3rd edition. New York: Elsevier.

KAPUR, S., CRAIK, F.I., TULVING, E., WILSON, A., HOULE, S., AND BROWN, G. (1994). Neuroanatomical correlates of encoding in episodic memory: Levels of processing effect. *Proc. Natl. Acad. Sci. U.S.A.* 91:2008–2011.

KASS-SIMON, G., AND FARNES, P. (1990). *Women of Science: Righting the Record.* Bloomington, IN: Indiana University Press.

KEELE, S. (1986). Motor Control. In J.K. Boff, L. Kaufman, and J.P. Thomas (Eds.), *Handbook of Human Perception and Performance,* Vol. II (pp. 1–60). New York: John Wiley and Sons.

KELLOGG, R.T. (1995). *Cognitive Psychology.* Thousand Oaks, CA: Sage.

KERETSZ, A., AND HOOPER, P. (1982). Praxis and language: The extent and variety of apraxia in aphasia. *Neuropsychologia* 20:275–286.

KIMURA, D. (1973). The Asymmetry of the human brain. *Sci. Am.* 228:70–78.

KINGSTONE, A., AND GAZZANIGA, M.S. (1995). Subcortical transfer of higher order information: More illusory than real? *Neuropsychology* 9:321–328.

KINGSTONE, A., AND KLEIN, R.M. (1993). Visual offsets facilitate saccadic latency: Does predisengagement of visuospatial attention mediate this gap effect? *J. Exp. Psychol. Hum. Percept. Perform.* 19:1251–1265.

KINSBOURNE, M. (1982). Hemispheric specialization and the growth of human understanding. *Am. Psychol.* 37:411–420.

KITTERLE, F., CHRISTMAN, S., AND HELLIGE, J. (1990). Hemispheric differences are found in identification, but not detection, of low versus high spatial frequencies. *Percept. Psychophysics* 48:297–306.

KLATT, D.H. (1989). Review of Selected Models of Speech Perception. In W. Marslen-Wilson (Ed.), *Lexical Representation and Process* (pp. 169–226). Cambridge, MA: MIT Press.

KNIGHT, R., SCABINI, D., WOODS, D., AND CLAYWORTH, C. (1989). Contributions of temporal-parietal junction to the human auditory P3. *Brain Res.* 502:109–116.

KNIGHT, R.T., AND GRABOWECKY, M. (1995). Escape from Linear Time: Prefrontal Cortex and Conscious Experience. In M.S. Gazzaniga (Ed.), *The Cognitive Neurosciences* (pp. 1357–1371). Cambridge, MA: MIT Press.

KOLB, B., AND WHISHAW, I.Q. (1996). *Fundamentals of Human Neuropsychology,* 4th edition. New York: W.H. Freeman and Co.

KONISHI, M. (1993). Listening with two ears. *Sci. Am.* 2681:66–73.

KOSSLYN, S., AND ANDERSEN, R. (Eds.) (1992). *Frontiers in Cognitive Neuroscience.* Cambridge, MA: MIT Press.

KOSSLYN, S.M. (1987). Seeing and imagining in the cerebral hemispheres: A computational approach. *Psychol. Rev.* 94:148–175.

KOSSLYN, S.M. (1988). Aspects of cognitive neuroscience of mental imagery. *Science* 240:1621–1626.

KOSSLYN, S.M., ALPERT, N.M., THOMPSON, W.L., MALJKOVIK, V., WEISE, S.B., CHABRIS, C.F., HAMILTON, S.E., RAUCH, S.L., AND BUONANNO, F.S. (1993). Visual mental imagery activates topographically organized visual cortex: PET investigations. *J. Cogn. Neurosci.* 5:263–287.

KOSSLYN, S.M., KOENIG, O., BARRET, A., CAVE, C.B., TANG, J., AND GABRIELI, J.D.E. (1989). Evidence for two types of spatial representations: Hemispheric specialization for categorical and coordinate relations. *J. Exp. Psychol. Hum. Percept. Perform.* 15:723–735.

KUFFLER, S., AND NICHOLLS, J. (1976). *From Neuron to Brain.* Sunderland, MA: Sinauer Associates.

KUSHCH, A., GROSS-GLENN, K., JALLAD, B., LUBS, H., RABIN, M., FELDMAN, E., AND DUARA, R. (1993). Temporal lobe surface area measurements on MRI in normal and dyslexic readers. *Neuropsychologia* 31:811–821.

KUTAS, M., AND HILLYARD, S.A. (1980). Reading senseless sentences: Brain potentials reflect semantic incongruity. *Science* 207:203–205.

LABERGE, D. (1990). Thalamic and cortical mechanisms of attention suggested by recent positron emission tomographic experiments. *J. Cogn. Neurosci.* 2:358–372.

LACHICA, E.A., BECK, P.D., AND CASAGRANDE, V.A. (1993). Intrinsic connections of layer III of striate cortex in squirrel monkey and bush baby: Correlations with patterns of cytochrome oxidase. *J. Comp. Neurol.* 328:163–187.

LAENG, B. (1994). Lateralization of categorical and coordinate spatial functions: A study of unilateral stroke patients. *J. Cogn. Neurosci.* 6:189–203.

LANGSTON, W.J. (1984). I. MPTP neurotoxicity: An overview and characterization of phases of toxicity. *Life Sci.* 36:201–206.

LE DOUX, J.E. (1994). Emotion, memory, and the brain. *Sci. Am.* 270:50–57.

LE DOUX, J.E. (1995). In Search of an Emotional System in the Brain: Leaping from Fear to Emotion and Consciousness. In M.S. Gazzaniga (Ed.), *The Cognitive Neurosciences* (pp. 1047–1061). Cambridge, MA: MIT Press.

LETTVIN, J.Y., MATURANA, H.R., MCCULLOCH, W.S., AND PITTS, W.H. (1959). What the frog's eye tells the frog's brain. *Proc. Inst. Radio Engineers* 47:1940–1951.

LEVELT, W.J.M. (1989). *Speaking: From Intention to Articulation.* CAMBRIDGE, MA: MIT PRESS.

LEVELT, W.J.M. (1993). The Architecture of Normal Spoken Language Use. In G. Blanken, J. Dittman, H. Grimm, J.C. Marshall and C-W. Wallesh (Eds.), *Linguistic Disorders and Pathologies: An International Handbook.* Berlin: Walter de Gruyter.

LEVELT, W.J.M. (1994). The Skill of Speaking. In P. Bertelson, P. Eelen, and G. d'Ydewalle (Eds.), *International Perspectives on Psychological Science.* Vol. 1: *Leading Themes* (pp. 89–103). Hove, England: Lawerence Erlbaum Associates.

LEWIS, D.A., AND LUND, J.S. (1990). Heterogeneity of chandelier neurons in monkey neocortex: Corticotropin-releasing factor and parvalbumin-immunoreactive populations. *J. Comp. Neurol.* 293:599–615.

LEY, R.G., AND BRYDEN, M.P. (1982). A dissociation of right and left hemispheric effects for recognizing emotional tone and verbal content. *Brain Cogn.* 1:3–9.

LHERMITTE, F. (1983). "Utilization behaviour" and its relation to lesions of the frontal lobes. *Brain* 106:237–255.

LHERMITTE, F., PILLON, B., AND SERDARU, M. (1986). Human autonomy and the frontal lobes. Part I: Imitation and utilization behavior: A neuropsychological study of 75 patients. *Ann. Neurol.* 19:326–334.

LINDVALL, O., BRUNDIN, P., WIDNER, H., REHNCRONA, S., GUSTAVII, B., FRACKOWIAK, R., LEENDERS, K.L., SAWLE, G., ROTHWELL, J.C., MARSDEN, C.D., AND BJORKLUND, A. (1990). Grafts of fetal dopamine neurons survive and improve motor function in Parkinson's disease. *Science* 247:574–577.

LISSAUER, H. (1890). Ein fall von seelenblindheit nebst einem Beitrage zur Theori derselben. *Archiv fur Psychiatrie und Nervenkrankheiten* 21:222–270.

LIVINGSTONE, M., AND HUBEL, D. (1988). Segregation of form, color, movement, and depth: Anatomy, physiology, and perception. *Science* 240:740–749.

LIVINGSTONE, M.S., AND HUBEL, D.H. (1984). Anatomy and physiology of a color system in the primate visual cortex. *J. Neurosci.* 4:309–356.

LOFTUS, E., AND GREENE, E. (1980). Warning: Even memory for faces may be contagious. *Law Hum. Behav.* 4:323–334.

LOFTUS, E., MILLER, D., AND BURNS, H. (1978). Semantic integration of verbal information into visual memory. *J. Exp. Psychol. Hum. Learn. Mem.* 4:19–31.

LOFTUS, W.C., TRAMO, M.J., THOMAS, C.E., GREEN, R.L., NORDGREN, R.A., AND GAZZANIGA, M.S. (1993). Three-dimensional quantitative analysis of hemispheric asymmetry in the human superior temporal region. *Cereb. Cortex* 3:348–355.

LOOMIS, J.M., FUJITA, N., DA SILVA, J.A., AND FUKUSIMA, S.S. (1992). Visual space perception and visually directed action. *J. Exp. Psychol.* 18:906–921.

LUCK, S.J., FAN, S., AND HILLYARD, S.A. (1993). Attention-related modulation of sensory-evoked brain activity in a visual search task. *J. Cogn. Neurosci.* 5:188–195.

LURIA, A.R. (1968). *The Mind of a Mnemonist: A Little Book About a Vast Memory.* New York: Basic Books.

MACCOBY, E., AND JACKLIN, C. (1974). *The Psychology of Sex Differences.* Stanford, CA: Stanford University Press.

MACKAY, D.G. (1987). *The Organization of Perception and Action: A Theory for Language and Other Cognitive Skills.* New York: Springer.

MACLEOD, C. (1991). Half a century of research on the Stroop effect: An integrative review. *Psych. Bull.* 109:163–203.

MALMO, R. (1942). Interference factors in delayed response in monkeys after removal of frontal lobes. *J. Neurophysiol.* 5:295–308.

MANGUN, G.R., AND HILLYARD, S.A. (1991). Modulations of sensory-evoked brain potentials indicate changes in perceptual processing during visual-spatial priming. *J. Exp. Psychol. Hum. Percept. Perform.* 17:1057–1074.

MANGUN, G.R., HILLYARD, S., AND LUCK, S. (1993). Electrocortical Substrates of Visual Selective Attention. In D.E. Meyer and S. Kornblum (Eds.), *Attention and Performance XIV: Synergies in Experimental Psychology, Artificial Intelligence, and Cognitive Neuroscience* (pp. 219–243). Cambridge, MA: MIT Press.

MARCEL, A. (1983a). Conscious and unconscious perception: Experiments on visual masking and word recognition. *Cogn. Psychol.* 15:197–237.

MARCEL, A. (1983b). Conscious and unconscious perception: An approach to the relations between phenomenal experience and perceptual processes. *Cogn. Psychol.* 15:238–300.

MARLER, P. (1991). Song-learning Behavior: The interface with neuroethology. *Trends Neurosci.* 14:199–206.

MARR, D. (1982). Vision: *A Computational Investigation into the Human Representation and Processing of Visual Information.* San Francisco: Freeman.

MARR, D., AND NISHIHARA, H.K. (1992). Visual Information Processing: Artificial Intelligence and the Sensorium of Sight. In S.M. Kosslyn and R.A. Andersen (Eds.), *Frontiers in Cognitive Neuroscience* (pp. 165–186). Cambridge, MA: MIT Press.

MARSLEN-WILSON, W., AND TYLER, L.K. (1980). The temporal structure of spoken language understanding. *Cognition* 8:1–71.

MARSOLEK, C., KOSSLYN, S., AND SQUIRE, L. (1992). Form-specific visual priming in the right cerebral hemisphere. *J. Exp. Psychol. Learn. Mem. Cogn.* 18:492–508.

MARSOLEK, C.J. (1995). Abstract visual-form representations in the left cerebral hemisphere. *J. Exp. Psychol. Hum. Percept. Perform.* 21:375–386.

MARSOLEK, C.J., KOSSLYN, S.M., AND SQUIRE, L.R. (1992). Form-specific visual priming in the right cerebral hemisphere. *J. Exp. Psychol. Learn. Mem. Cogn.* 8:492–508.

MARTIN, A., HAXBY, J.V., LALONDE, F.M., WIGGS, C.L., AND UNGERLEIDER, L.G. (1995). Discrete cortical regions associated with knowledge of color and knowledge of action. *Science* 270:102–105.

MAUNSELL, J.H.R., AND VAN ESSEN, D.C. (1983). Functional properties of neurons in middle temporal visual area of the macaque monkey. I. Selectivity for stimulus direction, speed, and orientation. *J. Neurophysiol.* 49:1127–1147.

MCCARTHY, G., BLAMIRE, A.M., PUCE, A., NOBE, A.C., BLOCH, G., HYDER, F., GOLDMAN-RAKIC, P., AND SHULMAN, R.G. (1994). Functional magnetic resonance imaging of human prefrontal cortex activation during a spatial working memory task. *Proc. Natl. Acad. Sci. U.S.A.* 91:8690–8694.

MCCARTHY, R., AND WARRINGTON, E.K. (1986). Visual associative agnosia: A clinico-anatomical study of a single case. *J. Neurol. Neurosurg. Psychiatry* 49:1233–1240.

MCCLELLAND, J.L., AND RUMMELHART, D.E. (1986). *Parallel Distributed Processing: Explorations in the Microstructure of Cognition. Vol. 2: Psychological and Biological Models.* Cambridge, MA: MIT Press.

MCEWEN, B.S. (1995). Stressful Experience, Brain, and Emotions: Developmental, Genetic, and Hormonal Influences. In M.S. Gazzaniga (Ed.), *The Cognitive Neurosciences* (pp. 1117–1135). Cambridge, MA: MIT Press.

MCGINN, C. (1991). *The problem of consciousness: Essays towards a resolution.* Cambridge, MA: Blackwell.

MCGUIRE, M.T., RALEIGH, M.J., AND BRAMMER, G.L. (1984). Adaptation, selection, and benefit-cost balances: Implications of behavioral-physiological studies of social dominance in male vervet monkeys. Symposium of the IXth International Congress of Primatology: The study of the adaptiveness of aggressive, dominance, and conflict resolution strategies in humans and nonhuman primates (1982, Atlanta, GA). *Ethnol. Sociobiol.* 5:269–277.

MCNEIL, J.E., AND WARRINGTON, E.K. (1993). Prosopagnosia: A face-specific disorder. *Q. J. Exp. Psychol.* A 46:1–10.

MEADOWS, J.C. (1974). Disturbed perception of colours associated with localized cerebral lesions. *Brain* 97:615–632.

MERZENICH, M., AND JENKINS, W.M. (1995). Cortical Plasticity, Learning and Learning Dysfunction. In B. Julesz and I. Kovacs (Eds.), *Maturational Windows and Adult Cortical Plasticity* (pp. 1–24). Addison-Wesley.

MERZENICH, M., RECANZONE, G., JENKINS, W., ALLARD, T., AND NUDO, R. (1988). Cortical Representational Plasticity. In P. Rakic and W. Singer (Eds.), *Neurobiology of Neocortex* (pp. 41–67). New York: John Wiley and Sons.

METTER, E.J. (1995). PET in Aphasia and Language. In H.S. Kirsner (Ed.), *Handbook of Neurological Speech and Language Disorders. Neurological Disease and Therapy. Vol. 33.* New York: Marcel Dekker.

MIDDLETON, F.A., AND STRICK, P.L. (1994). Anatomical evidence for cerebellar and basal ganglia involvement in higher cognitive function. *Science* 266:458–461.

MILBERG, W., AND BLUMSTEIN, S.E. (1981). Lexical decision and aphasia: Evidence for semantic processing. *Brain Lang.* 14:371–385.

MILLER, G. (1951). *Language and Communication.* New York: McGraw-Hill, Inc.

MILLER, G. (1962). *Psychology, the Science of Mental Life.* New York: Harper and Row.

MILLER, G. (1994). The magical number seven, plus or minus two: Some limits on our capacity for processing information. *Psychol. Rev.* 101:343–352.

MILNER, B. (1995). Aspects of human frontal lobe function. *Adv. Neurol.* 66:67–84.

MILNER, B., CORKIN, S., AND TEUBER, H. (1968). Further analysis of the hippocampal amnesic syndrome: 14-year follow-up study of HM. *Neuropsychologia* 6:215–234.

MILNER, B., CORSI, P., AND LEONARD, G. (1991). Frontal-lobe contributions to recency judgements. *Neuropsychologia* 29:601–618.

MISHKIN, M. (1978). Memory in monkeys severely impaired by combined but not by separate removal of amygdala and hippocampus. *Nature* 273:297–298.

MORAN, J., AND DESIMONE, R. (1985). Selective attention gates visual processing in extrastriate cortex. *Science* 229:782–784.

MORAY, N. (1959) Attention in dichotic listening: Effective cues and the influence of instructions. *Q. J. Exp. Psychol.* 9:56–60.

MORRIS, R.G.M., ANDERSON, E., LYNCH, G., AND BAUDRY, M. (1986). Selective impairment of learning and blockade of long-term potentiation by an N-methyl-D-aspartate receptor antagonist, AP5. *Nature* 319:774–776.

MORUZZI, G., AND MAGOUN, H.W. (1949). Brainstem reticular formation and activation of the EEG. *Electroencephalogr. Clin. Neurophysiol.* 1:455–473.

MOUNTCASTLE, V. (Ed.) (1980). *Medical Physiology*, 14th edition. St. Louis: Mosby.

MOUNTCASTLE, V.B. (1976).The world around us: Neural command functions for selective attention. *Neurosci. Res. Prog. Bull.* 14(suppl):1–47.

MUKERJEE, M. (1997). Trends in animal research. *Sci. Am.* 276:86–93.

MÜNTE, T.F., HEINZE, H.-J., AND MANGUN, G.R. (1993). Dissociation of brain activity related to semantic and syntactic aspects of language. *J. Cogn. Neurosci.* 5:335–344.

MUSHIAKE, H., MASAHIKO, I., AND TANJI, J. (1991). Neuronal activity in the primate premotor, supplementary, and precentral motor cortex during visually guided and internally determined sequential movements. *J. Neurophysiol.* 66:705–718.

MYERS, J.J., AND SPERRY, R.W. (1985). Interhemispheric communication after section of the forebrain commissures. *Cortex* 21:249–260.

MYERS, R.E., SWETT, C., AND MILLER, M. (1973). Loss of social group affinity following prefrontal lesions in free-ranging macaques. *Brain Res.* 64:257–269.

NAKAYAMA, K., AND SILVERMAN, G.H. (1986). Serial and parallel processing of visual feature conjunctions. *Nature* 320:264–265.

NASS, R.D., AND GAZZANIGA, M.S. (1987). Cerebral Lateralization and Specialization in Human Central Nervous System. In V.B. Mountcastle, F. Plum, and S.R. Geiger (Eds.), *Handbook of Physiology*, Vol. 5 (pp. 701–761). Bethesda: American Physiological Society.

NAVON, D. (1977). Forest before trees: The precedence of global features in visual perception. *Cogn. Psychol.* 9:353–383.

NEISSER, U. (1982). Snapshots or Benchmarks? In U. Neisser (Ed.), *Memory Observed: Remembering in Natural Contexts.* New York: W.H. Freeman.

NEISSER, U., AND HARSCH, N. (1992). Phantom Flashbulbs: False Recollections of Hearing the News about Challenger. In E. Winograd and U. Neisser (Eds.), *Affect and Accuracy in Recall: Studies of "Flashbulb" Memories* (pp. 9–31). New York: Cambridge University Press.

NEISSER, V. (1967). *Cognitive Psychology.* New York: Appleton, Century, Crofts.

NESSE, R.M., AND WILLIAMS, G.C. (1996). *Why we get sick: The new science of Darwinian medicine.* New York: Vintage Books.

NETTER, F.H. (1983). *The CIBA Collection of Medical Illustrations. Vol I: Nervous System, Part 1: Anatomy and Physiology.* Summit, NJ: CIBA Pharmaceutical.

NEVILLE, H. (1995). Developmental Specificity in Neurocognitive Development in Humans. In M.S. Gazzaniga (Ed.), *The Cognitive Neurosciences* (pp. 219–234). Cambridge, MA: MIT Press.

NEWSOME, W.T., AND PARE, E.B. (1988). A selective impairment of motion perception following lesions of the middle temporal visual area (MT). *J. Neurosci.* 8:2201–2211.

NEWSOME, W.T., SHADLEN, M.N., ZOHARY, E., BRITTEN, K.H., AND MOVSHON, J.A. (1995). Visual Motion: Linking Neuronal Activity to Psychophysical Performance. In M.S. Gazzaniga (Ed.), *The Cognitive Neurosciences* (pp. 401–414). Cambridge, MA: MIT Press.

NISBETT, R.E., ROSS, L. (1980). *Human inference: Strategies and shortcomings of social judgment. Englewood Cliffs, NJ:* Prentice-Hall.

NISSEN, M.J., KNOPMAN, D.S., AND SCHACTER, D.L. (1987). Neurochemical dissociation of memory systems. *Neurology* 37:789–794.

NORMAN, D., AND SHALLICE, T. (1980). *Attention to Action: Willed and Automatic Control of Behavior.* Center for Human Information Processing Report 99. La Jolla, CA: University of California, San Diego.

NORMAN, D.A., AND SHALLICE, T. (1986). Attention to Action: Willed and Automatic Control of Behavior. In R.J. Davidson, G.E. Schwartz, and D. Shapiro (Eds.), *Consciousness and Self-Regulation*, Vol. 4 (pp. 1–18). New York: Plenum Press.

NOTTEBOHM, F. (1980). Brain pathways for vocal learning in birds: A review of the first 10 years. *Prog. Psychobiol. Physiol. Psychol.* 9:85–124.

NYBERG, L., MCINTOSH, A., CABEZA, R., HABIB, R., HOULE, S., AND TULVING, E. (1996). General and specific brain regions involved in encoding and retrieval of events: What, where, and when. *Proc. Natl. Acad. Sci. U.S.A.* 93:11280–11285.

OJEMANN, G., OJEMANN, J., LETTICH, E., AND BERGER, M. (1989). Cortical language localization in left, dominant hemisphere. *J. Neurosurg.* 71:316–326.

OWEN, A.M., ROBERTS, A.C., HODGES, J.R., SUMMERS, B.A., POLKEY, C.E., AND ROBBINS, T.W. (1993). Contrasting mechanisms of impaired attentional set-shifting in patients with frontal lobe damage or Parkinson's disease. *Brain* 116:1159–1175.

PALLER, K., KUTAS, M., AND MCISAAC, H. (1995). Monitoring conscious recollection via the electrical activity of the brain. *Psychol. Sci.* 6:107–111.

PALLIS, C.A. (1955). Impaired identification of faces and places with agnosia for colors. *J. Neurol. Neurosurg. Psychiatry.* 18:218–224.

PASCUAL-LEONE, A., GOMEZ-TORTOSA, E., GRAFMAN, J., ALWAY, D.P.N., AND HALLETT, M. (1994). Induction of visual extinction by rapid-rate transcranial magnetic stimulation of parietal lobe. *Neurology* 44:494–498.

PASSINGHAM, R. (1993). *The Frontal Lobes and Voluntary Action.* New York: Oxford University Press.

PASSINGHAM, R.E. (1982). *The Human Primate.* Oxford, UK: W.H. Freeman.

PAULESU, E., FRITH, D.D., AND FRACKOWIAK, R.S.J. (1993). The neural correlates of the verbal component of working memory. *Nature* 362:342–345.

PENFIELD, W., AND JASPER, H. (1954). *Epilepsy and the Functional Anatomy of the Human Brain.* Boston: Little and Brown.

PERETZ, I., KOLINSKY, R., TRAMO, M., LABRECQUE, R., HUBLET, C., DEMEURISSE, G., AND BELLEVILLE, S. (1994). Functional dissociations following bilateral lesions of auditory cortex. *Brain* 117:1283–1301.

PERRETT, D.I., ORAM, M.W., HIETANEN, J.K., AND BENSON, P.J. (1994). Issues of Representations in Object Vision. In M.J. Farah and G. Ratcliff (Eds.), *The Neuropsychology of High-Level Vision: Collected Tu-*

torial Essays (pp. 33–62). Hillsdale, NJ: Lawrence Erlbaum Associates.

PERRETT, S., RUIZ, B., AND MAUK, M. (1993). Cerebellar cortex lesions disrupt learning-dependent timing of conditioned eyelid responses. *J. Neurosci.* 13:1708–1718.

PETERSEN, L.R., AND PETERSEN, M.R. (1959). Short-term retention of individual verbal items. *J. Exp. Psychol.* 58:193–198.

PETERSEN, S.E., AND FIEZ, J.A. (1993). The processing of single words studied with positron emission tomography. *Ann. Rev. Neurosci.* 16:509–530.

PETERSEN, S.E., FIEZ, J.A., AND CORBETTA, M. (1992). Neuroimaging. *Curr. Opin. Neurobiol.* 2:217–222.

PETERSEN, S.E., FOX, P.T., POSNER, M.I., MINTUN, M., AND RAICHLE, M. (1988). Positron emission tomographic studies of the cortical anatomy of single-word processing. *Nature* 331:585–589.

PETERSEN, S.E., FOX, P.T., SNYDER, A.Z., AND RAICHLE, M.E. (1990). Activation of extrastriate and frontal cortical areas by visual words and word-like stimuli. *Science* 249:1041–1044.

PETERSEN, S.E., ROBINSON, D.L., AND MORRIS, J.D. (1987). Contributions of the pulvinar to visual spatial attention. *Neuropsychologia* 25:97–105.

PETRIDES, M. (1994). Frontal lobes and behaviour. *Curr. Opin. Neurobiol.* 4:207–211.

PINKER, S. (1987). The Bootstrapping Problem in Language Acquisition. In B. MacWhinney (Ed.), *Mechanisms of Language Acquisition* (pp. 399–441). Hillsdale, NJ: Lawrence Erlbaum Associates.

PINKER, S. (1994). *The Language Instinct.* New York: W. Morrow. (pp. 370–403)

PINKER, S. (1995). Facts about Human Language Relevant to Its Evolution. In J. Changeux and J. Chavaillon (Eds.), *Origins of the Human Brain. Symposia of the Fyssen Foundation* (pp. 262–285). Oxford, UK: Clarendon Press/Oxford University Press.

PINKER, S. (1997a). *How the Mind Works.* New York: W.W. Norton.

PINKER, S.W. (1997b). Interview in M.S. Gazzaniga's *Conversations in Cognitive Neuroscience.* Cambridge, MA: MIT Press.

PODGORNY, P., AND SHEPARD, R. (1978). Functional representations common to visual perception and imagination. *J. Exp. Psychol. Hum. Percept. Perform.* 4:21–35.

POHL, W. (1973). Dissociation of spatial discrimination deficits following frontal and parietal lesions in monkeys. *J. Comp. Physiol. Psychol.* 82:227–239.

POSNER, M. (1994). Attention: The mechanisms of consciousness. *Proc. Natl. Acad. Sci. U.S.A.* 91:7398–7403.

POSNER, M.I. (1986). *Chronometric Explorations of Mind.* New York: Oxford University Press.

POSNER, M.I., AND RAICHLE, M.E. (1994). *Images of Mind.* New York: W.H. Freeman.

POSNER, M.I., AND ROTHBART, M. (1980). The development of attentional mechanisms. In J.H. Flowers (Ed.), *Nebraska Symposium on Motivation* (Volume 28). Lincoln, Nebraska: Univ. of Nebraska Press.

POSNER, M.I., SNYDER, C.R.R., AND DAVIDSON, J. (1980). Attention and the detection of signals. *J. Exp. Psychol. Gen.* 109:160–174.

POSNER, M.I., WALKER, J.A., FRIEDRICH, F.J., AND RAFAL, B.D. (1984). Effects of parietal injury on covert orienting of attention. *J. Neurosci.* 4:1863–1874.

POVEL, D.J., AND COLLARD, R. (1982). Structural factors in patterned finger tapping. *Acta Psychologia* 52:107–123.

POVINELLI, D.J., NELSON, K.E., AND BOYSEN, S.T. (1990). Inferences about guessing and knowing by chimpanzees (*Pan troglodytes*). *J. Comp. Psychol.* 104:203–210.

POVINELLI, D.J., RULF, A.B., AND BIERSCHWALE, D.T. (1994). Absence of knowledge attribution and self-recognition in young chimpanzees. *J. Comp. Psychol.* 108:74–80.

PREMACK, D., AND WOODRUFF, G. (1978). Does the chimpanzee have a theory of mind? *Behav. Brain Sci.* 1:515–526.

PREUSS, T.M. (1995). The Argument from Animals to Humans on Cognitive Neuroscience. In M.S. Gazzaniga (Ed.), *The Cognitive Neurosciences* (pp. 1227–1241). Cambridge, MA: MIT Press.

PREVIC, F.H. (1991). A general theory concerning the prenatal origins of cerebral lateralization in humans. *Psychol. Rev.* 98:299–334.

PTITO, A., LEPORE, F., PTITO, M., AND LASSONDE, M. (1991). Target detection and movement discrimination in the blind field of hemispherectomized patients. *Brain* 114:497–512.

RAFAL, R., AND POSNER, M.I. (1987). Deficits in human visual spatial field following thalamic lesions. *Proc. Natl. Acad. Sci. U.S.A.* 84:7349–7353.

RAFAL, R., SMITH, J., KRANTZ, J., COHEN, A., AND BRENNAN, C. (1990). Extrageniculate vision in hemianopic humans: Saccade inhibition by signals in the blind field. *Science* 250:118–121.

RAICHLE, M.E. (1994). Visualizing the mind. *Sci. Am.* 270:58–64.

RAICHLE, M.E., FIEZ, J.A., VIDEEN, T.O., MACLEOD, A.K., PARDO, J.V., FOX, P.T., AND PETERSEN, S.E. (1994). Practice-related changes in human brain functional anatomy during nonmotor learning. *Cerebral Cortex* 4:8–26.

RAKIC, P. (1995a). Corticogenesis in Human and Nonhuman Primates. In M.S. Gazzaniga (Ed.), *The Cognitive Neurosciences* (pp. 127–146). Cambridge, MA: MIT Press.

RAKIC, P. (1995b). A small step for the cell, a giant leap for mankind: A hypothesis of neocortical expansion during evolution. *Trends Neurosci.* 18:383–388.

RALEIGH, M.J. (1987). Differential behavioral effects of tryptophan and 5-hydroxytryptophan in vervet monkeys: Influence of catecholaminergic systems. *Psychopharmacol.* 93:44–50.

RAMACHANDRAN V.S. (1993). Behavioral and magnetoencephalographic correlates of plasticity in the adult human brain. *Proc. Natl. Acad. Sci. U.S.A.* 90:10413–10420.

RAMACHANDRAN, V.S. (1988). Perceiving shape from shading. *Sci. Am.* 259:76–83.

RAMOA A.S., CAMPBELL G., AND SHATZ, C.J. (1988). Dendritic growth and remodeling of cat retinal ganglion cells during fetal and postnatal development. *J. Neurosci.* 8:4239–4261.

RECANZONE, G., SCHREINER, C.E., AND MERZENICH, M. (1993). Plasticity in the frequency representation of primary auditory cortex following discrimination training in adult owl monkeys. *J. Neurosci.* 13:87–103.

REICHER, G.M. (1969). Perceptual recognition as a function of meaningfulness of stimulus material. *J. Exp. Psychol.* 81:275–280.

REMPEL-CLOWER, N., ZOLA, S., SQUIRE, L., AND AMARAL, D. (1996). Three cases of enduring memory impairment after bilateral damage limited to the hippocampal formation. *J. Neurosci.* 16:5233–5255.

RIDDOCH, G. (1917). Dissociation of visual perceptions due to occipital injuries, with especial reference to appreciation of movement. *Brain* 40:15–47.

RINGO, J.L., DOTY, R.W., DEMETER, S., AND SIMARD, P.Y. (1994). Time is of the essence: A conjecture that hemispheric specialization arises from interhemispheric conduction delays. *Cereb. Cortex* 4:331–343.

RIZZOLATTI, G., GENTILUCCI, M., FOGASSI, L., LUPPINO, G., MATELLI, M., AND CAMARDA, R. (1988). Functional organization of inferior area 6 in the macaque monkey. *Exp. Brain Res.* 71:465–490.

ROBERTSON, L.C., KNIGHT, R.T., RAFAL, R., AND SHIMAMURA, A.P. (1993). Cognitive neuropsychology is more than single-case studies. *J. Exp. Psychol. Learn. Mem. Cogn.* 19:710–717.

ROBERTSON, L.C., LAMB, M.R., AND KNIGHT, R.T. (1988).

Effects of lesions of temporal-parietal junction on perceptual and attentional processing in humans. *J. Neurosci.* 8:3757–3769.

ROBERTSON, L.C., LAMB, M.R., AND ZAIDEL, E. (1993). Inter-hemispheric relations in processing hierarchical patterns: Evidence from normal and commissurotomized subjects. *Neuropsychology* 7:325–342.

ROBINSON, D.L., AND PETERSEN, S. (1992). The pulvinar and visual salience. *Trends Neurosci.* 15:127–132.

ROBINSON, D.L., GOLDBERG, M.E., AND STANTON, G.B. (1978). Parietal association cortex in the primate: Sensory mechanisms and behavioral modulation. *J. Neurophysiol.* 41:910–932.

ROCK, I. (1995). *Perception.* New York: W.H. Freeman.

ROLAND, P.E. (1993). *Brain Activation.* New York: Wiley-Liss.

ROSE, J.E., HIND, J.E., ANDERSON, D.J., AND BRUGGE, J.F. (1971). Some effects of stimulus intensity on response of auditory nerve fibers in the squirrel monkey. *J. Neurophysiol.* 24:685–699.

ROSENBAUM, D.A., SLOTTA, J.D., VAUGHAN, J., AND PLAMON-DON, R. (1991). Optimal movement selection. *Psychol. Sci.* 2:86–91.

ROSENZWEIG, M.R., LEIMAN, A.L., AND BREEDLOVE, S.M. (1996). *Biological Psychology.* Sunderland, MA: Sinaur Associates.

ROTHWELL, J.C., TRAUB, M.M., DAY, B.L., OBESO, J.A., THOMAS, P.K., AND MARSDEN, C.D. (1982). Manual motor performance in a deafferented man. *Brain* 105:515–542.

ROVET, J., AND NETELY, C. (1982). Processing deficits in Turner's syndrome. *Dev. Psychol.* 18:77–94.

ROWAN, A.N., AND ROLLIN, B.E. (1983). Animal research—For and against: A philosophical, social, and historical perspective. *Perspect. Biol. Med.* 27:1–17.

RUMMELHART, D.E., McCLELLAND, J.L., and the PDP Research Group. (1986). *Parallel Distributed Processing: Explorations in the Microstructure of Cognition. Vol. 1: Foundations.* Cambridge, MA: MIT Press.

SADATO, N., PASCUAL-LEONE, A., GRAFMAN, J., IBANEZ, V., DEIBER, M-P., DOLD, G., AND HALLETT, M. (1996). Activation of the primary visual cortex by Braille reading in blind subjects. *Nature* 380:526–528.

SAMS, M., HARI, R., RIF, J., AND KNUUTILA, J. (1993). The human auditory sensory memory trace persists about 10 sec—Neuromagnetic evidence. *J. Cogn. Neurosci.* 5:363–370.

SATORI, G., AND JOB, R. (1988). The oyster with four legs: A neuropsychological study on the interaction of visual and semantic information. *Cog. Neuropsychol.* 5:105–132.

SAUCIER, D., AND CAIN, D.P. (1995). Spatial learning without NMDA receptor-dependent long-term potentiation. *Nature* 378:186–189.

SAYWITZ, K., GOODMAN, G., NICHOLAS, E., AND MOAN, S. (1991). Children's memories of a physical examination involving genital touch: Implications for reports of child sexual abuse. *J. Consult. Clin. Psychol.* 59:682–691.

SCHACTER, D., ALPERT, N., SAVAGE, C., RAUCH, S., et al. (1996). Conscious recollection and the human hippocampal formation—Evidence from positron emission tomography. *Proc. Natl. Acad. Sci. U.S.A.* 93:321–325.

SCHACTER, D., COOPER, L., AND DELANEY, S. (1990). Implicit memory for unfamiliar objects depends on access to structural descriptions. *J. Exp. Psychol. Gen.* 119:5–24.

SCHACTER, D.L. (1987). Implicit memory: History and current status. *J. Exp. Psychol. Learn. Mem. Cogn.* 113:501–518.

SCHILLER, P., AND LOGOTHETIS, N. (1990). The color-opponent and broad-band channels of the primate visual system. *Trends Neurosci.* 13:392–398.

SCHMIDT, R.A. (1987). The Acquisition of Skill: Some Modifica-

tions to the Perception-Action Relationship Through Practice. In H. Heuer and A.F. Sanders (Eds.), *Perspectives on Perception and Action* (pp. 77–103). Hillsdale, NJ: Lawrence Erlbaum Associates.

SCHNIEDER, G.E. (1969). Two visual systems. *Science* 163:895–902.

SCOVILLE, W.B. (1954). The limbic lobe in man. *J. Neurosurg.* 11:64–66.

SCOVILLE, W.B., AND MILNER, B. (1957). Loss of recent memory after bilateral hippocampal lesions. *J. Neurol. Neurosurg. Psychiatry* 20:11–21.

SEARLE, J. (1992). *The Rediscovery of Mind.* Cambridge, MA: MIT Press.

SEJNOWSKI, T.J., AND CHURCHLAND, P.S. (1989). Brain and Cognition. In M.I. Posner (Ed.), *Foundations of Cognitive Science* (pp. 301–356). Cambridge, MA: MIT Press.

SEKULER, R., AND BLAKE, R. (1990). *Perception,* 2nd edition. New York: McGraw-Hill, Inc.

SELFRIDGE, O.G. (1959). Pandemonium: A Paradigm for Learning. In *Proceedings of a Symposium on the Mechanisation of Thought Processes* (pp. 511–526). London: H.M. Stationary Office.

SERGENT, J. (1982). The cerebral balance of power: Confrontation or cooperation: *J. Exp. Psychol. Hum. Percept. Perform.* 8:253–272.

SERGENT, J. (1985). Influence of task and input factors on hemispheric involvement in face processing. *J. Exp. Psychol. Hum. Percept. Perform.* 11:846–861.

SHALLICE, T., AND BURGESS, W. (1991). Deficits in strategy application following frontal lobe damage in man. *Brain* 114:727–741.

SHALLICE, T., AND WARRINGTON, E. (1969). Independent functioning of verbal memory stores: A neuropsychological study. *Q. J. Exp. Psychol.* 22:261–273.

SHALLICE, T., BURGESS, P.W., SCHON, F., AND BAXTER, D.M. (1989). The origins of utilization behaviour. *Brain* 112:1587–1598.

SHEPHERD, G.M. (1992). *Foundations of the Neuron Doctrine.* New York: Oxford University Press.

SHEPHERD, G.M., WOOLF, T.B., AND CARNEVALE, N.T.L. (1989). Comparisons between active properties and distal dendritic branches and spines: Implications for neuronal computations. *J. Cogn. Neurosci.* 1:273–286.

SHERRINGTON, C. (1947). *The Integrative Action of the Nervous System,* 2nd edition. New Haven: Yale University Press.

SHERRINGTON, C.S. (1935). Santiago Ramón y Cajal 1852–1934. *Obit Not. R. Soc.* 4:425–441.

SHERRY, D.F., JACOBS, L.F., AND GAULIN, S.J. (1992). Spatial memory and adaptive specialization of the hippocampus. *Trends Neurosci.* 15:298–303.

SHIMAMURA, A.P. (1995). Memory and Frontal Lobe Function. In M.S. Gazzaniga (Ed.), *The Cognitive Neurosciences* (pp. 803–813). Cambridge, MA: MIT Press.

SIGNORET, J–L., CASTAIGNE, P., LEHERMITTE, F., ABELANET, R., and LAVOREL, P. (1984). Rediscovery of Legorgre's brain: Anatomical description with CT scan. *Brain Lang.* 22:303–319.

SKINNER, J.E., AND YINGLING, C.D. (1976). Regulation of slow potential shifts in nucleus reticularis thalami by the mesencephalic reticular formation and the frontal granular cortex. *Electroencephalogr. Clin. Neurophysiol.* 40:288–296.

SMITH, E.E., AND JONIDES, J. (1994). Working Memory in Humans: Neuropsychological Evidence. In M.S. Gazzaniga (Ed.), *The Cognitive Neurosciences* (pp. 1009–1020). Cambridge, MA: MIT Press.

SNODGRASS, J.G., AND VANDERWART, M. (1980). A standardized set of 260 pictures: Norms for name agreement, image agreement, familiarity, and visual complexity. *J. Exp. Psychol. Hum. Learn. Mem.* 6:174–215.

SNYDER, A.Z., ABDULLAEV, Y.G., POSNER, M.I., AND RAICHLE,

M.E. (1995). Scalp electrical potentials reflect regional cerebral blood flow responses during processing of written words. *Proc. Natl. Acad. Sci. U.S.A.* 92:1689–1693.

SPELKE, E., HIRST, W., AND NEISSER, U. (1976). Skills of divided attention. *Cognition* 4:215–230.

SPERLING, G. (1960). The information available in brief visual presentations. *Psychol. Monogr. Gen. Appl.* 74:1–29.

SPERRY, R.W., GAZZANIGA, M.S., AND BOGEN, J.E. (1969). Inter-hemispheric relationships: The neocortical commissures; syndromes of hemisphere disconnection. In P.J. Vinken and G.W. Bruyn (Eds.), *Handbook of Clinical Neurology, Vol. 4* (pp. 273–290). Amsterdam: North-Holland Publishing Company; New York: John Wiley and Sons.

SQUIRE, L. (1987). *Prefrontal Cortex, Memory and Brain.* New York: Oxford University Press.

SQUIRE, L.R. (1987). *Memory and Brain.* New York: Oxford University Press.

SQUIRE, L.R., AND KNOWLTON, B.J. (1995). Memory, Hippocampus, and Brain Systems. In M.S. Gazzaniga (Ed.), *The Cognitive Neurosciences* (pp. 825–837). Cambridge, MA: MIT Press.

SQUIRE, L.R., AND SLATER, P. (1983). Electroconvulsive therapy and complaints of memory dysfunction: A prospective three-year follow-up study. *Br. J. Psychiatry* 142:1–8.

SQUIRE, L.R., OJEMANN, J.G., MIEZIN, F.M., PETERSEN, S.E., VIDEEN, T.O., AND RAICHLE, M.E. (1992). Activation of the hippocampus in normal humans: A functional anatomical study of memory. *Proc. Natl. Acad. Sci. U.S.A.* 89:1837–1841.

STERNBERG, S. (1966). High speed scanning in human memory. *Science* 153:652–654.

STERNBERG, S. (1975). Memory scanning: New findings and current controversies. *Q. J. Exp. Psychol.* 27:1–32.

STROOP, J. (1935). Studies of interference in serial verbal reaction. *J. Exp. Psychol.* 18:643–662.

SWAAB, T.Y., BROWN, C.M., AND HAGOORT, P. (1997). Spoken sentence comprehension in aphasia: Event-related potential evidence for a lexical integration deficit. *J. Cogn. Neurosci.* 9:39–66.

TAUB, E., AND BERMAN, A.J. (1968). Movement and Learning in the Absence of Sensory Feedback. In S.J. Freedman (Ed.), *The Neuropsychology of Spatially Oriented Behavior* (pp. 173–191). Homewood, IL: Dorsey.

THACH, W.T. (1975). Timing of activity in cerebellar dentate nucleus and cerebral motor cortex during prompt volitional movements. *Brain Res.* 88:233–241.

THORNDIKE, E. (1911). Animal Intelligence: An Experimental Study of the Associative Processes in Animals. New York: MacMillian.

TOOBY, J., AND COSMIDES, L. (1995). Mapping the Evolved Functional Organization of Mind and Brain. In M.S. Gazzaniga (Ed.), *The Cognitive Neurosciences.* Cambridge, MA: MIT Press.

TOOTELL, R.B., REPPA, J.B., KWONG, K.K., MALACH, R., BORN, R.T., BRADY, T.J., ROSEN, B.R., AND BELLIVEAU, J.W. (1995). Functional analysis of human MT and related visual cortical areas during magnetic resonance imaging. *J. Neurosci.* 15:3215–3230.

TOOTELL, R.B., SILVERMAN, M.S., SWITKES, E., AND DEVALOIS, R.L. (1982). Deoxyglucose analysis of retinotopic organization in primate striate cortex. *Science* 218:902–904.

TREISMAN, A. (1988). Features and objects: The Fourteenth Bartlett Memorial Lecture. *Q. J. Exp. Psychol. A* 40:201–237.

TREISMAN, A., AND GELADE, G. (1980). A feature-integration theory of attention. *Cogn. Psychol.* 12:97–136.

TREISMAN, A.M. (1969). Strategies and models of selective attention. *Psychol. Rev.* 76:282–299.

TRIVERS, R.L. (1971). The evolution of reciprocal altruism. *Q. Rev. Biol.* 46:35–57.

TULVING, E. (1995). Organization of memory: Quo vadis? In M.S. Gazzaniga (Ed.), *The Cognitive Neurosciences* (pp. 839–847). Cambridge, MA: MIT Press.

TULVING, E., AND SHACTER, D.L. (1990). Priming and human memory systems. *Science* 247:301–306.

TULVING, E., GORDON HAYMAN, C.A., AND MACDONALD, C.A. (1991). Long-lasting perceptual priming and semantic learning in amnesia. A case experiment. *J. Exp. Psychol.* 17:595–617.

TULVING, E., KAPUR, S., CRAIK, F.I.M., MOSCOVITCH, M., AND HOULE, S. (1994). Hemispheric encoding/retrieval asymmetry in episodic memory: Positron emission tomography findings. *Proc. Natl. Acad. Sci. U.S.A.* 91:2016–2020.

UNGERLEIDER, L.G., AND HAXBY, J.V. (1994). "What" and "where" in the human brain. *Curr. Opin. Neurobiol.* 4:157–165.

UNGERLEIDER, L.G., AND MISHKIN, M. (1982). Two Cortical Visual Systems. In D.J. Engle, M.A. Goodale, and R.J. Mansfield (Eds.), *Analysis of Visual Behavior* (pp. 549–586). Cambridge, MA: MIT Press.

UPDIKE, J. (1989). *Self-consciousness: Memoirs.* New York: Knopf.

VALENSTEIN, E.S. (1986). *Great and Desperate Cures: The Rise and Decline of Psychosurgery and Other Radical Treatments for Mental Illness.* New York: Basic Books.

VAN ESSEN, D.C., AND DEYOE, E.A. (1995). Concurrent Processing in the Primate Visual Cortex. In M.S. Gazzaniga (Ed.), *The Cognitive Neurosciences* (pp. 383–400). Cambridge, MA: MIT Press.

VOLPE, B.T., LEDOUX, J.E., AND GAZZANIGA, M.S. (1979). Information processing of visual field stimuli in an "extinguished" field. *Nature* 282:722–724.

VON HELMHOLTZ, H. (1894). Handbuch der Physiologischen Optik. Leipzig: L. Vos., Hamburg, Germany. (See Van der Heijden, A.C.H. (1992). *Selective Attention in Vision* (pp. 32–33). London: Routledge.)

WAPNER, W., JUDD, T., AND GARDNER, H. (1978). Visual agnosia in an artist. *Cortex* 14:343–364.

WARRINGTON, E., AND SHALLICE, T. (1969). The selective impairment of auditory verbal short-term memory. *Brain* 92:885–896.

WARRINGTON, E.K. (1982). Neuropsychological studies of object recognition. *Phil. Transact. Royal Soc. London, Section B* 298:13–33.

WARRINGTON, E.K. (1985). Agnosia: The Impairment of Object Recognition. In P.J. Vinken, G.W. Bruyn, and H.L. Klawans (Eds.), *Handbook of Clinical Neurology* (pp. 333–349). New York: Elsevier Science.

WARRINGTON, E.K., AND SHALLICE, T. (1984). Category specific semantic impairments. *Brain* 107:829–854.

WARRINGTON, E.K., AND TAYLOR, A.M. (1978). Two categorical stages of object recognition. *Perception* 7:695–705.

WARRINGTON, E.K., AND MCCARTHY, R. (1983). Category specific access dysphasia. *Brain* 106:859–878.

WARRINGTON, E.K., AND MCCARTHY, R. (1987). Categories of knowledge: Further fractionation and an attempted integration. *Brain* 110:1273–1296.

WARRINGTON, E.K., AND MCCARTHY, R.A. (1994). Multiple meaning systems in the brain: A case for visual semantics. *Neuropsychologia* 32:1465–1473.

WARRINGTON, E.K., AND WHITELEY, A.M. (1977). Prosopagnosia: A clinical, psychological, and anatomical study of three patients. *J. Neurol. Neurosurg. Psychiatry* 40:395–403.

WAUGH, N.C., AND NORMAN, D.A. (1965). Primary memory. *Psychol. Rev.* 72:89–104.

WEINBERGER, D.R. (1988). Schizophrenia and the frontal lobes. *Trends Neurosci.* 11:367–370.

WEISKRANTZ, L. (1986). *Blindsight: A Case Study and Implications.* Oxford, UK: Oxford University Press.

WEISKRANTZ, L., WARRINGTON, E.K., SANDERS M.D., AND MARSHALL, J. (1974). Visual capacity in the hemianopic field following a restricted occipital ablation. *Brain* 97:709–728.

WENKE, R.J. (1980). *Patterns in Prehistory: Mankinds First Three Million Years.* New York: Oxford University Press.

WICHMANN, T., AND DELONG, M.R. (1996). Functional and pathophysiological models of the basal ganglia. *Curr. Opin. Neurobiol.* 6:751–758.

WIDNER, H., TZTRND, J., REHNERONA, S., SNOW, B.J., BRUMDIN, P., BJORKLURD, A., LINDVALL, O., AND LANGSTON, J. (1993). Fifteen months' follow-up on bilateral embryonic mesencephalic grafts in two cases of severe MPTP-induced parkinsonism. *Advances in Neurol.* 60:729–733.

WILKERSON, I. (August 21, 1987). Apparent lapse on wing flaps shocks experts. *New York Times* 136:A8.

WILLIAMS, G.C. (1966). *Adaptation and Natural Selection.* Princeton, NJ: Princeton University Press.

WILLIAMSON, A., SPENCER, D.D., AND SHEPHERD, G.M. (1993). Comparisons between the membrane and synaptic properties of human and rodent dentate granule cells. *Brain Res.* 622:194–202.

WILSON, E.O. (1994). *Naturalist.* Washington DC: Shearwater Books/Island Press.

WILSON, F.A., SCALAIDHE, S.P., AND GOLDMAN-RAKIC, P.S. (1993). Dissociation of object and spatial processing domains in primate prefrontal cortex. *Science* 260:1955–1958.

WILSON, M.A., AND MCNAUGHTON, B.L. (1994). Reactivation of hippocampal ensemble memories during sleep. *Science* 265:676–679.

WISE, S.P., DI PELLEGRINO, G., AND BOUSSAOUD, D. (1996). The premotor cortex and nonstandard sensorimotor mapping. *Can. J. Physiol. Pharmacol.* 74:469–482.

WOLDORFF, M.G., GALLEN, C.C., HAMPSON, S.A., HILLYARD, S.A., PANTEV, C., SOBEL, D., AND BLOOM, F.E. (1993). Modulation of early sensory processing in human auditory cortex during auditory selective attention. *Proc. Natl. Acad. Sci. U.S.A.* 90:8722–8726.

WOODARD, J.S. (1973). *Histologic Neuropathology: A Color Slide Set.* Orange, CA: California Medical Publications.

WURTZ, R.H., GOLDBERG, M.E., AND ROBINSON, D.L. (1982). Brain mechanisms of visual attention. *Sci. Am.* 246:124–135.

YINGLING, C.D., AND SKINNER, J.E. (1976). Selective regulation of thalamic sensory relay nuclei by nucleus reticularis thalami. *Electroencephalogr. Clin. Neurophysiol.* 41:476–482.

YOUDIM, M.B.H., AND RIEDERER, P. (1997). Understanding Parkinson's Disease. *Sci. Am.* 276:52–59.

ZEKI, S. (1993). *A Vision of the Brain.* Oxford, UK: Blackwell Scientific.

ZIHL, J., VON CRAMON, D., AND MAI, N. (1983). Selective disturbance of movement vision after bilateral brain damage. *Brain* 106:313–340.

ZOLA-MORGAN, S., SQUIRE, L.R., CLOWER, R.P., AND REMPEL, N.L. (1993). Damage to the perirhinal cortex exacerbates memory impairment following lesions to the hippocampal formation. *J. Neurosci.* 13:251–265.

ACKNOWLEDGMENTS AND CREDITS

About the cover Sean Scully, *Magdalena,* 1993. Oil on linen, 80 × 70". Courtesy of Mary Boone Gallery, New York.

PHOTOS

Chapter 1: **1.1A** Corbis-Bettmann. **1.2** General Research Division, New York Public Library, Astor, Lenox and Tilden Foundations. **1.3A** Mary Evans Picture Library. **1.3B** From Luciani, Luigi *Fisiologia del Homo.* Le Monnier, Firenze, 1901–1911. **1.4** Mary Evans Picture Library/Sigmund Freud Copyrights. **1.5A** New York Academy of Medicine. **1.6A** World Health Organization, Geneva, Switzerland. **1.6B** World Health Organization, Geneva, Switzerland. **1.6C** From *Arch. Anat. Physiol. Wiss. Medezin* (1852): 199–216. **1.8B** From Golgi, Camillo, *Untersuchungen über den Flineren Bau des Centralen und Peripherischen Nerven Systems.* Fisher, Jena, 1894. **1.9A** Corbis-Bettmann. **1.9B** From *Histologie du Système Nerveaux de l'Homme et de Vertébrés* by Santiago Ramón y Cajal. Maloine, Paris. 1909–1911. **1.11A** Science Photo Library/Photo Researchers, Inc. **1.12A** Courtesy National Library of Medicine, Bethesda, Maryland. **1.12B** From Sigmund Freud's Über den Bau der Nervenfasern und Nervenzellen beim Flusskrebs, *Sitz. Akad. Wiss.* 85 (1882): 9–14. Wien, Austria. **1.13A** Science Photo Library/Photo Researchers, Inc. **1.13B** From Budge, Julius, *Lehrbuch der Speciallen Physiologie des Menschen,* vol. 8 (1862). **1.14A,B, and C** Courtesy of Mary Brazier. **1.15** McHenry, L.C., Jr., *Garrison's History of Neurology.* Springfield, Illinois: Charles C. Thomas, Publisher, 1969, p. 206. © 1969 by Charles C. Thomas, Publisher. Courtesy of Professor O.L. Zangwill, Cambridge. **1.16** Courtesy National Library of Medicine, Bethesda,

Maryland. **1.17A** Underwood & Underwood/Corbis-Bettmann. **1.17B** Buckley, K.W., *Mechanical Man: John Broadus Watson and the Beginnings of Behaviorism.* New York: Guilford Press, 1989, figure 9. Courtesy Ben Harris. **1.18** Courtesy George Miller. **1.19** UPI/Corbis-Bettmann. **p. 10, left** © Copyright Museum Boerhaave, Leiden. **p. 10, right** Corbis-Bettmann. **p. 10,** Réunion des Musées Nationaux. **p. 10, left** Reprinted from *The Physiologist* (1981) with permission. **p. 10, right** From *Biological Bulletin* 40 (1921).

Chapter 2: **2.25** Finger, S., *Origins of Neuroscience.* Oxford University Press, 1994. Copyright © 1994 by Oxford University Press, Inc. Reprinted with permission. **2.30** Drury, H.A., Van Essen, D.C., Anderson, C.H., Lee, C.W., Coogan, T.A., and Lewis, J.W., Computerized Mappings of the Cerebral Cortex: A Multiresolution Flattening Method and a Surface-Based Coordinate System, *Journal of Cognitive Neuroscience* 8, no. 1 (1996): p. 13. © 1996 by the Massachusetts Institute of Technology. Reprinted by permission of MIT Press. **2.31** Wessinger, C.M., Buonocore, M.H., Kussmaul, C.L., and Mangun, G.R., Tonotopy in human auditory cortex examined with functional magnetic resonance imaging, *Human Brain Mapping* 5 (1997): 18–25. New York: John Wiley & Sons, Inc., 1997. Reprinted by permission of the authors. **2.37** Courtesy of David Amaral.

Chapter 3: **3.1A** Courtesy of Cindy Jordan, University of California, Berkeley. **3.1B, 3.1C** Courtesy Carla J. Shatz, University of California, Berkeley. **3.3** Woodard, J.S., *Histologic Neuropathology: A Color Slide Set.* Orange, CA: California Medical Publications, 1973. **3.2A, 3.2B** DeArmond, S.J.,

Fusco, M.M., and Dewey, M.M., *The Structure of the Human Brain: A Photographic Atlas,* 2nd edition. New York: Oxford University Press, 1976. Copyright © 1976 by Oxford University Press, Inc. Reprinted with permission. **3.8** Courtesy of Carla J. Shatz, University of California, Berkeley. **3.10A, 3.10B** Courtesy of John Walker, University of California, San Francisco. **3.12A** Reprinted with permission from Tootell, R.B., Silverman, M.S., Switkes, E., and De Valois, R.L., Deoxyglucose analysis of retinotopic organization in primate striate cortex, *Science* 218 (1982): 902–904. Copyright 1982 American Association for the Advancement of Science. **3.13B** Fig. 1–1 (A), Greenberg, J.O., and Adams, R.D. (Eds.), *Neuroimaging: A Companion to Adams and Victor's Principles of Neurology.* New York: McGraw-Hill, Inc., 1995. Reprinted by permission of McGraw-Hill, Inc. **3.14B** Fig. 1–1 (B), (C), and (D), Greenberg, J.O., and Adams, R.D. (Eds.), *Neuroimaging: A Companion to Adams and Victor's Principles of Neurology.* New York: McGraw-Hill, Inc., 1995. Reprinted by permission of McGraw-Hill, Inc. **3.15** DeArmond, S.J., Fusco, M.M., and Dewey, M.M., *The Structure of the Human Brain: A Photographic Atlas,* 2nd edition. New York: Oxford University Press, 1976. Copyright © 1976 by Oxford University Press, Inc. Reprinted with permission. **3.16** Woodard, J.S., *Histologic Neuropathology: A Color Slide Set.* Orange, CA: California Medical Publications, 1973. **3.17** Woodard, J.S., *Histologic Neuropathology: A Color Slide Set.* Orange, CA: California Medical Publications, 1973. **3.18A** Woodard, J.S., *Histologic Neuropathology: A Color Slide Set.* Orange, CA: California Medical Publications, 1973. **3.18B** Fig. 8.24 (B) and (C), Greenberg, J.O., and Adams, R.D. (Eds.), *Neuroimaging: A Companion to Adams and Victor's Principles of Neurology.* New York: McGraw-Hill, Inc., 1995. Reprinted by permission of McGraw-Hill, Inc. **3.19A** Woodard, J.S., *Histologic Neuropathology: A Color Slide Set.* Orange, CA: California Medical Publications, 1973. **3.19B** Holbourn, A.H.S., Mechanics of head injury, *The Lancet* 2: 177–180, © by *The Lancet* 1943. **3.21** These cartoons appeared in *Life,* 3 March 1947. Used by permission of the estate of Mina Turner. **3.31** Courtesy of Robert T. Knight, University of California, Davis. **3.37** Courtesy Marcus Raichle, M.D., School of Medicine, Washington University in St. Louis. **3.38** Figure 4, Fox et al., "Retinotopic Organization of Human Visual Cortex Mapped with Positron-emission Tomography," *The Journal of Neuroscience* 7 (3): 918, (1987). Reprinted with permission of The Society for Neuroscience. **p. 81** Courtesy of Foundation for Biomedical Research, Washington, D.C.

Chapter 4: **4.1A** Claude Monet, *Le Déjeuner sur l'Herbe,* detail. Paris, Musée d'Orsay. Photo: Giraudon/Art Resource, New York. **4.1B** Pablo Picasso, *Weeping Woman,* 1937. Copyright © 1998 Estate of Pablo Picasso/Artists Rights Society (ARS), New York. **4.6** Woodard, J.S., *Histologic Neuropathology: A Color Slide Set.* Orange, CA: California Medical Publications, 1973. **4.9** Woodard, J.S., *Histologic Neuropathology: A Color Slide Set.* Orange, CA: California Medical Publications, 1973. **p. 149** From Sadato, N., Pascual-Leone, A., Grafman, Jordan,

Ibañez, V., Deiber, M., Doid, G. and Hallett, M., Activation of the primary visual cortex by Braille reading in blind subjects, *Nature* 380, 11 April, 1996.

Chapter 5: **5.1A** Photograph © Craig Newbauer/Peter Arnold, Inc. **5.1B** Photograph © Helga Lade/Peter Arnold, Inc. **5.18** Sekuler, R., and Blake, R., *Perception,* 2nd edition. New York: McGraw-Hill, Inc., 1990. © 1990 by McGraw-Hill, Inc. Reprinted by permission of McGraw-Hill, Inc. **5.24** McCarthy, G., and Warrington, E.K., Visual associative agnosia: A Clinico-anatomical study of a single case, *Journal of Neurology, Neurosurgery and Psychiatry* 49 (1986): 1233–1240. **5.34** Wapner, W., Judd, T., and Gardner, H., Visual agnosia in an artist, *Cortex* 14 (1978): 343–364. Copyright 1978 by the Assoicazione per lo Sviluppo delle Recerche Neuropsicologiche. **5.35** Reprinted from *Brain Research* 342, Baylis, G.C., Rolls, E.T., and Leonard, C.M., Selectivity between faces in the responses of a population of neurons in the cortex in the superior temporal sulcus of the monkey, pp. 91–102, © 1985 with kind permission of Elsevier Science-NL, Sara Burgerhartstr 25, 1055 KV Amsterdam, The Netherlands. **5.36** McNeil, J.E., and Warrington, E.K., "Prosopagnosia: A Face Specific Disorder" in *The Quarterly Journal of Experimental Psychology* 46A (1993): 1–10. Copyright 1993. Reprinted by permission of The Experimental Psychology Society. **5.37** Block, J.R., and Yuker, H.E., *Can You Believe Your Eyes: Over 250 Illusions and Other Visual Oddities.* Mattituck, New York: Amereon Press, 1992. **p. 196** Behrmann, M., Moscovitch, M., and Winocur, G., Intact visual imagery and impaired visual perception in a patient with visual agnosia, *Journal of Experimental Psychology: Human Perception and Performance* 20 (1994): 1068–1087. Copyright © 1994 by the American Psychological Association. Reprinted with permission.

Chapter 6: **6.1** Courtesy National Library of Medicine, Bethesda, Maryland. **6.2 left** Corbis-Bettmann. **6.29B** Courtesy of Robert T. Knight, University of California, Davis. **6.31** Reproduced from *Scientific American* 246 (1982), p. 134. © 1998 Artists Rights Society (ARS), New York/VG Bild-Kunst, Bonn.

Chapter 7: **7.12** M.C. Escher, "Waterfall," © 1998 Cordon Art B.V. -Baarn-Holland. All rights reserved. **7.15** Courtesy of David Amaral. **7.29** Squire, L.R., Ojemann, J.G., Miezin, F.M., Petersen, S.E., Videen, T.O., and Raichle, M.E., Activation of the hipocampus in normal humans: A functional anatomical study of memory, *Proc. Natl. Acad. Sci. U.S.A.* 89 (1992): 1837–1841. Courtesy of Larry Squire.

Chapter 8: **8.24** Courtesy of Nina Dronkers.

Chapter 9: **9.4** Courtesy of Michael Gazzaniga. **9.5** Courtesy of Michael Gazzaniga. **9.30** Sergent, J., Influence of task and input factors on hemispheric involvement in face processing, *Journal of Experimental Psychology: Human Perception and Performance* 11 (1985): 846–861.

Chapter 10: **10.1 top** From Lewis P. Rowland (Ed.), *Merritt's Textbook of Neurology,* 8th edition. Philadelphia: Lea & Febiger, 1989, p. 661. Copyright © 1989 by Lea & Febiger. **10.1 bottom** From Jon Palfreman and J. William Langston, *The Case of the Frozen Addicts.* New York: Pantheon Books, 1995. Photograph by Russ Lee, © Pantheon Books, 1995. Used by permission. **10.9** From Taub, E., and Berman, A.J., Movement and Learning in the Absence of Sensory Feedback. In S.J. Freedman (Ed.), *The Neuropsychology of Spatially Oriented Behavior.* Homewood, IL: Dorsey, 1968, Figs. 2 and 8. Reprinted with permission. **10.10** Rothwell, J.C., Traub, M.M., Day, B.L., Obeso, J.A., Thomas, P.K., and Marsden, C.D., Manual motor performance in a deafferented man, *Brain* 105 (1982): 515–542. **10.43** Color plates 2 and 4 from Greenberg, J.O., and Adams, R.D. (Eds.), *Neuroimaging: A Companion to Adams and Victor's Principles of Neurology.* New York: McGraw-Hill, Inc., 1995. Reprinted by permission of McGraw-Hill, Inc.

Chapter 11: **11.1** Damasio, A.R., *Descartes' Error: Emotion, Reason, and the Human Brain.* New York: G.P. Putnam, 1994. Courtesy of Hanna Damasio. **11.6** McCarthy, G., Blamire, A.M., Puce, A., Nobe, A.C., Bloch, G., Hyder, F., Goldman-Rakic, P., and Shulman, R.G., Functional magnetic resonance imaging of human prefrontal cortex activation during a spatial working memory task, *Proc. Natl. Acad. Sci. U.S.A.* 91 (1994): 8690–8694. **11.9** Figure 5, Friedman et al., "Coactivation of Prefrontal Cortex and Inferior Parietal Cortex in Working Memory Tasks Revealed by 2DG Functional Mapping in the Rhesus Monkey," *The Journal of Neuroscience* 14 (5): 2782, (1994). Reprinted with permission of The Society for Neuroscience. **11.20A, B, C, and D** Lhermitte, F., Pillon, B., and Serdaru, M., Human Autonomy and the Frontal Lobes. Part I: Imitation and Utilization Behavior: A Neuropsychological Study of 75 Patients, *Annals of Neurology* 19 (1986): 326–334. **11.20E, F, and G** From Lhermitte, F., Utilization behavior and its relation to lesions of the frontal lobes, *Brain* 106 (1983): 237–255. Oxford Journals, Oxford University Press. **11.24** Courtesy of David Tranel. **11.32A** Janer, K.W., and Pardo, J.V., Deficits in selective attention following bilateral anterior cingulotomy, *Journal of Cognitive Neuroscience* 3 (1991): 231–241. © 1991 by the Massachusetts Institute of Technology. Reprinted by permission of MIT Press. **11.32B** Courtesy of Robert T. Knight, University of California, Davis. **p. 455, top** Cohen, R.M., Semple, W.E., Gross, M., and Nordhal, T.E., From syndrome to illness: Delineating the pathophysiology of schizophrenia with PET, *Schizophrenia Bulletin* 14 (1988): 169–176. U.S. Public Health Service, National Institute of Mental Health. **p. 455, bottom** From Drevets, W.C., Videen, T.O., Price, J.L., Preskorn, S.H., Carmichael, S.T., and Raichle, M.E., "A functional anatomical study of unipolar depression," *The Journal of Neuroscience* 12: 3628–3641, (1992). Reprinted with permission of The Society for Neuroscience. **p. 456, top** From the book *Great and Desperate Cures* by Elliot S. Valenstein. Reprinted by permission of the author. **p. 456, bottom** From

W. Freeman and J.W. Watts, *Psychosurgery: In the Treatment of Mental Disorders and Intractable Pain,* 2nd ed., Springfield, Illinois: Charles C. Thomas, Publisher, 1950. Courtesy of Charles C. Thomas, Publisher.

Chapter 12: **12.4** UPI/Corbis-Bettmann. **12.8** Photograph © Garvis Kerimian/Peter Arnold, Inc. **12.10B** Photo: Lennart Nilsson/Bonnier Alba AB. **p. 470** Courtesy of Linda Acredolo.

Chapter 13. **13.2A, 13.2B** Courtesy Todd M. Preuss, Department of Psychology, Vanderbilt University. **13.14** Haerer, A.F. (revised by), *DeJong's The Neurologic Examination,* 5th edition. Philadelphia, Pennsylvania: J. B. Lippincott Company, 1992. Copyright © 1992 by J.B. Lippincott Company. **13.15** Ekman, P. (1971), Universals and cultural differences in facial expressions of emotions. In J.K. Cole (Ed.), *Nebraska Symposium on Motivation,* 207–283. Lincoln, NE: University of Nebraska Press. © Paul Ekman, 1972. Reprinted by permission of the author. **p. 499** Robert Harding Picture Library, London.

FIGURES

Chapter 1: **1.7** Brodmann, K., *Vergleichende Lokalisationslehre der Grosshirnrinde in ihren Prinzipien dargestellt auf Grund des Zellenbaues.* Leipzig: J.A. Barth, 1909.

Chapter 2: **2.2** Carpenter, M., *Human Neuroanatomy,* 7th edition. Baltimore, Maryland: William & Wilkins, 1976. © 1976 by Williams & Wilkins. Adapted by permission of the publisher. **2.4** Adapted from Kandel, E.R. Schwartz, J.H., and Jessell, T.M. (Eds.), *Principles of Neural Science,* 3rd edition. Norwalk, Connecticut: Appleton & Lange, 1991. Copyright © 1991 by Appleton & Lange. **2.6 and 2.12** Netter, F.H., *The CIBA Collection of Medical Illustrations. Vol I: Nervous System, Part 1: Anatomy and Physiology.* Summit, NJ: CIBA Pharmaceutical Company, 1983. Adapted with permission of Novartis, formerly CIBA. **2.13A** Adapted from Kandel, E.R. Schwartz, J.H., and Jessell, T.M. (Eds.), *Principles of Neural Science,* 3rd edition. Norwalk, Connecticut: Appleton & Lange, 1991. Copyright © 1991 by Appleton & Lange. **2.13B** Adapted from Kuffler, S., and Nicholls, J., *From Neuron to Brain.* Sunderland, MA: Sinauer Associates, 1976. **2.16** Adapted from Kandel, E.R. Schwartz, J.H., and Jessell, T.M. (Eds.), *Principles of Neural Science,* 3rd edition. Norwalk, Connecticut: Appleton & Lange, 1991. Copyright © 1991 by Appleton & Lange. **2.18** Adapted from Kuffler, S., and Nicholls, J., *From Neuron to Brain.* Sunderland, MA: Sinauer Associates, 1976. **2.20** Adapted from Kandel, E.R. Schwartz, J.H., and Jessell, T.M. (Eds.), *Principles of Neural Science,* 3rd edition. Norwalk, Connecticut: Appleton & Lange, 1991. Copyright © 1991 by Appleton & Lange. **2.23** DeArmond, S.J., Fusco, M.M., and Dewey, M.M., *The Structure of the Human Brain: A Photographic Atlas,* 2nd edition. New York: Oxford University Press, 1976. Copyright © 1976 by Oxford University Press, Inc. Adapted with permission. **2.31** Wessinger, C.M., Buonocore,

M.H., Kussmaul, C.L., and Mangun, G.R., Tonotopy in human auditory cortex examined with functional magnetic resonance imaging, *Human Brain Mapping* 5 (1997): 18–25. New York: John-Wiley & Sons, Inc., 1997. Adapted by permission of the authors. **2.33** Adapted from Kandel, E.R. Schwartz, J.H., and Jessell, T.M. (Eds.), *Principles of Neural Science,* 3rd edition. Norwalk, Connecticut: Appleton & Lange, 1991. Copyright © 1991 by Appleton & Lange. **2.34** Carpenter, M., *Human Neuroanatomy,* 7th edition. Baltimore, Maryland: William & Wilkins, 1976. © 1976 by Williams & Wilkins. Adapted by permission of the publisher. **2.35** Adapted from Kandel, E.R. Schwartz, J.H., and Jessell, T.M. (Eds.), *Principles of Neural Science,* 3rd edition. Norwalk, Connecticut: Appleton & Lange, 1991. Copyright © 1991 by Appleton & Lange. **2.39 and 2.40** Netter, F.H., *The CIBA Collection of Medical Illustrations. Vol I: Nervous System, Part 1: Anatomy and Physiology.* Summit, NJ: CIBA Pharmaceutical Company, 1983. Adapted with permission of Novartis, formerly CIBA. **2.42, 2.43, and 2.44** Carpenter, M., *Human Neuroanatomy,* 7th edition. Baltimore, Maryland: William & Wilkins, 1976. © 1976 by Williams & Wilkins. Adapted by permission of the publisher. **p. 35** Netter, F.H., *The CIBA Collection of Medical Illustrations. Vol I: Nervous System, Part 1: Anatomy and Physiology.* Summit, NJ: CIBA Pharmaceutical Company, 1983. Adapted with permission of Novartis, formerly CIBA.

Chapter 3: **3.4** Kolb, B. and Whishaw, I.Q., *Fundamentals of Human Neuropsychology,* 4th edition. New York: W.H. Freeman and Company, 1996. © 1996 by W.H. Freeman and Company. Adapted by permission of W.H. Freeman and Company. **3.6** McClelland, J.L., and Rummelhart, D.E., *Parallel Distributed Processing: Explorations in the Microstructure of Cognition. Vol. 2: Psychological and Biological Models.* Cambridge, MA: MIT Press, 1986. Adapted with permission of MIT Press. **3.9 top** Kolb, B. and Whishaw, I.Q., *Fundamentals of Human Neuropsychology,* 4th edition. New York: W.H. Freeman and Company, 1996. © 1996 by W.H. Freeman and Company. Adapted by permission of W.H. Freeman and Company. **3.9 bottom** Adapted from Ramachandran, V.S., Behavioral and magnetoencephalographic correlates of plasticity in the adult human brain, *Proc. Natl. Acad. Sci. U.S.A.* 90 (1993): 10413–10420. **3.12C** Bear, M.F., Connors, B.W., and Paradiso, M.A., *Neuroscience: Exploring the Brain.* Baltimore, Maryland: William & Wilkins, 1996. © 1996 by Williams & Wilkins. Adapted by permission of the publisher. **3.20** Kolb, B. and Whishaw, I.Q., *Fundamentals of Human Neuropsychology,* 4th edition. New York: W.H. Freeman and Company, 1996. © 1996 by W.H. Freeman and Company. Adapted by permission of W.H. Freeman and Company. **3.22 and 3.23** Adapted from Posner, M.I., *Chronometric Explorations of Mind.* New York: Oxford University Press, 1986. **3.24** Adapted with permission from Sternberg, S., High speed scanning in human memory, *Science* 153 (1966): 652–654. Copyright 1966 American Association for the Advancement of Science. **3.27** Braitenberg, V., *Vehicles: Experiments in Synthetic Psychology.* Cambridge, MA: MIT Press, 1984. Adapted with permission of MIT Press. **3.32**

Kolb, B. and Whishaw, I.Q., *Fundamentals of Human Neuropsychology,* 4th edition. New York: W.H. Freeman and Company, 1996. © 1996 by W.H. Freeman and Company. Adapted by permission of W.H. Freeman and Company. **3.37** Posner, M.I., and Raichle, M.E., *Images of Mind.* New York: W.H. Freeman and Company, 1994. © 1994 by W.H. Freeman and Company. Adapted by permission of W.H. Freeman and Company.

Chapter 4: **4.2** Sekuler, R., and Blake, R., *Perception,* 2nd edition. New York: McGraw-Hill, Inc., 1990. © 1990 by McGraw-Hill, Inc. Adapted by permission of McGraw-Hill, Inc. **4.7 and 4.8** Bear, M.F., Connors, B.W., and Paradiso, M.A., *Neuroscience: Exploring the Brain.* Baltimore, Maryland: William & Wilkins, 1996. © 1996 by Williams & Wilkins. Adapted by permission of the publisher. **4.11** Zeki, S., *A Vision of the Brain.* Oxford, UK: Blackwell Scientific, 1993. **4.12** Adapted from Maunsell, J.H.R., and Van Essen, D.C., Functional properties of neurons in middle temporal visual area of the macaque monkey. I. Selectivity for stimulus direction, speed, and orientation, *Journal of Neurophysiology* 49 (1983): 1127–1147. **4.16** Treisman, A., "Features and objects: The Fourteenth Bartlett Memorial Lecture" in *The Quarterly Journal of Experimental Psychology* 40A (1988): 201–237. Copyright 1988. Adapted by permission of The Experimental Psychology Society. **4.17A** Adapted from Enns, J.T., and Rensink, R.A., Sensitivity to three-dimensional orientation in visual search, *Psychological Science* 1 (1990): 323–326. **4.20 and 4.21** Zeki, S., *A Vision f the Brain.* Oxford, UK: Blackwell Scientific, 1993. **4.23** Adapted from Heywood, C.A., Wilson, B., and Cowey, A., A case study of cortical colour blindness with relatively intact achromatic discrimination, *Journal of Neurology, Neurosurgery and Psychiatry* 50 (1987): 22–29. **4.27** Weiskrantz, L., *Blindsight: A Case Study and Implications.* Oxford, UK: Oxford University Press, 1986. Copyright © 1986 by Oxford University Press, Inc. Adapted with permission. **4.30 and 4.31** Bear, M.F., Connors, B.W., and Paradiso, M.A., *Neuroscience: Exploring the Brain.* Baltimore, Maryland: William & Wilkins, 1996. © 1996 by Williams & Wilkins. Adapted by permission of the publisher. **4.33** Adapted from Konishi, M., Listening with two ears, *Scientific American* 2681 (1993): 66–73. Copyright 1993 by Scientific American, Inc. All rights reserved. **p. 132C top** Adapted from Hubel, D., and Wiesel, T., Receptive fields and functional architecture of monkey striate cortex, *Journal of Physiology* 195 (1968): 215–243. Published by the Cambridge University Press for the Physiological Society, London. **p. 132C bottom** Bear, M.F., Connors, B.W., and Paradiso, M.A., *Neuroscience: Exploring the Brain.* Baltimore, Maryland: William & Wilkins, 1996. © 1996 by Williams & Wilkins. Adapted by permission of the publisher.

Chapter 5: **5.4** Adapted from Robinson, D.L., and Petersen, S., The pulvinar and visual salience, *Trends in Neuroscience* 15 (1992): 127–132. **5.5** Desimone et al., "Stimulus-selective properties of inferior temporal neurons in the macaque," *The Journal of Neuroscience* 4: 2051–2062, (1984). Adapted with permission of The Society for Neuroscience. **5.8** Pohl, W.,

Dissociation of spatial discrimination deficits following frontal and parietal lesions in monkeys, *Journal of Comparative and Physiological Psychology* 82 (1973): 227–239. Copyright © 1973 by the American Psychological Association. Adapted with permission. **5.9** Ungerleider, L.G., and Mishkin, M., Two Cortical Visual Systems, in Engle, D.J., Goodale, M.A., and Mansfield, R.J. (Eds.), *Analysis of Visual Behavior.* Cambridge, MA: MIT Press, 1982, pp. 549–586. Adapted with permission of MIT Press. **5.10** Haxby et al., "The functional organization of human extrastriate cortex: A PET-rCBF study of selective attention to faces and locations," *The Journal of Neuroscience* 14: 6336–6353, (1994). Adapted with permission of The Society for Neuroscience. **5.20** Biederman, I., Higher-Level Vision, in Osherson, D.N., Kosslyn, S.M., and Hollberbach, J.M. (Eds.), *Visual Cognition and Action: An Invitation to Cognitive Science,* vol. 2. Cambridge, MA: MIT Press, pp. 41–63. Adapted with permission of MIT Press. **5.22** Adapted from Warrington, E.K., Agnosia: The Impairment of Object Recognition, in Vinken, P.J., Bruyn, G.W., and Klawans, H.L. (Eds.), *Handbook of Clinical Neurology.* New York: Elsevier Science, 1985, pp. 333–349. **5.23** Adapted from Warrington, E.K., Neuropsychological studies of object recognition, *Philosophical Transactions of the Royal Society, London, Section B* 298 (1982): 13–33. **5.25 top** Adapted from Warrington, E.K., Neuropsychological studies of object recognition, *Philosophical Transactions of the Royal Society, London, Section B* 298 (1982): 13–33. **5.25 bottom** Warrington, E.K., and Taylor, A.M., Two categorical stages of object recognition, *Perception* 7 (1978): 695–705. **5.27** Adapted from Warrington, E.K., and McCarthy, R.A., Multiple meaning systems in the brain: A case for visual semantics, *Neuropsychologia* 32 (1994): 1465–1473. **5.29** Snodgrass, J.G., and Vanderwart, M., A standardized set of 260 pictures: Norms for name agreement, image agreement, familiarity, and visual complexity, *Journal of Experimental Psychology: Human Learning and Memory* 6 (1980): 174–215. Copyright © 1980 by the American Psychological Association. Adapted with permission. **5.31** Farah, M.J., and McClelland, J.L., A computational model of semantic memory impairment: Modality specificity and emergent category specificity, *Journal of Experimental Psychology: General* 120 (1991): 339–357. Copyright © 1991 by the American Psychological Association. Adapted with permission. **5.32** Adapted from Humphreys, G.W., Riddoch, M.J., Donnelly, N., Freeman, T., Boucart, M., and Muller, H.M., Intermediate Visual Processing and Visual Agnosia, in Farah, M.J., and Ratcliff, G. (Eds.), *The Neuropsychology of High-Level Vision: Collected Tutorial Essays.* Hillsdale, NJ: Lawrence Erlbaum Associates, 1994, pp. 63–102. **5.33** Behrmann, M., Moscovitch, M., and Winocur, G., Intact visual imagery and impaired visual perception in a patient with visual agnosia, *Journal of Experimental Psychology: Human Perception and Performance* 20 (1994): 1068–1087. Copyright © 1994 by the American Psychological Association. Adapted with permission. **5.35** Adapted from *Brain Research* 342, Baylis, G.C., Rolls, E.T., and Leonard, C.M., Selectivity between faces in the responses of a population of neurons in the cortex in the superior temporal sulcus of the monkey, pp. 91–102, © 1985 with kind permission of Elsevier Science - NL, Sara Burgerhartstr 25, 1055 KV Amsterdam, The Netherlands. **5.38** Adapted from Farah, M.J., Specialization Within Visual object Recognition: Clues from Prosopagnosia and Alexia, in Farah, M.J., and Ratcliff, G. (Eds.), *The Neuropsychology of High-Level Vision: Collected Tutorial Essays.* Hillsdale, NJ: Lawrence Erlbaum Associates, 1994, pp. 133–146. **p. 195** Podgorny, P., and Shepard, R., Functional representations common to visual perception and imagination, *Journal of Experimental Psychology: Human Perception and Performance* 4 (1978): 21–35. Copyright © 1978 by the American Psychological Association. Adapted with permission.

Chapter 6: **6.5** Adapted from fig. 2, Broadbent, D.A., *Perception and Communication.* New York: Pergamon, 1958. **6.8** Posner, M.I., Snyder, C.R.R., and Davidson, J., Attention and the detection of signals, *Journal of Experimental Psychology: General* 109 (1980): 160–174. Copyright © 1980 by the American Psychological Association. Adapted with permission. **6.11** Adapted with permission from Hillyard, S.A., Hink, R.F., Schwent, V.L., and Picton, T.W., Electrical signs of selective attention in the human brain, *Science* 182 (1973): 177–180. Copyright 1973 American Association for the Advancement of Science. **6.12** Adapted from Woldorff, M.G., Gallen, C.C., Hampson, S.A., Hillyard, S.A., Pantev, C., Sobel, D., and Bloom, F.E., Modulation of early sensory processing in human auditory cortex during auditory selective attention, *Proc. Natl. Acad. Sci. U.S.A.* 90 (1993): 8722–8726. **6.17** Adapted from Hopfinger, J., and Mangun, G.R., Effects of automatic attentional capture on visual processing. (submitted). **6.18** Luck, S.J., Fan, S., and Hillyard, S.A., Attention-related modulation of sensory-evoked brain activity in a visual search task, *Journal of Cognitive Neuroscience* 5 (1993): 188–195. © 1993 by the Massachusetts Institute of Technology. Adapted with permission of MIT Press. **6.19** Figs. 4, 5, and 6, Corbetta et al., "Selective and divided attention during visual discriminations of shape, color and speed: Functional anatomy by positron emission tomography, *The Journal of Neuroscience* 11: 2383–2402, (1991) Adapted with permission of The Society for Neuroscience. Adapted from Heinze, H.J., Mangun, G.R., Burchert, W., Hinrichs, H., Scholz, M., Münte, T.G., Gös, A., Scherg, M., Johannes, S., Hundeshagen, H., Gazzaniga, M.S. and Hillyard, S.A., Combined spatial and temporal imaging of brain activity during visual selective attention in humans, *Nature* 372 (1994): 543–546. **6.20** Figs. 1 and 4, Corbetta et al., "A PET study of visuospatial attention," *The Journal of Neuroscience* 13: 1202–1226, (1993). Adapted with permission of The Society for Neuroscience. **6.22** Adapted with permission from Moran, J., and Desimone, R., Selective attention gates visual processing in extrastriate cortex, *Science* 229 (1985): 782–784. Copyright 1985 American Association for the Advancement of Science. **6.24** Adapted from Wurtz, R.H., Goldberg, M.E., and Robinson, D.L., Brain mechanisms of visual attention, *Scientific American* 246 (1982): 124–135. Copyright © 1982 by Scientific American, Inc. All rights reserved. **6.25** Adapted from Desimone, R., Wessinger, M., Thomas, L., and Schneider, W., Attentional control of visual perception: Cortical and subcortical mechanisms, *Cold Spring Harbor Laboratory. Symposia on Quantitative Biology* 55 (1990): 963–971. **6.27** Adapted from Robinson, D.L., and Petersen, S., The pulvinar and visual salience, *Trends in Neuroscience* 15 (1992): 127–132. **6.28** Adapted from Wurtz, R.H., Goldberg, M.E., and Robinson, D.L., Brain mechanisms of visual attention, *Scientific American* 246 (1982): 124–135. Copyright © 1982 by Scientific American, Inc. All rights reserved. **6.29** Adapted from Knight, R., Scabini, D., Woods, D., and Clayworth, C., Contributions of temporal-parietal junction to the human auditory P3, *Brain Research* 502 (1989): 109–116. © 1989 with kind permission of Elsevier Science-NL. **6.32** Fig. 2, Posner et al., "Effects of parietal injury on covert orienting of attention," *The Journal of Neuroscience* 4: 1863–1874, (1984). Adapted with permission of The Society for Neuroscience. **6.34** Cohen, J.D., Romero, R.D., Servan-Schreiber, D., and Farah, M.J., Mechanisms of spatial attention: The relation of macrostructure to microstructure in parietal neglect, *Journal of Cognitive Neuroscience* 6 (1994): 377–387. © 1994 by the Massachusetts Institute of Technology. Adapted with permission of MIT Press. **6.35** Eglin, M. Robertson, L.C., and Knight, R.T., Visual search performance in the neglect syndrome, *Journal of Cognitive Neuroscience* 1 (1989): 372–385. © 1989 by the Massachusetts Institute of Technology. Adapted with permission of MIT Press. **6.36** Grabowecky, M., Robertson, L.C., and Treisman, A., Preattentive processes guide visual search, *Journal of Cognitive Neuroscience* 5 (1993): 288–302. © 1993 by the Massachusetts Institute of Technology. Adapted with permission of MIT Press. **6.38** Adapted from Bisiach, E., and Luzzatti, C., Unilateral neglect of representational space, *Cortex* 14 (1978): 129–133. **6.39** Behrmann, M., and Tipper, S.P., Object-Based Attentional Mechanisms: Evidence from Patients with Unilateral Neglect, in Umilta, C., and Moscovitch, M. (Eds.), *Attention and Performance 15: Conscious and Nonconscious Information Processing*. Cambridge, MA: MIT Press, 1994, pp. 351–375. Adapted with permission of MIT Press. **6.41** Adapted from Humphreys, G.W., and Riddoch, M.J., Interactions Between Objects and Space-Vision Revealed Through Neuropsychology, in Meyers, D.E., and Kornblum, S. (Eds.), *Attention and Performance XIV*. Hillsdale, NJ: Lawrence Erlbaum Associates, 1992, pp. 143–162.

Chapter 7: **7.1** Petersen, L.R., and Petersen, M.R., Short-term retention of individual verbal items, *Journal of Experimental Psychology* 58 (1959): 193–198. Copyright © 1959 by the American Psychological Association. Adapted with permission. **7.3** Waugh, N.C. and Norman, D.A., Primary memory, *Psychological Review* 72 (1965): 89–104. Copyright © 1965 by the American Psychological Association. Adapted with permission. **7.6** Atkinson, R.C., and Shiffrin, R.M., Human Memory: A Proposed System and Its Control Processes, in Spence, K.W., and Spence, J.T. (Eds.), *The Psychology of Learning and Motivation*, Vol. 2. New York: Academic Press, 1968, pp. 89–195. Adapted by permission of the publisher. **7.7** Bad-

deley, A., and Hitch, G., Working Memory, in Bower, G.H. (Ed.), *The Psychology of Learning and Motivation*, Vol. 8. New York, Academic Press, 1974, pp. 47–89. Adapted by permission of the publisher. **7.9 and 7.10** Adapted with permission from Tulving, E. and Shacter, D.L., Priming and human memory systems, *Science* 247 (1990): 301–306. Copyright 1990 American Association for the Advancement of Science. **7.13** Drachman, D.A., and Arbit, J., Memory and the hippocampal complex. II. Is memory a multiple process?, *Archives of Neurology* 15 (1966): 52–61. **7.14** Fig. 6.1, Corkin et al., "H.M.'s medial temporal lobe lesion: Findings from magnetic resonance imaging," *The Journal of Neuroscience* 17: 3964–3979, (1997). Adapted with permission of The Society for Neuroscience. **7.16** Adapted from Squire, L.R., and Slater, P., Electroconvulsive therapy and complaints of memory dysfunction: A prospective three-year follow-up study, *British Journal of Psychiatry* 142 (1983): 1–8. **7.18** Tulving, E., Gordon Hayman, C.A., and MacDonald, C.A., Long-lasting perceptual priming and semantic learning in amnesia. A case experiment, *Journal of Experimental Psychology* 17 (1991): 595–617. Copyright © 1991 by the American Psychological Association. Adapted with permission. **7.21** Adapted from Gabrieli, J., Fleischman, D., Keane, M., Reminger, S., and Morell, F., Double dissociation between memory systems underlying explicit and implicit memory in the human brain, *Psychological Science* 6 (1995): 76–82. **7.26** Figs. 2, 4, and 6, Zola-Morgan et al, "Damage to the perirhinal cortex exacerbates memory impairment following lesions to the hippocampal formation, *The Journal of Neuroscience* 13: 251–265, (1993).). Adapted with permission of The Society for Neuroscience. **7.27** Cohen, N.J., and Eichenbaum, H., *Memory, Amnesia and the Hippocampal System*. Cambridge, MA: MIT Press, 1993. Adapted with permission of MIT Press. **7.28** Grafton, S., Hazelttine, E., and Ivry, R., Functional mapping of sequence learning in normal humans, *Journal of Cognitive Neuroscience* 7 (1995): 497–510. © 1995 by the Massachusetts Institute of Technology. Adapted with permission of MIT Press. **7.32** Adapted from Schacter, D., Alpert, N., Savage, C., Rauch, S., et al., Conscious recollection and the human hippocampal formation—Evidence from positron emission tomography, *Proc. Natl. Acad. Sci. U.S.A.* 93 (1996): 321–325. Courtesy of Dr. Daniel Schacter. **7.33 and 7.34** Adapted from Kapur, S., Craik, F.I., Tulving, E., Wilson, A., Houle, S., and Brown, G., Neuroanatomical correlates of encoding in episodic memory: Levels of processing effect, *Proc. Natl. Acad. Sci. U.S.A.* 91 (1994): 2008–2011.

Chapter 8: **8.2 and 8.3** Adapted from Damasio, H., Grabowski, T.J., Tranel, D., Hichwa, R.D., and Damasio, A.R., A neural basis of lexical retrieval, *Nature* 380 (1996): 499–505. **8.4** Adapted from Caramazza, A., The brain's dictionary, *Nature* 380 (1996): 485–486. **8.6 and 8.7** Courtesy of Tamara Swaab. © 1997 by the Massachusetts Institute of Technology **8.8** Adapted from Coren, S., Ward, L.M., and Enns, J.T., *Sensation and Perception*, 4th edition. Ft. Worth, TX: Harcourt Brace College Publishers, 1994. **8.9** Adapted with permission from Petersen, S.E., Fox, P.T., Snyder, A.Z., and Raichle, M.E., Activation of extrastriate and frontal cortical areas by visual words and word-like stimuli, *Science* 249 (1990): 1041–1044. Copyright 1990 American Association for the Advancement of Science. **8.10** Klatt, D.H., Review of Selected Models of Speech Perception, in Marslen-Wilson, W. (Ed.), *Lexical Representation and Process.* Cambridge, MA: MIT Press, 1989, 169–226. Adapted with permission of MIT Press. **8.11** Adapted from Petersen, S.E., and Fiez, J.A., The processing of single words studied with positron emission tomography, *Annual Review of Neuroscience* 16 (1993), 509–530. **8.14** Adapted from Levelt, W.J.M., The Architecture of Normal Spoken Language Use, in Blanken, G., Dittman, J., Grimm, H., Marshall, J.C., and Wallesh, C-W. (Eds.), *Linguistic Disorders and Pathologies: An International Handbook.* Berlin: Walter de Gruyter, 1993. **8.15** Adapted from Levelt, W.J.M., The Skill of Speaking, in Bertelson, P., Eelen, P., and d'Ydewalle, G. (Eds.), *International Perspectives on Psychological Science.* Vol. 1: *Leading Themes.* Hove, England: Lawerence Erlbaum Associates, 1994. **8.19** Caplan, D., Language and the brain, in Gernsbacher, M.A. (Ed.), *Handbook of Psycholinguistics.* San Diego, CA: Academic Press, 1994, pp. 1023–1053. Adapted by permission of the publisher. **8.23** Adapted from Petersen, S.E., and Fiez, J.A., The processing of single words studied with positron emission tomography, *Annual Review of Neuroscience* 16 (1993), 509–530. **8.25** Adapted with permission from Kutas, M., and Hillyard, S.A., Reading senseless sentences: Brain potentials reflect semantic incongruity, *Science* 207 (1980): 203–205. Copyright 1980 American Association for the Advancement of Science. **8.26** Adapted from Hagoort, P., Brown, C., and Groothusen, J., The syntactic positive shift (SPS) as an ERP measure of syntactic processing. Special issue: Event-related brain potentials in the study of language, *Language and Cognitive Processes* 8 (1993):439–483. **8.27** Münte, T.F., Heinze, H.-J., and Mangun, G.R., Dissociation of brain activity related to semantic and syntactic aspects of language, *Journal of Cognitive Neuroscience* 5 (1993): 335–344. © 1993 by the Massachusetts Institute of Technology. Adapted with permission of MIT Press. **p. 317** Adapted from Ojemann, G., Ojemann, J., Lettich, E., and Berger, M., Cortical Language localization in left, dominant hemisphere, *Journal of Neurosurgery* 71 (1989): 316–326. **p. 318** Adapted from Swaab, T.Y., Brown, C.M., and Hagoort, P., Spoken sentence comprehension in aphasia: Event-related potential evidence for a lexical integration deficit, *Journal of Cognitive Neuroscience* 9 (1997): 39–66. © 1997 by the Massachusetts Institute of Technology. Adapted with permission of MIT Press.

Chapter 9: **9.17 top** Adapted from Kimura, D., The Asymmetry of the human brain, *Scientific American* 228 (1973): 70–78. Copyright 1973 by Scientific American, Inc. All rights reserved. **9.18** Adapted from Bartholomeus, B., Effects of task requirements on ear superiority for sung speech, *Cortex* 10 (1974): 215–223. **9.22** Sergent, J., The cerebral balance of power: Confrontation or cooperation, *Journal of Experimental Psychology: Human Perception and Performance* 8 (1982): 253–272. Copyright © 1982 by the American Psychological Association. Adapted with permission. **9.23** Adapted from Delis, D., Robertson, L., and Efron, R., Hemispheric specialization of memory for visual hierarchical stimuli, *Neuropsychologia* 24 (1986): 205–214. **9.28** Adapted from Kitterle, F., Christman, S., and Hellige, J., Hemispheric differences are found in identification, butt not detection of low versus high spatial frequencies, *Perception and Psychophysics* 48 (1990), 297–306. **9.31** Adapted from Deutsch, A., Dichotic listening to melodic patterns and its relationship to hemispheric specialization of function, *Music Perception* 3 (1985): 127–154. **9.32** Adapted from four speech contours. Courtesy of Susan Ravissa, University of California, Berkeley. **9.34** Kosslyn, S.M., Koenig, O., Barret, A., Cave, C.B., Tang, J., and Gabrieli, J.D.E., Evidence for two types of spatial representations: Hemispheric specialization for categorical and coordinate relations, *Journal of Experimental Psychology: Human Perception and Performance* 15 (1989): 723–735. Copyright © 1989 by the American Psychological Association. Adapted with permission. **9.35** Ivry, R.B., and Robertson, L.C., *The Two Sides of Perception.* Cambridge, MA: MIT Press, 1998 (in press). Adapted by permission of Dr. Richard Ivry. **9.36** Laeng, B., Lateralization of categorical and coordinate spatial functions: A study of unilateral stroke patients, *Journal of Cognitive Neuroscience* 6 (1994): 189–203. © 1994 by the Massachusetts Institute of Technology. Adapted with permission of MIT Press. **9.38** Marsolek, C.J., Abstract visual-form representations in the left cerebral hemisphere, *Journal of Experimental Psychology: Human Perception and Performance* 21 (1995): 375–386. Copyright © 1995 by the American Psychological Association. Adapted with permission. **9.40** Previc, F.H., A general theory concerning the prenatal origins of cerebral lateralization in humans, *Psychological Review* 98 (1991): 299–334. Copyright © 1991 by the American Psychological Association. Adapted with permission. **9.41 and 9.42** Kolb, B. and Whishaw, I.Q., *Fundamentals of Human Neuropsychology,* 4th edition. New York: W.H. Freeman and Company, 1996. © 1996 by W.H. Freeman and Company. Adapted by permission of W.H. Freeman and Company.

Chapter 10: **10.4** Bear, M.F., Connors, B.W., and Paradiso, M.A., *Neuroscience: Exploring the Brain.* Baltimore, Maryland: William & Wilkins, 1996. © 1996 by Williams & Wilkins. Adapted by permission of the publisher. **10.8** Adapted from Kandel, E.R. Schwartz, J.H., and Jessell, T.M. (Eds.), *Principles of Neural Science,* 3rd edition. Norwalk, Connecticut: Appleton & Lange, 1991. Copyright © 1991 by Appleton & Lange. **10.11 and 10.12** Bizzi, E., Accornero, N. Chappel, W., and Hogan, N., Posture control and trajectory formation during arm movement, *The Journal of Neuroscience* 4: 2738–2744, (1984). Reprinted with permission of The Society for Neuroscience. **10.14** Adapted from Abrams, R.A., and Landgraf, J.Z., Differential use of distance and location information for spatial localization, *Perception and Psychophysics* 47 (1990): 349–359. **10.15** Adapted from Povel, D.J., and Collard, R., Structure factors in patterned finger tapping, *Acta Psychologia* 52 (1982): 107–123. **10.18, 10.19, and 10.20** Adapted from Georgopoulos,

A.P., Neurophysiology of Reaching, in Jeannerod, M. (Ed.), *Attention and Performance XIII: Motor Representation and Control.* Hillsdale, NJ: Lawrence Erlbaum Associates, 1990, pp. 227–263. **10.21** Adapted from Ashe, J., Taira, M., Smyrnis, N., Pellizzer, G., Gerorakopoulos, T., Lurito, J.T., and Georgopoulos, A.P., Motor cortical activity preceding a memorized movement trajectory with an orthogonal bend, *Experimental Brain Research* 95 (1993): 118–130. **10.22** Adapted from Graziano, M.S.A., and Gross, C.G., Mapping space with neurons, *Current Directions in Psychological Science* 3 (1994): 164–167. **10.23** Adapted from Thach, W.T., Timing of activity in cerebellar dentate nucleus and cerebral motor cortex during prompt volitional movements, *Brain Research* 88 (1975): 233–241. © 1975 with kind permission of Elsevier Science-NL. **10.24** Adapted from Roland, P.E., *Brain Activation.* New York: Wiley-Liss, 1993. **10.27** Adapted from Mushiake, H., Masahiko, I., and Tanji, J., Neuronal activity in the primate premotor, supplementary, and precentral motor cortex during visually guided and internally determined sequential movements, *Journal of Neurophysiology* 66 (1991): 705–718. **10.28** Jenkins et al., "Motor sequence learning: A study with positron emission tomography," *The Journal of Neuroscience* 14 (1994): 3775–3790. Adapted with permission of The Society for Neuroscience. **10.31** Adapted from Keretz, A. and Hooper, P., Praxis and language: The extent and variety of apraxia in aphasia, *Neuropsychologia* 20 (1982): 275–286. **10.33** Adapted from Heilman, K.M., Rothi, L.J., and Valenstein, E., Two forms of ideomotor apraxia, *Neurology* 32 (1982): 342–346. **10.35** Adapted from Wise, S.P., Di Pellegrino, G., and Boussaoud, D., The premotor cortex and nonstandard sensorimotor mapping, *Canadian Journal of Physiology and Pharmacology* 74 (1996): 469–482. **10.40 and 10.42** Adapted from Wichmann, T., and DeLong, M.R., Functional and pathophysiological models of the basal ganglia, *Current Opinion in Neurobiology* 6 (1996): 751–758. **p. 409** Adapted from Franz, E., Eliassen, J., Ivry, R., and Gazzaniga, M., Dissociation of Spatial and Temporal Coupling in the Bimanual Movements of Callosotomy Patients, *Psychological Science* 7 (1996): 306–310.

Chapter 11: **11.3** Adapted from Fuster, J.M., *The Prefrontal Cortex: Anatomy, Physiology, and Neuropsychology of the Frontal Lobe,* 2nd edition. New York: Raven Press, 1989. **11.4** Adapted from Goldman-Rakic, P.S., Working memory and the mind, *Scientific American* 267 (1992): 111–117. Copyright 1992 by Scientific American, Inc. All rights reserved **11.6** Adapted from McCarthy, G., Blamire, A.M., Puce, A., Nobe, A.C., Bloch, G., Hyder, F., Goldman-Rakic, P., and Shulman, R.G., Functional magnetic resonance imaging of human prefrontal cortex activation during a spatial working memory task, *Proc. Natl. Acad. Sci. U.S.A.* 91 (1994): 8690–8694. **11.7** Adapted from Fuster, J.M., *The Prefrontal Cortex: Anatomy, Physiology, and Neuropsychology of the Frontal Lobe,* 2nd edition. New York: Raven Press, 1989. **11.11** Smith, E.E., and Jonides, J., Working Memory in Humans: Neuropsychological Evidence, in Gazzaniga, M.S. (Ed.), *The Cognitive Neurosciences.* Cambridge, MA: MIT Press, 1995, pp. 1009–1020.

© 1995 Massachusetts Institute of Technology. Adapted with permission of MIT Press. **11.12** Adapted from Milner, B., Corsi, P., and Leonard, G., Frontal-lobe contributions to recency judgements, *Neuropsychologia* 29 (1991): 601–618. **11.14** Glisky, E.L., Polster, M.R., and Routhuieaux, B.C., Double dissociation between item and source memory, *Neuropsychology* 9 (1995): 229–235. Copyright © 1995 by the American Psychological Association. Adapted with permission. **11.17** Knight, R.T., and Grabowecky, M., Escape from Linear Time: Prefrontal Cortex and Conscious Experience, in Gazzaniga, M.S. (Ed.), *The Cognitive Neurosciences.* Cambridge, MA: MIT Press, 1995, pp. 1357–1371. © 1995 Massachusetts Institute of Technology. Adapted with permission of MIT Press. **11.21** Le Doux, J.E., Emotion, memory, and the brain, *Scientific American* 270 (1994): 50–57. Copyright 1994 by Scientific American, Inc. All rights reserved. **11.24 bottom** Adapted from Damasio, A.R., *Descartes' Error: Emotion, Reason, and the Human Brain.* New York: G.P. Putnam, 1994. Courtesy of Hanna Damasio. **11.27** Adapted from Shallice, T., Burgess, P.W., Schon, F., and Baxter, D.M., The origins of utilization behaviour, *Brain* 112 (1989): 1587–1598. **11.28** Posner, M.I., and Raichle, M.E., *Images of Mind.* New York: W.H. Freeman and Company, 1994. © 1994 by W.H. Freeman and Company. Adapted by permission of W.H. Freeman and Company. **11.30** Adapted from Snyder, A.Z., Abdullaev, Y.G., Posner, M.I., and Raichle, M.E., Scalp electrical potentials reflect regional cerebral blood flow responses during processing of written words, *Proc. Natl. Acad. Sci. U.S.A.* 92 (1995): 1689–1693. **11.31** Adapted from Gehring, W.J., Goss, B., Coles, M.G.H., Meyer, D.E., and Donchin, E., A neural system for error detection and compensation, *Psychological Science* 43 (1993): 385–390. **p. 414** Adapted from Owen, A.M., Robert, A.C., Hodges, J.R., Summers, B.A., Polkey, C.E., and Robbins, T.W., Contrasting mechanisms of impaired attentional set-shifting in patients with frontal lobe damage or Parkinson's disease, *Brain* 116 (1993): 1159–1175.

Chapter 12: **12.3** Adapted from Kandel, E.R. Schwartz, J.H., and Jessell, T.M. (Eds.), *Principles of Neural Science,* 3rd edition. Norwalk, Connecticut: Appleton & Lange, 1991. Copyright © 1991 by Appleton & Lange. **12.9** Carpenter, M., *Human Neuroanatomy,* 7th edition. Baltimore, Maryland: William & Wilkins, 1976. © 1976 by Williams & Wilkins. Adapted by permission of the publisher. Adapted from Goldsby, R.A., *Basic Biology.* New York: Harper and Row Publishers, 1976, pp. 282–297. Adapted from Kandel, E.R. Schwartz, J.H., and Jessell, T.M. (Eds.), *Principles of Neural Science,* 3rd edition. Norwalk, Connecticut: Appleton & Lange, 1991. Copyright © 1991 by Appleton & Lange. **12.10A** Carpenter, M., *Human Neuroanatomy,* 7th edition. Baltimore, Maryland: William & Wilkins, 1976. © 1976 by Williams & Wilkins. Adapted by permission of the publisher. **12.12, 12.13, 12.15, and 12.16** Rakic, P., Corticogenesis in Human and Nonhuman Primates, in Gazzaniga, M.S. (Ed.), *The Cognitive Neurosciences.* Cambridge, MA: MIT Press, 1995, pp. 127–146. © 1995 Massachusetts Institute of Technology. Adapted with permission of MIT Press. **12.19** Adapted from Kandel, E.R. Schwartz, J.H., and Jessell, T.M. (Eds.), *Principles of Neural Science*, 3rd edition. Norwalk, Connecticut: Appleton & Lange, 1991. Copyright © 1991 by Appleton & Lange. **p. 483** Adapted from Caviness, V.S., Jr., and Rakic, P., Mechanisms of cortical development: A view from mutations in mice, *Annual Review of Neuroscience* 1 (1978): 297–326.

Chapter 13: **13.5 and 13.6** Adapted from Gaulin, S.J.C., and Fitzgerald, R.W., Sexual selection for spatial-learning ability, *Animal Behaviour* 37 (1989): 322–331. **13.7** Adapted from Jacobs, L.F., Gaulin, S.J.C., Sherry, D.F., and Hoffman, G.E., Evolution of spatial cognition: Sex-specific patterns of spatial behavior predict hippocampal size, *Proc. Natl. Acad. Sci. U.S.A.* 87 (1990): 6349–6352. **13.11** Le Doux, J.E., In Search of an Emotional System in the Brain: Leaping from Fear to Emotion and Consciousness, in Gazzaniga, M.S. (Ed.), *The Cognitive Neurosciences*. Cambridge, MA: MIT Press, 1995, pp. 1047–1061. © 1995 Massachusetts Institute of Technology. Adapted with permission of MIT Press. **13.12** McEwen, B.S., Stressful Experience, Brain, and Emotions: Developmental, Genetic, and Hormonal Influences, in Gazzaniga, M.S. (Ed.), *The Cognitive Neurosciences*. Cambridge, MA: MIT Press, 1995, pp. 1117–1135. © 1995 Massachusetts Institute of Technology. Adapted with permission of MIT Press. **13.16** Gallistel, C.R., The Replacement of General-Purpose Theories with Adaptive Specializations, in Gazzaniga, M.S. (Ed.), *The Cognitive Neurosciences*. Cambridge, MA: MIT Press, 1995, pp. 1255–1267. © 1995 Massachusetts Institute of Technology. Adapted with permission of MIT Press. **13.17** Adapted from Harkness, R.D., and Maroudas, N.G., Central place foraging by an ant (Cataglyphis bicolor Fab.): A model of searching, *Animal Behaviour* 33 (1985): 916–928. Gallistel,

C.R., The Replacement of General-Purpose Theories with Adaptive Specializations, in Gazzaniga, M.S. (Ed.), *The Cognitive Neurosciences*. Cambridge, MA: MIT Press, 1995, pp. 1255–1267. © 1995 Massachusetts Institute of Technology. Adapted with permission of MIT Press. **p. 505** Adapted from Lettvin, J.Y., Maturana, H.R., McCulloch, W.S., and Pitts, W.H., What the frog's eye tells the frog's brain, *Proc. Insti. Radio Engineers* 47 (1959): 1940–1951.

Chapter 14: **14.3** Adapted from Marcel, A., Conscious and unconscious perception: Experiments on visual masking and word recognition, *Cognitive Psychology* 15 (1983): 197–237. Adapted from Marcel, A., Conscious and unconscious perception: An approach to the relations between phenomenal experience and perceptual processes, *Cognitive Psychology* 15 (1983): 238–300. **14.4** Adapted from Weiskrantz, L., Warrington, E.K., Sanders, M.D., and Marshall, J., Visual capacity in the hemianopic field following a restricted occipital ablation, *Brain* 97 (1974): 709–728. **14.9** Newsome, W.T., and Pare, E.B., "A selective impairment of motion perception following lesions of the middle temporal visual area (MT), *The Journal of Neuroscience* 8: 2201–2211, (1988). Adapted with permission of The Society for Neuroscience

TABLES

Table 5.1 Adapted from Farah, M.J., *Visual Agnosia: Disorders of Object Recognition and What They Tell Us about Normal Vision*. Cambridge, MA: MIT Press, 1990. Adapted with permission of MIT Press. **Table 13.1** Adapted from Alcock, J., *Animal Behavior: An Evolutionary Approach*, 2nd edition. Sunderland, MA: Sinauer Associates, 1979.

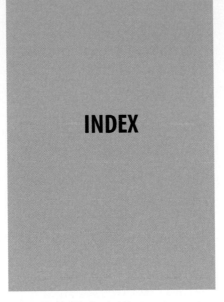

INDEX